WRITING LIVES
reading communities

SECOND EDITION

edited by

KAY HALASEK • EDGAR SINGLETON • BRENDA M. BOYLE • JENNIFER S. CLARK
ROBERT W. DUNKS • BRUCE MACHART • MICHAEL J. SASSO • LISA TATONETTI
REBECCA GREENBERG TAYLOR

Pearson
Custom
Publishing

Cover Art: "Reader," by Christian Stolte.

Printed in the United States of America

10 9 8 7 6 5 4 3 2 1

Please visit our website at www.pearsoncustom.com

ISBN 0–536–61444–X

BA 992414

PEARSON CUSTOM PUBLISHING
75 Arlington Street, Suite 300, Boston, MA 02116
A Pearson Education Company

Copyright Acknowledgments

PREFACE TO INSTRUCTORS

Writing Lives/Reading Communities, although a composition reader and not a rhetoric, is informed by a student-centered pedagogy in which writing is presented as a process with multiple opportunities for drafting, receiving responses from peers and instructors before revising, and eventually developing a final draft. *Writing Lives/Reading Communities* also provides numerous opportunities for informal writing, so students can reflect upon and challenge their ideas as they develop essays and projects. As Donald Murray and others might put it, we intend to give students the opportunity to write to learn.

Writing Lives/Reading Communities promotes critical reading, writing, and discussion as means of inquiry. Reading and writing, we recognize, are related activities. To assist students in understanding the relationship between reading and writing, we first encourage students to approach the readings in *Writing Lives/Reading Communities* as active respondents.

"Writing Before Reading" activities that precede selections in *Writing Lives/Reading Communities* are intended to initiate student inquiry about the issues raised in the readings. These activities give students a first opportunity to engage the subject of the selection by asking them to investigate the ways that their own opinions and experiences might already relate to the authors' ideas. By foregrounding the students' experiences in this fashion, we hope to illustrate to students that reading entails making personal connections to the texts they encounter. Instructors may wish to have students collect their responses to "Writing Before Reading" questions in a *writer's notebook,* an electronic or manuscript text in which students collect their responses to their reading and explore their thinking about their development as a writer. We've constructed the "Writing Before Reading" activities and "Explorations" as prompts for a writer's notebook should you wish to have students keep one. We anticipate that responses to these informal writing activities will serve students as valuable aids as they begin longer writing assignments.

The activities that follow reading selections continue the engagement begun in "Writing Before Reading" exercises. "Questions for Discussion," while diverse and wide-ranging in their content, generally ask students to reflect actively on the selections, to inquire about details, generalizations, voice, tone, and style, etc. and in doing so introduce concepts and generate class discussion. Such activities not only provide students with a more specific and sophisticated understanding of the rhetorical strategies authors employ in their texts but also enrich students' own resources as writers, helping them to consider the impact of their words on readers.

"Explorations" are intended to invite students to think about their own writing and reading processes and offer a variety of opportunities for students to extend their understanding of the texts through writing. In many cases, "Explorations" connect one selection to others in *Writing Lives/Reading Communities* (usually in the same unit). The "Explorations" may also help students consider a particular theme in reading or assist them in comparing how similar themes are treated differently by various authors. Such "Explorations" also often ask students to examine the selections in terms of discourse, community and other of the themes that run throughout the text: individual and cultural identity, race, class, technologies, etc. Teachers can use "Explorations" in a variety of ways. They can be used, in conjunction with "Questions for Discussion," as the basis for small or large group discussions, collaborative projects, short writing assignments, an on-going "Writer's Notebook," or the starting point for longer writing projects.

The reading and writing activities in *Writing Lives/Reading Communities* culminate in "Formal Writing Assignments." Constructed as extended writing projects, these activities provide teachers and students alike a means of further investigating the readings and their relationship to themes and issues that arise from "Writing Before Reading," "Questions for Discussion," and "Explorations." We include two formal writing assignments in an effort to illustrate to students that engagement with readings can lead to a variety of kinds of writing projects. These activities are not exhaustive, of course, but illustrate some of the ways we have begun to think about the reading selections and ways that they, individually and collectively, comment on the ways that discourse functions in home, academic, and public sites. These assignments offer general guidelines to instructors and students and are meant to be suggestive, not pre-scriptive. Instructors may assign these prompts as they are written or let students decide which aspects of the assignment on which to focus. You may also discuss the prompts with students and together con-struct a revised approach. In any case, we encourage instructors and students alike to revise prompts to emphasize those elements of the unit in which they're most interested.

We have attempted, in developing *Writing Lives/Reading Communities,* to provide first-year writ-ing students and their instructors with a range of materials that illuminate the relationships among var-ious discursive practices and individuals, communities, and cultures. If used in the order in which they're presented, the units of *Writing Lives/Reading Communities* moves students through three distinct but interrelated sections devoted to personal, academic, and public discourses. Although the readings explore the connections among culture and context evident in various discursive practices, the pedagogical appa-ratus of *Writing Lives/Reading Communities* challenges students to recognize the ways that language car-ries values and power and, in turn, to use this knowledge as writers themselves. The organization of the readings and pedagogical apparatus emphasizes this invitation to students to enter into a dialogue with their instructors, the readings, and each other.

The readings in Part I, "Personal Discourses," were selected to prompt students to recollect and ana-lyze their past language experiences within the context of particular communities. This unit encourages students to practice a stance that they will develop during the course—that of a self-reflective reader and writer—as they integrate the aims of the personal narrative with more common academic forms such as the expository essay. Although Part I encourages students to see the value of their experiences with lan-guage and the discourses of particular communities, it also suggests that they incorporate other voices—the voices of their communities and the authors that they're reading—into their writing.

Part II, "Academic Discourses," builds on the definitions of personal and communal discourses by examining how discourse is defined, constructed, and used in academic settings. Students consider social, political, and economic factors that influence how they negotiate the often difficult boundaries between home communities and the academy. In their writing, students examine the multiple discourses at work in the university.

Part III, "Public Discourses," promotes further attention to audience and point of view by exam-ining the significance of public discourses. The readings in this portion of *Writing Lives/Reading Com-munities* examine how public (e.g., consumer, media) discourses function and influence their intended audiences. The readings also offer students ways of effectively engaging and using public discourse in the academic sphere.

The readings themselves illustrate the complexity of discourses available to students as producers and consumers—non-fiction essays, poems, narratives, editorial opinions. As such, *Writing Lives/Read-ing Communities* provides a rich resource on discourse and language practices that can be used by students and instructors as a springboard for further research. We invite instructors and students to use the book to enter the ongoing conversations about discourse and language practice already underway in the pages of *Writing Lives/Reading Communities.*

PREFACE TO STUDENTS

Even as recently as the 1960s and 1970s, first-year writing courses in many colleges and universities across the country were notorious among entering students. Freshman English, upper class students told them, was a "flunk out" course, composition instructors the unofficial gatekeepers of the university. In some institutions, as many as 25% of incoming students were expected to fail their first-year writing courses. The activities in these classrooms were often devoted to sentence and paragraph work—grammar, mechanics, style, and organizational models. Campus lore included tales of students failing an entire essay because of one dangling modifier or a single misspelled word. The lore, of course, was fact. The focus in these "flunk out" writing courses was on detecting and eliminating error. The teacher found the errors and instructed students in the appropriate conventions; the students strived to produce error-free prose, often at the expense of learning the more important arts of analysis, interpretation, and persuasion.

All of this is not to say that grammar, mechanics and style are unimportant. To the contrary. Effective writing—that is, writing that achieves its implicit or explicit purpose—is expected by readers to be free from error that makes its meaning unclear or impedes reading. The conventions of and expectations for correctness shift, of course. What counts as "error" changes. Twenty or thirty years ago, students who neglected to use "whom" when called for were very likely chastised by instructors, their grades lowered. Today, a significant number of highly educated people do not follow the rule for the proper use of "who" and "whom," yet their writing is well-received and effective. Other errors continue to be more serious, more equal than others. These errors are those that impede meaning, detract from the writer's authority and expertise, or confound the reader. What is clear is that correctness is, to one degree or another, an element—but not the determiner—of effective writing.

Writing classes in the 1980s and 1990s turned from a focus on the sentence, paragraph and error to writing as a process and the practice of composing fully developed essays. The writing process, which is now a part of nearly every first-year writing course in the U.S., is founded on the belief that writers do their best work if they imagine a writing activity as a cumulative project, one that includes prewriting, drafting, revising, and editing. Rather than require students to submit a final paper for evaluation, instructors began collecting, responding, and returning to students drafts of essays, which were then revised, submitted, and graded. This development in writing instruction from a culture of correction to a culture of process was accompanied by a significant shift in the activity of the writing classroom. Many classrooms of the 1960s and early 1970s were taken up by lectures on literature, grammar, and style. By contrast, classrooms in the 1980s and 1990s more often revolved around in-class writing and collaborative activities, with explicit grammar instruction occurring more often than not in conferences with teachers and in tutorials in university writing centers.

Each year, the first-year writing programs across the nation offer thousands of sections of first-year writing to hundreds of thousands of students. As you might imagine, to generalize about them is an impossible task. Different instructors approach their teaching from a variety of pedagogical and even philosophical positions. Some, you may find, value creative approaches to writing assignments; others value well-organized essays and clear and precise language; others prefer essays that manage complex ideas in a sophisticated fashion. Still others expect student essays to accomplish all of these things. Students in one class may be asked to compose summaries, informal reflections and analyses, while assignments in an adjacent class may include researched essays and interpretations of films, advertisements, short stories, or poems.

What *can* be said about the majority of first-year writing courses in the U.S. is that they provide students with opportunities to practice and improve their writing abilities and reflect critically upon the writing process, types of academic writing, and methods of critical inquiry and problem-solving. *Writing Lives/Reading Communities* is designed to encourage students to develop just these kinds of skills.

The readings in *Writing Lives/Reading Communities* and the "Writing Before Reading" questions, "Discussion Questions," "Explorations," and "Formal Writing Assignments" that accompany each reading selection invite you to explore the ways that others have thought and written about how discourses—stories, official documents, advertisements, visual images—function within home or local communities, the academic community, and the larger public community of consumers.

Writing Lives/Reading Communities encourages you to think—and write—critically about discourses, noting how the concept of "discourse" shifts in various educational and cultural communities. You'll find that discourse itself serves as a frame for thinking about how people come to know and communicate knowledge in specific communities. You'll be asked to *investigate* how discourses have shaped your experiences. Through this investigation, you'll *describe* the relationship between your own beliefs and the discursive practices you've encountered (Unit 1), *analyze* what it means to receive and produce discourses in an academic setting (Unit 2), and *examine* critically the rhetorical and persuasive strategies of public consumer discourses (Unit 3). In its focus on discourses and language practices, *Writing Lives/Reading Communities* challenges you to understand, define, describe, analyze, interpret, argue, and communicate to others the ways that discourses function in these varied cultural arenas

As you work your way through *Writing Lives/Reading Communities,* you'll encounter numerous opportunities to explore and write about the personal, academic, and public sites in which discourses are formed and framed. Throughout *Writing Lives/Reading Communities* we offer questions to encourage you to think critically about the reading selections and your own writing. The activities that lead you through these inquiries are labeled "Writing Before Reading," "Questions for Discussion," "Explorations," and "Formal Writing Assignments." (If you'd like, you can also read our brief descriptions of these in the "Preface to Instructors.") "Writing Before Reading" prompts are meant to engage your own thoughts and experiences *before* you read. We also include "Questions for Discussion" and "Explorations" after each selection. These are designed to help you generate ideas for small or large group discussions and explore, through your own writing, your responses to what you read. "Questions for Discussion" typically direct your attention to specific features; "Explorations" invite you to reflect upon the reading in terms of themes or other readings in *Writing Lives/Reading Communities.* "Formal Writing Assignments" are just that, opportunities for you to construct in response to a reading or readings a lengthy, more formal piece of writing. These are the assignments that your instructor will most likely evaluate in a more formal manner, with comment, response, and (eventually) letter grades.

Active reading—the kind of reading we propose that you enact as you read the selections in *Writing Lives/Reading Communities*—requires that you read with a questioning mind. Your instructor will expect you to come to class with thoughtful questions about your reading. Learning to ask productive questions is part of learning to "do" school in higher education and has the added benefits of making you a better reader and writer. Being an active reader enables you to

- become more engaged with class readings and in class discussions,
- develop more focused papers, and
- carry out more productive and, ultimately, more interesting research projects.

Your instructor may ask that you compose and keep your written responses to any or all of the informal writing activities—the "Writing Before Reading" activities, "Questions for Discussion," and "Explorations"—in what we refer to as a Writer's Notebook. Such a notebook is a valuable aid as you participate in class discussions and as you begin longer writing assignments. Use your writer's notebook to write about your responses to the reading selections. In addition to responding to those activities that your instructor assigns, consider using the notebook as a site for your own lines of inquiry and response. You might begin by describing your gut level reaction to a text or its formal features. Any of the following kinds of questions would be useful prompts for your own entries into the writer's notebook:

- What is my emotional response to this piece of writing? Does it make me angry, enthusiastic, puzzled? Which passages seem to contribute most directly to this response?

- What did I find interesting about the piece, either in terms of the topic, writer's point of view, style, or other element?

- How well does the author develop ideas?

- How well does the author support claims with details and examples?

- Is the essay well organized?

- Do the tone and style of the essay seem appropriate for the writer's purpose and audience?

Try your hand at your first writer's notebook entry in response to the following prompt:

> *How do you define discourse? Who and what helped you arrive at this definition? How did you learn your discursive habits, your language practices? How do we recognize effective discourses?*

Share your responses with classmates. You may want to supplement your responses with several dictionary definitions of the term in an effort to complicate and broaden the notion of "discourse" that the group discusses.

As you read, write, and take part in classroom discussions about the topics raised in *Writing Lives/Reading Communities,* you'll notice that people—including many of the writers whose work you'll encounter here—do not agree on a single definition of discourse. As a first-year college student, you already possess tremendous skills in reading, writing, and other language practices, but at the same time, you may not be aware of the ways that those and other discourses that you encounter each day are shaped or how they affect you. As the organization of *Writing Lives/Reading Communities* itself suggests, we believe that discourses are constructed within the contexts of various communities and social situations—home, academia, and the larger public sphere. If you begin to think about discourses as shared by groups in certain situations, you will begin to see how many discourses are at work in U.S. culture.

We mean, in *Writing Lives/Reading Communities,* to give you a richer sense of your own uses of discourse by engaging you in the discussions that inform the reading selections that make up *Writing Lives/Reading Communities.* In one way or another, each of the writers whose work appears here addresses discourses and their relationship to the communities in which those discourses are developed and shared. Understanding discourses in this richer sense means understanding discourse as a complex network of language and culture, of recognizing how languages function within the communities to which we belong and how knowledge is valued in those communities.

ACKNOWLEDGMENTS

Writing Lives/Reading Communities is an extensive revision of *Writing Lives: Exploring Literacy and Community* (St. Martin's Press, 1996) and is, like that text, an intensely collaborative work undertaken by several groups of faculty, professional staff, graduate student administrators, and teachers in the First-Year Writing Program at Ohio State University under the direction of Kay Halasek and Eddie Singleton. As those of you familiar with *Writing Lives: Exploring Literacy and Community* will recognize immediately, this new edition bears a significant resemblance to that earlier text. Because of this, our editorial team wishes to acknowledge again the vision and material contributions provided by those people who worked on what was to become *Writing Lives: Exploring Literacy and Community*. Thanks to the editorial team of *Writing Lives: Exploring Literacy and Community*: Sara Garnes, David Humphries, Vic Mortimer, Jennifer Phegley, Kathleen Wallace. Thanks also to Carrie Dirmeikis, Theresa Doerfler, Suellynn Duffey, Victoria Dunn, Natalie Fields, Amy Goodburn, Jane Greer, Nathan Grey, Paul Hanstedt, Carrie Leverenz, Gianna Marsella, Lori Mathis, Chuck Schroeder, and Melinda Turnley.

Materials in *Writing Lives/Reading Communities* come from the desks of scores of writing teachers and administrators who have worked in the program over many years. The FYWP and the editorial team gratefully acknowledge the contributions of each of these people: Janet Badia, Jennifer Cognard-Black, Tinitia Coleman, Ben Feigert, Kate Gillespie, Melissa Goldthwaite, Gina Hicks, Nels Highberg, Mike Lohre, Emma Perry Loss, Sandee McGlaun, Kirk Robinson, and Jean Williams. Their expertise and commitment to writing instruction are commendable.

Many others at Ohio State have helped in a variety of ways. Melinda Bogarty, the FYWP administrative assistant, provided invaluable support and a steadfast good nature that kept the project enjoyable and on time. JB Blevins and Nikole Marzano, undergraduate work-study students, provided much needed manuscript and research support.

The editors also wish to thank Kurt Jaenicke, Jackie Grisvard, and Kevin Crossland of Pearson Custom Publishing and Steve McDonald of Ohio State University for their support of this project.

We hope that the contributions and inspiration provided to us by our colleagues—past and present—are done justice by the book that follows.

Royalties from *Writing Lives/Reading Communities* go to a fund that supports programs within the First-Year Writing Program at Ohio State University. These programs include the *Writing Lives* student essay awards and professional development grants. Funds also support special initiatives, speakers, and professional development workshops for instructors in the program.

DEDICATION

In Memorium
Edward P. J. Corbett
and
James L. Kinneavy

Contents

Unit I

Unit II

Contents

Unit III

Alternative Table of Contents

The following alternative table of contents provides instructors and students an additional means of organizing the readings in *Writing Lives/Reading Communities*. These are intended neither as exhaustive topics nor comprehensive lists; rather, they serve as points of departure. Within each topical category we have indicated the unit from which each reading comes. This allows instructors and students to further focus their readings within the three units of *Writing Lives/Reading Communities*. One might, for example, focus on identity and academic discourse by selecting Unit II readings from the "Identity" group. Similarly, one could focus on "Nation and Culture" in the public sphere by selecting readings from Unit III that appear in the "Nation and Culture" list.

IMAGES

IDENTITY

Hart (Unit II)
Hempel (Unit II)
hooks (Unit II)
Jones (Unit III)
LeGuin (Unit I)
Lorde (Unit II)
McIntosh (Unit I)
Meyers (Unit III)
Shen (Unit II)
Turkle (Unit III)

LANGUAGE

Anzaldúa (Unit II)
Bazerman (Unit III)
Berger (Unit III)
Devor (Unit III)
Douglass (Unit I)
Ewen (Unit III)
Freire (Unit II)
Gilyard (Unit II)
Herschberger (Unit III)
LeGuin (Unit I)
Meyers (Unit III)
Morales (Unit I)
O'Neill (Unit III)
Postman and Powers (Unit III)
Rodriguez (Unit I)
Samuelson (Unit III)
Scribner (Unit III)
Stern (Unit II)
Tan (Unit I)
Williams (Unit III)

NATION AND CULTURE

Angelou (Unit II)
Anyon (Unit II)
Anzaldúa (Unit I)
Cantor (Unit III)
Douglass (Unit I)
Earley (Unit I)
Gamson (Unit III)
Giroux (Unit III)
Goldberg (Unit III)
Hine (Unit III)

PERSONAL DISCOURSES

After years of working with words, writers often reflect on how they first became acquainted with language and how they came to understand language through their writing and experiences. These reflections, or personal literacy narratives, encourage writers to examine how their identity has been expressed and shaped through language. Writers, like all of us, explore and express their individuality through language. The literacy narrative, however, gives writers a vehicle for their examinations of how the values and beliefs of communities influence the rules and boundaries of language use and personal behavior. Personal literacy narratives, then, are stories of individual growth that reflect upon the factors that shaped that growth.

Consider for a moment how you have come to understand language. Perhaps as a child you had a favorite book or story that your parents read to you. This book or story may have helped you to learn about language by sparking your imagination or by making you curious about learning to read and write. While this story may be an intimate part of your personal history of becoming literate, it originated in a broader community. Children's stories such as "Little Red Riding Hood," or "Br'er Rabbit," and those of Dr. Seuss all reflect different communities and values that may or may not overlap. For example, several of the Dr. Seuss stories teach fundamental skills in counting and identifying colors. The story of "Little Red Riding Hood" teaches the lesson that appearances may be deceiving. The tales of "Br'er Rabbit" show how being cunning can lead the seemingly weak to triumph over the strong but stupid.

Different communities, different eras, and different authors are likely to have varied perspectives on the same issue, and in choosing to read or to tell particular stories, parents express their own sets of values. Your appreciation of a story's "importance" expresses both your own values and those of the communities to which you belong.

Understanding the language of a community and learning to read and write, then, are only one part of becoming literate. To become truly literate, you also need to know the values of the community in which you are trying to become literate. Tony Earley illustrates this kind of literacy in his essay "The Quare Gene." Earley writes of how his struggle to achieve acceptance in the academic community increased his appreciation for the dialect of his family and neighbors in the hills of western North Carolina. In gaining fluency in a more standardized dialect, Earley came to understand the richness of expression of his native dialect. He learned that language was inseparable from the character of the people who had settled that inaccessible land, and he now mourns the potential disappearance of that dialect as its speakers are inevitably engulfed by the broader society. In "Aria: Memory of a Bilingual Childhood," Richard Rodriguez writes of how is life was forever changed by his acquisition of English. The more literate he grew in this adopted language, the less able he was to maintain a close connection with his Spanish-speaking family. He discovered that language truly defined his identity.

Our memories and our histories are often housed in our stories, which we share through different uses of language. In some sense, we *are* the stories we create and tell; we are the language we use to understand and express ourselves. Literacy is more, then, than simply reading and writing. To be literate requires that we grasp the complexity of how discourse functions in communities.

The following readings illustrate these complex understandings of literacy. Some authors focus more on their own experiences with language and discourse. Others focus more on communities and the values behind different kinds of discourse. Each reading, though, will challenge you to consider not only *how* an author acquired a certain kind of literacy, but also *why* that literacy was valued by a particular community. In turn, you will be asked to reflect on your own process of acquiring discourses and how this process has been intertwined with your membership in different communities.

EXPLORATION

Think about your favorite childhood book. Which communities does it most reflect? Describe the community values or desires expressed by this book.

How to Tame a Wild Tongue

Gloria Anzaldúa

W hat we say and what we do," writes Gloria Anzaldúa, "ultimately comes back to us so let us own our responsibility, place it in our hands and carry it with dignity and strength." This quotation from Anzaldúa, a chicana/feminist/lesbian writer and cultural theorist, illustrates her understanding of the central importance of personal and collective responsibility in effecting change in a range of U.S. policies. An advocate for migrant workers, third world women, and lesbians, Anzaldúa is widely recognized as a leading voice against political and institutional oppression. Many of her writings are composed in both English and Spanish and combine poetry, autobiography, and essays, and in these Anzaldúa speaks to the need for improving social justice. A native Texan, Anzaldúa has spent the greatest share of her adult life as a teacher and practicing writer.

Anzaldúa's works include *Borderlands/La Frontera: The New Mestiza; This Bridge Called My Back: Writings by Radical Women of Color; Making Face, Making Soul/Hacieno Caras: Creative and Critical Perspectives by Women of Color; Friends from the Other Side/Amigos Del Otro Lado; Prietita has a Friend—Prietita tiene un Amigo* (a children's book), and most recently *La Prieta*, a novel. *Interviews/Entrevistas*, a series of interviews with Anzaldúa and edited by Analouise Keating, will be published in June 2000. Anzaldúa is the recipient of numerous awards, including the Before Columbus Foundation American Book Award and the Lambda Lesbian Small Press Book Award.

Writing Before Reading

1. Do you or any members of your family or immediate circle of friends speak more than one language? If so, what languages do you/they speak? Recount briefly one or two experiences they've described for you concerning their experiences as bi- or multilinguals in the United States.

2. In many cultures, the old cliché "children should be seen, not heard" still holds value. How do you respond to that adage? What do you believe its purpose is? Do you believe there is ever a time when children should, in fact, be seen and not heard? Why or why not?

3. Have you ever experienced negative reactions to your own "home" tongues or language practices? If so, in what contexts? Describe one of these experiences. If not, have you ever found yourself negatively responding to the language practices of someone else? In what contexts? How would you characterize this experience?

How to Tame a Wild Tongue

"We're going to have to control your tongue," the dentist says, pulling out all the metal from my mouth. Silver bits plop and tinkle into the basin. My mouth is a motherlode. The dentist is cleaning out my roots. I get a whiff of the stench when I gasp. I can't cap that tooth yet, you're still draining," he says. "We're going to have to do something about your tongue," I hear the anger rising in his voice. My tongue keeps pushing out the wads of cotton, pushing back the drills, the long thin needles. "I've never seen anything as strong or as stubborn," he says. And I think, how do you tame a wild tongue, train it to be quiet, how do you bridle and saddle it? How do you make it lie down?

"Who is to say that robbing a people of its language is less violent than war?"
-Ray Gwyn Smith

I remember being caught speaking Spanish at recess—that was good for three licks on the knuckles with a sharp ruler. I remember being sent to the corner of the classroom for "talking back" to the Anglo teacher when all I was trying to do was tell her how to pronounce my name. If you want to be American, speak 'American.' If you don't like it, go back to Mexico where you belong."

"I want you to speak English. *Pa' hallar buen trabajo tienes quo saber hablar el inglés bien. Qué vale toda tu educación si todavia hablas inglés con un* 'accent,'" my mother would say, mortified that I spoke English like a Mexican. At Pan American University, I, and all Chicano students were required to take two speech classes. Their purpose: to get rid of our accents.

Attacks on one's form of expression with the intent to censor are a violation of the First Amendment. *El Anglo con cara de inocente nos arrancó la lengua.* Wild tongues can't be tamed, they can only be cut out.

Overcoming the Tradition of Silence

> *Ahogadas, escupimos el oscuro.*
> *Peleando con nuestra propia sombra*
> *el silencio nos sepulta*

En boca cerrada no entran moscas. "Flies don't enter a closed mouth" is a saying I kept hearing when I was a child. *Ser habladora* was to be a gossip and a liar, to talk too much. *Muchachitas bien criadas,* well-bred girls don't answer back. *Es una falta de respeto* to talk back to one's mother or father. I remember one of the sins I'd recite to the priest in the confession box the few times I went to confession: talking back to my mother, *hablar pa' 'tras, repelar. Hocicona, repelona, chismosa,* having a big mouth, questioning, carrying tales are all signs of being *mal criada.* In my culture they are all words that are derogatory if applied to women—I've never heard them applied to men.

The first time I heard two women, a Puerto Rican and a Cuban, say the word *"nosotrars,"* I was shocked. I had not known the word existed. Chicanas use *nosotros* whether we're male or female. We are robbed of our female being by the masculine plural. Language is a male discourse.

> *And our tongues have become*
> *dry the wilderness has*
> *dried out our tongues and*
> *we have forgotten speech.*
> *-Irena Klepfisz*

Even our own people, other Spanish speakers *nos quieren poner candados en la boca.* They would hold us back with their bag of *reglas de academia.*
Oyé como ladra: el lenguaje de la frontera

> *Quien tiene boca se equivoca.*
> *-Mexican saying*

"*Pocho,* cultural traitor, you're speaking the oppressor's language by speaking English, you're ruining the Spanish language," I have been accused by various Latinos and Latinas. Chicano Spanish is considered by the purist and by most Latinos deficient, a mutilation of Spanish.

But Chicano Spanish is a border tongue which developed naturally. Change, *evolución, enriquecimiento de palabras nuevas por invención o adopción* have created variants of Chicano Spanish, *un nuevo lenguaje. Un lenguaje que corresponde a un modo de vivir.* Chicano Spanish is not incorrect, it is a living language.

For a people who are neither Spanish nor live in a country in which Spanish is the first language; for a people who live in a country in which English is the reigning tongue but who are not Anglo; for a people who cannot entirely identify with either standard (formal, Castillian) Spanish nor standard English, what recourse is left to them but to create their own language? A language which they can connect their identity to, one capable of communicating the realities and values true to themselves—a language with terms that are neither *español ni inglés,* but both. We speak a patois, a forked tongue, a variation of two languages.

Chicano Spanish sprang out of the Chicanos' need to identify ourselves as a distinct people. We needed a language with which we could communicate with ourselves, a secret language. For some of us, language is a homeland closer than the Southwest—for many Chicanos today live in the Midwest and the East. And because we are a complex, heterogeneous people, we speak many languages. Some of the languages we speak are:

1. Standard English

2. Working class and slang English

3. Standard Spanish

4. Standard Mexican Spanish

5. North Mexican Spanish dialect

6. Chicano Spanish (Texas, New Mexico, Arizona and California have regional variations)

7. Tex-Mex

8. Pachuco (called caló)

My "home" tongues are the languages I speak with my sister and brothers, with my friends. They are the last five listed, with 6 and 7 being closest to my heart. From school, the media and job situations, I've picked up standard and working class English. From Mamagrande Locha and from reading Spanish and Mexican literature, I've picked up Standard Spanish and Standard Mexican Spanish. From *los recién llegados,* Mexican immigrants, and *braceros,* I learned the North Mexican dialect. With Mexicans I'll try to speak either Standard Mexican Spanish or the North Mexican dialect. From my parents and Chicanos living in the Valley, I picked up Chicano Texas Spanish, and I speak it with my mom, younger brother (who married a Mexican and who rarely mixes Spanish with English), aunts and older relatives.

With Chicanas from Nuevo México or Arizona I will speak Chicano Spanish a little, but often they don't understand what I'm saying. With most California Chicanas I speak entirely in English (unless I forget). When I first moved to San Francisco, I would rattle off something in Spanish, unintentionally embarrassing them. Often it is only with another Chicana *tejana* that I can talk freely.

Words distorted by English are known as anglicisms or *pochismos.* The *pocho* is an anglicized Mexican or American of Mexican origin who speaks Spanish with an accent characteristic of North Americans and who distorts and reconstructs the language according to the influence of English. Tex-Mex, or Spanglish, comes most naturally to me. I may switch back and forth from English to Spanish in the same sentence or in the same word. With my sister and my brother Nune and with Chicano *tejano* contemporaries I speak in Tex-Mex.

From kids and people my own age I picked up *Pachuco*. Pachuco (the language of the zoot suiters) is a language of rebellion, both against Standard Spanish and Standard English. It is a secret language. Adults of the culture and outsiders cannot understand it. It is made up of slang words from both English and Spanish. *Ruca* means girl or woman, *vato* means guy or dude, *chale* means no, *simón* means yes, *churro* is sure, talk is *periquiar*, *pigionear* means petting, *que gacho* means how nerdy, *ponte águila* means watch out, death is called *la pelona*. Through lack of practice and not having others who can speak it, I've lost most of the *Pachuco* tongue.

Chicano Spanish

Chicanos, after 250 years of Spanish/Anglo colonization have developed significant differences in the Spanish we speak. We collapse two adjacent vowels into a single syllable and sometimes shift the stress in certain words such as *maiz/maiz, cohete/ cuete*. We leave out certain consonants when they appear between vowels: lado/lao, *mojado/mojao*. Chicanos from South Texas pronounce f as j as in *jue (fue)*. Chicanos use "archaisms," words that are no longer in the Spanish language, words that have been evolved out. We say *semos, truje, haiga, ansina,* and *naiden*. We retain the "archaic" j, as in *jalar*, that derives from an earlier *h*, (the French *halar* or the Germanic *halon* which was lost to standard Spanish in the 16th century), but which is still found in several regional dialects such as the one spoken in South Texas. (Due to geography, Chicanos from the Valley of South Texas were cut off linguistically from other Spanish speakers. We tend to use words that the Spaniards brought over from Medieval Spain. The majority of the Spanish colonizers in Mexico and the Southwest came from Extremadura—Hernán Cortés was one of them—and Andalucía. Andalucians pronounce ll like a y, and their d's tend to be absorbed by adjacent vowels: *tirado* becomes *tirao*. They brought *el lenguaje popular, dialectos y regionalismos*.)

Chicancos and other Spanish speakers also shift *ll* to *y* and *z* to *s*. We leave out initial syllables, saying *tar* for *estar*, *toy* for *estoy*, *hora* for *ahora (cubanos* and *puertorriqueños* also leave out initial letters of some words.) We also leave out the final syllable such as *pa* for *para*. The intervocalic *y*, the ll as in *tortilla, ella, botella*, gets replaced by *tortia* or *tortiya, ea, botea*. We add an additional syllable at the beginning of certain words: *atocar* for *tocar*, *agastar* for *gastar*. Sometimes we'll say *lavaste las vasijas*, other times *lavates* (substituting the *ates* verb endings for the *aste*).

We use anglicisms, words borrowed from English: *bola* from ball, *carpeta* from carpet, *máchina de lavar* (instead of *lavadora*) from washing machine. Tex-Mex argot, created by adding a Spanish sound at the beginning or end of an English word such as *cookiar* for cook, *watchar* for watch, *parkiar* for park, and *rapiar* for rape, is the result of the pressures on Spanish speakers to adapt to English.

We don't use the word *vosotros/as* or its accompanying verb form. We don't say *claro* (to mean yes), *imagínate*, or *me emociona*, unless we picked up Spanish from Latinas, out of a book, or in a classroom. Other Spanish-speaking groups are going through the same, or similar, development in their Spanish.

Linguistic Terrorism

Deslenguadas. *Somos los del español deficiente*. We are your linguistic nightmare, your linguistic aberration, your linguistic mestisaje, the subject of your *burla*. Because we speak with tongues of fire we are culturally crucified. Racially, culturally and linguistically *somos huérfanos*—we speak an orphan tongue.

Chicanas who grew up speaking Chicano Spanish have internalized the belief that we speak poor Spanish. It is illegitimate, a bastard language. And because we internalize how our language has been used against us by the dominant culture, we use our language differences against each other.

Chicana feminists often skirt around each other with suspicion and hesitation. For the longest time I couldn't figure it out. Then it dawned on me. To be close to another Chicana is like looking into the mirror. We are afraid of what we'll see there. *Pena.* Shame. Low estimation of self. In childhood we are told that our language is wrong. Repeated attacks on our native tongue diminish our sense of self. The attacks continue throughout our lives.

Chicanas feel uncomfortable talking in Spanish to Latinas, afraid of their censure. Their language was not outlawed in their countries. They had a whole lifetime of being immersed in their native tongue; generations, centuries in which Spanish was a first language, taught in school, heard on radio and TV, and read in the newspaper.

If a person, Chicana or Latina, has a low estimation of my native tongue, she also has a low estimation of me. Often with *mexicanas y latinas* we'll speak English as a neutral language. Even among Chicanas we tend to speak English at parties or conferences. Yet, at the same time, we're afraid the other will think we're *agringadas* because we don't speak Chicano Spanish. We oppress each other trying to out-Chicano each other, vying to be the "real" Chicanas, to speak like Chicinos. There is no one Chicano language just as there is no one Chicano experience. A monolingual Chicana whose first language is English or Spanish is just as much a Chicana as one who speaks several variants of Spanish. A Chicana from Michigan or Chicago or Detroit is just as much a Chicana as one from the Southwest. Chicano Spanish is as diverse linguistically as it is regionally.

By the end of this century, Spanish speakers will comprise the biggest minority group in the U.S., a country where students in high schools and colleges are encouraged to take French classes because French is considered more "cultured." But for a language to remain alive it must be used. By the end of this century English, and not Spanish, will be the mother tongue of most Chicanos and Latinos.

So, if you want to really hurt me, talk badly about my language. Ethnic identity is twin skin to linguistic identity—I am my language. Until I can take pride in my language, I cannot take pride in myself. Until I can accept as legitimate Chicano Texas Spanish, Tex-Mex and all the other languages I speak, I cannot accept the legitimacy of myself. Until I am free to write bilingually and to switch codes without having always to translate, while I still have to speak English or Spanish when I would rather speak Spanglish, and as long as I have to accommodate the English speakers rather than having them accommodate me, my tongue will be illegitimate.

I will no longer be made to feel ashamed of existing. I will have my voice: Indian, Spanish, white. I will have my serpent's tongue—my woman's voice, my sexual voice, my poet's voice. I will overcome the tradition of silence.

> *My fingers*
> *move sly against your palm*
> *Like women everywhere, we speak in code . . .*
> *-Melanie Kaye/Kantrowitz*

"Vistas," corridos, y comida: My Native Tongue

In the 1960s, I read my first Chicano novel. It was *City of Night* by John Rechy, a gay Texan, son of a Scottish father and a Mexican mother. For days I walked around in stunned amazement that a Chicano could write and could get published. When I read *I Am Joaquin* I was surprised to see a bilingual book by a Chicano in print. When I saw poetry written in Tex-Mex for the first time, a feeling of pure joy flashed through me. I felt like we really existed as a people. In 1971, when I started teaching High School English to Chicano students, I tried to supplement the required texts with works by Chicanos, only to be reprimanded and forbidden to do so by the principal. He claimed that I was supposed to teach "American" and English literature. At the risk of being fired, I swore my students to secrecy and slipped in Chicano short stories, poems, a play. In graduate school, while working toward a Ph.D., I had to "argue" with one advisor after the other, semester after semester, before I was allowed to make Chicano literature an area of focus.

Even before I read books by Chicanos or Mexicans, it was the Mexican movies I saw at the drive-in—the Thursday night special of $1.00 a carload—that gave me a sense of belonging. "*Vamonos a las Vistas,*" my mother would call out and we'd all—grandmother, brothers, sister and cousins—squeeze into the car. We'd wolf down cheese and bologna white bread sandwiches while watching Pedro Infante in melodramatic tear-jerkers like *Nosotros los pobres,* the first "real" Mexican movie (that was not an imitation of European movies). I remember seeing *Cuando los hijos se van* and surmising that all Mexican movies played up the love a mother has for her children and what ungrateful sons and daughters suffer when they are not devoted to their mothers. I remember the singing-type "westerns" of Jorge Negrete and Miguel Aceves Mejía. When watching Mexican movies, I felt a sense of homecoming as well as alienation. People who were to amount to something didn't go to Mexican movies, or *bailes* or tune their radios to *bolero, rancherita,* and *corrido* music.

The whole time I was growing up, there was *norteño* music sometimes called North Mexican border music, or Tex-Mex music, or Chicano music, or *cantina* (bar) music. I grew up listening to *conjuntos* three- or four-piece bands made up of folk musicians playing guitar, *bajo sexto,* drums and button accordion, which Chicanos had borrowed from the German immigrants who had come to Central Texas and Mexico to farm and build breweries. In the Rio Grande Valley, Steve Jordan and Little Joe Hernández were popular, and Flaco Jiménez was the accordian king. The rhythms of Tex-Mex music are those of the polka, also adapted from the Germans, who in turn had borrowed the polka from the Czechs and Bohemians.

I remember the hot, sultry evenings when *corridos*—songs of love and death on the Texas-Mexican borderlands—reverberated out of cheap amplifiers from the local cantinas and wafted in through my bedroom window.

Corridos first became widely used along the South Texas/Mexican border during the early conflict between Chicanos and Anglos. The *Corridos* are usually about Mexican heroes who do valiant deeds against the Anglo oppressors. Pancho Villa's song, "*La cucaracha,*" is the most famous one. *Corridos* of John F. Kennedy and his death are still very popular in the Valley. Older Chicanos remember Lydia Mendoza, one of the great border *corrido* singers who was called *la Gloria de Tejas.* Her "*El tango negro,*" sung during the Great Depression, made her a singer of the people. The everpresent *corridos* narrated one hundred years of border history, bringing news of events as well as entertaining. These folk musicians and folk songs are our chief cultural mythmakers, and they made our hard lives seem bearable.

I grew up feeling ambivalent about our music. Country-western and rock-and-roll had more status. In the 50s and 60s, for the slightly educated and *agringado* Chicanos, there existed a sense of shame at being caught listening to our music. Yet I couldn't stop my feet from thumping to the music, could not stop humming the words, nor hide from myself the exhilaration I felt when I heard it.

There are more subtle ways that we internalize identification, especially in the forms of images and emotions. For me food and certain smells are tied to my identity, to my homeland. Woodsmoke curling up to an immense blue sky; woodsmoke perfuming my grandmother's clothes, her skin. The stench of cow manure and the yellow patches on the ground; the crack of a .22 rifle and the reek of cordite. Homemade white cheese sizzling in a pan, melting inside a folded *tortilla.* My sister Hilda's hot, spicy *menudo, chile colorado* making it deep red, pieces of *panza* and hominy floating on top. My brother Carito barbequing fajitas in the backyard. Even now and 3,000 miles away, I can see my mother spicing the ground beef, pork and venison with *chile.* My mouth salivates at the thought of the hot steaming *tamales* I would be eating if I were home.

Si le preguntas a mi mamá, "¿Qué eres?"

"Identity is the essential core of who
we are as individuals,the conscious
experience of the self inside."—Kaufman

Nosotros los Chicanos straddle the borderlands. On one side of us, we are constantly exposed to the Spanish of the Mexicans, on the other side we hear the Anglos' incessant clamoring so that we forget our language. Among ourselves we don't say *nosotros los americanos, o nosotros los españoles, o nosotros los hispanos.* We say *nosotros los mexicanos* (by *mexicanos* we do not mean citizens of Mexico; we do not mean a national identity, but a racial one). We distinguish between *mexicanos del otro lado* and *Mexicanos de este lado.* Deep in our hearts we believe that being Mexican has nothing to do with which country one lives in. Being Mexican is a state of soul—not one of mind, not one of citizenship. Neither eagle nor serpent, but both. And like the ocean, neither animal respects borders.

> *Dime con quien andas y te diré quien eres.*
> *(Tell me who your friends are and I'll tell you who you are.)*
> —Mexican saying

Si le preguntas a mi mamá, "¿Qué eres?" te dirá, *"Soy mexicana."* My brothers and sister say the same. I sometimes will answer *"soy mexicana"* and at others will say *"soy Chicana"* o *"soy tejana."* But I identified as *"Raza"* before I ever identified as *"mexicana"* or "Chicana."

As a culture, we call ourselves Spanish when referring to ourselves as a linguistic group and when copping out. It is then that we forget our predominant Indian genes. We are 70–80% Indian. We call ourselves Hispanic or Spanish-American or Latin American or Latin when linking ourselves to other Spanish-speaking peoples of the Western hemisphere and when copping out. We call ourselves Mexican-American to signify we are neither Mexican nor American, but more the noun "American" than the adjective "Mexican" (and when copping out).

Chicanos and other people of color suffer economically for not acculturating. This voluntary (yet forced) alienation makes for psychological conflict, a kind of dual identity—we don't identify with the Anglo-American cultural values and we don't totally identify with the Mexican cultural values. We are a synergy of two cultures with various degrees of Mexicanness or Angloness. I have so internalized the borderland conflict that sometimes I feel like one cancels out the other and we are zero, nothing, no one. *A veces no soy nada ni nadie. Pero hasta cuando no lo soy, lo soy.* When not copping out, when we know we are more than nothing, we call ourselves Mexican, referring to race and ancestry; *mestizo* when affirming both our Indian and Spanish (but we hardly ever own our Black ancestry); Chicano when referring to a politically aware people born and/or raised in the U.S.; *Raza* when referring to Chicanos; *tejanos* when we are Chicanos from Texas.

Chicanos did not know we were a people until 1965 when Ceasar Chavez and the farmworkers united and *I Am Joaquín* was published and *la Raza Unida* party was formed in Texas. With that recognition, we became a distinct people. Something momentous happened to the Chicano soul—we became aware of our reality and acquired a name and a language (Chicano Spanish) that reflected that reality. Now that we had a name, some of the fragmented pieces began to fall together—who we were, what we were, how we had evolved. We began to get glimpses of what we might eventually become.

Yet the struggle of identities continues, the struggle of borders is our reality still. One day the inner struggle will cease and a true integration take place. In the meantime, *tenémos que hacer la lucha. ¿Quién está protegiendo los ranchos de mi gente? ¿Quién está tratando de cerrar la fisura entre la india y el blanco on nuestra sangre? El Chicano, si, el Chicano que anda como un ladrón en su propia casa.*

Los Chicanos, how patient we seem, how very patient. There is the quiet of the Indian about us. We know how to survive. When other races have given up their tongue, we've kept ours. We know what it is to live under the hammer blow of the dominant *norteamericano* culture. But more than we count the blows, we count the days the weeks the years the centuries the eons until the white laws and commerce and customs will rot in the deserts they've created, lie bleached. *Humildes* yet proud, *quietos* yet wild, *nosotros los mexicanos-Chicanos* will walk by the crumbling ashes as we go about our business. Stubborn, persevering, impenetrable as stone, yet possessing a malleability that renders us unbreakable, we, the *mestizas* and *mestizos,* will remain.

Questions for Discussion

1. In Anzaldúa's essay, the word "border" takes on multiple meanings. How does Anzaldúa use the term? How is it significant to her larger argument about the relationship between one's language and one's identity?

2. According to Anzaldúa, what is the "tradition of silence?" Within her various culture(s), who has been silenced most often? Why?

3. What is "linguistic terrorism?" How has linguistic terrorism functioned in Anzaldúa's life? Which incidents of linguistic terrorism described within the essay seem most powerful to you? Why?

Explorations

1. "How to Tame a Wild Tongue" blends a variety of languages, stylistic approaches, and forms in order to make a specific argument—or several arguments. For this exploration, respond to the following question in any form that you choose: How do Anzaldúa's rhetorical choices—style, vocabulary, form, argumentative strategies—"speak to" or reflect the subject matter of her piece?

2. Anzaldúa imports many other voices into her writing, using epigraphs (which appear before the piece even begins), extended quotations, and even excerpts from songs and poems, not all of which are in English. Choose three or four of these "other voices" and describe how they function in Anzaldúa's piece. What effects do they have on you as a reader?

3. In "Aria: A Memory of a Bilingual Childhood," Richard Rodriguez also describes his experiences as a bilingual in the United States. How would Anzaldúa respond to Rodriguez? Draft a brief response—using a form or forms that you believe Anzaldúa would find appropriate or useful—to Rodriguez in Anzaldúa's voice.

Formal Writing Assignments

1. The "English Only" movement has gained strength in recent years in the United States, particularly in communities where many non-native speakers of English have settled. Using the World Wide Web, locate at least two web sites devoted to the discussion of this movement or its opposition. Once you have studied the sites, draft an essay in which you define and discuss one of the concepts raised by Anzaldúa (i.e. "linguistic terrorism," "borderlands," "Chicano/a Spanish"), using the information gleaned from your web sites as an additional resource. Be sure to use the conventions for citation preferred by your composition teacher/ composition program.

2. In "How to Tame a Wild Tongue," Gloria Anzaldúa shares personal experiences that have helped

her to understand the relationship between her language and her identity. Anzaldúa has often referred to her own texts as "montage" or "assemblage" of stories arranged in a "mosaic pattern." For this assignment, draft your own "montage" of personal experiences designed to help you illustrate your own understanding of the relationship between your language practices and your identity.

Why Write?

Paul Auster

Paul Auster was born in New Jersey in 1947. Though he is best known as a novelist, his literary endeavors also include poetry, criticism, translations, and film. In addition to writing, Auster has held a variety of jobs in his lifetime, including work as a seaman, a teacher, and even a census taker. Readers often comment that Auster's novels are difficult to categorize because they do not fit our expectations. Though his novel *City of Glass* was nominated for an Edgar Award for best mystery of 1986, it is not like most mystery novels. For example, one of the story's characters is named Paul Auster, which asks the reader to consider the relationship between the author and his creation. In the following essay, Auster explores his own calling as a writer by considering several seemingly unrelated events in his life through writing.

Writing Before Reading

1. Recall a moment in your life that stands out in your memory and, you now realize, has changed your life in some way. Summon as many of the accompanying details as possible and describe that moment in writing. As you write, consider how each of your senses contributes to your recollection of that moment.

2. There are times when some people feel that they must respond to events in their lives by writing about them. If you have ever experienced the need to write like this, consider now the value to you of that writing. Did your writing help you cope with a difficult situation or experience more fully? A joyous one? Did you share your writing with anyone?

3. Have you ever read an account, say in a newspaper, of a moment you witnessed yourself, and wondered how the writer's version of events could be so different from your own memory? How did the other version differ from your own? What factors account for that difference?

Why Write?

1

A German friend tells of the circumstances that preceded the births of her two daughters.

Nineteen years ago, hugely pregnant and already several weeks past due, A. sat down on the sofa in her living room and turned on the television set. As luck would have it, the opening credits of a film were just coming onscreen. It was "The Nun's Story," a nineteen-fifties Hollywood drama starring Audrey Hepburn. Glad for the distraction, A. settled in to watch the movie and immediately got caught up in it. Halfway through, she went into labor. Her husband drove her to the hospital, and she never learned how the film turned out.

Three years later, pregnant with her second child, A. sat down on the sofa and turned on the television set once again. Once again a film was playing, and once again it was "The Nun's Story," with Audrey Hepburn. Even more remarkable (and A. was very emphatic about this point), she had tuned in to the film at the precise moment where she had left off three years earlier. This time, she was able to see the film through to the end. Less than fifteen minutes later, her water broke, and she went off to the hospital to give birth for the second time.

These two daughters are A.'s only children. The first labor was extremely difficult (my friend nearly didn't make it and was ill for many months afterward), but the second delivery went smoothly, with no complications of any kind.

2

Five years ago, I spent the summer with my wife and children in Vermont, renting an old, isolated farmhouse on the top of a mountain. One day, a woman from the next town stopped by to visit, along with her two children, a girl of four and a boy of eighteen months. My daughter had just turned three, and she and the girl enjoyed playing with each other. My wife and I sat down in the kitchen with our guest, and the children ran off to amuse themselves.

Five minutes later, there was a loud crash. The little boy had wandered into the front hall at the other end of the house. Since my wife had put a vase of flowers in that hall just two hours earlier, it wasn't difficult to guess what had happened. I didn't have to look to know that the floor would be covered with broken glass and a pool of water—along with the stems and petals of a dozen scattered flowers.

I was annoyed. "Goddam kids," I said to myself. "Goddam people with their goddam clumsy kids. Who gave them the right to drop by without calling first?"

I told my wife that I'd clean up the mess, and so while she and our visitor continued their conversation I gathered up a broom, a dustpan, and some towels and marched off to the front of the house.

My wife had put the flowers on a wooden trunk that sat just below the staircase railing. This staircase was especially steep and narrow, and there was a large window not more than a yard from the bottom step. I mention this geography because it's important. Where things were has everything to do with what happened next.

I was about half finished with the cleanup job when my daughter rushed out from her room onto the second-floor landing. I was close enough to the foot of the stairs to catch a glimpse of her (a couple of steps back and she would have been blocked from view), and in that brief moment I saw that she had that high-spirited, utterly happy expression that has filled my middle age with such overpowering gladness. Then, an instant later, before I could even say hello, she tripped. The toe of her sneaker had caught on the landing, and just like that, without any cry or warning, she was sailing through air. I don't mean to suggest that she was falling or tumbling or bouncing down the steps. I mean to say that she was flying. The stumble had literally launched her into space, and from the trajectory of her flight I could see that she was heading straight for the window.

What did I do? I don't know what I did. I was on the wrong side of the bannister when I saw her trip. By the time she was midway between the landing and the window I was standing on the bottom step of the staircase. How did I get there? It was no more than a question of several feet, but it hardly seems possible to cover that distance in that amount of time which is next to no time at all. Nevertheless, I was there, and the moment I got there I looked up, opened my arms, and caught her.

3

I was fourteen. For the third year in a row, my parents had sent me to a summer camp in New York State. I spent the bulk of my time playing basketball and baseball, but as it was a coed camp there were other activities as well: evening "socials," the first awkward grapplings with girls, panty raids, the usual adolescent shenanigans. I also remember smoking cheap cigars on the sly, "Frenching" beds, and massive water-balloon fights.

None of this is important. I simply want to underscore what a vulnerable age fourteen can be. No longer a child, not yet an adult, you bounce back and forth between who you were and who you are about to become. In my own case, I was still young enough to think that I had a legitimate shot at playing in the major leagues, but old enough to be questioning the existence of God. I had read the "Communist Manifesto," and yet I still enjoyed watching Saturday-morning cartoons. Every time I saw my face in the mirror, I seemed to be looking at someone else.

There were about sixteen or eighteen boys in my group. Most of us had been together for several years, but a couple of newcomers had also joined us that summer. One was named Ralph. He was a quiet kid without much enthusiasm for dribbling basketballs and hitting the cutoff man, and while no one gave him a particularly hard time, he had trouble blending in. He had flunked a couple of subjects that year, and most of his free periods were spent being tutored by one of the counsellors. It was a little sad, and I felt sorry for him— but not too sorry, not sorry enough to lose any sleep over it.

Our counsellors were all New York college students from Brooklyn and Queens. Wisecracking basketball players, future dentists, accountants, and teachers, city kids to their very bones. Like most true New Yorkers, they persisted in calling the ground the "floor," even when all that was under their feet was grass, pebbles, and dirt. The trappings of traditional summer-camp life were as alien to them as the I.R.T. is to an Iowa farmer. Canoes, lanyards, mountain climbing, pitching tents, singing around the campfire were nowhere to be found in the inventory of their concerns. They could drill us on the finer points of setting picks and boxing out for rebounds; otherwise they horsed around and told jokes.

Imagine our surprise, then, when one afternoon our counsellor announced that we were going for a hike in the woods. He had been seized by an inspiration and wasn't going to let anyone talk him out of it. Enough basketball, he said. We're surrounded by nature, and it's time we took advantage of it and started acting like real campers—or words to that effect. And so, after the rest period that followed lunch, the whole gang of sixteen or eighteen boys, along with two counsellors, set off into the woods.

It was late July, 1961. Everyone was in a fairly buoyant mood, I remember, and half an hour or so into the trek most people agreed that the outing had been a good idea. No one had a compass, of course, or the slightest clue as to where we were going, but we were all enjoying ourselves, and if we happened to get lost, what difference would that make? Sooner or later we'd find our way back.

Then it began to rain. At first, it was barely noticeable, a few light drops falling between the leaves and branches, nothing to worry about. We walked on, unwilling to let a little water spoil our fun, but a couple minutes later it started coming down in earnest. Everyone got soaked, and the counsellors decided we that we should turn around and head back. The only problem was that no one knew where the camp was. The woods were thick, dense with clusters of trees and thorn-studded bushes, and we had woven this way and that, abruptly shifting directions in order to move on. To add to the confusion, it was becoming hard to see. The woods had been dark to begin with, but, with the rain falling and the sky turning black, it felt more like night than three or four in the afternoon.

Then the thunder started. And after the thunder the lightning started. The storm was directly on top of us, and it turned out to be the summer storm to end all summer storms. I have never seen weather like that before or since. The rain poured down on us so hard that it actually hurt; each time the thunder exploded, you could feel the noise vibrating inside your body. When the lightning came, it danced around us like spears. It was as if weapons had materialized out if thin air—a sudden flash that turned everything a bright, ghostly white. Trees were struck, and their branches began to smolder. Then it would go dark again for a moment, there would be another crash in the sky, and the lightning would return in a different spot.

The lightning was what scared all of us, of course, and in our panic we tried to run away from it. But the storm was too big, and everywhere we went we were met by more lightning. It was a helter-skelter stampede, a headlong rush in circles. Then, suddenly, someone spotted a clearing in the woods. A brief dispute broke out whether it was it was safer to go into the open or continue to stand under the trees. The voice arguing for the open won, and we ran in the direction of the clearing.

It was a small meadow, most likely a pasture that belonged to a local farm, and to get to it we had to crawl under a barbed-wire fence. One by one, we got down on our bellies and and inched our way through. I was in the middle of the line, directly behind Ralph. Just as he went under the barbed wire, there was another flash of lightning. I was two or three feet away, but, because of the rain pounding against my eyelids, I had trouble making out what happened. All I knew was that Ralph had stopped moving. I figured that he had been stunned, so I crawled past him under the fence. Once I was on the other side, I took hold of his arm and dragged him through.

I don't know how long we stayed in the that field. An hour, I would guess, and the whole time we were there the rain and lightning and thunder continued to crash down upon us. It was a storm ripped from the pages of the Bible, and it went on and on and on, as if it would never end.

Two or three boys were hit by something—perhaps by lightning, perhaps by the shock of the lightning as it struck the ground near them—and the meadow began to fill with their moans. Other boys wept and prayed. Still others, fear in their voices, tried to give sensible advice. Get rid of everything metal, they said; metal attracts the lightning. We took off our belts and threw them away from us.

I don't remember saying anything. I don't remember crying. Another boy and I kept ourselves busy trying to take care of Ralph. He was still unconscious. We rubbed his hands and arms, we held down his tongue so he wouldn't swallow it, we told him to hang in there. After a while, his skin began to take on a bluish tinge. His body seemed colder to the touch, but in spite of the mounting evidence it never occurred to me that he wasn't going to come around. I was only fourteen years old, after all, and what did I know? I had never seen a dead person before.

It was the barbed wire that did it, I suppose. The other boys hit by the lightning went numb, felt pain in their limbs for an hour or so, and then recovered. But Ralph had been under the fence when the lightning struck and he had been electrocuted on the spot.

Later on, when they told me he was dead, I learned that there was an eight-inch burn across his back. I remember trying to absorb this news and telling myself that life would never feel the same to me again. Strangely enough, I didn't think about how I had been right next to him when it happened. I didn't think, "One or two seconds later and it would have been me." What I thought about was holding his tongue and looking down at his teeth. His mouth had been set in a slight grimace, and, with his lips partly open, I had spent an hour looking down at the tips of his teeth. Thirty-four years later, I still remember them. And his half-closed, half-open eyes. I remember those, too.

4

Not many years ago, I received a letter from a woman who lives in Brussels. In it, she told me the story of a friend of hers, a man she has known since childhood.

In 1940, this man joined the Belgian Army. When the country fell to the Nazis later that year, he was captured and sent to a prisoner-of-war camp in Germany. He remained there until the war ended, in 1945.

Prisoners were allowed to correspond with Red Cross workers back in Belgium. The man was arbitrarily assigned a pen pal—a Red Cross nurse from Brussels—and for the next five years he and this woman exchanged letters every month, Over the course of time, they became fast friends. At a certain point (I'm not exactly sure how long this took), they understood that something more than friendship had developed between them. The correspondence went on, growing more intimate with each exchange, and at last they declared their love for each other. Was such a thing possible? They had never seen each other, had never spent a minute in each other's company.

After the war was over, the man was released from prison and returned to Brussels. He met the nurse, the nurse met him, and neither was disappointed. A short time later, they were married.

Years went by. They had children, they grew older, the world became a slightly different world. Their son completed his studies in Belgium and went off to do graduate work in Germany. At the university there, he fell in love with a young German woman. He wrote his parents and told them that he intended to marry her.

The parents on both sides couldn't have been happier for their children. The two families arranged to meet, and on the appointed day the German family showed up at the house of the Belgian family in Brussels. As the German father walked into the living room and the Belgian father rose to welcome him, the two men looked into each other's eyes and recognized each other. Many years had passed, but neither one was in any doubt as to who the other was. At one time in their lives, they had seen each other every day. The German father had been a guard in the prison camp, where the Belgian father had spent the war.

As the woman who wrote me the letter hastened to add, there was no bad blood between them. However monstrous the German regime might have been, the German father had done nothing during those five years to turn the Belgian father against him.

These two men are now the best of friends. The greatest joy in both their lives is the grandchildren they have in common.

5

I was eight years old. At that moment in my life, nothing was more important to me than baseball. My team was the New York Giants, and I followed the doings of those men in the black-and-orange caps with all the devotion of a true believer. Even now, remembering that team—which no longer exists, which played in a ballpark that no longer exists—I can reel off the names of nearly every player on the roster. Alvin Dark, Whitey Lockman, Don Mueller, Johnny Antonelli, Monte Irvin. Hoyt Wilhelm. But none was greater, none more perfect nor more deserving of worship than Willie Mays, the incandescent Say Hey kid.

That spring, I was taken to my first big league game. Friends of my parents had box seats at the Polo Grounds, and one April night a group of us went to watch the Giants play the Millwaukee Braves. I don't know who won. I can't recall a single detail of the game, but I do remember that after the game was over, my parents and their friends sat talking in their seats until all the other spectators had left. It got so late that we had to walk across the diamond and leave by the center field exit, which was the only one still open. As it happened, that exit was right below the players' locker rooms.

Just as we approached the wall, I caught sight of Willie Mays. There was no question about who it was. It was Willie Mays, already out of uniform and standing there in his street clothes not ten feet away from me. I managed to keep my legs moving in his direction and then, mustering every ounce of my courage, I forced some words out of my mouth. "Mr. Mays," I said, "could I please have your autograph?"

He had to have been all of twenty-four years old, but I couldn't bring myself to pronounce his first name.

His response to my question was brusque but amiable. "Sure, kid, sure," he said. "You got a pencil?" He was so full of life, I remember, so full of youthful energy, that he kept bouncing up and down as he spoke.

I didn't have a pencil, so I asked my father if I could borrow his. He didn't have one, either. Nor did my mother. Nor, as it turned out, did any of the other grownups.

The great Willie Mays stood there watching in silence. When it became clear that no one in the group had anything to write with, he turned to me and shrugged. "Sorry, kid," he said. "Ain't got no pencil, can't give no autograph." And then he walked out of the ballpark into the night.

I didn't want to cry, but tears started falling down my cheeks, and there was nothing I could do to stop them. Even worse, I cried all the way home in the car. Yes, I was crushed with disappointment, but I was also revolted at myself for not being able to control those tears. I wasn't a baby. I was eight years old, and big kids weren't supposed to cry over things like that. Not only did I not have Willie Mays' autograph, I didn't have anything else, either. Life had put me to the test and in all respects I had found myself wanting.

After that night, I started carrying a pencil with me wherever I went. It became a habit of mine never to leave the house with out making sure I had a pencil in my pocket. It's not that I had any particular plans for that pencil, but I didn't want to be unprepared. I had been caught empty-handed once, and I wasn't about to let it happen again.

If nothing else the years have taught me this: If there is a pencil in your pocket, there's a good chance that one day you'll feel tempted to start using it. As I like to tell my children, that's how I became a writer.

Questions for Discussion

1. In this essay, Paul Auster writes that he tells his children he became a writer thanks to his habit of carrying around a pencil, which he developed after losing the opportunity to get an autograph from Willie Mays. In fact, Auster is saying much more about why he writes. Though he does not answer the question "Why Write?" directly, what does the essay suggest that Auster's real answer to this question would be?

2. What, if any, are the threads that connect sections 1, 2, 3, 4, and 5 of this essay? What similarities do you see in their form? Their content? How are the sections different from each other? Why do you think Auster chose to put these five sections in the order in which they appear?

3. The events Auster describes in the sections of this essay would have occurred whether or not Auster wrote about them. How might a writer's perception of events such as these be changed by the process of writing about them? Are people's memories of events altered by the act of writing about them? Is the writer changed by this process?

Explorations

1. Each of the vignettes that make up "Why Write?" could be viewed as an interesting story from the author's past. Each one, however, also reveals something about the author's beliefs and values. All of the essays, for example, touch in some way on the issue of family. Identify some of the other themes Auster develops through this essay.

2. Recall a moment from your life that you consider to have been life-defining in some way, and in writing describe that moment in as much detail as possible. When you have completed this description, add a sentence specifying exactly what this moment meant to you. Which version of your writing do you believe to be more effective, the version with or without the concluding sentence?

3. The title of this essay implies that the author's purpose is to say something about his motivation for expressing himself in written form. How do you believe Auster's motivation for writing differs from that of other authors in this unit? Why does Gloria Anzaldua write? John Hockenberry? Beth Brant? Explore your thoughts on how written expression differs from spoken expression.

Formal Writing Assignments

1. In an essay modeled after "Why Write?," choose three seemingly disparate moments from your life and describe them with the same level of detail and description you found in Auster's essay. Try to make clear to a reader through your choice of these moments something about who you are and what you believe to be important.

2. Find a photograph of you, taken when you were very young but old enough to have some memory of the moment when the photo was taken. Describe not only the photograph but also the events that led up to it. What other memories does the photograph trigger for you? In an essay, argue for or against the importance of recording one's past in photography or writing. Try to answer these questions: Which is a more accurate version of past events, the written or photographic? What elements of an event are missing from written or photographic records of that event?

"Vietnam Revisited"

Earl S. Braggs

Earl Braggs, a native of Wilmington, North Carolina, now teaches at the University of Tennessee, Chattanooga. At UTC, Braggs teaches fiction writing, poetry, and African-American literature; he is also a practitioner of writing, as evidenced by this poem, which is selected from his 1992 collection, *Hat Dancer Blue*. Additional publications include his recent collection of poems, *Walking Back from Woodstock*, and a novel-in-progress entitled *Looking for Jack Kerouac*.

Writing Before Reading

1. What do you know about the Vietnam War? How have you received this information? Write down as much as you can recall of what you know.

2 Think of a memory which means a lot to you. Which senses predominate in your memory? Record the memory on paper, paying special attention to those senses. How would you convey those senses to someone else, so that she could re-experience your original memory?

3. What does personal experience mean? If someone has experienced firsthand, does that make the experience true? Write a few sentences about how you think experience should be valued.

Vietnam Revisited

"I spent a year in the mouth of a dragon before they shipped me here,"
was all he said as I took a seat
across the aisle from him.
Maybe fifty miles of horses and cows passed before I turned
to look at him.

The war was never real to me until I looked
into those wild army-green eyes
scanning the purple red horizon, blazing
like an M-16 with a full metal jacket.
Those eyes say he sees everything—things that are there
and things that are not there. He smiles at me, blinking
he shoots at anything that hints a move.

The day turned dusty gray and then pitch black and haunting.
We talked from Macon until we were lost in the red Georgia hills
of Southeast Asia. He told me about the night sky over Danang
and how the stars are always brightest just before the clouds come
and color the night fleshtone pink.
The sky was so light you could see the face of the enemy
like a flash photograph.

He told how you couldn't smell heroin burning
until it burned you in two and how he was a tunnel rat,
the bravest man in his platoon crawling down into that black hole,
not coming up until the full moon showed its face on the other end.
Listening, I heard grenades

rolling around on the floor beneath my feet. I could see war
raging in his twenty-two-year-old face like a wild horse captured
in the Saigon heat, a street covered with broken bottles
of fear spilling onto the rear view mirror face of the bus driver
driving troops into the mouth of the Tet Offensive.

Into the eyes of your foxhole mate who turned out to be Charlie,
tapping you on the shoulder to wake you with a single round
between the eyes point blank, straight as a dart thrown at a bull
paralyzed from the head down, painted dead red on a board
in a front street Vietnam bar full of drunk soldiers and sailors
unaware that tomorrow they will wake up dead
with purple hearts dangling around their necks
decked out in navy and army dress blue,
taking the slow train back to Georgia.
Your mother will not recognize you
laid out and draped in blood, white and
"Boo! I scared you," he said loud enough for the driver to hear.

Somewhere along the way he opened a bottle and passed
it back and forth until everyone seated near had moved
into those red Georgia hills hiding their faces behind tall seats.

We talked about the WHITE ONLY bars on Tu Do Street and the
NOBODY-EVER-CALLED-ME-A-NIGGER-WHILE-I-WAS-TOTING-A-
BAZOOKA soulbrothers that kicked the door in like John Wayne,
how he used to smoke marijuana laced with mace and how he'd kick
Charlie in the ass and shoot him in the face and not blink an eye.
Then after a long silence, he told me about the night he died,
the night he got a telegram from home that read:

YOUR BABY BROTHER WAS KILLED YESTERDAY-STOP
THE POLICE SAID IT WAS SELF-DEFENSE-STOP

He turned and looked at me with those wild army-green eyes
and said
I was supposed to be the one to die I was supposed to be the one . . .

The words echoed and faded into the humming of the highway.
Everyone is asleep now except two cigarettes glowing orange
in the pitch black Vietnam night.

Questions for Discussion

1. Examine the language that Braggs uses. Are there any terms you don't understand? Is it important that you not understand them? Are you able to understand them from their context, and is that somehow significant?

2. Think about the genre of poetry and its conventions. Why is this genre more or less appropriate to the story being told? In what ways does it convey images and ideas? To what extent does the poem have rhythm and rhyme? How might these presences or absences be significant?

3. Look closely at Braggs' use of pronouns. Where do the shifts occur, and what do those signify about the meaning being told by the teller and heard by the listener? What do the pronouns indicate about the power of language to transport?

Explorations

1. In "Feathers a Thousand Li Away," Amy Tan suggests that language has the power to determine culture. That is, because the mother cannot speak the perfect American English she feels she needs to speak meaningfully to her daughter about Chinese culture, she never does speak to her. As a result, the daughter knows very little about her mother's culture and, arguably, about the mother herself. What kinds of language and consequent culture gaps like these can be found in Braggs' poem?

2. Braggs uses references to geographical areas as though the reader should know what these are and what they mean. What do these assumptions suggest about cultural memory? What does it mean if you know what Tu Do Street is, even though you've never experienced it yourself? What does it mean if you don't know what Tu Do Street is?

3. In her personal narrative, Peggy McIntosh suggests that when we do not challenge our assumptions about the way things are, we become complacent and "the way things are" become "the way things should be." How is Braggs challenging "the way things are"?

Formal Writing Assignments

1. Write an essay elaborating on Exploration #3. Look at Braggs' poem from a very specific level—use of pronouns, imagery, use of white space—to a more general level, in terms of message conveyed. Use McIntosh's point about challenging complacency to bolster your own argument.

2. Think about how Tim O'Brien in "How to Tell a True War Story" suggests how truth can be conveyed. Both Braggs and O'Brien want to convey something about the war; which is a "truer" way of telling?

3. Interview someone who has had firsthand experience of the Vietnam War. Record the results on paper. Then reflect: How does the story compare to Braggs' or O'Brien's? To what extent do you want, but feel unable, to challenge his or her story? How do that person's experience and your non-experience conflict or complement one another?

A Long Story

Beth Brant

A member of the Turtle Clan, a practitioner of Earth religion, and an advocate for environmental justice, Beth Brant has concerns about Native American traditions and social situations that serve as dominant themes in her writing. A writer and teacher of creative writing and native women's writing, Brant came to her occupation later in life. Not until the age of forty, after experiencing a vision of a bald eagle instructing her to become a writer, did Brant begin to write. After her marriage ended at the age of thirty-three, Brant came to terms with her lesbian sexuality, another prevalent theme in her writing. In her first published volume, *Mohawk Trail*, Brant writes about her multiple identities: her Mohawk heritage, her experiences as a woman, her early family life, and her sexual experiences. The following piece, "A Long Story," is part of this collection. In her efforts to persuade audiences to understand and sympathize with contemporary Native American culture, gay and lesbian communities, and working-class people, Brant believes that when "human beings feel, it changes things."

Writing Before Reading

1. Describe a family. Who is part of the family? How are they related to one another? Why did you choose to describe this type of family? What assumptions about family units shaped your description? Describe another family that challenges your assumptions.

2. Consider what it means to be a "good" parent and define the criteria for this person. In your writing, address the following questions: Who deserves to be a parent? Who decides who is allowed to be a parent? Is everyone afforded the same opportunity to have children? If there are differences among people's rights to parent, what are they?

3. Briefly outline your understanding of Native American history. How did the United States relate to Native Americans in establishing the country? Through what means did native peoples become "Americans"?

A Long Story

Dedicated to my great-grandmothers,
Eliza Powless and Catherine Brant

About 40 Indian children took the train at this depot for the Philadelphia
Indian School last Friday. They were accompanied by the government
agent, and seemed a bright looking lot.
—The Northern Observer
(Massena, New York, July 20, 1892)

*I am only beginning to understand what it means for a mother to lose
a child.*
—Anna Demeter, *Legal Kidnapping*
(Beacon Press, Boston, 1977)
1890

It has been two days since they came and took the children away. My body is greatly chilled. All our blankets have been used to bring me warmth. The women keep the fire blazing. The men sit. They talk among themselves. We are frightened by this sudden child-stealing. We signed papers, the agent said. This gave them rights to take our babies. It is good for them, the agent said. It will make them civilized, the agent said. I do not know *civilized.*

I hold myself tight in fear of flying apart in the air. The others try to feed me. Can they feed a dead woman? I have stopped talking. When my mouth opens, only air escapes. I have used up my sound screaming their names—She Sees Deer! He Catches The Leaves! My eyes stare at the room, the walls of scrubbed wood, the floor of dirt. I know there are people here, but I cannot see them. I see a darkness, like the lake at New Moon. Black, unmoving. In the center, a picture of my son and daughter being lifted onto the train. My daughter wearing the dark blue, heavy dress. All of the girls dressed alike. Never have I seen such eyes! They burn into my head even now. My son. His hair cut. Dressed as the white men, his arms and legs covered by cloth that made him sweat. His face, streaked with tears. So many children crying, screaming. The sun on our bodies, our heads. The train screeching like a crow, sounding like laughter. Smoke and dirt pumping out of the insides of the train. So many people. So many children. The women, standing as if in prayer, our hands lifted, reaching. The dust sifting down on our palms. Our palms making motions at the sky. Our fingers closing like the claws of the bear.

I see this now. The hair of my son held in my hands. I rub the strands, the heavy braids coming alive as the fire flares and casts a bright light on the black hair. They slip from my fingers and lie coiled on the ground. I see this. My husband picks up the braids, wraps them in cloth; he takes the pieces of our son away. He walks outside, the eyes of the people on him. I see this. He will find a bottle and drink with the men. Some of the women will join him. They will end the night by singing or crying. It is all the same. I see this. No sounds of children playing games and laughing. Even the dogs have ceased their noise. They lay outside each doorway, waiting. I hear this. The voices of children. They cry. They pray. They call me. *Nisten ha.** I hear this. *Nisten ha.*

1978

I am wakened by the dream. In the dream my daughter is dead. Her father is returning her body to me in pieces. He keeps her heart. I thought I screamed … *Patricia!* I sit up in bed, swallowing air as if for nourishment. The dream remains in the air. I rise to go to her room. Ellen tries to lead me back to bed, but I have to see once again. I open her door. She is gone. The room empty, lonely. They said it was in her best interests. How can that be? She is only six, a baby who needs her mothers. She loves us. This has not happened. I will not believe this. Oh, god I think I have died.

Night after night, Ellen holds me as I shake. Our sobs stifling the air in our room. We lie in our bed and try to give comfort. My mind can't think beyond last week when she left. I would have killed him if I'd had the chance! He took her hand and pulled her to the car. The look in his eyes of triumph. It was a contest to him, Patricia the prize. He will teach her to hate us. He will! I see her dear face. That face looking out the back window of his car. Her mouth forming the words *Mommy, Mama.* Her dark braids tied with red yarn. Her front teeth missing. Her overalls with the yellow flowers on the pocket, embroidered by Ellen's hands. So lovingly she sewed the yellow wool. Patricia waiting quietly until she

---

* Mother.

was finished. Ellen promising to teach her designs—chain stitch, french knot, split stitch. How Patricia told everyone that Ellen made the flower just for her. So proud of her overalls.

I open the closet door. Almost everything is gone. A few things hang there limp, abandoned. I pull a blue dress from the hanger and take it back to my room. Ellen tries to take it from me, but I hold on, the soft blue cotton smelling of my daughter. How is it possible to feel such pain and live? "Ellen?!" She croons my name. "Mary, Mary, I love you." She sings me to sleep.

1890

The agent was here to deliver a letter. I screamed at him and sent curses his way. I threw dirt in his face as he mounted his horse. He thinks I'm a crazy woman and warns me, "You better settle down, Annie." What can they do to me? I am a crazy woman. This letter hurts my hand. It is written in their hateful language. It is evil, but there is a message for me.

I start the walk up the road to my brother. He works for the whites and understands their meanings. I think about my brother as I pull the shawl closer to my body. It is cold now. Soon there will be snow. The corn has been dried and hangs from our cabin, waiting to be used. The corn never changes. My brother is changed. He says that I have changed and bring shame to our clan. He says I should accept the fate. But I do not believe in the fate of child-stealing. There is evil here. There is much wrong in our village. My brother says I am a crazy woman because I howl at the sky every evening. He is a fool. I am calling the children. He says the people are becoming afraid of me because I talk to the air and laugh like the raven overhead. But I am talking to the children. They need to hear the sound of me. I laugh to cheer them. They cry for us.

This letter burns my hands. I hurry to my brother. He has taken the sign of the wolf from over the doorway. He pretends to be like those who hate us. He gets more and more like the child-stealers. His eyes move away from mine. He takes the letter from me and begins the reading of it. I am confused. This letter is from two strangers with the names Martha and Daniel. They say they are learning civilized ways. Daniel works in the fields, growing food for the school. Martha cooks and is being taught to sew aprons. She will be going to live with the schoolmaster's wife. She will be a live-in girl. What is a *live-in girl?* I shake my head. The words sound the same to me. I am afraid of Martha and Daniel, these strangers who know my name. My hands and arms are becoming numb.

I tear the letter from my brother's fingers. He stares at me, his eyes traitors in his face. He calls after me, "Annie! Annie!" That is not my name! I run to the road. That is not my name! There is no Martha! There is no Daniel! This is witch work. The paper burns and burns. At my cabin, I quickly dig a hole in the field. The earth is hard and cold, but I dig with my nails. I dig, my hands feeling weaker. I tear the paper and bury the scraps. As the earth drifts and settles, the names Martha and Daniel are covered. I look to the sky and find nothing but endless blue. My eyes are blinded by the color. I begin the howling.

1978

When I get home from work, there is a letter from Patricia. I make coffee and wait for Ellen, pacing the rooms of our apartment. My back is sore from the line, bending over and down, screwing the handles on the doors of the flashy cars moving by. My work protects me from questions, the guys making jokes at my expense. But some of them touch my shoulder lightly and briefly as a sign of understanding. The few women, eyes averted or smiling in sympathy. No one talks. There is no time to talk. No room to talk, the noise taking up all space and breath.

I carry the letter with me as I move from room to room. Finally I sit at the kitchen table, turning the paper around in my hands. Patricia's printing is large and uneven. The stamp has been glued on half–heartedly and is coming loose. Each time a letter arrives, I dread it, even as I long to hear from my child. I hear Ellen's key in the door. She walks into the kitchen, bringing the smell of the hospital with her. She comes toward me, her face set in new lines, her uniform crumpled and stained, her brown hair pulled back in an imitation of a french twist. She knows there is a letter. I kiss her and bring mugs of coffee to the table. We look at each other. She reaches for my hand, bringing it to her lips. Her hazel eyes are steady in her round face.

I open the letter. *Dear Mommy. I am fine. Daddy got me a new bike. My big teeth are coming in. We are going to see Grandma for my birthday. Daddy got me new shoes. Love, Patricia.* She doesn't ask about Ellen. I imagine her father standing over her, coaxing her, coaching her. The letter becomes ugly. I tear it in bits and scatter them out the window. The wind scoops the pieces into a tight fist before strewing them in the street. A car drives over the paper, shredding it to garbage and mud.

Ellen makes a garbled sound. " I'll leave. If it will make it better, I'll leave." I quickly hold her as the dusk moves into the room and covers us. "Don't leave. Don't leave." I feel her sturdy back shiver against my hands. She kisses my throat, and her arms tighten as we move closer. "Ah, Mary, I love you so much." As the tears threaten our eyes, the taste of salt is on our lips and tongues. We stare into ourselves, touching the place of pain, reaching past the fear, the guilt, the anger, the loneliness.

We go to our room. It is beautiful again. I am seeing it new. The sun is barely there. The colors of cream, brown, green mixing with the wood floor. The rug with its design of wild birds. The black ash basket glowing on the dresser, holding a bouquet of dried flowers bought at a vendor's stand. I remember the old woman, laughing and speaking rapidly in Polish as she wrapped the blossoms in newspaper. Ellen undresses me as I cry. My desire for her breaking through the heartbreak we share. She pulls the covers back, smoothing the white sheets, her hands repeating the gestures done at work. She guides me onto the cool material. I watch her remove the uniform of work. An aide to nurses. A healer of spirit.

She comes to me full in flesh. My hands are taken with the curves and soft roundness of her. She covers me with the beating of her heart. The rhythm steadies me. Heat is centering me. I am grounded by the peace between us. I smile at her face above me, round like a moon, her long hair loose and touching my breasts. I take her breast in my hand, bring it to my mouth, suck her as a woman—in desire, in faith. Our bodies join. Our hair braids together on the pillow. Brown, black, silver, catching the last light of the sun. We kiss, touch, move to our place of power. Her mouth, moving over my body, stopping at curves and swells of skin, kissing, removing pain. Closer, close, together, woven, my legs are heat, the center of my soul is speaking to her. I am sliding into her, her mouth is medicine, her heart is the earth, we are dancing with flying arms, I shout, I sing, I weep salty liquid, sweet and warm it coats her throat. This is my life. I love you, Ellen, I love you, Mary, I love, we love.

1891

The moon is full. The air is cold. This cold strikes at my flesh as I remove my clothes and set them on fire in the withered cornfield. I cut my hair, the knife sawing through the heavy mass. I bring the sharp blade to my arms, legs, and breasts. The blood trickles like small red rivers down my body. I feel nothing. I throw the tangled webs of my hair into the flames. The smell, like a burning animal, fills my nostrils. As the fire stretches to touch the stars, the people come out to watch me—the crazy woman. The ice in the air touches me.

They caught me as I tried to board the train and search for my babies. The white men tell my husband to watch me. I am dangerous. I laugh and laugh. My husband is good only for tipping bottles and swallowing anger. He looks at me, opening his month and making no sound. His eyes are dead. He wanders from the cabin and looks out on the corn. He whispers our names. He calls after the children. He is a dead man.

Where have they taken the children? I ask the question of each one who travels the road past our door. The women come and we talk. We ask and ask. They say there is nothing we can do. The white man is like a ghost. He slips in and out where we cannot see. Even in our dreams he comes to take away our questions. He works magic that resists our medicine. This magic has made us weak. What is the secret about them? Why do they want our children? They sent the Blackrobes many years ago to teach us new magic. It was evil! They lied and tricked us. They spoke of gods who would forgive us if we believed as they do. They brought the rum with the cross. This god is ugly! He killed our masks. He killed our men. He sends the women screaming at the moon in terror. They want our power. They take our children to remove the inside of them. Our power. They steal our food, our sacred rattle, the stories, our names. What is left?

I am a crazy woman. I look to the fire that consumes my hair and see their faces. My daughter. My son. They still cry for me, though the sound grows fainter. The wind picks up their keening and brings it to me. The sound has bored into my brain. I begin howling. At night I dare not sleep. I fear the dreams. It is too terrible, the things that happen there. In my dream there is wind and blood moving as a stream. Red, dark blood in my dream. Rushing for our village. The blood moves faster. There are screams of wounded people. Animals are dead, thrown in the blood stream. There is nothing left. Only the air echoing nothing. Only the earth soaking up blood, spreading it in the four directions, becoming a thing there is no name for. I stand in the field watching the fire. The People watching me. We are waiting, but the answer is not clear yet. A crazy woman. That is what they call me.

1979

After taking a morning off work to see my lawyer, I come home, not caring if I call in. Not caring, for once, at the loss in pay. Not caring. My lawyer says there is nothing more we can do. I must wait. As if there has been something other than waiting. He has custody and calls the shots. We must wait and see how long it takes for him to get tired of being a mommy and a daddy. So I wait.

I open the door to Patricia's room. Ellen and I keep it dusted and cleaned in case my baby will be allowed to visit us. The yellow and blue walls feel like a mockery. I walk to the windows, begin to systematically tear down the curtains. I slowly start to rip the cloth apart. I enjoy hearing the sounds of destruction. Faster, I tear the material into strips. What won't come apart with my hands, I pull at with my teeth. Looking for more to destroy, I gather the sheets and bedspread in my arms and wildly shred them to pieces. Grunting and sweating, I am pushed by rage and the searing wound in my soul. Like a wolf, caught in a trap, gnawing at her own leg to set herself free, I begin to beat my breasts to deaden the pain inside. A noise gathers in my throat and finds the way out. I begin a scream that turns to howling, then becomes hoarse choking. I want to take my fists, my strong fists, my brown fists, and smash the world until it bleeds. Bleeds! And all the judges in their flapping robes, and the fathers who look for revenge, are ground, ground into dust and disappear with the wind.

The word *lesbian*. Lesbian. The word that makes them panic, makes them afraid, makes them destroy children. The word that dares them. Lesbian. *I am one.* Even for Patricia, even for her, *I will not cease to be!* As I kneel amid the colorful scraps, Raggedy Ann's smiling up at me, my chest gives a sigh. My heart slows to its normal speed. I feel the blood pumping outward to my veins, carrying nourishment and life. I strip the room naked. I close the door.

Thanks so much to Chrystos for the title. Thanks to Gloria Anzaldúa for encouraging the writing of this story.

Reprinted by permission of Firebrand Books from *Mohawk Trail* (Ithaca, NY: Firebrand Books, 1985).

Questions for Discussion

1. What is the significance of the title? What is the "long story"?

2. Brant's twin narratives are divided by eighty-eight years. What is the rhetorical impact of separating the two women's stories by this amount of time? What do the stories have in common?

3. Both stories contain a letter from the children to their mothers. What do these letters convey or symbolize? What do they reveal about the childrens' relationship to their mothers?

Explorations

1. Brant employs an unconventional narrative structure of time to convey the point of her story. In this instance, form affects meaning. Select another story from Unit I that challenges writing conventions. Does its message have any connections to Brant's? Are certain types of stories more effective if they are told in non-traditional ways? Who might employ these methods and why?

2. The narrator of the 1979 section ends her story by identifying the word lesbian as the "word that makes them afraid, makes them destroy children . . . [t]he word that dares them." (24) The narrator of the 1890 story calls herself a "crazy woman" (23). Why does each woman's identity evoke the reactions that they do? What is powerful about these particular identities, given the particular historical contexts of the stories?

3. Why is the name "lesbian" so important to the 1979 narrator? Reread "She Unnames Them" and speculate as to what Ursula Le Guin's narrator would say about the value of this attachment to a name. Is naming oneself "lesbian" a different type of naming from Adam's methods of labeling the animals? Why or why not?

Formal Writing Assignments

1. In the 1891 story, the narrator is a Native American woman relating the loss of her children to the Blackcoats. Research this period in history using a variety of sources. Did you find any historical account that would explain this scenario? If you did, what was the source? If you did not, why was it missing? Use your research findings to explain the importance of this story in a historical context.

2. Using a media source (television, film, magazine, music, advertisement), find some representation of sexuality that challenges mainstream notions. What is challenging about this representation? What values would you associate with the representation? What does your interpretation of this image say about your values?

Call to A.G. Bell

Brenda Brueggemann

Brenda Brueggemann serves as director of the University Writing Center at Ohio State University, where she is also an Associate Professor of English. A graduate of the University of Louisville, Brueggemann has in only a few years established herself as a leading voice in the interdisciplinary field of disability studies. "Call to A.G. Bell," which appears as an Interlude in *Lend Me Your Ear: Rhetorical Constructions of Deafness*, illustrates the range of Brueggemann's skills as a writer. A poet, essayist, and theorist, her academic interests include qualitative research, literacy, rhetoric, deaf and disability studies. She is also co-editor of *Disability Discourses: A Sourcebook on Disability Studies in Language and Literature*.

Writing Before Reading

1. In what ways did your primary and secondary educational experiences function to shape your thinking on social issues? For example, did education on drugs, alcohol, or sexuality change your values or behaviors?

2. Write about a time when someone expected you to know more about a subject then you actually did. Who was the person you had this exchange with? A parent? A teacher? A friend? A stranger? What type of knowledge did he/she expect you to have and why might they have had unrealistic expectations? How did it feel to find yourself unable to meet those expectations? How did you handle the situation?

3. How do you define poetry? Imagine a poem. Describe its length, its style, its layout on the page. What kind of tone do you imagine most poetry to have? What kinds of issues have been most commonly addressed in the poetry you've come across? After reading Bruggemann's work, look back at this list and consider the ways in which her poetry did or did not meet your expectations.

Call to A.G. Bell

Got a quarter
so I call you up on the telephone
ring-ring-ring
but only your wife and mother are home,
so no one answers.
You out charting and graphing
marriages and progeny
of the deaf,
while only your wife and mother-
deaf—
are home. (ringed in)
So I leave a message
after the beep—
but actually,
it's before the beep because

the beep
I can not hear.
So, you miss half of it.
I start again.
This time, I mouth the message—
so you can lipread.
But you don't get it,
can't tell my b's from my p's,
my f's from my v's.
So I try again
Slowing . . .   down . . .
emph-a-siz-ing
each
W-O-R-D,
my face contorted, clown-like.
still,
that won't do.
(What are you, dumb?)
I try signing,
hands across space
in your face,
but you are horrified
by the spectacle of my body
moving
beyond speech,
and you avert your eyes.
Too late.
I have burned your retina,
salt-pillared you,
left you speechless.
And oh, the time is up,
message too long.
(It's taken 120 years to
get this call through.)
Sorry.

No wait—
I'll fax you the facts;
I'll send a video,
documentary of my life,
caption and all,
interpreter on standby;
or perhaps TTY or relay service;
an e-mail even,
coming through.

Let's "talk."

But oh—
now that I've gotten my medium,
I've forgotten my message.
(It wasn't important after all.)

-Brenda Jo Brueggemann

Poet's Note. A.G. Bell, inventor of the telephone, was also a foremost and formidable advocate of "oralism" for educating deaf people; he was involved in the Milan Conference of 1880, which succeeded in banishing sign language from deaf schools. He also conducted "research" that sought to verify his argument for not allowing deaf people to marry other deaf people—fueled by the fear that they would only have more deaf children and thereby, pollute the human race. His own mother and wife were deaf.

Questions for Discussion

1. Brueggemann uses Alexander Graham Bell as the named audience for this poem. In what ways is Brueggemann addressing Bell? To what others is the poem aimed? What in the poem suggests this to you?

2. Brueggemann ends her poem with a "Poet's Note" that outlines some rather disturbing information about Bell's political and social beliefs about deafness. What kind of effect did this note have on your readng? Why do you think Brueggemann placed it at the end of the poem? What would its effect have been if it had appeared as a head note?

3. What kinds of arguments does Brueggemann's poem make about the relationship between technology and deafness?

Explorations

1. The telephone, for hearing people, is a technological achievement of great significance, yet as Brueggemann's poem reminds us, that same technology further marginalizes members of the deaf community. What other scientific or technological advancements have disadvantaged people with disabilities?

2. Brueggemann's poem relates a number of means by which the poet/narrator attempts to communicate with Bell when simple telephone technology fails. What other means of communication does the poet attempt? What is Bell's response?

3. Brueggemann, like Hockenberry in his condemnation of an *Oprah* broadcast focusing on disabled couples, speaks with great power and conviction. What elements of Bell's politics and his technologies are most problematic for her? What do you make of her parenthetical comments, "(ringed in)" and "(What are you, dumb?)"

Formal Writing Assignments

1. Brueggemann's poem, like those of Jerome Stern in the next unit, is a cultural commentary and critique. Working with Brueggemann's poem as an outline of arguments, construct a prosaic version of her poem.

2. The issue of deafness has been widely discussed from medical, social, and political perspectives. There are those who argue that deafness is not a disability at all, but merely a different way of perceiving the environment. As a starting point for an inquiry into Deaf culture and the deaf rights movement, visit the website of Gallaudet University (www.gallaudet.edu) in Washington DC, an institution created to enhance the lives of the deaf and hard of hearing. In an essay based on your research, summarize history of the deaf rights movement and analyze its impact on all Americans, not just the deaf.

Cathedral

Raymond Carver

Raymond Carver was born in Catskanie, Oregon, in 1939, and lived in Port Angeles, Washington, until his death in 1988. He was a Guggenheim Fellow in 1979 and was twice awarded grants from the National Endowment for the Arts. Considered by many to be both a contemporary master and innovator of the American short story, Carver was elected to the American Academy and Institute of Arts and Letters, and, in 1988, received a Brandeis Citation for fiction. He is the author of five story collections, five books of poetry, and two prose/poetry collections.

In various interviews, Carver and his friends discussed the autobiographical impulse behind the story "Cathedral." His wife, poet Tess Gallagher, and presumably the real-life model for the wife in the story, wrote and published her own fictionalized account of the events. As is so often the case, this story is, then, an intersection of personal history and fiction and, like O'Brien's "How to Tell a True War Story," blurs the boundaries between historical/factual truth and remembered/reported truth. The title selection of Carver's fourth collection, "Cathedral" was selected for *The Best American Short Stories 1982*.

Writing Before Reading

1. Write about a time when you found it necessary to communicate with someone who was in some way drastically different from you. How did it feel to be in that position, and how did you attempt (successfully or unsuccessfully) to relate to the person in question?

2. Imagine that your audience has never seen a cathedral (or even a picture of one). In a few paragraphs, try to describe one as vividly as possible.

3. Imagine that you've been blind since birth. Try, without using any visual details, to describe the face of someone you know well.

Cathedral

This blind man, an old friend of my wife's, he was on his way to spend the night. His wife had died. So he was visiting the dead wife's relatives in Connecticut. He called my wife from his in-laws'. Arrangements were made. He would come by train, a five-hour trip, and my wife would meet him at the station. She hadn't seen him since she worked for him one summer in Seattle ten years ago. But she and the blind man had kept in touch. They made tapes and mailed them back and forth. I wasn't enthusiastic about his visit. He was no one I knew. And his being blind bothered me. My idea of blindness came from the movies. In the movies, the blind moved slowly and never laughed. Sometimes they were led by seeing-eye dogs. A blind man in my house was not something I looked forward to.

That summer in Seattle she had needed a job. She didn't have any money. The man she was going to marry at the end of the summer was in officers' training school. He didn't have any money, either. But she was in love with the guy, and he was in love with her, etc. She'd seen something in the paper: HELP WANTED—*Reading to Blind Man*, and a telephone number. She phoned and went over, was hired on the spot. She'd worked with this blind man all summer. She read stuff to him, case studies, reports, that sort of thing. She helped him organize his little office in the county social-service department. They'd become good friends, my wife and the blind man. How do I know these things? She told me. And she told me something else. On her last day in the office, the blind man asked if he could touch her face. She agreed to this. She told me he touched his fingers to every part of her face, her nose—even her neck! She never forgot it. She even tried to write a poem about it. She was always trying to write a poem. She wrote a poem or two every year, usually after something really important had happened to her.

When we first started going out together, she showed me the poem. In the poem, she recalled his fingers and the way they had moved around over her face. In the poem, she talked about what she had felt at the time, about what went through her mind when the blind man touched her nose and lips. I can remember I didn't think much of the poem. Of course, I didn't tell her that. Maybe I just don't understand poetry. I admit it's not the first thing I reach for when I pick up something to read.

Anyway, this man who'd first enjoyed her favors, the officer-to-be, he'd been her childhood sweetheart. So okay. I'm saying that at the end of the summer she let the blind man run his hands over her face, said good-bye to him, married her childhood etc., who was now a commissioned officer, and she moved away from Seattle. But they'd kept in touch, she and the blind man. She made the first contact after a year or so. She called him up one night from an Air Force base in Alabama. She wanted to talk. They talked. He asked her to send him a tape and tell him about her life. She did this. She sent the tape. On the tape, she told the blind man about her husband and about their life together in the military. She told the blind man she loved her husband but she didn't like it where they lived and she didn't like it that he was a part of the military-industrial thing. She told the blind man she'd written a poem and he was in it. She told him that she was writing a poem about what it was like to be an Air Force officer's wife. The poem wasn't finished yet. She was still writing it. The blind man made a tape. He sent her the tape. She made a tape. This went on for years. My wife's officer was posted to one base and then another. She sent tapes from Moody AFB, McGuire, McConnell, and finally Travis, near Sacramento, where one night she got to feeling lonely and cut off from people she kept losing in that moving-around life. She got to feeling she couldn't go it another step. She went in and swallowed all the pills and capsules in the medicine chest and washed them down with a bottle of gin. Then she got into a hot bath and passed out.

But instead of dying, she got sick. She threw up. Her officer—why should he have a name? He was the childhood sweetheart, and what more does he want?—came home from somewhere, found her, and called the ambulance. In time, she put it all on a tape and sent the tape to the blind man, Over the years, she put all kinds of stuff on tapes and sent the tapes off lickety-split. Next to writing a poem every year, I think it was her chief means of recreation. On one tape, she told the blind man she'd decided to live away from her officer for a time. On another tape, she told him about her divorce. She and I began going out, and of course she told her blind man about it. She told him everything, or so it seemed to me. Once she asked me if I'd like to hear the latest tape from the blind man. This was a year ago. I was on the tape, she said. So I said okay, I'd listen to it. I got us drinks and we settled down in the living room. We made ready to listen. First she inserted the tape into the player and adjusted a couple of dials. Then she pushed a lever. The tape squeaked and someone began to talk in this loud voice. She lowered the volume.

After a few minutes of harmless chitchat, I heard my own name in the mouth of this stranger, this blind man I didn't even know! And then this: "From all you've said about him, I can only conclude—" But we were interrupted, a knock at the door, something, and we didn't ever get back to the tape. Maybe it was just as well. I'd heard all I wanted to.

Now this same blind man was coming to sleep in my house.

"Maybe I could take him bowling," I said to my wife. She was at the draining board doing scalloped potatoes. She put down the knife she was using and turned around.

"If you love me," she said, "you can do this for me. If you don't love me, okay. But if you had a friend, any friend, and the friend came to visit, I'd make him feel comfortable." She wiped her hands with the dishtowel.

"I don't have any blind friends," I said.

"You don't have any friends," she said. "Period. Besides," she said, "goddamn it, his wife just died! Don't you understand that? The man's lost his wife!"

I didn't answer. She'd told me a little about the blind man's wife. Her name was Beulah. Beulah! That's a name for a colored woman.

"Was his wife a Negro?" I asked.

"Are you crazy?" my wife said. "Have you just flipped or something?" She picked up a potato. I saw it hit the floor, then roll under the stove. "What's wrong with you?" she said. "Are you drunk?"

"I'm just asking," I said.

Right then my wife filled me in with more detail than I cared to know. I made a drink and sat at the kitchen table to listen. Pieces of the story began to fall into place.

Beulah had gone to work for the blind man the summer after my wife had stopped working for him. Pretty soon Beulah and the blind man had themselves a church wedding. It was a little wedding—who'd want to go to such a wedding in the first place?—just the two of them, plus the minister and the minister's wife. But it was a church wedding just the same. It was what Beulah had wanted, he'd said. But even then Beulah must have been carrying the cancer in her glands. After they had been inseparable for eight years—my wife's word, *inseparable*— Beulah's health went into a rapid decline. She died in a Seattle hospital room, the blind man sitting beside the bed and holding on to her hand. They'd married, lived and worked together, slept together—had sex, sure—and then the blind man had to bury her. All this without his having ever seen what the goddamned woman looked like. It was beyond my understanding. Hearing this, I felt sorry for the blind man for a little bit. And then I found myself thinking what a pitiful life this woman must have led. Imagine a woman who could never see herself as she was seen in the eyes of her loved one. A woman who could go on day after day and never receive the smallest compliment from her beloved. A woman whose husband could never read the expression on her face, be it misery or something better. Someone who could wear makeup or not—what difference to him? She could, if she wanted, wear green eye-shadow around one eye, a straight pin in her nostril, yellow slacks, and purple shoes, no matter. And then to slip off into death, the blind man's hand on her hand, his blind eyes streaming tears—I'm imagining now—her last thought maybe this: that he never even knew what she looked like, and she on an express to the grave. Robert was left with a small insurance policy and half of a twenty-peso Mexican coin. The other half of the coin went into the box with her. Pathetic.

So when the time rolled around, my wife went to the depot to pick him up. With nothing to do but wait—sure, I blamed him for that—I was having a drink and watching the TV when I heard the car pull into the drive. I got up from the sofa with my drink and went to the window to have a look.

I saw my wife laughing as she parked the car. I saw her get out of the car and shut the door. She was still wearing a smile. Just amazing. She went around to the other side of the car to where the blind man was already starting to get out. This blind man, feature this, he was wearing a full beard! A beard on a blind man! Too much, I say. The blind man reached into the backseat and dragged out a suitcase. My wife took his arm, shut the car door, and, talking all the way, moved him down the drive and then up the steps to the front porch. I turned off the TV. I finished my drink, rinsed the glass, dried my hands. Then I went to the door.

My wife said, "I want you to meet Robert. Robert, this is my husband. I've told you all about him." She was beaming. She had this blind man by his coat sleeve.

The blind man let go of his suitcase and up came his hand.

I took it. He squeezed hard, held my hand, and let it go.

"I feel like we've already met," he boomed.

"Likewise," I said. I didn't know what else to say. Then I said, "Welcome. I've heard a lot about you." We began to move then, a little group, from the porch into the living room, my wife guiding him by the arm. The blind man was carrying his suitcase in his other hand. My wife said things like, "To your left here, Robert. That's right. Now watch it, there's a chair. That's it. Sit down right here. Here is the sofa. We just bought this sofa two weeks ago."

I started to say something about the old sofa. I'd liked that old sofa. But I didn't say anything. Then I wanted to say something else, small-talk, about the scenic ride along the Hudson. How going to New York, you should sit on the right-hand side of the train, and coming from New York, the left-hand side.

"Did you have a good train ride?" I said. "Which side of the train did you sit on, by the way?"

"What a question, which side!" my wife said. "What's it matter which side?" she said.

"I just asked," I said.

"Right side," the blind man said. "I hadn't been on a train in nearly forty years. Not since I was a kid. With my folks. That's been a long time. I'd nearly forgotten the sensation. I have winter in my beard now," he said. "So I've been told, anyway. Do I look distinguished, my dear?" the blind man said to my wife.

"You look distinguished, Robert," she said. "Robert," she said. "Robert, it's just so good to see you."

My wife finally took her eyes off the blind man and looked at me. I had the feeling she didn't like what she saw. I shrugged.

I've never met, or personally known, anyone who was blind. This blind man was late forties, a heavy-set, balding man with stooped shoulders, as if he carried a great weight there. He wore brown slacks, brown shoes, a light-brown shirt, a tie, a sports coat. Spiffy. He also had this full beard. But he didn't use a cane and he didn't wear dark glasses. I'd always thought dark glasses were a must for the blind. Fact was, I wished he had a pair. At first glance, his eyes looked like anyone else's eyes. But if you looked close, there was something different about them. Too much white in the iris, for one thing, and the pupils seemed to move around in the sockets without his knowing it or being able to stop it. Creepy. As I stared at his face, I saw the left pupil turn in toward his nose while the other made an effort to keep in one place. But it was only an effort, for that eye was on the roam without his knowing it or wanting it to be.

I said, "Let me get you a drink. What's your pleasure? We have a little of everything. It's one of our pastimes."

"Bub, I'm a Scotch man myself," he said fast enough in this big voice.

"Right," I said. Bub! "Sure you are. I knew it."

He let his fingers touch his suitcase, which was sitting alongside the sofa. He was taking his bearings. I didn't blame him for that.

"I'll move that up to your room," my wife said.

"No, that's fine," the blind man said loudly. "It can go up when I go up."

"A little water with the Scotch?" I said.

"Very little," he said.

"I knew it," I said.

He said, "Just a tad. The Irish actor, Barry Fitzgerald? I'm like that fellow. When I drink water, Fitzgerald said, I drink water. When I drink whiskey, I drink whiskey." My wife laughed. The blind man brought his hand up under his beard. He lifted his beard slowly and let it drop.

I did the drinks, three big glasses of Scotch with a splash of water in each. Then we made ourselves comfortable and talked about Robert's travels. First the long flight from the West Coast to Connecticut, we covered that. Then from Connecticut up here by train. We had another drink concerning that leg of the trip.

I remembered having read somewhere that the blind didn't smoke because, as speculation had it, they couldn't see the smoke they exhaled. I thought I knew that much and that much only about blind people. But this blind man smoked his cigarette down to the nubbin and then lit another one. This blind man filled his ashtray and my wife emptied it.

When we sat down at the table for dinner, we had another drink. My wife heaped Robert's plate with cube steak, scalloped potatoes, green beans. I buttered him up two slices of bread. I said, "Here's bread and butter for you." I swallowed some of my drink. "Now let us pray," I said, and the blind man lowered his head. My wife looked at me, her mouth agape. "Pray the phone won't ring and the food doesn't get cold," I said.

We dug in. We ate everything there was to eat on the table. We ate like there was no tomorrow. We didn't talk. We ate. We scarfed. We grazed that table. We were into serious eating. The blind man had right away located his foods, he knew just where everything was on his plate. I watched with admiration as he used his knife and fork on the meat. He'd cut two pieces of meat, fork the meat into his mouth, and then go all out for the scalloped potatoes, the beans next, and then he'd tear off a bunk of buttered bread and eat that. He'd follow this up with a big drink of milk. It didn't seem to bother him to use his fingers once in a while, either.

We finished everything, including half a strawberry pie. For a few moments, we sat as if stunned. Sweat beaded on our faces. Finally, we got up from the table and left the dirty plates. We didn't look back. We took ourselves into the living room and sank into our places again. Robert and my wife sat on the sofa. I took the big chair. We had us two or three more drinks while they talked about the major things that had come to pass for them in the past ten years. For the most part, I just listened. Now and then I joined in. I didn't want him to think I'd left the room, and I didn't want her to think I was feeling left out. They talked of things that had happened to them—to them!—these past ten years. I waited in vain to hear my name on my wife's sweet lips: "And then my dear husband came into my life"—something like that. But I heard nothing of the sort. More talk of Robert. Robert had done a little of everything, it seemed, a regular blind jack-of-all-trades. But most recently he and his wife had had an Amway distributorship, from which, I gathered, they'd earned their living, such as it was. The blind man was also a ham radio operator. He talked in his loud voice about conversations he'd had with fellow operators in Guam, in the Philippines, in Alaska, and even in Tahiti. He said he'd have a lot of friends there if he ever wanted to go visit those places. From time to time, he'd turn his blind face toward me, put his hand under his beard, ask me something. How long had I been in my present position? (Three years.) Did I like my work? (I didn't.) Was I going to stay with it? (What were the options?) Finally, when I thought he was beginning to run down, I got up and turned on the TV.

My wife looked at me with irritation. She was heading toward a boil. Then she looked at the blind man and said, "Robert, do you have a TV?" The blind man said, "My dear, I have two TVs. I have a color set and a black-and-white thing, an old relic. It's funny, but if I turn the TV on, and I'm always turning it on, I turn on the color set. It's funny, don't you think?" I didn't know what to say to that. I had absolutely nothing to say to that. No opinion. So I watched the news program and tried to listen to what the announcer was saying.

"This is a color TV," the blind man said. "Don't ask me how, but I can tell."

"We traded up a while ago," I said.

The blind man had another taste of his drink. He lifted his beard, sniffed it, and let it fall. He leaned forward on the sofa. He positioned his ashtray on the coffee table, then put the lighter to his cigarette. He leaned back on the sofa and crossed his legs at the ankles.

My wife covered her mouth, and then she yawned. She stretched. She said, "I think I'll go upstairs and put on my robe. I think I'll change into something else. Robert, you make yourself comfortable," she said.

"I'm comfortable," the blind man said.

"I want you to feel comfortable in this house," she said.

"I am comfortable," the blind man said.

After she'd left the room, he and I listened to the weather report and then to the sports roundup. By that time, she'd been gone so long I didn't know if she was going to come back. I thought she might have gone to bed. I wished she'd come back downstairs. I didn't want to be left alone with a blind man. I asked him if he wanted another drink, and he said sure. Then I asked if he wanted to smoke some dope with me. I said I'd just rolled a number. I hadn't, but I planned to do so in about two shakes.

"I'll try some with you," he said.

"Damn right," I said. "That's the stuff."

I got our drinks and sat down on the sofa with him. Then I rolled us two fat numbers. I lit one and passed it. I brought it to his fingers. He took it and inhaled.

"Hold it as long as you can," I said. I could tell he didn't know the first thing.

My wife came back downstairs wearing her pink robe and her pink slippers.

"What do I smell?" she said.

"We thought we'd have us some cannabis," I said.

My wife gave me a savage look. Then she looked at the blind man and said, "Robert, I didn't know you smoked."

He said, "I do now, my dear. There's a first time for everything. But I don't feel anything yet."

"This stuff is pretty mellow," I said. "This stuff is mild. It's dope you can reason with," I said. "It doesn't mess you up.

"Not much it doesn't, bub," he said, and laughed.

My wife sat on the sofa between the blind man and me. I passed her the number. She took it and toked and then passed it back to me. "Which way is this going?" she said. Then she said, "I shouldn't be smoking this. I can hardly keep my eyes open as it is. That dinner did me in. I shouldn't have eaten so much."

"It was the strawberry pie," the blind man said. "That's what did it," he said, and he laughed his big laugh. Then he shook his head.

"There's more strawberry pie," I said.

"Do you want some more, Robert?" my wife said.

"Maybe in a little while," he said.

We gave our attention to the TV. My wife yawned again. She said, "Your bed is made up when you feel like going to bed, Robert. I know you must have had a long day. When you're ready to go to bed, say so." She pulled his arm. "Robert?"

He came to and said, "I've had a real nice time. This beats tapes, doesn't it?"

I said, "Coming at you," and I put the number between his fingers. He inhaled, held the smoke, and then let it go. It was like he'd been doing it since he was nine years old.

"Thanks, bub," he said. "But I think this is all for me. I think I'm beginning to feel it," he said. He held the burning roach out for my wife.

"Same here," she said. "Ditto. Me, too." She took the roach and passed it to me. "I may just sit here for a while between you two guys with my eyes closed. But don't let me bother you, okay? Either one of you. If it bothers you, say so. Otherwise, I may just sit here with my eyes closed until you're ready to go to bed," she said. "Your bed's made up, Robert, when you're ready. It's right next to our room at the top of the stairs. We'll show you up when you're ready. You wake me up now, you guys, if I fall asleep." She said that and then she closed her eyes and went to sleep.

The news program ended. I got up and changed the channel. I sat back down on the sofa. I wished my wife hadn't pooped out. Her head lay across the back of the sofa, her mouth open. She'd turned so that her robe had slipped away from her legs, exposing a juicy thigh. I reached to draw her robe back over her, and it was then that I glanced at the blind man. What the hell! I flipped the robe open again.

"You say when you want some strawberry pie," I said.

"I will," he said.

I said, "Are you tired? Do you want me to take you up to your bed? Are you ready to hit the hay?"

"Not yet," he said. "No, I'll stay up with you, bub. If that's all right. I'll stay up until you're ready to turn in. We haven't had a chance to talk. Know what I mean? I feel like me and her monopolized the evening." He lifted his beard and he let it fall. He picked up his cigarettes and his lighter.

"That's all right," I said. Then I said, "I'm glad for the company."

And I guess I was. Every night I smoked dope and stayed up as long as I could before I fell asleep. My wife and I hardly ever went to bed at the same time. When I did go to sleep, I had these dreams. Sometimes I'd wake up from one of them, my heart going crazy.

Something about the church and the Middle Ages was on the TV. Not your run-of-the-mill TV fare. I wanted to watch something else. I turned to the other channels. But there was nothing on them, either. So I turned back to the first channel and apologized.

"Bub, it's all right," the blind man said. "It's fine with me. Whatever you want to watch is okay. I'm always learning something. Learning never ends. It won't hurt me to learn something tonight. I got ears," he said.

He didn't say anything for a time. He was leaning forward with his head turned at me, his right ear aimed in the direction of the set. Very disconcerting. Now and then his eyelids drooped and then they snapped open again. Now and then he put his fingers into his beard and tugged, like he was thinking about something he was hearing on the television.

On the screen, a group of men wearing cowls was being set upon and tormented by men dressed in skeleton costumes and men dressed as devils. The men dressed as devils wore devil masks, horns, and long tails. This pageant was part of a procession. The Englishman who was narrating the thing said it took place in Spain once a year. I tried to explain to the blind man what was happening.

"Skeletons," he said. "I know about skeletons," he said, and he nodded.

The TV showed this one cathedral. Then there was a long, slow look at another one. Finally, the picture switched to the famous one in Paris, with its flying buttresses and its spires reaching up to the clouds. The camera pulled away to show the whole of the cathedral rising above the skyline.

There were times when the Englishman who was telling the thing would shut up, would simply let the camera move around over the cathedrals. Or else the camera would tour the countryside, men in fields walking behind oxen. I waited as long as I could. Then I felt I had to say something. I said, "They're showing the outside of this cathedral now. Gargoyles. Little statues carved to look like monsters. Now I guess they're in Italy. Yeah, they're in Italy. There's paintings on the walls of this one church."

"Are those fresco paintings, bub?" he asked, and he sipped from his drink.

I reached for my glass. But it was empty. I tried to remember what I could remember. "You're asking me are those frescoes?" I said. "That's a good question. I don't know."

The camera moved to a cathedral outside Lisbon. The differences in the Portuguese cathedral compared with the French and Italian were not that great. But they were there. Mostly the interior stuff. Then something occurred to me, and I said, "Something has occurred to me. Do you have any idea what a cathedral is? What they look like, that is? Do you follow me? If somebody says cathedral to you, do you have any notion what they're talking about? Do you know the difference between that and a Baptist church, say?"

He let the smoke dribble from his mouth. "I know they took hundreds of workers fifty or a hundred years to build," he said. "I just heard the man say that, of course. I know generations of the same families worked on a cathedral. I heard him say that, too. The men who began their life's work on them, they never lived to see the completion of their work. In that wise, bub, they're no different from the rest of us, right?" He laughed. Then his eyelids drooped again. His head nodded. He seemed to be snoozing. Maybe he was imagining himself in Portugal. The TV was showing another cathedral now. This one was in Germany. The Englishman's voice droned on. "Cathedrals," the blind man said—He sat up and rolled his head back and forth. "If you want the truth, bub, that's about all I know. What I just said. What I heard him say. But maybe you could describe one to me? I wish you'd do it. I'd like that. If you want to know, I really don't have a good idea."

I stared hard at the shot of the cathedral on the TV. How could I even begin to describe it? But say my life depended on it. Say my life was being threatened by an insane guy who said I had to do it or else.

I stared some more at the cathedral before the picture flipped off into the countryside. There was no use. I turned to the blind man and said, "To begin with, they're very tall." I was looking around the room for clues. "They reach way up. Up and up. Toward the sky. They're so big, some of them, they have to have these supports. To help hold them up, so to speak. These supports are called buttresses. They remind me of viaducts, for some reason. But maybe you don't know viaducts, either? Sometimes the cathedrals have devils and such carved into the front. Sometimes lords and ladies. Don't ask me why this is," I said.

He was nodding. The whole upper part of his body seemed to be moving back and forth.

"I'm not doing so good, am I?" I said.

He stopped nodding and leaned forward on the edge of the sofa. As he listened to me, he was running his fingers through his beard. I wasn't getting through to him, I could see that. But he waited for me to go on just the same. He nodded, like he was trying to encourage me. I tried to think what else to say. "They're really big," I said. "They're massive. They're built of stone. Marble, too, sometimes. In those olden days, when they built cathedrals, men wanted to be close to God. In those olden days, God was an important part of everyone's life. You could tell this from their cathedral building. I'm sorry," I said, "but it looks like that's the best I can do for you. I'm just not good at it."

"That's all right, bub," the blind man said. "Hey, listen. I hope you don't mind my asking you. Can I ask you something? Let me ask you a simple question, yes or no. I'm just curious and there's no offense. You're my host. But let me ask if you are in any way religious? You don't mind my asking?"

I shook my head. He couldn't see that, though. A wink is the same as a nod to a blind man. "I guess I don't believe in it. In anything. Sometimes it's hard. You know what I'm saying?"

"Sure, I do," he said.

"Right," I said.

The Englishman was still holding forth. My wife sighed in her sleep. She drew a long breath and went on with her sleeping.

"You'll have to forgive me," I said. "But I can't tell you what a cathedral looks like. It just isn't in me to do it. I can't do any more than I've done." The blind man sat very still, his head down, as he listened to me.

I said, "The truth is, cathedrals don't mean anything special to me. Nothing. Cathedrals. They're something to look at on late-night TV. That's all they are." It was then that the blind man cleared his throat. He brought something up. He took a handkerchief from his back pocket. Then he said, "I get it, bub. It's okay. It happens. Don't worry about it," he said. "Hey, listen to me. Will you do me a favor? I got an idea. Why don't you find us some heavy paper? And a pen. We'll do something. We'll draw one together. Get us a pen and some heavy paper. Go on, bub, get the stuff," he said. So I went upstairs. My legs felt like they didn't have any strength in them. They felt like they did after I'd done some running. In my wife's room, I looked around. I found some ballpoints in a little basket on her table. And then I tried to think where to look for the kind of paper he was talking about.

Downstairs, in the kitchen, I found a shopping bag with onionskins in the bottom of the bag. I emptied the bag and shook it. I brought it into the living room and sat down with it near his legs. I moved some things, smoothed the wrinkles from the bag, spread it out on the coffee table

The blind man got down from the sofa and sat next to me on the carpet.

He ran his fingers over the paper. He went up and down the sides of the paper. The edges, even the edges. He fingered the corners.

"All right," he said. "All right, let's do her."

He found my hand, the hand with the pen. He closed his hand over my hand. "Go ahead, bub, draw," he said. "Draw. You'll see. I'll follow along with you. It'll be okay. Just begin now like I'm telling you. You'll see. Draw," the blind man said.

So I began. First I drew a box that looked like a house. It could have been the house I lived in. Then I put a roof on it. At either end of the roof, I drew spires. Crazy.

"Swell," he said. "Terrific. You're doing fine," he said.

"Never thought anything like this could happen in your lifetime, did you, bub? Well, it's a strange life, we all know that. Go on now. Keep it up."

I put in windows with arches. I drew flying buttresses. I hung great doors. I couldn't stop. The TV station went off the air. I put down the pen and closed and opened my fingers. The blind man felt around over the paper. He moved the tips of his fingers over the paper, all over what I had drawn, and he nodded.

"Doing fine," the blind man said.

I took up the pen again, and he found my hand. I kept at it. I'm no artist. But I kept drawing just the same.

My wife opened up her eyes and gazed at us. She sat up on the sofa, her robe hanging open. She said, "What are you doing? Tell me, I want to know."

I didn't answer her.

The blind man said, "We're drawing a cathedral. Me and him are working on it. Press hard," he said to me. "That's right. That's good," he said. "Sure. You got it, bub. I can tell. You didn't think you could. But you can, can't you? You're cooking with gas now. You know what I'm saying? We're going to really have us something here in a minute. How's the old arm?" he said. "Put some people in there now. What's a cathedral without people?"

My wife said, "What's going on? Robert, what are you doing? What's going on?"

"It's all right," he said to her. "Close your eyes now," the blind man said to me.

I did it. I closed them just like he said.

"Are they closed?" he said. "Don't fudge."

"They're closed," I said.

"Keep them that way," he said. He said, "Don't stop now. Draw."

So we kept on with it. His fingers rode my fingers as my hand went over the paper. It was like nothing else in my life up to now. Then he said, "I think that's it. I think you got it," he said. "Take a look. What do you think?"

But I had my eyes closed. I thought I'd keep them that way for a little longer. I thought it was something I ought to do.

"Well?" he said. "Are you looking?"

My eyes were still closed. I was in my house. I knew that. But I didn't feel like I was inside anything.

"It's really something," I said.

Where I'm Calling From. Raymond Carver. Vintage Books, Random House. NY: 1988.

Questions for Discussion

1. In many cultures, even today, the blind are believed to have supernatural powers, which allow them to "see" the future and communicate with the dead. Why might people believe this? What might be gained or lost in the process of having such a belief?

2. Discuss the narrator's apparent fascination with seemingly ordinary details about the blind man, Robert. Why is he so interested in, say, the way Robert smokes his cigarettes or the fact that he wears a long beard?

3. Compare the narrator's attitude toward blind people throughout the story. List the characteristics he associates with blind people before he meets Robert. Where do you think the narrator obtained his understanding of blind people? Discuss the role of television as a cultural phenomenon, as living room entertainment for a blind visitor, and as a force in the narrator's personal relationship with Robert.

Explorations

1. Via e-mail, correspond with a classmate and describe someone your partner doesn't know. After receiving each other's descriptions, draw a picture of the person described. In class, compare your drawings to a photograph provided by your partner. Other than artistic ability, what factors contributed to the successes and short-comings of your drawings?

2. Early in the story, the narrator refers to Robert as "her [his wife's] blind man." What can we deduce about the narrator by his use of the possessive pronoun "her" in this sentence? How is your assertion complicated by the fact that, in reference to his wife's first husband, the narrator also uses the possessive pronoun to describe "her officer"?

3. Describe a time when, like the narrator at the end of the story, you didn't "feel like [you] were inside anything." What caused this feeling of physical freedom? In particular, what senses (or lack thereof) allowed for this feeling?

Formal Writing Assignments

1. Using as much detail as possible, tell the story of a time when an interaction with a stranger allowed you to learn something important about yourself. In the first draft, concentrate on getting the story down as fully and vividly as you can. In revision, add commentary throughout the story, reflecting on things that, because of hindsight, you've come to understand about the occurrence. In the end, the reader should have a feel not only for what transpired and how it affected you, but also for how your memory of the event allows you to reflect on the situation in complex ways. How has your memory been altered by time and what you've learned from the experience?

2. Using on-line and/or traditional resources, research the personal life and writing life of Raymond Carver. "Cathedral," like many of his stories, is based on an actual personal experience. In a narrative, try to reconstruct the actual events of Carver's experience with a blind man, then compare and contrast it with the plot of "Cathedral." In your analysis, either interrogate or defend Carver's decision to fictionalize the story, rather than writing about the event in a creative, non-fiction account.

Narrative of the Life of Frederick Douglass, an American Slave: Written by Himself

Frederick Douglass

Frederick Douglass is recognized as one of the great American intellectuals of the nineteenth century. A speaker, writer, and activist, Douglass was born a slave in Maryland in 1818 and originally named Frederick Bailey. He was the son of Harriet Bailey, whom he saw only a few times before her death. His father was a white man, probably the plantation overseer. While in Baltimore, he taught himself to read and write, and in 1838 he escaped to the North, where he renamed himself Frederick Douglass. In 1841, Douglass gave his first abolitionist speech, and he soon achieved acclaim as a powerful speaker.

Douglass entreated President Lincoln to free the slaves and he helped recruit African-American troops for the Civil War. As an abolitionist, he lectured throughout the North and in England. He also co-founded the abolitionist periodical *North Star* with Martin Delany. Douglass served as the *North Star's* editor for sixteen years. Douglass' activism extended beyond the abolitionist movement of the Civil War. He was also an active voice on behalf of women's suffrage and served as ambassador to Haiti (1889–91).

The first edition of Douglass' *Narrative*, which is excerpted below, was published in 1845. The publication of the *Narrative* was considered by most readers of the time to be an act of authentication, a way of "proving" his intelligence and his humanity, of justifying his very identity. As you read Douglass' discussion of how and why he became literate, you may want to consider how other writers within the unit speak to the relationship between one's literacy and one's identity. Have other writers in Unit One viewed their own literacy practices as "evidence" of other aspects of their identities?

Writing Before Reading

1. Using the prewriting method of your choice (i.e. brainstorming, listing, clustering, freewriting, etc.), take a few minutes to record as much as you know about the abolitionist movement in the United States. What was abolition? Who was active within the movement? How did it achieve its goals?

2. Education is often considered to be empowering. Is this necessarily true? Why or why not? Think of contemporary examples of this argument—who uses it most often? Where do you hear it voiced? To what effect?

3. Describe an incident in your own life when the act of reading or writing helped you to achieve a particular goal. Were others involved in this situation? If so, who? Did these others help or hinder you?

Narrative of the Life of Frederick Douglass, an American Slave: Written by Himself

I lived in Master Hugh's family about seven years. During this time, I succeeded in learning to read and write. In accomplishing this, I was compelled to resort to various stratagems. I had no regular teacher. My mistress, who had kindly commenced to instruct me, had, in compliance with the advice and direction of her husband, not only ceased to instruct, but had set her face against my being instructed by any one else. It is due, however, to my mistress to say of her, that she did not adopt this course of treatment immediately. She at first lacked the depravity indispensable to shutting me up in mental darkness. It was at least necessary for her to have some training in the exercise of irresponsible power, to make her equal to the task of treating me as though I were a brute.

My mistress was, as I have said, a kind and tender-hearted woman; and in the simplicity of her soul she commenced, when I first went to live with her, to treat me as she supposed one human being ought to treat another. In entering upon the duties of a slaveholder, she did not seem to perceive that I sustained to her the relation of a mere chattel, and that for her to treat me as a human being was not only wrong, but dangerously so. Slavery proved as injurious to her as it did to me. When I went there, she was a pious, warm, and tender-hearted woman. There was no sorrow or suffering for which she had not a tear. She had bread for the hungry, clothes for the naked, and comfort for every mourner that came within her reach. Slavery soon proved its ability to divest her of these heavenly qualities. Under its influence, the tender heart became stone, and the lamblike disposition gave way to one of tiger-like fierceness. The first step in her downward course was in her ceasing to instruct me. She now commenced to practise her husband's precepts. She finally became even more violent in her opposition than her husband himself. She was not satisfied with simply doing as well as he had commanded; she seemed anxious to do better. Nothing seemed to make her more angry than to see me with a newspaper. She seemed to think that here lay the danger. I have had her rush at me with a face made all up of fury, and snatch from me a newspaper, in a manner that fully revealed her apprehension. She was an apt woman; and a little experience soon demonstrated, to her satisfaction, that education and slavery were incompatible with each other.

From this time I was most narrowly watched. If I was in a separate room any considerable length of time, I was sure to be suspected of having a book and was at once called to give an account of myself. All this, however, was too late. The first step had been taken. Mistress, in teaching me the alphabet, had given me the *inch*, and no precaution could prevent me from taking the *ell*.

The plan which I adopted, and the one by which I was most successful, was that of making friends of all the little white boys whom I met in the street. As many of these as I could, I converted into teachers. With their kindly aid, obtained at different times and in different places, I finally succeeded in learning to read. When I was sent of errands, I always took my book with me, and by going one part of my errand quickly, I found time to get a lesson before my return. I used also to carry bread with me, enough of which was always in the house, and to which I was always welcome; for I was much better off in this regard than many of the poor white children in our neighborhood. This bread I used to bestow upon the hungry little urchins, who, in return, would give me that more valuable bread of knowledge. I am strongly tempted to give the names of two or three of those little boys, as a testimonial of the gratitude and affection I bear them; but prudence forbids; —not that it would injure me, but it might embarrass them; for it is almost an unpardonable offence to teach slaves to read in this Christian country. It is enough to say of the dear little fellows, that they lived on Philpot Street, very near Durgin and Bailey's ship-yard. I used to talk this matter of slavery over with them. I would sometimes say to them, I wished I could be as free as they would be when they got to be men. "You will be free as soon as you are twenty-one, but *I am a slave for life!* Have not I as good a right to be free as you have?" These words used to trouble them; they would express for me the liveliest sympathy, and console me with the hope that something would occur by which I might be free.

I was now about twelve years old, and the thought of being a *slave for life* began to bear heavily upon my heart. Just about this time, I got hold of a book entitled "The Columbian Orator." Every opportunity I got, I used to read this book. Among much of other interesting matter, I found in it a dialogue between a master and his slave. The slave was represented as having run away from his master three times. The dialogue represented the conversation which took place between them, when the slave was retaken the third time. In this dialogue, the whole argument in behalf of slavery was brought forward by the master, all of which was disposed of by the slave. The slave was made to say some very smart as well as impressive things in reply to his master—things which had the desired though unexpected effect; for the conversation resulted in the voluntary emancipation of the slave on the part of the master.

In the same book, I met with one of Sheridan's mighty speeches on and in behalf of Catholic emancipation. These were choice documents to me. I read them over and over again with unabated interest. They gave tongue to interesting thoughts of my own soul, which had frequently flashed through my mind, and died away for want of utterance. The moral which I gained from the dialogue was the power of truth over the conscience of even a slaveholder. What I got from Sheridan was a bold denunciation of slavery, and a powerful vindication of human rights. The reading of these documents enabled me to utter my thoughts, and to meet the arguments brought forward to sustain slavery; but while they relieved me of one difficulty, they brought on another even more painful than the one of which I was relieved. The more I read, the more I was led to abhor and detest my enslavers. I could regard them in no other light than a band of successful robbers, who had left their homes, and gone to Africa, and stolen us from our homes, and in a strange land reduced us to slavery. I loathed them as being the meanest as well as the most wicked of men. As I read and contemplated the subject, behold! that very discontentment which Master Hugh had predicted would follow my learning to read had already come, to torment and sting my soul to unutterable anguish. As I writhed under it, I would at times feel that learning to read had been a curse rather than a blessing. It had given me a view of my wretched condition, without the remedy. It opened my eyes to the horrible pit, but to no ladder upon which to get out.

In moments of agony, I envied my fellow-slaves for their stupidity. I have often wished myself a beast. I preferred the condition of the meanest reptile to my own. Any thing, no matter what, to get rid of thinking! It was this everlasting thinking of my condition that tormented me. There was no getting rid of it. It was pressed upon me by every object within sight or hearing, animate or inanimate. The silver trump of freedom had roused my soul to eternal wakefulness. Freedom now appeared, to disappear no more forever. It was heard in every sound, and seen in every thing. It was ever present to torment me with a sense of my wretched condition. I saw nothing without seeing it, I heard nothing without hearing it, and felt nothing without feeling it. It looked from every star, it smiled in every calm, breathed in every wind, and moved in every storm.

I often found myself regretting my own existence, and wishing myself dead; and but for the hope of being free, I have no doubt but that I should have killed myself, or done something for which I should have been killed. While in this state of mind, I was eager to hear any one speak of slavery. I was a ready listener. Every little while, I could hear something about the abolitionists. It was some time before I found what the word meant. It was always used in such connections as to make it an interesting word to me. If a slave ran away and succeeded in getting clear, or if a slave killed his master, set fire to a barn, or did any thing very wrong in the mind of a slaveholder, it was spoken of as the fruit of *abolition*. Hearing the word in this connection very often, I set about learning what it meant. The dictionary afforded me little or no help. I found it was "the act of abolishing;" but then I did not know what was to be abolished. Here I was perplexed. I did not dare to ask any one about its meaning, for I was satisfied that it was something they wanted me to know very little about. After a patient waiting, I got one of our city papers, containing an account of the number of petitions from the north, praying for the abolition of slavery in the District of Columbia, and of the slave trade between the States. From this time I understood the words *abolition* and *abolitionist*, and always drew near when that word was spoken, expecting to hear something of importance to myself and fellow-slaves. The light broke in upon me by degrees. I went one day down on the wharf of Mr. Waters; and seeing two Irishmen unloading a scow of stone, I went, unasked, and helped them. When we had finished, one of them came to me and asked me if I were a slave. I told him I was. He asked, "Are ye a slave for life?" I told him that I was. The good Irishman seemed to be deeply affected by the statement. He said to the other that it was a pity so fine a little fellow as myself should be a slave for life. He said it was a shame to hold me. They both advised me to run away to the north; that I should find friends there, and that I should be free. I pretended not to be interested in what they said, and treated them as if I did not understand them; for I feared they might be treacherous. White men have been known to encourage slaves to escape, and then, to get the reward, catch them and return them to their masters. I was afraid that these seemingly good men might use me so; but I nevertheless remembered their advice, and from that time I resolved to run away. I looked forward to a time at which it would be safe for me to escape. I was too young to think of doing so immediately; besides, I wished to learn how to write, as I might have occasion to write my own pass. I consoled myself with the hope that I should one day find a good chance. Meanwhile, I would learn to write.

The idea as to how I might learn to write was suggested to me by being in Durgin and Bailey's shipyard, and frequently seeing the ship carpenters, after hewing, and getting a piece of timber ready for use, write on the timber the name of that part of the ship for which it was intended. When a piece of timber was intended for the larboard side, it would be marked thus "L." When a piece was for the starboard side, it would be marked thus "S." A piece for the larboard side forward, would be marked thus "L. F." When a piece was for starboard side forward., it would be marked thus "S. F." For larboard aft? it would be marked thus "L. A." For starboard aft, it would be marked thus "S. A." I soon learned the names of these letters, and for what they were intended when placed upon a piece of timber in the ship-yard. I immediately commenced copying them, and in a short time was able to make the four letters named. After that, when I met with any boy who I knew could write, I would tell him I could write as well as he. The next word would be, "I don't believe you. Let me see you try it." I would then make the letters which I had been so fortunate as to learn, and ask him to beat that. In this way I got a good many lessons in writing, which it is quite possible I should never have gotten in any other way. During this time, my copy-book was the board fence, brick wall, and pavement; my pen and ink was a lump of chalk. With these, I learned mainly how to write. I then commenced and continued copying the Italics in Webster's Spelling Book, until I could make them all without looking on the book. By this time, my little Master Thomas had gone to school, and learned how to write, and had written over a number of copy-books. These had been brought home, and shown to some of our near neighbors, and then laid aside. My mistress used to go to class meeting at the Wilk Street meetinghouse every Monday afternoon, and leave me to take care of the house. When left thus, I used to spend the time in writing in the spaces left in Master Thomas's copy-book, copying what he had written. I continued to do this until I could write a hand very similar to that of Master Thomas. Thus, after a long, tedious effort for years, I finally succeeded in learning how to write.

Questions for Discussion

1. Why is Mistress Hugh so violently opposed to Douglass learning to read and write? Why does she think that education and slavery are incompatible?

2. Why is it significant that Douglass teaches himself to write? How do others help him with his efforts? How would you characterize the relationships between Douglass and others within this chapter of the narrative?

3. Describe the content of *The Columbian Orator*. Why is this book so powerful for Douglass? What does it teach him about communication? About freedom? What does Douglass mean when he says, "it had given me a view of my wretched condition"?

Explorations

1. Frederick Douglass' narrative exhibits many of the formal qualities associated with several oral and literate traditions, including religious or sermonic discourse and nineteenth century serial narratives (often published within periodicals and designed to leave the audience longing for more after reading each periodical issue). For this Exploration, reflect upon Douglass' stylistic and formal choices within this chapter. Try to find examples that remind you of other forms/genres you may have encountered as a reader or listener.

2. As a member of the abolitionist movement, Frederick Douglass was considered a masterful speaker and writer with a keen ability to persuade. Choose a particular passage from Douglass' work and analyze its use of persuasive strategies. You may want to consider, for instance, Douglass' use of the rhetorical appeals—logos (appeals to logic), ethos (appeals to the character of the speaker), and pathos (appeals to the emotions), his use of metaphor or imagery, the way he positions his audience, etc.

3. For many students who have used *Writing Lives* in the past, the idea that literacy is a complicated concept that may go well beyond the ability to read and write is both intriguing and troubling. For this Exploration, consider what Douglass might say if, for instance, you introduced him to Lars Eighner's "On Dumpster Diving" or Raymond Carver's "Cathedral," telling him that both pieces were literacy narratives. How do you think Douglass would respond? Write a response to Eighner, Carver—or another writer within the unit who complicates your notion of literacy—as you believe Douglass would.

Formal Writing Assignments

1 The genre most commonly associated with Frederick Douglass' and many other freed and former slaves' work of the 19th century is the literacy narrative, a story written explicitly about how the slave learned to read and write. Draft your own literacy narrative in which you describe a powerful incident involving reading and/or writing in your own life and analyze the significance of that incident to your development as a literate individual. Successful essays will carefully balance narration, description, and analysis so that the narrative is both vivid and reflective.

2 Draft an essay in which you describe and analyze Douglass' rhetorical choices. You may want to consider issues such as relationship to an imagined or invoked audience; use of appeals (to reason, emotion, and/or the good will and character of the speaker and listeners); use of rhythm, style, and tone; use of imagery; storytelling skills, etc. Your goal is to construct a particular thesis based upon your own "take" on Douglass' work—how it functions, if it functions successfully, which sections seem most successful, etc.

The Quare Gene: What Will Happen to the Secret Language of the Appalachians?

Tony Earley

Tony Earley teaches creative writing at Vanderbilt University in Nashville, TN. He was born in San Antonio, TX and received his Master of Fine Arts degree at the University of Alabama. He has published many articles and stories, including a highly-praised collection of short stories called *Here We Are in Paradise*. He is currently writing a novel.

Writing Before Reading

1. Consider conversations you have had with your grandparents. How does their speech differ from your own? Write down as many terms or turns of phrase as you can that you have heard your grandparents (or someone you know from their generation) use but that are not part of your personal voice. Do any of these phrases reveal something about the speaker's view of the world that is different from yours?

2. Is there an individual in your family who can be identified as its matriarch or patriarch? How does your relationship with this person determine or affect your role as a member of your extended family?

3. Since coming to college, you have no doubt noticed differences between your speech and that of some of your fellow students. Would you say your speech is close to the standard, or much different from it? For you, are the differences in your speech a source of pride or a source of embarrassment?

The Quare Gene

What will happen to the secret language of the Appalachians?

I do not like, I have never liked, nor do I expect to like watermelon. For the record, I consider this a private, dietary preference, not a political choice, neither a sign of failing character nor a renunciation of Southern citizenship. I simply do not like watermelon. Nor, for that matter, do I like grits, blackberries, cantaloupe, buttermilk, okra, baked sweet potatoes, rhubarb, or collard greens. Particularly collard greens. I don't even like to look at collard greens. But, because I am a Southerner—a North Carolinian, of Appalachian, Scots-Irish descent, the offspring of farming families on both sides—my family finds my refusal to like the foods they like somehow distressing. When I eat at my grandmother's red-roofed, high-ceilinged Victorian barn of a house, in Polk County, North Carolina, my relatives earnestly strive to persuade me that I am making a big mistake by not sampling this or that, that I should just try the greens, have just a little slice of watermelon, a small bite of cantaloupe. They tell me that I will get used to the seeds in blackberries, the mealiness of grits, the swampy odor of greens boiled too long in a big pot. And when I passionately and steadfastly refuse, as I have done for the last thirty-seven years, they stare at me for a few seconds as if they didn't know me, their mouths set sadly, before looking down at their plates as if preparing to offer up a second grace. Then my grandmother pronounces, "Tony Earley, you're just quare."

According to my edition of the *Shorter Oxford English Dictionary*, "quare" is an Anglo-Irish adjective from the early nineteenth century meaning "queer, strange, eccentric." Most other dictionaries, if they list the word at all, will tell you that it is dialectical, archaic, or obsolete, an anachronism, a muted, aging participant in the clamoring riot of the English language. But when spoken around my grandmother's table, by my parents and aunts and uncles and cousins, "quare" is as current as the breath that produces it, as pointed as a sharpened stick. In my family's lexicon, "quare" packs a specificity of meaning which "queer," "strange," "eccentric," "odd," "unusual," "unconventional," and "suspicious" do not. The only adjective of synonymous texture would be "squirrelly," but we are a close bunch and would find the act of calling one another squirrelly impolite. So, in my grandmother's dining room, when "quare" is the word we need, "quare" is the word we use.

Nor is "quare" the only word still hiding out in my grandmother's house which dictionaries assure us lost currency years ago. If I brought a quare person to Sunday dinner at Granny's and he ate something that disagreed with him, we might say that he looked a little peaked. Of course, we might decide that he was peaked not because he had eaten something that disagreed with him but because he had eaten a bait of something he liked. We would say, Why, he was just too trifling to leave the table. He ate almost the whole mess by himself. And now we have this quare, peaked, trifling person on our hands. How do we get him to leave? Do we job him in the stomach? Do we hit him with a stob? No, we are kinder than that. We tell him, "Brother, you liked to have stayed too long." We put his dessert in a poke and send him on his way.

When I was a child, I took these words for granted. They were part of the language I heard around me, and I breathed them in like air. Only when I began to venture away from the universe that revolved around my grandmother's table did I to come to realize that the language of my family was not the language of the greater world. I was embarrassed and ashamed when my town-bred classmates at Rutherfordton Elementary School corrected my speech, but by the time I entered college and signed up for an Appalachian-studies class I wasn't surprised to learn that my family spoke a dialect. I had begun to suspect as much, and was, by that time, bilingual: I spoke in the Appalachian vernacular when I was with my family and spoke standard English when I wasn't. This tailoring of speech to audience, which still feels a shade ignoble to me, is not uncommon among young people from my part of the world. In less generous regions of the greater American culture, the sound of Appalachian dialect has come to signify ignorance, backwardness, intransigence, and, in the most extreme examples, toothlessness, rank stupidity, and an alarming propensity for planting flowers in painted tractor tires.

This is not some sort of misguided, Caucasian appeal for ethnicity, nor is it a battle cry from the radical left against the patriarchal oppression of grammar, but the fact is that for me standard English has always been something of a second language. I have intuitively written it correctly from the time I started school, but speaking it still feels slightly unnatural, demands just enough conscious thought on my part to make me question my fluency. When I am introduced to a stranger, when I meet a more showily educated colleague in the English department at Vanderbilt, when I go to parties at which I feel unsure of my place in the evening's social pecking order, I catch myself proofreading sentences before I speak them—adding "g"s to the ends of participles, scanning clauses to make sure they ain't got no double negatives, clipping long vowels to affectless, Midwestern dimensions, and making sure I use "lay" and "lie" in a manner that would not embarrass my father-in-law, who is a schoolteacher from California. Occasionally, even my wife, whose Southern accent is significantly more patrician than my own, will smile and ask, "What did you just say?" And I'll realize that I have unwittingly slipped into the language of my people, that I have inadvertently become "colorful." I'll rewind my sentence in my head so that I can save it as an example of how not to speak to strangers. Only in the sanctity of Granny's house can I speak my mother tongue with anything resembling peace of mind.

In 1904, a librarian and writer named Horace Kephart, having recently left his wife and children and suffered a nervous breakdown, moved to the mountains around Bryson City, North Carolina. Although he traveled there initially to distance himself from human contact, he soon recovered enough to take an active interest in the world in which he found himself. An avid gatherer of information and a compulsive list-maker, Kephart spent the rest of his life compiling exhaustive journals and records detailing the geography, history, culture, and language of the southern Appalachians—a pursuit that resulted in countless magazine articles, a celebrated handbook, "Camping and Woodcraft," and two editions of a book entitled "Our Southern Highlanders."

Although Kephart had chosen the Appalachians over the deserts of the Southwest somewhat randomly, he arrived in western North Carolina at a particularly fortuitous time for a man of his particular talents. In the roadless hollows of the Blue Ridge and the Smokies, Kephart found a people isolated by their hostile, vertical geography and living largely as their ancestors had, in the later half of the eighteenth century, when the great Scots-Irish migration out of Pennsylvania first filled the region with people of European descent.

"No one can understand the attitude of our highlanders toward the rest of the earth," Kephart wrote, until he realizes their amazing isolation from all that lies beyond the blue, hazy skyline of their mountains. Conceive a shipload of emigrants cast away on some unknown island, far from the regular track of vessels, and left there for five or six generations, unaided and untroubled by the growth of civilization. Among the descendants of such a company we would expect to find customs and ideas unaltered from the time of their forefathers. The mountain folk still live in the eighteenth century. The progress of mankind from that age to this is no heritage of theirs.

Because the Scots-Irish settlers had spoken to and been influenced by so few outsiders, the language they brought with them from Scotland and Ireland, by way of Pennsylvania, had been preserved remarkably intact. And the English dialect that Kephart encountered in North Carolina was in many ways closer to the Elizabethan English of Shakespeare or the Middle English of Chaucer than to anything that had been spoken in England for centuries. Coincidentally, had Kephart come to these mountains a generation later, his research would have been less definitive. Within a few years after his death, in 1931, road-building initiatives, radio, and the Sears, Roebuck catalogue had begun to open even the darkest hollows of the Appalachians to twentieth-century America. In a very short time, the resulting cultural homogenization had turned the southern highlands into a vastly different world from the one that Kephart had originally discovered.

When I first read "Our Southern Highlanders," late last year, it held for me the power of revelation. It told who I was—or at least where I came from—in a way that I had never fully understood before. All the words I had thought specific to my family had entries in a dictionary compiled from Kephart's research. And all of them—with the exception of "quare," which is a mere two hundred years old—were words of Middle English origin, which is to say anywhere from five hundred to eight hundred years old. Although most of the people I meet today wouldn't have any idea what it's like to eat a bait, Chaucer would have.

Of course, words of Middle English origin are mere babes compared with the words of Latin, Greek, and Hebrew etymology that constitute much of our language. The Latin and Greek roots of the words "agriculture" and "barbarian" were old long before the primitive tribes of the British Isles painted their faces blue and grunted in a dialect resembling English. So I am less taken by the age of the words of the Appalachian vernacular which found their way into my grandmother's house than I am by the specific history they hold.

The word "quare," for me, contains sea voyages and migrations. It speaks of families stopping after long journeys and saying, for any one of a thousand reasons, "This is far enough." It speaks to me of generations of farmers watching red dirt turn below plow blades, of young men stepping into furrows when old men step out. It speaks to me of girls fresh from their mothers' houses crawling into marriage beds and becoming mothers themselves. It bears witness to the line of history, most of it now unmappable, that led to my human waking beneath these particular mountains. If language is the mechanism through which we inherit history and culture, then each individual word functions as a type of gene, bearing with it a small piece of the specific information that makes us who we are, and tells us where we have been. My first cousin Greg and I came down with the same obscure bone disease in the same knee at the same age. For us, the word "quare" is no less a genetic signifier of the past than the odd, bone-eating chromosome carried down through history by one wonders how many limping Scots-Irish.

The last time I remember talking to my great-grandfather Womack, he was well into his nineties, and our whole family had gathered on the porch of the house he built as a young man, along Walnut Creek, in the Sunny View community of Polk County. When I tell this story, I choose to remember it as a spring day—although it may not have been—simply because I like to think that the daffodils in his yard were blooming. (My grandmother, who is eighty-three now, helped him plant them when she was a little girl.) At some point, everyone else got up and went inside, leaving Paw Womack and me alone on the porch. I was in high school, a freshman or sophomore, and was made self-conscious by his legendary age. He had been born in another century. His father had been wounded at Gettysburg. A preacher's son, he had never uttered a swear word or tasted alcohol. He had farmed with a mule until he was well into his eighties, and he had never got another car after one that he bought in 1926 wore out. He voted for Woodrow Wilson. He was *historical*. I felt that the family had somehow chosen me to sit with him; I felt that I needed to say something. I got out of my chair and approached him as one would a sacred relic. I sat down on the porch rail facing him. I remember his immense, knotted farmer's hands spread out on the arms of his rocker. We stared at each other for what seemed like a long time. Eventually, I blushed. I smiled at him and nodded. He smiled back and said, "Who *are* you?"

I said, "I'm Reba's boy. Clara Mae's grandson."

Oh," he said. "Reba's boy."

If we ever spoke again, I don't remember it.

It seems significant to me now that when I told Paw Womack who I was I didn't give him my name. My position as an individual was secondary to my place in the lineage that had led to my sitting on his porch. I identified myself as a small part of a greater whole. *Who are you?* I'm Reba's boy, Clara Mae's grandson, Tom Womack's great-grandson. *Where are you from?* Over yonder. *Why don't you like watermelon?* I don't know. I guess I'm just quare.

Ironically, just as I have learned to appreciate the history contained in the word "quare," I have also had to accept the fact that it is passing out of my family with my generation. Neither I nor my cousins use it outside Granny's house unless we temper it first with irony—a sure sign of a word's practical death within a changing language. Of course, no language is a static property: the life cycles of words mirror the life cycles of the individuals who speak them. Every language, given enough time, will replace each of its words, just as the human body replaces each of its cells every seven years. The self-appointed guardians of English who protest that the word "celibate" means "unmarried," and not "abstaining from sexual intercourse," are wasting their time. "Sounds are too volatile and subtle for legal restraints," Samuel Johnson wrote in the 1755 Preface to his "Dictionary of the English Language"; "to enchain syllables, and to lash the wind, are equally the undertakings of pride."

I tell myself that the passing of Appalachian vernacular from my family's vocabulary is not a tragedy, or a sign of our being assimilated into a dominant culture, but simply the arrival of an inevitable end. "Tongues, like governments," Dr. Johnson wrote, "have a natural tendency to degeneration." I tell myself that it is a natural progression for my children to speak a language significantly different from that of my ancestors, but the fact that it has happened so suddenly, within the span of a single generation—my generation—makes me wonder if I have done something wrong, if I have failed the people who passed those words down. Sometimes the truest answer to the question "Who are you?" is "I don't know."

Words and blood are the double helix that connect us to our past. As a member of a transitional generation, I am losing those words and the connection they make. I am losing the small comfort of shared history. I compensate, in the stories I write, by sending people up mountains to look, as Horace Kephart did, for the answers to their questions, to look down from a high place and see what they can see. My characters, at least, can still say the words that bind them to the past without sounding queer, strange, eccentric, odd, unusual, unconventional, or suspicious. "Stories," says the writer Tim O'Brien, "can save us." I have put my faith in the idea that words, even new ones, possess that kind of redemptive power. Writers write about a place not because they belong there, but because they want to belong. It's a quare feeling.

Questions for Discussion

1. Why do you think some people are particularly judgmental about the speech patterns and vocabulary of others? Do you believe that speech patterns such as those used by Tony Earley's family signify a lack of intelligence on the part of the speakers? Do you think that speakers of a non-standard dialect of English face any of the same barriers faced by non-English speakers in American society?

2. Why would a person who had learned in school the spoken and written forms of Standard American English choose not to use that version of English in certain circumstances? Is your personal literacy broad enough to include more than one version of the language—one for home and another for work or school, for example?

3. For the individual, what is gained through fluency in Standard American English? For society, what is lost when non-standard dialects such as "the secret language of the Appalachians" disappear?

Explorations

1. In his essay, Earley writes that he has intuitively written standard English from the beginning of his education, but that he still struggles to use it in speech. What do you think accounts for the differences between his spoken and written discourses? Analyze the differences between your own written and spoken speech, and explore what you believe accounts for those differences. On the world wide web or at the library, find what has been written about the regional dialect in your area of the country. Do you feel that your own speech pattern fits the description you find? What other influences have shaped the way you speak and write? To what extent does your language define who you are?

2. Gloria Anzaldúa, in "How to Tame a Wild Tongue," writes of the difficulties she has faced as a person who feels torn between cultures, especially when language is one of the defining characteristics of those cultures. The Chicano Spanish she speaks is disdained by both speakers of standard Spanish and the English speakers of the dominant culture. How is Anzaldúa's experience like that of Tony Earley? How is it different?

Formal Writing Assignments

1. In an essay, analyze the differences between the characteristics of your speech and that of someone from the generation of your grandparents. As part of this assignment, interview someone from that generation. How do that person's perceptions of the importance of "correctness" in speech differ from your own? What speech characteristics can you identify that may be lost to your generation? What is the significance of that loss?

2. Have you ever found yourself making an erroneous assumption about someone's intellectual abilities or social skills based on that person's speech patterns or dialect? In an essay that begins with a description of this situation, analyze why you were wrong and how you came to understand and reassess your perceptions. What role does an individual's dialect play in your perception of that individual?

On Dumpster Diving

Lars Eighner

Lars Eighner was born in Corpus Christi, Texas, in 1948, and he later studied at The University of Texas. He worked for a drug-crisis program and as an attendant and ward worker at the Austin State Hospital from 1980 to 1987 before becoming homeless for three years. *Travels with Lizbeth* (1993), the book that includes "On Dumpster Diving," recounts these years. It began as letters to friends explaining his circumstances and evolved into a series of essays on equipment that he found in the garbage. Eighner later sent essays to the *Threepenny Review* for publication. "On Dumpster Diving" show Eighner's uniquely powerful insights and unconventional yet elegant prose style. Eighner is also the author of several novels, including *Pawn to Queen Four* and *Whispered in the Dark*.

Writing Before Reading

1. Think about a subject or activity about which you could consider yourself an expert. How did you become an expert? How would you go about explaining this experience to someone else?

2. Explore your own assumptions about the subject of this essay—Dumpster diving, or scavenging, for food and supplies. What generalizations—both positive and negative—do you make about people you encounter sorting through trash cans near a college campus? Now turn the question around: What kinds of assumptions do you think Dumpster divers might make about you?

3. Reflect for a few moments on what it means to be "homeless." What, in addition to simple shelter from the elements, is lost when a person finds himself or herself homeless?

On Dumpster Diving

Long before I began Dumpster diving I was impressed with Dumpsters, enough so that I wrote the Merriam-Webster research service to discover what I could about the word "Dumpster." I learned from them that "Dumpster" is a proprietary word belonging to the Dempsey Dumpster company.

Since then I have dutifully capitalized the word although it was lowercased in almost all of the citations Merriam-Webster photocopied for me. Dempsey's word is too apt. I have never heard these things called anything but Dumpsters. I do not know anyone who knows the generic name for these objects. From time to time, however, I hear a wino or hobo give some corrupted credit to the original and call them Dipsy Dumpsters.

I began Dumpster diving about a year before I became homeless.

I prefer the term "scavenging" and use the word "scrounging" when I mean to be obscure. I have heard people, evidently meaning to be polite, using the word "foraging," but I prefer to reserve that word for gathering nuts and berries and such which I do also according to the season and the opportunity. "Dumpster diving" seems to me to be a little too cute and, in my case, inaccurate because I lack the athletic ability to lower myself into the Dumpster as the true divers do, much to their increased profit.

I like the frankness of the word "scavenging," which I can hardly think of without picturing a big black snail on an aquarium wall. I live from the refuse of others. I am a scavenger. I think it a sound and honorable niche, although if I could I would naturally prefer to live the comfortable consumer life, perhaps—and only perhaps—as a slightly less wasteful consumer owing to what I have learned as a scavenger.

While my dog Lizbeth and I were still living in the house on Avenue B in Austin, as my savings ran out, I put almost all of my sporadic income into rent. The necessities of daily life I began to extract from Dumpsters. Yes, we ate from Dumpsters. Except for jeans, all my clothes came from Dumpsters. Boom boxes, candles, bedding, toilet paper, medicine, books, a typewriter, a virgin male love doll, change sometimes amounting to many dollars: I have acquired many things from the Dumpsters.

I have learned much as a scavenger. I mean to put some of what I have learned down here, beginning with the practical art of dumpster diving and proceeding to the abstract.

What is safe to eat?

After all, the finding of objects is becoming something of an urban art. Even respectable employed people will sometimes find something tempting sticking out of a Dumpster or standing beside one. Quite a number of people, not all of them of the bohemian type, are willing to brag that they found this or that piece in the trash. But eating from Dumpsters is the thing that separates the dilettanti from the professionals.

Eating safely from the Dumpsters involves three principles: using the senses and common sense to evaluate the condition of the found materials, knowing the Dumpsters of a given area and checking them regularly, and seeking always to answer the question, "Why was this discarded?"

Perhaps everyone who has a kitchen and a regular supply of groceries has, at one time or another, made a sandwich and eaten half of it before discovering mold on the bread or got a mouthful of milk before realizing the milk had turned. Nothing of the sort is likely to happen to a Dumpster diver because he is constantly reminded that most food is discarded for a reason. Yet a lot of perfectly good food can be found in Dumpsters.

Canned goods, for example, turn up fairly often in the Dumpsters I frequent. All except the most phobic people would be willing to eat from a can even if it came from a Dumpster. Canned goods are among the safest of foods to be found in Dumpsters, but are not utterly foolproof.

Although very rare with modern canning methods, botulism is a possibility. Most other forms of food poisoning seldom do lasting harm to a healthy person. But botulism is almost certainly fatal and often the first symptom is death. Except for carbonated beverages, all canned goods should contain a slight vacuum and suck air when first punctured. Bulging, rusty, dented cans and cans that spew when punctured should be avoided, especially when the contents are not very acidic or syrupy.

Heat can break down the botulin, but this requires much more cooking than most people do to canned goods. To the extent that botulism occurs at all, of course, it can occur in cans on pantry shelves as well as in cans from Dumpsters. Need I say that home-canned goods found in Dumpsters are simply too risky to be recommended.

From time to time one of my companions, aware of the source of my provisions, will ask, "Do you think these crackers are really safe to eat?" For some reason it is most often the crackers they ask about.

The question always makes me angry. Of course I would not offer my companion anything I had doubts about. But more than that I wonder why he cannot evaluate the condition of the crackers for himself. I have no special knowledge and I have been wrong before. Since he knows where the food comes from, it seems to me he ought to assume some of the responsibility for deciding what he will put in his mouth.

For myself I have few qualms about dry foods such as crackers, cookies, cereal, chips, and pasta if they are free of visible contaminates and still dry and crisp. Most often such things are found in the original packaging, which is not so much a positive sign as it is the absence of a negative one.

Raw fruits and vegetables with intact skins seem perfectly safe to me, excluding of course the obviously rotten. Many are discarded for minor imperfections which can be pared away. Leafy vegetables, grapes, cauliflower, broccoli, and similar things may be contaminated by liquids and may be impractical to wash.

Candy, especially hard candy, is usually safe if it has not drawn ants. Chocolate is often discarded only because it has become discolored as the cocoa butter de-emulsified. Candying after all is one method of food preservation because pathogens do not like very sugary substances.

All of these foods might be found in any Dumpster and can be evaluated with some confidence largely on the basis of appearance. Beyond these are foods which cannot be correctly evaluated without additional information.

I began scavenging by pulling pizzas out of the Dumpster behind a pizza delivery shop. In general prepared food requires caution, but in this case I knew when the shop closed and went to the Dumpster as soon as the last of the help left.

Such shops often get prank orders, called "bogus." Because help seldom stays long at these places pizzas are often made with the wrong topping, refused on delivery for being cold, or baked incorrectly. The products to be discarded are boxed up because inventory is kept by counting boxes: a boxed pizza can be written off; an unboxed pizza does not exist.

I never placed a bogus order to increase the supply of pizzas and I believe no one else was scavenging in this Dumpster. But the people in the shop became suspicious and began to retain their garbage in the shop overnight.

While it lasted I had a steady supply of fresh, sometimes warm pizza. Because I knew the Dumpster I knew the source of the pizza, and because I visited the Dumpster regularly I knew what was fresh and what was yesterday's.

The area I frequent is inhabited by many affluent college students. I am not here by chance; the Dumpsters in this area are very rich. Students throw out many good things, including food. In particular they tend to throw everything out when they move at the end of a semester, before and after breaks, and around midterm when many of them despair of college. So I find it advantageous to keep an eye on the academic calendar.

The students throw food away around the breaks because they do not know whether it has spoiled or will spoil before they return. A typical discard is a half jar of peanut butter. In fact nonorganic peanut butter does not require refrigeration and is unlikely to spoil in any reasonable time. The student does not know that, and since it is Daddy's money, the student decides not to take a chance.

Opened containers require caution and some attention to the question "Why was this discarded?" But in the case of discards from student apartments, the answer may be that the item was discarded through carelessness, ignorance, or wastefulness. This can sometimes be deduced when the item is found with many others, including some that are obviously perfectly good.

Some students, and others, approach defrosting a freezer by chucking out the whole lot. Not only do the circumstances of such a find tell the story, but also the mass of frozen goods stays cold for a long time and items may be found still frozen or freshly thawed.

Yogurt, cheese, and sour cream are items that are often thrown out while they are still good. Occasionally I find a cheese with a spot of mold, which of course I just pare off, and because it is obviously why such a cheese was discarded, I treat it with less suspicion than an apparently perfect cheese found in similar circumstances. Yogurt is often discarded, still sealed, only because the expiration date on the carton has passed. This is one of my favorite finds because yogurt will keep for several days, even in warm weather.

Students throw out canned goods and staples at the end of semesters and when they give up college at midterm. Drugs, pornography, spirits, and the like are often discarded when parents are expected—Dad's day, for example. And spirits also turn up after big party weekends, presumably discarded by the newly reformed. Wine and spirits, of course, keep perfectly well even after opened.

My test for carbonated soft drinks is whether they still fizz vigorously. Many juices or other beverages are too acid or too syrupy to cause much concern provided they are not visibly contaminated. Liquids, however, require some care.

One hot day I found a large jug of Pat O'Brien's Hurricane mix. The jug had been opened, but it was still ice cold. I drank three large glasses before it became apparent to me that someone had added the rum to the mix, and not a little rum. I never tasted the rum and by the time I began to feel the effects I had already ingested a very large quantity of the beverage. Some divers would have considered this a boon, but being suddenly and thoroughly intoxicated in a public place in the early afternoon is not my idea of a good time.

I have heard of people maliciously contaminating discarded food and even handouts, but mostly I have heard of this from people with vivid imaginations who have had no experience with Dumpsters themselves. Just before the pizza shop stopped discarding its garbage at night, jalapenos began showing up on most of the discarded pizzas. If indeed this was meant to discourage me it was a wasted effort because I am a native Texan.

For myself, I avoid game, poultry, pork, and egg-based foods, whether I find them raw or cooked. I seldom have the means to cook what I find, but when I do I avail myself of plentiful supplies of beef which is often in very good condition. I suppose fish becomes disagreeable before it becomes dangerous. The dog is happy to have any such thing that is past its prime in and, in fact, does not recognize fish as food until it is quite strong.

Home leftovers, as opposed to surpluses from restaurants, are very often bad. Evidently, especially among students, there is a common type of personality that carefully wraps up even the smallest leftover and shoves it into the back of the refrigerator for six months or so before discarding it. Characteristic of this type are the reused jars and margarine tubs which house the remains.

I avoid ethnic foods I am unfamiliar with. If I do not know what it is supposed to look like when it is good, I cannot be certain I will be able to tell if it is bad.

No matter how careful I am I still get dysentery at least once a month, often in warm weather. I do not want to paint too romantic a picture. Dumpster diving has serious drawbacks as a way of life.

I learned to scavenge gradually, on my own. Since then I have initiated several companions into the trade. I have learned that there is a predictable series of stages a person goes through in learning to scavenge.

At first the new scavenger is filled with disgust and self-loathing. He is ashamed of being seen and may lurk around, trying to duck behind things, or he may try to dive at night.

(In fact, most people instinctively look away from a scavenger. By skulking around, the novice calls attention to himself and arouses suspicion. Diving at night is ineffective and needlessly messy.)

Every grain of rice seems to be a maggot. Everything seems to stink. He can wipe the egg yolk off the found can, but he cannot erase the stigma of eating garbage out of his mind.

That stage passes with experience. The scavenger finds a pair of running shoes that fit and look and smell brand new. He finds a pocket calculator in perfect working order. He finds pristine ice cream, still frozen, more than he can eat or keep. He begins to understand: people do throw away perfectly good stuff, a lot of perfectly good stuff.

At this stage, Dumpster shyness begins to dissipate. The diver, after all, has the last laugh. He is finding all manner of good things which are his for the taking. Those who disparage his profession are the fools, not he.

He may begin to hang onto some perfectly good things for which he has neither a use nor a market. Then he begins to take note of the things which are not perfectly good but are nearly so. He mates a Walkman with broken earphones and one that is missing a battery cover. He picks up things which he can repair.

At this stage he may become lost and never recover. Dumpsters are full of things of some potential value to someone and also of things which never have much intrinsic value but are interesting. All the Dumpster divers I have known come to the point of trying to acquire everything they touch. Why not take it, they reason, since it is all free.

This is, of course, hopeless. Most divers come to realize that they must restrict themselves to items of relatively immediate utility. But in some cases the diver simply cannot control himself. I have met several of these pack-rat types. Their ideas of the values of various pieces of junk verge on the psychotic. Every bit of glass may be a diamond, they think, and all that glistens, gold.

I tend to gain weight when I am scavenging. Partly this is because I always find far more pizza and doughnuts than water-packed tuna, nonfat yogurt, and fresh vegetables. Also I have not developed much faith in the reliability of Dumpsters as a food source, although it has been proven to me many times. I tend to eat as if I have no idea where my next meal is coming from. But mostly I just hate to see food go to waste and so I eat much more than I should. Something like this drives the obsession to collect junk.

As for collecting objects, I usually restrict myself to collecting one kind of small object at a time, such as pocket calculators, sunglasses, or campaign buttons. To live on the street I must anticipate my needs to a certain extent: I must pick up and save warm bedding I find in August because it will not be found in Dumpsters in November. But even if I had a home with extensive storage space I could not save everything that might be valuable in some contingency.

I have proprietary feelings about my Dumpsters. As I have suggested, it is no accident that I scavenge from Dumpsters where good finds are common. But my limited experience with Dumpsters in other areas suggests to me that it is the population of competitors rather than the affluence of the dumpers that most affects the feasibility of survival by scavenging. The large number of competitors is what puts me off the idea of trying to scavenge in places like Los Angeles.

Curiously, I do not mind my direct competition, other scavengers, so much as I hate the can scroungers.

People scrounge cans because they have to have a little cash. I have tried scrounging cans with an able-bodied companion. Afoot a can scrounger simply cannot make more than a few dollars a day. One can extract the necessities of life from the Dumpsters directly with far less effort than would be required to accumulate the equivalent value in cans.

Can scroungers, then, are people who *must* have small amounts of cash. These are drug addicts and winos, mostly the latter because the amounts of cash are so small.

Spirits and drugs do, like all other commodities, turn up in dumpsters and the scavenger will from time to time have a half bottle of a rather good wine with his dinner. But the wino cannot survive on these occasional finds; he must have his daily dose to stave off the DTs. All the cans he can carry will buy about three bottles of Wild Irish Rose.

I do not begrudge them the cans, but can scroungers tend to tear up the Dumpster, mixing the contents and littering the area. They become so specialized that they can see only cans. They earn my contempt by passing up change, canned goods, and readily hockable items.

There are precious few courtesies among scavengers. But is a common practice to set aside surplus items: pairs of shoes, clothing, canned goods, and such. A true scavenger hates to see good stuff go to waste and what he cannot use he leaves in good condition in plain sight.

Can scroungers lay waste to everything in their path and will stir one of a pair of good shoes to the bottom of a Dumpster, to be lost or ruined in the muck. Can scroungers will even go through individual garbage cans, something I have never seen a scavenger do.

Individual garbage cans are set out on the public easement only on garbage days. On other days going through them requires trespassing close to a dwelling. Going through individual garbage cans without scattering litter is almost impossible. Litter is likely to reduce the public's tolerance of scavenging. Individual garbage cans are simply not as productive as Dumpsters; people in houses and duplexes do not move as often and for some reason do not tend to discard as much useful material. Moreover, the time required to go through one garbage can that serves one household is not much less than the time required to go through a Dumpster that contains the refuse of twenty apartments.

But my strongest reservation about going through individual garbage cans is that this seems to me a very personal kind of invasion to which I would object if I were a householder. Although many things in Dumpsters are obviously meant never to come to light, a Dumpster is somehow less personal.

I avoid trying to draw conclusions about the people who dump in the Dumpsters I frequent. I think it would be unethical to do so, although I know many people will find the idea of scavenger ethics too funny for words.

Dumpsters contain bank statements, bills, correspondence, and other documents, just as anyone might expect. But there are also less obvious sources of information. Pill bottles, for example. The labels pill bottles contain the name of the patient, the name of the doctor, and the name of the drug. AIDS drugs and antipsychotic medicines, to name but two groups, are specific and are seldom prescribed for any other disorders. The plastic compacts for birth control pills usually have complete label information.

Despite all of this sensitive information, I have had only one apartment resident object to my going through the Dumpster. In that case it turned out the resident was a university athlete who was taking bets and was afraid I would turn up his wager slips.

Occasionally a find tells a story. I once found a small paper bag containing some unused condoms, several partial tubes of flavored sexual lubricant, a partially used compact of birth control pills, and the torn pieces of a picture of a young man. Clearly she was through with him and planning to give up sex altogether.

Dumpster things are often sad—abandoned teddy bears, shredded wedding books, despaired-of sales kits. I find many pets lying in state in Dumpsters. Although I hope to get off the streets so that Lizbeth can have a long and comfortable old age, I know this hope is not very realistic. So I suppose when her time comes she too will go into a Dumpster. I will have no better place for her. And after all, for most of her life her livelihood has come from the Dumpster. When she finds something I think is safe that has been spilled into the Dumpster I let her have it. She already knows the route around the best Dumpsters. I like to think that if she survives me she will have a chance of evading the dog catcher and of finding her sustenance on the route.

Silly vanities also come to rest in the Dumpsters. I am a rather accomplished needleworker. I get a lot of materials from the Dumpsters. Evidently sorority girls, hoping to impress someone, perhaps themselves, with their mastery of a womanly art, buy a lot of embroider-by-number kits, work a few stitches horribly, and eventually discard the whole mess. I pull out their stitches, turn the canvas over, and work original design. Do not think I refrain from chuckling as I make original gifts from these kits.

I find diaries and journals. I have often thought of compiling a book of literary found objects. And perhaps I will one day. But what I find is hopelessly commonplace and bad without being, even unconsciously, camp. College students also discard their papers. I am horrified to discover the kind of paper which now merits an A in an undergraduate course. I am grateful, however, for the number of good books and magazines the students throw out.

In the area I know best I have never discovered vermin in the Dumpster, but there are two kinds of kitty surprise. One is alley cats which I meet as they leap, claws first, out of Dumpsters. This is especially thrilling when I have Lizbeth in tow. The other kind of kitty surprise is a plastic garbage bag filled with some ponderous, amorphous mass. This always proves to be used cat litter.

City bees harvest doughnut glaze and this makes the Dumpster at the doughnut shop more interesting. My faith in the instinctive wisdom of animals is always shaken whenever I see Lizbeth attempt to catch a bee in her mouth, which she does whenever bees are present. Evidently some birds find Dumpsters profitable, for birdie surprise is almost as common as kitty surprise of the first kind. In hunting season all kinds of small game turn up in Dumpsters, some of it, sadly, not entirely dead. Curiously, summer and winter, maggots are uncommon.

The worst of the living and near-living hazards of the Dumpsters are the fire ants. The food that they claim is not much of a loss, but they are vicious and aggressive. It is very easy to brush against some surface of the Dumpster and pick up half a dozen or more fire ants, usually in some sensitive area such as the underarm. One advantage of bringing Lizbeth along as I make Dumpster rounds is that, for obvious reasons, she is very alert to ground-based fire ants. When Lizbeth recognizes the signs of fire ant infestation around our feet she does the Dance of the Zillion Fire Ants. I have learned not to ignore this warning from Lizbeth, whether I perceive the tiny ants or not, but to remove ourselves at Lizbeth's first pas de bourrée. All the more so because the ants are the worst in the months I wear flip-flops, if I have them.

(Perhaps some will misunderstand the above. Lizbeth does the Dance of the Zillion Fire Ants when she recognizes more fire ants than she cares to eat, not when she is being bitten. Since I have learned to react promptly, she does not get bitten at all. It is the isolated patrol of fire ants that falls in Lizbeth's range that deserve pity. Lizbeth finds them quite tasty.)

By far the best way to go through a Dumpster is to lower yourself into it. Most of the good stuff tends to settle at the bottom because it is usually weightier than the rubbish. My more athletic companions have often demonstrated to me that they can extract much good material from a Dumpster I have already been over.

To those psychologically or physically unprepared to enter a Dumpster, I recommend a stout stick, preferably with some barb or hook at one end. The hook can be used to grab plastic garbage bags. When I find canned goods or other objects loose at the bottom of a Dumpster I usually can roll them into a small bag that I can then hoist up. Much Dumpster diving is a matter of experience for which nothing will do except practice.

Dumpster diving is outdoor work, often surprisingly pleasant. It is not entirely predictable; things of interest turn up every day and some say there are finds of great value. I am always very pleased when I can turn exactly the thing I most wanted to find. Yet in spite of the element of chance, scavenging more than most other pursuits tends to yield returns in some proportion to the effort and intelligence brought to bear. It is very sweet to turn a few dollars in change from a Dumpster that has just been gone over by a wino.

The land is now covered with cities. The cities are full of Dumpsters. I think of scavenging as a modern form of self-reliance. In any event, after ten years of government service, where everything is geared to the lowest common denominator, I find work that rewards initiative and effort refreshing. Certainly I would be happy to have a sinecure again, but I am not heartbroken not to have one anymore.

I find from the experience of scavenging two rather deep lessons. The first is to take what I can use and let the rest go by. I have come to think that there is no value in the abstract. A thing I cannot use or make useful, perhaps by trading, has no value however fine or rare it may be. I mean useful in a broad sense—so, for example, some art I would think useful and valuable, but other art might be otherwise for me.

I was shocked to realize that some things are not worth acquiring, but now I think it is so. Some material things are white elephants that eat up the possessor's substance.

The second lesson is of the transience of material being. This has not quite converted me to a dualist, but it has made some headway in that direction. I do not suppose that ideas are immortal, but certainly mental things are longer-lived than other material things.

Once I was the sort of person who invests material objects with sentimental value. Now I no longer have those things, but I have the sentiments yet.

Many times in my travels I have lost everything but the clothes I was wearing and Lizbeth. The things I find in Dumpsters, the love letters and ragdolls of so many lives, remind me of this lesson. Now I hardly pick a thing without envisioning the time I will cast it away. This I think is a healthy state of mind. Almost everything I have now has already been cast out at least once, proving that what I own is valueless to someone.

Anyway, I find my desire to grab for the gaudy bauble has been largely sated. I think this is all attitude I share with the very wealthy—we both know there is plenty more where what we have came from. Between us are the rat-race millions who have confounded their selves with the objects they grasp and who nightly scavenge the cable channels looking for they know not what.

I am sorry for them.

Questions for Discussion

1. Consider the various skills Eighner developed and deployed as a Dumpster diver. What does he suggest one must know or do to become an effective Dumpster diver? What values must one assume? Why is Eighner a successful Dumpster diver?

2. Describe Eighner's attitude toward students. Do you think he was writing specifically to students in this essay? What elements of the text suggest that he was (or was not) directing his comments to students?

3. In what ways did Eighner meet or change your expectations about Dumpster divers? Why do you think that Eighner ended his essay by expressing sympathy for other kinds of scavengers?

Explorations

1. Comment on Eighner's use of lists. What is the rhetorical or narrative effect of the listing?

2. In a review of *Travels with Lizbeth*, that appeared in *Booklist*, one critic wrote that "Eighner fills his pages with vivid descriptions, perceptive observations, humor, and writing that carries the reader easily over troublesome issues." Explore and examine Eighner's stylistic choices. How does his style contribute to his aims in writing this piece? What were the effects of Eighner's stylistic choices on you as a reader?

3. Although the underlying theme of this essay is homelessness, Eighner also uses "Dumpster Diving" as a means of investigating waste, poverty, and uncertainty. Outline his philosophy or commentary on these and related issues as he presents them. What's his opinion of the possibility of generosity in an affluent society?

Formal Writing Assignments

1 Take on the role of "urban anthropologist," as Eighner does in "On Dumpster Diving," by participating in an activity that allows you insight into a group of people or an activity with which you're not currently familiar. Spend several hours observing a group of people lawn bowling in a public park, take a "trash walk" along a city street, or cruise through neighborhoods on trash day. Record your initial findings in the form of a list or extended notes. What kinds of patterns emerge in people's behavior? What kinds of rituals do they follow? What observations can you make about the waste that people leave behind? Modeling your work on Eighner's, compose an essay in which you provide vivid and rich details of scenes and people and at the same time identify the principles that guide the human behavior you've observed.

2. Compose a reply to Eighner in which you address his comments on college students. Draft it as if it were a direct response to Eighner's essay to be published in your college newspaper. Assume that your readers, like your classmates, are familiar with Eighner's argument. (You will probably still want to quote Eighner as a means of illustrating his ideas and claims.) You needn't take an oppositional stance in this response. That is, you may compose a response in which you largely agree with Eighner's assessment of college students. If this is the case, be sure that your essay includes a call to action, an appeal to college students to do something to change their wasteful habits. Conversely, you may elect to disagree with Eighner's assessments. If you do, use your response as an opportunity to illustrate (with examples from your own experiences) that Eighner's observations and claims are not universal.

I Lost It at the Movies

Jewelle Gomez

Jewelle Gomez was born in Boston in 1948, and she has written short stories, poetry, and novels. Gomez has also worked as teacher, a television producer, and a social activist. Her most recent book, *Don't Explain: Short Stories* was published in 1998.

Writing Before Reading:

1. Recall a time when you believe a truth has gone unspoken but understood between you and your parents or someone close to you. Did you wish to be able to speak about this truth but, for one reason or another, could not? How did you know that this truth was understood if no words were used to express it?

2. Communication between parents and their grown or college-age children can sometimes be difficult. What are some of the barriers to communication between these groups? How are those barriers made even more difficult when the topic is sexuality?

3. The "coming out" story has become a part of the literacy of our society, especially in the gay and lesbian community. No one's story is exactly the same as another's, yet similarities run through them and tie them to the experiences of others. Are there other kinds of "coming out" stories? Recall a time when you had to make clear to another person something true about yourself and write about the effect the experience of making that revelation had on you.

I Lost It at the Movies

My grandmother, Lydia, and my mother, Dolores, were both talking to me from their bathroom stalls in the Times Square movie theatre. I was washing butter from my hands at the sink and didn't think it at all odd. The people in my family are always talking; conversation is a life force in our existence. My great-grandmother, Grace, would narrate her life story from 7 A.M. until we went to bed at night. The only break was when we were reading or the reverential periods when we sat looking out of our tenement windows, observing the neighborhood, which we naturally talked about later.

So it was not odd that Lydia and Dolores talked non-stop from their stalls, oblivious to everyone except us. I hadn't expected it to happen there, though. I hadn't really expected an "it" to happen at all. To be a lesbian was part of who I was, like being left-handed—even when I'd slept with men. When my great-grandmother asked me in the last days of her life if I would be marrying my college boyfriend I said yes, knowing I would not, knowing I was a lesbian.

It seemed a fact that needed no expression. Even my first encounter with the word "bulldagger" was not charged with emotional conflict. As a teen in the 1960s my grandmother told a story about a particular building in our Boston neighborhood that had gone to seed. She described the building's past through the experience of a party she'd attended there thirty years before. The best part of the evening had been a woman she'd met and danced with. Lydia had been a professional dancer and singer on the black theater circuit; to dance with women was who she was. They'd danced, then the woman walked her home and asked her out. I heard the delicacy my grandmother searched for even in her retelling of how she'd explained to the "bulldagger," as she called her, that she liked her fine but she was more interested in men. I was struck with how careful my grandmother had been to make it clear to that woman (and in effect to me) that there was no offense taken in her attentions, that she just didn't "go that way," as they used to say. I was so happy at thirteen to have a word for what I knew myself to be. The word was mysterious and curious, as if from a new language that used some other alphabet which left nothing to cling to when touching its curves and crevices. But still a word existed and my grandmother was not flinching in using it. In fact she'd smiled at the good heart and good looks of the bulldagger who'd liked her.

Once I had the knowledge of a word and a sense of its importance to me, I didn't feel the need to explain, confess, or define my identity as a lesbian. The process of reclaiming my ethnic identity in this country was already all consuming. Later, of course, in moments of glorious self-righteousness, I did make declarations. But they were not usually ones I had to make. Mostly they were a testing of the waters. A preparation for the rest of the world which, unlike my grandmother, might not have a grounding in what true love is about. My first lover, the woman who'd been in my bed once a week most of our high school years, finally married. I told her with my poems that I was a lesbian. She was not afraid to ask if what she'd read was about her, about my love for her. So there, amidst her growing children, errant husband, and bowling trophies I said yes, the poems were about her and my love for her, a love I'd always regret relinquishing to her reflexive obeisance to tradition. She did not flinch either. We still get drunk together when I go home to Boston.

During the 1970s I focused less on career than on how to eat and be creative at the same time. Graduate school and a string of non-traditional jobs (stage manager, mid-town messenger, etc.) left me so busy I had no time to think about my identity. It was a long time before I made the connection between my desire, my isolation, and the difficulty I had with my writing. I thought of myself as a lesbian between girlfriends —except the between had lasted five years. After some anxiety and frustration I deliberately set about meeting women. Actually, I knew many women, including my closest friend at the time, another black woman also in the theatre. She became uncharacteristically obtuse when I tried to open up and explain my frustration at going to the many parties we attended and being too afraid to approach women I was attracted to, certain I would be rejected either because the women were straight and horrified or gay and terrified of being exposed. For my friend theoretical homosexuality was acceptable, even trendy. Any uncomfortable experience was irrelevant to her. She was impatient and unsympathetic. I drifted away from her in pursuit of the women's community, a phrase that was not in my vocabulary yet, but I knew it was something more than just "women." I fell into that community by connecting with other women writers, and that helped me to focus on my writing and on my social life as a lesbian.

Still, none of my experiences demanded that I bare my soul. I remained honest but not explicit. Expediency, diplomacy, discretion, are all words that come to mind now. At that time I knew no political framework through which to filter my experience. I was more preoccupied with the Attica riots than with Stonewall. The media helped to focus our attentions within a proscribed spectrum and obscure the connections between the issues. I worried about who would shelter Angela Davis, but the concept of sexual politics was remote and theoretical.

I'm not certain exactly when and where the theory and reality converged.

Being a black woman and a lesbian unexpectedly blended like that famous scene in Ingmar Bergman's film *Persona*. The different faces came together as one, and my desire became part of my heritage, my skin, my perspective, my politics, and my future. And I felt sure that it had been my past that helped make the future possible. The women in my family had acted as if their lives were meaningful. Their lives were art. To be a lesbian among them was to be an artist. Perhaps the convergence came when I saw the faces of my great-grandmother, grandmother, and mother in those of the community of women I finally connected with. There was the same adventurous glint in their eyes; the same determined step; the penchant for breaking into song and for not waiting for anyone to take care of them.

I need not pretend to be other than who I was with any of these women. But did I need to declare it? During the holidays when I brought home best friends or lovers my family always welcomed us warmly, clasping us to their magnificent bosoms. Yet there was always an element of silence in our neighborhood, and surprisingly enough in our family, that was disturbing to me. Among the regulars in my father, Duke's, bar, was Maurice. He was eccentric, flamboyant, and still ordinary. He was accorded the same respect by neighborhood children as every other adult. His indiscretions took their place comfortably among the cyclical, Saturday night, man/woman scandals of our neighborhood. I regret never having asked my father how Maurice and he had become friends.

Soon I felt the discomforting silence pressing against my life more persistently. During visits home to Boston it no longer sufficed that Lydia and Dolores were loving and kind to the "friend" I brought home. Maybe it was just my getting older. Living in New York City at the age of thirty in 1980, there was little I kept deliberately hidden from anyone. The genteel silence hat hovered around me when I entered our home was palpable but I was unsure whether it was already there when I arrived or if I carried it home within myself. It cut me off from what I knew was a kind of fulfillment available only from my family. The lifeline from Grace, to Lydia, to Dolores, to Jewelle was a strong one. We were bound by so many things, not the least of which was looking so much alike. I was not willing to be orphaned by silence.

If the idea of cathedral weddings and station wagons held no appeal for me, the concept of an extended family was certainly important. But my efforts were stunted by our inability to talk about the life I was creating for myself, for all of us. It felt all the more foolish because I thought I knew how my family would react. I was confident they would respond with their customary aplomb just as they had when I'd first had my hair cut as an Afro (which they hated) or when I brought home friends who were vegetarians (which they found curious). While we had disagreed over some issues, like the fight my mother and I had over Vietnam when I was nineteen, always when the deal went down we sided with each other. Somewhere deep inside I think I believed that neither my grandmother nor my mother would ever censure my choices. Neither had actually raised me; my great-grandmother had done that, and she had been a steely barricade against any encroachment on our personal freedoms and she'd never disapproved out loud of anything I'd done.

But it was not enough to have an unabashed admiration for these women. It is one thing to have pride in how they'd so graciously survived in spite of the odds against them. It was something else to be standing in a Times Square movie theater faced with a chance to say "it" out loud and risk the loss of their brilliant and benevolent smiles.

My mother had started reading the graffiti written on the wall of the bathroom stall. We hooted at each of her dramatic renderings. Then she said (not breaking her rhythm since we all know timing is everything), "Here's one I haven't seen before—'Dykes Unite'." There was that profound silence again, as if the frames of my life had ground to a halt. We were in a freeze-frame and options played themselves out in my head in rapid successions: Say nothing? Say something? Say what?

I laughed and said, "Yeah, but have you seen the rubber stamp on my desk at home?"

"No," said my mother with a slight bit of puzzlement. "What does it say?"

"I saw it," my grandmother called out from her stall. "It says: 'Lesbian Money!'"

"What?"

"*Lesbian Money*," Lydia repeated.

"I just stamp it on my big bills," I said tentatively, and we all screamed with laughter. The other woman at the sinks tried to pretend we didn't exist.

Since then there has been little discussion. There have been some moments of awkwardness, usually in social situations where they feel uncertain. Although we have not explored the "it," the shift in our relationship is clear. When I go home it is with my lover and she is received as such. I was lucky. My family was as relieved as I to finally know who I was.

Questions for Discussion

1. What is the significance of the title of this work? What did Gomez "lose"? What did she gain? What are the possible connotations of the phrase "lose it" in relation to the essay?

2. How would you describe the relationship between Gomez and her mother and grandmother? Did that relationship make it easier or more difficult for Gomez to talk with them about her sexuality? How did this relationship compare to the relationship with her friend who could accept "theoretical" homosexuality? What do you believe Gomez means by the phrase "theoretical"?

3. What does Gomez mean when she declares her unwillingness to be "orphaned by silence"?

Explorations

1. Recall other "coming out" stories you have heard or read. Are they like Jewelle Gomez's story? How are they different? the same?

2. Ellen Louis Hart ("Literacy and the Lesbian/Gay Lerner"), argues that homosexual students face special challenges in the classroom. What could be the consequences of "coming out" in an academic setting? Could there be negative repercussions? How could the benefits outweigh the negative consequences?

3. At the library or on the internet, learn more about the varied writing career of Jewelle Gomez. Her best known work, "The Gilda Stories," is a novel about lesbian vampires who work for social justice. What other literary expectations are challenged by Gomez in her poetry and short stories?

Formal Writing Assignments

1. Write about a time when you found yourself in a position of revealing a difficult truth to your parents or someone close to you. How did you prepare for conversation, if at all? What rhetorical choices did you make—either to make sure your point was understood or to make the task easier for yourself? What did you learn from this experience? How was your life changed?

2. In her essay, Gomez writes "My family was as relieved as I to finally know who I was." What she means by this is that her family cannot really know her without understanding her homosexuality. In an essay, explore the ways in which our sexuality defines who we are in relation to others and society. In a predominantly heterosexual society, heterosexuals have little at stake in "revealing" their sexuality. How might the life of a homosexual be affected by the choice of "coming out" or remaining silent?

Fear of Bees

John Hockenberry

John Hockenberry was born in 1956 in Dayton, OH. Though he has been a wheelchair user since an automobile accident in 1976 injured his spine, he has enjoyed a varied and highly successful career as a correspondent for National Public Radio, ABC, and NBC news. He currently appears on NBC's "Dateline NBC" and on the cable networks MSNBC and CNBC. For NPR, Hockenberry covered the Middle East from 1988-90, reporting from Israel, Jordan, Egypt, Iran, Lebanon, and Iraq. He also covered the Gulf War and its aftermath in 1991, once riding a mule into the mountains on the border between Turkey and Iraq to report on Kurdish refugees.

"Fear of Bees" is a part of Hockenberry's book *Moving Violations*, which chronicles his life and career as a journalist.

Writing Before Reading

1. Have you ever seen John Hockenberry on television or heard his reports on the radio? If so, were you aware that he is a wheelchair user? Does your knowledge of his disability change the way you perceive his reporting or media persona?

2. If you are not a wheelchair user, what do you believe would be the greatest daily challenges of wheelchair use? What activities would be off limits to you? What elements of your life would be altered if you were in a wheelchair? What elements would stay the same?

3. The Americans with Disabilities Act mandates that both public and private locations (other than private homes) be made accessible to the disabled through such things as architectural changes to buildings and the provision of information—such as menu selections—in Braille. You have probably noticed many of changes that have come about through this Act, including designated parking spaces and restroom facilities for the disabled, ramp entrances to buildings, and lifts on city buses. Beyond improving access for the disabled to employment, shopping, and schools, do you believe that the Americans with Disabilities Act has changed the attitude of society as a whole toward the disabled? If so, how?

Fear of Bees

People often ask me what I would prefer to be called. Do they think I have an answer?

I'm a crip for life. I cannot walk. I have "lost the use of my legs." I am paralyzed from the waist down. I use a wheelchair. I am wheelchair-bound. I am confined to a wheelchair. I am a paraplegic. I require "special assistance for boarding." I am a gimp, crip, physically challenged, differently abled, paralyzed. I am a T-5 para. I am sick. I am well. I have T4-6 incomplete dural lesion, a spinal cord injury, a broken back, "broken legs" to Indian cabbies in New York who always ask, "What happened to your legs, Mister?"

I have a spastic bladder, pneumatic tires, and air in all four of my tires. Solid wheelchair tires are for hospitals and weenies. No self-respecting crip would be caught dead in one. I use a catheter to take a whiz. I require no leg bag. That's for the really disabled. I have no van with a wheelchair lift anymore.

Those are for the really disabled, and thank God I'm not one of them. I need no motor on my wheelchair. Those are for the really disabled, and I am definitely not one of those. From mid-chest down I have no sensation. I am numb all the way to my toes.

I know what they're all thinking. My dick doesn't work. The truth? My dick works sometimes. My dick works without fail. I have two dicks. I have totally accepted my sexuality. I have massive problems with my sexuality. Actually, there is no problem with sexuality. It's just not a problem. I think we can just drop this subject of sexuality because it's not an issue. Not at all. The truth? I had a little problem there in the beginning, then I learned how to compensate. Now everything is fine. It's actually better than fine. To be perfectly honest, I am the sexual version of crack. There are whole clinics set up for people who became addicted to sleeping with me. All right, the truth? Not so fast.

You do not have to feel guilty for causing my situation even though your great-great-grandparents may have been slave owners. You do have to feel guilty and fawning and contrite if I ever catch you using a wheelchair stall in an airport men's room or parking in a disabled space. I feel as though I caused my situation and deserve to be cast from society, on which I am a burden. I am a poster boy demanding a handout. I am the 800 number you didn't call to donate money. I am the drum major in Sally Struther's parade of wretches. I watch the muscular dystrophy telethon every year without fail. I would like to have Jerry Lewis sliced thinly and packed away in Jeffrey Dahmer's freezer. I am not responsible for my situation and roll around with a chip on my shoulder ready to lash out at and assault any person making my life difficult, preferably with a deadly weapon.

I have unlimited amounts of "courage," which is evident to everyone but myself and other crips. I get around in a wheelchair. I am a wheelchair "racer." I am just rolling to work. I am in denial. I have accepted my disability and have discovered within myself a sublime reservoir of truth. I can't accept my disability, and the only truth I am aware of is that my life is shit and that everyone is making it worse. I am a former food stamp recipient. I am in the 35 percent tax bracket. I am part of the disability rights movement. I am a sell-out wannabe TV star media scumbag who has turned his broken back on other crips.

I am grateful for the Americans with Disabilities Act, which has heralded a new era of civil rights in this country. I think the Americans with Disabilities Act is the most useless, empty, unenforceable law of the last quarter-century. It ranks up there as one of the most pansy-assed excuses for a White House news conference in U.S. history. I think that the disabled community is a tough, uncompromising coalition of activists. I think the disabled community is a back-biting assembly of noisy, mutually suspicious clowns who would eagerly sell out any revolution just to appear on a telethon, or in the White House Rose Garden, or in a Levi's commercial.

I cannot reach the cornflakes in my cupboard. I cannot do a hand stand. I cannot use most revolving doors. I cannot rollerblade. Bowling is more of a waste of time than it used to be. (One of the chief advantages of being in a wheelchair is always having an excuse not to go bowling, even though I do miss the shoes.) I'm telling you these things because I want us to share, and for you to understand my experiences and then, together, bridge the gulf between us. I want you all to leave me alone.

I'm a guy in a chair, crip for life. Everything you think about me is right. Everything you think is wrong.

What is "normal" but another stereotype, no different than "angry black man," "Asian math genius," "welfare mother," or "gay man with a lisp"? Each stereotype thrives in direct proportion to the distance from each class of persons it claims to describe. Get close to the real people and these pretend images begin to break up, but they don't go easily. As each stereotype breaks down, it reveals a pattern of wrongs. Losing a stereotype is about being wrong retroactively. For a person to confront such assumptions they must admit an open-ended wrong for as long as those assumptions have lived inside them. There is the temptation to hold on to why you believed in stereotypes. "I was told gays were like that as a child." "I never knew many blacks, and that's what my parents believed about them." "I was once frightened and disgusted by a person in a wheelchair," To relinquish a stereotype is to lose face by giving up a mask.

We trade in masks in America. Especially in politics. Politicians love to talk about the "American people" and what they allegedly want or don't want. But who are they, really? The America evoked most often today by politicians and pundits is a closet full of masks denoting race, nationality, and a host of other characteristics. America's definitive social unit of measurement is no longer the family, nor is it the extended family. On the other end of the scale, it is not the village or hamlet, neighborhood or block, city, state, or region. I grew up in America at a time when its logo was the racially balanced commercial image of four or five children, one black, white, Asian, female, and disabled (optional) romping in an idyllic, utopian, and quite nonexistent playground.

You can still occasionally see this image in the children's fashion supplement to *The New York Times Magazine*. These are happy measuring sticks of a demographic formula, perfect faces of social equilibrium to distract from the fact that each child is usually clad in the designer fabric hard currency equivalent of the GNP of Guyana or Cameroon. In the eighties the fashion chain Benetton crossed the old American emblem with the UN General Assembly and produced its own utopian logo of a meticulously integrated, multiracial youth army, no disabled (not optional).

We once portrayed these idealized young people as seeds of a racially harmonious society we dreamed would come. Now those children shout down the long narrow lenses of music video cameras, or gun each other down on the streets. Our communities have become multiracial, just as the dream foretold. But they are not utopias. Integration is no guarantee of harmony. It is what most of the world has known since the end of World War Two. It is this nation's last, cruel lesson of the twentieth century.

Today, if one measures America at all, it is in audience units, America is the union of all the multiracial groups of ostensibly "normal" people, ranging from submissive and polite to angry and aggressive, who can be seated in a television studio in front of a talk-show host. There they stare at, and react to, the famous hosts, the famous guests, or anyone else on stage. Mad people, older people, teenagers, victims, predators, all of the species in America's great political aviary pass in front of the audience, America turns its thumbs up or down, then goes to a commercial break. There is no verdict. There is just the din of many verdicts. As the camera scans the audience, the people who can be anticipated to have a distinct opinion, or more likely, an outrage, are handed the microphone. "Why don't you just leave him if he beats you?" "It's people like you skinheads who spread hate in this country." America punctuates each of these outraged questions and challenges with applause, jeers, and shouts.

I caught the delivery of verdicts from one such clump of Americana between commercial breaks on the "Oprah Winfrey" show some time after my accident. I had always thought of myself as a face in the audience. On this show I saw myself on the stage with a group of four married couples, each with a disabled partner. Three of the couples contained a partner in a wheelchair; the other was a blind woman and her sighted husband. The theme of the show that day was something like "One of them is fine and the other one is defective. How do they manage?" The audience applauded with an enthusiasm they reserved for First Ladies, and Oprah herself had that deep, breathy voice that television talk-show hosts reserve for the inspirational subjects—the serious themes that justify all of those celebrity interviews and fluff. Here, Crips and Their Spouses" was gripping television.

The couples represented an odd composite of the crip population. This was Oprah's idea of the crips next door, and that next door, in this case, was not necessarily the static institution. Just your average run-of-the mill crip and spouse combo package. There were no Vietnam vets on this panel, no wheelchair jocks, no quadriplegics, no gunshot ghetto homies with their stripped-down Quickie ultra-lights, and, of course, they had neglected to call me.

Three of the couples might as well have had lamp shades on their heads. They were nonthreatening, overweight, jolly, well-adjusted types with a hint of acne, all wearing loud, baggy shirts. These are the people the audience was used to giving a wide berth on the bus and then ignoring. One of the women was in a dented, ill-fitting wheelchair with gray hospital wheels. They said things like, "Hey, Oprah, it just takes more planning. It's no big deal." They laughed a lot. The audience imagined working near one of these people; it did not have to imagine being one.

One of the couples was different; a thin guy in a wheelchair and his pretty, young, unparalyzed wife. They had dated in college before his "accident." They were neatly dressed and clearly held the most fascination for the audience members. "How difficult was it for you after his accident?" Oprah addressed herself to the young woman when she wanted to know some detail. No, she had never thought of breaking up with him after the accident. "It's no different than anything else that might make a relationship difficult." The audience began to applaud while Oprah nodded. On their faces was a kind of sentimental approval. The audience wanted her to know that she could have left him. . . she would have had the perfect excuse . . . no jury would have convicted, certainly not in that audience. She seemed slightly sensitive about this point because she insisted again that she had not thought of breaking up the relationship, and that it really was just another thing, like a joint checking account, for a couple to deal with.

The joint checking account line really got them. "I just want to say that I think you are such an inspiration to us all," an audience member addressed the panel. It didn't really matter what the panelists said, especially the young couple. It only mattered what the audience thought about the young man's plight and his courageous girlfriend. It was far more important to assume that he was broken, that she was tied to him now selflessly, and that they would make the best of things. "Yes, Oprah; we manage just fine," she said in her small voice with her husband's nodding assent. Oprah addressed the young man once. "You must be so happy to have someone like Amy," or whatever her name was.

I was rooting for these folks to hold their own. Though I was just a little older I could tell that I had logged lots more wheelchair time than the young guy on TV. I could feel what was coming. I saw the audience greedily looking them up and down. I saw what we were supposed to think about them. He: strong, brave, and struck down in his youth. She: stronger and braver for spending her youth with him. On their faces you could see that the conditions of this public execution were just beginning to dawn on them.

But it was just Oprah. It was all in good fun. I was making too much of a television talk show. They weren't forced to go out onto that stage. A voice inside said, "If you weren't so angry and dysfunctional, John, maybe you would be invited to go on 'Oprah' too."

It didn't take long for Oprah to deliver. "So there's one thing I want to know." She looks directly at the young girl as the hungry crowd buzzes with anticipation, Oh, my god, she's going to ask. Like a car accident in the movies, the world slows down at this point. I can see the smile freeze on the face of the young woman. The crowd goes wild. The camera cuts away to Oprah.

"What I want to know is . . ."

She pauses for sincerity. The crowd is totally with her. The woman must know what's about to happen. She must have been asked a million times. I wondered if the guy knew. The guy probably had no idea. Or maybe it was a condition for going on the show. I'm screaming at the TV now: "Tell her it's none of her damn business. We're counting on you out here. Tell Oprah to stuff it!"

Oprah delivers.

"Amy, can he do it?"

Loud gasp from the crowd. I imagine that it must have sounded this way when Sydney Carton's head was lopped off in *A Tale of Two Cities*. The camera immediately cuts to the woman's face, which has blushed a deep red. She tries something of a laugh, glances at her husband, who is out of the shot. Eventually, when the noise dies down, she says, "Yes, he can, Oprah." She giggles.

The camera pulls wide, and the two onstage seem very small. He takes her hand for comfort. The crowd bursts into applause. Even the other crips on stage are applauding. He withdraws his hand, as though it had been placed in hot oil. The camera cuts back to Orphan, who is nodding to the crowd halfheartedly, trying to get them to stop clapping. She looks somewhere between a very satisfied Perry Mason and a champion mud wrestler. Now we know what the show was really about. It wasn't just Oprah; the whole crowd seemed to care only about this. The oddest thing was that after the question and the embarrassed answer the audience seemed to think they now knew how "it" was done. What did they know? They knew that they had the guts to ask this question; they didn't really care about the answer.

Oprah, there is something I have always wanted to know. Do black guys really have giant dicks? The angry voice yelled at the television and then turned it off. Is that what people think when they stare? What constitutes "doing it"? There was no answer for them. There was no answer for me. Questions like these were the weapon. They need no real answer and apparently are always loaded in the chambers of people's curiosity. Stereotypes bring forth righteous anger and deep humiliation. At the same time, they are completely understandable, like an old piece of furniture you have walked by every day of your life.

Once on a very hot day on the Washington, D.C., subway a woman sat looking at me for a long time. She was smiling. I suspected that she knew about me from the radio, that she had seen some picture of me, somewhere. I am rarely recognized in public, but it was the only plausible explanation for why she kept watching me with a look of some recognition. Eventually she walked up to me when the train stopped, said hello, then proceeded in a very serious voice.

"Your legs seem to be normal."

"They are normal, I just can't move them."

"Right, I know that. I mean, I can see that you are paralyzed." I was beginning to wonder where she was going with this. "Why aren't you shriveled up more?" she asked, as though she was inquiring about the time of day. "I notice that your legs aren't shrunken and all shriveled up. Why is that?" I was wearing shorts. She looked at my legs as though she was pricing kebab at the market. "I mean, I thought paralyzed legs got all shriveled up after a while. Were you just injured recently?"

"Uh . . . twelve years ago."

This was a line of questioning I was unprepared for. I continued to smile and listen. I wondered under what circumstances I would ever roll up to a perfect stranger and ask the question, "Why aren't you shriveled up more?" I really didn't have an answer for her. I said something like I try to stay active, eat plenty of salads, vitamins.

She said she knew people in wheelchairs who were much more shriveled up. I can only assume that the expression on my face was one of extreme annoyance and skepticism. Her reaction was to redouble her efforts to convince me that she had some degree of expertise in these matters. She started to click off her credentials. She had worked for the outpatient clinic at a local hospital. She had been responsible for wheelchair access at some community women's health film festival, and she was once roommates with a woman who signed for the hearing impaired. I should accept her as a progressive, hip, knowledgeable person where disability was concerned, and acknowledge her theories on shriveled muscle.

I wondered if these disabled people she claimed to know were close friends and if that's what she called them, her "shriveled-up" friends. This was a whole constituency I had failed to encounter. I looked around the train and wondered if everyone who saw me in shorts was thinking, What's this guy trying to prove by not being more shriveled up?

In quite another context, I was once on the other end of this transaction. I was interviewing African musician Hugh Masekele and critic Greg Tate on the radio around the time Nelson Mandela was released from a South African prison. It was a moment of dramatic change, and I wanted to know if American blacks and black South Africans would become closer now, even to the point of some musicians feeling free to visit South Africa to perform. I can recall that Tate smiled and told me something to the effect that black Africans and black Americans are as close as they need to be and, in any case, were not interested in performing some sentimental act of reunion for the benefit of whites in the media. In my follow-up I tried to reassure him that this was NPR and that I wasn't one of those insensitive journalists who was ignorant about the black struggle. He was aggressively unmoved. "We don't need white people to tell us when it's time to go home to Africa." No amount of cajoling him into accepting that I was progressive and hip was going to change that point. It was just as true that events in South Africa would bring great changes in political outlook and identity for blacks on both continents, but we didn't get into any of that on the radio that night in 1990. Was there a correct answer or a correct question? Whatever lessons might been drawn from the encounter, it was a minor milestone in nationally broadcast awkwardness.

All stereotypes have some, albeit distorted, basis in fact. With the lady on the Washington, D.C., subway, I had to admit that I knew what she was talking about even if I had no shriveled-up friends, or if I was not prepared to admit that she was anything more than an ignorant boob. People in wheelchairs do lose muscle tone, and legs can become quite thin, especially in neuromuscular disease. My legs are intact even though they cannot be controlled by me. Their own muscles move around spastically. Because this movement happens fairly regularly, the muscles are exercised and therefore they retain their tone and shape. Discussing the clinical details of muscle-tone retention was one thing. I was just wondering how anyone could ask such questions of a perfect stranger.

"Hi, I notice that you have been out jogging, and I'm wondering if you're developing a red chafing rash along your groin right about now?

"I have a lot of chafed friends with groin rashes, and it looks to me as though your legs are not stiff. You are not holding them wide apart as though you're in pain, and I'm noticing that you are not grabbing at your underwear discreetly to ease your discomfort. Am I right in concluding that you are not experiencing a burning, itching sensation in your groin area at this moment?" Not everyone would want to call the police immediately if I rolled up and inquired about their groin discomfort, but I bet I wouldn't have any long conversations on this subject.

If I were not so haunted by these experiences I could simply dismiss each intrusive questioner as just another dangerous psychopath or ignorant clown. More often than not, the intrusions are humorous, and they usually contain nuggets of some elusive truth. Each encounter is a parable about the increasing distance we humans all hail from even as we are more closely packed together on this planet. Perhaps the correct answer to the woman on the train was to take a deep breath and calmly explain the details of my legs and muscles as I understood them. Yet to do so I would have had to admit that there was a category of shriveled up people, and that I was not one of them. I would also have had to concede that it was perfectly permissible for her to walk up to me and say something outrageous when that was the last thing I believed.

In her question she was demanding that I acknowledge a relationship with her that I wasn't prepared to admit I had. At the very least, I did not realize that I was a part of her own confrontation with the experience of disability. I was a part of this woman's experience of disabled people. That experience was so powerful that she suspected I might be having it along with her. But I was not. "No, I am John! I am a person, not a wheelchair. You must deal with me as I think of myself." This was how I responded. I could dismiss her even though I completely understood what she was talking about.

Encounters with strangers who claimed the right to ask bizarre detailed questions about disability had long ago become common for me when, in 1993, a man boarded a commuter train in New York bound for Long Island. He opened fire on the passengers and killed seven people. The event was a headline for the people of New York City and part of the footnoted background noise of crime for much of the rest of the country. His murderous rampage was psychotic and horrific to be sure; yet trapped within the bloody savagery was a plaintive cry that someone acknowledge his relationship with the rest of the world. He surely had no cause to express that relationship in lead and gunpowder, but what was not reported about the LIRR killings, and which was reflected in extensive conversations with people of every race and occupation for weeks later, is that no one in 1993 was in the least surprised by the fact that a black man in America would be angry, that he might be carrying a gun on the train, that he might look at the faces of people around him with unreasoning hatred even though he did not know them.

We accept our masks so completely that we scarcely recognize the faces of the real people behind them, including our own. Getting beyond them requires a leap that people are rarely prepared to take. For me to accept why someone might have had their own preconceived notion about shriveled-up people in wheelchairs is to accept that it was somehow natural for crips to be considered diseased. For an African-American to enthusiastically accept a white person's celebration over seeing black Africans and black Americans coming together is for them to concede that slavery and apartheid were some brief natural mistakes of history and that all some white guys need to do is adjust the political control panel and everyone will be free to kiss and make up . . . preferably on "Oprah," "Dinah," or "Nightline."

Often these meetings of the mask end in anger or bitterness. It is much harder to use such encounters to inform. In order to convince you that another view is possible, I have to accept your degrading stereotype about wheelchairs for a moment. That is the one thing I have declared at the outset that I will not do. I can explain myself to the drivers on the road who honk or presume that I am lost, to the woman inspecting me to see if my legs are shriveled up, or I can dismiss them angrily. It is their choice to be curious or dogmatic. It is my choice to inform or punish.

It is the rare encounter in which both parties leave feeling that they know more about the other. Usually, the stereotype remains real along with the accumulated bits of anger from each face-off. In America in this half-century, we can claim to have made the effort to integrate our communities and to learn more about the diversity within them. But along with these changes it has also become clear that we, in America, are all experiencing this slow accumulation of anger. The tide rises, droplets at a time. Each failed encounter is a capillary tied off, raising the pressure to the heart and denying oxygen to the brain. It has been this way for a long time. It gets harder to laugh at all of this, but it is still possible.

Once a flight attendant noted how adept I seemed to be in getting on planes. She had seen me move from my wheelchair to a small movable seat, to be rolled down the narrow aisle of the airliner; then she saw me move with quick, confident arm motions into the passenger seat.

"You really don't let anything stop you, do you? I saw you get on that plane and you just didn't stop at all. I just think that is great."

"I travel a lot."

"I guess you are the first handicapped person I have ever seen up close. Have you ever thought of killing yourself?"

I wondered if this question appeared in this flight attendant's official training manual under the heading of "Handicapped Patrons: Suggested Conversation Starters."

"Do you ask lots of people on your airline if they think of suicide?"

"Oh, goodness no, that would be crazy. I was just wondering about you because you get around so well that you must have really done a lot of praying to get this great attitude."

My great attitude was eroding fast. There was nothing to do but say something like, "Well, you know, I just think that if you take the energy to do things instead of just staring into space, life can be pretty interesting." Brilliant, John. No wonder you can't get on "Oprah." I was hoping that she would just take my word about not committing suicide during the flight and leave the pilot, standing nearby, out of this conversation when she came out with her other big question.

"Can you, I mean, can your body, I mean are you able to do it with a woman?"

This line did not sound like one from the manual. Some business-class passengers had gotten up from their seats and were slowly walking up toward the lavatory. She continued to look at me, expecting an answer. I could say yes and giggle like on "Oprah"; I could take some time and clinically explain the situation and perhaps gain the attention of the business-class passengers, or we could exchange phone numbers. But what is the real correct answer?

"Paralyzed from the waist down" describes so little of the experience of a spinal-cord injury that most crips use it as a kind of shorthand joke. In my case I am paralyzed from the nipples down. When people learn of this they are shocked that there is no international checkpoint at the waist. It is an arbitrary demarcation. In actual fact, relatively few people are paralyzed from the waist down. Everyone has their particular line separating sensation from numbness. Each line of separation is invisible to the eye. In some people the aspects of temperature and pressure and muscle control are separate. Some spinal-cord-injured people can feel pressure but not temperature in some parts of their body, and vice versa. There are people with almost total sensation but with no motor control ... a partially damaged fiber-optic cable ... picture but no sound ... bad reception. All of these metaphors aid understanding, but none is precise. The trace of each paraplegic and quadriplegic's sensory border zone is as unique as a fingerprint. Each person has a different answer to the question: What does paralysis feel like?

Not being able to sense the rhythms of your body is to be cast off from the familiar. But the shock is in learning that nothing physical has really changed beneath the skin. Your body is your body whether you can feel it or not. There is actually no reason to believe that loss of feeling makes you any different from the same old bag of water and flesh that you have always known. The bag fills. The bag empties. Life goes on.

In sensation there is the illusion that we are complicit in the body's biology. It is sensation that lures humans into endowing their bodily processes with intent and intelligence. Sensation makes a heart "burn," puts butterflies in the stomach, and a frog in the throat. Sensation creates the little gatekeeper in the brain working the body's control panels. Sensation is the neural confirmation that the brain needs the body more than the other way around. In feelings, the brain is permitted to believe that it gets to vote on processes it has no part of. The body requires no brain to get most of its work done. The infuriating truth about a brain dead person is that they are perfectly alive. The fact that they cannot have a conversation is a requirement only another brain would demand; the same brain would make no such demand of a pet fish and yet continue to feed and take care of it. When people no longer want their fish, they flush them down the toilet with no attendant scandal, or simply eat them with some nice steamed vegetables on the side. But there is no endless Kevorkianesque discussion of the "brain dead fish" and the necessity of removing its life support. You kill the fish, you kill the person. It's your call. The brain is capable of making such decisions. People make life and death decisions all the time. The brain wants more, though. It wants the world to act as though what has no brain is not alive. This is folly, and just a trifle arrogant.

The brain can neither explain life, nor explain it away. While consciousness is something of a mystery, it is not permitted to intervene in the mechanics of the body. The identity of limbs and organs is mechanical, and in the case of the large intestine and bladder, fluid mechanics. Loss of sensation reveals these mechanics.

A friend visited me in the hospital shortly after my accident, and as she sat on the bed next to me and we talked, I placed my hand on her leg, which was next to mine. I had assumed that it was my leg I was touching, but when I looked down and saw hers I realized that without sensation I could not tell the difference between my leg and someone else's. Her leg is not the same as mine. But because of an injury to my spinal cord, her leg and my leg felt the same to my hand, that is to say, numb. I recall with a hearty Protestant blush the times, and there have been many, when I have placed my hand on a leg under the bed sheets and while caressing its skin realized that it was my own leg, not that of a companion sleeping beside me. Guiltily, I withdrew my hand from my own leg which, truth be told, gets relatively little attention. To have been tricked by one's own body is unsettling. On the other hand, part of the attraction of touching someone else's leg, assuming they were not also paralyzed, is that it would respond to my touch. My own will not. It is the strangest sensation of all.

The spine is a knotted code of evolutionary ladder. There, in a mysterious order, the functions of the body are laid out on a schematic. At the bottom is sensation for the feet, move upward and you encounter nerves for the muscles of the leg, the buttocks, hips, abdomen, chest, arms, and neck. In the fine print is another message. One of the lowest set of nerves just above the tailbone controls sensation of the bladder and genitals. Just above are the nerves of sensation for the muscles of the large intestines. The abdominal muscles fall silent one by one as you proceed up the verttebrae until about the fifth vertebra in the thorax.

At this point there is an additional nerve connected to the genitals. It controls some involuntary functions. The toggle switches that open the bladder sphincter, that open the rectum, and that control orgasm are on this 220-volt nerve. The strictly voluntary nerves at the bottom can control things until certain physical limits are met. But when the limit is reached there is no more discussion. The higher nerve fires.

The childhood battle between release and anal retention takes place between the sacral vertebrae and the thoracic. The higher nerve always wins. Orgasm works in this way. Foreplay happens in the lower nerves, then at a perfect moment the higher nerve takes over and in men, at least, one decisive little sphincter opens like clockwork. An orgasm arrives with the rush of a train and the control of a free fall. It has nothing to do with sensation. Sensation is only the illusion of control. What we think of as advanced—our sensation—is on the bottom of the ladder.

The crucial functioning of these systems has to do with the loop between the voluntary nerves on the bottom of the spine and the involuntary nerves in the middle. If the loop is unbroken, then sphincters remain closed. If the loop is broken, then neither voluntary nor involuntary systems are available. Lower injuries between the base and the middle of the spine generally mean that while the body retains more muscle control, more use of legs and abdominals, it is incontinent, impotent, and incapable of having an orgasm. Injuries above the middle mean more severe paralysis in terms of pure muscle loss, but because the voluntary and involuntary nerves can talk to each other on what's left of the spinal cord, bladders stay closed and an orgasm is possible if difficult.

The effect of this curious neural ordering is to divide the wheelchair crips (males particularly) into jocks and sex gods. The lower injuries make all of the lay-ups on the basketball courts . . . the higher injuries, the quadriplegics, get all of the dates. In my case the injury was in the middle. My bladder is spastic, which means it is closed until opened by a catheter. Sexual function is erratic, unpredictable, but orgasm and ejaculation are reliably achieved through some aggressive manual stimulation. Without sensation, though, making this happen can be frustrating. It is hard to know what I did right, or if it doesn't happen, what I did wrong.

There is a kind of harrowing ambiguity about a body without the familiar warning sensations associated with the control of bodily functions. The body is suddenly a saboteur. To be in public becomes a trip behind enemy lines with a time bomb taped quite literally to one's abdomen. To go out and have a large meal and a few drinks in public is a kind of intestinal roulette until one becomes fluent in decoding far subtler and more direct messages and warnings about what is going on in the body.

Much of the independence seen among spinal-cord-injured people today stems not from any new-found magnanimity on the part of society or a breakthrough in wheelchair technology, but from the development of plastic. During World War One the souls whose chest and spinal fractures could be stabilized could look forward to a short life of gradual kidney failure. After just a few weeks, the kidneys would back up or become infected from uncontrolled draining. Death would come within a year in most cases.

Plastic was a material that could be fashioned into tubes and inserted up into the bladder to empty it. It revolutionized the prognosis for the spinal-cord injuries in World War Two, and the victims of polio. More details buried inside the cold phrase, "paralyzed from the waist down." What inkling was there that an injury to the spine even involved the bladder? Bladder stuck shut . . . wait a minute. The nurse told me that I should be thankful that it was stuck shut and not stuck open. She was right.

It makes all the difference in the world if paralysis results in an uncontrolled bladder that is stuck in the open position versus an uncontrolled bladder stuck in the closed position. Mine is closed. It means that I will fill until emptied. But I must insert a tube inside just as the nurse did, every four hours or so for the rest of my life. Why some bladders are stuck open and others are stuck closed reveals some crucial details about the spinal cord, to say nothing of the laundromat.

Loss of control is a dark fear, particularly in America. Why we should so fear losing control in a world that we have no control over anymore is one of the central questions of American culture. The notions of control and power are themes of American policy. Going with the flow and becoming attentive to the subtleties of one's economy or politics are not themes of American policy anywhere in the world. The frustrations in our superpower identity, the frustrations of homelessness, bankruptcy, and in continence are all facets of the same fear. People who lose control are deviants or failures. People who have control are heroes, role models, victors over adversity, people "with their shit together."

It is the keenest insight gained from a loss of sensation to discover that the icons of control over the body are illusions. For all its urgent tangibility, sensation is the illusion of control over the body rather than the mechanism for that control. Sensation in the body is more a curtain than a window. It hides more about the body than it purports to reveal. The nerves in the skin and muscles give you the "sense" that your limbs are extensions of the brain, which they most assuredly are not. Phantoms of pain and pleasure determine our actions, while the body's processes inexorably continue. Sensation is life's ultimate mask, at life's ultimate costume party: consciousness.

In demanding simple names for complex experiences, our society loses the precious details. A person asked to define the word paraplegic will undoubtedly remark that it is someone who has lost the use of his or her legs. The handicapped, the disabled, the confined to a wheelchair, the mobile in a wheelchair, the physically challenged, the mobility-impaired, the broken in half, the chronically stared at, the person with disability, the about to wet his pants, the intestinally challenged, the numb from the nipples down, the shrapnelly challenged, the amputee, the confined to a car wreck: all of these names could also accurately describe someone in a wheelchair, on a wheelchair, or with a wheelchair. The obsession with finding the right name leads us away from the unique. The whole is diminished by ignoring its parts.

My seven-year-old niece, Sarah, was once sitting on my lap, having long ago gotten used to Uncle John never walking. As a child whose notions of normal had not solidified in concrete, she was free to think far and wide about the implications of my physical condition. Much farther and wider than even I. She grabbed my thigh and looked into my eyes with a questioning, probing gaze that only a child can give. "Can you feel that, Uncle John?" she asked.

"No," I told her incredulous, shaking head. She moved her hands up on my legs and pounded with a force that she was convinced would have caused her own leg pain. The look in her eyes was exhilarating, as though she were on the edge of some experimental breakthrough. "Can you feel that, Uncle John?" She tried a fist out on her own thigh and winced. "Wow." She thought for a moment and then pinched a loose bit of skin above my left knee. "You feel nothing, Uncle John?" "Nothing, Sarah."

She was deep in thought, examining the implications of such a truth. She was satisfied that I had no sensation, but she still needed further elaboration. She suddenly burst out with a last question: "So if a bee stung you right here, Uncle John. . . ." She pointed to a place on my thigh where one summer she had been stung. It was her ultimate test, her ultimate definition of pain. I shook my head. "Nothing, Sarah. Ten bees could sting me there."

She turned around on my lap. "Mommy, Uncle John can't even feel a bee stinging him on his leg." Her mom was occupied with making sandwiches or having a rare conversation with an adult. She had noted with some alarm Sarah's blows to my legs, wondering if her persistent daughter might continue the investigation with a fork or other sharp object. "That's right, Sarah. Uncle John can't feel anything on his legs, but it's not all right to hit him." Sarah was lost in thought until she said triumphantly, "Then you aren't afraid of bees."

In a future world where the thoughts of little girls can matter as much as those of presidents and generals, the fear of bees as a metaphor for spinal-cord injury might even be an appropriate topic for "Oprah." It would truly be an indication of the millennium if in supermarket parking lots in the twenty-first century the signs on the parking spaces in the front said: RESERVED FOR PEOPLE UNAFRAID OF BEES. If you need a name for me, call me John. If you want to know if I can "do it," perhaps that can be discreetly arranged. If you want to say one thing more about me, you may comfortably note that I am a person not afraid of bees.

Questions for Discussion

1. "Fear of Bees" begins with two pages of seemingly contradictory statements: "Everything you think about me is right. Everything you think is wrong." Is it possible for each of Hockenberry's statements to be true? What rhetorical purpose is served by opening the essay this way? How do these paragraphs relate to the rest of the essay?

2. How can a disability such as John Hockenberry's be considered part of his "personal literacy"? What are some examples of how the language of disability affects our perception of the disabled? What, for example, is the difference between a "crips" and a "wheelchair user"? Why might it seem insulting for an able-bodied person to call a wheelchair user a "cripple," but not for one wheelchair user to use the same word in reference to another wheelchair user?

3. Hockenberry spares nothing in his condemnation of an Oprah broadcast focusing on disabled couples. What elements of the program inspire his anger? Do you believe he is right to be so angry? What points does he believe Oprah has missed? What does Hockenberry mean when he says that "stereotypes bring forth righteous anger and deep humiliation. At the same time, they are completely understandable"?

Explorations

1. Recall some images of the disabled you have encountered in the media, such as characters in television programs, movies, or advertisements. Do you believe there is a tendency to portray disabled people in ways that are limiting? Are they portrayed, for example, as pitiable? heroic? resourceful? Is it possible to say that a person who cannot walk is "just like everyone else, only happens to be in a wheelchair"?

2. In one of his seemingly contradictory sentence pairings, John Hockenberry writes "I am grateful for the Americans with Disabilities Act, which has heralded a new era of civil rights in this country. I think the Americans with Disabilities Act is the most useless, empty, unenforceable law of the last quarter-century." On the web or at the library, find evidence that a person would need to back up either or both of these claims.

3. What visible steps has your university taken to comply with the Americans with Disabilities Act? Consult your institution's web site or visit the student services office to find out what less-visible steps have been taken. Do you believe that your university has done enough to ensure equal access and opportunity for disabled students, faculty, and staff?

Formal Writing Assignments

1. Return to the third exploration above and write an essay that chronicles your college or university's efforts to comply with the Americans with Disabilities Act. Evaluate the effectiveness of actions taken so far, and suggest what further steps should be taken. As part of this essay, consider interviewing a disabled student, staff member, or faculty member, as well as the person at your institution who is responsible for assuring compliance with the ADA.

2. Write an essay analyzing the effect on the disabled and on society as a whole of the phrases used to describe disability. For example, what is the difference in the impact of the terms "crippled," "handicapped," and "disabled"? What about other terms, from the negatively-connotated "spastic" or "retarded," to the seemingly clinical diagnosis of cerebral palsy or Down syndrome? If you, a family member, or friend are disabled, how have any of these terms altered your perception of yourself? How are they a part of your personal literacy?

The Circuit

Francisco Jimenez

Francisco Jimenez is a professor of modern languages at Santa Clara University in California. Though "The Circuit" is written in the style of a short story, it chronicles real events in the author's life. His family immigrated to the United States from Mexico when Jimenez was four years old, and their lives as migrant farm workers did not allow him to attend school regularly until high school. His early understanding of the power of language to change lives, however, drove him to excel as a student. He became the student body president of his high school and ultimately earned college degrees at Santa Clara University and Columbia University.

Writing Before Reading

1. Children's lives are often affected by decisions or circumstances completely beyond their control. Write about the frustration you may have experienced as a result of your family moving or your parents' changing jobs.

2. Write about a time when you felt yourself to be caught between two cultures. Perhaps the language, values, or traditions of your family came into conflict with those of your school or friends. How did you negotiate this conflict?

3. If you grew up in an area where migrant laborers harvest crops—or if you are a member of a migrant labor family—describe the relationship you witnessed in school between the children of migrant families and other students.

The Circuit

It was that time of year again. Ito, the strawberry sharecropper, did not smile. It was natural. The peak of the strawberry season was over and the last few days the workers, most of them braceros, were not picking as many boxes as they had during the months of June and July.

As the last days of August disappeared, so did the number of braceros. Sunday, only one—the best picker—came to work. I liked him. Sometimes we talked during our half-hour lunch break. That is how I found out he was from Jalisco, the same state in Mexico my family was from. That Sunday was the last time I saw him.

When the sun had tired and sunk behind the mountains, Ito signaled us that it was time to go home. "Ya esora," he yelled in his broken Spanish. Those were the words I waited for twelve hours a day, every day, seven days, a week, week after week. And the thought of not hearing them again saddened me.

As we drove home Papa did not say a word. With both hands on the wheel, he stared at the dirt road. My older brother, Roberto, was also silent. He leaned his head back and closed his eyes. Once in a while he cleared from his throat the dust that blew in from outside.

Yes, it was that time of year. When I opened the front door to the shack, I stopped. Everything we owned was neatly packed in cardboard boxes. Suddenly I felt even more the weight of hours, days, weeks, and months of work. I sat down on a box. The thought of having to move to Fresno and knowing what was in store for me there brought tears to my eyes.

That night I could not sleep. I lay in bed thinking about how much I hated this move.

A little before five o'clock in the morning, Papá woke everyone up. A few minutes later, the yelling and screaming of my little brothers and sisters, for whom the move was a great adventure, broke the silence of dawn. Shortly, the barking of the dogs accompanied them.

While we packed the breakfast dishes, Papá went outside to start the "Carcanchita." That was the name Papá gave his old '38 black Plymouth. He bought it in a used-car lot in Santa Rosa in the winter of 1949. Papá was very proud of his little jalopy. He had a right to be proud of it. He spent a lot of time looking at other cars before buying this one. When he finally chose the "Carcanchita," he checked it thoroughly before driving it out of the car lot. He examined every inch of the car. He listened to the motor, tilting his head from side to side like a parrot, trying to detect any noises that spelled car trouble. After being satisfied with the looks and sounds of the car, Papá then insisted on knowing who the original owner was. He never did find out from the car salesman, but he bought the car anyway. Papá figured the original owner must have been an important man because behind the rear seat of the car he found a blue necktie.

Papá parked the car out in front and left the motor running. "Listo," he yelled. Without saying a word, Roberto and I begin to carry the boxes out to the car. Roberto carried the two big boxes and I carried the two smaller ones. Papá then threw the mattress on top of the car roof and tied it with ropes to the front and rear bumpers.

Everything was packed except Mamá's pot. It was an old large galvanized pot she had picked up at an army surplus store in Santa Maria the year I was born. The pot had many dents and nicks, and the more dents and nicks it acquired the more Mamá liked it. "Mi olla," she used to say proudly.

I held the front door open as Mamá carefully carried out her pot by both handles, making sure not to spill the cooked beans. When she got to the car, Papá reached out to help her with it. Roberto opened the rear car door and Papá gently placed it on the floor behind the front seat. All of us then climbed in. Papá sighed, wiped the sweat off his forehead with his sleeve, and said wearily: "Es todo."

As we drove away, I felt a lump in my throat. I turned around and looked at our little shack for the last time.

At sunset we drove into a labor camp near Fresno. Since Papá did not speak English, Mamá asked the camp foreman if he needed any more workers. "We don't need no more," said the foreman, scratching his head. "Check with Sullivan down the road. Can't miss him. He lives in a big white house with a fence around it."

When we got there, Mamá walked up to the house. She went through a white gate, past a row of rose bushes, up the stairs to the front door. She rang the doorbell. The porch light went on and a tall husky man came out. They exchanged a few words. After the man went in, Mamá clasped her hands and hurried back to the car. "We have work! Mr. Sullivan said we can stay there the whole season," she said, gasping and pointing to an old garage near the stables.

The garage was worn out by the years. It had no windows. The walls, eaten by termites, strained to support the roof full of holes. The dirt floor, populated by earthworms, looked like a gray road map.

That night, by the light of kerosene lamp, we unpacked and cleaned our new home. Roberto swept away the loose dirt, leaving the hard ground. Papá plugged the holes in the walls with old newspapers and tin can tops. Mamá fed my little brothers and sisters. Papá and Roberto then brought in the mattress and placed it on the far corner of the garage. "Mamá, you and the little ones sleep on the mattress. Roberto, Panchito, and I will sleep outside under the trees," Papá said.

Early next morning Mr. Sullivan showed us where his crop was, and after breakfast, Papá, Roberto, and I headed for the vineyard to pick.

Around nine o'clock the temperature had risen to almost one hundred degrees. I was completely soaked in sweat and my mouth felt as if I had been chewing on a handkerchief. I walked over to the end of the row, picked the jug of water we had brought, and began drinking. "Don't drink too much, you'll get sick," Roberto shouted. No sooner had he said that than I felt sick to my stomach. I dropped to my knees and let the jug roll off my hands. I remained motionless with my eyes glued on the hot, sandy ground. All I could hear was the drone of insects. Slowly I began to recover. I poured water over my face and neck and watched the dirty water run down my arms to the ground.

I still felt a little dizzy when we took a break to eat lunch. It was past two o'clock and we sat underneath a large walnut tree that was on the side of the road. While we ate, Papá jotted down the number of boxes we had picked. Roberto drew designs on the ground with a stick. Suddenly I noticed Papá's face turn pale as he looked down the road. "Here comes the school bus," he whispered loudly in alarm. Instinctively, Roberto and I ran and hid in the vineyards. We did not want to get in trouble for not going to school. The neatly dressed boys about my age got off. They carried books under their arms. After they crossed the street, the bus drove away. Roberto and I came out from hiding and joined Papá. "Tienen que tener cuidado," he warned us.

After lunch we went back to work. The sun kept beating down. The buzzing insects, the wet sweat, and the hot dry dust made the afternoon seem to last forever. Finally the mountains around the valley reached out and swallowed the sun. Within an hour it was too dark to continue picking.

The vines blanketed the grapes, making it difficult to see the bunches. "Vámonos," said Papá, signaling to us that it was time to quit work. Papá then took out a pencil and began to figure out how much we had earned our first day. He wrote down numbers, crossed some out, wrote down some more. "Quince," he murmmured.

When we arrived home, we took a cold shower underneath a water hose. We then sat down to eat dinner around some wooden crates that served as a table. Mamá had cooked a special meal for us. We had rice and tortillas with "carne con chile," my favorite dish.

The next morning I could hardly move. My body ached all over. I felt little control over my arms and legs. This feeling went on for days until my muscles finally got used to the work.

It was Monday, the first week of November. The grape season was over and I could now go to school. I woke up early that morning and lay in bed, looking at the stars and savoring the thought of not going to work and of starting sixth grade for the first time that year. Since I could not sleep, I decided to get up and join Papá and Roberto at breakfast. I sat at the table across from Roberto, but I kept my head down. I did not want to look up and face him. I knew he was sad. He was not going to school today. He was not going tomorrow, or the next week, or next month. He would not go until the cotton season was over, and that was sometime in February. I rubbed my hands together and watched the dry, acid stained skin fall to the floor in little rolls.

When Papá and Roberto left for work, I felt relief. I walked to the top of a small grade next to the shack and watched the "Carcanchita" disappear in the distance in a cloud of dust.

Two hours later, around eight o'clock, I stood by the side of the road waiting for school bus number twenty. When it arrived I climbed in. Everyone was busy either talking or yelling. I sat in an empty seat in the back.

When the bus stopped in front of the school, I felt very nervous. I looked out the bus window and saw boys and girls carrying books under their arms. I put my hands in my pants pockets and walked to the principal's office. When I entered I heard a women's voice say: "May I help you?" I was startled. I looked at the lady who waited for an answer. My first instinct was to answer her in Spanish, but I held back. Finally, after struggling for English words, I managed to tell her I wanted to enroll in the sixth grade. After answering many questions, I was led to the classroom.

Mr. Lema, the sixth grade teacher, greeted me and assigned me a desk. He then introduced me to the class. I was so nervous and scared at that moment when everyone's eyes were on me that I wished I were with Papá and Roberto picking cotton. After taking roll, Mr. Lema gave the class the assignment for the first hour. "The first thing we have to do this morning is finish reading the story we began yesterday," he said enthusiastically. He walked up to me, handed me an English book, and asked me to read. "We are on page 125," he said politely. When I heard this, I felt my blood rush to my head; I felt dizzy. "Would you like to read?" he asked hesitantly. I opened the book to page 125. My mouth was dry. My eyes began to water. I could not begin. "You can read later," Mr. Lema said understandingly.

For the rest of the reading period I kept getting angrier and angrier with myself. I should have read, I thought to myself.

During recess I went into the restroom and opened my English book to page 125. I began to read in low voice, pretending I was in class. There were many words I did not know. I closed the book and headed back to the classroom.

Mr. Lema was sitting at his desk correcting papers. When I entered he looked up at me and smiled. I felt better. I walked up to him and asked if he could help me with the new words. "Gladly," he said.

The rest of the month I spent my lunch hours working on English with Mr. Lema, my best friend at school.

One Friday during lunch hour Mr. Lema asked me to take a walk with him to the music room. "Do you like music?" he asked me as we entered the building.

"Yes. I like corridos," I answered. He then picked up a trumpet, blew on it and handed it to me. The sound gave me goose bumps. I knew that sound. I had heard it in many corridos. "How would you like to learn how to play it?" he asked. He must have read my face because before I could answer, he added: "I'll teach you how to play it during our lunch hours."

That day I could hardly wait to get home to tell Papá and Mamá the great news. As I got off the bus, my little brothers and sisters ran up to meet me. They were yelling and screaming. I thought they were happy to see me, but when I opened the door to our shack, I saw that everything we owned was neatly packed in cardboard boxes.

Questions for Discussion

1. The voice of the narrator in this story is that of a grown person remembering events through the eyes of child. As a result, readers are likely to identify with the viewpoint of the child. How does this narrative voice alter our perception of the events as they are described? How would these same events have been described differently through the eyes of another character, such as the writer's father? siblings? mother?

2. What factors do you believe drove the author to want to learn English? Why did he experience such a strong sense of guilt that he was able to attend school while his brother Roberto could not?

3. The title of this work refers to circuit of travel that migrant workers follow as crops become ready for harvesting. Keeping in mind that a "circuit" is generally considered to be a closed or circular route, to what circuits other than his family's actual travel could Jimenez be referring?

Explorations

1. Do some research into the creation of the United Farm Workers Union (UFW) and its founder, Cesar Chavez. How has the creation of the Union changed the lives of migrant laborers across the United States? How have advances in farming technology further altered the lives of these workers and families?

2. Though Gloria Anzaldúa ("How to Tame a Wild Tongue") also writes of the struggle between Hispanic and Anglo culture in California, how does her experience differ from that of Francisco Jimenez? What are the similarities between them? Jimenez found himself anxious to master English, Anzaldúa less so. Why?

3. How do you believe Jimenez would define "literacy"? Why?

Formal Writing Assignments

1. In an essay, argue that a person's personal literacy goes beyond mastery of language and is inextricably connected to that person's culture, family, and upbringing. Using your own experience as an example, demonstrate how your use of language is defined by and helps define who you are. If the language or dialect of your schooling is different from that of your home, which do you consider to be your real literacy? Can both versions be real?

2. Describe some of the many "circuits" that make up a person's life. Sometimes we are liberated when a circuit is broken; sometimes our lives are enriched through the tradition and knowledge cycled from one generation to the next. What circuits have you traveled in your life, and how have they had an impact on who you are?

She Unnames Them

Ursula LeGuin

Most famous for her science fiction novels, Ursula LeGuin's writing covers a broad spectrum of themes and genres, including children's fiction, poetry, literary criticism and history, fantasy fiction, novels and short stories. Critics find it difficult to pigeonhole her style; LeGuin herself avoids narrow categorization of her writing, claiming the categories of fantasy, realism, magical realism, and science fiction to describe her works. Her range of interests can be attributed to her scholarly training at Columbia University as well as to the influence of her parents. LeGuin's mother, writer Theodora Kroeber, chronicled the life of Ishi, the last Yahi Indian, and loved myths and legends from around the world.

Noted anthropologist Alfred Kroeber, LeGuin's father, told her campfire tales he collected from Northern California tribes. LeGuin absorbed her parents' interest in the study of different cultures and combined them with her academic background in Renaissance history to create the backdrop for many of her stories. Along with her knowledge of cultures outside of her own, LeGuin experienced religion in ways different from many Americans. During the late nineteenth century, LeGuin's father was a member of the Ethical Culture movement, a nonreligious, but highly moral system of thought. In the following story, "She Unnames Them," LeGuin's understanding of cultural practices, history, and religion comes together to revise a story familiar to many Western readers.

Writing Before Reading:

1. Compose a journal entry or other piece of informal writing that considers the significance of names. Do names affect our daily lives? Why or why not? Remember, there are place names, proper names, nicknames, pet names, team names, car names, brand names, screen names—the list is innumerable, try to consider at least a few different types in your answer.

2. Think about your given name, your nickname, or the name of someone close to you. Tell the story of that name. Who gave it? Why? What kind of links exist between names and stories?

3. Almost all cultures have a history of storytelling: personal and public histories are retold and rewritten; fairy tales and urban legends are revised; books are made into movies; movies are then remade; histories are fictionalized, while "actual" events of years are transformed into five-minute segments of the daily news or single paragraphs in textbooks. Write a journal entry that examines the human drive to retell, revise, and refashion life into language. If you're unsure of where to begin, consider the following questions—Why are stories important? Why might someone choose to radically revise a traditional or canonical story? What types of stories hold the most weight in current US culture?

She Unnames Them

Most of them accepted namelessness with the perfect indifference with which they had so long accepted and ignored their names. Whales and dolphins, seals and sea otters consented with particular grace and alacrity, sliding into anonymity as into their element. A faction of yaks, however, protested. They said that "yak" sounded right, and that almost everyone who knew they existed called them that. Unlike the ubiquitous creatures such as rats and fleas, who had been called by hundreds or thousands of different names since Babel, the yaks could truly say, they said, that they had a *name*. They discussed the matter all summer. The councils of the elderly females finally agreed that though the name might be useful to others it was so redundant from the yak point of view that they never spoke it themselves and hence might as well dispense with it. After they presented the argument in this light to their bulls, a full consensus was delayed only by the onset of severe early blizzards. Soon after the beginning of the thaw, their agreement was reached and the designation "yak" was returned to the donor.

Among the domestic animals, few horses had cared what anybody called them since the failure of Dean Swift's attempt to name them from their own vocabulary. Cattle, sheep, swine, asses, mules, and goats, along with chickens, geese, and turkeys, all agreed enthusiastically to give their names back to the people to whom—as they put it—they belonged.

A couple of problems did come up with pets. The cats, of course, steadfastly denied ever having had any name other than those self-given, unspoken, ineffably personal names which, as the poet named Eliot said, they spend long hours daily contemplating—though none of the contemplators has ever admitted that what they contemplate is their names and some onlookers have wondered if the object of that meditative gaze might not in fact be the Perfect, or Platonic, Mouse. In any case, it is a moot point now. It was with the dogs, and with some parrots, lovebirds, ravens, and mynahs, that the trouble arose. These verbally talented individuals insisted that their names were important to them, and flatly refused to part with them. But as soon as they understood that the issue was precisely one of individual choice, and that anybody who wanted to be called Rover, or Froufrou, or Polly, or even Birdie in the personal sense, was perfectly free to do so, not one of them had the least objection to parting with the lowercase (or, as regards German creatures, uppercase) generic appellations "poodle," "parrot," "dog," or "bird," and all the Linnaean qualifiers that had trailed along behind them for two hundred years like tin cans tied to a tail.

The insects parted with their names in vast clouds and swarms of ephemeral syllables buzzing and stinging and humming and flitting and crawling and tunnelling away.

As for the fish of the sea, their names dispersed from them in silence throughout the oceans like faint, dark blurs of cuttlefish ink, and drifted off on the currents without a trace.

None were left now to unname, and yet how close I felt to them when I saw one of them swim or fly or trot or crawl across my way or over my skin, or stalk me in the night, or go along beside me for a while in the day. They seemed far closer than when their names had stood between myself and them like a clear barrier: so close that my fear of them and their fear of me became one same fear. And the attraction that many of us felt, the desire to smell one another's smells, feel or rub or caress one another's scales or skin or feathers or fur, taste one another's blood or flesh, keep one another warm—that attraction was now all one with the fear, and the hunter could not be told from the hunted, nor the eater from the food.

This was more or less the effect I had been after. It was somewhat more powerful than I had anticipated, but I could not now, in all conscience, make an exception for myself. I resolutely put anxiety away, went to Adam, and said, "You and your father lent me this—gave it to me, actually. It's been really useful, but it doesn't exactly seem to fit very well lately. But thanks very much! It's really been very useful."

It is hard to give back a gift without sounding peevish or ungrateful, and I did not want to leave him with that impression of me. He was not paying much attention, as it happened, and said only, "Put it down over there, O.K.?" and went on with what he was doing.

One of my reasons for doing what I did was that talk was getting us nowhere, but all the same I felt a little let down. I had been prepared to defend my decision. And I thought that perhaps when he did notice he might be upset and want to talk. I put some things away and fiddled around a little, but he continued to do what he was doing and to take no notice of anything else. At last I said, "Well, goodbye, dear. I hope the garden key turns up."

He was fitting parts together, and said, without looking around. "O.K., fine, dear. When's dinner?"

"I'm not sure," I said. "I'm going now. With the . . ." I hesitated, and finally said, "With them, you know," and went on out. In fact, I had only just then realized how hard it would have been to explain myself. I could not chatter away as I used to do, taking it all for granted. My words now must be as slow, as new, as single, as tentative as the steps I took going down the path away from the house, between the dark-branched, tall dancers motionless against the winter shining.

Questions for Discussion

1. What story is LeGuin using as the basis of her piece? Is an understanding of this allusion necessary for real understanding of this piece? Why or why not?

2. After the unnaming, the speaker describes a new relationship with the animals, saying, "They seemed far closer than when their names had stood between myself and them like a clear barrier." This is an interesting, but rather opaque or ambiguous statement. What are some ways you might interpret the speaker's observation? What does it mean for names to be a "clear barrier"?

3. Many of the essays in *Writing Lives* examine the intersections between discourse and power. Do you see any of these intersections in "She Unnames Them"? How is power defined in this piece? Who has it? Who doesn't? How do your answers relate to questions of language and literacy?

Explorations

1. Poet Amy Lowell has been quoted as having said: "All books are either dreams or swords." Compose an exploration that places LeGuin's short story in one category or the other. Be sure to provide both an analytical explanation and textual proof for your choice. Once the entire class has completed this assignment discuss your various stances and evidence in either large or small groups.

2. The speaker and the animals reject the language of Adam's naming system because it does not suit their understanding of themselves. How does the system of language described in this text compare to Ruth Herschberger's theory of gender-biased language in "Society Writes Biology"? Are the problems of scientific discourse the same as those of Adam's naming? What is the problem in both?

3. Although the speaker and many of the animals consider unnaming to be a beneficial practice, some animals defend their proper names, revealing contested relationships to the value of names. Compare the importance Toni Morrison places on naming in remembering people in "The Site of Memory" with the value LeGuin's speaker places on names. Do you think Morrison's argument and LeGuin's point conflict or agree? Why? If you feel they represent two different arguments, support one and explain your position.

Formal Writing Assignments

1. Take a myth or foundational story you feel shapes a part of your culture and explain its importance. What does it reveal about your culture's values? Once you have established its value, then rewrite the story to challenge these values. What would change if the original story became your story? What would change in your world?

2. Try to describe a person or group of people who are important in your life without naming them or using traditional language to connote identity categories. What difficulties does this absence of naming pose? Why? How would your relationship with these people change if you no longer thought about them according to these labels?

A Voice

Barry Lopez

Barry Lopez is perhaps best known as a fiction writer and essayist on the environment and natural history and for his contributions to *Outside* magazine. In addition to writing full time for thirty years, Lopez has taught at numerous institutions, including Eastern Washington University, the University of Iowa, Columbia, and Notre Dame. The excerpt below, "A Voice" is the introduction to his most recent book, *About This Life: Journies on the Threshold of Memory*. He is the author of numerous books, including *Of Wolves and Men*, *Winter Count*, and *Arctic Dreams: Imagination and Desire in a Northern Landscape*. He's been awarded the John Burroughs Medal for distinguished natural history writing, Christopher Medal for humanitarian writing, and National Book Award in nonfiction.

Lopez, in interviews, has commented that as a writer he finds himself often engaging the "issues of tolerance and dignity" and that these themes often present themselves through his writing on the environment. He lives in western Oregon.

Writing Before Reading

1. What does it mean to have a "voice" as a writer? What elements do you believe make up "voice"? In what ways have you, in the writing that you have done on your own or for creative writing classes, worked to cultivate a distinctive voice?

2. Reflect upon those people in your life who have made significant contributions to your development as a reader or writer. Who were these people and how did they influence you?

3. Take a few moments to commit to paper a scene, place, or event from your distant past that carries with it a special significance or magic. Be as detailed as possible, trying to call up from memory as many images as possible.

A Voice

I was born east of the heights of New Rochelle in the watershed of New York's Mamaroneck River in the winter of 1945. In the spring of 1948 my father, a billboard advertising executive, would move us away, to a home in rural California at the foot of the Santa Susana Mountains in the San Fernando Valley, far from this suburban landscape just thirty miles from New York City. I would never know why. Perhaps the move was an effort to save a marriage gone awry, or maybe he hoped to capitalize on prospects in southern California after the war.

For a long time I thought of California as the beginning, the place where my life took a distinctive shape, but something had already begun. When I recall incidents from those first three years in New York, some still vivid as a bowl of oranges on a summer windowsill, several seem to bear directly on my later life, to be adumbration's. Or perhaps that is only how memory works.

We lived on the second floor of a six-story apartment building situated on Orienta Point in the town of Mamaroneck. It faced onto Mamaroneck Harbor, an embayment of Long Island Sound. My parents, avid sailors, had a membership in the Nanhook Yacht Club, which was affiliated with "The Orienta"— a primary attraction for people who chose to live there.

A great lawn sloped north from the building down to a seawall and a narrow beach, off which sailboats were moored. My earliest memories are of crawling off a blanket onto this cool, prickly turf under a huge elm. Flowerbeds had been planted along the building's east side, and I remember walking in them with my mother to pick flowers as tall as I was. I remember the aroma of the soil in summer and the way the bare earth puckered to a dry crust after an early morning watering.

The odor and the flowers' colors in the garden attracted me. To ensure visits there with Mother, I'd sometimes line my alphabet blocks up on a windowsill—our windows were right above the gardens—and push them out. She'd take me along to retrieve them while she gathered bouquets.

I also remember the glare of light on the harbor and the snap of white sails coming taut in a breeze. In warm weather I was closely watched like other children on the beach, but I recall wading out into the water as if I were alone, and wanting to go farther. I could see across to Shootfly Island and the estuary of Otter Creek. Away to the east, where Turkey Rock and Hen Island stood out, low lying Peningo Neck protected the harbor from the open waters of the Sound.

Standing in seawater stirred to wavelets by the wind, my head thrown back, I'd turn slowly to gaze at the towering crown of the elm, backlit and twinkling in noon light, turn and catch the long horizon of the sound to the east, keep turning to follow scudding sailboats on that wind. On the hottest days I sought out the shade of the big elm, but I would go back in the water again to experience that peculiar yearning—to swim, to sail, to go. I would wait in the water for something to emerge, to appear in that empty space, above its surface.

Shortly after my brother was born in 1948, my father drove out to California. My mother and brother and I flew west afterward in a Constellation. (I remember a living-room-like atmosphere at the rear of this plane, where couch seats were arranged in a horseshoe around a table, and going into the terminal at Love Field in Dallas with one of the stewardesses to eat dinner while my mother attended to my infant brother.) My parents divorced two years later, and my mother began raising us with a dedication I would not understand or appreciate for years. She taught home economics during the day at a junior high school; twice a week she taught night school at a junior college. She also worked at home as a dressmaker.

My images of our first house, when I was three or four and my father still lived with us, are of the way it sat apart, surrounded by alfalfa hay fields. Our street was a macadam-surfaced ditch meant to funnel heavy winter rains into the Los Angeles River. It also served as a corridor for heading sheep to summer pastures in the Santa Susanas. On different days we might be stuck in the car for either reason.

After my father left, not to be seen again, Mother bought a small one-bedroom house on a half-acre of land in the town of Reseda. For boys my age growing up then in the northern San Fernando Valley, adventure unfolded in fruit orchards and wisteria hedges, in horse pastures and haylofts, and around farming operations, truck gardens, and chicken ranches. During these same years the Los Angeles River channel, another haunt, was floored and walled in concrete, so we saw the last of that river's natural days. We hiked in the Santa Monica Mountains and we caught rides on slow freights west from Reseda to Canoga Park and back. We rode our bikes out as far as Porter Ranch, the rural fringes of valley settlement where braceros worked the fields and where encounters with coyotes, jackrabbits, and even rattlesnakes were not unusual.

Mother frequently drove my brother, Dennis, and me into the Mojave Desert on weekends, or up to Antelope Valley or away to one of a dozen beaches from Zuma, west of Malibu, to Pismo, up north near San Luis Obispo. We spent summer weeks in camp at Big Bear Lake or with Mother's friends at Lake Arrowhead in the San Bernardino Mountains.

One advantage of growing up in a single-parent home (it wasn't called that back then, of course; "broken home" was the preferred term) is that if your mother is an interesting or handsome woman, she can attract the attention of interesting men. My brother and I knew several such men, all but one in my memory impeccable in their conduct and generous toward us. I remember picnics at the home of a movie stuntman who kept a rambling, jerrybuilt house in an unspoiled part of the Calabasas hills, where he'd dammed a creek to create a swimming hole. And picnics at the summer house of a man who was the gentlest person I ever knew, a horticulturalist at the Santa Barbara Botanic Garden whom for a long time I wished my mother would marry. With them and Mother I experienced the crash of Pacific storm surf on the deserted beaches of Los Angeles and Ventura Counties. I felt the hysteria that came with brush fires fanned by Santa Ana winds and caught the astringent smell of creosote bush after a desert rain.

In the middle of what was, for me, this intensely physical landscape, another man emerged who engaged a different part of my mind. He was an aeronautical engineer at Hughes Aircraft and also an artist. He'd taught my mother painting in college in Alabama and had been her first husband. After their divorce, he moved to California and remarried. When my father left he became like a father to me. He drove a blue-gray sports car, an Austin Healey convertible, and I rode with him swiftly along winding Mulholland Drive above the city and down the broad promenade of the Pacific Coast Highway with the top down. One Christmas he built a large layout for my trains, a landscape of paper-maché mountains and tunnels with a handcrafted bridge and a scenic backdrop he'd painted.

For years I believed my childhood nothing out of the ordinary, but it was a sort of bohemian existence. Mother was strict with Dennis and me about table and social manners. She disciplined us and was conscientious about our schooling and protective of our emotional lives. But I remember no impatience, no indifference toward imagination. She embraced our drawings, our stories, and our Tinkertoy kingdoms, and she drove us to many intriguing places in our green 1934 Ford coupe—to Boulder (later, Hoover) Dam, the La Brea Tar Pits. And she invited engaging, independent men and women to the house for dinner.

The parents of some of my classmates and some of Mother's friends worked in the motion picture industry and in television, but I do not remember that their professions colored my life in any untoward way. Work in Hollywood, like work at Lockheed or other aircraft companies, didn't seem any more remarkable to us as children then than farming or teaching. I was more interested, actually, in farming and in what was done by people who worked astride a horse, a mysterious and magnificent beast, with its shuddering flanks and high nickers.

One unusual thing about those years was that I raised pigeons. Many of them were tumblers, a kind of bird that folds its wings and then plummets from a height, only to pull up sharply inches from the ground. A tumbler then beats its way back up into the sky from which it plummets again. Sometimes a dozen or more will tumble together, careening past each other as they fall.

Watching the pigeons fly was an experience so exhilarating I would turn slowly under them in circles of glee. They would spiral above the house before flying off every day, and the tumblers would fall toward an adjacent field. They'd disappear behind lofty banks of aging eucalyptus north and south of the house in flocks of thirty and forty. When they returned in the afternoon, I found that faithfulness, their soft cooing at dusk in the pigeon coop, as soothing as my mother's fingers running through my hair.

I could not have understood at this age of course, only eight or nine, what it might mean to have a voice one day, to speak as a writer speaks. I would have been baffled by the thought. The world I inhabited-the emotions I imagined horses to have, the sound of a night wind clattering ominously in the dry leaves of eucalyptus trees—I imagined as a refuge, one that would be lost to me if I tried to explain it. The countryside around me was a landscape full of small, wild animals. When I walked alone down windbreaks of Russian olives or up sandy washes and met them, I'd stand still until they went on. They did not seem to my mind animals that wanted to be known.

My future, as I vaguely pictured it then, would include going to high school in the valley, maybe Stanford University afterward, and then perhaps I would work toward owning a farm. Like my friends, though, I had few concrete thoughts beyond repairing my bike and being included at the periphery of the circle of older boys, the ones who possessed such gleaming, loud, extraordinarily powerful, and customized automobiles.

When I was eleven my mother married again, and we moved back East to an apartment in the Murray Hill section of Manhattan on East Thirty-fifth Street. I would live there for six years before going away to college. This change was wrenching: socially, economically, and geographically. I was bewildered by it—a penthouse apartment, Jesuit prep school, Saturday afternoon trapshooting at the New York Athletic Club's Travers Island range, debutante balls at the Plaza and the Pierre. Gone were the rural, agricultural, and desert landscapes to which I was so attached. They were replaced by summers on the Jersey shore and by visits to eastern Alabama, where my mother had grown up. But, for the first time, I had an allowance. And I began to grasp from my new classmates, all boys, what went with this new life with no cars, where no one bicycled alone at night to the sound of big sprinklers slow-chucking water over alfalfa fields.

I recall a moment that first eastern summer of 1956, a scene I've come back to often. My parents put Dennis and me in a summer camp on the North Fork of eastern Long Island for a few weeks. Among my bunkmates were Thom and John Steinbeck, the writer's two sons. On parents' day, John and Elaine Steinbeck would come over from their home in Sag Harbor in a cabin cruiser. He would row a dinghy in to shore to fetch the boys and take them back out for the afternoon to the moored boat. I might have been reading "The Red Pony" or other stories in The Long Valley then. What I most remember, though, was that this man had come here from California, like me, and that things seemed to be going well for him. I was having a difficult time that first summer adjusting to city life. I missed the open-endedness of the other landscape, with its hay fields and its perimeter of unset-unsettled mountains.

And what I missed was embodied somehow in burly man, rowing the boat away with his boys. Before I left for college I read all of Steinbeck's books. I drew from them a sense of security.

Later that same summer my parents rented a house for a few weeks near Montauk Point, at the tip of Long Island. My father, as I would always refer to him later, took my brother and me fishing several times on charter boats. As it happened, Peter Matthiessen—a writer I would later come to admire and get to know—was captaining just such a boat out of Montauk that August. Thirty years later, crossing Little Peconic Bay to the west of Montauk with him, in a boat he was thinking of buying, we tried to determine whether it could have been his boat that my father had hired one of those times.

I thrived in the city in spite of the change in landscape. I focused on my studies—Latin, history, English literature, French, art (a class taught by the painter John Sloan's widow)—a standard Jesuit regimen, light in the sciences. I developed into a fast, strong athlete, and graduated with letters in three varsity, sports and a scholastic average high enough to have gained me entry to almost any university.

I felt privileged rather than deserving of all this. I understood that my Jesuit education, my social and economic class, my good grades, my trained and confident young man's voice, my white skin and the hegemony of my religion all pointed toward being well received in the world. In my private heart, though, thinking back to the years in California and forgetting those early days of privilege at Orienta Point, I felt I was dressed in borrowed clothes. How did I come to be here?

The summer after I graduated from high school I traveled to Europe with fifteen of my classmates. We flew to Lisbon and then spent two months being driven in a small Fiat tour bus with huge windows through Spain, France, Italy, Switzerland, Austria, and West Germany. Later we crossed the Channel and toured England and Ireland. Among hundreds of things I did, I remember laying my hand on the thigh of Agesander's statue of Laocoon in the Vatican Museums and feeling the sinew of muscle in the white marble; seeing a matador gored and then spun like a pinwheel on a bull's horn in the corrida in Pamplona; an ethereal light that seemed to bathe Napoleon's catafalque in blue in Paris; and a vast cemetery of identical white crosses, ranked over green hills in northern France, a bucolic landscape lovely, benign, and enormously sad.

In the fall of 1962 I entered the University of Notre Dame in northern Indiana with the intention of becoming an aeronautical engineer. Once I got my driver's license I began leaving school on weekends, camping out or sleeping in the cars I borrowed, whatever was necessary to see the surrounding country from Michigan's Upper Peninsula to West Virginia. I once drove to Mississippi and back with my room-mate over a weekend—eleven hundred miles—just to see it, drawn by little more than the lure of the Natchez Trace.

During my sophomore and junior years I started writing stories that had nothing to do with class-room assignments. I understood the urge to write as a desire to describe what happened, what I saw, when I went outside. The book that engaged me most along these lines was *Moby-Dick*, which I read three times before I entered college.

Story, as I understood it by reading Faulkner, Hardy, Cather, and Hemingway, was a powerful and clarifying human invention. The language alone, as I discovered it in Gerard Manley Hopkins and Faulkner, was exquisitely beautiful, also weirdly and mysteriously evocative.

My attitude toward language and story crystallized on a single afternoon in my sophomore year. I cut a class to hear Robert Fitzgerald read from his new translation of *The Odyssey*. I'd heard the transla-tion was brilliant; what was spellbinding about his reading, however, was the way the audience became galvanized in beauty by his presentation. History, quest, longing, metered prose, moral consternation, and fantastic image all came together in that room. The feeling broadened and calmed us. Whatever Fitzger-ald did in that hour, that's what I wanted to do.

I was driven to write, but of course anguished over my efforts. Who was I to speak? What had I to say? As a college student of nineteen, I was being encouraged in the idea that if I spoke I would be heard. The privilege that ensured this, however, was the accident of my mother's third marriage. It was nothing I'd earned. And much of what seemed to me so worth addressing psychological draw of landscape, that profound mystery I sensed in wild animals (which reading Descartes had done nothing to dissuade)—was regarded as peculiar territory, by other nascent writers at the university.

In my senior year at Notre Dame, at bat in an intramural baseball game, I took a high inside pitch that shattered the stone in my senior ring. I left the setting empty. The emptiness came to symbolize doubts I'd developed about my education. I'd learned a lot, but I had not learned it in the presence of women blacks or Jews or Koreans. Something important, those refinements and objections, had been omitted.

When I departed the university in 1966 (with a degree in Communication Arts) I left in order to discover a voice and a subject, though this was not at all clear then. I floundered in two jobs for a year, married, finished a graduate degree with the thought that I would teach prep school, and then entered the master of fine arts program in writing at the University of Oregon. I left that program after only a semester, but matriculated at the university for more than a year, during which time I met a singular teacher in the English department, a man named Barre Toelken. He helped frame the questions seething inside me then about how justice, education, and other Enlightenment ideals could be upheld against the depth of prejudice and the fields of ignorance I saw everywhere around me.

Toelken pointed me toward anthropological research which demonstrated that other cultures approached questions of natural history and geography in the same way I preferred. They did not sepa-rate humanity and nature. They recognized the immanence of the divine in both. And they regarded land-scape as a component as integral to the development of personality and social order as we take the Oedipus complex and codified law to be.

As a guest in the Toelkens' home, I frequently met scholars and other insightful people from out-side white, orthodox, middleclass culture. I didn't consider that these people spoke a truth no one else possessed; but, listening to them, I saw the inadequacy of my education. It lacked any suggestion that these voices were necessary, that they were relevant. Further, it became clear to me in the Toelkens' home that their stories, despite the skilled dramatizing of human triumph and failure, were destined for quar-antine in the society of which I was a part. I was not going to find these voices in American magazines.

In the years after those first encounters with senior Native American men, itinerant Asian poets, black jazz musicians, and translators, I deliberately began to seek the company of people outside my own narrow cultural bounds. I was drawn especially to men and women who had not dissociated themselves from the passionate and spiritual realms of life, people for whom mystery was not a challenge to intelligence but a bosom.

The effect of these encounters was not a belief that I was now able to speak for such people—a notion I find dangerous as well as absurd—but an understanding that my voice, steeped in Jung, Dante, Heisenberg, Melville, and Merton, was not the only voice. My truth was not the one truth. My tongue did not compose a pinnacle language. These other voices were as indispensable to our survival as variations in our DNA.

In my earliest essays, I wanted to report what others were thinking, and I was driven by a feeling that these other voices were being put asunder by "progress" in its manifold forms.

Although I'm wary of pancultural truths, I believe in all human societies there is a desire to love and be loved, to experience the full fierceness of human emotion, and to make a measure of the sacred part of one's life. Wherever I've traveled—Kenya, Chile, Australia, Japan—I've found that the most dependable way to preserve these possibilities is to be reminded of them in stories. Stories do not give instruction, they do not explain how to love a companion or how to find God. They offer, instead, patterns of sound and association, of event and image. Suspended as listeners and readers in these patterns, we might reimagine our lives. It is through story that we embrace the great breadth of memory, that we can distinguish what is true, and that we may glimpse, at least occasionally, how to live without despair in the midst of the horror that dogs and unhinges us.

As long as it took for me to see that a writer's voice had to grow out of his own knowledge and desire, that it could not rise legitimately out of the privilege of race or gender or social rank, so did it take time to grasp the depth of cruelty inflicted upon all of us the moment voices are silenced, then for prejudicial reasons people are told their stories are not valuable, not useful. Anyone educated in the existence and history of metaphorical expression—Schrödinger's or Li Po's—cannot help but recoil before such menace, such ignorance.

Once I was asked by a seatmate on a trans-Pacific flight, a man who took the liberty of glancing repeatedly at the correspondence in my lap, what instruction he should give his fifteen-year-old daughter, who wanted to be a writer. I didn't know how to answer him, but before I could think I heard myself saying, "Tell your daughter three things." Tell her to read, I said. Tell her to read whatever interests her, and protect her if someone declares what she's reading to be trash. No one can fathom what happens between a human being and written language. She may be paying attention to things in the words beyond anyone else's comprehension, things that feed her curiosity, her singular heart and mind. Tell her to read classics like *The Odyssey*. They've been around a long time because the patterns in them have proved endlessly useful, and, to borrow Evan Connell's observation, with a good book you never touch bottom. But warn your daughter that ideas of heroism, of love, of human duty and devotion that women have been writing about for centuries will not be available to her in this form. To find these voices she will have to search. When, on her own, she begins to ask, make her a present of George Eliot, or the travel writing of Alexandra David-Neel, or *To the Lighthouse*.

Second, I said, tell your daughter that she can learn a great deal about writing by reading and by studying books about grammar and the organization of ideas, but that if she wishes to write well she will have to become someone. She will have to discover her beliefs, and then speak to us from within those beliefs. If her prose doesn't come out of her belief, whatever that proves to be, she will only be passing along information, of which we are in no great need. So help her discover what she means.

Finally, I said, tell your daughter to get out of town, and help her do that. I don't necessarily mean to travel to Kazakhstan, or wherever, but to learn another language, to live with people other than her own, to separate herself from the familiar. Then when she returns, she will be better able to understand why she loves the familiar, and will give us a fresh sense of how fortunate we are to share these things.

Read. Find out what you truly believe. Get away from the familiar. Every writer, I told him, will offer you thoughts about writing that are different, but these are three I trust.

In the pages that follow, you will see how this thinking has played out for me. My beliefs will be apparent, but not, I hope, obtrusive. And it will be obvious that I have left town, or tried to, and that I've wanted to put to work what I saw. I've chosen these essays to give a sense of how one writer proceeds, and they are reflective of my notion of what it means to travel. The order is not chronological, and I've not included all the work of recent years.

If I were asked what I want to accomplish as a writer, I would say it's to contribute to a literature of hope. With my given metaphors, rooted in a childhood spent outdoors in California and which take much of their language from Jesuit classrooms in New York City, I want to help create a body of stories in which men and women can discover trustworthy patterns.

Every story is an act of trust between a writer and a reader; each story, in the end, is social. Whatever a writer sets down can harm or help the community of which he or she is a part. When I write, I can imagine a child in California wishing to give away what he's just seen—a wild animal fleeing through creosote cover in the desert, casting a bright-eyed backward glance. Or three lines of overheard conversation that seem to contain everything we need understand to repair the gaping rift between body and soul. I look back at that boy turning in glee beneath his pigeons, and know it can take a lifetime to convey what you mean, to find the opening. You watch, you set it down. Then you try again.

Questions for Discussion

1. Compare and contrast Lopez's narrative of coming to voice with Mellix's. Do the two share common events? In what ways do race, class, and/or gender play a role in their struggles and achievements as language users, as writers coming to voice?

2. Lopez's narrative is quite sensual, his descriptions detailed and dynamic. Select two or three sentences or paragraphs that struck you as presenting particularly powerful images. Take a few moments to analyze, to break down and then piece back together Lopez's use of figurative and descriptive language.

3. Each of the scenes or events that Lopez relates reveals something about his beliefs and values about writing, family, home. Identify some of the themes Lopez develops through his narrative and how they relate to one another.

Explorations

1. In what ways does Lopez's reading and acquaintances with writers propel him to become a writer? What role does the natural world play in his development as a writer?

2. When speaking with an airline passenger seated next to him, Lopez articulates three necessities for young people wishing to become writers: read what interests you, "become someone" by understanding your own beliefs and desires, "get out of town," travel, and place yourself in the unfamiliar. What might be the reasons behind each piece of Lopez's advice? Why do you think he chose these suggestions over the hundreds of other ones he might have made?

3. Lopez argues (as does Keith Gilyard in the next unit) that writers bear a responsibility to their readers, that "each story, in the end, is social." Do you agree with his claim that "whatever a writer sets down can harm or help the community of which he or she is a part"? What kinds of responsibilities do writers have to their readers?

Formal Writing Assignments

1. Lopez writes near the beginning of "A Voice" that "For a long time I thought of California as the beginning, the place where my life took a distinctive shape, but something had already begun. When I recall incidents from . . . New York . . . several seem to bear directly on my later life, to be adumbrations. Or perhaps that is only how memory works." Look to your own history and compose an reflective essay in which you explore adumbrations, those events that foreshadow, or those incidents, people, or places to which you might point as having great significance on your later life.

2. Return to either the second or third "Writing Before Reading" question that precedes Lopez's essay. Before extending the narrative, identify one or more themes that reside in or are implied by the text. Working from that response and your thoughts on them, explore and articulate through a narrative essay the significance of those people, places, or events.

White Privilege and Male Privilege: A Personal Account of Coming to See Correspondences Through Work in Women's Studies

Peggy McIntosh

As a personal narrative, this essay differs from most of those in this unit but is faithful to McIntosh's professional commitment. That is, much of her work in the last decade and a half at the Wellesley College Center for Research on Women has focused on ways to make more inclusive school curricula, from grade school through college. As a co-founder of the National S.E.E.D. Project, McIntosh believes that teachers themselves need to be retaught, that most have had debilitating schooling in terms of social issues like gender and race, and so need to inspect closely their own assumptions. The S.E.E.D. manifesto reads: "Unless we as teachers reopen our own backgrounds to look anew at how we were schooled to deal with diversity and connection, we will be unable to create school climates and curriculum which more adequately help students to deal with diversity and connection." To this end, McIntosh and her Co-Director, Emily Style, conduct year-long seminars in teachers' own schools. But to begin with, and perhaps to model the sort of investigation McIntosh hopes for the teachers in the seminars, she probes in this essay her own deeply embedded assumptions about her position as a white woman.

Writing Before Reading

1. How do you think of the word "privilege"? How have you heard it used by other people, and how do you use it yourself? Brainstorm a list of the ways you think the word can be understood and the factors that may impact those different meanings.

2. When the topic of race is brought up, who is usually being referred to? Recall an instance in one of your classes when race became the issue and reconstruct on paper the conversation that followed. What do you think about this conversation?

3. Think about the use of personal experience in writing. Recall whether you were permitted to use it in your high school writing. Or were you required to use it? Write a brief paragraph outlining your recollection, and comment on whether you think this was or was not beneficial to you.

White Privilege and Male Privilege: A Personal Account of Coming to See Correspondences Through Work in Women's Studies

Through work to bring materials and perspectives from Women's Studies into the rest of the curriculum, I have often noticed men's unwillingness to grant that they are overprivileged in the curriculum, even though they may grant that women are disadvantaged. Denials that amount to taboos surround the subject of advantages that men gain from women's disadvantages. These denials protect male privilege from being fully recognized, acknowledged, lessened, or ended.

Thinking through unacknowledged male privilege as a phenomenon with a life of its own, I realized that since hierarchies in our society are interlocking, there was most likely a phenomenon of white privilege that was similarly denied and protected, but alive and real in its effects. As a white person, I realized I had been taught about racism as something that puts others at a disadvantage, but had been taught not to see one of its corollary aspects, white privilege, which puts me at an advantage.

I think whites are carefully taught not to recognize white privilege, as males are taught not to recognize male privilege. So I have begun in an untutored way to ask what it is like to have white privilege. This paper is a partial record of my personal observations and not a scholarly analysis. It is based on my daily experiences within my particular circumstances.

I have come to see white privilege as an invisible package of unearned assets that I can count on cashing in every day, but about which I was "meant" to remain oblivious. White privilege is like an invisible weightless knapsack of special provisions, assurances, tools, maps, guides, code books, passports, visas, clothes, compass, emergency gear, and blank checks.

Since I have had trouble facing white privilege, and describing its results in my life, I saw parallels here with men's reluctance to acknowledge male privilege. Only rarely will a man go beyond acknowledging that women are disadvantaged to acknowledging that men have unearned advantage, or that unearned privilege has not been good for men's development as human beings, or for society's development, or that privilege systems might ever be challenged and *changed*.

I will review here several types or layers of denial that I see at work protecting, and preventing awareness about, entrenched male privilege. Then I will draw parallels, from my own experience, with the denials that veil the facts of white privilege. Finally, I will list forty-six ordinary and daily ways in which I experience having white privilege, by contrast with my African American colleagues in the same building. This list is not intended to be generalizable. Others can make their own lists from within their own life circumstances.

Writing this paper has been difficult, despite warm receptions for the talks on which it is based.[1] For describing white privilege makes one newly accountable. As we in Women's Studies work reveal male privilege and ask men to give up some of their power, so one who writes about having white privilege must ask, "Having described it, what will I do to lessen or end it?"

The denial of men's overprivileged state takes many forms in discussions of curriculum change work. Some claim that men must be central in the curriculum because they have done most of what is important or distinctive in life or in civilization. Some recognize sexism in the curriculum but deny that it makes male students seem unduly important in life. Others agree that certain *individual* thinkers are male oriented but deny that there is any *systemic* tendency in disciplinary frameworks or epistemology to overempower men as a group. Those men who do grant that male privilege takes institutionalized and embedded forms are still likely to deny that male hegemony has opened doors for them personally. Virtually all men deny that male overreward alone can explain men's centrality in all the inner sanctums of our most powerful institutions. Moreover, those few who will acknowledge that male privilege systems have overempowered them usually end up doubting that we could dismantle these privilege systems. They may say they will work to improve women's status, in the society or in the university, but they can't or won't support the idea of lessening men's. In curricular terms, this is the point at which they say that they regret they cannot use any of the interesting new scholarship on women because the syllabus is full. When the talk turns to giving men less cultural room, even the most thoughtful and fair-minded of the men I know will tend to reflect, or fall back on, conservative assumptions about the inevitability of present gender relations and

---

1. This paper was presented at the Virginia Women's Studies Association Conference in Richmond in April, 1996, and the American Educational Research Association Conference in Boston in October, 1986, and discussed with two groups of participants in the Dodge seminars for Secondary School Teachers in New York and Boston in the spring of 1987.

distributions of power, calling on precedent or sociobiology and psychobiology to demonstrate that male domination is natural and follows inevitably from evolutionary pressures. Others resort to arguments from "experience" or religion or social responsibility or wishing and dreaming.

After I realized, through faculty development work in Women's Studies, the extent to which men work from a base of unacknowledged privilege, I understood that much of their oppressiveness was unconscious. Then I remembered the frequent charges from women of color that white women whom they encounter are oppressive. I began to understand why we are justly seen as oppressive, even when we don't see ourselves that way. At the very least, obliviousness of one's privileged state can make a person or group irritating to be with. I begin to count the ways in which I enjoy unearned skin privilege and have been conditioned into oblivion about its existence, unable to see that it put me "ahead" in any way, or put my people ahead, overrewarding us and yet also paradoxically damaging us, or that it could or should be changed.

My schooling gave me no training in seeing myself as an oppressor, as an unfairly advantaged person, or as a participant in a damaged culture. I was taught to see myself as an individual whose moral state depended on her individual moral will. At school, we were not taught about slavery in any depth; we were not taught to see slaveholders as damaged people. Slaves were seen as the only group at risk of being dehumanized. My schooling followed the pattern which Elizabeth Minnich has pointed out: whites are taught to think of their lives as morally neutral, normative, and average, and also ideal, so that when we work to benefit others, this is seen as work that will allow "them" to be more like "us." I think many of us know how obnoxious this attitude can be in men.

After frustration with men who would not recognize male privilege, I decided to try to work on myself at least by identifying some of the daily effects of white privilege in my life. It is crude work, at this stage, but I will give here a list of special circumstances and conditions I experience that I did not earn but that I have been made to feel are mine by birth, by citizenship, and by virtue of being a conscientious law-abiding "normal" person of goodwill. I have chosen those conditions that I think in my case *attach somewhat more to skin-color privilege* than to class, religion, ethnic status, or geographical location, though these other privileging factors are intricately intertwined. As far as I can see, my Afro-American co-workers, friends, and acquaintances with whom I come into daily or frequent contact in this particular time, place, and line of work cannot count on most of these conditions.

1. I can, if I wish, arrange to be in the company of people of my race most of the time.

2. I can avoid spending time with people whom I was trained to mistrust and who have learned to mistrust my kind or me.

3. If I should need to move, I can be pretty sure of renting or purchasing housing in an area which I can afford and in which I would want to live.

4. I can be reasonably sure that my neighbors in such a location will be neutral or pleasant to me.

5. I can go shopping alone most of the time, fairly well assured that I will not be followed or harassed by store detectives.

6. I can turn on the television or open to the front page of the paper and see people of my race widely and positively represented.

7. When I am told about our national heritage or about "civilization," I am shown that people of my color made it what it is.

8. I can be sure that my children will be given curricular materials that testify to the existence of their race.

9. If I want to, I can be pretty sure of finding a publisher for this piece on white privilege.

10. I can be fairly sure of having my voice heard in a group in which I am the only member of my race.

11. I can be casual about whether or not to listen to another woman's voice in a group in which she is the only member of her race.

12. I can go into a book shop and count on finding the writing of my race represented, into a supermarket and find the staple foods that fit with my cultural traditions, into a hairdresser's shop and find someone who can deal with my hair.

13. Whether I use checks, credit cards, or cash, I can count on my skin color not to work against the appearance that I am financially reliable.

14. I could arrange to protect our young children most of the time from people who might not like them.

15. I did not have to educate our children to be aware of systemic racism for their own daily physical protection.

16. I can be pretty sure that my children's teachers and employers will tolerate them if they fit school and workplace norms; my chief worries about them do not concern others' attitudes toward their race.

17. I can talk with my mouth full and not have people put this down to my color.

18. I can swear, or dress in secondhand clothes, or not answer letters, without having people attribute these choices to the bad morals, the poverty, or the illiteracy of my race.

19. I can speak in public to a powerful male group without putting my race on trial.

20. I can do well in a challenging situation without being called a credit to my race.

21. I am never asked to speak for all the people of my racial group.

22. I can remain oblivious to the language and customs of persons of color who constitute the world's majority without feeling in my culture any penalty for such oblivion.

23. I can criticize our government and talk about how much I fear its policies and behavior without being seen as a cultural outsider.

24. I can be reasonably sure that if I ask to talk to "the person in charge," I will be facing a person of my race.

25. If a traffic cop pulls me over or if the IRS audits my tax return. I can be sure I haven't been singled out because of my race.

26. I can easily buy posters, postcards, picture books, greeting cards, dolls, toys, and children's magazines featuring people of my race.

27. I can go home from most meetings of organizations I belong to feeling somewhat tied in, rather than isolated, out of place, outnumbered, unheard, held at a distance, or feared.

28. I can be pretty sure that an argument with a colleague of another race is more likely to jeopardize her chances for advancement than to jeopardize mine.

29. I can be fairly sure that if I argue for the promotion of a person of another race, or a program centering on race, this is not likely to cost me heavily within my present setting, even if my colleagues disagree with me.

30. If I declare there is a racial issue at hand, or there isn't a racial issue at hand, my race will lend me more credibility for either position than a person of color will have.

31. I can choose to ignore developments in minority writing and minority activist programs, or disparage them, or learn from them, but in any case, I can find ways to be more or less protected from negative consequences of any of these choices.

32. My culture gives me little fear about ignoring the perspectives and powers of people of other races.

33. I am not made acutely aware that my shape, bearing, or body odor will be taken as a reflection on my race.

34. I can worry about racism without being seen as self-interested or self-seeking.

35. I can take a job with an affirmative action employer without having my co-workers on the job suspect that I got it because of my race.

36. If my day, week, or year is going badly, I need not ask of each negative episode or situation whether it has racial overtones.

37. I can be pretty sure of finding people who would be willing to talk with me and advise me about my next steps, professionally.

38. I can think over many options, social, political, imaginative, or professional, without asking whether a person of my race would be accepted or allowed to do what I want to do.

39. I can be late to a meeting without having the lateness reflect on my race.

40. I can choose public accommodation without fearing that people of my race cannot get in or will be mistreated in the places I have chosen.

41. I can be sure that if I need legal or medical help, my race will not work against me.

42. I can arrange my activities so that I will never have to experience feelings of rejection owing to my race.

43. If I have low credibility as a leader, I can be sure that my race is not the problem.

44. I can easily find academic courses and institutions that give attention only to people of my race.

45. I can expect figurative language and imagery in all of the arts to testify to experiences of my race.

46. I can choose blemish cover or bandages in "flesh" color and have them more or less match my skin.

I repeatedly forgot each of the realizations on this list until I wrote it down. For me, white privilege has turned out to be an elusive and fugitive subject. The pressure to avoid it is great, for in facing it I must give up the myth of meritocracy. If these things are true, this is not such a free country, one's life is not what one makes it many doors open for certain people through no virtues of their own. These perceptions mean also that my moral condition is not what I had been led to believe. The appearance of being a good citizen rather than a troublemaker comes in large part from having all sorts of doors open automatically because of my color.

A further paralysis of nerve comes from literary silence protecting privilege. My clearest memories of finding such analysis are in Lillian Smith's unparalleled *Killers of the Dream* and Margaret Andersen's review of Karen and Mamie Fields' *Lemon Swamp*. Smith, for example, wrote about walking toward black children on the street and knowing they would step into the gutter; Andersen contrasted the pleasure that she, as a white child, took on summer driving trips to the south with Karen Fields' memories of driving in a closed car stocked with all necessities lest, in stopping, her black family should suffer "insult, or worse." Adrienne Rich also recognizes and writes about daily experiences of privilege, but in my observation, white women's writing in this area is far more often on systemic racism than on our daily lives as light-skinned women.[2]

In unpacking this invisible knapsack of white privilege, I have listed conditions of daily experience that I once took for granted, as neutral, normal, and universally available to everybody, just as I once thought of a male-focused curriculum as the neutral or accurate account that can speak for all. Nor did I think of any of these perquisites as bad for the holder. I now think that we need a more finely differentiated taxonomy of privilege, for some of these varieties are only what one would want for everyone in a just society, and others give license to be ignorant, oblivious, arrogant, and destructive. Before proposing some more finely tuned categorization, I will make some observations about the general effects of these conditions on my life and expectations.

In this potpourri of examples, some privileges make me feel at home in the world. Others allow me to escape penalties or dangers that others suffer. Through some, I escape fear, anxiety, insult, injury, or a sense of not being welcome, not being real. Some keep me from having to hide, to be in disguise, to feel sick or crazy, to negotiate each transaction from the position of being an outsider or, within my group, a person who is suspected of having too close links with a dominant culture. Most keep me from having to be angry.

I see a pattern running through the matrix of white privilege, a pattern of assumptions that were passed on to me as a white person. There was one main piece of cultural turf; it was my own turf, and I was among those who could control the turf. I could measure up to the cultural standards and take advantage of the many options I saw around me to make what the culture would call a success of my life. *My skin color was an asset for any move I was educated to want to make.* I could think of myself as "belonging" in major ways and of making social systems work for me. I could freely disparage, fear, neglect, or be oblivious to anything outside of the dominant cultural forms. Being of the main culture, I could also criticize it fairly freely. My life was reflected back to me frequently enough so that I felt, with regard to my race, if not to my sex, like one of the real people.

Whether through the curriculum or in the newspaper, the television, the economic system, or the general look of people in the streets, I received daily signals and indications that my people counted and

---

2. Andersen, Margaret, "Race and the Social Science Curriculum: A Teaching and Learning Discussion." *Radical Teaching,* November 1984, pp. 17–20. Smith, Lillian, *Killers of the Dream,* New York: W. W. Norton, 1949.

that others *either didn't exist or must be trying, not very successfully, to be like people of my race*. I was given cultural permission not to hear voices of people of other races or a tepid cultural tolerance for hearing or acting on such voices. I was also raised not to suffer seriously from anything that darker-skinned people might say about my group, "protected," though perhaps I should more accurately say *prohibited*, through the habits of my economic class and social group, from living in racially mixed groups or being reflective about interactions between people of differing races.

In proportion as my racial group was being made confident, comfortable, and oblivious, other groups were likely being made unconfident, uncomfortable, and alienated. Whiteness protected me from many kinds of hostility, distress, and violence, which I was being subtly trained to visit in turn upon people of color.

For this reason, the word "privilege" now seems to me misleading. Its connotations are too positive to fit the conditions and behaviors which "privilege systems" produce. We usually think of privilege as being a favored state, whether earned, or conferred birth or luck. School graduates are reminded they are privileged and urged to use their (enviable) assets well. The word "privilege" carries the connotation of being something everyone must want. Yet some of the conditions I have described here work to systemically overempower certain groups. Such privilege simply *confers dominance*, gives permission to control, because of one's race or sex. The kind of privilege that gives license to some people to be, at best, thoughtless and, at worst, murderous should not continue to be referred to as a desirable attribute. Such "privilege" may be widely desired without being in any way beneficial to the whole society.

Moreover, though "privilege" may confer power, it does not confer moral strength. Those who do not depend on conferred dominance have traits and qualities that may never develop in those who do. Just as Women's Studies courses indicate that women survive their political circumstances to lead lives that hold the human race together, so "underprivileged" people of color who are the world's majority have survived their oppression and lived survivors' lives from which the white global minority can and must learn. In some groups, those dominated have actually become strong through *not* having all of these unearned advantages, and this gives them a great deal to teach the others. Members of so-called privileged groups can seem foolish, ridiculous, infantile, or dangerous by contrast.

I want, then, to distinguish between earned strength and unearned power conferred systemically. Power from unearned privilege can look like strength when it is, in fact, permission to escape or to dominate. But not all of the privileges on my list are inevitably damaging. Some, like the expectation that neighbors will be decent to you, or that your race will not count against you in court, should be the norm in a just society and should be considered as the entitlement of everyone. Others, like the privilege not to listen to less powerful people, distort the humanity of the holders as well as the ignored groups. Still others, like finding one's staple foods everywhere, may be a function of being a member of a numerical majority in the population. Others have to do with *not* having to labor under pervasive negative stereotyping and mythology.

We might at least start by distinguishing between positive advantages that we can work to spread, to the point where they are not advantages at all but simply part of the normal civic and social fabric, and negative types of advantage that unless rejected will always reinforce our present hierarchies. For example, the positive "privilege" of belonging, the feeling that one belongs within the human circle, as Native Americans say, fosters development and should not be seen as privilege for a few. It is, let us say, an entitlement that none of us should have to claim; ideally it is an *unearned entitlement*. At present, since only a few have it, it is an *unearned advantage* for them. The negative "privilege" that gave me cultural permission not to take darker skinned Others seriously can be seen as arbitrarily conferred dominance and should not be desirable for anyone. This paper results from a process of coming to see that Some of the power that I originally saw as attendant on being a human being in the United States consisted in *unearned advantage* and *conferred dominance*, as well as other kinds of special circumstance not universally taken for granted.

In writing this paper I have also realized that white identity and status (as well as class identity and status) give me considerable power to choose whether to broach this subject and its trouble. I can pretty well decide whether to disappear and avoid and not listen and escape the dislike I may engender in other people through this essay, or interrupt, answer, interpret, preach, correct, criticize, and control to some extent what goes on in reaction to it. Being white, I am given considerable power to escape many kinds of danger or penalty as well as to choose which risks I want to take.

There is an analogy here, once again, with Women's Studies. Our male colleagues do not have a great deal to lose in supporting Women's Studies, but they do not have a great deal to lose if they oppose it either. They simply have the power to decide whether to commit themselves to more equitable distributions of power. They will probably feel few penalties whatever choice they make; they do not seem, in any obvious short-term sense, the ones at risk, though they and we are all at risk because of the behaviors that have been rewarded in them.

Through Women's Studies work I have met very few men who are truly distressed about systemic, unearned male advantage and conferred dominance. And so one question for me and others like me is whether we will be like them, or whether we will get truly distressed, even outraged, about unearned race advantage and conferred dominance and if so, what we will do to lessen them. In any case, we need to do more work in identifying how they actually affect our daily lives. We need more down-to-earth writing by people about these taboo subjects. We need more understanding of the ways in which white "privilege" damages white people, for these are not the same ways in which it damages the victimized. Skewed white psyches are an inseparable part of the picture, though I do not want to confuse the kinds of damage done to the holders of special assets and to those who suffer the deficits. Many, perhaps most, of our white students in the United States think that racism doesn't affect them because they are not people of color; they do not see "whiteness" as a racial identity. Many men likewise think that Women's Studies does not bear on their own existences because they are not female; they do not see themselves as having gendered identities. Insisting on the universal "effects" of "privilege" systems, then, becomes one of our chief tasks, and being more explicit about the *particular* effects in particular contexts is another. Men need to join us in this work.

In addition, since race and sex are not the only advantaging systems at work, we need to similarly examine the daily experience of having age advantage, or ethnic advantage, or physical ability, or advantage related to nationality, religion, or sexual orientation. Professor Marnie Evans suggested to me that in many ways the list I made also applies directly to heterosexual privilege. This is a still more taboo subject than race privilege: the daily ways in which heterosexual privilege makes some persons comfortable or powerful, providing supports, assets, approvals, and rewards to those who live or expect to live in heterosexual pairs. Unpacking that content is still more difficult, owing to the deeper embeddedness of heterosexual advantage and dominance and stricter taboos surrounding these.

But to start such an analysis I would put this observation from my own experience: The fact that I live under the same roof with a man triggers all kinds of societal assumptions about my worth, politics, life, and values and triggers a host of unearned advantages and powers. After recasting many elements from the original list I would add further observations like these:

1. My children do not have to answer questions about why I live with my partner (my husband).

2. I have no difficulty finding neighborhoods where people approve of our household.

3. Our children are given texts and classes that implicitly support our kind of family unit and do not turn them against my choice of domestic partnership.

4. I can travel alone or with my husband without expecting embarrassment or hostility in those who deal with us.

5. Most people I meet will see my marital arrangements as an asset to my life or as a favorable comment on my likability, my competence, or my mental health.

6. I can talk about the social events of a weekend without fearing most listeners' reactions.

7. I will feel welcomed and "normal" in the usual walks of public life, institutional and social.

8. In many contexts, I am seen as "all right" in daily work on women because I do not live chiefly with women.

Difficulties and dangers surrounding the task of finding parallels are many. Since racism, sexism, and heterosexism are not the same, the advantages associated with them should not be seen as the same. In addition, it is hard to isolate aspects of unearned advantage that derive chiefly from social class, economic class, race, religion, region, sex, or ethnic identity. The oppressions are both distinct and interlocking, as the Combahee River Collective statement of 1977 continues to remind us eloquently.[3]

One factor seems clear about all of the interlocking oppressions. They take both active forms that we can see and embedded forms that members of the dominant group are taught not to see. In my class and place, I did not see myself as racist because I was taught to recognize racism only in individual acts of meanness by members of my group, never in invisible systems conferring racial dominance on my group from birth. Likewise, we are taught to think that sexism or heterosexism is carried on only through intentional, individual acts of discrimination, meanness, or cruelty, rather than in invisible systems conferring unsought dominance on certain groups. Disapproving of the systems won't be enough to change them. I was taught to think that racism could end if white individuals changed their attitudes; many men think sexism can be ended by individual changes in daily behavior toward women. But a man's sex provides advantage for him whether or not he approves of the way in which dominance has been conferred on his group. A "white" skin in the United States opens many doors for whites whether or not we approve of the way dominance has been conferred on us. Individual acts can palliate, but cannot end, these problems. To redesign social systems, we need first to acknowledge their colossal unseen dimensions. The silences and denials surrounding privilege are the key political tool here. They keep the thinking about equality or equity incomplete, protecting unearned advantage and conferred dominance by making these taboo subjects. Most talk by whites about equal opportunity seems to me now to be about equal opportunity to try to get into a position of dominance while denying that *systems* of dominance exist.

Obliviousness about white advantage, like obliviousness about male advantage, is kept strongly inculturated in the United States so as to maintain the myth of meritocracy, the myth that democratic choice is equally available to all. Keeping most people unaware that freedom of confident action is there for just a small number of people props up those in power and serves to keep power in the hands of the same groups that have most of it already. Though systemic change takes many decades, there are pressing questions for me and I imagine for some others like me if we raise our daily consciousness on the perquisites of being light-skinned. What will we do with such knowledge? As we know from watching men, it is an open question whether we will choose to use unearned advantage to weaken invisible privilege systems and whether we will use any of our arbitrarily awarded power to try to reconstruct power systems on a broader base.

---

3. "A Black Feminist Statement," The Combahee River Collective. pp. 13-22 in G. Hull, P. Scott, B. Smith, Eds., All the Women Are White, All the Blacks Are Men, But Some of Us Are Brave: Black Women's Studies, Old Westbury, NY: The Feminist Press, 1982.

4. I have appreciated commentary on this paper from the Working Papers Committee of the Wellesley College for Research on Women, from members of the Dodge seminar, and from many individuals, including Margaret Andersen, Sorel Berman, Joanne Braxton, Johnella Butler, Sandra Dickerson, Marnie Evans, Beverly Guy-Sheftall, Sandra Harding, Eleanor Hinton Hoytt, Pauline Houston, Paul Lauter, Joyce Miller, Mary Norris, Gloria Oden, Beverly Smith, and John Walter.

Questions for Discussion

1. McIntosh compares her position as privileged white person to that of the slaveholder and claims that dehumanization occurs on both sides of this relationship: to the oppressor as well as to the oppressed. What does she mean by this?

2. Take a close look at the list of forty-six unearned privileges that McIntosh enjoys simply because of her skin color. Which of these surprise you? Which of these sound familiar to you? Which of these anger you? Which of these do you disbelieve?

3. After the "knapsack" list, McIntosh makes a distinction between "unearned privilege" and "unearned advantage," further arguing that there should be such a thing as "unearned entitlement." What does McIntosh mean by these terms? How does she propose some be eliminated and others be encouraged?

Explorations

1. Toni Morrison's "Site of Memory" asserts that it is the bits and pieces of memory, mixed with imagination, that fuel fiction. How are the "bits and pieces" of McIntosh's memory useful to her? Though Morrison calls her work fiction and McIntosh calls hers personal narrative, is it possible that both writers are more involved in imagination and actual personal experience than either would admit? In other words, how is memory working in each piece?

2. Amy Tan's "Feathers from a Thousand Li Away" suggests that keepsakes have a value to their owner that should be questioned; that is, keepsakes usually have meaning only for the bearer. Can the privileges in McIntosh's knapsack be thought of as keepsakes? For whom? How can they be questioned?

3. Earl Braggs' "Vietnam Revisited" raises the issue of language's ability to transport the hearer and the deliverer. Amy Tan's story also queries the power of language, only in this case, to estrange people. How might McIntosh's use of language be characterized? What does she think language can do?

Formal Writing Assignments

1. Review McIntosh's list, taking note of where she is positioned in each of the "privileges." Position yourself in an unearned privileged position—as a white person, as a male, as a heterosexual, as a college student, as an upper-class citizen, as an American—and construct your own list. Then, reflect on the meaning of each of these privileges and postulate about whether these could or should be unearned entitlements.

2. As part of the S.E.E.D. project, teachers are required to inspect through personal narrative and story-telling their own assumptions about issues of diversity. Think about the impact that this personal aspect has on whether you believe and/or agree with McIntosh. Survey the places in McIntosh's essay where she makes most use of her personal experience and personal argument, analyze whether this is an effective strategy, and postulate about what the narrative may have looked and sounded like had McIntosh not used the personal.

From Outside, In

Barbara Mellix

Barbara Mellix received her M.F.A. in creative writing in 1986 from the University of Pittsburgh. Mellix continues to live and work in Pittsburgh, where she is the Executive Assistant Dean of the College of Arts and Sciences (CAS) and Interim Director of the CAS Advising Center. She has also edited Pitt's award-winning arts and sciences alumni magazine. A composition teacher at Pitt, Mellix gets great pleasure and satisfaction from teaching first-year students and "helping them discover through writing who they are and who they can be." Her courses often revolve around the theme of making choices (in the same way *Writing Lives* revolves around writing about and reading communities and discourses). She's taken her students on outings and lecture tours to such sites as the Trail of Tears and the Museum of the Cherokee Indian in Cherokee, North Carolina.

Mellix is currently working on a murder mystery, which she describes as a "coming of age story set in South Carolina in 1959," and notes that "writing is still very much a part of my life, and one of my passions."

Writing Before Reading

1. Write about a time when you changed or adjusted your language practices for a given setting or occasion. What changes did you make and why?

2. Reflect in writing on an occasion in which you attended carefully to what someone was saying because of the beauty, creativity, or uniqueness of their expression. What was it that captured your attention? Their descriptive skills? An accent? A lilt or tone to their voice? Their expressiveness?

3 Try your hand at recreating in writing an informal conversation that you recently had with a friend or group of friends. Use apostrophes, invented spellings, slang, sentence fragments, and other mechanisms for illustrating as accurately as possible the sounds and structures of the conversation.

From Outside, In

Two years ago, when I started writing this paper, trying to bring order out of chaos, my ten-year-old daughter was suffering from an acute attack of boredom. She drifted in and out of the room complaining that she had nothing to do, no one to "be with" because none of her friends were at home. Patiently I explained that I was working on something special and needed peace and quiet, and I suggested that she paint, read, or work with her computer. None of these interested her. Finally, she pulled up a chair to my desk and watched me, now and then heaving long, loud sighs. After two or three minutes (nine or ten sighs), I lost my patience. "Looka here, Allie," I said, "you are too old for this kinda carryin' on. I done told you this is important. You wronger than dirt to be in here haggin' me like this and you know it. Now git on outta here and leave me off before I put my foot all the way down."

I was at home, alone with my family, and my daughter understood that this way of speaking was appropriate in that context. She knew, as a matter of fact, that it was almost inevitable; when I get angry at home, I speak some of my finest, most cherished black English. Had I been speaking to my daughter in this manner in certain other environments, she would have been shocked and probably worried that I had taken leave of my sense of propriety.

Like my children, I grew up speaking what I considered two distinctly different languages—black English and standard English (or as I thought of them then, the ordinary everyday speech of "country" coloreds and "proper" English)—and in the process of acquiring these languages, I developed an understanding of when, where, and how to use them. But unlike my children, I grew up in a world that was primarily black. My friends, neighbors, minister, teachers—almost everybody I associated with every day—were black.

And we spoke to one another in our own special language: *That sho is a pretty dress you got on. If she don' soon leave me off I'm gon tell her head a mess. I was so mad I could'a pissed a blue rod. He all the time trying to low-rate somebody. Ain't that just about the nastiest thing you ever set ears on?*

Then there were the "others," the "proper" blacks, transplanted relatives and one-time friends who came home from the city for weddings, funerals, and vacations. To these we spoke standard English. "Ain't?" my mother would yell at me when I used the term in the presence of "others." "You *know* better than that." And I would hang my head in shame and say the "proper" word.

I remember one summer sitting in my grandmother's house in Greeleyville, South Carolina, when it was full of the chatter of city relatives who were home on vacation. My parents sat quietly, only now and then volunteering a comment or answering a question. My mother's face took on a strained expression when she spoke. I could see that she was being careful to say just the right words in just the right way. Her voice sounded thick, muffled. And when she finished speaking, she would lapse into silence, her proper smile on her face. My father was more articulate, more aggressive. He spoke quickly, his words sharp and clear. But he held his proud head higher, a signal that he, too, was uncomfortable. My sisters and brothers and I stared at our aunts, uncles, and cousins, speaking only when prompted. Even then, we hesitated, formed our sentences in our minds, then spoke softly, shyly.

My parents looked small and anxious during those occasions, and I waited impatiently for our leave-taking when we would mock our relatives the moment we were out of their hearing. "Reeely, " we would say to one another, flexing our wrists and rolling our eyes, "how dooo you stan' this heat? Chile, it just too hyooo-mid for words." Our relatives had made us feel "country," and this was our way of regaining pride in ourselves while getting a little revenge in the bargain. The words bubbled in our throats and rolled across our tongues, a balming.

As a child I felt this same doubleness in uptown Greeleyville where the whites lived. "Ain't that a pretty dress you're wearing!" Toby, the town policeman, said to me one day when I was fifteen. "Thank you very much," I replied, my voice barely audible in my own ears. The words felt wrong in my mouth, rigid, foreign. It was not that I had never spoken that phrase before—it was common in black English, too—but I was extremely conscious that this was an occasion for proper English. I had taken out my English and put it on as I did my church clothes, and I felt as if I were wearing my Sunday best in the middle of the week. It did not matter that Toby had not spoken grammatically correct English. He was white and could speak as he wished. I had something to prove. Toby did not.

Speaking standard English to whites was our way of demonstrating that we knew their language and could use it. Speaking it to standard-English-speaking blacks was our way of showing them that we, as well as they, could "put on airs." But when we spoke standard English, we acknowledged (to ourselves and to others—but primarily to ourselves) that our customary way of speaking was inferior. We felt foolish, embarrassed, somehow diminished because we were ashamed to be our real selves. We were reserved, shy in the presence of those who owned and/or spoke *the* language.

My parents never set aside time to drill us in standard English. Their forms of instruction were less formal. When my father was feeling particularly expansive, he would regale us with tales of his exploits in the outside world. In almost fluent English, complete with dialogue and flavored with gestures and embellishment, he told us about his attempt to get a haircut at a white barbershop; his refusal to acknowledge one of the town merchants until the man addressed him as "Mister"; the time he refused to step off the sidewalk uptown to let some whites pass; his airplane trip to New York City (to visit a sick relative) during which the stewardess and porters—recognizing that he was a "gentleman"—addressed him as "Sir." I did not realize then—nor, I think, did my father—that he was teaching us, among other things, standard English and the relationship between language and power.

My mother's approach was different. Often, when one of us said, "I'm gon wash off my feet," she would say, "And what will you walk on if you wash them off?" Everyone would laugh at the victim of my mother's "proper" mood. But it was different when one of us children was in a proper mood. "You think you are so superior," I said to my oldest sister one day when we were arguing and she was winning. "Superior!" my sister mocked. "You mean I am acting 'biggidy'?" My sisters and brothers sniggered, then joined in teasing me. Finally, my mother said, "Leave your sister alone. There's nothing wrong with using proper English." There was a half-smile on her face, I had gotten "uppity," had "put on airs" for no good reason. I was at home, alone with the family, and I hadn't been prompted by one of my mother's proper moods. But there was also a proud light in my mother's eyes; her children were learning English very well.

Not until years later, as a college student, did I begin to understand our ambivalence toward English, our scorn of it, our need to master it to be owned by it—an ambivalence that extended to the public-school classroom. In our school, where there were no whites, my teachers taught standard English but used black English to do it. When my grammar school teachers wanted us to write, for example, they usually said something like, "I want y'all to write five sentences that make a statement. Anybody get done before the rest can color." It was probably almost those exact words that led me to write these sentences in 1953 when I was in the second grade:

The white clouds are pretty.
There are only 15 people in our room.
We will go to gym.
We have a new poster.
We may go out doors.

Second grade came after "Little First" and "Big First," so by then I knew the implied rules that accompanied all writing assignments. Writing was an occasion for proper English. I was not to write in the way we spoke to one another: The white clouds pretty; There ain't but 15 people in our room; We going to gym; We got a new poster; We can go out in the yard. Rather I was to use the language of "other": clouds *are*, there *are*, we will, we *may*.

My sentences were short, rigid, perfunctory, like the letters my mother wrote to relatives:

Dear Papa,
How are you? How is Mamie? Fine I hope. We are all fine. We will come to see you Sunday. Cousin Ned will give us a ride.
Love,
Daughter

The language was not ours. It was something from outside us, something we used for special occasions.

But my coloring on the other side of that second-grade paper is different. I drew three hearts and a sun. The sun has a smiling face that radiates and envelops everything it touches. And although the sun and its world are enclosed in a circle, the colors I used—red, blue, green, purple, orange, yellow, black—indicates that I was less restricted with drawing and coloring than I was with writing standard English. My valentines were not just red. My sun was not just a yellow ball in the sky.

By the time I reached the twelfth grade, speaking and writing standard English had taken on new importance. Each year, about half of the newly graduated seniors of our school moved to large cities—particularly in the North—to live with relatives and find work. Our English teacher constantly corrected our grammar: "Not ain't,' but 'isn't.' "We seldom wrote papers, and even those few were usually plot summaries of short stories. When our teacher returned the papers, she usually lectured on the importance of using standard English: "I *am*; you *are*; he, she, or it *is*," she would say, writing on the chalkboard as she spoke. "How you gon git a job talking about 'I is,' or 'I isn't' or 'I ain't' ?"

In Pittsburgh, where I moved after graduation, I watched my aunt and uncle—who had always spoken standard English when in Greeleyville—switch from black English to standard English to a mixture of the two, according to where they were or who they were with. At home and with certain close relatives, friends, and neighbors, they spoke black English. With those less close, they spoke a mixture. In public and with strangers, they generally spoke standard English.

In time, I learned to speak standard English with ease and to switch smoothly from black to standard or a mixture, and back again. But no matter where I was, no matter what the situation or occasion, I continued to write as I had in school:

Dear Mommie,
How are you? How is everybody else? Fine I hope. I am fine. So are Aunt and Uncle. Tell everone I said hello. I will write again soon.
Love,
Barbara

At work, at a health insurance company, I learned to write letters to customers. I studied form letters and letters written by co-workers, memorizing the phrases and the ways in which they were used. I dictated:

Thank you for your letter of January 5. We have made the changes in your coverage you requested. Your new premium will be $150 every three months. We are pleased to have been of service to you.

In a sense, I was proud of the letters I wrote for the company: they were proof of my ability to survive in the city, the outside world—all indication of my growing mastery of English. But they also indicate that writing was still mechanical for me, something that didn't require much thought.

Reading also became a more significant part of my life during those early years in Pittsburgh. I had always liked reading, but now I devoted more and more of my spare time to it. I read romances, mysteries, popular novels. Looking back, I realized that the books I liked best were simple, unambiguous: good versus bad and right versus wrong with right rewarded and wrong punished, mysteries unraveled and all set right in the end. It was how I remembered life in Greeleyville.

Of course I was romanticizing. Life in Greeleyville had not been so very uncomplicated. Back there I had been—first as a child, then as a young woman with limited experience in the outside world—living in a relatively closed-in society. But there were implicit and explicit principles that guided our way of life and shaped our relationships with one another and the people outside—principles that a newcomer would find elusive and baffling. In Pittsburgh, I had matured, become more experienced: I had worked at three different jobs, associated with a wider range of people, married, had children. This new environment with different prescripts for living required that I speak standard English much of the time, and slowly, imperceptibly, I had ceased seeing a sharp distinction between myself and "others." Reading romances and mysteries, characterized by dichotomy, was a way of shying away from change, from the person I was becoming.

But that other part of me—that part which took great pride in my ability to hold a job writing business letters—was increasingly drawn to the new developments in my life and the attending possibilities, opportunities for even greater change. If I could write letters for a nationally known business, could I not also do something better, more challenging, more important? Could I not, perhaps, go to college and become a school teacher? For years, afraid and a little embarrassed, I did no more than imagine this different me, this possible me. But sixteen years after coming north, when my younger daughter entered kindergarten, I found myself unable—or unwilling—to resist the lure of possibility. I enrolled in my first college course: Basic Writing, at the University of Pittsburgh.

For the first time in my life, I was required to write extensively about myself. Using the most formal English at my command, I wrote these sentences near the beginning of the term:

> One of my duties as a homemaker is simply picking up after others. A day seldom passes that I don't search for a mislaid toy, book, or gym shoe, etc. I change the Ty-D-Bol, fight "ring around the collar," and keep our laundry smelling "April fresh." Occasionally, I settle arguments between my children and suggest things to do when they're bored. Taking telephone messages for my oldest daughter is my newest (and sometimes most aggravating) chore. Hanging the toilet paper is my most insignificant.

My concern was to use "appropriate" language, to sound as if I belonged in a college classroom. But I felt separate from the language—as if it did not and could not belong to me. I couldn't think and feel genuinely in that language, couldn't make it express what I thought and felt about being a housewife. A part of me resented, among other things, being judged by such things as the appearance of my family's laundry and toilet bowl, but in that language I could only imagine and write about a conventional housewife.

For the most part, the remainder of the term was a period of adjustment, a time of trying to find my bearings as a student in a college composition class, to learn to shut out my black English whenever I composed, and to prevent it from creeping into my formulations; a time for trying to grasp the language of the classroom and reproduce it in my prose; for trying to talk about myself in that language, reach others through it. Each experience of writing was like standing naked and revealing my imperfection, my "otherness." And each new assignment was another chance to make myself over in language, reshape myself, make myself "better" in my rapidly changing image of a student in a college composition class.

But writing became increasingly unmanageable as the term progressed, and by the end of the semester, my sentences sounded like this:

> My excitement was soon dampened, however, by what seemed like a small voice in the back of myhead saying that I should be careful with my long awaited opportunity. I felt frustrated and thisseemed to make it difficult to concentrate.

There is a poverty of language in these sentences. By this point, I knew that the clichéd language of my Housewife essay was unacceptable, and I generally recognized trite expressions. At the same time, I hadn't yet mastered the language of the classroom, hadn't yet come to see it as belonging to me. Most notable is the lifelessness of the prose, the apparent absence of a person behind the words. I wanted those sentences—and the rest of the essay—to convey the anguish of yearning to, at once, become something more and yet remain the same. I had the sensation of being split in two, part of me going into a future the other part didn't believe possible. As that person, the student writer at that moment, I was essentially mute. I could not—in the process of composing—use language of the old me, yet I couldn't imagine myself in the language of "others."

I found this particularly discouraging because at midsemester I had been writing in a much different way. Note the language of this introduction to an essay I had written then, near the middle of the term:

> Pain is a constant companion to the people in "Footwork." Their jobs are physically damaging. Employers are insensitive to their feelings and in many cases add to their problems.

The general public wounds them further by treating them with disgrace because of what they do for a living. Although the workers are as diverse as they are similar, there is a definite link between them. They suffer a great deal of abuse.

The voice here is stronger, more confident, appropriate terms like "physically damaging," "wounds them further," "insensitive," "diverse"—terms I couldn't have imagined using when writing about my own experience—and shaping them into sentences like "Although the workers are as diverse as they are similar, there is a definite link between them." And there is the sense of a personality behind the prose, someone who sympathizes with the workers. "The general public wounds them further by treating them with disgrace because of what they do for a living."

What causes these differences? I was, I believed, explaining other people's thoughts and feelings, and I was free to move about in the language of "others" so long as I was speaking of others. I was unaware that I was transforming into my best classroom language my own thoughts and feelings about people whose experiences and ways of speaking were in many ways similar to mine.

The following year, unable to turn back or to let go of what had become something of an obsession with language (and hoping to catch and hold the sense of control that had eluded me in Basic Writing), I enrolled in a research writing course. I spent most of the term learning how to prepare for and write a research paper. I chose sex education as my subject and spent hours in libraries, searching for information, reading, taking notes. Then (not without messiness and often demoralizing frustration) I organized my information into categories, wrote a thesis statement, and composed my paper—a series of paragraphs and quotations spaced between carefully constructed transitions. The process and results felt artificial, but as I would later come to realize I was passing through a necessary stage. My sentences sounded like this:

This reserve becomes understandable with examination of who the abusers are. In an overwhelming number of cases, they are people the victims know and trust. Family members, relatives, neigbors, and close family friends commit seventy-five percent of all reported sex crimes against children, and parents, parent substitutes and relatives are the offenders in thirty to eighty percent of all reported cases. While assault by strangers does occur, it is less common, and is usually a single episode. But abuse by family members, relatives and acquaintances may continue for an extended period of time. In cases of incest, for example, children are abused repeatedly for an average of eight years. In such cases, "the use of physical force is rarely necessary because of the child's trusting, dependent relationship with the offender. The child's cooperation is often facilitated by the adult's position of dominance, an offer of material goods, a threat of physical violence, or a misrepresentation of moral standards."

The completed paper gave me a sense of profound satisfaction, and I read it often after my professor returned it. I know now that what I was pleased with was the language I used and the professional voice it helped me maintain. "Use better words," my teacher had snapped at me one day after reading the notes I'd begun accumulating from my research, and slowly I began taking on the language of my sources. In my next set of notes, I used the word "vacillating" my professor applauded. And by the time I composed the final draft, I felt at ease with terms like "overwhelming number of cases," "single episode," and "reserve," and I shaped them into sentences similar to those of my "expert" sources.

If I were writing the paper today, I would of course do some things differently. Rather than open with an anecdote—as my teacher suggested—I would begin simply with a quotation that caught my interest as I was researching my paper (and which I scribbled, without its source, in the margin of my notebook): "Truth does not do so much good in the world as the semblance of truth does evil." The quotation felt right because it captured what was for me the central idea of my essay—an idea that emerged gradually during the making of my paper—and expressed it in a way I would like to have said it. The anecdote, a hypothetical situation I invented to conform to the information in the paper, felt forced and insincere because it represented—to a great degree—my teacher's understanding of the essay, her idea of what in it was most significant. Improving upon my previous experiences with writing, I was beginning to think and feel in the language I used, to find my own voices in it, to sense that how one speaks influences how one means. But I was not yet secure enough, comfortable enough with the language to trust my intuition.

Now that I know that to seek knowledge, freedom, and autonomy means always to be in the concentrated process of becoming—always to be venturing into new territory, feeling one's way at first, then getting one's balance, negotiating, discovering one's self in ways that previously defined "others"—I sometimes get tired. And I ask myself why I keep on participating in this highbrow form of violence, this slamming against perplexity. But there is no real futility in the question, no hint of that part of the old me who stood outside standard English, hugging to herself a disabling mistrust of a language she thought could not represent a person with her history and experience. Rather, the question represents a person who faces the consequences of her education, the weight of her possibilities as a teacher and writer and human being, a voice in society. And I would not change that person, would not give back the good burden that accompanies my growing expertise, my increasing power to shape myself in language and share that self with "others."

"To speak," says Frantz Fanon, "means to be in a position to use a certain syntax, to grasp the morphology of this or that language, but it means above all to assume a culture, to support the weight of civilization." To write means to do the same, but in a more profound sense. However, Fanon also says that to achieve mastery means to "get" in a position of power, to "grasp," to—assume." This I have learned both as a student and subsequently as a teacher—can involve tremendous emotional and psychological conflict for those attempting to master academic disclosure. Although as a beginning student writer I had a fairly good grasp of ordinary spoken English and was proficient at what Labov calls "code-switching" (and what John Baugh in *Black Street Speech* terms "style shifting"), when I came face to face with the demands of academic writing, I grew increasingly self-conscious, constantly aware of my status as a black and a speaker of one of the many black English vernaculars—a traditional outsider. For the first time, I experienced my sense of doubleness as something menacing, a built-in enemy. Whenever I turned inward for salvation, the balm so available during my childhood, I found instead this new fragmentation which spoke to me in many voices. It was the voice of my desire to prosper, but at the same time it spoke of what I had relinquished and could not regain: a safe way of being, a state of powerlessness which exempted me from responsibility for who I was and might be. And it accused me of betrayal, of turning away from blackness. To recover balance, I had to take on the language of the academy, the language of "others." And to do that, I had to learn to imagine myself as a part of the culture of that language, and therefore someone free to manage that language, to take liberties with it. Writing and rewriting, practicing, experimenting, I came to comprehend more fully the generative power of language. I discovered—with the help of some especially sensitive teachers—that through writing one can continually bring new selves into being, each with new responsibilities and difficulties, but also with new possibilities. Remarkable power, indeed. I write and continually give birth to myself.

Questions for Discussion

1. Compare and contrast Mellix's and Rodriguez's opinions about and experiences with language(s). What fundamental differences do you find in their conclusions about language diversity? How might you account for these differences?

2. Examine the ways that Mellix has written her speaking "selves" into this essay. How does her position as speaker/writer affect how she deals with the subjects of language, literacy, and discourse?

3. As a child, Mellix's choice of how and when to speak is governed more by her community's sense of propriety than by her sense of what constitutes effective or expressive speech. Who determines what this proper speech is, and how does Mellix come to know this? How does Mellix determine when to use different kinds of language or discourse?

Explorations

1. Mellix says that she realized "the implied rules that accompany all writing assignments," namely that teachers expect (and that essays therefore require students to employ) standardized American English. What do you think are the "rules" for language use in your first-year writing class? Were you familiar with these rules before coming to college? If so, in what settings and through what kinds of learning did you become familiar with them?

2. In what ways does Mellix come to feel a sense of ownership of and comfort with different discourses? Is she able, ever, to choose which kinds of language she would like to "own"? If so, how does she claim ownership? If not, what prevents her from this ownership?

3. Mellix writes that to "seek knowledge, freedom, and autonomy means always to be in the concentrated process of becoming—always venturing into new territory, feeling one's way at first, then getting one's balance, negotiating, accommodating, discovering one's self." In what ways and on what subjects do you find yourself now, in college, seeking, venturing, negotiating, accommodating, and/or discovering?

Formal Writing Assignments

1. Write an essay in which you, like Mellix, take a retrospective look at the developments and revisions you've made in your own speaking or writing. Allow yourself the time and space to recreate these changes in the essay. (You may want to return to essays, diary entries, letters, poems, or stories you wrote as a middle school or high school student to illustrate the kinds of writing you composed.) As you draft, analyze the contexts for those developments. What kinds of familial, cultural, or educational demands exerted pressure on you? Were you aware of these pressures at the time?

2. Compose an essay in which you (a) compare and contrast Mellix's opinions on the value of language diversity and bilingualism (or bidialectism) with those of another author (e.g., Anzaldúa, Earley, Rodriguez) in this or the next unit and then (b) articulate your own stance on this issue.

How to Become a Writer

Lorrie Moore

At the ripe old age of nineteen, Lorrie Moore won first prize from a *Seventeen* magazine short story contest in 1976 for her story "Raspberries." Born in Glen Falls, New York, she is currently Professor of English at the University of Wisconsin-Madison. A widely read and widely published author, Moore is the author of *Self-Help* and *Like Life,* both collections of short stories; *Anagrams* and *Who Will Run the Frog Hospital*, both novels.

Moore's short stories are particularly known for their wry sense of humor and offbeat characterizations. *Self-Help,* the collection of short stories in which "How to Become a Writer" appears, has been described by Moore as one of several "stylistic experiments" with second person narration. Moore claims that she wanted to "see what happens when one eliminates the subject, leaves the verb shivering at the start of a clause; what happens when one appropriates the 'how- to' form for a fiction, for an irony, for a 'how-not-to.'" As you read "How to Become a Writer," pay attention to that use of the second person, an unusual approach for a short story writer to take. How does it affect your understanding of Moore's audience? How does it make possible (or not make possible) credibility for the narrator?

Writing Before Reading

1. How have your career plans changed (or not changed) since you were a young adolescent? To what do you attribute the change in plans? If your plans stayed the same, how were you able to maintain them?

2. How do you define "creative" writing? What makes it different from other kinds of writing? Have you ever studied creative writing formally? Practiced creative writing publicly or privately? What were those experiences like?

3. What were your parents' or guardians' goals for you as a child? How did they communicate those goals? How did you respond?

How to Become a Writer

First, try to be something, anything, else. A movie star/astronaut. A movie star/missionary. A movie star/kindergarten teacher. President of the World. Fail miserably. It is best if you fail at an early age—say, fourteen. Early, critical disillusionment is necessary so that at fifteen you can write long haiku sequences about thwarted desire. It is a pond, a cherry blossom, a wind brushing against sparrow wing leaving for mountain. Count the syllables. Show it to your mom. She is tough and practical. She has a son in Vietnam and a husband who may be having an affair. She believes in wearing brown because it hides spots. She'll look briefly at your writing, then back up at you with a face blank as a donut. She'll say: "How about emptying the dishwasher?" Look away. Shove the forks in the fork drawer. Accidentally break one of the freebie gas station glasses. This is the required pain and suffering. This is only for starters.

In your high school English class look only at Mr. Killian's face. Decide faces are important. Write a villanelle about pores. Struggle. Write a sonnet. Count the syllables: nine, ten, eleven, thirteen. Decide to experiment with fiction. Here you don't have to count syllables. Write a short story about an elderly man and woman who accidentally shoot each other in the head, the result of an inexplicable malfunction of a shotgun which appears mysteriously in their living room one night. Give it to Mr. Killian as your final project. When you get it back, he has written on it: "Some of your images are quite nice, but you have no sense of plot." When you are home, in the privacy of your own room, faintly scrawl in pencil beneath his black-inked comments: "Plots are for dead people, pore-face."

Take all the babysitting jobs you can get. You are great with kids. They love you. You tell them stories about old people who die idiot deaths. You sing them songs like "Blue Bells of Scotland," which is their favorite. And when they are in their pajamas and have finally stopped pinching each other, when they are fast asleep, you read every sex manual in the house, and wonder how on earth anyone could ever do those things with someone they truly loved. Fall asleep in a chair reading Mr. McMurphy's *Playboy*. When the McMurphys come home, they will tap you on the shoulder, look at the magazine in your lap, and grin. You will want to die. They will ask you if Tracey took her medicine all right. Explain, yes, she did, that you promised her a story if she would take it like a big girl and that seemed to work out just fine. "Oh, marvelous," they will exclaim.

Try to smile proudly.

Apply to college as a child psychology major.

As a child psychology major, you have some electives. You've always liked birds. Sign up for something called "The Ornithological Field Trip." It meets Tuesdays and Thursdays at two. When you arrive at Room 134 on the first day of class, everyone is sitting around a seminar table talking about metaphors. You've heard of these. After a short, excruciating while, raise your hand and say diffidently, "Excuse me, isn't this Birdwatching One-oh-one?" The class stops and turns to look at you. They seem to all have one face—giant and blank as a vandalized clock. Someone with a beard booms out, "No, this is Creative Writing." Say: "Oh—right," as if perhaps you knew all along. Look down at your schedule. Wonder how the hell you ended up here. The computer, apparently, has made an error. You start to get up to leave and then don't. The lines at the registrar this week are huge. Perhaps you should stick with this mistake. Perhaps your creative writing isn't all that bad. Perhaps it is fate. Perhaps this is what your dad meant when he said, "It's the age of computers, Francie, it's the age of computers."

Decide that you like college life. In your dorm you meet many nice people. Some are smarter than you. And some, you notice, are dumber than you. You will continue, unfortunately, to view the world in exactly these terms for the rest of your life.

The assignment this week in creative writing is to narrate a violent happening. Turn in a story about driving with your Uncle Gordon and another one about two old people who are accidentally electrocuted when they go to turn on a badly wired desk lamp. The teacher will hand them back to you with comments: "Much of your writing is smooth and energetic. You have, however, a ludicrous notion of plot." Write another story about a man and a woman who, in the very first paragraph, have their lower torsos accidentally blitzed away by dynamite. In the second paragraph, with the insurance money, they buy a frozen yogurt stand together. There are six more paragraphs. You read the whole thing out loud in class. No one likes it. They say your sense of plot is outrageous and incompetent. After class someone asks you if you are crazy.

Decide that perhaps you should stick to comedies. Start dating someone who is funny, someone who has what in high school you called a "really great sense of humor" and what now your creative writing class calls "self-contempt giving rise to comic form." Write down all of his jokes, but don't tell him you are doing this. Make up anagrams of his old girlfriend's name and name all of your socially handicapped characters with them. Tell him his old girlfriend is in all of your stories and then watch how funny he can be, see what a really great sense of humor he can have.

Your child psychology advisor tells you, you are neglecting courses in your major. What you spend the most time on should be what you're majoring in. Say yes, you understand.

In creative writing seminars over the next two years, everyone continues to smoke cigarettes and ask the same things: "But does it work?" "Why should we care about this character?" "Have you earned this cliché?" These seem like important questions.

On days when it is your turn, you look at the class hopefully as they scour your mimeographs for a plot. They look back up at you, drag deeply, and then smile in a sweet sort of way.

You spend too much time slouched and demoralized. Your boyfriend suggests bicycling. Your roommate suggests a new boyfriend. You are said to be self-mutilating and losing weight, but you continue writing. The only happiness you have is writing something new, in the middle of the night, armpits damp, heart pounding, something no one has yet seen. You have only those brief, fragile, untested moments of exhilaration when you know: you are a genius. Understand what you must do. Switch majors. The kids in your nursery project will be disappointed, but you have a calling, an urge, a delusion, an unfortunate habit. You have, as your mother would say, fallen in with a bad crowd.

Why write? Where does writing come from? These are questions to ask yourself. They are like: Where does dust come from? Or: Why is there war? Or: If there's a God, then why is my brother now a cripple?

These are questions that you keep in your wallet, like calling cards. These are questions, your creative writing teacher says, that are good to address in your journals but rarely in your fiction.

The writing professor this fall is stressing the Power of the Imagination. Which means he doesn't want long descriptive stories about your camping trip last July, he wants you to start in a realistic context but then to alter it. Like recombinant DNA. He wants you to let your imagination sail, to let it grow big-bellied in the wind. This is a quote from Shakespeare.

Tell your roommate your great idea, your great exercise of imaginative power: a transformation of Melville to contemporary life. It will be about monomania and the fish-eat-fish world of life insurance in Rochester, New York. The first line will be "Call me Fishmeal," and it will feature a menopausal suburban husband named Richard, who because he is so depressed all the time is called "Mopey Dick" by his witty wife Elaine. Say to your roommate: "Mopey Dick, get it?" Your roommate looks at you, her face blank as a large Kleenex. She comes up to you, like a buddy, and puts an arm around your burdened shoulders. "Listen, Francie," she says, slow as speech therapy. "Let's go out and get a big beer."

The seminar doesn't like this one either. You suspect they are beginning to feel sorry for you. They say: "You have to think about what is happening. Where is the story here?"

The next semester the writing professor is obsessed with writing from personal experience. You must write from what you know, from what has happened to you. He wants death, he wants camping trips. Think about what has happened to you. In three years there have been three things: you lost your virginity; your parents got divorced; and your brother came home from a forest ten miles from the Cambodian border with only half a thigh, a permanent smirk nestled into one corner of his mouth.

About the first you write: "It created a new space, which hurt and cried in a voice that wasn't mine, 'I'm not the same anymore, but I'll be okay.'"

About the second you write an elaborate story of an old married couple who stumble upon an unknown land mine in their kitchen and accidentally blow themselves up. You call it: "For Better or for Liverwurst."

About the last you write nothing. There are no words for this. Your typewriter hums. You can find no words.

At undergraduate cocktail parties, people say, "Oh, you write? What do you write about?" Your roommate, who has consumed too much wine, too little cheese, and no crackers at all, blurts: "Oh, my god, she always writes about her dumb boyfriend."

Later on in life you will learn that writers are merely open, helpless texts with no real understanding of what they have written and therefore must half-believe anything and everything that is said of them. You, however, have not yet reached this stage of literary criticism. You stiffen and say, "I do not," the same way you said it when someone in the fourth grade accused you of really liking oboe lessons and your parents really weren't just making you take them.

Insist you are not very interested in any one subject at all, that you are interested in the music of language, that you are interested in—in—syllables, because they are the atoms of poetry, the cells of the mind, the breath of the soul. Begin to feel woozy. Stare into your plastic wine cup.

"Syllables?" you will hear someone ask, voice trailing off, as they glide slowly toward the reassuring white of the dip.

Begin to wonder what you do write about. Or if you have anything to say. Or if there even is such a thing as a thing to say. Limit these thoughts to no more than ten minutes a day; like sit-ups, they can make you thin.

You will read somewhere that all writing has to do with one's genitals. Don't dwell on this. It will make you nervous.

Your mother will come visit you. She will look at the circles under your eyes and hand you a brown book with a brown briefcase on the cover. It is entitled: *How to Become a Business Executive*. She has also brought the *Names for Baby* encyclopedia you asked for; one of your characters, the aging clown—schoolteacher, needs a new name. Your mother will shake her head and say: "Francie, Francie, remember when you were going to be a child psychology major?"

Say: "Mom, I like to write."

She'll say: "Sure you like to write. Of course. Sure you like to write."

Write a story about a confused music student and title it: "Schubert Was the One with the Glasses, Right?" It's not a big hit, although your roommate likes the part where the two violinists accidentally blow themselves up in a recital room. "I went out with a violinist once," she says, snapping her gum.

Thank god you are taking other courses. You can find sanctuary in nineteenth-century ontological snags and invertebrate courting rituals. Certain globular mollusks have what is called "Sex by the Arm." The male octopus, for instance, loses the end of one arm when placing it inside the female body during intercourse. Marine biologists call it "Seven Heaven." Be glad you know these things. Be glad you are not just a writer. Apply to law school.

From here on in, many things can happen. But the main one will be this: you decide not to go to law school after all, and, instead, you spend a good, big chunk of your adult life telling people how you decided not to go to law school after all. Somehow you end up writing again. Perhaps you go to graduate school. Perhaps you work odd jobs and take writing courses at night. Perhaps you are working on a novel and writing down all the clever remarks and intimate personal confessions you hear during the day. Perhaps you are losing your pals, your acquaintances, your balance.

You have broken up with your boyfriend. You now go out with men who, instead of whispering "I love you," shout: "Do it to me, baby." This is good for your writing.

Sooner or later you have a finished manuscript more or less. People look at it in a vaguely troubled sort of way and say, "I'll bet becoming a writer was always a fantasy of yours, wasn't it?" Your lips dry to salt. Say that of all the fantasies possible in the world, you can't imagine being a writer even making the top twenty. Tell them you were going to be a child psychology major. "I bet," they always sigh, "you'd be great with kids." Scowl fiercely. Tell them you're a walking blade.

Quit classes. Quit jobs. Cash in old savings bonds. Now you have time like warts on your hands. Slowly copy all of your friends' addresses into a new address book.

> Vacuum. Chew cough drops. Keep a folder full of fragments.
> An eyelid darkening sideways.
> World as conspiracy.
> Possible plot? A woman gets on a bus.
> Suppose you threw a love affair and nobody came?

At home drink a lot of coffee. At Howard Johnson's order the cole slaw. Consider how it looks like the soggy confetti of a map: where you've been, where you're going—"You Are Here," says the red star on the back of the menu.

Occasionally a date with a face blank as a sheet of paper asks you whether writers often become discouraged. Say that sometimes they do and sometimes they do. Say it's a lot like having polio.

"Interesting," smiles your date, and then he looks down at his arm hairs and starts to smooth them, all, always, in the same direction.

Questions for Discussion

1. Revisit your response to Writing Before Reading question two. How does your idea of what constitutes "creative writing" compare with Moore's? What portions of Moore's description of her creative writing seminars in college struck a chord with you? Why?

2. While Moore's piece is clearly humorous and satirical, it is possible to also identify a more serious or even a persuasive edge. Locate a passage or several passages that seem to perform this persuasive function for you. How do these passages work? What makes them different from other passages in the story?

3. Moore's experiences in her creative writing seminar suggest that the notion of different audiences valuing different kinds of written texts is true for creative, as well as expository, writing. Describe an instance where you have encountered two or more readers who value your writing differently. What were those experiences like? How did you negotiate your readers' needs with your own interests?

Explorations

1. Browse your college's web site and navigate your way to any available course descriptions. Once you find them, locate your major field's list of course offerings. Read the descriptions on the web, and then revise three or four of the course descriptions, doing your best to imitate or mimic Moore's style. How, for instance, would Moore describe an Introduction to Chemistry class? A golf seminar offered by the physical education department?

2. Reflect on your own choice of major/career. Draft your own brief, second person "how to guide" designed to help new students at your university become a member of that major field or profession. What advice would you give them?

3. Like Lorrie Moore, Paul Auster ("Why Write?") discusses his own reasons for being a writer. How might Moore's and Auster's reasons/experiences be similar? How do their uses of writing differ from the reasons outlined by Frederick Douglass in his narrative? Spend some time tracing connections and disjunctions amongst the three writers.

Formal Writing Assignments

1. Lorrie Moore is clearly not the only writer in Unit One who writes very selfconsciously about the act of writing. The notion of writing or even story-telling also serves as subject matter for Paul Auster, Beth Brant, Frederick Douglass, Ursula LeGuin, Barbara Mellix, Toni Morrison, Leslea Newman, Tim O'Brien, and Leslie Silko. Draft an essay in which you compare and contrast Lorrie Moore's discussion of how to become a writer—paying particular attention to the methods she outlines—with the methods and rationales described by one other writer within the unit. You may want to think about the essay as a kind of conversation between these two writers, with your voice acting as a moderator for the discussion. How do you situate yourself and your methods of writing within this conversation?

2. Draft an essay in which you analyze the rhetorical choices made by Lorrie Moore In "How to Become a Writer." Your goal is to delineate how Moore's piece achieves the effect that it does by discussing explicitly the choices she makes as a writer. You may want to consider Moore's use of form; voice; point of view; vocabulary; style; tone; appeals to reason, emotion, or character (logos, pathos, ethos); imagery; dialogue; etc.

I Recognize You

Rosario Morales

Rosario Morales is a poet and writer whose work grows from her Puerto Rican heritage. Her best known collection of poetry and prose, *Getting Home Alive*, was published in 1986 and was co-written with her daughter, Aurora Levins Morales. This poem, from that collection, addresses the difficulties faced by learners of English as a second language who face a loss of cultural identity even as they become fluent in their new language.

Writing Before Reading

1. Create a definition of poetry by listing its characteristic elements.

2. Describe an experience in which you had to speak a language other than your primary one or in which you were silenced because you weren't able to speak a language other than your primary one. Narrate how this experience affected your social interaction at the time.

3. List as many words, phrases, and constructions in the English language that you know or suspect have their origin in some other language. How did you become aware of these terms or groups of terms?

I Recognize You

I recognize you. Spitting out four, five, six-syllable English words, your tongue turning a tight grammatical sentence, flipping adjectives and adverbs into line faster than you can say *Oxford Unabridged Dictionary* and pinning all of it in place with commas, colons, semicolons, and parentheses.

You were one I couldn't beat at spelling bees, the other girl who got *A* in grammar two semesters in a row. You're the one who went on to college, or maybe didn't, but took classes after work, who reads and reads and worries whether you're reading enough or the right thing.

I know without meeting you that you're working class, or a woman of color, or an immigrant, or child of immigrants. That you keep your mama language for the kitchen, hardly ever pronounce it in public, never on the written page.

You're proud. You've done this by yourself, or with your family behind you. And I'm impressed. You can make the English language roll over, bark on command, sit up and beg, you—who were raised on spuds, grits, rice, or tortillas.

But I'm sad, too. For the English language robbed of the beat your home talk could give it, the words you could lend, the accent, the music, the word-order reordering, the grammatical twist. I'm sad for you, too, for the shame with which you store away—hide—a whole treasure box of other, mother, language. It's too rough-mannered, you say, too strange, too exotic, too untutored, too low class.

You're robbing us, robbing the young one saying her first sentence, reading her first book, writing her first poem. You're confirming her scorn of her cradle tongue. You're robbing her of a fine brew of language, a stew of words and ways that could inspire her to self-loving invention.

And you're robbing yourself . . . no, we're robbing ourselves, of selfness, of wholeness, of the joys of writing with *all* our words, of the sound of your Mama's voice, my Papa's voice, of the smell of the kitchen on the page.

Questions for Discussion

1. To what genre does this text belong? Is Morales writing poetry or prose? Point to elements in the text, like its structure and grammar, that support your answer. Then discuss why you think Morales wrote the text in this form. How does the form affect the meaning of the piece?

2. Discuss the boundaries, as you see them, of the English language. What factors define the language and differentiate it from, say, Spanish, Chinese or Yiddish? Are these factors, and other definitive characteristics, stable over time? If so, how can we account for the difference between our English and, for example, Shakespeare's English? If not, describe how you think the process of change in the English language works.

3. What is "standard" English in America today? Discuss the variety of differences in "standard" English that you see illustrated in our diversity of class, cultural background, geographic region, in other words, in what Morales calls "home talk." How can we account for these differences within a "standard" language system?

Explorations

1. Consider your unique way of using language. Do you use particular words or slang, particular constructions or accents that differentiate your way of expressing yourself from, say, the way your parents express themselves? Do these types of differences help to express who you are? In other words, do the differences between your language and your parents' language illustrate how your identity differs from theirs? How would it affect your identity if you were told how to express yourself? What might you lose if you had to express yourself according to a standard?

2. This poem addresses many of the same issues raised by Richard Rodriguez in "Aria: Memory of a Bilingual Childhood." There are important differences in genre and style between these two works, but consider the points where they intersect. How are the writers' perspectives similar? How do they differ?

3. Find the book *Getting Home Alive* at your local library or book store, and compare this poem with other works in the collection. How does "I Recognize You" compare to other poems in the collection in style? in theme? Is it representative of Morales' work, or does it represent a shift away from most of her writing?

Formal Writing Assignments

1. Elaborate on your findings for questions two and three in Questions for Discussion. Discuss how we account for differences over time and between spaces in English: a system that is supposedly stable or "standard"? Then discuss the importance or lack of importance difference has in American English. Is the existence of a standard for American English possible? Is it necessary?

2. Relate an experience of yours that illustrates your feelings and thoughts about Explorations question one. In other words, tell a story about a time when you noticed how some difference in the way you expressed yourself helped differentiate your personality from another's. Did this experience happen when you were forced to conform to another's standard, making you feel that you had to abandon some part of who you are?

The Site of Memory

Toni Morrison

Recognized by both a popular and a scholarly audience, Toni Morrison's writing has been adapted to film, selected for Oprah Winfrey's book club, and has received the National Book Award, Pulitzer Prize, and Nobel Prize. Born in Lorain, Ohio, Morrison set her first novel, *The Bluest Eye*, in her hometown. *The Bluest Eye* is both the story of a small-town family and a pointed criticism of the self-hatred African Americans feel in a world dominated by white standards of beauty and worth. Fiction, to Morrison, should be "beautiful and powerful, but it should also work. It should have something in it that enlightens; something in it that opens the door and points the way. Something in it that suggests what the conflicts are, what the problems are. But it need not solve those problems because it is not a case study, it is not a recipe." In addition to her fiction, Morrison has written several non-fiction essays that deal with issues similar to those raised in her novels; one such issue is the condition of African Americans in a history that marginalizes their experiences. Morrison deals explicitly with this theme in "The Site of Memory," an essay that discusses Morrison's technique of recovering experiences erased by traditional historical texts.

Writing Before Reading

1. What's the difference between self-recollections (autobiographies, memoirs) and fiction? If you don't view them as differerent, discuss your reasons.

2. What self-recollections have you read? For what purpose, do you think, did the authors write self-recollections?

3. Can self-recollections be used as historical studies? If so, how? If not, why not?

The Site of Memory

My inclusion in a series of talks on autobiography and memoir is not entirely a misalliance. Although it's probably true that a fiction writer thinks of his or her work as alien in that company, what I have to say may suggest why I'm not completely out of place here. For one thing, I might throw into relief the differences between self-recollection (memoir) and fiction, and also some of the similarities—the places where those two crafts embrace and where that embrace is symbiotic.

But the authenticity of my presence here lies in the fact that a very large part of my own literary heritage is the autobiography. In this country the print origins of black literature (as distinguished from the oral origins) were slave narratives. These book-length narratives (autobiographies, recollections, memoirs), of which well over a hundred were published, are familiar texts to historians and students of black history. They range from the adventure-packed life of Olaudah Equiano's *The Interesting Narrative of the Life of Olaudah Equiano, or Gustavus Vassa, the African, Written by Himself* (1769) to the quiet desperation of *Incidents in the Life of a Slave Girl: Written by Herself* (1861), in which Harriet Jacob ("Linda Brent") records hiding for seven years in a room too small to stand up in; from the political savvy of Frederick Douglass's *Narrative of the Life of Frederick Douglass, an American Slave, Written by Himself* (1845) to the subtlety and modesty of Henry Bibb, whose voice, in *Life and Adventures of Henry Bibb, an American Slave, Written by Himself* (1849), is surrounded by ("loaded with" is a better phrase) documents attesting to its authenticity. Bibb is careful to note that his formal schooling (three weeks) was short, but that he was "educated in the school of adversity, whips, and chains." Born in Kentucky, he put aside his plans to escape in order to marry. But when he learned that he was the father of a slave and watched the degradation of his wife and child, he reactivated those plans.

Whatever the style and circumstances of these narratives, they were written to say principally two things. One: "This is my historical life—my singular, special example that is personal, but that also represents the race." Two: "I write this text to persuade other people—you, the reader, who is probably not black—that we are human beings worthy of God's grace and the immediate abandonment of slavery." With these two missions in mind, the narratives were clearly pointed.

In Equiano's account, the purpose is quite up-front. Born in 1745 near the Niger River and captured at the age of ten, he survived the Middle Passage, American plantation slavery, wars in Canada and the Mediterranean; learned navigation and clerking from a Quaker named Robert King, and bought his freedom at twenty-one. He lived as a free servant, traveling widely and living most of his latter life in England. Here he is speaking to the British without equivocation: "I hope to have the satisfaction of seeing the renovation of liberty and justice resting on the British government . . . I hope and expect the attention of gentlemen of power . . . May the time come—at least the speculation is to me pleasing—when the sable people shall gratefully commemorate the auspicious era of extensive freedom." With typically eighteenth-century reticence he records his singular and representative life for one purpose: to change things. In fact, he and his coauthors *did* change things. Their works gave fuel to the fires that abolitionists were setting everywhere.

More difficult was getting the fair appraisal of literary critics. The writings of church martyrs and confessors are and were read for the eloquence of their message as well as their experience of redemption, but the American slaves' autobiographical narratives were frequently scorned as "biased," "inflammatory" and "improbable." These attacks are particularly difficult to understand in view of the fact that it was extremely important, as you can imagine, for the writers of these narratives to appear as objective as possible—not to offend the reader by being too angry, or by showing too much outrage, or by calling the reader names. As recently as 1966, Paul Edwards, who edited and abridged Equiano's story, praises the narrative for its refusal to be "inflammatory."

"As a rule," Edwards writes, "he (Equiano) puts no emotional pressure on the reader other than that which the situation itself contains—his language does not strain after our sympathy, but expects it to be given naturally and at the proper time. This quiet avoidance of emotional display produces many of the best passages in the book." Similarly, an 1836 review of Charles Bell's *Life and Adventures of a Fugitive Slave*, which appeared in the "Quarterly Anti-Slavery Magazine," praised Bell's account for its objectivity. "We rejoice in the book the more, because it is not a partisan work . . . It broaches no theory in regard to [slavery], nor proposes any mode or time of emancipation."

As determined as these black writers were to persuade the reader of the evil of slavery, they also complimented him by assuming his nobility of heart and his high-mindedness. They tried to summon up his finer nature in order to encourage him to employ it. They knew that their readers were the people who could make a difference in terminating slavery. Their stories—of brutality, adversity and deliverance—had great popularity in spite of critical hostility in many quarters and patronizing sympathy in others. There was a time when the hunger for "slave stories" was difficult to quiet, as sales figures show. Douglass's *Narrative* sold five thousand copies in four months; by 1847 it had sold eleven thousand copies. Equiano's book had thirty six editions between 1789 and 1850. Moses Roper's book had ten editions from 1837 to 1856; William Wells Brown's was reprinted four times in its first year. Solomon Northrop's book sold twenty-seven thousand copies before two years had passed. A book by Josiah Henson (argued by some to be the model for the "Tom" of Harriet Beecher Stowe's *Uncle Tom's Cabin*) had a pre-publication sale of five thousand.

In addition to using their own lives to expose the horrors of slavery, they had a companion motive for their efforts. The prohibition against teaching a slave to read and write (which in many Southern states carried severe punishment) and against a slave's learning to read and write had to be scuttled at all costs. These writers knew that literacy was power. Voting, after all, was inextricably connected to the ability to read; literacy was a way of assuming and proving the "humanity" that the Constitution denied them. That is why the narratives carry the subtitle "written by himself," or "herself," and include introductions and prefaces by white sympathizers to authenticate them. Other narratives, "edited by" such well known anti-slavery figures as Lydia Maria Child and John Greenleaf Whittier, contain prefaces to assure the reader how little editing was needed. A literate slave was supposed to be a contradiction in terms.

One has to remember that the climate in which they wrote reflected not only the Age of Enlightenment but its twin, born at the same time, the Age of Scientific Racism. David Hume, Immanuel Kant and Thomas Jefferson, to mention only a few, had documented their conclusions that blacks were incapable of intelligence. Frederick Douglass knew otherwise, and he wrote refutations of what Jefferson said in "Notes on the State of Virginia": "Never yet could I find that a black had uttered a thought above the level of plain narration, never see even an elementary trait of painting or sculpture" a sentence that I have always thought ought to be engraved at the door to the Rockefeller Collection of African Art. Hegel, in 1813, had said that Africans had no "history" and couldn't write in modern languages. Kant disregarded a perceptive observation by a black man by saying, "This fellow was quite black from head to foot, a clear proof that what he said was stupid."

Yet no slave society in the history of the world wrote more—or more thoughtfully—about its own enslavement. The milieu, however, dictated the purpose and the style. The narratives are instructive, moral and obviously representative. Some of them are patterned after the sentimental novel that was in vogue at the time. But whatever the level of eloquence or the form, popular taste discouraged the writers from dwelling too long or too carefully on the more sordid details of their experience. Whenever there was an unusually violent incident, or a scatological one, or something "excessive," one finds the writer taking refuge in the literary conventions of the day. "I was left in a state of distraction not to be described" (Equiano). "But let us now leave the rough usage of the field . . . and turn our attention to the less repulsive slave life as it existed in the house of my childhood" (Douglass). "I am not about to harrow the feelings of my readers by a terrific representation of the untold horrors of that fearful system of oppression. . . . It is not my purpose to descend deeply into the dark and noisome caverns of the hell of slavery" (Henry Box Brown).

Over and over, the writers pull the narrative up short with a phrase such as, "But let us drop a veil over these proceedings too terrible to relate." In shaping the experience to make it palatable to those who were in a position to alleviate it, they were silent about many things, and they "forgot" many other things. There was a careful selection of the instances that they would record and a careful rendering of those that they chose to describe. Lydia Maria Child identified the problem in her introduction to "Linda Brent's" tale of sexual abuse: "I am well aware that many will accuse me of indecorum for presenting these pages to the public; for the experiences of this intelligent and much-injured woman belong to a class which some call delicate subjects, and others indelicate. This peculiar phase of Slavery has generally been kept veiled; but the public ought to be made acquainted with its monstrous features, and I am willing to take the responsibility of presenting them with the veil drawn [aside]."

But most importantly—at least for me—there was no mention of their interior life.

For me—a writer in the last quarter of the twentieth century, not much more than a hundred years after Emancipation, a writer who is black and a woman—the exercise is very different. My job becomes how to rip that veil drawn over "proceedings too terrible to relate." The exercise is also critical for any person who is black, or who belongs to any marginalized category, for, historically, we were seldom invited to participate in the discourse even when we were its topic.

Moving that veil aside requires, therefore, certain things. First of all, I must trust my own recollections. I must also depend on the recollections of others. Thus memory weighs heavily in what I write, in how I begin and in what I find to be significant. Zora Neale Hurston said, "Like the dead-seeming cold rocks, I have memories within that came out of the material that went to make me." These "memories within" are the subsoil of my work. But memories and recollections won't give me total access to the unwritten interior life of these people. Only the act of the imagination can help me.

If writing is thinking and discovery and selection and order and meaning, it is also awe and reverence and mystery and magic. I suppose I could dispense with the last four if I were not so deadly serious about fidelity to the milieu out of which I write and in which my ancestors actually lived. Infidelity to that milieu—the absence of the interior life, the deliberate excising of it from the records that the slaves themselves told—is precisely the problem in the discourse that proceeded without us. How I gain access to that interior life is what drives me and is the part of this talk which both distinguishes my fiction from autobiographical strategies and which also embraces certain autobiographical strategies. It's a kind of literary archeology: On the basis of some information and a little bit of guesswork you journey to a site to see what remains were left behind and to reconstruct the world that these remains imply. What makes it fiction is the nature of the imaginative act: my reliance on the image—on the remains—in addition to recollection, to yield up a kind of a truth. By "image," of course, I don't mean "symbol"; I simply mean "picture" and the feelings that accompany the picture.

Fiction, by definition, is distinct from fact. Presumably it's the product of imagination—invention —and it claims the freedom to dispense with "what really happened," or where it really happened, or when it really happened, and nothing in it needs to be publicly verifiable, although much in it can be verified. By contrast, the scholarship of the biographer and the literary critic seems to us only trustworthy when the events of fiction can be traced to some publicly verifiable fact. It's the research of the "Oh, yes, this is where he or she got it from" school, which gets its own credibility from excavating the credibility of the sources of the imagination, not the nature of the imagination.

The work that I do frequently falls, in the minds of most people, into that realm of fiction called fantastic, or mythic, or magical, or unbelievable. I'm not comfortable with these labels. I consider that my single gravest responsibility (in spite of that magic) is not to lie. When I hear someone say, "Truth is stranger than fiction," I think that old chestnut is truer than we know, because it doesn't say that truth is truer than fiction; just that it's stranger, meaning that it's odd. It may be excessive, it may be more interesting, but the important thing is that it's random—and fiction is not random.

Therefore the crucial distinction for me is not the difference between fact and fiction, but the distinction between fact and truth. Because facts can exist without human intelligence, but truth cannot. So if I'm looking to find and expose a truth about the interior life of people who didn't write it (which doesn't mean that they didn't have it); if I'm trying to fill in the blanks that the slave narrative left—to part the veil that was so frequently drawn, to implement the stories that I heard–then the approach that's most productive and most trustworthy for me is the recollection that moves from the image to the text. Not from the text to the image.

Simone de Beauvoir, in *A Very Easy Death,* says, "I don't know why I was so shocked by my mother's death." When she heard her mother's name being called at the funeral by the priest, she says, "Emotion seized me by the throat . . . . 'Françoise de Beauvoir': the words brought her to life; they summed up her history, from birth to marriage to widowhood to the grave. Françoise de Beauvoir—that retiring woman, so rarely named, became an *important* person." The book becomes an exploration both into her own grief and into the images in which the grief lay buried.

Unlike Mme. de Beauvoir, Frederick Douglass asks the reader's patiences for spending about half a page on the death of his grandmother—and he apologizes by saying, in effect, "It really was very important to me. I hope you aren't bored by my indulgence." He makes no attempt to explore that death: its images or its meaning. His narrative is as close to factual as he can make it, which leaves no room for subjective speculation. James Baldwin, on the other hand, in *Notes of a Native Son,* says in recording his father's life and his own relationship with his father, "All of my father's Biblical texts and songs, which I had decided were meaningless, were ranged before me at his death like empty bottles, waiting to hold the meaning which life would give them for me." And then his text fills those bottles. Like Simone de Beauvior, he moves from the event to the image that it left. My route is the reverse: The image comes first and tells me what the "memory" is about.

I can't tell you how I felt when my father died. But I was able to write *Song of Soloman* and imagine, not him, and not his specific interior life, but the world that he inhabited and the private or interior life of the people in it. And I can't tell you how I felt reading to my grandmother while she was turning over and over in her bed (because she was dying, and she was not comfortable), but I could try to reconstruct the world she lived in. And I have suspected, more often than not, that *I know* more than she did, that *I know* more than my grandfather and my great-grandmother did, but I also know that I'm no wiser than they were. And whenever I have tried earnestly to diminish their vision and prove to myself that I know more, and when I have tried to speculate on their interior life and match it up to my own, I have been overwhelmed every time by the richness of theirs compared to my own. Like Frederick Douglass talking about his grandmother, and James Baldwin talking about his father, and Simone de Beauvoir talking about her mother, these people are my access to me; they are my entrance into my own interior life. Which is why the images that float around them—the remains, so to speak, at the archeological site—surface first, and they surface so vividly and so compellingly that I acknowledge them as my route to reconstruction of a world, to an exploration of an interior life that was not written and to the revelation of a kind of truth.

So the nature of my research begins with something as ineffable and as flexible as a dimly recalled figure, the corner of a room, a voice. I began to write my second book, which was called *Sula,* because of my preoccupation with a picture of a woman and the way in which I heard her name pronounced. Her name was Hannah, and I think she was a friend of my mother's. I don't remember seeing her very much, but what I do remember is the color around her—a kind of violet, a suffusion of something violet—and her eyes, which appeared to be half closed. But what I remember most is how the women said her name: how they said "Hannah Peace" and smiled to themselves, and there was some secret about her that they knew, which they didn't talk about, at least not in my hearing, but it seemed *loaded* in the way in which they said her name. And I suspected that she was a little bit of an outlaw but that they approved in some way.

And then, thinking about their relationship to her and the way in which they talked about her, the way in which they articulated her name, made me think about friendship between women. What is it that they forgive each other for? And what it is that is unforgivable in the world of women. I don't want to know any more about Miss Hannah Peace, and I'm not going to ask my mother who she really was and what did she do and what were you laughing about and why were you smiling? Because my experience when I do this with my mother is so crushing: She will give you *the* most pedestrian information you ever heard, and I would like to keep all of my remains and my images intact in their mystery when I begin. Later I will get to the facts. That way I can explore two worlds—the actual and the possible.

What I want to do in this talk is to track an image from picture to meaning to text—a journey which appears in the novel that I'm writing now, which is called *Beloved.*

I'm trying to write a particular kind of scene, and I see corn on the cob. To "see" corn on the cob doesn't mean that it suddenly hovers; it only means that it keeps coming back. And in trying to figure out "What is all this corn doing?" I discover what it is doing.

I see the house where I grew up in Lorain, Ohio. My parents had a garden some distance away from our house, and they didn't welcome me and my sister there, when we were young, because we were not able to distinguish between the things that they wanted to grow and the things that they didn't, so we were not able to hoe, or weed, until much later.

I see them walking, together, away from me. I'm looking at their backs and what they're carrying in their arms: their tools, and maybe a peck basket. Sometimes when they walk away from me they hold hands, and they go to this other place in the garden. They have to cross some railroad tracks to get there.

I also am aware that my mother and father sleep at odd hours because my father works many jobs and works at night. And these naps are times of pleasure for me and my sister because nobody's giving us chores, or telling us what to do, or nagging us in any way. In addition to which, there is some feeling of pleasure in them that I'm only vaguely aware of. They're very rested when they take these naps.

And later on in the summer we have an opportunity to eat corn, which is the one plant that I can distinguish from the others, and which is the harvest that I like the best; the others are the food that no child likes—the collards, the okra, the strong, violent vegetables that I would give a great deal for now. But I do like the corn because it's sweet, and because we all sit down to eat it, and it's finger food, and it's hot, and it's even good cold, and there are neighbors in, and there are uncles in, and it's easy, and it's nice.

The picture of the corn and the nimbus of emotion surrounding it became a powerful one in the manuscript I'm now completing.

Authors arrive at text and subtext in thousands of ways, learning each time they begin anew how to recognize a valuable idea and how to render the texture that accompanies, reveals or displays it to its best advantage. The process by which this is accomplished is endlessly fascinating to me. I have always thought that as an editor for twenty years I understood writers better than their most careful critics, because in examining the manuscript in each of its subsequent stages I knew the author's process, how his or her mind worked, what was effortless, what took time, where the "solution" to a problem came from. The end result—the book—was all that the critic had to go on.

Still, for me, that was the least important aspect of the work. Because, no matter how "fictional" the account of these writers, or how much it was a product of invention, the act of imagination is bound up with memory. You know, they straightened out the Mississippi River places, to make room for houses and livable acreage. Occasionally the river floods these places. "Floods" is the word they use, but in fact it is not flooding; it is remembering. Remembering where it used to be. All water has perfect memory and is forever trying to get back to what it was. Writers are like that: remembering where we were, what valley we ran through, what the banks were like, the light that was there and the route back to our original place. It is emotional memory—what the nerves and the skin remember as well as how it appeared. And a rush of imagination is our "flooding."

Along with personal recollection, the matrix of the work I do is the wish to extend, fill in and complement slave autobiographical narratives. But only the matrix. What comes of all that is dictated by other concerns, not least among them the novel's own integrity. Still, like water I remember where I was before I was "straightened out."

Questions for Discussion

1. Do you think that authors adopt a persona when they write self-recollections? Why or why not? How could an author's adopted persona be seen as a rhetorical strategy? In other words, what end would be served by an author adopting a persona in order to write a self-recollection?

2. In what ways are the literacy practices of the authors Morrison discusses important for the success of their works? How do they display their forms of literacy to their audiences? What other strategies do the authors use to prove their authority?

3. How does Morrison, through recollection, go about "moving [the] veil aside" that obscures the history of marginalized people, who more often than not were not able to relate their "interior lives" in print? How does she uncover the historical riches found in self-recollections?

Explorations

1. Discuss the difference Morrison sees between fiction and self-recollection. How are the two genres both similar and different? Are they more similar than different or more different than similar?

2. What is the importance in our reading self-recollections—specifically those of marginalized people? How can contemporary authors' identity and work be shaped by reading self-recollections of their literary ancestors? How can we all be shaped by these self-recollections for that matter?

3. How might the speaker from Langston Hughes' "Theme from English B" be treated in his/her instructor's written account of the success of the class? Reread Hughes' poem with "The Site of Memory" in mind in order to speculate about the representation of the poem's speaker. Will her/his experience in the class be truthfully recorded?

Formal Writing Assignments

1. Analyze several different historical accounts of a single event in order to answer the following questions: Whose accounts are these? How are the accounts raced, gendered, classed? Whose stories do these stories erase? How can your reading of the different account contribute to a composite reading? Does that composite adequately fill the gaps in the separate accounts? Feel free to analyze history books, movies, current magazines, or any other source you feel is appropriate.

2. Write a *fictional* narrative account of one individual's experience with the event you have analyzed for question one. Express who this person is and your (the narrator's) reasons for relating her story. Will you be explicit about your own identity in the piece you create? Why or why not?

A Letter to Harvey Milk

Leslea Newman

Leslea Newman has gained national prominence as a writer, columnist, speaker, and humorist whose works focus on issues of lesbian and Jewish identity. She has written more than thirty books and received awards including the *Highlights for Children* Fiction Writing Award and the James Baldwin Award for Cultural Achievement. Perhaps her best known work is the children's book *Heather Has Two Mommies,* one of the first books to shine a positive light on lesbian and gay families. "A Letter to Harvey Milk" is a short story that touches on many issues, from the relationship between the generations to memories of the Holocaust to our shared human capacity for acceptance of those different from ourselves.

Writing Before Reading

1. As a child or teenager growing up, did your family/parents/guardians ever give you the sense that a particular behavior or action was considered "unforgivable" or "unacceptable" on your part? If so, describe it. How did you respond to your family's admonitions? Do you believe that any behavior or action is ever unacceptable or unforgivable? How come?

2. Use a prewriting technique (clustering, listing, brainstorming, freewriting, etc.) to explore your own familiarity with the Holocaust. What do you know about this period of time? Where does your knowledge come from?

3. Have you ever directly experienced the "generation gap" between you and an older friend or relative? Describe that experience and speculate about its causes and effects.

A Letter to Harvey Milk

for Harvey Milk 1930–1978

The teacher says we should write about our life, everything that happened today. So *nu,* what's there to tell? Why should today be different than any other day? May 5, 1986. I get up, I have myself a coffee, a little cottage cheese, half an English muffin. I get dressed. I straighten up the house a little, nobody should drop by and see I'm such a slob. I go down to the Senior Center and see what's doing. I play a little cards. I have some lunch, a bagel with cheese. I read a sign in the cafeteria. Writing Class 2:00. I think to myself, why not, something to pass the time. So at two o'clock I go in. The teacher says we should write about our life.

Listen, I want to say to this teacher, I. B. Singer I'm not. You think anybody cares what I did all day? Even my own children, may they live and be well, don't call. You think the whole world is waiting to see what Harry Weinberg had for breakfast?

The teacher is young and nice. She says everybody has something important to say. Yeah, sure, when you're young you believe things like that. She has short brown hair and big eyes, a nice figure, *zaftig* like my poor Fannie, may she rest in peace. She's wearing a Star of David around her neck, hanging from a purple string, that's nice. She gave us all notebooks and told us we're gonna write something every day, and if we want we can even write at home. Who'd a thunk it, me—Harry Weinberg, seventy-seven years old—scribbling in a notebook like a schoolgirl. Why not, it passes the time.

So after the class I go to the store. I pick myself up a little orange juice, a few bagels, a nice piece of chicken. I shouldn't starve to death. I go up, I put on the slippers, I eat the chicken, I watch a little TV, I write in this notebook, I get ready for bed. *Nu*, for this somebody should give me a Pulitzer Prize?

Today the teacher tells us something about herself. She's a Jew, this we know from the *Mogen David* she wears around her neck. She tells us she wants to collect stories from old Jewish people, to preserve our history. *Oy*, such stories that I could tell her, shouldn't be preserved by nobody, She tells us she's learning Yiddish. For what, I wonder. I can't figure this teacher out. She's young, she's pretty, she shouldn't be with the old people so much. I wonder is she married. She doesn't wear a ring. Her grandparents won't tell her stories, she says, and she's worried that the Jews her age won't know nothing about the culture, about life in the *shtetls*. Believe me, life in the *shtetl* is nothing worth knowing about. Hunger and more hunger. Better off we're here in America, the past is past.

Then she gives us our homework, the homework we write in the class, it's a little *meshugeh*, but alright. She wants us to write a letter to somebody from our past, somebody who's no longer with us. She reads us a letter a child wrote to Abraham Lincoln, like an example. Right away I see everybody's getting nervous. So I raise my hand. "Teacher," I say, "you can tell me maybe how to address such a letter? There's a few things I've wanted to ask my wife for a long time." Everybody laughs. Then they start to write.

I sit for a few minutes, thinking about Fannie, thinking about my sister Frieda, my mother, my father, may they all rest in peace. But it's the strangest thing, the one I really want to write to is Harvey.

Dear Harvey:

You had to go get yourself killed for being a *faygeleh?* You couldn't let somebody else have such a great honor? Alright, alright, so you liked the boys, I wasn't wild about the idea. But I got used to it. I never said you wasn't welcome in my house, did I?

Nu, Harvey, you couldn't leave well enough alone. You had your own camera store, your own business, what's bad? You, couldn't keep still about the boys, you weren't satisfied until the whole world knew? Harvey Milk, with the big ears and the big ideas, had to go make himself something, a big politician. I know, I know, I said, "Harvey, make something of yourself, don't be an old *shmegeggie* like me, Harry the butcher." So now I'm eating my words, and they stick like a chicken bone in my old throat.

It's a rotten world, Harvey, and rottener still without you in it. You know what happened to that *momzer*, Dan White? They let him out of jail, and he goes and kills himself so nobody else should have the pleasure. Now you know me, Harvey, I'm not a violent man. But this was too much, even for me. In the old country, I saw things you shouldn't know from, things you couldn't imagine one person could do to another. But here in America, a man climbs through the window, kills the Mayor of San Francisco, kills Harvey Milk, and a couple years later he's walking around on the street? This I never thought I'd see in my whole life. But from a country that kills the Rosenbergs, I should expect something different.

Harvey, you should be glad you weren't around for the trial. I read about it in the papers. The lawyer, that son of a bitch, said Dan White ate too many Twinkies the night before he killed you, so his brain wasn't working right. Twinkies, *nu*, I ask you. My kids ate Twinkies when they were little, did they grow up to be murderers, God forbid? And now, do they take the Twinkies down from the shelf, somebody else shouldn't go a little crazy, climb through a window, and shoot somebody? No, they leave them right there next to the cupcakes and the donuts, to torture me every time I go to the store to pick up a few things, I shouldn't starve to death.

Harvey, I think I'm losing my mind. You know what I do every week? Every week I go to the store, I buy a bag of jelly beans for you, you should have something to *nosh* on, I remember what a sweet tooth you have. I put them in a jar on the table, in case you should come in with another crazy petition for me to sign. Sometimes I think you're gonna just walk through my door and tell me it was another *meshugeh* publicity stunt.

Harvey, now I'm gonna tell you something. The night you died the whole city of San Francisco cried for you. Thirty thousand people marched in the street, I saw it on TV. Me, I didn't go down. I'm an old man, I don't walk so good, they said there might be riots. But no, there were no riots. Just people walking in the street, quiet, each one with a candle, until the street looked like the sky all lit up with a million stars. Old people, young people, black people, white people, Chinese people. You name it, they were there. I remember thinking, Harvey must be so proud, and then I remembered you were dead and such a lump rose in my throat, like a grapefruit it was, and then the tears ran down my face like rain. Can you imagine, Harvey, an old man like me, sitting alone in his apartment, crying and carrying on like a baby? But it's the God's truth. Never did I carry on so in all my life.

And then all of a sudden I got mad. I yelled at the people on TV: for getting shot you made him into such a hero? You couldn't march for him when he was alive, he couldn't *shep* a little *naches*?

But *nu*, what good does getting mad do, it only makes my pressure go up. So I took myself a pill, calmed myself down.

Then they made speeches for you, Harvey. The same people who called you a *shmuck* when you were alive, now you were dead, they were calling you a *mensh*. You were a *mensh*, Harvey, a *mensh* with a heart of gold. You were too good for this rotten world. They just weren't ready for you.

> *Oy Harveleh, alav ha-sholom,*
> *Harry*

Today the teacher asks me to stay for a minute after class. *Oy*, what did I do wrong now, I wonder. Maybe she didn't like my letter to Harvey? Who knows?

After the class she comes and sits down next to me. She's wearing purple pants and a white T-shirt. *"Feh,"* I can just hear Fannie say. "God forbid she should wear a skirt? Show off her figure a little? The girls today dressing like boys and the boys dressing like girls—this I don't understand."

"Mr. Weinberg," the teacher says.

"Call me Harry," I says.

"O.K., Harry," she says. "I really liked the letter you wrote to Harvey Milk. It was terrific, really. It meant a lot to me. It even made me cry."

I can't even believe my own ears. My letter to Harvey Milk made the teacher cry?

"You see, Harry," she says, "I'm gay, too. And there aren't many Jewish people your age that are so open-minded. At least that I know. So your letter gave me lots of hope. In fact, I was wondering if you'd consider publishing it."

Publishing my letter? Again I couldn't believe my own ears. Who would want to read a letter from Harry Weinberg to Harvey Milk? No, I tell her. I'm too old for fame and glory. I like the writing class, it passes the time. But what I write is my own business. The teacher looks sad for a moment, like a cloud passes over her eyes. Then she says, "Tell me about Harvey Milk. How did you meet him? What was he like?" *Nu*, Harvey, you were a pain in the ass when you were alive, you're still a pain in the ass now that you're dead. Everybody wants to hear about Harvey.

So I tell her. I tell her how I came into the camera shop one day with a roll of film from when I went to visit the grandchildren. How we started talking and I said, "Milk, that's not such a common name. Are you related to the Milks in Woodmere?" And so we found out we were practically neighbors forty years ago, when the children were young, before we moved out here. Gracie was almost the same age as Harvey, a couple years older, maybe, but they went to different schools. Still, Harvey leans across the counter and gives me such a hug, like I'm his own father.

I tell her more about Harvey, how he didn't believe there was a good *kosher* butcher in San Francisco, how he came to my store just to see. But all the time I'm talking I'm thinking to myself, no, it can't be true. Such a gorgeous girl like this goes with the girls, not with the boys? Such a *shanda*. Didn't God in His wisdom make a girl a girl and a boy a boy—boom they should meet, boom they should get married, boom they should have babies, and that's the way it is? Harvey I loved like my own son, but this I never could understand. And *nu*, why was the teacher telling me this, it's my business who she sleeps with? She has some sadness in her eyes, this teacher. Believe me I've known such sadness in my life, I can recognize it a hundred miles away. Maybe she's lonely. Maybe after class one day I'll take her out for a coffee, we'll talk a little bit, I'll find out.

It's 3:00 in the morning, I can't sleep. So *nu*, here I am with this crazy notebook. Who am I kidding, maybe I think I'm Yitzhak Peretz? What would the children think, to see their old father sitting up in his bathrobe with a cup of tea, scribbling in his notebook? *Oy, meyn kinder,* they should only live and be well and call their old father once in a while.

Fannie used to keep up with them. She could be such a *nudge*, my Fannie. "What's the matter, you're too good to call your old mother once in a while?" she'd yell into the phone. Then there'd be a pause. "Busyshmusy," she'd yell even louder. "Was I too busy to change your diapers? Was I too busy to put food into your mouth?" *Oy*, I haven't got the strength, but Fannie could she yell and carry on.

You know sometimes, in the middle of the night, I'll reach across the bed for Fannie's hand. Without even thinking, like my hand got a mind of its own, it creeps across the bed, looking for Fannie's hand. After all this time, fourteen years she's been dead, but still, a man gets used to a few things. Forty-two years, the body doesn't forget. And my little *Faigl* had such hands, little *hentelehs*, tiny like a child's. But strong. Strong from kneading *challah*, from scrubbing clothes, from rubbing the children's backs to put them to sleep. My Fannie, she was so ashamed from those hands. After thirty-five years of marriage when finally, I could afford to buy her a diamond ring, she said no. She said it was too late already, she'd be ashamed. A girl needs nice hands to show off a diamond, her hands were already ruined, better yet buy a new stove.

Ruined? *Feh*. To me her hands were beautiful. Small, with veins running through them like rivers, and cracks in the skin like the desert. A hundred times I've kicked myself for not buying Fannie that ring.

Today in the writing class the teacher read my notebook. Then she says I should make a poem about Fannie. "A poem," I says to her, "now Shakespeare you want I should be?" She says I have a good eye for detail. I says to her, "Excuse me, Teacher, you live with a woman for forty-two years, you start to notice a few things."

She helps me. We do it together, we write a poem called "Fannie's Hands"

Fannie's hands are two little birds
that fly into her lap.
Her veins are like rivers.
Her skin is cracked like the desert.
Her strong little hands
baked *challah*, scrubbed clothes,
rubbed the children's backs.
Her strong little hands
and my big clumsy hands
fit together in the night
like pieces of a jigsaw puzzle
made in Heaven, by God.

So *nu*, who says you can't teach an old dog new tricks? I read it to the class and such a fuss they made. "A regular Romeo," one of them says. "If only my husband, may he live and be well, would write such a poem for me," says another. I wish Fannie was still alive, I could read it to her. Even the teacher was happy, I could tell, but still, there was a ring of sadness around her eyes.

After the class I waited till everybody left, they shouldn't get the wrong idea, and I asked the teacher would she like to go get a coffee. "*Nu*, it's enough writing already," I said. "Come, let's have a little treat."

So we take a walk, it's a nice day. We find a diner, nothing fancy, but clean and quiet. I try to buy her a piece of cake, a sandwich maybe, but no, all she wants is coffee.

So we sit and talk a little. She wants to know about my childhood in the old country, she wants to know about the boat ride to America, she wants to know did my parents speak Yiddish to me when I was growing up. "Harry," she says to me, "when I hear old people talking Yiddish, it's like a love letter blowing in the wind. I try to run after them, and sometimes I catch a phrase that makes me cry or a word that makes me laugh. Even if I don't understand, it always touches my heart."

Oy, this teacher has some strange ideas. "Why do you want to speak Jewish?" I ask her. "Here in America, everybody speaks English. You don't need it. What's done is done, what's past is past. You shouldn't go with the old people so much. You should go out, make friends, have a good time. You got some troubles you want to talk about? Maybe I shouldn't pry," I say, "but you shouldn't look so sad, a young girl like you. When you're old you got plenty to be sad. You shouldn't think about the old days so much, let the dead rest in peace. What's done is done."

I took a swallow of my coffee, to calm down my nerves. I was getting a little too excited.

"Harry, listen to me," the teacher says. "I'm thirty years old and no one in my family will talk to me because I'm gay. It's all Harvey Milk's fault. He made such an impression on me. You know, when he died, what he said, 'If a bullet enters my brain, let that bullet destroy every closet door.' So when he died, I came out to everyone—the people at work, my parents. I felt it was my duty, so the Dan Whites of the world wouldn't be able to get away with it. I mean, if every single gay person came out—just think of it—everyone would see they had a gay friend or a gay brother or a gay cousin or a gay teacher. Then they couldn't say things like 'Those gays should be shot.' Because they'd be saying you should shoot my neighbor or my sister or my daughter's best friend."

I never saw the teacher get so excited before. Maybe a politician she should be. She reminded me a little bit of Harvey.

"So *nu*, what's the problem?" I ask.

"The problem is my parents," she says with a sigh, and such a sigh I never heard from a young person before. "My parents haven't spoken to me since I told them I was gay. 'How could you do this to us they said. I wasn't doing anything to them. I tried to explain I couldn't help being gay, like I couldn't help being a Jew, but that they didn't want to hear. So I haven't spoken to them in eight years."

"Eight years, *Gottenyu*," I say to her. This I never heard in my whole life. A father and a mother cut off their own daughter like that. Better they should cut off their own hand. I thought about Gracie, a perfect daughter she's not, but your child is your child. When she married the *Goy*, Fannie threatened to put her head in the oven, but she got over it. Not to see your own daughter for eight years, and such a smart, gorgeous girl, such a good teacher, what a *shanda*.

So what can I do, I ask. Does she want me to talk to them, a letter maybe I could write. Does she want I should adopt her, the hell with them, I make a little joke. She smiles. "Just talking to you makes me feel better," she says. So *nu*, now I'm Harry the social worker, She says that's why she wants the old people's stories so much, she doesn't know nothing from her own family history, She wants to know about her own people, maybe write a book. But it's hard to get the people to talk to her, she says, she doesn't understand.

"Listen, Teacher," I tell her. "These old people have stories you shouldn't know from. What's there to tell? Hunger and more hunger. Suffering and more suffering. I buried my sister over twenty years ago, my mother, my father—all dead. You think I could just start talking about them like I just saw them yesterday? You think I don't think about them every day? Right here I keep them," I say, pointing to my heart. "I try to forget them, I should live in peace, the dead are gone. Talking about them won't bring them back. You want stories, go talk to somebody else. I ain't got no stories. "

I sat down then, I didn't even know I was standing up, I got so excited. Everybody in the diner was looking at me, a crazy man shouting at a young girl.

Oy, and now the teacher was cryin. "I'm sorry," I says to her. "You want another coffee?"

"No thanks, Harry," she says. "I'm sorry, too."

"Forget it. We can just pretend it never happened," I say, and then we go.

All this crazy writing has shaken me up inside a little bit. Yesterday I was walking home from the diner, I thought I saw Harvey walking in front of me. No, it can't be, I says to myself, and my heart started to pound so, I got afraid I shouldn't drop dead in the street from a heart attack. But then the man turned around and it wasn't Harvey. It didn't even look like him at all.

I got myself upstairs and took myself a pill, I could feel my pressure was going up. All this talk about the past—Fannie, Harvey, Frieda, my mother, my father—what good does it do? This teacher and her crazy ideas. Did I ever ask my mother, my father, what their childhood was like? What nonsense. Better I shouldn't know.

So today is Saturday, no writing class, but still I'm writing in this crazy notebook. I ask myself, Harry, what can I do to make you feel a little better? And I answer myself, make me a nice chicken soup.

You think an old man like me can't make chicken soup? Let me tell you, on all the holidays it was Harry that made the soup. Every *Pesach* it was Harry skimming the *shmaltz* from the top of the pot, it was Harry making the *kreplach*. I ask you, where is it written that a man shouldn't know from chicken soup?

So I take myself down to the store, I buy myself a nice chicken, some carrots, some celery, some parsley—onions I already got, parsnips I can do without. I'm afraid I shouldn't have a heart attack *shlepping* all that food up the steps, but thank God, I make it alright.

I put up the pot with water, throw everything in one-two-three, and soon the whole house smells from chicken soup.

I remember the time Harvey came to visit and there I was with my apron on, skimming the *shmaltz* from the soup. Did he kid me about that! The only way I could get him to keep still was to invite him to dinner. "Listen, Harvey," I says to him. "Whether you're a man or a woman, it doesn't matter. You gotta learn to cook. When you're old, nobody cares. Nobody will do for you. You gotta learn to do for yourself."

"I won't live past fifty, Har," he says, smearing a piece of rye bread with *shmaltz*. "Nobody wants to grow old, believe me, I know," I says to him. "But listen, it's not so terrible. What's the alternative? Nobody wants to die young, either." I take off my apron and sit down with him.

"No, I mean it Harry," he says to me with his mouth full. "I won't make it to fifty. I've always known it. I'm a politician. A gay politician. Someone's gonna take a pot shot at me. It's a risk you gotta take."

The way he said it, I tell you, a chill ran down my back like I never felt before. He was forty-seven at the time, just a year before he died.

Today after the writing class, the teacher tells us she's going away for two days. Everyone makes a big fuss, the class they like so much already. She tells us she's sorry, something came up she has to do. She says we can come have class without her, the room will be open, we can read to each other what we write in our notebooks. Someone asks her what we should write about.

"Write me a letter," she says. "Write a story called 'What I Never Told Anyone.' "

So, after everyone leaves, I ask her does she want to go out, have a coffee, but she says no, she has to go home and pack.

I tell her wherever she's going she should have a good time.

"Thanks, Harry," she says. "You'll be here when I get back?"

"Sure," I tell her. "I like this crazy writing. It passes the time."

She swings a big black bookbag onto her shoulder, a regular Hercules this teacher is, and she smiles at me. "I gotta run, Harry. Have a good week." She turns and walks away and something on her book-bag catches my eye. A big shiny pin that spells out her name all fancy-shmancy in rhinestones: Barbara. And under that, right away I see sewn onto her bookbag an upside-down pink triangle.

I stop in my tracks, stunned. No, it can't be, I says to myself. Maybe it's just a design? Maybe she doesn't know from this? My heart is beating fast now, I know I should go home, take myself a pill, my pressure, I can feel it going up.

But I just stand there. And then I get mad. What, she thinks maybe I'm blind as well as old. I can't see what's right in front of my nose? Or maybe we don't remember such things? What right does she have to walk in here with that, that thing on her bag, to remind us of what we been through? Haven't we seen enough?

Stories she wants. She wants we should cut our hearts open and give her stories so she could write a book. Well, alright, now I'll tell her a story.

This is what I never told anyone. One day, maybe seven, eight years ago—no, maybe longer, I think Harvey was still alive—one day Izzie comes knocking on my door. I open the door and there's Izzie, standing there, his face white as a sheet. I bring him inside, I make him a coffee. "Izzie, what is it," I says to him. "Something happened to the children, to the grandchildren, God forbid?"

He sits down, he doesn't drink his coffee. He looks through me like I'm not even there. Then he says, "Harry, I'm walking down the street, you know I had a little lunch at the Center, and then I come outside, I see a young man, maybe twenty-five, a good-looking guy, walking toward me. He's wearing black pants, a white shirt, and on his shirt he's got a pink triangle."

"So," I says. "A pink triangle, a purple triangle, they wear all kinds of crazy things these days."

"*Heshel*," he tells me, "don't you understand? The gays are wearing pink triangles just like the war, just like in the camps."

No, this I can't believe. Why would they do a thing like that? But if Izzie says it, it must be true. Who would make up such a thing?

"He looked a little bit like *Yussl*," Izzie says, and then he begins to cry, and such a cry like I never heard. Like a baby he was, with the tears streaming down his cheeks and his shoulders shaking with great big sobs. Such moans and groans I never heard from a grown man in all my life. I thought maybe he was gonna have a heart attack the way he was carrying on. I didn't know what to do. I was afraid the neighbors would hear, they shouldn't call the police, such sounds he was making. Fifty-eight years old he was, but he looked like a little boy sitting there, sniffling. And who was *Yussl*? Thirty years we'd been friends, and I never heard from *Yussl*.

So finally, I put my arms around him, and I held him, I didn't know what else to do. His body was shaking so, I thought his bones would crack from knocking against each other. Soon his body got quiet, but then all of sudden his mouth got noisy.

"Listen, *Heshel*, I got to tell you something, something I never told nobody in my whole life. I was young in the camps, nineteen, maybe twenty when they took us away." The words poured from his mouth like a flood. "*Yussl* was my best friend in the camps. Already I saw my mother, my father, my Hannah marched off to the ovens. *Yussl* was the only one I had to hold on to.

"One morning, during the selection, they pointed me to the right, *Yussl* to the left. I went a little crazy, I ran after him. 'No, he stays with me, they made a mistake,' I said, and I grabbed him by the hand and dragged him back in line. Why the guard didn't kill us right then, I couldn't tell you. Nothing made sense in that place.

"*Yussl* and I slept together on a wooden bench. That night I couldn't sleep. It happened pretty often in that place. I would close my eyes and see such things that would make me scream in the night, and for that I could get shot. I don't know what was worse, asleep or awake. All I saw was suffering.

"On this night, *Yussl* was awake, too. He didn't move a muscle, but I could tell. Finally he said my name, just a whisper, but something broke in me and I began to cry. He put his arms around me and we cried together, such a close call we'd had.

"And then he began to kiss me. 'You saved my life,' he whispered, and he kissed my eyes, my cheeks, my lips. And Harry, I kissed him back. Harry, I never told nobody this before. I, we . . . we, you know, that was such a place that hell, I couldn't help it. The warmth of his body was just too much for me and Hannah was dead already and we would soon be dead too, probably, so what did it matter?"

He looked up at me then, the tears streaming from his eyes. "It's O.K., Izzie," I said. "Maybe I would have done the same."

"There's more, Harry," he says, and I got him a tissue, he should blow his nose. What more could there be?

"This went on for a couple of months maybe, just every once in a while when we couldn't sleep. He'd whisper my name and I'd answer with his, and then we'd, you know, we'd touch each other. We were very, very quiet, but who knows, maybe some other boys in the barracks were doing the same.

"To this day I don't know how it happened, but somehow someone found out. One day *Yussl* didn't come back to the barracks at night. I went almost crazy, you can imagine, all the things that went through my mind, the things they might have done to him, those lousy Nazis. I looked everywhere, I asked everyone, three days he was gone. And then on the third day, they lined us up after supper and there they had *Yussl*. I almost collapsed on the ground when I saw him. They had him on his knees with his hands tied behind his back. His face was swollen so, you couldn't even see his eyes. His clothes were stained with blood. And on his uniform they had sewn a pink triangle, big, twice the size of our yellow stars.

"*Oy*, did they beat him but good. 'Who's your friend?' they yelled at him. 'Tell us and we'll let you live.' But no, he wouldn't tell. He knew they were lying, he knew they'd kill us both. They asked him again and again, 'Who's your friend? Tell us which one he is.' And every time he said no, they'd crack him with a whip until the blood ran from him like a river. Such a sight he was, like I've never seen. How he remained conscious I'll never know.

"Everything inside me was broken after that. I wanted to run to his side, but I didn't dare, so afraid I was. At one point he looked at me, right in the eye, as though he was saying, *Izzie, save yourself. Me, I'm finished, but you, you got a chance to live through this and tell the world our story.*

"Right after he looked at me, he collapsed, and they shot him, Harry, right there in front of us. Even after he was dead they kicked him in the head a little bit. They left his body out there for two days, as a warning to us. They whipped us all that night, and from then on we had to sleep with all the lights on and with our hands on top of the blankets. Anyone caught with their hands under the blankets would be shot.

"He died for me, Harry, they killed him for that, was it such a terrible thing? *Oy*, I haven't thought about Yussl for twenty-five years maybe, but when I saw that kid on the street today, it was too much." And then he started crying again, and he clung to me like a child.

So what could I do? I was afraid he shouldn't have a heart attack, maybe he was having a nervous breakdown, maybe I should get the doctor. *Vay iss mir*, I never saw anybody so upset in my whole life. And such a story, *Gottenyu*.

"Izzie, come lie down," I says, and I took him by the hand to the bed. I laid him down, I took off his shoes, and still he was crying. So what could I do? I lay down with him, I held him tight. I told him he was safe, he was in America. I don't know what else I said, I don't think he heard me, still he kept crying.

I stroked his head, I held him tight. "Izzie, it's alright," I said. "Izzie, Izzie, *Izzaleh*." I said his name over and over, like a lullaby, until his crying got quiet. He said my name once softly, *Heshel*, or maybe he said *Yussl*, I don't remember, but thank God he finally fell asleep. I tried to get up from the bed, but Izzie held onto me tight. So what could I do? Izzie was my friend for thirty years, for him I would do anything. So I held him all night long, and he slept like a baby.

And this is what I never told nobody, not even Harvey. That there in that bed, where Fannie and I slept together for forty-two years, me and Izzie spent the night. Me, I didn't sleep a wink, such a lump in my throat I had, like the night Harvey died.

Izzie passed on a couple months after that. I saw him a few more times, and he seemed different somehow. How, I couldn't say. We never talked about that night. But now that he had told someone his deepest secret, he was ready to go, he could die in peace. Maybe now that I told, I can die in peace, too?

Dear Teacher:

You said write what you never told nobody, and write you a letter. I always did all my home-work, such a student I was. So *nu*, I got to tell you something. I can't write in this notebook no more, I can't come no more to the class. I don't want you should take offense, you're a good teacher and a nice girl. But me, I'm an old man, I don't sleep so good at night, these stories are like a knife in my heart. Harvey, Fannie, Izzie, Yussi, my father, my mother, let them all rest in peace. The dead are gone. Better to live for today. What good does remem-bering do, it doesn't bring back the dead. Let them rest in peace.

But Teacher, I want you should have my notebook. It doesn't have nice stories in it, no love letters, no happy endings for a nice girl like you. A bestseller it ain't, I guarantee. Maybe you'll put it in a book someday, the world shouldn't forget.

Meanwhile, good luck to you, Teacher. May you live and be well and not get shot in the head like poor Harvey, may he rest in peace. Maybe someday we'll go out, have a coffee again, who knows? But me, I'm too old for this crazy writing. I remember too much, the pen is like a knife twisting in my heart.

One more thing, Teacher. Between parents and children, it's not so easy. Believe me, I know. Don't give up on them. One father, one mother, it's all you got. If you were my *tochter*, I'd be proud of you.

Harry

Questions for Discussion

1. Why does Harry feel such a kinship to the young teacher? What events in Harry's life contribute to his desire to connect with her?

2. How does Harry's letter to Harvey Milk affect the teacher? Why does she respond to it the way that she does?

3. Discuss the significance of the pink triangle in the story. How does that triangle function for Izzie? For the teacher? For Harry? How would you explain the triangle's significance to an "outsider," a person who is neither gay/Lesbian nor Jewish?

Explorations

1. There are several "real life" references within "A Letter to Harvey Milk." Harvey Milk, for instance, is a real person with a real history, and the Holocaust serves as a kind of backdrop for the piece, as does the Gay Rights Movement. Working with a small group of three or four students, choose a particular "real life" aspect of the short story to explore via the World Wide Web or another electronic resource, perhaps one linked to your university's library system. Once you've explored the resource or web site, construct a brief "mini-presentation" for the rest of the class to help contextualize the short story.

2. Several other writers within the unit consider the issue of sexuality and society's acceptance or rejection of gays and Lesbians. Consider the couple who lose their daughter in Brant's "A Long Story," or Jewelle Gomez's experience of coming out in "I Lost it At the Movies," for instance. For this exploration, consider how the issue of Gay and lesbian identity is discussed in one or more of the pieces within the unit. In particular, think about the importance of naming within these pieces—how do the narrators name themselves, and how do others respond to those acts of naming?

3. The idea of writing itself is an important theme within Newman's short story. For this exploration, discuss how writing functions within "A Letter to Harvey Milk." Who does it? Why do they do it? How is it read and received? How is it shared with others? What genres of writing are present/discussed?

Formal Writing Assignments

1. Return to one of the four Explorations above and revisit your response to the question. Using your response as a springboard, construct a more formal essay about this particular subject (i.e. historical events/figures in the story; identities within the story; the function of the act of writing within the story). As you draft the essay, you should construct a specific argument about one of these subjects as it intersects the story. Your goal is to develop a thesis that propels your argument. The thesis may be based upon your Exploration; for example, you might pose a specific argument about the importance of Harry's writing to the telling of the story, or how the pink triangle issue affects Harry's relationship with his teacher.

2. For this assignment, revisit the story in order to focus upon the "writing within the writing" that takes place here: Harry's letters, poems, and other writings. Once you have studied these pieces, draft an essay in which you describe and analyze Harry's work as a writer within the story. Discuss the kinds of writing choices Harry makes. What do you see as Harry's strengths? How does he achieve the effects that he does? How do those pieces of Harry's writing contribute to Newman's story as a whole? Which genres does he seem to use most effectively? How? How does Newman allow Harry to have his own voice as a writer?

How to Tell a True War Story

Tim O'Brien

Tim O'Brien is the author of five novels, a memoir of his experiences as a soldier in Vietnam, and *The Things They Carried*, a collection of interrelated short stories in which the following selection appeared. He received the National Book Award for *Going After Cacciato* in 1979, and *The Things They Carried* was selected by the editors of the *New York Times Book Review* as one of the best books of 1990.

The following selection explicitly challenges many of our preconceptions about truth and storytelling as a vehicle for exposing the truth. In the work of fiction, *The Things They Carried*, from which this story is taken, O'Brien presents us with a narrator named Tim O'Brien who serves in Vietnam (as did the author), is a writer, and comments freely on both the fictionalization of "true" events and on the inherent "truth" of memory. In a work both realistic and postmodern, O'Brien even dedicates the book to his fictional characters, calling attention to the fictional conceit most authors try to veil. "How to Tell a True War Story," both as a personal narrative and a study of storytelling, examines the inseparability of memory and history and fiction and truth.

Writing Before Reading

1. Tell the story of a time when you remembered something vividly (from childhood, for instance), only to find out later that the events did not or could not have occurred the way you remembered them? How did you reconcile yourself to these discrepancies?

2. Sometimes true stories are too strange or outlandish to believe. Write about something that really happened but rarely tell to others because you don't think it's believable. Do you hesitate to tell the story because the facts themselves are incredible or because you don't trust your own ability to tell it convincingly?

How to Tell a True War Story

THIS IS TRUE

I had a buddy in Vietnam. His name was Bob Kiley, but everybody called him Rat.

A friend of his gets killed, so about a week later Rat sits down and writes a letter to the guy's sister. Rat tells her what a great brother she had, how together the guy was, a number one pal and comrade. A real soldier's soldier, Rat says. Then he tells a few stories to make the point, how her brother would always volunteer for stuff nobody else would volunteer for in a million years, dangerous stuff, like doing recon or going out on these really badass night patrols. Stainless steel balls, Rat tells her. The guy was a little crazy, for sure, but crazy in a good way, a real daredevil, because he liked the challenge of it, he liked testing himself, just man against gook. A great, great guy, Rat says.

Anyway, it's a terrific letter, very personal and touching. Rat almost bawls writing it. He gets all teary telling about the good times they had together, how her brother made the war seem almost fun, always raising hell and lighting up villes and bringing smoke to bear every which way. A great sense of humor, too. Like the time at this river when he went fishing with a whole damn crate of hand grenades. Probably the funniest thing in world history, Rat says, all that gore, about twenty zillion dead gook fish. Her brother, he had the right attitude. He knew how to have a good time. On Halloween, this real hot spooky night, the dude paints up his body all different colors and puts on this weird mask and hikes over to a ville and goes trick-or-treating almost stark naked, just boots and balls and an M-16. A tremendous human being, Rat says. Pretty nutso sometimes, but you could trust him with your life.

And then the letter gets very sad and serious. Rat pours his heart out. He says he loved the guy. He says the guy was his best friend in the world. They were like soul mates, he says, like twins or something, they had a whole lot in common. He tells the guy's sister he'll look her up when the war's over.

So what happens?

Rat mails the letter. He waits two months. The dumb cooze never writes back.

A true war story is never moral. It does not instruct, nor encourage virtue, nor suggest models of proper human behavior, nor restrain men from doing the things men have always done. If a story seems moral, do not believe it. If at the end of a war story you feel uplifted, or if you feel that some small bit of rectitude has been salvaged from the larger waste, then you have been made the victim of a very old and terrible lie. There is no rectitude whatsoever. There is no virtue. As a first rule of thumb, therefore, you can tell a true war story by its absolute and uncompromising allegiance to obscenity and evil. Listen to Rat Kiley. Cooze, he says. He does not say bitch. He certainly does not say woman, or girl. He says cooze. Then he spits and stares. He's nineteen years old—it's too much for him—so he looks at you with those big sad gentle killer eyes and says cooze, because his friend is dead and because it's so incredibly sad and true: she never wrote back.

You can tell a true war story if it embarrasses you. If you don't care for obscenity, you don't care for the truth; if you don't care for the truth, watch how you vote. Send guys to war, they come home talking dirty.

Listen to Rat: "Jesus Christ, man, I write this beautiful fuckin' letter, I slave over it, and what happens? The dumb cooze never writes back."

The dead guy's name was Curt Lemon. What happened was, we crossed a muddy river and marched west into the mountains, and on the third day we took a break along a trail junction in deep jungle. Right away, Lemon and Rat Kiley started goofing. They didn't understand about the spookiness. They were kids; they just didn't know. A nature hike, they thought, not even a war, so they went off into the shade of some giant trees - quadruple canopy, no sunlight at all- and they were giggling and calling each other yellow mother and playing a silly game they'd invented. The game involved smoke grenades, which were harmless unless you did stupid things, and what they did was pull out the pin and stand a few feet apart and play catch under the shade of those huge trees. Whoever chickened out was a yellow mother. And if nobody chickened out, the grenade would make a light popping sound and they'd be covered with smoke and they'd laugh and dance around and then do it again.

It's all exactly true.

It happened, to me, nearly twenty years ago, and I still remember that trail junction and those giant trees and a soft dripping sound somewhere beyond the trees. I remember the smell of moss. Up in the canopy there were tiny white blossoms, but no sunlight at all, and I remember the shadows spreading out under the trees where Curt Lemon and Rat Kiley were playing catch with smoke grenades. Mitchell Sanders sat flipping his yo-yo. Norman Bowker and Kiowa and Dave Jensen were dozing, or half dozing, and all around us were those ragged green mountains.

Except for the laughter things were quiet.

At one point, I remember, Mitchell Sanders turned and looked at me, not quite nodding, as if to warn me about something, as if he already knew, then after a while he rolled up his yo-yo and moved away.

It's hard to tell you what happened next.

They were just goofing. There was a noise, I suppose, which must've been the detonator, so I glanced behind me and watched Lemon step from the shade into bright sunlight. His face was suddenly brown and shining. A handsome kid, really. Sharp gray eyes, lean and narrow-waisted, and when he died it was almost beautiful, the way the sunlight came around him and lifted him up and sucked him high into a tree full of moss and vines and white blossoms.

In any war story, but especially a true one, it's difficult to separate what happened from what seemed to happen. What seems to happen becomes its own happening and has to be told that way. The angles of vision are skewed. When a booby trap explodes, you close your eyes and duck and float outside yourself. When a guy dies, like Curt Lemon, you look away and then look back for a moment and then look away again. The pictures get jumbled; you tend to miss a lot. And then afterward, when you go to tell about it, there is always that surreal seemingness, which makes the story seem untrue, but which in fact represents the hard and exact truth as it seemed.

In many cases a true war story cannot be believed. If you believe it, be skeptical. It's a question of credibility. Often the crazy stuff is true and the normal stuff isn't, because the normal stuff is necessary to make you believe the truly incredible craziness.

In other cases you can't even tell a true war story. Sometimes it's just beyond telling.

I heard this one, for example, from Mitchell Sanders. It was near dusk and we were sitting at my foxhole along a wide muddy river north of Quang Ngai. I remember how peaceful the twilight was. A deep pinkish red spilled out on the river, which moved without sound, and in the morning we would cross the river and march west into the mountains. The occasion was right for a good story.

"God's truth," Mitchell Sanders said. "A six-man patrol goes up into the mountains on a basic listening-post operation. The idea's to spend a week up there, just lie low and listen for enemy movement. They've got a radio along, so if they hear anything suspicious—anything—they're supposed to call in artillery or gunships, whatever it takes. Otherwise they keep strict field discipline. Absolute silence. They just listen."

Sanders glanced at me to make sure I had the scenario. He was playing with his yo-yo, dancing it with short, tight little strokes of the wrist.

His face was blank in the dusk.

"We're talking regulation, by-the-book LP. These six guys, they don't say boo for a solid week. They don't got tongues. All ears."

"Right," I said.

"Understand me?"

"Invisible."

Sanders nodded.

"Affirm," he said. "Invisible. So what happens is, these guys get themselves deep in the bush, all camouflaged up, and they lie down and wait and that's all they do, nothing else, they lie there for seven straight days and just listen. And man, I'll tell you—it's spooky. This is mountains. You don't know spooky till you been there. Jungle, sort of, except it's way up in the clouds and there's always this fog - like rain, except it's not raining—everything's all wet and swirly and tangled up and you can't see jack, you can't find your own pecker to piss with. Like you don't even have a body. Serious spooky. You just go with the vapors—the fog sort of takes you in . . . And the sounds, man. The sounds carry forever. You hear stuff nobody should ever hear."

Sanders was quiet for a second, just working the yo-yo, then he smiled at me.

"So after a couple days the guys start hearing this real soft, kind of wacked-out music. Weird echoes and stuff. Like a radio or something, but it's not a radio, it's this strange gook music that comes right out of the rocks. Faraway, sort of, but right up close, too. They try to ignore it. But it's a listening post, right? So they listen. And every night they keep hearing that crazyass gook concert. All kinds of chimes and xylophones. I mean, this is wilderness—no way, it can't be real—but there it is, like the mountains are tuned in to Radio fucking Hanoi. Naturally they get nervous. One guy sticks Juicy Fruit in his ears. Another guy almost flips. Thing is, though, they can't report music. They can't get on the horn and call back to base and say, 'Hey, listen, we need some firepower, we got to blow away this weirdo gook rock band.' They can't do that. It wouldn't go down. So they lie there in the fog and keep their mouths shut. And what makes it extra bad, see, is the poor dudes can't horse around like normal. Can't joke it away. Can't even talk to each other except maybe in whispers, all hush-hush, and that just revs up the willies. All they do is listen."

Again there was some silence as Mitchell Sanders looked out on the river. The dark was coming on hard now, and off to the west I could see the mountains rising in silhouette, all the mysteries and unknowns.

"This next part," Sanders said quietly, "you won't believe."

"Probably not," I said.

"You won't. And you know why?" He gave me a long, tired smile. "Because it happened. Because every word is absolutely dead-on true."

Sanders made a sound in his throat, like a sigh, as if to say he didn't care if I believed him or not. But he did care. He wanted me to feel the truth, to believe by the raw force of feeling. He seemed sad, in a way.

"These six guys," he said, "they're pretty fried out by now, and one night they start hearing voices. Like at a cocktail party. That's what it sounds like, this big swank gook cocktail party somewhere out there in the fog. Music and chitchat and stuff. It's crazy, I know, but they hear the champagne corks. They hear the actual martini glasses. Real hoity-toity, all very civilized, except this isn't civilization. This is Nam.

"Anyway, the guys try to be cool. They just lie there and groove, but after a while they start hearing—you won't believe this—they hear chamber music. They hear violins and cellos. They hear this terrific mama-san soprano. Then after a while they hear gook opera and a glee club and the Haiphong Boys Choir and a barbershop quartet and all kinds of weird chanting and Buddha-Buddha stuff. And the whole time, in the background, there's still that cocktail party going on. All these different voices. Not human voices, though. Because it's the mountains. Follow me? The rock—it's talking. And the fog, too, and the grass and the goddamn mongooses. Everything talks. The trees talk politics, the monkeys talk religion. The whole country. Vietnam. The place talks. It talks. Understand? Nam—it truly talks.

"The guys can't cope. They lose it. They get on the radio and report enemy movement—a whole army, they say—and they order up the firepower. They get arty and gunships. They call in air strikes. And I'll tell you, they fuckin' crash that cocktail party. All night long, they just smoke those mountains. They make jungle juice. They blow away trees and glee clubs and whatever else there is to blow away. Scorch time. They walk napalm up and down the ridges. They bring in the Cobras and F-4s, they use Willie Peter and HE and incendiaries. It's all fire. They make those mountains burn.

"Around dawn things finally get quiet. Like you never even heard quiet before. One of those real thick, real misty days—just clouds and fog, they're off in this special zone—and the mountains are absolutely dead-flat silent. Like Brigadoon—pure vapor, you know? Everything's all sucked up inside the fog. Not a single sound, except they still hear it.

"So they pack up and start humping. They head down the mountain, back to base camp, and when they get there they don't say diddly. They don't talk. Not a word, like they're deaf and dumb. Later on this fat bird colonel comes up and asks what the hell happened out there. What'd they hear? Why all the ordnance? The man's ragged out, he gets down tight on their case. I mean, they spent six trillion dollars on firepower, and this fatass colonel wants answers, he wants to know what the fuckin' story is.

"But the guys don't say zip. They just look at him for a while, sort of funny like, sort of amazed, and the whole war is right there in that stare. It says everything you can't ever say. It says, man, you got wax in your ears. It says, poor bastard, you'll never know—wrong frequency—you don't even want to hear this. Then they salute the fucker and walk away, because certain stories you don't ever tell."

You can tell a true war story by the way it never seems to end. Not then, not ever. Not when Mitchell Sanders stood up and moved off into the dark.

It all happened.

Even now, at this instant, I remember that yo-yo. In a way, I suppose, you had to be there, you had to hear it, but I could tell how desperately Sanders wanted me to believe him, his frustration at not quite getting the details right, not quite pinning down the final and definitive truth.

And I remember sitting at my foxhole that night, watching the shadows of Quang Ngai, thinking about the coming day and how we would cross the river and march west into the mountains, all the ways I might die, all the things I did not understand.

Late in the night Mitchell Sanders touched my shoulder.

"Just came to me," he whispered. "The moral, I mean. Nobody listens. Nobody hears nothin'. Like that fatass colonel. The politicians, all the civilian types. Your girlfriend. My girlfriend. Everybody's sweet little virgin girlfriend. What they need is to go out on LP. The vapors, man. Trees and rocks—you got to listen to your enemy."

And then again, in the morning, Sanders came up to me. The platoon was preparing to move out, checking weapons, going through all the little rituals that preceded a day's march. Already the lead squad had crossed the river and was filing off toward the west.

"I got a confession to make," Sanders said. "Last night, man, I had to make up a few things."

"I know that."

"The glee club. There wasn't any glee club."

"Right."

"No opera."

"Forget it, I understand."

"Yeah, but listen, it's still true. Those six guys, they heard wicked sound out there. They heard sound you just plain won't believe."

Sanders pulled on his rucksack, closed his eyes for a moment, then almost smiled at me. I knew what was coming.

"All right," I said, "what's the moral?"

"Forget it."

"No, go ahead."

For a long while he was quiet, looking away, and the silence kept stretching out until it was almost embarrassing. Then he shrugged and gave me a stare that lasted all day.

"Hear that quiet, man?" he said. "That quiet—just listen. There's your moral."

In a true war story, if there's a moral at all, it's like the thread that makes the cloth. You can't tease it out. You can't extract the meaning without unraveling the deeper meaning. And in the end, really, there's nothing much to say about a true war story, except maybe "Oh."

True war stories do not generalize. They do not indulge in abstraction or analysis.

For example: War is hell. As a moral declaration the old truism seems perfectly true, and yet because it abstracts, because it generalizes, I can't believe it with my stomach. Nothing turns inside.

It comes down to gut instinct. A true war story, if truly told, makes the stomach believe.

This one does it for me. I've told it before—many times, many versions—but here's what actually happened.

We crossed that river and marched west into the mountains. On the third day, Curt Lemon stepped on a boobytrapped 105 round. He was playing catch with Rat Kiley, laughing, and then he was dead. The trees were thick; it took nearly an hour to cut an LZ for the dustoff.

Later, higher in the mountains, we came across a baby VC water buffalo. What it was doing there I don't know—no farms or paddies—but we chased it down and got a rope around it and led it along to a deserted village where we set up for the night. After supper Rat Kiley went over and stroked its nose.

He opened up a can of C rations, pork and beans, but the baby buffalo wasn't interested.

Rat shrugged.

He stepped back and shot it through the right front knee. The animal did not make a sound. It went down hard, then got up again, and Rat took careful aim and shot off an ear. He shot it in the hindquarters and in the little hump at its back. He shot it twice in the flanks. It wasn't to kill; it was to hurt. He put the rifle muzzle up against the mouth and shot the mouth away. Nobody said much. The whole platoon stood there watching, feeling all kinds of things, but there wasn't a great deal of pity for the baby water buffalo. Curt Lemon was dead. Rat Kiley had lost his best friend in the world. Later in the week he would write a long personal letter to the guy's sister, who would not write back, but for now it was a question of pain. He shot off the tail. He shot away chunks of meat below the ribs. All around us there was the smell of smoke and filth and deep greenery, and the evening was humid and very hot. Rat went to automatic. He shot randomly, almost casually, quick little spurts in the belly and butt. Then he reloaded, squatted down, and shot it in the left front knee. Again the animal fell hard and tried to get up, but this time it couldn't quite make it. It wobbled and went down sideways. Rat shot it in the nose. He bent forward and whispered something, as if talking to a pet, then he shot it in the throat. All the while the baby buffalo was silent, or almost silent, just a light bubbling sound where the nose had been. It lay very still. Nothing moved except the eyes, which were enormous, the pupils shiny black and dumb.

Rat Kiley was crying. He tried to say something, but then cradled his rifle and went off by himself.

The rest of us stood in a ragged circle around the baby buffalo. For a time no one spoke. We had witnessed something essential, something brand-new and profound, a piece of the world so startling there was not yet a name for it.

Somebody kicked the baby buffalo.

It was still alive, though just barely, just in the eyes.

"Amazing," Dave Jensen said. "My whole life, I never seen anything like it."

"Never?"

"Not hardly. Not once."

Kiowa and Mitchell Sanders picked up the baby buffalo. They hauled it across the open square, hoisted it up, and dumped it in the village well.

Afterward, we sat waiting for Rat to get himself together.

"Amazing," Dave Jensen kept saying. "A new wrinkle. I never seen it before."

Mitchell Sanders took out his yo-yo. "Well, that's Nam," he said. "Garden of Evil. Over here, man, every sin's real fresh and original."

How do you generalize?

War is hell, but that's not the half of it, because war is also mystery and terror and adventure and courage and discovery and holiness and pity and despair and longing and love. War is nasty; war is fun. War is thrilling; war is drudgery. War makes you a man; war makes you dead.

The truths are contradictory. It can be argued, for instance, that war is grotesque. But in truth war is also beauty. For all its horror, you can't help but gape at the awful majesty of combat. You stare out at tracer rounds unwinding through the dark like brilliant red ribbons. You crouch in ambush as a cool, impassive moon rises over the nighttime paddies. You admire the fluid symmetries of troops on the move, the harmonies of sound and shape and proportion, the great sheets of metal-fire streaming down from a gunship, the illumination rounds, the white phosphorus, the purply orange glow of napalm, the rocket's red glare. It's not pretty, exactly. It's astonishing. It fills the eye. It commands you. You hate it, yes, but your eyes do not. Like a killer forest fire, like cancer under a microscope, any battle or bombing raid or artillery barrage has the aesthetic purity of absolute moral indifference—a powerful, implacable beauty —and a true war story will tell the truth about this, though the truth is ugly.

To generalize about war is like generalizing about peace. Almost everything is true. Almost nothing is true. At its core, perhaps, war is just another name for death, and yet any soldier will tell you, if he tells the truth, that proximity to death brings with it a corresponding proximity to life. After a firefight, there is always the immense pleasure of aliveness. The trees are alive. The grass, the soil—everything. All around you things are purely living, and you among them, and the aliveness makes you tremble. You feel an intense, out-of-the-skin awareness of your living self—your truest self, the human being you want to be and then become by the force of wanting it. In the midst of evil you want to be a good man. You want decency. You want justice and courtesy and human concord, things you never knew you wanted. There is a kind of largeness to it, a kind of godliness. Though it's odd, you're never more alive than when you're almost dead. You recognize what's valuable. Freshly, as if for the first time, you love what's best in yourself and in the world, all that might be lost. At the hour of dusk you sit at your foxhole and look out on a wide river turning pinkish red, and at the mountains beyond, and although in the morning you must cross the river and go into the mountains and do terrible things and maybe die, even so, you find yourself studying the fine colors on the river, you feel wonder and awe at the setting of the sun, and you are filled with a hard, aching love for how the world could be and always should be, but now is not.

Mitchell Sanders was right. For the common soldier, at least, war has the feel—the spiritual texture—of a great ghostly fog, thick and permanent. There is no clarity. Everything swirls. The old rules are no longer binding, the old truths no longer true. Right spills over into wrong. Order blends into chaos, love into hate, ugliness into beauty, law into anarchy, civility into savagery. The vapors suck you in. You can't tell where you are, or why you're there, and the only certainty is overwhelming ambiguity.

In war you lose your sense of the definite, hence your sense of truth itself, and therefore it's safe to say that in a true war story nothing is ever absolutely true.

Often in a true war story there is not even a point, or else the point doesn't hit you until twenty years later, in your sleep, and you wake up and shake your wife and start telling the story to her, except when you get to the end you've forgotten the point again. And then for a long time you lie there watching the story happen in your head. You listen to your wife's breathing. The war's over. You close your eyes. You smile and think, Christ, what's the point?

This one wakes me up.

In the mountains that day, I watched Lemon turn sideways. He laughed and said something to Rat Kiley. Then he took a peculiar half step, moving from shade into bright sunlight, and the booby-trapped 105 round blew him into a tree. The parts were just hanging there, so Dave Jensen and I were ordered to shinny up and peel him off. I remember the white bone of an arm. I remember pieces of skin and something wet and yellow that must've been the intestines. The gore was horrible, and stays with me. But what wakes me up twenty years later is Dave Jensen singing "Lemon Tree" as we threw down the parts.

You can tell a true war story by the questions you ask. Somebody tells a story, let's say, and afterward you ask, "Is it true?" and if the answer matters, you've got your answer.

For example, we've all heard this one. Four guys go down a trail. A grenade sails out. One guy jumps on it and takes the blast and saves his three buddies.

Is it true?

The answer matters.

You'd feel cheated if it never happened. Without the grounding reality, it's just a trite bit of puffery, pure Hollywood, untrue in the way all such stories are untrue. Yet even if it did happen—and maybe it did, anything's possible—even then you know it can't be true, because a true war story does not depend upon that kind of truth. Absolute occurrence is irrelevant. A thing may happen and be a total lie; another thing may not happen and be truer than the truth. For example: Four guys go down a trail. A grenade sails out. One guy jumps on it and takes the blast, but it's a killer grenade and everybody dies anyway. Before they die, though, one of the dead guys says, "The fuck you do that for?" and the jumper says, "Story of my life, man," and the other guy starts to smile but he's dead.

That's a true story that never happened.

Twenty years later, I can still see the sunlight on Lemon's face. I can see him turning, looking back at Rat Kiley, then he laughed and took that curious half step from shade into sunlight, his face suddenly brown and shining, and when his foot touched down, in that instant, he must've thought it was the sunlight that was killing him. It was not the sunlight. It was a rigged 105 round. But if I could ever get the story right, how the sun seemed to gather around him and pick him up and lift him high into a tree, if I could somehow recreate the fatal whiteness of that light, the quick glare, the obvious cause and effect, then you would believe the last thing Curt Lemon believed, which for him must've been the final truth.

Now and then, when I tell this story, someone will come up to me afterward and say she liked it. It's always a woman. Usually it's an older woman of kindly temperament and humane politics. She'll explain that as a rule she hates war stories; she can't understand why people want to wallow in all the blood and gore. But this one she liked. The poor baby buffalo, it made her sad. Sometimes, even, there are little tears. What I should do, she'll say, is put it all behind me. Find new stories to tell.

I won't say it but I'll think it.

I'll picture Rat Kiley's face, his grief, and I'll think, You dumb cooze.

Because she wasn't listening.

It wasn't a war story. It was a love story.

But you can't say that. All you can do is tell it one more time, patiently, adding and subtracting, making up a few things to get at the real truth. No Mitchell Sanders, you tell her. No Lemon, no Rat Kiley. No trail junction. No baby buffalo. No vines or moss or white blossoms. Beginning to end, you tell her, it's all made up. Every goddamn detail—the mountains and the river and especially that poor dumb baby buffalo. None of it happened. None of it. And even if it did happen, it didn't happen in the mountains, it happened in this little village on the Batangan Peninsula, and it was raining like crazy, and one night a guy named Stink Harris woke up screaming with a leech on his tongue. You can tell a true war story if you just keep on telling it.

And in the end, of course, a true war story is never about war. It's about sunlight. It's about the special way that dawn spreads out on a river when you know you must cross the river and march into the mountains and do things you are afraid to do. It's about love and memory. It's about sorrow. It's about sisters who never write back and people who never listen.

Questions for Discussion

1. In the story, the narrator evokes the common claim that "maybe you had to be there." Assuming that storytellers are not trying to deceive us, how does personal experience strengthen or weaken the authority of their stories?

2. How might stories, as O'Brien suggests, be made truer by retelling them over and over, changing names and places and events with each retelling?

3. Considering that our entire system of juris prudence relies on "truthful testimony," on witnesses telling "the truth, the whole truth, and nothing but the truth," what are the ramifications of O'Brien's vision of narrative truth? How would our judicial system be affected (for better or worse) if we all saw truth as the personal, flexible, constantly changing sense of understanding that O'Brien describes?

Explorations

1. Tell the story of an event that dramatically changed either who you are or how you thought of yourself. Next, change as many of the facts (who's, when's, where's, what's) as possible without changing the "main point" of your personal evolution. Why is it that some of the details are negligible? What details cannot, in your opinion, be changed? Why not?

2. Using O'Brien's rules for telling a true war story (e.g. "A true war story is never moral."), replace the words "war story" with some other type of narrative. Defend your statement by analyzing it in terms of O'Brien's rules.

3. Search for and identify the contradictions in O'Brien's assertions about "true war stories." How, in your own words, might the narrator justify the apparent inconsistencies in his argument?

Formal Writing Assignments

1. Compose a narrative about a significant moment in your childhood and, specifically, about something that happened before you were old enough to remember it vividly. Use as many specific details as possible, whether they come from first-hand memory or not. As you compose your narrative, make reflexive statements about the sources of details you choose to include. Do they come from memory, from childhood photographs, from stories your family has told you? In the end, analyze your own story, defending its validity as a "true story."

2. Using on-line and/or traditional library resources, compile several "first-hand" accounts of a controversial historical occurrence (e.g. The alleged UFO cover-up at Roswell, NM, or the Massacre of Vietnamese civilians at Mi Lai). Next, construct your own narrative of the event, borrowing freely from the "first-hand" accounts of your sources, while making sure to cite them. Next, construct an analysis of your sources, either interrogating or defending the differences in their respective "memories." Explain, in light of this analysis, why you have constructed your narrative the way you have, why you have privileged certain "first-hand" accounts over others. Be sure to consider and address the possibility that all the accounts are, in some way, true.

Aria: A Memoir of a Bilingual Childhood

Richard Rodriguez

Born to Mexican immigrants in Sacramento, California, Richard Rodriguez describes his experiences with language and education in his 1982 autobiographical study, *Hunger of Memory*. For Rodriguez, the transition from Spanish (the private language of his home and family) to English (the public language of school) was necessary for his intellectual and individual growth. In the following selection, he examines both the losses and gains of this transition.

Writing Before Reading

1. Have you ever been in a situation where you did not speak the language being used by most of the people around you? How did you communicate?

2. In recent years, there has been much debate about the use of bilingual education in US schools. Describe what you know about bilingual education. In your approximation, what might be the pros and cons of this approach?

3. Many times, siblings and close friends develop idiosyncratic ways of speaking or otherwise communicating that cannot be readily understood by others. Have you ever been able to communicate with someone else in such a way? Why did you choose to do so?

Aria: A Memoir of a Bilingual Childhood

I remember, to start with, that day in Sacramento, in a California now nearly thirty years past, when I first entered a classroom—able to understand about fifty stray English words. The third of four children, I had been preceded by my older brother and sister to a neighborhood Roman Catholic school. But neither of them had revealed very much about their classroom experiences. They left each morning and returned each afternoon, always together, speaking Spanish as they climbed the five steps to the porch. And their mysterious books, wrapped in brown shopping-bag paper, remained on the table next to the door, closed firmly behind them.

An accident of geography sent me to a school where all my classmates were white and many were the children of doctors and lawyers and business executives. On that first day of school, my classmates must certainly have been uneasy to find themselves apart from their families, in the first institution of their lives. But I was astonished. I was fated to be the "problem student" in class.

The nun said, in a friendly but oddly impersonal voice: "Boys and girls, this is Richard Rodriguez." (I heard her sound it out: *Richheard Road-ree-guess.*) It was the first time I had heard anyone say my name in English. "Richard," the nun repeated more slowly, writing my name down in her book. Quickly I turned to see my mother's face dissolve in a watery blur behind the pebbled-glass door.

Now, many years later, I hear of something called "bilingual education"—a scheme proposed in the late 1960s by Hispanic American social activists, later endorsed by a congressional vote. It is a program that seeks to permit non-English-speaking children (many from lower class homes) to use their "family language" as the language of school. Such, at least, is the aim its supporters announce. I hear them, and am forced to say no: It is not possible for a child, any child, ever to use his family's language in school.

Not to understand this is to misunderstand the public uses of schooling and to trivialize the nature of intimate life.

Memory teaches me what I know of these matters. The boy reminds the adult. I was a bilingual child, but of a certain kind: "socially disadvantaged," the son of working-class parents, both Mexican immigrants.

In the early years of my boyhood, my parents coped very well in America. My father had steady work. My mother managed at home. They were nobody's victims. When we moved to a house many blocks from the Mexican-American section of town, they were not intimidated by those two or three neighbors who initially tried to make us unwelcome. ("Keep your brats away from my sidewalk!") But despite all they achieved, or perhaps because they had so much to achieve, they lacked any deep feeling of ease, of belonging in public. They regarded the people at work or in crowds as being very distant from us. Those were the others, *los gringos*. That term was interchangeable in their speech with another, even more telling: *los americanos*.

I grew up in a house where the only regular guests were my relations. On a certain day, enormous families of relatives would visit us, and there would be so many people that the noise and the bodies would spill out to the backyard and onto the front porch. Then for weeks no one would come. (If the doorbell rang, it was usually a salesman.) Our house stood apart—gaudy yellow in a row of white bungalows. We were the people with the noisy dog, the people who raised chickens. We were the foreigners on the block. A few neighbors would smile and wave at us. We waved back. But until I was seven years old, I did not know the name of the old couple living next door or the names of the kids living across the street.

In public, my father and mother spoke a hesitant, accented, and not always grammatical English. And then they would have to strain, their bodies tense, to catch the sense of what was rapidly said by *los gringos*. At home, they returned to Spanish. The language of their Mexican past sounded in counterpoint to the English spoken in public. The words would come quickly, with ease. Conveyed through those sounds was the pleasing, soothing, consoling reminder that one was at home.

During those years when I was first learning to speak, my mother and father addressed me only in Spanish; in Spanish I learned to reply. By contrast, English (*inglés*) was the language I came to associate with gringos, rarely heard in the house. I learned my first words of English overhearing my parents speaking to strangers. At six years of age, I knew just enough words for my mother to trust me on errands to stores one block away—but no more.

I was then a listening child, careful to hear the very different sounds of Spanish and English. Wide-eyed with hearing, I'd listen to sounds more than to words. First, there were English (gringo) sounds. So many words still were unknown to me that when the butcher or the lady at the drugstore said something, exotic polysyllabic sounds would bloom in the midst of their sentences. Often the speech of people in public seemed to me very loud, booming with confidence. The man behind the counter would literally ask, "What can I do for you?" But by being so firm and clear, the sound of his voice said that he was a gringo; he belonged in public society. There were also the high, nasal notes of middle-class American speech —which I rarely am conscious of hearing today because I hear them so often, but could not stop hearing when I was a boy. Crowds at Safeway or at bus stops were noisy with the birdlike sounds of *los gringos*. I'd move away from them all—all the chirping chatter above me.

My own sounds I was unable to hear, but I knew that I spoke English poorly. My words could not extend to form complete thoughts. And the words I did speak I didn't know well enough to make distinct sounds. (Listeners would usually lower their heads to hear better what I was trying to say.) But it was one thing for me to speak English with difficulty; it was more troubling to hear my parents speaking in public: their high-whining vowels and guttural consonants; their sentences that got stuck with "eh" and "ah" sounds; the confused syntax; the hesitant rhythm of sounds so different from the way gringos spoke. I'd notice, moreover, that my parents' voices were softer than those of gringos we would meet.

I am tempted to say now that none of this mattered. (In adulthood I am embarrassed by childhood fears.) And, in a way, it didn't matter very much that my parents could not speak English with ease. Their linguistic difficulties had no serious consequences. My mother and father made themselves understood at the county hospital clinic and at government offices. And yet, in another way, it mattered very much. It was unsettling to hear my parents struggle with English. Hearing them, I'd grow nervous, and my clutching trust in their protection and power would be weakened.

There were many times like the night at a brightly lit gasoline station (a blaring white memory) when I stood uneasily hearing my father talk to a teenage attendant. I do not recall what they were saying, but I cannot forget the sounds my father made as he spoke. At one point his words slid together to form one long word—sounds as confused as the threads of blue and green oil in the puddle next to my shoes. His voice rushed through what he had left to say. Toward the end, he reached falsetto notes, appealing to his listener's understanding. I looked away at the lights of passing automobiles. I tried not to hear any more. But I heard only too well the attendants reply, his calm, easy tones. Shortly afterward, headed for home, I shivered when my father put his hand on my shoulder. The very first chance that I got, I evaded his grasp and ran on ahead into the dark, skipping with feigned boyish exuberance.

But then there was Spanish: *español*, the language rarely heard away from the house; *español*, the language which seemed to me therefore a private language, my family's language. To hear its sounds was to feel myself specially recognized as one of the family, apart from *los otros*. A simple remark, an inconsequential comment could convey that assurance. My parents would say something to me and I would feel embraced by the sounds of their words. Those sounds said: *I am speaking with ease in Spanish. I am addressing you in words I never use with los gringos. I recognize you as someone special, close, like no one outside. You belong with us. In the family. Ricardo.*

At the age of six, well past the time when most middle-class children no longer notice the difference between sounds uttered at home and words spoken in public, I had a different experience. I lived in a world compounded of sounds. I was a child longer than most. I lived in a magical world, surrounded by sounds both pleasing and fearful. I shared with my family a language enchantingly private—different from that used in the city around us.

Just opening or closing the screen door behind me was an important experience. I'd rarely leave home all alone or without feeling reluctance. Walking down the sidewalk, under the canopy of tall trees, I'd warily notice the (suddenly) silent neighborhood kids who stood warily watching me. Nervously, I'd arrive at the grocery store to hear there the sounds of the gringo, reminding me that in this so-big world I was a foreigner. But if leaving home was never routine, neither was coming back. Walking toward our house, climbing the steps from the sidewalk, in summer when the front door was open, I'd hear voices beyond the screen door talking in Spanish. For a second or two I'd stay, linger there listening. Smiling, I'd hear my mother call out, saying in Spanish, "is that you, Richard ? " Those were her words, but all the while her sounds would assure me: *You are home now. Come closer—inside. With us.* "*Sí,* "I'd reply.

Once more inside the house, I would resume my place in the farmly. The sounds would grow harder to hear. Once more at home, I would grow less conscious of them. It required, however, no more than the blurt of the doorbell to alert me all over again to listen to sounds. The house would turn instantly quiet while my mother went to the door. I'd hear her hard English sounds. I'd wait to hear her voice turn to soft-sounding Spanish, which assured me, as surely as did the clicking tongue of the lock on the door, that the stranger was gone.

Plainly, it is not healthy to hear such sounds often. It is not healthy to distinguish public from private sounds so easily. I remained cloistered by sounds, timid and shy in public, too dependent on the voices at home. And yet I was a very happy child when I was at home. I remember many nights when my father would come back from work, and I'd hear him call out to my mother in Spanish, sounding relieved. In Spanish, his voice would sound the light and free notes that he never could manage in English. Some nights I'd jump up just hearing his voice. My brother and I would come running into the room where he was with our mother. Our laughing (so deep was the pleasure!) became screaming. Like others who feel the pain of public alienation, we transformed the knowledge of our public separateness into a consoling reminder of our intimacy. Excited, our voices joined in a celebration of sounds. *We are speaking now the way we never speak out in public—we are together,* the sounds told me. Some nights no one seemed willing to loosen the hold that sounds had on us. At dinner we invented new words that sounded Spanish, but made sense only to us. We pieced together new words by taking, say, an English verb and giving it Spanish endings. My mother's instructions at bedtime would be lacquered with mock urgent tones. Or a word like *sí,* sounded in several notes, would convey added measures of feeling. Tongues lingered around the edges of words, especially fat vowels, and we happily sounded that military drum roll, the twirling roar of the Spanish *r.* Family language, my family's sounds: the voices of my parents and sisters and brother. Their voices insisting: *You belong here. We are family members. Related. Special to one another. Listen!* Voices singing and sighing, rising and straining, then surging, teeming with pleasure which burst syllables into fragments of laughter. At times it seemed there was steady quiet only when, from another room, the rustling whispers of my parents faded and I edged closer to sleep.

Supporters of bilingual education imply today that students like me miss a great deal by not being taught in their family's language. What they seem not to recognize is that, as a socially disadvantaged child, I regarded Spanish as a private language. The odd truth is that my first-grade classmates could have become bilingual, in the conventional sense of the word, more easily than I. Had they been taught early (as upper middle-class children often are taught) a "second language" like Spanish or French, they could have regarded it simply as another public language. In my case, such bilingualism could not have been so quickly achieved. What I did not believe was that I could speak a single public language.

Without question, it would have pleased me to have heard my teachers address me in Spanish when I entered the classroom. I would have felt much less afraid. I would have imagined that my instructors were somehow "related" to me: I would indeed have heard their Spanish as my family's language. I would have trusted them and responded with ease. But I would have delayed—postponed for how long?—having to learn the language of public society. I would have evaded—and for how long?—learning the great lesson of school: that I had a public identity.

Fortunately, my teachers were unsentimental about their responsibility. What they understood was that I needed to speak public English. So their voices would search me out, asking me questions. Each time I heard them I'd look up in surprise to see a nun's face frowning at me. I'd mumble, not really meaning to answer. The nun would persist. "Richard, stand up. Don't look at the floor. Speak up. Speak to the entire class, not just to me!" But I couldn't believe English could be my language to use. (In part, I did not want to believe it.) I continued to mumble. I resisted the teacher's demands. (Did I somehow suspect that once I learned this public language my family life would be changed?) Silent, waiting for the bell to sound, I remained dazed, diffident, afraid.

Because I wrongly imagined that English was intrinsically a public language and Spanish was intrinsically private, I easily noted the difference between classroom language and the language at home. At school, words were directed to a general audience of listeners. ("Boys and girls . . .") Words were meaningfully ordered. And the point was not self-expression alone, but to make oneself understood by many others. The teacher quizzed: "Boys and girls, why do we use that word in this sentence? Could we think of a better word to use there? Would the sentence change its meaning if the words were differently arranged? Isn't there a better way, of saying much the same thing?" (I couldn't say. I wouldn't try to say.)

Three months passed. Five. A half year. Unsmiling, ever watchful, my teachers noted my silence. They began to connect my behavior with the slow progress my brother and sisters were making. Until, one Saturday morning, three nuns arrived at the house to talk to our parents. Stiffly they sat on the blue living-room sofa. From the doorway of another room, spying on the visitors, I noted the incongruity, the clash of two worlds, the faces and voices of school intruding upon the familiar setting of home. I overheard one voice gently wondering, "Do your children speak only Spanish at home, Mrs. Rodriguez?" While another voice added, "That Richard especially seems so timid and shy. "

That Rich-heard!

With great tact, the visitors continued, "Is it possible for you and your husband to encourage your children to practice their English when they are home?" Of course my parents complied. What would they not do for their children's well-being? And how could they question the Church's authority which those women represented? In an instant they agreed to give up the language (the sounds) which had revealed and accentuated our family's closeness. The moment after the visitors left, the change was observed. "*Ahora, speak to us only en inglés,* " my father and mother told us.

At first, it seemed a kind of game. After dinner each night, the family gathered together to practice "our" English. It was still then inglés, a language foreign to us, so we felt drawn to it as strangers. Laughing, we would try to define words we could not pronounce. We played with strange English sounds, often overanglicizing our pronunciations. And we filled the smiling gaps of our sentences with familiar Spanish sounds. But that was cheating, somebody shouted, and everyone laughed.

In school, meanwhile, like my brother and sister, I was required to attend a daily tutoring session. I needed a full year of this special work. I also needed my teachers to keep my attention from straying in class by calling out, "*Rich –heard*"—their English voices slowly loosening the ties to my other name, with its three notes, Ri-car-do. Most of all, I needed to hear my mother and father speak to me in a moment of seriousness in "broken"—suddenly heartbreaking English. This scene was inevitable. One Saturday morning I entered the kitchen where my parents were talking, but I did not realize that they were talking in Spanish until, the moment they saw me, their voices changed and they began speaking English. The gringo sounds they uttered startled me. Pushed me away. In that moment of trivial misunderstanding and profound insight, I felt my throat twisted by unsounded grief. I simply turned and left the room. But I had no place to escape to where I could grieve in Spanish. My brother and sisters were speaking English in another part of the house.

Again and again in the days following, as I grew increasingly angry, I was obliged to hear my mother and father encouraging me: "Speak to us *en inglés*. " Only then did I determine to learn classroom English. Thus, sometime afterward it happened: one day in school, I raised my hand to volunteer an answer to a question. I spoke out in a loud voice and I did not think it remarkable when the entire class understood. That day I moved very far from being the disadvantaged child I had been only days earlier. Taken hold at last was the belief, the calming assurance, that I *belonged* in public.

Shortly after, I stopped hearing the high, troubling sounds of *los gringos*. A more and more confident speaker of English, I didn't listen to how strangers sounded when they talked to me. With so many English-speaking people around me, I no longer heard American accents. Conversations quickened. Listening to persons whose voices sounded eccentrically pitched, I might note their sounds for a few seconds, but then I'd concentrate on what they were saying. Now when I heard someone's tone of voice—angry or questioning or sarcastic or happy or sad—I didn't distinguish it from the words it expressed. Sound and word were thus tightly wedded. At the end of each day I was often bemused, and always relieved, to realize how "soundless," though crowded with words, my day in public had been. An eight-year-old boy, I finally came to accept what had been technically true since my birth: I was an American citizen.

But diminished by then was the special feeling of closeness at home. Gone was the desperate, urgent, intense feeling of being at home among those with whom I felt intimate. Our family remained a loving family, but one greatly changed. We were no longer so close, no longer bound tightly together by the knowledge of our separateness from *los gringos*. Neither my older brother nor my sisters rushed home after school any more. Nor did I. When I arrived home, often there would be neighborhood kids in the house. Or the house would be empty of sounds.

Following the dramatic Americanization of their children, even my parents grew more publicly confident—especially my mother. First she learned the names of all the people on the block. Then she decided we needed to have a telephone in our house. My father, for his part, continued to use the word gringo, but it was no longer charged with bitterness or distrust. Stripped of any emotional content, the word simply became a name for those Americans not of Hispanic descent. Hearing him, sometimes, I wasn't sure if he was pronouncing the Spanish word *gringo*, or saying gringo in English.

There was a new silence at home. As we children learned more and more English, we shared fewer and fewer words with our parents. Sentences needed to be spoken slowly when one of us addressed our mother or father. Often the parent wouldn't understand. The child would need to repeat himself. Still the parent misunderstood. The young voice, frustrated, would end up saying, "Never mind"—the subject was closed. Dinners would be noisy with the clinking of knives and forks against dishes. My mother would smile softly between her remarks; my father, at the other end of the table, would chew and chew his food while he stared over the heads of his children.

My mother! My father! After English became my primary language, I no longer knew what words to use in addressing my parents. The old Spanish words (those tender accents of sound) I had earlier used—mamá and papá couldn't use any more. They would have been all-too-painful reminders of how much had changed in my life. On the other hand, the words I heard neighborhood kids call their parents seemed equally unsatisfactory. "mother" and "father" "ma," "papa," "pa," "dad," "pop" (how I hated the all American sound of that last word)—all these I felt were unsuitable terms of address for my parents. As a result, I never used them at home. Whenever I'd speak to my parents, I would try to get their attention by looking at them. In public conversations, I'd refer to them as my "parents" or my "mother" and "father. "

My mother and father, for their part, responded differently, as their children spoke to them less. My mother grew restless, seemed troubled and anxious at the scarceness of words exchanged in the house. She would question me about my day when I came home from school. She smiled at my small talk. She pried at the edges of my sentences to get me to say something more. ("What . . . ? ") She'd join conversations she overheard, but her intrusions often stopped her children's talking. By contrast, my father seemed to grow reconciled to the new quiet. Though his English somewhat improved, he tended more and more to retire into silence. At dinner he spoke very little. One night his children and even his wife helplessly giggled at his garbled English pronunciation of the Catholic "Grace Before Meals." Thereafter he made his wife recite the prayer at the start of each meal, even on formal occasions when there were guests in the house.

Hers became the public voice of the family. On official business it was she, not my father, who would usually talk to strangers on the phone or in stores. We children grew so accustomed to his silence that years later we would routinely refer to his "shyness." (My mother often tried to explain: both of his parents died when he was eight. He was raised by an uncle who treated him as little more than a menial servant. He was never encouraged to speak. He grew up alone—a man of few words.) But I realized my father was not shy whenever I'd watch him speaking Spanish with relatives. Using Spanish, he was quickly effusive. Especially when talking with other men, his voice would spark, flicker, flare alive with varied sounds. In Spanish he expressed ideas and feeling he rarely revealed when speaking English. With firm Spanish sounds he conveyed a confidence and authority that English would never allow him.

The silence at home, however, was not simply the result of fewer words passing between parents and children. More profound for me was the silence created by inattention to sounds. At about the time I no longer bothered to listen with care to the sounds of English in public, I grew careless about listening to the sounds made by the family when they spoke. Most of the time I would hear someone speaking at home and didn't distinguish his sounds from the words people uttered in public. I didn't even pay much attention to my parents' accented and ungrammatical speech—at least not at home. Only when I was with them in public would I become alert to their accents. But even then their sounds caused me less and less concern. For I was growing increasingly confident of my own public identity.

I would have been happier about my public success had I not recalled, sometimes, what it had been like earlier, when my family conveyed its intimacy through a set of conveniently private sounds. Sometimes in public, hearing a stranger, I'd hark back to my lost past. A Mexican farm worker approached me one day downtown. He wanted directions to some place. "*Hijito, . . .* " he said. And his voice stirred old longings. Another time I was standing beside my mother in the visiting room of a Carmelite convent, before the dense screen which rendered the nuns shadowy figures. I heard several of them speaking Spanish in their busy, singsong, overlapping voices, assuring my mother that yes, yes, we were remembered, all our family was remembered, in their prayers. Those voices echoed faraway family sounds. Another day a dark-faced old woman touched my shoulder lightly to steady herself as she boarded a bus. She murmured something to me I couldn't quite comprehend. Her Spanish voice came near, like the face of a never-before-seen relative in the instant before I was kissed. That voice, like so many of the Spanish voices I'd hear in public, recalled the golden age of my childhood.

Bilingual educators say today that children lose a degree of "individuality" by becoming assimilated into public society. (Bilingual schooling is a program popularized in the seventies, that decade when middle-class "ethics" began to resist the process of assimilation—the "American melting pot.") But the bilingualists oversimplify when they scorn the value and necessity of assimilation. They do not seem to realize that a person is individualized in two ways. So they do not realize that, while one suffers a diminished sense of private individuality by being assimilated into public society, such assimilation makes possible the achievement of public individuality.

Simplistically again, the bilingualist insist that a student should be reminded of his difference from others in mass society, of his "heritage." But they equate mere separateness with individuality. The fact is that only in private—with intimates—is separateness from the crowd a prerequisite for individuality; an intimate "tells" me that I am unique, unlike all others, apart from the crowd. In public, by contrast, full individuality is achieved, paradoxically by those who are able to consider themselves members of the crowd. Thus it happened for me. Only when I was able to think of myself as all American, no longer an alien in gringo society, could I seek the rights and opportunities necessary for full public individuality. The social and political advantages I enjoy as a man began on the day I came to believe that my name is indeed *Rich-heard Road-ree-guess*. It is true that my public society today is often impersonal; in fact, my public society is usually mass society. But despite the anonymity of the crowd, and despite the fact that the individuality I achieve in public is often tenuous—because it depends on my being one in a crowd— I celebrate the day I acquired my new name. Those middleclass ethnics who scorn assimilation seem to me filled with decadent self-pity, obsessed by the burden of public life. Dangerously, they romanticize public separateness and trivialize the dilemma of those who are truly socially disadvantaged.

If I rehearse here the changes in my private life after my Americanization, it is finally to emphasize a public gain. The loss implies the gain. The house I returned to each afternoon was quiet. Intimate sounds no longer greeted me at the door. Inside there were other noises. The telephone rang. Neighborhood kids ran past the door of the bedroom where I was reading my schoolbooks—covered with brown shopping-bag paper. Once I learned the public language, it would never again be easy for me to hear intimate family voices. More and more of my day was spent hearing words, not sounds. But that may only be a way of saying that on the day I raised my hand in class and spoke loudly to an entire roomful of faces, my childhood started to end.

Questions for Discussion

1. Rodriguez describes a sense of security he felt when he exited the English-speaking public world and entered the Spanish-speaking private world of his home. Is it possible, then, for non-bilingual children to experience similar feelings of security because of language? If so, how? If not, why?

2. When Rodriguez's parents, in an attempt to foster their children's assimilation into English-speaking society, insisted that the kids speak to them in English, Rodriguez notes that the special sense of family security he'd felt before was diminished. Is English literacy, then, more important than the cultural bonds of family? Why or why not?

3. Rodriguez states that, as a child, English was just "chirping chatter." Often, people just learning a new language complain that native speakers talk very quickly, making it difficult for them to understand. How, in light of this, do you think comprehension or familiarity color our preferences for certain kinds of sounds?

Explorations

1. If you're unfamiliar with the word, look up "aria" in the dictionary. Then consider the title. What significance is revealed by Rodriguez's choice of the word?

2. How does Rodriguez associate language and power with his parents? When, in your experience, have you been made to feel proud or embarrassed by your parents' use of language? Why?

3. In responding to the proponents of "bilingual education," Rodriguez writes: "It is not possible for a child, any child, ever to use his family's language in school." What might he mean by this? Do you agree with this statement? Why or why not?

Formal Writing Assignments

1. Tell the story of a time when, because of your education or the nature of the situation, you felt inadequate in your ability to communicate with those around you. While telling the story, try to analyze the situation. What were the factors that contributed to your perceived inability to make yourself understood? How did you (or didn't you) resolve the problem? What impact did it have on your desire to become more proficient in certain kinds of communication skills? How, looking back on the event, did it affect your views of language and social interaction?

2. In an essay, describe and analyze how language is used in school and in your home. How do these public and private modes of communication differ? Develop your thesis around your view of WHY we interact differently with our families and our classmates and teachers. Use specific details to illustrate the differences and consider how your home life would change if your family made the switch to more academic modes of discourse, if everyone at school spoke like your family does at home. What can you learn from the differences and from your assertions about the factors that contribute to these difference?

Literacy in Three Metaphors

Sylvia Scribner

Sylvia Scribner has enjoyed a long and varied career. A social scientist who has spent a great deal of time in West Africa and who is currently affiliated with the Graduate Center of the City University of New York, Scribner is the co-author of *The Psychology of Literacy* and other works in which she examines the relationships between the social and the individual. She has served as the research director for the United Electrical, Radio, and Machine Workers of America and the associate director for Mental Health programs at the National Institute of Labor Education. Scribner received her B.A. from Smith College in 1943 and her Ph.D. from the New School for Social Research in 1970.

Scribner once told an interviewer that her research "has always involved the complex interplay between social and cultural factors and the psychological development of the individual. I have been awed by the immensity of the enterprise, yet have enjoyed it so much that I am not content merely to report findings to a professional audience. I want to write about the hunt itself and to bring others in on the day-to-day research process. That objective leads to books as well as scientific papers. I write light poetry on the side, but only to fill my files. Thus, regardless of the work Scribner undertakes, the act of writing itself remains central for her.

"Literacy in Three Metaphors" begins with the examination of the relationship between the cultural/social and the individual and addresses how various definitions of literacy affect how individuals are perceived and how they respond to the world around them. As you consider each of Scribner's metaphors (literacy as power, adaptation, state of grace), think about how these metaphors do or do not operate in your own definition of literacy.

Writing Before Reading

1. Think back to the first days of this writing course. In what ways have your ideas about literacy changed since then? How would you define the term now?

2. What kind of knowledge do you believe today's U.S. citizen needs in order to survive? Is there a minimum amount of knowledge? A maximum amount? Upon what evidence or experience do you base your response?

3. Have you ever traveled to a foreign country? What was the most fulfilling part of that trip? The most frustrating part? If you've never left the United States, describe a trip to a region of the U. S. that *felt* foreign to you. What was that experience like?

Literacy in Three Metaphors

Although literacy is a problem of pressing national concern, we have yet to discover or set its boundaries. This observation, made several years ago by a leading political spokesman (McGovern 1978), echoes a long-standing complaint of many policymakers and educators that what counts as literacy in our technological society is a matter "not very well understood" (Advisory Committee on National Illiteracy 1929).

A dominant response of scholars and researchers to this perceived ambiguity has been to pursue more rigorously the quest for definition and measurement of the concept. Many approaches have been taken (among them, Adult Performance Level Project 1975; Bormuth 1975; Hillerich 1976; Kirsch and

Guthrie 1977-78; Miller 1973, Powell 1977), and at least one attempt (Hunter and Harman 1979) has been made to put forward an "umbrella definition." Each of these efforts has identified important parameters of literacy, but none has yet won consensual agreement (for a thoughtful historical and conceptual analysis of shifting literacy definitions, see Radwin [1978]).

The definitional controversy has more than academic significance. Each formulation of an answer to the question "What is literacy?" leads to a different evaluation of the scope of the problem (i.e., the extent of illiteracy) and to different objectives for programs aimed at the formation of a literate citizenry. Definitions of literacy shape our perceptions of individuals who fall on either side of the standard (what a "literate" or "nonliterate" is like) and thus in a deep way affect both the substance and style of educational programs. A chorus of clashing answers also creates problems for literacy planners and educators. This is clearly evident in the somewhat acerbic comments of Dauzat and Dauzat (1977, p. 37), who are concerned with adult basic education: "In spite of all of the furor and the fervor for attaining literacy . . . few have undertaken to say what they or anyone else means by literacy. Those few professional organizations, bureaus and individuals who have attempted the task of explaining 'what is literacy?' generate definitions that conflict, contradict but rarely complement each other. . . . These 'champions of the cause of literacy' crusade for a national effort to make literacy a reality without establishing what that reality is."

What lies behind the definitional difficulties this statement decries? The authors themselves provide a clue. They suggest that literacy is a kind of reality that educators should be able to grasp and explain, or, expressed in more classical terms, that literacy has an "essence" that can be captured through some Aristotelian-like enterprise. By a rational process of discussion and analysis, the "true" criterial components of literacy will be identified, and these in turn can become the targets of education for literacy.

Many, although by no means all, of those grappling with the problems of definition and measurement appear to be guided by such a search for the "essence"—for the "one best" way of conceptualizing literacy. This enterprise is surely a useful one and a necessary component of educational planning. Without denigrating its contribution, I would like to suggest, however, that conflicts and contradictions are intrinsic to such an essentialist approach.

Consider the following. Most efforts at definitional determination are based on a conception of literacy as an attribute of *individuals*; they aim to describe constituents of literacy in terms of individual abilities. But the single most compelling fact about literacy is that it is a *social* achievement; individuals in societies without writing systems do not become literate. Literacy is an outcome of Cultural transmission; the individual child or adult does not extract the meaning of written symbols through personal interaction with the physical objects that embody them. Literacy abilities are acquired by individuals only in the course of participation in socially organized activities with written language (for a theoretical analysis of literacy as a set of socially organized practices, see Scribner and Cole [1981]. It follows that individual literacy is relative to social literacy. Since social literacy practices vary in time (Resnick [1983] contains historical studies) and space (anthropological studies are in Goody [1968]), what qualifies as individual literacy varies with them. At one time, the ability to write one's name was a hallmark of literacy; today in some parts of the world, the ability to memorize a sacred text remains the modal literacy act. Literacy has neither a static nor a universal essence.

The enterprise of defining literacy, therefore, becomes one of assessing what counts as literacy in the modern epoch in some given social context. If a nation-society is the context, this enterprise requires that consideration be given to the functions that the society in question has invented for literacy and their distribution throughout the populace. Grasping what literacy "is" inevitably involves social analysis: What activities are carried out with written symbols? What significance is attached to them, and what status is conferred on those who engage in them? Is literacy a social right or a private power? These questions are subject to empirical determination. But others are not: Does the prevailing distribution of literacy conform to standards of social justice and human progress? What social and educational policies might promote such standards? Here we are involved, not with fact but with considerations of value, philosophy, and ideology similar to those that figure prominently in debates about the purposes and goals of schooling. Points of view about literacy as a social good, as well as a social fact, form the ground of the definitional enterprise. We may lack consensus on how best to define literacy because we have differing views about literacy's social purposes and values.

These differing points of view about the central meaning of literacy warrant deeper examination. In this essay, I will examine some of them, organizing my discussion around three metaphors: literacy as adaptation, literacy as power, and literacy as a state of grace. Each of these metaphors is rooted in certain assumptions about the social motivations for literacy in this country, the nature of existing literacy practices, and judgments about which practices are critical for individual and social enhancement. Each has differing implications for educational policies and goals. I will be schematic in my discussion; my purpose is not to marshal supporting evidence for one or the other metaphor but to show the boundary problems of all. My argument is that any of the metaphors, taken by itself, gives us only a partial grasp of the many and varied utilities of literacy and of the complex social and psychological factors sustaining aspirations for and achievement of individual literacy. To illustrate this theme, I will draw on the literacy experiences of a Third World people who, although remaining at an Iron Age level of technology, have nevertheless evolved varied functions for written language; their experience demonstrates that, even in some traditional societies, literacy is a "many-meaninged thing."

Literacy as Adaption

This metaphor is designed to capture concepts of literacy that emphasize its survival or pragmatic value. When the term "functional literacy" was originally introduced during World War I (Harman 1970), it specified the literacy skills required to meet the tasks of modern soldiering. Today, functional literacy is conceived broadly as the level of proficiency necessary for effective performance in a range of settings and customary activities.

This concept has a strong commonsense appeal. The necessity for literacy skills in daily life is obvious; on the job, riding around town, shopping for groceries, we all encounter situations requiring us to read or produce written symbols. No justification is needed to insist that schools are obligated to equip children with the literacy skills that will enable them to fulfill these mundane situational demands. And basic educational programs have a similar obligation to equip adults with the skills they must have to secure jobs or advance to better ones, receive the training and benefits to which they are entitled, and assume their civic and political responsibilities. Within the United States, as in other nations, literacy programs with these practical aims are considered efforts at human resource development and, as such, contributors to economic growth and stability.

In spite of their apparent commonsense grounding, functional literacy approaches are neither as straightforward nor as unproblematic as they first appear. Attempts to inventory "minimal functional competencies" have floundered on lack of information and divided perceptions of functionality. Is it realistic to try to specify some uniform set of skills as constituting functional literacy for all adults? Two subquestions are involved here. One concerns the choice of parameters for defining a "universe of functional competencies." Which literacy tasks (e.g., reading a newspaper, writing a check) are "necessary," and which are "optional"? The Adult Performance Level Project test (1975), one of the best conceptualized efforts to specify and measure competencies necessary for success in adult life, has been challenged on the grounds that it lacks content validity: "The APL test fails to meet this [validity] criterion . . . not necessarily because test development procedures were technically faulty, but because it is not logically possible to define this universe of behaviors [which compose functional competence] without respect to a value position which the test developers have chosen not to discuss" (Cervero 1980, 1). 163).

An equally important question concerns the concept of uniformity. Do all communities and cultural groups in our class-based and heterogeneous society confront equivalent functional demands? If not, how do they differ? Some experts (e.g., Gray 1965; Hunter and Harman 1979) maintain that the concept of functional literacy makes sense only with respect to the proficiencies required for participation in the actual life conditions of particular groups or communities. But how does such a relativistic approach mesh with larger societal needs? If we were to consider the level of reading and writing activities carried out in small and isolated rural communities as the standard for functional literacy, educational objectives would be unduly restricted. At the other extreme, we might not want to use literacy activities of college teachers as the standard determining the functional competencies required for high school graduation. Only in recent years has research been undertaken on the range of literacy activities practiced in different communities or settings within the United States (e.g., Heath 1980, 1981; Scribner 1982a), and we still know little about how, and by whom, required literacy work gets done. Lacking such knowledge, public discussions fluctuate between narrow definitions of functional skills pegged to immediate vocational and personal needs, and sweeping definitions that virtually reinstate the ability to cope with college subject matter as the hallmark of literacy. On the other hand, adopting different criteria for different regions or communities would ensure the perpetuation of educational inequalities and the differential access to life opportunities with which these are associated.

Adapting literacy standards to today's needs, personal or social, would be shortsighted. The time-limited nature of what constitutes minimal skill is illustrated in the "sliding scale" used by the U. S. Bureau of Census to determine literacy. During World War I, a fourth-grade education was considered sufficient to render one literate; in 1947, a U. S. Census sample survey raised that figure to five years; and by 1952 six years of school was considered the minimal literacy threshold. Replacing the school-grade criterion with a functional approach to literacy does not eliminate the time problem. Today's standards for functional competency need to be considered in the light of tomorrow's requirements. But not all are agreed as to the nature or volume of literacy demands in the decades ahead. Some (e.g., Naisbitt 1982) argue that, as economic and other activities become increasingly subject to computerized techniques of production and information handling, even higher levels of literacy will be required of all. A contrary view, popularized by McLuhan (1962, 1964) is that new technologies and communication media are likely to reduce literacy requirements for all. A responding argument is that some of these technologies are, in effect, new systems of literacy. The ability to use minicomputers as information storage and retrieval devices requires mastery of symbol systems that build on numeral language literacy; they are second-order literacies as it were. One possible scenario is that in coming decades literacy may be increased for some and reduced for others, accentuating the present uneven, primarily class-based distribution of literacy functions.

From the perspective of social needs, the seemingly well-defined concept of functional competency becomes fuzzy at the edges. Equally as many questions arise about functionality from the individual's point of view. Functional needs have not yet been assessed from the perspective of those who purportedly experience them. To what extent do adults whom tests assess as functionally illiterate perceive themselves as lacking the necessary skills to be adequate parents, neighbors, workers? Inner-city youngsters may have no desire to write letters to each other; raising one's reading level by a few grades may not be seen as a magic ticket to a job; not everyone has a bank account that requires the mastery of unusual forms (Heath 1980). Appeals to individuals to enhance their functional skills might founder on the different subjective utilities communities and groups attach to reading and writing activities.

The functional approach has been hailed as a major advance over more traditional concepts of reading and writing because it takes into account the goals and settings of people's activities with written language. Yet even tender probing reveals the many questions of fact, value, and purpose that complicate its application to educational curricula.

We now turn to the second metaphor.

Literacy as Power

While functional literacy stresses the importance of literacy to the adaptation of the individual, the literacy-as-power metaphor emphasizes a relationship between literacy and group or community advancement.

Historically, literacy has been a potent tool in maintaining the hegemony of elites and dominant classes in certain societies, while laying the basis for increased social and political participation in others (Resnick 1983; Goody 1968). In a contemporary framework, expansion of literacy skills is often viewed as a means for poor and politically powerless groups to claim their place in the world. The International Symposium for Literacy, meeting in Persepolis, Iran (Bataille 1976), appealed to national governments to consider literacy as an instrument for human liberation and social change. Paulo Freire (1970) bases his influential theory of literacy education on the need to make literacy a resource for fundamental social transformation. Effective literacy education, in his view, creates a critical consciousness through which a community can analyze its conditions of social existence and engage in effective action for a just society. Not to be literate is a state of victimization.

Yet the capacity of literacy to confer power or to be the primary impetus for significant and lasting economic or social change has proved problematic in developing countries. Studies (Gayter, Hall, Kidd, and Shivasrava 1979; United Nations Development Program 1976) of UNESCO's experimental world literacy program have raised doubts about earlier notions that higher literacy rates automatically promote national development and improve the social and material conditions of the very poor. The relationship between social change and literacy education, it is now suggested (Harman 1977), may be stronger in the other direction. When masses of people have been mobilized for fundamental changes in social conditions—as in the USSR, China, Cuba, and Tanzania—rapid extensions of literacy have been accomplished (Gayter et al. 1979; Hammiche 1976; Scribner 1982b). Movements to transform social reality appear to have been effective in some parts of the world in bringing whole populations into participation in modern literacy activities. The validity of the converse proposition—that literacy per se mobilizes people for action to change their social reality—remains to be established.

What does this mean for us? The one undisputed fact about illiteracy in America is its concentration among poor, black, elderly, and minority-language groups—groups without effective participation in our country's economic and educational institutions (Hunter and Harman 1979). Problems of poverty and political powerlessness are, as among some populations in developing nations, inseparably intertwined with problems of access to knowledge and levels of literacy skills. Some (e.g., Kozol 1980) Suggest that a mass and politicized approach to literacy education such as that adopted by Cuba is demanded in these conditions. Others (e.g., Hunter and Harman 1979) advocate a more action-oriented approach that views community mobilization around practical, social, and political goals as a first step in creating the conditions for effective literacy instruction and for educational equity.

The possibilities and limits of the literacy-as-power metaphor within our present-day social and political structure are not at all clear. To what extent can instructional experiences and programs be lifted out of their social contexts in other countries and applied here? Do assumptions about the functionality and significance of literacy in poor communities in the United States warrant further consideration? Reder and Green's (1984) research and educational work among West Coast immigrant communities reveals that literacy has different meanings for members of different groups. How can these cultural variations be taken into account? How are communities best mobilized for literacy—around local needs and small-scale activism? or as part of broader political and social movements? If literacy has not emerged as a priority demand, should government and private agencies undertake to mobilize communities around this goal? And can such efforts be productive without the deep involvement of community leaders?

Literacy as a State of Grace

Now we come to the third metaphor. I have variously called it literacy as salvation and literacy as a state of grace. Both labels are unsatisfactory because they give a specific religious interpretation to the broader phenomenon I want to depict—that is, the tendency in many societies to endow the literate person with special virtues. A concern with preserving and understanding scripture is at the core of many religious traditions, Western and non-Western alike. As studies by Resnick and Resnick (1977) have shown, the literacy-as-salvation metaphor had all almost literal interpretation in the practice of post-Luther Protestant groups to require of the faithful the ability to read and remember the Bible and other religious material. Older religious traditions—Hebraic and Islamic—have also traditionally invested the written word with great power and respect. 'This is a perfect book. There is no doubt in it," reads a passage from the Qur'an. Memorizing the Qur'an—literally taking its words into you and making them part of yourself—is simultaneously a process of becoming both literate and holy.

The attribution of special powers to those who are literate has its ancient secular roots as well. Plato and Aristotle strove to distinguish the man of letters from the poet of oral tradition. In the perspective of Western humanism, literateness has come to be considered synonymous with being "cultured," using the term in the old-fashioned sense to refer to a person who is knowledgeable about the content and techniques of the sciences, arts, and humanities as they have evolved historically. The term sounds elitist and archaic, but the notion that participation in a literate–that is, bookish–tradition enlarges and develops a person's essential self is pervasive and still undergirds the concept of a liberal education (Steiner 1973). In the literacy-as-a-state-of-grace concept, the power and functionality of literacy is not bounded by political or economic parameters but in a sense transcends them; the literate individual's life derives its meaning and significance from intellectual, aesthetic, and spiritual participation in the accumulated creations and knowledge of humankind, made available through the written word.

The self-enhancing aspects of literacy are often given a cognitive interpretation (Greenfield and Bruner 1969; Olson 1977). For centuries, and increasingly in this generation, appeals have been made for increased attention to literacy as a way of developing minds. An individual who is illiterate, a UNESCO (1972) publication states, is bound to concrete thinking and cannot learn new material. Some teachers of college English in the United States (e.g., Farrell 1977) urge greater prominence for writing in the curriculum as a way of promoting logical reasoning and critical thinking. Literate and nonliterate individuals presumably are not only in different states of grace but in different stages of intellectual development as well. Although evidence is accumulating (Scribner and Cole 1981) refuting this view, the notion that literacy per se creates a great divide in intellectual abilities between those who have and those who have not mastered written language is deeply entrenched in educational circles of industrialized countries.

The metaphor of literacy- as- grace, like the others, has boundary problems. For one thing, we need to know how widely dispersed this admiration of book knowledge is in our society. To what extent are beliefs about the value of literateness shared across social classes and ethnic and religious groups? How does book culture—more accurately, how do book cultures—articulate with the multiple and diverse oral cultures flourishing in the United States? Which people value literacy as a preserver of their history or endow their folk heroes with book learning? Are there broad cultural supports for book learning among wide sectors of the population? McLuhan and others have insisted that written literacy is a vestige of a disappearing "culture." Is this point of view defensible? And if so, what implications does it pose for our educational objectives?

I have described some current views of the meaning of literacy in terms of three metaphors. I have tried to indicate that each metaphor embraces a certain set of, sometimes unexamined, values; moreover, each makes assumptions about social facts in our society—the utilities of literacy and the conditions fostering individual attainment of literacy status. These metaphors are often urged on us as competitive; some choice of one or the other does in fact seem a necessary starting point for a definitional enterprise. But for purposes of social and educational planning, none need necessarily become paramount at the expense of the others; all may have validity. To illustrate this argument, I will briefly describe research on the social meaning of literacy among a West African people. Learning how literacy functions among a people far removed from us culturally and geographically may help us take a new look at its functions here at home.

Social Meaning of Literacy: A Case Study

My own consideration of the question "What is literacy?" was prompted by research experiences in a traditional West African society. Together with colleagues, I spent five years studying the social and intellectual consequences of literacy among the Vai people of West Africa (Scribner and Cole 1981). The material conditions of Vai life are harsh. Rural villages lack electricity and public water supplies; clinics and schools are scarce; dirt roads, often impassable in the rainy season, restrict social and economic exchanges. To the casual observer, Vai society is the very prototype of traditional nonliterate subsistence farming societies. Yet the Vai have practiced literacy for over 150 years, initially in a syllabic writing system of their own invention. The Vai script has been passed on from one generation to another in tutorial fashion without benefit of a formal institution such as a school and without the constitution of a professional teacher group. In addition to this indigenous script, literacy in the Arabic and Roman alphabets also flourishes in the countryside. The Vai are a Muslim people, and the Arabic script is the literacy for religious practice and theological learning. Missionaries and, more recently, the Liberian government have been disseminating English literacy, the official government literacy, through the establishment of Western-style schools. About one-third of the Vai male population is literate in one of these scripts, the majority in the Vai script. Many read and write both Vai and Arabic, and some outstanding scholars are literate in all three scripts. Since each writing system has a different orthography, represents a different language and is learned in a different setting, becoming literate in two or more scripts is an impressive intellectual accomplishment. Why do people take the trouble to do it?

Certain obvious answers are ruled out. Literacy is not a necessity for personal survival. As far as we could determine, nonliteracy status does not exclude a person from full participation in economic activities or in town or society life. As we look around Vai country and see major activities and institutions continuing to function in the traditional oral mode, we are at a loss to define the literacy competencies that might be useful in everyday life. But Vai literates have not been at such a loss and have found no end of useful functions for writing.

Commonly they engage in extensive personal correspondence, which for some involves the composition of 30–40 letters per month. Since Vai society, like other traditional societies, maintains an effective oral grapevine system, reasons for the popularity of letter writing are not self-evident, especially since all letters must be personally sent and hand-delivered. Yet literates find the advantage of secrecy and guarantee of delivery more than compensation for the time and trouble spent in writing. Scholars (Hair 1963; Holsoe 1967) speculate that the usefulness of the Vai script in protecting secrets and allowing clandestine resistance to the central governing machinery of Liberia, whose official literacy was English, were important factors in its invention and longevity.

On closer study, we find that Vai script literacy also serves many personal and public record-keeping functions. Household heads keep albums for family births, deaths, and marriages; some maintain lists of dowry items and death feast contributions that help to regulate kinship exchanges. Records also enlarge the scope and planful aspects of commercial transactions. Artisans maintain lists of customers; farmers record the yield and income from cash-crop farming. The script also serves a variety of administrative purposes such as recording house tax payments and political contributions. Some fraternal and religious organizations maintain records in Vai script. All of these activities fit nicely into the metaphor of literacy as functional adaptation; the only surprising aspect is that so many varieties of pragmatic uses occur in an economic and social milieu in which modern institutions (schools, cash markets) still play a limited role.

Not all literacy uses are devoted to practical ends. Although the Vai script has not been used to produce public books or manuscripts, in the privacy of their homes, many Vai literates engage in creative acts of composition. Almost everyone keeps a diary; some write down maxims and traditional tales in copybooks; others maintain rudimentary town histories; some record their dreams and tales of advice to children; a few who might qualify as scholars produce extended family and clan histories. Townspeople, when questioned about the value of the script, will often cite its utilitarian functions, but will equally as often speak about its importance for self-education and knowledge. Vai script literates are known in the community, are accorded respect, and are sought out for their information and help as personal scribes or as town clerks. A Vai parable about the relative merits of money, power, and book learning for success in this world concludes with the judgment that the "man who knoweth book passeth all."

Why this excursion into a case of African literacy after our metaphoric discussion of the goals of literacy education in a technological society? Perhaps because Vai society, much simpler than ours in the range of literacy functions it calls for, nonetheless serves to highlight unnecessary simplicities in our attempts to define the one best set of organizing principles for literacy education. If we were called on as experts to devise literacy education programs for the Vai people, which metaphor would dominate our recommendations? Would we emphasize the spread of functional competencies, urging all farmers to keep crop records and all carpenters to list customers? This would be an effective approach for some, but it would neglect the interests and aspirations of others. Should we appeal to the cultural pride of the populace, suggesting Vai script literacy be extended as an instrument for group cohesion and social change? We might count on support for this appeal, but resistance as well; Qur'anic schools and the network of Muslim teachers and scholars are a powerful counterforce to the Vai script and a countervailing center for cultural cohesion. Moreover, families participating in the Vai script tradition do not necessarily repudiate participation in English literacy; some find it prudent to have one or more children in English school as well as Qur'anic school. As for literacy as a state of grace, aspirations for self-improvement and social status clearly sustain many aspects of Vai literacy both in the Arabic religious and Vai secular traditions. A diversity of pragmatic, ideological, and intellectual factors sustains popular literacy among the Vai.

The sociohistorical processes leading to multiple literacies among the Vai are not unique. In their research in Alaska, Reder and Green (1983) found community members practicing literacy in any one (or, occasionally, a combination) of three languages. Sonic used the Cyrillic script, introduced by the Russian Orthodox Church, for reading and writing Russian; others used that script for literacy activities in their native Eskimo language; and still others participated in English literacy. Each of these literacies, they report, occurred through distinct socialization processes and in well-defined nonoverlapping domains of activity, and each had a distinctive social meaning. Wagner (in press) similarly documents the multiple meanings of literacy in contemporary Moroccan society, and other reports might be cited.

This is not to suggest, of course, that all cultural groups have elaborated rich functions for literacy, nor that all groups strive for participation in the official literacy of their state (as, for example, English in Alaska and throughout the United States). The value of the growing body of ethnographic studies for the "What is literacy?" question is twofold. First, it promotes skepticism of the "one best answer" approach to the improvement of literacy in our society. Second, it urges the need for understanding the great variety of beliefs and aspirations that various people have developed toward literacy in their particular historical and current life circumstances.

What implications does this analysis have for literacy policy and education? This is a question that calls for the continued, sustained, and thoughtful attention of educators and others in our society. One implication that I find compelling is the need to "disaggregate" various levels and kinds of literacy. If the search for all essence is futile, it might appropriately be replaced by serious attention to varieties of literacy and their place in social and educational programs. In this disentangling process, I would place priority on the need to extricate matters of value and policy from their hidden position in the definitional enterprise and to address them head on. The International Symposium for Literacy, closing UNESCO's Experimental World Literacy Program, declared that literacy is a fundamental human right (Bataille 1976). Literacy campaigns need no other justification. Setting long-range social and educational goals, however, pushes us farther toward an inquiry into the standard of literacy that is a desirable (valued) human right in our highly developed technological society, whose policies have such a powerful impact on the world's future. What is *ideal* literacy in our society? If the analysis by metaphor presented here contributes some approach to that question, it suggests that ideal literacy is simultaneously adaptive, socially empowering, and self-enhancing. Enabling youth and adults to progress toward that ideal would be a realization of the spirit of the symposium in Persepolis reflective of the resources and literacy achievements already available in our society. This suggests that long-term social and educational policies might be directed at maximum literacy objectives; minimal literacy standards would serve a useful function, not as goals but as indicators of our progress in equipping individuals and communities with the skills they need for "takeoff" in continuing literacy careers.

Recognition of the multiple meanings and varieties of literacy also argues for a diversity of educational approaches, informal and community-based as well as formal and school-based. As ethnographic research and practical experience demonstrate, effective literacy programs are those that are responsive to perceived needs, whether for functional skills, social power, or self-improvement. Individual objectives may be highly specific: to qualify for a promotion at work, to help children with their lessons, to record a family history. Anzalone and McLaughlin (1982) have coined the term "specific literacies" to designate such special-interest or special-purpose literacy skills. The road to maximal literacy may begin for some through the feeder routes of a wide variety of specific literacies.

These are speculative and personal views; others will have different conceptions. The notions offered here of ideal and specific literacies do not simplify the educational issues nor resolve the definitional dilemmas. I hope, however, that these concepts and the metaphoric analysis from which they flowed suggest the usefulness of "dissecting literacy" into its many forms and, in the process, clarifying the place of fact and value in discussions of the social meaning of literacy.

Note

This paper is based on a planning document for research on literacy that I prepared when associate director of the National Institute of Education. Eugene Radwin made many helpful comments on that document and contributed a number of bibliographic references cited here.

References

Adult Performance Level Project. *Adult Functional Competency: A Summary*. Austin: University of Texas, Division of Extension, 1975.

Advisory Committee on National Illiteracy. "Report." *School and Society* 30 (1929): 708.

Anzalone, S., and S. McLaughlin. *Literacy for Specific Situations*. Amherst: University of Massachusetts, Center for International Education, 1982.

Bataille, L., ed. *A Turning Point for Literacy: Proceedings of the International Symposium for Literacy, Persepolis, Iran, 1975*. Oxford: Pergamon Books, 1976.

Bormuth, J. R. "Reading Literacy: Its Definition and Assessment." *In Toward a Literate Society: 'The Report of the Committee on Reading of the National Academy of Education*, edited by J . B. Carroll and J. S. Chall. New York: McGraw-Hill Book Co., 1975.

Cervero, R. M. "Does the Texas Adult Performance Level Test Measure Functional Competence?" *Adult Education* 30 (1980): 152-65.

Dauzat, S. J., and J. Dauzat. "Literacy in Quest of a Definition." *Convergence* 10 (1977): 37-41.

Farrell, L. J. "Literacy, the Basics, and All that Jazz." *College English* 38 (1977): 443-59.

Freire, P. *Cultural Action for Freedom* (Monograph Series no. 1). Cambridge, Mass.: Harvard Educational Review, 1970.

Cayter, M., B. Hall, J. R. Kidd, and V. Shivasrava. *The World of Literacy: Policy, Research and Action.* Toronto: International Development Centre, 1979.

Goody, J., ed. Literacy in Traditional Societies. Cambridge: Cambridge University Press, 1968.

Gray, W. *The Teaching of Reading and Writing: An International Survey.* Chicago: Scott, Foresman & Co./UNESCO, 1965.

Greenfield, P. M., and J. S. Bruner. "Culture and Cognitive Growth." *In Handbook of Socialization: Theory and Research*, edited by D. A. Goslin. New York: Rand McNally & Co., 1969.

Hair, P. E. H. "Notes on the Discovery of the Vai Script." *Sierra Leone Language Review* 2 (1963): 36-49.

Hammiche, B. "Functional Literacy and Educational Revolution." *In A Turning Point for literacy: Proceedings of the International Symposium for Literacy, Persepolis Iran, 1975*, edited by L. Bataille. Oxford: Pergamon Press, 1976.

Harman, D. "Review of *The Experimental World Literacy Program*." Harvard Educational Review 47 (1977): 444-46.

Heath, S. B. "The Functions and Uses of Literacy. " *Journal of Communication* 30 (1980): 123-33.

Heath, S. B. "Toward an Ethnohistory of Writing in American Education." *In Writing: The Nature, Development and Teaching of Written Communication*, vol. 1, edited by M. F. Whiteman. Hillsdale, N. J.: Lawrence Erlbaum Associates, 1981.

Hillerich, R. L. "Toward an Assessable Definition of Literacy. " *English Journal* 65 (1976): 50-55.

Holsoc, S. E. "Slavery and Economic Response among the Vai." *In Slavery in Africa: Historical and Anthropological Perspectives*, edited by S. Miers and I. Kopytoff. Madison: University of Wisconsin Press, 1977.

Hunter, C. S. J., and D. Harman. *Adult Illiteracy in the United States*, New York: McGraw-Hill Book Co., 1979.

Kirsch, I., and J. T. Guthrie. "The Concept and Measurement of Functional Literacy." *Reading Research Quarterly* 13 (1977-78): 485-507.

Kozol, J. *Prisoners of Silence: Breaking the Bonds of Adult Illiteracy in the United States.* New York: Continuum Publishing Corp., 1980.

McGovern, G. *Congressional Record* (September 1978), p. 14,834.

McLuhan, M. *The Gutenberg Galaxy.* Toronto: University of Toronto Press, 1962.

McLuhan, M. *Understanding Media: The Extensions of Man.* New York: McGraw-Hill Book Co., 1964.

Miller, G. A., ed. *Linguistic Communication: Perspectives for Research.* Newark, Del.: International Reading Association, 1973.

Naisbett, J. Megatrends: *Ten New Directions Transforming Our Lives.* New York: Warner Books, 1982.

Olson, D. R. "From Utterance to Text: The Bias of Language in Speech and Writing." *Harvard Educational Review* 47 (1977): 257-81.

Powell, W. R. "Levels of Literacy." *Journal of Reading* 20 (1977): 488-92.

Radwin, E. "Literacy—What and Why." Unpublished manuscript, Harvard University, 1978.

Reder, S., and K. R. Green. "Literacy as a Functional Component of Social Structure in an Alaska Fishing Village." *International Journal of the Sociology of Language* 42 (1983): 122-41.

Resnick, D. P., ed. *Literacy in Historical Perspective.* Washington, D. C.: Library of Congress, 1983.

Resnick, D. P., and L. B. Resnick. "The Nature of Literacy: An Historical Exploration." *Harvard Educational Review* 47 (1977): 370-85.

Scribner, S. "Industrial Literacy" (Final Report to the Ford Foundation). New York: CUNY, Graduate School and University Center, 1982. (a) [Scribner, S. "Observations on Literacy Education in China." *Linguistic Reporter* 25 (1982): 1-4. (b)]

Scribner, S., and M. Cole. *The Psychology of Literacy*. Cambridge, Mass.: Harvard University Press, 1981.

Steiner, G. "After the Book." *In The Future of Literacy*, edited by R. Disch. Englewood Cliffs, N. J.: Prentice-Hall, Inc. 1973.

United Nations Development Program. *The Experimental World Literacy Programme: A Critical Assessment. Paris: UNESCO, 1976.* [UNESCO. *Regional Report on Literacy.* Teheran: UNESCO, 1972.]

Wagner, D. A., B. M. Messick, and J. Spratt. "Studying Literacy in Morocco." In The *Acquisition of Literacy: Ethnographic Perspectives*, edited by B. B. Schieffelin and P. Gilmore. Norwood, N. J.: Ablex, in press.

Questions for Discussion

1. Who do you believe was Scribner's intended audience for this piece? Upon what kinds of context or reading cues or linguistic and stylistic choices do you base your answer?

2. Work with a small group of other students. Have each group member summarize a major section of the essay: the introductory pages, the first metaphor, the second metaphor, the third metaphor, and the case study section. Present your summaries to one another, delineating what you feel are Scribner's most important claims in each section. When your group is finished, compare your summaries and lists of claims with those produced by other groups within the class.

3. The case study of Vai literacy helps many readers connect with Scribner's more theoretical discussion in the earlier pages of the essay. Working in the word processing program available to you in your classroom, summarize and/or annotate the case study portion of Scribner's essay. How does it function to explain earlier concepts and the three metaphors? What portions of the case study leave questions unanswered?

Explorations

1. Which of Scribner's three metaphors is most compelling to you? Why? For this Exploration, take some time to respond to the metaphor that speaks to you most strongly. Can you think of examples from your own life, print media, films, television, billboards, etc. that have helped exemplify this metaphor for literacy?

2. Using Scribner's metaphors as a frame or interpretive lens, revisit one of the earlier selections from Unit 1. How does this metaphor help you to understand the selection? For example, you might revisit Frederick Douglass' narrative and discuss the "literacy as power" metaphor. Does the use of Scribner's metaphor complicate or clarify your understanding of literacy in the selection you chose?

3. Scribner's "Literacy in Three Metaphors" draws upon the conventions of the social science community. For this Exploration, work descriptively with Scribner's essay to reflect upon your understanding of those conventions and how they may differ from the conventions valued within your first-year writing classroom. What do you notice about Scribner's voice, style, use of point of view, vocabulary, argumentative strategies, etc.? How do those aspects of her work seem different from the conventions valued in your writing class?

Formal Writing Assignments

1. Return to your response to Exploration one, which asks you to consider which of Scribner's metaphors (literacy as adaptation, literacy as power, literacy as state of grace) is most compelling to you. Using that Exploration response as a prewriting activity, draft an essay that develops your discussion of this metaphor by focusing upon the act of analysis: telling how and why this metaphor functions as it does in your immediate line of vision. Your goal is to draw upon evidence available to you from television, film, newspaper, billboards, the world wide web, the classroom, and your personal experience in order to analyze how this metaphor "works" in your immediate cultural context.

2. Sylvia Scribner explored her theories of literacy via a case study of the literate behaviors of the Vai people. Choose a particular group or community (you may choose one that you belong to or one to which you do not belong) as a site for your own exploration of how literacy works in a particular context. Spend approximately one week collecting "thick descriptions"—extremely detailed descriptive pieces of writing—of how this particular group or community utilizes its literacy practices. In the process, you will be developing your own definition of literacy and, perhaps, comparing that definition to the definition that is forwarded by the community you are studying. Once you have collected your data, draft a report of your findings that shares your definition and summarizes/responds to your thick descriptions.

Excerpt from Yellow Woman and a Beauty of the Spirit

Leslie Marmon Silko

A novelist, essayist, and poet, Leslie Marmon Silko has established herself as a leading author of writings about Native Americans. In her writing, she concentrates not only on themes of identity, loss, and the place of humanity in the cosmos but also on native religious and cultural rituals, narratives, and storytelling traditions. She is perhaps most well-known for two books, *Ceremony* (a novel) and *Storyteller* (poems and stories). The selection below comes from *Yellow Woman and a Beauty of the Spirit: Essays on Native American Life Today,* which one critic described as a "carefully controlled blend of pride in Pueblo heritage and anger over the perpetuation of injustice against Native Americans" and focuses in the collection on "how integral place is to the Pueblo ethos and sense of identity, and how stories are a vibrant part of everyday Pueblo life." Silko lives in Tucson, Arizona.

Writing Before Reading

1. Stories serve many purposes in families and local communities or groups. Consider the ways that stories function in your immediate or extended family. What stories do you recall hearing from parents, grandparents, or other relatives during your childhood? Why do you think that these stories were told and retold?

2. Of what importance is *place* for you, your family, or community? What places are of greatest significance? What kinds of cultural, social, or religious meaning do you attribute to these particular places?

3. The selection below from Silko's *Yellow Woman and a Beauty of the Spirit* relates the communal nature of storytelling among Pueblo tribes. Although storytelling remains a central means of disseminating information within cultural groups, many groups in a print—and technologically—enhanced world find other means of developing a sense of community. What are some of the ways that members of a group to which you belong strive to achieve a sense of community?

Excerpt from Yellow Woman and a Beauty of the Spirit

THROUGH THE STORIES WE HEAR WHO WE ARE

All summer the people watch the west horizon, scanning the sky from south to north for rain clouds. Corn must have moisture at the time the tassels form. Otherwise pollination will be incomplete, and the ears will be stunted and shriveled. An inadequate harvest may bring disaster. Stories told at Hopi, Zuñi, and at Acoma and Laguna describe drought and starvation as recently as 1900. Precipitation in west-central New Mexico averages fourteen inches annually. The western pueblos are located at altitudes over 5,600 feet above sea level, where winter temperatures at night fall below freezing. Yet evidence of their presence in the high desert and plateau country goes back ten thousand years. The ancient Pueblo not only survived in this environment, but for many years they also thrived. In A.D. 1100 the people at Chaco Canyon had built cities with apartment buildings of stone five stories high. Their sophistication as sky watchers was surpassed only by Mayan and Inca astronomers. Yet this vast complex of knowledge and belief, amassed for thousands of years, was never recorded in writing.

Instead, the ancient Pueblo people depended upon collective memory through successive generations to maintain and transmit an entire culture, a worldview complete with proven strategies for survival. The oral narrative, or story, became the medium through which the complex of Pueblo knowledge and belief was maintained. Whatever the event or the subject, the ancient people perceived the world and themselves within that world as part of an ancient, continuous story composed of innumerable bundles of other stories.

The ancient Pueblo vision of the world was inclusive. The impulse was to leave nothing out. Pueblo oral tradition necessarily embraced all levels of human experience. Otherwise, the collective knowledge and beliefs comprising ancient Pueblo culture would have been incomplete. Thus, stories about the Creation and Emergence of human beings and animals into this world continue to be retold each year for four days and four nights during the winter solstice. The *hummah-hah* stories related events from the time long ago when human beings were still able to communicate with animals and other living things. But beyond these two preceding categories, the Pueblo oral tradition knew no boundaries. Accounts of the appearance of the first Europeans (Spanish) in Pueblo country or of the tragic encounters between Pueblo people and Apache raiders were no more and no less important than stories about the biggest mule deer ever taken or adulterous couples surprised in cornfields and chicken coops. Whatever happened, the ancient people instinctively sorted events and details into a loose narrative structure. Everything became a story.

Traditionally everyone, from the youngest child to the oldest person, was expected to listen and be able to recall or tell a portion of, if only a small detail from, a narrative account or story. Thus, the remembering and the retelling were a communal process. Even if a key figure, an elder who knew much more than others, were to die unexpectedly, the system would remain intact. Through the efforts of a great many people, the community was able to piece together valuable accounts and crucial information that might otherwise have died with an individual.

Communal storytelling was a self-correcting process in which listeners were encouraged to speak up if they noted an important fact or detail omitted. The people were happy to listen to two or three different versions of the same event of the same *hummah-hah* story. Even conflicting versions of an incident were welcomed for the entertainment they provided. Defenders of each version might joke and tease one another, but seldom were there any direct confrontations. Implicit in the Pueblo oral tradition was the awareness that loyalties, grudges, and kinship must always influence the narrator's choices as she emphasizes to listeners that this is the way *she* has always heard the story told. The ancient Pueblo people sought a communal truth, not an absolute truth. For them this truth lived somewhere within the web of differing versions, disputes over minor points, and outright contradictions tangling with old feuds and village rivalries.

A dinner-table conversation recalling a deer hunt forty years ago, when the largest mule deer ever was taken, inevitably stimulates similar memories in listeners. But hunting stories were not merely after-dinner entertainment. These accounts contained information of critical importance about the behavior and migration patterns of mule deer. Hunting stories carefully described key landmarks and locations of fresh water. Thus, a deer-hunt story might also serve as a map. Lost travelers and lost piñon-nut gatherers have been saved by sighting a rock formation they recognize only because they once heard a hunting story describing this rock formation.

The importance of cliff formations and water holes does not end with hunting stories. As offspring of the Mother Earth, the ancient Pueblo people could not conceive of themselves within a specific landscape, but location, or place, nearly always plays a central role in the Pueblo oral narratives. Indeed, stories are most frequently recalled as people are passing by a specific geographical feature or the exact location where a story took place. The precise date of the incident often is less important than the place or location of the happening. "Long, long ago," "a long time ago," "not too long ago," and "recently" are usually how stories are classified in terms of time. But the places where the stories occur are precisely located, and prominent geographical details recalled, even if the landscape is well known to listeners, often because the turning point in the narrative involved a peculiarity of the special quality of a rock or tree or plant found only at that place. Thus, in the case of many of the Pueblo narratives, it is impossible to determine which came first, the incident or the geographical feature that begs to be brought alive in a story that features some unusual aspect of this location.

There is a giant sandstone boulder about a mile north of Old Laguna, on the road to Paguate. It is ten feet tall and twenty feet in circumference. When I was a child and we would pass this boulder driving to Paguate village, someone usually made reference to the story about Kochininako, Yellow Woman, and the Estrucuyo, a monstrous giant who nearly ate her. The Twin Hero Brothers saved Kochininako, who had been out hunting rabbits to take home to feed her mother and sisters. The Hero Brothers had heard her cries just in time. The Estrucuyo had cornered her in a cave too small to fit its monstrous head. Kochininako had already thrown to the Estrucuyo all her rabbits, as well as her moccasins and most of her clothing. Still the creature had not been satisfied. After killing the Estrucuyo with her bows and arrows, the Twin Hero Brothers slit open the Estrucuyo and cut out its heart. They threw the heart as far as they could.

The monster's heart landed there, beside the old trail to Paguate village, where the sandstone boulder rests now.

It may be argued that the existence of the boulder precipitated the creation of a story to explain it. But sandstone boulders and sandstone formations of strange shapes abound in the Laguna Pueblo area. Yet, most of them do not have stories. Often the crucial element in a narrative is the terrain—some specific detail of the setting.

A high, dark mesa rises dramatically from a grassy plain, fifteen miles southeast of Laguna, in an area known as Swahnee. On the grassy plain 140 years ago, my greatgrandmother's uncle and his brother-in-law were grazing their herd of sheep. Because visibility on the plain extends for over twenty miles, it wasn't until the two sheepherders came near the high, dark mesa that the Apaches were able to stalk them. Using the mesa to obscure their approach, the raiders swept around from both ends of the mesa. My great-grandmother's relatives were killed, and the herd was lost. The high, dark mesa played a critical role: the mesa had compromised the safety that the openness of the plains had seemed to assure.

Pueblo and Apache alike relied upon the terrain, the very earth herself, to give them protection and aid. Human activities or needs were maneuvered to fit the existing surroundings and conditions. I imagine the last afternoon of my distant ancestors as warm and sunny for late September. They might have been traveling slowly, bringing the sheep closer to Laguna in preparation for the approach of colder weather. The grass was tall and only beginning to change from green to a yellow that matched the late afternoon sun shining off it. There might have been comfort in the warmth and the sight of the sheep fattening on good pasture that lulled my ancestors into their fatal inattention. They might have had a rifle, whereas the Apaches had only bows and arrows. But there would have been four or five Apache raiders, and the surprise attack would have canceled any advantage the rifles gave them.

Survival in any landscape comes down to making the best use of all available resources. On that particular September afternoon, the raiders made better use of the Swahnee terrain than my poor ancestors did. Thus, the high, dark mesa and the story of the two lost Laguna herders became inextricably linked. The memory of them and their story resides in part with the high, dark mesa. For as long as the mesa stands, people within the family and clan will be reminded of the story of that afternoon long ago. Thus, the continuity and accuracy of the oral narratives are reinforced by the landscape—and the Pueblo interpretation of that landscape is *maintained.*

Questions for Discussion

1. Why is place (as opposed to time) such a significant element in Pueblo narratives? In what other ways do the narratives Silko relates illustrate the relationship between the Pueblo people and their natural world?

2. Why do you believe Silko elects to tell the stories she does in this selection? What purposes do the stories serve for her? What function, in other words, do the stories serve in Silko's own essay?

3. Silko uses narrative to weave an argument. What argument is implied or stated in the essay? In what ways do the narrative form and the specific retellings of the Pueblo stories illustrate or "prove" her argument?

Explorations

1. Within the very stories told by the Pueblos were keys to their cultural values and beliefs. Select one or more stories from your own family or community and explore what they say about your cultural values and beliefs.

2. The advent of writing in any culture, anthropologists argue, necessarily changes the narrative dynamic of the people. Once writing is introduced, the need to relate stories orally diminishes because those same stories can be committed to paper. Examine the ways that you're dependent upon writing as a means of remembering. For what, if anything, do you continue to rely on memory alone?

3. Silko writes here about the powerful oral traditions of her ancestors. Other scholars and essayists write with a similar sense of nostalgia and loss about the print culture of the late nineteenth and early twentieth centuries. Computer technologies (like print) necessarily change our ways of communicating with one another. Draw parallels between the oral culture about which Silko writes and the print culture of the late-nineteenth and early-twentieth centuries and the forces that disrupt them.

Formal Writing Assignments

1. Interview one or more older relatives, preferably some who came of age before the advent of television. Inquire about storytelling, family gatherings, and the ways that community members shared their narratives and passed on beliefs. Did they do it through stories? Song? After completing the interview, compose an interview-based essay in which you relate the details of the conversations and articulate a working theory about the role that discourses played in your family.

2. Investigate through internet and/or library resources prominent myths, tales, or narratives from your ethnic, regional, racial, or religious heritage. Relate in an essay the substance of a story or stories and then analyze the content and its relationship to larger communal beliefs.

Feathers from a Thousand Li Away

Amy Tan

Accused of being a workaholic by even the best of her friends, Amy Tan (b. 1952) took up writing fiction as a form of therapy. As a freelance technical writer, she'd often worked ninety hour weeks, and so looked for other outlets of expression that were not "work." Her first novel, *The Joy Luck Club*, was an immediate success and was made into a Hollywood movie. In the novel, from which this selection is taken, Tan explores the cultural and generational conflict amongst Chinese and Chinese-American women. The Chinese-American women are especially ambivalent about their Chinese background. Written as a fable, the story only alludes to potential interpretations, making it possible for many readers, not just Chinese or Chinese-American women, to understand the tale.

Writing Before Reading

1. Many people enjoy keepsakes that remind them of important times or aspects of their lives. Make a list of objects you keep that symbolize something important to you.

2. Have you ever felt that one of your parents wishes certain achievements for you that he or she had originally wanted but was unable to realize? What are they?

3. Write briefly about either your own difficulties in adapting after moving to another country or what you imagine might be difficult for immigrants in the United States.

Feathers from a Thousand Li Away

The old woman remembered a swan she had bought many years ago in Shanghai for a foolish sum. This bird, boasted the market vendor, was once a duck that stretched its neck in hopes of becoming a goose, and now look!—it is too beautiful to eat.

Then the woman and the swan sailed across an ocean many thousands of *Li* wide, stretching their necks toward America. On her journey she cooed to the swan: "In America I will have a daughter just like me. But over there nobody will say her worth is measured by the loudness of her husband's belch. Over there nobody will look down on her, because I will make her speak only perfect American English. And over there she will always be too full to swallow any sorrow! She will know my meaning, because I will give her this swan—a creature that became more than what was hoped for."

But when she arrived in the new country, the immigration officials pulled her swan away from her, leaving the woman fluttering her arms and with only one swan feather for a memory. And then she had to fill out so many forms she forgot why she had come and what she had left behind.

Now the woman was old. And she had a daughter who grew up speaking only English and swallowing more Coca-Cola than sorrow. For a long time now the woman had wanted to give her daughter the single swan feather and tell her, "This feather may look worthless, but it comes from afar and carries with it all my good intentions." And she waited, year after year, for the day she could tell her daughter this in perfect American English.

Questions for Discussion

1. Building on question one from Writing Before Reading, trade your list of keepsakes with a classmate. Try to guess what meaning his or her keepsakes have and then list probable reasons for these meanings. Then trade lists again. How close were your partner's guesses? How close were your guesses?

2. What effect does Tan achieve by writing this story as a vignette? How would the effects of the piece have differed if Tan had expanded the vignette into a short story? What effects might the piece have had if written in verse?

3. Discuss the literacies and communities about which Tan writes. How does moving between two cultural/linguistic communities impact language acquisition in this story? How does the move impact the old woman's intentions?

Explorations

1. Write a vignette about a significant experience from which you have a keepsake. Use images and metaphors to illustrate the importance of your experience. Show how that keepsake symbolizes the experience or some important aspect of it.

2. Write about an achievement your parents strongly wish or wished for you. Did their wish have a positive or a negative affect on your own desire for that achievement? What was positive about the way they encouraged you toward this end and how could it have become negative? Or, what was negative about their method and how could it have been made positive?

3. Both Earl Braggs in "Vietnam Revisited" and Peggy McIntosh in "White Privilege, Male Privilege" emphasize the way language can be used to suit one's purpose. In the former, language has transportative abilities; in the latter, language has the power to determine our identities. Tan's story also conveys a message about the impact of language: what is it, and how does it compare to the other two?

Formal Writing Assignments

1. Expand on the vignette you wrote for "Explorations" question number one. Write the story in explicit detail that your vignette had illustrated through imagery. Use your vignette as a sort of epigraph that introduces your longer story.

2. In an essay, compare the theories of language use in Braggs, McIntosh, and Tan. What are they, what are the advantages and disadvantages of each, and which is most effective?

ACADEMIC DISCOURSES

Although most Americans probably agree that education is necessary for the well-being of both individuals and society as a whole, the history of American education has been characterized by contending visions of the purposes of education. In "Academic Discourses," for example, Frederick Douglass portrays education as part of the American ideal of self-reliance and progress. At the same time, many of the writers in this unit of *Writing Lives/Reading Communities,* such as Fan Shen and Mike Rose, suggest that teachers and schools often fail to accept and learn from the discourse practices that many students bring with them to classrooms. The selections in "Academic Discourses" discuss and challenge the purposes of education, its importance in U.S. culture, and the different discourses that are privileged and learned at the college level.

How do discourses function in the academy? What does it mean to acquire new discourses within this rarified community? Are different discourses at work at different kinds of post-secondary institutions—community colleges, four-year schools, universities? Using discourses in a college or university setting involves becoming literate in the particular discourse practices of one or (most likely) more academic disciplines. Acquiring academic discourses—those language practices shared by members of particular disciplinary groups—also entails becoming part of an academic community. You'll no doubt find yourself negotiating the differences between the language practices of your home communities and those of college or the university. The language practices of our home communities are not always valued by colleges and universities, as many writers in this unit argue and as Barbara Mellix and Richard Rodriguez implied in Unit I. How, then, are people to succeed in college without losing touch with the places where they grew up? Just as important, how can a college or university learn from and accommodate the variety of discourses and language practices that teachers *and* students bring with them to campus?

The readings in "Academic Discourses" ask you to consider these "boundary crossings" between home communities and the academy. They also encourage you to reflect critically upon education and educational settings, to look at *what, how,* and *where* you are being taught. In "The Banking Concept of Education," Brazilian educator Paulo Freire argues against teaching methods that assume students are little more than passive receptacles for the knowledge of their teachers. Keith Gilyard examines the responsibilities of writers and writing instructors in making a difference through their discourses. Ellen Louise Hart illustrates the tensions faced by gays and lesbians as students that can arise when students from working class and minority backgrounds learn to speak the language of the academy. Jean Anyon turns our attention to the intellectual and educational implications of a public schooling system driven by economic privilege. E.D. Hirsch argues that we, collectively, need to pay more attention to the content of education. All Americans, he claims—if they're to read and write effectively—must know certain ideas and traditions. But as Sherman Alexie, bell hooks, Herbert Kohl, and Audre Lorde argue, the question of whose traditions and stories are taught in schools involves difficult and often painful political and social struggles.

You will notice that all of the writers in "Academic Discourses" argue (implicitly or explicitly) that the process of education should be changed. Consider for yourself the following questions as you read:

- What kinds of changes does a given author advocate?

- On which issues do they agree or disagree?

- How do these writers define "academic discourse"?

- Is a single definition even possible or desirable?

- Do you think that there will always be a need to change the process of education in the United States?

- Are there any changes in educational processes or institutions that you would like to see made? If so, who would benefit from such changes?

- What would have to happen for such changes to occur?

The readings in "Academic Discourses" are often deliberately provocative, and you will probably find yourself applying these writers' observations and arguments to your own educational experiences. In the end, you may find that your goals and expectations for college have been affirmed, changed, or complicated.

EXPLORATION

Drawing on your own experiences as a high school or college student, develop a definition of academic discourse. You might consider the following questions. What were your expectations of the kinds of reading and writing you'd encounter at college? In what ways have those expectations been met, challenged, or modified? What kinds of discourses do your instructors expect from you already? How do the academic discourses you've encountered in college differ from the language practices and discourses in your high school or home community?

The Joy of Reading: Superman and Me

Sherman Alexie

Sherman Alexie, who is of Coeur d'Alene and Spokane Indian ancestry, was born in October 1966 in Wellpinit, on the Spokane Indian Reservation, 50 miles northwest of Spokane, Washington. To date, he has published more than three hundred poems, stories, essays, reviews and translations and is considered one of the most talented young writers of his generation. While still an undergraduate at Washington State University in 1990, Alexie published his first work in the Brooklyn literary magazine *Hanging Loose*. Two years later, the magazine's ancillary, Hanging Loose Press, published Alexie's first book, *The Business of Fancydancing,* a collection of short stories and poetry. A short story in Alexie's next major publication, *The Lone Ranger and Tonto Fistfight in Heaven,* became the basis for the recently acclaimed movie *Smoke Signals,* while two of his later novels, *Reservation Blues* and *Indian Killer,* are currently the subject of ongoing film negotiations.

Alexie desribes the inception of his career in this way: "I started writing because I kept fainting in human anatomy class and needed a career change. The only class that fit where the human anatomy class had been was a poetry writing workshop. I always liked poetry. I'd never heard of . . . a book written by a First Nations person, ever. I got into the class and my professor, Alex Kwo, gave me an anthology of contemporary Native American poetry called *Songs From This Earth on Turtle's Back.* I opened it up and—oh my gosh—I saw my life in poems and stories for the very first time." This focus on the contemporary experiences of Native Americans on and off reservations forms the basis for much of Alexie's own work, as his piece in *Writing Lives* illustrates. Like Shorris' "On the Uses of a Liberal Education as a Weapon in the Hands of the Restless Poor" and the excerpt from Audre Lorde's *Zami,* "Superman and Me" examines the intersections between discourse and power. "Superman and Me" is taken from Michael Dorris' *The Most Wonderful Books,* a collection of writers' literacy narratives.

Writing Before Reading

1. Make a list of the qualities that you believe are necessary for success in school and in life. What was expected of you by your teachers and other adults around you? What was expected of you by your friends? If these two sets of expectations differed, how did you resolve this conflict?

2. What was the first book you remember reading? Describe as much about the characters and the situations as you can. For example, what did the characters look like? What was their gender? Race? Sexuality? Where did they live? Take a moment to consider whether your answers mirror or conflict with your own identity. What is the significance of such intersections?

3. What connections do you see between race and education?

The Joy of Reading: Superman and Me

I learned to read with a Superman comic book. Simple enough, I suppose. I cannot recall which particular Superman comic book I read, nor can I remember which villain he fought in that issue. I cannot remember the plot, nor the means by which I obtained the comic book. What I can remember is this: I was 3 years old, a Spokane Indian boy living with his family on the Spokane Indian Reservation in eastern Washington state. We were poor by most standards, but one of my parents usually managed to find some minimum-wage job or another, which made us middle-class by reservation standards. I had a brother and three sisters. We lived on a combination of irregular paychecks, hope, fear and government surplus food.

My father, who is one of the few Indians who went to Catholic school on purpose, was an avid reader of westerns, spy thrillers, murder mysteries, gangster epics, basketball player biographies and anything else he could find. He bought his books by the pound at Dutch's Pawn Shop, Goodwill, Salvation Army and Value Village. When he had extra money, he bought new novels at supermarkets, convenience stores and hospital gift shops. Our house was filled with books. They were stacked in crazy piles in the bathroom, bedrooms and living room. In a fit of unemployment-inspired creative energy, my father built a set of bookshelves and soon filled them with a rare assortment of books about the Kennedy assassination, Watergate, the Vietnam War and the entire 23-book series of the Apache westerns. My father loved books, and since I loved my father with an aching devotion, I decided to love books as well.

I can remember picking up my father's books before I could read. The words themselves were mostly foreign, but I still remember the exact moment when I first understood, with a sudden clarity, the purpose of a paragraph. I didn't have the vocabulary to say "paragraph," but I realized that a paragraph was a fence that held words. The words inside a paragraph worked together for a common purpose. They had some specific reason for being inside the same fence. This knowledge delighted me. I began to think of everything in terms of paragraphs. Our reservation was a small paragraph within the United States. My family's house was a paragraph, distinct from the other paragraphs of the LeBrets to the north, the Fords to our south and the Tribal School to the west. Inside our house, each family member existed as a separate paragraph but still had genetics and common experiences to link us. Now, using this logic, I can see my changed family as an essay of seven paragraphs: mother, father, older brother, the deceased sister, my younger twin sisters and our adopted little brother.

At the same time I was seeing the world in paragraphs, I also picked up that Superman comic book. Each panel, complete with picture, dialogue and narrative was a three-dimensional paragraph. In one panel, Superman breaks through a door. His suit is red, blue and yellow. The brown door shatters into many pieces. I look at the narrative above the picture. I cannot read the words, but I assume it tells me that "Superman is breaking down the door." Aloud, I pretend to read the words and say, "Superman is breaking down the door." Words, dialogue, also float out of Superman's mouth. Because he is breaking down the door, I assume he says, "I am breaking down the door." Once again, I pretend to read the words and say aloud, "Superman is breaking down the door" In this way, I learned to read.

This might be an interesting story all by itself. A little Indian boy teaches himself to read at an early age and advances quickly. He reads "Grapes of Wrath" in kindergarten when other children are struggling through "Dick and Jane." If he'd been anything but an Indian boy living on the reservation, he might have been called a prodigy. But he is an Indian boy living on the reservation and is simply an oddity. He grows into a man who often speaks of his childhood in the third-person, as if it will somehow dull the pain and make him sound more modest about his talents.

A smart Indian is a dangerous person, widely feared and ridiculed by Indians and non-Indians alike. I fought with my classmates on a daily basis. They wanted me to stay quiet when the non-Indian teacher asked for answers, for volunteers, for help. We were Indian children who were expected to be stupid. Most lived up to those expectations inside the classroom but subverted them on the outside. They struggled with basic reading in school but could remember how to sing a few dozen powwow songs. They were monosyllabic in front of their non-Indian teachers but could tell complicated stories and jokes at the dinner table. They submissively ducked their heads when confronted by a non-Indian adult but would slug it out with the Indian bully who was 10 years older. As Indian children, we were expected to fail in the non-Indian world. Those who failed were ceremonially accepted by other Indians and appropriately pitied by non-Indians.

I refused to fail. I was smart. I was arrogant. I was lucky. I read books late into the night, until I could barely keep my eyes open. I read books at recess then during lunch, and in the few minutes left after I had finished my classroom assignments. I read books in the car when my family traveled to pow-wows or basketball games. In shopping malls, I ran to the bookstores and read bits and pieces of as many books as I could. I read the books my father brought home from the pawnshops and secondhand. I read the books I borrowed from the library. I read the backs of cereal boxes. I read the newspaper. I read the bulletins posted on the walls of the school, the clinic, the tribal offices, the post office. I read junk mail. I read auto-repair manuals. I read magazines. I read anything that had words and paragraphs. I read with equal parts joy and desperation. I loved those books, but I also knew that love had only one purpose. I was trying to save my life.

Despite all the books I read, I am still surprised I became a writer. I was going to be a pediatrician. These days, I write novels, short stories, and poems. I visit schools and teach creative writing to Indian kids. In all my years in the reservation school system, I was never taught how to write poetry, short stories or novels. I was certainly never taught that Indians wrote poetry, short stories and novels. Writing was something beyond Indians. I cannot recall a single time that a guest teacher visited the reservation. There must have been visiting teachers.

Who were they? Where are they now? Do they exist? I visit the schools as often as possible. The Indian kids crowd the classroom. Many are writing their own poems, short stories and novels. They have read my books. They have read many other books. They look at me with bright eyes and arrogant wonder. They are trying to save their lives. Then there are the sullen and already defeated Indian kids who sit in the back rows and ignore me with theatrical precision. The pages of their notebooks are empty. They carry neither pencil nor pen. They stare out the window. They refuse and resist. "Books," I say to them. "Books," I say. I throw my weight against their locked doors. The door holds. I am smart. I am arrogant. I am lucky. I am trying to save our lives.

Questions for Discussion

1. How do the intersections of race and class affect education according to Alexie's narrative? What specific circumstances does Alexie attribute to class? What circumstances does he attribute to race? Is it possible to separate the two in this narrative?

2. How can we situate "Superman and Me" within the conversation on education that is the subject of this unit? Would the classrooms described by Alexie resemble any of those analyzed by Jean Anyon? In what ways does Paulo Freire's "The Banking Concept of Education" impact your reading of "Superman and Me"? How might Alexie respond to Hirsch's call for a common "cultural literacy"? What evidence supports your claims?

3. Why might some students "refuse and resist" the notion that books can save their lives?

Explorations

1. After reading "Superman and Me," compile a list of the qualities that Alexie describes as necessary for success within his home community. Compare this with the list you compiled for the first "Writing Before Reading" question. How and why are the two lists similar or different?

2. Map a home, school, or work community of your own choosing using Alexie's definition of a paragraph. What delineates the boundaries between the paragraphs of your community? What are the connections/transitions between the paragraphs that make up the entire essay of community? What makes the essay of your community distinct from another, such as Alexie's?

3. In *The Lone Ranger and Tonto*, Alexie writes: "Survival equals anger times imagination, and imagination is the only weapon on the reservation." Give your own interpretation of the meaning of this statement and write about the connections between this philosophy and Alexie's own autobiography as it is presented in "Superman and Me."

Formal Writing Assignments

1. A great deal of mythology in the US surrounds what has been called "The American Dream" and the role of education in that dream. Write a draft examining the connections between education and the American Dream using Alexie's piece as a basis for your argument. It will be necessary to first arrive at a coherent definition or definitions of what the American Dream symbolizes. Of what does it consist? How has it changed over the years? How does the American dream intersect with the US system of education? On the WWW or in magazines, search for images of the "average" American student or the "average" American family. Working from "Superman and Me" and these texts, make an argument that considers the correlations between your observations about the American dream and Alexie's stories about education on the reservation.

2. The history of US governmental policy toward Indian education is a vexed one. For most of our nation's history, government policies on assimilation (the absorption of a minority culture into a dominant one) required large numbers of Indian children to leave their homes and families in order to study at government-run schools. These institutions, such as the Carlisle school in Pennsylvania, attempted to indoctrinate Indian students into an "American" way of life by prohibiting students from speaking their native languages or wearing their native dress. Keeping this information in mind, write an essay examining the ways that such a history plays into "Superman and Me." You might consider doing library or WWW research on these schools to gain a better understanding of the history before making your claims. To help you begin, look back at the ways that Alexie characterizes both his and his peers' reactions to education. How does their native culture influence their attitudes toward education? How might their knowledge of the history of White/Indian conflict influence their attitudes?

On the Pulse of Morning

Maya Angelou

Maya Angelou was born Marguerite Johnson on April 4, 1928 in St. Louis. She was raised in segregated rural Arkansas, and has come to be one of the most recognized cultural figures of our time. The list of Angelou's accomplishments is lengthy. An author, poet, historian, conductor, actress, singer, songwriter, playwright, film director, and civil rights activist, Angelou was the first black woman to have an original screenplay produced, *Georgia, Georgia* (1971). She has also published ten best-selling books and numerous magazine articles culminating in a Pulitzer Prize and National Book Award nominations.

Currently Reynolds Professor of American Studies at Wake Forest University in North Carolina, Angelou has led a multi-faceted life. Drama and dance formed the basis for her early forays into the arts. This focus expanded during her time in Cairo, where she moved after her marriage to a South African freedom fighter. In Cairo, Angelou became editor of *The Arab Observer*, the only English-language news weekly in the Middle East. Later she moved to Ghana, where she taught at the University of Ghana and was feature editor of *The African Review*. During this time, the 1960s, Angelou also served as the northern coordinator for the Southern Christian Leadership Conference at the request of Dr. Martin Luther King, Jr. In the 1970s, President Gerald Ford appointed Angelou to the Bicentennial Commission, and President Jimmy Carter appointed her to the National Commission on the Observance of International Women's Year. The poem "On the Pulse of Morning" was delivered at the 1993 inauguration of President Bill Clinton.

Writing Before Reading

1. If you're familiar with other of Angelou's work—her films (*Down in the Delta*), memoirs (*I Know Why the Caged Bird Sings*) or poetry ("Africa"), summarize what you believe to be the central themes, issues, and images of her work.

2. What are your expectations for this poem, knowing that it was written for and delivered at President Clinton's Inaugural? What topics or themes do you anticipate a poet would address at such an occasion?

3. What role do you believe poets should play in politics in the U.S.? Should they enter social and political debates through their poems? Why or why not?

Inaugural Poem [Excerpt]

. . . Lift up your faces, you have a piercing need
   For this bright morning dawning for you.

   History, despite its wrenching pain,
   Cannot be unlived, and if faced
   With courage, need not be lived again.

   Lift up your eyes upon
   The day breaking for you. . . .

. . . The horizon leans forward,
    Offering you space to place new steps of change.
    Here, on the pulse of this fine day
    You may have the courage
    To look up and out upon me, the
    Rock, the River, the Tree, your country. . . .

. . . Here on the pulse of this new day
    You may have the grace to look up and out
    And into your sister's eyes, into
    Your brother's face, your country
    And say simply
    Very simply
    With hope
    Good morning.

Questions for Discussion

1. As the headnote to "On the Pulse of Morning" indicates, Angelou wrote and delivered the poem for the occasion of President Bill Clinton's first inaugural. What effect does that information have on your reception and interpretation of the poem?

2. The point of view of the narrator shifts several times during "On the Pulse of Morning." From what perspectives does the narrator speak and to whom is the narrator speaking? What effect does this shifting perspective have on the poem?

3. If you were to articulate a single purpose or "message" for this poem, what would it be?

Explorations

1. In "The Social Responsibility That Writing Is—and Writing Instruction Too", Keith Gilyard writes that "Writing is social responsibility. . . . You can be irresponsible as a writer, but you cannot be non-responsible." In making this claim, Gilyard states that art can rightly serve propagandistic or social ends. Reflect on what you believe to be the social or political ends that Angelou's poem serves. To whom or what is she being responsible?

2. Angelou alludes to other texts and other events and poetic images in her poem. What allusions or explicit references did you find as you read? What was the effect of these allusions on your reading and interpretation of the poem?

3. Read the other poetry in this unit—Hughes' "Theme for English B" and Stern's "Mad" and "What They Learn in School." What common themes do you find among these poems related to schooling and cultural values?

Formal Writing Assignments

1. Compose an essay in which you analyze some element or elements of "On the Pulse of Morning." In writing the essay, you may elect to focus on one or more of any number of issues: metaphors and other figurative language and imagery, the use of allusions and references, the relationship between the poem and the occasion of its composition.

2. Using Angelou's poem as an example of the kind of poetry that Jayne Cortez (cited by Gilyard) refers to as that which captures "significant experiences that . . . allow a person to use her or his imagination, intelligence, and emotions to gain a greater awareness and understanding of self," write an essay that argues for the importance and value of poetry as a social, cultural, and political voice of the people.

Social Class and the Hidden Curriculum of Work

Jean Anyon

Jean Anyon is a professor of education at Rutgers University. She has published several scholarly articles on social class, gender, and race in education. In 1997, Anyon published *Ghetto Schooling: A Political Economy of Urban Educational Reform,* which elaborates on many of the themes in "Social Class and the Hidden Curriculum of Work." *Ghetto Schooling,* like much of Anyon's work, was well-received, with critics noting its powerful argument, sound reasoning, and stunning illustrations of the inequities within U.S. educational systems. In his review of *Ghetto Schooling,* Larry Cuban of *The New York Times Book Review* lauds Anyon for "return[ing] our attention to the tougher issues of race, class, and urban neglect that have helped to produce the institutions that have failed ghetto students time and again."

Although her attention is turned in "Social Class and the Hidden Curriculum of Work" on schools from a range of socioeconomic classes, Anyon's concerns remain trained on the social and economic inequities that accompany public policy decisions on educational spending.

Writing Before Reading

1. Reflect on the "work" you do in a classroom and the "work" you do on the job (or anticipate that you'll do on the job after graduation). What similarities or differences do you notice between the two types of "work"?

2. What do you believe to be the goals of primary and secondary education in the U.S.? What methods or activities might schools use to best reach these goals? (You may limit your response to either primary or secondary education or even focus on a particular grade level.)

3. What differences do you believe currently exist between public schools that enroll a significant number of students from working-class families and those enrolling students from affluent families?

Social Class and the Hidden Curriculum of Work

Scholars in political economy and the sociology of knowledge have recently argued that public schools in complex industrial societies like our own make available different types of educational experience and curriculum knowledge to students in different social classes. Bowles and Gintis (1976), for example, have argued that students from different social class backgrounds are rewarded for classroom behaviors that correspond to personality traits allegedly rewarded in the different occupational strata—the working classes for docility and obedience, the managerial classes for initiative and personal assertiveness. Basil Bernstein (1977), Pierre Bourdieu (Bourdieu and Passeron 1977), and Michael W. Apple (1979), focusing on school knowledge, have argued that knowledge and skills leading to social power and reward (e.g., medical, legal, managerial) are made available to the advantaged social groups but are withheld from the working classes, to whom a more "practical" curriculum is offered (e.g., manual skills, clerical knowledge). While there has been considerable argumentation of these points regarding education in England, France, and North America, there has been little or no attempt to investigate these ideas empirically in elementary or secondary schools and classrooms in this country.

This article offers tentative empirical support (and qualification) of the above arguments by providing illustrative examples of differences in student work in classrooms in contrasting social class communities. The examples were gathered as part of an ethnographical study of curricular, pedagogical and pupil evaluation practices in five elementary schools. The article attempts a theoretical approach to social class analysis.

THE SAMPLE OF SCHOOLS

The social class designation of each of the five schools will be identified, and the income, occupation, and other relevant available social characteristics of the students and their parents will be described. The first three schools are in a medium-sized city district in northern New Jersey, and the other two are in a nearby New Jersey suburb.

The first two schools I will call *Working-class Schools*. Most of the parents have blue-collar jobs. Less than a third of the fathers are skilled, while the majority are in unskilled or semiskilled jobs. During the period of the study (1978–1979) approximately 15 percent of the fathers were unemployed. The large majority (85 percent) of the families are white. The following occupations are typical: platform, storeroom, and stockroom workers; foundrymen, pipe welders, and boilermakers; semiskilled and unskilled assembly-line operatives; gas station attendants, auto mechanics, maintenance workers, and security guards. Less then 30 percent of the women work, some part-time and some full-time, oil assembly lines, in storerooms and stockrooms, as waitresses, barmaids, or sales clerks. Of the fifth grade parents, none of the wives of the skilled workers had jobs. Approximately 15 percent of the families in each school are at or below the federal "poverty" level; most of the rest of the family incomes are at or below $12,000, except some of the skilled workers whose incomes are higher. The incomes of the majority of the families in these two schools (i.e., at or below $12,000) are typical of 38.6 percent of the families in the United States (U. S. Bureau of the Census, 1979, p. 2, table A).

The third school is called the *Middle-class School*, although because of neighborhood residence patterns, the population is a mixture of several social classes. The parents' occupations can be divided into three groups: a small group of blue-collar "rich," who are skilled, well-paid workers such as printers, carpenters, plumbers, and construction workers. The second group is composed of parents in working-class and middle-class white-collar jobs: women in office jobs, technicians, supervisors in industry, and parents employed by the city (such as firemen, policemen, and several of the school's teachers). The third group is composed of occupations such as personnel directors in local firms, accountants, "middle management," and a few small capitalists (owners of shops in the area). The children of several local doctors attend this school. Most family incomes are between $13,000 and $25,000 with a few higher. This income range is typical of 38.9 percent of the families in the United States (U. S. Bureau of the Census, 1979, p. 2, table A).

The fourth school has a parent population that is at the upper income level of the upper middle class, and is predominantly professional. This school will be called the *Affluent Professional School*. Typical jobs are: cardiologist, interior designer, corporate lawyer or engineer, executive in advertising or television. There are some families who are not as affluent as the majority (e.g., the family of the superintendent of the district's schools, and the one or two families in which the fathers are skilled workers). In addition, a few of the families are more affluent than the majority, and can be classified in the capitalist class (e.g., a partner in a prestigious Wall Street stock brokerage firm). Approximately 90 percent of the children in this school are white. Most family incomes are between $40,000 and $80,000. This income span represents approximately 7 percent of the families in the United States.

192

In the fifth school the majority of the families belong to the capitalist class. This school will be called the *Executive Elite School* because most of the fathers are top executives (e.g., presidents and vice presidents) in major U.S.-based multinational corporations—for example, ATT, RCA, City Bank, American Express, U.S. Steel. A sizable group of fathers are top executives in financial firms on Wall Street. There are also a number of fathers who list their occupations as "general counsel" to a particular corporation, and these corporations are also among the large multinationals. Many of the mothers do volunteer work in the Junior League, Junior Fortnightly, or other service groups; some are intricately involved in town politics; and some are themselves in well-paid occupations. There are no minority children in the school. Almost all family incomes are over $100,000 with some in the $500,000 range. The incomes in this school represent less than 1 percent of the families in the United States (see Smith and Franklin, 1974).

Since each of the five schools is only one instance of elementary education in a particular social class context, I will not generalize beyond the sample. However, the examples of school work which follow will suggest characteristics of education in each social setting that appear to have theoretical and social significance and to be worth investigation in a larger number of schools.

The Working-Class School. In the two working-class schools, work is following the steps of a procedure. The procedure is usually mechanical, involving rote behavior and very little decision making or choice. The teachers rarely explain why the work is being assigned, how it might connect to other assignments, or what the idea is that lies behind the procedure or gives it coherence and perhaps meaning or significance. Available textbooks are not always used, and the teachers often prepare their own dittoes or put work examples on the board. Most of the rules regarding work are designations of what the children are to do; the rules are steps to follow. These steps are told to the children by the teachers and often written on the board. The children are usually told to copy the steps as notes. These notes are to be studied. Work is often evaluated not according to whether it is right or wrong, but according to whether the children followed the right steps.

The following examples illustrate these points. In math, when two-digit division was introduced, the teacher in one school gave a four-minute lecture on what the terms are called (i.e., which number is the divisor, dividend, quotient, and remainder). The children were told to copy these names in their notebooks. Then the teacher told them the steps to follow to do the problems, saying, "This is how you do them." The teacher listed the steps on the board, and then appeared several days later as a chart hung in the middle of the front wall: "Divide; Multiply; Subtract; Bring Down." The children often did examples of two-digit division. When the teacher went over the examples with them, he told them for each problem what the procedure was, rarely asking them to conceptualize or explain it themselves: "3 into 22 is 7; do your subtraction and one is left over." During the week that two-digit division was introduced (or at any other time), the investigator did not observe any discussion of the idea of grouping involved in division, any use of manipulables, or any attempt to relate two-digit division to any other mathematical process. Nor was there any attempt to relate the steps to an actual or possible thought process of the children. The observer did not hear the terms dividend, quotient, etc., used again. The math teacher in the other working-class school followed similar procedures regarding two-digit division, and at one point her class seemed confused. She said, "You're confusing yourselves. You're tensing up, Remember, when you do this, it's the same steps over and over again—and that's the way division always is." Several weeks later, after a test, a group of her children " still didn't get it," and she made no attempt to explain the concept of dividing things into groups, or to give them manipulables for their own investigation. Rather, she went over the steps with them again and told them that they "needed more practice."

In other areas of math, work is also carrying out often unexplained, fragmented procedures. For example, one of the teachers led the children through a series of steps to make a one-inch grid on their paper *without* telling them that they were making a one-inch grid, or that it would be used to study scale. She said, "Take your ruler. Put it across the top. Make a mark at every number. Then move your ruler down to the bottom. No, put it across the bottom. Now make a mark on top of every number. Now draw a line from. . . ." At this point a girl said that she has a faster way to do it and the teacher said, "No, you don't; you don't even know what I'm making yet. Do it this way, or it's wrong." After they had made the lines up and down and across, the teacher told them she wanted them to make a figure by connecting some dots and to measure that, using the scale of one inch equals one mile. Then they were to cut it out. She said, "Don't cut until I check it."

In both working-class schools, work in language arts is mechanics of punctuation (commas, periods, question marks, exclamation points), capitalization, and the four kinds of sentences. One teacher explained to me, "Simple punctuation is all they'll ever use." Regarding punctuation, either a teacher or a ditto stated the rules for where, for example, to put commas. The investigator heard no classroom discussion of the aural context of punctuation (which, of course, is what gives each mark its meaning). Nor did the investigator hear any statement or inference that placing a punctuation mark could be a decision-making process, depending, for example, on one's intended meaning. Rather, the children were told to follow the rules. Language arts did not involve creative writing. There were several writing assignments throughout the year, but in each instance the children were given a ditto, and they wrote answers to questions on the sheet. For example, they wrote their "autobiography" by answering such questions as "Where were you born?" "What is your favorite animal?" on a sheet entitled, "All About Me."

In one of the working-class schools the class had a science period several times a week. On the three occasions observed, the children were not called upon to set up experiments or to give explanations for facts or concepts. Rather, on each occasion the teacher told them in his own words what the book said. The children copied the teacher's sentences from the board. Each day that preceded the day they were to do a science experiment, the teacher told them to copy the directions from the book for the procedure they would carry out the next day, and to study the list at home that night. The day after each experiment, the teacher went over what they had "found" (they did the experiments as a class, and each was actually a class demonstration led by the teacher). Then the teacher wrote what they "found" on the board, and the children copied that in their notebooks. Once or twice a year there are science projects. The project is chosen and assigned by the teacher from a box of three-by-five-inch cards. On the card the teacher has written the question to be answered, the books to use, and how much to write. Explaining the cards to the observer, the teacher said, "It tells them exactly what to do, or they couldn't do it."

Social studies in the working-class schools is also largely mechanical, rote work that was given little explanation or connection to larger contexts. In one school, for example, although there was a book available, social studies work was to copy the teacher's notes from the board. Several times a week for a period of several months, the children copied these notes. The fifth grades in the district were to study U. S. history. The teacher used a booklet she had purchased called "The Fabulous Fifty States." Each day she put information from the booklet in outline form on the board and the children copied it. The type of information did not vary: the name of the state, its abbreviation, state capital, nickname of the state, its main products, main business, and a "Fabulous Fact" (e.g., "Idaho grew 27 billion potatoes in one year. That's enough potatoes for each man, woman and . . ."). As the children finished copying the sentences, the teacher erased them and wrote more. Children would occasionally go to the front to pull down the wall map in order to locate the states they were copying, and the teacher did not dissuade them. But the observer never saw her refer to the map; nor did the observer ever hear her make other than perfunctory remarks concerning the information the children were copying. Occasionally the children colored in a ditto and cut it out to make a stand-up figure (representing, for example, a man roping a cow in the Southwest). These were referred to by the teacher as their social studies "projects."

Rote behavior was often called for in classroom oral work. When going over math and language arts skills sheets, for example, as the teacher asked for the answer to each problem, he fired the questions rapidly, staccato, and the scene reminded the observer of a sergeant drilling recruits: above all, the questions demanded that you stay at attention: "the next one? What do I put here? . . . Here? Give us the next." Or "How many commas in this sentence? Where do I put them . . . The next one?"

The (four) fifth grade teachers observed in the working-class schools attempted to control classroom time and space by making decisions without consulting the children and without explaining the basis for their decisions. The teacher's control thus often seemed capricious. Teachers, for instance, very often ignored the bells to switch classes—deciding among themselves to keep the children after the period was officially over, to continue with the work, or for disciplinary reasons, or so they (the teachers) could stand in the hall and talk. There were no clocks in the rooms in either school, and the children often asked, "What period is this?" "When do we go to gym?" The children had no access to materials. These were handed out by teachers and closely guarded. Things in the room "belonged" to the teacher: "Bob, bring me my garbage can." The teachers continually gave the children orders. Only three times did the investigator hear a teacher in either working-class school preface a directive with an unsarcastic "please," or "let's" or "would you." Instead, the teachers said, "Shut up," "Shut your mouth," "Open your books," "Throw your *gum* away—if you want to rot your teeth, do it on your own time." Teachers made every effort to control the movement of the children, and often shouted, "Why are you out of your *seat??!!*". If the children got permission to leave the room they had to take a written pass with the date and time.

The control that the teachers have is less than they would like. It is a result of constant struggle with the children. The children continually resist the teachers' orders and the work itself. They do not directly challenge the teachers' authority or legitimacy, but they make indirect attempts to sabotage and resist the flow of assignments:

TEACHER:	I will put some problems on the board. You are to divide.
CHILD:	We got to divide?
TEACHER:	Yes.
SEVERAL CHILDREN:	(Groan) Not again. Mr. B., we done this yesterday.
CHILD:	Do we put the date?
TEACHER:	Yes. I hope we remember we work in silence. You're supposed to do it on white paper. I'll explain it later.
CHILD:	Somebody broke my pencil. (Crash—a child falls out of his chair.)
CHILD:	(repeats) Mr. B., somebody broke my *pencil!*
CHILD:	Are we going to be here all morning?
	(Teacher comes to the observer, shakes his head and grimaces, then smiles.)

The children are successful enough in their struggle against work that there are long periods where they are not asked to do any work, but just to sit and be quiet. Very often the work that the teachers assign is "easy," that is, not demanding, and thus receives less resistance. Sometimes a compromise is reached where, although the teachers insist that the children continue to work, there is a constant murmur of talk. The children will be doing arithmetic examples, copying social studies notes, or doing punctuation or other dittoes, and all the while there is muted but spirited conversation about somebody's broken arm, an afterschool disturbance of the day before, etc. Sometimes the teachers themselves join in the conversation because, as one teacher explained to me, "It's a relief from the routine."

Middle-class School. In the middle-class school, work is getting the right answer. If one accumulates enough right answers one gets a good grade. One must follow the directions in order to get the right answers, but the directions often call for some figuring, some choice, some decision making. For example, the children must often figure out by themselves what the directions ask them to do, and how to get the answer: what do you do first, second, and perhaps third? Answers are usually found in books or by listening to the teacher. Answers are usually words, sentences, numbers, or facts and dates; one writes them on paper, and one should be neat. Answers must be in the right order, and one can not make them up.

The following activities are illustrative. Math involves some choice: one may do two-digit division the long way, or the short way and there are some math problems that can be done "in your head." When the teacher explains how to do two-digit division, there is recognition that a cognitive process is involved; she gives several ways, and says, "I want to make sure you understand what you're doing—so you get it right"; and, when they go over the homework, she asks the *children* to tell how they did the problem and what answer they got.

In social studies the daily work is to read the assigned pages in the textbook and to answer the teacher's questions. The questions are almost always designed to check on whether the students have read the assignment and understood it: who did so-and-so; what happened after that; when did it happen, where, and sometimes, why did it happen? The answers are in the book and in one's understanding of the book; the teacher's hints when one doesn't know the answer are to "read it again," or to look at the picture or at the rest of the paragraph. One is to search for the answer in the "context," in what is given.

Language arts is "simple grammar, what they need for everyday life." The language arts teacher says, "They should learn to speak properly, to write business letters and thank-you letters, and to understand what nouns and verbs and simple subjects are." Here, as well, the actual work is to choose the right answers, to understand what is given. The teacher often says, "Please read the next sentence and then I'll question you about it." One teacher said in some exasperation to a boy who was fooling around in class, "If you don't know the answers to the questions I ask, then you can't stay in this *class!* (pause) You *never* know the answers to the questions I ask, and it's not fair to me—and certainly not to you!"

Most lessons are based on the textbook. This does not involve a critical perspective on what is given there. For example, a critical perspective in social studies is perceived as dangerous by these teachers because it may lead to controversial topics; the parents might complain. The children, however, are often curious, especially in social studies. Their questions are tolerated, and usually answered perfunctorily. But after a few minutes the teacher will say, "All right, we're not going any farther. Please open your social studies workbook." While the teachers spend a lot of time explaining and expanding on what the textbooks say, there is little attempt to analyze how or why things happen, or to give thought to how pieces of a culture, or, say, a system of numbers or elements of a language fit together or can be analyzed. What has happened in the past, and what exists now may not be equitable or fair, but (shrug) that is the way things are, and one does not confront such matters in school. For example, in social studies after a child is called on to read a passage about the pilgrims, the teacher summarizes the paragraph and then says, "So you can see how strict they were about everything." A child asks, "Why?" "Well, because they felt that if you weren't busy you'd get into trouble." Another child asks, "Is it true that they burned women at the stake? " The teacher says, "Yes, if a woman did anything strange, they handed them. [sic] What would a woman do, do you think, to make them burn them? [sic] See if you can come up with better answers than my other [social studies] class." Several children offer suggestions, to which the teacher nods but does not comment. Then she says, "OK, good," and calls on the next child to read.

Work tasks do not usually request creativity. Serious attention is rarely given in school work to *how* the children develop or express their own feelings and ideas, either linguistically or in graphic form. On the occasions when creativity or self-expression is requested, it is peripheral to the main activity, or it is "enrichment," or "for fun." During a lesson on what similes are, for example, the teacher explains what they are, puts several on the board, gives some other examples herself, and then asks the children if they can "make some up." She calls on three children who give similes, two of which are actually in the book they have open before them. The teacher does not comment on this, and then asks several others to choose similes from the list of phrases in the book. Several do so correctly, and she says, "Oh good! You're picking them out! See how good we are?" Their homework is to pick out the rest of the similes from the list.

Creativity is not often requested in social studies and science projects, either. Social studies projects, for example, are given with directions to "find information on your topic," and write it up. The children are not supposed to copy, but to "put it in your own words." Although a number of the projects subsequently went beyond the teacher's direction to find information and had quite expressive covers and inside illustrations, the teacher's evaluative comments had to do with the amount of information, whether they had "copied," and if their work was neat.

The style of control of the three fifth grade teachers observed in this school varied from somewhat easygoing to strict, but in contrast to the working-class schools, the teachers' decisions were usually based on external rules and regulations, for example, on criteria that were known or available to the children. Thus, the teachers always honor the bells for changing classes, and they usually evaluate children's work by what is in the textbooks and answer booklets.

There is little excitement in school work for the children, and the assignments are perceived as having little to do with their interests and feelings. As one child said, what you do is "store facts in your head like cold storage-until you need it later for a test, or your job." Thus, doing well is important because there are thought to be other likely rewards: a good job, or college.

Affluent Professional School. In the affluent professional school, work is creative activity carried out independently. The students are continually asked to express and apply ideas and concepts. Work involves individual thought and expressiveness, expansion and illustration of ideas, and choice of appropriate method and material. (The class is not considered an open classroom, and the principal explained that because of the large number of discipline problems in the fifth grade this year they did not departmentalize. The teacher who agreed to take part in the study said she is "more structured" this year than she usually is.) The products of work in this class are often written stories, editorials and essays, or representations of ideas in mural, graph, or craft form. The products of work should not be like everybody else's and should show individuality. They should exhibit good design, and (this is important), they must also fit empirical reality. Moreover, one's work should attempt to interpret or "make sense" of reality. The relatively few rules to be followed regarding work are usually criteria for, or limits on, individual activity. One's product is usually evaluated for the quality of its expression and for the appropriateness of its conception to the task. In many cases one's own satisfaction with the product is an important criterion for its evaluation. When right answers are called for, as in commercial materials like SRA (Science Research Associates) and math, it is important that the children decide on an answer as a result of thinking about the idea involved in what they're being asked to do. Teacher's hints are to "think about it some more."

The following activities are illustrative. The class takes home a sheet requesting each child's parents to fill in the number of cars they have, the number of television sets, refrigerators, games, or rooms in the house, etc. Each child is to figure the average number of a type of possession owned by the fifth grade. Each child must compile the "data" from all the sheets. A calculator is available in the classroom to do the mechanics of finding the average. Some children decide to send sheets to the fourth grade families for comparison. Their work should be "verified" by a classmate before it is handed in.

Each child and his or her family has made a geoboard. The teacher asks the class to get their geoboards from the side cabinet, to take a handful of rubber bands, and then to listen to what she would like them to do. She says, "I would like you to design a figure and then find the perimeter and area. When you have it, check with your neighbor. After you've done that, please transfer it to graph paper and tomorrow I'll ask you to make up a question about it for someone. When you hand it in, please let me know whose it is, and who verified it. Then I have something else for you to do that's really fun. (pause) Find the average number of chocolate chips in three cookies. I'll give you three cookies, and you'll have to eat your way through, I'm afraid!" Then she goes around the room and gives help, suggestions, praise, and admonitions that they are getting noisy. They work sitting, or standing up at their desks, at benches in the back, or on the floor. A child hands the teacher his paper and she comments, "I'm not accepting this paper. Do a better design." To another child she says, "That's fantastic! But you'll never find the area. Why don't you draw a figure inside [the big one] and subtract to get the area?"

The school district requires the fifth grades to study ancient civilizations (in particular, Egypt, Athens, and Sumer). In this classroom, the emphasis is on illustrating and re-creating the culture of the people of ancient times. The following are typical activities: The children made an 8mm film on Egypt, which one of the parents edited. A girl in the class wrote the script, and class acted it out. They put the sound on themselves. They read stories of those days. They wrote essays and stories depicting the lives of the people and the societal and occupational divisions. They chose from a list of projects, all of which involved graphic representations of ideas: for example, "Make a mural depicting the division of labor in Egyptian society."

Each child wrote and exchanged a letter in hieroglyphics with a fifth grader in another class, and they also exchanged stories they wrote in cuneiform. They made a scroll and singed the edges so it looked authentic. They each chose an occupation and made an Egyptian plaque representing that occupation, simulating the appropriate Egyptian design. They carved their design on a cylinder of wax, pressed the wax into clay, and then baked the clay. Although one girl did not choose an occupation, but carved instead a series of gods and slaves, the teacher said, "That's all right, Amber, it's beautiful." As they were working the teacher said, "don't cut into your clay until you're satisfied with your design."

Social studies also involves almost daily presentation by the children of some event from the news. The teacher's questions ask the children to expand what they say, to give more details, and to be more specific. Occasionally she adds some remarks to help them see connections between events.

The emphasis on expressing and illustrating ideas in social studies is accompanied in language arts by an emphasis on creative writing. Each child wrote a rhebus story for a first grader whom they had interviewed to see what kind of story the child liked best. They wrote editorials on pending decisions by the school board, and radio plays, some of which were read over the school intercom from the office, and one of which was performed in the auditorium. There is no language arts textbook because, the teacher said, "The principal wants us to be creative." There is not much grammar, but there is punctuation. One morning when the observer arrived the class was doing a punctuation ditto. The teacher later apologized for using the ditto. "It's just for review," she said. "I don't teach punctuation that way. We use their language." The ditto had three unambiguous rules for where to put commas in a sentence. As the teacher was going around to help the children with the ditto, she repeated several times, "Where you put commas depends on how you say the sentence; it depends on the situation and what you want to say. " Several weeks later the observer saw another punctuation activity. The teacher had printed a five-paragraph story on an oak tag and then cut it into phrases. She read the whole story to the class from the book, then passed out the phrases. The group had to decide how the phrases could best be put together again. (They arranged the phrases on the floor.) The point was not to replicate the story, although that was not irrelevant, but to "decide what you think the best way is." Punctuation marks on cardboard pieces were then handed out and the children discussed, and then decided, what mark was best at each place they thought one was needed. At the end of each paragraph the teacher asked, "Are you satisfied with the way the paragraphs are now? Read it to yourself and see how it sounds. " Then she read the original story again, and they compared the two.

Describing her goals in science to the investigator, the teacher said, "We use ESS (Elementary Science Study). It's very good because it gives a hands-on experience—so they can make sense out of it. It doesn't matter whether it [what they find] is right or wrong. I bring them together and there's value in discussing their ideas."

The products of work in this class are often highly valued by the children and the teacher. In fact, this was the only school in which the investigator was not allowed to take original pieces of the children's work for her files. If the work was small enough, however and was on paper, the investigator could duplicate it on the copying machine in the office.

The teacher's attempt to control the class involves constant negotiation. She does not give direct orders unless she is angry because the children have been too noisy. Normally, she tries to get them to foresee the consequences of their actions and to decide accordingly. For example, lining them up to go see a play written by the sixth graders, she says, "I presume you're lined up by someone with whom you want to sit. I hope you're lined up by someone you won't get in trouble with." The following two dialogues illustrate the process of negotiation between student and teacher.

TEACHER:	Tom, you're behind in your SRA this marking period.
TOM:	So what!
TEACHER:	Well, last time you had a hard time catching up.
TOM:	But I have my [music] lesson at 10:00.
TEACHER:	Well, that doesn't mean you're going to sit here for twenty minutes.
TOM:	Twenty minutes! OK. (He goes to pick out a SRA booklet and chooses one, puts it back, then takes another, and brings it to her.)
TEACHER:	OK, this is the one you want, right?
TOM:	Yes.
TEACHER:	OK, I'll put tomorrow's date on it so you can take it home tonight or finish it tomorrow if you want.
TEACHER:	(to a child who is wandering around during reading) Kevin, why don't you do *Reading for Concepts*?
KEVIN:	No, I don't like *Reading for Concepts*.
TEACHER:	Well, what are you going to do?
KEVIN:	(pause) I'm going to work on my DAR. (The DAR had sponsored an essay competition on "Life in the American Colonies.")

One of the few rules governing the children's movement is that no more than three children may be out of the room at once. There is a school rule that anyone can go to the library at any time to get a book. In the fifth grade I observed, they sign their name on the chalkboard and leave. There are no passes. Finally, the children have a fair amount of officially sanctioned say over what happens in the class. For example, they often negotiate what work is to be done. If the teacher wants to move on to the next subject, but the children say they are not ready, they want to work on their present projects some more, she very often lets them do it.

Executive Elite School. In the executive elite school, work is developing one's analytical intellectual powers. Children are continually asked to reason through a problem, to produce intellectual products that are both logically sound and of top academic quality. A primary goal of thought is to conceptualize rules by which elements may fit together in systems, and then to apply these rules in solving a problem. School work helps one to achieve, to excel, to prepare for life.

The following are illustrative. The math teacher teaches area and perimeter by having the children derive formulae for each. First she helps them, through discussion at the board, to arrive at $A = W \times L$ as a formula (not *the* formula) for area. After discussing several, she says, "Can anyone make up a formula for perimeter? Can you figure that out yourselves? (pause) Knowing what we know, can we think of a formula?" She works out three children's suggestions at the board, saying to two, "Yes, that's a good one," and then asks the class if they can think of any more. No one volunteers. To prod them, she says, "If you use rules and good reasoning, you get many ways. Chris, can you think up a formula?"

She discusses two-digit division with the children as a decision-making process. Presenting a new type of problem to them, she asks, "What's the first decision you'd make if presented with this kind of example? What is the first thing you'd think? Craig?" Craig says, "To find my first partial quotient." She responds, "Yes, that would by your first decision. How would you do that?" Craig explains, and then the teacher says, "OK, we'll see how that works for you." The class tries his way. Subsequently, she comments on the merits and shortcomings of several other children's decisions. Later, she tells the investigator that her goals in math are to develop their reasoning and mathematical thinking and that, unfortunately, "there's no time for manipulables."

While right answers are important in math, they are not "given" by the book or by the teacher, but may be challenged by the children. Going over some problems in late September the teacher says, "Raise your hand if you do not agree." A child says, "I don't agree with 64." the teacher responds, "OK, there's a question about 64. (to class) Please check it. Owen, they're disagreeing with you. Kristen, they're checking yours." The teacher emphasized this repeatedly during September and October with statements like, "Don't be afraid to say if you disagree. In the last [math] class, somebody disagreed, and they were right. Before you disagree, check yours, and if you still think we're wrong, then we'll check it out." By Thanksgiving, the children did not often speak in terms of right and wrong math problems, but of whether they agreed with the answer that had been given.

There are complicated math mimeos with many word problems. Whenever they go over the examples, they discuss how each child has set up the problem. The children must explain it precisely. On one occasion the teacher said, "I'm more—just as interested in how you set up the problem as in what answer you find. If you set up a problem in a good way, the answer is easy to find."

Social studies work is most often reading and discussion of concepts and independent research. There are only occasional artistic, expressive, or illustrative projects. Ancient Athens and Sumer are, rather, societies to analyze. The following questions are typical of those which guide the children's independent research: "What mistakes did Pericles make after the war?" "What mistakes did the citizens of Athens, make?" "What are the elements of a civilization?" "How did Greece build an economic empire?" "Compare the way Athens chose its leaders with the way we choose ours." Occasionally the children are asked to make up sample questions for their social studies tests. On an occasion when the investigator was present the social studies teacher rejected a child's question by saying, "That's just fact. If I asked you that question on a test, you'd complain it was just memory! Good questions ask for concepts."

In social studies—but also in reading, science, and health—the teachers initiate classroom discussions of current social issues and problems. These discussions occurred on every one of the investigator's visits, and a teacher told me, "These children's opinions are important—it's important that they learn to reason things through." The classroom discussions always struck the observer as quite realistic and analytical, dealing with concrete social issues like the following: "Why do workers strike?" "Is that right or wrong?" "Why do we have inflation, and what can be done to stop it" "Why do companies put chemicals in food when the natural ingredients are available?" etc. Usually the children did not have to be prodded to give their opinions. In fact, their statements and the interchanges between them struck the observer as quite sophisticated conceptually and verbally, and well-informed. Occasionally the teachers would prod with statements such as, "Even if you don't know [the answers], if you think logically about it, you can figure it out." And "I'm asking you [these] questions to help you think this through."

Language arts emphasizes language as a complex system, one that should be mastered. The children are asked to diagram sentences of complex grammatical construction, to memorize irregular verb conjugations (he lay, he has lain, etc. . . .), and to use the proper participles, conjunctions, and interjections in their speech. The teacher (the same one who teaches social studies) told them, "It is not enough to get these right on tests; you must use what you learn [in grammar classes] in your written and oral work. I will grade you on that."

Most writing assignments are either research reports and essays for social studies, or experiment analyses and write-ups for science. There is only an occasional story or other "creative writing" assignment. On the occasion observed by the investigator (the writing of a Halloween story), the points the teacher stressed in preparing the children to write involved the structural aspects of a story rather than the expression of feelings or other ideas. The teacher showed them a filmstrip, "The Seven Parts of a Story," and lectured them on plot development, mood setting, character development, consistency, and the use of a logical or appropriate ending. The stories they subsequently wrote were, in fact, well-structured, but many were also personal and expressive. The teacher's evaluative comments, however, did not refer to the expressiveness or artistry, but were all directed toward whether they had "developed" the story well.

Language arts work also involved a large amount of practice in presentation of the self and in managing situations where the child was expected to be in charge. For example, there was a series of assignments in which each child had to be a "student teacher." The child had to plan a lesson in grammar, outlining, punctuation, or other language arts topics and explain the concept to the class. Each child was to prepare a worksheet or game and a homework assignment as well. After each presentation, the teacher and other children gave a critical appraisal of the "student teacher's" performance. Their criteria were: whether the student spoke clearly; whether the lesson was interesting; whether the student made any mistakes; and whether he or she kept control of the class. On an occasion when a child did not maintain control, the teacher said, "When you're up there, you have authority, and you have to use it. I'll back you up."

The teacher of math and science explained to the observer that she likes the ESS program because "the children can manipulate variables. They generate hypotheses and devise experiments to solve the problem. They have to explain what they found."

The executive elite school is the only school where bells do not demarcate the periods of time. The two fifth grade teachers were very strict about changing classes on schedule, however, as specific plans for each session had been made. The teachers attempted to keep tight control over the children during lessons, and the children were sometimes flippant, boisterous, and occasionally, rude. However, the children may be brought into line by reminding them that "it is up to you." "You must control yourself", "you are responsible for your work," you must "set your priorities." One teacher told a child, "You are the only driver of your car—and only you can regulate your speed." A new teacher complained to the observer that she had thought "these children" would have more control.

While strict attention to the lesson at hand is required, the teachers make relatively little attempt to regulate the movement of the children at other times. For example, except for the kindergartners, the children in this school do not have to wait for the bell to ring in the morning; they may go to their classroom when they arrive at school. Fifth graders often came early to read, to finish work, or to catch up. After the first two months of school the fifth grade teachers did not line the children up to change classes or to go to gym, etc., but, when the children were ready and quiet, they were told they could go—sometimes without the teachers.

In the classroom, the children could get materials when they needed them and took what they needed from closets and from the teacher's desk. They were in charge of the office at lunchtime. During class they did not have to sign out or ask permission to leave the room; they just got up and left. Because of the pressure to get work done, however, they did not leave the room very often. The teachers were very polite to the children, and the investigator heard no sarcasm, no nasty remarks, and few direct orders. The teachers never called the children "honey," or "dear," but always called them by name. The teachers were expected to be available before school, after school, and for part of their lunch time to provide extra help if needed.

The foregoing analysis of differences in school work in contrasting social class contexts suggests the following conclusion: the "hidden curriculum" of school work is tacit preparation for relating to the process of production in a particular way. Differing curricular, pedagogical, and pupil evaluation practices emphasize different cognitive and behavioral skills in each social setting and thus contribute to the development in the children of certain potential relationships to physical and symbolic capital, to authority, and to the process of work. School experience, in the sample of schools discussed here, differed qualitatively by social class. These differences may not only contribute to the development in the children in each social class of certain types of economically significant relationships and not others, but would thereby help to reproduce this system of relations in society. In the contribution to the reproduction of unequal social relations lies a theoretical meaning, and social consequence, of classroom practice.

The identification of different emphases in classrooms in a sample of contrasting social class contexts implies that further research should be conducted in a large number of schools to investigate the types of work tasks and interactions in each, to see if they differ in the ways discussed here, and to see if similar potential relationships are uncovered. Such research could have as a product the further elucidation of complex but not readily apparent connections between everyday activity in schools and classrooms and the unequal structure of economic relationships in which we work and live.

Notes

1. But see, in a related vein, Apple and King (1977) and Rist (1973).

2. The U. S. Bureau of the Census defines "poverty" for a nonfarm family of four as a yearly income of $6,191 a year or less. U.S. Bureau of the Census, *Statistical Abstract of the United States: 1978* (Washington, D.C.: U.S. Government Printing Office, 1978, p. 465, table 754).

3. This figure is an estimate. According to the Bureau of the Census, only 2.6 percent of families in the United States have money income of $50,000 or over. U. S. Bureau of the Census, *Current Population Reports*, series P-60, no. 118, "Money Income in 1977 of Families and Persons in the United States." [Washington, D.C.: U.S. Government Printing Office, 1979, p. 2, table A). For figures on income at these higher levels, see Smith and Franklin (1974).

4. A dominant feeling, expressed directly and indirectly by teachers in this school, was boredom with their work. They did, however, in contrast to the working-class schools, almost always carry out lessons during class times.

References

Althusser, L. Ideology and ideological state apparatuses. In L. Althusser,
Lenin and philosophy and other essays. Ben Brewster, Trans. New York: Monthly Review Press, 1971.

Anyon, J. Elementary social studies textbooks and legitimating knowledge.
Theory and Research in Social Education, 1978, 6, 40-55.

Anyon, J. Ideology and United States history textbooks.
Harvard Educational Review, 1979, 49, 36 1-386.

Apple, M. W. *Ideology and curriculum*. Boston: Routledge and Kegan Paul, 1979.

Apple, M. W., & King, N. What do schools teach? *Curriculum Inquiry*, 1977, 6, 341-358.

Aronowitz, S. Marx, Braverman, and the logic of capital.
The Insurgent Sociologist, 1978, 8, 126-146.

Benson, S. The clerking sisterhood: rationalization and the work culture of saleswomen in American department stores, 1890-1960. *Radical America*, 1978, 12, 4 1- 5 5.

Berstein, B. *Class, codes and control, Vol. 3. Towards a theory of educational transmission*.
2nd ed. London: Routledge and Kegan Paul, 1977.

Bourdieu. P. and Passeron, J. *Reproduction in education, society, and culture*. Beverly Hills, Calif.: Sage, 1977.

Bowles, S. & Gintis, H. *Schooling in capitalist America: educational reform and the contradictions of economic life*. New York: Basic Books, 1976.

Braverman, H. Labor and monopoly capital: the degradation of work in the twentieth century. New York: Monthly Review Press, 1974.

Dreeben, R. *On what is learned in school.* Reading, Mass.: Addison-Wesley, 1968.

Jackson, P. *Life in classrooms.* Holt, Reinhart & Winston, 1968.

Lampman, R. J. The share of top wealth-holders in national wealth, 1922-1956: A study of the National Bureau of Economic Research. Princeton, N. J.: Princeton University Press, 1962.

Levison, A. *The working-class majority.* New York: Penguin Books, 1974.

New York Stock Exchange. *Census.* New York: New York Stock Exchange, 1975.

Rist, R. C. *The urban school: a factory for failure.* Cambridge, Mass.: MIT Press, 1973.

Sarasan, S. *The culture of school and the problem of change.* Boston: Allyn and Bacon, 1971.

Smith, J. D. and Franklin, S. The concentration of personal wealth 1922-1969. *American Economic Review*, 1974, *64*, 162-167

U.S. Bureau of the Census. Current population reports. Series P-60, no. 118. Money income in 1977 of families and persons in the United States. Washington, D.C.: U.S. Government Printing Office, 1979.

U.S. Bureau of the Census. *Statistical abstract of the United States: 1978* Washington, D.C.: U.S. Government Printing Office, 1978.

Williams, R. *Marxism and literature.* New York: Oxford University Press, 1977.

Wright, E. O. *Class, crisis and the state.* London: New Left Books, 1978.

Questions for Discussion

1. What is the "hidden curriculum" of Anyon's title?

2. Look carefully at Anyon's descriptions of language arts and writing instruction in each of the four types of schools. What differences do you notice among the methods and activities? What influence might these different approaches have on the developing literacy of the students?

3. In the middle-class school, Anyon observed that students were not asked to take a "critical perspective on" the topics covered in their social studies work. Such a goal, Anyon believes, is ignored by teachers in these schools because "it may lead to controversial topics; the parents might complain." What are the implications of not encouraging students' critical awareness and critical thinking? Why might avoiding confrontation and controversy be in the school's (and society's) interest?

Explorations

1. What do the everyday activities of college classrooms you're in this term reveal about the educational goals of the university and the instructors who teach there? Do the activities and expectations differ from course to course? If so, what might account for the differences?

3. In her description of the working-class schools, Anyon records that one teacher commented that she has to provide students strict instructions for their work because without them, "they couldn't do it." (Rose makes a similar comment when he writes that "students will float to the mark" teachers set.) What are the implications of this teacher's practice of scripting every move her students make?

4. Anyon's essay provides some interesting data from which to determine the extent to which socio-economic class and educational concept coincide. To what degree can Freire's banking and problem-posing concepts illuminate differences between the schools? What methods in each school suggest that it espouses a banking or problem posing approach to education?

Formal Writing Assignments

1. Anyon argues that there is very likely a connection "between everyday activity in schools and classrooms and the unequal structure of economic relationships in which we work and live." In an essay, describe and analyze the everyday activities in an elementary or secondary classroom with which you are familiar. What do these activities tell you about what teachers and schools think is important for students to learn? What kinds of out-of-school activities do they seem to be preparing students for?

2. Locate and read the websites of two or three school districts in your home state or in the state in which you're attending college. You may select schools from three districts with different socio-economic demographics (e.g., working-class, middleclass, and affluent professional) or schools from districts with similar demographics. The information you search for and questions you ask will be determined a good deal by the districts you select and the sophistication of their websites, but in many cases, information about the districts' stated educational goals and philosophy will prove useful. After reviewing the websites, compare and contrast the information, analyzing it for an audience of citizens in the state interested in knowing how the districts characterize their expectations.

America Skips School

Benjamin R. Barber

Benjamin R. Barber (b. 1939) teaches political science at Rutgers University in New Brunswick, New Jersey. In addition to scholarly articles and books, Barber has published five plays and a novel. His most recent books, *A Passion for Democracy: American Essays* and *A Place for Us: Civilizing Society and Domesticating the Marketplace,* were published in 1998. "America Skips School" was published in *Harper's* in 1993. In this essay, Barber wonders if society has lost sight of the original goals of public education.

Writing Before Reading

1. Which has had a greater influence on shaping your values and beliefs: school or television? Which has better prepared you to participate in our democratic form of government?

2. How would the working challenges faced by a teacher in an elementary school be different from those faced by an attorney who analyzes tax law for a major corporation? Typically, an attorney would be paid a higher salary than a teacher. Could an argument be made that the attorney also contributes more to the well-being of our society?

3. What would you say to someone who defines "freedom" as "lack of responsibility"? Are these two things one and the same?

America Skips School

On September 8, the day most of the nation's children were scheduled to return to school, the Department of Education Statistics issued a report, commissioned by Congress, on adult literacy and numeracy in the United States. The results? More than 90 million adult Americans lacked simple literacy. Fewer than 20 percent of those surveyed could compare two metaphors in a poem; not 4 percent could calculate the cost of carpeting at a given price for a room of a given size, using a calculator. As the DOE report was being issued, as if to echo its findings, two of the nation's largest school systems had delayed their openings: in New York, to remove asbestos from aging buildings; in Chicago, because of a battle over the budget.

Inspired by the report and the delays, pundits once again began chanting the familiar litany of the education crisis. We've heard it all many times before: 130,000 children bring guns along with their pencils and books to school each morning; juvenile arrests for murder increased by 85 percent from 1987 to 1991; more than 3,000 youngsters will drop out today and every day for the rest of the school year, until about 600,000 are lost by June—in many urban schools, perhaps half the enrollment. A lot of the dropouts will end up in prison, which is a surer bet for young black males than college: one in four will pass through the correctional system, and at least two out of three of those will be dropouts.

In quiet counterpoint to those staggering facts is another set of statistics: teachers make less than accountants, architects, doctors, lawyers, engineers, judges, health professionals, auditors, and surveyors, They can earn higher salaries teaching in Berlin, Tokyo, Ottawa, or Amsterdam than in New York or Chicago. American children are in school only about 180 days a year, as against 240 days or more for children in Europe or Japan. The richest school districts (school financing is local, not federal) spend twice as much per student as poorer ones do. The poorer ones seem almost beyond help: children with venereal disease or AIDS (2.5 million adolescents annually contract a sexually transmitted disease), gangs in the schoolyard, drugs in the classroom, children doing babies instead of homework, playground fire-fights featuring Uzis and Glocks.

Clearly, the social contract that obliges adults to pay taxes so that children can be educated is in imminent danger of collapse. Yet for all the astonishing statistics, more astonishing still is that no one seems to be listening. The education crisis is kind of like violence on television: the worse it gets the more inert we become, and the more of it we require to rekindle our attention. We've had a "crisis" every dozen years or so at least since the launch of *Sputnik*, in 1957, when American schools were accused of falling behind the world standard in science education. Just ten years ago, the National Commission on Excellence in Education warned that America's pedagogical inattention was putting America "at risk." What the com-mission called "a rising tide of mediocrity" was imperiling "our very future as a Nation and a people." What was happening to education was an "act of war."

Since then, countless reports have been issued decrying the condition of our educational system, the DOE report being only the most recent. They have come from every side, Republican as well as Democrat, from the private sector as well as the public. Yet for all the talk, little happens. At times, the schools look more like they are being dismantled than rebuilt. How can this be? If Americans over a broad political spectrum regard education as vital, why has nothing been done?

I have spent thirty years as a scholar examining the nature of democracy, and even more as a citizen optimistically celebrating its possibilities, but today I am increasingly persuaded that the reason for the country's inaction is that Americans do not really care about education—the country has grown comfort-able with the game of "let's pretend we care."

As America's educational system crumbles, the pundits, instead of looking for solutions, search busily for scapegoats. Some assail the teachers—those "Profscam" pedagogues trained in the licentious Sixties who, as aging hippies, are supposedly still subverting the schools—for producing a dire illiteracy. Others turn on the kids themselves, so that at the same moment as we are transferring our responsibilities to the shoulders of the next generation, we are blaming them for our generation's most conspicuous failures. Allan Bloom was typical of the many recent critics who have condemned the young as vapid, lazy, selfish, complacent, self-seeking, materialistic, small-minded, apathetic, greedy, and, of course, illiterate. E. D. Hirsch in his *Cultural Literacy* and Diane Ravitch and Chester E. Finn Jr. in their *What Do Our Seventeen-Year-Olds Know?* have lambasted the schools, the teachers, and the children for betraying the adult generation from which they were to inherit, the critics seemed confident, a precious cultural legacy.

How this captious literature reeks of hypocrisy! How sanctimonious all the hand-wringing over still another "education crisis" seems. Are we ourselves really so literate? Are our kids stupid or smart for ignor-ing what we preach and copying what we practice? The young, with their keen noses for hypocrisy, are in fact adept readers—but not of books. They are society-smart rather than school-smart, and what they read so acutely are the social signals emanating from the world in which they will have to make a living. Their teachers in that world, the nation's true pedagogues, are television, advertising, movies, politics, and the celebrity domains they define. We prattle about deficient schools and the gullible youngsters they turn out, so vulnerable to the siren song of drugs, but think nothing of letting the advertisers into the classroom to fashion what an *Advertising Age* essay calls "brand and product loyalties through classroom-centered, peer-powered lifestyle patterning."

Our kids spend 900 hours a year in school (the ones who go to school) and from 1,200 to 1,800 hours a year in front of the television set. From which are they likely to learn more? Critics such as Hirsch and Ravitch want to find out what our seventeen-year-olds know, but it's really pretty simple: they know exactly what our forty-seven-year-olds know and teach them by example—on television, in the boardroom, around Washington, on Madison Avenue, in Hollywood. The very first lesson smart kids learn is that it is much more important to heed what society teaches implicitly by its deeds and reward structures than what school teaches explicitly in its lesson plans and civic sermons. Here is a test for adults that may help reveal what the kids see when they look at our world.

REAL-WORLD CULTURAL LITERACY

1. According to television, having fun in America means

    a) going blond
    b) drinking Pepsi
    c) playing Nintendo
    d) wearing Air Jordans
    e) reading Mark Twain

2. A good way to prepare for a high-income career and to acquire status in our society is to

    a) win a slam-dunk contest
    b) take over a company and sell off its assets
    c) start a successful rock band
    d) earn a professional degree
    e) become a kindergarten teacher

3. Book publishers are financially rewarded today for publishing

    a) mega-cookbooks
    b) mega-cat books
    c) megabooks by Michael Crichton
    d) megabooks by John Grisham
    e) mini-books by Voltaire

4. A major California bank that advertised "no previous credit history required" in inviting Berkeley students to apply for Visa cards nonetheless turned down one group of applicants because

    a) their parents had poor credit histories
    b) they had never held jobs
    c) they had outstanding student loans
    d) they were "humanities majors"

5. Colleges and universities are financially rewarded today for

    a) supporting bowl-quality football games
    b) forging research relationships with large corporations
    c) sustaining professional programs in law and business
    d) stroking wealthy alumni
    e) fostering outstanding philosophy departments

6. Familiarity with *Henry, IV Part II* is likely to be of vital importance in

    a) planning a corporate takeover
    b) evaluating budget cuts in the Department of Education
    c) initiating a medical-malpractice lawsuit
    d) writing an impressive job résumé
    c) taking a test on what our seventeen-year-olds know

7. To help the young learn that "history is a living thing," Scholastic, Inc., a publisher of magazines and paper-backs, recently distributed to 40,000 junior and senior high school classrooms

   a) a complimentary video of the award-winning series *The Civil War*
   b) free copies of Plato's *Dialogues*
   c) an abridgment of Alexis Tocqueville's *Democracy in America*
   d) a wall-size Periodic Table of the Elements
   e) gratis copies of Billy Joel's hit single "We Didn't Start the Fire" (which recounts history via a vaguely chronological list of warbled celebrity names)

My sample of forty-seven-year-olds scored very well on the test. Not surprisingly, so did their seventeen-year-old children. (For each question, either the last entry is correct or all responses are correct except the last one.) The results of the test reveal again the deep hypocrisy that runs through our lamentations about education. The illiteracy of the young turns out to be our own reflected back to us with embarrassing force. We honor ambition, we reward greed, we celebrate materialism, we worship acquisitiveness, we cherish success, and we commercialize the classroom—and then we bark at the young about the gentle arts of the spirit. We recommend history to the kids but rarely consult it ourselves. We make a fuss about ethics but are satisfied to see it taught as an "add-on," as in "ethics in medicine" or "ethics in business"—as if Sunday morning in church could compensate for uninterrupted sinning from Monday to Saturday.

The children are onto this game. They know that if we really valued schooling, we'd pay teachers what we pay stockbrokers; if we valued books, we'd spend a little something on the libraries so that adults could read, too; if we valued citizenship, we'd give national service and civic education more than pilot status; if we valued children, we wouldn't let them be abused, manipulated, impoverished, and killed in their beds by gang-war cross fire and stray bullets. Schools can and should lead, but when they confront a society that in every instance tells a story exactly opposite to the one they are supposed to be teaching, their job becomes impossible. When the society undoes each workday what the school tries to do each day, schooling can't make much of a difference.

Inner-city children are not the only ones who are learning the wrong lessons. TV sends the same messages to everyone, and the success of Donald Trump, Pete Rose, Henry Kravis, or George Steinbrenner makes them potent role models, whatever their values. Teen dropouts are not blind; teen drug sellers are not deaf; teen college students who avoid the humanities in favor of pre-business or pre-law are not stupid. Being apt pupils of reality, they learn their lessons well. If they see a man with a rubber arm and an empty head who can throw a ball at 95 miles per hour pulling down millions of dollars a year while a dedicated primary-school teacher is getting crumbs, they will avoid careers in teaching even if they can't make the major leagues. If they observe their government spending up to $35,000 a year to keep a young black behind bars but a fraction of that to keep him in school, they will write off school (and probably write off blacks as well).

Our children's illiteracy is merely our own, which they assume with commendable prowess. They know what we have taught them all too well: there is nothing in Homer or Virginia Woolf, in Shakespeare or Toni Morrison, that will advantage them in climbing to the top of the American heap. Academic credentials may still count, but schooling in and of itself is for losers. Bookworms. Nerds. Inner-city rappers and fraternity-house wise guys are in full agreement about that. The point is to start pulling down the big bucks. Some kids just go into business earlier than others. Dropping out is the national pastime, if by dropping out we mean giving up the precious things of the mind and the spirit in which America shows so little interest and for which it offers so little payback. While the professors argue about whether to teach the ancient history of a putatively white Athens or the ancient history of a putatively black Egypt, the kids are watching televised political campaigns driven by mindless image-mongering and inflammatory polemics that ignore history altogether. Why, then, are we so surprised when our students dismiss the debate over the origins of civilization, whether Eurocentric or Afrocentric, and concentrate on cash-and-carry careers? Isn't the choice a tribute not to their ignorance but to their adaptive intelligence? Although we can hardly be proud of ourselves for what we are teaching them, we should at least be proud of them for how well they've learned our lessons.

Not all Americans have stopped caring about the schools, however. In the final irony of the educational endgame, cynical entrepreneurs like Chris Whittle are insinuating television into the classroom itself, bribing impoverished school boards by offering free TV sets on which they can show advertising for children—sold to sponsors at premium rates. Whittle, the mergers and acquisitions mogul of education, is trying to get rich off the poverty of public schools and the fears of parents. Can he really believe advertising in the schools enhances education? Or is he helping to corrupt public schools in ways that will make parents even more anxious to use vouchers for private schools—which might one day be run by Whittle's latest entrepreneurial venture, the Edison Project.

According to Lifetime Learning Systems, an educational software company, "kids spend 40 percent of each day... where traditional advertising can't reach them." Not to worry, says Lifetime Learning in an *Advertising Age* promo: "Now, you can enter the classroom through custom-made learning materials created with your specific marketing objectives in mind. Communicate with young spenders directly and, through them, their teachers and families as well." If we redefine young learners as "young spenders," are the young really to be blamed for acting like mindless consumers? Can they become young spenders and still become young critical thinkers, let alone informed citizens? If we are willing to give TV cartoons the government's imprimatur as "educational television" (as we did a few years ago, until the FCC changed its mind), can we blame kids for educating themselves on television trash?

Everyone can agree that we should educate our children to be something more than young spenders molded by "lifestyle patterning." But what should the goals of the classroom be? In recent years it has been fashionable to define the educational crisis in terms of global competition and minimal competence, as if schools were no more than vocational institutions. Although it has talked sensibly about education, the Clinton Administration has leaned toward this approach, under the tutelage of Secretary of Labor Robert Reich.

The classroom, however, should not be merely a trade school. The fundamental task of education in a democracy is what Tocqueville once called the apprenticeship of liberty: learning to be free. I wonder whether Americans still believe liberty has to be learned and that its skills are worth learning. Or have they been deluded by two centuries of rhetoric into thinking that freedom is "natural" and can be taken for granted?

The claim that all men are born free, upon which America was founded, is at best a promising fiction. In real life, as every parent knows, children are born fragile, born needy, born ignorant, born unformed, born weak, born foolish, born dependent—born in chains. We acquire our freedom over time, if at all. Embedded in families, clans, communities, and nations, we must learn to be free. We may be natural consumers and born narcissists, but citizens have to be made. Liberal-arts education actually means education in the arts of liberty; the "servile arts" were the trades learned by unfree men in the Middle Ages, the vocational education of their day. Perhaps this is why Thomas Jefferson preferred to memorialize his founding of the University of Virginia on his tombstone rather than his two terms as president; it is certainly why he viewed his Bill for the More General Diffusion of Knowledge in Virginia as a centerpiece of his career (although it failed passage as legislation—times were perhaps not so different). John Adams, too, boasted regularly about Massachusetts's high literacy rates and publicly funded education.

Jefferson and Adams both understood that the Bill of Right offered little protection in a nation without informed citizens. Once educated, however, a people was safe from even the subtlest tyrannies. Jefferson's democratic proclivities rested on his conviction that education could turn a people into a safe refuge—indeed "the only safe depository" for the ultimate powers of society. "Cherish therefore the spirit of our people," he wrote to Edward Carrington in 1787, "and keep alive their attention. Do not be severe upon their errors, but reclaim them by enlightening them. If once they become inattentive to public affairs, you and I and Congress and Assemblies, judges and governors, shall all become wolves."

The logic of democracy begins with public education, proceeds to informed citizenship, and comes to fruition in the securing of rights and liberties. We have been nominally democratic for so long that we presume it is our natural condition rather than the product of persistent effort and tenacious responsibility. We have decoupled rights from civic responsibilities and severed citizenship from education on the false assumption that citizens just happen. We have forgotten that the "public" in public schools means not just paid for by the public but procreative of the very idea of a public. Public schools are how a public—a citizenry—is forged and how young, selfish individuals turn into conscientious, community-minded citizens.

Among the several literacies that have attracted the anxious attention of commentators, civic literacy has been the least visible. Yet this is the fundamental literacy by which we live in a civil society. It encompasses the competence to participate in democratic communities, the ability to think critically and act with deliberation in a pluralistic world, and the empathy to identify sufficiently with others to live with them despite conflicts of interest and differences in character. At the most elementary level, what our children suffer from most, whether they're hurling racial epithets from fraternity porches or shooting one another down in schoolyards, is the absence of civility. Security guards and metal detectors are poor surrogates for civility, and they make our schools look increasingly like prisons (though they may be less safe than prisons). Jefferson thought schools would produce free men: we prove him right by putting dropouts in jail.

Civility is a work of the imagination, for it is through the imagination that we render others sufficiently like ourselves for them to become subjects of tolerance and respect, if not always affection. Democracy is anything but a "natural" form of association. It is an extraordinary and rare contrivance of cultivated imagination. Give the uneducated the right to participate in making collective decisions, and what results is not democracy but, as best, mob rule: the government of private prejudice once known as the tyranny of opinion. For Jefferson, the difference between the democratic temperance he admired in agrarian America and the rule of the rabble he condemned when viewing the social unrest of Europe's teeming cities was quite simply education. Madison had hoped to "filter" out popular passion through the device of representation. Jeferson saw in education a filter that could be installed within each individual, giving to each the capacity to rule prudently. Education creates a ruling aristocracy constrained by temperance and wisdom; when that education is public and universal, it is an aristocracy to which all can belong. At its best, the American dream of a free and equal society governed by judicious citizens has been this dream of an aristocracy of everyone.

To dream this dream of freedom is easy, but to secure it is difficult as well as expensive. Notwithstanding their lamentations, Americans do not appear ready to pay the price. There is no magic bullet for education. But I no longer can accept that the problem lies in the lack of consensus about remedies—in a dearth of solutions. There is no shortage of debate over how to repair our educational infrastructure. National standards or more local control? Vouchers or better public schools? More parental involvement or more teacher autonomy? A greater federal presence (only 5 or 6 percent of the nation's education budget is federally funded) or fairer local school taxes? More multicultural diversity or more emphasis on what Americans share in common? These are honest disputes. But I am convinced that the problem is simpler and more fundamental. Twenty years ago, writer and activist Frances Moore Lappé captured the essence of the world food crisis when she argued that starvation was caused not by a scarcity of food but by a global scarcity in democracy. The education crisis has the same genealogy. It stems from a dearth of democracy: an absence of democratic will and a consequent refusal to take our children, our schools, and our future seriously.

Most educators, even while they quarrel among themselves, will agree that a genuine commitment to any one of a number of different solutions could help enormously. Most agree that although money can't by itself solve problems, without money few problems can be solved. Money also can't win wars or put men in space, but it is the crucial facilitator. It is also how America has traditionally announced, We are serious about this!

If we were serious, we would raise teachers' salaries to levels that would attract the best young professionals in our society: starting lawyers get from $70,000 to $80,000—why don't starting kindergarten teachers get the same? Is their role in vouchsafing our future less significant? And although there is evidence suggesting that an increase in general educational expenditures doesn't translate automatically into better schools, there is also evidence that an increase aimed specifically at instructional service does. Can we really take in earnest the chattering devotion to excellence of a country so wedded in practice to mediocrity, a nation so ready to relegate teachers—conservators of our common future—to the professional backwaters?

If we were serious, we would upgrade physical facilities so that every school met the minimum standards of our better suburban institutions. Good buildings do not equal good education, but can any education at all take place in leaky, broken-down habitats of the kind described by Jonathan Kozol in his *Savage Inequalities*? If money is not a critical factor, why are our most successful suburban school districts funded at nearly twice the level of our inner-city schools? Being even at the starting line cannot guarantee that the runners will win or even finish the race, but not being even pretty much assures failure. We would rectify the balance not by penalizing wealthier communities but by bringing poorer communities up to standard, perhaps by finding other sources of funding for our schools besides property taxes.

If we were serious, we'd extend the school year by a month or two so that learning could take place throughout the year. We'd reduce class size (which means more teachers) and nurture more cooperative learning so that kids could become actively responsible for their own education and that of their classmates. Perhaps most important, we'd raise standards and make teachers and students responsible for them. There are two ways to breed success: to lower standards so that everybody "passes" in a way that loses all meaning in the real world; and to raise standards and then meet them, so that school success translates into success beyond the classroom. From Confucian China to Imperial England, great nations have built their success in the world upon an education of excellence. The challenge in a democracy is to find a way to maintain excellence while extending educational opportunity to everyone.

Finally, if we were serious, parents, teachers, and students would be the real players while administrators, politicians, and experts would be secondary, at best advisers whose chief skill ought to be knowing when and how to facilitate the work of teachers and then get out of the way. If the Democrats can clean up federal government bureaucracy (the Gore plan), perhaps we can do the same for educational bureaucracy. In New York up to half of the city's teachers occupy jobs outside the classroom. No other enterprise is run that way: Half the soldiers at company headquarters? Half the cops at stationhouse desks? Half the working force in the assistant manager's office? Once the teachers are back in the classroom, they will need to be given more autonomy, more professional responsibility for the success or failure of their students. And parents will have to be drawn in not just because they have rights or because they are politically potent but because they have responsibilities and their children are unlikely to learn without parental engagement. How to define the parental role in the classroom would become serious business for educators.

Some Americans will say this is unrealistic. Times are tough, money's short, and the public is fed up with almost all of its public institutions: the schools are just one more frustrating disappointment. With all the goodwill in the world, it is still hard to know how schools can cure the ills that stem from the failure of so many other institutions. Saying we want education to come first won't put it first.

America, however, has historically been able to accomplish what it sets its mind to. When we wish it and will it, what we wish and will has happened. Our successes are willed; our failures seem to happen when will is absent. There are, of course, those who benefit from the bankruptcy of public education and the failure of democracy. But their blame is no greater than our own: in a world where doing nothing has such dire consequences, complacency has become a greater sin than malevolence.

In wartime, whenever we have known why we were fighting and believed in the cause, we have prevailed. Because we believe in profits, we are consummate salespersons and efficacious entrepreneurs. Because we love sports, ours are the dream teams. Why can't a Chicago junior high school be as good as the Chicago Bulls? Because we cherish individuality and mobility, we have created a magnificent (if costly) car culture and the world's largest automotive consumer market. Even as our lower schools are among the worst in the Western world, our graduate institutions are among the very best because professional training in medicine, law, and technology is vital to our ambitions and because corporate America backs up state and federal priorities in this crucial domain. Look at the things we do well and observe how very well we do them: those are the things that as a nation we have willed.

Then observe what we do badly and ask yourself, Is it because the challenge is too great? Or is it because, finally, we aren't really serious? Would we will an end to the carnage and do whatever it took—more cops, state militias, federal marshals, the Marines?—if the dying children were white and middle class? Or is it a disdain for the young—white, brown, and black—that inures us to the pain? Why are we so sensitive to the retirees whose future (however foreshortened) we are quick to guarantee—don't worry, no reduced cost-of-living allowances, no taxes on social security except for the well-off—and so callous to the young? Have you noticed how health care is on every politician's agenda and education on no one's?

To me, the conclusion is inescapable: we are not serious. We have given up on the public schools because we have given up on the kids; and we have given up on the kids because we have given up on the future—perhaps because it looks too multicolored or too dim or too hard. "Liberty," said Jean-Jacques Rousseau, "is a food easy to eat but hard to digest." America is suffering from a bad case of indigestion. Finally, in giving up on the future, we have given up on democracy. Certainly there will be no liberty, no equality, no social justice without democracy, and there will be no democracy without citizens and the schools that forge civic identity and democratic responsibility. If I am wrong (I'd like to be), my error will be easy to discern, for before the year is out we will put education first on the nation's agenda. We will put it ahead of the deficit, for if the future is finished before it starts, the deficit doesn't matter. Ahead of defense, for without democracy, what liberties will be left to defend? Ahead of all the other public issues and public goods, for without public education there can be no public and hence no truly public issues or public goods to advance. When the polemics are spent and we are through hyperventilating about the crisis in education, there is only one question worth asking: are we serious? If we are, we can begin by honoring that old folk homily and put our money where for much too long our common American mouth has been. Our kids, for once, might be grateful.

Questions for Discussion

1. In what way does Barber use his "Real World Cultural Literacy" test to advance his argument? How does it reveal the "deep hypocrisy that runs through our lamentations about education" that Barber claims it does?

2. How does Barber portray American students? Do you believe that this portrayal is accurate? Why or why not? How does Barber's portrayal of American students differ from that of Mark Edmundsen or Frederick Busch?

3. According to Barber, product marketers see students as potential customers, and hope to gain access to those students through programs such as the Edison Project, which would place advertising in schools. Do you consider yourself to be vulnerable to this "lifestyle patterning" that Barber warns could damage teaching even further when advertisers are allowed into the classroom?

Explorations

1. Barber claims that the fundamental task of education is learning to be free. He calls this civic literacy, "the fundamental literacy by which we live in a civil society." What kind of freedom is Barber talking about?

2. Barber concludes in his essay that Americans are not serious about education. What evidence does he use to support his claim? Do you feel that your community was serious about education when you were in high school? According to Barber, who should be blamed for this lack of seriousness?

3. Thomas Jefferson believed that an educated populace was the strongest guarantee of freedom. Barber goes further, specifying the type of education America needs to remain true to democratic principles. He claims that schools must provide much more than mere vocational education. What type of coursework do you believe would be most valuable in "learning to be free"?

Formal Writing Assignments

1. In an essay, explain how your education influenced your decision to vote or not vote in the most recent election. If you did not vote, what factors might have encouraged you to participate? If you voted, what do you believe was accomplished through your participation?

2. Barber believes that our national priorities are skewed when it is possible for professional athletes to command salaries in the millions of dollars, while those entrusted with teaching our children are compensated with "crumbs." These disparities, however, were created by a free market that responds to the law of supply and demand. Can you, in an essay, argue that the contributions of a professional athlete to our society in fact merit a salary in the millions?

Ralph the Duck

Frederick Busch

Author of twelve novels and six collections of short stories, Frederick Busch has been heralded as a "writer's writer," a "a novelist who focuses on domestic life and the everyday hardships of ordinary people." "Ralph the Duck," which was selected by the Best American Short Stories series for 1989, portrays the educational experience of a nontraditional student whose current and past real-life experiences intersect with his pursuit of a college education.

Writing Before Reading

1. What, in your experience, might be the reaction of young college students to older, "non-traditional" classmates? What qualities do such students seem to bring to the classroom? How are these qualities either valued or discounted by their classmates and/or professors?

2. Before reading the story, imagine that a middle-aged man is enrolled in your English class. What observations might he make about students of younger generations? What stereotypes might he rely upon, and how accurate would these be?

3. Taking into consideration the other readings you've done in this unit (i.e. hooks, Freire, Edmundson, or Rose), make a list of ways a teacher can abuse his/her position of authority in the academic community. Next, try to determine which of these abuses would be more likely to occur with young students than with older, non-traditional students, and vice-versa? What factors, other than age, might account for these differences?

Ralph the Duck

I woke up at 5:25 because the dog was vomiting. I carried seventy-five pounds of heaving golden retriever to the door and poured him onto the silver, moonlit snow. "Good boy," I said because he'd done his only trick. Outside he retched, and I went back up, passing the sofa on which Fanny lay. I tiptoed with enough weight on my toes to let her know how considerate I was while she was deserting me. She blinked her eyes. I swear I heard her blink her eyes. Whenever I tell her that I hear her blink her eyes, she tells me I'm lying; but I can hear the damp slap of lash after I have made her weep.

In bed and warm again, noting the red digital numbers (5:29) and certain that I wouldn't sleep, I didn't. I read a book about men who kill each other for pay or for their honor. I forget which, and so did they. It was 5:45, the alarm would buzz at 6:00, and I would make a pot of coffee and start the wood stove; I would call Fanny and pour her coffee into her mug; I would apologize because I always did. And then she would forgive me if I hadn't been too awful—I didn't think I'd been that bad—and we would stagger through the day, exhausted but pretty sure we were all right, and we'd sleep that night, probably after sex, and then we'd waken in the same bed to the alarm at 6:00, or the dog, if he'd returned to the frozen deer carcass he'd been eating in the forest on our land. He loved what made him sick. The alarm went off. I got into jeans and woolen socks and a sweatshirt, and I went downstairs to let the dog in. He'd be hungry, of course.

I was the oldest college student in America, I thought. But of course I wasn't. There were always ancient women with parchment for skin who graduated at seventy-nine from places like Barnard and the University of Alabama. I was only forty-two and I hardly qualified as a student. I patrolled the college at night in a Bronco with a leaky exhaust system, and I went from room to room in the classroom building, kicking out students who were studying or humping in chairs—they'd do it *anywhere*—and answering emergency calls with my little blue light winking on top of the truck. I didn't carry a gun or a billy, but I had a flashlight that took six batteries and I'd used it twice on some of my overprivileged northeastern-playboy part-time classmates. On Tuesdays and Thursdays I would waken at 6:00 with my wife, and I'd do my homework, and work around the house, and go to school at 11:30 to sit there for an hour and a half while thirty-five stomachs growled with hunger and boredom, and this guy gave instruction about books. Because I was on the staff, the college let me take a course for nothing every term. I was getting educated, in a kind of slow-motion way—it would have taken me something like fifteen or sixteen years to graduate, and I would no doubt get an F in gym and have to repeat—and there were times when I respected myself for it. Fanny often did, and that was fair incentive.

I am not unintelligent. *You are not an unintelligent writer*, my professor wrote on my paper about Nathaniel Hawthorne. We had to read short stories, I and the other students, and then we had to write little essays about them. I told how I saw Kafka and Hawthorne in a similar light, and I was not unintelligent, he said. He ran into me at dusk one time, when I answered a call about a dead battery and found out it was him. I jumped his Buick from the Bronco's battery, and he was looking me over, I could tell, while I clamped onto the terminals and cranked it up. He was a tall, handsome guy who never wore a suit. He wore khakis and sweaters, loafers or sneaks, and he was always talking to the female students with the brightest hair and best builds. But he couldn't get a Buick going on an ice-cold night, and he didn't know enough to look for cells going bad. I told him he was going to need a new battery and he looked me over the way men sometimes do with other men who fix their cars for them.

"Vietnam?"

I said, "Too old."

"Not at the beginning. Not if you were an adviser. So-called. Or one of the Phoenix Project fellas?"

I was wearing a watch cap made of navy wool and an old Marine fatigue jacket. Slick characters like my professor like it if you're a killer or at least a onetime middleweight fighter. I smiled like I knew something. "Take it easy," I said, and I went back to the truck to swing around the cemetery at the top of the campus. They'd been known to screw in down-filled sleeping bags on horizontal stones up there, and the dean of students didn't want anybody dying of frostbite while joined at the hip to a matriculating fellow resident of our northeastern camp for the overindulged.

He blinked his high beams at me as I went. "You are not an unintelligent driver," I said.

Fanny had left me a bowl of something made with sausages and sauerkraut and potatoes, and the dog hadn't eaten too much more than his fair share. He watched me eat his leftovers and then make myself a king-size drink composed of sourmash whiskey and ice. In our back room, which is on the northern end of the house, and cold for sitting in that close to dawn, I sat and watched the texture of the sky change. It was going to snow and I wanted to see the storm come up the valley. I woke up that way—sitting in the rocker with its loose right arm, holding a watery drink, and thinking right away of the girl I'd convinced to go back inside. She'd been standing outside her dormitory, looking up at a window that was dark in the midst of all those lighted panes—they never turned a light off and often let the faucets run half the night—crying onto her bathrobe. She was barefoot in shoe-pacs, the brown ones so many them wore unlaced, and for all I know she was naked under the robe. She was beautiful, I thought, and she was somebody's redheaded daughter, standing in a quadrangle how many miles from home and weeping.

"He doesn't love anyone," the kid told me. "He doesn't love his wife—I mean his ex-wife. And he doesn't love the ex-wife before that, or the one before that. And you know what? He doesn't love me. I don't know anyone who *does!*"

"It isn't your fault if he isn't smart enough to love you," I said, steering her toward the truck.

She stopped. She turned. "You know him?"

I couldn't help it. I hugged her hard, and she let me, and then she stepped back, and of course I let her go. "Don't you touch me! Is this sexual harassment? Do you know the rules? Isn't this sexual harassment?"

"I'm sorry," I said at the door to the truck, "But I think I have to be able to give you a grade before it counts as harassment."

She got in. I told her we were driving to the dean of students' house. She smelled like marijuana and something very sweet, maybe one of those coffee-with-cream liqueurs you don't buy unless you hate to drink.

As the heat of the truck struck her, she started going kind of clay-gray-green, and I reached across her to open the window.

"You touched my breast!" she said.

"It's the smallest one I've touched all night, I'm afraid."

She leaned out the window and gave her rendition of my dog.

But in my rocker, waking up, at whatever time in the morning in my silent house, I thought of her as someone's child. Which made me think of ours, of course. I went for more ice, and I started on a wet breakfast. At the door of the dean of students' house, she'd turned her chalky face to me and asked. "What grade would you give me, then?"

It was a week composed of two teachers locked out of their offices late at night, a Toyota with a flat and no spare, an attempted rape on a senior girl walking home from the library, a major fight outside a fraternity house (broken wrist and significant concussion), and variations on breaking-and-entering. I was scolded by the director of nonacademic services for embracing a student who was drunk; I told him to keep his job, but he called me back because I was right to hug her, he said, and also wrong, but what the hell, and he'd promised to admonish me, and now he had, and would I please stay. I thought of the fringe benefits—graduation in only sixteen years—so I went back to work.

My professor assigned a story called "A Rose for Emily," and I wrote him a paper about the mechanics of corpse fucking, and how, since she clearly couldn't screw her dead boyfriend, she was keeping his rotten body in bed because she truly loved him. I called the paper "True Love." He gave me a B and wrote *See me, pls.* In his office after class, his feet up on his desk, he trimmed a cigar with a giant folding knife he kept in his drawer.

"You got to clean the hole out," he said, "or they don't draw."

"I don't smoke," I said.

"Bad habit. Real *habit*, though. I started smoking'em in Georgia, in the service. My C.O. smoked'em. We collaborated on a brothel inspection one time, and we ended up smoking these with a couple of women—" He waggled his eyebrows at me now that his manhood was established.

"Were the women smoking them too?"

He snorted laughter through his nose while the greasy smoke came curling off his thin, dry lips. "They were pretty smoky, I'll tell ya!" Then he propped his feet—he was wearing cowboy boots that day—and he sat forward. "It's a little hard to explain. But—hell. You just don't say *fuck* when you write an essay for a college prof. Okay?" Like a scoutmaster with a kid he'd caught in the outhouse jerking off. "All right? You don't wanna do that."

"Did it shock you?"

"Fuck, no, it didn't shock me. I just told you. It violates certain proprieties."

"But if I'm writing it to you, like a letter—"

"You're writing it for posterity. For some mythical reader someplace, not just me. You're making a *statement.*"

"Right. My statement said how hard it must be for a woman to fuck with a corpse."

"And a point worth making. I said so. Here."

"But you said I shouldn't say it."

"No. Listen. just because you're talking about fucking, you don't have to say *fuck.* Does that make it any clearer?"

"No."

"I wish you'd lied to me just now," he said.

I nodded. I did too.

"Where'd you do your service?" he asked.

"Baltimore. Baltimore, Maryland."

"What's in Baltimore?"

"Railroads. I liaised on freight runs of army matériel. I killed a couple of bums on the rod with my bare hands, though."

He snorted again, but I could see how disappointed he was. He'd been banking on my having been a murderer. Interesting guy in one of my classes, he must have told some terrific woman at an over-priced meal: I just *know* the guy was a rubout specialist in the Nam, he had to have said. I figured I should come to work wearing my fatigue jacket and a red bandanna tied around my head. Say "Man" to him a couple of times, hang a fist in the air for grief and solidarity, and look terribly worn, exhausted by experiences he was fairly certain that he envied me. His dungarees were ironed, I noticed.

On Saturday we went back to the campus because Fanny wanted to see a movie called *The Seven Samurai.* I fell asleep, and I'm afraid I snored. She let me sleep until the auditorium was almost empty. Then she kissed me awake. "Who was screaming in my dream?" I asked her.

"Kurosawa," she said.

"Who?"

"Ask your professor friend."

I looked around, but he wasn't there. "Not an un-weird man," I said. We went home and cleaned up after the dog and put him out. We drank a little Spanish brandy and went upstairs and made love. I was fairly premature, you might say, but one way and another by the time we fell asleep we were glad to be there with each other, and glad that it was Sunday coming up the valley toward us, and nobody with it. The dog was howling at another dog someplace, or at the moon, or maybe just his moon-thrown shadow on the snow. I did not strangle him when I opened the back door and he limped happily past me and stumbled up the stairs. I followed him into our bedroom and groaned for just being satisfied as I got into bed. You'll notice I didn't say fuck.

He stopped me in the hall after class on a Thursday, and asked me How's it goin, just one of the kickers drinking sour beer and eating pickled eggs and watching the tube in a country bar. How's it goin, I nodded. I wanted a grade from the man, and I did want to learn about expressing myself. I nodded and made what I thought was a smile. He'd let his mustache grow out and his hair grow longer. He was starting to wear dark shirts with lighter ties. I thought he looked like someone in *The Godfather.* He still wore those light little loafers or his high-heeled cowboy boots. His corduroy pants looked baggy. I guess he wanted them to look that way. He motioned me to the wall of the hallway, and he looked up and said, "How about the Baltimore stuff?"

I said, "Yeah?"

"Was that really true?" He was almost blinking, he wanted so much for me to be a damaged Vietnam vet just looking for a bell tower to climb into and start firing from. The college didn't have a bell tower you could get up into, though I'd once spent an ugly hour chasing a drunken ATO down from the roof of the observatory. "You were just clocking through boxcars in Baltimore?"

I said, "Nah."

"I thought so!" He gave a kind of sigh.

"I killed people," I said.

"You know, I could have sworn you did," he said.

I nodded, and he nodded back. I'd made him so happy.

The assignment was to write something to influence somebody. He called it Rhetoric and Persuasion. We read an essay by George Orwell and "A Modest Proposal" by Jonathan Swift. I liked the Orwell better, but I wasn't comfortable with it. He talked about "niggers," and I felt him saying it two ways.

I wrote "Ralph the Duck."

Once upon a time, there was a duck named Ralph who didn't have any feathers on either wing. So when the cold wind blew, Ralph said, Brr, and shivered and shook.

What's the matter? Ralph's mommy asked.

I'm *cold*, Ralph said.

Oh, the mommy said. Here. I'll keep you warm.

So she spread her big, feathery wings, and hugged Ralph tight, and when the cold wind blew, Ralph was warm and snuggly, and fell fast asleep.

The next Thursday, he was wearing canvas pants and hiking boots. He mentioned kind of casually to some of the girls in the class how whenever there was a storm he wore his Lake District walking outfit. He had a big, hairy sweater on. I kept waiting for him to make a noise like a mountain goat. But the girls seemed to like it. His boots made a creaky squeak on the linoleum of the hall when he caught up with me after class.

"As I told, you," he said, "it isn't unappealing. It's just—not a college theme."

"Right." I said. "Okay. You want me to do it over?"

"No," he said. "Not at all. The D will remain your grade. But I'll read something else if you want to write it."

"This'll be fine," I said.

"Did you understand the assignment?"

"Write something to influence someone—Rhetoric and Persuasion."

We were at his office door and the redheaded kid who had gotten sick in my truck was waiting for him. She looked at me like one of us was in the wrong place, which struck me as accurate enough. He was interested in getting into his office with the redhead, but he remembered to turn around and flash me a grin he seemed to think he was known for.

Instead of going on shift a few hours after class, the way I'm supposed to, I told my supervisor I was sick, and I went home. Fanny was frightened when I came in, because I don't get sick and I don't miss work. She looked at my face and she grew sad. I kissed her hello and went upstairs to change. I always used to change my clothes when I was a kid, as soon as I came home from school. I put on jeans and a flannel shirt and thick wool socks, and I made myself a dark drink of sourmash. Fanny poured herself some wine and came into the cold northern room a few minutes later. I was sitting in the rocker, looking over the valley. The wind was lining up a lot of rows of cloud so that the sky looked like a baked trout when you lift the skin off. "It'll snow," I said to her.

She sat on the old sofa and waited. After a while, she said. "I wonder why they always call it a mackerel sky?"

"Good eating, mackerel," I said.

Fanny said, "Shit! You're never that laconic unless you feel crazy. What's wrong? Who'd you punch out at the playground?"

"We had to write a composition," I said.

"Did he like it?"

"He gave me a D."

"Well, you're familiar enough with D's. I never saw you get this low over a grade."

"I wrote about Ralph the Duck."

She said, "You did?" She said, "Honey." She came over and stood beside the rocker and leaned into me and hugged my head and neck. "Honey," she said. "Honey."

It was the worst of the winter's storms, and one of the worst in years. That afternoon they closed the college, which they almost never do. But the roads were jammed with snow over ice, and now it was freezing rain on top of that, and the only people working at the school that night were the operator who took emergency calls and me. Everyone else had gone home except the students, and most of them were inside. The ones who weren't were drunk, and I kept on sending them in and telling them to act like grown-ups. A number of them said they were, and I really couldn't argue. I had the bright beams on, the defroster set high, the little blue light winking, and a thermos of sourmash and hot coffee that I sipped from every time I had to get out of the truck or every time I realized how cold all that wetness was out there.

About eight o'clock, as the rain was turning back to snow and the cold was worse, the roads impossible, just as I was done helping a county sander on the edge of the campus pull a panel truck out of a snow bank, I got the emergency call from the college operator. We had a student missing. The roommates thought the kid was headed for the quarry. This meant I had to get the Bronco up on a narrow road above the campus, above the old cemetery, into all kinds of woods and rough track that I figured would be choked with ice and snow. Any kid up there would really have to want to be there, and I couldn't go in on foot, because you'd only want to be there on account of drugs, booze, or craziness, and either way I'd be needing blankets and heat, and then a fast ride down to the hospital in town. So I dropped into four-wheel drive to get me up the hill above the campus, bucking snow and sliding on ice, putting all the heater's warmth up onto the windshield because I couldn't see much more than swarming snow. My feet were still cold from the tow job, and it didn't seem to matter that I had on heavy socks and insulated boots I'd coated with waterproofing. I shivered, and I thought of Ralph the Duck.

I had to grind the rest of the way, from the cemetery, in four-wheel low, and in spite of the cold I was smoking my gearbox by the time I was close enough to the quarry—they really did take a lot of the rocks for the campus buildings from there—to see I'd have to make my way on foot to where she was. It was a kind of hollowed-out shape, maybe four or five stories high, where she stood—well, wobbled is more like it. She was as chalky as she'd been the last time, and her red hair didn't catch the light anymore. It just lay on her like something that had died on top of her head. She was in a white nightgown that was plastered to her body. She had her arms crossed as if she wanted to be warm. She swayed, kind of, in front of the big, dark, scooped-out rock face, where the trees and brush had been cleared for trucks and earthmovers. She looked tiny against all the darkness. From where I stood, I could see the snow driving down in front of the lights I'd left on, but I couldn't see it near her. All it looked like around her was dark. She was shaking with the cold, and she was crying.

I had a blanket with me, and I shoved it down the front of my coat to keep it dry for her, and because I was so cold. I waved. I stood in the lights and I waved. I don't know what she saw—a big shadow, maybe. I surely didn't reassure her, because when she saw me she backed up, until she was near the face of the quarry. She couldn't go any farther.

I called, "Hello! I brought a blanket. Are you cold? I thought you might want a blanket."

He roommates had told the operator about pills, so I didn't bring her the coffee laced with mash. I figured I didn't have all that much time, anyway, to get her down and pumped out. The booze with whatever pills she'd taken would make her die that much faster.

I hated that word. Die. It made me furious with her. I heard myself seething when I breathed. I pulled my scarf and collar up above my mouth. I didn't want her to see how close I might come to wanting to kill her because she wanted to die.

I called, "Remember me?" I was closer now. I could see the purple mottling of her skin. I didn't know if it was cold or dying. It probably didn't matter much to distinguish between them right now, I thought. That made me smile. I felt the smile, and I pulled the scarf down so she could look at it. She didn't seem awfully reassured. "You're the sexual harassment guy," she said. She said it very slowly. Her lips were clumsy. It was like looking at a ventriloquist's dummy.

"I gave you an A," I said.

"When?"

"It's a joke," I said. "You don't want me making jokes. You want me to give you a nice warm blanket, though. And then you want me to take you home."

She leaned against the rock face when I approached. I pulled the blanket out, then zipped my jacket back up. The snow had stopped, I realized, and that wasn't really a very good sign. It felt like an arctic cold descending in its place. I held the blanket out to her, but she only looked at it.

"You'll just have to turn me in," I said. "I'm gonna hug you again." She screamed, "No more! I don't want any more hugs!"

But she kept her arms on her chest, and I wrapped the blanket around her and stuffed a piece into each of her tight, small fists. I didn't know what to do for her feet. Finally, I got down on my haunches in front of her. She crouched down too, protecting herself.

"No," I said. "No. You're fine."

I took off the woolen mittens I'd been wearing. Mittens keep you warmer than gloves because they trap your hand's heat around the fingers and palms at once. Fanny had knitted them for me. I put a mitten as far onto each of her feet as I could. She let me. She was going to collapse, I thought.

"Now, let's go home," I said. "Let's get you better."

With her funny, stiff lips, she said, "I've been very self-indulgent and weird and I'm sorry. But I'd really like to die." She sounded so reasonable that I found myself nodding in agreement as she spoke.

"You can't just die," I said.

"Aren't I dying already? I took all of them, and then," she giggled like a child, which of course is what she was, "I borrowed different ones from other people's rooms. See, this isn't some teenage cry for like *help*. Understand? I'm seriously interested in death and I have to stay out here a little longer and fall asleep. All right?"

"You can't do that," I said. "You ever hear of Vietnam?"

"I saw that movie," she said. "With the opera in it? Apocalypse? Whatever."

"I was there!" I said. "I killed people! I helped to kill them! And, when they die, you see their bones later on. You dream about their bones and blood on the ends of the splintered ones, and this kind of mucous stuff coming out of their eyes. You probably heard of guys having dreams like that, didn't you? Whacked-out Vietnam vets? That's me, see? So I'm telling you, I know about dead people and their eyeballs and everything falling out. And people keep dreaming about the dead people they knew, see? You can't make people dream about you that like that! It isn't fair!"

"You dream about me?" She was ready to go. She was ready to fall down, and I was going to lift her up and get her to the truck.

"I will," I said. "If you die."

"I want you to," she said. Her lips were hardly moving now. Her eyes were closed. "I want you all to."

I dropped my shoulder and put it into her waist and picked her up and carried her down to the Bronco. She was talking, but not a lot, and her voice leaked down my back. I jammed her into the truck and wrapped the blanket around her better and then put another one down around her feet. I strapped her in with the seat belt. She was shaking, and her eyes were closed and her mouth open. She was breathing. I checked that twice, once when I strapped her in, and then again when I strapped myself in and backed up hard into a sapling and took it down. I got us into first gear, held the clutch in, leaned over to listen for breathing, heard it—shallow panting, like a kid asleep on your lap for a nap—and then I put the gear in and howled down the hillside on what I thought might be the road.

We passed the cemetery. I told her that was a good sign. She didn't respond. I found myself panting too, as if we were breathing for each other. It made me dizzy, but I couldn't stop. We passed the highest dorm, and I dropped the truck into four-wheel high. The cab smelled like burnt oil and hot metal. We were past the chapel now, and the observatory, the president's house, then the bookstore. I had the blue light winking and the V-6 roaring, and I drove on the edge of out-of-control, sensing the skids just before I slid into them, and getting back out of them as I needed to. I took a little fender off once, and a bit of the corner of a classroom building, but I worked us back on course, and all I needed to do now was to negotiate the sharp left turn around the Administration Building past the library, then floor it for the straight run to the town's main street and then the hospital.

I was panting into the mike, and the operator kept saying. "Say again?"

I made myself slow down some, and I said we'd need stomach pumping, and to get the names of the pills from her friends in the dorm, and I'd be there in less than five or we were crumpled up someplace and dead.

"Roger," the radio said. "Roger all that." My throat tightened and tears came into my eyes. They were helping us, they'd told me: Roger.

I said to the girl, whose head was slumped and whose face looked too blue all through its whiteness, "You know, I had a girl once. My wife, Fanny. She and I had a small girl one time."

I reached over and touched her check. It was cold. The truck swerved, and I got my hands on the wheel. I'd made the turn past the Ad Building using just my left. "I can do it in the dark," I sang to no tune I'd ever learned. "I can do it with one hand." I said to her. "We had a girl child, very small. Now, I do *not* want you dying."

I came to the campus gates doing fifty on the ice and snow, smoking the engine, grinding the clutch and I bounced off a wrought iron fence to give me the curve going left that I needed. On a pool table, it would have been a bank shot worth applause. The town cop picked me up and got out ahead of me. He used his growler and siren and horn alternately, and I leaned on the horn. We banged up to the emergency room entrance and I was out and at the other door before the cop on duty, Elmo St. John, could loosen his seat belt. I loosened hers, and I carried her into the lobby of the ER. They had a gurney and doctors, and they took her away from me. I tried to talk to them, but they made me sit down and do my shaking on a dirty sofa decorated with drawings of little spinning wheels. Somebody brought me hot coffee, I think it was Elmo, but I couldn't hold it.

"They won't," he kept saying to me. "They won't."

"What?"

"You just been sitting there for a minute and a half like St. Vitus dancing, telling me, 'Don't let her die. Don't let her die.'"

"Oh. "

"You all right?"

"How about the kid?"

"They'll tell us soon."

"She better be all right."

"That's right."

"She—somebody's gonna have to tell me plenty if she isn't."

"That's right."

"She better not die this time," I guess I said.

Fanny came downstairs to look for me. I was at the northern windows, looking through the mullions down the valley to the faint red line along the mounds and little peaks of the ridge beyond the valley. The sun was going to come up, and I was looking for it.

Fanny stood behind me. I could hear her. I could smell her hair and the sleep on her. The crimson line widened, and I squinted at it. I heard the dog limp in behind her, catching up. He panted and I knew why his panting sounded familiar. She put her hands on my shoulders and arms. I made muscles to impress her with, and then I let them go, and let my head drop down until my chin was on my chest.

"I didn't think you'd be able to sleep after that," Fanny said.

"I brought enough adrenaline home to run a football team."

"But you hate being a hero, huh? You're hiding in here because somebody's going to call, or come over, and want to talk to you—her parents for shooting sure, sooner or later. Or is that supposed to be part of the service up at the playground? Saving their suicidal daughters. Almost dying to find them in the woods and driving too fast for any weather, much less what we had last night. Getting their babies home. The bastards." She was crying. I knew she would be, sooner or later. I could hear the soft sound of her lashes. She sniffed and I could feel her arm move as she felt for the tissues on the coffee table.

"I have them over here," I said. "On the windowsill."

"Yes." She blew her nose, and the dog thumped his tail. He seemed to think it one of Fanny's finer tricks, and he had wagged for her for thirteen years whenever she'd done it. "Well, you're going to have to talk to them."

"I will," I said. "I will." The sun was in our sky now, climbing. We had built the room so we could watch it climb. "I think that jackass with the smile, my prof? She showed up a lot at his office, the last few weeks. He called her 'my advisee,' you know? The way those guys sound about what they're achieving by getting up and shaving and going to work and saying the same thing every day? Every year? Well, she was his advisee, I bet. He was shoving home the old advice."

"She'll be okay," Fanny said. "Her parents will take her home and love her up and get her some help." She began to cry again, then she stopped. She blew her nose, and the dog's tail thumped. She kept a hand between my shoulder and my neck. "So tell me what you'll tell a waiting world. How'd you talk her out?"

"Well, I didn't, really. I got up close and picked her up and carried her is all."

"You didn't say *anything?*"

"Sure I did. Kid's standing in the snow outside of a lot of pills, you're gonna say something."

"So what'd you *say?*"

"I told her stories," I said. "I did Rhetoric and Persuasion."

Fanny said, "Then you go in early on Thursday, you go in half an hour early, and you get that guy to jack up your grade."

Questions for Discussion

1. As a class, discuss the significance of the story's title. The professor suggests that the narrator's efforts in a previous paper had "violated certain proprieties." What academic propriety or convention was violated by the narrator's paper about Ralph the Duck?

2. The narrator of this story holds some strong opinions about college-aged students. How are his generalizations realistic or unrealistic?

3. In the story, the narrator has received a D grade on a paper he had submitted earlier. If the story "Ralph the Duck" is the narrator's revision of that paper, what statement do you believe the narrator is trying to make?

Explorations

1. The narrator of this story makes many statements about "college-aged" students. How does he characterize such students, and how might his generalizations be viewed by Edmundson, hooks, or Freire?

2. "Ralph the Duck" is, essentially, a story of an educational struggle. Consider how it differs in this regard from the stories told by Rose, Lohre, and Edmundson. Write your own personal narrative about a time when you struggled in a class, then propose how the lesson might have been more successfully taught. How did your teacher's preconceptions about his/her students affect your ability to succeed?

3. Imagine that you are a forty-something-year-old student in one of your current college classes. Write a description of your traditional classmates from this point-of-view. What characteristics would stand out most: dress, speech-patterns, the way they interact with the teacher? If possible, share this writing with someone from a previous generation. What are their responses to your imagined perceptions? How accurate did this exercise enable you to be?

Formal Writing Assignments

1. The narrator of "Ralph the Duck" finds it conspicuous that his English professor tries to connect with him through discussion of his service in Vietnam, yet the professor seeks to "instruct" the girl in the story by relating to her on a personal level. Tell the story of a successful teacher you've had in the past, and then analyze how that teacher forged "personal connections" with his/her students. What assumptions about you as a student were evident in your teacher's tactics? How do such assumptions influence the ways that teachers teach? What kinds of students might have been neglected by this teacher's approach?

2. Think about the ways that your university seeks to "relate" to its students. Go to the admissions office and browse the brochures; do a study of materials and advertisements in the student union. How, if at all, are these materials geared toward "traditional," 18-22 year-old students? How might they fail to accomplish their goals if presented to students from earlier generations? Write an analytical essay in which you examine these materials and formulate a thesis about the characteristics of students the university is "targeting" with its advertisements and propaganda. Consider why the target audience is given priority in the marketing strategies of the school, and whether or not such a marketing focus neglects the interest of certain nontraditional students.

On the Uses of a Liberal Education I: As Lite Entertainment for Bored College Students

Mark Edmundson

Mark Edmundson is a professor of English at the University of Virginia and contributing editor at *Raritan, Civilization Magazine*, and *Harper's Magazine*. His publications include books and essays on romanticism, Freud, philosophy, Bob Dylan, and James Dickey. His most recent book, *Terror's Reign: Angels, Sado-Masochism, and the Culture of Gothic* (1997)—like the essay that follows—speaks to the powerful force of popular culture in the U.S.

"On the Uses of a Liberal Education I: As Lite Entertainment for Bored College Students," which appears in the September 1997 issue of *Harper's Magazine,* is a companion to Earl Shorris' "On the Uses of a Liberal Education II: In the Hands of the Restless Poor."

Writing Before Reading

1. Edmundson writes in this essay of the current attitudes of college students toward education. Before reading his essay, characterize for yourself students' attitudes and expectations about universities' responsibility to their students in providing classes, programs, extracurricular activities, etc.

2. Oftentimes, persons of one age group generalize about people in other age groups. You, in fact, might have been wrongfully characterized by someone older. Describe a moment when you or people of your age group were inaccurately described or characterized by someone older because of your age, appearance, or actions.

3. Reflect on why you made the decision to attend the college in which you're currently enrolled. What programs, financial packages, information, or materials from the college were most influential in leading you to the decision?

On the Uses of a Liberal Education I: As Lite Entertainment for Bored College Students

Today is evaluation day in my Freud class, and everything has changed. The class meets twice a week, late in the afternoon, and the clientele, about fifty undergraduates, tends to drag in and slump, looking disconsolate and a little lost, waiting for a jump start. To get the discussion moving, they usually require a joke, an ancedote, an off-the-wall question—When you were a kid, were your Halloween getups ego costumes, or superego costumes? That sort of thing. But today, as soon as I flourish the forms, a buzz rises in the room. Today they write their assessments of the course, their assessments of me, and they are without a doubt wide-awake. "What is your evaluation of the instructor?" asks question number eight, entreating them to circle a number between five (excellent) and one (poor, poor). Whatever interpretive subtlety they've aquired during the term is now out the window. Edmundson: one to five, stand and shoot.

And they do. As I retreat through the door—I never stay around for this phase of the ritual—I look over my shoulder and see them toiling away like the devil's auditors. They're pitched into high writing gear, even the ones who struggle to squeeze out their journal entries word by word, stoked on a procedure they have by now supremely mastered. They're playing the informed consumer, letting the provider know where he's come through and where he's not quite up to snuff.

But why am I so distressed, bolting like a refugee out of my own classroom, where I usually hold easy sway? Chances are the evaluations will be much like what they've been in the past—they'll be just fine. It's likely that I'll be commended for being "interesting" (and I am commended, many times over), that I'll be cited for my relaxed and tolerant ways (that happens, too), that my sense of humor and capacity to connect the arcana of the subject matter with current culture will come in for some praise (yup). I've been hassled this term, finishing a manuscript, and so haven't given their journals the attention I should have, and for that I'm called—quite civilly, though—to account. Overall, I get off pretty well.

Yet I have to admit that I do not much like the image of myself that emerges from these forms, the image of knowledgeable, humorous detachment and bland tolerance. I do not like the forms themselves, with their number ratings, reminiscent of the sheets circulated after the TV pilot has just played to its sample audience in Burbank. Most of all I dislike the attitude of calm consumer expertise that pervades the responses. I'm disturbed by the serene belief that my function—and, more important, Freud's, or Shakespeare's, or Blake's—is to divert, entertain, and interest. Observes one respondent, not at all unrepresentative: "Edmundson has done a fantastic job of presenting this difficult, important & controversial material in an enjoyable and approachable way."

Thanks but no thanks. I don't teach to amuse, to divert, or even, for that matter, to be merely interesting. When someone says she "enjoyed" the course—and that word crops up again and again in my evaluations—somewhere at the edge of my immediate complacency I feel encroaching self-dislike. That is not at all what I had in mind. The off-the-wall questions and the sidebar jokes are meant as leadins to stronger stuff—in the case of the Freud course to a complexly tragic view of life. But the affability and the one-liners often seem to be all that land with the students; their journals and evaluations leave me little doubt.

I want some of them to say that they've been changed by the course. I want them to measure themselves against what they've read. It's said that some time ago a Columbia University instructor used to issue a harsh two-part question. One: What book did you most dislike in the course? Two: What intellectual or characterological flaws in you does that dislike point to? The hand that framed that question was surely heavy. But at least it compels one to see intellectual work as confrontation between two people, student and author, where the stakes matter. Those Columbia students were being asked to relate the quality of an *encounter*, not rate the action as though it had unfolded on the big screen.

Why are my students decribing the Oedipus complex and the death drive as being interesting and enjoyable to contemplate? And why am I coming across as an urbane, mildly ironic, endlessly affable guide to this intellectual territory, operating without intensity, generous, funny, and loose?

Because that's what works. On evaluation day, I reap the rewards of my partial compliance with the culture of my students and, too, with the culture of the university as it now operates. It's a culture that's gotten little exploration. Current critics tend to think that liberal-arts education is in crisis because universities have been invaded by professors with peculiar ideas: deconstruction, Lacanianism, feminism, queer theory. They believe that genius and tradition are out and that P.C., multiculturalism, and identity politics are in because of an invasion by tribes of tenured radicals, the late millennial equivalents of the Visigoth hordes that cracked Rome's walls.

But mulling over my evaluations and then trying to take a hard, extended look at campus life both here at the University of Virginia and around the country eventually led me to some different conclusions. To me, liberal-arts education is as ineffective as it is now not chiefly because there are a lot of strange theories in the air. (Used well, those theories can be illuminating.) Rather, it's that university culture, like American culture writ large, is, to put it crudely, ever more devoted to consumption and entertainment, to the using and using up of goods and images. For someone growing up in America now, there are few available alternatives to the cool consumer worldview. My students didn't ask for that view, much less create it, but they bring a consumer weltanschauung to school, where it exerts a powerful, and largely unacknowledged, influence. If we want to understand current universities, with their multiple woes, we might try leaving the realms of expert debate and fine ideas and turning to the classrooms and campuses, where a new kind of weather is gathering.

From time to time I bump into a colleague in the corridor and we have what I've come to think of as a Joon Lee fest. Joon Lee is on of the best students I've taught. He's endlessly curious, has read a small library's worth, seen every movie, and knows all about showbiz and entertainment. For a class of mine he wrote an essay using Nietzsche's Apollo and Dionysus to analyze the pop group The Supremes. A trite, cultural-studies bonbon? Not at all. He said striking things about conceptions of race in America and about how they shape our ideas of beauty. When I talk with one of his other teachers, we run on about the general splendors of his work and presence. But what inevitably follows a JL fest is a mournful reprise about the divide that separates him and a few other remarkable students from their contemporaries. It's not that some aren't nearly as bright—in terms of intellectual ability, my students are all that I could ask for. Instead, it's that Joon Lee has decided to follow his interests and let them make him into a singular and rather eccentric man; in his charming way, he doesn't mind being at odds with most anyone.

It's his capacity for enthusiasm that sets Joon apart from what I've come to think of as the reigning generational style. Whether the students are sorority/fraternity types, grunge aficionados, piercer/tattooers, black or white, rich or middle class (alas, I teach almost no students from truly poor backgrounds), they are, nearly across the board, very, very self-contained. On good days they display a light, appealing glow; on bad days, shuffling disgruntlement. But there's little fire, little passion to be found.

This point came home to me a few weeks ago when I was wandering across the university grounds. There beneath a classically cast portico, were two students, male and female, having a rip-roaring argument. They were incensed, bellowing at each other, headstrong, confident, and wild. It struck me how rarely I see this kind of full-out feeling in students anymore. Strong emotional display is forbidden. When conflicts arise, it's generally understood that one of the parties will say something sarcastically propitiating ("whatever" often does it) and slouch away.

How did my students reach this peculiar state in which all passion seems to be spent? I think that many of them have imbibed their sense of self from consumer culture in general and from the tube in particular. They're the progeny of 100 cable channels and omnipresent Blockbuster outlets. TV, Marshall McLuhan famously said, is a cool medium. Those who play best on it are low-key and nonassertive; they blend in. Enthusiasm, à la Joon Lee, quickly looks absurd. The form of character that's most appealing on TV is calmly self-interested though never greedy, attuned to the conventions, and ironic. Judicious timing is preferred to sudden self-assertion. The TV medium is inhospitable to inspiration, improvisation, failures, slipups. All must run perfectly.

Naturally, a cool youth culture is a marketing bonanza for producers of the right products, who do all they can to enlarge that culture and keep it grinding. The Internet, TV, and magazines now teem with what I call persona ads, ads for Nikes and Reeboks and Jeeps and Blazers that don't so much endorse the capacities of the product per se as show you what sort of person you will be once you've acquired it. The Jeep ad that features hip, outdoorsy kids whipping a Frisbee from mountaintop to mountaintop isn't so much about what Jeeps can do as it is the kind of people who own them. Buy a Jeep and be one of them. The ad is of little consequence in itself, but expand its message exponentially and you have the central thrust of current consumer culture—buy in order to be.

Most of my students seem desperate to blend in, to look right, not to make a spectacle of themselves. (Do I have to tell you that those two students having the argument under the portico turned out to be acting in a role-playing game?) The specter of the uncool creates a subtle tyranny. It's apparently an easy standard to subscribe to, this Letterman-like, Tarantino-like cool, but once commited to it, you discover that matters are rather different. You're inhibited, except on ordained occasions, from showing emotion, stifled from trying to achieve anything original. You're made to feel that even the slightest departure from the reigning code will get you genially ostracized. This is a culture tensely committed to a laid-back norm.

Am I coming off like something of a crank here? Maybe. Oscar Wilde, who is almost never wrong, suggested that it is perilous to promiscuously contradict people who are much younger than yourself. Point taken. But one of the lessons that consumer hype tries to insinuate is that we must never rebel against the new, never even question it. If it's new—a new need, a new product, a new show, a new style, a new generation—it must be good. So maybe, even at the risk of winning the withered, brown laurels of crankdom, it pays to resist newness-worship and cast a colder eye.

Praise for my students? I have some of that too. What my students are, at their best, is decent. They are potent believers in equality. They help out at the soup kitchen and volunteer to tutor poor kids to get a stripe on their résumés, sure. But they also want other people to have a fair shot. And in their commitment to fairness they are discerning; there you see them at their intellectual best. If I were on trial and innocent, I'd want them on the jury.

What they will not generally do, though, is indict the current system. They won't talk about how the exigencies of capitalism lead to a reserve army of the unemployed and nearly inevitable misery. That would be getting too loud, too brash. For the pervading view is the cool consumer perspective, where passion and strong admiration are forbidden. "To stand in awe of nothing, Numicus, is perhaps the one and only thing that can make a man happy and keep him so," says Horace in the *Epistles*, and I fear that his lines ought to hang as a motto over the university in this era of high consumer capitalism.

It's easy to mount one's high horse and blame the students for this state of affairs. But they didn't create the present culture of consumption. (It was largely my own generation, that of the Sixties, that let the counterculture search for pleasure devolve into a quest for commodities.) And they weren't the ones responsible, when they were six and seven and eight years old, for unplugging the TV set from time to time or for hauling off and kicking a hole through it. It's my generation of parents who sheltered these students, kept them away from the hard knocks of everyday life, making them cautious and overfragile, who demanded that their teachers, from grade school on, flatter them endlessly so that the kids are shocked if their college profs don't reflexively suck up to them.

Of course, the current generational style isn't simply derived from culture and environment. It's also about dollars. Students worry that taking too many chances with their educations will sabotage their future prospects. They're aware of the fact that a drop that looks more and more like one wall of the Grand Canyon separates the top economic tenth from the rest of the population. There's a sentiment currently abroad that if you step aside for a moment, to write, to travel, to fall too hard in love, you might lose position permanently. We may be on a conveyor belt, but it's worse down there on the filth-strewn floor. So don't sound off, don't blow your chance.

But wait. I teach at the famously conservative University of Virginia. Can I extend my view from Charlottesville to encompass the whole country, a whole generation of college students? I can only say that I hear comparable stories about classroom life from colleagues everywhere in America. When I visit other schools to lecture, I see a similar scene unfolding. There are, of course, terrific students everywhere. And they're all the better for the way they've had to strive against the existing conformity. At some of the small liberal-arts colleges, the tradition of strong engagement persists. But overall, the students strike me as being sweet and sad, hovering in a nearly suspended animation.

Too often now the pedagogical challenge is to make a lot from a little. Teaching Wordsworth's "Tintern Abbey," you ask for comments. No one responds. So you call on Stephen. Stephen: "The sound, this poem really flows." You: "Stephen seems interested in the music of the poem. We might extend his comment to ask if the poem's music coheres with its argument. Are they consistent? Or is there an emotional pain submerged here that's contrary to the poem's appealing melody?" All right, it's not usually that bad. But close. One friend describes it as rebound teaching: they proffer a weightless comment, you hit it back for all your worth, then it comes dribbling out again. Occasionally a professor will try to explain away this intellectual timidity by describing the students as perpetrators of postmodern irony, a highly sophisticated mode. Everything's a slick counterfeit, a simulacrum, so by no means should any phenomenon be taken seriously. But the students don't have the urbane, Oscar Wilde-type demeanor that should go with this view. Oscar was cheerful, funny, confident, strange. (Wilde, mortally ill, living in a Paris flophouse: "My wallpaper and I are fighting a duel to the death. One or the other of us has to go.") This generation's style is considerate, easy to please, and a touch depressed.

Granted, you might say, the kids come to school immersed in a consumer mentality—they're good Americans, after all—but then the university and the professors do everything in their power to fight that dreary mind-set in the interest of higher ideals, right? So it should be. But let us look at what is actually coming to pass.

Over the past few years, the physical layout of my university has been changing. To put it a little indecorously, the place is looking more like a retirement spread for the young. Our funds go to construction, into new dorms, into renovating the student union. We have a new aquatics center and ever-improving gyms, stocked with Stairmasters and Nautilus machines. Engraved on the wall in the gleaming aquatics building is a line by our founder, Thomas Jefferson, declaring that everyone ought to get about two hours exercise a day. Clearly even the author of the Declaration of Independence endorses the turning of his university into sports-and-fitness emporium.

But such improvements shouldn't be surprising. Universities need to attract the best (that is, the smartest *and* the richest) students in order to survive in an ever more competitive market. Schools want kids whose parents can pay the full freight, not the ones who need scholarships or want to bargain down the tuition costs. If the marketing surveys say that the kids require sports centers, then, trustees willing, they shall have them. In fact, as I began looking around, I came to see that more and more of what's going on in the university is customer driven. The consumer pressures that beset me on evaluation day are only a part of an overall trend.

From the start, the contemporary university's relationship with students has a solicitous, nearly servile tone. As soon as someone enters his junior year in high school, and especially if he's living in a prosperous zip code, the informational material—the advertising—comes flooding in. Pictures, testimonials, videocassettes, and CD ROMs (some bidden, some not) arrive at the door from colleges across the country, all trying to capture the student and his tuition cash. The freshman-to-be sees photos of well-appointed dorm rooms; of elaborate phys-ed facilities; of fine dining rooms; of expertly kept sports fields; of orchestras and drama troupes; of students working alone (no overbearing grown-ups in range), peering with high seriousness into computer and microscopes; or of students arrayed outdoors in attractive conversational garlands.

Occasionally—but only occasionally, for we usually photograph rather badly; in appearance we tend at best to be styleless—there's a professor teaching a class. (The college catalogues I received, by my request only, in the late Sixties were austere affairs full of professors' credentials and course descriptions; it was clear on whose terms the enterprise was going to unfold.) A college financial officer recently put matters to me in concise, if slightly melodramatic, terms: "Colleges don't have admissions offices anymore, they have marketing departments." Is it suprising that someone who has been approached with photos and tapes, bells and whistles, might come in thinking that the Freud and Shakespeare she had signed up to study were also going to be agreeable treats?

How did we reach this point? In part the answer is a matter of demographics and (surprise) of money. Aided by the G.I. bill, the college-going population in America dramatically increased after the Second World War. Then came the baby boomers, and to accommodate them, schools continued to grow. Universities expand easily enough, but with tenure locking faculty in for lifetime jobs, and with the general reluctance of administrators to eliminate their own slots, it's not easy for a university to contract. So after the baby boomers had passed through—like a fat meal digested by a boa constrictor—the colleges turned to energetic promotional strategies to fill the empty chairs. And suddenly college became a buyer's market. What students and their parents wanted had to be taken more and more into account. That usually meant creating more comfortable, less challenging environments, places where almost no one failed, everything was enjoyable, and everyone was nice.

Just as universities must compete with one another for students, so must the individual departments. At a time of rank economic anxiety, the English and history majors have to contend for students against the more success-insuring branches, such as the sciences and the commerce school. In 1968, more than 21 percent of all the bachelor's degrees conferred in America were in the humanities; by 1993, that number had fallen to about 13 percent. The humanities now must struggle to attract students, many of whose parents devoutly wish they would study something else.

One of the ways we've tried to stay attractive is by loosening up. We grade much more softly than our colleagues in science. In English, we don't give many Ds, or Cs for that matter. (The rigors of Chem 101 create almost as many English majors per year as do the splendors of Shakespeare.) A professor at Stanford recently explained grade inflation in the humanities by observing that the undergraduates were getting smarter every year; the higher grades simply recorded how much better they were than their predecessors. Sure.

Along with softening the grades, many humanities departments have relaxed major requirements. There are some good reasons for introducing more choice into curricula and requiring fewer standard courses. But the move, like many others in the university now, jibes with a tendency to serve—and not challenge—the students. Students can also float in and out of classes during the first two weeks of each term without making any commitment. The common name for this time span—shopping period— speaks volumes about the consumer mentality that's now in play. Usually, too, the kids can drop courses up until the last month with only an innocuous "W" on their transcripts. Does a course look too challenging? No problem. Take it pass-fail. A happy consumer is, by definition, one with multiple options, one who can always have what he wants. And since a course is something the students and their parents have bought and paid for, why can't they do with it pretty much as they please?

A sure result of the university's widening elective leeway is to give students more power over their teachers. Those who don't like you can simply avoid you. If the clientele dislikes you en masse, you can be left without students, period. My first term teaching I walked into my introduction to poetry course and found it inhabited by one student, the gloriously named Bambi Lynn Dean. Bambi and I chatted amiably awhile, but for all that she and the pleasure of her name could offer, I was fast on the way to meltdown. It was all a mistake, luckily, a problem with the scheduling book. Everyone was waiting for me next door. But in a dozen years of teaching I haven't forgotten that feeling of being ignominiously marooned. For it happens to others, and not always because of scheduling glitches. I've seen older colleagues go through hot embarrassment at not having enough students sign up for courses: they graded too hard, demanded too much, had beliefs too far out of keeping with the existing disposition. It takes only a few such instances to draw other members of the professoriat further into line.

And if what's called tenure reform—which generally just means the abolition of tenure—is broadly enacted, professors will be yet more vulnerable to the whims of their customer-students. Teach what pulls the kids in, or walk. What about entire departments that don't deliver? If the kids say no to Latin and Greek, is it time to dissolve classics? Such questions are being entertained more and more seriously by university administrators.

How does one prosper with the present clientele? Many of the most successful professors now are the ones who have "decentered" their classrooms. There's a new emphasis on group projects and on computer-generated exchanges among the students. What they seem to want most is to talk to one another. A classroom now is frequently an "environment," a place highly conducive to the exchange of existing ideas, the students' ideas. Listening to one another, students sometimes change their opinions. But what they generally can't do is aquire a new vocabulary, a new perspective, that will cast issues in a fresh light.

The Socratic method—the animated, sometimes impolite give-and-take between student and teacher—seems too jagged for current sensibilities. Students frequently come to my office to tell me how intimidated they feel in class; the thought of being embarrassed in front of the group fills them with dread. I remember a student telling me how humiliating it was to be corrected by the teacher, by me. So I asked the logical question: "Should I let a major factual error go by so as to save discomfort?" The student—a good student, smart and earnest—said that was a tough question. He'd need to think about it.

Disturbing? Sure. But I wonder, are we getting students ready for Socratic exchange with professors when we push them off into vast lecture rooms, two and three hundred to a class, sometimes face them with only grad students until their third year, and signal in our myriad professorial ways that we often have much better things to do than sit in our offices and talk with them? How bad will the student-faculty ratios have to become, how teeming the lecture courses, before we hear students righteously complaining, as they did thirty years ago, about the impersonality of their schools, about their decline into knowledge factories? "This is a firm," said Mario Savio at Berkeley during the Free Speech protests of the Sixties, "and if the Board of Regents are the board of directors, …then…the faculty are a bunch of employees and we're the raw material. But we're a bunch of raw material that don't mean…to be made into any product."

Teachers who really do confront students, who provide significant challenges to what they believe, can be very successful, granted. But sometimes such professors generate more than a little trouble for themselves. A controversial teacher can send students hurrying to the deans and the counselors, claiming to have been offended. ("Offensive" is the preferred term of repugnance today, just as "enjoyable" is the summit of praise.) Colleges have brought in hordes of counselors and deans to make sure that everything is smooth, serene, unflustered, that everyone has a good time. To the counselor, to the dean, and to the university legal squad, that which is normal, healthy and prudent is best.

An air of caution and deference is everywhere. When my students come to talk with me in my office, they often exhibit a Franciscan humility. "Do you have a moment?" "I know you're busy. I won't take up much of your time." Their presences tend to be very light; they almost never change the temperature of the room. The dress is nondescript: clothes are in earth tones; shoes are practical—cross-trainers, hiking boots, work shoes, Dr. Martens, with now and then a stylish pair of raised-sole boots on one of the young women. Many, male and female both, peep from beneath the bills of monogrammed baseball caps. Quite a few wear sports, or even corporate, logos, sometimes on one piece of clothing but occasionally (and disconcertingly) on more. The walk is slow; speech is careful, sweet, a bit weary, and without strong inflection. (After the first lively week of the term, most seem far in debt to sleep.) They are almost unfailingly polite. They don't want to offend me; I could hurt them, savage their grades.

Naturally, there are exceptions, kids I chat animatedly with, who offer a joke, or go on about this or that new CD (almost never a book, no). But most of the traffic is genially sleepwalking. I have to admit that I'm a touch wary, too. I tend to hold back. An unguarded remark, a joke that's taken to be off-color, or simply an uncomprehended comment can lead to difficulties. I keep it literal. They scare me a little, these kind and melancholy students, who themselves seem rather frightened of their own lives.

Before they arrive, we ply the students with luscious ads, guaranteeing them a cross between summer camp and lotusland. When they get here, flattery and nonstop entertainment are available, if that's what they want. And when they leave? How do we send our students out into the world? More and more, our administrators call the booking agents and line up one or another celebrity to usher the graduates into the millennium. This past spring, Kermit the Frog won himself an honorary degree at Southampton College on Long Island; Bruce Willis and Yogi Berra took credentials away at Montclair State; Arnold Schwarzenegger scored at the University of Wisconsin-Superior. At Wellesley, Oprah Winfrey gave the commencement address. (*Wellesley*—one of the most rigorous academic colleges in the nation.) At the University of Vermont, Whoopi Goldberg laid down the word. But why should a worthy administrator contract the likes of Susan Sontag, Christopher Hitchens, or Robert Hughs—someone who might actually say something, something disturbing, something "offensive"—when he can get what the parents and kids apparently want and what the newspapers will softly commend—more lite entertainment, more TV?

It is a surprise then, that this generation of students—steeped in consumer culture before going off to school, treated as potent customers by the universty well before their date of arrival, then pandered to from day one until the morning of the final kiss-off from Kermit or one of his kin—are inclined to see the books they read as a string of entertainments to be placidly enjoyed or languidly cast down? Given the way universities are now administered (which is more and more to say, given the way that they are currently marketed), is it a shock that the kids don't come to school hot to learn, unable to bear their own ignorance? For some measure of self-dislike, or self-discontent—which is much different than simple depression—seems to me to be a prerequisite for getting an education that matters. My students, alas, usually lack the confidence to acknowledge what would be their most precious asset for learning: their ignorance.

Not long ago, I asked my Freud class a question that, however hoary, never fails to solicit intriguing responses: Who are your heroes? Whom do you admire? After one remarkable answer, featuring T.S. Eliot as a hero, a series of generic replies rolled in, one gray wave after the next: my father, my best friend, a doctor who lives in our town, my high school history teacher. Virtually all the heroes were people my students had known personally, people who had done something local, specific, and practical, and had done it for them. They were good people who had delivered the goods.

My students' answers didn't exhibit any philosophical resistance to the idea of greatness. It's not that they had been primed by their professors with complex arguments to combat genius. For the truth is that these students don't need debunking theories. Long before college, skepticism became their habitual mode. They are the progeny of Bart Simpson and David Letterman, and the hyper-cool ethos of the box. It's insane to say that theorizing professors have created them, as many conservative critics like to do. Rather, they have substantially created a university environment in which facile skepticisim can thrive without being substantially contested.

Skeptical approaches have *potential* value. If you have no all-encompassing religious faith, no faith in historical destiny, the future of the West, or anything comparably grand, you need to acquire your vision of the world somewhere. If it's from literature, then the various visions literature offers have to be inquired into skeptically. Surely it matters that women are denigrated in Milton and in Pope, that some novelistic voices assume an overbearing godlike authority, that the poor are, in this or that writer, inevitably cast as clowns. You can't buy all of literature wholesale if it's going to help draw your patterns of belief.

But demystifying theories are now overused, applied mechanically. It's all logocentrism, patriarchy, ideology. And in this the student environment—laid-back, skeptical, knowing—is, I believe, central. Full-out debunking is what plays with this clientele. Some have been doing it nearly as long as, if more crudely than, their deconstructionist teachers. In the context of the contemporary university, and cool consumer culture, a useful intellectual skepticism has become exaggerated into a fundamentalist caricature of itself. The teachers have buckled to their students' views.

At its best, multiculturalism can be attractive as well-deployed theory. What could be more valuable than encountering the best work of far-flung cultures and becoming a citizen of the world? But in the current consumer environment, where flattery plays so well, the urge to encounter the other can devolve into the urge to find others who embody and celebrate the right ethnic origins. So we put aside the African novelist Chinua Achebe's abrasive, troubling *Things Fall Apart* and gravitate toward hymns on Africa, cradle of all civilizations.

What about the phenomenon called political correctness? Raising the standard of civility and tolerance in the university has been—who can deny it?—a very good thing. Yet this admirable impulse has expanded to the point where one is enjoined to speak well—and only well—of women, blacks, gays, the disabled, in fact of virtually everyone. And we can owe this expansion in many ways to the student culture. Students now do not wish to be criticized, not in any form. (The culture of consumption never criticizes them, at least not *overtly*.) In the current university, the movement for urbane tolerance has devolved into an imperative against critical reaction, turning much of the intellectual life into a dreary Sargasso Sea. At a certain point, professors stopped being usefully sensitive and became more like careful retailers who have it as a cardinal point of doctrine never to piss the customers off.

To some professors, the solution lies in the movement called cultural studies. What students need, they believe, is to form a critical perspective on pop culture. It's a fine idea, no doubt. Students should be able to run a critical commentary against the stream of consumer stimulations in which they're immersed. But cultural-studies programs rarely work, because no matter what you propose by way of analysis, things tend to bolt downhill toward an uncritical discussion of students' tastes, into what they like and don't like. If you want to do a Frankfurt School-style analysis of *Braveheart*, you can be pretty sure that by mid-class Adorno and Horkheimer will be consigned to the junk heap of history and you'll be collectively weighing the charms of Mel Gibson. One sometimes wonders if cultural studies hasn't prospered because, under the guise of serious intellectual analysis, it gives the customers what they most want—easy pleasure, more TV. Cultural studies becomes nothing better than what its detractors claim it is—Madonna studies—when students kick loose from the critical perspective and groove to the product, and that, in my experience teaching film and pop culture, happens plenty.

On the issue of genius, as on multiculturalism and political correctness, we professors of the humanities have, I think, also failed to press back against our students' consumer tastes. Here we tend to nurse a pair of—to put it charitably—disparate views. In one mode, we're inclined to a programmatic debunking criticism. We call the concept of genius to question. But in our professional lives per se, we aren't usually disposed against the idea of distinguished achievement. We argue animatedly about the caliber of potential colleagues. We support a star system, in which some professors are far better paid, teach less, and under better conditions than the rest. In our own profession, we are creating a system that is the mirror image of the one we're dismantling in the curriculum. Ask a professor what she thinks of the work of Stephen Greenblatt, a leading critic of Shakespeare, and you'll hear it for an hour. Ask her what her views are on Shakespeare's genius and she's likely to begin questioning the term along with the whole "discourse of evaluation." This dual sensibility may be intellectually incoherent. But in its awareness of what plays with students, it's conducive to good classroom evaluations and, in its awareness of where and how the professional bread is buttered, to self-advancement as well.

My overall point is this: It's not that a left-wing professional coup has taken over the university. It's that at American universities, left-liberal politics have collided with the ethos of consumerism. The consumer ethos is winning.

Then how do those who at least occasionally promote genius and high literary ideals look to current students? How do we appear, those of us who take teaching to be something of a performance art and who imagine that if you give yourself over completely to your subject you'll be rewarded with insight beyond what you individually command?

I'm reminded of an old piece of newsreel footage I saw once. The speaker (perhaps it was Lenin, maybe Trotsky) was haranguing a large crowd. He was expostulating, arm waving, carrying on. Whether it was flawed technology or the man himself, I'm not sure, but the orator looked like an intricate mechanical device that had sprung into fast-forward. To my students, who mistrust enthusiasm in every form, that's me when I start riffing about Freud or Blake. But more and more, as my evaluations showed, I've been replacing enthusiasm and intellectual animation with stand-up routines, keeping it all at arm's length, praising under the cover of irony.

It's too bad that the idea of genius has been denigrated so far, because it actually offers a live alternative to the demoralizing culture of hip in which most of my students are mired. By embracing the works and lives of extraordinary people, you can adapt new ideals to revise those that came courtesy of your parents, your neighborhood, your clan—or the tube. The aim of a good liberal-arts education was once, to adapt an observation by the scholar Walter Jackson Bate, to see that "we need not be the passive victims of what we deterministically call 'circumstances' (social, cultural, or reductively psychological-personal), but that by linking ourselves through what Keats calls an "immortal free-masonry" with the great we can become freer—freer to be ourselves, to be what we most want and value."

But genius isn't just a personal standard; genius can also have political effect. To me, one of the best things about democratic thinking is the conviction that genius can spring up anywhere. Walt Whitman is born into the working class and thirty-six years later we have a poetic image of America that gives a passionate dimension to the legalistic brilliance of the Constitution. A democracy needs to constantly develop, and to do so it requires the most powerful visionary minds to interpret the present and to propose possible shapes for the future. By continuing to notice and praise genius, we create a culture in which the kind of poetic gamble that Whitman made—a gamble in which failure would have entailed rank humiliation, depression, maybe suicide—still takes place. By rebelling against established ways of seeing and saying things, genius helps us to apprehend how malleable the present is and how promising and fraught with danger is the future. If we teachers do not endorse genius and self-overcoming, can we be surprised when our students find their ideal images in TV's latest persona ads?

A world uninterested in genius is a despondent place, whose sad denizens drift from coffee bar to Prozac dispensary, unfired by ideals, by the glowing image of the self that one might become. As Northrop Frye says in a beautiful and now dramatically unfashionable sentence, "The artist who uses the same energy and genius that Homer and Isaiah had will find that he not only lives in the same palace of art as Homer and Isaiah, but lives in it at the same time." We ought not to deny the existence of such a place simply because we, or those we care for, find the demands it makes intimidating, the rent too high.

What happens if we keep trudging along this bleak course? What happens if our most intelligent students never learn to strive to overcome what they are? What if genius, and the imitation of genius, become silly, outmoded ideas? What you're likely to get are more and more one-dimensional men and women. These will be people who live for easy pleasures, for comfort and prosperity, who think of money first, then second, and third, who hug the status quo; people who believe in God as a sort of insurance policy (cover your bets); people who are never surprised. They will be people so pleased with themselves (when they're not in despair at the general pointlessness of their lives) that they cannot imagine humanity could do better. They'll think it their highest duty to clone themselves as frequently as possible. They'll claim to be happy, and they'll live a long time.

It is probably time now to offer a spate of inspiring solutions. Here ought to come a list of reforms, with due notations about a core curriculum and various requirements. What the traditionalists who offer such solutions miss is that no matter what our current students are given to read, many of them will simply translate it into melodrama, with flat characters and predictable morals. (The unabated capitalist culture that conservative critics so often endorse has put students in a position to do little else.) One can't simply wave a curricular wand and reverse acculturation.

Perhaps it would be a good idea to try firing the counselors and sending half the deans back into their classrooms, dismantling the football team and making the stadium into a playground for local kids, emptying the fraternities, and boarding up the student-activities office. Such measures would convey the message that American colleges are not northern outposts of Club Med. A willingness on the part of the faculty to defy student conviction and affront them occasionally—to be usefully offensive—also might not be a bad thing. We professors talk a lot about subversion, which generally means subverting the views of people who never hear us talk or read our work. But to subvert the views of our students, our customers, that would be something else again.

Ultimately, though, it is up to individuals—and individual students in particular—to make their own way against the current sludgy tide. There's still the library, still the museum, there's still the occasional teacher who lives to find things greater than herself to admire. There are still fellow students who have not been cowed. Universities are inefficient, cluttered, archaic places, with many unguarded corners where one can open a book or gaze out onto the larger world and construe it freely. Those who do as much, trusting themselves against the weight of current opinion, will have contributed something to bringing this sad dispensation to an end. As for myself, I'm canning my low-key one-liners; when the kid's TV-based tastes come to the fore, I'll aim and shoot. And when it's time to praise genius, I'll try to do it in the right style, full-out, with faith that finer artistic spirits (maybe not Homer and Isaiah quite, but close, close), still alive somewhere in the ether, will help me out when my invention flags, the students doze, or the dean mutters into the phone. I'm getting back to a more exuberant style; I'll be expostulating and arm waving straight into the millennium, yes I will.

Questions for Discussion

1. Edmundson places blame for the current state of affairs in higher education on U. S. consumer culture. In what ways does Edmundson support this claim? What "evidence" does he cite?

2. Economics, Edmundson argues, determines universities' decisions about nearly every facet of its educational enterprise. The modern university is driven by the "customer." Is this so bad? (Edmundson thinks so, of course.) What are the advantages and disadvantages of allowing students a voice in determining the content, form, and rigor of their educational experiences? Are they capable of making these kinds of decisions? Why or why not?

3. What kinds of "promotional strategies" did universities use to encourage you to consider their institutions? Which strategies were most successful in your case? What finally determined your decision to attend your college?

Explorations

1. Although he makes few explicit statements about how college professors might best approach their teaching to combat the consumerist modes held by their students, Edmundson articulates a few characteristics near the end of his essay when he writes that he will be "canning" the "low-key one-liners." What characteristics do you believe make an effective teacher? Are they some of the ones Edmundson condemns or embraces?

2. Compare Edmundson's characterization of students to those of Barber, Rose or Shorris. How do they differ? Barber, for example, also makes claims about the forces that shape U. S. students. Do you agree with Barber? Edmundson? Are their characterizations accurate? Why or why not? How do you think Rose or Shorris would respond to Edmundson's essay?

3. Edmundson writes rather disparagingly about students' clothing, interactions with professors, and their "shopping" habits as they look for courses early in a term. Why do you make the choices you do for the clothing you wear? The ways you interact with professors? The courses you take? In what ways does consumerism affect these decisions?

Formal Writing Assignments

1. Compose an analysis of Edmundson's argument in which you address one or more of the central elements of his essay (e.g., argumentative form; literary or popular culture allusions; rhetorical appeals to logic, emotion, and authority) and analyze their role in the essay and effect on his claims.

2. Write an essay that rebuts Edmundson. In the essay, use your own college or university and its faculty and students as the "proof" for your case against Edmundson's argument.

The Banking Concept of Education

Paulo Freire

Paulo Freire (pronounced "Frair-uh") was born in Recife, Brazil in 1929. Until his death of a heart attack in Sao Paulo in May 1997, Freire was considered a world leader in literacy studies, founding adult literacy programs worldwide in third world and developing countries. In the course of his nearly half-century long teaching and writing career, Freire endured a fifteen year exile from Brazil but returned in 1980, eventually to serve as Brazil's secretary of education and general coordinator of the National Plan of Adult Literacy. Once a visiting professor at Harvard, consultant to the Office of Education at the World Council of Churches and UNESCO, and professor of education at Catholic University in Sao Paulo, Freire published more than a dozen books in (or translated into) English on such topics as liberatory education, Christianity and education, adult education, and literacy and culture.

Much of Freire's early career, however, was devoted to working in poverty-stricken areas of Brazil, where he developed methods for teaching illiterate adults to read and write and, in the process, to take power over their own lives by learning to think critically about their political and economic positions. This work led to his exile in 1964 but also initiated a call for a significant shift in educational and political policies aimed at combating the illiteracy of Brazil's poorest citizens. In Freire's view, education should be a collaborative process in which teachers and students work together as co-investigators of their cultures. "The Banking Concept of Education" is taken from *Pedagogy of the Oppressed* (1970), the book that brought Freire's name to the forefront of literacy education in the U.S.

Writing Before Reading

1. Describe what is for you an ideal learning situation. You can either describe a class or other learning situation (e.g., tae kwon do, guitar, dance, band) in the past that was extremely successful or construct a hypothetical context. What is (or was) the teacher's role? the students'? What methods were used to engage students? encourage learning?

2. Characterize yourself as a student. Are you typically quiet? passive? boisterous? engaged? Does your disposition or attitude shift depending on the course? the teacher's approach?

3. What are your expectations for teachers? What do you expect them to do or provide? How do you expect them to relate to you? How do your expectations for college teachers differ from your expectations for high school teachers? Why have your expectations changed?

The Banking Concept of Education

A careful analysis of the teacher-student relationship at any level, inside or outside the school, reveals its fundamentally *narrative* character. This relationship involves a narrating Subject (the teacher) and patient, listening objects (the Students). The contents, whether values or empirical dimensions of reality, tend in the process of being narrated to become lifeless and petrified. Education is suffering from narration sickness.

The teacher talks about reality as if it were motionless, static, compartmentalized, and predictable. Or else he expounds on a topic completely alien to the existential experience of the students. His task is to "fill" the students with the contents of his narration—contents which are detached from reality, disconnected from the totality that engendered them and could give them significance. Words are emptied of their concreteness and become a hollow, alienated, and alienating verbosity.

The outstanding characteristic of this narrative education, then, is the sonority of words, not their transforming power. "Four times four is sixteen; the capital of Pará is Belém." The student records, memorizes, and repeats these phrases without perceiving what four times four really means, or realizing the true significance of "capital" in the affirmation "the capital of Pará is Belém," that is, what Belém means for Pará and what Pará means for Brazil.

Narration (with the teacher as narrator) leads the students to memorize mechanically the narrated content. Worse yet, it turns them into "containers," into "receptacles" to be "filled" by the teacher. The more completely he fills the receptacles, the better a teacher he is. The more meekly the receptacles permit themselves to be filled, the better students they are.

Education thus becomes an act of depositing, in which the students are the depositories and the teacher issues communiqués and makes deposits which the students patiently receive, memorize, and repeat. This is the "banking" concept of education, in which the scope of action allowed to the students extends only as far as receiving, filing, and storing the deposits. They do, it is true, have the opportunity to become collectors or cataloguers of the things they store. But in the last analysis, it is men themselves who are filed away through the lack of creativity, transformation, and knowledge in this (at best) misguided system. For apart from inquiry, apart from the praxis, men cannot be truly human. Knowledge emerges only through invention and re-invention, through the restless, impatient, continuing, hopeful inquiry men pursue in the world, with the world, and with each other.

In the banking concept of education, knowledge is a gift bestowed by those who consider themselves knowledgeable upon those whom they consider to know nothing. Projecting an absolute ignorance onto others, a characteristic of the ideology of oppression, negates education and knowledge as processes of inquiry. The teacher presents himself to his students as their necessary opposite; by considering their ignorance absolute, he justifies his own existence. The students, alienated like the slave in the Hegelian dialectic, accept their ignorance as justifying the teacher's existence—but, unlike the slave, they never discover that they educate the teacher.

The *raison d'être* of libertarian education, on the other hand, lies in its drive towards reconciliation. Education must begin with the solution of the teacher-student contradiction, by reconciling the poles of the contradiction so that both are simultaneously teachers *and* students.

This solution is not (nor can it be) found in the banking concept. On the contrary, banking education maintains and even stimulates the contradiction through the following attitudes and practices, which mirror oppressive society as a whole:

(a) the teacher teaches and the students are taught;

(b) the teacher knows everything and the students know nothing;

(c) the teacher thinks and the students are thought about;

(d) the teacher talks and the students listen—meekly;

(e) the teacher disciplines and the students are disciplined;

(f) the teacher chooses and enforces his choice, and the students comply;

(g) the teacher acts and the students have the illusion of acting through the action of the teacher;

(h) the teacher chooses the program content, and the students (who were not consulted) adapt to it;

(i) the teacher confuses the authority of knowledge with his own

    professional authority, which he sets in opposition to the freedom of the students;

(j) the teacher is the Subject of the learning process, while the pupils are mere objects

It is not surprising that the banking concept of education regards men as adaptable, manageable beings. The more students work at storing the deposits entrusted to them, the less they develop the critical consciousness which would result from their intervention in the world as transformers of that world. The more completely they accept the passive role imposed on them, the more they tend simply to adapt to the world as it is and to the fragmented view of reality deposited in them.

The capability of banking education to minimize or annul the students' creative power and to stimulate their credulity serves the interests of the oppressors, who care neither to have the world revealed nor to see it transformed. The oppressors use their "humanitarianism" to preserve a profitable situation. Thus they react almost instinctively against any experiment in education which stimulates the critical facilities and is not content with a partial view of reality but always seeks out the ties which link one point to another and one problem to another.

Indeed, the interests of the oppressors lie in "changing the consciousness of the oppressed, not the situation which oppresses them";[1] for the more the oppressed can be led to adapt to that situation, the more easily they can be dominated. To achieve this end, the oppressors use the banking concept of education in conjunction with a paternalistic social action apparatus, within which the oppressed receive the euphemistic title of "welfare recipients." They are treated as individual cases, as marginal men who deviate from the general configuration of a "good, organized, and just" society. The oppressed are regarded as the pathology of the healthy society, which must therefore adjust these "incompetent and lazy" folk to its own patterns by changing their mentality. These marginals need to be "integrated," "incorporated" into the healthy society they have "forsaken."

The truth is, however, that the oppressed are not "marginals," are not men living "outside" society. They have always been "inside"—inside the structure which made them "beings for others." The solution is not to "integrate" them into the structure of oppression, but to transform that structure so that they can become "beings for themselves." Such transformation, of course, would undermine the oppressors' purposes; hence their utilization of the banking concept of education to avoid the threat of student *conscientização*.

The banking approach to adult education, for example, will never propose to students that they critically consider reality. It will deal instead with such vital questions as whether Roger gave green grass to the goat, and insist upon the importance of learning that, on the contrary, *Roger* gave green grass to the rabbit. The "humanism" of the banking approach masks the effort to turn men into automatons— the very negation of their ontological vocation to be more fully human.

Those who use the banking approach, knowingly or unknowingly (for there are innumerable well-intentioned bank-clerk teachers who do not realize that they are serving only to dehumanize), fail to perceive that the deposits themselves contain contradictions about reality. But, sooner or later, these contradictions may lead formerly passive students to turn against their domestication and the attempt to domesticate reality. They may discover through existential experience that their present way of life is irreconcilable with their vocation to become fully human. They may perceive through their relations with reality that reality is really a process, undergoing constant transformation. If men are searchers and their ontological vocation is humanization, sooner or later they may perceive the contradiction in which banking education seeks to maintain them, and then engage themselves in the struggle for their liberation.

But the humanist, revolutionary educator cannot wait for this possibility to materialize. From the outset, his efforts must coincide with those of the students to engage in critical thinking and the quest for mutual humanization. His efforts must be imbued with a profound trust in men and their creative power. To achieve this, he must be a partner of the students in his relations with them.

The banking concept does not admit to such partnership—and necessarily so. To resolve the teacher-student contradiction, to exchange the role of depositor, prescriber, domesticator, for the role of student among students would be to undermine the power of oppression and serve the cause of liberation.

Implicit in the banking concept is the assumption of a dichotomy between man and the world: man is merely in the world, not with the world or with others; man is spectator, not re-creator, In this view, man is not a conscious being *(corpo consciente)*; he is rather the possessor of a consciousness: an empty "mind" passively open to the reception of deposits of reality from the world outside. For example, my desk, my books, my coffee cup, all the objects before me—as bits of the world which surrounds me—would be "inside" me, exactly as I am inside my study right now. This view makes no distinction between being accessible to consciousness and entering consciousness. The distinction, however, is essential: the objects which surround me are simply accessible to my consciousness, not located within it. I am aware of them, but they are not inside me.

It follows logically from the banking notion of consciousness that the educator's role is to regulate the way the world "enters into" the students. His task is to organize a process which already occurs spontaneously to "fill" the students by making deposits of information which he considers to constitute true knowledge.[2] And since men "receive" the world as passive entities, education should make them more passive still, and adapt them to the world. The educated man is the adapted man, because he is better "fit" for the world. Translated into practice, this concept is well suited to the purposes of the oppressors, whose tranquility rests on how well men fit the world the oppressors have created, and how little they question it.

The more completely the majority adapt to the purposes which the dominant minority prescribe for them (thereby depriving them of the right to their own purposes), the more easily the minority can continue to prescribe. The theory and practice of banking education serve this end quite efficiently. Verbalistic lessons, reading requirements,[3] the methods for evaluating "knowledge," the distance between the teacher and the taught, the criteria for promotion: everything in this ready-to-wear approach serves to obviate thinking.

The bank-clerk educator does not realize that there is no true security in his hypertrophied role, that one must seek to live *with* others in solidarity. One cannot impose oneself, nor even merely coexist with one's students. Solidarity requires true communication, and the concept by which such an educator is guided fears and proscribes communication.

Yet only through communication can human life hold meaning. The teacher's thinking is authenticated only by the authenticity of the students' thinking. The teacher cannot think for his students, nor can he impose his thought on them. Authentic thinking, thinking that is concerned about *reality*, does not take place in ivory tower isolation, but only in communication. If it is true that thought has meaning only when generated by action upon the world, the subordination of students to teachers becomes impossible.

Because banking education begins with a false understanding of men as objects, it cannot promote the development of what Fromm calls "biophily," but instead produces its opposite: "Necrophily."

> While life is characterized by growth in a structured, functional manner, the necrophilous person loves all that does not grow, all that is mechanical. The necrophilous person is driven by the desire to transform the organic into the inorganic, to approach life mechanically, as if all living persons were things. . . . Memory, rather than experience; having, rather than being, is what counts. The necrophilous person can relate to an object—a flower or a person—only if he possesses it; hence a threat to his possession is a threat to himself, if he loses

possession he loses contact with the world . . . He loves control, and in the act of controlling he kills life.[4]

Oppression—overwhelming control—is necrophilic; it is nourished by love of death, not life. The
banking concept of education, which serves the interests of oppression, is also necrophilic. Based on a
mechanistic, static, naturalistic, spatialized view of consciousness, it transforms students into receiving
objects. It attempts to control thinking and action, leads men to adjust to the world, and inhibits their
creative power.

When their efforts to act responsibly are frustrated, when they find themselves unable to use their
faculties, men suffer. "This suffering due to impotence is rooted in the very fact that the human equilibrium has been disturbed."[5] But the inability to act which causes men's anguish also causes them to reject
their impotence, by attempting

> . . . to restore [their] capacity to act. But can [they], and how? One way is to submit to and
> identify with a person or group having power. By this symbolic participation in another per-
> son's life, [men have] the illusion of acting, when in reality [they] only submit to and become
> a part of those who act.[6]

Populist manifestations perhaps best exemplify this type of behavior by the oppressed, who, by
identifying with charismatic leaders, come to feel that they themselves are active and effective. The rebellion they express as they emerge in the historical process is motivated by that desire to act effectively. The
dominant elites consider the remedy to be more domination and repression, carried out in the name of
freedom, order, and social peace (that is, the peace of the elites). Thus they can condemn—logically,
from their point of view—"the violence of a strike by workers and [can] call upon the state in the same
breath to use violence in putting down the strike."[7]

Education as the exercise of domination stimulates the credulity of students, with the ideological
intent (often not perceived by educators) of indoctrinating them to adapt to the world of oppression. This
accusation is not made in the naïve hope that the dominant elites will thereby simply abandon the practice. Its objective is to call the attention of true humanists to the fact that they cannot use banking educational methods in the pursuit of liberation. For they would only negate that very pursuit. Nor may a
revolutionary society inherit these methods from an oppressor society. The revolutionary society which
practices banking education is either misguided or mistrusting of men. In either event, it is threatened
by the specter of reaction.

Unfortunately, those who espouse the cause of liberation are themselves surrounded and influenced by the climate which generates the banking concept, and often do not perceive its true significance
or its dehumanizing power. Paradoxically, then, they utilize this same instrument of alienation in what
they consider an effort to liberate. Indeed, some "revolutionaries" brand as "innocents," "dreamers," or
even "reactionaries" those who would challenge this educational practice. But one does not liberate men
by alienating them. Authentic liberation—the process of humanization—is not another deposit to be made
in men. Liberation is a praxis: the action and reflection of men upon their world in order to transform
it. Those truly committed to the cause of liberation can accept neither the mechanistic concert of consciousness as an empty vessel to be filled, nor the use of banking methods of domination (propaganda,
slogans—deposits) in the name of liberation,

Those truly committed to liberation must reject the banking concept in its entirety, adopting
instead a concept of men as conscious beings, and consciousness as consciousness intent upon the world.
They must abandon the educational goal of deposit-making and replace it with the posing of the problems of men in their relations with the world. "Problem-posing" education, responding to the essence of
consciousness—*intentionality*—rejects communiqués and embodies communication. It epitomizes the spe-

cial characteristic of consciousness: being *conscious of*, not only as intent on objects but as turned in upon itself in a Jasperian "split"—consciousness as consciousness *of* consciousness.

Liberating education consists in acts of cognition, not transferrals of information. It is a learning situation in which the cognizable object (far from being the end of the cognitive act) intermediates the cognitive actors—teacher on the one hand and students on the other. Accordingly, the practice of problem-posing education entails at the outset that the teacher-student contradiction be resolved. Dialogical relations—indispensable to the capacity of cognitive actors to cooperate in perceiving the same cognizable object—are otherwise impossible.

Indeed, problem-posing education, which breaks with the vertical patterns characteristic of banking education, can fulfill its functions as the practice of freedom only if it can overcome the above contradiction. Through dialogue, the teacher-of-the-students and the students-of-the-teacher cease to exist and a new term emerges: teacher-student with students-teachers. The teacher is no longer merely the-one-who-teaches, but one who is himself taught in dialogue with the students, who in turn while being taught also teach. They become jointly responsible for a process in which all grow. In this process, arguments based on "authority" are no longer valid; in order to function, authority must be *on the side of freedom*, not *against* it. Here, no one teaches another, nor is anyone self-taught. Men teach each other, mediated by the world, by the cognizable objects which in banking education are "owned" by the teacher.

The banking concept (with its tendency to dichotomize everything) distinguishes two stages in the action of the educator. During the first, he cognizes a cognizable object while he prepares his lessons in his study or his laboratory; during the second, he expounds to his students about that object. The students are not called upon to know, but to memorize the contents narrated by the teacher. Nor do the students practice any act of cognition, since the object towards which that act should be directed is the property of the teacher rather than a medium evoking the critical reflection of both teacher and students. Hence in the name of the "preservation of culture and knowledge" we have a system which achieves neither true knowledge nor true culture.

The problem-posing method does not dichotomize the activity of the teacher-student: he is not "cognitive" at one point and "narrative" at another. He is always "cognitive," whether preparing a project or engaging in dialogue with the students. He does not regard cognizable objects as his private property, but as the object of reflection by himself and the students. In this way, the problem posing educator constantly re-forms his reflections in the reflection of the students. The students—no longer docile listeners— are now critical co-investigators in dialogue with the teacher. The teacher presents the material to the students for their consideration, and reconsiders his earlier considerations as the students express their own. The role of the problem-posing educator is to create, together with the students, the conditions under which knowledge at the level of the *doxa* is superseded by true knowledge, at the level of the *logos*.

Whereas banking education anesthetizes and inhibits creative power, problem-posing education involves a constant unveiling of reality. The former attempts to maintain the *submersion* of consciousness; the latter strives for the *emergence* of consciousness and *critical intervention* in reality.

Students, as they are increasingly posed with problems relating to themselves in the world and with the world, will feel increasingly challenged and obliged to respond to that challenge. Because they apprehend the challenge as interrelated to other problems within a total context, not as a theoretical question, the resulting comprehension tends to be increasingly critical and thus constantly less alienated. Their response to the challenge evokes new challenges, followed by new understandings; and gradually the students come to regard themselves as committed.

Education as the practice of freedom—as opposed to education as the practice of domination—denies that man is abstract, isolated, independent, and unattached to the world; it also denies that the world exists as a reality apart from men. Authentic reflection considers neither abstract men nor the world without men, but men in their relations with the world. In these relations consciousness and world are simultaneous: consciousness neither precedes the world nor follows it.

> La conscience et le monde sont dormés d'un même coup: extérieur par essence à la conscience, le monde est, par essence relatif à elle.[8]

In one of our culture circles in Chile, the group was discussing (based on a codification[9]) the anthropological concept of culture. In the midst of the discussion, a peasant who by banking standards was completely ignorant said: "Now I see that without man there is no world." When the educator responded: "Let's say, for the sake of argument, that all the men on earth were to die, but that the earth itself remained, together with trees, birds, animals, rivers, seas, the stars . . . wouldn't all this be a world?" "Oh no," the peasant replied emphatically. "There would be no one to say: 'This is a world'."

The peasant wished to express the idea that there would be lacking the consciousness of the world which necessarily implies the world of consciousness. *I* cannot exist without a *not-I*. In turn, the *not-I* depends on that existence. The world which brings consciousness into existence becomes the world of that consciousness. Hence, the previously cited affirmation of Sartre: *"La conscience et le monde sont dormés d'un même coup. "*

As men, simultaneously reflecting on themselves and on the world, increase the scope of their perception, they begin to direct their observations toward previously inconspicuous phenomena:

> In perception properly so-called, as an explicit awareness [*Gewahren*], I am turned towards the object, to the paper, for instance. I apprehend it as being this here and now. The apprehension is a singling out, every object having a background in experience. Around and about the paper lie books, pencils, ink-well, and so forth, and these in a certain sense are also "perceived," perceptually there, in the "field of intuition"; but whilst I was turned towards the paper there was no turning in their direction, nor any apprehending of them, not even in a secondary sense. They appeared and yet were not singled out, were not posited on their own account. Every perception of a thing has such a zone of background intuitions or background awareness, if "intuiting" already includes the state of being turned towards, and this also is a "conscious experience," or more briefly a "consciousness of" all indeed that in point of fact lies in the co-perceived objective background.[10]

That which had existed objectively but had not been perceived in its deeper implications (if indeed it was perceived at all) begins to "stand out," assuming the character of a problem and therefore of challenge. Thus, men begin to single out elements from their "background awareness" and to reflect upon them. These elements are not objects of men's consideration, and, as such, objects of their actions and cognition.

In problem-posing education, men develop their power to perceive critically *the way they exist* in the world *with which* and *in which* they find themselves; they come to see the world not as a static reality, but as a reality in process, in transformation. Although the dialectical relations of men with the world exist independently of how these relations are perceived (or whether or not they are perceived at all), it is also true that the form of action men adopt is to a large extent a function of how they perceive themselves in the world. Hence, the teacher-student and the students-teachers reflect simultaneously on themselves and the world without dichotomizing this reflection from action, and thus establish an authentic form of thought and action.

Once again, the two educational concepts and practices under analysis come into conflict. Banking education (for obvious reasons) attempts, by mythicizing reality, to conceal certain facts which explain the way men exist in the world; problem-posing education sets itself the task of demythologizing. Banking education resists dialogue; problem-posing education regards dialogue as indispensable to the act of cognition which unveils reality. Banking education treats students as objects of assistance; problem-posing education makes them critical thinkers. Banking education inhibits creativity and domesticates (although it cannot completely destroy) the *intentionality* of consciousness by isolating consciousness from the world, thereby denying men their ontological and historical vocation of becoming more fully human. Problem-posing education bases itself on creativity and stimulates true reflection and action upon reality thereby responding to the vocation of men as beings who are authentic only when engaged in inquiry and creative transformation. In sum: banking theory and practice, as immobilizing and fixating forces, fail to acknowledge men as historical beings; problem-posing theory and practice take man's historicity as their starting point.

Problem-posing education affirms men as being in the process of *becoming*—as unfinished, uncompleted beings in and with a likewise unfinished reality. Indeed, in contrast to other animals who are unfinished, but not historical, men know themselves to be unfinished; they are aware of their incompletion. In this incompletion and this awareness lie the very roots of education as all exclusively human manifestation. The unfinished character of men and the transformational character of reality necessitate that education be an ongoing activity.

Education is thus constantly remade in the praxis. In order to *be*, it must *become*. Its "duration" (in the Bergsonian meaning of the word) is found in the interplay of the opposites *permanence* and *change*. The banking method emphasizes permanence and becomes reactionary; problem-posing education—which accepts neither a "well-behaved" present nor a predetermined future—roots itself in the dynamic present and becomes revolutionary.

Problem-posing education is revolutionary futurity. Hence it is prophetic (and, as such, hopeful). Hence, it corresponds to the historical nature of man. Hence, it affirms men as beings who transcend themselves, who move forward and look ahead, for whom immobility represents a fatal threat, for whom looking at the past must only be a means of understanding more clearly what and who they are so that they can more wisely build the future. Hence, it identifies with the movement which negates men as being aware of their incompletion—an historical movement which has its point of departure, its subjects and its objective.

The point of departure of the movement lies in men themselves. But since men do not exist apart from the world, apart from reality, the movement must begin with the men-world relationship. Accordingly, the point of departure must always be with men in the "here and now," which constitutes the situation within which they are submerged, from which they emerge, and in which they intervene. Only by starting from this situation—which determines their perception of it—can they begin to move. To do this authentically they must perceive their state not as fated and unalterable, but merely as limiting—and therefore challenging.

Whereas the banking method directly or indirectly reinforces men's fatalistic perception of their situation, the problem-posing method presents this very situation to them as a problem. As the situation becomes the object of their cognition, the naïve or magical perception which produced their fatalism gives way to perception which is able to perceive itself even as it perceives reality, and can thus be critically objective about that reality.

A deepened consciousness of their situation leads men to apprehend that situation as an historical reality susceptible of transformation. Resignation gives way to the drive for transformation and inquiry, over which men feel themselves to be in control. If men, as historical beings necessarily engaged with other men in a movement of inquiry, did not control that movement, it would be (and is) a violation of men's humanity. Any situation in which some men prevent others from engaging in the process of inquiry is one of violence. The means used are not important; to alienate men from their own decision-making is to change them into objects.

This movement of inquiry must be directed towards humanization—man's historical vocation. The pursuit of full humanity, however, cannot be carried out in isolation or individualism, but only in fellowship and solidarity; therefore it cannot unfold in the antagonistic relations between oppressors and oppressed. No one can be authentically human while he prevents others from being so. Attempting to be *more* human, individualistically, leads to *having more*, egotistically: a form of dehumanization. Not that it is not fundamental to *have* in order to *be* human. Precisely because it *is* necessary, some men's *having* must not be allowed to constitute an obstacle to others' having, must not consolidate the power of the former to crush the latter.

Problem-posing education, as a humanist and liberating praxis, posits as fundamental that men subjected to domination must fight for their emancipation. To that end, it enables teachers and students to become Subjects of the educational process by overcoming authoritarianism and an alienating intellectualism; it also enables men to overcome their false perception of reality. The world—no longer something to be described with deceptive words—becomes the object of that transforming action by men which results in their humanization.

Problem-posing education does not and cannot serve the interests of the oppressor. No oppressive order could permit the oppressed to begin to question: Why? while only a revolutionary society can carry out this education in systematic terms, the revolutionary leaders need not take full power before they can employ the method. In the revolutionary process, the leaders cannot utilize the banking method as an interim measure, justified on grounds of expediency, with the intention of *later* behaving in a genuinely revolutionary fashion. They must be revolutionary—that is to say, dialogical—from the outset.

Notes

1. Simone de Beauvoir, *La Pensée de Droite, Aujord'hui* Paris; ST, *El Pensamiento Politico de la Derecha* (Buenos Aires, 1963), p. 34.

2. This concept corresponds to what Sartre calls the "digestive" or "nutritive" concept of education, in which knowledge is "fed" by the teacher to the students to "fill them out." See Jean-Paul Sartre, "Une idée fundamentale de la phénomenologie de Husserl: L'internationalite," *Situations* I (Paris, 1947).

3. For example, some professors specify in their reading lists that a book should be read from pages 10 to 15—and do this to "help" their students!

4. Fromm, *op. cit.,* p. 41.

5. *Ibid., P.* 3 1.

6. *Ibid.*

7. Reinhold Niebuhr, *Moral Man and Immoral Society* (New York, 1960), p. 130.

8. Sarte, *op. cit.,* p. 32.

9. See Chapter 3—Translator's note.

10. Edmund Husserl, *Ideas—General Introduction to Pure Phenomenology* (London, 1969), pp. 105-106.

Questions for Discussion

1. What is the "banking concept" of education? In a banking classroom, what are the "rules of the game" and what are the roles of participants?

2. What is "problem-posing" education? In a problem-posing classroom, what are the "rules of the game" and what are the roles of participants? How, in other words, are "students" and "teachers" redefined in problem-posing education?

3. What kinds of classes (e.g., humanities, social sciences, engineering, the arts, hard sciences) are most conducive to problem-posing approaches? Why do some classes lend themselves to a problem-posing approach while others do not?

Explorations

1. Freire's essay is remarkable, even in translation to English, in its use of terminology. The language is deeply philosophical and sometimes quite abstract. To engage the text more fully, it is often helpful to investigate and amplify the meaning of some of the key phrases. Consider and then write about the following phrases. Freire writes that "[s]olidarity requires true communication." What is this "solidarity'? What is "true communication" and why is it necessary for the development of solidarity? What, to Freire, does it mean to be "truly human"? What does it mean to you to be truly human? How does your definition compare with Freire's?

2. Freire and Rose (as well as other writers in this unit) discuss how education has traditionally worked against the needs of many working-class and "underprepared" students. What cultural attitudes and economic or political principles uphold the traditional system? Is the traditional system as easy to identify as Freire implies? Why or why not?

3. Apply Freire's two concepts of education to the types of schools described by Anyon. Which of the school descriptions are more oriented toward a banking concept of education? Which are more oriented toward a problem-posing concept? Given your observations, what conclusions might you draw about the relationship between economics and educational approaches?

Formal Writing Assignments

1. Compose an essay directed toward the teachers and administrators of your local high school district in which you explain to them Freirean theories of education, analyze your own experiences as a student in the district, and suggest changes in the district that will offer students more "problem-posing" opportunities.

2. Working from your response to the second Exploration above, construct an essay in which you theorize about some part of the learning environment in U.S. schools. Base your essay on your own and your classmates' educational experiences from elementary school through high school. As you draft, begin by identifying a specific subject (e.g., teacher approaches, student learning styles or attitudes, learning environments). Next, identify categories, as Freire does when he develops the banking and problem-posing concepts of education. The essay should, as well, illustrate each of the categories with specific and concrete examples.

The Social Responsibility that Writing Is—And Writing Instruction, Too

Keith Gilyard

Keith Gilyard is currently Professor of English at The Pennsylvania State University, and he is the former Director of the Writing Program at Syracuse University. Born, raised, and educated in New York City, Gilyard is a poet, critic, activist, educator, and administrator. He earned his BS at CUNY, his MFA at Columbia, and his Doctorate at NYU; no doubt the variety of educational institutions he attended helped him develop his keen understanding of how educational contexts reflect the identities of those who matriculate there. Gilyard is also currently the Associate Chair of the Conference on College Composition and Communication, the largest and most influential organization for writing teachers in the United States.

He is the author and editor of seven books, including *Voices of the Self: A Study of Language Competence* (1991) and *Let's Flip the Script: An African American Discourse on Language, Literature, and Learning* (1996). His most recent book is titled *Race, Rhetoric, and Composition* (1999). The essay you are about to read, "The Social Responsibility That Writing Is—and Writing Instruction Too" was originally presented orally in February, 1993 at the Conference of CUNY Writing Centers Association. Later, the piece was published in the journal *Community Review*.

As you read, consider the political implications of Gilyard's essay. Like Rose, Shorris, hooks, and others, Gilyard sees the classroom as a highly politicized space where teachers, texts, and students all interact with one another in ways that have real consequences.

Writing Before Reading

1. When you write, how do you imagine your audience? Do you most often write for yourself, or for others? How would you describe your responsibilities—as a communicator, a thinker, a sharer of ideas—to those for whom you write?

2. Describe a time when you believe something that you wrote had real consequences. Who did your writing affect? What kind of effect did it have? What end results came out of your writing?

3. Choose another selection you've read during the Academic Literacies unit and skim it briefly. Do you believe that writer handled his/her issue responsibly? Why or why not? What was your own response to the writer's treatment of the issues addressed?

The Social Responsiblity that Writing Is— And Writing Instruction Too

Writing is not an activity that features social responsibility as an option. Writing *is* social responsibility. When you write, you are being responsible to some social entity even if that entity is yourself. You can be irresponsible as a writer, but you cannot be nonresponsible.

This issue probably has been discussed most in literary circles, couched in the long-running debate between those who view art as propaganda and those who subscribe to the notion of art for art's sake. I am obviously in the former camp and feel, for example, that the late critic Addison Gayle spoke compellingly when he asserted at the National Black Writers Conference in 1986 that "if Black people are being shipped to die in Grenada and you choose to write poems and novels about sunsets and trees, you are being responsible. You are just being responsible to the status quo."

At the same gathering, the poet Jayne Cortez reasoned:

> If information is a resource for advancement and development and is the basis by which people make their decisions, then one of the responsibilities of the poet to the community is to provide information. I don't mean merely news reports, statistics, advertisements, or the kind of information some leaders use to assault and manipulate the public, but information detailing significant experiences that would allow a person to use her or his imagination, intelligence, and emotions to gain a greater awareness and understanding of self and the outside world.

Inauguration poetry is certainly intended to be socially responsible writing, whether it is Maya Angelou's official inaugural poem, "On the Pulse of Morning," which seems to fit the Cortez prescription, given Angelou's heartfelt vision of who we are and ought to become as a nation, or Allen Ginsberg's "New Democracy Wish List," the entry, published the same day, that Ginsberg would have read at the ceremony had he been invited. I offer a brief extract:

> Purge U.S. military death squad subsidies in Salvador,
> Guatemala, etc. We backed up dictators in Zaire, So-
> malia, Liberia, Sudan, Angola, Haiti, Iran, Iraq, Salva-
> dor, we're responsible: admit it then figure ways out.
> Encourage international trade in Eco-technology in
> place of enabling codependency on weapons trade.
> Open CIA & FBI & NSA archives on Cointelpro raids,
> Government drug dealing, Kennedy/King assassina-
> tions, Iranian Contragate, Panama Deception, Vati-
> can, Hand & Lavoro Bank thuggery, etc. including
> Bush-Noriega relations and other CIA client-agent scandals. (78)

Ginsberg harbors no illusions about art for art's sake. While some readers surely will want to discuss the quality of form, Ginsberg as poet is clearly more interested in the quality of the presidency and other political matters.

Other viewpoints on writing and responsibility, ones more directly related to our work in composition, are revealed in the academic discourse on literacy. Several are touched upon by James Paul Gee in his review of Harvey Graff's *The Legacies of Literacy: Continuities and Contradictions in Western Culture and Society.* Gee first takes up Graff's idea of the literacy myth, that is, the popular notion that literacy is not only requisite for higher-order consciousness but ensures critical thinking, governmental complexity, economic development, and social equity. Concerning the strictly cognitive claims supporting the literacy myth, Gee points to the work of Sylvia Scribner and Michael Cole, *The Psychology of Literacy,* which demonstrates that literacy is not a key variable in the development of ability to reason abstractly. Context proves more salient than the mere fact of literacy.

Graff himself provides ample historical evidence to debunk the social constructs underpinning the literacy myth. For example, the fact that Sweden was the first Western nation to achieve near-universal literacy did not lead to tremendous economic development or social progress. However, one need not scour historical texts very much on this point. Most of us would agree—we know Ginsberg would—that overall development hasn't been ideal in the latter-day United States, where, although the rate of illiteracy is alarming to many, a lot of our most important bad decisions are made by literate people. Even where major social gains have taken place, and the United States fits in here as well, the causes are quite complex. Literacy cannot be extracted from the social matrix—and highlighted as the determining factor. In fact, it has been argued that because it privileges certain language interaction, school-based literacy is not a means of ameliorating social inequity but a tool for reproducing it, serving mainly the purposes of the elite. Their particular brands of speech and writing are celebrated; other types are undervalued, discouraged, and penalized. Students generating the latter patterns realize early on, sometimes quite clearly, that the linguistic playing field is tilted against them. Some relish the uphill climb. Many don't even bother, thus falling victim to school systems that purportedly serve their best interests.

The argument being traced here is not that formal literacy instruction has no merit. We should not cease writing and resign our jobs. It is one thing to recognize that some claims about literacy and cognition have been exaggerated, but one need never to have considered literacy and orality a hierarchal proposition, much less one of either/or. Americans of African descent, for example, spring from a tremendous oral tradition but know full well the power of literacy, know it to be strong medicine if for no other reason than the fact that it was in large measure legislated away from them. We're not ambivalent about needing to master both the spoken and the written word. We need to be empowered in as many ways as we can. I would not want to choose between dialogue and writing, between oral tradition and text, between the Negro spirituals that clearly form the basis for Angelou's poem and that poem itself, between this paper I am presenting and the oral exchange I hope will ensue. Literacy has no monopoly on profundity but unmistakably contributes to it—as I am sure any academic who feels he or she has written a brilliant and insightful critique of literacy would agree. Scholars and others are right to warn against abuses of literacy and to rage against language practices that are exclusionary and exploitative. This has been a focus of my own professional endeavors. But any written argument against literacy, including any academic argument against academic literacy, is ultimately, as a philosopher-colleague of mine would say, self-refuting. It reminds me of the paper I heard arguing against the further spread of the English language being delivered, in English, at a conference of English teachers.

This is not a criticism of Gee. He has not taken the position, either in the review essay or in his own book, *Social Linguistics and Literacies*, that literacy is irrelevant. Far from being "anti-literacy, " his goals are to force a more careful examination of issues surrounding literacy instruction based upon the understanding that such instruction per se guarantees no particular form of social activity or organization and to keep open the question of how literacy instruction can best contribute to the public good. Gee is as aware as anyone—argues explicitly, in fact—that there never is a neutral literacy agenda. Just as there is no nonresponsible writing, there is no nonresponsible writing instruction. In every act of teaching there is complicity. Or, as he phrases it:

> A text, whether written on paper, on the soul (Plato), or on the world (Freire), is a loaded weapon. The person, the educator, who hands over the gun, hands over the bullets (the perspective), and must own up to the consequences. There is no way out of having an opinion, an ideology, and a strong one. . . . Literacy education is not for the timid. ("The Legacies of Literacy" 208)

What Gee fails to point out, but conceivably could have, is that revolts do occur. Perspectives fall into disfavor. Rulers are toppled. Slaves do forge freedom papers. Personal radicalization can, like Richard Wright's, begin in libraries. In other words, the process of initially becoming literate does not overdetermine how we continue to proceed in our "literateness" since potentially at least, we are always becoming. Reading, writing, and instruction do act powerfully upon us; at the same time, we can act powerfully on and through reading, writing, and instruction. This is the heart of the matter. The urgent query is not whether we can or cannot write or teach devoid of social responsibility, but whether we dare specify a role for ourselves in situating students in the strongest possible positions relative to our teaching (which means, of course, that in a sense they can overthrow us). Do we deliberately encourage students to be agents of social change? How often, in fact, is the idea that students should change things spelled out in curricula. And I don't mean anything really controversial at this point. (My thing is to restructure society so that material profit for the few is not more important than mass human need, but I know I can't sell this to everybody.) I am merely suggesting that social change is always necessary because, at the very least, what exists is not perfect. But even this mild form of agitation is not championed enough in schools.

In *Writing and Sense of Self*, Robert Brooke distinguishes between the roles of writing students and the roles of writers. In the student role, one habitually follows the dictates of the instructor, learning the strategies and values—both stated and implied—that are issued forth. However, Brooke finds this arrangement unsuitable, possibly debilitating, because it is an attempt to teach writing that has little in common with what motivates practicing writers or how they produce work. He argues, instead:

> Learning to write meaningfully in our culture requires developing an understanding of the self as writer, as someone who uses writing to further personal thinking and to help solve public problems. The development of such a role, such a self-understanding, is more important than developing any set of procedural competencies. Developing such a role, however, depends crucially on connecting the role of self as writer with other roles in the culture outside the classroom, especially writers' roles in the culture at large—including roles for the self as reflective thinker and community influencer. (5)

To Brooke, writers' roles—along with writing itself—are best promoted in a workshop setting steeped in writing-process methodology (multiple drafts, collaboration, alternative purposes and audiences, deferred emphasis on correctness, etc.), and over the years he has shifted his courses in that direction and away from a sequential curriculum emphasizing rhetorical principles. However, because they function within a university, none of Brooke's workshop members fully escape the student role. But in Brooke's view they are able to minimize and/or benefit from the tension involved in negotiating identities relative to both student and writer roles. Joy Ritchie, a participant-observer in a class taught by Brooke, writes that "the workshop classroom values personal experience and self-reflection, tolerance and consideration for plural perspectives, dialogue, responsibility, and commitment to action" (Brooke 139).

Brooke's workshop is admirable, undoubtedly in line with a significant strand of thought in the profession, and is an approach I generally endorse. There is, though, a disturbing aspect. For all their talk about "influencers" and "commitment to action," Brooke and Ritchie avoid indicating what deeds they find commendable. They forward a vague notion of democratic participation as a desirable outcome for their student writers or writer students. Beyond that, they adopt a politically neutral posture, which by now we understand is not an apolitical stance at all, merely one that reflects an unwillingness to articulate political persuasion. To simply advocate social responsibility, once we understand all professional educational activity to be socially responsible, is to advocate nothing. I have asserted the same nothingness many times—quite recently, for that matter—so I am not ridiculing anyone else for doing the same. But I now feel that teachers, including myself, should embrace the honesty that comes with delineating their political views. The point is to truly model mature literacy, to show that literacy always means something in particular. Recalling Gayle, we may pose a question: to whom are you being responsible? Gee causes us to question which type of ammunition is being used. Or, as Richard Bullock, John Trimbur, and Charles Schuster, editors of *The Politics of Writing: Postsecondary*, explain, "we prefer a disciplinary perspective that makes its politics explicit so that all involved—from students and instructors to administrators and theorists—can make intelligent, knowledgeable, informed choices about their own actions" (xviii).

Trimbur closes his own essay in the volume, "Literacy and the Discourse of Crisis" (the literacy crisis is an intellectual kin of the literacy myth), by maintaining that "To counter the growing privatization of education, we need to revive the movement of the late 1960s and early 1970s to democratize higher education through open admissions to *all* colleges and universities, free tuition, and a liveable student stipend" (294).

I don't think this referendum will fly. I think public institutions should remain or become tuition-free, open-admissions entities. I will continue to argue this even though the fight possibly will be lost. I won't, on the other hand, invest much energy debating the stipend issue or the status of private colleges because, though Trimbur's ideas appeal to me, I don't think there is the remotest possibility that fundamental changes will be made in those areas, at least not preceding greater equity and access to quality education in public schools. Although, like Trimbur, I range so far left that I wouldn't register a blip on the radar of what passes for fashionable political conversation in our country these days, there are some struggles I am actually trying to win. But the most important point regarding Trimbur's writing and my pondering it is that his writing about education is expressly political, as must be any response. Writing and writing instruction are socially, not naturally, occurring phenomena. They are never heading nowhere.

Works Cited

Brooke, Robert E. *Writing and Sense of Self: Identity Negotiation in Writing Workshops.* Urbana, IL; NCTE, 1991.

Bullock, Richard, John Trimbur, and Charles Schuster, eds. Preface. *The Politics of Writing: Postsecondary.* Portsmouth, NH: Boynton/Cook, 1991. xvii-xx.

Cortez, Jayne. Speech at First National Black Writers Conference at Medgar Evers College, CUNY, March 22,1986.

Gayle, Addison. Speech at First National Black Writers Conference at Medgar Evers College, CUNY, March 22, 1986.

Gee, James Paul. *Social Linguistics and Literacies: Ideology in Discourses.* New York: Falmer Press, 1990.

—"The Legacies of Literacy: From Plato to Freire through Harvey Graff." *Harvard Educational Review* 58, No. 2 (1988): 195-212.

Ginsberg, Allen. "New Democracy Wish List." *Newsday*, January 20, 1993. 44,78.

Graff, Harvey G. *The Legacies of Literacy: Continuities and Contradictions in Western Culture and Society.* Bloomington: Indiana UP, 1987.

Scribner, Sylvia, and Michael Cole. *The Psychology of Literacy.* Cambridge, MA.: Harvard UP, 1981.

Trimbur, John. "Literacy and the Discourse of Crisis." In Richard Bullock et al., eds., *The Politics of Writing Instruction: Postsecondary.* Portsmouth, NH: Boynton/Cook, 1991. 277-95.

Presented February 6, 1993, at the Conference of CUNY Writing Centers Association. The conference theme was "Writing and Social Responsibility." Later published in *Community Review* 13.

Questions for Discussion

1. In this essay, Gilyard talks a great deal about the "literacy myth"—the idea that "literacy is not only requisite for higher-order consciousness, but ensures critical thinking, governmental complexity, economic development, and social equity." What does Gilyard mean by a "literacy myth?" Why is that concept important to him?

2. Turn to Maya Angelou's "On the Pulse of Morning," which Gilyard mentions in his essay. Read the poem again. What do you think Gilyard would say about Angelou's poem? How is this poem an example of what Gilyard would call "socially responsible writing?"

3. Working with a partner or a small group, visit the web site of your college or university (provided that one is available). After surfing that site, studying carefully its representation of your school, and discuss whether or not you believe that web site has accurately portrayed your school. Evaluate that web site in terms of its responsibility to prospective and current students.

Explorations

1. Keith Gilyard argues that "when you write, you are being responsible to some social entity even if that entity is yourself." Take a few minutes to reflect on your own writing this quarter. How would you describe your written responses (formal and informal) using Gilyard's terms? To whom have you been socially responsible in your writing? How have you imagined your audience? What impact, if any, have you intended your writing to have upon that audience?

2. Take a few moments to reflect upon a class that you are currently taking. How has or hasn't this class encouraged students to be "agents of social change?" If it hasn't encouraged students this way, how might you reimagine the class so that such encouragement would be possible? Would it involve changing assignments? Classroom structure? Textbooks?

3. In some ways, Freire and Gilyard might be seen as having similar educational views, but the forms of their essays differ a great deal. Use this exploration to consider how the forms of these two essays affected your reading of them. What reading strategies did you use in order to read both selections? How did issues of style, voice, vocabulary, sentence structure, etc. affect your ability to read them?

Formal Writing Assignments

1. Draft an essay in which you describe a time in your life when a particular piece of writing has mattered to you—or when a piece of writing that you authored had great effect on its audience. Use the act of describing in order to help you move into the realm of analysis—taking apart the experience to see what it's made of. What features of this writing made it so persuasive or significant? How did the writer/subject/audience relationship play itself out in this piece of writing? What happened when you shared this piece of writing with others?

2. Keith Gilyard clearly argues that teachers and their courses have political values, that it is impossible for teachers or their subject matter to remain neutral. Draft an essay that responds to Gilyard's argument in some way. Your essay should include evidence to support your position; evidence may be gleaned from personal experience, from Gilyard's and/or other readings within the unit, or from resources you've discovered outside of *Writing Lives*.

Literacy and the Gay/Lesbian Learner

Ellen Louise Hart

Ellen Louise Hart teaches writing at the University of California–Santa Cruz, where she received her Ph.D. in 1996. Her dissertation focused on new ways of editing the work of poet Emily Dickinson, and in 1998 she published with Martha Nell Smith a book called *Open Me Carefully: Emily Dickinson's Intimate Letters to Susan Huntington Dickinson.* Hart also maintains special interests in lesbian poetry and the representations of lesbians and gay men in fiction. She was born in Maine and has lived in Vermont and California. In this essay, which appeared in the collection *The Lesbian In Front of the Classroom* (1988), Hart advances literacy "beyond the performance of concrete tasks to the creation of self, world, and identity."

Writing Before Reading

1. If you have ever found yourself in a situation where you were afraid to voice your opinion in a classroom, describe that time. Do you now think your fears were well-grounded?

2. Why do you think it would be important for a gay or lesbian student to be able to speak and write openly about sexuality in the classroom? Why might it be important to the heterosexual students in the classroom that the gay or lesbian students be free to express themselves?

3. How would a gay or lesbian student's perspective on a class discussion of the issue of marriage be different from that of a heterosexual student?

Literacy and the Gay/Lesbian Learner

Millions of Americans have never learned to read and write. How many are lesbians and gay men and how might homophobia be helping to enforce their illiteracy? As teachers what can we do? Before I address these questions I want to present some premises about homosexuality and education and follow with a definition of literacy. I want to make clear that homosexuality is not a "controversial issue"; it is a way of loving, living, creating homes and rituals, communities, cultures and cultural artifacts. Homosexuality can not be reduced to a private act that belongs in the bedroom and not in the classroom. Sexuality is much more than sex; it is integral to identity, culture, and all of life. It is personal, and the personal, as we know, is the political. Then, as teachers it is essential for us to recognize that since an estimated ten percent of the population is lesbian or gay, at any given time in any given classroom, from kindergarten to the university, ten percent of our students will be, or will become, lesbian or gay. Others will be bisexual, and twenty-five per cent will have a lesbian or gay family member. Education that is true to its name presents accurate information about homosexuality and includes lesbian, gay, and bisexual perspectives throughout the entire curriculum. This integration provides opportunity for our students to raise their self-esteem, to develop values based on knowledge rather than prejudice and dogma, and to learn.

By literacy I mean the ability to function independently in the society as a reader and writer, not only being able to read road signs and the ingredients on packages of food, to read bills and write checks, but to read, with comprehension and ease, newspapers and magazines, stories and poems and textbooks, to write, fluently, letters, journals, stories, and papers. Then there is another level of literacy that moves beyond the performance of concrete tasks to the creation of self, world, and identity. What is different about this process of becoming literate for a lesbian or gay man? The most fundamental difference is the need for particular texts that represent lesbian and gay experience and consciousness, the experience and consciousness of individual lesbians and gay men. Our lesbian and gay students need to know that they exist and that they exist in print. Literacy also requires the writing skills to enable the continuing creation of these representations. The claims I bring to this discussion of literacy are that the acts of reading and writing are acts of creation, not peripheral but essential to all education and all learning. Gay and lesbian students have special needs as learners in a patriarchal, heterosexist, homophobic society where their lives and experience are largely absent or misrepresented.

A Classroom Climate Survey, conducted in 1984 at Berkeley by the Associated Students of the University of California (ASUC), found that lesbian and gay students were the most uncomfortable in class, more than any other ethnic minority group, women, or the disabled. While I am ill at ease with this comparison of oppressions and do not believe that this kind of suffering can ever be measured, the ASUC Study supports my claim that throughout elementary, secondary, and post-secondary education, lesbian and gay students are deeply hurt. Like any other people, lesbians and gay men have an overwhelming need to see themselves made visible. Not only are these needs not being attended to, lesbian and gay students frequently must sit in silence while abusive comments about homosexuality and homosexuals made by their peers are tolerated, condoned, echoed by their teachers. The same ASUC study found that "82% of lesbian and gay students surveyed had been subjected to pejorative stereotypical comments about homosexuals by instructors."[2] A 1983 University of California Lesbian and Gay Intercampus Network (UCLGIN) Study found that only thirteen per cent of student, faculty, staff, and alumni surveyed at the nine U. C. campuses considered that lesbian and gay topics "had been adequately covered in courses where they should have been treated."[3] The Berkeley Multicultural Lesbian and Gay Studies Program (MLGS), a student organization, has been working for the past five years to encourage faculty to develop courses and curriculum on lesbian and gay issues. They argue:

> The lesbian and gay perspective has been systematically omitted from the University's course offerings. . . The roots of the omission. . . are not hard to find. The UCLGIN survey revealed that thirty-six percent of the faculty responding that lesbian/gay topics were appropriate to their fields had refrained from doing research on these topics because of fear of negative reaction from colleagues, while forty-one percent had refrained from including such material in their courses. Forty-four percent of students refrained from doing research or coursework for the same reason, and fourteen percent were advised by faculty not to pursue these topics.[4]

These UC surveys are useful for establishing a view of the censorship and the suffering of lesbian and gay students. And yet, it is at this end of the educational process, a place only the most select group ever reaches, where it is possible to find any opportunity to take a course and engage in a discussion concerning homosexuality; the picture in elementary and secondary schools is far worse.

I now want to turn to the classroom to consider the contradictions of a theory of teaching writing based on the idea of freedom of expression for a student, lesbian or gay, who is not free, who is taboo, silenced and made invisible. In *Writing Without Teachers* (1973) and *Writing With Power* (1981), Peter Elbow pioneered the technique of an automatic, nonstop, timed, restrictionless writing called "free writing." "Even if someone reads it, it doesn't send any ripples," Elbow writes.[5] "Free" is also a key word for educator John Holt: "People get better at using language when they use it to say things they really want to say to people they really want to say them to, in a context in which they can express themselves freely and honestly."[6] On the one hand how "free" is any student ever in a class that is part of a program that is part of an institution that is part of a system that is hierarchical, authoritarian, racist, classist, sexist, and so on? Still, for some students there can be something freeing about freewriting, particularly because students need not share the ideas they have generated with an audience. But this exercise is often followed by a sharing exercise that is part of the process of developing the idea. As Elbow puts it, the next step after freewriting, sharing, is the "essential human act at the heart of writing."

My point here is that a student who is lesbian or gay may not feel that she can express herself freely and honestly and she will therefore censor herself. She may fear "ripples" from the teacher or even more from her peers in the class. And so she will divert her first and best, her most vital idea, and the work of getting better at using language is getting undone. A non-gay student may be more likely than the gay student to feel free. To illustrate this point I will use an experience I had teaching in a community college adult literacy program.

A woman came into my beginning writing class. I gave her paper and asked her to write a letter introducing herself. She began to write and by the end of the class had four or five pages to read to me. She had written about a man in the Navy she'd married, about how unhappy she'd been cooped up alone when he wouldn't let her go out at night, how he brought his friends home and demanded she fix dinner for them, how she began to break away from him, had a relationship secretly with another man and finally left her husband, how he tried to get her back and she wouldn't go. "Whew!" she said as she went out the door. "I just had to get that down on paper. " I never saw the student again. But somehow this had been an important moment for her. She felt the need to tell her story in writing and she had presumed that she would be free to do it.

How many of my students did not feel free? How many censored their topics? Kept their journal writing secret or separate from school writing? Gave up on their writing because they didn't know what to say? In the literacy program students first learning to write describe family reunions and wedding anniversaries (some community college writing programs actually call a section of their program emphasizing personal experience writing "the engagement ring unit"), but they do not write coming out stories or portraits of gay relationships. And I know there are gay and lesbian students in the class, not only because of statistics, but because gays are not as invisible to themselves as they are to others. I decide that the man getting teased by other students in the class, who is thrilled to be interviewing someone who used to know Prince (the pre-"Purple Rain" androgynous Prince), has to be gay; that the teacher and counselor who helped Gina get off drugs and finish high school was a woman and Gina is probably a lesbian. And sure enough. There they are in the gay bar, at the gay pride and freedom day parade, along with others I've recognized, none of whom ever wrote anything explicit about being gay. I don't know if that was a conscious decision or how painful it was, how much it hurt their development as a writer, when the split between the speakable and the unspeakable will catch up with them, how much longer they will stay in school, keep writing, keep reading, keep encouraging their children, their parents to read and to write.

Luis, who dropped out of the program, sees me one morning in a local, lesbian owned and operated breakfast spot. "I'm thinking of coming back to school," he tells me. "I can't understand what I read in the newspaper. And I talk so fast I can't write. This is the right time for me. You know, I've got no kids, no wife"—he's talking fast and watching me— "no husband to support." Luis is coming out to me. And he's checking out how safe and comfortable my classroom might be.

Another example of how self-censorship affects a gay student is Walter, whose work I followed over a period of several years. He repeatedly cycled through the college writing courses, dropping out at the highest level and re-enrolling himself in entry level classes. In my intermediate course, he wrote his papers in the third person, referring to himself as "junior." His first essay described a suicide attempt which he explained was a plea for attention from his father. In his last essay he researched the founding of the Sears Roebuck Company. (His reason for the project was to find out whether or not Roebuck was black since he had found contradictory information about this.) The essay took him a year to write; he took an incomplete in the course and finally turned in a report that said very little. A year later Walter came into a beginning writing class I was teaching because he had taken an incomplete in a literature course and he wanted an opportunity to work on an essay on Huckleberry Finn. After two weeks of pouring over criticism, unable to put a word of his own on paper, he dropped out.

I use Walter as an example of a motivated and ambitious student (he often talked about transferring to a four year university and becoming a teacher) afraid to have an idea of his own. I don't want to appear to be simplifying the complexity of his problems with school and with writing which clearly amount to a deeply rooted psychological block. I would like research to be available that will help to explain how his position in the world as a gay man—and as a gay black man—influences his ability to write and to learn.

I want to use one more example from my teaching—a University of California Student enrolled in a composition and rhetoric course. On the first day of class Nathan is describing a night at a gay bar, responding to an assignment to describe a recent event showing something about his values, traditions, or culture. He watches closely as I glance over the paper, measuring my reaction to his subject, a topic he can censor in the future depending on my response. Later he writes essays, oblique, and convoluted about "universal oppressions" and how we all "have to struggle against them," until I call him into a writing conference. "Why don't you be more clear?" I ask him. "I've been afraid to," he says. While others lucidly defend abortion rights, civil rights, religious freedom, only Nathan is writing about gay rights, and he writes vaguely and self-consciously.

Homophobia advises our students not to write clearly. Self-censorship and fear of our response keep lesbian and gay students from "getting power through voice."[8] "Real voice," Peter Elbow calls it. "Nothing stops you," he writes, "from writing now, today words that people will want to read. Nothing stops you, that is, but your fear or unwillingness or lack of familiarity with what I am calling your real voice." As the quarter progressed Nathan became increasingly vocal about his politics, in class discussions never specifically mentioning gay issues, but coming close as he spoke about gender stereotyping and oppression. Neither did I encourage him to be more specific in these discussions, even though I know that specificity is at the root of critical thinking.

How might things have been different for Nathan, Walter, Gina, Luis, and others? For one thing, I was not "out" in the classroom; I included no readings on lesbian and gay issues; I reinforced their silence as well as the split in their lives: for them, like them, I was gay in the bars and at the parades, but never in the classroom. As I write this, I'm aware of a sense that I failed these students and that I now must ask myself—that as lesbian and gay teachers and academics we all must ask ourselves: what are our attitudes toward our gay and lesbian students? What kind of responsibility do we have? How are we similar to and different from other members of the profession who identify with students like themselves; male teachers, male students; feminist teachers, feminist students; black teachers, black students? As lesbian and gay teachers how does our invisibility affect our teaching and our students' lives?

I am reminded of an English professor I had in the mid-seventies, a formidable woman who lived with another formidable woman, also of the English Department. This professor raised an eyebrow at me one morning as I excused myself from her survey of great literature (all of it written by men) in order to attend "Women's Day" activities. On the program I held out to her, she pointed first to the "Lesbian Workshop" at the college that day, then to the "Lesbian Workshop" to follow during "Women's Weekend" at a neighboring college. "I see you're both using the same language," she said, her face a mask. Puzzled and embarrassed, I hastily assured her we didn't want to exclude anyone, and she nodded me away.

Looking back I would say that in three years I read two pieces of "lesbian literature" with this professor who travelled to far away midwestern universities to lecture on Willa Cather and Gertrude Stein. Our class session on *Three Women* was devoted entirely to Stein's use of grammar. During our discussion of Henry James' *The Bostonians*—her favorite women's writer, she told us—there was no mention of the lesbian relationship between the two main characters, and I could only get up the nerve, finally, to approach her after class one day to ask if she would please stop using the term "women's lib." Her housemate and colleague used similar tactics: she was primarily responsible for the department's veto of Virginia Woolf as required reading. When I asked about some earlier writing she had done on Edna St. Vincent Millay, she told me shortly that she preferred to disclaim it. The picture of these two women shows most poignantly my experience with teachers who refrain from openly conducting or encouraging discussion of love between women. When I speak of the intellectual growth denied lesbian and gay students, I speak from my own memory of suffocating censorship.

In her "Foreword" to *The Coming Out Stories*, Adrienne Rich asks the reader to view in her mind millions of pages of women's writing censored, concealed, lost, burned:

> As you read the stories in this book I would like you to think of those piles of ash, those cages behind which women's words, lesbian words, lie imprisoned. . . . This is poverty. This is starvation. This is cultural imperialism—the decision made by one group of people that another group shall be cut off from their past, shall be kept from the power of memory, context, continuity. This is why lesbians, meeting, need to tell and retell stories like the ones in this book. In the absence of the books we needed, the knowledge of woman whose lives were like our own, an oral tradition—here set down on paper—has sustained us.[9]

Like Rich I believe that the "coming out story," the lesbian narrative, has a central position in the making of lesbian history and culture. (An interesting question, and subject for research, is whether the coming out story has a similar role in the making of gay male culture.) But I wonder about the notion of an oral tradition. Lesbians do tell their stories to each other, in small private circles; yet it seems to me that peculiar to lesbian culture is its extreme dependence on writing.

Because of the taboo surrounding lesbian experience and the profound isolation surrounding many lesbian women, writing has a special place in the coming out process, and this is not only true for women who have access to education. I suspect that the coming out story is shared with one other, the woman with whom the experience is lived, and then very often the story is put down in writing—in the form of a poem, journal entry, a letter. I believe that lesbians rarely have access to the power Paule Marshall attributes to "the poets in the kitchen," the "set of giants" who taught "the first lesson in the narrative art. "[10] Describing her mother and her mother's friends who "suffered a triple invisibility, being black, female and foreigner," Marshall writes: "Given the kind of women they were, they couldn't tolerate the fact of their invisibility, their powerlessness. And they fought back using the only weapon at their command: the spoken word."[11] Lesbians do not have the kitchen table tradition Marshall shows us here, or Cherríe Moraga describes in "La Güera," "the sounds of my mother and aunts gossiping—half in English, half in Spanish—while drinking cerveza in the kitchen."[12] We do not have the words of our mothers, aunts, grandmothers around us. We inherit invisibility and silence.

There is a shared language among lesbians and often it originates from books. In the "Preface" to *Another Mother Tongue: Gay Words, Gay Worlds*, Judy Grahn, lesbian poet and cultural worker, describes sources for her research:

> I have recalled my utter isolation at sixteen, when I looked up *Lesbian* in the dictionary, having no one to ask about such things, terrified, elated, painfully self-aware, grateful it was there at all. Feeling the full weight of the social silence surrounding it. I have gone over and over in my mind the careful teaching my first lover Von gave me, as she recited in strictest secrecy the litany of words and phrases related to the forbidden subject of our being.[13]

This list, Grahn remembers, included a "mysterious word she had no definition for: *catafoil. . . . Catafoil* I now believe, came from a Gay book Von read while standing in a drugstore—a habit she had, especially with Gay books since it was socially embarrassing if not dangerous to buy them."[14] Grahn argues that an oral tradition exists among lesbians and she traces origins of that tradition. What is striking is that much of the oral tradition has its roots in writing.

Grahn followed *Another Mother Tongue* with *The Highest Apple: Sappho and the Lesbian Poetic Tradition*, which began as a chapter of the first book and grew too large. In her introduction she writes:

> Poetry is important to women, and it is especially important to Lesbians. More than one Lesbian has been kept from floundering on the rocks of alienation from her own culture, her own center, by having access, at least, to lesbian poetry. We owe a great deal to poetry; two of our most important names, for instance: Lesbian and Sapphic. When has a larger group of humans, more pervasive behavior, and much more than this, the tradition of women's secret powers that such names imply, ever been named for a single poet?[15]

Writing sustains lesbians. Our "weapon" against our isolation and oppression has traditionally been the written word. For lesbians, then, the consistent culture is the written culture—and we have had to he very vigilant to keep that culture consistent, to sift through the ashes of women's writing, to piece together Sappho's fragments, to keep the books on our kitchen tables and beside our beds. Lesbian and gay cultures have a unique dependency on literacy, and lesbians and gay men must be able to read and to write their own stories if the culture and the people are to survive.

Finally, I want to focus on necessity. There are many questions I can explore here about how need manifests itself for lesbian and gay learners. Jonathan Kozol writes about the cycle of illiteracy in *Illiterate America*. How many of those parents who pass illiteracy to their children are gay and lesbian? What might the relationship be of illiteracy to the spread of AIDS in terms of accessibility to information about the disease? And what about the relationship of literacy to healing? Journal writing is often used in workshops for incest survivors. (see Ellen Bass's work, especially *I Never Told Anyone: Writings by Women Survivors of Child Sexual Abuse*) and in work on recovering from alcoholism and substance abuse (see Jean Swallow, ed., *Out From Under: Sober Dykes and Our Friends*) and in work on healing from abusive relationships (see *Naming the Violence: Speaking Out About Lesbian Battering*, ed. Kerry Lobel for the National Coalition Against Domestic Violence Lesbian Task Force). And what role might literacy have in healing from Sex and Love Addiction, from depression? (I think of the last verse of a song Bonnie Raitt has recorded:

Tonight I'm sitting learning how to read

Because in school I never liked to

It's just one of the little things I'm going to need

As I go on living my life without you.)

These are questions that can open up new areas in the study of literacy in America.

I want to end with the words of two participants in a summer writing workshop for teachers who expressed their need when I pushed the group to begin to think about how lesbian and gay students are being censored. What I wanted to do as a member of that group was create a space in which the lesbian and gay students (there were five of us in a class of twenty) could voice our particular concerns, could speak and write our experience as gay and lesbian teachers. What happened was that I tried for three days in a row to bring the issue to the table. The first day no one responded. The second day someone agreed that it was an important subject but it then got lost. On the third day, late in the morning the group leader asked me to bring the matter up after a break. Here are two freewritings that came out of that moment. Sam wrote:

My father is gay. He has lived with the same man for almost fourteen years, one year less than my parents' marriage lasted. Ellen tells me that 25% of the population has an immediate family member who is gay, 10% are gay themselves. I never knew this as a teenager. No one ever talked about it. We never dealt with it in school.

For me, in adolescence—a time of great pain and change for even the happiest of us, my father's homosexuality was something I had to bear alone. It was something I discussed with no one. It increased my sense of isolation. Running was my place of belonging and to a great extent my coach played the role of my father. I believe if I could have written about this, it would have helped me to accept my father on his own terms much sooner.

Homophobia is a prejudice that must be dealt with in the classroom. To ignore it is criminal.

Alice wrote:

The room grew strangely silent. This group of expressive, committed, open-minded people seemed suddenly uncomfortable. My heart leaped into my throat, all my blood began to tingle. And I too remained silent. I who love to say what I think, especially regarding issues I know something about.

They have murdered us, burned us at the stake and in the gas chambers. They have taken our children from us. They have fired us from jobs and blacklisted us. They have cross- referenced us in the card catalogs with abnormal psychology, "see also suicide and depression." They have separated us from our mates, our lovers. They have arrested and incarcerated us. They have banned us from public participation. They have silenced us.

And that's the overt oppression.

The covert oppression is standing next to my lover at my brother's wedding and having to listen to my uncle making cracks about my not being married. Or watching a young person in school struggle with her sexual identity, wanting to offer myself as an example, but remaining mute.

Realizations are stirring me to the core. I can no longer sit here in silence.

Gay issues are issues which affect us all. These are issues not of sexuality and lifestyle alone. They are issues of political, religious and intellectual freedom.

The writings by these two teachers are coming out stories, just as the writing I am doing now is part of my own continuing story. Clearly, we can not tell or teach any one else's story until we are free to tell and to be told our own.

Notes

1. Helping to inform these premises are *Demystifying Homosexuality: A Teaching Guide about Lesbians and Gay Men*, published by the Human Rights Foundation, and Alicia Abramson's "TA's Guide for Overcoming Homophobia in the Classroom," UC Berkeley.

2. Proposal to Vice-Chancellor Roderic Park for campus funding of the Multicultural Lesbian and Gay Studies Program, UC Berkeley, June 30, 1986.

3. Ibid.

4. Ibid.

5. Peter Elbow, *Writing Without Teachers* (New York: Oxford University Press, 1973) p. 3.

6. *Handbook for Planning An Effective Writing Program* (California State Department of Education, 1983) p. 69.

7. Peter Elbow, *Writing With Power* (New York: Oxford University Press, 1981) p. 20.

8. Ibid. p. 304.

9. Adrienne Rich, "Foreword," *The Coming Out Stories*, eds. Julia Penelope Stanley and Susan J. Wolfe, (Watertown, Massachusetts: Persephone Press, 1980) xi-xii.

10. Paule Marshall, from "The Poets in the Kitchen," *The Borzoi College Reader*, eds. Charles Muscatine and Marlene Griffith (New York: Alfred Knopf, 1984) p. 81.

11. Marshall, p. 78.

12. Cherríe Moraga, "La Güera," *This Bridge Called My Back: Writings By Radical Women of Color*, eds. Cherríe Moraga and Gloria Anzaldúa (New York: Kitchen Table Women of Color Press, 1981) p. 31.

13. Judy Grahn, *Another Mother Tongue: Gay Words, Gay Worlds* (Boston: Beacon Press, 1984) xii.

14. Ibid.

15. Judy Grahn, *The Highest Apple: Sappho and the Lesbian Poetic Tradition* (San Francisco: Spinsters Ink, 1985) xii.

Questions for Discussion

1. What does Ellen Louise Hart mean when she claims that "sexuality is much more than sex; it is integral to identity, culture, and all of life"? According to Hart, how would a person's sexuality affect that person's literacy?

2. To conclude her essay, Hart includes relatively lengthy excerpts from students writing about their personal experiences. What role do these excerpts play in strengthening Hart's central argument?

3. The Classroom Climate Survey that Hart cites, which documents the discomfort experienced by homosexual students in the classroom situation, was conducted in 1984. Do you think that homosexual students are more likely to feel comfortable discussing their sexuality now than they were then? If so, what events or changes in society might account for this shift?

Explorations

1. Hart states that for gay and lesbian learners to gain more complete literacy, they need access to "particular texts that represent lesbian and gay experience and consciousness, the experience and consciousness of individual lesbians and gay men." She goes on to say that "our lesbian and gay students need to know that they exist and that they exist in print." Consider portrayals of the experience of gay and lesbian people you have read or seen in movies or on television. Would you consider these portrayals to be generally positive or generally negative? In your experience, are these portrayals accurate representations of societal attitudes?

2. Hart seems at times to be more concerned with the effects of gay and lesbian self-censorship than with overt censorship by schools or instructors. What factors outside the classroom might cause gay or lesbian students to censor their own writing and speech?

3. According to Hart, why is writing particularly important in the lesbian community? In what ways does silence restrict individuals and the power of a community? How does writing allow Hart to identify with the values of a certain community? In the communities to which you belong, does language act to create a sense of cohesion and belonging? If so, how? You might also consider how silence functions within these communities.

Formal Writing Assignments

1. You probably consider yourself as belonging to more than one community of people with similar interests, abilities, backgrounds, or professional goals. Some of these communities you have chosen to join (such as a fraternity or sorority, campus organization, or workplace); others include you because of who you are (such as an ethnic group or your extended family). Consider two of the communities in which you consider yourself a member, one by choice and one not. In responding to the following questions, write an essay that focuses on the importance you place on a sense of belonging to these communities. In what ways are these communities alike? How are they different? Is each community aware of the other? Do these communities ever come into conflict, and if so, how have you negotiated that conflict? What are the types of literacy that hold these communities together?

2. In an essay, explore the ways in which society is organized around the notion that heterosexuality is the "normal" state of being. How does this societal orientation affect families? employment? How are the lives of both homosexuals and heterosexuals affected?

Why I'm Here

Amy Hempel

Born in Chicago (1951), Amy Hempel studied at Whittier College, San Francisco State University and Columbia University. She pursued her writing career in New York where, for a time, she was a contributing editor for *Vanity Fair* magazine. Her story collections include *At the Gates of the Animal Kingdom* (1990), *Tumble Home* (1997), and *Reasons to Live* (1985), from which "Why I'm Here" is excerpted. Noted for her minimalist technique and her interest in characters who exist in worlds of sadness, Hempel once told an interviewer: "Dr. Christian Barnard said, 'Suffering isn't ennobling, recovery is.' If I have a motto for this particular bunch of stories, that's what it is."

Writing Before Reading

1. Hempel's narrator relates an experience during which he/she appeals to a vocational guidance counselor for help in deciding on a career. Describe an instance when a counselor helped or attempted to help you decide on a new direction for your life. Was the consultation successful? Why or why not? How were your interests and needs revealed and/or categorized by the counselor?

2. Oftentimes, job placement services attempt to categorize the personality, motivations, interests and needs of their clients. Why do you think this is so? Do you see this type of categorization as liberating or confining? Why? What other organizations/institutions categorize individuals?

3. How important for your long-range plans is your own happiness? Describe the role your happiness will play when you plan(ned) your academic future. What other factors in your plans are either more important or less important than your happiness?

Why I'm Here

"Name a time when you are happy," is one of the questions. I am taking a test to find out what to do. The way to do this is to find out what you like. This is not obvious, the way it sounds. For example, the questions that say, "Would you prefer . . ." "Would you prefer to: (a) Answer questions about what you do, (b) Answer questions about what you know, (c) Answer questions about what you think?"

My answer is, "Depends." But it's not one of the choices. I am having to think in terms of Always, Sometimes, Never.

You cannot pass or fail this test; your grade is more of a profile.

After the written part of the test, I talk to the vocational-guidance counselor. She is fifty or so, a short, square woman in a dress like a blender cozy. Mrs. Deane is the one who asks me when I'm happy. She says, "Tell me the thing you do *anyway*, and let's find a way to get you paid for that."

I ask about a job throwing sticks for dogs to fetch, and she says, "Oh, now," and gives me the courtesy laugh.

I'm the wrong age to be doing this.

You take this test in college if you can't pick a major. Or you take it to help you change your life— later, after you've *had* a life. Somewhere in the middle is the reason why I'm here.

So—The Time When I Am Happy.

It starts with the sign that says "Open House," and the colored cellophane flags on a string across the walk. Then the unlocked door into a furnished model home, or, even better, unfurnished rooms. Here you have to imagine the lives the way you see characters in a book as you read.

It doesn't stop here, with inspecting the rooms. The thing that I do anyway—I move into new apartments.

First, I get rid of most of what I have. My friends are loaded up with ironing boards and sofa-beds. I hand out records and wicker and lamps. Never mind the plants.

The books alone!

When the place is pared down, I spell my new number. It works like this: you take your telephone prefix, say it's 7-7-6. That's P-r-o. Then you start dialing words until you reach a disconnect, an available number: Pro-mise, Pro-digy, Pro-verb, Pro-blem, Pro-voke, Pro-tect, Pros-per . . .

I buy a few beers for the "Two Guys with Van" who will load up what is left. I hope for the best, though you can count on this for damage: three moves equals a fire.

The new place brings a rush of settlement. Paper towels and spray cleaners, plastic bags to line plastic wastebaskets. There is glossy shelf paper to cut for the cabinets, and my name to put on the mailbox. It's the same thing again, three months later. Move enough times and you will never defrost a freezer.

I'm telling this to Mrs. Deane.

She says the key thing here is process—what she looks for on the Happiness Question. Does this happiness come from a person, place, or process?

I tell her I don't know, that sometimes I just have to move.

The place before this, this is what it was. I took a small apartment on the top floor of a house. It was a narrow gray Victorian with amber stained-glass windows on the landing.

The manager apologized for the faulty showerhead. He said he would fix it, and he did—the next day. He said that he used to live in the house. He said that he and his brother used to play in my apartment where they set up their H.O. trains.

On my way out one morning, I said hello to the manager. He was down on his knees on the carpeted stairs, suctioning lint with a special vacuum attachment. But something was different when I got home that night. It took me a minute. Nothing was moved. Then I noticed the rug. It covered the space between the fireplace and couch. Since I had been gone, that rug had been vacuumed.

That wasn't all.

There was something the manager said, the day he fixed the shower. He said now that the stream was strong, I could "really lather up."

"Lather up!" I repeat to Mrs. Deane.

Mrs. Deane scans the written portion of my test. She says I skipped a question, the one that says, "Would you prefer to: (a) Think about your plans for tomorrow, (b) Think about what you would do if you had a million dollars, (c) Think about how it would feel to be held up at gunpoint?"

I say, "I want the job for the person who picks (b)."

Mrs. Deane says, "What do you suppose would happen if you just stayed put? If you just stayed still long enough to think a thing through?"

"I don't know," I say. "I won't feel like myself."

"Oh," she says, "but you will—you are."

Questions for Discussion

1. What is the rhetorical significance of the passage about the narrator's apartment manager? What is its purpose in relation to the rest of the story?

2. What difference does it make that the narrator is middle-aged? How would the story be different if the narrator were in college? Or retired?

3. Compare the exploratory techniques displayed by Levine's M. Degas and Mrs. Deane. What are the differences/similarities? Which of the two seems to be more effective for its particular situation? Which of the two would be more effective for your learning process? Why?

Explorations

1. Describe methods by which you have taught someone something. Or, describe how you imagine you would teach your favorite course. What factors have you considered or will you consider when forming a teaching method?

2. In what ways does the narrator's near constant process of moving compare to the process of drafting in writing? In both processes, what is more valuable: starting over from scratch when the going gets tough, or working to make right where you are in the process currently? How might Hempel be indirectly commenting on various unnamed processes by illustrating the narrator's need to always be on the move?

3. What is Mrs. Deane's position of authority in the story? How does Hempel establish her character? How would you feel about taking career advice from Mrs. Deane? With these thoughts in mind, how important is establishing your own authority over a subject when you write for an audience other than yourself?

Formal Writing Assignments

1. Building on your response to Writing Before Reading question two, write an essay in which you briefly describe and then analyze some institution at your university or college that works by categorizing those it serves. Argue either for or against this type of categorization. Is it limiting or liberating? If you find the categorization limiting, how might this particular institution better serve its clientele given the number and variety of people it helps? If you find it liberating, what would be the effect on the system if all categorization was stopped?

2. In an essay, compare/contrast Mrs. Deane's pedagogy with that displayed in Barber, Busch, Edmundson, Hart, hooks, Hughes, Kohl, Levine, Lohre, Lorde or Stern ("Mad"). How do each of the two pedagogies reveal the other's strengths and weaknesses? Which method would you rather use for teaching? Why? Describe how each might be incorporated in a writing class. Which would be more effective for the teaching of various factors in writing such as audience, authority, voice, revision, invention, style, et cetera? Finally, adapt the better of the two pedagogies for the writing class you would like to teach or see taught at your university or college.

Cultural Literacy

E. D. Hirsch, Jr.

E. D. Hirsch is a professor of English at the University of Virginia. Though the focus of his scholarly work has been literary theory and the Romantic Period, he is perhaps best known for his notion of "cultural literacy." The essay printed here first appeared in *The American Scholar* in 1983. Four years later, he published *Cultural Literacy: What Every American Needs to Know*. The book was a best seller that sparked a heated debate about the purposes of education. Hirsch argues that readers and writers must share a body of core knowledge if they are to be understood, and that many Americans do not have that knowledge. Following this essay in *Writing Lives/Reading Communities*, you will find excerpts from the 63-page appendix to Hirsch's book. The full appendix lists 5,000 names, terms, and phrases that Hirsch believes are essential to cultural literacy. In 1989, Hirsch published *A First Dictionary of Cultural Literacy*, which provides brief definitions of the terms he introduced in the earlier book. In his latest book, *The Schools We Need and Why We Don't Have Them*, Hirsch argues that American schools have failed students in part by relying on the idea of formalism, which privileges the teaching of skill-learning over the teaching of factual knowledge.

In 1986, Hirsch founded the Core Knowledge Foundation. This not-for-profit foundation publishes and sells classroom curricula, lesson plans, and other teaching resources based on Hirsch's books and articles.

Writing Before Reading

1. Think of a time when you found yourself in a conversation where you sensed yourself to be the only person who did not understand the particular terminology or vocabulary of the discussion. What techniques did you use to try to grasp the meaning of the words or terms that were not familiar to you?

2. In the 19th century and the early part of the 20th century, elementary and secondary teaching relied much more heavily on rote memorization of facts and entire sections of texts. Who do you feel received a stronger high school education: your grandparents or you?

3. The weight of public opinion has recently been strongly in favor of holding public schools accountable for educational outcomes as measured by standardized test scores. Do you think that standardized testing is a fair measure of the success or failure of the teaching at your high school?

Cultural Literacy

For the past twelve years I have been pursuing technical research in the teaching of reading and writing. I now wish to emerge from my closet to declare that technical research is not going to remedy the national decline in our literacy that is documented in the decline of verbal SAT scores. We already know enough about methodology to do a good job of teaching reading and writing. Of course we would profit from knowing still more about teaching methods, but better teaching techniques alone would produce only a marginal improvement in the literacy of our students. Raising their reading and writing levels will depend far less on our methods of instruction (there are many acceptable methods) than on the specific contents of our school curricula. Commonsensical as this proposition might seem to the man in the street, it is regarded as heresy by many (I hope by ever fewer) professional educators. The received and dominant view of educational specialists is that the specific materials of reading and writing instruction are interchangeable so long as they are "appropriate," and of "high quality. "

But consider this historical fact. The national decline in our literacy has accompanied a decline in our use of common, nationwide materials in the subject most closely connected with literacy, "English." From the 1890s to 1900 we taught in English courses what amounted to a national core curriculum. As Arthur Applebee observes in his excellent book *Tradition and Reform in the Teaching of English*, the following texts were used in those days in more than 25 percent of our schools: *The Merchant of Venice, Julius Caesar*, "First Bunker Hill Oration," *The Sketch Book, Evangeline*, "The Vision of Sir Launfal," "Snow-Bound," *Macbeth*, "The Lady of the Lake," *Hamlet*, "The Deserted Village," Gray's "Elegy," "Thanatopsis," *As You Like It*. Other widely used works will strike a resonance in those who are over fifty: "The Courtship of Miles Standish," "Il Penseroso," *Paradise Lost*, "L'Allegro," "Lycidas," *Ivanhoe, David Copperfield, Silas Marner*, etc., etc. Then in 1901 the College Entrance Examinations Board issued its first "uniform lists" of texts required to be known by students in applying to colleges. This core curriculum, though narrower, became even more widespread than the earlier canon. Lest anyone assume that I shall urge a return to those particular texts, let me at once deny it. By way of introducing my subject, I simply want to claim that the decline in our literacy and the decline in commonly shared knowledge that we acquire in school are causally related facts. Why this should be so and what we might do about it are my twin subjects.

That a decline in our national level of literacy has occurred few will serious doubt. The chief and decisive piece of evidence for it is the decline in verbal SAT scores among the white middle class. (This takes into account the still greater lowering of scores caused by an increased proportion of poor and minority students taking the tests.) Now scores on the verbal SAT show a high correlation with reading and writing skills that have been tested independently by other means. So, as a rough index to the literacy levels of our students, the verbal SAT is a reliable guide. That is unsurprising if we accept the point made by John Carroll and others that the verbal SAT is chiefly a vocabulary test, for no one is surprised by a correlation between a rich vocabulary and a high level of literacy. A rich vocabulary is not a purely technical or rote-learnable skill. Knowledge of words is an adjunct to knowledge of cultural realities signified by words, and to whole domains of experience to which words refer. Specific words go with specific knowledge. And when we begin to contemplate how to teach specific knowledge, we are led back inexorably to the contents of the school curriculum, whether or not those contents are linked, as they used to be, to specific texts.

From the start of our national life, the school curriculum has been an especially important formative element of our national culture. In the schools we not only tried to harmonize the various traditions of our parent cultures, we also wanted to strike out on our own within the dominant British heritage. Being rebellious children, we produced our own dictionary, and were destined, according to Melville, to produce our own Shakespeare. In this self-conscious job of culture making, the schools played a necessary role. That was especially true in the teaching of history and English, the two subjects central to culture making. In the nineteenth century we held national conferences on school curricula. We formed the College Board, which created the "uniform lists" already referred to. The dominant symbol for the role of the school was the symbol of the melting pot.

But from early times we have also resisted this narrow uniformity in our culture. The symbol of the melting pot was opposed by the symbol of the stew pot, where our national ingredients kept their individual characteristics and contributed to the flavor and vitality of the whole. That is the doctrine of pluralism. It has now become the dominant doctrine in our schools, especially in those subjects, English and history, that are closest to culture making. In math and science, by contrast, there is wide agreement about the contents of a common curriculum. But in English courses, diversity and pluralism now reign without challenge. I am persuaded that if we want to achieve a more literate culture than we now have, we shall need to restore the balance between these two equally American traditions of unity and diversity. We shall need to restore certain common contents to the humanistic side of the school curriculum. But before we can make much headway in that direction, we shall also need to modify the now-dominant educational principle that holds that any suitable materials of instruction can be used to teach the skills of reading and writing. I call this the doctrine of educational formalism.

The current curriculum guide to the study of English in the state of California is a remarkable document. In its several pages of advice to teachers I do not find the title of a single recommended work. Such "curricular guides" are produced on the theory that the actual contents of English courses are simply vehicles for inculcating formal skills, and that contents can be left to local choice. But wouldn't even a dyed-in-the-wool formalist concede that teachers might be saved time if some merely illustrative, non-compulsory titles were listed? Of course; but another doctrine, in alliance with formalism, conspires against even that concession to content—the doctrine of pluralism. An illustrative list put out by the state would imply official sanction of the cultural and ideological values expressed by the works on the list. The California Education Department is not in the business of imposing cultures and ideologies. Its business is to inculcate "skills" and "positive self-concepts," regardless of the students' cultural backgrounds. The contents of English should be left to local communities.

This is an attractive theory to educators in those places where spokesmen for minority cultures are especially vocal in their attack on the melting-pot idea. That concept, they say, is nothing but cultural imperialism (true), which submerges cultural identities (true) and gives minority children a sense of inferiority (often true). In recent years such attitudes have led to attacks on teaching school courses exclusively in standard English; in the bilingual movement (really a monolingual movement) it has led to attacks on an exclusive use of the English language for instruction. This kind of political pressure has encouraged a retreat to the extreme and untenable educational formalism reflected in the California curriculum guide.

What the current controversies have really demonstrated is a truth that is quite contrary to the spirit of neutrality implied by educational formalism. Literacy is not just a formal skill; it is also a political decision. The decision to want a literate society is a value-laden one that carries costs as well as advantages. English teachers by profession are committed to the ideology of literacy. They cannot successfully avoid the political implications of that ideology by hiding behind the skirts of methodology and research. Literacy implies specific contents as well as formal skills. Extreme formalism is misleading and evasive. But allow me to illustrate that point with some specific examples.

During most of the time that I was pursuing research in literacy I was, like others in the field, a confirmed formalist. In 1977 I came out with a book on the subject, *The Philosophy of Composition*, that was entirely formalistic in outlook. One of my arguments, for instance, was that the effectiveness of English prose as an instrument of communication gradually increased, after the invention of printing, through a trial-and-error process that slowly uncovered some of the psycholinguistic principles of efficient communication in prose. I suggested that freshmen could learn in a semester what earlier writers had taken centuries to achieve, if they were directly taught those underlying psycholinguistic principles. (With respect to certain formal structures of clauses, this idea still seems valid.) I predicted further that we could learn how to teach those formal principles still more effectively if we pursued appropriately controlled pedagogical research.

So intent was I upon this idea that I undertook some arduous research into one of the most important aspects of writing pedagogy—evaluation. After all, in order to decide upon the best methods of inculcating the skills of writing, it was essential to evaluate the results of using the different teaching methods. For that we needed non-arbitrary, reliable techniques for evaluating student writing. In my book I had made some suggestions about how we might do this, and those ideas seemed cogent enough to a National Endowment for the Humanities panel to get me a grant to go forward with the research. For about two years I was deeply engaged in this work. It was this detailed engagement with the realities of reading and writing under controlled conditions that caused me finally to abandon my formalistic assumptions. (Later I discovered that experimentation on a much bigger scale had brought Richard C. Anderson, the premier scholar in reading research, to similar conclusions.)

The experiments that changed my mind were, briefly, these: To get a non-arbitrary evaluation of writing, we decided to base our evaluations on actual audience effects. We devised a way of comparing the effects of well-written and badly written versions of the same paper. Our method was to pair off two large groups of readers (about a hundred in each group), each of which, when given the same piece of writing, would read it collectively with the same speed and comprehension. In other words, we matched the reading skills of these two large groups. Then, when one group was given a good version and the other given a degraded version, we measured the overall effect of these stylistic differences on speed and accuracy of comprehension. To our delight, we discovered that good style did make an appreciable difference, and that the degree of difference was replicable and predictable. So far so good. But what became very disconcerting about these results was that they came out properly only when the subjects of the papers were highly familiar to our audiences. When, later in the experiments, we introduced unfamiliar materials, the results were not only messy, they were "counterintuitive," the term of art for results that go against one's expectations. (Real scientists generally like to get counterintuitive results, but we were not altogether disinterested onlookers and were dismayed.) For what we discovered was that good writing makes very little difference when the subject is unfamiliar. We English teachers tend to believe that a good style is all the more helpful when the content is difficult, but it turns out that we are wrong. The reasons for this unexpected result are complex, and I will not pause to discuss them at length, since the important issues lie elsewhere.

Briefly, good style contributes little to our reading of unfamiliar material because we must continually backtrack to test out different hypotheses about what is being meant or referred to. Thus, a reader of a text about Grant and Lee who is unsure just who Grant and Lee are would have to get clues from later parts of the text, and then go back to re-read earlier parts in the light of surer conjectures. This trial-and-error backtracking with unfamiliar material is so much more time-consuming than the delays caused by a bad style alone that style begins to lose its importance as a factor in reading unfamiliar material. The contribution of style in such cases can no longer be measured with statistical confidence.

The significance of this result is, first of all, that one cannot, even in principle, base writing evaluations on audience effects—the only non-arbitrary principle that makes any sense. The reading skill of an audience is not a constant against which prose can be reliably measured. Audience reading skills vary unpredictably with the subject matter of the text. Although we were trying to measure our prose samples with the yardstick of paired audiences, the contrary had, in effect, occurred; our carefully contrived prose samples were measuring the background knowledge of our audiences. For instance, if the subject of a text was "Friendship," all audience pairs, everywhere we gave the trials, exhibited the same differentials. Also, for all audiences, if the subject was "Hegel's Metaphysics," the differential between good and bad writing tended to disappear. Also, so long as we used university audiences, a text on Grant and Lee gave the same sort of appropriate results as did a text on friendship. But for one community college audience (in, no less, Richmond, Virginia) "Grant and Lee" turned out to be as unfamiliar as "Hegel's Metaphysics"—a complacency-shattering result.

While the variability of reading skills within the same person was making itself disconcertingly known to me, I learned that similar variability was showing up in formal writing skills—and for the same reasons. Researchers at the City University of New York were finding that when a topic is unfamiliar, writing skill declines in all of its dimension—including grammar and spelling—not to mention sentence structure, parallelism, unity, focus, and other skills taught in writing courses. One part of the explanation for such results is that we all have limited attention space, and cannot pay much heed to form when we are devoting a lot of our attention to unfamiliar content. But another part of the explanation is more interesting. Part of our skill in reading and in writing is skill not just with linguistic structures but with words. Words are not purely formal counters of language; they represent large underlying domains of content. Part of language skill is content skill. As Apeneck Sweeney profoundly observed: "I gotta use words when I talk to you."

When I therefore assert that reading and writing skills are content-bound, I mean also to make the corollary assertion that important aspects of reading and writing skills are *not* transferable. Of course some skills are carried over from task to task; we know that broad strategies of reading and writing can become second nature, and thereby facilitate literary skills at all levels. But the content-indifferent, how-to approach to literacy skills is enormously oversimplified. As my final example of this, I shall mention an ingenious experiment conducted by Richard C. Anderson and his colleagues at the University of Illinois. It, too, was an experiment with paired audiences and paired texts. The texts were two letters, each describing a wedding, each of similar length, word-familiarity, sentence complexity, and number of idea units. Each audience was similarly paired according to age, educational level, marital status, sex, professional specialty, etc. Structurally speaking, the texts were similar and the audiences were similar. The crucial variables were these: one letter described a wedding in America, the other a wedding in India. One audience was American, the other Indian. Both audiences read both letters. The results were that the reading skills of the two groups—their speed and accuracy of comprehension—were very different in reading the two linguistically similar letters. The Americans read about an American wedding skillfully, accurately, and with good recall. They did poorly with the letter about the Indian wedding. The reverse was the case with the group of Indian readers. Anderson and his colleagues concluded that reading is not just a linguistic skill, but involves translinguistic knowledge beyond the abstract sense of words. They suggested that reading involves both "linguistic-schemata" (systems of expectation) and "content-schemata" as well. In short, the assumptions of educational formalism are incorrect.

Every writer is aware that the subtlety and complexity of what can be conveyed in writing depends on the amount of relevant tacit knowledge that can be assumed in readers. As psycholinguists have shown, the explicitly stated words on the page often represent the smaller part of the literary transaction. Some of this assumed knowledge involves such matters as generic conventions, that is, what to expect in a business letter, a technical report, a detective story, etc. An equally significant part of the assumed knowledge— often a more significant part—concerns tacit knowledge of the experiential realities embraced by the discourse. Not only have I gotta use words to talk to you, I gotta assume you know *something* about what I am saying. If I had to start from scratch, I couldn't start at all.

We adjust for this in the most casual talk. It has been shown that we always explain ourselves more fully to strangers than to intimates. But, when the strangers being addressed are some unknown collectivity to whom we are writing, how much shall we then need to explain? This was one of the most difficult authorial problems that arose with the advent of printing and mass literacy. Later on, in the eighteenth century, Dr. Johnson confidently assumes he could predict the knowledge possessed by a personage whom he called "'the common reader." Some such construct is a necessary fiction for every writer in every literate culture and subculture. Even a writer for an astrophysics journal must assume a "common reader" for the subculture being addressed. A newspaper writer must also assume a "common reader" but for a much bigger part of the culture, perhaps for the literate culture as a whole. In our own culture, Jefferson wanted to create a highly informed "common reader," and he must have assumed the real existence of such a personage when he said he would prefer newspapers without government to government without newspapers. But, without appropriate, tacitly shared background knowledge, people cannot understand newspapers. A certain extent of shared, canonical knowledge is inherently necessary to a literate democracy.

For this canonical information I have proposed the term "cultural literacy." It is the translinguistic knowledge on which linguistic literacy depends. You cannot have the one without the other. Teachers of foreign languages are aware of this interdependency between linguistic proficiency and translinguistic, cultural knowledge. To get very far in reading or writing French, a student must come to know facets of French culture quite different from his own. By the same token, American children learning to read and write English get instruction in aspects of their own national culture that are as foreign to them as French. National Culture always has this "foreignness" with respect to family culture alone. School materials contain unfamiliar materials that promote the "acculturation" that is a universal part of growing up in any tribe or nation. Acculturation into a national literate culture might be defined as learning what the "common reader" of a newspaper in a literate culture could be expected to know. That would include knowledge of certain values (whether or not one accepted them), and knowledge of such things as (for example) the First Amendment, Grant and Lee, and DNA. In our own culture, what should these contents be? Surely our answer to that should partly define our school curriculum. Acculturation into a literate culture (the minimal aim of schooling; we should aim still higher) could be defined as the gaining of cultural literacy.

Such canonical knowledge could not be fixed once and for all. "Grant and Lee" could not have been part of it in 1840, or "DNA" in 1940. The canon changeth. And in our media-paced era, it might change from month to month—faster at the edges, more slowly at the center, and some of its contents would be connected to events beyond our control. But much of it is within our control and is part of our traditional task of culture making. One reassuring feature of our responsibilities as makers of culture is the implicit and automatic character of most canonical cultural knowledge; we get it through the pores. Another reassuring aspect is its vagueness. How much do I *really* have to know about DNA in order to comprehend a newspaper text directed to the common reader? Not much. Such vagueness in our background knowledge is a feature of cultural literacy that Hilary Putnam has analyzed brilliantly as "the division of linguistic labor." An immensely literate person, Putnam claims that he does not know the difference between a beech tree and an elm. Still, when reading those words he gets along acceptably well because he knows that under the division of linguistic labor somebody in the culture could supply more precise knowledge if it should be needed. Putnam's observation suggests that the school curriculum can be vague enough to leave plenty of room for local choice regarding what things shall be studied in detail, and what things shall be touched on just far enough to get us by. This vagueness in cultural literacy permits a reasonable compromise between lockstep, Napoleonic prescription of texts on the one side, and extreme laissez-faire Pluralism on the other. Between these two extremes we have a national responsibility to take stock of the contents of schooling.

Although I have argued that a literate society depends upon shared information, I have said little about what that information should be. This is chiefly a political question. Estimable cultures exist that are ignorant of Shakespeare and the First Amendment. Indeed, estimable cultures exist that are entirely ignorant of reading and writing. On the other hand, no culture exists that is ignorant of its own traditions. In a literate society, culture and cultural literacy are nearly synonymous terms. American culture, always large and heterogeneous, and increasingly lacking a common acculturative curriculum, is perhaps getting fragmented enough to lose its coherence as a culture. Television is perhaps our only national curriculum, despite the justified complaints against it as a partial cause of the literacy decline. My hunch is that this complaint is overstated. The decline in literacy skills, I have suggested, is mainly a result of cultural fragmentation. Within black culture, for instance, blacks are more literate than whites, a point that was demonstrated by Robert L. Williams, as I learned from a recent article on the SAT by Jay Amberg (*The American Scholar*, Autumn 1982). The big political question that has to be decided is whether we want a broadly literate culture that unites our cultural fragments enough to allow us to write to one another and read what our fellow citizens have written. Our traditional, Jeffersonian answer has been yes. But even if that political decision remains the dominant one, as I very much hope, we still face the much more difficult political decision of choosing the contents of cultural literacy.

The answer to this question is not going to be supplied by theoretical speculation and educational research. It will be worked out, if at all, by discussion, argument, and compromise. Professional educators have understandably avoided this political arena. Indeed, educators should not be left to decide so momentous an issue as the canonical contents of our culture. Within a democracy, educational technicians do not want and should not be awarded the function that Plato reserved for philosopher kings. But who is making such decisions at a national level? Nobody, I fear, because we are transfixed by the twin doctrines of pluralism and formalism.

Having made this technical point where I have some expertise, I must now leave any pretense of authority, except as a parent and citizen. The question of guidance for our national school curriculum is a political question on which I have only a citizen's opinion. For my own part, I wish we could have a National Board of Regents—our most successful and admirable body for educational leadership. This imposing body of practical idealists is insulated by law from short-term demagogic pressures. It is a pluralistic group, too, with representation for minority as well as majority cultures. Its influence for good may be gauged by comparing the patterns of SAT scores in New York with those in California, two otherwise comparable states. To give just one example of the Regents' leadership in the field of writing, they have instituted a requirement that no New Yorker can receive a high school diploma before passing a statewide writing test that requires three types of prose composition.

Of course I am aware that the New York Regents have powers that no National Board in this country could possibly gain. But what a National Board could hope to achieve would be the respect of the country, a respect that could give it genuine influence over our schools. Such influence, based on leadership rather than compulsion, would be quite consistent with our federalist and pluralist principles. The Board, for instance, could present broad lists of suggested literary works for the different grades, lists broad enough to yield local freedom but also to yield a measure of commonality in our literary heritage. The teachers whom I know, while valuing their independence, are eager for intelligent guidance in such matters.

But I doubt that such a Curriculum Board would ever be established in this country. So strong is our suspicion of anything like a central "ministry of culture," that the Board is probably not a politically feasible idea. But perhaps a consortium of universities, or of national associations, or of foundations could make ongoing recommendations that arise from broadly based discussions of the national curriculum. In any case, we need leadership at the national level, and we need specific guidance.

It would be useful, for instance, to have guidance about the words that high school graduates ought to know—a lexicon of cultural literacy. I am thinking of a special sort of lexicon that would include not just ordinary dictionary words, but would also include proper names, important phrases, and conventions. Nobody likes word lists as objects of instruction; for one thing, they don't work. But I am not thinking of such a lexicon as an object of instruction. I am thinking of it rather as a guide to objects of instruction. Take the phrase "First Amendment," for instance. That is a lexical item that can hardy be used without bringing in a lot of associated information. Just what are the words and phrases that our school graduates should know? Right now, this seems to be decided by the makers of the SAT, which is, as I have mentioned, chiefly a vocabulary test. The educational technicians who choose the words that appear on the SAT are already the implicit makers of our national curriculum. Is then the Educational Testing Service our hidden National Board of Education? Does it sponsor our hidden national curriculum? If so, the ETS is rather to be praised than blamed. For if we wish to raise our national level of literacy, a hidden national curriculum is far better than no curriculum at all.

Where does this leave us? What issues are raised? If I am right in my interpretation of the evidence—and I have seen no alternative interpretation in the literature—then we can only raise our reading and writing skills significantly by consciously redefining and extending our cultural literacy. And yet our current national effort in the schools is largely run on the premise that the best way to proceed is through a culturally neutral, skills-approach to reading and writing. But if skill in writing and in reading comes about chiefly through what I have termed cultural literacy, then radical consequences follow. These consequences are not merely educational but social and political in their scope—and that scope is vast. I shall not attempt to set out these consequences here, but it will be obvious that acting upon them would involve our dismantling and casting aside the leading educational assumptions of the past half century.

Excerpt from "Appendix: What Literate Americans Need to Know"

Oakland, CA

Oakley, Annie

Oak Ridge

object

objet d'art

oboe

O brave new world!

obscenity laws

obsolescence

obtuse angle

O Captain! my Captain! (text)

Occident

O Come All Ye Faithful (Adeste Fideles) (song)

October Revolution ode

Ode on a Grecian Urn (text)

Odyssey, The (title)

Oedipus complex

Oedipus Rex (title)

oeuvre

off-Broadway

Office of Economic Opportunity(OEO)

offshore drilling

Off with her head!

O'Hara, Scarlett

Oh beautiful for spacious skies.

Ohio

Ohio River

ohm

Oil and water don't mix.

oil sands (tar shales)

Okinawa

Oklahoma

Oklahoma! (title)

Oklahoma City, OK

old boy network

Old Glory

Old King Cole

Old Mother Hubbard

Old soldiers never die; they just fade away.

Old Testament

Old World

oligarchy

oligopoly

Oliver Twist (title)

Olympian heights

Omaha, NE

Omar Khayyám

ombudsman

omnivore

Once bitten twice shy.

once in a blue moon

Once more into the breach, dear friends.

one for all and all for one

One good turn deserves another.

One if by land, two if by sea.

O'Neill, Eugene

One man's meat is another man's poison.

One picture is worth a thousand words.

One rotten apple spoils the barrel.

One swallow does not make a summer.

one that loved not wisely but too well

on its last legs

only thing we have to fear is fear itself., The

Ontario

on tenterhooks

on the Hill

Ontogeny recapitulates phylogeny.

On Top of Old Smokey (song)

op art

OPEC

Open Door policy

open primary

open sesame

open shop

opera

operetta

Oppenheimer, J. Robert

opposable thumbs

optic nerve

optics

oral personality

orbit

order of magnitude

ore (ore deposit)

Oregon

Oregon Trail

Orestes

organic chemistry

organic molecule

organization man

Organization of American States (OAS)

Orient

original sin

Origin of Species, The (title)

Orion

O Romeo, Romeo! wherefore art thou Romeo?

Orpheus

Orwell, George

Oslo

osmosis

ostracism

Oh! Susannah (song)

Othello (title)

Ottawa

Ottoman Empire

ounce of prevention is worth a pound of cure., An

our country, right or wrong

Out, damned spot!

Out of sight, out of mind.

out of the frying pan into the fire

Oval Office

ovarian cycle

ovary

overdraft

overhead

overkill

Over There (song)

overture

Ovid

ovum (ova)

Owens, Jesse

Oxford and Cambridge universities (Oxbridge)

oxidation

oxygen

oxymoron

ozone layer

Sabbath, the

Sacco-Vanzetti Case

sacrament

Sacramento, CA

Sacramento Valley

sacred cow

Sade, Marquis de

sadism

Sahara Desert

Saigon

Saint George and the dragon

Saint Lawrence River

Saint Louis, MO

Saint Paul, MN

Saint Paul's Cathedral

Saint Petersburg, FL

Saint Peter's Church

Saint Sophia (basilica)

salad days

Salem witch trials

Salk vaccine

Salome

salon

Salt Lake City, UT

salt of the earth

salt on a bird's tail

salvation

Salvation Army

Samson and Delilah

San Andreas Fault

San Antonio, TX

sanctions

sanctum sanctorum

Sand, George

Sandburg, Carl

San Diego, CA

San Francisco, CA

San Francisco Bay

sang froid

San Joaquin Valley

San Jose, CA

San Salvador

Sanskrit

Santa Fe, NM

Santa Fe Trail

Santiago

São Paulo

Sappho

Sarajevo

Saratoga, NY

sarcasm

Sardinia

Sartre, Jean-Paul

Satan

satellite (politics)

satellite (technology)

satire

saturated fatty acid

Saturn (myth)

Saturn (planet)

satyr

Saudi Arabia

savanna

savings and loan association

savings bond

savoir-faire

Savonarola, Girolamo

saxophone

scab (labor)

Scandinavia

scapegoat

Scarlet Letter, The (title)

Scheherazade

Schiller, Friedrich von

schism

schizophrenia

scholasticism

Schubert, Franz

Schweitzer, Albert

sciatica

science fiction

scientific method

Scopes trial (monkey trial)

Scotland

Scotland Yard

Scott, Sir Walter

Scrooge

Scylla and Charybdis

sea legs

seamy side

seasonal unemployment

Seattle, WA

secession

Second Coming, the

Second Inaugural Address

second sight

second wind

Secret Life of Walter Mitty, The (title)

Secret Service

sect

secular

Securities and Exchange Commission (SEC)

Security Council

sedimentary rock (sedimentation)

sedition

Seeing is believing.

segregation

Seine River, the

seismology (seismograph)

Seize the day. (Carpe diem.)

Selective Service

self-incrimination

Self-Reliance (title)

seller's market

Selma, AL

semantics

semicolon (;)

Seminole Indians

Semite, Semitic

semper fidelis

Senate, the U.S.

seniority

señor

señora

señorita

sentence

Seoul

separate but equal

separation of church and state

separation of powers

Sequoyah, Chief

serfdom

Sermon on the Mount

Serpent, the

Serra, Junipero

service industry

Sesame Street (title)

settlement houses

set your teeth on edge

Seuss, Dr.

seven deadly sins

Seventh-Day Adventists

Seven Wonders of the World

Seville

sexism

sex-linked trait

sexual reproduction

Shakespeare, William

shale

Shall I compare thee to a summer's day?

shalom

Shanghai

Shangri-la

sharecropping

Shaw, George Bernard (GBS)

Shawnee Indians

Shelley, Percy Bysshe

Sherman Anti-Trust Act

Sherman's march to the sea

Sherwood Forest

shibboleth

shipshape

ships that pass in the night

shock therapy

Shoot, if you must, this old gray head

short circuit

short story

shout fire in a crowded theater

show must go on., The

Shreveport, LA

Siberia

sic

Sicily

sickle-cell anemia

Sic transit gloria mundi.

Sierra Madre

Sierra Nevada

siesta

sign of the cross

signor

signora

signorina

Silence is golden. (Speech is silver.)

silent majority

Silent Night (song)

silicates

silicon chip

Silicon Valley

simile

simple sentence

Simple Simon (text)

Sinai

Sinatra, Frank

sine die

sine qua non

Singapore

Sing a Song
   of Sixpence (song)

singular

sinking fund

Sink or swim.

Sioux Indians

Sirens, the

Sistine Chapel

Sisyphus

sitcom (situation comedy)

sit-ins

sit on the fence

Sitting Bull

skepticism

Skinner, B. F.

skin of your teeth

skull and crossbones

skyscrapers

slang

slavery

slave trade, the

Sleeping Beauty (title)

sliding scale

slow but sure

smallpox

smell a rat

Smith, Adam

Smith, Captain John

Smithsonian Institution

smog

Snow White (title)

social gospel

socialism

social science

Social Security

Society of Friends

sociobiology

sociology

sociopath

Socrates

Sodom and Gomorrah

soft answer turneth away wrath.,
   A

software

solar cell

solar system, the

solid South

solipsism

Solomon

Something is rotten in the state of
   Denmark.

sonata

sonic boom

sonnet

sophist

Sophocles

soprano

Sorbonne

sound mind in a sound body, a

soup to nuts

sour grapes

Sousa, John Philip

Sousa marches

South Africa

South America

South Carolina

South Dakota

Southeast Asia

Southern Hemisphere

South Korea

South Sea Islands

South Seas

sovereignty

Soviet bloc

Soviet Union

space shuttle

space station

space telescope

Spain

Spanish-American War

Spanish Armada

Spanish Civil War

Spanish Inquisition

Spare the rod and spoil the child.

Sparta

Speaker of the House

Speak softly and carry a big stick.

Speech is silver; silence is golden.

speed of light

sperm whale

sphere

Sphinx, the

Spinoza, Baruch

Spirit Of '76 (image)

Spirit of St. Louis

split hairs

split infinitive

Spock, Dr. Benjamin

spoils system

spontaneous combustion

spore

spreading yourself too thin

sputnik

Sri Lanka

staccato

staff of life

stagflation

stalactite

stalagmite

Stalin, Josef

Stalingrad, Battle of

Stalinism

stamen

Stamp Act

standard deviation

standard of living

standing orders

stanza

Star Chamber

star-crossed lovers

stare decisis

Stars and Stripes Forever (song)

Star-Spangled Banner, The (song)

Star Trek (title)

Star Wars (title)

State of the Union Address

states' rights

static electricity

statistics

Statue of Liberty

status quo

status symbol

statute of limitations

steal (someone's) thunder

Stein, Gertrude

Stendhal

Step on a crack, break your mother's back.

steppe

stereotype

Stevenson, Robert Louis

Stewart, Jimmy
Still waters run deep.
stitch in time saves nine., A
stock exchange/stock market
stoicism
stomach (anatomy)
Stone Age
Stonehenge
Stone walls do not a prison make.
Stopping by Woods on a Snowy
    Evening (title)
storage battery
Stowe, Harriet Beecher
Stradivarius
strain at a gnat and swallow a camel
strange bedfellows
Strategic Arms Limitation Treaty
    (SALT)
strategic defense initiative (SDI)
strategy/tactics
stratification
stratosphere
stratus clouds
Strauss, Johann
Strauss, Richard
Strauss waltzes
Stravinsky, Igor
straw in the wind
straw man
streamline
stream of consciousness
Streetcar Named Desire, A (title)
strike
strikebreaker
Strike while the iron is hot.
Strindberg, August
string quartet
strip mining
Stuart, Gilbert
Stuttgart
Sturm und Drang
Stuyvesant, Peter

Styx, River
subconsciousness
subject (grammar)
subjunctive
sublimation (chemistry)
sublimation (psychology)
subordination (grammar)
subpoena
subsidy
subsistence farming
suffer fools gladly
suffix
suffrage
suffragette
sui generis
sulfa drug
summa cum laude
summit meeting
Sumter, Fort
Sun Also Rises, The (title)
Sun King
superconductor
superego
superlative (grammar)
Superman
supernova
supersonic
supply and demand
supply-side economics
Supreme Court
surface tension
surrealism
surtax
swastika
sweatshop
Sweden
sweetness and light
Swift, Jonathan
swing
Swing Low, Sweet Chariot (song)
Switzerland

Sword of Damocles
Sydney
symphony
synagogue
syndrome
synfuel
synonym
syntax
syphilis
Syracuse, NY
Syria

U-boats
UFO
Uganda
Ugly Duckling, The (title)
UHF (ultrahigh frequency)
ukelele
ulcer
Ulster
ultimatum
Ulysses
umbilical cord
un-American
uncertainty principle
Uncle Remus stories
Uncle Sam (image)
Uncle Tom
Uncle Tom's Cabin (title)
underdog
Underground Railroad
understatement

Uneasy lies the head that wears the crown.
UNESCO (United Nations Educational, Scientific, and Cultural Organization)
unicorn
unilateral
Union, the
union shop
Unitarian church
United Kingdom
United Nations
United States Information Agency (USIA)
universal gravitation
unsaturated fatty acid
uppercase
uppercrust
upward mobility
uranium
Uranus
urbanization
urban renewal
Ursa Major
Ursa Minor
usury
Utah
uterus
utilitarianism
utility (business)
utopia
utopianism

Questions for Discussion

1. Based on the essay and your knowledge of the items included in the excerpt from his list, would Hirsch find you to be a culturally literate person?

2. Based on the items you have seen, can you predict two or three other items that are probably on the list? Can you think of two or three items that you consider important elements of our national culture that probably are NOT on Hirsch's list?

3. What events or developments that have occurred since 1993 (the most recent publication date of *The Dictionary of Cultural Literacy*) are likely to be included on the next list? Of those, which are likely to still be of importance 50 years from now?

Explorations

1. Choose a college textbook and use some of the following questions to analyze the textbook. Consider the textbook carefully. What does the cover look like? Does the body of the text contain pictures, charts, diagrams? Does it have a preface, appendix, or glossary? What effect does the overall appearance of the textbook have on the reader? Describe the organization of the textbook. How is the information contained in it presented and organized? Sequentially, categorically, hierarchically? Are there sections, subheadings, boldfaced words? Why might the authors have organized it as they did? Based on your analysis of this textbook, what kind of knowledge do you think is most valued in the class in which it is used? And, how does it appear that you are expected to go about learning the information contained in this text?

2. Who is Hirsch's audience? Unlike other authors in this book, he does not use footnotes or provide a list of works cited. Speculate about why this might be so. What does that say about his intended audience and about his purposes in writing this particular essay?

3. Hirsch suggests that there is a body of knowledge that every American must know in order to read and write well. How would such content be determined? Who would decide? What are the political, social, and economic stakes involved in such decisions?

Formal Writing Assignments

1. Choose an element of popular culture that is very familiar to you but which for one reason or another is unlikely to be known to the broader American public. For example, there are popular songs that members of each generation identify with very closely but which are virtually unknown to their parents. You may also consider books, dance styles, slang phrases—virtually anything that defines and separates your generation from the preceding (or succeeding) one. Describe this item and how it reflects or captures the essence of an important segment of our society. Where does it fit in the larger picture of American culture? Are you willing to make the case for including it on everyone's "cultural literacy" list, or does the power of this particular cultural phenomenon depend on its exclusivity?

2. Critics of E. D. Hirsch, Jr. argue that his list amounts to a kind of "cultural imperialism," where the cultures of smaller groups in our country are subordinated to the predominantly Eurocentric historical and cultural view of the majority. Hirsch does not disagree with this argument; he simply states that there are values and ideas that in his estimation ought to be shared by everyone who claims to be an American. He sees himself taking a political stand in favor of his version of cultural literacy and wants his critics to see that through their opposition they are also taking a political stand. Have you ever found your own values to be at odds with that of the majority of people you know? Were you willing to take a public stand in favor of your viewpoint? Is there a way for your view to co-exist with that of the majority?

Discovering the Forms of Academic Discourse

Robert M. Holland, Jr.

Professor Robert Holland is currently a Master of the University Honors Program at the University of Akron, where he served as the Director of Composition from 1978–1984 and the Director of the Early English Composition Assessment Program from 1984–1988. Born in Waltham, Massachusetts, this graduate of Dartmouth (BA), Harvard (GSEd MAT), and Indiana (Ph.D.) has enjoyed a long career as both a teacher and an administrator in Higher Education. He also enjoys translating Plato, flying, and spending time with his grandchildren.

The dual emphasis in Holland's career upon classroom teaching and administration, perhaps, shapes his interest in the issue of academic discourse, the subject of his essay, "Discovering the Forms of Academic Discourse." Holland's essay might be seen as a continuation of the conversation begun by Sherman Alexie ("Superman and Me"), who describes learning to read—an "academic" enterprise" by using a Superman comic book—an "unacademic" form. Holland's piece asks these kinds of questions about academic discourse: What forms can it take? Who uses it and to what ends? How does it get evaluated in different contexts?

The selection below is excerpted from "Discovering the Forms of Academic Discourse," an essay published in *Audits of Meaning* (1988), a book edited by Louise Z. Smith.

Writing Before Reading

1. Describe a classroom experience for which you felt your previous "academic training" hadn't really prepared you. How did you react to this new task? What did you do in order to face it?

2. Have you ever been subjected to what you might label a "trick question" in your own classroom experience? Reflect on that experience. What was that like? How did you react to the teacher's strategy at the time? What do you think about that strategy now?

3. There are countless forms of "academic discourse" that we encounter in our lives as students: lab reports, the research paper, the personal essay, the flow chart. What else might count as academic discourse? In "Superman and Me," for instance, Sherman Alexie describes learning to read by using comic books. Can a comic book be seen as a form of "academic discourse"? Why or why not?

Discovering the Forms of Academic Discourse

Plato has Socrates define the ideal of academic discourse in the *Phaedrus*: "true written rhetoric" must not be a creation of fantasy or something aimed merely at creating belief without any attempt at instruction by question and answer; it must be more than a record or mnemonic device; it is written by one who has knowledge of the truth he writes, who can defend what he has written by submitting to an interrogation on the subject, and who makes it evident as soon as he speaks how comparatively inferior are his writings. A scholar teaches what he knows; inquires, through dialectic, into what he does not know; and not only submits to but *seeks* the best interrogation, refutation, or criticism that may be developed by other scholars. Academic discourse, at its best, is both dialectic and didactic.

Such is the case with ideal academic discourse. In the world of school, however, from the earliest "sharing" or pre-school through doctoral dissertations, the academic writer may choose an *eidolon*, a "dream-image" of academic discourse; furthermore, he or she may be quite unaware of having made such a choice. Format and formula may become primary, for they often appear to be the observable determiners of esteem or success. Teachers also (whether aware of it or not) may invite either the idea or the eidolon of academic discourse by the way they design their writing assignments.

Let me illustrate this concept of eidolon with a story from my own early schooling. In September of 1955 our high school chemistry class went to the chemistry laboratory for the first time. We had been told that there was to be no talking while we were in the lab; we were to follow the written instructions on how to work with the material assembled at our stations and to submit a written report before leaving the lab. At each station were four numbered beakers containing clear liquid, two pads of litmus paper (blue, pink), and this assignment: "Use only the litmus paper to find out what you can about the contents of the beakers. Write a report of your findings and what you think those findings mean."

Of course, none of us was entirely in the dark at that point: we had had some experience with "chemistry sets," we "knew" the simple magic of litmus. We set to work, systematically dipping little strips of blue and pink litmus into the series of beakers. For me, as I recall, it went like this: with beaker #1, the pink litmus became blue and the blue litmus became merely damp; with beaker #2, the pink litmus became damp and the blue litmus became pink; with beaker #3, both the blue and the pink litmus paper became damp, neither of them changing color; with beaker #4, both the blue and pink litmus paper turned white.

Now, I hadn't the slightest idea what was happening with beaker #4. I peeked about the lab to see how my classmates were doing and found them peeking about, too: we all had before us, from one or another of our beakers, pink and blue litmus paper strips which had both turned white. Since we had been prohibited from discussing our work, we each turned to the task of composing a written report.

Though puzzled by the whitened litmus, we did know something about writing reports. We each drew up a chart or table (columns for the beakers, rows for the litmus, that sort of thing) and wrote in our findings. We added an introduction, repeating the written instructions at our stations, and we made some sentences about how we had done what we had been told to do. But here is the curious part: *not one of us included the information about both the blue and the pink litmus strips turning white.* (I believe I wrote in my report of both blue and pink litmus for beaker #4: "No change." Others, wrote, "Both became damp," or, "Nothing happened.")

The following day, the chemistry teacher began by asking each of us in turn what we had experienced with the litmus and the liquid in a particular beaker (he asked me, of course, about beaker #4). One after another we stated not what we had seen, but what we had written in our reports. The teacher then asked whether any of us had noticed litmus paper turning white. Well, we all had, and now we said so. But none of us, he pointed out, had reported that; how, he asked, did we account for this phenomenon of our concurrence in a fiction? Why had we all written what was untrue?

We replied as best we could, explaining that we had been afraid of being wrong and admitting a shared belief that every finding must be explained; since we had no idea of what was happening with the whitened litmus, we had chosen to describe that occurrence by redefining it. Our replies, taken all together, made clear to us that our reports were not academic discourse but an imitation of academic discourse. While none of us had pretended not to see the litmus paper turn white, we all had pretended so in our reports.

We had missed the point of the laboratory assignment, which had been designed to enable us to discover for ourselves the dialectic of chemistry, and we had chosen to substitute our eidolon of academic discourse. Having assumed that the true subject of our exercise was "Using Litmus Paper," we then formulated our "learning" to fit our expectations. We formatted our findings to fit the fantasy of our waking dream of science—*in spite of* our first-hand experience that called into question the very tool we imagined we had mastered. (Beaker #4, it turned out, contained commercial bleach, which subverted the dye system of the litmus paper itself.)

We had used format and formulation to excuse ourselves from the learning of form, creating an illusion of knowledge based on an absurd and unspoken premise: "What you do not understand, hide." In imitating scientists, we had behaved as no true scientist ever would. What made the exercise nonetheless useful for us, in spite of our failure, was that our reports were in writing: having created ignorance (or, more generously, having made a predictable student error), we had to confront, in the written testimony of our reports, the consequences of our creation. Written discourse made possible a scene for learning that would have been impossible through vocal discussion. By discovering ourselves as a community of *non*scholars we were able to see what it might mean to become a community of scholars.

The lesson was not learned all at once, of course. In another year, doing physics, we went about the business of heating metal rods, viewing salt and other things in a flame, and rolling steel balls down troughs—and then looked up in handbooks the correct coefficient of expansion or wavelength of light or acceleration of gravity and worked our calculations backwards, leaving what we called a "margin of error." In biology we knew better than to try to draw precisely the protozoa we tracked through our microscopes; no, we traced perfect circles into our laboratory reports and drew within them adaptations of what our textbooks showed. If you were "seeing" a paramecium, it better have a fringe of cilia all around; if an amoeba, include one contractile vacuole.

And so it went in other school subjects: we told back history as it was told to us—never mentioning an open question or an unresolved doubt, and never imagining that it was all right *not* to know the significance of everything. We wrote school discourse, not academic discourse but an eidolon of academic discourse. We dealt in formulas and format, not in form, not in meaning-making dialectic.

Questions for Discussion

1. Holland claims there is a discernible difference between an "eidolon," or "dream image" of academic discourse and the real thing. How does Holland define those terms? Why does he consider the lab reports written by him and his classmates to be eidolon, rather than real academic discourse? What evidence does he supply to support his claim?

2. Holland argues that he and his classmates "missed the point" of the assignment. What do you think the point of that assignment really was? How did you arrive at that conclusion?

3. How does Holland's experience as a student compare with the speakers' experiences in Jerome Stern's "Mad?" Likewise, can you make connections to Audre Lorde's experience as a student in the excerpt from *Zami?* To Mike Rose's experiences in "I Just Wanna Be Average"? Working with a partner or a small group, try to map out the connections you see; feel free to categorize patterns that may arise as you work.

Explorations

1. According to Holland, the written report required him and his classmates to "confront . . . the consequences of our creation. Written discourse made possible a scene for learning that would have been impossible through vocal discussion. By discovering ourselves as a community of *non*-scholars we were able to see what it might mean to become a community of scholars." Draft a response to Holland's claim in which you describe/evaluate the role that writing plays in Holland's essay. How does writing help him to "confront" those consequences?

2. If Holland were to use Freire's terms to write about this experience, what might he say? Use Freire's vocabulary in order to draft a "review" of both the teacher's and the students' approaches to the chemistry experiment.

3. Describe an activity from one of your high school classes that you consider memorable or important. After describing that activity, take a critical step back and evaluate it. What were the teacher's goals in assigning it? What were your goals in completing the activity? Speculate a bit about how those goals might reflect larger goals held by your high school or school system.

Formal Writing Assignments

1. Spend some time "taking stock" of the readings you've encountered in this unit thus far. Calling upon evidence (summary, quotation, or paraphrase) from at least two of those readings, draft an essay in which you formulate your own definition of "academic discourse." How does your definition differ from the definitions that various authors within this unit might provide? How does your definition connect with the definitions of others?

2. Choose a professor/teacher with whom you are currently studying and interview that teacher about his/her favorite classroom activity or lesson plan. Your goal as a researcher is to encourage the professor to describe the activity and to discuss how and why s/he uses it in the classroom. Once your interview is complete, draft an essay in which you share the results of your interview and evaluate the teacher's activity. Be sure to address your own system of evaluation: how did you decide whether or not the teacher's activity was useful, pertinent, creative?

Engaged Pedagogy

bell hooks

bell hooks (1955–) is the pen name of Gloria Watkins; "bell hooks" was the name of her great-grand-mother, whose wisdom Watkins wanted to honor. She is currently Distinguished professor of English at City College in New York. Her work has explored how factors such as African-American womanhood, feminism, the civil rights movement, and critical theory clash in the world at large, in her own life, and, perhaps most importantly, in the classroom. "Engaged Pedagogy," which appeared as the opening chapter of *Teaching to Transgress* in 1994, calls into question the traditional role of the "teacher" in our educational system, and asserts that teachers who are "engaged" must be concerned with their students' well being, and with their own.

Writing Before Reading

1. Write about a time when a teacher cared about you as an individual. How did you know? How did this personal concern affect the way he/she taught?

2. How could we "revise" the classroom to give students more control of their educations? What adjustments would the teacher have to make if these "revisions" were to be adopted? Why might some teachers balk at such plans?

3. Why should (or shouldn't) teachers share personal information/experiences with their students?

Engaged Pedagogy

To educate as the practice of freedom is a way of teaching that anyone can learn. That learning process comes easiest to those of us who teach who also believe that there is an aspect of our vocation that is sacred; who believe that our work is not merely to share information but to share in the intellectual and spiritual growth of our students. To teach in a manner that respects and cares for the souls of our students is essential if we are to provide the necessary conditions where learning can most deeply and intimately begin.

Throughout my years as student and professor, I have been most inspired by those teachers who have had the courage to transgress those boundaries that would confine each pupil to a rote, assembly-line approach to learning. Such teachers approach students with the will and desire to respond to our unique beings, even if the situation does not allow the full emergence of a relationship based on mutual recognition. Yet the possibility of such recognition is always present.

Paulo Freire and the Vietnamese Buddhist monk Thich Nhat Hanh are two of the "teachers" who have touched me deeply with their work. When I first began college, Freire's thought gave me the support I needed to challenge the "banking system" of education, that approach to learning that is rooted in the notion that all students need to do is consume information fed to them by a professor and be able to memorize and store it. Early on, it was Freire's insistence that education could be the practice of freedom that encouraged me to create strategies for what he called "conscientization" in the classroom. Translating that term to critical awareness and engagement, I entered the classrooms with the conviction that it was crucial for me and every other student to be an active participant, not a passive consumer. Education as the practice of freedom was continually undermined by professors who were actively hostile to the notion of student participation. Freire's work affirmed that education can only be liberatory when everyone claims knowledge as a field in which we all labor. That notion of mutual labor was affirmed by Thich Nhat Hanh's philosophy of engaged Buddhism, the focus on practice in conjunction with contemplation. His philosophy was similar to Freire's emphasis on "praxis"–action and reflection upon the world in order to change it.

In his work Thich Nhat Hanh always speaks of the teacher as a healer. Like Freire, his approach to knowledge called on students to be active participants, to link awareness with practice. Whereas Freire was primarily concerned with the mind, Thich Nhat Hanh offered a way of thinking about pedagogy which emphasized wholeness, a union of mind, body, and spirit. His focus on a holistic approach to learning and spiritual practice enabled me to overcome years of socialization that had taught me to believe a classroom was diminished if students and professors regarded one another as "whole" human beings, striving not just for knowledge in books, but knowledge about how to live in the world.

During my twenty years of teaching, I have witnessed a grave sense of dis-ease among professors (irrespective of their politics) when students want us to see them as whole human beings with complex lives and experiences rather than simply as seekers after compartmentalized bits of knowledge. When I was an undergraduate, Women's Studies was just finding a place in the academy. Those classrooms were the one space where teachers were willing to acknowledge a connection between ideas learned in university settings and those learned in life practices. And, despite those times when students abused that freedom in the classroom by only wanting to dwell on personal experience, feminist classrooms were, on the whole, one location where I witnessed professors striving to create participatory spaces for the sharing of knowledge. Nowadays, most women's studies professors are not as committed to exploring new pedagogical strategies. Despite this shift, many students still seek to enter feminist classrooms because they continue to believe that there, more than in any other place in the academy, they will have an opportunity to experience education as the practice of freedom.

Progressive, holistic education, "engaged pedagogy" is more demanding than conventional critical or feminist pedagogy. For, unlike these two teaching practices, it emphasizes well-being. That means that teachers must be actively committed to a process of self-actualization that promotes their own well-being if they are to teach in a manner that empowers students. Thich Nhat Hanh emphasized that "the practice of a healer, therapist, teacher or any helping professional should be directed toward his or herself first because if the helper is unhappy, he or she cannot help many people." In the United States it is rare that anyone talks about teachers in university settings as healers. And it is even more rare to hear anyone suggest that teachers have any responsibility to be self-actualized individuals.

Learning about the work of intellectuals and academics primarily from nineteenth-century fiction and nonfiction during my pre-college years, I was certain that the task for those of us who chose this vocation was to be holistically questing for self-actualization. It was the actual experience of college that disrupted this image. It was there that I was made to feel as though I was terribly naive about "the profession." I learned that far from being self-actualized, the university was seen more as a haven for those who are smart in book knowledge but who might be otherwise unfit for social interaction. Luckily, during my undergraduate years I began to make a distinction between the practice of being an intellectual/teacher and one's role as a member of the academic profession.

It was difficult to maintain fidelity to the idea of the intellectual as someone who sought to be whole—well-grounded in a context where there was little emphasis on spiritual well-being, on care of the soul. Indeed, the objectification of the teacher within bourgeois educational structures seemed to denigrate notions of wholeness and uphold the idea of a mind/body split, one that promotes and supports compartmentalization.

This support reinforces the dualistic separation of public and private, encouraging teachers and students to see no connection between life practices, habits of being, and the roles of professors. The idea of the intellectual questing for a union of mind, body, and spirit had been replaced with notions that being smart meant that one was inherently emotionally unstable and that the best in oneself emerged in one's academic work. This meant that whether academics were drug addicts, alcoholics, batterers, or sexual abusers, the only important aspect of our identity was whether or not our minds functioned, whether we were able to do our jobs in the classroom. The self was presumably emptied out the moment the threshold was crossed, leaving in place only an objective mind—free of experiences and biases. There was fear that the conditions of that self would interfere with the teaching process. Part of the luxury and privilege of the role of teacher/professor today is the absence of any requirement that we be self-actualized. Not surprisingly, professors who are not concerned with inner well-being are the most threatened by the demand on the part of students for liberatory education, for pedagogical processes that will aid them in their own struggle for self-actualization.

Certainly it was naive for me to imagine during high school that I would find spiritual and intellectual guidance in university settings from writers, thinkers, scholars. To have found this would have been to stumble across a rare treasure. I learned, along with other students, to consider myself fortunate if I found an interesting professor who talked in a compelling way. Most of my professors were not the slightest bit interested in enlightenment. More than anything they seemed enthralled by the exercise of power and authority within their mini-kingdom, the classroom.

This is not to say that there were not compelling, benevolent dictators, but it is true to my memory that it was rare—absolutely, astonishingly rare—to encounter professors who were deeply committed to progressive pedagogical practices. I was dismayed by this; most of my professors were not individuals whose teaching styles I wanted to emulate.

My commitment to learning kept me attending classes. Yet, even so, because I did not conform—would not be an unquestioning, passive student—some professors treated me with contempt. I was slowly becoming estranged from education. Finding Freire in the midst of that estrangement was crucial to my survival as a student. His work offered both a way for me to understand the limitations of the type of education I was receiving and to discover alternative strategies for learning and teaching. It was particularly disappointing to encounter white male professors who claimed to follow Freire's model even as their pedagogical practices were mired in structures of domination, mirroring the styles of conservative professors even as they approached subjects from a more progressive standpoint.

When I first encountered Paulo Freire, I was eager to see if his style of teaching would embody the pedagogical practices he described so eloquently in his work. During the short time I studied with him, I was deeply moved by his presence, by the way in which his manner of teaching exemplified his pedagogical theory. (Not all students interested in Freire have had a similar experience.) My experience with him restored my faith in liberatory education. I had never wanted to surrender the conviction that one could teach without reinforcing existing systems of domination. I needed to know that professors did not have to be dictators in the classroom.

While I wanted teaching to be my career, I believed that personal success was intimately linked with self-actualization. My passion for this quest led me to interrogate constantly the mind/body split that was so often taken to be a given. Most professors were often deeply antagonistic toward, even scornful of, any approach to learning emerging from a philosophical standpoint emphasizing the union of mind, body, and spirit, rather than the separation of these elements. Like many of the students I now teach, I was often told by powerful academics that I was misguided to seek such a perspective in the academy. Throughout my student years I felt deep inner anguish. Memory of that pain returns as I listen to students express the concern that they will not succeed in academic professions if they want to be well, if they eschew dysfunctional behavior or participation in coercive hierarchies. These students are often fearful, as I was, that there are no spaces in the academy where the will to be self-actualized can be affirmed.

This fear is present because many professors have intensely hostile responses to the vision of liberatory education that connects the will to know with the will to become. Within professorial circles, individuals often complain bitterly that students want classes to be "encounter groups." While it is utterly unreasonable for students to expect classrooms to be therapy sessions, it is appropriate for them to hope that the knowledge received in these settings will enrich and enhance them.

Currently, the students I encounter seem far more uncertain about the project of self-actualization than my peers and I were twenty years ago. They feel that there are no clear ethical guidelines shaping actions. Yet, while they despair, they are also adamant that education should be liberatory. They want and demand more from professors than my generation did. There are times when I walk into classrooms overflowing with students who feel terribly wounded in their psyches (many of them see therapists), yet I do not think that they want therapy from me. They do want an education that is healing to the uninformed, unknowing spirit. They do want knowledge that is meaningful. They rightfully expect that my colleagues and I will not offer them information without addressing the connection between what they are learning and their overall life experiences.

This demand on the students' part does not mean that they will always accept our guidance. This is one of the joys of education as the practice of freedom, for it allows students to assume responsibility for their choices. Writing about our teacher/student relationship in a piece for the *Village Voice*, "How to Run the Yard: Off-Line and into the Margins at Yale," one of my students, Gary Dauphin, shares the joys of working with me as well as the tensions that surfaced between us as he began to devote his time to pledging a fraternity rather than cultivating his writing:

> People think academics like Gloria [my given name] are all about difference: but what I learned from her was mostly about sameness, about what I had in common as a black man to people of color; to women and gays and lesbians and the poor and anyone else who wanted in. I did some of this learning by reading but most of it came from hanging out on the fringes of her life. I lived like that for a while, shuttling between high points in my classes and low points outside. Gloria was a safe haven . . . Pledging a fraternity is about as far away as you can get from her classroom, from the yellow kitchen where she used to share her lunch with students in need of various forms of sustenance.

This is Gary writing about the joy. The tension arose as we discussed his reason for wanting to join a fraternity and my disdain for that decision. Gary comments, "They represented a vision of black manhood that she abhorred, one where violence and abuse were primary ciphers of bonding and identity." Describing his assertion of autonomy from my influence he writes, "But she must have also known the limits of even her influence on my life, the limits of books and teachers."

Ultimately, Gary felt that the decision he had made to join a fraternity was not constructive, that I "had taught him openness" where the fraternity had encouraged one-dimensional allegiance. Our interchange both during and after this experience was an example of engaged pedagogy.

Through critical thinking—a process he learned by reading theory and actively analyzing texts—Gary experienced education as the practice of freedom. His final comments about me: "Gloria had only mentioned the entire episode once after it was over, and this to tell me simply that there are many kinds of choices, many kinds of logic. I could make those events mean whatever I wanted as long as I was honest." I have quoted his writing at length because it is testimony affirming engaged pedagogy. It means that my voice is not the only account of what happens in the classroom.

Engaged pedagogy necessarily values student expression. In her essay, "Interrupting the Calls for Student Voice in Liberatory Education: A Feminist Poststructuralist Perspective," Mimi Orner employs a Foucauldian framework to suggest that

> Regulatory and punitive means and uses of the confession bring to mind curricular and pedagogical practices which call for students to publicly reveal, even confess, information about their lives and cultures in the presence of authority figures such as teachers.

When education is the practice of freedom, students are not the only ones who are asked to share, to confess. Engaged pedagogy does not seek simply to empower students. Any classroom that employs a holistic model of learning will also be a place where teachers grow, and are empowered by the process. That empowerment cannot happen if we refuse to be vulnerable while encouraging students to take risks. Professors who expect students to share confessional narratives but who are themselves unwilling to share are exercising power in a manner that could be coercive. In my classrooms, I do not expect students to take any risks that I would not take, to share in any way that I would not share. When professors bring narratives of their experiences into classroom discussions it eliminates the possibility that we can function as all-knowing, silent interrogators. It is often productive if professors take the first risk, linking confessional narratives to academic discussions so as to show how experience can illuminate and enhance our understanding of academic material. But most professors must practice being vulnerable in the classroom, being wholly present in mind, body, and spirit.

Progressive professors working to transform the curriculum so that it does not reflect biases or reinforce systems of domination are most often the individuals willing to take the risks that engaged pedagogy requires and to make their teaching practices a site of resistance. In her essay, "On Race and Voice: Challenges for Liberation Education in the 1990s," Chandra Mohanty writes that

> resistance lies in self-conscious engagement with dominant, normative discourses and representations and in the active creation of oppositional analytic and cultural spaces. Resistance that is random and isolated is clearly not as effective as that which is mobilized through systemic politicized practices of teaching and learning. Uncovering and reclaiming subjugated knowledge is one way to lay claims to alternative histories. But these knowledges need to be understood and defined pedagogically, as questions of strategy and practice as well as of scholarship, in order to transform educational institutions radically.

Professors who embrace the challenge of self-actualization will be better able to create pedagogical practices that engage students, providing them with ways of knowing that enhance their capacity to live fully and deeply.

Questions for Discussion

1. In her essay, hooks undermines the concept of professional objectivity, calling the attempt to free the mind of "experiences and biases" a "mind/body split." Why do we hold "objectivity" in such esteem? Is pure objectivity possible? Is it more desirable in some academic fields than in others?

2. Consider hooks' involvement with her student who is considering joining a fraternity. Does hooks' influence on the student and shared "disdain" for his decision exhibit what she calls "engaged pedagogy"?

3. hooks contends that when "education is the practice of freedom," teachers join their students in classroom "confessions." Are there certain kinds of confessions that would not be appropriate in the classroom? Why or why not?

Explorations

1. Using email, students and teachers should be assigned a "send to" address of one classmate's email address. They should compose what hooks would call "confessional narratives" and send them to their assigned address. Next, the narratives should be forwarded (without the name of the original contributor) to the recipients' assigned "send to" addresses. This process should be repeated several times until the narratives are "shuffled" and seemingly anonymous. Using email, the final recipient should respond to the narrative, both emotionally and critically, and then send it back down the email "chain" until it reaches its original source. How does anonymity affect the way you react to other's work? How does it affect the way you react to criticism and feedback?

2. In her essay, hooks praises Freire's discussion of the "Banking Concept of Education" and cites it as a source of inspiration for her own pedagogy. At first glance, their approaches seem quite different—for example, in a perfect world Freire would advocate that there be no teachers, that students take charge of their own educations, while hooks would argue that the teachers need to be involved completely: bodily, intellectually, and spiritually. Imagine a situation in which a teacher tried to construct a classroom by combining the theories of hooks and Freire. Describe how you envision that classroom.

3. Imagine that you are a college professor. Write a letter to hooks in which you argue that her ideas about personal involvement of teachers are preposterous. Describe the class you teach, and the reasons you hold for the separation of things personal and intellectual. Make sure that your argument asserts that your approach is most beneficial for the students of your class.

Formal Writing Assignments

1. According to hooks, the ideal educational environment is one in which we, as students and teachers, acknowledge the equal importance of intellect and emotion (or spirit, or "soul") as components of our education. In an attempt to test her thesis, write an essay in which you react to her argument in two different ways. First, write a reaction that excludes any personal or emotional content; in other words, write a strictly analytical, intellectual response. Second, write a reaction that is composed entirely of subjective, emotional response. Finally, analyze these approaches to academic writing and consider the following questions: What are the benefits and limitations to each approach? What ways is your writing strengthened or weakened by the restrictions of each approach? Were you ever truly successful in writing exclusively objectively or subjectively?

2. Choose a class in which you are currently enrolled and analyze the environment and instructor using hooks' criteria for "engaged pedagogy." If possible, after having completed your evaluation, ask to interview the teacher about his or her pedagogy. Before the interview, try to determine what the instructor will claim to value in education, what his/her priorities are in the classroom. Next, analyze the responses of the instructor, trying to account for any discrepancies between your presumptions and the instructors' views.

Theme for English B

Langston Hughes

One of the central figures of the Harlem Renaissance, James Mercer Langston Hughes (1902–1967) continued influencing literature throughout his life, including in the Black Arts Movement of the late 1960s. Hughes mingled with such writers as Zora Neale Hurston and Countee Cullen, and helped inspire young writers Margaret Walker and Gwendolyn Brooks. He educated himself at Columbia University and Lincoln University. Known for the idiom and rhythm he expressed in his work, Hughes incorporates the cadence of jazz in "Theme for English B." The poem articulates one "colored" student's experience of discourse in an otherwise all "white" classroom community.

Writing Before Reading

1. Reflect on a time when you tried to fulfill an assignment in ways that kept your own identity in the writing.

2. List elements of your experience that you feel have help shaped your identity. In other words, what places, people and things have influenced or currently influence who you are.

3. Describe your feelings about the "truth" of your academic writing. Is the writing you do for school always and completely true to who you are?

Theme for English B

The instructor said,

> Go home and write
> a page tonight.
> And let that page come out of you—
> Then, it will be true.

I wonder if it's that simple?
I am twenty-two, colored, born in Winston-Salem.
I went to school there, then Durham, then here
to this college on the hill above Harlem.
I am the only colored student in my class.
The steps from the hill lead down into Harlem,
through a park, then I cross St. Nicholas,
Eighth Avenue, Seventh, and I come to the Y,
the Harlem Branch Y, where I take the elevator
up to my room, sit down, and write this page:

It's not easy to know what is true for you or me
at twenty-two, my age. But I guess I'm what
I feel and see and hear, Harlem, I hear you:

hear you, hear me—we two—you, me, talk on this page.
(I hear New York, too.) Me—who?
Well, I like to eat, sleep, drink, and be in love.
I like to work, read, learn and understand life.
I like a pipe for a Christmas present,
or records—Bessie, bop, or Bach.
I guess being colored doesn't make me *not* like
 the same things other folks like who are other races.
So will my page be colored that I write?

Being me, it will not be white.
But it will be
a part of you, instructor.
You are white—
yet a part of me, as I am a part of you.
That's American.
Sometimes perhaps you don't want to be a part of me.
Nor do I often want to be a part of you.
But we are, that's true!
As I learn from you,
I guess you learn from me—
although you're older—and white—
and somewhat more free.

This is my page for English B.

Questions for Discussion

1. List some of the themes that Hughes develops in this poem. How does he link them? How does the structure of the poem work to support and highlight these themes and their relationships?

2. How can the educational authorities of this poem and Amy Hempel's "Why I'm Here" (the instructor and Mrs. Deane) be compared? Do you think that they are aware of their students'/clients' true identities and true needs?

3. What rhetorical impact does this theme have because it takes place in an academic setting? Describe how important you believe identity in the classroom is to Hughes. For what reasons would Hughes be interested in this theme?

Explorations

1. Hughes wrote this theme as a poem. Rewrite his poem in prose. Does the change in form create a change in meaning? How would you evaluate this "theme" if you received a copy of it in a peer-response group?

2. Identify elements of Hughes's "Theme . . ." that stand out to you as "poetic." What effect do they create in you as a reader?

3. Why is it not so simple to write "a page that comes out of you," especially one that is "true"? How is the speaker "true" to himself/herself in this poem? How does the speaker include various aspects of his/her identity in the completion of this assignment?

Formal Writing Assignments

1. Have you ever felt yourself to be an "outsider" in a classroom? What do you feel to be the source of your alienation? Can you identify in some way with Hughes's speaker, or have you always felt at home in classrooms? What's the significance of your particular experience? Write an essay in which you describe your feelings of alienation or comfort, and analyze the situation to discover the reasons behind your experience.

2. Do you think that the academy needs changing to accommodate the feelings of individual students? If so, what changes would have to occur in the academy before all students felt themselves to be members of the classroom community? If not, what structures are in place that ensure the comfort of students? Analyze academic situations you have experienced in order to comment on the state of inclusiveness in the academy today.

The Story of Rosa Parks and the Montgomery Bus Boycott Revisited

Herbert Kohl

Herbert Kohl is a native New Yorker, born in the Bronx. He is a pioneer of the Open Classroom movement, which seeks to reform the American educational system by placing more emphasis upon students as independent choice-makers and de-emphasizes rigid, teacher-determined classroom structures. An avid student himself, Kohl was educated at Harvard University and University College, Oxford as an undergraduate.

He is the author of several books, with subject matter ranging from Deaf student education to how to teach children in urban settings. His publications include *Shall We Burn Babar: Essays on Children's Literature and the Power of Stories* (1995), which is the source for "The Story of Rosa Parks and the Montgomery Bus Boycott Revisited," below. Kohl has taken particular interest throughout his career in issues of systemic racism as they affect African American children growing up in large urban areas.

As you read Kohl, think about the other writers in this unit who have also served as educational administrators and teachers: Robert Holland, Keith Gilyard, bell hooks, Benjamin Barber, E.D. Hirsch, Mike Rose, and others. How might that dual perspective influence their theories of education? In what ways do these writers ask us to think not only about what goes on in individual classrooms, but what goes on in our education system as a whole?

Writing Before Reading

1. Take ten minutes and write—in any form (brainstorming, clustering, freewriting)—as much as you can remember about Rosa Parks and the Montgomery Bus Boycott. Once you've finished, try to characterize the information you see. Is it mostly factual? Descriptive? Evaluative? Where did this information come from?

2. Write about a time when your understanding of an historical event was challenged by a revision, or revised story. How did you respond to that revision? What did you feel you gained or lost by reading it?

3. What do you believe that authors of textbooks and books for children should take into account when they try to represent historical events to their young audiences? How "realistic" should books for children be?

The Story of Rosa Parks and the Montgomery Bus Boycott Revisited

Racism, and the direct confrontation between African American and European American people in the United States, is an issue that is usually considered too sensitive to be dealt with directly in the elementary school classroom. When confrontation between African Americans and European Americans occurs in children's literature, it is routinely described as a problem between individuals that can be worked out on a personal basis. In the few cases where racism is addressed as a social problem, there has to be a happy ending. This is most readily apparent in the biographical treatment of Rosa Parks, one of the two names that most children in the United States associate with the Civil Rights movement in the southern United States during the 1960s; the other is Martin Luther King, Jr.

Over the past few years, during visits to schools, I've talked with children about the Civil Rights movement. One of the things I ask the children is what they know of Rosa Parks and her involvement in the Montgomery bus boycott. This focus developed after I observed a play about civil rights in a fourth-grade classroom in southern California several years ago. One scene in the play took place on a bus in Montgomery, Alabama. A tired Rosa Parks got on the bus and sat down. The child portraying Mrs. Parks was dressed in shabby clothes and carried two worn shopping bags. She sat down next to the driver, and other children got on the bus until all the seats in front were filled up. Then a boy got on and asked her to move. She refused, and the bus driver told her he didn't want any trouble. Politely he asked her to move to the back of the bus. She refused again and the scene ended. In the next scene we see a crowd of students, African American and European American, carrying signs saying Don't Ride the Buses, We Shall Overcome, and Blacks and Whites Together. One of the students, playing Martin Luther King, Jr., addressed the rest of the class, saying something to the effect that African American and European American people in Montgomery got angry because Rosa Parks was arrested for not moving to the back of the bus, and that they were boycotting the buses until all people could ride wherever they wanted. The play ended with a narrator pointing out that the bus problem in Montgomery was solved by people coming together to protest peacefully for justice.

Before talking to the children about their perceptions of Rosa Parks and her motivations, I had a moment to talk with the teacher about a major misrepresentation of facts in the play: there were no European Americans involved in boycotting the buses in Montgomery. The struggle was organized and maintained by the African American community, and to represent it as an interracial struggle was to take the power and credit away from that community. The teacher agreed that the play took some liberty with history but said that since his class was interracial, it was better for all the children to do the play as an integrated struggle. Otherwise, he said, the play might lead to racial strife in the classroom. I disagreed and pointed out that by showing the power of organized African Americans, it might lead all the children to recognize and appreciate the strength oppressed people can show when confronting their oppressors. In addition, the fact that European Americans joined the struggle later on could lead to very interesting discussions about social change and struggles for justice, and could be related to the current situation in South Africa and the resurgence of overt racism in the United States. He disagreed and ended our chat by telling me how hard it was to manage an integrated classroom.

I contented myself with asking the children about Rosa Parks. The girl who played Mrs. Parks, Anna, told me that she imagined "Rosa," as she called Mrs. Parks, to be a poor woman who did tiring and unpleasant work. She added that she imagined Rosa was on her way home to a large family that she had to take care of all by herself when she refused to move to the back of the bus. In other words, Rosa Parks was, in her mind, a poor, single parent with lots of children, and an unskilled worker. I asked her how she got that idea, and she replied that's just the kind of person she felt Rosa Parks must be. She added that nobody had ever told her that her view was wrong, so she never bothered to question it. Her teacher backed her up and claimed that she had made reasonable assumptions about Rosa Parks, ones that he felt were true to the way Rosa Parks was portrayed in the books they had in class. I couldn't argue with that last comment.

I changed the subject and asked Anna why Rosa Parks's arrest led to a boycott. She said she didn't know. Maybe Rosa had a friend who told everybody, or maybe it was in the newspaper. One of the other students suggested that her arrest was on TV and everybody came out to protest because they didn't think it was right to arrest someone just for not moving to the back of the bus. The boycott was, to them, some form of spontaneous action that involved no planning or strategy.

All the children admired Rosa Parks for not moving. Some said she must be a very stubborn person, others that she had to be so angry that she didn't care what happened to her. They agreed that it took a special person to be so courageous and wondered if they would be able to muster such courage. I got the impression that Mrs. Parks's exceptional courage might be an excuse for them to not act.

I decided to push the issue a bit and asked the class why Rosa Parks had to move to the back of the bus anyway. One of the African American children said it was segregated in the South back then, and African Americans and European Americans couldn't do things together. When I asked why there was segregation in those days there was absolute silence. I shifted a bit and asked if the African Americans and European Americans in their classroom could do things together. One of the boys answered, "In school they do, mostly." Since I was just a guest I left it at that. However, it was clear to me that issues of racial conflict were not explicitly discussed in this classroom, and that the play about the Montgomery bus boycott left the children with some vague sense of unity and victory, but with no sense of the risk and courage of the African American people who originated the struggle for civil rights in the United States or of the history and nature of segregation. I have no idea whether there was any racism manifest in the everyday lives of the children in that classroom, but wondered whether they or the teacher were at all prepared to deal with it if it erupted.

The children's visualization of Rosa Parks, whom they felt free to call by her first name, was particularly distressing. As well as poor, they imagined her to be without education or sophistication, a person who acted on impulse and emotion rather than intelligence and moral conviction. There was no sense of her as a community leader or as part of an organized struggle against oppression. I decided to find out how common this view was, and I have been astonished to find that those children's view of Rosa Parks is not at all different from that of most European American adults and almost all the school children I have questioned.

The image of "Rosa the Tired," and the story that goes with it, exists on the level of a national cultural icon in the United States. School textbooks and children's books are major perpetuators of this myth, but none of them I've seen quote sources for their distorted personal information about Mrs. Parks. Yet, most American children's first encounter with the Civil Rights movement comes through these writings. Dozens of children's books and textbooks I've looked at present the same version of Rosa Parks and the Montgomery bus boycott. This version can be reduced to the following generic story, which I fabricated and could be titled:

"ROSA WAS TIRED: THE STORY OF THE MONTGOMERY BUS BOYCOTT"

Rosa Parks was a poor seamstress. She lived in Montgomery, Alabama, during the 1950s. In those days there was still segregation in parts of the United States. That meant that African Americans and European Americans were not allowed to use the same public facilities such as restaurants or swimming pools. It also meant that whenever it was crowded on the city buses African Americans had to give up seats in front to European Americans and move to the back of the bus.

One day on her way home from work Rosa was tired and sat down in the front of the bus. As the bus got crowded she was asked to give up her seat to a European American man, and she refused. The bus driver told her she had to go to the back of the bus, and she still refused to move. It was a hot day, and she was tired and angry, and became very stubborn.

The driver called a policeman, who arrested Rosa.

When other African Americans in Montgomery heard this they became angry too, so they decided to refuse to ride the buses until everyone was allowed to ride together. They boycotted the buses.

The boycott, which was led by Martin Luther King, Jr., succeeded. Now African Americans and European Americans can ride the buses together in Montgomery.

Rosa Parks was a very brave person.

This story seems innocent enough. Rosa Parks is treated with respect and dignity and the African American community is given credit for running the boycott and winning the struggle. It reflects the view of Mrs. Parks often found in adult literature as well as writings for children. For example, in the book by eminent psychiatrist Robert Coles, *The Moral Life of Children* (Boston: Houghton Mifflin, 1986), we find the following quote:

> We had come to know . . . a group of poor and poorly educated people, who, nevertheless, acquitted themselves impressively in pursuit of significant ethical objectives. I think of Rosa Parks, a seamstress, whose decision to sit where she pleased on a Montgomery, Alabama, bus in the middle 1950s preceded the emergence of the so-called Civil Rights movement and of Dr. King and Ralph Abernathy as leaders of it.

A more recent example of this can be found in Robert Fulghum's best-selling book, *It Was on Fire When I Lay Down on It* (Ivy Books, 1988):

> I write this on the first day of December in 1988, the anniversary of a moment when someone sat still and lit the fuse to social dynamite. On this day in 1955, a forty-two-year-old woman was on her way home from work. Getting on a public bus, she paid her fare and sat down on the first vacant seat. It was good to sit down—her feet were tired. As the bus filled with passengers, the driver turned and told her to give up her seat and move on back in the bus. She sat still. The driver got up and shouted, "MOVE IT!" She sat still. Passengers grumbled, cursed her, pushed at her. Still she sat. So the driver got off the bus, called the police, and they came to haul her off to jail and into history.
>
> Rosa Parks. Not an activist or a radical. Just a quiet, conservative, churchgoing woman with a nice family and a decent job as a seamstress. For all the eloquent phrases that have been turned about her place in the flow of history, she did not get on that bus looking for trouble or trying to make a statement. Going home was all she had in mind, like everybody else. She was anchored to her seat by her own dignity. Rosa Parks simply wasn't going to be a "nigger" for anybody anymore. And all she knew to do was to sit still.

And here's a current textbook version of the Montgomery bus boycott story written for elementary school children. It comes from the Heath Social Studies series for elementary school, *Exploring My World* by Jeff Passe and Evangeline Nicholas (Lexington, MA: 1991, D.C. Heath, reproduced on page 188 of the Teachers' Guide), and is similar in content to my generic tale:

> When Rosa Parks rode on a bus, she had to sit all the way in the back.
> Her city had a law. It said black people could not sit in the front of a bus.
> One day Rosa was tired. She sat in the front. The bus driver told her to move. She did not. He called the police. Rosa was put in jail.
> Some citizens tried to help. One of them was Martin Luther King, Jr.
> The citizens decided to stop riding buses until the law was changed.
> Their plan worked. The law was changed. Soon, many other unfair laws were changed.
> Rosa Parks led the way!

The Teachers' Guide to this text informs teachers that "Mrs. Parks' single act brought about the desegregation of buses all over the country." In a lesson plan referring to Rosa Parks's being told to move to the back of the bus, it informs teachers to "tell children they will be reading about a woman who became angry when this happened to her. She decided she was not being treated fairly, and she was not going to put up with that kind of treatment anymore. Have children read to find out how the actions of Rosa Parks helped to change the way black people were treated."

This book was published in 1991 and is certainly still in use. It encourages presenting the Montgomery bus boycott as the single act of a person who was tired and angry. Intelligent and passionate opposition to racism is simply not part of the story. In the entire part of the guide dealing with the Montgomery bus boycott, there is no mention of racism at all. Instead the problem is unfairness, a more generic and softer form of abuse that avoids dealing with the fact that the great majority of White people in Montgomery were racist and capable of being violent and cruel to maintain segregation. Thus we have an adequate picture of neither the courage of Rosa Parks nor the intelligence and resolve of the African American community in the face of racism.

Research into the history of the Montgomery bus boycott, however, reveals some distressing characteristics of this generic story, which misrepresents an organized and carefully planned movement for social change as a spontaneous outburst based upon frustration and anger. The following annotations on "Rosa Was Tired" suggest that we need a new story, one more in line with the truth and directed at showing the organizational intelligence and determination of the African American community in Birmingham, as well as the role of the bus boycott in the larger struggle to desegregate Birmingham and the South.

THE ANNOTATED "ROSA WAS TIRED"

Rosa Parks was a seamstress who was poor. She lived in Montgomery, Alabama, during the 1950s.

Rosa Parks was one of the first women in Montgomery to join the NAACP and was its secretary for years. At the NAACP she worked with E. D. Nixon, vice president of the Brotherhood of Sleeping Car Porters, who was president of the Montgomery NAACP, and learned about union struggles from him. She also worked with the youth division of the NAACP, and she took a youth NAACP group to visit the Freedom Train when it came to Montgomery in 1954. The train, which carried the originals of the U.S. Constitution and the Declaration of Independence, was traveling around the United States promoting the virtues of democracy. Since its visit was a federal project, access to the exhibits could not legally be segregated. Mrs. Parks took advantage of that fact to visit the train. There, Rosa Parks and the members of the youth group mingled freely with European Americans from Montgomery who were also looking at the documents. This overt act of crossing the boundaries of segregation did not endear Rosa Parks to the Montgomery political and social establishment.

Her work as a seamstress in a large department store was secondary to her community work. As she says in an interview in *My Soul Is Rested* by Howard Raines (New York: Bantam, 1978, p. 35), she had "almost a life history of being rebellious against being mistreated because of my color." She was well known to all of the African American leaders in Montgomery for her opposition to segregation, her leadership abilities, and her moral strength. Since 1954 and the Supreme Court's *Brown v. Topeka Board of Education* decision, she had been working on the desegregation of the Montgomery schools. In addition, she was good friends with Clifford and Virginia Durr, European Americans who were well known opponents of segregation. She had also attended an interracial meeting at the Highlander Folk School in Tennessee a few months before the boycott. Highlander was known throughout the South as a radical education center that was overtly planning for the total desegregation of the South, and Rosa Parks was aware of that when she attended the meeting. At that meeting, which dealt with plans for school desegregation in the South, she indicated that she intended to become an active participant in other attempts to break down the barriers of segregation. Finally, Rosa Parks had the active support of her mother and her husband in her civil rights activities. To call Rosa Parks a poor, tired seamstress and not talk about her role as a community leader as well is to turn an organized struggle for freedom into a personal act of frustration. It is a thorough misrepresentation of the Civil Rights movement in Montgomery, Alabama, and an insult to Mrs. Parks as well. Here is a more appropriate way of beginning a children's version of the Montgomery bus boycott:

It was 1955. Everyone in the African American community in Montgomery, Alabama, knew Rosa Parks. She was a community leader, and people admired her courage. All throughout her life she had opposed prejudice, even if it got her into trouble.

In those days there was still segregation in parts of the United States. That meant that African Americans and European Americans were not allowed to use the same public facilities . . .

The existence of legalized segregation in the South during the 1950s is integral to the story of the Montgomery bus boycott, yet it is an embarrassment to many school people and difficult to explain to children without accounting for the moral corruption of the majority of the European American community in the South. The sentence I composed is one way of avoiding direct confrontation with the moral issues of segregation. First it says, "In those days there was still segregation" as if segregation were no longer an issue. However, as recently as July 1, 1990, an article by Ron Rapaport of the *Los Angeles Daily News* (reprinted in the Santa Rosa, CA, *Press Democrat*, July 1, 1990) focused on the current segregation of private golf clubs in Birmingham and other parts of the United States. In the article he says:

> It certainly isn't a secret that Shoal Creek Country Club has no black members because, in the words of its founder, Hall Thompson, "that's just not done in Birmingham."

> There are lots of places where it's just not done and not just in the South, either. Many of the golf courses that host PGA (Professional Golfers Association) events are restricted and while it may not often become a public issue, that does not mean people are not aware of it.

> As for shame, well, that is a commodity that is in short supply as well.

> "The country club is our home," Thompson said, "and we pick and choose who we want."

To this day the club still has only one African American member, who has special status as a guest member. Ironically, in 1994 a young African American golfer won a tournament at the club while other African Americans demonstrated outside its gates protesting the club's segregationist policies.

Locating segregation in the past is a way of avoiding dealing with its current manifestations and implying that racism is no longer a major problem in the United States. This is particularly pernicious at a time when overt racism is once again becoming a common phenomenon and when children have to be helped to understand and eliminate it.

Describing integration passively ("there was still segregation" instead of "European Americans segregated facilities so that African Americans couldn't use them") avoids the issue of activist racist activity on the part of some Whites. Since there was legalized segregation in Alabama, and Mrs. Parks was arrested for a violation of the Alabama state law that institutionalized segregation in public facilities, there must have been racists to have passed those laws. Yet they are absent from the narrative, which doesn't talk overtly about racism. The avoidance of direct discussion of what to do about individuals who are racist is all too characteristic of school programs and children's literature.

This avoidance of dealing directly with racism is also evident in the next sentence, which says that "African Americans and European Americans were not allowed to use the same public facilities." It puts African Americans and European Americans on the same footing, as if there were some symmetry and both were punished by the segregation laws. A more appropriate way of describing the situation would be:

> African American people were prevented by law from using the same public facilities as European Americans. In addition, the African American facilities were vastly inferior to the ones made available to European Americans.

Even this rewriting is too generous given the pervasive, brutal, and absolute nature of segregation in the pre–civil rights South. Perhaps the best analogy that could be used here is apartheid, as legalized segregation in the South hardly differed from South Africa's policy of total separation of the races to ensure White dominance.

I've raised the question with a number of educators, both African American and European American, of how to expose children to the reality of segregation and racism. Most of the European American and a few of the African American educators felt that young children do not need to be exposed to the harsh and violent history of segregation in the United States.

They worried about the effects such exposure would have on race relations in their classrooms, and especially about provoking rage on the part of African American students. The other educators felt that, given the resurgence of overt racism in the United States these days, allowing rage and anger to come out was the only way African American and European American children could work from the reality of difference and separation toward a common life. They felt that conflict was a positive thing that could be healing when confronted directly, and that avoiding the horrors of racism was just another way of perpetuating them. I agree with this second group and believe that some recasting of the third and fourth sentences of "Rosa Was Tired" is called for:

> In those days Alabama was legally segregated. That means that African American people were prevented by the state law from using the same swimming pools, schools, and other public facilities as European Americans. There also were separate entrances, toilets, and drinking fountains for African Americans and European Americans in places such as bus and train stations. The facilities African Americans were allowed to use were not only separate from the ones European Americans used but were also very inferior. The reason for this was racism, the belief that European Americans were superior to African Americans and that therefore European Americans deserved better facilities.

. . .whenever it was crowded on the city buses African Americans had to give up seats in front to European Americans and move to the back of the bus.

Actually African Americans were never allowed to sit in the front of the bus in the South in those days. The front seats were reserved for European Americans. Between five and ten rows back the "Colored" section began. When the front of the bus filled up, African Americans seated in the "Colored" section had to give up their seats and move toward the back of the bus. Thus, for example, an elderly African American woman would have to give up her seat to a European American teenage male at the peril of being arrested. Consistent with the comments I've been making so far, and with the truth of the experience of segregation, this sentence should be expanded as follows:

> In those days public buses were divided into two sections, one at the front for European Americans, which was supposed to be "for Whites only." From five to ten rows back the section for African Americans began. That part of the bus was called the "Colored" section.

> Whenever it was crowded on the city buses African American people were forced to give up seats in the "Colored" section to European Americans and move to the back of the bus. For example, an elderly African American woman would have to give up her seat to a European American teenage male. If she refused she could be arrested for breaking the segregation laws.

One day on her way home from work Rosa was tired and sat down in the front of the bus.

Rosa Parks did not sit in the front of the bus. She sat in the front row of the "Colored" section. When the bus got crowded she refused to give up her seat in the "Colored" section to a European American. It is important to point this out, as it indicates quite clearly that it was not her intent, on that day, to break the segregation laws.

At this point the story lapses into the familiar and refers to Rosa Parks as "Rosa." The question of whether to use the first name for historical characters in a factual story is complicated. One argument in favor of doing so is that young children will more readily identify with characters who are presented in a personalized and familiar way. However, given that it was a sanctioned social practice in the South during the time of the story for European Americans to call African American adults by their first names as a way of reinforcing the African Americans' inferior status (African Americans could never call European Americans by their first names without breaking the social code of segregation), it seems unwise to use that practice in the story.

In addition, it's reasonable to assume that Rosa Parks was not any more tired on that one day than on other days. She worked at an exhausting full-time job and was also active full-time in the community. To emphasize her being tired is another way of saying that her defiance of segregation was an accidental result of her fatigue and consequent short temper on that particular day. However, rage is not a one-day thing, and Rosa Parks acted with full knowledge of what she was doing.

It is more respectful and historically accurate to make these changes:

December 1, 1955, on her way home from work, Rosa Parks took the bus as usual. She sat down in the front row of the "Colored" section.

As the bus got crowded she was asked to give up her seat to a European American man, and she refused. The bus driver told her she had to go to the back of the bus, and she still refused to move. It was a hot day, and she was tired and angry and became very stubborn.

The driver called a policeman, who arrested Rosa.

Rosa Parks described her experiences with buses in her own words (*My Soul Is Rested*):

I had problems with bus drivers over the years because I didn't see fit to pay my money into the front and then go around to the back. Sometimes bus drivers wouldn't permit me to get on the bus, and I had been evicted from the bus. But, as I say, there had been incidents over the years. One of the things that made this . . . [incident] . . . get so much publicity was the fact that the police were called in and I was placed under arrest. See, if I had just been evicted from the bus and he hadn't placed me under arrest or had any charges brought against me, it probably could have been just another incident.

More recently, in *Voices of Freedom* by Henry Hampton and Steve Fayer (New York: Bantam, 1990), she described her thoughts that day in the following way:

Having to take a certain section [on a bus] because of your race was humiliating, but having to stand up because a particular driver wanted to keep a white person from having to stand was, to my mind, most inhumane.

More than seventy-five, between eighty-five and I think ninety, percent of the patronage of the buses were black people, because more white people could own and drive their own cars than blacks. I happened to be the secretary of the Montgomery branch of the NAACP as well as the NAACP Youth Council adviser. Many cases did come to my attention that nothing came out of because the person that was abused would be too intimidated to sign an affidavit, or to make a statement. Over the years, I had had my own problems with the bus drivers. In fact, some did tell me not to ride their buses if I felt that I was too important to go to the back door to get on. One had evicted me from the bus in 1943, which did not cause anything more than just a passing glance.

On December 1, 1955, I had finished my day's work as a tailor's assistant in the Montgomery Fair Department store and I was on my way home. There was one vacant seat on the Cleveland Avenue bus, which I took, alongside a man and two women across the aisle. There were still a few vacant seats in the white section in the front, of course. We went to the next stop without being disturbed. On the third, the front seats were occupied and this one man, a white man, was standing. The driver asked us to stand up and let him have those seats, and when none of us moved at his first words, he said, "You all make it light on yourselves and let me have those seats." And the man who was sitting next to the window stood up, and I made room for him to pass by me. The two women across the aisle stood up and moved out. When the driver saw me still sitting, he asked if I was going to stand up and I said, "No, I'm not."

And he said, "Well, if you don't stand up, I'm going to call the police and have you arrested."

I said, "You may do that."

He did get off the bus, and I still stayed where I was. Two policemen came on the bus. One of the policemen asked me if the bus driver had asked me to stand and I said yes.

He said, "Why don't you stand up?"

And I asked him, "Why do you push us around?"

He said, "I do not know, but the law is the law and you're under arrest." (pp. 19, 20)

Mere anger and stubbornness could not account for the clear resolve with which Rosa Parks acted. Nor was she, as Robert Fulghum says in the selection from his book quoted at the beginning of this [essay], "Not an activist or a radical. Just a quiet, conservative, churchgoing woman with a nice family and a decent job as a seamstress." She knew what she was doing, understood the consequences, and was prepared to confront segregation head on at whatever sacrifice she had to make. A more accurate account of the event, taking into consideration Rosa Parks's past history, might be:

As the bus got crowded the driver demanded that she give up her seat to a European American man, and move to the back of the bus. This was not the first time that this had happened to Rosa Parks. In the past she had refused to move, and the driver had simply put her off the bus. Mrs. Parks hated segregation, and along with many other African American people, refused to obey many of its unfair rules. On this day she refused to do what the bus driver demanded.

The bus driver commanded her once more to go to the back of the bus and she stayed in her seat, looking straight ahead and not moving an inch. He got angry at her and became very stubborn. He called a policeman, who arrested Mrs. Parks.

When other African Americans in Montgomery heard this they became angry too, so they decided to refuse to ride the buses until everyone was allowed to ride together. They boycotted the buses.

The connection between Rosa Parks's arrest and the boycott is a mystery in most accounts of what happened in Montgomery. Community support for the boycott is portrayed as being instantaneous and miraculously effective the very day after Mrs. Parks was arrested. Things don't happen that way, and it is an insult to the intelligence and courage of the African American community in Montgomery to turn their planned resistance to segregation into a spontaneous emotional response. The actual situation was more interesting and complex. Not only Rosa Parks had defied the bus segregation laws in the past: According to E. D. Nixon, in the three months preceding Mrs. Parks's arrest at least three other African American people had been arrested in Montgomery for refusing to give up their bus seats to European American people. In each case, Nixon and other people in leadership positions in the African American community in Montgomery investigated the background of the person arrested. They were looking for someone who had the respect of the community and the strength to deal with the racist police force as well as all the publicity that would result from being at the center of a bus boycott. This leads to the most important point left out in popularized accounts of the Montgomery bus boycott: the boycott had been planned and organized before Rosa Parks was arrested. It was an event waiting to take place, and that is why it could be mobilized so quickly. Rosa Parks's arrest brought it about because she was part of the African American leadership in Montgomery and was trusted not to cave in under the pressure everyone knew she would be exposed to, including threats to her life.

But the story goes back even farther than that. There was an African American women's organization in Montgomery called the Women's Political Council (WPC). It was headed those days by Jo Ann Gibson Robinson, who was a professor of English at Alabama State University in Montgomery, an all-African American university. In 1949 Ms. Gibson was put off a bus in Montgomery for refusing to move from her seat in the fifth row of an almost empty bus to the back of the bus. She and other women in Montgomery resolved to do something about bus segregation. As she says in her book *The Montgomery Bus Boycott and the Women Who Started It: The Memoir of Jo Ann Gibson Robinson* (Knoxville: University of Tennessee Press, 1987), "It was during the period of 1949–1955 that the Women's Political Council of Montgomery—founded in 1946 with Dr. Mary Burks as president and headed from 1950 on by me—prepared to stage a bus boycott when the time was ripe and the people were ready. The right time came in 1985."

This story of collective decision making, willed risk, and coordinated action is more dramatic than the story of an angry individual who sparked a demonstration; it has more to teach children who themselves may have to organize and act collectively against oppressive forces in the future. Here's one way to tell this complex story to young children:

Mrs. Parks was not the first African American person to be arrested in Montgomery for refusing to move to the back of the bus. In the months before her refusal, at least three other people were arrested for the same reason. In fact, African American leaders in Montgomery were planning to overcome segregation. One way they wanted to do this was to have every African American person boycott the buses. Since most of the bus riders in the city were African American, the buses would go broke if they refused to let African Americans and European Americans ride the buses as equals.

From 1949 right up to the day Mrs. Parks refused to move, the Women's Political Council of Montgomery prepared to stage a bus boycott because of how African Americans were treated on the bus. African American people in Montgomery were ready to support the boycott. They were just waiting for the time to be ripe. Nineteen fifty-five was the time.

However, none of the people who were arrested before Mrs. Parks was were leaders. She was a leader, and the day she was arrested the leadership called a meeting at the Dexter Avenue Baptist Church. They decided to begin their refusal to ride the buses the next morning. They knew Mrs. Parks had the courage to deal with the pressure of defying segregation and would not yield even if her life was threatened.

The next day the Montgomery bus boycott began.

The boycott, which was led by Martin Luther King Jr., succeeded. Now African American and European Americans can ride the buses together in Montgomery. Rosa Parks was a very brave person.

The boycott was planned by the WPC, E. D. Nixon, and others in Montgomery. Martin Luther King Jr. was a new member of the community. He had just taken over the Dexter Avenue Baptist Church, and when Nixon told him that Rosa Parks's arrest was just what everybody was waiting for to kick off a bus boycott and assault the institution of segregation, King was at first reluctant. However, the community people chose him to lead, and he accepted their call. The boycott lasted 381 inconvenient days, something not usually mentioned in children's books. It did succeed and was one of the events that sparked the entire Civil Rights movement. People who had been planning an overt attack on segregation for years took that victory as a sign that the time was ripe, even though the people involved in the Montgomery boycott did not themselves anticipate such results. Here's one possible way to convey this to children:

There was a young new minister in Montgomery those days. His name was Martin Luther King Jr. People in the community felt that he was a special person and asked him to lead the boycott. At first he wasn't sure. He worried about the violence that might result from the boycott. However, he quickly made up his mind that it was time to destroy segregation and accepted the people's call for him to be their leader.

The Montgomery bus boycott lasted 381 days. For over a year the African American people of Montgomery, Alabama, stayed off the buses. Some walked to work, others rode bicycles or shared car rides. It was very hard for them, but they knew that what they were doing was very important for all African American people in the South.

The boycott succeeded, and by the end of 1956 African Americans and European Americans could ride the buses in Montgomery as equals. However, the struggle for the complete elimination of segregation had just begun.

We all owe a great deal to the courage and intelligence of Rosa Parks and the entire African American community of Montgomery, Alabama. They took risks to make democracy work for all of us.

Concluding Thoughts

What remains, then, is to retitle the story. The revised version is still about Rosa Parks, but it is also about the African American people of Montgomery, Alabama. It takes the usual, individualized version of the Rosa Parks tale and puts it in the context of a coherent, community-based social struggle. This does not diminish Rosa Parks in any way. It places her, however, in the midst of a consciously planned movement for social change, and reminds me of the freedom song "We shall not be moved," for it was precisely Rosa Parks's and the community's refusal to be moved that made the boycott possible. For that reason the new title, "She Would Not Be Moved: The Story of Rosa Parks and the Montgomery Bus Boycott" makes sense.

As it turns out, my retelling of the story of Rosa Parks and the Montgomery bus boycott is not the only recent one. In 1990, thirty-five years after the event, we finally have a full, moving, and historically accurate 124 page retelling of the story written for young people. The book, *Rosa Parks: The Movement Organizes* by Kai Friese (Englewood Cliffs, NJ: Silver Burdett, 1990), is one of nine volumes in a series edited by the scholar Eldon Morris entitled *The History of the Civil Rights Movement.* Other volumes in the series, such as those about Ella Baker and Fannie Lou Hamer, also provide a fuller, more accurate look at people's struggles during the Civil Rights movement of the 1960s than has been available to young people until now. These volumes are gifts to all of us from a number of African American scholars who have reclaimed history from the distortions and omissions of years of irresponsible writing for children about the Civil Rights movement. They are models of how history and biography can directly confront racial conflict and illuminate social struggle. This is particularly true of the Rosa Parks volume, which takes us up to date in Mrs. Parks's life and informs us that she remained active over the years, working for social and economic justice in Congressman John Conyer's office in Detroit.

The book, which credits all the people involved in making the Montgomery boycott possible, provides a portrait of a community mobilized for justice. It also leaves us with a sense of the struggle that still needs to be waged to eliminate racism in the United States.

Rosa Parks has also written an autobiography (with Jim Haskins), which presents a more personal version of the story given here.

When the story of the Montgomery bus boycott is told merely as a tale of a single heroic person, it leaves children hanging. Not everyone is a hero or heroine. Of course, the idea that only special people can create change is useful if you want to prevent mass movements and keep change from happening. Not every child can be a Rosa Parks, but everyone can imagine her or himself as a participant in the boycott. As a tale of a social movement and a community effort to overthrow injustice, the Rosa Parks story as I've tried to rewrite it opens the possibility of every child identifying her- or himself as an activist, as someone who can help make justice happen. And it is that kind of empowerment that people in the United States desperately need.

References

The following quotes are taken from recent children's books and school textbooks. The publication date of the earliest of them is 1976; the rest were published in their current form in the 1980s. However, two of the children's books were copyrighted in 1969 and reissued in the 1980s with new illustrations. No attempt was made in these two cases to update the material in the books.

The sample of quotes included is representative of dozens I've read, and cumulatively represents all the different aspects of the Rosa Parks myth I portrayed in "Rosa Was Tired." Some of the other texts and the specific lines that related to my text are listed at the end of this appendix. The passages quoted more fully here are from the most progressive texts and trade books I've found. I have avoided citing texts no longer in print.

1. From Valerie Schloredt, *Martin Luther King Jr: America's Great Nonviolent Leader in the Struggle for Human Rights* (Harrisburg, PA: Morehouse Publishing, 1990).

    On the evening of Dec. 1, 1955, a black lady named Rosa Parks left the downtown department store where she worked as a seamstress and walked to the bus stop to catch the bus that would take her home.

The book goes on to describe what happened when Mrs. Parks refused to move to the back of the bus: Mrs. Parks was tired. She had a long, hard day. . . . Something snapped in Mrs. Parks at that moment. Perhaps the patience with which she had endured years of sub-servience and insult. . . . Mrs. Parks didn't look like a person to challenge the law of Montgomery. She was a quiet looking lady, wearing small steel rimmed spectacles; but like thousands of other black people who rode the buses day after day, she was weary of being treated with such contempt.

Much later she was asked if she had planned her protest. "No," she answered. "I was just plain tired, and my feet hurt."

Mrs. Parks' patience had given way, had she but known it, at the best possible moment.

2. Here is the Random House version for first-to third-graders from James T. Kay, *Meet Martin Luther King Jr.* (New York: Random House, Step-up Books, 1969), reprinted with new cover in 1989.

On Dec. 1, 1955, a woman named Rosa Parks did something about the Jim Crow buses.

Mrs. Parks was black. She worked in a department store. That evening she climbed on the bus and sat down. Each time the bus stopped, more people got on. Soon no seats were left in the white part of the bus.

At the next stop some white people got on. The driver got up and walked over to Mrs. Parks. He told her to give her seat to a white woman.

But Rosa Parks was tired. She did something she had never done before. She just stayed in her seat . . . .

Black people all over the city heard about Rosa Parks. They were very angry. They were mad at the Jim Crow laws. They were mad at the police. They were mad at the bus company. But what could they do?

Then one man said, "Why don't we boycott the buses?" This meant that all the black people would stop riding the buses. Soon the bus company would lose money. Maybe then the owners would be fair to blacks. (not paged)

3. This selection is from Dharathula H. Millender's *Martin Luther King, Jr.: Young Man with a Dream* (New York: Bobbs-Merrill, 1969; Macmillan, Alladin Books, 1986). It is one of the finest of the older children's books about the Civil Rights movement.

Things came to a head over bus segregation on December 1, 1955. Mrs. Rosa Parks, an attractive negro seamstress, boarded a bus in downtown Montgomery. This was the same bus she had boarded many times after a hard day's work. Today she was tired and eager to get off her aching feet. Accordingly she sat down in the first seat in the Negro section behind the section reserved for white passengers. . . .

At first the driver was surprised (when she refused to move) wondering whether he had heard correctly. When Mrs. Parks clung to her seat, however, and held her head proudly in the air, he realized that he was facing trouble. Accordingly, he stopped his bus, called the police and had her arrested. Her arrest attracted wide attention because she was one of the most respected people in the Negro community. It helped to start a Negro revolt not only in Montgomery but all across the nation.

4. This is from the upper elementary grades social studies textbook *The United States and the Other Americas* by Allan King, Ida Dennis, and Florence Potter, in the Macmillan Social Studies Series (New York: Macmillan, 1982).

In 1955 Rosa Parks, a black, refused to give up her bus seat to a white in Montgomery, Alabama. She was arrested because of this. Other blacks, led by Dr. Martin Luther King Jr., of Atlanta, Georgia, refused to ride the city buses. The following year a federal Court ruled that segregated buses were no longer allowed.

In the teacher's edition the following instructions are given to teachers:

Have the pupils read the rest of page 413. Draw their attention to the photograph of Rosa Parks. Explain that on December 1, 1955, Rosa Parks boarded a bus in Montgomery, Alabama. Her arms were full of groceries, so she sat in the front row of the section of the bus in which blacks were permitted to sit. As the bus filled up, more white people got on, and the bus driver told Rosa to give up her seat to a white person. Rosa looked out the window and pretended not to hear him. She refused to give up her seat, and because of this she was arrested. In protest against her arrest, the black people of Montgomery refused to ride the bus. They formed car pools, walked, rode mules and horses and buggies. On April 23, the Supreme Court declared that state and local laws that required segregation of buses were unconstitutional.

5. This is taken from Allan O. Kownslar and William R. Fielder's *Inquiring About American History* (New York: Holt, Rinehart and Winston, 1976), in the Holt Databank System. This is a "modern" series based on inquiry and is considered too liberal for many school districts. It is for upper elementary and junior high students.

For the black citizens of Montgomery, Alabama, some of the "separate but equal" laws had been changed by 1955. . . . But, in spite of these changes, many people still refused to treat blacks and whites equally. Rosa Parks, a black woman who lived in Montgomery in 1955, had to deal with this problem.

One evening, Rosa Parks was coming home from work on a Montgomery city bus. She had been working hard all day at her job in a downtown department store. Rosa was quite tired. She took a seat toward the back of the bus, where black passengers normally sat. The bus began to fill quickly. As whites got on, they took what seats there were, and soon the bus was full.

Rosa realized that some of the blacks would be asked to give up their seats and move to the back of the bus. They would be asked to stand so that white passengers could sit. She felt that this was unfair. Why should she have to move?

Suddenly the driver turned and asked her, and some other blacks, to move to the rear of the bus. Rosa argued with the driver, but he still insisted that she leave her seat and stand in the back. Rosa paused. She had to make a decision quickly. Should she give up her seat or remain seated?

What would you have done if you had been Rosa Parks? What do you think she did?

Rosa Parks made her choice. She decided to remain seated on the bus. Her action led to the Montgomery Bus Boycott—and eventually, to a Supreme Court ruling against the separation of blacks and whites on all buses.

6. This selection is from another upper elementary text, *The United States and Its Neighbors* by Timothy Helmus, Val Arnsdorf, Edgar Toppin, and Norman Pounds (Morristown, NJ: Silver Burdett, 1984), in the series *The World and Its People*.

Dr. King gained nationwide fame in Montgomery, Alabama, in 1955. At that time blacks had to sit in the back of public buses. But one day a quiet woman named Rosa Parks decided to sit in the "whites only" part of the bus. She was arrested. Dr. King led a boycott of Montgomery buses to protest her arrest. People who supported Dr. King would not use the buses until anyone could sit wherever she or he pleased. The boycott worked.

Finally, here is a list of quotes from a sampling of texts for all grade levels dealing with Rosa Parks and the Montgomery bus boycott. I've only quoted eighteen of the dozens of books consulted, though I think the unity of their tale comes across quite clearly. The word *racism* was not used in any of them.

1. Karen McAuley et al., *The United States Past to Present*, Teacher's Ed. (Lexington, MA: D.C. Heath, 1987), p. 405. Grade 5.

    "It had been a long, hard day and she was tired."

2. Susan Williams McKay, *The World of Mankind* (Chicago: Follet Publishing, 1973), p. 221. Grade 3

    "Mrs. Parks sat alone. She was tired. She decided not to move."

3. *The United States: Its History and Neighbors*, Teacher's Ed. (Orlando, FL: Harcourt Brace Jovanovich, 1988), p. 507. Grade 5.

    "On Dec. 1, 1955, Rosa Parks sank wearily to her seat on the bus in Montgomery, Alabama . . . ."As the bus filled up, Rosa Parks was asked to give up her seat. She refused. The bus driver called the police, and she was taken to jail."

4. Leonard C. Wood et al., *America: Its People and Values,* Teacher's Ed. 1985, p. 721. Junior High.

    "On that day a black seamstress named Rosa Parks refused to give up her seat in the white section of the bus. . . .

    "There as in many other parts of the south, local laws kept public places strictly segregated. Restaurants, businesses, and all forms of public transportation had separate sections for blacks and whites."

5. Allan O. Kownslar et al., *Inquiring About American History* (New York: Holt, Rinehart and Winston, 1976), p. 301. Grade 5.

    "One evening, Rosa Parks was coming home from work on a Montgomery city bus. She had been working hard all day at her job . . . Rosa was quite tired. . ."

    "Suddenly, the driver turned and asked her, and some other blacks, to move to the rear of the bus. Rosa argued with the driver . . ."

6. JoAnn Cangemi, *Our History*, 1983, pp. 388–89. Grade 5.

    "In 1955, a black woman named Rosa Parks sat down in the front of the bus in Montgomery, Alabama. Parks refused to get up from the seat so that a white person could sit down and she was arrested."

    "Angry about the arrest, Montgomery Blacks refused to ride city buses."

    "The bus boycott was led by Dr. Martin Luther King, Jr."

7. Beverly J. Armento et al., *This Is My Country* (Boston: Houghton Mifflin, 1991), p. 68. Grade 4.

    She was tired and her feet hurt"

    "At that time, black and white people had to sit in separate sections on the bus. Other places were divided too, such as restrooms, waiting rooms, movie theatres and restaurants."

8. Henry F. Graff, *America: The Glorious Republic*, vol. 1, 1985, pp. 717–718. Jr./Sr. High.

   "The next day the 50,000 black citizens of Montgomery began a bus boycott of the city's buses: choosing to walk rather than ride under humiliating conditions."

9. Henry F. Graff, America: *The Glorious Republic,* vol. 2, 1986, pp. 349–50. Jr./Sr. High.

   " . . . a seamstress named Rosa Parks took a courageous and fateful step."

   "The next day the 50,000 black citizens of Montgomery began a boycott of city buses. "

10. John Edward Wiltz, The Search for Identity: Modern American History (Philadelphia: J. B. Lippincott, 1973), p. 684. Jr. High.

    "When Mrs. Parks, a small, soft-spoken woman boarded the Cleveland Avenue bus she was tired and her feet hurt."

11. Beverly Jeanne Armento et at., *Living in Our Country* (River Forest, IL: Laidlaw Brothers, 1988), pp. 417-18. Grade 5.

    "In Montgomery, Alabama, a black woman was arrested for using a seat in the front of a bus.
    "For this reason many black people refused to ride the buses in Montgomery."

12. Glen M. Linden et al., *Legacy of Freedom: A History of the United States*, 1986, 670 Jr./Sr. High.

    "Tired after a long clay's work, Mrs. Parks boarded a bus for home and refused to give up her seat to a white passenger when asked to do so by the bus driver."
    The leaders of Montgomery's black community were outraged. Almost at once, they organized a boycott of the Montgomery transit system."

13. Ernest R. May, *A Proud Nation*, Teacher's Ed. (Evanston, IL: McDougal, Littell, 198"), p. 69, Jr. High.

    "On Dec. 1, Rosa Parks, a black woman, refused to give up her seat in the front of a bus to a white person. She had simply worked all day, Parks said, and her feet hurt."

14. Alma Graham et al., United States: Our Nation and Neighbors (New York: McGraw-Hill, 1980), p. 340. Grade 5.

    "The bus boycott was led by Dr. Martin Luther King Jr."

15. George Vuicich et al., *United States*, 1983, p. 322. Grade 5.

    "In 1955, a black woman, Rosa Parks, refused to give up her seat on a bus in Montgomery, Alabama. She was arrested. Some people became determined to do something. Blacks in Montgomery began a boycott of the city's buses."
    "The bus boycott was led by Dr. Martin Luther King, Jr., . . ."

16. Henry F. Graff et al., *The Promise of Democracy: The Grand Experiment* (Chicago: Rand McNally, 1978), pp. 365–66. Jr./Sr. High.

    ". . . in many southern communities, black people had to sit at the back of the city buses. "
    ". . . and she was tired."

17. Roger M. Berg, *Social Studies* (Glenview, IL: Scott, Foresman, 1979), p. 335. Grade S.

    "In some cities, blacks were forced to ride in separate parts of buses.

In 1955, in Montgomery, Alabama, Rosa Parks wanted to sit in a part of a public bus set aside for whites. She was arrested. The black people of Montgomery refused to ride the city buses until they could sit where they wanted."

18. Richard H. Loftin et al., *Our Country's Communities* (Morristown, NJ: Silver Burdett and Ginn, 1988), p. 246. Grade 3.

"One day a black woman named Rosa Parks got on a bus and found the back seats filled. She had been working all day and was tired. She sat down in another seat and was arrested."

"With Dr. King as their leader, the black people of Montgomery refused to ride on the bus until they had the same rights as the other riders."

"They did as he (King) said and finally won out."

Questions for Discussion

1. What kinds of representations of Rosa Parks does Kohl find disturbing? How does he account for those representations? What purposes do they serve? Whom do they serve?

2. Describe the nature of the evidence Kohl uses and trace his argument. What aspects of Kohl's argument are most compelling to you? How were you persuaded by this evidence?

3. Herbert Kohl argues that racism is rarely addressed "as a social problem" in children's texts. Instead, he claims that "it is routinely described as a problem between individuals that can be worked out on a personal basis." Working with a small group, list examples—from popular culture/media, school situations, or other locations—that portray racism this way. What might be the danger in portraying racism as an individual, rather than a social, problem?

Explorations

1. Using a common search engine on the World Wide Web (Yahoo, Infoseek, Excite, etc.), do a word search on "Rosa Parks" and "The Montgomery Bus Boycott." How many sites do you find? Describe the nature of the information available to you at those web sites. What is your evaluation of the web sites?

2. Think about Kohl's essay in relation to the four poems in this unit: Hughes' "Theme for English B," Levine's "M. Degas Teaches Art and Science at Durfee Intermediate School," Stern's "Mad," and Stern's "What They Learn in School." What links can you make? How might Hughes respond to the textbooks Kohl critiques? Are the "facts" that Stern's students don't know the same "facts" that surface again in Kohl's textbooks? Use this exploration as an opportunity to explore connections.

Formal Writing Assignments

1. Draft an essay in which you describe a time in your life when something you believed to be true was challenged—by a teacher, a textbook, a film, a news report, another authoritative source. How did you respond to that challenge? How did this experience change or not change your point of view?

2. Choose a recent event that has affected your school's community. Select a small sampling of students, teachers, support staff, or other university community members and ask them to give you their personal account of that event. Once you have collected your data, draft a report that 1) summarizes the various accounts and 2) analyzes those accounts in order to come to some conclusion about the nature of that campus event. That conclusion should synthesize a variety of perspectives.

M. Degas Teaches Art & Science at Durfee Intermediate School

Philip Levine

Philip Levine was born in Detroit (1928) and studied at Wayne State University and Iowa University. A self-proclaimed anarchist both politically and religiously, Levine worked at "a succession of industrial jobs" before becoming a visiting professor and writer at universities across the United States. His poetry has often chronicled the lives of the working class, in part because he wants to provide a voice for people whom he sees as all too often "voiceless." In addition to winning the Pulitzer Prize in Poetry (1995), Levine earned the National Book Award for Poetry (1991) for *What Work Is*, the collection in which "M. Degas Teaches Art & Science at Durfee Intermediate School" appears. Levine's poem offers a glimpse of one instructor's pedagogical method while showing its effect, or lack of it, on students.

Writing Before Reading

1. What makes a teacher effective or ineffective?

2. Describe courses you have taken in which the instructor provides answers and those courses you have taken in which the instructor asked the class to discover answers for themselves. Discuss the suitability or lack of it for each teaching style in terms of the situation.

3. Have you ever relied on outspoken students to do the responding in a class? For what reasons did you remain silent? How does your silence affect your classroom experience? Is silence in a classroom a positive or negative experience for you?

M. Degas Teaches Art & Science at Durfee Intermediate School

He made a line on the blackboard,
one bold stroke from right to left
diagonally downward and stood back
to ask, looking as always at no one
in particular, "What have I done?"
From the back of the room Freddie
shouted, "You've broken a piece
of chalk." M. Degas did not smile.
"What have I done?" he repeated.
The most intellectual students
looked down to study their desks
except for Gertrude Bimmler, who raised
her hand before she spoke, "M. Degas,
you have created the hypotenuse

of an isosceles triangle." Degas mused.
Everyone knew that Gertrude could not
be incorrect. "It is possible,"
Louis Warshowsky added precisely,
"that you have begun to represent
the roof of a barn. " I remember
that it was exactly twenty minutes
past eleven, and I thought at worst
this would go on another forty
minutes. It was early April,
the snow had all but melted on
the playgrounds, the elms and maples
bordering the cracked walks shivered
in the new winds, and I believed
that before I knew it I'd be
swaggering to the candy store
for a Milky Way. M. Degas
pursed his lips, and the room
stilled until the long hand
of the clock moved to twenty one
as though in complicity with Gertrude,
who added confidently, "You've begun
to separate the dark from the dark."
I looked back for help, but now,
the trees bucked and quaked, and I
knew this could go on forever.

Questions for Discussion

1. Students offer various interpretations of the line that M. Degas draws on a chalkboard. What do their interpretations tell us about the students and their perception of the learning process?

2. What does the narrator of the poem know "could go on forever"?

3. How would you describe M. Degas' "teaching methods"? How does Levine describe the knowledge created in the classroom?

Explorations

1. How do the instructors impact the students—who are the speakers—in Hughes's "*Theme for English B*" and the Levine poem? How could you compare and contrast these different effects?

2. What do you think M. Degas' purpose is in pursuing his line of questioning? Is his method of questioning effective or ineffective in terms of achieving this goal? What are the benefits and detriments of his approach?

3. What is the level of commitment the speaker shows for the classroom? How does Levine illustrate the speaker's feelings? How do elements of the poem's construction (point of view, setting, external and internal dialogue, image) support your read of the speaker's feelings?

Formal Writing Assignments

1. Describe and analyze an instructor's methods of teaching. Does he/she lecture, ask questions, lead class discussions, or use some other method? What do you see as the intended outcome of this method? How effective is it? How would you change it for the better?

2. Write a companion piece, in either verse or prose, of Levine's poem from the instructor's perspective. What is going through M. Degas' mind as he teaches this class? Consider how the very same moment can be reevaluated according to the speaker's position in the situation. In other words, how might the instructor's authority and personal investment in education affect his assessment of the lesson?

What We Are Best At

Mike Lohre

Mike Lohre is a poet and fiction writer who received his MFA from Ohio State University in 1998. He has received the Acadamy of American Poets Award as well as a grant from the Ohio Arts Council to support his fiction writing. Now a senior lecturer and teacher of basic writing, Lohre grew up on a cash crop and livestock farm in Southwestern Minnesota, and this story, which originally appeared in the Winter 1998 issue of *The Kenyon Review*, takes its life from that rural experience.

Writing Before Reading

1. Before reading the story, write about a time when you were "kept out of school" for a day by your parents or guardians. What was the reason? How was your absence justified? What, if anything, were you taught in place of that day's schooling?

2. These days, many school-aged children are kept out of public schools and "home-schooled" by their parents. What areas of study, in your opinion, should be included in all home-schooling curriculums? Why?

3. Write about a time when you were asked to perform a task in a way that seemed outdated or outmoded or unnecessarily difficult. What, if anything, did you learn from the experience?

What We Are Best At

At eight years old I could kill rats with a gun because my Pa showed me how to use the old single-shot .22 with the pine stock and the bolt action. A young boy attaches himself to words like bolt and action, and when my town friends at school asked me what kind of gun a farmboy uses when he hunts rats, I tried to say to them just as casually as I could: Just an old bolt action .22.

Then one fall Minnesota morning Pa says we must go out to the cattletank and kill rats. Pa says we must make ourselves a club. But Pa, why not with guns, I ask, and he says because you already know how to kill rats with a gun.

And this was true. When we first had problems with rats, it was because of the chicks that were dying out in the chickenshed. Ma would pace out there in the morning and find chicks every day that didn't anymore have either one or both of their legs. Chicks are real tender and loose at the joints, like young things are, and what had happened was that the rats under the floorboards would wait for those chicks' little leafstem legs to drop through the cracks and tiny knotholes and then just teeth on and rip those legs off. That left the chicks flopping yellow on the boards up top and that's how we'd find them.

Nine baby chicks in two days had to be killed before Pa figured the rats out and kept me home from school one full day to help move all the chickens and then clean and gum every inch of that old wood floor. He also found a burrow under the steps that the rats ran from and set me up with the rifle by the grain bin to wait and shoot them. I shot four in one afternoon and Pa, when I fetched him, came and picked them heavy off the dirt by their tails and I could hardly stand to look. I didn't mind shooting them but their long slick tails put me to fidget.

Even after we'd shot some of the rats and the floorboards were fixed, Pa said those rats were multiplying and because I already hated any word associated with math I was glad when Pa said he'd have to spend money for poison and no rats were going to make a home on his farm. Ma said she supposed he'd have to keep me home from school for that too and all Pa was going to do was drive them off somewhere else. Pa said the granary was their real target and once winter set in they'd soon be up in the grain bins and working bushels and bushels of corn back to their lair. How would she feel about the money then, Pa asked, and Ma just shook her head and said, But don't you dare keep that boy home from school.

The poison only killed a few of the rats before they knew better and Pa said that rats have been around the world a long time for a reason. The rats had moved from under the chickenshed by the end of the summer, but Ma was right that they'd camped themselves off somewhere else, multiplying.

So Pa on that cold autumn morning declares we must go out to the cattletank and kill rats.

Pa and I eat quietly and then leave the kitchen and walk to the back porch on the east side of our house. Ma won't let us wear our boots past the porch so morning, noon, and past supper we dig them from the bell of an old milk ceramic taking up a corner and step outside, boots in hand.

The air is very cool on this morning, the kind of morning so crisp and alive that the first sound your voice makes in it surprises you. I clear my throat and we sit down on the steps like always so we can put our boots on. Pa rubs his hands together fast and then starts digging in the pocket of his heavy coat for snoose. I am wearing my denim work coat and it has a much thinner lining than Pa's coat, so while Pa puts in his snoose I wait and tilt my head back some so that my face can catch the best angles of low breaking sun.

When Pa spits I know he is ready to put his boots on so I get ready too. Pa's boots have all kinds of laces and hooks and it takes him a lot longer to put his on, so I always wait until he has one boot on before I start to put mine on. When we went to the Country Store to get boots, I begged for the cowboy ones and Pa said that farmers didn't wear cowboy boots but OK anyway and they better last for two years like his did.

I hear Ma clanking pans around in the kitchen and I know she must have a burr about something because she makes me wash and wipe those pans as if they're glass. Pa says I don't know what that woman's rattling about this time and he winks at me before he stands up. He opens the door about two feet and yells back in to Ma, asking her is there something on her mind that she couldn't spit out at the breakfast table.

Ma comes to the door and her mouth is screwed up like about to laugh and she's pulling hard to make knots in the kerchief she's got her hair up in. Summer vacation's long over and are you going to get that boy missing school again today, she asks, and her smile fades in half when she brings her hands away from those knots and drops them down to her sides.

Pa says there is work to be done and work to be taught and we might be done in time for me to go to school today and we might not. Ma crouches down as if to pick at some imaginary dirt chunks on the floor and her face through the screen door is right even across from me when she says to Pa—well, he's only in third grade.

And Pa laughs and says he knows and it's a shame what I ain't already come to learn but he'll fix that and Ma stands up again and says OK Curtis, and she only says his full name like that when she knows she'll just have to trust him.

Then Ma kind of breathes like there is no air good enough to make more words with and shuts the wood door tight behind us. We stand and start to walk across the acreage toward the barn. The lawn is scattered with leaves and fallen walnuts and I like the sound of my heels as we hush across the dead grass and then thumpaclick our way across the packed dirt and stones leading south to the barn: thumpa-click, thumpa-click, thumpa-click, thumpa-click, thumpa-click.

At the barn, Pa tugs to open the heavy slide door and when it finally starts to come loose he heaves at it. The rollers down their track make a short, loud scream, like a chicken when you press its neck before butchering, and suddenly the way is clear into Pa's workshop.

We walk into the small section of room penned off in the front of the barn, built right off the bed-down area for the cattle and I notice that our three black Angus feeder steers have already wandered out into the south cattleyard for the morning. Pa tells me to sit down on a stump while he goes to get some two-by-fours and a hatchet and as I sit there and wait for him I wonder why those three Angus would want to stumble out into the cattleyard so early in the morning. Why don't they just stay in the soft dirt and straw in the bedding area, I think, instead of nuzzling endlessly the hoof-trod turf left in the small cattleyard behind the barn.

So when Pa comes with the hatchet and two-by-fours, I ask him and he laughs and asks did I want to stay in bed all day too? I say no and feel a little embarrassed. Pa sees that I am and tells me I was right about there being nothing left in the dirt for the cattle. He pulls a stump up across from me and before he sits down he looks over and tells me that the cattle get up and out in the morning because they drink a hell of a lot more water than a young boy does, and they are thirsty.

That makes sense to me—the cattletank lies to the west outside the back of the barn so they had to go out to get to it—and I nod at Pa and smile. Pa laughs and sits down on his stump. He says another thing to learn about those three cows is that even when they get a belly full of water they'll still stand out in that yard all day till nightfall because what cattle are best at is grazing and when there ain't that then they do what they are next best at, which is standing.

I try to be smart and say, Outside, in the open you mean? . . . It don't make sense to stand around in a barn, right? Pa says yes, that's just right.

I say that what rats must be best at is growing tails and Pa spits snoose and says yes, that, stealing, and living underground are indeed what rats are best at.

Pa weighs the hatchet in his hand, bobbing the sharp head of it up and down with the motion of his wrist, then leans forward and pulls a two-by-four off the ground and into his lap. Pa then stands the two-by-four up in front of him and steadies it into the ground with one hand, like he's reaching out to press his hand on top of a young boy's head. I think that because the board is almost as tall as me and I ask Pa if that's his club.

He says no, it'll be mine, and he strikes a crisp stroke of the hatchet from the middle down on one side of the two-by-four. A very thin strip of yellow-white pine curls off the board. I think out loud to Pa that it looks like the inside of an orange peel. He nods and smiles a work smile, one where a person doesn't show any teeth.

I say that it looks like he's making a stake and he says yes, this is about the same way we do that, except now we're just trying to take some thickness off the board so a boy like me can take a proper grip with it. Pa says he's going to make us both a nice round handle to grasp.

Pa spins the two-by-four a little bit at a time, around and around, shaving pine as he goes, slowly, until the wood starts to take on a cobbled roundness at the bottom instead of the awkward rectangle it was in before. I lean forward on my stump and rock my heels with the rhythm of Pa's hatchet as he carefully gleans wood from wood. It doesn't mean to come out but I say that maybe I could almost use something like that for a baseball bat since I didn't yet have one.

Pa slows his pace, keeps staring at the handle he's making like he can't decide if he's quite finished or not. Or maybe I could just hit rocks with it, I say. He's just still there and when he finally looks over to me I notice how pale his eyes are, and how dark and loose the skin rests underneath them. I feel like I hurt Pa's feelings and suddenly I feel bad too. I shouldn't have mentioned anything about the baseball bat again. Or wasting time hitting rocks off the driveway.

Hand me that other board, Pa says, and I try to do it too fast and rap it against his shin swinging it over to him. Goddamnit, Pa says, what gets you in a hurry all of a sudden now? He's frowning when he asks if I think to learn more at school than from my own father.

I wasn't thinking about being late for school at all but I just sit there and figure it's better to say nothing. Pa starts swinging the hatchet and splintering wood off in chunks. He hits the board too high sometimes and at bad angles but it only buckles a little bit in the middle due to his hand force pinning it into the ground. Pa starts talking fast to me like he's trying to get something out strange to him, something that can't come in his usually deliberate way. Pa starts working fever pitch—being close to reckless with the hatchet—and says he had to quit school when he was in third grade. Pa says maybe he would just stop sending me to school too if these damn teachers didn't stop calling to ask where I was, says he needs me during busy time and he can educate me more proper than any goddamn schoolteacher living off the taxpayers' dollar in town, says didn't farmers pay more tax in Cottonwood County than anybody and what if he did decide to keep his boy home from school for help. Pa says when his Pa died there was no question of him going to school anymore because somebody had to work and that's the only thing to learn in this world anyway.

Pa stops and puts the hatchet on his lap for a moment, wipes with his sleeve the sweat that's started in his hairline. He says it's vital important to learn how to work, and sometimes the best way is just to shut up about it and do it. Says if there's one thing in the world he hates it's a rat and he doesn't look forward to this any better than I do but it's work that's gotta be done and do I understand?

I nod. Grip the board long across my knees tight by the middle. Like usual, Pa's temper isn't very big and he soon settles down to smooth out the unevens in his club, swinging the short accurate strokes of the hatchet again and putting me at ease with the noise of the handle coming rounder. I watch as now delicate shavings fly off and nest around the bottom of the board in a small, even circle. When Pa finishes his club, he hangs the hatchet in the gate slat next to him and tells me to listen as careful as I can.

Pa says that school is good when you can get it and he don't want me to not finish school—a boy's got to have school he says, but you'll need more than that to be a man. Pa says you need experience to make you a man.

I say yes and tell Pa that the clubs are awful nice and I like the way the wood looks nested up on the floor, like the way it smells when you cut it fresh.

That's right, Pa says, there is something beautiful and useful always about wood.

Pa puts his hand down on my shoulder and squeezes tight once before turning around and walking outside. His club is about half as long as his body and he stands outside the doorway, practicing swinging it side to side, then up and down high over his head, using the same motion Ma does when she beats dust from the rugs out on the lawn.

He looks a little stiff doing that with his coat on and I go out and try to swing my long club a few times for practice. I have to grip the handle tight when I put it high over my head or I almost lose my balance. Once it starts to come down I have no problem controlling where I hit and I practice marking a few rocks about as big as my fist, pretending that they're rat heads.

We are ready to kill rats and we walk around the barn to the rise where the pump and the cattle-tank are and sure enough the three Angus are right there at the cattletank. getting their fill. The Angus are chest up to the tankrim and the water is so low that the steers are reaching their heads way down to get it. I watch as they powerfully suck it into their mouths, the water in each gulp traveling smoothly up their stretched necks like a slow zipper. Pa yells them off and they galumph over to the far south fence and do their standing there.

Pa has lined up a half dozen five-gallon pails and he takes them to the well pump, the iron heights stretching up and down in its orbit, bringing water up from down below to fill the pails.

The pails are soon full and as we get ready to lift the cattletank and expose the dark dirt surely below, I notice my breath in the cold air where I did not notice before. Pa says, OK, let's tip the tank up and he and I both lean our clubs against a gate to the right of the cattletank so we can.

I ask does he think we can lift it and he says yes, he's seen to it that the water's almost gone. I look around the base of the cattletank on our side and I don't see any digging anyplace. I've never seen one rat near the pump at all, but Pa tells me while we're bucking up beneath the tank that he's seen them crawl out from under it and they're surely there. I start to get a little nervous, my hands damp as the wood on the cattletank. I imagine some of those rats I'd shot by the bins being as large as tomcats even when I know in truth they weren't quite that big. In my mind I picture myself standing over a rat and trying to club it, but the rat's tail fights me like a snake and I wonder how you can kill a tail when it's supposed to be dead on the rat in the first place.

Pa heaves. I'm trying to help push too but the round underside of steelbanded wood is going up and away with Pa. He balances the tank on its side and rolls it away a few steps, releasing his hands slowly then to test whether the tank has settled the curve of its spine firmly into the ground. All I feel is the need to step quick to the gate for my club. I don't look to the ground under the tank yet for fear rats are already huddled gray around my tan cowboy boots.

Pa laughs and says, Don't worry, the rats aren't dumb enough to be right there when they hear us coming. I turn around, club now in hand, and see the perfect circle of gloss black dirt. It looks nearly wet with its shine, like something brand new to both wind and sun.

There are three holes under the cattletank—the mouth of each hole nearly the size of a coffee can's. Two of the holes are close to each other and just a few feet inside the outer curve of the cattletank border. One hole is set off a little bit from those two and seems to mark the center of the circle. It looks too organized.

I keep counting the holes one, two, three, and the counting reminds me of math. I'm poorly at math. I'm thinking poorly of those three holes as I count.

Pa carries over from behind the pump a tub and rests it too down next to the holes. Says this is old tractor oil he topped off by changing the Case last week and he'll use it and water. They'll hate the oil, he says. They'll come out.

They have a whole community, Pa says, there might be a hundred of them. The number one hundred overwhelms me a little and I ask can we kill that many and does that mean including baby rats, too?

Yes, says Pa twice, but the big ones will come first. Pa says get ready, Pa says I should just worry about one hole, here, and he'll stand over by the two closer together.

I stand there pretty nervous and Pa pours about a third of the tub oil down my hole. It disappears and it's as if the hole goes straight down to the center of the earth. I don't want to stand exactly over the hole to check for movement so I stand back two steps and raise my club over my head. Pa says, Good, but it will require water also, and he finishes the other holes with the oil and hustles for the water. He comes to my hole and splashes an entire pail down easily, the hole never backing up or the water getting ahead of itself at all.

I am waiting and I am scared and I imagine all sorts of things underneath the ground that might come up this hole, but nothing as terrible as the rats I know must be right now winding their tails below, building their courage to climb.

Pa finishes with the water on his holes and he has his club and is waiting and I am waiting.

There is a soft sound like a gurgle and then the rats come. The rats come and they appear suddenly and before I can see one I see three over by Pa scurrying and escaping and shaking their heads running off toward the woodpile. The rats from Pa's holes flow forward in one black-gray line like a liquid and Pa begins crushing many terribly, even as they flee everywhere around him. I watch him swing at one fidgeting rat's head as it slips, trying for traction in the smattered dirt around the hole. The sound of the board on that rat's skull is the sound of a baseball bat smacking hard green walnuts.

I can't look down to my hole because I have the feeling the first rat forward is still there and silent and fierce and beadily staring and waiting for me to swing my club so he can make me miss.

I stand back and I watch Pa. He can't afford to take his eyes off his holes, the rats seem to propel each other from below up out of the openings. When will the big ones stop, I wonder, when will the leaders no longer lead, their heads slick and black? I don't like the way they come up from the mouths of the holes. I don't like the wild marks of the oil and the shake in their eyes, like invaders come scrawling the banks of a new land from a dirty, underground river. The rats look fierce and confused and terrible and frightened and bold. Oil and water beads the air around them when they hesitate to quiver their coats.

At last I look to my hole and there are no rats there and by the looks of the smooth dirt around it they have not come this way.

Pa by the busy holes still swings and swings and swings, the thud and crack of his club as regular as the pistoned vapors that seem to crank out of my mouth watching him. The bodies of rats large and small lie collapsed on the ground everywhere gray and brown and black like exploded sections from a huge tractor tire innertube.

The rats are pulling their tails along everywhere, they are confused, they are furious, they are weaving around the corpses of the fallen, and Pa is fighting hard. Pa is standing there in his boots and one is crawling up his shoelace and he clubs it, he clubs it, he clubs it, then one gets his slimy head inside Pa's cuffs and disappears up his toughs so far that the end of the rat's tail hangs down like a shoelace. The rat is inside his pant leg. The oiled rat is on his shin and is biting him, I can feel it. I see its tail wagging in with his boot laces and I stare only at that tail and those boots: Red Wings, been in mud, not very new, laces the color of leather but more the color of earth.

I keep my eyes low. I do not look at Pa. The rat's tail hangs there in the knot of mud-clay shoelaces and I know for the rest of my life if I have to say what color a rat's tail is, if I have to say what a rat's tail looks like, I can say it looks like the shoelaces of my Pa's old workboots that day we went out to the cattletank to club rats.

And then I get in there. These are rats. These are rats, and we must kill them.

Questions for Discussion

1. In many states with large rural populations, school years are still cut short to allow students to help on their farms and ranches at harvest time. What other "economic" reasons might justify the temporary suspension of a school term? What reasons are sometimes used by parents to remove their students from school temporarily? How are these (or aren't these) "economic" in nature?

2. How might one's generation determine or affect one's value of traditional, school-based education? What would, in your opinion, be the position of the narrator's grandfather on keeping the boy home from school? How might this differ from the opinions of the narrator's future children?

3. We often judge people by the way they communicate. Think about the language used by the narrator of the story. How does his language stray from traditional conventions or grammatical 'correctness'? How might these idiosyncrasies of language affect his authority as a story-teller?

Explorations

1. Several times during the story, Lohre aligns the narrator and his father against the more traditional educational values of the mother. How, if at all, do you think gender influences our perception of education?

2. Compare Lohre's depiction of education to those of Rose or Edmundson. How are their views on the relationship of student and teacher similar? How are they different? What characteristics of teachers and students are privileged over others, and how does the educational environment influence which of these characteristics are seen as most important?

3. With a partner, browse the web for information about homeschooling. How do the representations of this educational alternative seem to differ from more traditional curriculums/ programs? How do they differ from the scenario depicted in Lohre's story? How are they similar?

Formal Writing Assignments

1. Interview someone who was of "school age" before 1950. Have them describe to you their educational experiences both "in" and "out" of the classroom. Try to determine what kinds of knowledge were most valued by their teachers and parents. Next, write an essay which first compares and contrasts that person's educational experience with your own. Next, use your findings to identify any generational shifts in educational priorities. What "subject matter" has come into educational vogue? What has been dropped from our curriculums? Consider what your educational experiences might have looked like without these shifts in priorities. How, had you been educated at the time of your interviewee, would you be more or less prepared for today's social and professional interactions?

2. Lohre's story is written in a way that reveals much about the narrator's level of formal education. Where we might laugh at phrases such as, "I'm poorly at math," the language of the story functions in many ways to foster our trust of the narrator. Choose a narrative piece of writing that you completed in the previous unit and do a close reading of your style and voice. How much of your personality and/or educational background are revealed by your writing? Now pretend the writing is that of a stranger. Write an essay in which you make assertions about the personality and educational background of the author or narrator, supporting your assertions (whether true or false, only you will know) with examples from the text.

Zami: A New Spelling of My Name

Audre Lorde

Audre Lorde was a prolific poet, essayist, novelist, activist, critic, and memoirist. Lorde's work reflects her own racial, cultural, and gender identity as a Black woman writer, a descendant of West Indians, a lesbian, a mother, a librarian, a teacher, a victim of cancer. Her education took her to the National University of Mexico and Hunter College as an undergraduate, and she earned an M.L.S. from Columbia University in 1961. She worked as a librarian before she began teaching, first as a lecturer in creative writing at City College (1968), and later as a professor of English at Hunter College, CUNY (1980–87). Lorde was also founder of the Kitchen Table Women of Color Press. She is known for her critique of racism, sex discrimination, and heterosexism.

Lorde's published works include nonfiction collections, such as *The Cancer Journals* (1980) and *Sister Outsider* (1984). Her novel *Zami: A New Spelling of My Name* (1982), provides us with the excerpt you are about to read, and she also authored several collections of poetry, including *Cables to Rage* (1970), *The Black Unicorn* (1978), and *Our Dead Behind Us* (1986). According to Lorde, her first published poem appeared in *Seventeen* magazine when she was still in high school, but that poem was actually rejected by her own high school newspaper.

The publishers of *Zami: A New Spelling of My Name* once labeled it a "biomythography, combining elements of history, biography and myth." This label may be important to bear in mind as you read the excerpt below. How might a "biomythography" differ from a memoir like Rose's or Alexie's? How important is the actual genre of the piece to your understanding of how to read it? What kinds of statements does Lorde make about the educational system in the United States using this genre? How do you respond to those statements?

Writing Before Reading

1. How are public and private schools perceived in the community where you grew up? What assumptions did you have while you were growing up about what a private school education entailed? A public school education? How have your assumptions changed, if at all?

2. When you were a young student, did you "color in the lines," following the directions given to you by your teachers and other authority figures? Why/why not?

3. A popular book in the early 1990's was *Everything I Needed to Know I Learned in Kindergarten*. What does that title mean to you? What values were instilled in you via your kindergarten class?

From Zami: A New Spelling of My Name

When I was five years old and still legally blind, I started school in a sight-conservation class in the local public school on 135th Street and Lenox Avenue. On the corner was a blue wooden booth where white women gave away free milk to Black mothers with children. I used to long for some Hearst Free Milk Fund milk, in those cute little bottles with their red and white tops, but my mother never allowed me to have any, because she said it was charity, which was bad and demeaning, and besides the milk was warm and might make me sick.

The school was right across the avenue from the catholic school where my two older sisters went, and this public school had been used as a threat against them for as long as I could remember. If they didn't behave and get good marks in schoolwork and deportment, they could be "transferred." A "transfer" carried the same dire implications as "deportation" came to imply decades later.

Of course everybody knew that public school kids did nothing but "fight," and you could get "beaten up" every day after school, instead of being marched out of the schoolhouse door in two neat rows like little robots, silent but safe and unattacked, to the corner where the mothers waited.

But the catholic school had no kindergarten, and certainly not one for blind children.

Despite my nearsightedness, or maybe because of it, I learned to read at the same time I learned to talk, which was only about a year or so before I started school. Perhaps *learn* isn't the right word to use for my beginning to talk, because to this day I don't know if I didn't talk earlier because I didn't know how, or if I didn't talk because I had nothing to say that I would be allowed to say without punishment. Self-preservation starts very early in West Indian families.

I learned how to read from Mrs. Augusta Baker, the children's librarian at the old 135th Street branch library, which has just recently been torn down to make way for a new library building to house the Schomburg Collection on African-American History and Culture. If that was the only good deed that lady ever did in her life, may she rest in peace. Because that deed saved my life, if not sooner, then later, when sometimes the only thing I had to hold on to was knowing I could read, and that that could get me through.

My mother was pinching my ear off one bright afternoon, while I lay spreadeagled on the floor of the Children's Room like a furious little brown toad, screaming bloody murder and embarrassing my mother to death. I know it must have been spring or early fall, because without the protection of a heavy coat, I can still feel the stinging soreness in the flesh of my upper arm. There, where my mother's sharp fingers had already tried to pinch me into silence. To escape those inexorable fingers I had hurled myself to the floor, roaring with pain as I could see them advancing toward my ears again. We were waiting to pick up my two older sisters from story hour, held upstairs on another floor of the dry-smelling quiet library. My shrieks pierced the reverential stillness.

Suddenly, I looked up, and there was a library lady standing over me. My mother's hands had dropped to her sides. From the floor where I was lying, Mrs. Baker seemed like yet another mile-high woman about to do me in. She had immense, light, hooded eyes and a very quiet voice that said, not damnation for my noise, but "Would you like to hear a story, little girl?"

Part of my fury was because I had not been allowed to go to that secret feast called story hour since I was too young, and now here was this strange lady offering me my own story.

I didn't dare to look at my mother, half-afraid she might say no, I was too bad for stories. Still bewildered by this sudden change of events, I climbed up upon the stool which Mrs. Baker pulled over for me, and gave her my full attention. This was a new experience for me and I was insatiably curious.

Mrs. Baker read me *Madeline*, and *Horton Hatches the Egg*, both of which rhymed and had huge lovely pictures which I could see from behind my newly acquired eyeglasses, fastened around the back of my rambunctious head by a black elastic band running from earpiece to earpiece. She also read me another storybook about a bear named Herbert who ate up an entire family, one by one, starting with the parents. By the time she had finished that one, I was sold on reading for the rest of my life.

I took the books from Mrs. Baker's hands after she was finished reading, and traced the large black letters with my fingers, while I peered again at the beautiful bright colors of the pictures. Right then I decided I was going to find out how to do that myself. I pointed to the black marks which I could now distinguish as separate letters, different from my sisters' more grown-up books, whose smaller print made the pages only one grey blur for me. I said, quite loudly, for whoever was listening to hear, "I want to read."

My mother's surprised relief outweighed whatever annoyance she was still feeling at what she called my whelpish carryings-on. From the background where she had been hovering while Mrs. Baker read, my mother moved forward quickly, mollified and impressed. I had spoken. She scooped me up from the low stool, and to my surprise, kissed me, right in front of everybody in the library, including Mrs. Baker.

This was an unprecedented and unusual display of affection in public, the cause of which I did not comprehend. But it was a warm and happy feeling. For once, obviously, I had done something right.

My mother set me back upon the stool and turned to Mrs. Baker, smiling.

"Will wonders never cease to perform!" Her excitement startled me back into cautious silence.

Not only had I been sitting still for longer than my mother would have thought possible, and sitting quietly. I had also spoken rather than screamed, something that my mother, after four years and a lot of worry, had despaired that I would ever do. Even one intelligible word was a very rare event for me. And although the doctors at the clinic had clipped the little membrane under my tongue so I was no longer tongue-tied, and had assured my mother that I was not retarded, she still had her terrors and her doubts. She was genuinely happy for any possible alternative to what she was afraid might be a dumb child. The ear-pinching was forgotten. My mother accepted the alphabet and picture books Mrs. Baker gave her for me, and I was on my way.

I sat at the kitchen table with my mother, tracing letters and calling their names. Soon she taught me how to say the alphabet forwards and backwards as it was done in Grenada. Although she had never gone beyond the seventh grade, she had been put in charge of teaching the first grade children their letters during her last year at Mr. Taylor's School in Grenville. She told me stories about his strictness as she taught me how to print my name.

I did not like the tail of the Y hanging down below the line in Audrey, and would always forget to put it on, which used to disturb my mother greatly. I used to love the evenness of AUDRELORDE at four years of age, but I remembered to put on the Y because it pleased my mother, and because, as she always insisted to me, that was the way it had to be because that was the way it was. No deviation was allowed from her interpretations of correct.

So by the time I arrived at the sight-conservation kindergarten, braided, scrubbed, and bespectacled, I was able to read large-print books and write my name with a regular pencil. Then came my first rude awakening about school. Ability had nothing to do with expectation.

There were only seven or eight of us little Black children in a big classroom, all with various serious deficiencies of sight. Some of us were crosseyed, some of us were nearsighted, and one little girl had a patch over one of her eyes.

We were given special short wide notebooks to write in, with very widely spaced lines on yellow paper. They looked like my sister's music notebooks. We were also given thick black crayons to write with. Now you don't grow up fat, Black, nearly blind, and ambidextrous in a West Indian household, particularly my parents' household, and survive without being or becoming fairly rigid fairly fast. And having been roundly spanked on several occasions for having made that mistake at home, I knew quite well that crayons were not what you wrote with, and music books were definitely not what you wrote in.

I raised my hand. When the teacher asked me what I wanted, I asked for some regular paper to write on and a pencil. That was my undoing. "We don't have any pencils here," I was told.

Our first task was to copy down the first letter of our names in those notebooks with our black crayons. Our teacher went around the room and wrote the required letter into each one of our notebooks. When she came around to me, she printed a large A in the upper left corner of the first page of my notebook, and handed me the crayon.

"I can't," I said, knowing full well that what you do with black crayons is scribble on the wall and get your backass beaten, or color around the edges of pictures, but not write. To write, you needed a pencil. "I can't!" I said, terrified, and started to cry.

"Imagine that, a big girl like you. Such a shame, I'll have to tell your mother that you won't even try. And such a big girl like you!"

And it was true. Although young, I was the biggest child by far in the whole class, a fact that had not escaped the attention of the little boy who sat behind me, and who was already whispering "fatty, fatty!" whenever the teacher's back was turned.

"Now just try, dear. I'm sure you can try to print your A. Mother will be so pleased to see that at least you tried." She patted my stiff braids and turned to the next desk.

Well, of course, she had said the magic words, because I would have walked over rice on my knees to please Mother. I took her nasty old soft smudgy crayon and pretended that it was a nice neat pencil with a fine point, elegantly sharpened that morning outside the bathroom door by my father, with the little penknife that he always carried around in his bathrobe pocket.

I bent my head down close to the desk that smelled like old spittle and rubber erasers, and on that ridiculous yellow paper with those laughably wide spaces I printed my best AUDRE. I had never been too good at keeping between straight lines no matter what their width, so it slanted down across the page something like this: A

      U

         D

           R

            E

The notebooks were short and there was no more room for anything else on that page. So I turned the page over, and wrote again, earnestly and laboriously, biting my lip, L

                      O

                        R

                          D

                            E

half-showing off, half-eager to please.

By this time, Miss Teacher had returned to the front of the room.

"Now when you're finished drawing your letter, children," she said, "Just raise your hand high." And her voice smiled a big smile. It is surprising to me that I can still hear her voice but I can't see her face, and I don't know whether she was Black or white. I can remember the way she smelled, but not the color of her hand upon my desk.

Well, when I heard that, my hand flew up in the air, wagging frantically. There was one thing my sisters had warned me about school in great detail: you must never talk in school unless you raised your hand. So I raised my hand, anxious to be recognized. I could imagine what teacher would say to my mother when she came to fetch me home at noon. My mother would know that her warning to me to "be good" had in truth been heeded.

Miss Teacher came down the aisle and stood beside my desk, looking down at my book. All of a sudden the air around her hand beside my notebook grew very still and frightening.

"Well I never!" Her voice was sharp. "I thought I told you to draw this letter? You don't even want to try and do as you are told. Now I want you to turn that page over and draw your letter like everyone . . . " and turning to the next page, she saw my second name sprawled down across the page.

There was a moment of icy silence, and I knew I had done something terribly wrong. But this time, I had no idea what it could be that would get her so angry, certainly not being proud of writing my name.

She broke the silence with a wicked edge to her voice. "I see." she said. "I see we have a young lady who does not want to do as she is told. We will have to tell her mother about that." And the rest of the class snickered, as the teacher tore the page out of my notebook.

"Now I am going to give you one more chance," she said, as she printed another fierce A at the head of the new page. "Now you copy that letter exactly the way it is, and the rest of the class will have to wait for you." She placed the crayon squarely back into my fingers.

By this time I had no idea at all what this lady wanted from me, and so I cried and cried for the rest of the morning until my mother came to fetch me home at noon. I cried on the street while we stopped to pick up my sisters, and for most of the way home, until my mother threatened to box my ears for me if I didn't stop embarrassing her on the street.

That afternoon, after Phyllis and Helen were back in school, and I was helping her dust, I told my mother how they had given me crayons to write with and how the teacher didn't want me to write my name. When my father came home that evening, the two of them went into counsel. It was decided that my mother would speak to the teacher the next morning when she brought me to school, in order to find out what I had done wrong. This decision was passed on to me, ominously, because of course I must have done something wrong to have made Miss Teacher so angry with me.

The next morning at school, the teacher told my mother that she did not think that I was ready yet for kindergarten, because I couldn't follow directions, and I wouldn't do as I was told.

My mother knew very well I could follow directions, because she herself had spent a good deal of effort and arm-power making it very painful for me whenever I did not follow directions. And she also believed that a large part of the function of school was to make me learn how to do what I was told to do. In her private opinion, if this school could not do that, then it was not much of a school and she was going to find a school that could. In other words, my mother had made up her mind that school was where I belonged.

That same morning, she took me off across the street to the catholic school, where she persuaded the nuns to put me into the first grade, since I could read already, and write my name on regular paper with a real pencil. If I sat in the first row I could see the blackboard. My mother also told the nuns that unlike my two sisters, who were models of deportment, I was very unruly, and that they should spank me whenever I needed it. Mother Josepha, the principal, agreed, and I started school.

My first grade teacher was named Sister Mary of Perpetual Help, and she was a disciplinarian of the first order, right after my mother's own heart. A week after I started school she sent a note home to my mother asking her not to dress me in so many layers of clothing because then I couldn't feel the strap on my behind when I was punished.

Sister Mary of Perpetual Help ran the first grade with an iron hand in the shape of a cross. She couldn't have been more than eighteen. She was big, and blond, I think, since we never got to see the nuns' hair in those days. But her eyebrows were blonde, and she was supposed to be totally dedicated, like all the other Sisters of the Blessed Sacrament, to caring for the Colored and Indian children of America. Caring for was not always caring about. And it always felt like Sister MPH hated either teaching or little children.

She had divided up the class into two groups, the Fairies and the Brownies. In this day of heightened sensitivity to racism and color usage, I don't have to tell you which were the good students and which were the baddies. I always wound up in the Brownies, because either I talked too much, or I broke my glasses, or I perpetrated some other awful infraction of the endless rules of good behavior.

But for two glorious times that year, I made it into the Fairies for brief periods of time. One was put into the Brownies if one misbehaved, or couldn't learn to read. I had learned to read already, but I couldn't tell my numbers. Whenever Sister MPH would call a few of us up to the front of the room for our reading lesson, she would say, "All right, children, now turn to page six in your readers." or, "Turn to page nineteen, please, and begin at the top of the page."

Well, I didn't know what page to turn to, and I was ashamed of not being able to read my numbers, so when my turn came to read I couldn't, because I didn't have the right place. After the prompting of a few words, she would go on to the next reader, and soon I wound up in the Brownies.

This was around the second month of school, in October. My new seatmate was Alvin, and he was the worst boy in the whole class. His clothes were dirty and he smelled unwashed, and rumor had it he had once called Sister MPH a bad name, but that couldn't have been possible because he would have been suspended permanently from school.

Alvin used to browbeat me into lending him my pencil to draw endless pictures of airplanes dropping huge penile bombs. He would always promise to give me the pictures when he was finished. But of course, whenever he was finished, he would decide that the picture was too good for a girl, so he would have to keep it, and make me another. Yet I never stopped hoping for one of them, because he drew airplanes very well.

He also would scratch his head and shake out the dandruff onto our joint spelling book or reader, and then tell me the flakes of dandruff were dead lice. I believed him in this, also, and was constantly terrified of catching cooties. But Alvin and I worked out our own system together for reading. He couldn't read, but he knew all his numbers, and I could read words, but I couldn't find the right page.

The Brownies were never called up to the front of the room; we had to read in anonymity from our double seats, where we scrunched over at the edges, ordinarily, to leave room in the middle for our two guardian angels to sit. But whenever we had to share a book our guardian angels had to jump around us and sit on the outside edge of our seats. Therefore, Alvin would show me the right pages to turn to when Sister called them out, and I would whisper the right words to him whenever it came his turn to read. Inside of a week after we devised this scheme of things, we had gotten out of the Brownies together. Since we shared a reader, we always went up together to read with the Fairies, so we had a really good thing going there for a while.

But Alvin began to get sick around Thanksgiving, and was absent a lot, and he didn't come back to school at all after Christmas. I used to miss his dive-bomber pictures, but most of all I missed his page numbers. After a few times of being called up by myself and not being able to read, I landed back in the Brownies again.

Years later I found out that Alvin had died of tuberculosis over Christmas, and that was why we all had been X-rayed in the auditorium after Mass on the first day back to school from Christmas vacation.

I spent a few more weeks in the Brownies with my mouth almost shut during reading lesson, unless the day's story fell on page eight, or ten, or twenty, which were the three numbers I knew.

Then, over one weekend, we had our first writing assignment. We were to look in our parents' newspaper and cut out words we knew the meaning of, and make them into simple sentences. We could only use one "the." It felt like an easy task, since I was already reading the comics by this time.

On Sunday morning after church, when I usually did my homework, I noticed an ad for White Rose Salada Tea on the back of the New York Times Magazine which my father was reading at the time. It had the most gorgeous white rose on a red background, and I decided I must have that rose for my picture—our sentences were to be illustrated. I searched through the paper until I found an "I," and then a "like," which I dutifully clipped out along with my rose, and the words "White," "Rose," "Salada," and "Tea." I knew the brand-name well because it was my mother's favorite tea.

On Monday morning, we all stood our sentence papers up on the chalk channels, leaning them against the blackboards. And there among the twenty odd "The boy ran," "it was cold," was "I like White Rose Salada Tea" and my beautiful white rose on a red background.

That was too much coming from a Brownie. Sister Mary of PH frowned.

"This was to be our own work , children," she said. "Who helped you with your sentence, Audre?" I told her I had done it alone.

"Our guardian angels weep when we don't tell the truth, Audre. I want a note from your mother tomorrow telling me that you are sorry for lying to the baby Jesus."

I told the story at home, and the next day I brought a note from my father saying that the sentence had indeed been my own work. Triumphantly, I gathered up my books and moved back over to the Fairies.

The thing that I remember best about being in the first grade was how uncomfortable it was, always having to leave room for my guardian angel on those tiny seats, and moving back and forth across the room from Brownies to Fairies and back again.

This time I stayed in the Fairies for a long time, because I finally started to recognize my numbers. I stayed there until the day I broke my glasses. I had taken them off to clean them in the bathroom and they slipped out of my hand. I was never to do that, and so I was in disgrace. My eyeglasses came from the eye clinic of the medical center, and it took three days to get a new pair made. We could not afford to buy more than one pair at a time, nor did it occur to my parents that such an extravagance might be necessary. I was almost sightless without them, but my punishment for having broken them was that I had to go to school anyway, even though I could see nothing. My sisters delivered me to my classroom with a note from my mother saying I had broken my glasses despite the fact they were tied to me by the strip of elastic.

I was never supposed to take my glasses off except just before getting into bed, but I was endlessly curious about these magical circles of glass that were rapidly becoming a part of me, transforming my universe, and remaining movable. I was always trying to examine them with my naked, nearsighted eyes, usually dropping them in the process.

Since I could not see at all to do any work from the blackboard, Sister Mary of PH made me sit in the back of the room on the window seat with a dunce cap on. She had the rest of the class offer up a prayer for my poor mother who had such a naughty girl who broke her glasses and caused her parents such needless extra expense to replace them. She also had them offer up a special prayer for me to stop being such a wicked-hearted child.

I amused myself by counting the rainbows of color that danced like a halo around the lamp on Sister Mary of PH's desk, watching the starburst patterns of light that the incandescent light bulb became without my glasses. But I missed them, and not being able to see. I never once gave a thought to the days when I believed that bulbs were starburst patterns of color, because that was what all light looked like to me.

It must have been close to summer by this time. As I sat with the dunce cap on, I can remember the sun pouring through the classroom window hot upon my back, as the rest of the class dutifully entoned their Hail Marys for my soul, and I played secret games with the distorted rainbows of light, until Sister noticed and made me stop blinking my eyes so fast.

Questions for Discussion

1 *Zami: A New Spelling of My Name*, is often treated as a novel, a piece of fiction. The book has also been called a "biomythography, combining elements of history, biography, and myth." Regardless of how the genre of the text is named, it clearly takes a position on a variety of issues. What issues are raised by this excerpt? What are Lorde's positions on those issues? Try to tease out the argument(s) you see in this piece.

2. A variety of teacher/student relationships are explored in this selection. How would you characterize them? What roles do the other adult characters play in the selection? How are the adult/child relationships shaping the narrative?

3. How does Lorde's account of the educational system in the United States compare with the accounts offered by Mike Rose in "I Just Wanna Be Average?" What aspects of Anyon's research in "Social Class and the Hidden Curriculum of Work" play themselves out in Lorde's narrative? Earl Shorris's teaching?

Explorations

1. Audre Lorde is a poet as well as a novelist and essayist, and her keen attention to issues of style, word choice, and usage marks her work. Choose a passage from *Zami: A New Spelling of My Name* that you feel is particularly powerful or compelling, and reflect upon the writerly choices Lorde makes in that passage. How is she able to achieve the effect you describe? What aspects of her writing do you most engage with?

2. Lorde suggests that the labeling of the two groups, the "Fairies" and the "Brownies," is clearly problematic because of the racial implications. What other portions of the piece demonstrate how race and culture impact the events Lorde describes? Explore the identity issues involved in this selection.

3. Choose another essay/short story/poem/editorial within the Academic Literacies unit and compare and contrast this piece with Lorde's. How might you articulate the relationship between the two pieces? You may want to consider issues of style, genre, argumentative strategies, imagery, voice, content, politics, authorial position, or other factors.

Formal Writing Assignments

1. Select an educational experience (you define the parameters of this term) from your own personal history and draft your own "biomythography," using that event as a focus. Your goal is to blend autobiography, mythology, and history as you represent this event from your own educational life. Before you begin, you might ask yourself questions: What are the "myths" about education that I'd like to address? What parts of my personal history might intersect those myths? How do I want to represent myself in this piece of writing? How do I want others to see me?

2. Draft an essay in which you analyze the role played by issues of identity within Audre Lorde's selection. What facets of identity seem to matter for Lorde and the other characters in the selection. Where do those facets matter most? How do they operate in conjunction with each other? Use evidence (summary, paraphrase, and/ or quotation) from the selection in order to support your analysis.

I Just Wanna Be Average

Mike Rose

Mike Rose, himself a student once labeled as under prepared, writes movingly in "I Just Wanna Be Average" of events surrounding his years as a student in East L.A. Now a faculty member in the UCLA School of Education and Information Studies, Rose is widely recognized as a leader in the field of composition studies. Although he has published widely in scholarly journals, *Lives on the Boundary* (1989), the book from which "I Just Wanna Be Average" is taken, brought Rose to the attention of the nation as a leader in educational policy. His more recent book, *Possible Lives,* recounts his travels across the country in search of inspired and effective teaching. Rose finds it at every turn in elementary, middle, and high schools, as well as colleges and universities.

Lives on the Boundary chronicles Rose's own difficult journey through the public schools and the university. The book, however, is also an argument against viewing under prepared students as "remedial," "illiterate," or "intellectually deficient." Instead, Rose argues that the difficulties that many students face in school have as much to do with the economic, political, and social realities of their lives as with the ways teachers and schools respond to under prepared students. Rose combines his serious critique of education in the U.S. with demonstrations of what is possible at all levels of education and with all students. "I Just Wanna Be Average" appears early in the book, as chapter two. In this portion of the book, we find that as a student Rose faced many of the same economic challenges as the students attending the schools Anyon describes.

Writing Before Reading

1. All of us, at one time or another, have found ourselves unprepared for the demands of school. For some, it might be for a math or science class, for others, phys ed or music class that were most stressful for us. Describe a time during elementary, middle, or high school when you felt unprepared. To what did you attribute your feelings?

2. Rose writes in this essay about the complex relationships between success at school and economics and politics. To what degree do you believe that the degree of economic affluence and political power influence the kind of education students receive?

3. Political decisions, at the state level in particular, exert considerable influence on both public and private schooling in the U.S. Take a few minutes to describe two or three recent political debates in your home state (or state where you're attending college) that have affected (or have the potential to affect) schooling.

I Just Wanna Be Average

Between 1880 and 1920, well over four million Southern Italian peasants immigrated to America. Their poverty was extreme and hopeless—twelve hours of farm labor would get you one lira, about twenty cents—so increasing numbers of desperate people booked passage for the United States, the country where, the steamship companies claimed, prosperity was a way of life. My father left Naples before the turn of the century; my mother came with her mother from Calabria in 1921. They met in Altoona,

Pennsylvania at the lunch counter of Tom and Joe's, a steamy diner with twangy-voiced waitresses and graveyard stew.

For my mother, life in America was not what the promoters had told her father it would be. She grew up very poor. She slept with her parents and brothers and sisters in one room. She had to quit school in the seventh grade to care for her sickly younger brothers. When her father lost his leg in a railroad accident, she began working in a garment factory where women sat crowded at their stations, solitary as penitents in a cloister. She stayed there until her marriage. My father had found a freer route. He was closemouthed about his past, but I know that he had been a salesman, a tailor, and a gambler; he knew people in the mob and had, my uncles whisper, done time in Chicago. He went through a year or two of Italian elementary school and could write a few words—those necessary to scribble measurements for a suit—and over the years developed a quiet urbanity, a persistence, and a slowly debilitating arteriosclerosis.

When my father proposed to my mother, he decided to open a spaghetti house, a venture that lasted through the war and my early years. The restaurant collapsed in bankruptcy in 1951 when Altoona's major industry, the Pennsylvania Railroad, had to shut down its shops. My parents managed to salvage seven hundred dollars and, on the advice of the family doctor, headed to California, where the winters would be mild and where I, their seven-year-old son, would have the possibility of a brighter future.

At first we lived in a seedy hotel on Spring Street in downtown Los Angeles, but my mother soon found an ad in the *Times* for cheap property on the south side of town. My parents contacted a woman named Mrs. Jolly, used my mother's engagement ring as a down payment, and moved to 9116 South Vermont Avenue, a house about one and one-half miles northwest of Watts. The neighborhood was poor, and it was in transition. Some old white folks had lived there for decades and were retired. Younger black families were moving up from Watts and settling by working class white families newly arrived from the South and the Midwest. Immigrant Mexican families were coming in from Baja. Any such demographic mix is potentially volatile, and as the fifties wore on, the neighborhood would be marked by outbursts of violence.

I have many particular memories of this time, but in general these early years seem a peculiar mix of physical warmth and barrenness: a gnarled lemon tree, thin rugs, a dirt alley, concrete in the sun. My uncles visited a few times, and we went to the beach or to orange groves. The return home, however, left the waves and spray, the thick leaves and split pulp far in the distance. I was aware of my parents watching their money and got the sense from their conversations that things could quickly take a turn for the worse. I started taping pennies to the bottom of a shelf in the kitchen.

My father's health was bad, and he had few readily marketable skills. Poker and pinochle brought in a little money, and he tried out an idea that had worked in Altoona during the war: He started a "suit club." The few customers he could scare up would pay two dollars a week on a tailor-made suit. He would take the measurements and send them to a shop back East and hope for the best. My mother took a job at a café in downtown Los Angeles, a split shift 9:00 to 12:00 and 5:00 to 9:00, but her tips were totaling sixty cents a day, so she quit for a night shift at Coffee Dan's. This got her to the bus stop at one in the morning, waiting on the same street where drunks were urinating and hookers were catching the last of the bar crowd. She made friends with a Filipino cook who would scare off the advances of old men aflame with the closeness of taxi dancers. In a couple of years, Coffee Dan's would award her a day job at the counter. Once every few weeks my father and I would take a bus downtown and visit with her, sitting at stools by the window, watching the animated but silent mix of faces beyond the glass.

My father had moved to California with faint hopes about health and a belief in his child's future, drawn by that far edge of America where the sun descends into green water. What he found was a city that was warm, verdant, vast, and indifferent as a starlet in a sports car. Altoona receded quickly, and my parents must have felt isolated and deceived. They had fallen into the abyss of Paradise—two more poor settlers trying to make a go of it in the City of the Angels.

Let me tell you about our house. If you entered the front door and turned right you'd see a small living room with a couch along the east wall and one along the west wall—one couch was purple, the other tan, both bought used and both well worn. A television set was placed at the end of the purple couch, right at arm level. An old Philco radio sat next to the TV, its speaker covered with gold lamé. There was a small coffee table in the center of the room on which sat a murky fishbowl occupied by two listless guppies. If, on entering, you turned left you would see a green Formica dinner table with four chairs, a cedar chest given as a wedding present to my mother by her mother, a painted statue of the Blessed Virgin Mary, and a black trunk. I also had a plastic chaise longue between the door and the table. I would lie on this and watch television.

A short hallway leading to the bathroom opened on one side to the kitchen and, on the other, to the bedroom. The bedroom had two beds, one for me and one for my parents, a bureau with a mirror, and a chest of drawers on which we piled old shirt boxes and stacks of folded clothes. The kitchen held a refrigerator and a stove, small older models that we got when our earlier (and newer) models were repossessed by two silent men. There was one white wooden chair in the corner beneath wall cabinets. You could walk in and through a tiny pantry to the backyard and to four one-room rentals. My father got most of our furniture from a secondhand store on the next block; he would tend the store two or three hours a day as payment on our account.

As I remember it, the house was pretty dark. My mother kept the blinds in the bedroom drawn—there were no curtains there—and the venetian blinds in the living room were, often as not, left closed. The walls were bare except for a faded picture of Jesus and a calendar from the *Altoona Mirror*. Some paper carnations bent out of a white vase on the television. There was a window on the north side of the kitchen that had no blinds or curtains, so the sink got good light. My father would methodically roll up his sleeves and show me how to prepare a sweet potato or avocado seed so it would sprout. We kept a row of them on the sill above the sink, their shoots and vines rising and curling in the morning sun.

The house was on a piece of land that rose about four feet up from heavily trafficked Vermont Avenue. The yard sloped down to the street, and three steps and a short walkway led up the middle of the grass to our front door. There was a similar house immediately to the south of us. Next to it was Carmen's Barber Shop. Carmen was a short, quiet Italian who, rumor had it, had committed his first wife to the crazy house to get her money. In the afternoons, Carmen could be found in the lot behind his shop playing solitary catch, flinging a tennis ball high into the air and running under it. One day the police arrested Carmen on charges of child molesting. He was released but became furtive and suspicious. I never saw him in the lot again. Next to Carmen's was a junk store where, one summer, I made a little money polishing brass and rewiring old lamps. Then came a dilapidated real estate office, a Mexican restaurant, an empty lot, and an appliance store owned by the father of Keith Grateful, the streetwise, chubby boy who would become my best friend.

Right to the north of us was a record shop, a barber shop presided over by old Mr. Graff, Walt's Malts, a shoe repair shop with a big Cat's Paw decal in the window, a third barber shop, and a brake shop. It's as I write this that I realize for the first time that three gray men could have had a go at your hair before you left our street.

Behind our house was an unpaved alley that passed, just to the north, a power plant the length of a city block. Massive coils atop the building hissed and cracked through the day, but the doors never opened. I used to think it was abandoned—feeding itself on its own wild arcs—until one sweltering afternoon a man was electrocuted on the roof. The air was thick and still as two firemen—the only men present—brought down a charred and limp body without saying a word.

The north and south traffic on Vermont was separated by tracks for the old yellow trolley cars, long since defunct. Across the street was a huge garage, a tiny hot dog stand run by a myopic and reclusive man named Freddie, and my dreamland, the Vermont Bowl. Distant and distorted behind thick lenses, Freddie's eyes never met yours; he would look down when he took your order and give you your change with a mumble. Freddie slept on a cot in the back of his grill and died there one night, leaving tens of thousands of dollars stuffed in the mattress.

My father would buy me a chili dog at Freddie's, and then we would walk over to the bowling alley where Dad would sit at the lunch counter and drink coffee while I had a great time with pinball machines, electric shooting galleries, and an ill-kept dispenser of cheese corn. There was a small, dark bar abutting the lanes, and it called to me. I would devise reasons to walk through it: "Scuse me, is the bathroom in here?" or "Anyone see my dad?" though I can never remember my father having a drink. It was dark and people were drinking and I figured all sorts of mysterious things were being whispered. Next to the Vermont Bowl was a large vacant lot overgrown with foxtails and dotted with car parts, bottles, and rotting cardboard. One day Keith heard that the police had found a human head in the brush. After that we explored the lot periodically, coming home with stickers all the way up to our waists. But we didn't find a thing. Not even a kneecap.

When I wasn't with Keith or in school, I would spend most of my day with my father or with the men who were renting the one-room apartments behind our house. Dad and I whiled away the hours in the bowling alley, watching TV, or planting a vegetable garden that never seemed to take. When he was still mobile, he would walk the four blocks down to St. Regina's Grammar School to take me home to my favorite lunch of boiled wieners and chocolate milk. There I'd sit, dunking my hot dog in a jar of mayonnaise and drinking my milk while Sheriff John tuned up the calliope music on his "Lunch Brigade." Though he never complained to me, I could sense that my father's health was failing, and I began devising child's ways to make him better. We had a box of rolled cotton in the bathroom, and I would go in and peel off a long strip and tape it around my jaw. Then I'd rummage through the closet, find a sweater of my father's, put on one of his hats—and sneak around to the back door. I'd knock loudly and wait. It would take him a while to get there. Finally, he'd open the door, look down, and quietly say, "Yes, Michael?" I was disappointed. Every time. Somehow I thought I could fool him. And, I guess, if he had been fooled, I would have succeeded in redefining things: I would have been the old one, he much younger, more agile, with strength in his legs.

The men who lived in the back were either retired or didn't work that much, so one of them was usually around. They proved to be, over the years, an unusual set of companions for a young boy. Ed Gionotti was the youngest of the lot, a handsome man whose wife had run off and who spoke softly and never smiled. Bud Hall and Lee McGuire were two out-of-work plumbers who lived in adjacent units and who weekly drank themselves silly, proclaiming in front of God and everyone their undying friendship or their unequivocal hatred. Old Cheech was a lame Italian who used to hobble along grabbing his testicles and rolling his eyes while he talked about the women he claimed to have on a string. There was Lester, the toothless cabbie, who several times made overtures to me and who, when he moved, left behind a drawer full of syringes and burnt spoons. Mr. Smith was a rambunctious retiree who lost his nose to an untended skin cancer. And there was Mr. Berryman, a sweet and gentle man who eventually left for a retirement hotel only to be burned alive in an electrical fire.

Except for Keith, there were no children on my block and only one or two on the immediate side streets. Most of the people I saw day to day were over fifty. People in their twenties and thirties working in the shoe shop or the garages didn't say a lot; their work and much of what they were working for drained their spirits. There were gang members who sauntered up from Hoover Avenue, three blocks to the east, and occasionally I would get shoved around, but they had little interest in me either as member or victim. I was a skinny, bespectacled kid and had neither the coloring nor the style of dress or carriage that marked me as a rival. On the whole, the days were quiet, lazy, lonely. The heat shimmering over the asphalt had no snap to it; time drifted by. I would lie on the couch at night and listen to the music from the record store or from Walt's Malts. It was new and quick paced, exciting, a little dangerous (the church had condemned Buddy Knox's "Party Doll"), and I heard in it a deep rhythmic need to be made whole with love, or marked as special, or released in some rebellious way. Even the songs about lost love—and there were plenty of them—lifted me right out of my socks with their melodious longing:

> Came the dawn,
> and my heart and her love and the night
> were gone.
> But I know I'll never forget
> her kiss in the moonlight Oooo . . .
> such a kiss Oooo Oooo such a night . . .

In the midst of the heat and slow time the music brought the promise of its origins, a promise of deliverance, a promise that, if only for a moment, life could be stirring and dreamy.

But the anger and frustration of South Vermont could prove too strong for music's illusion; then it was violence that provided deliverance of a different order. One night I watched as a guy sprinted from Walt's to toss something on our lawn. The police were right behind, and a cop tackled him, smashing his face into the sidewalk. I ducked out to find the packet: a dozen glassine bags of heroin. Another night, one August midnight, an argument outside the record store ended with a man being shot to death. And the occasional gang forays brought with them some fated kid who would fumble his moves and catch a knife.

It's popular these days to claim you grew up on the streets. Men tell violent tales and romanticize the lessons violence brings. But, though it was occasionally violent, it wasn't the violence in South L.A. that marked me, for sometimes you can shake that ugliness off. What finally affected me was subtler, but more pervasive: I cannot recall a young person who was crazy in love or lost in work or one old person who was passionate about a cause or an idea. I'm not talking about an absence of energy—the street toughs and, for that fact, old Cheech had energy. And I'm not talking about an absence of decency, for my father was a thoughtful man. The people I grew up with were retired from jobs that rub away the heart or were working hard at jobs to keep their lives from caving in or were anchorless and in between jobs and spouses or were diving headlong into a barren tomorrow: junkies, alcoholics, and mean kids walking along Vermont looking to throw a punch. I developed a picture of human existence that rendered it short and brutish or sad and aimless or long and quiet with rewards like afternoon naps, the evening newspaper, walks around the block, occasional letters from children in other states. When, years later, I was introduced to humanistic psychologists like Abraham Maslow and Carl Rogers, with their visions of self-actualization, or even Freud with his sober dictum about love and work, it all sounded like a glorious fairy tale, a magical account of a world full of possibility, full of hope and empowerment. Sindbad and Cinderella couldn't have been more fanciful.

Some people who manage to write their way out of the working class describe the classroom as an oasis of possibility. It became their intellectual playground, their competitive arena. Given the richness of my memories of this time, it's funny how scant are my recollections of school. I remember the red brick building of St. Regina's itself, and the topography of the playground: the swings and basketball courts and peeling benches. There are images of a few students: Erwin Petschaur, a muscular German boy with a strong accent; Dave Sanchez, who was good in math; and Sheila Wilkes, everyone's curly-haired heart-throb. And there are two nuns: Sister Monica, the third-grade teacher with beautiful hands for whom I carried a candle and who, to my dismay, had wedded herself to Christ; and Sister Beatrice, a woman truly crazed, who would sweep into class, eyes wide, to tell us about the Apocalypse.

All the hours in class tend to blend into one long, vague stretch of time. What I remember best, strangely enough, are the two things I couldn't understand and over the years grew to hate: grammar lessons and mathematics. I would sit there watching a teacher draw her long horizontal line and her short, oblique lines and break up sentences and put adjectives here and adverbs there and just not get it, couldn't see the reason for it, turned off to it. I would hide by slumping down in my seat and page through my reader, carried along by the flow of sentences in a story. She would test us, and I would dread that, for I always got Cs and Ds. Mathematics was a bit different. For whatever reasons, I didn't learn early math very well, so when it came time for more complicated operations, I couldn't keep up and started day-dreaming to avoid my inadequacy. This was a strategy I would rely on as I grew older. I fell further and further behind. A memory: The teacher is faceless and seems very far away. The voice is faint and is discussing an equation written on the board. It is raining, and I am watching the streams of water form patterns on the windows.

I realize now how consistently I defended myself against the lessons I couldn't understand and the people and events of South L.A. that were too strange to view head-on. I got very good at watching a blackboard with minimum awareness. And I drifted more and more into a variety of protective fantasies. I was lucky in that although my parents didn't read or write very much and had no more than a few books around the house, they never debunked my pursuits. And when they could, they bought me what I needed to spin my web.

One early Christmas they got me a small chemistry set. My father brought home an old card table from the secondhand store, and on that table I spread out my test tubes, my beaker, my Erlenmeyer flask, and my gas-generating apparatus. The set came equipped with chemicals, minerals, and various treated papers—all in little square bottles. You could send away to someplace in Maryland for more, and I did, saving pennies and nickels to get the substances that were too exotic for my set, the Junior Chemcraft: Congo red paper, azurite, glycerine, chrome alum, cochineal—this from female insects!—tartaric acid, chameleon paper, logwood. I would sit before my laboratory and play for hours. My father rested on the purple couch in front of me watching wrestling or *Gunsmoke* while I measured powders or heated crystals or blew into solutions that my breath would turn red or pink. I was taken by the blends of names and by the colors that swirled through the beaker. My equations were visual and phonetic. I would hold a flask up to the hall light, imagining the veils of a million atoms dancing. Sulfur and alcohol hung in the air. I wanted to shake down the house.

One day my mother came home from Coffee Dan's with an awful story. The teenage brother of one of her waitress friends was in the hospital. He had been fooling around with explosives in his garage "where his mother couldn't see him," and something happened, and "he blew away part of his throat. For God's sake, be careful," my mother said. "Remember poor Ada's brother." Wow! I thought. How neat! Why couldn't my experiments be that dangerous? I really lost heart when I realized that you could probably eat the chemicals spread across my table.

I knew what I had to do. I saved my money for a week and then walked with firm resolve past Walt's Malts, past the brake shop, across Ninetieth Street, and into Palazzolla's market. I bought a little bottle of Alka-Seltzer and ran home. I chipped up the wafers and mixed them into a jar of white crystals. When my mother came home, dog tired, and sat down on the edge of the couch to tell me and Dad about her day, I gravely poured my concoction into a beaker of water, cried something about the unexpected, and ran out from behind my table. The beaker foamed ominously. My father swore in Italian. The second time I tried it, I got something milder—in English. And by my third near-miss with death, my parents were calling my behavior cute. Cute! Who wanted cute? I wanted to toy with the disaster that befell Ada Pendleton's brother. I wanted all those wonderful colors to collide in ways that could blow your voice box right off.

But I was limited by the real. The best I could do was create a toxic antacid. I loved my chemistry set—its glassware and its intriguing labels—but it wouldn't allow me to do the things I wanted to do. St. Regina's had an all-purpose room, one wall of which was lined with old books—and one of those shelves held a row of plastic-covered space novels. The sheen of their covers was gone, and their futuristic portraits were dotted with erasures and grease spots like a meteor shower of the everyday. I remember the rockets best. Long cylinders outfitted at the base with three stick fins, tapering at the other end to a per-fect conical point, ready to pierce out of the stratosphere and into my imagination: X-fifteens and Mach 1, the dark side of the moon, the Red Planet, Jupiter's Great Red Spot, Saturn's rings—and beyond the solar system to swirling wisps of galaxies, to stardust.

I would check out my books two at a time and take them home to curl up with a blanket on my chaise longue, reading, sometimes, through the weekend, my back aching, my thoughts lost between galaxies. I became the hero of a thousand adventures, all with intricate plots and the triumph of good over evil, all many dimensions removed from the dim walls of the living room. We were given time to draw in school, so, before long, all this worked itself onto paper. The stories I was reading were reshaping themselves into pictures. My father got me some butcher paper from Palazolla's, and I continued to draw at home. My collected works rendered the Horsehead Nebula, goofy space cruisers, robots, and Saturn. Each had its crayon, a particular waxy pencil with mood and meaning: rust and burnt sienna for Mars, yellow for the Sun, lime and rose for Saturn's rings, and bright red for the Jovian spot. I had a little sharp-ener to keep the points just right. I didn't write any stories; I just read and drew. I wouldn't care much about writing until late in high school.

The summer before the sixth grade, I got a couple of jobs. The first was at a pet store a block or so away from my house. Since I was still small, I could maneuver around in breeder cages, scraping the heaps of parakeet crap from the tin floor, cleaning the water troughs and seed trays. It was pretty awful. I would go home after work and fill the tub and soak until all the fleas and bird mites came floating to the surface, little Xs in their multiple eyes. When I heard about a job selling strawberries door-to-door, I jumped at it. I went to work for a white-haired Chicano named Frank. He would carry four or five kids and dozens of crates of strawberries in his ramshackle truck up and down the avenues of the better neigh-borhoods: houses with mowed lawns and petunia beds. We'd work all day for seventy-five cents, Frank dropping pairs of us off with two crates each, then picking us up at pre-assigned corners. We spent lots of time together, bouncing around on the truck bed redolent with strawberries or sitting on a corner, cold, listening for the sputter of Frank's muffler. I started telling the other kids about my books, and soon it was my job to fill up that time with stories.

Reading opened up the world. There I was, a skinny bookworm drawing the attention of street kids who, in any other circumstances, would have had me for breakfast. Like an epic tale-teller, I developed the stories as I went along, relying on a flexible plot line and a repository of heroic events. I had a great time. I sketched out trajectories with my finger on Frank's dusty truck bed. And I stretched out each story's climax, creating cliffhangers like the ones I saw in the Saturday serials. These stories created for me a tem-porary community.

It was around this time that fiction started leading me circuitously to a child's version of science. In addition to the space novels, St. Regina's library also had half a dozen books on astronomy—*The Golden Book of the Planets* and stuff like that—so I checked out a few of them. I liked what I read and wheedled enough change out of my father to enable me to take the bus to the public library. I discov-ered star maps, maps of lunar seas, charts upon charts of the solar system and the planetary moons: Rhea, Europa, Callisto, Miranda, Io. I didn't know that most of these moons were named for women—I didn't know classical mythology—but I would say their names to myself as though they had a woman's power to protect: Europa, Miranda, Io. . . The distances between stars fascinated me, as did the sizes of the big telescopes. I sent away for catalogs. Then prices fascinated me too. I wanted to drape my arm over a thousand-dollar scope and hear its motor drive whirr. I conjured a twelve-year-old's life of the astronomer: sitting up all night with potato chips and the stars, tracking the sky for supernovas, humming "Earth Angel" with the Penguins. What was my mother to do but save her tips and buy me a telescope?!

It was a little reflecting job, and I solemnly used to carry it out to the front of the house on warm summer nights, to find Venus or Alpha Centauri or trace the stars in Orion or lock onto the moon. I would lay out my star maps on the concrete, more for their magic than anything else, for I had trouble figuring them out. I was no geometer of the constellations; I was their balladeer. Those nights were very peaceful. I was far enough away from the front door and up enough from the sidewalk to make it seem as if I rested on a mound of dark silence, a mountain in Arizona, perhaps, watching the sky alive with points of light. Poor Freddie, toothless Lester whispering promises about making me feel good, the flat days, the gang fights—all this receded, for it was now me, the star child, lost in an eyepiece focused on a reflecting mirror that cradled, in its center, a shimmering moon.

The loneliness in Los Angeles fosters strange arrangements. Lou Minton was a wiry man with gaunt, chiseled features and prematurely gray hair, combed straight back. He had gone to college in the South for a year or two and kicked around the country for many more before settling in L.A. He lived in a small downtown apartment with a single window and met my mother at the counter of Coffee Dan's. He had been alone too long and eventually came to our house and became part of the family. Lou repaired washing machines, and he had a car, and he would take me to the vast, echoing library just west of Pershing Square and to the Museum of Science and Industry in Exposition Park. He bought me astronomy books, taught me how to use tools, and helped me build model airplanes from balsa wood and rice paper. As my father's health got worse, Lou took care of him.

My rhapsodic and prescientific astronomy carried me into my teens, consumed me right up till high school, losing out finally, and only, to the siren call of pubescence—that endocrine hoodoo that transmogrifies nice boys into gawky flesh fiends. My mother used to bring home *Confidential* magazine, a peepshow rag specializing in the sins of the stars, and it beckoned me mercilessly: Jayne Mansfield's cleavage, Gina Lollobrigida's eyes, innuendos about deviant sexuality, ads for Frederick's of Hollywood—spiked heels, lacy brassieres, the epiphany of silk panties on a mannequin's hips. Along with Phil Everly, I was through with counting the stars above.

Budding manhood. Only adults talk about adolescence budding. Kids have no choice but to talk in extremes; they're being wrenched and buffeted, rabbit-punched from inside by systemic thugs. Nothing sweet and pastoral here. Kids become ridiculous and touching at one and the same time: passionate about the trivial, fixed before the mirror, yet traversing one of the most important rites of passage in their lives—liminal people, silly and profoundly human. Given my own expertise, I fantasized about concocting the fail-safe aphrodisiac that would bring Marianne Bilpusch, the cloakroom monitor, rushing into my arms or about commanding a squadron of bosomy, linguistically mysterious astronauts like Zsa Zsa Gabor. My parents used to say that their son would have the best education they could afford. Maybe I would be a doctor. There was a public school in our neighborhood and several Catholic schools to the west. They had heard that quality schooling meant private, Catholic schooling, so they somehow got the money together to send me to Our Lady of Mercy, fifteen or so miles southwest of Ninety-first and Vermont. So much for my fantasies. Most Catholic secondary schools then were separated by gender.

It took two buses to get to Our Lady of Mercy. The first started deep in South Los Angeles and caught me at midpoint. The second drifted through neighborhoods with trees, parks, big lawns, and lots of flowers. The rides were long but were livened up by a group of South L.A. veterans whose parents also thought that Hope had set up shop in the west end of the county. There was Christy Biggars, who, at sixteen, was dealing and was, according to rumor, a pimp as well. There were Bill Cobb and Johnny Gonzales, grease-pencil artists extraordinaire, who left Nembutal-enhanced swirls of "Cobb" and "Johnny" on the corrugated walls of the bus. And then there was Tyrrell Wilson. Tyrrell was the coolest kid I knew. He ran the dozens like a metric halfback, laid down a rap that outrhymed and outpointed Cobb, whose rap was good but not great—the curse of a moderately soulful kid trapped in white skin. But it was Cobb who would sneak a radio onto the bus, and thus underwrote his patter with Little Richard, Fats Domino, Chuck Berry, the Coasters, and Ernie K. Doe's mother-in-law, an awful woman who was "sent from down below." And so it was that Christy and Cobb and Johnny G. and Tyrrell and I and assorted others picked up along the way passed our days in the back of the bus, a funny mix brought together by geography and parental desire.

Entrance to school brings with it forms and releases and assessments. Mercy relied on a series of tests, mostly the Stanford-Binet, for placement, and somehow the results of my tests got confused with those of another student named Rose. The other Rose apparently didn't do very well, for I was placed in the vocational track, a euphemism for the bottom level. Neither I nor my parents realized what this meant. We had no sense that Business Math, Typing, and English-Level D were dead ends. The current spate of reports on the schools criticizes parents for not involving themselves in the education of their children. But how would someone like Tommy Rose, with his two years of Italian schooling, know what to ask? And what sort of pressure could an exhausted waitress apply? The error went undetected, and I remained in the vocational track for two years. What a place.

My homeroom was supervised by Brother Dill, a troubled and unstable man who also taught freshman English. When his class drifted away from him, which was often, his voice would rise in paranoid accusations, and occasionally he would lose control and shake or smack us. I hadn't been there two months when one of his brisk, face-turning slaps had my glasses sliding down the aisle. Physical education was also pretty harsh. Our teacher was a stubby ex-lineman who had played old-time pro ball in the Midwest. He routinely had us grabbing our ankles to receive his stinging paddle across our butts. He did that, he said, to make men of us. "Rose," he bellowed on our first encounter; me standing geeky in line in my baggy shorts. "'Rose'? What the hell kind of name is that?"

"Italian, sir," I squeaked.

"Italian! Ho. Rose, do you know the sound a bag of shit makes when it hits the wall?"

"No, sir."

"Wop!"

Sophomore English was taught by Mr. Mitropetros. He was a large, bejeweled man who managed the parking lot at the Shrine Auditorium. He would crow and preen and list for us the stars he'd brushed against. We'd ask questions and glance knowingly and snicker, and all that fueled the poor guy to brag some more. Parking cars was his night job. He had little training in English, so his lesson plan for his day work had us reading the district's required text, *Julius Caesar*, aloud for the semester. We'd finish the play way before the twenty weeks was up, so he'd have us switch parts again and again and start again: Dave Snyder, the fastest guy at Mercy, muscling through Caesar to the breathless squeals of Calpurnia, as interpreted by Steve Fusco, a surfer who owned the school's most envied paneled wagon. Week ten and Dave and Steve would take on new roles, as would we all, and render a water-logged Cassius and a Brutus that are beyond my powers of description.

Spanish I—taken in the second year—fell into the hands of a new recruit. Mr. Montez was a tiny man, slight, five foot six at the most, soft-spoken and delicate. Spanish was a particularly rowdy class, and Mr. Montez was as prepared for it as a doily maker at a hammer throw. He would tap his pencil to a room in which Steve Fusco was propelling spitballs from his heavy lips, in which Mike Dweetz was taunting Billy Hawk, a half-Indian, half-Spanish, reed-thin, quietly explosive boy. The vocational track at Our Lady of Mercy mixed kids traveling in from South L.A. with South Bay surfers and a few Slavs and Chicanos from the harbors of San Pedro. This was a dangerous miscellany: surfers and hodads and South-Central blacks all ablaze to the metronomic tapping of Hector Montez's pencil.

One day Billy lost it. Out of the corner of my eye I saw him strike out with his right arm and catch Dweetz across the neck. Quick as a spasm, Dweetz was out of his seat, scattering desks, cracking Billy on the side of the head, right behind the eye. Snyder and Fusco and others broke it up, but the room felt hot and close and naked. Mr. Montez's tenuous authority was finally ripped to shreds, and I think everyone felt a little strange about that. The charade was over, and when it came down to it, I don't think any of the kids really wanted it to end this way. They had pushed and pushed and bullied their way into a freedom that both scared and embarrassed them.

Students will float to the mark you set. I and the others in the vocational classes were bobbing in pretty shallow water. Vocational education has aimed at increasing the economic opportunities of students who do not do well in our schools. Some serious programs succeed in doing that, and through exceptional teachers—like Mr. Gross in *Horace's Compromise*—students learn to develop hypotheses and troubleshoot, reason through a problem, and communicate effectively—the true job skills. The vocational track, however, is most often a place for those who are just not making it, a dumping ground for the disaffected. There were a few teachers who worked hard at education; young Brother Slattery, for example, combined a stern voice with weekly quizzes to try to pass along to us a skeletal outline of world history. But mostly the teachers had no idea of how to engage the imaginations of us kids who were scuttling along at the bottom of the pond.

And the teachers would have needed some inventiveness, for none of us was groomed for the classroom. It wasn't just that I didn't know things—didn't know how to simplify algebraic fractions, couldn't identify different kinds of clauses, bungled Spanish translations—but that I had developed various faulty and inadequate ways of doing algebra and making sense of Spanish. Worse yet, the years of defensive tuning out in elementary school had given me a way to escape quickly while seeming at least half alert. During my time in Voc. Ed., I developed further into a mediocre student and a somnambulant problem solver, and that affected the subjects I did have the wherewithal to handle: I detested Shakespeare; I got bored with history. My attention flitted here and there. I fooled around in class and read my books indifferently—the intellectual equivalent of playing with your food. I did what I had to do to get by, and I did it with half a mind.

But I did learn things about people and eventually came into my own socially. I liked the guys in Voc. Ed. Growing up where I did, I understood and admired physical prowess, and there was an abundance of muscle here. There was Dave Snyder, a sprinter and halfback of true quality. Dave's ability and his quick wit gave him a natural appeal, and he was welcome in any clique, though he always kept a little independent. He enjoyed acting the fool and could care less about studies, but he possessed a certain maturity and never caused the faculty much trouble. It was a testament to his independence that he included me among his friends—I eventually went out for track, but I was no jock. Owing to the Latin alphabet and a dearth of R and S, Snyder sat behind Rose, and we started exchanging one-liners and became friends.

There was Ted Richard, a much-touted Little League pitcher. He was chunky and had a baby face and came to Our Lady of Mercy as a seasoned street fighter. Ted was quick to laugh and he had a loud, jolly laugh, but when he got angry he'd smile a little smile, the kind that simply raises the corner of the mouth a quarter of an inch. For those who knew, it was an eerie signal. Those who didn't found themselves in big trouble, for Ted was very quick. He loved to carry on what we would come to call philosophical discussions: What is courage? Does God exist? He also loved words, enjoyed picking up big ones like *salubrious* and *equivocal* and using them in our conversations—laughing at himself as the word hit a chuckhole rolling off his tongue. Ted didn't do all that well in school—baseball and parties and testing the courage he'd speculated about took up his time. His textbooks were *Argosy* and *Field and Stream*, whatever newspapers he'd find on the bus stop—from the *Daily Worker* to pornography—conversations with uncles or hobos or businessmen he'd meet in a coffee shop, *The Old Man and the Sea*. With hindsight, I can see that Ted was developing into one of those rough-hewn intellectuals whose sources are a mix of the learned and the apocryphal, whose discussions are both assured and sad.

And then there was Ken Harvey. Ken was good-looking in a puffy way and had a full and oily ducktail and was a car enthusiast . . . a hodad. One day in religion class, he said the sentence that turned out to be one of the most memorable of the hundreds of thousands I heard in those Voc. Ed. years. We were talking about the parable of the talents, about achievement, working hard, doing the best you can do, blah-blah-blah, when the teacher called on the restive Ken Harvey for an opinion. Ken thought about it, but just for a second, and said (with studied, minimal affect), "I just wanna be average." That woke me up. Average?! Who wants to be average? Then the athletes chimed in with the clichés that make you want to laryngectomize them, and the exchange became a platitudinous melee. At the time, I thought Ken's assertion was stupid, and I wrote him off. But his sentence has stayed with me all these years, and I think I am finally coming to understand it.

Ken Harvey was gasping for air. School can be a tremendously disorienting place. No matter how bad the school, you're going to encounter notions that don't fit with the assumptions and beliefs that you grew up with—maybe you'll hear these dissonant notions from teachers, maybe from the other students, and maybe you'll read them. You'll also be thrown in with all kinds of kids from all kinds of backgrounds, and that can be unsettling—this is especially true in places of rich ethnic and linguistic mix, like the L.A. basin. You'll see a handful of students far excel you in courses that sound exotic and that are only in the curriculum of the elite: French, physics, trigonometry. And all this is happening while you're trying to shape an identity; your body is changing, and your emotions are running wild. If you're a working-class kid in the vocational track, the options you'll have to deal with this will be constrained in certain ways: You're defined by your school as "'slow"; you're placed in a curriculum that isn't designed to liberate you but to occupy you, or, if you're lucky, train you, though the training is for work the society does not esteem; other students are picking up the cues from your school and your curriculum and interacting with you in particular ways. If you're a kid like Ted Richard, you turn your back on all this and let your mind roam where it may. But youngsters like Ted are rare. What Ken and so many others do is protect themselves from such suffocating madness by taking on with a vengeance the identity implied in the vocational track. Reject the confusion and frustration by openly defining yourself as the Common Joe. Champion the average. Rely on your own good sense. Fuck this bullshit. Bullshit, of course, is everything you—and the others—fear is beyond you: books, essays, tests, academic scrambling, complexity, scientific reasoning, philosophical inquiry.

The tragedy is that you have to twist the knife in your own gray matter to make this defense work. You'll have to shut down, have to reject intellectual stimuli or diffuse them with sarcasm, have to cultivate stupidity, have to convert boredom from a malady into a way of confronting the world. Keep your vocabulary simple, act stoned when you're not or act more stoned than you are, flaunt ignorance, materialize your dreams. It is a powerful and effective defense—it neutralizes the insult and the frustration of being a vocational kid and, when perfected, it drives teachers up the wall, a delightful secondary effect. But like all strong magic, it exacts a price.

My own deliverance from the Voc. Ed. world began with sophomore biology. Every student, college prep to vocational, had to take biology, and unlike the other courses, the same person taught all sections. When teaching the vocational group, Brother Clint probably slowed down a bit or omitted a little of the fundamental biochemistry, but he used the same book and more or less the same syllabus across the board. If one class got tough, he could get tougher. He was young and powerful and very handsome, and looks and physical strength were high currency. No one gave him any trouble.

I was pretty bad at the dissecting table, but the lectures and the textbook were interesting: plastic overlays that, with each turned page, peeled away skin, then veins and muscle, then organs, down to the very bones that Brother Clint, pointer in hand, would tap out on our hanging skeleton. Dave Snyder was in big trouble, for the study of life—versus the living of it—was sticking in his craw. We worked out a code for our multiple-choice exams. He'd poke me in the back: once for the answer under A, twice for B, and so on; and when he'd hit the right one, I'd look up to the ceiling as though I were lost in thought. Poke: cytoplasm. Poke, poke: methane. Poke, poke, poke: William Harvey. Poke, poke, poke, poke: islets of Langerhans. This didn't work out perfectly, but Dave passed the course, and I mastered the dreamy look of a guy on a record jacket. And something else happened. Brother Clint puzzled over this Voc. Ed. kid who was racking up 98s and 99s on his tests. He checked the school's records and discovered the error. He recommended that I begin my junior year in the College Prep program. According to all I've read since, such a shift, as one report put it, is virtually impossible. Kids at that level rarely cross tracks. The telling thing is how chancy both my placement into and exit from Voc. Ed. was; neither I nor my parents had anything to do with it. I lived in one world during spring semester, and when I came back to school in the fall, I was living in another.

Switching to College Prep was a mixed blessing. I was an erratic student. I was undisciplined. And I hadn't caught onto the rules of the game: Why work hard in a class that didn't grab my fancy? I was also hopelessly behind in math. Chemistry was hard; toying with my chemistry set years before hadn't prepared me for the chemist's equations. Fortunately, the priest who taught both chemistry and second-year algebra was also the school's athletic director. Membership on the track team covered me; I knew I wouldn't get lower than a C. U.S. history was taught pretty well, and I did okay. But civics was taken over by a football coach who had trouble reading the textbook aloud—and reading aloud was the centerpiece of his pedagogy. College Prep at Mercy was certainly an improvement over the vocational program—at least it carried some status—but the social science curriculum was weak, and the mathematics and physical sciences were simply beyond me. I had a miserable quantitative background and ended up copying some assignments and finessing the rest as best I could. Let me try to explain how it feels to see again and again material you should once have learned but didn't.

You are given a problem. It requires you to simplify algebraic fractions or to multiply expressions containing square roots. You know this is pretty basic material because you've seen it for years. Once a teacher took some time with you, and you learned how to carry out these operations. Simple versions, anyway. But that was a year or two or more in the past, and these are more complex versions, and now you're not sure. And this, you keep telling yourself, is ninth- or even eighth-grade stuff.

Next it's a word problem. This is also old hat. The basic elements are as familiar as story characters: trains speeding so many miles per hour or shadows of buildings angling so many degrees. Maybe you know enough, have sat through enough explanations, to be able to begin setting up the problem: "If one train is going this fast . . ." or "This shadow is really one line of a triangle. . . ." Then: "Let's see . . ." "How did Jones do this?" "Hmmmm." "No." "No, that won't work." Your attention wavers. You wonder about other things: a football game, a dance, that cute new checker at the market. You try to focus on the problem again. You scribble on paper for a while, but the tension wins out and your attention flits elsewhere. You crumple the paper and begin daydreaming to ease the frustration.

The particulars will vary, but in essence this is what a number of students go through, especially those in so-called remedial classes. They open their textbooks and see once again the familiar and impenetrable formulas and diagrams and terms that have stumped them for years. There is no excitement here. *No* excitement. Regardless of what the teacher says, this is not a new challenge. There is, rather, embarrassment and frustration and, not surprisingly, some anger in being reminded once again of longstanding inadequacies. No wonder so many students finally attribute their difficulties to something inborn, organic: "That part of my brain just doesn't work." Given the troubling histories many of these students have, it's miraculous that any of them can lift the shroud of hopelessness sufficiently to make deliverance from these classes possible.

Through this entire period, my father's health was deteriorating with cruel momentum. His arteriosclerosis progressed to the point where a simple nick on his shin wouldn't heal. Eventually it ulcerated and widened. Lou Minton would come by daily to change the dressing. We tried renting an oscillating bed—which we placed in the front room—to force blood through the constricted arteries in my father's legs. The bed hummed through the night, moving in place to ward off the inevitable. The ulcer continued to spread, and the doctors finally had to amputate. My grandfather had lost his leg in a stockyard accident. Now my father too was crippled. His convalescence was slow but steady, and the doctors placed him in the Santa Monica Rehabilitation Center, a sun-bleached building that opened out onto the warm spray of the Pacific. The place gave him some strength and some color and some training in walking with an artificial leg. He did pretty well for a year or so until he slipped and broke his hip. He was confined to a wheelchair after that, and the confinement contributed to the diminishing of his body and spirit.

I am holding a picture of him. He is sitting in his wheelchair and smiling at the camera. The smile appears forced, unsteady, seems to quaver, though it is frozen in silver nitrate. He is in his mid-sixties and looks eighty. Late in my junior year, he had a stroke and never came out of the resulting coma. After that, I would see him only in dreams, and to this day that is how I join him. Sometimes the dreams are sad and grisly and primal: my father lying in a bed soaked with his suppuration, holding me, rocking me. But sometimes the dreams bring him back to me healthy: him talking to me on an empty street, or buying some pictures to decorate our old house, or transformed somehow into someone strong and adept with tools and the physical.

Jack MacFarland couldn't have come into my life at a better time. My father was dead, and I had logged up too many years of scholastic indifference. Mr. MacFarland had a master's degree from Columbia and decided, at twenty-six, to find a little school and teach his heart out. He never took any credentialing courses, couldn't bear to, he said, so he had to find employment in a private system. He ended up at Our Lady of Mercy teaching five sections of senior English. He was a beatnik who was born too late. His teeth were stained, he tucked his sorry tie in between the third and fourth buttons of his shirt, and his pants were chronically wrinkled. At first, we couldn't believe this guy, thought he slept in his car. But within no time, he had us so startled with work that we didn't much worry about where he slept or if he slept at all. We wrote three or four essays a month. We read a book every two to three weeks, starting with the *Iliad* and ending up with Hemingway. He gave us a quiz on the reading every other day. He brought a prep school curriculum to Mercy High.

MacFarland's lectures were crafted, and as he delivered them he would pace the room jiggling a piece of chalk in his cupped hand, using it to scribble on the board the names of all the writers and philosophers and plays and novels he was weaving into his discussion. He asked questions often, raised everything from Zeno's paradox to the repeated last line of Frost's "Stopping by Woods on a Snowy Evening." He slowly and carefully built up our knowledge of Western intellectual history—with facts, with connections, with speculations. We learned about Greek philosophy, about Dante, the Elizabethan world view, the Age of Reason, existentialism. He analyzed poems with us, had us reading sections from John Ciardi's *How Does a Poem Mean?*, making a potentially difficult book accessible with his own explanations. We gave oral reports on poems Ciardi didn't cover. We imitated the styles of Conrad, Hemingway, and *Time* magazine. We wrote and talked, wrote and talked. The man immersed us in language.

Even MacFarland's barbs were literary. If Jim Fitzsimmons, hung over and irritable, tried to smart-ass him, he'd rejoin with a flourish that would spark the indomitable Skip Madison—who'd lost his front teeth in a hapless tackle—to flick his tongue through the gap and opine, "good chop," drawing out the single "o" in stinging indictment. Jack MacFarland, this tobacco-stained intellectual, brandished linguistic weapons of a kind I hadn't encountered before. Here was this *egghead*, for God's sake, keeping some pretty difficult people in line. And from what I heard, Mike Dweetz and Steve Fusco and all the notorious Voc. Ed. crowd settled down as well when MacFarland took the podium. Though a lot of guys groused in the schoolyard, it just seemed that giving trouble to this particular teacher was a silly thing to do. Tomfoolery, not to mention assault, had no place in the world he was trying to create for us, and instinctively everyone knew that. If nothing else, we all recognized MacFarland's considerable intelligence and respected the hours he put into his work. It came to this: The troublemaker would look foolish rather than daring. Even Jim Fitzsimmons was reading *On the Road* and turning his incipient alcoholism to literary ends.

There were some lives that were already beyond Jack MacFarland's ministrations, but mine was not. I started reading again as I hadn't since elementary school. I would go into our gloomy little bedroom or sit at the dinner table while, on the television, Danny McShane was paralyzing Mr. Moto with the atomic drop, and work slowly back through *Heart of Darkness,* trying to catch the words in Conrad's sentences. I certainly was not MacFarland's best student; most of the other guys in College Prep, even my fellow slackers, had better backgrounds than I did. But I worked very hard, for MacFarland had hooked me. He tapped my old interest in reading and creating stories. He gave me a way to feel special by using my mind. And he provided a role model that wasn't shaped on physical prowess alone, and something inside me that I wasn't quite aware of responded to that. Jack MacFarland established a literacy club, to borrow a phrase of Frank Smith's, and invited me—invited all of us—to join.

There's been a good deal of research and speculation suggesting that the acknowledgment of school performance with extrinsic rewards—smiling faces, stars, numbers, grades—diminishes the intrinsic satisfaction children experience by engaging in reading or writing or problem solving. While it's certainly true that we've created an educational system that encourages our best and brightest to become cynical grade collectors and, in general, have developed an obsession with evaluation and assessment, I must tell you that venal though it may have been, I loved getting good grades from MacFarland. I now know how subjective grades can be, but then they came tucked in the back of essays like bits of scientific data, some sort of spectroscopic readout that said, objectively and publicly, that I had made something of value. I suppose I'd been mediocre for too long and enjoyed a public redefinition. And I suppose the workings of my mind, such as they were, had been private for too long. My linguistic play moved into the world; like the intergalactic stories I told years before on Frank's berry-splattered truck bed, these papers with their circled, red B-pluses and A-minuses linked my mind to something outside it. I carried them around like a club emblem.

One day in the December of my senior year, Mr. MacFarland asked me where I was going to go to college. I hadn't thought much about it. Many of the students I teach today spent their last year in high school with a physics text in one hand and the Stanford catalog in the other, but I wasn't even aware of what "entrance requirements" were. My folks would say that they wanted me to go to college and be a doctor, but I don't know how seriously I ever took that; it seemed a sweet thing to say, a bit of supportive family chatter, like telling a gangly daughter she's graceful. The reality of higher education wasn't in my scheme of things: No one in the family had gone to college; only two of my uncles had completed high school. I figured I'd get a night job and go to the local junior college because I knew that Snyder and Company were going there to play ball. But I hadn't even prepared for that. When I finally said, "I don't know," MacFarland looked down at me—I was seated in his office—and said, "'Listen, you can write."

My grades stank. I had A's in biology and a handful of B's in a few English and social science classes. All the rest were C's—or worse. MacFarland said I would do well in his class and laid down the law about doing well in the others. Still, the record for my first three years wouldn't have been acceptable to any four-year school. To nobody's surprise, I was turned down flat by USC and UCLA. But Jack MacFarland was on the case. He had received his bachelor's degree from Loyola University, so he made calls to old professors and talked to somebody in admissions and wrote me a strong letter. Loyola finally accepted me as a probationary student. I would be on trial for the first year, and if I did okay, I would be granted regular status. MacFarland also intervened to get me a loan, for I could never have afforded a private college without it. Four more years of religion classes and four more years of boys at one school, girls at another. But at least I was going to college. Amazing.

In my last semester of high school, I elected a special English course fashioned by Mr. MacFarland, and it was through this elective that there arose at Mercy a fledgling literati. Art Mitz, the editor of the school newspaper and a very smart guy, was the kingpin. He was joined by me and by Mark Dever, a quiet boy who wrote beautifully and who would die before he was forty. MacFarland occasionally invited us to his apartment, and those visits became the high point of our apprenticeship: We'd clamp on our training wheels and drive to his salon.

He lived in a cramped and cluttered place near the airport, tucked away in the kind of building that architectural critic Reyner Banham calls a *dingbat*. Books were all over: stacked, piled, tossed, and crated, underlined and dog eared, well worn and new. Cigarette ashes crusted with coffee in saucers or spilled over the sides of motel ashtrays. The little bedroom had, along two of its walls, bricks and boards loaded with notes, magazines, and oversized books. The kitchen joined the living room, and there was a stack of German newspapers under the sink. I had never seen anything like it: a great flophouse of language furnished by City Lights and Café le Metro. I read every title. I flipped through paperbacks and scanned jackets and memorized names: Gogol, *Finnegan's Wake*, Djuna Barnes, Jackson Pollock, *A Coney Island of the Mind*, F.O. Matthiessen's *American Renaissance*, all sorts of Freud, *Troubled Sleep*, Man Ray, *The Education of Henry Adams*, Richard Wright, *Film as Art*, William Butler Yeats, Marguerite Duras, *Red-burn*, *A Season in Hell*, *Kapital.* On the cover of Alain-Fournier's *The Wanderer* was an Edward Gorey drawing of a young man on a road winding into dark trees. By the hotplate sat a strange Kafka novel called *Amerika*, in which an adolescent hero crosses the Atlantic to find the Nature Theater of Oklahoma. Art and Mark would be talking about a movie or the school newspaper, and I would be consuming my English teacher's library. It was heady stuff. I felt like a Pop Warner athlete on steroids.

Art, Mark, and I would buy stogies and triangulate from MacFarland's apartment to the Cinema, which now shows X-rated films but was then L.A.'s premiere art theater, and then to the musty Cherokee Bookstore in Hollywood to hobnob with beatnik homosexuals—smoking, drinking bourbon and coffee, and trying out awkward phrases we'd gleaned from our mentor's bookshelves. I was happy and precocious and a little scared as well, for Hollywood Boulevard was thick with a kind of decadence that was foreign to the South Side. After the Cherokee, we would head back to the security of MacFarland's apartment, slaphappy with hipness.

Let me be the first to admit that there was a good deal of adolescent passion in this embrace of the avant-garde: self-absorption, sexually charged pedantry, an elevation of the odd and abandoned. Still it was a time during which I absorbed an awful lot of information: long lists of titles, images from expressionist paintings, new wave shibboleths, snippets of philosophy, and names that read like Steve Fusco's misspellings—Goethe, Nietzsche, Kierkegaard. Now this is hardly the stuff of deep understanding. But it was an introduction, a phrase book, a Baedeker to a vocabulary of ideas, and it felt good at the time to know all these words. With hindsight I realize how layered and important that knowledge was.

It enabled me to do things in the world. I could browse bohemian bookstores in far-off, mysterious Hollywood; I could go to the Cinema and see events through the lenses of European directors; and, most of all, I could share an evening, talk that talk, with Jack MacFarland, the man I most admired at the time. Knowledge was becoming a bonding agent. Within a year or two, the persona of the disaffected hipster would prove too cynical, too alienated to last. But for a time it was new and exciting: It provided a critical perspective on society, and it allowed me to act as though I were living beyond the limiting boundaries of South Vermont.

Questions for Discussion

1. Rose describes throughout this essay the debilitating effects on students who are constantly reminded of their deficiencies and errors. What scenes from Rose's essay are most revealing to you in presenting this belief? What do those scenes of schooling illustrate and how do they support Rose's implied claims?

2. Why is Ken Harvey's desire to just be "average" so troubling to Rose? Of what problems in the U.S. educational system is it emblematic?

3. Rose's parents are genuinely supportive of education, earnestly desiring his academic and economic success, yet they are also ineffectual in many ways. What economic, social, or political circumstances contribute to their inability to effect change in Rose's educational experiences?

Explorations

1. Many states (e.g., Michigan, Ohio, Texas) have passed or are considering passage of legislation that will redistribute state and local taxes more equitably across school districts. Such a redistribution will increase funding in poorer districts and, legislators and educators claim, lead to great access and success among students in the poorer districts. What effect do you believe such legislative responses will have on students' educational opportunities? What problems will likely go unaddressed?

2. Rose describes life in South L.A. as "short and brutish or sad and aimless or long and quiet," that there was little in the way of enthusiasm for life. This communal social attitude, he implies, is far different from that required of people who succeed academically and socially. In what ways was life in neighborhoods you grew up in different from or similar to Rose's? What effect do you believe the relative advantages and disadvantages of your growing up years have on your experiences in school?

3. In elementary school, Rose found solace and excitement in his chemistry set and books on astronomy. He began drawing and was soon entertaining his friends with stories. What toys, games, or books from childhood stand out for you? What was the significance of those items in your growing up?

Formal Writing Assignments

1. Describe and evaluate the rhetorical techniques in Rose's essay. It might be helpful to begin by brainstorming about the general organizational structure. How many parts does the selection seem to have? What is the purpose or point of each part? Do the parts work cumulatively? In what ways? You may also wish to address the various methods of development that Rose uses in the essay: prose narration, argumentation, persuasion. Which does he use most often? When do the other modes enter into the discourse? What kinds of persuasive appeals does Rose use? Which appeals are more or less frequent in the narrative sections of the selection? Why do you think that's the case? Because you're to describe and evaluate, be sure to use your observations about organizational and rhetorical techniques as evidence for your evaluative assessment of the essay.

2. Investigate the placement practices at your college or former high. High schools often track higher achieving students into "college prep" courses and all other students into vocational or standard tracks. Universities reward high achievers through honors programs and will most often have placement policies in math and English. What are the differences between curricula in the various programs? What are the demographics in each track? Is there a higher percentage of students of color and working-class students in the high school vocational or standard tracks? Are students from affluent households more likely to be placed in the college prep courses? What advantages do students in honors programs have? How many additional hours do students in a remedial track have to take in English or math to satisfy general education or graduation requirements? Much of the information you seek may be available on-line at a school's website or through the counselor's office or office of admissions. Once you've located the information, write an informative position essay in which you explain to parents and students the economic and academic significance of placement into remedial or vocational programs.

The Classroom and the Wider Culture: Identity as a Key to Learning English Composition

Fan Shen

Before moving to the United States to pursue graduate work in English Studies, Fan Shen completed a BA in literature and linguistics at Lanzhou University in China. Fan Shen experienced the Chinese Cultural Revolution firsthand, working as a farm laborer after spending seven years working in an aircraft factory. The essay you are about to read, "The Classroom and the Wider Culture: Identity as a Key to Learning English Composition," was written while Fan Shen was a Ph.D. student at Marquette University in Milwaukee. This piece was first published in a journal called College Composition and Communication (1989), one of the most important and influential journals available for writing teachers in the United States.

As you read, think about your own experiences encountering "academic discourse" for the first time at the university level. How did your background (cultural, racial, gender, regional, etc.) affect your way of learning this new form of writing? Likewise, consider how Fan Shen's experience might complicate the argument made by Holland. Are there ever times when a kind of imitation is necessary for a student's survival? Can a student use critical thinking skills and imitate the forms s/he encounters at the same time?

Writing Before Reading

1. Take a few minutes and freewrite/reflect upon a time in your own academic life when you were asked to write in a way that felt somehow "unnatural" to you. What was that experience like? What did you learn from it?

2. Have you ever been in a situation where your definition of good writing did not match the teacher's or the textbooks? If so, describe that experience. If not, why do you suppose you've often shared such definitions with your teachers and textbooks?

3. Describe what you believe counts as the "acceptable" or "expected" form of an essay in your current composition course. How did you come to understand this? How are the conventions of writing such essays communicated to you explicitly in the course? Implicitly?

The Classroom and the Wider Culture: Identity as a Key to Learning English Composition

One day in June 1975, when I walked into the aircraft factory where I was working as an electrician, I saw many large-letter posters on the walls and many people parading around the workshops shouting slogans like "Down with the word 'I'!" and "Trust in masses and the Party!" I then remembered that a new political campaign called "Against Individualism" was scheduled to begin that day. Ten years later, I got back my first English composition paper at the University of Nebraska–Lincoln. The professor's first comments were: "Why did you always use 'we' instead of 'I'?" and "Your paper would be stronger if you eliminated some sentences in the passive voice." The clashes between my Chinese background and the requirements of English composition had begun. At the center of this mental struggle, which has lasted several years and is still not completely over, is the prolonged, uphill battle to recapture "myself."

In this paper I will try to describe and explore this experience of reconciling my Chinese identity with an English identity dictated by the rules of English composition. I want to show how my cultural background shaped—and shapes—my approaches to my writing in English and how writing in English redefined—and redefines—my *ideological* and *logical* identities. By "ideological identity" I mean the system of values that I acquired (consciously and unconsciously) from my social and cultural background. And by "logical identity" I mean the natural (or Oriental) way I organize and express my thoughts in writing. Both had to be modified or redefined in learning English composition. Becoming aware of the process of redefinition of these different identities is a mode of learning that has helped me in my efforts to write in English, and, I hope, will be of help to teachers of English composition in this country. In presenting my case for this view, I will use examples from both my composition courses and literature courses, for I believe that writing papers for both kinds of courses contributed to the development of my "English identity." Although what I will describe is based on personal experience, many Chinese students whom I talked to said that they had had the same or similar experiences in their initial stages of learning to write in English.

IDENTITY OF THE SELF: IDEOLOGICAL AND CULTURAL

Starting with the first English paper I wrote, I found that learning to compose in English is not an isolated classroom activity, but a social and cultural experience. The rules of English composition encapsulate values that are absent in, or sometimes contradictory to, the values of other societies (in my case, China). Therefore, learning the rules of English composition is, to a certain extent, learning the values of Anglo-American society. In writing classes in the United States I found that I had to reprogram my mind, to redefine some of the basic concepts and values that I had about myself, about society, and about the universe, values that had been imprinted and reinforced in my mind by my cultural background, and that had been part of me all my life.

Rule number one in English composition is: Be yourself. (More than one composition instructor has told me, "Just write what *you* think.") The values behind this rule, it seems to me, are based on the principle of protecting and promoting individuality (and private property) in this country. The instruction was probably crystal clear to students raised on these values, but, as a guideline of composition, it was not very clear or useful to me when I first heard it. First of all, the image or meaning that I attached to the word "I" or "myself" was, as I found out, different from that of my English teacher. In China, "I" is always subordinated to "We"—be it the working class, the Party, the country, or some other collective body. Both political pressure and literary tradition require that "I" be somewhat hidden or buried in writings and speeches; presenting the "self" too obviously would give people the impression of being disrespectful of the Communist Party in political writings and boastful in scholarly writings. The word "I" has often been identified with another "bad" word, "individualism," which has become a synonym for selfishness in China. For a long time the words "self" and "individualism" have had negative connotations in my mind, and the negative force of the words naturally extended to the field of literary studies. As a result, even if I had brilliant ideas, the "I" in my papers always had to show some modesty by not competing with or trying to stand above the names of ancient and modern authoritative figures. Appealing to Mao or other Marxist authorities became the required way (as well as the most "forceful" or "persuasive" way) to prove one's point in written discourse. I remember that in China I had even committed what I can call "reversed plagiarism"—here, I suppose it would be called "forgery"—when I was in middle school: willfully attributing some of my thoughts to "experts" when I needed some arguments but could not find a suitable quotation from a literary or political "giant."

Now, in America, I had to learn to accept the words "I" and "Self" as something glorious (as Whitman did), or at least something not to be ashamed of or embarrassed about. It was the first and probably biggest step I took into English composition and critical writing. Acting upon my professor's suggestion, I intentionally tried to show my "individuality" and to "glorify" "I" in my papers by using as many "I's" as possible—"I think," "I believe," "I see"—and deliberately cut out quotations from authorities. It was rather painful to hand in such "pompous" (I mean immodest) papers to my instructors. But to an extent it worked. After a while I became more comfortable with only "the shadow of myself." I felt more at ease to put down *my* thoughts without looking over my shoulder to worry about the attitudes of my teachers or the reactions of the Party secretaries, and to speak out as "bluntly" and "immodestly" as my American instructors demanded.

But writing many "I's" was only the beginning of the process of redefining myself. Speaking of redefining myself is, in an important sense, speaking of redefining the word "I." By such a redefinition I mean not only the change in how I envisioned myself, but also the change in how *I* perceived the world. The old "I" used to embody only one set of values, but now it had to embody multiple sets of values. To be truly "myself," which I knew was a key to my success in learning English composition, meant *not to be my Chinese* self at all. That is to say, when I write in English I have to wrestle with and abandon (at least temporarily) the whole system of ideology which previously defined me in myself. I had to forget Marxist doctrines (even though I do not see myself as a Marxist by choice) and the Party lines imprinted in my mind and familiarize myself with a system of capitalist/bourgeois values. I had to put aside an ideology of collectivism and adopt the values of individualism. In composition as well as in literature classes, I had to make a fundamental adjustment: if I used to examine society and literary materials through the microscopes of Marxist dialectical materialism and historical materialism, I now had to learn to look through the microscopes the other way around, i.e., to learn to look at and understand the world from the point of view of "idealism." (I must add here that there are American professors who use a Marxist approach in their teaching.)

The word "idealism," which affects my view of both myself and the universe, is loaded with social connotations, and can serve as a good example of how redefining a key word can be a pivotal part of redefining my ideological identity as a whole.

To me, idealism is the philosophical foundation of the dictum of English composition: "Be yourself." In order to write good English, I knew that I had to be myself, which actually meant not to be my Chinese self. It meant that I had to create an English self and be *that* self. And to be that English self, I felt, I had to understand and accept idealism the way a Westerner does. That is to say, I had to accept the way a Westerner sees himself in relation to the universe and society. On the one hand, I knew a lot about idealism. But on the other hand, I knew nothing about it. I mean I knew a lot about idealism through the propaganda and objections of its opponent, Marxism, but I knew little about it from its own point of view. When I thought of the word "materialism"—which is a major part of Marxism and in China has repeatedly been "shown" to be the absolute truth—there were always positive connotations, and words like "right," "true," etc., flashed in my mind. On the other hand, the word "idealism" always came to me with the dark connotations that surround words like "absurd," "illogical," "wrong," etc. In China "idealism" is depicted as a ferocious and ridiculous enemy of Marxist philosophy. Idealism, as the simplified definition imprinted in my mind had it, is the view that the material world does not exist; that all that exists is the mind and its ideas. It is just the opposite of Marxist dialectical materialism which sees the mind as a product of the material world. It is not too difficult to see that idealism, with its idea that mind is of primary importance, provides a philosophical foundation for the Western emphasis on the value of individual human minds, and hence individual human beings. Therefore, my final acceptance of myself as of primary importance—an importance that overshadowed that of authority figures in English composition—was, I decided, dependent on an acceptance of idealism.

My struggle with idealism came mainly from my efforts to understand and to write about works such as Coleridge's *Biographia Literaria* and Emerson's "Over-Soul." For a long time I was frustrated and puzzled by the idealism expressed by Coleridge and Emerson—given their ideas, such as "I think, therefore I am" (Coleridge obviously borrowed from Descartes) and "the transparent eyeball" (Emerson's view of himself)—because in my mind, drenched as it was in dialectical materialism, there was always a little voice whispering in my ear "You are, therefore you think." I could not see how human consciousness, which is not material, could create apples and trees. My intellectual conscience refused to let me believe that the human mind is the primary world and the material world secondary. Finally, I had to imagine that I was looking at a world with my head upside down. When I imagined that I was in a new body (born with the head upside down) it was easier to forget biases imprinted in my subconsciousness about idealism, the mind, and my former self. Starting from scratch, the new inverted self—which I called my "English Self" and into which I have transformed myself—could understand and *accept*, with ease, idealism as "the truth" and "himself" (i.e., my English Self) as the "creator" of the world.

Here is how I created my new "English Self." I played a "game" similar to ones played by mental therapists. First I made a list of (simplified) features about writing associated with my old identity (the Chinese Self), both ideological and logical, and then beside the first list I added a column of features about writing associated with my new identity (the English Self). After that I pictured myself getting out of my old identity, the timid, humble, modest Chinese "I," and creeping into my new identity (often in the form of a new skin or a mask), the confident, assertive, and aggressive English "I." The new "Self" helped me to remember and accept the different rules of Chinese and English composition and the values that underpin these rules. In a sense, creating an English Self is a way of reconciling my old cultural values with the new values required by English writing, without losing the former.

An interesting structural but not material parallel to my experiences in this regard has been well described by Min-zhan Lu in her important article, "From Silence to Words: Writing as Struggle" (*College English* 49 [April 1987]: 437–48). Min-zhan Lu talks about struggles between two selves, an open self and a secret self, and between two discourses, a mainstream Marxist discourse and a bourgeois discourse her parents wanted her to learn. But her struggle was different from mine. Her Chinese self was severely constrained and suppressed by mainstream cultural discourse, but never interfused with it. Her experiences, then, were not representative of those of the majority of the younger generation who, like me, were brought up on only one discourse. I came to English composition as a Chinese person, in the fullest sense of the term, with a Chinese identity already fully formed.

Identity of the Mind: Illogical and Alogical

In learning to write in English, besides wrestling with a different ideological system, I found that I had to wrestle with a logical system very different from the blueprint of logic at the back of my mind. By "logical system" I mean two things: the Chinese way of thinking I used to approach my theme or topic in written discourse, and the Chinese critical/logical way to develop a theme or topic. By English rules, the first is illogical, for it is the opposite of the English way of approaching a topic; the second is alogical (non-logical), for it mainly uses mental pictures instead of words as a critical vehicle.

The Illogical Pattern. In English composition, an essential rule for the logical organization of a piece of writing is the use of a "topic sentence." In Chinese composition, "from surface to core" is an essential rule, a rule which means that one ought to reach a topic gradually and "systematically" instead of "abruptly."

The concept of a topic sentence, it seems to me, is symbolic of the values of a busy people in an industrialized society, rushing to get things done, hoping to attract and satisfy the busy reader very quickly. Thinking back, I realized that I did not fully understand the virtue of the concept until my life began to rush at the speed of everyone else's in this country. Chinese composition, on the other hand, seems to embody the values of a leisurely paced rural society whose inhabitants have the time to chew and taste a topic slowly. In Chinese composition, an introduction explaining how and why one chooses this topic is not only acceptable, but often regarded as necessary. It arouses the reader's interest in the topic little by little (and this is seen as a virtue of composition) and gives him/her a sense of refinement. The famous Robert B. Kaplan "noodles" contrasting a spiral Oriental thought process with a straight-line Western approach ("Cultural Thought Patterns in Inter-Cultural Education," *Readings on English as a Second Language,* Ed. Kenneth Croft, 2nd ed., Winthrop, 1980, 403–10) may be too simplistic to capture the preferred pattern of writing in English, but I think they still express some truth about Oriental writing. A Chinese writer often clears the surrounding bushes before attacking the real target. This bush clearing pattern in Chinese writing goes back two thousand years to Kong Fuzi (Confucius). Before doing anything, Kong says in his *Luen Yu (Analects)*, one first needs to call things by their proper names (expressed by his phrase "Zheng Ming"正名). In other words, before touching one's main thesis, one should first state the "conditions" of composition: how, why, and when the piece is being composed. All of this will serve as a proper foundation on which to build the "house" of the piece. In the two thousand years after Kong, this principle of composition was gradually formalized (especially through the formal essays required by imperial examinations) and became known as "Ba Gu," or the eight-legged essay. The logic of Chinese composition, exemplified by the eight-legged essay, is like the peeling of an onion: layer after layer is removed until the reader finally arrives at the central point, the core.

Ba Gu still influences modern Chinese writing. Carolyn Matalene has an excellent discussion of this logical (or illogical) structure and its influence on her Chinese students' efforts to write in English ("Contrastive Rhetoric: An American Writing Teacher in China," *College English* 47 [November 1985]: 789–808). A Chinese textbook for composition lists six essential steps (factors) for writing a narrative essay, steps to be taken in this order: time, place, character, event, cause, and consequence *(Yuwen Jichu Zhishi Liushi Jiang [Sixty Lessons on the Basics of the Chinese Language],* Ed. Beijing Research Institute of Education, Beijing Publishing House, 1981,525–609). Most Chinese students (including me) are taught to follow this sequence in composition.

The straightforward approach to composition in English seemed to me, at first, illogical. One could not jump to the topic. One had to walk step by step to reach the topic. In several of my early papers I found that the Chinese approach—the bush-clearing approach—persisted, and I had considerable difficulty writing (and in fact understanding) topic sentences. In what I deemed to be topic sentences, I grudgingly gave out themes. Today, those papers look to me like Chinese papers with forced or false English openings. For example, in a narrative paper on a trip to New York, I wrote the forced/false topic sentence, "A trip to New York in winter is boring." In the next few paragraphs, I talked about the weather, the people who went with me, and so on, before I talked about what I learned from the trip. My real thesis was that one could always learn something even on a boring trip.

The Alogical Pattern. In learning English composition, I found that there was yet another cultural blueprint affecting my logical thinking. I found from my early papers that very often I was unconsciously under the influence of a Chinese critical approach called the creation of "yijing," which is totally non-Western. The direct translation of the word "yijing" is: yi, "mind or consciousness," and jing, "environment." An ancient approach which has existed in China for many centuries and is still the subject of much discussion, yijing is a complicated concept that defies a universal definition. But most critics in China nowadays seem to agree on one point, that yijing is the critical approach that separates Chinese literature and criticism from Western literature and criticism. Roughly speaking, yijing is the process of creating a pictorial environment while reading a piece of literature. Many critics in China believe that yijing is a creative process of inducing oneself, while reading a piece of literature or looking at a piece of art, to create mental pictures, in order to reach a unity of nature, the author, and the reader. Therefore, it is by its very nature both creative and critical. According to the theory, this nonverbal, pictorial process leads directly to a higher ground of beauty and morality. Almost all critics in China agree that yijing is not a process of logical thinking—it is not a process of moving from the premises of an argument to its conclusion, which is the foundation of Western criticism. According to yijing, the process of criticizing a piece of art or literary work has to involve the process of creation on the reader's part. In yijing, verbal thoughts and pictorial thoughts are one. Thinking is conducted largely in pictures and then "transcribed" into words (Ezra Pound once tried to capture the creative aspect of yijing in poems such as "In a Station of the Metro." He also tried to capture the critical aspect of it in his theory of imagism and vorticism, even though he did not know the term "yijing.") One characteristic of the yijing approach to criticism, therefore, is that it often includes a description of the created mental pictures on the part of the reader/critic and his/her mental attempt to bridge (unite) the literary work, the pictures, with ultimate beauty and peace.

In looking back at my critical papers for various classes, I discovered that I unconsciously used the approach of yijing, especially in some of my earlier papers when I seemed not yet to have been in the grip of Western logical critical approaches. I wrote, for instance, an essay entitled "Wordsworth's Sound and Imagination: The Snowdon Episode." In the major part of the essay I described the pictures that flashed in my mind while I was reading passages in Wordsworth's long poem, *The Prelude*.

I saw three climbers (myself among them) winding up the mountain in silence "at the dead of night," absorbed in their "private thoughts." The sky was full of blocks of clouds of different colors, freely changing their shapes, like oily pigments disturbed in a bucket of water. All of a sudden, the moonlight broke the darkness "like a flash," lighting up the mountain tops. Under the "naked moon," the band saw a vast sea of mist and vapor, a silent ocean. Then the silence was abruptly broken, and we heard the "roaring of waters, torrents, streams/ Innumerable, roaring with one voice" from a "blue chasm," a fracture in the vapor of the sea. It was a joyful revelation of divine truth to the human mind: the bright, "naked" moon sheds the light of "higher reasons" and "spiritual love" upon us; the vast ocean of mist looked like a thin curtain through which we vaguely saw the infinity of nature beyond; and the sounds of roaring waters coming out of the chasm of vapor cast us into the boundless spring of imagination from the depth of the human heart. Evoked by the divine light from above, the human spring of imagination is joined by the natural spring and becomes a sustaining source of energy, feeding "upon infinity" while transcending infinity at the same time. . . .

Here I was describing my own experience more than Wordsworth's. The picture described by the poet is taken over and developed by the reader. The imagination of the author and the imagination of the reader are thus joined together. There was no "because" or "therefore" in the paper. There was little *logic*. And I thought it was (and it is) criticism. This seems to me a typical (but simplified) example of the yijing approach. (Incidentally, the instructor, a kind professor, found the paper interesting, though a bit "strange.")

In another paper of mine, "The Note of Life: Williams's 'The Orchestra,'" I found myself describing my experiences of pictures of nature while reading William Carlos Williams's poem "The Orchestra." I "painted" these fleeting pictures and described the feelings that seemed to lead me to an understanding of a harmony, a "common tone," between man and nature. A paragraph from that paper reads:

The poem first struck me as a musical fairy tale. With rich musical sounds in my ear, I seemed to be walking in a solitary, dense forest on a spring morning. No sound from human society could be heard. I was now sitting under a giant pine tree, ready to hear the grand concert of Nature. With the sun slowly rising from the east, the cello (the creeping creek) and the clarinet (the rustling pine trees) started with a slow overture. Enthusiastically the violinists (the twittering birds) and the French horn (the mumbling cow) "interpose[d] their voices," and the bass (bears) got in at the wrong time. The orchestra did not stop, they continued to play. The musicians of Nature do not always play in harmony. "Together, unattuned," they have to seek "a common tone" as they play along. The symphony of Nature is like the symphony of human life: both consist of random notes seeking a "common tone."

For the symphony of life
Love is that common tone
   shall raise his fiery head
   and Sound his note.

Again, the logical pattern of this paper, the "pictorial criticism," is illogical to Western minds but "logical" to those acquainted with yijing. (Perhaps I should not even use the words "logical" and "think" because they are so conceptually tied up with "words" and with culturally based conceptions, and therefore very misleading if not useless in a discussion of yijing. Maybe I should simply say that yijing is neither illogical nor logical, but alogical.)

I am not saying that such a pattern of "alogical" thinking is wrong—in fact some English instructors find it interesting and acceptable—but it is very non-Western. Since I was in this country to learn the English language and English literature, I had to abandon Chinese "pictorial logic," and to learn Western "verbal logic."

If I had to Start Again

The change is profound: through my understanding of new meanings of words like "individualism," "idealism," and "I," I began to accept the underlying concepts and values of American writing, and by learning to use "topic sentences" I began to accept a new logic. Thus, when I write papers in English, I am able to obey all the general rules of English composition. In doing this I feel that I am writing through, with, and because of a new identity. I welcome the change, for it has added a new dimension to me and to my view of the world. I am not saying that I have entirely lost my Chinese identity. In fact I feel that I will never lose it. Any time I write in Chinese, I resume my old identity, and obey the rules of Chinese composition such as "Make the 'I' modest," and "Beat around the bush before attacking the central topic." It is necessary for me to have such a Chinese identity in order to write authentic Chinese. (I have seen people who, after learning to write in English, use English logic and sentence patterning to write Chinese. They produce very awkward Chinese texts.) But when I write in English, I imagine myself slipping into a new "skin," and I let the "I" behave much more aggressively and knock the topic right on the head. Being conscious of these different identities has helped me to reconcile different systems of values and logic, and has played a pivotal role in my learning to compose in English.

Looking back, I realize that the process of learning to write in English is in fact a process of creating and defining a new identity and balancing it with the old identity. The process of learning English composition would have been easier if I had realized this earlier and consciously sought to compare the two different identities required by the two writing systems from two different cultures. It is fine and perhaps even necessary for American composition teachers to teach about topic sentences, paragraphs, the use of punctuation, documentation, and so on, but can anyone design exercises sensitive to the ideological and logical differences that students like me experience—and design them so they can be introduced at an early stage of an English composition class? As I pointed out earlier, the traditional advice "just be yourself" is not clear and helpful to students from Korea, China, Vietnam, or India. From "Be yourself" we are likely to hear either "Forget your cultural habit of writing" or "Write as you would write in your own language." But neither of the two is what the instructor meant or what we want to do. It would be helpful if he or she pointed out the different cultural/ideological connotations of the word "I," the connotations that exist in a group-centered culture and an individual-centered culture. To sharpen the contrast, it might be useful to design papers on topics like "The Individual vs. The Group: China vs. America" or "Different 'I's' in Different Cultures."

Carolyn Matalene mentioned in her article (789) an incident concerning American businessmen who presented their Chinese hosts with gifts of cheddar cheese, not knowing that the Chinese generally do not like cheese. Liking cheddar cheese may not be essential to writing English prose, but being truly accustomed to the social norms that stand behind ideas such as the English "I" and the logical pattern of English composition—call it "compositional cheddar cheese"—is essential to writing in English. Matalene does not provide an "elixir" to help her Chinese students like English "compositional cheese," but rather recommends, as do I, that composition teachers not be afraid to give foreign students English "cheese," but to make sure to hand it out slowly, sympathetically, and fully realizing that it tastes very peculiar in the mouths of those used to a very different cuisine.

Questions for Discussion

1. Revisit your response to the first Writing Before Reading question above. Now that you've read Shen's essay, do you see your own "unnatural" writing situation as different from or similar to Shen's experience? How so?

2. How does Fan Shen see the political climates of both China and the United States impacting the forms of discourse that are privileged in those two countries? In other words, what does Shen say about the relationship between a country's politics and the written forms students are expected to produce within that country?

3. Working in small groups, break Fan Shen's essay down into smaller "chunks" and summarize his argument within each of those chunks. You may want to use the essay's subheadings to help you divide the essay. Then, draft a collaboratively authored summary of that chunk and post it to your class listserv or web-based discussion site. Read the other groups' summaries. How does this new form of Shen's essay compare with the original form in Writing Lives? What were you able to learn from these summaries? What couldn't you learn from them?

Explorations

1. Shen writes, "Looking back, I realize that the process of learning to write in English is in fact a process of creating and defining a new identity and balancing it with the old identity." Use this exploration as a chance to respond to that statement and apply it to your own experiences as a student adapting to this college writing course. How have you experienced a process of identity formation or reformation as a college writer? What aspects of your pre-college self have you preserved? What aspects have you de-emphasized?

2. Shen uses a variety of complex terms in his essay, including "ideological identity," "logical identity," "individuality," "idealism," etc. Choose one or two of these terms and trace them in Shen's essay in order to define them for yourself. What do the terms mean to you? To Shen? How do the terms function in the essay? How do they/don't they help you understand Shen's argument?

3. Using Shen's terms/theories about the conventions of good writing in United States classrooms, analyze another selection in the Academic Literacies unit. How does this piece "measure up" to Shen's understanding of such conventions? How does the piece deviate from those conventions?

Formal Writing Assignments

1. Think of a time in your own educational history when your gender, culture, race, geographical region, age, class, or other aspect of your identity has somehow come into conflict with a particular classroom task or goal. Draft an essay in which you narrate the story of that conflict and reflect upon how you resolved or responded to it. Work to really acknowledge the complexities of the situation, to help your audience—who may not share this aspect of your identity with you—understand the situation and its effect on you.

2. Draft an essay in which you review Fan Shen's "The Classroom and the Wider Culture: Identity as a Key to Learning English Composition." Your goal is to establish criteria that you will use to evaluate the essay, explain those criteria, and then review the piece accordingly. You may want to consider your audience to be students who will soon read the essay OR teachers who must decide whether or not to teach the essay in their composition classes.

On the Uses of a Liberal Education II: As a Weapon in the Hands of the Restless Poor

Earl Shorris

Earl Shorris was born in 1936 in Chicago, IL and attended the University of Chicago. He has worked in many fields, but always as a writer. Shorris has written novels, full-length non-fiction works, and numerous articles for journals and magazines. He has been employed as a journalist and advertiser. His most recent book, *New American Blues: The Private Life of the Poor*, develops in greater detail the ideas behind the following essay. To write it, Shorris returned to the neighborhood in Chicago where he was born and lived more than fifty years earlier. In the book, he studies the changes the decades have brought and documents the lives of the extremely poor residents of the neighborhood.

Writing Before Reading

1. You may have taken a humanities course, such as philosophy, history, or literature, in which the course material seemed removed or distant from your experiences and interests. Have you ever discovered, months or even years after taking the course, a real-life application for something you learned in that course?

2. Since 1964, the United States has waged a "war on poverty," which has been deemed by many to be a failure. What are some of the reasons you believe make poverty so prevalent in our society, the richest in the world?

3. Why do you think universities often insist that students take elective courses outside their majors, particularly in the humanities?

On the Uses of a Liberal Education II: As a Weapon in the Hands of the Restless Poor

Next month I will publish a book about poverty in America, but not the book I intended. The world took me by surprise—not once, but again and again. The poor themselves led me in directions I could not have imagined, especially the one that came out of a conversation in a maximum-security prison for women that is set, incongruously, in a lush Westchester suburb fifty miles north of New York City.

I had been working on the book for about three years when I went to the Bedford Hills Correctional Facility for the first time. The staff and inmates had developed a program to deal with family violence, and I wanted to see how their ideas fit with what I had learned about poverty.

Numerous forces—hunger, isolation, illness, landlords, police, abuse, neighbors, drugs, criminals, and racism, among many others—exert themselves on the poor at all times and enclose them, making up a "surround of force" from which, it seems, they cannot escape. I had come to understand that this was what kept the poor from being political and that the absence of politics in their lives was what kept them poor. I don't mean "political" in the sense of voting in an election but in the way Thucydides used the word: to mean activity with other people at every level, from the family to the neighborhood to the broader community to the city-state.

By the time I got to Bedford Hills, I had listened to more than six hundred people, some of them over the course of two or three years. Although my method is that of the *bricoleur*, the tinkerer who assembles a thesis of the bric-a-brac he finds in the world, I did not think there would be any more surprises. But I had not counted on what Viniece Walker was to say.

It is considered bad form in prison to speak of a person's crime, and I will follow that precise etiquette here. I can tell you that Viniece Walker came to Bedford Hills when she was twenty years old, a high school dropout who read at the level of a college sophomore, a graduate of crackhouses, the streets of Harlem, and a long alliance with a brutal man. On the surface Viniece has remained as tough as she was on the street. She speaks bluntly, and even though she is HIV positive and the virus has progressed during her time in prison, she still swaggers as she walks down the long prison corridors. While in prison, Niecie, as she is known to her friends, completed her high school requirements and began to pursue a college degree (psychology is the only major offered at Bedford Hills, but Niecie also took a special interest in philosophy). She became a counselor to women with a history of family violence and a comforter to those with AIDS.

Only the deaths of other women cause her to stumble in the midst of her swaggering step, to spend days alone with the remorse that drives her to seek redemption. She goes through life as if she had been imagined by Dostoevsky, but even more complex than his fictions, alive, a person, a fair-skinned and freckled African-American woman, and in prison. It was she who responded to my sudden question, "Why do you think people are poor?"

We had never met before. The conversation around us focused on the abuse of women. Niecie's eyes were perfectly opaque—hostile, prison eyes. Her mouth was set in the beginning of a sneer.

"You got to begin with the children," she said, speaking rapidly, clipping out the street sounds as they came into her speech.

She paused long enough to let the change of direction take effect, then resumed the rapid, rhythmless speech. "You've got to teach the moral life of downtown to the children. And the way you do that, Earl, is by taking them downtown to plays, museums, concerts, lectures, where they can learn the moral life of downtown."

I smiled at her, misunderstanding, thinking I was indulging her. "And then they won't be poor anymore?"

She read every nuance of my response, and answered angrily, "And they won't be poor *no more*."

"What you mean is what I said—"

"What I mean is what I said—a moral alternative to the street."

She didn't speak of jobs or money. In that, she was like the others I had listened to. No one had spoken of jobs or money. But how could the "moral life of downtown" lead anyone out from the surround of force? How could a museum push poverty away? Who can dress in statues or eat the past? And what of the political life? Had Niecie skipped a step or failed to take a step? The way out of poverty was politics, not the "moral life of downtown." But to enter the public world, to practice the political life, the poor had first to learn to reflect. That was what Niecie meant by the "moral life of downtown." She did not make the error of divorcing ethics from politics. Niecie had simply said, in a kind of shorthand, that no one could step out of the panicking circumstance of poverty directly into the public world.

Although she did not say so, I was sure that when she spoke of the "moral life of downtown" she meant something that had happened to her. With no job and no money, a prisoner, she had undergone a radical transformation. She had followed the same path that led to the invention of politics in ancient Greece. She had learned to reflect. In further conversation it became clear that when she spoke of "the moral life of downtown" she meant the humanities, the study of human constructs and concerns, which has been the source of reflection for the secular world since the Greeks first stepped back from nature to experience wonder at what they beheld. If the political life was the way out of poverty, the humanities provided an entrance to reflection and the political life. The poor did not need anyone to release them; an escape route existed. But to open this avenue to reflection and politics a major distinction between the preparation for the life of the rich and the life of the poor had to be eliminated.

Once Niecie had challenged me with her theory, the comforts of tinkering came to an end; I could no longer make an homage to the happenstance world and rest. To test Niecie's theory, student, faculty, and facilities were required. Quantitative measures would have to be developed; anecdotal information would also be useful. And the ethics of the experiment had to be considered: I resolved to do no harm. There was no need for the course to have a "sink or swim" character; it could aim to keep as many afloat as possible.

When the idea for an experimental course became clear in my mind, I discussed it with Dr. Jaime Inclán, director of the Roberto Clemente Family Guidance Center in lower Manhattan, a facility that provides counseling to poor people, mainly Latinos, in their own language and in their own community. Dr. Inclán offered the center's conference room for a classroom. We would put three metal tables end to end to approximate the boat-shaped tables used in discussion sections at the University of Chicago of the Hutchins era, which I used as a model for the course. A card table in the back of the room would hold a coffeemaker and a few cookies. The setting was not elegant, but it would do. And the front wall was covered by a floor-to-ceiling blackboard.

Now the course lacked only students and teachers. With no funds and a budget that grew every time a new idea for the course crossed my mind, I would have to ask the faculty to donate its time and effort. Moreover, when Hutchins said, "The best education for the best is the best education for us all," he meant it: he insisted that full professors teach discussion sections in the college. If the Clemente Course in the Humanities was to follow the same pattern, it would require a faculty with the knowledge and prestige that students might encounter in their first year at Harvard, Yale, Princeton, or Chicago.

I turned first to the novelist Charles Simmons. He had been assistant editor of *The New York Times Book Review* and had taught at Columbia University. He volunteered to teach poetry, beginning with simple poems, Housman, and ending with Latin poetry. Grace Glueck, who writes art news and criticism for the *New York Times*, planned a course that began with cave paintings and ended in the late twentieth century. Timothy Koranda, who did his graduate work at MIT, had published journal articles on mathematical logic, but he had been away from his field for some years and looked forward to getting back to it. I planned to teach the American history course through documents, beginning with the Magna Carta, moving on to the second of Locke's *Two Treatises of Government*, the Declaration of Independence, and so on through the documents of the Civil War. I would also teach the political philosophy class.

Since I was a naif in this endeavor, it did not immediately occur to me that recruiting students would present a problem. I didn't know how many I needed. All I had were criteria for selection: Age: 18–35.

Household income: Less than 150 percent of the Census Bureau's Official Poverty Threshold (though this was to change slightly).

Educational level: Ability to read a tabloid newspaper.

Educational goals: An expression of intent to complete the course.

Dr. Inclán arranged a meeting of community activists who could help recruit students. Lynette Lauretig of The Door, a program that provides medical and educational services to adolescents, and Angel Roman of the Grand Street Settlement, which offers work and training and GED programs, were both willing to give us access to prospective students. They also pointed out some practical considerations. The course had to provide bus and subway tokens, because fares ranged between three and six dollars per class per student, and the students could not afford sixty or even thirty dollars a month for transporation. We also had to offer dinner or a snack, because the classes were to be held from 6:00 to 7:30 P.M.

The first recruiting session came only a few days later. Nancy Mamis-King, associate executive director of the Neighborhood Youth & Family Services program in the South Bronx, had identified some Clemente Course candidates and had assembled about twenty of her clients and their supervisors in a circle of chairs in a conference room. Everyone in the room was black or Latino, with the exception of one social worker and me.

After I explained the idea of the course, the white social worker was the first to ask a question: "Are you going to teach African history?"

"No. We'll be teaching a section on American history, based on documents, as I said. We want to teach the ideas of history so that—."

"You have to teach African history."

"This is America, so we'll teach American history. If we were in Africa, I would teach African history, and if we were in China, I would teach Chinese history."

"You're indoctrinating people in Western culture."

I tried to get beyond her. "We'll study African art," I said, "as it affects art in America. We'll study American history and literature; you can't do that without studying African-American culture, because culturally all Americans are black as well as white, Native American, Asian, and so on." It was no use; not one of them applied for admission to the course.

A few days later Lynette Lauretig arranged a meeting with some of her staff at The Door. We disagreed about the course. They thought it should be taught at a much lower level. Although I could not change their views, they agreed to assemble a group of Door members who might be interested in the humanities.

On an early evening that same week, about twenty prospective students were scheduled to meet in a classroom at The Door. Most of them came late. Those who arrived first slumped in their chairs, staring at the floor or greeting me with sullen glances. A few ate candy or what appeared to be the remnants of a meal. The students were mostly black and Latino, one was Asian, and five were white; two of the whites were immigrants who had severe problems with English. When I introduced myself, several of the students would not shake my hand, two or three refused even to look at me, one girl giggled, and the last person to volunteer his name, a young man dressed in a Tommy Hilfiger sweatshirt and wearing a cap turned sideways, drawled, "Henry Jones, but they call me Sleepy, because I got these sleepy eyes—"

"In our class, we'll call you Mr. Jones."

He smiled and slid down in his chair so that his back was parallel to the floor.

Before I finished attempting to shake hands with the prospective students, a waiflike Asian girl with her mouth half-full of cake said, "Can we get on with it? I'm bored."

I liked the group immediately.

Having failed in the South Bronx, I resolved to approach these prospective students differently. "You've been cheated," I said. "Rich people learn the humanities; you didn't. The humanities are a foundation for getting along in the world, for thinking, for learning to reflect on the world instead of just reacting to whatever force is turned against you. I think the humanities are one of the ways to become political, and I don't mean political in the sense of voting in an election but in the broad sense." I told them Thucydides' definition of politics.

"Rich people know politics in that sense. They know how to negotiate instead of using force. They know how to use politics to get along, to get power. It doesn't mean that rich people are good and poor people are bad. It simply means that rich people know a more effective method for living in this society.

"Do all rich people, or people who are in the middle, know the humanities? Not a chance. But some do. And it helps. It helps to live better and enjoy life more. Will the humanites make you rich? Yes. Absolutely. But not in terms of money. In terms of life.

"Rich people learn the humanities in private schools and expensive universities. And that's one of the ways in which they learn the political life. I think that is the real difference between the haves and have-nots in this country. If you want real power, legitimate power, the kind that comes from the people and belongs to the people, you must understand politics. The humanities will help.

"Here's how it works: We'll pay your subway fare; take care of your children, if you have them; give you a snack or a sandwich; provide you with books and any other materials you need. But we'll make you think harder, use your mind more fully, than you ever have before. You'll have to read and think about the same kinds of ideas you would encounter in a first-year course at Harvard or Yale or Oxford.

"You'll have to come to class in the snow and the rain and the cold and the dark. No one will coddle you, no one will slow down for you. There will be tests to take, papers to write. And I can't promise you anything but a certificate of completion at the end of the course. I'll be talking to colleges about giving credit for the course, but I can't promise anything. If you come to the Clemente Course, you must do it because you want a certain kind of life, a richness of mind and spirit. That's all I offer you: philosophy, poetry, art history, logic, rhetoric, and American history.

"Your teachers will all be people of accomplishment in their fields," I said, and I spoke a little about each teacher. "That's the course. October through May, with a two-week break at Christmas. It is generally accepted in America that the liberal arts and the humanities in particular belong to the elites. I think you're the elites."

The young Asian woman said, "What are you getting out of this?"

"This is a demonstration project. I'm writing a book. This will be proof, I hope, of my idea about the humanities. Whether it succeeds or fails will be up to the teachers and you."

All but one of the prospective students applied for admission to the course.

I repeated the new presentation at the Grand Street Settlement and at other places around the city. There were about fifty candidates for the thirty positions in the course. Personal interviews began in early September.

Meanwhile, almost all of my attempts to raise money had failed. Only the novelist Starling Lawrence, who is also editor in chief of W.W. Norton, which had contracted to publish the book; the publishing house itself; and a small, private family foundation supported the experiment. We were far short of our budgeted expenses, but my wife, Sylvia, and I agreed that the cost was still very low, and we decided to go ahead.

Of the fifty prospective students who showed up at the Clemente Center for personal interviews, a few were too rich (a postal supervisor's son, a fellow who claimed his father owned a factory in Nigeria that employed sixty people) and more than a few could not read. Two home-care workers from Local 1199 could not arrange their hours to enable them to take the course. Some of the applicants were too young: a thirteen-year-old and two who had just turned sixteen.

Lucia Medina, a woman with five children who told me that she often answered the door at the single-room occupancy hotel where she lived with a butcher knife in her hand, was the oldest person accepted into the course. Carmen Quiñones, a recovering addict who had spent time in prison, was the next eldest. Both were in their early thirties.

The interviews went on for days.

Abel Lomas[1] shared an apartment and worked part-time wrapping packages at Macy's. His father had abandoned the family when Abel was born. His mother was murdered by his stepfather when Abel was thirteen. With no one to turn to and no place to stay, he lived on the streets, first in Florida, then back in New York City. He used the tiny stipend from his mother's Social Security to keep himself alive.

After the recruiting session at The Door, I drove up Sixth Avenue from Canal Street with Abel, and we talked about ethics. He had a street tough's delivery, spitting out his ideas in crudely formed

---

[1] *Not his real name.*

sentences of four, five, eight words, strings of blunt declarations, with never a dependent clause to qualify his thoughts. He did not clear his throat with badinage, as timidity teaches us to do, nor did he waste his breath with tact.

"What do you think about drugs?" he asked, and the strangely breathless delivery further coarsened by his Dominican accent. "My cousin is a dealer."

"I've seen a lot of people hurt by drugs."

"Your family has nothing to eat. You sell drugs. What's worse? Let your family starve or sell drugs?"

"Starvation and drug addiction are both bad, aren't they?"

"Yes," he said, not "yeah" or "uh-huh" but a precise, almost formal "yes."

"So it's a question of the worse of two evils? How shall we decide?"

The question came up near Thirty-fourth Street, where Sixth Avenue remains hellishly traffic-jammed well into the night. Horns honked, people flooded into the street against the light. Buses and trucks and taxicabs threatened their way from one lane to the next where the overcrowded avenue crosses the equally crowded Broadway. As we passed Herald Square and made our way north again, I said, "There are a couple of ways to look at it. One comes from Immanuel Kant, who said that you should not do anything unless you want it to become a universal law; that is, unless you think it's what everybody should do. So Kant wouldn't agree to selling drugs *or* letting your family starve."

Again he answered with a formal "Yes."

"There's another way to look at it, which is to ask what is the greatest good for the greatest number: in this case, keeping your family from starvation or keeping tens, perhaps hundreds of people from losing their lives to drugs. So which is the greatest number?"

"That's what I think," he said.

"What?"

"You shouldn't sell drugs. You can always get food to eat. Welfare. Something."

"You're a Kantian."

"Yes."

"You know who Kant is?"

"I think so."

We had arrived at Seventy-seventh Street, where he got out of the car to catch the subway before I turned east. As he opened the car door and the light came on, the almost military neatness of him struck me. He had the newly cropped hair of a cadet. His clothes were clean, without a wrinkle. He was an orphan, a street kid, an immaculate urchin. Within a few weeks he would be nineteen years old, the Social Security payments would end, and he would have to move into a shelter.

Some of those who came for interviews were too poor. I did not think that was possible when we began, and I would like not to believe it now, but it was true. There is a point at which the level of forces that surround the poor can become insurmountable, when there is no time or energy left to be anything but poor. Most often I could not recruit such people for the course; when I did, they soon dropped out.

Over the days of interviewing, a class slowly assembled. I could not then imagine who would last the year and who would not. One young woman submitted a neatly typed essay that said, "I was homeless once, then I lived for some time in a shelter. Right now, I have got my own space granted by the Partnership for the Homeless. Right now, I am living alone with very limited means. Financially I am overwhelmed by debts. I cannot afford all the food I need. . . ."

A brother and sister, refugees from Tashkent, lived with their parents in the farthest reaches of Queens, far beyond the end of the subway line. They had no money, and they had been refused admission by every school to which they had applied. I had not intended to accept immigrants or people who had difficulty with the English language, but I took them into the class.

I also took four who had been in prison, three who were homeless, three who were pregnant, one who lived in a drugged dream-state in which she was abused, and one whom I had known for a long time and who was dying of AIDS. As I listened to them, I wondered how the course would affect them. They had no public life, no place; they lived within the surround of force, moving as fast as they could, driven by necessity, without a moment to reflect. Why should they care about fourteenth-century Italian painting or truth tables or the death of Socrates?

Between the end of recruiting and the orientation session that would open the course, I made a visit to Bedford Hills to talk with Niecie Walker. It was hot, and the drive up from the city had been unpleasant. I didn't yet know Niecie very well. She didn't trust me, and I didn't know what to make of her. While we talked, she held a huge white pill in her hand. "For AIDS," she said.

"Are you sick?"

"My T-cell count is down. But that's neither here nor there. Tell me about the course, Earl. What are you going to teach?"

"Moral philosophy."

"And what does that include?"

She had turned the visit into an interrogation. I didn't mind. At the end of the conversation I would be going out into "the free world"; if she wanted our meeting to be an interrogation, I was not about to argue. I said, "We'll begin with Plato: the *Apology*, a little of the *Crito*, a few pages of the *Phaedo* so that they'll know what happened to Socrates. Then we'll read Aristotle's *Nicomachean Ethics*. I also want them to read Thucydides, particularly Pericles' Funeral Oration in order to make the connection between ethics and politics, to lead them in the direction I hope the course will take them. Then we'll end with *Antigone*, but read as moral and political philosophy as well as drama."

"There's something missing," she said, leaning back in her chair, taking on an air of superiority.

The drive had been long, the day was hot, the air in the room was dead and damp. "Oh, yeah," I said, "and what's that?"

"Plato's Allegory of the Cave. How can you teach philosophy to poor people without The Allegory of the Cave? The ghetto is the cave. Education is the light. Poor people can understand that."

At the beginning of the orientation at the Clemente Center a week later, each teacher spoke for a minute or two. Dr. Inclán and his research assistant, Patricia Vargas, administered the questionnaire he had devised to measure, as best he could, the role of force and the amount of reflection in the lives of the students. I explained that each class was going to be videotaped as another way of documenting the project. Then I gave out the first assignment: "In preparation for our next meeting, I would like you to read a brief selection from Plato's *Republic*: the Allegory of the Cave."

I tried to guess how many students would return for the first class. I hoped for twenty, expected fifteen, and feared ten. Sylvia, who had agreed to share the administrative tasks of the course, and I prepared coffee and cookies for twenty-five. We had a plastic container filled with subway tokens. Thanks to Starling Lawrence, we had thirty copies of Bernard Knox's *Norton Book of Classical Literature*, which contained all of the texts for the philosophy section except the *Republic* and the *Nicomachean Ethics*.

At six o'clock there were only ten students seated around the long table, but by six-fifteen the number had doubled, and a few minutes later two more straggled in out of the dusk. I had written a time line on the blackboard, showing them the temporal progress of thinking—from the role of myth in Neolithic societies to *The Gilgamesh Epic* and forward to the Old Testament, Confucius, the Greeks, the New Testament, the Koran, the *Epic of SonJara*, and ending with Nahuatl and Maya poems, which took us up to the contact between Europe and America, where the history course began. The time line served as context and geography as well as history: no race, no major culture was ignored. "Let's agree," I told them, "that we are all human, whatever our origins. And now let's go into Plato's cave."

I told them that there would be no lectures in the philosophy section of the course; we would use the Socratic method, which is called maieutic dialogue. 'Maieutic' comes from the Greek work for midwifery. I'll take the role of midwife in our dialogue. Now, what do I mean by that? What does a midwife do?"

It was the beginning of a love affair, the first moment of their infatuation with Socrates. Later, Abel Lomas would characterize that moment in his no-nonsense fashion, saying that it was the first time anyone had ever paid attention to their opinions.

Grace Glueck began the art history class in a darkened room lit with slides of the Lascaux caves and next turned the students' attention to Egypt, arranging for them to visit the Metropolitan Museum of Art to see the Temple of Dendur and the Egyptian Galleries. They arrived at the museum on a Friday evening. Darlene Codd brought her two-year-old son. Pearl Lau was late, as usual. One of the students, who had told me how much he was looking forward to the museum visit, didn't show up, which surprised me. Later I learned that he had been arrested for jumping a turnstile in a subway station on his way to the museum and was being held in a prison cell under the Brooklyn criminal courthouse. In the Temple of Dendur, Samantha Smoot asked questions of Felicia Blum, a museum lecturer. Samantha was the student who had burst out with the news, in one of the first sessions of the course, that people in her neighborhood believed it "wasn't no use goin' to school, because the white man wouldn't let you up no matter what." But in a hall where the statuary was of half-human, half-animal female figures, it was Samantha who asked what the glyphs meant, encouraging Felicia Blum to read them aloud, to translate them into English. Toward the end of the evening, Grace led the students out of the halls of antiquities into the Rockefeller Wing, where she told them of the connection of culture and art in Mali, Benin, and the Pacific Islands. When the students had collected their coats and stood together near the entrance to the museum, preparing to leave, Samantha stood apart, a tall, slim young woman, dressed in a deerstalker cap and dark blue peacoat. She made an exaggerated farewell wave at us and returned to Egypt—her ancient mirror.

Charles Simmons began the poetry class with poems as puzzles and laughs. His plan was to surprise the class, and he did. At first he read the poems aloud to them, interrupting himself with footnotes to bring them along. He showed them poems of love and of seduction, and satiric commentaries on those poems by later poets. "Let us read," the students demanded, but Charles refused; He tantalized them with the opportunity to read poems aloud. A tug-of-war began between him and the students, and the standoff was ended not by Charles directly but by Hector Anderson. When Charles asked if anyone in the class wrote poetry, Hector raised his hand.

"Can you recite one of your poems for us?" Charles said.

Until that moment, Hector had never volunteered a comment, though he had spoken well and intelligently when asked. He preferred to slouch in his chair, dressed in full camouflage gear, wearing a nylon stocking over his hair and eating slices of fresh cantaloupe or honeydew melon.

In response to Charles' question, Hector slid up to a sitting position. "If you turn that camera off," he said. "I don't want anybody using my lyrics." When he was sure the red light of the video camera was off, Hector stood and recited verse after verse of a poem that belonged somewhere in the triangle formed by Ginsberg's *Howl*, the Book of Lamentations, and hip-hop. When Charles and the students finished applauding, they asked Hector to say the poem again, and he did. Later Charles told me, "That kid is the real thing." Hector's discomfort with Sylvia and me turned to ease. He came to our house for a small Christmas party and at other times. We talked on the telephone about a scholarship program and about what steps he should take next in his education. I came to know his parents. As a student, he began quietly, almost secretly, to surpass many of his classmates.

Timothy Koranda was the most professorial of the professors. He arrived precisely on time, wearing a hat of many styles—part fedora, part Borsalino, part Stetson, and at least one-half World War I campaign hat. He taught logic during class hours, filling the blackboard from floor to ceiling, wall to wall, drawing the inter-sections of sets here and truth tables there and a great square of oppositions in the middle of it all. After class, he walked with students to the subway, chatting about Zen or logic or Heisenberg.

On one of the coldest nights of the winter, he introduced the students to logic problems stated in ordinary language that they could solve by reducing the phrases to symbols. He passed out copies of a problem, two pages long, then wrote out some of the key phrases on the blackboard. "Take this home with you," he said, "and at our next meeting we shall see who has solved it. I shall also attempt to find the answer."

By the time he finished writing out the key phrases, however, David Iskhakov raised his hand. Although they listened attentively, neither David nor his sister Susana spoke often in class. She was shy, and he was embarrassed at his inability to speak perfect English.

"May I go to blackboard?" David said. "And will see if I have found correct answer to zis problem."

Together Tim and David erased the blackboard, then David began covering it with signs and symbols. "If first man is earning this money, and second man is closer to this town…"he said, carefully laying out the conditions. After five minutes or so, he said, "And the answer is: B will get first to Cleveland!

Samantha Smoot shouted, "That's not the answer. The mistake you made is in the first part there, where it says who earns more money."

Tim folded his arms across his chest, happy. "I shall let you all take the problem home," he said.

When Sylvia and I left the Clemente Center that night, a knot of students was gathered outside, huddled against the wind. Snow had begun to fall, a slippery powder on the gray ice that covered all but a narrow space down the center of the sidewalk. Samantha and David stood in the middle of the group, still arguing over the answer to the problem. I leaned in for a moment to catch the character of the argument. It was even more polite than it had been in the classroom, because now they governed themselves.

One Saturday morning in January, David Howell telephoned me at home. "Mr. Shores," he said, Anglicizing my name, as many of the students did.

"Mr. Howell," I responded, recognizing his voice.

"How you doin', Mr. Shores?"

"I'm fine. How are you?"

"I had a little problem at work."

Uh-oh, I thought, bad news was coming. David is a big man, generally good-humored but with a quick temper. According to his mother, he had a history of violent behavior. In the classroom he had been one of the best students, a steady man, twenty-four years old, who always did the reading assignments and who often made interesting connections between the humanities and daily life. "What happened?"

"Mr. Shores, there's a woman at my job, she said some things to me and I said some things to her. And she told my supervisor I had said things to her, and he called me in about it. She's forty years old and she don't have no social life, and I have a good social life and she's jealous of me."

"And then what happened?" The tone of his voice and the timing of the call did not portend good news.

"Mr. Shores, she made me so mad, I wanted to smack her up against the wall. I tried to talk to some friends to calm myself down a little, but nobody was around."

"And what did you do?" I asked, fearing this was his one telephone call from the city jail.

"Mr. Shores, I asked myself, 'What would Socrates do?'"

David Howell had reasoned that his co-worker's envy was not his problem after all, and he had dropped his rage.

One evening, in the American history section, I was telling the students about Gordon Wood's ideas in *The Radicalism of the American Revolution*. We were talking about the revolt by some intellectuals against classical learning at the turn of the eighteenth century, including Benjamin Franklin's late-life change of heart, when Henry Jones raised his hand.

"If the Founders loved the humanities so much, how come they treated the natives so badly?"

I didn't know how to answer this question. There were confounding explanations to offer about changing attitudes toward Native Americans, vaguely useful references to views of Rousseau and James Fenimore Cooper. For a moment I wondered if I should tell them about Heidegger's Nazi past. Then I saw Abel Lomas's raised hand at the far end of the table. "Mr. Lomas," I said.

Abel said, "That's what Aristotle means by incontinence, when you know what's morally right but you don't do it, because you're overcome by your passions."

The other students nodded. They were all inheritors of wounds caused by the incontinence of educated men; now they had an ally in Aristotle, who had given them a way to analyze the actions of their antagonists.

Those who appreciate ancient history understand the radical character of the humanities. They know that politics did not begin in a perfect world but in a society even more flawed than ours: one that embraced slavery, denied the rights of women, practiced a form of homosexuality that verged on pedophilia, and endured the intrigues and corruption of its leaders. The genius of that society originated in man's re-creation of himself through the recognition of his humanness as expressed in art, literature, rhetoric, philosophy, and the unique notion of freedom. At that moment, the isolation of the private life ended and politics began.

The winners in the game of modern society, and even those whose fortune falls in the middle, have other means to power: they are included at birth. They know this. And they know exactly what to do to protect their place in the economic and social hierarchy. As Allan Bloom, author of the nationally best-selling tract in defense of elitism, *The Closing of the American Mind*, put it, they direct the study of the humanities exclusively at those young people who "have been raised in comfort and with the expectation of ever increasing comfort."

In the last meeting before graduation, the Clemente students answered the same set of questions they'd answered at orientation. Between October and May, students had fallen to AIDS, pregnancy, job opportunities, pernicious anemia, clinical depression, a schizophrenic child, and other forces, but of the thirty students admitted to the course, sixteen had completed it, and fourteen had earned credit from Bard College. Dr. Inclán found that the students' self-esteem and their abilities to divine and solve problems had significantly increased; their use of verbal aggression as a tactic for resolving conflicts had significantly decreased. And, they all had notably more appreciation for the concepts of benevolence, spirituality, universalism, and collectivism.

It cost about $2,000 for a student to attend the Clemente Course. Compared with unemployment, welfare, or prison, the humanities are a bargain. But coming into possession of the faculty of reflection and the skills of politics leads to a choice for the poor—and whatever they choose, they will be dangerous: they may use politics to get along in a society based on the game, to escape from the surround of force into a gentler life, to behave as citizens, and nothing more; or they may choose to oppose the game itself. No one can predict the effect of politics, although we all would like to think that wisdom goes our way. That is why the poor are so often mobilized and so rarely politicized. The possibility that they will adopt a moral view other than that of their mentors can never be discounted. And who wants to run that risk?

On the night of the first Clemente Course graduation, the students and their families filled the eighty-five chairs we crammed into the conference room where classes had been held. Robert Martin, associate dean of Bard College, read the graduates' names. David Dinkins, the former mayor of New York City, handed out the diplomas. There were speeches and presentations. The students gave me a plaque on which they had misspelled my name. I offered a few words about each student, congratulated them, and said finally, "This is what I wish for you: May you never be more active than when you are doing nothing..." I saw their smiles of recognition at the words of Cato, which I had written on the blackboard early in the course. They could recall again too the moment when we had come to the denouement of Aristotle's brilliantly constructed thriller, the *Nicomachean Ethics*—the idea that in the contemplative life man was most like God. One or two, perhaps more of the students, closed their eyes. In the momentary stillness of the room it was possible to think.

The Clemente Course in the Humanities ended a second year in June 1997. Twenty-eight new students had enrolled; fourteen graduated. Another version of the course will begin this fall in Yucatán, Mexico, using classical Maya literature in Maya.

On May 14,1997, Viniece Walker came up for parole for the second time. She had served more than ten years of her sentence, and she had been the best of prisoners. In a version of the Clemente Course held at the prison, she had been my teaching assistant. After a brief hearing, her request for parole was denied. She will serve two more years before the parole board will reconsider her case.

A year after graduation, ten of the first sixteen Clemente Course graduates were attending four-year colleges or going to nursing school; four of them had received full scholarships to Bard College. The other graduates were attending community college or working full-time. Except for one: she had been fired from her job in a fast-food restaurant for trying to start a union.

Questions for Discussion

1. Near the beginning of Shorris' essay, he introduces us to Viniece Walker, a prisoner at Bedford Hills Correctional Institute. How does her response to the question "Why do think people are poor?" inspire the creation of the Clemente Course? What is Shorris' purpose in returning to Viniece Walker at the end of the essay?

2. What does Shorris mean when he claims that a liberal education is "dangerous"?

3. When Earl Shorris first conceived the Clemente Course, he hoped to make it more possible for his students to be more "political." What did he mean by this? How do you think a course in the humanities will make students more political by Shorris' definition?

Explorations

1. Viniece Walker tells Shorris he must include Plato's Allegory of the Cave in his course. Plato's Allegory of the Cave is from a larger work called *The Republic*. At your library or on the internet, find a copy of Plato's Allegory of the Cave, then try to determine why Walker was so insistent on its inclusion in the Clemente Course.

2. This essay was published in companion with Mark Edmundson's "*On the Uses of a Liberal Education 1: As Lite Entertainment for Bored College Students*," which is also included in *Writing Lives*. Though the subject matter in the courses described by Edmundson is much like that taught in the Clemente Course, the students come from much different circumstances. How do you imagine the consequences of learning will be different for the students Shorris describes than for the students at the University of Virginia?

3. Many training programs designed to help people break the cycle of poverty through educational and professional achievement focus on specific job skills such as typing, mechanical repair, or health care assistance. Shorris seems to believe that knowledge of the humanities will make a greater difference in the lives of the poor. How would you construct an argument in favor of Shorris' point of view? How would you convince a potential funder to support such a project?

Formal Writing Assignments

1. In an essay, analyze the college or high school course that you feel has made the greatest impact on your life. Describe the physical setting of the class, the coursework itself, your classmates, and the instructor's approach to teaching. How has what you learned in that class changed how your view of the world? Did the class make you a better person, or just a more knowledgeable one? Do you think that this course has made you more "political" by Shorris' definition?

2. Near many urban college campuses, students must pass homeless and poverty-stricken individuals on the sidewalk each day. Imagine that you are charged with designing a course that these people could attend free of charge with the hope that what they learn will improve the quality of their lives. In an essay, describe what would you include in this course and how would you defend your decisions. Work to convince the reader that your expectations are realistic.

MAD & What They Learn in School

Jerome Stern

Jerome Stern was the director of the writing program at Florida State University and the creator of the World's Best Short Short Story contest (no story over 250 words). He contributed to *Harper's* Magazine and to *Playboy*. His short monologues, known as "Radios" made him a much-beloved commentator on National Public Radio (NPR). Stern's poetry and fiction carries with it an irrepressible wit that allows us to laugh at everyday ironies even as we see them in a new light.

Writing Before Reading

1. In what ways did your primary and secondary educational experiences function to shape your thinking on social issues? For example, did education on drugs, alcohol, or sexuality change your values or behaviors?

2. Write about a time when someone expected you to know more about a subject than you actually did. Who was the person you had this exchange with? A parent? A teacher? A friend? A stranger? What type of knowledge did they expect you to have and why might they have had unrealistic expectations? How did it feel to find yourself unable to meet those expectations? How did you handle the situation?

3. How do you define poetry? Imagine a poem. Describe its length, its style, its layout on the page. What kind of tone do you imagine most poetry to have? What kind of issues have been most commonly addressed in the poetry you've come across? After reading Stern's work, look back at this list and consider the ways in which his poetry did or did not meet your expectations.

MAD

So I don't know, I don't know what the teacher wants from us, I
   mean the teacher gives us these notes on John Milton and
   then he asks us if we have any questions and we can't have
   any questions because we don't know what to ask and so we
   are quiet and then he gets mad at us,

And then he asks us if we heard of Jean Paul Sartre and
   Reinhold Niebuhr who we never heard of and are not on the
   syllabus, and then he gets mad at us for not having heard of
   people no one ever told us about,

And then he says what about *Crime and Punishment* and *War
   and Peace?* which it turns out are books that nobody even
   ever mentioned in our lives, and then he gets mad at us.

And then he gives us things to read which are very sad and confusing and then he gets mad at us because we don't like things that are sad and confusing.

Then he says life doesn't have happy endings and we say why does it have to be that way, and that's why we want to read things that have happy endings and then he gets mad at us.

And we tell him we would do what we are supposed to, but he won't tell us what we are supposed to do.

Think he says, think, why don't you think. And then, when we tell him what we think is that we don't understand what he is saying, and what will be on the exam, and will we be responsible for everything in the syllabus, or just what we cover in class, then he gets mad at us, and says all we care about is grades and money.

And then he gets sarcastic and asks us when World War II was, and then he gets unhappy because we don't know, and never heard of Mussolini or Mao or Molotov cocktails, and we don't know why we should have heard of those things so there doesn't seem to be any reason to know these things

And then he gets mad at us and says all we care about is ourselves and we don't even know who we are, and that is not the way it was at some time before, but what that time was is not clear.

We do not know that time because it was a time maybe before we were born, and he seems mad at us because we were not born when he was, and did not do the things he said he did, and that it is all our fault.

He does not like what we like and is mad at us for liking the things we do like instead of other things which no one ever told us about, and so he is almost always mad, but we hope he likes us and gives us good grades anyway.

What They Learn in School

In the schools now, they want them to know all about marijuana, crack, heroin, and amphetamines,

Because then they won't be interested in marijuana, crack, heroin, and amphetamines,

But they don't want to tell them anything about sex because if the schools tell them about sex, then they will be interested in sex,

But if the schools don't tell them anything about sex,

Then they will have high morals and no one will get pregnant, and everything will be all right,

And they do want them to know a lot about computers so they will outcompete the Japanese,

But they don't want them to know anything about real science because then they will lose their faith and become secular humanists,

And they do want them to know all about this great land of ours so they will be patriotic,

But they don't want them to learn about the tragedy and pain in its real history because then they will be critical about this great land of ours and we will be passively taken over by a foreign power

And they want them to learn how to think for themselves so they can get good jobs and be successful,

But they don't want them to have books that confront them with real ideas because that will confuse their values,

And they'd like them to be good parents,

But they can't teach them about families because that takes them back to how you get to be a family,

And they want to warn them about how not to get AIDS

But that would mean telling them how not to get AIDS,

And they'd like them to know the Constitution,

But they don't like some of those amendments except when they are invoked by the people they agree with,

And they'd like them to vote,

But they don't want them to discuss current events because it might be controversial and
upset them and make them want to take drugs which they already have told them
all about,

And they want to teach them the importance of morality,

But they also want them to learn that Winning is not everything—it is the Only Thing,

And they want them to be well-read,

But they don't want them to read Chaucer or Shakespeare or Aristophanes or Mark Twain
or Ernest Hemingway or John Steinbeck, because that will corrupt them,

And they don't want them to know anything about art because that will make them weird,

But they do want them to know about music so they can march in the band,

And they mainly want to teach them not to question, not to challenge, not to imagine,
but to be obedient and behave well so that they can hold them forever as children to
their bosoms as the second millennium lurches toward its panicky close.

Questions for Discussion

1. How do "What They Learn in School" and "MAD" speak to each other? Are there commonalities of voice or style in the two pieces? Are there commonalities of purpose?

2. Who would you imagine to be the target audience(s) for these pieces? What is their age range? Their gender? Their occupations? Their political leanings? What textual details bring you to your conclusions?

3. Pick out the passage in the poem to which you reacted most strongly. Why did you have such a response?

Explorations

1. Write about the effect of first-person narration in "MAD." Is this poem more or less effective because it is told from the perspective of a single student? Why? What would happen if the poet had instead used the third-person as he did in "What They Learn in School"? You can extend this exploration by considering the effect of the speaker's shift from the singular pronoun, "I," to the collective pronoun, "we."

2. Get into groups and rewrite "What They Learn in School." Can you keep any of Stern's claims about learning? Which would your group cut? Which would they keep? And, most importantly, what new "lessons" could your group add to individualize your poem to each of your different experiences in the educational system? When you finish either read the revised piece to the class or post it to the class listserv for further discussion.

3. Where might you place Stern in a debate on education? Write an exploration describing your interpretation of Stern's stand using quotes from the poems as evidence and then place yourself within that debate. When do you agree with Stern? When do you disagree? What evidence or ideology provides the basis for your beliefs?

Formal Writing Assignments

1. Stern's poems could be read as a commentary on the U.S. system of education. Write an essay that compares and contrasts these two poems' views of education. Are they calling for the same type of student? The same type of teacher? What implicit or explicit demands does each make on the educational system in the U.S.? Feel free to bring in the work of other authors in this unit as evidence for your argument.

2. The generation gap plays a large role in both "MAD" and "What They Learn in School." Write an essay that examines the educational expectations of people from various age groups. For this essay you will want to interview a number of people from a range of backgrounds in order to gain varying perspectives. Talk with your parents, with older or younger friends or members of your class, call or email current or past teachers, coaches, mentors. Take notes on their responses to your questions on education. There are any number of questions you can ask. Here are a few examples: What should be taught in school? What shouldn't be taught in school? What is the ultimate goal of an education? In your opinion, how has the U.S. education system changed in the past five, ten, fifteen, or twenty years? Keeping in mind that your interviews can give you only a small sample of perspectives, carefully examine your collected responses and present them in a paper that both discusses the process of data collection and gives an analysis of the ways in which your results compare to the scenarios of Stern's poetry.

PUBLIC DISCOURSES

Public discourse includes all the myths, legends, stories, and slogans through which society shapes us and by which we shape society. It includes the ways we talk about and understand the world—from public conversations about politics and education to casual chatter about sports or music. Public discourse takes all kinds of forms: magazines, newspapers, talk shows on radio and television, books, the Internet, political speeches and debates, advertising, sermons in churches and on street corners, and demonstrations. These forms and discourses are interdependent; a change in one effects a change in the other.

This unit illustrates a variety of public discourses currently evolving. Several authors in the unit suggest generic methods of interpreting consumer texts. For instance, Neil Postman and Steve Powers, in "The Bias of Language, the Bias of Pictures," offer a systematic way of viewing television. Though their argument is intended to empower a viewing audience, the argument is arguably based on a single type of audience and a single means of interpretation. Other authors in this unit challenge these assumptions when they contend that audiences are multiple, varied, and constantly changing, offering through these audiences alternative interpretive strategies. An example of this school of thought is Paul Gamson's "Why I Love Trash," as he counters the prevailing perception of daytime talk shows, re-reading them as valuable for audiences rarely represented in consumer culture. In comparison, Patricia Williams' discussion of talk radio shows suggests that there are some discourses and audiences that claim to represent democratic values, but ultimately create a community of racist "dittoheads." What these two examples demonstrate are the range of discourses in and outside of the unit, and the complexity of their meanings.

You encounter and create public discourses on a daily basis; taking part in chat room or newsgroup conversations on the Internet, for instance, both place you in a pre-existing discourse and ask you to contribute to its growth. You also participate in discourse when you attend public spaces such as shopping malls, as you leaf through a magazine, and as you interpret media messages in advertising or on television. You might also find yourself decoding the nuances of body language in the gym, similar to Stuart Ewen's approach in "Hard Bodies." What Ewen does further, however, is interpret working out in a social context outside the confines of the gym, suggesting that the "hard body" is not only part of a culture of beauty, but also part of an economic system. What Ewen's approach exemplifies is an awareness of how discourses overlap, even within a single cultural text and in not always apparent ways.

Public discourses influence many of our decisions—the college or university we choose to attend, the bank we put our money in, the clubs and organizations we join, and even the brand of laundry detergent we purchase. Their influence is not one-way, however; we play a part in forming, sustaining, and sometimes resisting these public conversations. Because the media and other forums for public discourse are so pervasive, though, they often pass unnoticed as subjects for study. Advertising, television, fashion, and even the physical arrangement of space within public buildings convey silent or ignored messages, messages to which we should reply because they influence our everyday lives.

EXPLORATION

Observe and record as many examples as possible of public discourse you are exposed to in a single day. Your list might include written examples (such as junk mail and the campus newspaper), visual examples (like television ads and billboards), and spoken examples (including an instructor's lecture, or a speaker for a campus organization), as well as combinations of these types. Record what you see and hear as well as where the discourse takes place and how it is presented. Then think about the relationships between content and the medium used to communicate the content. Is there a relationship between the medium with which a message is delivered and the message itself? Are there mediums that mark their messages as public? Are there messages that mark their mediums as public? Which of your examples are overtly public? Which are not?

379

A Gentleman and a Consumer

Diane Barthel

A sociologist by training and education, and a professor at SUNY Stony Brook, Diane Barthel (b. 1949) is particularly interested in the sociology of nonprofit organizations, of symbolic communities, of art, and of gender. In this selection from *Putting on Appearances: Gender and Advertising* (1988), Barthel begins by assuming that gender structures consumer behavior, but concludes that gendered advertising can also reciprocate by impacting common notions of appropriate gender behavior. In her analysis, Barthel finds that the advertising rhetoric used to address males is predictably masculine, but that the rhetoric is also being altered for the purpose of selling more consumable goods—especially fashion products—to men.

Writing Before Reading

1. Envision a recent beer commercial on television. Is the appeal gendered? Write a short paragraph detailing the ways in which gender is "said" in the commercial.

2. What do you think is the purpose of advertisements? Make a list of your reasons.

3. Contemplate in a few sentences the use of beauty products. If you are a male, what do you think of males using beauty products? If you are a female, what do you think of males using beauty products? Should these viewpoints differ?

A Gentleman and a Consumer

There are no men's beauty and glamour magazines with circulations even approaching those of the women's magazines. The very idea of men's beauty magazines may strike one as odd. In our society men traditionally were supposed to make the right appearance, to be well groomed and neatly tailored. What they were *not* supposed to do was to be overly concerned with their appearance, much less vain about their beauty. That was to be effeminate, and not a "real man." Male beauty was associated with homosexuals, and "real men" had to show how red-blooded they were by maintaining a certain distance from fashion.

Perhaps the best-known male fashion magazine is *GQ* founded in 1957 and with a circulation of 446,000 in 1986. More recently, we have seen the launching of *YMF* and *Young Black Male*, which in 1987 still [had] few advertising pages. *M* magazine, founded in 1983, attracts an audience "a cut above" that of *GQ*.[1]

Esquire Magazine, more venerable (founded in 1933), is classified as a general interest magazine. Although it does attract many women readers, many of the columns and features and much of the advertising are definitely directed toward attracting the attention of the male readers, who still make up the overwhelming majority of the readership.

The highest circulations for men's magazines are for magazines specializing either in sex (*Playboy*, circulation 4.1 million; *Penthouse*, circulation nearly 3.8 million; and *Hustler*, circulation 1.5 million) or sports (*Sports Illustrated*, circulation 2.7 million).[2] That these magazines share an emphasis on power — either power over women or over other men on the playing field—should not surprise. In fact, sociologist John Gagnon would argue that sex and sports now represent the major fields in which the male role, as defined by power, is played out, with physical power in work, and even in warfare, being less important than it was before industrialization and technological advance.[3]

If we are looking for comparative evidence as to how advertisements define gender roles for men and women we should not then see the male role as defined primarily through beauty and fashion. This seems an obvious point, but it is important to emphasize how different cultural attitudes toward both the social person and the physical body shape the gender roles of men and women. These cultural attitudes are changing, and advertisements are helping to legitimate the use of beauty products and an interest in fashion for men, as we shall see. As advertisements directed toward women are beginning to use male imagery, so too advertisements for men occasionally use imagery resembling that found in advertisements directed toward women. We are speaking of two *modes*, then. As Baudrillard[4] writes, these modes "do not result from the differentiated nature of the two sexes, but from the differential logic of the system. The relationship of the Masculine and the Feminine to real men and women is relatively arbitrary."[5] Increasingly today, men and women use both modes. The two great terms of opposition (Masculine and Feminine) still, however, structure the forms that consumption takes; they provide identities for products and consumers.

Baudrillard agrees that the feminine model encourages a woman to please herself, to encourage a certain complacency and even narcissistic solicitude. But by pleasing herself, it is understood that she will also please others, and that she will be chosen. "She never enters into direct competition. . . . If she is beautiful, that is to say, if this woman is a woman, she will be chosen. If the man is a man, he will choose his woman as he would other objects/signs (HIS car, HIS woman, HIS eau de toilette)."[6]

Whereas the feminine model is based on passivity, complacency, and narcissism, the masculine model is based on exactingness and choice.

All of masculine advertising insists on rule, on choice, in terms of rigor and inflexible minutiae. He does not neglect a detail . . . It is not a question of just letting things go, or of taking pleasure in something, but rather of distinguishing himself. To know how to choose, and not to fail at it, is here the equivalent of the military and puritanical virtues: intransigence, decision, "virtus."[7]

This masculine model, these masculine virtues, are best reflected in the many car advertisements. There, the keywords are masculine terms: *power, performance, precision*. Sometimes the car is a woman, responding to the touch and will of her male driver, after attracting him with her sexy body. "Pure shape, pure power, pure Z. It turns you on." But, as the juxtaposition of shape and power in this advertisement suggests, the car is not simply other; it is also an extension of the owner. As he turns it on, he turns himself on. Its power is his power; through it, he will be able to overpower other men and impress and seduce women.

How well does it perform?
How well can you drive? (Merkur XR4Ti)
The 1987 Celica GT-S has the sweeping lines and aggressive stance that promise performance. And Celica keeps its word.
Renault GTA:
Zero to sixty to zero in 13.9 sec.
It's the result of a performance philosophy where acceleration and braking are equally important.
There's a new Renault sports sedan called GTA. Under its slick monochromatic skin is a road car with a total performance attitude.
. . . It's our hot new pocket rocket.

In this last example, the car, like the driver, has a total performance attitude. That is what works. The slick monochromatic skin, like the Bond Street suit, makes a good first impression. But car, like owner, must have what it takes, must be able to go the distance faster and better than the competition. This point is explicitly made in advertisements in which the car becomes a means through which this masculine competition at work is extended in leisure. Some refer directly to the manly sport of auto racing "The Mitsubishi Starion ESI-R. Patiently crafted to ignite your imagination. Leaving little else to say except . . . gentlemen, start your engines." Others refer to competition in the business world: "To move ahead fast in this world, you've got to have connections. The totally new Corolla FX 16 GT-S has the right ones." Or in life in general. "It doesn't take any [Japanese characters] from anyone. It won't stand for any guff from 300ZX. Or RX-7. Introducing Conquest Tsi, the new turbo sport coupe designed and built by Mitsubishi in Japan." Or Ferrari, which says simply, "We are the competition." In this competition between products, the owners become almost superfluous. But the advertising of course, suggest that the qualities of the car will reflect the qualities of the owner, as opposed to the purely abstract, apersonal quality of money needed for purchase. Thus, like the would-be owner, the BMW also demonstrates a "relentless refusal to compromise." It is for "those who thrive on a maximum daily requirement of high performance." While the BMW has the business attitude of the old school ("aggression has never been expressed with such dignity"), a Beretta suggests what it takes to survive today in the shark-infested waters of Wall Street. In a glossy three-page cover foldout, a photograph of a shark's fin cutting through Indigo waters is accompanied by the legend "Discover a new species from today's Chevrolet." The following two pages show a sleek black Beretta similarly cutting through water and, presumably, through the competition: "Not just a new car, but a new species . . . with a natural instinct for the road . . . Aggressive stance. And a bold tail lamp. See it on the road and you won't soon forget. Drive it, and you never will."

And as with men, so with cars. "Power corrupts. Absolute power corrupts absolutely" (Maserati). Not having the money to pay for a Maserati, to corrupt and be corrupted, is a source of embarrassment. Advertisements reassure the consumer that he need not lose face in this manly battle. Hyundai promises, "It's affordable. (But you'd never know it.)"

> On first impression, the new Hyundai Excel GLS Sedan might seem a trifle beyond most people's means. But that's entirely by design. Sleek European design, to be exact.

Many advertisements suggest sexual pleasure and escape, as in "Pure shape, pure power, pure Z. It turns you on." Or "The all-new Chrysler Le Baron. Beauty . . . with a passion for driving." The Le Baron may initially suggest a beautiful female, with its "image of arresting beauty" and its passion "to drive. And drive it does!" But it *is* "Le Baron," not "La Baronness." And the advertisement continues to emphasize how it "*attacks* [emphasis mine] the road with a high torque, 2.5 fuel-injected engine. And its turbo option can blur the surface of any passing lane." Thus the object of the pleasure hardly has to be female if it is beautiful or sleek. The car is an extension of the male that conquers and tames the (female) road: "Positive-response suspension will calm the most demanding roads." The car becomes the ultimate lover when, like the Honda Prelude, it promises to combine power, "muscle," with finesse. Automobile advertisements thus play with androgyny and sexuality; the pleasure is in the union and confusion of form and movement, sex and speed. As in any sexual union, there is ultimately a merging of identities, rather than rigid maintenance of their separation. Polymorphous perverse? Perhaps. But it sells.

Though power, performance, precision as a complex of traits find their strongest emphasis in automobile advertisements, they also appear as selling points for products as diverse as shoes, stereos, and sunglasses. The car performs on the road, the driver performs for women, even in the parking lot, as Michelin suggests in its two-page spread showing a male front waist down resting on his car and chatting up a curvaceous female: "It performs great. And looks great. So, it not only stands out on the road. But in the parking lot. Which is one more place you're likely to discover how beautifully it can handle the curves" (!).

As media analyst Todd Gitlin points out, most of the drivers shown in advertisements are young white males, loners who become empowered by the car that makes possible their escape from the everyday. Gitlin stresses the advertisements' "emphasis on surface, the blankness of the protagonist; his striving toward self-sufficiency, to the point of displacement from the recognizable world."[8] Even the Chrysler advertisements that coopt Bruce Springsteen's "Born in the USA" for their "Born in America" campaign lose in the process the original political message, "ripping off Springsteen's angry anthem, smoothing it into a Chamber of Commerce ditty as shots of just plain productive-looking folks, black and white . . . whiz by in a montage-made community." As Gitlin comments, "None of Springsteen's losers need apply —or rather, if only they would roll up their sleeves and see what good company they're in, they wouldn't feel like losers any longer."[9]

This is a world of patriarchal order in which the individual male can and must challenge the father. He achieves identity by breaking loose of the structure and breaking free of the pack. In the process he recreates the order and reaffirms the myth of masculine independence. Above all, he demonstrates that he knows what he wants; he is critical, demanding, and free from the constraints of others. What he definitely does not want, and goes to some measure to avoid, is to appear less than masculine, in any way weak, frilly, feminine.

Avoiding the Feminine

Advertisers trying to develop male markets for products previously associated primarily with women must overcome the taboo that only women wear moisturizer, face cream, hair spray, or perfume. They do this by overt reference to masculine symbols, language and imagery, and sometimes by confronting the problem head-on.

There is not so much of a problem in selling products to counteract balding—that traditionally has been recognized as a male problem (a bald woman is a sexual joke that is not particularly amusing to the elderly.) But other hair products are another story, as the March 1987 GQ cover asks, "Are you man enough for mousse?" So the advertisements must make their products seem manly, as with S-Curl's "wave and curl kit" offering "The Manly Look" on its manly model dressed in business suit and carrying a hard hat (a nifty social class compromise), and as in college basketball sportscaster Al McGuire's testimonial for Consort hair spray:

> "Years ago, if someone had said to me, "Hey Al, do you use hair spray?" I would have said, 'No way, baby!'"
> "That was before I tried Consort Pump."
> "Consort adds extra control to my hair without looking stiff or phony. Control that lasts clean into overtime and post-game interviews . . ."
> Grooming Gear for Real Guys. *Consort.*

Besides such "grooming gear" as perms and hair sprays, Real Guys use "skin supplies" and "shaving resources." They adopt a "survival strategy" to fight balding, and the "Fila philosophy"— "products with a singular purpose: performance"—for effective "bodycare." If they wear scent, it smells of anything but flowers: musk, woods, spices, citrus, and surf are all acceptable. And the names must be manly, whether symbolizing physical power ("Brut") or financial power ("Giorgio VIP Special Reserve," "The Baron. A distinctive fragrance for men," "Halston—For the privileged few").

As power/precision/performance runs as a theme throughout advertising to men, so too do references to the business world. Cars, as we have seen, promise to share their owner's professional attitude and aggressive drive to beat out the competition. Other products similarly reflect the centrality of business competition to the male gender role. And at the center of this competition itself, the business suit.

At the onset of your business day, you choose the suit or sport coat that will position you
    front and center . . .
The Right Suit can't guarantee he'll see it your way. The wrong suit could mean not seeing him
    at all.

Along with the Right Suit, the right shirt. "You want it every time you reach across the conference
table, or trade on the floor, or just move about. You want a shirt that truly fits, that is long enough to
stay put through the most active day, even for the taller gentleman." The businessman chooses the right
cologne—Grey Flannel, or perhaps Quorum.

He wears a Gucci "timepiece" as he conducts business on a cordless telephone from his poolside—
or prefers the "dignity and styling" promised by Raymond Weil watches, "a beautiful way to dress for success."

Men's products connect status and success; the right products show that you have the right stuff,
that you're one of them. In the 1950s C. Wright Mills[10] described what it took to get ahead, to become
part of the "power elite":

The fit survive, and fitness means, not formal competence . . . but conformity with the criteria of those who have already succeeded. To be compatible with the top men is to act like
them, to look like them, to think like them: to be of and for them—or at least to display oneself to them in such a way as to create that impression. This, in fact, is what is meant by "creating"—a well-chosen word—"a good impression." This is what is meant—and nothing
else—by being a "sound man," as sound as a dollar.[11]

Today, having what it takes includes knowing "the difference between dressed, and well dressed"
(Bally shoes). It is knowing that "what you carry says as much about you is what you put inside it" (Hart-
mann luggage). It is knowing enough to imitate Doug Fout, "member of one of the foremost equestrian
families in the country."

Because of our adherence to quality and the natural shoulder tradition, Southwick clothing
was adopted by the Fout family years ago. Clearly, they have as much appreciation for good
lines in a jacket as they do in a thoroughbred.

There it is, old money. There is no substitute for it, really, in business or in advertising, where
appeals to tradition form one of the mainstays guaranteeing men that their choices are not overly fashionable or feminine, not working class or cheap, but, rather, correct, in good form, above criticism. If,
when, they achieve this status of gentlemanly perfection, then, the advertisement suggests, they may be
invited to join the club.

When only the best of associations will do

Recognizing style as the requisite for membership, discerning men prefer the natural shoulder styling of Racquet Club. Meticulously tailored in pure wool, each suit and sportcoat is
the ultimate expression of the clubman's classic good taste.

Ralph Lauren has his Polo University Club, and Rolex picks up on the polo theme by sponsoring
the Rolex Gold Cup held at the Palm Beach Polo and Country Club, where sixteen teams and sixty-four
players competed for "the pure honor of winning, the true glory of victory":

It has added new lustre to a game so ancient, its history is lost in legend Tamerlane is said to have been its patriarch. Darius's Persian cavalry, we're told, played it. It was the national sport of 16th-century India, Egypt, China, and Japan. The British rediscovered and named it in 1857.

The linking of polo and Rolex is uniquely appropriate. Both sponsor and sport personify rugged grace. Each is an arbiter of the art of timing.

In the spring of 1987, there was another interesting club event—or nonevent. The prestigious New York University Club was ordered to open its doors to women. This brought the expected protests about freedom of association—and of sanctuary. For that has been one of the points of the men's club. It wasn't open to women. Members knew women had their place, and everyone knew it was not there. In the advertisements, as in the world of reality, there is a place for women in men's lives, one that revolves around:

Sex and Seduction

The growing fascination with appearances, encouraged by advertising, has led to a "feminization" of culture. We are all put in the classic role of the female: manipulable, submissive, seeing ourselves as objects. This "feminization of sexuality" is clearly seen in men's advertisements, where many of the promises made to women are now made to men. If women's advertisements cry, "Buy (this product) and he will notice you," men's advertisements similarly promise that female attention will follow immediately upon purchase, or shortly thereafter. "They can't stay away from Mr. J." "Master the Art of Attracting Attention." She says, "He's wearing my favorite Corbin again." Much as in the advertisements directed at women, the advertisements of men's products promise that they will do the talking for you. "For the look that says come closer." "All the French you'll ever need to know."

Although many advertisements show an admiring and/or dependent female, others depict women in a more active role. "I love him—but life in the fast lane starts at 6 A.M.," says the attractive blonde tying on her jogging shoes, with the "him" in question very handsome and very asleep on the bed in the background. (Does this mean he's in the slow lane?) In another, the man slouches silhouetted against a wall; the woman leans aggressively toward him. He: "Do you always serve Tia Maria . . . or am I special?" She: "Darling, if you weren't special . . . you wouldn't be here."

The masculine role of always being in charge is a tough one. The blunt new honesty about sexually transmitted diseases such as AIDS appears in men's magazines as in women's, in the same "I enjoy sex, but I'm not ready to die for it" condom advertisement. But this new fear is accompanied by old fears of sexual embarrassment and/or rejection. The cartoon shows a man cringing with embarrassment in a pharmacy as the pharmacist yells out, "Hey, there's a guy here wants some information on Trojans." ("Most men would like to know more about Trojan brand condoms. But they're seriously afraid of suffering a spectacular and terminal attack of embarrassment right in the middle of a well-lighted drugstore.") Compared with such agony and responsibility, advertisements promising that women will *want* whatever is on offer, and will even meet the male halfway, must come as blessed relief. Men can finally relax, leaving the courting to the product and seduction to the beguiled woman, which, surely, must seem nice for a change.

Masculine Homilies

A homily is a short sermon, discourse, or informal lecture, often on a moral topic and suggesting a course of conduct. Some of the most intriguing advertisements offer just that, short statements and bits of advice on what masculinity is and on how real men should conduct themselves. As with many short sermons, many of the advertising homilies have a self-congratulatory air about th.m; after all, you do not want the consumer to feel bad about himself.

What is it, then, to be a man? It is to be *independent.* "There are some things a man will not relinquish." Among them says the advertisement his Tretorn tennis shoes.

It is to *savor freedom.* "Dress easy, get away from it all and let Tom Sawyer paint the fence," advises Alexander Julian, the men's designer.

"Because man was meant to fly, we gave him wings" (even if only on his sunglasses).

It is to live a life of *adventure.* KL Homme cologne is "for the man who lives on the edge." Prudential Life Insurance preaches. "If you can dream it, you can do it." New Man sportswear tells the reader, "Life is more adventurous when you feel like a New Man."

It is to *keep one's cool.* "J. B. Scotch. A few individuals know how to keep their heads, even when their necks are on the line."

And it is to stay one step *ahead of the competition.* "Altec Lansing. Hear what others only imagine." Alexander Julian again: "Dress up a bit when you dress down. They'll think you know something they don't."

What is it, then to be a woman? It is to be *dependent.* "A woman needs a man," reads the copy in the Rigolletto advertisement showing a young man changing a tire for a grateful young woman.

The America cowboy as cultural model was not supposed to care for or about appearances. He was what he was, hard-working, straightforward, and honest. He was authentic. Men who cared "too much" about how they looked did not fit this model; the dandy was effete, a European invention, insufficient in masculinity and not red-blooded enough to be a real American. The other cultural model, imported from England, was the gentleman. A gentleman did care about his appearance, in the proper measure and manifestation, attention to tailoring and to quality, understatement rather than exaggeration."

From the gray flannel suit of the 1950s to the "power look" of the 1980s, clothes made the man fit in with his company's image. Sex appeal and corporate correctness merged in a look that spelled success, that exuded confidence.

Whether or not a man presumed to care about his appearance, he did care about having "the right stuff," as Tom Wolfe and *Esquire* call it, or "men's toys," as in a recent special issue of *M* magazine. Cars, motorcycles, stereos, sports equipment: These are part of the masculine appearance. They allow the man to demonstrate his taste, his special knowledge his affluence: to extend his control. He can be and is demanding, for only the best will do.

He also wants to be loved, but he does not want to appear needy. Advertisements suggest the magic ability of products ranging from cars to hair creams to attract female attention. With the right products, a man call have it all, with no strings attached: no boring marital ties, hefty mortgages, corporate compromises.

According to sociologist Barbara Ehrenreich, *Playboy* magazine did much to legitimate this image of male freedom. The old male ethos, up to the postwar period, required exchanging bachelor irresponsibility for married responsibility, which also symbolized entrance into social adulthood.[13] The perennial bachelor, with his flashy cars and interchangeable women, was the object of both envy and derision; he had fun, but . . . he was not fully grown up. There was something frivolous in his lack of purpose and application.

This old ethos has lost much of its legitimacy. Today's male can, as Baudrillard suggests, operate in both modes: the feminine mode of indulging oneself and being indulged and the masculine mode of exigency and competition. With the right look and the right stuff, he can feel confident and manly in boardroom or suburban backyard. Consumer society thus invites both men and women to live in a world of appearances and to devote ever more attention to them.

Notes

1. Katz and Katz, *Magazine*, pp. 703-5.

2. Ibid.

3. John Gagnon, "Physical Strength: Once of Significance," in Joseph H. Pleck and Jack Sawyer, eds., *Men and Masculinity* (Englewood Cliffs, NJ.: Prentice-Hall, 1974), pp. 139-49.

4. **Jean Baudrillard** (b. 1929) French semiologist.—EDS.

5. Baudrillard, *La société de consommation*. pp. 144-47.

6. Ibid.

7. Ibid.

8. Todd Gitlin; "We Build Excitement," in Todd Gitlin, ed., *Watching Television* (New York: Pantheon, 1986), pp. 139-40.

9. Ibid.

10. **C. Wright Mills** (1916-1962) American sociologist.—EDS.

11. C. Wright Mills, *The Power Elite* (NewYork: Oxford University Press, 1956), p 141.

12. See Diane Barthel. "A Gentleman and a Consumer: A Sociological Look at Man at His Best," paper presented at the annual meeting of the Eastern Sociological Society, March 1983, Baltimore.

13. Barbara Ehrenreich, *The Hearts of Men: American Dreams and the Flight from Commitment* (New York: Anchor Books, 1983).

Questions for Discussion

1. How does Barthel characterize the "masculine model" of advertising? What does she have to say about the "feminine" model?

2. On page 385, Barthel says that "Men's products connect status and success; the right products show that you have the right stuff, that you're one of them." Who is "them"? How could you characterize "them" in terms of race, class, gender, and sexuality?

3. In her conclusion, Barthel contends that males "can operate in both modes," using qualities of both the masculine and feminine models. Do you agree with her? Can females also operate in both modes? Are there advantages to operating in both modes?

Explorations

1. The core assumption of Barthel's argument is that advertising has the power not only to influence collective and individual behaviors, but also to construct them. In "AIDS, Ads and Us vs. Them," Michael Meyers makes a similar assertion, though his conclusion is that ads, in reflecting social boundaries, can fashion destructive behaviors. In what ways are the authors' arguments similar, and how do they differ?

2. Though Barthel premises her discussion of the effect of advertising on a combination of visual and textual rhetoric in ads, she concentrates most on the textual, or written, components of advertisements. How could Robert Scholes' essay, "On Reading a Video Text" or John Berger's "Ways of Seeing" complement the analysis Barthel has already done?

3. Barthel seems to equate masculine with male and feminine with female. How does Holly Devor's reading of gender in "Gender Role Behaviors and Attitudes" complicate Barthel's equation?

Formal Writing Assignments

1. Barthel is strongly urging the reader to feel helpless in the face of an all-powerful advertising industry. Consider closely your own conception of your gender, and then compare it to the way in which you have been conceived by an advertisement or commercial. Do they differ or resemble one another? How and why?

2. Examine closely the argument that Barthel makes. Where are the holes, the places where she could have said more but did not, or the places where her argument is not well supported. Find another theorist in this book who might strengthen Barthel's argument, or one who might refute her argument altogether.

The Production of Technology and the Production of Human Meaning

Charles Bazerman

Charles Bazerman (b. 1945) has engaged for most of his career in studying the nature of language and the interrelationships among communities of language. He spent the major part of his academic career at Baruch College of CUNY, publishing *The Reading Skills Handbook, The Informed Writer,* and *Shaping Written Knowledge.* As a full professor, Bazerman left Baruch in 1990 for Georgia Tech, where he continued his work with rhetoric through texts such as *Constructing Experience.* His most recent move has been to the English Department at University of California, Santa Barbara, where he now teaches such undergraduate courses as "Discourse, Social Action, Culture and Consciousness" and "Theories of Genre: The Shape of Communicative Action." His most recent book, *The Languages of Edison's Light,* concerns the development of a discourse about electricity through words and symbols. The following essay demonstrates the interdisciplinarity of Bazerman's interests and work, particularly his interest in the rhetoric of science, and provides distinctions between rhetorics of science and technology that may be useful to a discussion of either.

Writing Before Reading

1. Recall and record one of your first experiences with technology. Did you feel prepared to use it? Did you feel that it was "user-friendly"?

2. List the languages you use in science and math classes. Think about your reactions to those languages. Are the languages ones that you can use outside of those environments?

3. Some people have a great need for language to have fixed and stable meanings. Others need language to be fluid and shifting. Yet others seem never to think about language. Ponder your own attitude and write a brief paragraph addressing what you need from and find in language?

The Production of Technology and the Production of Human Meaning

What is a rhetoric of technology? How would rhetoric help us understand technology? How would a rhetoric of technology differ from a rhetoric of science? How would it be distinctive from other domains of rhetorical practice? How would it deepen our understanding of rhetoric? How would a rhetoric of technology help us understand our current way of life? These are some of the questions I encountered while working on *The Languages of Edison's Light,* a book about the symbolic, representational, and rhetorical work that accompanied the emergence of the incandescent light as an everyday technology.

On the face of it, my Edison project is a study about the rhetoric of technology because it examines the rhetorical productions that surround a material technology. So just as people have examined the rhetoric of science, economics, sociology, psychology, presidential campaigns, and legal briefs, I now explore the rhetoric of technology. But this project on Edisonian rhetoric turned out to be as much a project in the rhetoric of the patent system and civil court proceedings, in the rhetoric of financial investment and stock market reports, in the rhetoric of the nineteenth-century newspaper and mass circulation magazines, in the rhetoric of the new technical and financial press, in the rhetoric of small group collaboration and large corporate communications, and in the rhetoric of civic regulation, regional boosterism, and Tammany Hall politics as it was in the rhetoric of technology. The electrical technology must make its presence felt in all these discursive arenas, must take on value and meaning in the language and discursive interaction of each. So in what sense is my study of the representations of Edison's incandescent light especially a project in the rhetoric of technology? And in what sense, if any, can there be a specialized realm of rhetorical studies called a rhetoric of technology?

Three Distinctions

These last two questions can be put in greater relief if we make three distinctions between the rhetorical studies of technology and those of science. The first distinction concerns the identification of the fields; the second, the degree of enclosure that bounds the fields; and the last, the effect of materiality on the symbolic activity.

First, the rhetoric of science in the short run has seemed to be relatively unproblematic to define as a special area, although in the long run that may not be the case. The only recurrent definitional issue that has troubled the rhetoric of science has been precisely whether, and to what extent, science is rhetorical. I will not rehearse here the now-familiar arguments and history of the issue but only point out that some rhetoricians and scientists still would like to consider science as knowledge that is privileged and therefore free of rhetoric, knowledge that rises above the situated and purposeful use of language. Throughout the history of the rise of modern science, from the time of Francis Bacon to the time of Hans Reichenbach and Karl Popper, there have been explicit attempts to distance natural philosophy and then science from rhetoric. We can even trace to Plato and Aristotle the impulse to distinguish the uncertain persuasions of rhetoric from those domains of philosophic inquiry that provided access to certain knowledge. At various times, experimentation, methodology, objectivity, and mathematical formulations have been seen as the key ingredients that demarcate science from other less certain endeavors.

In a way, the very surprise of the title rhetoric of science defines it as a field and has driven the kinds of questions that attracted the field's early controversialists. Is the title an oxymoron or a tautology? The intrigue of the field's title allows even those people who would simply subsume science into prior forms of rhetoric, such as Alan Gross or Lawrence Prelli, to still identify their work as rhetoric of science instead of just rhetoric that happens to be examining some texts appearing in science journals. I think the real question is, How does the phrase "rhetoric of science" manage to be both oxymoron and tautology? That is, how can science-working through human symbolic means that are faulted, imprecise, and multiple perspectival, nonetheless establish a high level of agreement, stability, mutual alignment to symbolic representations, and reliability in guiding behavior? Furthermore, how can the symbolic representations of science facilitate unimagined material projects and counterintuitive investigations? What set of historical developments engendered a form of discourse within specialized systems of discourse circulation, distinct from other discursive practices and networks, with a consequence of reorganizing relations with the material world and with other social discursive systems?

Although science has gained the appearance of distinctiveness from other realms of rhetoric, technology has always been part of the rhetorical barnyard, part of commerce and finances, customers and vendors, partnerships and corporations, suppliers and production, lawyers and courts. Even more, technology has always been fundamentally designed to meet human ends. Thus, technology, as a human-made object, has always been part of human needs, desires, values, and evaluation, articulated in language and at the very heart of rhetoric. Although science has at times been able to wrap itself in a mantle of disinterested curiosity, free of overt interests (although we know this is never the case—scientists' curiosities are driven by who they are, and societies fund the kind of knowledge they need and want), technology must always overtly appeal to the marketplace, political ambitions, and personal desire.

That brings us to our second distinction, which is as rough and loose as the first, filled with exceptions and qualifications, but nonetheless as recognizably true. In the past few centuries, science has been an increasingly enclosed specialized communication system, explicitly creating distances between itself and other systems of communication. Tom Gieryn has pointed toward the boundary work by which scientists at particular moments (e.g., during the Scopes trial), to assert science's authority as a privileged way of knowing, have engaged in public campaigns to create strong boundaries between science and other sources of knowledge and belief. Within the bounded discursive world of science, an intertext of cited works or a literature defines a gradually transforming discursive space within which new claims vie for acceptance, judged by an epistemic court of insider specialists. This enclosed communication system must then represent itself and its knowledge outward to the other public realms, to spread its influence, to petition for resources, and to establish and maintain its boundaries and authority. So a rhetoric of science can study an internal discourse of claim making, a socially contentious discourse of boundary creation and maintenance, and an outward-facing, interest-driven discourse of professional representation. The discursive communities and directions are rather clearly drawn, even though recent developments in computing and genetic sciences have overtly transgressed these socially constructed boundaries.

In contrast, although some producers of technology work within discursive enclosures of professions, corporations, and specialties, these enclosures are smaller, more recent, and more permeable. Furthermore, the technology itself moves rapidly outward from the small worlds of the expert innovators into the lives of many different kinds of people. The technology, as in the case of Edison's incandescent light and central power, must often enlist the support of numerous publics (financial, legal, corporate, public, technical) long before it becomes anything like a material reality. Certainly, scientists and science laboratories do need support from academic sponsors and granting agencies, but usually this support is mediated through science-controlled peer review, with the intended consequence that the arguments for the value of the projected work can be largely cast in terms of internal scientific values. The words of technology, however, seem to flow all over the discursive landscape, arguing for value in the terms of business, law, government, the public, and consumers (Bijker; Bijker, Hughes, and Pinch; Latour). Even the professional knowledges of engineering sciences are permeable interdisciplinary spaces that are organized around practical problems and projects rather than the advancement of a disciplinary account. The discourse of technology is as pervasive as the electricity that comes out of all our walls. Even the discourses of law or journalism, both of which comprise representation spaces that draw the entire world into them, are more enclosed than technological discourse. Both law and journalism require that the world be translated into their terms to be regulated or to become news, but technology is translated into the terms of the world so as to gain the support and use it requires for its existence.

The enclosure of scientific discourse versus the profligacy of discourse about the technical that accompanies technological objects around the world is related to a third distinction: Technology for the most part produces objects and material processes; science for the most part produces symbols. Science generally produces claims as its end product—mathematical, graphic, or verbal symbols. So once you argue that those symbols are rhetorical—that is, the strategic result of human processes of contention, fought out with words (although also in relation to the material practices of data gathering and experiments)—then the entire project becomes deeply rhetorical, calling for examination of its language at every turn. Technology, on the other hand, generally circulates objects and material processes, not words. Words, pictures, and numbers may accompany—in the fundraising, the contracts, the manuals, or the advertising-but the technology itself has a seemingly physical obduracy. Of course, as the history of technology has always shown, the material embodies intentions and plans and perceived uses—armaments are built for wars with specific perceived enemies with known weapons, and bicycles are designed for users with specific leisure or transportation needs. Moreover, recent constructivist studies show how technologies embody interests, negotiations, and struggles, as well as the enlistment of users, so that different constituencies contend for design control of arms or bicycles. So there is a kind of material rhetoric in whether a company produces daredevil racing cycles or safe and comfortable bikes for everyday transport. But, ultimately, it is the material object that conveys the primary rhetoric and not the language that went into forming the technology and conceiving its uses and meanings.

A Rhetoric of Technology

So what is a rhetoric of technology? It is the rhetoric that accompanies technology and makes it possible—the rhetoric that makes technology fit into the world and makes the world fit with technology. There is a dialectic between rhetoric and the material design as the technology is made to fit the imaginably useful and valuable, to fit into people's understanding of the world. Technological discourse is a special coalescence of the many discourses of the world. Consider how the technology of architecture brings new buildings to life in the midst of proposals to clients, legal codes, contractual relations, financial discussions, blueprints and materials specifications, negotiations with contractors, and postmodern theories of aesthetics. Of course, science discourse also intersects at many points with other differentiated discourses from the legal and even criminal to the political, financial, or cultural—but yet we can still perceive those in relation to a primary discourse of knowledge production among specialists.

So given that the rhetoric of technology encompasses such a promiscuous and varied range of practices—whose only defining feature is its relation to the material technology being imagined, projected, advanced, managed, coped with, or that is emergent in the world of multiple affairs—why is the rhetoric of technology special in character or importance? Why does it not just decompose into the separate discourses that it engages? What is there separate to study that is not a rhetoric of law, finance, journalism, or corporate organizations? First, the obduracy of the technological object, although it may be plastic in its uses, meanings, and interpretations, challenges the discourses it intersects with to assimilate its otherness. The rhetoric of technology shows how the objects of the built environment become part of our systems of goals, values, and meaning, part of our articulated interests, struggles, and activities. The technological object, its circulation in many social worlds, and the impact it has on our daily lives give rise to the further discourses of new corporations; social communication among enthusiasts, expert users, and aficionados (e.g., computer user groups and auto collectors); and talk by people simply living in the wake of the new technology.

The changed conditions of life made possible by the introductions of new technology create new realms of discussion as we try to figure out what these changed conditions mean, what problems they pose, and what we can accomplish within them. Technology constantly invites social, legal, personal, and economic discussions that shape how that technology becomes incorporated into new ways of life. This strong discursive force of technology—the fact that we cannot seem to stop talking about the latest technological presence in our life—may make it seem that the technology is determining our life, and we are only reacting. All that talk, however, determines what the technology becomes and what our society becomes with the new tools of technology.

Nonetheless, the course of that technological development is necessarily interactant with many other powerful discursive systems, and if there seems to be an inevitable trajectory it is not technologically determined in itself, it is in the alliance of the several discourses that provide major meanings for the technology. For example, consider the way patent monopolies, corporate imperatives, and government planning and policy values came together with citizen desires in a post-World War II period, ideological competitions, booming economies and international economic competition, and domestic and international political talk about international security to foster nuclear and rocket technology in the middle of this century. The inevitability of the arms race, if it was inevitable, lay in the coming together of these many systems of meaning and not just in the demonstrated possibilities of big explosions and distant, delivery (see MacKenzie).

Because we are living at a time when our lives seem so caught up in the apparent opportunities and imperatives of technology, the rhetoric of technology—that is, the rhetoric of all the discourses that surround and embed technology—is a particularly useful endeavor. By picking apart the conjunction of the powerful discursive forces that create value for and give shape to technological developments and their uses, we can begin to regain some of our choices about the technological future we will live in.

References

Bazerman, Charles. *The Languages of Edison's Light*. Cambridge. MA: MIT Press, forthcoming.

Bijker, Wiebe. *Of Bicycles, Bakelite, and Bulbs*. Cambridge, MA: MIT Press, 1995.

Bijker, Wiebe, Thomas Hughes, and Trevor Pinch. *The Social Construction of Technological Systems*. Cambridge, MA: MIT Press, 1987.

Gieryn, Tom. "Boundary-Work and the Demarcation of Science from Non-Science: Strains and Interests in Professional Ideologies of Scientists." *American Sociological Review* 48 (1983): 781–95.

Gross, Alan G. *The Rhetoric of Science*. Cambridge, MA: Harvard University Press, 1990.

Latour, Bruno. *Aramis or the Love of Technology*. Cambridge, MA: Harvard University Press, 1996.

MacKenzie, Donald A. *Inventing Accuracy: An Historical Sociology of Nuclear Missile Guidance*. Cambridge, MA: MIT Press, 1990.

Prelli, Lawrence J. *A Rhetoric of Science: Inventing Scientific Discourse*. Columbia: University of South Carolina Press, 1989.

Questions for Discussion

1. In his first distinction between a rhetoric of technology and a rhetoric of science, Bazerman raises the issue of science's supposed freedom from rhetoric. How does Bazerman refute that argument, and how does he then set apart the rhetoric of technology?

2. In his second distinction, Bazerman claims that "technology is translated into the terms of the world." Later, towards his conclusion, he argues that our talk about technology "determines what technology becomes and what our society becomes with the new tools of technology." In the first quote, it appears that technology serves us; in the second, technology seems to serve us but ultimately also shapes us ("what our society becomes"). What roles does a rhetoric of technology play in shaping and reflecting identities, and for what is Bazerman arguing?

3. Bazerman finally suggests that understanding the complicated network of discourses that is a rhetoric of technology can help us understand other rhetorics as well. Do you agree?

Explorations

1. Bazerman challenges the notion that science is free from rhetoric. Think about his challenge in relation to Ruth Herschberger's "Society Writes Biology," where Herschberger unequivocally asserts that even biology can be considered a construction. How are their arguments similar? Dissimilar?

2. Central to Bazerman's argument is that the rhetoric of technology is a synthetic one, taking bits and pieces from multiple discourses, and that this is its strength. Robert Samuelson makes the point in "Technology in Reverse," however, that not all technologies are valuable but some are "retarded." Could the fragmentedness of technology rhetoric be related to Samuelson's retardedness?

3. Bazerman's essay argues for distinctions between rhetorics of science and technology, setting up the rhetoric of technology as a more democratic and socially active medium than that of science. Yet Cynthia Selfe points out in "Lest We Think The Revolution is a Revolution" that technology can be simply a more sophisticated medium for delivering the same old messages. Can both of these arguments be valid? How?

Formal Writing Assignments

1. Choose a rhetoric with which you are familiar—for instance, a rhetoric of the first year student, or a rhetoric of avant-garde movies, or a rhetoric of popular music—and examine its qualities. Is it a closed system, as Bazerman says science is, or are its boundaries as permeable as Bazerman's technology? Is its nature a valuable trait, or one that needs dismantling?

2. In his conclusion, Bazerman suggests that it is in knowing about and understanding "the powerful discursive forces that create value for and give shape to technological developments and their uses" that we "regain" power over our lives. What does the use of "regain" mean about our lives? If rhetoric is so pervasive, can we hope to control it?

Ways of Seeing

John Berger

Born in London in 1926, John Berger has been instrumental in influencing the way we in the modern western world think about images, words, and their intersections. He was educated at London's Central School of Art and the Chelsea School of Art but has worked in a variety of genres: novels and short stories, art, art criticism, literary criticism and history, sociology, non-fiction, poetry, screenwriting, translations, and acting. Most of his work in art history reflects the interdisciplinarity of his interests, demonstrated by a multi-media approach in books such as *Ways of Seeing* (1972), *About Looking* (1980), and *Another Way of Telling* (1982). Since 1973, Berger has lived in a remote peasant village in an un-trendy part of the French Alps; this locale and its inhabitants have informed most of the fiction he has written in the last nearly three decades, including his most recent work, the 1996 *Photocopies*. The following essay is the introductory chapter from *Ways of Seeing*, written collaboratively and based on the BBC series of the same name.

Writing Before Reading

1. Describe in a few sentences your perception of an art museum, and on what this perception is based: experience, hearsay, or a combination? How do you think of the art, and what role do you imagine it playing in your life?

2. Recall two advertisements, one including images and written text, the other only images. Using lists, itemize how each of the ads' images is affected by the presence or absence of words.

3. Write a brief paragraph defining what you think the role of an artist should be.

Ways of Seeing

Seeing comes before words. The child looks and recognizes before it can speak.

But there is also another sense in which seeing comes before words. It is seeing which establishes our place in the surrounding world; we explain that world with words, but words can never undo the fact that we are surrounded by it. The relation between what we *see* and what we know is never settled. Each evening we see the sun set. We *know* that the earth is turning away from it. Yet the knowledge, the explanation, never quite fits the sight. The Surrealist painter Magritte commented on this always-present gap between words and seeing in a painting called *The Key of Dreams*.

The Key of Dreams By Magritte 1898-1967

The way we see things is affected by what we know or what we believe. In the Middle Ages when men believed in the physical existence of Hell the sight of fire must have meant something different from what it means today. Nevertheless their idea of Hell owed a lot to the sight of fire consuming and the ashes remaining—as well as to their experience of the pain of burns.

When in love, the sight of the beloved has a completeness which no words and no embrace can match: a completeness which only the act of making love can temporarily accommodate.

Yet this seeing which comes before words, and can never be quite covered by them, is not a question of mechanically reacting to stimuli. (It can only be thought of in this way if one isolates the small part of the process which concerns the eye's retina.) We only see what we look at. To look is an act of choice. As a result of this act, what we see is brought within our reach—though not necessarily within arm's reach. To touch something is to situate oneself in relation to it. (Close your eyes, move round the room and notice how the faculty of touch is like a static, limited form of sight.) We never look at just one thing; we are always looking at the relation between things and ourselves. Our vision is continually active, continually moving, continually holding things in a circle around itself, constituting what is present to us as we are.

Soon after we can see, we are aware that we can also be seen. The eye of the other combines with our own eye to make it fully credible that we are part of the visible world.

If we accept that we can see that hill over there, we propose that from that hill we can be seen. The reciprocal nature of vision is more fundamental then that of spoken dialogue. And often dialogue is an attempt to verbalize this—an attempt to explain how, either metaphorically or literally, 'you see things', and an attempt to discover how 'he sees things'.

In the sense in which we use the word in this book, all images are man-made.

An image is a sight which has been recreated or reproduced. It is an appearance, or a set of appearances, which has been detached from the place and time in which it first made its appearance and preserved—for a few moments or a few centuries. Every image embodies a way of seeing. Even a photograph. For photographs are not, as is often assumed, a mechanical record. Every time we look at a photograph, we are aware, however slightly, of the photographer selecting that sight from an infinity of other possible sights. This is true even in the most casual family snapshot. The photographer's way of seeing is reflected in his choice of subject. The painter's way of seeing is reconstituted by the marks he makes on the canvas or paper. Yet, although every image embodies a way of seeing, our perception or appreciation of an image depends also upon our own way of seeing. (It may be, for example, that Sheila is one figure among twenty; but for our own reasons she is the one we have eyes for.)

*   *   *

Images were first made to conjure up the appearances of something that was absent. Gradually it became evident that an image could outlast what it represented; it then showed how something or somebody had once looked—and thus by implication how the subject had once been seen by other people. Later still the specific vision of the image-maker was also recognized as part of the record. An image became a record of how X had seen Y. This was the result of an increasing consciousness of individuality, accompanying an increasing awareness of history. It would be rash to try to date this last development precisely. But certainly in Europe such consciousness has existed since the beginning of the Renaissance.

No other kind of relic or text from the past can offer such a direct testimony about the world which surrounded other people at other times. In this respect images are more precise and richer than literature. To say this is not to deny the expressive or imaginative quality of art, treating it as mere documentary evidence; the more imaginative the work, the more profoundly it allows us to share the artist's experience of the visible.

Yet when an image is presented as a work of art, the way people look at it is affected by a whole series of learnt assumptions about art. Assumptions concerning:

Beauty
Truth
Genius
Civilization
Form
Status
Taste, etc.

Many of these assumptions no longer accord with the world as it is. (The world-as-it-is is more than pure objective fact, it includes consciousness.) Out of true with the present, these assumptions obscure the past. They mystify rather than clarify. The past is never there waiting to be discovered, to be recognized for exactly what it is. History always constitutes the relation between a present and its past. Consequently fear of the present leads to mystification of the past. The past is not for living in; it is a well of conclusions from which we draw in order to act. Cultural mystification of the past entails a double loss. Works of art are made unnecessarily remote. And the past offers us fewer conclusions to complete in action.

When we 'see' a landscape, we situate ourselves in it. If we 'saw' the art of the past, we would situate ourselves in history. When we are prevented from seeing it, we are being deprived of the history which belongs to us. Who benefits from this deprivation? In the end, the art of the past is being mystified because a privileged minority is striving to invent a history which can retrospectively justify the role of the ruling classes, and such a justification can no longer make sense in modern terms. And so, inevitably, it mystifies.

Let us consider a typical example of such mystification. A two-volume study was recently published on Frans Hals. It is the authoritative work to date on this painter. As a book of specialized art history it is no better and no worse than the average.

* Seymour Slive, *Frans Hals* (Phaidon, London)

The last two great paintings by Frans Hals portray the Governors and the Governesses of an Alms House for old paupers in the Dutch seventeenth-century city of Haarlem. They were officially commissioned portraits. Hals, an old man of over eighty, was destitute. Most of his life he had been in debt. During the winter of 1664, the year he began painting these pictures, he obtained three loads of peat on public charity, otherwise he would have frozen to death. Those who now sat for him were administrators of such public charity.

The author records these facts and then explicitly says that it would be incorrect to read into the paintings any criticism of the sitters. There is no evidence, he says, that Hals painted them in a spirit of bitterness. The author considers them, however, remarkable works of art and explains why. Here he writes of the Regentesses:

> Each woman speaks to us of the human condition with equal importance. Each woman stands out with equal clarity against the *enormous* dark surface, yet they are linked by a firm rhythmical arrangement and the subdued diagonal pattern formed by their heads and hands. Subtle modulations of the *deep*, glowing blacks contribute to the *harmonious fusion* of the whole and form an *unforgettable contrast* with the *powerful* whites and vivid flesh tones where the detached strokes reach *a peak of breadth and strength*. (our italics)

The compositional unity of a painting contributes fundamentally to the power of its image. It is reasonable to consider a painting's composition. But here the composition is written about as though it were in itself the emotional charge of the painting. Terms like harmonious fusion, unforgettable contrast, reaching a peak of breadth and strength transfer the emotion provoked by the image from the plane of lived experience, to that of disinterested 'art appreciation'. All conflict disappears. One is left with the unchanging 'human condition', and the painting considered as a marvellously made object. Very little is known about Hals or the Regents who commissioned him. It is not possible to produce circumstantial evidence to establish what their relations were. But there is the evidence of the paintings themselves: the evidence of a group of men and a group of women as seen by another man, the painter. Study this evidence and judge for yourself.

The art historian fears such direct judgement:

As in so many other pictures by Hals, the penetrating characterizations almost seduce us into believing that we know the personality traits and even the habits of the men and women portrayed.

What is this 'seduction' he writes of ? It is nothing less than the paintings working upon us. They work upon us because we accept the way Hals saw his sitters. We do not accept this innocently. We accept it in so far as it corresponds to our own observation of people, gestures, faces, institutions. This is possible because we still live in a society of comparable social relations and moral values. And it is precisely this which gives the paintings their psychological and social urgency. It is this — not the painter's skill as a 'seducer' — which convinces us that we can know the people portrayed. The author continues:

In the case of some critics the seduction has been a total success. It has, for example, been asserted that the Regent in the tipped slouch fiat, which hardly covers any of his long, lank hair, and whose curiously set eyes do not focus, was shown in a drunken state.

This, he suggests, is a libel. He argues that it was a fashion at that time to wear hats on the side of the head. He cites medical opinion to prove that the Regent's expression could well be the result of a facial paralysis. He insists that the painting would have been unacceptable to the Regents if one of them had been portrayed drunk. One might go on discussing each of these points for pages. (Men in seventeenth-century Holland wore their hats on the side of their heads in order to be thought of as adventurous and pleasure-loving. Heavy drinking was an approved practice. Etcetera.) But such a discussion would take us even farther away from the only confrontation which matters and which the author is determined to evade.

In this confrontation the Regents and Regentesses stare at Hals, a destitute old painter who has lost his reputation and lives off public charity; he examines them through the eyes of a pauper who must nevertheless try to be objective, i.e., must try to surmount the way he sees as a pauper. This is the drama of these paintings. A drama of an 'unforgettable contrast'.

Mystification has little to do with the vocabulary used. Mystification is the process of explaining away what might otherwise be evident. Hals was the first portraitist to paint the new characters and expressions created by capitalism. He did in pictorial terms what Balzac did two centuries later in literature. Yet the author of the authoritative work on these paintings sums up the artist's achievement by referring to

> Hals's unwavering commitment to his personal vision, which enriches our consciousness of our fellow men and heightens our awe for the ever-increasing power of the mighty impulses that enabled him to give us a close view of life's vital forces.

That is mystification. In order to avoid mystifying the past (which can equally well suffer pseudo-Marxist mystification) let us now examine the particular relation which now exists, so far as pictorial images are concerned, between the present and the past. If we can see the present clearly enough, we shall ask the right questions of the past.

Today we see the art of the past as nobody saw it before. We actually perceive it in a different way. This difference can be illustrated in terms of what was thought of as perspective. The convention of perspective, which is unique to European art and which was first established in the early Renaissance, centres everything on the eye of the beholder. It is like a beam from a lighthouse — only instead of light travelling outwards, appearances travel in. The conventions called those appearances *reality*. Perspective makes the single eye the centre of the visible world. Everything converges on to the eye as to the vanishing point of infinity. The visible world is arranged for the spectator as the universe was once thought to be arranged for God.

According to the convention of perspective there is no visual reciprocity. There is no need for God to situate himself in relation to others: he is himself the situation. The inherent contradiction in perspective was that it structured all images of reality to address a single spectator who, unlike God, could only be in one place at a time.

After the invention of the camera this contradiction gradually became apparent.

Still From Man With A Movie Camera By Vertov

I'm an eye. A mechanical eye. I, the machine, show you a world the way only I can see it. I free myself for today and forever from human immobility. I'm in constant movement. I approach and pull away from objects. I creep under them. I move alongside a running horse's mouth. I fall and rise with the falling and rising bodies. This is I, the machine, manoeuvring in the chaotic movements, recording one movement after another in the most complex combinations.

Freed from the boundaries of time and space, I co-ordinate any and all points of the universe, wherever I want them to be. My way leads towards the creation of a fresh perception of the world. Thus I explain in a new way the world unknown to you.*

*This quotation is from an article written in 1923 by Dziga Vertov, the revolutionary Soviet film director

The camera isolated momentary appearances and in so doing destroyed the idea that images were timeless. Or, to put it another way, the camera showed that the notion of time passing was inseparable from the experience of the visual (except in paintings). What you saw depended upon where you were when. What you saw was relative to your position in time and space. It was no longer possible to imagine everything converging on the human eye as on the vanishing point of infinity.

This is not to say that before the invention of the camera men believed that everyone could see everything. But perspective organized the visual field as though that were indeed the ideal. Every drawing or painting that used perspective proposed to the spectator that he was the unique centre of the world. The camera — and more particularly the movie camera — demonstrated that there was no centre.

The invention of the camera changed the way men saw. The visible came to mean something different to them. This was immediately reflected in painting.

For the Impressionists the visible no longer presented itself to man in order to be seen. On the contrary, the visible, in continual flux, became fugitive. For the Cubists the visible was no longer what confronted the single eye, but the totality of possible views taken from points all round the object (or person) being depicted.

Still Life With Wicker Chair By Picasso 1881

The invention of the camera also changed the way in which men saw paintings painted long before the camera was invented. Originally paintings were an integral part of the building for which they were designed. Sometimes in an early Renaissance church or chapel one has the feeling that the images on the wall are records of the building's interior life, that together they make up the building's memory—so much are they part of the particularity of the building.

Church of St. Francis At Assisi

The uniqueness of every painting was once part of the uniqueness of the place where it resided. Sometimes the painting was transportable. But it could never be seen in two places at the same time. When the camera reproduces a painting, it destroys the uniqueness of its image. As a result its meaning changes. Or, more exactly, its meaning multiplies and fragments into many meanings.

This is vividly illustrated by what happens when a painting is shown on a television screen. The painting enters each viewer's house. There it is surrounded by his wallpaper, his furniture, his mementoes. It enters the atmosphere of his family. It becomes their talking point. It lends its meaning to their meaning. At the same time it enters a million other houses and, in each of them, is seen in a different context. Because of the camera, the painting now travels to the spectator rather than the spectator to the painting. In its travels, its meaning is diversified.

One might argue that all reproductions more or less distort, and that therefore the original painting is still in a sense unique. Here is a reproduction of the *Virgin of the Rocks* by Leonardo da Vinci.

Virgin of the Rocks By Leonardo Da Vinci 1452-1519
National Gallery

Having seen this reproduction, one can go to the National Gallery to look at the original and there discover what the reproduction lacks. Alternatively one can forget about the quality of the reproduction and simply be reminded, when one sees the original, that it is a famous painting of which somewhere one has already seen a reproduction. But in either case the uniqueness of the original now lies in it being the original of a reproduction. It is no longer what its image shows that strikes one as unique; its first meaning is no longer to be found in what it says, but in what it is.

This new status of the original work is the perfectly rational consequence of the new means of reproduction. But it is at this point that a process of mystification again enters. The meaning of the original work no longer lies in what it uniquely says but in what it uniquely is. How is its unique existence evaluated and defined in our present culture? It is defined as an object whose value depends upon its rarity. This value is affirmed and gauged by the price it fetches on the market. But because it is nevertheless 'a work of art'—and art is thought to be greater than commerce—its market price is said to be a reflection of its spiritual value. Yet the spiritual value of an object, as distinct from a message or an example, can only be explained in terms of magic or religion. And since in modern society neither of these is a living force, the art object, the 'work of art', is enveloped in an atmosphere of entirely bogus religiosity. Works of art are discussed and presented as though they were holy relics: relics which are first and foremost evidence of their own survival. The past in which they originated is studied in order to prove their survival genuine. They are declared art when their line of descent can be certified.

Before the *Virgin of the Rocks* the visitor to the National Gallery would be encouraged by nearly everything he might have heard and read about the painting to feel something like this: 'I am in front of it. I can see it. This painting by Leonardo is unlike any other in the world. The National

Gallery has the real one. If I look at this painting hard enough, I should somehow be able to feel its authenticity. The *Virgin of the Rocks* by Leonardo da Vinci: it is authentic and therefore it is beautiful.'

To dismiss such feelings as naive would be quite wrong. They accord perfectly with the sophisticated culture of art experts for whom the National Gallery catalogue is written. The entry on the *Virgin of the Rocks* is one of the longest entries. It consists of fourteen closely printed pages. They do not deal with the meaning of the image. They deal with who commissioned the painting, legal squabbles, who owned it, its likely date, the families of its owners. Behind this information lie years of research. The aim of the research is to prove beyond any shadow of doubt that the painting is a genuine Leonardo. The secondary aim is to prove that an almost identical painting in the Louvre is a replica of the National Gallery version.

National Gallery

Virgin of the Rocks By Leonardo Da Vinci 1452-1519 Louvre

French art historians try to prove the opposite.

The Virgin and Child with St Ann and St. John the Baptist
By Leonardo Da Vinci 1452-1519

The National Gallery sells more reproductions of Leonardo's cartoon of *The Virgin and Child with St Anne and St John the Baptist* than any other picture in their collection. A few years ago it was known only to scholars. It became famous because an American wanted to buy it for two and a half million pounds.

Now it hangs in a room by itself. The room is like a chapel. The drawing is behind bullet-proof perspex. It has acquired a new kind of impressiveness. Not because of what it shows—not because of the meaning of its image. It has become impressive, mysterious, because of its market value.

The bogus religiosity which now surrounds original works of art, and which is ultimately dependent upon their market value, has become the substitute for what paintings lost when the camera made them reproducible. Its function is nostalgic. It is the final empty claim for the continuing values of an oligarchic, undemocratic culture. If the image is no longer unique and exclusive, the art object, the thing, must be made mysteriously so.

The majority of the population do not visit art museums. The following table shows how closely an interest in art is related to privileged education.

National proportion of art museum visitors according to level of education:
Percentage of each educational category who visit art museums

	Greece	Poland	France	Holland		Greece	Poland	France	Holland
With no educational qualification	0.02	0.12	0.15	—	Only secondary education	10.5	10.4	10	20
Only primary education	0.30	1.50	0.45	0.50	Further and higher education	11.5	11.7	12.5	17.3

Source: Pierre Bourdieu and Alain Darbel, *L'Amour de L'Art*, Editions de Minuit, Paris 1969, Appendix 5, table 4

The majority take it as axiomatic that the museums are full of holy relics which refer to a mystery which excludes them: the mystery of unaccountable wealth. Or, to put this another way, they believe that original masterpieces belong to the preserve (both materially and spiritually) of the rich. Another table indicates what the idea of an art gallery suggests to each social class.

Of the places listed below which does a museum remind you of most?		
	Manual Workers	Skilled and white collar worker	Professional and upper managerial
	%	%	%
Church	66	45	30.5
Library	9	34	28
Lecture hall	—	4	4.5
Department store or enterance hall in public building	—	7	2
Church and library	9	2	4.5
Church and lecture hall	4	2	—
Library and lecture hall	—	—	2
None of these	4	2	19.5
No reply	8	4	9
	100 (n=53)	100 (n=98)	100 (n=99)

In the age of pictorial reproduction the meaning of paintings is no longer attached to them; their meaning becomes transmittable: that is to say it becomes information of a sort, and, like all information, it is either put to use or ignored; information carries no special authority within itself. When a painting is put to use, its meaning is either modified or totally changed. One should be quite clear about what this involves. It is not a question of reproduction failing to reproduce certain aspects of an image faithfully; it is a question of reproduction making it possible, even inevitable, that an image will be used for many different purposes and that the reproduced image, unlike an original work, can lend itself to them all. Let us examine some of the ways in which the reproduced image lends itself to such usage.

Venus and Mars
By Botticelli 1445-1510

Reproduction isolates a detail of a painting from the whole. The detail is transformed. An allegorical figure becomes a portrait of a girl.

When a painting is reproduced by a film camera it inevitably becomes material for the film-maker's argument.

A film which reproduces images of a painting leads the spectator, through the painting, to the film-maker's own conclusions. The painting lends authority to the film-maker.

In a painting all its elements are there to be seen simultaneously. The spectator may need time to examine each element of the painting but whenever he reaches a conclusion, the simultaneity of the whole painting is there to reverse or qualify his conclusion. The painting maintains its own authority.

Procession to Calvary By Breughel 1525-1569

Paintings are often reproduced with words around them.

This is a landscape of a cornfield with birds flying out of it. Look at it for a moment. Then turn the page.

Wheatfield With Crows
By Van Gogh 1853-1890

Wheatfield With Crows
By Van Gogh 1853-1890

This is the last picture that Van Gogh painted before he killed himself.

It is hard to define exactly how the words have changed the image but undoubtedly they have. The image now illustrates the sentence.

In this essay each image reproduced has become part of an argument which has little or nothing to do with the painting's original independent meaning. The words have quoted the paintings to confirm their own verbal authority. (The essays without words in this book may make that distinction clearer.)

Reproduced paintings, like all information, have to hold their own against all the other information being continually transmitted.

Consequently a reproduction, as well as making its own references to the image of its original, becomes itself the reference point for other images. The meaning of an image is changed according to what one sees immediately beside it or what comes immediately after it. Such authority as it retains, is distributed over the whole context in which it appears.

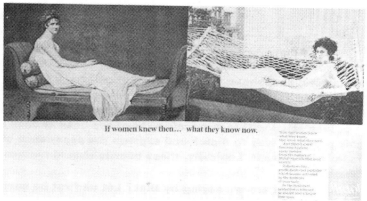

If women knew then... what they know now.

Because works of art are reproducible, they can, theoretically, be used by anybody. Yet mostly—in art books, magazines, films or within gilt frames in living-rooms—reproductions are still used to bolster the illusion that nothing has changed, that art, with its unique undiminished authority, justifies most other forms of authority, that art makes inequality seem noble and hierarchies seem thrilling. For example, the whole concept of the National Cultural Heritage exploits the authority of art to glorify the present social system and its priorities.

The means of reproduction are used politically and commercially to disguise or deny what their existence makes possible. But sometimes individuals use them differently.

Adults and children sometimes have boards in their bedrooms or living-rooms on which they pin pieces of paper: letters, snapshots, reproductions of paintings, newspaper cuttings, original drawings, post-cards. On each board all the images belong to the same language and all are more or less equal within it, because they have been chosen in a highly personal way to match and express the experience of the room's inhabi-tant. Logically, these boards should replace museums.

What are we saying by that? Let us first be sure about what we are not saying.

We are not saying that there is nothing left to experience before original works of art except a sense of awe because they have survived. The way original works of art are usually approached—through museum cat-alogues, guides, hired cassettes, etc.—is not the only way they might be approached. When the art of the past ceases to be viewed nostalgically, the works will cease to be holy relics—although they will never re-become what they were before the age of reproduction. We are not saying original works of art are now useless.

Woman Pouring Milk By Vermeer 1632-1675

Original paintings are silent and still in a sense that information never is. Even a reproduction hung on a wall is not comparable in this respect for in the original the silence and stillness permeate the actual material, the paint, in which one follows the traces of the painter's immediate gestures. This has the effect of closing the distance in time between the painting of the picture and one's own act of looking at it. In this special sense all paintings are contemporary. Hence the immediacy of their testimony. Their historical moment is literally there before our eyes. Cézanne made a similar observation from the painter's point of view. 'A minute in the world's life passes! To paint it in its reality, and forget everything for that! To become that minute, to be the sensitive plate . . . give the image of what we see, forgetting everything that has appeared before our time . . .' What we make of that painted moment when it is before our eyes depends upon what we expect of art, and that in turn depends today upon how we have already experienced the meaning of paintings through reproductions.

Nor are we saying that all art can be understood spontaneously. We are not claiming that to cut out a magazine reproduction of an archaic Greek head, because it is reminiscent of some personal experience, and to pin it on to a board beside other disparate images, is to come to terms with the full meaning of that head.

The idea of innocence faces two ways. By refusing to enter a conspiracy, one remains innocent of that conspiracy. But to remain innocent may also be to remain ignorant. The issue is not between innocence and knowledge (or between the natural and the cultural) but between a total approach to art which attempts to relate it to every aspect of experience and the esoteric approach of a few specialized experts who are the clerks of the nostalgia of a ruling class in decline. (In decline, not before the proletariat, but before the new power of the corporation and the state.) The real question is: to whom does the meaning of the art of the past properly belong? To those who can apply it to their own lives, or to a cultural hierarchy of relic specialists?

The visual arts have always existed within a certain preserve; originally this preserve was magical or sacred. But it was also physical: it was the place, the cave, the building, in which, or for which, the work was made. The experience of art, which at first was the experience of ritual, was set apart from the rest of life—precisely in order to be able to exercise power over it. Later the preserve of art became a social one. It entered the culture of the ruling class, whilst physically it was set apart and isolated in their palaces and houses. During all this history the authority of art was inseparable from the particular authority of the preserve.

What the modern means of reproduction have done is to destroy the authority of art and to remove it—or, rather, to remove its images which they reproduce—from any preserve. For the first time ever, images of art have become ephemeral, ubiquitous, insubstantial, available, valueless, free. They surround us in the same way as a language surrounds us. They have entered the mainstream of life over which they no longer, in themselves, have power.

Yet very few people are aware of what has happened because the means of reproduction are used nearly all the time to promote the illusion that nothing has changed except that the masses, thanks to reproductions, can now begin to appreciate art as the cultured minority once did. Understandably, the masses remain uninterested and sceptical.

If the new language of images were used differently, it would, through its use, confer a new kind of power. Within it we could begin to define our experiences more precisely in areas where words are inadequate. (Seeing comes before words.) Not only personal experience, but also the essential historical experience of our relation to the past: that is to say the experience of seeking to give meaning to our lives, of trying to understand the history of which we can become the active agents.

The art of the past no longer exists as it once did. Its authority is lost. In its place there is a language of images. What matters now is who uses that language for what purpose. This touches upon questions of copyright for reproduction, the ownership of art presses and publishers, the total policy of public art galleries and museums. As usually presented, these are narrow professional matters. One of the aims of this essay has been to show that what is really at stake is much larger. A people or a class which is cut off from its own past is far less free to choose and to act as a people or class than one that has been able to situate itself in history. This is why—and this is the only reason why—the entire art of the past has now become a political issue.

Questions for Discussion

1. Early in this essay, Berger says "The way we see things is affected by what we know or believe." How does he apply that notion to art?

2. What does Berger mean by "seeing comes before words"? Is it possible to separate meaning-making/seeing from language/words? Is Berger able to convey your understanding of the artwork included in his words?

3. Berger urges his reader to believe that each original piece of art has a "unique" image; and the uniqueness is destroyed in reproducing the image. Does Berger persuade you of these two points? How or how not?

Explorations

1. In "Radio Hoods," Patricia Williams makes a case for some talk radio as a vehicle for explicitly hateful verbal rhetoric. Berger attempts to convince the reader, however, that the rhetoric of images is a more powerful force. Which author presents a more compelling argument, and how?

2. Neil Postman and Steve Powers contend in "The Bias of Language, the Bias of Pictures" that "unlike words and sentences, a picture does not present to us an idea or concept about the world, except as we use language itself to convert the idea" (page 574). Does this dispute or confirm Berger's suggestions that images can have meaning apart from words?

3. Both Stuart Ewen in "Hard Bodies" and Thomas Hine in "What's in a Package?" argue that an understanding of packaging extends beyond selling consumer products, but is still under the influence of "market forces." Would Berger find this idea of packaging and its influences a useful way to think about art?

Formal Writing Assignments

1. Make a visit to a museum, keeping in mind Berger's argument that art is ideological, or "affected by what we know or believe." Do you see ideologies displayed in the museum? In what forms? Are you influenced in what you see by your own ways of seeing, by the image-makers, or a combination of both?

2. Find some advertisements which have appropriated works of art, and then identify and locate (copies of) the originals. Is the meaning of the original work changed in the ad? If so, in what way(s)?

Body Language

Katherine Betts

Katherine Betts (b. 1964), a graduate of Princeton University and native of New York City, recently left *Vogue* after an eight-year tenure to become the editor of another women's fashion magazine, *Harper's Bazaar*. It was her work on the fashionable life—as opposed to high fashion design and photography—that made her attractive to *Harper's*. She was educated in the fashionable life early, though. Highlights of her Manhattan childhood included seeing Liza Minelli and Andy Warhol at the local butcher's, and living across the street from the famous designer Halston. Betts began her career in journalism after college as an assistant at *The International Herald Tribune* in Paris, and then as a writer for *W*. She returned to the States in 1991, when she began writing for *Vogue*. The following essay typifies Betts' writing: sophisticated style combined with a deep sense of popular culture.

Writing Before Reading

1. Consider, by listing, your own fashion habits. Annotate them to indicate whether you think of them as ways to fit in to social expectations, as ways to resist those expectations, or as neither option.

2. Think about a time when you've seen someone with remarkable tattoos or body piercings. Describe your response to that person's body alterations.

3. Many people think of themselves in terms of a group: a social club, interest group, or team. Think of your own group affiliations and the extent to which they impact your identity. Answer these questions in a brief paragraph: Does membership in the group require anything of you which you would not do were you not a member? Conversely, does your identity have an impact on the group's identity?

Body Language

The two English girls poring over the neat rows of barbell and hoop-shaped jewelry in the black-velvet-lined display cases at Manhattan's Gauntlet piercing parlor look worried. Maybe they're not worried, just nervous. I definitely am worried, and my name's not even listed in the Gauntlet's appointment calendar to get one of those increasingly popular $35 navel piercings. I'm just here to interview the manager.

"Just sit down and we're gonna show you the after-care video we've put together to teach you how to care for your navel while it's healing," says a superpolite piercer called Bobby who will be doing the damage (literally) on these two relatively prissy-looking girls. I sit down to watch the video with them, but when a close-up of some guy's nipple ring flashes on the screen, I'm already averting my eyes. Unfortunately, there's little else to look at in this preeminent parlor without cringing, from the raunchy photos of pierced models lining the walls to the heavily pierced employees behind the jewelry counter to the clients themselves—a peculiar mix of long-haired heavymetal types, Generation-Xers with major grunge hangovers, a few daffy New Agers from Silicon Valley, and a handful of very well groomed European tourists.

This is not the East Village, by the way; this is Fifth Avenue, one block down from Emporio Armani.

"We get all types in here," says manager Mark Seitchik, the senior piercer with several of his own badges of courage placed strategically around his face—nose, ear, lip (he had his tongue pierced too but

419

felt there was too much metal going on around his mouth, so he took it out). "From 18-year-old street punks to 80-year-old retired judges. I wouldn't say piercing's gone mainstream, but it's definitely attracting a pretty diverse crowd lately." Likewise, Leo Zulueta, a co-owner of the Black Wave tattoo parlor on Los Angeles's La Brea, says he has tattooed every type—from dental instructors to federal prosecutors, and even a Catholic priest.

Indeed, five years ago body piercing was to the downtown gay and punk-rock scenes of big cities like New York and San Francisco what tattooing was to the Harley-Davidson biker crowd. Back then the act of tattooing or piercing had its own kind of clan or tribal identification, which was resolutely underground and usually, in the case of piercing, sexual. But if the streets of New York and San Francisco or the runways of Paris and Milan are any indication, body piercings have replaced tattoos—and even hairstyles—as the latest expression of individuality. And it's a different kind of clanning—now one ascribed to the hip and very diverse tribes of MTV, rap music, fashion, sports, and megamalls.

Like hairstyles, tattoos have been around forever. As far back as the Crusades, men were tattooed with crucifixes to ensure a Christian burial should they die on foreign soil. And for centuries the Maori of New Zealand, Tahitians, Japanese, and Native Americans tattooed for religious, tribal social, or superstitious reasons. Although tattooing has always had deviant connotations (think circus acts, sailors, bikers, gangs, and prison inmates), some surprisingly staid historical figures have been "inked," including Winston Churchill's mother, Lady Randolph Churchill, who had herself tattooed to commemorate Edward VII's coronation. Other European crowned heads, including Edward VII and George V, had royal emblems etched discreetly on their arms. And even former secretary of state George Schultz had a tiger tattooed on his posterior while a student at Princeton.

Of course those small tattoos, tucked away underneath clothing, were meant for intimate admirers' eyes only. It wasn't until the eighties, when supermodels like Stephanie Seymour and Carré Otis and Hollywood actresses like Julia Roberts and Drew Barrymore began flaunting very public "pieces" on their shoulders, ankles, and lower backs, that tattooing took a decidedly glamorous turn. (Call me conservative, but I still do a double take when I see tattooed limbs on the likes of squeaky-clean teenagers like Niki Taylor.)

In the nineties tattooing has become so routine that jaded fashion watchers barely flinch when more elaborately tattooed models like one-time car mechanic Jenny Shimizu (who has a bawdy tattoo of a near-naked woman riding a wrench on her upper arm) or the buzz-cut model Eve Salvail (who has a large tattoo of a serpent across one side of her head) strut down the Chanel, Versace, and Calvin Klein runways of Paris, Milan, and New York. Although many tattoo artists still discourage visible pieces that can jeopardize employment, it's now common to see tattoos prominently displayed in television commercials, on lawyers in courtrooms, or even peeking out of waiters' sleeves at renowned New York City restaurants.

Tattoo "studios" have responded by upgrading their image and treating their service as an art. Places like the Inkspot II in Linden, New Jersey, cater to an elite clientele, which co-owner Steve Ferguson defines as "business-class people." "We also get our share of housewives," he adds."They feel comfortable here, they bring the kids. It's not a freaky atmosphere like you might find on the Lower East Side. There's none of that piercing going on here; that stuff's just for shock value. Tattooing for me is an art."

In a society that rewards shock value with dollars, it makes sense that tattooing would make way for piercing. And, thanks to media vehicles like MTV and high-profile personalities like football players, piercing is everywhere, not just on the Lower East Side. At a recent Buffalo Bills game, fans and players alike flaunted multiple earrings. Models like Stella Tennant stare out from Versace couture ads with conspicuous nose rings; kids roam through malls across the country sporting hoops all over their ears and studs on their lips; and Howard Stern has invited volunteers to pierce their tongues live on television. With the blessing of fashion, piercing—like makeup, tanning, plastic surgery, and tattooing—is shedding its sexual connotations and moving from the underground to the mainstream. Let's not forget that applying makeup, now an everyday ritual for most women, was initially done to inspire erotic arousal. And tans, once a mark of lower-class status or south-of-the-border eroticism, became the height of chic when Coco Chanel and company began taking sun on the French Riviera in the 1920s (only to go out of fashion again in the 1980s because of the threat of bodily harm).

Nobody seems to be able to pinpoint the exact moment that piercing went from wrong to right—and, yes, the jury's still out—but two milestones at the European collections last October provide clues: (1) Jean Paul Gaultier's Paris runway show and (2) the morning Christy Turlington called a professional piercer to her London hotel room to pierce her navel. Gaultier, French fashion's veritable outlaw, is one thing. But Christy Turlington? The clean-cut Audrey Hepburn of supermodels piercing her navel? "I just wanted to try it," she told me sheepishly backstage at a London show hours after the deed was done. "Why not?"

Why not indeed. That's what I said to my mom when I was fifteen and desperate to get my ears pierced, and she pleaded, "Why do you want to destroy your body that way? Why do you want to put holes through your skin?" I had no real answer, it was just the thing to do. And besides, deep down I felt that urge to decorate myself. Let's face it, at fifteen the idea of wearing earrings is enchanting.

After seasons of drab black minimalism, after women quietly tucked their jewelry away so they wouldn't stand out as beacons for burglars, Gaultier's body-art show of real tattoo and piercing "collectors," followed by supermodels wearing clip-on face jewelry and sheer T-shirts decorated to look like tattoos, was enchanting too. If nothing else, he succeeded in reigniting an interest in ornamentation at a time in fashion when the slightest trace of decoration has been scorned. Then Christy took the plunge, and before you knew it couturiers like Christian Lacroix were turning out couture suits cut to expose the navel. Despite the deviant connotations, body piercing has, indirectly, helped reinstate a certain degree of femininity and sexiness in fashion—whether that means simple decoration with jewelry or more exposure of skin.

Ever since Gaultier's show and Christy's daring move, places like the Gauntlet in New York, San Francisco, and L.A. have seen a steady stream of young women between the ages of 18 and 30 signing up for navel-piercing appointments (you have to be at least 18). Nonetheless, Seitchik and his staff caution people about getting pierced just because it's trendy. "It's not a haircut, it's not a piece of clothing. You can't just throw it away," insists Seitchik. "Piercing and tattooing are things you have to be passionate about," agrees 22-year-old Shimizu, who has four substantial tattoos and a pierced navel. "You can't just do it to be trendy or you will definitely regret it. These are two things you have to live with for the rest of your life."

True. Tattoos don't come out without expensive and very painful laser surgery. And although piercings seem less complicated because they're easier to undo, the holes require cleaning at least twice a day while they heal, which can take up to nine months—and, if mistreated or neglected, can lead to infection. Gaultier's show was beautiful, but it was a show. Christy is a model; perhaps for that reason she can get away with a navel ring. But beyond those two examples, what makes a woman pierce her nose, her tongue, or her navel? Not to mention that face and body jewelry is not like your standard earring for pierced ears—the posts are much, much thicker, which means the hole is much, much bigger. Strangely, vanity is the most common answer to that nagging question.

"You can play with your body in ways other than plastic surgery," says Gaultier, who has several piercings on his ears. "It's a kind of art, it's not only sexual or sensual. People do it for beauty." Although I personally still can't see the beauty in it, I can see Gaultier's point. Piercing has been around for a long time and has meant different things to different cultures. In ancient Egypt, a navel ring indicated royalty, while in India a nose ring still signifies Hindu and Muslim devotion. Even in proper Victorian England women pierced their nipples so they could wear jewels in them.

"It's just like buying a beautiful dress," explains Maria Tashjian, an owner of Venus Modern Body Arts, a piercing studio in Manhattan's East Village. "Why do you buy a beautiful dress? Because it makes you feel beautiful, it enhances your natural features; and that's what piercing does." This comes from someone who has enhanced her natural features a lot: Tashjian has long, wild Tallulah Bankhead hair with green stripes through it and major piercings along her earlobes, in her nose, and on her lower lip. "When I first started getting into piercing, my mother asked, 'Why do you want to mutilate yourself?' But I think it's a natural human tendency to decorate."

"I pierced my tongue because I think it looks beautiful," echoes nineteen-year-old Anouche Wise, a waiflike freshman at New York University who was also contemplating getting the skin on her collarbone pierced. "It's not that permanent; it's just not that big a deal," she says, even though she admits that she couldn't eat for three days afterward and that the jewelry ripped up the bottom of her mouth. Why go through that kind of pain? "For vanity. So many things women do for beauty are painful. It's the same thing as getting your legs waxed or having a facelift. You just have to really want to do it."

"When you look back over history, every period is connected to some sort of body modification," Seitchik agrees. "Whether it's the plastic surgery and breast implants of the eighties or the corsets of Victorian times. This idea of falsely enhancing your beauty is human. Some parents won't let their kid get their nose pierced, but they'll pay a lot of money for them to get a nose job."

There is an important, if superficial, difference between nose jobs and piercings: The former satisfies social standards while the latter intentionally flouts them. Similarly, most body modifications in the past were practiced in order to fit in, not stand out. Piercing may be increasingly popular, but it's still a statement. Tennant, for one, says she pierced her nose as an in-your-face gesture. "Piercing has become a lot like wearing a leather jacket," says Valerie Steele, a professor at the Fashion Institute of Technology who is currently working on a book about fashion and fetishism. "For a lot of people, piercing symbolizes being a sex radical: it's a very antibourgeois gesture, and fashion is more and more about that. It's part of an ongoing fascination with the look of deviance in our society. More and more people are drawing on sadomasochistic themes in fashion without being involved with them or conscious of them."

What keeps piercing exotic is the pain factor. Unlike plastic surgeons, piercers cannot offer any kind of anesthetic, because they're not licensed, and, essentially, a shot of Novocain would probably be as painful as a piercing. "In a way, that's what makes it more attractive to some," says Harold Koda, associate curator of the Metropolitan Museum of Art's Costume Institute. "Pain is implicit, so there's always that forbidden zone, that danger."

Although the idea of putting a piece of metal through some part of the body as decoration may sound exotic, consider the fact that no one thinks twice about pierced earlobes anymore.

Decoration and vanity aside, some aficionados see piercing and tattooing as a modern rite of passage or a form of outlaw bonding for an alienated generation. "For me, getting pierced was not about taking part in a fashion trend," explains Shimizu. "It was about going from a delinquent to a mature person." In a mass-market culture so immune to nudity or vulgarity, it makes sense that kids—even adults— would alter their physical appearance so blatantly in order to express and enhance their individuality. Soon nobody will think twice about visible piercings, either.

"Piercing is not really mutilation anymore, it's decorating an object," says Barbara Ilardi, a professor of psychology at the University of Rochester, who explains piercing as the result of society's objectification of the body. "In advertising and in the movies, body parts have been taken out of context as if they don't belong to the person. In doing this, we've created a culture of persons whose bodies don't belong to them." Body manipulation is now a means of gaining social acceptance, which makes it an accessory of sorts, argues Ilardi. "The message is: If you don't like the body you were given, get another one."

Questions for Discussion

1. Betts suggests that a new sort of tribalism is developing by way of "MTV, rap music, fashion, sports, and megamalls." How is it that these particular media are able to form clans? What do these media indicate about the clannishness Betts is describing? How might these kinds of tribes differ from earlier ones in history?

2. What is the purpose of Betts' historicization of tattooing? What does its history have to do with body piercing? To what other fashion habits does Betts relate piercing, and why?

3. Tattooing, according to Betts, made room for body piercing because ours is a culture that "rewards shock value with dollars." This implies that our mainstream fashion happens as a result of capitalism, and that was it not for the blessing of capital, a method of ornamentation would not become popular. Is Betts exaggerating?

Explorations

1. In its concluding paragraphs, "Body Language" strongly urges the reader to view body piercing as a naturally human activity and as one of many types of ornamentation, both of which contest the notion of fashion as driven primarily by money. In his essay "Hard Bodies," Stuart Ewen contends that it is the look of financial success that one is after in packaging one's body. Betts advocates for nature, Ewen for nurture. Is either a more persuasive argument?

2. Betts raises an issue about the formation of identity: that our exteriors are not necessarily indicative of who we are, that the meaning of appearance may not largely be in the eyes of the beholder. This contradicts what many social critics (like Diane Barthel with "A Gentleman and a Consumer") assert: that citizens have little ability to resist the power of consumer culture, and so we are how we look. Do any of these viewpoints approximate your own experience as a citizen and consumer?

3. In "Call and Response: Sports, Talk Radio, and the Death of Democracy," David Goldberg asserts that talk radio builds community, but a community of racialized and gendered privilege. Katherine Betts also argues for community, except in her case, communities of tattooers and body-piercers who seem to be more inclusive than those of sports talk radio. Compare the two arguments; which community seems more representative of the American ideal?

Formal Writing Assignments

1. Choose another form of fashion or behavior that you think has worked its way from marginal culture into mainstream culture. Using Betts's essay as a model, analyze how your fashion or behavior has arrived in mainstream culture, through historicization, analogies with other fashions or behaviors, and the implications for identity formation that the fashion or behavior presents.

2. In her concluding paragraph, Betts quotes a professor of psychology explaining piercing as a result of " 'society's objectification of the body'." This quote raises issues that Betts has not addressed directly in the body of her essay. What does including that quote do to the rest of Betts's argument? Why do you think she included it? How could Betts have elaborated further on this point?

Gay Men's Revenge

Susan Bordo

Susan Bordo (b. 1947) is a professor of English and Women's Studies at the University of Kentucky. It has been said that her work began the new interdisciplinary field known as "body studies." Bordo's 1993 *Unbearable Weight* broke ground in calling attention to the profound role of cultural images in the spread of eating problems across race and class, and garnered a Pulitzer Prize nomination. She continues that examination of popular culture's influence on bodies with her 1999 *The Male Body: A New Look at Men in Public and in Private*, from which this section is taken. In an interview, Bordo claims that "edification, relief, and communication become possible when we talk openly (and intelligently) about those aspects of life that hold the most shame for us, that are most taboo." This piece typifies Bordo's talking openly, her irreverence for the traditional way of dealing with scholarly topics, and for many social mores.

Writing Before Reading

1. Recall a movie, TV show, or advertisement that featured explicitly the "bodyness" of a male body. How did you respond to this depiction? Describe the depiction in a few sentences, including such elements as lighting, color, positioning, location, the product being marketed, story line, and then list your responses to it.

2. Besides "happily ever after," how do you expect a romantic comedy film to end? Write a brief paragraph outlining that ending.

3. Think of specific instances of popular culture's representations of male-female relationships that are not sexual and those that are. List those in two columns, and annotate them, indicating how some representations are similar and how some are different.

Gay Men's Revenge

It finally happened in the summer of 1997, and just where you'd least expect it: in a date movie. Rupert Everett as Julianne's—or Jules, as she's usually called (Julia Roberts)—mentor and editor George in *My Best Friend's Wedding* was a first for a major Hollywood production: an openly gay actor playing a gay male who is the moral center of the movie and the best-adjusted, happiest person in it. As urbane as James Bond (but without Bond's misogyny), as homespun-wise as Gramma Walton (but without the sermons), a goofy cutup but also a serious intellectual who spends time at book readings not the gym, George also has all those "caring" virtues usually reserved for female characters. He's tolerant even when Jules interrupts his dinner parties with hysterical phone calls, and drops everything to run to her side when she needs him. But unlike the kindly-gay-male-friend-of-the-heroine as, for example, Harvey Fierstein might play him, it isn't because he hasn't anything better to do. George isn't an ersatz mom or perennially rejected sad sack. God no, this man could get any date he wants, of any sexual orientation.

Even those critics who didn't care for the movie raved about Everett's performance, describing him as a "charismatic male presence . . . who brazenly swipes every scene that he's in," and predicting that he would become the "first openly gay sex symbol in Hollywood." Viewers concurred; there's now a thriving "Crazy About Rupert Everett" Internet site, complete with pics, bios, interviews, and other fan-club paraphernalia. It may be the first openly multisexual fan club in history, with Everett himself Hollywood's first fully realized success at what fashion merchandisers refer to as "dual marketing"—the creation of images which embody elements of strong appeal to different sexual "gazes," gay and straight, male and female. Unlike the sophisticated fashion world, Hollywood has hit on dual-appeal characters only by chance (or through the covert codings of gay screenwriters and actors), and their appeal has been an underground phenomenon. Usually, too, it's been gay and lesbian audiences who have had to eke their pleasures out of slightly "queer" representations of straight characters: a certain outfit worn by Joan Crawford, a sly look of Lauren Bacall's, James Dean or Brad Pitt slouching flirtatiously in T-shirt and jeans.

Everett's George, on the other hand, represented a stolen delight for straight women. There have, of course, been other gay male characters in the movies with appeal to women. But George was more than just appealing; something about him spoke directly—and powerfully—to women. Unlike the well-hung men in the underwear ads, he doesn't flaunt his pecs. (He's beautiful to look at, but the closest we get to his body in the movie is when he wears a sexy black jersey; the rest of the time he's in well-cut suits.) Yet his sex appeal, as co-star Roberts describes it, was "enormous." "We were dancing in one scene," she recalled in an interview, "and he was being all sexy with me, saying hilarious things like 'Darling, can't you see it? My last ray of heterosexuality is shining on you.'" Yes, and on the fantasies of every straight woman who saw the movie.

Those fantasies, moreover, are written right into the movie. At the very end of the film, when all Jules's schemes to recapture ex-boyfriend Michael (Dermot Mulroney) have miserably failed and he has married sugary Kimmy (Cameron Diaz), George makes a surprise appearance at the wedding reception in an effort to cheer Jules up. He is (as he accurately describes himself) "sleek, stylish, and radiant with charisma." He rises from his chair, and takes the hand of the beautiful but depressed heroine, pulls her to him, and leads her into a ballroom dance that within minutes has her flushed and bubbling over with delight. He dips and twirls her; they glide across the screen, glamorous and happy, a matched pair of dazzling creatures. Life, as at the end of all comedies, is renewed, refreshed by their being together. For a moment, we might imagine that we are at a revival of screwball comedy, that this is a modern incarnation of Irene Dunne and Cary Grant, a future of (re)wedded bliss ahead of them.

The beautiful heroine doesn't get her man; she gets a dance with her gay male editor. *That* was the happy ending of one of 1997s biggest hits. What did it mean? Reviewers didn't seriously ponder this question, but instead took *My Best Friend's Wedding* at face value, as a somewhat quirky attempt to refresh the "boy meets girl, boy loses girl, boy gets girl" scenario, which departs from the usual formula only in the fact that the boy (in this case a girl) doesn't get her heart's desire in the end. I want to suggest a more culturally informative reading than that. *My Best Friend's Wedding*, as I read it, very deliberately means to "queer" representations of gender and cast doubt on the viability or durability of the fifties version of happily-ever-after. It's not just the character of George that functions this way in the film, but George is essential—not only to challenge stereotypes of homosexuality but also to reveal the inadequacies of *straight* masculinity. This was something critics missed, for all that they raved about Everett, and it was truly something new for Hollywood—a gay male serving up instruction to straight men.

The ideal that Everett/George offered was not an absolutely new one, but a revival of qualities postwar Hollywood in its anxieties about masculinity had buried. Contemporary reviewers have frequently described Everett as a "gay" Cary Grant. None seem to have noticed, as Pauline Kael did in an essay on Grant, that Cary Grant, if only (or perhaps not only) in his screen relations with women, was a bit "gay" himself. Here, Kael contrasts him with Clark Gable:

> With Gable, sex is inevitable: What is there but sex? Basically, he thinks women are good for only one thing. Grant is interested in the qualities of a particular woman—her sappy expression, her nonsequiturs, the way her voice bobbles. She isn't going to be pushed to the wall as soon as she's alone with him. With Grant, the social, urban man, there are infinite possibilities for mutual entertainment. They might dance the night away or stroll or go to

a carnival—and nothing sexual would happen unless she wanted it to . . . [I]f the roof leaks, or the car stalls, or you don't know how to get the super to keep his paws off you, you may long for a Clark Gable to take charge, but when you think of going out, Cary Grant is your dream date. . . . How could the heroine ever consider marrying a rich rube from Oklahoma and leaving Cary Grant and the night spots? . . . When [women] look at him, they see a man they could have fun with.

"A man [a woman] could have fun with"—that seems like a pretty superficial appeal. But in the screwball comedies that Grant set his stamp on, having fun is far from a superficial accomplishment. You can't have fun with just anyone, and most men in these films don't really want to; they want to get down to the serious business of finding an "appropriate" mate who will help them to lead respectable, successful lives. As the man a woman could have fun with, Cary Grant is also the man who *wants* to have fun with a woman, who values her "particular" qualities, her independence and vitality, and is uninterested in taming her and turning her into a domestic "helpmate." The rich rube from Oklahoma (a reference to Ralph Bellamy in Leo McCarey's 1937 *The Awful Truth*) is shocked and calls the whole thing off when Lucy Warriner (Irene Dunne) appears to have been carrying on in a less than proper manner. But Jerry Warriner (Gary Grant) smiles admiringly, adoringly at his ex-wife's spirit and nerve, as she mimics the vulgar dance of a singer for the prissy relatives of his new (but not for long) girlfriend.

I didn't realize until I discovered the movies of the thirties and forties that there had been a genre which actually considered playfulness and equality of wit and style between men and women to be a romantic ideal, even an ideal of marriage. That ideal was rooted in class privilege rather than (as in the fifties) gender difference; it didn't matter whether you were a man or a woman in the classic screwball comedy, no one went to work or wore an apron, and everyone had time to fiddle and scheme over their relationships. Cary Grant and Irene Dunne in *The Awful Truth* were a matched set—wisecrack for wisecrack, scheme for scheme, glamour for glamour. They were made for each other not as the positive and negative poles of a magnet, but by virtue of an intimacy and mutual recognition so subtle and implicit that it was slightly incestuous. (Often, the heroes and heroines of screwball comedies have known each other since childhood.) But even such intimacy does not come easily and is certainly not guaranteed for the life of a relationship; it has to be renewed. Dejected by a failure of mutual understanding, the hero and heroine of the screwball comedy may decide to attempt a life with a more conventional person (e.g., the "rube"). It can't work, and learning that—learning who one really is and whom one needs to be with in order to fully realize that—is the arc of the comedy.

Sex was not the focus of the screwball comedy. Rather, it was the implicit consequence of intimacy. That the hero and heroine *did* have sex (never on-screen in those days, but it was often quite clearly alluded to) inspired, in the viewer, the remarkable notion that perhaps sexuality could be grounded in permission to be fully oneself, with someone who truly, deeply knows you, and is mad about you all the same. "I'll be yar, I promise to be yar!" Tracy (Katharine Hepburn) swears to Dexter (Grant), who's just proposed to marry her again. "Be whatever you want. You're my redhead," he replies. That one line (from *The Philadelphia Story*) speaks volumes to the difference between a thirties happily-ever-after and a fifties one, in which everyone, having ironed out the kinks in their personalities and sowed their wild oats, settles down and takes their conventional gender places.

The line from *The Philadelphia Story* is one that always brings tears to my eyes. And, watching the film again recently, I realized that the moment when Tracy and Dexter recommit was sexually evocative for me too. Had it always been that way? I doubt it. When I was a teenager I paid hardly any attention to these movies. By the time I came to appreciate them, it was the seventies and the cinematic codes were different. Deep, mutual recognition had dropped out as a prelude to sex in the movies. And so, in a curious and perverse way (for this was the era of women's liberation), had a certain ideal of equality as a precondition of real intimacy. In those days, I expected that love would result magically from sex, and

I certainly didn't require much in the way of respect or recognition from the one-night stands that were my laboratories. I suspect my experience was fairly typical.

Rupert Everett's George, like a Cary Grant character, radiates elegance, wit, charm, and playfulness—an importation of the old "class" values of the screwball comedy into a contemporary Hollywood movie. And, like Grant in *The Awful Truth* and *The Philadelphia Story*, his rapport with the movie's heroine is premised on recognition of who she is and deep affection for her unique qualities—maddening though they may sometimes be. George and Jules understand each other (or, at least, George understands Jules). And—a fact not noted by any reviewers—more touching and nuzzling goes on between George and Jules than between any other characters in the movie, including Michael and Kim. True, some of George's touching of Jules occurs when he is playing the part of her fiancé. But his tenderness for her generates sparks of intimacy nonetheless, not unlike those generated between Cary Grant and Katharine Hepburn at the end of *The Philadelphia Story*.

Audiences believed in these moments of contact, in the feeling behind them. In an earlier version of the movie—a revision of Ronald Bass's original screenplay, demanded by studio bosses who didn't think audiences would accept a gay best friend as compensation for not getting a husband—Jules ends up with a new heterosexual boyfriend. It bombed with preview audiences. The final version deposited the straight boyfriend "on the cutting-room floor" (as Bass has put it). Audiences preferred the specific "chemistry" (or perhaps "alchemy" is a better term) between Roberts and Everett to the conventionally happy ending.

Queering the Happily-ever-after

Even if we grant that the time was ripe for a reincarnation of Cary Grant and a revival of the screwball comedy, why did Bass and director P. J. Hogan choose to re-create Grant in the persona of a gay man and a friend—not a potential lover—of the heroine? "If this were a vintage screwball comedy [Jules] would have walked off happily ever after on George's exquisitely tailored arm," notes Rick Groen of the *Toronto Globe and Mail*. That she didn't disappointed many reviewers and seemed inexplicable to them. "For some reason," wrote Ruthe Stein of the *San Francisco Chronicle*, "the filmmakers have chosen to make George gay and therefore unavailable. Roberts and Everett are so right for each other," Stein goes on, "it is easy to imagine him as Michael [the longed-for boyfriend]. Now that would have been a movie as irresistible as its star."

Would it? I'm not sure that we *would* believe, in the nineties, in the same gestures as performed by a couple bound for the altar. Our cultural imagination is too cluttered with hundreds of contrived Hollywood happily-ever-afters between Michaels and Kimmys, and marriage as a metaphor for finding one's true self in another just doesn't ring as true as it may have in the thirties. Hogan's first film, *Muriel's Wedding*, certainly took a sardonic view of marriage, and although Hogan makes Michael and Kimmy fairly likable characters in *My Best Friend's Wedding*, he has his tongue firmly in his cheek when it comes to the happily-ever-after part.

Hogan's wry, although not mean-spirited, attitude toward the fifties fantasy is evident from the unmistakably satirical opening credits, featuring a girl group dressed as a bride and her bridesmaids, all sugarcoated and dripping softness, singing "Wishing and Hoping" (the deliberately precious little voice on the soundtrack is actually Ani DeFranco's), to the scene where Michael and Kimmy, newly married, drive off in their car as huge spurting fountains announce their triumph. Viewers may wish and hope that they'll be forever happy, but we know there's trouble down that road.

What reviewers like Ruthe Stein seem to have missed is that George's gayness is an essential ingredient in *My Best Friend's Wedding's* ironic, deconstructive take on gender. From the opening credits (the lead singer's gestures clearly inspired by Ann-Margret's opening credit number in *Bye Bye Birdie*), the movie signals its intention to send up the conventional gender roles that are our inheritance from the fifties. George plays an important part in this. Like the parody of the girl group, in his most hilarious scenes he's a fun-house mirror, reflecting in comic form the highly gendered world around him. Asked by Julianne to pretend that he's her ardent, straight fiancé, he grabs at her breast in the cab and shakes male relatives' hands with wristbreaking gusto ("Just in time for a quick preconjugal visit, if you catch my drift," he winks, man to man). But approached by squealing Kimmy and her mother (who trips daintily down the aisle like a drag queen and who often speaks in the droll bitchy tone of one), he sends *their* "femininity" right back at them: "Love the bags, love the shoes, love everything!" he exclaims.

My Best Friend's Wedding may not want to totally topple the little Barbie/Ken couple from the wedding cake, but it certainly intends that the legacy of the fifties make room (once again) for other kinds of intimacy, other styles of being men and women. In the nineties, that may first require figuring out who one is vis-à-vis a cultural inheritance of gender expectations and sexual roles. Homosexual *or* heterosexual, some people are "queer"—they don't fit easily into those pigeonholes. Jules, although played by a gorgeous Julia Roberts, is much less a Pretty Woman and more like a typical male from the self-help guides written for frustrated wives and girlfriends. Jules can't commit. A workaholic who doesn't like to smooch in public (when people embrace her, she cringes a bit) and who has cried only three times in her life, she was too self-contained for Michael, who wants someone more cuddly—which Kimmy, always on the verge of tears, giggles, or a hug, certainly is. Until she is provoked by the prospect of losing Michael to Kimmy, Jules hasn't been interested in "female priorities" like love and marriage; she can't stand "yucky love stuff."

Kimmy, on the other hand, is so stereotypically feminine that she's virtually a whole other gender. (Except for her frail blondness, Kimmy could be Elizabeth Taylor in *Father of the Bride*.) When Jules likens Kimmy to crème brûlée, suggesting that Michael might be more of a Jell-O man, Kimmy replies tearfully, "I can be Jell-O! I *have* to be Jell-O!" This is another moment when it's hard to believe that Bass and Hogan want us to admire Kimmy as wholeheartedly as reviewers seem to have thought. (Reviewers described her as "a spunky, ingenious, kindly spirit," "dainty, friendly," "goodness and warmth," "delightfully daffy," and so on.) But more important than whether Kimmy is "smart and spunky" or a sap is the fact that whatever her virtues, they are utterly different from Julianne's. When Kim wins over a karaoke bar with her off-key, tremulous rendition of (appropriately enough), "I just don't know what to do with myself," it's clear from Jules's astonished face, watching Kimmy perform, that she realizes she is in the presence of something utterly and bafflingly "other" to herself.

Although she sings that she doesn't, in actual fact Kimmy *does* know what to do with herself; it's Jules who doesn't. Jules is determined to become the girl on top of the wedding cake, even if it means resisting the truth of her own personality. The movie, of course, won't let her, and George is integral to that resolution, not just because he is the one who gets Jules to "do the right thing" and give up Michael, but because he shows us—by being "Cary Grant," the man a girl would *really* like to play with—just how boring a fifties-style happily-ever-after would be for high-spirited, independent Julianne. "It would never have worked out" with Michael, George tells Jules. "Different temperaments." But it's really George's "radiant charisma" and not his dispensed wisdom that disabuses us—the viewers—of any misguided notion we may have that Jules would be happy in a conventional mating with a conventional man. Kim and Michael—who even look like a little toy couple when they're side by side—do indeed belong together on top of the wedding cake. But not everyone is as comfortably fitted in his or her gender skin as Michael and Kimmy. In a world that's organized for those who are, it's a painful recognition to realize that one isn't—and Jules struggles against it.

George is proof, however, that letting go of gender rules has its compensations. Like Jules in the karaoke bar, conventional Michael has a moment of self-recognition when George's sultry, comic rendition of "Say a Little Prayer for You" transforms an entire restaurant into the Supremes. At that moment Michael begins to suspect that he, Michael, is the rube from Oklahoma (so to speak)—a nice, square dude but utterly without George's exuberant charm. Hollywood's obsessive exorcism of the shadow of homosexuality has finally caught up with the straight male hero, revealing to him the boring bland character that he has become. Other scenes too show that being queer can be fun. Before the wedding, Michael's little brother and a few other young guys (one with an earring in his ear), blowing up helium balloons, perform a chipmunk version of "You Fill Up My Senses." They don't crack up, as we might expect from a bunch of young boys, but close their eyes dreamily, sweetly crooning together, enjoying the chance to play at being something other than "guys." Their rendition is touching, an absurd moment turned luminous for the viewer—as the restaurant scene is too—by the uninhibited willingness of the characters to step outside the norms of behavior, to expand rather than to contract, to go for eros, even in unconventional forms.

And then there's the dance at the end of the movie. Early in *My Best Friend's Wedding*, we're told that Jules can't dance. It is Michael who tells us. "You can't dance! When did you learn how to dance?" he bursts out when Jules mentions that the best man (Michael's little brother) must dance with the maid of honor. "I've got moves you haven't seen . . ." Jules replies, and wiggles playfully. The moment strongly recalls the moment in *The Awful Truth* in which Dan, the rube, tells Jerry that Lucy "doesn't care much about dancing." But Jerry knows better, and watches smiling as Dan drags Lucy onto the dance floor and forces her into an unromantic, inelegant jitterbug. From Jerry's self-satisfied face as he watches them dance, we know he knows that Dan will never last. For Lucy *can* dance ("We used to call her twinkle-toes," says Jerry); she just needs the right man to dance with.

So, it appears, does Jules. But in 1998, perhaps, a girl can't have everything.* As George takes her hand and pulls her to him, in a dance that is no less romantic for the fact that they twirl each other by turns, he admits that there are limits to their relationship. "Maybe there won't be marriage, maybe there won't be sex," he admits, exaggerating a grimace, "but by God, there will be dancing!" Thousands of straight women watching him found this a pretty good bargain—a just and fitting revenge for the gay male's Hollywood career as the shadow of straight male sexuality.

*Since *My Best Friend's Wedding*, the gay male/straight female relationship has become something of a cultural paradigm, as other movies—*Object of My Affection*—and even prime-time television—*Will and Grace*—play with its possibilities for new models of male-female intimacy.

Questions for Discussion

1. Bordo argues that Rupert Everett's character both challenges "stereotypes of homosexuality" and also "reveals the inadequacies of *straight* masculinity." How does she support this argument?

2. How does Bordo contrast 1930's, 1950's, 1970's, and current conceptions of "happily-ever-after"?

3. What does Bordo mean when she uses the word "queer"?

Explorations

1. In Paul Gamson's "Why I Love Trash," he says that talk shows redraw the lines between normal and abnormal (page 467). How does this reading of a video text resemble or differ from Bordo's?

2. Robert Scholes suggests in "On Reading a Video Text" that the right sort of analysis will allow a reader to "recover from the surrender to the text" (page 595). What does Bordo offer as a means of recovery?

3. In the conclusion to "Children's Culture and Disney's Animated Films," Henry Giroux maintains that these films "work to secure particular forms of authority and social relations" (page 492). Given that pre-release audiences vetoed the heterosexual happy ending for *My Best Friend's Wedding*, could Giroux's argument pertain to Bordo's?

Formal Writing Assignments

1. Bordo asserts that, rather than *My Best Friend's Wedding* creating a new version of male-female relationship, it has revived one depicted in 1930's screwball comedies. Discuss the effect this historicizing has on your understanding of the film. Then choose another romantic comedy text and analyze it using a historical approach.

2. Think of another film which features a character who does not fit into prescribed "gender skin." Using Robert Scholes' model of "recovery from the surrender to the text," analyze the character's role in the relationships depicted in that other film.

That Lean and Hungry Look

Suzanne Britt Jordan

In her 1982 book, *Skinny People Are Dull and Crunchy Like Carrots*, Suzanne Britt Jordan uses humor to contest the values American culture places on body types, just as she does in the following essay. Jordan's pithy and wry journalistic style can be attributed to her career as a columnist for the *Raleigh News and Observer* as well as the European edition of *Stars and Stripes*. Besides working as a journalist, Jordan has worked as a professor of English and a freelance writer. All of Jordan's career paths have involved the written word, but each job has employed language differently and for different purposes. Taken from *Newsweek*'s "My Turn" column, this essay of Jordan's uses cliché, comparison and contrast, and humor to consider American prejudices about weight.

Writing Before Reading

1. What assumptions do you make about a person based on their physical appearance? Is this a fair method of assessing a person? Accurate? What personal experiences do you have that contradict traditional assumptions about body types and personality?

2. Consider the ways in which your actions are modified by your physical appearance. Does your body type affect your behavior? Do you feel that you are allowed to or prevented from acting in particular ways because of your body?

3. Write a brief personal narrative, describing yourself in clichéd terms. Talk about your personality, your emotions, or your physical appearance, but try to incorporate worn-out expressions whenever possible. How does this style of writing affect this depiction of yourself? What effect does clichéd writing have on your self-portrait?

That Lean and Hungry Look

Caesar was right. Thin people need watching. I've been watching them for most of my adult life, and I don't like what I see. When these narrow fellows spring at me, I quiver to my toes. Thin people come in all personalities, most of them menacing. You've got your "together" thin person, your mechanical thin person, your condescending thin person, your tsk-tsk thin person, your efficiency-expert thin person. All of them are dangerous.

In the first place, thin people aren't fun. They don't know how to goof off, at least in the best, fat sense of the word. They've always got to be a-doing. Give them a coffee break, and they'll jog around the block. Supply them with a quiet evening at home, and they'll fix the screen door and lick S&H green stamps. They say things like "There aren't enough hours in the day." Fat people never say that. Fat people think the day is too damn long already.

Thin people make me tired. They've got speedy little metabolisms that cause them to bustle briskly. They're forever rubbing their bony hands together and eyeing new problems to "tackle." I like to surround myself with sluggish, inert, easygoing fat people, the kind who believe that if you clean it up today, it'll just get dirty again tomorrow.

Some people say the business about the jolly fat person is a myth, that all of us chubbies are neurotic, sick, sad people. I disagree. Fat people may not be chortling all day long, but they're a hell of a lot *nicer* than the wizened and shriveled. Thin people turn surly, mean and hard at a young age because they never learn the value of a hot-fudge sundae for easing tension. Thin people don't like gooey soft things because they themselves are neither gooey nor soft. They are crunchy and dull, like carrots. They go straight to the heart of the matter while fat people let things stay all blurry and hazy and vague, the way things actually are. Thin people want to face the truth. Fat people know there is no truth. One of my thin friends is always staring at complex, unsolvable problems and saying, "The key thing is. . . ." Fat people never say that. They know there isn't any such thing as the key thing about anything.

Thin people believe in logic. Fat people see all sides. The sides fat people see are rounded blobs, usually gray, always nebulous and truly not worth worrying about. But the thin person persists. "If you consume more calories than you burn," says one of my thin friends, "you will gain weight. It's that simple." Fat people always grin when they hear statements like that. They know better.

Fat people realize that life is illogical and unfair. They know very well that God is not in his heaven and all is not right with the world. If God was up there, fat people could have two doughnuts and a big orange drink anytime they wanted it.

Thin people have a long list of logical things they are always spouting off to me. They hold up one finger at a time as they reel off these things, so I won't lose track. They speak slowly as if to a young child. The list is long and full of holes. It contains tidbits like "get a grip on yourself," "cigarettes kill," "cholesterol clogs," "fit as a fiddle," "ducks in a row," "organize," and "sound fiscal management." Phrases like that.

They think these 2000-point plans lead to happiness. Fat people know happiness is elusive at best and even if they could get the kind thin people talk about, they wouldn't want it. Wisely, fat people see that such programs are too dull, too hard, too off the mark. They are never better than a whole cheesecake.

Fat people know all about the mystery of life. They are the ones acquainted with the night, with luck, with fate, with playing it by ear. One thin person I know once suggested that we arrange all the parts of a jigsaw puzzle into groups according to the size, shape and color. He figured this would cut the time needed to complete the puzzle by at least 50 percent. I said I wouldn't do it. One, I like to muddle through. Two, what good would it do to finish early? Three, the jigsaw puzzle isn't the important thing. The important thing is the fun of four people (one thin person included) sitting around a card table, working a jigsaw puzzle. My thin friend had no use for my list. Instead of joining us, he went outside and mulched the boxwoods. The three remaining fat people finished the puzzle and made chocolate, double-fudged brownies to celebrate.

The main problem with thin people is they oppress. Their good intentions, bony torsos, tight ships, neat corners, cerebral machinations and pat solutions loom like dark clouds over the loose, comfortable, spread-out, soft world of the fat. Long after fat people have removed their coats and shoes and put their feet up on the coffee table, thin people are still sitting on the edge of the sofa, looking neat as a pin, discussing rutabagas. Fat people are heavily into fits of laughter, slapping their thighs and whooping it up, while thin people are still politely waiting for the punch line.

Thin people are downers. They like math and morality and reasoned evaluation of the limitations of human beings. They have their skinny little acts together. They expound, prognose, probe and prick.

Fat people are convivial. They will like you even if you're irregular and have acne. They will come up with a good reason why you never wrote the great American novel. They will cry in your beer with you. They will put your name in the pot. They will let you off the hook. Fat people will grab, giggle, guffaw, gallumph, gyrate and gossip. They are generous, giving and gallant. They are gluttonous and goodly and great. What you want when you're down is soft and jiggly, not muscled and stable. Fat people know this. Fat people have plenty of room. Fat people will take you in.

Questions for Discussion

1. Although Jordan uses a humorous tone throughout her essay, do you think she may be saying something serious about body type, social perception, and the ways we value other people? If Jordan is making a commentary on an important social and personal issue, then why does she use humor? How does it affect the argument of this piece?

2. Jordan attempts to reverse the cultural stereotypes about fatness and thinness. How effective is her inversion of values? Does it effectively challenge the prejudices about fat bodies? What other methods could Jordan have used to challenge cultural standards of the body?

3. In her assessment of skinny and fat people, Jordan links personality and behavior to body type. Do you think experiencing the world through a particular body type could change your attitude? Can you see ways in which your physical state influences your personality?

Explorations

1. Consider the different ways authors in this unit write about bodies. For instance, how would Stuart Ewen's assessment of the cultural obsession with muscular bodies compare with Jordan's criticism of thin bodies? In "Hard Bodies," Ewen talks about the frustrations in achieving the perfectly toned body, claiming that "photogenic majesty is elusive" (page 452). Does Jordan's article address this frustration with our bodies in a different way? Or does she assume that physically fit people feel superior? Is Jordan insensitive to the problems "thin" people face?

2. Jordan talks about thin people and fat people in generic terms; bodies are no more specific than their weight and shape. What would happen if Jordan considered a more specific body? For instance, if the fat body is also a woman's body, does that make Jordan's revaluation of fatness more radical? Take a look at Diane Barthel's distinction between men and women's appearances and the system within which women who are beautiful "will be chosen" by men who are afforded active decision making (page 382). If you consider more particular bodily identity in terms of sex, race, age, and ability, how would it change Jordan's ideas?

3. In this article, thin people and fat people are described in oppositional terms, both in appearance and in personality. Are there any drawbacks to this model of setting up and comparing irreconcilable differences? Imagine how someone like Patricia Williams or Holly Devor would respond to Britt's style of comparison. What are the positive and negative aspects of using two categories of people and contrasting their differences with one another?

Formal Writing Assignments

1. Take something about a traditionally undervalued part of your appearance and revalue it in positive terms. Feel free to experiment with tone and topic; use humor to explain a serious topic or use formal language to elevate a trivialized subject.

2. Try to imagine your body in another way. If you consider yourself to be fit, then imagine yourself out of shape. If you think you're tall, then imagine yourself to be short. Change your sex. Write about your imagined experiences in this body. Would you be treated differently? Would you treat others differently? Why?

Pro Wrestling and the End of History

Paul A. Cantor

With a Ph.D. from Harvard and a job as a professor at the University of Virginia, Paul Cantor may seem like an unlikely writer for an article on pro wrestling. While he has written extensively on Shakespeare and the literary movement known as Romanticism, his current interests align with the issues raised in the following article. In the following piece, Cantor infuses his study of a low cultural form with a serious examination of issues surrounding nationalism and power. In his most recent work, a collection of essays entitled *Gilligan Unbounded*, Cantor takes an extensive look at popular culture.

Writing Before Reading

1. What are your impressions of professional wrestling? What political or social messages do you think it sends its audience?

2. How have you formed your opinion of the United States and other counties in times of conflict or war? Is the U.S. generally seen in a positive light? Describe the ways in which this country is characterized, either positively or negatively, in a particular historical moment.

3. What impressions do you have of other nations? What do you rely upon to inform your opinions about them? Are there certain "types" of countries or characteristics you match up with particular nations?

Pro Wrestling and the End of History

When the great Parisian Hegelian Alexandre Kojève searched for an image of the end of history, he finally hit upon the Japanese tea ceremony. Coming from Brooklyn, I am a bit less sophisticated and turn to American professional wrestling instead. For wrestling has been as much a victim of the end of the Cold War as the military-industrial complex. It is not just that the demise of the Soviet Union deprived wrestling of one set of particularly despicable villains. The end of the Cold War signaled the end of an era of nationalism that had dominated the American psyche for most of this century. Like much else in the United States, including the power and prestige of the federal government itself, wrestling had fed off this nationalism. It drew upon ethnic hostilities to fuel the frenzy of its crowds and give a larger meaning to the confrontations it staged.

The state of professional wrestling today thus provides clues as to what living at the end of history means. It suggests how a large segment of American society is trying to cope with the emotional letdown that followed upon the triumph of capitalism and liberal democracy. If the vast wrestling audience (some 35 million people tune in to cable programs each week) is a barometer of American culture, then the nation is in trouble. Indeed, the very idea of the nation-state has become problematic. For wrestling has been denationalizing itself over the past decade, replacing the principle of the nation with the principle of the tribe.

The erosion of national identity in wrestling reflects broader trends in American society. If one wants to see moral relativism and even nihilism at work in American culture, one need only tune in to the broadcasts of either of the two main wrestling organizations, Vince McMahon's Worldwide Wrestling Federation and Ted Turner's World Championship Wrestling. (It is no accident that one of the pillars of

437

professional wrestling is Turner's cable TV empire, which also brings us CNN, the anti-nation-state, global news channel.) Both the WWF and the WCW offer the spectacle of an America that has lost its sense of national purpose and turned inward, becoming wrapped up in manufactured psychological crises and toying with the possibility of substituting class warfare for international conflict. And yet we should remain open to the possibility that contemporary wrestling may have some positive aspects; for one thing, the decline of the old nationalism may be linked to a new kind of creative freedom.

II.

The history of pro wrestling as we know it begins after World War II and is roughly contemporary—not coincidentally—with the rise of television. Wrestling provided relatively cheap and reliable programming and soon became a staple for fledgling television stations. By the 1950s—and well into the '60s and '70s—wrestling was filling the airwaves with ethnic stereotypes, playing off national hostilities that had been fired up by World War II and restoked during the Korean conflict. Wrestling villains—always the key to whatever drama the bouts have—were often defined by their national origin, which branded them as enemies of the American way of life.

Many of the villains were at first either German or Japanese, but as memories of World War II faded, pro wrestling turned increasingly to Cold War themes. I wish I had a ruble for every wrestling villain who was advertised as the "Russian Bear," but the greatest of all who bore that nickname was Ivan Koloff. Looking for all the world like Lenin pumped up on steroids, he eventually spawned a whole dynasty of villainous wrestling Koloffs.

The fact that the most successful of them was named Nikita shows that it was actually Khrushchev and not Lenin or Stalin who provided the model for the Russian wrestling villain. Time and again the Russian wrestler's pre-fight interview was a variation on "Ve vill bury you." Nikolai Volkoff used to infuriate American opponents and fans alike by waving a Soviet flag in the center of the ring and insisting on his right to sing the Soviet national anthem before his bout began.

To supplement its Russian villains, wrestling turned to the Arab Middle East, where a long tradition of ethnic stereotyping was readily available. During the years of tension between the United States and Iran, wrestling hit paydirt with a villain known as the Iron Sheik, who made no secret of his admiration for and close personal ties to the Ayatollah Khomeini. His pitched battles with the All-American G.I., Sgt. Slaughter, became the stuff of wrestling legend. Not to be left behind by the march of history, during the Gulf War the Iron Sheik reinvented himself as Colonel Mustafa, and suddenly Americans had an Iraqi wrestler to hate.

The extent to which wrestling relied on national identity to manufacture its villains should not be overstated. Some of the greatest villains were home-grown, like Nature Boy Buddy Rogers, and some of the greatest heroes were foreign-born, like Bruno Sammartino. But although ethnic stereotyping was not essential to the emotional dynamics of wrestling, it did play a crucial role. That is why the end of the Cold War threatened to deliver a serious if not mortal blow to the whole enterprise. Suddenly audiences could not be counted upon to treat a given wrestler automatically as a villain simply because he was identified as a Russian. There was a brief, almost comic era of wrestling *glasnost*, during which the promoters tried to see if they could generate drama out of the shifting political allegiances of the Russian wrestlers. The extended Koloff family was riven by internal dissent, as some sided with Gorbachev and the reformers, while others remained hardliners and stuck by the old regime. But since Kremlinology has never been a popular spectator sport outside academia, the public quickly grew bored with trying to sort out the internal politics of the Koloff family, and it began to dawn on the wrestling moguls that the end of the Cold War was a threat to their franchise.

This problem was compounded by the fact that at roughly the same time as the Cold War was ending, ethnic stereotyping began to be anathematized. By the early '90s, the WWF even seemed to be testing whether it could capitalize on the new era of political correctness. With Russia and virtually every other country ruled out as a source of villains, Vince McMahon and his brain trust searched the globe to see if any ethnic group remained an acceptable object of hatred. The result was a new villain named Colonel DeBeers—a white, South African wrestler with an attitude, who spoke in favor of apartheid during interviews. One can almost hear the wheels grinding in McMahon's head: "Russians may no longer be fair game, but no one will object to a little Boer-bashing." But wrestling fans did not take the bait. This was one of the few times the WWF misjudged its audience, proceeding as if its fans were sipping chardonnay and sampling brie instead of guzzling beer and munching on nachos. Colonel DeBeers was a flop as a villain and in some ways marked the end of a wrestling era—a last, desperate attempt to base physical conflict in the ring on political conflict outside it.

III.

Wrestling promoters have always been concerned that theirs is not a team sport and thus threatens to lack that extra measure of fan commitment that group solidarity can extract. Exploiting nationalist feeling had been one way of turning wrestling into something more than single combat. Instead of rooting for the home team, fans viewing a Sgt. Slaughter/Iron Sheik bout got to root for America. Or rather, America became the home team.

But there was also a germ of a team concept in wrestling's peculiar institution of the tag team—a bout in which two wrestlers pair up against a couple of opponents. And as ethnicity faded as a principle in wrestling, the WWF and the WCW began to expand tagteam partnerships into larger groupings that might best be described as extended families or tribes. The wrestlers in such tribes pool their resources to advance their careers, often illegally entering the ring to come to each other's aid, softening up each other's opponents for future matches, and generally creating trouble for any wrestler not within the tribe. These wrestling tribes adopt an outlaw pose within their larger leagues, refusing to conform to league rules and challenging the duly constituted wrestling authorities. The most famous of these groups is the New World Order (the nWo) within the WCW, which was headed by Hollywood Hulk Hogan and is constantly trying to outwit the league owners and take over the organization. It is surely one of the ironies of the end of history that in the aftermath of the Gulf War, that "vision thing" of George Bush's has left no more lasting monument than the name of a group of renegade wrestlers.

Tribal organization gives wrestling something intermediate between national identity and a purely individual identity. Fans almost have the sense of rooting for teams, since the wrestling tribes often have their own logos, uniforms, slogans, theme songs, cheerleaders, and other badges of communal or team identity. The wrestling brain trusts create ongoing storylines involving the various tribes, so that the future of the whole league, perhaps its very ownership, can seem to depend on the outcome of a given bout.

Thus the newly created tribal identities in wrestling can serve as substitutes for the old national identities. But one thing is missing—any sense of stability, the reassuring feeling of continuity that used to be provided by ethnic stereotyping in wrestling. Once a Russian, always a Russian, and, until the era of *glasnost*, that also meant always a villain as well. National identity is not a matter of choice; one is born into it and stuck with it, unless one chooses to betray one's national origins (at the height of the Koloff confusions, charges of "traitor" were routinely hurled back and forth in interviews). But in the world of wrestling today, which group a wrestler affiliates with appears to be a matter of personal choice (though in fact these "choices" are still scripted by the league). As it happens, the traditional national identities in wrestling were often made up. Both the "Manchurian" Gorilla Monsoon and the "Oklahoma Indian" Chief Jay Strongbow were in actuality Italian-Americans (Robert Marella and Joe Scarpa respectively), and the wrestler known as Nikolai Volkoff began his career as Bepo Mongol. In the contemporary era, though, wrestling virtually acknowledges that it is manufacturing its villains, and their roles are presented as a matter of personal choice rather than national destiny.

Thus pro wrestling takes its place along with the plays of Samuel Beckett and the buildings of Michael Graves as an example of the dominant cultural mode of our age, postmodernism. The characters in Beckett's plays are not meant to represent real-live human beings, who might be said to lead an existence independent of the drama. Rather they are revealed to be fictions, consciously constructed characters who are themselves sometimes dimly aware that they are merely characters on stage. Graves's buildings are not meant to be "true" in the way the triumphs of modernist architecture were. Abandoning the modernist dogma that form follows function, Graves returns to architectural decoration, reminding us that his buildings are after all human constructions and thereby "deconstructing" them before our eyes. Pro wrestling has similarly entered its postmodern phase, in which it deliberately subverts any claims to truth and naturalness it ever had. Of course, at least since the era of television, pro wrestling has always been entertainment rather than real sport. But for decades pro wrestling at least pretended it was real. It now admits its fictionality, and indeed, like most forms of postmodernism, revels in it.

But can we confidently say that wrestling simply mirrors broader movements in our culture and politics? It is difficult to look at developments in politics and culture today and not see them as in turn mirroring developments in wrestling. Was Hulk Hogan, who dominated the 1980s, perhaps our first taste of Bill Clinton? The Hulkster—who could never talk about anything but himself, his own career, and his standing with his Hulkamaniac fans—was the model of a roguish, narcissistic, utterly unprincipled performer. While changing his stance from moment to moment, he was never held accountable by his adoring public, to the point where he seems to have gotten away with anything. If postmodern wrestling was not a forerunner of postmodern politics, why is Jesse "The Body" Ventura now the governor of Minnesota?

IV.

When the villainy of wrestlers was rooted in their national identity, their evil was presented as inherent in their natures. Related to genuine political conflicts in the actual world, the evil of a Russian wrestler seemed real. But villainy has become something more fluid and elusive in the era of postmodern tribalism. Since the contemporary wrestler appears to choose his tribal affiliations, he also gets to choose whether to be a hero or a villain (again, these matters are carefully scripted by the WWF and the WCW authorities, but we are talking about how things are meant to appear to the wrestling public). The most striking characteristic of post-Cold War wrestling is the dizzying rapidity with which today's wrestlers switch from hero to villain and back again. Wrestlers used to spend their whole careers defined as either good guys or bad guys. Now they alter their natures so often that it no longer makes sense to speak of them as natural heroes or villains in the first place. The contemporary wrestler exemplifies the thoroughly postmodern idea that human identity is purely a construction, a matter of choice, not nature.

With its underpinnings in traditional notions of morality, heroism, and patriotism eroded, wrestling has turned to new sources to hold the interest of its fans. Generally these sources have been found in the dramas of private life. Televised wrestling has always had much in common with soap operas. Fans identify heroes and villains and get wrapped up in ongoing struggles between them and especially the working out of longstanding and complex feuds. Throughout its history, pro wrestling has occasionally sought to involve fans in the private lives of its warriors. Once in a while a wrestler has gotten married in the ring to his female manager or valet. (More recently—reflecting a loosening of morality—female companions of wrestlers have been at stake in matches, with the winner claiming the right to take possession of his opponent's woman.) Personal grudges have always been central to wrestling, but over the last decade they have gotten ever more personal, often involving family members who somehow get drawn into conflict inside or outside the ring.

In short, wrestling conflicts have come increasingly to resemble the appalling family feuds aired on *The Jerry Springer Show*. This is only fair, since Springer seems to have modeled his show on wrestling interviews. Wrestlers used to get angry with each other because one represented the Soviet Union and the other the United States, and the two ways of life were antithetical. Now when wrestlers scream at each other, dark domestic secrets are more likely to surface—sordid tales of adultery, sexual intrigue, and child abuse.

Here a wrestler with the evocative name of Kane is emblematic. Kane was introduced in the WWF as the counterpart of a well-established villain called the Undertaker, who often punishes his defeated opponents by stuffing them into coffins (a nasty case of adding interment to injury). Kane's aptly named manager, Paul Bearer, soon revealed that Kane is in fact the Undertaker's younger brother. Kane wears a mask to hide the frightening facial burns he suffered as a child in a fire set by his older brother, which killed their parents. Thus the stage is set for a series of epic battles between Kane and the Undertaker, as the younger brother seeks revenge against the older. Paul Bearer then reveals that Kane and the Undertaker are actually only half-brothers, and that he himself fathered the younger boy, though he neglected him for years and is only now acknowledging paternity. With its Kane storyline, the WWF crafted a myth for the '90s. All the elements are there: sibling rivalry, disputed parentage, child neglect and abuse, domestic violence, family revenge.

McMahon and his brain trust have once again proven that they have a finger on the pulse of America. In the wake of years of psychotherapy, Twinkie defenses, and the O.J. trial, they have reinvented the villain as himself a victim. No one ever felt a need to explain the evil of Russian wrestlers—they were presented as villainous by nature. But unlike his biblical counterpart, Kane is supplied with motivation for his evil, and therefore inevitably becomes a more sympathetic figure. After all, his problems started when he was just a little kid. Kane is in fact a huge man named Glen Jacobs: six-feet seven-inches tall and weighing 345 pounds. Yet when he climbs into the ring, he stands as the poster boy for the '90s—the victimized wrongdoer, the malefactor who would not be evil *if only someone had loved him as a child*.

The other victim of society now celebrated by pro wrestling is the poor, abused working man, symbolized by "Stone Cold" Steve Austin, currently enmeshed in a bitter feud with Vince McMahon and the entire power structure of the WWF. In his unceasing search for suitable villains, McMahon finally hit upon the most villainous person he could think of—himself. In the ultimate postmodern convolution, wrestling now focus on itself as a business and makes its own corruption the central theme of its plots.

McMahon has decided to build his storylines around ongoing labor-management disputes in the WWF. He is in constant public conflict with his wrestlers, trying to force them to do his bidding and above all to make his on-again, off-again champion Austin toe the corporate line.

In his quest to gain an edge on Turner's WCW, McMahon realized he could tap into the resentment the average working man feels against his boss. McMahon is always threatening to downsize the WWF wrestling staff and has surrounded himself with corporate yes-men. Austin is his perfect working class opponent—a beer drinkin', foot-stompin', truck-drivin', hell-raisin' Texas son-of-a-gun, always prepared to tell McMahon: "You can take this job and shove it." With this storyline, wrestling has completed its turn inward, moving from the Cold War to class war. Ironically, even at the height of the Cold War, wrestling never went after Russian communism with half the fervor it now devotes to pillorying American big business. If wrestling is any indication, the United States—deprived of any meaningful external enemy—seems to have nothing better to do than attack itself. Why not go after a bunch of tobacco companies, for example?

The McMahon-Austin feud proved to be so successful that Turner's WCW soon began imitating it, using its chief executive, Eric Bischoff (a former wrestler himself) to play the role of corporate bad guy. Always one step ahead of his competition, McMahon went on to fuse the family soap opera aspect of wrestling with the class warfare element by involving his son, his daughter, and eventually even his wife in his corporate struggles. These storylines have become increasingly bizarre, with McMahon's son Shane first seeming to betray him and then revealed to have been secretly acting on his behalf all along, and his daughter Stephanie set up for a kind of wrestling dynastic marriage and then kidnapped under weird circumstances. Who would have thought a century ago when wrestling began with a simple full nelson and a stepover toehold that it would eventually culminate in a proxy fight? But that is exactly what happened when McMahon's wife and daughter shocked him by voting their shares in the WWF to make Austin CEO, thereby transforming the board meetings back in Connecticut beyond recognition. (Austin brought a case of beer to his first session as president.) No wonder McMahon is about to take his corporation public.

Every time I think wrestling has reached rock bottom, either the WWF or the WCW finds its way to a new moral depth. A recent plot line culminated in Austin holding a gun to McMahon's head in the center of the ring, as the nattily attired owner/operator of the WWF appeared to wet himself in terror. When one looks at wrestling's "progress" from the 1950s to the 1990s, one really has to be concerned about America's future. If wrestling tells us anything about our country—and its widespread and sustained popularity suggests that it does—for the past three decades we have been watching a steady erosion of the country's moral fiber, and America's growing incapacity to offer functional models of heroism.

On the other hand, perhaps we should cease being moralistic for a moment, recognize that wrestling is only entertainment, and try to look beyond its admittedly grotesque antics. Though it is tempting to become nostalgic for the good old days of American patriotism in wrestling, let's face it: The traditional national stereotypes did become tired, overused, and predictable. In that sense, the end of the Cold War actually proved to be liberating for wrestling, as one might hope it could be for all American society. What appeared to be a loss of ethnic stereotyping proved to be a gain in creative freedom, as wrestling was forced to scour popular culture to come up with alternatives to traditional villains. Wrestling may not be more moral these days, but it certainly is more interesting and inventive. This development suggests that maybe we all need to be thinking beyond the nation-state as our chief cultural unit.

After all, the nation-state has not always been the dominant form of cultural or even political organization. It is largely a development out of 16th-century France, and has never as fully prevailed around the world as historians would have us think. There is no reason to believe that the nation-state as we know it is the perfect or even the best unit of political organization. When Aristotle made his famous statement usually translated as "man is a political animal," what he really was saying is that man is an animal whose nature it is to live in the *polis*—the Greek city conceived as the comprehensive human community, on a scale much smaller than a modern nation state. Thus Aristotle would have said that the nation-state is an unnaturally large and even overblown form of community.

Perhaps what appears to be the end of history is only the end of the nation-state, and humanity is now groping confusedly toward new modes of political organization, which may be at once more global and more local in their scope. Today's professional wrestling points in these two directions simultaneously. At any moment of deep historical change, it is easy to become fixated on what is being lost and fail to see what is being gained. The way wrestling has been struggling to find some kind of postnational identity reflects a deeper confusion in our culture as a whole, but one that may portend a profound and even beneficial reorganization of our lives in the coming century. Perhaps, then, when we watch—and enjoy—the WWF and the WCW, we really are wrestling with the end of history.

Questions for Discussion

1. In the era of nationalism during the Cold War between the United States and the Soviet Union, how did professional wrestling help create and support national identities, according to Cantor?

2. Cantor's article points out the shift in professional wrestling at the end of nationalism. Rather than relying upon inherent villainy or heroism, post-Cold War wrestling uses the "postmodern idea that human identity is purely a construction, a matter of choice, not nature". What are the ways that wrestling represents this postmodern concept?

3. To Cantor, what are the advantages of the post-nationalist state? With the fall of concrete national identities, what are the possibilities for U.S. culture in the postmodern condition?

Explorations

1. Cantor reveals the differences between a naturalized identity (like the villains and heroes of Cold War wrestling) and one that is constructed (like the postmodern wrestler). He seems to prefer the notion of a constructed identity. Holly Devor, in "Gender Roles Behavior and Attitudes," also values the notion of identity as learned and unnatural. Do Cantor and Devor agree about the benefits of a postmodern identity? Compare the benefits of examining supposedly "inherent" identities, according to each author.

2. By warning us against longing for the "good old days of American patriotism in wrestling," Cantor suggests that, in general, "traditional national stereotypes did become tired, overused, and predictable." What are the dangers of stereotyping other nations to bolster U.S. patriotism? Why do you think some people still long for the good old days?

3. Cantor suggests that the U.S. is progressing beyond the nation-state and its accompanying Cold War patriotism. Describe the current style of patriotism in the United States. What possibilities does this new conceptualization of the nation offer? What could be lost with the fall of the nation-state?

Formal Writing Assignments

1. Find a current example (a news story, advertisement, Armed Forces campaign, film) of U.S. patriotism that depends upon vilifying other nations. Does it contradict Cantor's study of the nation-state, its accompanying patriotism, and its eventual downfall? Are we done with the nation-state and its dependence on stereotyping other countries? What are the reasons for using negative images of other countries to bolster U.S. patriotism? In analyzing your example, talk about the potential value and pitfalls of this method in creating national identities.

2. Take a "low" cultural event or text and analyze in terms of national identity and/or individualism. What values does this cultural product convey? Through what means? Discuss your example and the potential importance of pop cultural in creating political opinions and beliefs.

Gender Role Behaviors and Attitudes

Holly Devor

Dedicated to questions of gender, sex, and sexuality, Professor Holly Devor's research examines sites of "gender blending" (a phrase coined by Devor), whether it be in our everyday behaviors, in transsexual and lesbian communities, or in the masculinity of women. The following piece exemplifies Devor's approach to gender. To her, gender is neither inevitable nor natural, but is constructed and taught to us. In her public lectures, Devor suggests that there may be more possibilities for our identities than masculinity and femininity, that two sexes and genders are not enough to describe how many people act and feel. Devor's interest in our sex/gender system extends beyond the academy. She works as a public speaker, educator, and legal consultant on issues concerning transsexual or transgendered people.

Writing Before Reading

1. Reflect on your perception of your gender attributes. Do you think your masculinity or femininity is inevitable and inherent? Or is it open to interpretation and choice?

2. What behaviors do you associate with femininity and masculinity? Are there advantages to either feminine or masculine behaviors? What are these advantages?

3. Recall a time when you or someone you know has challenged traditional gender behaviors. What was the general reaction of people who observed this non-traditional behavior? How do you account for their reactions?

Gender Role Behaviors and Attitudes

The clusters of social definitions used to identify persons by gender are collectively known as "femininity" and "masculinity." Masculine characteristics are used to identify persons as males, while feminine ones are used as signifiers for femaleness. People use femininity or masculinity to claim and communicate their membership in their assigned, or chosen, sex or gender. Others recognize our sex or gender more on the basis of these characteristics than on the basis of sex characteristics, which are usually largely covered by clothing in daily life.

These two clusters of attributes are most commonly seen as mirror images of one another with masculinity usually characterized by dominance and aggression, and femininity by passivity and submission. A more even-handed description of the social qualities subsumed by femininity and masculinity might be to label masculinity as generally concerned with egoistic dominance and femininity as striving for cooperation or communion.[1] Characterizing femininity and masculinity in such a way does not portray the two clusters of characteristics as being in a hierarchical relationship to one another but rather as being two different approaches to the same question, that question being centrally concerned with the goals, means, and use of power. Such an alternative conception of gender roles captures the hierarchical and competitive masculine thirst for power, which can, but need not, lead to aggression, and the feminine quest for harmony and communal well-being, which can, but need not, result in passivity and dependence.

Many activities and modes of expression are recognized by most members of society as feminine. Any of these can be, and often are, displayed by persons of either gender. In some cases, cross-gender behaviors are ignored by observers, and therefore do not compromise the integrity of a person's gender display. In other cases, they are labeled as inappropriate gender role behaviors. Although these behaviors are closely linked to sexual status in the minds and experiences of most people, research shows that dominant persons of either gender tend to use influence tactics and verbal styles usually associated with men and masculinity, while subordinate persons, of either gender, tend to use those considered to be the province of women.[2] Thus it seems likely that many aspects of masculinity and femininity are the result, rather than the cause, of status inequalities.

Popular conceptions of femininity and masculinity instead revolve around hierarchical appraisals of the "natural" roles of males and females. Members of both genders are believed to share many of the same human characteristics, although in different relative proportions; both males and females are popularly thought to be able to do many of the same things, but most activities are divided into suitable and unsuitable categories for each gender class. Persons who perform the activities considered appropriate for another gender will be expected to perform them poorly; if they succeed adequately, or even well, at their endeavors, they may be rewarded with ridicule or scorn for blurring the gender dividing line.

The patriarchal gender schema currently in use in mainstream North American society reserves highly valued attributes for males and actively supports the high evaluation of any characteristics which might inadvertently become associated with maleness. The ideology underlying the schema postulates that the cultural superiority of males is a natural outgrowth of the innate predisposition of males toward aggression and dominance, which is assumed to flow inevitably from evolutionary and biological sources. Female attributes are likewise postulated to find their source in innate predispositions acquired in the evolution of the species. Feminine characteristics are thought to be intrinsic to the female facility for childbirth and breastfeeding. Hence, it is popularly believed that the social position of females is biologically mandated to be intertwined with the care of children and a "natural" dependency on men for the maintenance of mother-child units. Thus the goals of femininity and, by implication, of all biological females are presumed to revolve around heterosexuality and maternity.[3]

Femininity, according to this traditional formulation, "would result in warm and continued relationships with men, a sense of maternity, interest in caring for children, and the capacity to work productively and continuously in female occupations."[4] This recipe translates into a vast number of proscriptions and prescriptions. Warm and continued relations with men and an interest in maternity require that females be heterosexually oriented. A heterosexual orientation requires women to dress, move, speak, and act in ways that men will find attractive. As patriarchy has reserved active expressions of power as a masculine attribute, femininity must be expressed through modes of dress, movement, speech, and action which communicate weakness, dependency, ineffectualness, availability for sexual or emotional service, and sensitivity to the needs of others.

Some, but not all, of these modes of interrelation also serve the demands of maternity and many female job ghettos. In many cases, though, femininity is not particularly useful in maternity or employment. Both mothers and workers often need to be strong, independent, and effectual in order to do their jobs well. Thus femininity, as a role, is best suited to satisfying a masculine vision of heterosexual attractiveness.

Body postures and demeanors which communicate subordinate status and vulnerability to trespass through a message of "no threat" make people appear to be feminine. They demonstrate subordination through a minimizing of spatial use: People appear feminine when they keep their arms closer to their bodies, their legs closer together, and their torsos and heads less vertical than do masculine-looking individuals. People also look feminine when they point their toes inward and use their hands in small or childlike gestures. Other people also tend to stand closer to people they see as feminine, often invading their personal space, while people who make frequent appeasement gestures, such as smiling, also give the appearance of femininity. Perhaps as an outgrowth of a subordinate status and the need to avoid conflict with more socially powerful people, women tend to excel over men at the ability to correctly interpret, and effectively display, nonverbal communication cues.[5]

Speech characterized by inflections, intonations, and phrases that convey nonaggression and subordinate status also make a speaker appear more feminine. Subordinate speakers who use more polite expressions and ask more questions in conversation seem more feminine. Speech characterized by sounds of higher frequencies are often interpreted by listeners as feminine, childlike, and ineffectual.[6] Feminine styles of dress likewise display subordinate status through greater restriction of the free movement of the body, greater exposure of the bare skin, and an emphasis on sexual characteristics. The more gender distinct the dress, the more this is the case.

Masculinity, like femininity, can be demonstrated through a wide variety of cues. Pleck has argued that it is commonly expressed in North American society through the attainment of some level of proficiency at some, or all, of the following four main attitudes of masculinity. Persons who display success and high status in their social group, who exhibit "a manly air of toughness, confidence, and self-reliance" and "the aura of aggression, violence, and daring," and who conscientiously avoid anything associated with femininity are seen as exuding masculinity.[7] These requirements reflect the patriarchal ideology that masculinity results from an excess of testosterone, the assumption being that androgens supply a natural impetus toward aggression, which in turn impels males toward achievement and success. This vision of masculinity also reflects the ideological stance that ideal maleness (masculinity) must remain untainted by female (feminine) pollutants.

Masculinity, then, requires of its actors that they organize themselves and their society in a hierarchical manner so as to be able to explicitly quantify the achievement of success. The achievement of high status in one's social group requires competitive and aggressive behavior from those who wish to obtain it. Competition, which is motivated by a goal of individual achievement, or egoistic dominance, also requires of its participants a degree of emotional insensitivity to feelings of hurt and loss in defeated others, and a measure of emotional insularity to protect oneself from becoming vulnerable to manipulation by others. Such values lead those who subscribe to them to view feminine persons as "born losers" and to strive to eliminate any similarities to feminine people from their own personalities. In patriarchally organized societies, masculine values become the ideological structure of the society as a whole. Masculinity thus becomes "innately" valuable and femininity serves a contrapuntal function to delineate and magnify the hierarchical dominance of masculinity.

Body postures, speech patterns, and styles of dress which demonstrate and support the assumption of dominance and authority convey an impression of masculinity. Typical masculine body postures tend to be expansive and aggressive. People who hold their arms and hands in positions away from their bodies, and who stand, sit, or lie with their legs apart—thus maximizing the amount of space that they physically occupy—appear most physically masculine. Persons who communicate an air of authority or a readiness for aggression by standing erect and moving forcefully also tend to appear more masculine. Movements that are abrupt and stiff, communicating force and threat rather than flexibility and cooperation, make an actor look masculine. Masculinity can also be conveyed by stern or serious facial expressions that suggest minimal receptivity to the influence of others, a characteristic which is an important element in the attainment and maintenance of egoistic dominance.[8]

Speech and dress which likewise demonstrate or claim superior status are also seen as characteristically masculine behavior patterns. Masculine speech patterns display a tendency toward expansiveness similar to that found in masculine body postures. People who attempt to control the direction of conversations seem more masculine. Those who tend to speak more loudly, use less polite and more assertive forms, and tend to interrupt the conversations of others more often also communicate masculinity to others. Styles of dress which emphasize the size of upper body musculature, allow freedom of movement, and encourage an illusion of physical power and a look of easy physicality all suggest masculinity. Such appearances of strength and readiness to action serve to create or enhance an aura of aggressiveness and intimidation central to all appearance of masculinity. Expansive postures and gestures combine with these qualities to insinuate that a position of secure dominance is a masculine one.

Gender role characteristics reflect the ideological contentions underlying the dominant gender schema in North American society. That schema leads us to believe that female and male behaviors are the result of socially directed hormonal instructions which specify that females will want to have children and will therefore find themselves relatively helpless and dependent on males for support and protection. The schema claims that males are innately aggressive and competitive and therefore will dominate over females. The social hegemony of this ideology ensures that we are all raised to practice gender roles which will confirm this vision of the nature of the sexes. Fortunately, our training to gender roles is neither complete nor uniform. As a result, it is possible to point to multitudinous exceptions to, and variations on, these themes. Biological evidence is equivocal about the source of gender roles; psychological androgyny is a widely accepted concept. It seems most likely that gender roles are the result of systematic power unbalances based on gender discrimination.[9]

Notes

1. Eleanor Maccoby, Social Development: Psychological Growth and tile Parent-Child Relationship (New York: Harcourt, Brace, Jovanovich, 1980), p. 217. Egoistic dominance is a striving for superior rewards for oneself or a competitive striving to reduce the rewards for one's competitors even if such action will not increase one's own rewards. Persons who are motivated by desires for egoistic dominance not only wish the best for themselves but also wish to diminish the advantages of others whom they may perceive as competing with them.

2. Judith Howard, Philip Blumstein, and Pepper Schwartz, "Sex, Power, and Influence Tactics in Intimate Relationships," *Journal of Personality and Social Psychology* 51 (1986), pp. 102–109; Peter Kollock, Philip Blumstein, and Pepper Schwartz, "Sex and Power in Interaction: Conversation Priviledges and Duties," *American Sociological Review* 50 (1985), pp. 34–46.

3. Nancy Chodorow, *The Reproduction of Mothering: Psychoanalysis and the Reproduction of Mothering* (Berkeley: University of California Press, 1978), p. 134.

4. Jon K. Meyer and John E. Hoopes, "The Gender Dysphoroa Syndromes: A Position Statement on So-Called 'Transsexualism'," *Plastic and Reconstructive Surgery* 54 (Oct. 1974), pp. 444–51.

5. Erving Goffman, *Gender Advertisements* (New York: Harper Colophon Books, 1976); Judith A. Hall, *Non-Verbal Sex Differences: Communication Accuracy and Expressive Style* (Baltimore: John Hopkins University Press, 1984); Nancy M. Henley, *Body Politics: Power, Sex and Non-Verbal Communication* (Englewood Cliffs, N. J.: Prentice-Hall, 1979); Marianne Wex, *"Let's Take Back Our Space": "Female" and "Male" Body Language as a Result of Patriarchal Structures* (Berlin: Frauenliteraturverlag Hermine Fees, 1979).

6. Karen L. Adams, "Sexism and the English Language: The Linguistic Implications of Being a Woman," in *Women: A Feminist Perspective*, 3rd ed., ed. Jo Freeman (Palo Alto, Calif.: Mayfield, 1984), pp. 478–91; Hall, pp. 37, 130–137.

7. Joseph H. Pleck, *The Myth of Masculinity* (Cambridge, Mass.: MIT Press, 1981), p. 139.

8. Goffman; Hall; Henley; Wex.

9. Howard, Blumstein, and Schwartz; Kollock, Blumstein, and Schwartz.

Questions for Discussion

1. Although our gender identity is constructed by social rules, our gender training is "neither complete nor uniform," according to Devor (pg.). Explain what this means for gender identity. Why does Devor think this is positive?

2. How is gender characteristically demonstrated, according to Devor? She claims that particular gender characteristics garner financial and social rewards. What are these?

3. Devor talks about gender in terms of femininity and masculinity, as well as in female and male behaviors. What is the difference between gender and sex ("woman" and "man")? Why would it be important to distinguish between the two, given Devor's arguments about gender roles?

Explorations

1. In "A Gentleman and a Consumer," Diane Barthel identifies advertising appeals to masculinity in men, claiming that "power/precision/performance run as a theme throughout advertising to men" (page 384). Compare Barthel and Devor on their positions concerning gender. Do you think Barthel finds the masculinity of men inevitable or does she agree with Devor's conception of gender as constructed? Could gender training fail in Barthel's argument or does advertising appeal to an essential masculinity inherent in men?

2. Compare Devor's outlook on gender possibilities and Cynthia Selfe's criticism of the "Ungendered Utopia story" of technology (306). Is Devor's argument a utopian one? Can Devor's theory be put into practice or does it ignore the inevitable patterns of our social structures? Does Devor's call for a gender-neutral society equate to Selfe's depiction of technology's idealistic promises? In what way does gender blending appeal to us? Romantically, theoretically, practically? Or do we, as Selfe claims, fail to conceptualize gender "outside the contexts of our familiar historical and cultural set of experiences" (307)?

3. Devor's examination of gender behaviors suggests a critique of femininity's link with maternity and heterosexuality. More overtly tying sexuality with gender roles, Susan Bordo joins challenges to the sexual order with the gender order of dominant culture. To Bordo, gayness is part of an "ironic, deconstructive take on gender," which offers us "other styles of being men and women"(164). Would Devor agree with Bordo's assessment? Do you think gender construction depends upon and/or supports the stability of other social categories? What other naturalized, socially constructed categories would come under question if we were to overturn traditional concepts of gender?

Formal Writing Assignments

1. Look at a public text (a magazine ad, billboard, TV commercial) and investigate the ways in which gender is represented and put on display. Describe the visual and behavioral signs of gender in this text. What does this gender behavior "say" to you as a consumer?

2. Keep a log of your most important daily activities and briefly describe your feelings and behaviors within each activity. How many of these activities are influenced by your gender? Do you find yourself behaving according to socially sanctioned gender standards or do you find yourself transgressing gender roles? What would you do differently if you did not "have to" act in a feminine or masculine manner?

Hard Bodies

Stuart Ewen

As a political activist, social critic, and professor in Media, History, Sociology, and American Studies departments, Stuart Ewen approaches the study of culture from a number of vantage points, both scholarly and political. In the following article, Ewen examines mass media images and their impact on individuals and culture. These concerns relate to those he and his wife, Elizabeth Ewen, raise in their co-authored "In the Shadow of the Image," which also appears in this unit. Taken from *All Consuming Images: The Politics of Style in Contemporary Culture*, "Hard Bodies" makes connections between the human body and industrialized labor. The book *All Consuming Images* served as a foundation for the Emmy, Peabody, and NEA Awards winning PBS series, "The Public Mind." Ewen appears on-camera for Part I of the series to discuss the points he raises here.

Writing Before Reading

1. List as many reasons for exercising as you can. How many of these reasons are related to health? To standards of physical attractiveness? What does your list suggest about the meaning of working out?

2. Describe the physical appearance of a successful person. Are there certain body types that you associate with success?

3. Are there different cultural expectations for men's and women's bodies? If so, why?

Hard Bodies

Writing in 1934, the sociologists George A. Lundberg, Mirra Komarovsky, and Mary Alice McInerny addressed the question of "leisure" in the context of an emerging consumer society. Understanding the symbiotic relationship between mass-production industries and a consumerized definition of leisure, they wrote of the need for society to achieve a compatibility between the worlds of work and daily life. "The ideal to be sought," they proposed, "is undoubtedly the gradual obliteration of the psychological barrier which today distinguishes work from leisure."[1]

That ideal has been realized in the daily routine of Raymond H——, a thirty-four-year-old middle-management employee of a large New York City investment firm. He is a living cog in what Felix Rohatyn has termed the new "money culture," one in which "making things" no longer counts; "making money," as an end in itself, is the driving force.[2] His days are spent at a computer terminal, monitoring an endless flow of numerical data.

When his workday is done, he heads toward a local health club for the relaxation of a "workout." Three times a week this means a visit to the Nautilus room, with its high, mirrored walls, and its imposing assembly line of large, specialized "machines." The workout consists of exercises for his lower body and for his upper body, twelve "stations" in all. As he moves from Nautilus machine to Nautilus machine, he works on his hips, buttocks, thighs, calves, back, shoulders, chest, upper arms, forearms, abdomen, and neck, body part by body part.

At the first station, Raymond lies on the "hip and back machine," making sure to align his hip joints with the large, polished, kidney shaped cams which offer resistance as he extends each leg downward over the padded roller under each knee. Twelve repetitions of this, and he moves on to the "hip abduction machine," where he spreads his legs outward against the padded restraints that hold them closed. Then leg extensions on the "compound leg machine" are followed by leg curls on the "leg curl machine." From here, Raymond H— proceeds to the "pullover/torso arm machine," where he begins to address each piece of his upper body. After a precise series of repetitions on the "double chest machine," he completes his workout on the "four-way neck machine."

While he alternates between different sequential workouts, and different machines, each session is pursued with deliberate precision, following exact instructions.

Raymond H— has been working on his body for the past three years, ever since he got his last promotion. He is hoping to achieve the body he always wanted. Perhaps it is fitting that this quintessential, single, young, urban professional—whose life has become a circle of work, money culture, and the cultivation of an image—has turned himself, literally, into a piece of work. If the body ideal he seeks is *lean*, devoid of fatty tissue, it is also *hard*. "Soft flesh," once a standard phrase in the American erotic lexicon, is now—within the competitive, upscale world he inhabits—a sign of failure and sloth. The hard shell is now a sign of achievement, visible proof of success in the "rat race." The goal he seeks is more about *looking* than *touching*.

To achieve his goal, he approaches his body piece by piece; with each machine he performs a discrete task. Along the way he also assumes the job of inspector, surveying the results of each task in the mirrors that surround him. The division of labor, the fragmentation of the work process, and the regulating function of continual measurement and observation—all fundamental to the principles of "scientific management—are intrinsic to this form of recreation. Like any assembly line worker, H— needs no overall knowledge of the process he is engaged in, only the specific tasks that comprise that process. "You don't have to understand *why* Nautilus equipment works," writes bodybuilder Mike Mentzer in the foreword to one of the most widely read Nautilus manuals. "With a tape measure in hand," he promises, "you will see what happens."[3]

The body ideal Raymond H— covets is, itself, an aestheticized tribute to the broken-down work processes of the assembly line. "I'm trying to get better definition," H— says. "I'm into Nautilus because it lets me do the necessary touchup work. Free weights [barbells] are good for building up mass, but Nautilus is great for definition."[4] By "definition," H— is employing the lingo of the gym, a reference to a body surface upon which each muscle, each muscle group, appears segmented and distinct. The perfect body is one that ratifies the fragmentary process of its construction, one that mimics—in flesh—the illustrative qualities of a schematic drawing, or an anatomy chart.

Surveying his work in the mirror, H— admires the job he has done on his broad, high pectorals, but is quick to note that his quadriceps "could use some work." This ambivalence, this mix of emotions, pursues him each time he comes for a workout, and the times in between. He is never quite satisfied with the results. The excesses of the weekend-past invariably leave their blemish. An incorrectly struck pose reveals an over-measure of loose skin, a sign of weakness in the shell. Despite all efforts, photogenic majesty is elusive.

The power of the photographic idiom, in his mind's eye, is reinforced again and again, by the advertisements and other media of style visible everywhere. The ideal of the perfectly posed machine—the cold, hard body in response—is paraded, perpetually, before his eyes and ours. We see him, or her, at every glance.

An advertisement for home gym equipment promises a "Body By Soloflex." Above is the silent, chiaroscuro portrait of a muscular youth, his torso bare, his elbows reaching high, pulling a thin-ribbed undershirt up over his head, which is faceless, covered by shadow. His identity is situated below the neck, an instrumentally achieved study in brawn. The powerful expanse of his chest and back is illuminated from the right side. A carefully cast shadow accentuates the paired muscle formations of his abdominal wall. The airbrush has done its work as well, effecting a smooth, standardized, molded quality, what John

Berger has termed "the skin without a biography." A silent, brooding hulk of a man, he is the unified product of pure engineering. His image is a product of expensive photographic technology, and expensive technical expertise. His body—so we are informed—is also a technical achievement. He has reached this captured moment of perpetual perfection on a "machine that fits in the corner" of his home. The machine, itself, resembles a stamping machine, one used to shape standardized, industrial products. Upon this machine, he has routinely followed instructions for "twenty-four traditional iron pumping exercises, each correct in form and balance." The privileged guidance of industrial engineering, and the mindless obedience of work discipline, have become legible upon his body; yet as it is displayed, it is nothing less than a thing of beauty, a transcendent aspiration.

This machine-man is one of a generation of desolate, finely tuned loners who have cropped up as icons of American style. Their bodies, often lightly oiled to accentuate definition, reveal their inner mechanisms like costly, open-faced watches, where one can see the wheels and gears moving inside, revealing—as it were—the magic of time itself. If this is eroticism, it is one tuned more to the mysteries of technology than to those of the flesh.

In another magazine advertisement, for Evian spring water from France, six similarly anatomized figures stand across a black and white two-page spread. From the look of things, each figure (three men and three women) has just completed a grueling workout, and four of the are partaking of Evian water as part of their recovery. The six are displayed in a lineup, each one displaying a particularly well-developed anatomical region. These are the new icons of beauty, precisely defined, powerful machines. Below, on the left, is the simple caption: "Revival of the Fittest." Though part of a group, each figure is conspicuously alone.

Once again, the modern contours of power, and the structures of work discipline, are imprinted upon the body. In a world of rampant careerism, self-absorption is a rule of thumb. If the division of labor sets each worker in competition with every other, here that fragmentation is aestheticized into the narcissism of mind and body.

Within this depiction, sexual equality is presented as the meeting point between the anorectic and the "nautilized." True to gender distinctions between evanescent value and industrial work discipline, the three women are defined primarily by contour, by the thin lines that their willowy bodies etch upon the page. Although their muscles are toned, they strike poses that suggest pure, disembodied form. Each of the men, situated alternately between the women, gives testimony on behalf of a particular fraction of segmented flesh: abdomen, shoulders and upper-arms, upper back. In keeping with the assembly line approach to muscle building, each man's body symbolizes a particular station within the labor process.

Another ad, for a health and fitness magazine, contains an alarmingly discordant statement: "Today's women workers are back in the sweat shop." There is a basis to this claim. In today's world, powerful, transnational corporations search the globe looking for the cheapest labor they can find. Within this global economy, more and more women—from Chinatown to Taiwan—are employed at tedious, low-paying jobs, producing everything from designer jeans to computer parts.

Yet this is not the kind of sweatshop the ad has in mind. The photographic illustration makes this clear. Above the text, across the two-page color spread, is the glistening, heavily muscled back of a woman hoisting a chrome barbell. Her sweat is self-induced, part of a "new woman" lifestyle being promoted in *Sport* magazine, "the magazine of the new vitality." Although this woman bears the feminine trademark of blonde, braided hair, her body is decidedly masculine, a new body aesthetic in the making. Her muscles are not the cramped, biographically induced muscles of menial labor. Hers is the brawn of the purely symbolic, the guise of the middle-class "working woman."

While the text of the advertisement seems to allude to the real conditions of female labor, the image transforms that truth into beauty, rendering it meaningless. Real conditions are copywritten into catchy and humorous phrases. The harsh physical demands of women's work are reinterpreted as regimented, leisure-time workouts at a "health club." Real sweat is reborn as photogenic body oil.

The migration of women into the social structures of industrial discipline is similarly aestheticized in an ad for Jack LaLanne Fitness Centers. A black and white close-up of a young woman wrestling with a fitness "machine" is complemented by the eroticized grimace on her face. Once again, the chiaroscuro technique accentuates the straining muscles of her arms. The high-contrast, black and white motif may also suggest the "night and day" metamorphosis that will occur when one commits to this particular brand of physical discipline.

In large white letters, superimposed across the shadowy bottom of the photograph, are the words: "Be taut by experts." With a clever play on words the goal of education moves from the mind to the body. Muscle power is offered as an equivalent substitute for brain power. No problem. In the search for the perfectly regulated self, it is implicit that others will do the thinking. This woman, like the Soloflex man, is the product of pure engineering, of technical expertise:

> We were building bodies back when you were building blocks. . . . We know how to perfectly balance your workout between swimming, jogging, aerobics and weight training on hundreds of the most advanced machines available. . . . Sure it may hurt a little. But remember. *You only hurt the one you love.* [Emphasis added.]

These advertisements, like Raymond H—'s regular visits to the Nautilus room, are part of the middle class bodily rhetoric of the 1980s. Together they mark a culture in which self-absorbed careerism, conspicuous consumption, and a conception of *self* as an object of competitive display have fused to become the preponderant symbols of achievement. The regulated body is the nexus where a cynical ethos of social Darwinism, and the eroticism of raw power, meet.

Notes

1. George A. Lundberg et al., *Leisure: A Suburban Study* (1934), p. 3.

2. *New York Time,* 3 June 1987, p. A27.

3. Ellington Darden, *The Nautilus Bodybuilding Book* (1986), pp. viii–ix.

4. Style Project, interview 1–13.

Questions for Discussion

1. Ewen writes about the relationship between work and the body. What is the connection between current labor conditions and social preoccupations with physical fitness? What connections can you make between the workout Ewen describes and a typical corporate job?

2. In spite of the labor involved in working out, Raymond H— feels "ambivalence" and dissatisfaction with his body. Ewen asserts that "ideal of the perfectly posed machine—the cold, hard body in response—is paraded, perpetually" before us (page 452). Given this pervasiveness of this ideal, can Raymond ever be satisfied? Is dissatisfaction important to maintaining the ideal body image?

3. What happens when the body is imagined as "the perfectly posed machine"? (page 452). What beliefs about humanity does this concept challenge? Is there anything to be gained by attaining this ideal? Drawbacks?

Explorations

1. In his assessment of the new body ideal, Ewen employs the word "hard" to describe both the muscular body and the personality of the successful corporate worker. With the "hard shell" as a "sign of achievement," the muscular body equates with the competitive nature of a worker; the physical represents personality traits (page 452). In "That Lean and Hungry Look," Suzanne Britt Jordan also compares body types to behaviors and personalities. How do you think Jordan's analysis compares to Ewen's? What are the significant differences and/or similarities among their arguments?

2. Linking the world of industrialized labor and the body ideal as the "aestheticized tribute to the broken-down work processes of the assembly line," Ewen identifies the effects of production on human conditions. In "Ways of Seeing," John Berger examines the results when images are mass-produced through reproduction. To Berger, reproducing an image diversifies its uses and its "meaning is either modified or totally changed" (page 407). Characterize the effects of mass production described in Ewen's and Berger's analysis. Do the two authors agree about the results of mass production? Are there different values for this type of production according to its product (human versus image)? Does Berger find any value in mass-production?

3. Ewen links labor conditions and human bodies, calling attention to the similar attitudes we hold about assembly line labor and the creation of perfect bodies. Other authors in this unit forge similar relationships between the human condition and the conditions of production. Use another author's argument about technology and humans, perhaps Charles Bazerman's "The Production of Technology" or Robert Samuelson's "Technology in Reverse," to create your own scenario of the human machine relationship. How do certain types of technology shape how we regard ourselves? What connections can you make between the technological present and the state of human behavior?

Formal Writing Assignments

1. Find several advertisements that fortify a particular message across a range of products, contexts, or implied audiences. What is this message? What forms can it take? Why is it important that this message is insistent?

2. Visit a gym and study its atmosphere. Describe how you feel there. Welcomed? Alienated? Embarrassed? What types of people do and don't belong there? Write an analytic essay that examines the purposes and cultural influences of a gym.

In the Shadow of the Image

Stuart Ewen and Elizabeth Ewen

As a wife and husband writing team, Stuart and Elizabeth Ewen bring their shared scholarly interests to bear on the following piece. A professor of American Studies at SUNY, Elizabeth's research deals with the cultural history of specific settings in American women's lives. Whether it be immigrant women living in the Lower East Side or late-20thC women living in the suburbs, Elizabeth's focus on the everydayness of lives marks her writing. Stuart Ewen works as a professor of Film and Media Studies at Hunter College as well as a History and Sociology professor at SUNY's Graduate Center. Concerned with the political and social effects of media, Stuart works under the name of Archie Bishop as a photographer, activist, and graphic artist. Much of his work protests economic cutbacks for the arts and demonstrates an accessible message and forum. Using billboards, street installations, and New York City blocks, Stuart's art brings his political message to highly visible spaces to reach the general public. Like Elizabeth's focus on ordinary lives, Stuart's activist art challenges the lofty tradition of scholarly work and "high" art.

Writing Before Reading

1. Think about your most recent purchase, regardless of its cost or personal value. What was it? Why were you persuaded to buy it? Write a personal narrative about the influences that led you to buy this item.

2. Write about a particular moment in your drive, walk, or bus ride to work or school when you see an advertisement. Why does it catch your eye? How do you react to this advertisement? Does the ad stay with you beyond that particular moment?

3. What are the purposes of advertising? How does it influence "real life"?

In the Shadow of the Image

Maria Aguilar was born twenty-seven years ago near Mayagüez, on the island of Puerto Rico. Her family had lived off the land for generations. Today she sits in a rattling IRT[1] subway car, speeding through the iron-and-rock guts of Manhattan. She sits on the train, her ears dazed by the loud outcry of wheels against tracks. Surrounded by a galaxy of unknown fellow strangers, she looks up at a long strip of colorful signboards placed high above the bobbing heads of the others. All the posters call for her attention.

Looking down at her, a blond-haired lady cabdriver leans out of her driver's side window. Here is the famed philosopher of this strange urban world, and a woman she can talk to. The tough-wise eyes of the cabby combine with a youthful beauty, speaking to Maria Aguilar directly:

Estoy sentada 12 horas al dia.
Lo último que necesito son hemorroides.

(I sit for twelve hours a day. The last thing I need are hemorrhoids.)

Under this candid testimonial lies a package of Preparation H ointment, and the promise "Alivia dolores y picasonas. Y ayuda a reducir la hinchazón." (Relieves pain and itching. And helps reduce swelling.) As her mind's eye takes it all in, the train sweeps into Maria's stop. She gets out; climbs the stairs to the street; walks to work where she will spend her day sitting, on a stool in a small garment factory, sewing hems on pretty dresses.

Every day, while Benny Doyle drives his Mustang to work along State Road Number 20, he passes a giant billboard along the shoulder. The billboard is selling whisky and features a woman in a black velvet dress stretching across its brilliant canvas.

As Benny Doyle downshifts by, the lounging beauty looks out to him. Day after day he sees her here. The first time he wasn't sure, but now he's convinced that her eyes are following him.

The morning sun shines on the red-tan forehead of Bill O'Conner as he drinks espresso on his sun deck, alongside the ocean cliffs of La Jolla, California. Turning through the daily paper, he reads a story about Zimbabwe.

"Rhodesia," he thinks to himself.

The story argues that a large number of Africans in Zimbabwe are fearful about black majority rule, and are concerned over a white exodus. Two black hotel workers are quoted by the article. Bill puts this, as a fact, into his mind.

Later that day, over a business lunch, he repeats the story to five white business associates, sitting at the restaurant table. They share a superior laugh over the ineptitude of black African political rule. Three more tellings, children of the first, take place over the next four days. These are spoken by two of Bill O'Conner's luncheon companions; passed on to still others in the supposed voice of political wisdom.[2]

Barbara and John Marsh get into their seven-year-old Dodge pickup and drive twenty-three miles to the nearest Sears in Cedar Rapids. After years of breakdowns and months of hesitation they've decided to buy a new washing machine. They come to Sears because it is there, and because they believe that their new Sears machine will be steady and reliable. The Marshes will pay for their purchase for the next year or so.

Barbara's great-grandfather, Elijah Simmons, had purchased a cream separator from Sears, Roebuck in 1897 and he swore by it.

When the clock-radio sprang the morning affront upon him, Archie Bishop rolled resentfully out of his crumpled bed and trudged slowly to the john. A few moments later he was unconsciously squeezing toothpaste out of a mess of red and white Colgate packaging. A dozen scrubs of the mouth and he expectorated a white, minty glob into the basin.

Still groggy, he turned on the hot water, slapping occasional palmfuls onto his gray face.

A can of Noxzema shave cream sat on the edge of the sink, a film of crud and whiskers across its once neat label. Archie reached for the bomb and filled his left hand with a white creamy mound, then spread it over his beard. He shaved, then looked with resignation at the regular collection of cuts on his neck.

Stepping into a shower, he soaped up with a soap that promised to wake him up. Groggily, he then grabbed a bottle of Clairol Herbal Essence Shampoo. He turned the tablet-shaped bottle to its back label, carefully reading the "Directions."

"Wet hair."

He wet his hair.

"Lather."

He lathered.

"Rinse."

He rinsed.

"Repeat if necessary."

Not sure whether it was altogether necessary, he repeated the process according to directions.

Late in the evening, Maria Aguilar stepped back in the subway train, heading home to the Bronx after a long and tiring day. This time, a poster told her that "The Pain Stops Here!"

She barely noticed, but later she would swallow two New Extra Strength Bufferin tablets with a glass of water from a rusty tap.

Two cockroaches in cartoon form leer out onto the street from a wall advertisement. The mail cockroach is drawn like a hipster, wearing shades and a cockroach zoot-suit. He strolls hand-in-hand with a lady cockroach, who is dressed like a floozy and blushing beet-red. Caught in the midst of their cockroach-rendezvous, they step sinfully into a Black Flag Roach Motel. Beneath them, in Spanish, the words:

Los Cucarachas entran . . . pero non pueden salir. (In the English version: Cockroaches check in . . . but they don't check out.)

The roaches are trapped; sin is punished. Salvation is gauged by one's ability to live roach-free. The sinners of the earth shall be inundated by roaches. Moral tales and insects encourage passersby to rid their houses of sin. In their homes, sometimes, people wonder whether God has forsaken them.

Beverly Jackson sits at a metal and tan Formica table and looks through the *New York Post*. She is bombarded by a catalog of horror. Children are mutilated . . . subway riders attacked. . . . Fanatics are marauding and noble despots lie in bloody heaps. Occasionally someone steps off the crime infested streets to claim a million dollars in lottery winnings.

Beverly Jackson's skin crawls; she feels a knot encircling her lungs. She is beset by immobility, hopelessness, depression.

Slowly she walks over to her sixth-floor window, gazing out into the sooty afternoon. From the empty street below, Beverly Jackson imagines a crowd yelling "Jump! . . . Jump!"

Between 1957 and 1966 Frank Miller saw a dozen John Wayne movies, countless other westerns, and war dramas. In 1969 he led a charge up a hill without a name in Southeast Asia. No one followed; he took a bullet in the chest.

Today he sits in a chair and doesn't get up. He feels that images betrayed him, and now he camps out across from the White House while another movie star cuts benefits for veterans. In the morning newspaper he reads of a massive weapons buildup taking place.

Gina Concepcion now comes to school, wearing the Jordache look. All this has been made possible by weeks and weeks of afterschool employment at a supermarket checkout counter. Now, each morning, she tugs the decorative denim over her young legs, sucking in her lean belly to close the snaps.

These pants are expensive compared to the "no-name" brands, but they're worth it, she reasons. They fit better, and she fits better.

The theater marquee, stretching out over a crumbling, garbage-strewn sidewalk, announced "The Decline of Western Civilization." At the ticket window a smaller sign read "All Seats $5.00."

It was ten in the morning and Joyce Hopkins stood before a mirror next to her bed. Her interview at General Public Utilities, Nuclear Division, was only four hours away and all she could think was "What to wear?"

A half hour later Joyce stood again before the mirror, wearing a slip and stockings. On the bed, next to her, lay a two-foot-high mountain of discarded options. Mocking the title of a recent bestseller, which she hadn't read, she said aloud to herself, "Dress for Success, . . . What *do* they like?"

At one o'clock she walked out the door wearing a brownish tweed jacket, a cream-colored Qiana blouse, full-cut with a tied collar; a dark beige skirt, fairly straight and hemmed (by Maria Aguilar) two inches below the knee; sheer fawn stockings, and simple but elegant reddish-brown pumps on her feet. Her hair was to the shoulder, her look tawny.

When she got the job she thanked her friend Millie, a middle manager, for the tip not to wear pants.

Joe Davis stood at the endless conveyor, placing caps on a round-the-clock parade of automobile radiators. His nose and eyes burned. His ears buzzed in the din. In a furtive moment he looked up and to the right. On the plant wall was a large yellow sign with THINK! printed on it in bold type. Joe turned back quickly to the radiator caps.

Fifty years earlier, in another factory, in another state, Joe's grandfather, Nat Davis, had looked up and seen another sign:

A *Clean* Machine Runs Better.
Your Body is a Machine.
KEEP IT CLEAN.

Though he tried and tried, Joe Davis' grandfather was never able to get the dirt out from under his nails. Neither could his great grandfather, who couldn't read.

In 1952 Mary Bird left her family in Charleston to earn money as a maid in a Philadelphia suburb. She earned thirty-five dollars a week, plus room and board, in a dingy retreat of a ranch-style tract house.

Twenty-eight years later she sits on a bus, heading toward her small room in North Philly. Across from her, on an advertising poster, a sumptuous meal is displayed. Golden fried chicken, green beans glistening with butter and flecked by pimento, and a fluffy cloud of rice fill the greater part of a calico-patterned dinner plate. Next to the plate sit a steaming boat of gravy, and an icy drink in an amber tumbler. The plate is on a quilted blue placemat, flanked by a thick linen napkin and colonial silverware.

As Mary Bird's hungers are aroused, the wording on the placard instructs her: *"Come home to Carolina."*

SHOPPING LIST
paper towels
milk
egg
rice crispies
chicken
snacks for kids (twinkies, chips, etc.)
potatoes
coke, ginger ale, plain soda
cheer
brillo
peanut butter
bread

ragu (2 jars)
spaghetti
saran wrap
salad
get cleaning, bank, *must pay electric!!!*

On his way to Nina's house, Sidney passed an ad for Smirnoff vodka. A sultry beauty with wet hair and beads of moisture on her smooth, tanned face looked out at him. "Try a Main Squeeze." For a teenage boy the invitation transcended the arena of drink; he felt a quick throb-pulse at the base of his belly and his step quickened.

In October of 1957, at the age of two and a half, Aaron Stone was watching television. Suddenly, from the black screen, there leaped a circus clown, selling children's vitamins and yelling "Hi! boys and girls!" He ran, terrified, from the room, screaming.

For years after, Aaron watched television in perpetual fear that the vitamin clown would reappear. Slowly his family assured him that the television was just a mechanical box and couldn't really hurt him, that the vitamin clown was harmless.

Today, as an adult, Aaron Stone takes vitamins, is ambivalent about clowns, and watches television, although there are occasional moments of anxiety.

These are some of the facts of our lives; disparate moments, disconnected, dissociated. Meaningless moments. Random incidents. Memory traces. Each is an unplanned encounter, part of day-to-day existence. Viewed alone, each by itself, such spaces of our lives seem insignificant, trivial. They are the decisions and reveries of survival; the stuff of small talk; the chance preoccupations of our eyes and minds in a world of images-soon forgotten.

Viewed together, however, as an ensemble, an integrated panorama of social life, human activity, hope and despair, images and information, another tale unfolds from these vignettes. They reveal a pattern of life, the structures of perception.

As familiar moments in American life, all of these events bear the footprints of a history that weighs upon us, but is largely untold. We live and breathe an atmosphere where mass images are everywhere in evidence; mass produced, mass distributed. In the streets, in our homes, among a crowd, or alone, they speak to us, overwhelm our vision. Their presence, their messages are givens; unavoidable. Though their history is still relatively short, their prehistory is, for the most part, forgotten, unimaginable.

The history that unites the seemingly random routines of daily life is one that embraces the rise of an industrial consumer society. It involves explosive interactions between modernity and old ways of life. It includes the proliferation, over days and decades, of a wide, repeatable vernacular of commercial images and ideas. This history spells new patterns of social, productive, and political life.

Notes

1. Interborough Rapid Transit.
2. This newspaper article was brought to our attention by journalist Les Payne, speaking at the American Writers Congress, New York City, october 10, 1981. [Author's note]

Questions for Discussion

1. Why do the Ewens write the majority of this article about the lives of other people? Does this form support the argument of the concluding paragraphs?

2. How would you characterize the influence advertising has on the various people depicted in this text? Are any of their experiences positive? Are they conscious of the power media has in their choices and emotions?

3. In the conclusion of the article, the Ewens emphasize the importance of seeing and understanding events that "bears the footprints of a history that weighs upon us" (page 461). What is this history? What is history's relationship to the series of events the article describes?

Explorations

1. The people described in this article are differently raced, gendered, and classed. Are their reactions to advertising different from one another's? Does this article suggest that different people experience the world of images differently?

2. According to John Berger, "[t]he way we see things is affected by what we know or what we believe," yet this article illustrates the different ways viewers of an image are influenced by that image. Do you think Berger challenges the Ewens' perspective on beliefs and ways of seeing? Do you think what we see affects how we think or does what we think affect how we see? What does your answer reveal about the influences of images and the viewers' power to act independently?

3. In "The Site of Memory," Toni Morrison looks to a forgotten and unwritten history of slave narratives to recover and validate individual experiences. The Ewens conclude their article by asking us to consider seemingly trivial moments of individual experience within a larger context of history. Do you think Morrison's approach coincides with the Ewens'? What are the differences between them? What might these approaches to viewing the personal reveal about the larger social and political world?

Formal Writing Assignments

1. Select an advertisement, directions on the back of a product, or a newspaper/magazine article. Imagine how this text would affect a particular viewer, either yourself or a character you create. Write a fictional account about the impact of this cultural message, tracing its influence on behavior, identity, and/or emotions as far as you can.

2. Use a creative writing format (other than a traditional essay) to convey the power of media messages and the buying public. Refer to the Ewens' text for ideas. In your writing, experiment with the relationship of humans to the cultural environment that surrounds them. Choose the form(s) that will best convey the critical message you're making about consumerism.

Why I Love Trash

Paul Gamson

As a fan of popular culture, celebrity gossip, and supermarket tabloids, Paul Gamson writes about commonly overlooked sources of social commentary. One of his most recent articles analyzes the game show "Who Wants to Be a Millionaire." In this article, taken from his book *Freaks Talk Back: Television Shows and Sexual Nonconformity*, Gamson reveals the personal connection he has to trash TV and the scholarly potentials of a seemingly laughable topic. The merits of talk shows, and perhaps of lowbrow culture in general, for Gamson, outweigh their detriments. A second-generation sociologist, Gamson is a professor at Yale University and specializes in contemporary Western commercial culture and mass media. His other book, *Claims to Fame: Celebrity in Contemporary America*, was inspired by his love of *People Magazine* and *Entertainment Tonight*.

Writing Before Reading

1. If you watch television talk shows, what is your attraction to them? If you don't watch them, why not? Regardless of your reaction, what do you think talk shows offer their viewing public?

2. Do you think television can act as a forum for non-traditional perspectives? What, if anything on TV challenges your perceptions? Has television ever caused you to reconsider your opinion on an issue?

3. What kinds of people are represented on television? Does this representation change according to types of television shows? Write about who you see on TV and how it varies according to channel, genre of show, time of day, or any other factor you deem important.

Why I Love Trash

One can only imagine what this constant attention to the fringes of society, to those who break rules, is doing to our society's ability to define and constrain deviance. One thing seems fairly certain: law-abiding, privacy-loving, ordinary people who have had reasonably happy childhoods and are satisfied with their lives, probably won't get to tell their stories on Phil, Sally, or Oprah. . . . Television talk shows are not interested in adequately reflecting or representing social reality, but in highlighting and trivializing its underside for fun and profit.

Professors Vicki Abt and Mel Seesholtz

Nobody wants to watch anything that's smarmy or tabloid or silly or unseemly—except the audience.

Talk show host Sally Jessy Raphael

Doesn't she look like a weird, scary drag queen?

Filmmaker Gregg Araki, on talk show host Sally Jessy Raphael

Let's begin here: talk shows are bad for you, so bad you could catch a cold. Turn them off, a women's magazine suggested in 1995, and turn on Mother Teresa, since watching her "caring feelings" radiate from the screen, according to psychologist Dr. David McClelland of Harvard, has been shown to raise the level of an antibody that fights colds. "It stands to reason," reasons the *First* magazine writer, "that viewing threatening, confrontational images could create an opposite reaction." In fact, given that talk shows "create feelings of frustration" and fear, "shatter our trust and faith" in our expectations of people's behavior, and "give us a false perception of reality," it is perhaps best to watch game shows or soaps while nursing that cold. Watching daytime talk shows could conceivably send you into a decline into pathologies of all sorts: scared, angry, disgusted, convinced that you are abnormal for not fitting in with the "cast of misfits and perverts," susceptible to both perversion and more colds.

While the Mother Teresa versus Jerry Springer match up is out there enough to be camp, the hand-wringing it represents is only an exaggerated version of the many criticisms and political rallying cries aimed at talk shows over the last few years. Experts of all sorts can be found issuing warnings about talk show dangers. Before bringing out Dr. McClelland, for instance the *First* article quotes George Gerbner, dean emeritus of the Annenberg School for Communication ("These shows are virtually destroying the goodness of America"), Harvard psychiatrist Alvin Poussaint ("it does not bode well for the future generation of young people growing up on a steady diet of this drivel"), and Fred Strassberger, once chair of the media task force of the American Psychological Association ("It's now becoming alarmingly clear that talk shows are adding greatly to the fear, tensions and stress in our society"); later, TV critic Tom Shales joins in ("These shows are portraying Americans as shallow monsters"), along with psychologist Robert Simmermon ("cruel exploitation of people's deepest wounds to entertain viewers who could very well wind up believing such aberrant behavior is normal"). Goodness, normality, and stability, if we buy these arguments, are all threatened by the drivel, exploitation, and monstrosities of daytime TV talk shows.

One person's trash, though, is another person's gold mine. Sure, I sometimes hate these shows. What's not to hate? They can be among the most shrill, mean, embarrassing, fingernails-on-the-chalkboard, one-note, pointless jabber. But I can't help it; I love them just the same. In part, I love them because they are so peculiar, so American, filled with fun stuff like "relationship experts" (who are not actually required to have any credentialed expertise; it's almost enough just to declare "I'm a people person") and huge emotions, and hosts who wear their hypocrisies on their tailored sleeves, shedding tears for the people whose secrets they extract for profit while attacking them for revealing secrets on national television, riling up their guests and then scolding them for being so malicious. Silly as they can be, daytime TV talk shows are filled with information about the American environment in which they take root, in which expertise and authenticity and rationality are increasingly problematic, and in which the lines between public and private are shifting so strangely. And they embody that information with Barnumesque gusto. I like what talk shows make us think about.

But there's more to my affinity. Although you might not know it from looking at me, and although in many ways my behaviors and tastes are embarrassingly, conventional—a good story, a comfortable pair of jeans, hugs—I identify with the misfits, monsters, trash, and perverts. From that perspective, talk shows look rather different. If you are lesbian, bisexual, gay, or transgendered, watching daytime TV talk shows is pretty spooky. (Indeed, it must be unnerving and exciting for pretty much anyone whose behavior or identity does not conform to the dominant conventions of goodness, decency, and normality.) While you might get a few minutes on national news every once in a while, or a spot on a sitcom looking normal as can be, almost everywhere else in media culture you are either unwelcome, written by somebody else, or heavily edited.

On television talk shows, you are more than welcome. You are begged and coached and asked to tell, tell, tell, in an absurd, hyper enactment of what Michel Foucault called the "incitement to discourse," that incessant modern demand that we voice every this-and-that of sexuality. Here you are testifying, dating, getting laughs, being made over, screaming, performing, crying, not just talking but talking back, and you are doing these things in front of millions of people. The last few years have seen shows on "lipstick lesbians," gay teens, gay cops, lesbian cops, cross-dressing hookers, transsexual call girls, gay and lesbian gang members, straight go-go dancers pretending to be gay, people who want their relatives to stop cross-dressing, lesbian and gay comedians, gay people in love with straight ones, women who love gay men, same-sex marriage, drag queen makeovers, drag kings, same-sex sexual harassment, homophobia, lesbian mothers, gay twins, gay beauty pageants, transsexual beauty pageants, people who are fired for not being gay, gay men reuniting with their high school sweethearts, bisexual teens, bisexual couples, bisexuals in general, gays in the military, same-sex crushes, hermaphrodites, boys who want to be girls, female-to-male transsexuals, male-to-female transsexuals and their boyfriends, and gay talk shows—to mention just a few. Watching all this, be it tap-dancing drag queens or married gay bodybuilders or self-possessed bisexual teenagers, I sometimes get choked up. For people whose life experience is so heavily tilted toward invisibility, whose nonconformity, even when it looks very much like conformity, discredits them and disenfranchises them, daytime TV talk shows are a big shot of visibility and media accreditation. It looks, for a moment, like you own this place.

Indeed, listening closely to the perspectives and experiences of sex and gender nonconformists—people who live, in one way or another, outside the boundaries of heterosexual norms and gender conventions—sheds a different kind of light on talk shows. Dangers begin to look like opportunities; spotlights start to feel like they're burning your flesh. Exploiting the need for visibility and voice, talk shows provide them, in distorted but real, hollow but gratifying, ways. They have much to tell about those needs and those contradictions, about the weird and changing public sphere in which people are talking. Just as important for my purposes, talk shows shed a different kind of light on sex and gender conformity. They are spots not only of visibility but of the subsequent redrawing of the lines between the normal and the abnormal. They are, in a very real sense, battlegrounds over what sexuality and gender can be in this country: in them we can see most clearly the kinds of strategies, casualties, and wounds involved, and we can think most clearly about what winning these kinds of battles might really mean. These battles over media space allow us to get a grip on the ways sex and gender conformity is filtered through the daily interactions between commercial cultural industries and those making their lives within and around media culture. I watch talk shows for a laugh and a jolt of recognition, but also for what they can tell me about a society that funnels such large questions—indeed, that funnels entire *populations* nearly wholesale—into the small, loopy spectacle of daytime talk.

Defecating in Public

It is a long, twisted road that takes us toward insight, but the controversy over the talk show genre in general—a genre itself largely composed of controversy and conflict—is a promising first step. On the one side, cultural critics, both popular and scholarly, point adamantly toward the dangers of exploitation, voyeurism, pseudotherapy, and the "defining down" of deviance, in which the strange and unacceptable are made to seem ordinary and fine. On the other side, defenders both within and outside the television industry argue that talk shows are democracy at work—flawed democracy but democracy nonetheless—giving voice to the socially marginalized and ordinary folks, providing rowdy commonsense counterpoints to elite authority in mass-mediated culture. Beneath each position, and in the space between them, is a piece of the puzzle with which this book is playing.

The list of dangers is well worth considering. There is, to begin with, concern for the people who go on the shows, who are offered and accept a deal with the devil. They are manipulated, sometimes lied to, seduced, used, and discarded; pick 'em up in a limo, producer's joke, send 'em home in a cab. They are sometimes set up and surprised—"ambushed," as critics like to call it—which can be extremely damaging, even to the point of triggering lawsuits and murderous impulses, as in the case of Scott Amedure, who revealed his secret crush for Jonathan Schmitz on a never-aired *Jenny Jones Show,* including his fantasy of tying Schmitz up in a hammock and spraying him with whipped cream and champagne. Amedure was murdered several days later by Schmitz, who, after receiving an anonymous love note, went to his admirer's trailer home near Detroit and shot him at close range with a 12-gauge shotgun. Schmitz complained that the show had set him up to be humiliated. "There was no ambush," a spokeswoman for *Jenny Jones* owner Warner Brothers said, "that's not our style." Amedure, Schmitz proclaimed, had "fucked me on national TV."

Although most survive without bodily harm, guests often do considerable damage to themselves and others. They are offered airfare and hotel room in New York, Los Angeles, or Chicago, a bit of television exposure, a shot of attention and a microphone, some free "therapy." In exchange, guests publicly air their relationship troubles, deep secrets, and intimate life experiences, usually in the manners most likely to grab ratings: exaggerated, loud, simplified, and so on. Even more disturbing, perhaps, it is those who typically do not feel entitled to speak, or who cannot afford or imagine therapy, who are most vulnerable to the seduction of television. This is, critics suggest, not a great deal for the guests, since telling problems and secrets in front of millions of people is a poor substitute for actually working them out. Not to mention, critics often add, a bit undignified. "Therapy is not a spectator sport," says sociologist and talk show critic-at-large Vicki Abt. Telling secrets on television is "like defecating in public."

While it is worth challenging the equation of talking and defecating, all this, we will see, is basically the case. But it is also the easy part: talk shows are show business, and it is their mission to exploit. They commodify and use talkers to build an entertainment product, which is then used to attract audiences, who then are sold to advertisers, which results in a profit for the producers. Exploitation thus ought to be the starting point for analysis and not, as it so often is, its conclusion. The puzzling thing is not the logic of commercial television, which is well documented, well understood, and extremely powerful, but why so many people, many of them fully aware of what's expected of them on a talk show, make the deal.

Yet it is not really the guests, generally dismissed as dysfunctional losers on display, who concern talk show critics most centrally. It is the audience, either innocent or drawn in by appeals to their most base interests, that preoccupies critics the most. For some, the problem is the model of problem solving offered. Psychologists Jeanne Heaton and Nona Wilson argue in *Tuning in Trouble*, for instance, that talk shows provide "bad lessons in mental health," offer "bad advice and no resolutions for problems," and wind up "reinforcing stereotypes rater than defusing them." "Credible therapeutic practice aimed at catharsis or confrontation," they point out, "is quite different from the bastardized Talk TV version." Indeed, they suggest that viewers avoid "the temptation to apply other people's problems or solutions to your own life," avoid using "the shows as a model for how to communicate" or as tools for diagnosing friends and relatives, and so on. The advice is sound, if a bit elementary: talk shows are not a smart place to look for either therapy or problem solving.

Beyond the worry that audiences will adopt therapeutic technique from daytime talk, critics are even more troubled by the general social effects of talk shows. Here and there, a critic from the Left, such as Jill Nelson writing in *The Nation*, assails the casting of "a few pathological individuals" as representatives of a population, distracting from social, political, and economic conditions in favor of stereotypes such as "stupid, sex-addicted, dependent, baby-makers, with an occasional castrating bitch thrown in" (women of all colors) and "violent predators out to get you with their penis, their gun, or both" (young black men). More commonly, though, critics make the related argument that talk shows indulge voyeuristic tendencies that, while perhaps offering the opportunity to feel superior, are ugly. *"Exploitation, voyeurism, peeping Toms, freak shows,* all come to mind in attempting to characterize these happenings," write Vicki Abt and Mel Seesholtz, for instance. "For the audience," *Washington Post* reporter Howard Kutz adds in *Hot Air,* "watching the cavalcade of deviant and dysfunctional types may serve as a kind of group therapy, a communal exercise in national voyeurism. These "fairground-style freak shows" are just a modern-day version of throwing Christians to the lions, psychologists Heaton and Wilson assert: in place of Christians we have "the emotionally wounded or the socially outcast," in place of lions are "psychic demons," in place of blood there is psychological damage, in place of crowds yelling "Kill, kill, kill!" we have crowds yelling "Why don't you cut his balls off?" Even if such events serve to unite the Romans among us, offering what Neal Gabler calls "the reassurance of our superiority over the guests and over the programs themselves," they do so at significant costs. "Perhaps the sight of so many people with revolting problems makes some folks feel better about their own rather humdrum lives," Kurtz argues, but "we become desensitized by the endless freak show." Talk shows are puriently addictive, the argument goes, like rubbernecking at car wrecks: daytime talk shows are to public information what pornography is to sexual intimacy.

I will have more to say about the ceaseless characterization of talk shows as "freak shows," but for now it is enough to note that the lines are drawn so starkly: between Christians and Romans, between 'deviant and dysfunctional types" and "some folks," the guests and "us," between "the fringes of society, those who break rules" and "law-abiding, privacy-loving, ordinary people who have had reasonably happy childhoods and are satisfied with their lives." These are important lines, and plainly political ones, and the ones critics most fiercely act to protect. And as one who falls both within and outside the lines, I find the confidence with which critics draw them in need of as much careful consideration as the genre's alarming exploitations.

In fact, the lines of difference and normality are the centerpiece of the arguments against talk shows: talk shows, critics repeat over and over, redefine deviance and abnormality, and this is not a good thing. "The lines between what is bizarre and alarming and what is typical and inconsequential are blurred," point out psychologists Heaton and Wilson; talk shows "exaggerate abnormality" by suggesting that "certain problems are more common than they are, thus exaggerating their frequency," and by embellishing "the symptoms and outcomes of problems, thus exaggerating their consequences." Viewers are left with images of "drag queens getting makeovers and transsexuals' surprising transformations blended together with normal adolescent development." Kurtz, himself a regular on political talk shows, is a little less clinical in his assessment: "This is more than just harmless diversion. It is, all too often, a televised exercise in defining deviancy down. By parading the sickest, the weirdest, the most painfully afflicted before an audience of millions, these shows bombard us with sleaze to the point of numbness. The abnormal becomes ordinary, the pathetic merely another pause in our daily channel surfing."

This boundary between the normal and the abnormal, tightly linked to those between decent and vulgar, sacred and profane, healthy and unhealthy, and moral and immoral, is the key not only for critics in journalism, but for those in politics as well. "This is the world turned upside down," former secretary of education William Bennett complained of daytime talk. "We've forgotten that civilization depends on keeping some of this stuff under wraps." As a reminder, Bennett offered his own tamer, secularized version of the Mother Teresa versus the freaks argument: this place is owned by perverts, and decent people must retrieve it. Launching a campaign to "clean-up" the "cultural rot" of daytime TV, pressuring advertisers to withdraw from shows that "parade perversity into our living rooms," Bennett, with Connecticut senator Joseph Lieberman and the public-interest group Empower America, emphasized the degenerative moral impact of talk shows, which "increasingly make the abnormal normal, and set up the most perverse role models for our children and adults." The entertainment industry, Lieberman told a press conference, is "degrading our culture and ultimately threatening our children's future," through both "sexual deviancy" and "constant hyperemotional confrontation." The reality is that these shows are at the front lines," he continued, echoing the *Post*'s Kurtz nearly word for word, "distorting our perceptions of what is normal and acceptable," adding to "the tendency of our country to define deviancy down." Our living rooms, our children, our normality, all under threat.

The interesting thing here is not just that talk shows are seen as a threat to norms and normality—as we will see, they are indeed just that, and the fight is often between those who think this is a good thing and those who think it is not—but just who threatens whom here, who is "us" and who is "them." Sexual nonconformists are only the most obvious specter. Consider the common strategy of listing topics to demonstrate the degraded status of talk shows: "Maury Povich has done women who leave husbands for other women, student-teacher affairs, and a woman who says she was gang-raped at fourteen. Geraldo Rivera has done transsexuals and their families, teen prostitutes, mud-wrestling women, swinging sexual suicide, power dykes, girls impregnated by their stepfathers, serial killers, kids who kill, and battered women who kill." One need not deny the prurience and sensationalism of talk shows to see the connections being made by critics. Serial killers and bisexual women, transsexuals and mud wrestlers, dykes and battered women: "the sickest, the weirdest, the most painfully afflicted." New York *Daily News* columnist Linda Stasi, not shy about telling us what she really thinks, provides a further, complicating hint of the threatening categories: talk shows, she says, have become "a vast, scary wasteland where the dregs of society—sociopaths, perverts, uneducated lazy scum who abuse their children and sleep with anyone who'll have them—become stars for fifteen minutes." That list is a typical and fascinating mix: perverts and those lacking education, lazy people and people who have a lot of sex. Kurtz backs up Stasi, for instance, asserting that, "after all, middle-class folks who work hard and raise their children in a reasonable fashion don't get invited on *Donahue* or *Geraldo*. They do not exist on daytime television. Instead, we are bombarded with negative images of the sort of losers most of us would avoid at the local supermarket."

The "dregs of society" argument, in fact, almost always lumps together indecency, sexual difference, lack of education, and social class—through class is typically coded as "uneducated" or "inarticulate," or, when linked to race, as "trash" or "urban." Take this passage from a book on talk shows and mental health: "Pulitzer prize–winning author David Halberstam used to call Donahue a 'televised Ph.D. course.' Now he says that Donahue has 'lost its soul.' Likewise, Art Buchwald used to receive regular invitations to talk about his essays and books on *Donahue*. But now 'Buchwald claims he can't get an invitation . . . unless he gets a sex-change operation.'" You used to be able to get an education, listening to men like Halberstam and Buchwald; now, talk shows have replaced educated men with transsexuals, resulting in the loss of the talk show soul. The examples continue, but after even just a taste the equations start to come clear; uneducated is lazy is sex-loving is sexually perverted is non-middle-class is soulless losers.

Puzzle pieces begin to emerge from these criticisms. How exactly do poverty and lack of education, sex and gender nonconformity, and race come to be lumped together and condemned as monstrosities? What are we to make of these equations? Are they the result of exploitative programming that scripts and markets weird people most of "us" wouldn't talk to in a supermarket, selling the middle-class audience its own superiority? Are they the result of willful distortions by guardians of middle-class morality and culture, part and parcel of the ongoing "culture wars" in the United States? Are they, as defenders of the genre suggest, the result of a democratization process that threatens those who are used to the privilege of owning and defining public discourse?

The Chatter of the Dispossessed

Audiences and participants sit in a circular form and —this is the only TV format in which this happens—speak out, sometimes without being called on. They yell at each other, disagree with experts, and come to no authoritative conclusions. There is something exhilarating about watching people who are usually invisible—because of class, race, gender, status—having their say and, often, being wholly disrespectful of their "betters."

Professor Elayne Rapping

Audience discussion programs adopt an anti-elitist position which implicitly draws on . . . alternative epistemological traditions, offering a revaluation of the life-world, repudiating criticism of the ordinary person as incompetent or ignorant, questioning the deference traditionally due to experts through their separation from the life-world and their incorporation into the system, and asserting instead the worth of the "common man."

Professors Sonia Livingstone and Peter Lunt

As long as they speak the King's English, we say it's O.K. but then you get someone who isn't wealthy, who doesn't have title or position, and they come on and talk about something that's important to them—all of a sudden we call that trash.

Talk show host Jerry Springer

Just as exploitation is an obvious component of talk shows, so is democratization. Where critics choose one Greco-Roman analogy, defenders tout another: in place of the Christian-eating spectacle, they see, although not always so simply, a democratic forum. Where critics see "freaks" and "trash," defenders see "have-nots" and "common people." These are important counterpoints, and raise important questions suppressed by critics, of voice, visibility, and inclusion. But this line of thinking, too, on its own tends to run in an unhelpful direction, simplifying the conditions of visibility, the distortions of voice, and the restrictions on inclusion that daytime talk involves. Just because people are talking back does not mean we are witnessing democratic impulses and effects.

It is easy enough to discern the elitism in criticisms of talk shows, or any other popular genre, and defenders of talk shows from within the industry push up against it with a defense of the masses, painting themselves as both defenders of free speech and friends of the common folk. "I think it's a shame that we've got so many people who claim to talk to God everyday," Phil Donahue complained to Larry King, "coming down from the mountain to tell their neighbors what they ought to see." Charles Perez, a young former *Ricki Lake Show* producer who had a short stint as host of his own show, while perhaps not quite as impressed with the tastes of his neighbors, took a similar "the people have chosen" approach to talk. "I put this a lot in the hands of the public," he said. "The same way you have a corner grocer and he should be selling mostly vegetables, but he's selling Hershey candy bars because that's what all the kids on the block want." Talk shows may not be nutritious, but viewers should not be faulted for wanting what they want.

This populist defense of talk shows, familiar from arguments about popular culture in general, is taken many steps beyond the shoulder-shrugging, "it's a free country" line. Talk shows, defenders claim, give voice to common folks and visibility to invisible folks, and it is this characteristic that elicits such hostility. Indeed, Donahue and others assert, the talk show genre was and is a "revolutionary" one. "It's called democracy," Donahue argues, 'but [before my program] there were no shows that—every day, let just folks stand up and say what-for. I'm proud of the democracy of the show." Ellen Willis, writing in *The Nation,* makes a similar, although much more complex, point: "Social conservatives have been notably unsuccessful at stemming the democratization of culture, the breakdown of those class, sex and race-bound conventions that once reliably separated high from low, 'news' from 'gossip,' public from unspeakable private, respectable from deviant. Talk shows are a product of this democratization; they let people who have been largely excluded from the public conversation appear on national TV and talk about their sex lives, their family fights, sometimes their literal dirty laundry. . . . On talk shows, whatever their drawbacks, the proles get to talk." When the proles get the microphone, when the excluded become included, there is always a fight. The nastiness of critics toward talk shows, the argument goes, is simply a veiled anxiety about cultural democratization—and especially about the assertive, rowdy space taken on talk shows by usually silent classes of people. Talk shows "operate at the level of everyday life, where real people live and breathe," Donna Gaines writes. 'Bennett's morality squad may see talk shows as carnival freak shows, but all that means is that the shows have the power to drag us statistical outcasts in from the margins." "Do you ever call a Congressman trash?" asks Jerry Springer. "It's a euphemism for trailer park, minorities, space between their teeth. We all know it. They don't want to hear about them, they don't want to see them." Springer argues that he is giving unpopular people "access to the airwaves" ("as if embarrassing them before millions," snorts Howard Kurtz, "were some kind of public service"). Princess Di with bulimia is news on *20/20* with Barbara Walters, Yale-educated host Richard Bey complains, but his own show—which, on the day I attended, included a "freeloader" named Rob lying on his back on a spinning "Wheel of Torture" while his dorm-mates poured buckets of paint and baked beans on him—is trash. "They don't think these people deserve to be heard or seen," he suggests, taking a sort of working-person's hero pose. "Mine is a working class audience. It's very representative of America."

Many academics echo this line of thinking, emphasizing the democratic aspects of the genre. Audience-participation talk shows, Sonia Livingstone and Peter Lunt claim, for instance, "are a forum in which people can speak in their own voice, which . . . is vital for the construction of a gendered or cultural identity." Oprah Winfrey herself, Gloria-Jean Masciarotte suggests in the journal *Genders,* is "a device of identity that organizes new antagonisms in the contemporary formations of democratic struggle." Talk shows "constitute a 'contested space'" in which new discursive practices are developed," Paolo Carpignano and his colleagues argue in the journal *Social Text,* "in contrast to the traditional modes of political and ideological representation." "The talk show can be seen as a terrain of struggle of discursive practices. . . . [What] is conceived as a confrontational device becomes an opening for the empowerment of an alternative discursive practice. These discourses don't have to conform to civility nor to the dictates of the general interest. They can be expressed for what they are: particular, regional, one-sided, and for that reason politically alive. . . . The talk show rejects the arrogance of a discourse that defines itself on the basis of its difference from common sense." Talk shows embrace everyday common sense against elite expertise, privileging "the storied life over the expert guest," emphasizing "'ordinary' experience," and the "'authentic' voice of the everyday people, or street smarts of the working class." They provide "a space in which ordinary experiences are collected together as grounding for a decision."

Indeed, daytime talk, as a woman-oriented genre, is arguable rooted in social movement–generated changes of the sixties and seventies, especially those pushed by feminism. Defenders point to the genre's predominantly female audience, and in particular to its feminist-inspired reworking of what counts as legitimate public discussion, as evidence that it is a genre of "empowerment." Most significantly, TV talk is built on a radical departure from what has traditionally been seen to belong in the public sphere: drawing on "the personal is political" charge of feminism, talk shows move personal lives to the forefront of public discussion. Their popularity, Carpignano and others argue, are a symptom of "a transformation in the nature of the political," and "the means of expression of these new areas of political struggle are quite different from those of formal politics." Talk shows, such arguments suggest, are politics by other means.

Moreover, such talk show analysts claim, the political effects are empowering for those who have traditionally been defined as outside of public discussion, whose lives were, until recently, kept private by both choice and coercion—in particular, women and sex and gender minorities. Phil Donahue argues, for instance, "these programs cumulatively make a contribution toward the empowerment of women especially"; *Village Voice* writer Richard Goldstein points out that talk shows "were the first mass-cultural arena where homosexuals could get beyond polemics and simply justify their love." The same basic claim comes through in the sparse academic literature on TV talk: that talk shows "afford women the political gesture of overcoming their alienation through talking about their particular experience as women in society," promote "an unnatural or perverse sexual identity," and can be seen as "a celebration of outlaw culture" (a point, of course, on which the critics concur). Daytime TV talk shows are thus "the lever in the dislocation of universal, natural difference," disrupting traditional sex and gender categories. "It is to that epic dislocation in categories and knowledge," Masciarotte claims, "that the talk shows' most recent, combative forms speak."

Previously silenced people speaking in their own voices, spaces for "alternative epistemologies" opening up, common sense battling the politics and ideology of traditional elites, political arenas expanding, "epic dislocations" and rethinking of social categories: these would all seem to be significant, healthy contributions of the talk show genre to democratic practice. Indeed, it would seem, talk shows, even if they aren't exactly good for you, are at least good for us—especially those of us with an investment in social change. Yet even setting aside the tendency to romanticize "the masses" and the near gibberish of claims such as "*The Oprah Winfrey Show* functions as a new bildungsroman that charts the irritant in the system through an endless narrative of discomfort" and so forth, something seems a bit fishy here. If you have ever actually watched a few hours of talk shows, they seem about as much about democracy as *The Price Is Right* is about mathematics. Sniffing around this territory more closely, digging through some of its assumptions, clarifies further where we have to go.

Two claims in particular hide within the defenses of talk shows, even the critical defenses: that talk shows "give voice" and that they operate as some kind of "forum." Pushing at them a little uncovers more interesting questions. It is certainly true that, more than anywhere else on television, talk shows invite people to speak for themselves. But do people on daytime talk really wind up speaking in a voice that they and others recognize as somehow authentically their own? How do the medium and the genre structure the "voices" that come out? What sorts of speaking voices are available, and in what ways are they distorted? How could we even tell a "real" voice from a "false" one? Second, there is the question of the "forum." It is certainly true that talk shows come closer than anywhere else on American television to providing a means for a wide range of people, credentialed but especially not so credentialed, to converse about all sorts of things. But is daytime talk really a forum, a set of conversations? How do the production and programming strategies shape the capacity for discussion, and the content of conversation? If, as Wayne Munson has put it, talk shows are simultaneously spectacle and conversation, what is the relationship here between the circus and the symposium, and what is the political significance of their combination?

It is tempting to choose sides in all of this, and often I do. Depending on my mood, I might be annoyed by the paternalistic moralizing critics and tout defiant perversity, or I might find myself overwhelmed by the willful, wasteful stupidity of TV talk and recommend V-chip brain implants. But I have now gone a different route, guided by the Big Issues running through the talk show debates and by my own gnawing ambivalence, both as scholar and as just a guy.

What critics and defenders, both inside my brain and outside of it, agree upon is that talk shows are consumed with blurring old distinctions (while often reaffirming them), with making differences harder to tell (while often asserting them with ease): the deviant isn't readily distinguished from the regular person, class stereotypes melt into the hard realities on which they rest, what belongs in private suddenly seems to belong in front of everybody, airing dirty laundry looks much like coming clean. Talk shows wreak special havoc with the "public sphere," moving private stuff into a public spotlight, arousing all sorts of questions about what the public sphere can, does, and should look like. In doing so, they mess with the "normal," giving hours of play and often considerable sympathy to stigmatized populations, behaviors, and identities, and at least partly muddying the waters of normality. And since those brought into the public sphere of TV talk are increasingly distant from the white middle-class guests of earlier years, talk shows wind up attaching class difference to the crossing of public/private and normal/abnormal divides. It is around this stirred pot, in which humdrum and freaky, off-limits and common property, high status and low, sane and crazed, all brew together, that the anxious flies swarm. This seething brew, and not just the talk shows themselves, is what is so powerful and intriguing, and it is this brew on which I myself am feeding, using the close study of TV talk to investigate the broader, linked activities of line-drawing between public and private, classy and trashy, normal and abnormal.

I have long been especially interested in how the lines between normal and abnormal sexual beings are drawn and redrawn: the ways those lines restrict me personally, from the question of whom I can touch to the question of where I can work; the dilemmas confronted by social movements trying to gain rights by claiming the mantle of normality, even as they are also celebrating their "queer" difference and criticizing the oppressive constraints imposed by a hetero-as-normal society; the ways sexual categories intersect with others (race, class, gender) with their own hierarchies of natural and defective people, and the permutations of perversion pile up and multiply. The mass media are plainly very central to these processes of sexual meaning-making, and talk shows are hot spots for the processes, and so my attention is driven toward them.

Indeed, many of the key terms of talk show controversy—the themes of health and pathology, of sacred and profane—speak with special force to people who cross or have crossed gender lines, and to people who form same-sex partnerships, who have been deemed ill or immoral for most of recent history, and who have been subject to often brutal forms of medical and religious control. But if talk shows speak to us, they certainly speak with forked tongues. Listening to them means living with the fact that they never quite make sense. On this trip into their country, as I offer a translation of their noisy, eager language into my own, you will see that it turns out to be a dialect filled with the syntax of savage contradiction. With careful listening, ambivalence about talk shows begins to sound just about right. At the heart of this book, where sexual meaning-making, sexual politics, and the redrawing of key social boundaries meet up, are the *paradoxes of visibility* that talk shows dramatize with such fury: democratization through exploitation, truths wrapped in lies, normalization through freak show. There is in fact no choice here between manipulative spectacle and democratic forum, only the puzzle of a situation in which one cannot exist without the other, and the challenge of seeing clearly what this means for a society at war with its own sexual diversity.

The Way In

How do we push our way into this weird world? Other people's ideas have certainly helped pave the road. There is by now much scholarly writing about both the construction of sexuality and gender, and the media representation of sexual minorities. Put simply, from theory and research on sexuality construction, I lift the idea that sexual categories and statuses are under continual negotiation, and the question of when and how these categories and statuses become open to change and challenge. From theory and research on mass media, I take the notion that media representations are part of a more general system of oppression of nonheterosexuals, operating most commonly to justify continued prejudice, violence, and discrimination against lesbian, gay, bisexual, and transgendered people, and the question of when and how media institutions become sites at which oppression can be combated.

"Sexuality is as much a human product as are diets, methods of transportation, systems of etiquette, forms of labor, types of entertainment, processes of production, and modes of oppression," Gayle Rubin wrote fifteen years ago. Although still subject to debate, the premise that sexuality and gender are "socially constructed," rather than simply reflecting categories and beings found in and fixed by nature, has become commonplace in academic analysis since the 1980s. Sexual categories and gender categories, theorists and researchers have persuasively demonstrated, vary dramatically across time and across cultures. Moreover, social scientists have suggested that within any given social structure, sexual attitudes, behaviors, and roles are produced and reproduced through everyday interactions and social "scripts." "Gender is a human invention, like language, kinship, religion, and technology; like them, gender organizes human social life in culturally patterned ways," as Judith Lorber put it recently.

This general framework has yielded an important set of questions, both intellectual and political. If sexuality is indeed constructed and negotiated through social processes, how exactly do these processes work? Under what conditions do sexual categories and meanings change? If we wanted to intervene in this process, where and how might we go about it? While the first question has been effectively approached, the latter two have not been terribly well answered, mainly because sexuality has typically been analyzed in abstraction from its institutional and organizational carriers. Studies of the construction of sexuality only rarely look in detail at the opportunities and constraints associated with particular institutional settings, proceeding instead as if sexual categories and meanings exist in free-floating "discourse," the everyday, practical activities through which sexual meanings are produced and reproduced tend to fade into the background.

Sociologists of culture, however, have long argued that cultural attitudes and cultural content cannot be understood divorced from the organizational contexts in which they are produced. One cannot understand the homogenization of much television culture, for example, without understanding the political economy of television entertainment production; one cannot understand the tip of television news toward the "official story" without understanding the norms and routines of journalists. The same goes for public discourse on sexuality and gender: in order to understand how sex and gender categories, and conformity to those categories, are put together, it helps a good deal to look at the concrete, structured settings where they are being negotiated. Daytime TV talk shows, with their unusual and tremendous attention to sex and gender nonconformity, are rich, juicy places to look at the link between cultural production and sexual meanings.

Partly because they are attentive to the relationship between institutional practice and cultural discourse, studies of commercial media's roles, in reproducing and justifying antigay prejudice have also lent a helpful, rattling hand here. Taking off with Vito Russo's ground-breaking *The Celluloid Closet,* in fact, studies of the portrayals of gay men and lesbians in film and television have soundly demonstrated how homosexual lives have been subject to systematic exclusion and stereotyping as victims and villains, how "aspects of gay and lesbian identity, sexuality, and community that are not compatible or that too directly challenge the heterosexual regime are excluded" from mainstream television, how television has produced "stereotypical conceptualization of AIDS that vilify gays and legitimate homophobia," how even "positive" portrayals of lesbians "serve as mechanisms to perpetuate hetero/sexism." At best, Larry Gross suggests of network television, the constraints of "public pressure and advertiser timidity" lead to "well-meaning approaches that plead for tolerance" but require "complete asexuality."

These studies have congealed into conventional, often sacred-cow ways of thinking about media visibility that are now begging for challenge. Vito Russo's "invisibility is the great enemy," for instance, is still the going line in lesbian and gay media activism: more exposure is the answer. Yet at a time when a major sitcom character and the lesbian playing her have come out amidst a coterie of gay and lesbian supporting characters, when a drag queen has her own talk show on VH-1, when big movie stars no longer see gay roles as career poison, when one soap opera has had a transsexual story line and another, thrillingly, a gay talk show–murder story line, it may no longer be enough to think so simply about invisibility and stereotyping. With their extraordinary interest in gay, lesbian, bisexual, and transgender topics (which predates the recent miniexplosion of gay visibility in commercial media by two decades), talk shows are a fabulous chance to see what happens when lesbian, gay, bisexual, and transgender people are highly visible subjects in a commercial cultural arena.

The most arresting challenge comes not just from the exceptional visibility daytime television brings to sex and gender nonconformity, but even more from the potential *agency* of gay men, lesbians, bisexuals, and transgendered people within the genre. "Gays have always been visible," after all, Russo argued in the afterword to the revised edition of *The Celluloid Closet.* "It's *how* they've been visible that has remained offensive for almost a century." Russo was right: until very recently, lesbians and gay men had little input into our own representation. Almost without exception, the literature on homosexuality and the media has therefore treated the process of representation as one-sided. Larry Gross captures this approach very well.

> Representation in the mediated "reality" of our mass culture is in itself power; certainly it is the case that nonrepresentation maintains the powerless status of groups that do not possess significant material or political power bases. Those who are the bottom of the various hierarchies will be kept in their place in part through their relative invisibility; this is a form of symbolic annihilation. When groups or perspectives do attain visibility, the manner of that representation will itself reflect the biases and interests of those elites who define the public agenda. And those elites are mostly white, mostly middle-aged, mostly male, mostly middle- and upper-middle class, and (at least in public) entirely heterosexual.

They annihilate us, or deform us, because it serves them well—and because they can.

It is not so much that this perspective is wrong, but that it sidesteps some of the most telling complexities. Missing from these analyses of lesbian and gay media representation is precisely what is interesting about talk shows: what happens to media representations of nonconforming sexualities when lesbians and gay men are actively invited to participate, to "play themselves" rather than be portrayed by others, to refute stereotypes rather than simply watch them on the screen? That is the twist talk shows provide. They allow us to witness tightly linked, media-generated battles over sexual norms and morality—struggles themselves closely tied to class cultural and public-private divisions—in which transgender, lesbian, gay, and bisexual people are vigorous, visible, sometimes agile, participants. They mess up our thinking about the difficulties and delights of becoming visible—and, in a more general sense, about the political benefits and dilemmas of cultural representation. And as the dust settles, they can clear up our thinking.

My takes on other people's ideas have planted not only these intellectual guideposts but also methodological ones, leading me to a wide range of places to dig for the information that feeds this book. The charge that discourse and institutional practice are not separable phenomena, for instance, prompted me to study the practices of talk show producers, organizations, and guests alongside the thematic, narrative, and representational content of the programs. Thus I wound up in studios, where I sat in the audience at least once in most of the New York-based programs, watching the production of the shows from that perspective; in offices and restaurants in New York and Los Angeles, where I interviewed production staff; in cafes and in people's homes in New York, Washington, Boston, San Francisco, and Los Angeles, and on the phone to smaller towns, where I interviewed people who had appeared as talk show guests. The details are all in the appendix, but here are the vitals: I interviewed a total of twenty production staff and forty-four guests. (In an ironic, if unsurprising, reversal of their daily routine, almost all of the production staff spoke on the condition that they not be identified, and I therefore sometimes use pseudonyms in the discussion. Almost all of the former guests spoke on the record.) Taken together, these interviews cover experience on just about every topic-driven daytime talk show that has had a life: *Bertice Berry, Richard Bey, Carnie, Donahue, Gordon Elliott, Gabrielle, M. Gaffney, Geraldo, Jenny Jones, Ricki Lake, Leeza, Oprah, The Other Side, Charles Perez, Maury Povich, Jane Pratt, Sally Jessy Raphael, Joan Rivers, Rolonda, Jerry Springer, Tempestt, Mark Walberg, Jane Whitney,* and *Montel Williams.*

At the same time, I collected all the available transcripts in which lesbian, gay, bisexual, and gender-crossing subjects made a significant appearance, for the years 1984-86 and 1994-95; with the assistance of interview subjects, the Gay and Lesbian Alliance against Defamation, and my own VCR, I collected as many videotapes on these subjects as I could get my hands on. Although not all programs are transcribed, the sample of more than 160 transcripts includes *Beatrice Berry, Donahue, Geraldo, Jenny Jones, Oprah, Maury Povich, Susan Powter, Dennis Prager, Sally Jessy Raphael, Rolonda, Jerry Springer, Jane Whitney,* and *Montel Williams.* The 100-odd hours of videos include most from that list, along with *Richard Bey, Danny Bonaduce, Carnie, Gordon Elliott, Gabrielle, Jenny Jones, Ricki Lake, Leeza, Marilu, The Other Side, Charles Perez, Jane Pratt, Joan Rivers, Tempestt,* and *Mark Walberg.* The transcripts were coded on a number of key dimensions—guest composition, program topic, thematic content, and so on—from which an outline of talk show content began to emerge: those outlines were then filled in with close readings of all of the transcripts and videos.

I swamped myself with more than enough data about talk show production and content, and much of the book teases out connections between these two strands of research: how producers' needs for both spontaneity and predictability lead to contradictions in the sexual politics of talk show programming, how some guests covertly strategize to change the framing of shows in which they are being used, and so on. But linking talk show content to institutional practices still leaves an important set of actors out of the loop: audience and viewers who, as much recent work on "cultural reception" has demonstrated, encounter cultural products with their own practices and interpretive lenses, often shaped by their location in the matrix of social hierarchies. The insufficiency of assertions about content is illustrated nicely in the debate over talk shows, in which critics and defenders alike assert that talk shows have this or that effect on viewers, or that viewers are getting such and such from them, but never actually *talk* to the people who are allegedly affected.

With that in mind, and backed also by my periodic participant-observation among talk show audiences, I facilitated thirteen group discussions with regular talk show viewers (a total of about seventy-five people). The first nine, conducted in suburban New Jersey, were with heterosexually identified viewers; some groups were mixed, and others were organized according to educational background and/or gender. The next three, which met in Manhattan, were with lesbians and gay men (one group of lesbians, one of gay men, and one mixed men and women). I also visited the Manhattan Gender Network, a transgender organization, and spoke with the group's members about their understandings of television talk shows. There are limits on this information, for sure: nearly all participants were middle-class, and the lesbian and gay viewers were all urban and mostly highly educated. Still, much of what I heard allows me to check the unanchored contentions running through the talk show debates, bouncing the content of the programming off the way viewers think about talk shows, and audience practices and thoughts off producers' routines and claims.

What has emerged from all this watching, reading, questioning, listening, and participating is the curious story of how talk shows and sex and gender nonconformity interact, how gay, lesbian, bisexual, and transgender people make their ways through the genre as subjects and objects, how what seems to be, and often is, a world of goofy lightness turns out to be heavily enmeshed in complicated, contradictory processes of social change. For now, a brief preview. Chapters 2 and 3 offer both a critical grounding in the history and production practices of television talk shows and important evidence of the complex, crisscrossing tracks on which queer visibility rides. Chapter 2 traces the history of TV talk, and the subhistory of sex and gender minorities within them, demonstrating that the genre is built on an awkward combination of class cultures; thus the visibility of lesbian, gay, transgender, and bisexual people is always shaped by the class friction that inheres in daytime TV talk. Chapter 3 takes up the vexed questions of truth and reality on talk shows, and in the process exposes the ins and outs of TV talk production: producers simultaneously pursue big moments of truth and revelation, and scramble, often to the exclusion of anything recognizably "real" or "true," to control the direction of a show; performance and dishonesty are built into the production of talk television, yet the shows are shot through with jarring breakthrough moments. Sex and gender nonconformity topics ride this wave, largely by fitting into a rhetoric of truth telling ("be true to yourself") which dovetails with both producers' needs and the coming-out strategy of bisexual, gay, lesbian, and transgender movements.

The next chapters move more explicitly onto political tracks. Chapter 4 wanders through the struggles over sexual morality playing out on talk shows, and especially the fate of the political and moral right on the shows. The shows, loosely guided by a combination of liberal, therapeutic, and bottom-line ideologies, wind up for the most part turning the tables on the antigay right, so that the bigots become the freaks; the result is an unusual, conditional, and unstable acceptance of gay and lesbian, and to a much lesser degree transgender and bisexual, people. Chapter 5 turns to the pulling apart and putting together of sex and gender categories, which are both a source of oppression and a resource for empowerment. Talk shows make a habit of raising the issue of "telling the difference" (between gay and straight, male and female), encouraged by their production needs both to raise the possibility that such differences are spurious and to then close down that possibility in a variety of ways; yet the issue is raised more often, and more frequent opportunities are given to talking "monsters" or "freaks" who defy categorization, than anywhere else in media culture.

Chapter 6 watches the disparate ways political battles are encouraged and reworked by TV talk; the often-successful attempts by activist guests to gain some control over the production process; the exacerbation of internal tensions within lesbian, gay, transgender, and bisexual political organizing, in particular and the sharpening of lines between those pursuing "mainstream" assimilation and those emphasizing "queer" difference; and the amplification of larger battles over the lines between public and private, into which sex and gender nonconformists, often interpreted as 'flaunting" on talk shows, are swallowed. In chapter 7, I bring together these funny dilemmas, ripe and sometimes rotten, squeezing out their implications for the important, dangerous, and necessary changes in the cultural representation of sex and gender differences.

But that is the end, where my mind left me after countless hours devoted to the somewhat unlikely, dangerously cold-inducing task of talk show immersion. As host, it seems only fair to start by telling you, in a nutshell, what I really think of talk shows. As gayman, I think they're a wretched little place, emptied of so much wisdom and filled, thank God, with inadvertent camp, but they're the place most enthusiastically afforded us—a measure of our cultural value. We are taking, and are being given, much more public media space now, but only because talk shows forged a path in there, and we had best understand what we can from the wretched little space where we were once honored guests. As scholarman, I think they're rich and interesting, like a funny, lively, slightly frightening room in a museum: dwell in them for a bit, think about their significance from a bunch of different angles, and you come out knowing more about the world, this current one, in which so much of how people see and feel themselves oozes into shape inside the sticky, narrow walls of commerce. Scholarman and gayman meet, for sure, in their common desire for a collective life in which, on a good day, people really take care of one another, and laugh; but it is really the restless coexistence of the two, one measured and the other lacking the luxury of distance, one concerned with culture in general and the other just filled with such odd couplings, packed with paradox, with double-edged swords, with painful pleasures and vapid depths and normal perverts. This book cavorts on the tips of those swords.

Questions for Discussion

1. Gamson defends talk shows because he likes "what talk shows make us think about" (page 464). According to this article, what topics do talk shows present to their audiences? Why are talk shows a unique source of knowledge to Gamson?

2. What groups of people gain visibility through talk shows? Why does this particular venue lend itself to recognizing these groups? What other issues/groups do talk shows reveal that are typically underrepresented? Are there issues talk shows conceal? Unfairly represent?

3. Gamson refutes anti-talk show critics who reject talk shows because they are bad for us. What are some reasons Gamson offers for people's rejection and fear of talk shows? How does he refute this rejection? How does he criticize talk shows?

Explorations

1. Some defendants of talk shows claim that these shows are "democracy at work" (page 465). Do you agree? Use examples, either from Gamson's text or from your own experience, to support your claim. What other television shows seem democratic to you? How do they compare to talk shows?

2. Gamson claims that talk shows can educate audiences about socially marginalized people. John Berger discusses the limitations of representation and how the "way we see things is affected by what we know or what we believe" (pg.). Discuss the power of images and the power of social beliefs. What is the potential for talk shows to change people's minds about socially devalued issues? How does Gamson account for people's interpretations of visual text of television? Can seeing representations of marginalized social groups overcome prevailing beliefs about them?

3. Talk shows, to Gamson, "shed different kind of light on sex and gender conformity" to redraw the "lines between normal and the abnormal" (page 467). Do you think Susan Bordo's interpretation of *My Best Friend's Wedding* reveals how movies can redraw these boundaries? Review "Gay Men's Revenge" to provide support for an argument for or against films as another forum for rethinking sex and gender norms. Would *My Best Friend's Wedding* do the same type of work that a talk show does? Does the medium affect the message?

Formal Writing Assignments

1. Take a look at a talk show and a more traditional television program (like the nightly news). What are the differences and similarities between the two shows? Does the traditional program sustain or threaten the prevailing social order? What about talk shows?

2. Gamson presents arguments that both defend talk shows as democratic and criticize them for their exploitative elements. Which side do you take? Or do you think they do both? Compare the open nature or repressive nature of talk shows with another television program. Is the talk show more or less welcoming to a variety of social groups than the other program?

Children's Culture and Disney's Animated Films

Henry A. Giroux

Henry Giroux is widely recognized as a leading educational critic and theorist. He has in his career turned his attention to a wide variety of subjects, including race, schooling for cultural change, television, multiculturalism, resistance through education, cultural studies, popular culture, corporate culture, and violence and youth. *The Mouse That Roared,* in which "Children's Culture and Disney's Animated Films" appears as chapter three, also includes chapters on cultural politics, national identity and family, and consumerism. Giroux is, by all counts a "public intellectual," a scholar and educator dedicated to bringing his work to bear on larger cultural discussions of education and schooling. Giroux is Waterbury Professor in curriculum and instruction at Penn State University.

Writing Before Reading

1. Recall the Disney films that you saw as a child. Which were they? What kind of messages do you recall the films sending? In what ways do you believe films and television programs generally influenced elements of your culture as a child?

2. Think back again to your childhood and the toys that you had. Did you accumulate any product tie-ins related to the films that you saw or television programs you watched? If so, what were they? Lunch boxes? Clothing? Games? Food? What changes have you noticed in this element of children's culture in the recent past?

3. If you've ever been to Disneyworld or Disneyland, write for a few moments about the most salient memories. Who worked there? How did they present themselves? Describe the scenes and what they represent, historically and culturally. If you've not been to one of these theme parks, describe the scenes at those sites.

Children's Culture and Disney's Animated Films

> Animation as a form of historical memory has entered real space. After all, any space or film that uses manipulated, interactive imagery must be called, by definition, a form of animation; and we are increasingly being submerged in life as a video game, even while our political crises deepen, and our class difference widens. . . . We act out stories inside cartoons now.
> —Norman M. Klein, *Seven Minutes: The Life and Death of the American Animated Cartoon*

As a single father of three young boys, I found myself somewhat reluctantly being introduced to the world of Hollywood animated films and, in particular, to those produced by Disney. Before becoming an observer of this form of children's culture, I accepted the largely unquestioned assumption that animated films stimulate imagination and fantasy, create a feeling of innocence and healthy adventure, and in general are "good" for kids. In other words, such films appeared to be wholesome vehicles of amusement, a highly regarded source of fun and joy for children.

However, within a very short period of time, it became clear to me that these films do more than entertain.[1] Needless to say, animated films operate on many registers, but one of the most persuasive is the role they play as the new "teaching machines." I soon found that for my children, and I suspect for many others, these films possess at least as much cultural authority and legitimacy for teaching roles, values, and ideals as more traditional sites of learning, such as the public schools, religious institutions, and the family. Disney films combine enchantment and innocence in narrating stories that help children understand who they are, what societies are about, and what it means to construct a world of play and fantasy in an adult environment. The authority of such films, in part, stems from their unique form of representation and their ever-growing presence. But such authority is also produced and secured within a media apparatus equipped with dazzling technology, sound effects, and imagery packaged as entertainment, spin-off commercial products, and "huggable" stories.

The significance of Disney's animated films as a site of learning is heightened by the widespread recognition that schools and other public sites are increasingly beset by a crisis of vision, purpose, and motivation. The mass media, especially the world of Hollywood films, constructs a dreamlike world of security, coherence, and childhood innocence in which kids find a place to situate themselves in their emotional lives. Unlike the often hard, joyless reality of schooling, children's films provide a high-tech visual space in which adventure and pleasure meet in a fantasy world of possibilities and a commercial sphere of consumerism and commodification. The educational relevance of animated films became especially clear to me as my kids experienced the vast entertainment and teaching machine embodied by Disney. Increasingly, as I watched a number of Disney films first in the movie theater and then on video, I became aware of how necessary it was to move beyond treating these films as transparent entertainment and to question the diverse messages that constitute Disney's conservative view of the world.

Trademarking Innocence

Kids learn from Disney films, so maybe it's time parents and educators paid closer attention to what these films are saying. I realize that this heresy, especially at a time when kids are being subjected to increasing violence in Hollywood blockbusters, video games, and other commercial forms of entertainment. But while Disney films do not promote the violence that has become central to many other forms of popular and mass culture, they do carry cultural and social messages that need to be scrutinized. After all, "the happiest place on earth" has traditionally gained its popularity in part through its trademark image of innocence, which has largely protected it from the interrogation of critics.

Left-wing criticism of Disney is often ignored by the popular press. Yet the recent charge by conservative Southern Baptists that Disney films promote a seditious, anti-Christian ideology received enormous publicity in the mainstream media. The reason is that such criticism appears so extreme as to be comical and, therefore, safe for the media to cover. The more liberal critiques often ignore entirely the racist, sexist, and antidemocratic ethos that permeates Disney films. For instance, the *New York Times* critic Michiko Kakutani argues that if anything is wrong with Disney's animated films it is that the characters of late are too preachy and promote "wholesome messages" that "only an ogre or bigot could hate."[2] One can't help wondering what is wholesome about Disney's overt racism toward Arabs displayed in *Aladdin*, the retrograde gender roles at work in *The Little Mermaid* and *Beauty and the Beast,* and the undisguised celebration of antidemocratic governments and racism (remember the hyenas, who sounded like poor blacks and Hispanics?) evident in *The Lion King.* (I discuss these films in detail later in this chapter.)

There is more at work here than a successful public relations campaign intent on promoting Disney's claim to goodness and morality. There is also the reality of a powerful economic and political empire, which in 1997 made more than $22.5 billion in revenues from all of its divisions.[3] Disney is more than a corporate giant; it is also a cultural institution that fiercely protects its legendary status as purveyor of innocence and moral virtue.

Quick to mobilize its legal representatives, public relations spokespersons, and professional cultural critics to safeguard the borders of its "magic kingdom," Disney has aggressively prosecuted violations of its copyrights and has a reputation for bullying authors who use the Disney archives but refuse to allow Disney censors to approve their manuscripts before they are actually published.[4] For example, in its zeal to protect its image and extend its profits, Disney has threatened legal action against three South Florida day care centers for using Disney cartoon characters on their exterior walls. In this instance, Disney's role as an aggressive defender of conservative family values was undermined through its aggressive endorsement of property rights. While Disney's reputation as an undisputed moral authority on American values has taken a beating in the last few years, the power of Disney's mythological status cannot be underestimated.

Disney's image as an icon of American culture is consistently reinforced through the penetration of the Disney empire into every aspect of social life. Disney's $22 billion empire shapes children's experiences through box office movies, home videos, theme parks, hotels, sports teams, retail stores, classroom instructional films, compact discs, radio programs, television shows, internet servers, and family restaurants.[5] Through the use of public visual space, Disney's network of power relations promotes the construction of an all-encompassing world of enchantment allegedly free from ideology, politics, and power.[6] At the same time, Disney goes to great lengths to boost its civic image. Defining itself as a vehicle for education and civic responsibility, Disney has sponsored teacher of the year awards, provided Doer and Dreamer scholarships, and offered financial aid, internships, and other learning opportunities to disadvantaged urban youth through educational and work programs, such as its ice-skating program called Goals. Intent on defining itself as a purveyor of ideas rather than commodities, Disney is aggressively developing its image as a public service industry.[7] For example, Disney has become a partner in a public school venture in Celebration, Florida. No longer content to spread its values through media entertainment and theme parks, Disney has now inserted itself into the growing lucrative market of the public school system.

What is interesting here is that Disney no longer simply dispenses the fantasies through which childhood innocence and adventure are produced, experienced, and affirmed. Disney now provides prototypes for families, schools, and communities. From the seedy urban haunts of New York City to the spatial monuments of consumption-shaping Florida, Disney is refiguring the social and cultural landscape while spreading its corporate ideology through the inventions of its imagineers. Disney transformed large sections of West Forty-second Street in New York City into an advertisement for a cleaned-up Disney version of America. It has also created the town of Celebration, Florida, designed after the "main streets of small-town America and reminiscent of Norman Rockwell images."[8] What Disney leaves out of its upbeat promotional literature is the rather tenuous notion of democracy that informs its view of municipal government, since Celebration is "premised upon citizens not having control over the people who plan for them and administer the policies of the city."[9]

But Disney does more than provide prototypes for upscale communities; it also makes a claim on the future through its nostalgic view of the past. The French theorist Jean Baudrillard provides an interesting theoretical twist on the scope and power of Disney's influence, arguing that Disneyland is more "real" than fantasy because it now provides the image on which America constructs itself. For Baudrillard, Disneyland functions as a "deterrent" designed to "rejuvenate in reverse the fiction of the real." "Disneyland is there to conceal the fact that it is the 'real' country, all of 'real' America, which is Disneyland (just as prisons are there to conceal the fact that it is the social in its entirety, in its banal omnipresence, which is carceral). Disneyland is presented as imaginary in order to make us believe that the rest is real, when in fact all of Los Angeles and the America surrounding it are no longer real but of the order of the hyperreal and of simulation."[10] Examples of the Disnification of America abound. For instance, the Houston airport modeled its monorail after the one at Disneyland. New housing developments throughout America appropriate a piece of nostalgia by imitating the Victorian architecture of Disneyland's Main Street, USA. Moreover, throughout America, shopping malls imitate Disney's approach to retailing so "that shopping takes place in themed environments."[11] It seems that the real policy makers are not in Washington, D.C., but in California, and they call themselves the Disney imagineers. The boundaries between entertainment, education, and commercialization collapse through Disney's sheer reach into everyday life. The scope of the Disney empire reveals both shrewd business practices and a sharp eye for providing dreams and products through forms of popular culture in which kids are willing to materially and emotionally invest.

Popular audiences tend to reject any link between ideology and the prolific entertainment world of Disney. And yet Disney's pretense of innocence appears to some critics as little more than a promotional mask that covers its aggressive marketing techniques and its influence in educating children to become active consumers. Eric Smoodin, editor of *Disney Discourse,* a book critical of Disney's role in American culture, argues that "Disney constructs childhood so as to make it entirely compatible with consumerism."[12] Even more disturbing is the widespread belief that Disney's "innocence" renders it unaccountable for the way it shapes children's sense of reality: its sanitized notions of identity, difference, and history in the seemingly apolitical cultural universe of the "magic kingdom." Jon Wiener argues that Disneyland's version of Main Street America harks back to an "image of small towns characterized by cheerful commerce, with barbershop quartets and ice cream sundaes and glorious parades." For Wiener, this view not only fictionalizes and trivializes the real Main Streets of the turn of the century, it also appropriates the past to legitimate a portrayal of a world "without tenements or poverty or urban class conflict. . . . It's a native white Protestant dream of a world without blacks or immigrants."[13]

Critiquing Disney Films

Some of Disney's animated films produced since 1989 are important because they have received enormous praise from the dominant press and have achieved blockbuster status.[14] For many children, they represent an entrance into the world of Disney. Moreover, the financial success and popularity of these films, rivaling many adult films, do not engender the critical analyses that adult films usually do. In short, critics and audiences are more willing to suspend critical judgment about children's films. Animated fantasy and entertainment films appear to fall outside of the world of values, meaning, and knowledge often associated with documentaries, art films, and even wide-circulation adult films. Elizabeth Bell, Lynda Haas, and Laura Sells capture this sentiment: "Disney audiences . . . legal institutions, film theorists, cultural critics, and popular audiences all guard the borders of Disney film as 'off limits' to the critical enterprise, constructing Disney as a metonym for 'America'—clean, decent, industrious—'the happiest place on earth.'"[15]

Given the influence that the Disney ideology has on children, it is imperative for parents, teachers, and other adults to understand how such films influence the values of the children who view them. As a producer of children's culture, Disney should not be given an easy pardon because it is defined as a citadel of fun and good cheer. On the contrary, as one of the primary institutions constructing childhood culture in the United States, Disney warrants healthy suspicion and critical debate. Such a debate should not be limited to the home but should be centered in schools and other public sites of learning.

It is important not to address Disney's animated films by simply condemning Disney as an ideological reactionary corporation promoting a conservative world view under the guise of entertainment. It is equally important not to celebrate Disney as the animated version of Mr. Rogers, doing nothing more than providing joy and happiness to children all over the world.[16] Disney does both. Disney does offer children visual stimulation and joy: dramatic thunderstorms, kaleidoscopic musical numbers, and the transformation of real life into wondrous spectacles. Disney's films offer children opportunities to locate themselves in a world that resonates with their desires and interests. Pleasure is one of the defining principles of what Disney produces, and children are both its subjects and objects. Hence, Disney's animated films have to be interrogated and mined as an important site for the production of children's culture. At the same time, these films are often filled with contradictory messages. Disney's influence and power must be situated within the broader understanding of the company's role as a corporate giant intent on spreading the conservative and commercial values that erode civil society while proclaiming to restructure it.

The role that Disney plays in shaping individual identities and in controlling the fields of social meaning through which children negotiate the world is far more complex than simple reactionary politics. If educators and other cultural workers are to include the culture of children as an important site of contestation and struggle, then it is imperative to analyze how Disney's animated films influence the way America's cultural landscape is imagined. Disney's scripted view of childhood and society needs to be engaged and challenged as "a historically specific matter of social analysis and intervention."[17] This is particularly important since Disney's animated films provoke and inform children's imaginations, desires, roles, and dreams while simultaneously sedimenting affect and meaning.

The wide distribution and popular appeal of Disney's animated films provide diverse audiences the opportunity for critical viewing. Critically analyzing how Disney films work to construct meaning, induce pleasure, and reproduce ideologically loaded fantasies is not meant as mere film criticism. Like any educational institution, Disney's view of the world needs to be discussed in terms of how it narrates children's culture and how it can be held accountable for what it does as a significant cultural public sphere—a space in which ideas, values, audiences, markets, and opinions create different publics and social formations. Of course, Disney's self-proclaimed innocence, inflexibility in dealing with social criticism, and paranoid attitude are now legendary and provide more reason that Disney be both challenged and engaged critically. Moreover, as a multi billion-dollar company, Disney's corporate and cultural influence is too enormous and far-reaching to allow it to define itself exclusively within the imaginary discourse of innocence, civic pride, and entertainment.[18]

The question of whether Disney's animated films are good for kids has no easy answer and resists simple analysis within the traditional and allegedly nonideological registers of fun and entertainment. Disney's most recent films—*The Little Mermaid* (1989), *Beauty and the Beast* (1991), *Aladdin* (1992), *The Lion King* (1994), *Pocahontas* (1995), *The Hunchback of Notre Dame* (1996), *Hercules* (1997), and *Mulan* (1998)—provide ample opportunity to address how Disney constructs a culture of joy and innocence for children out of the intersection of entertainment, advocacy, pleasure, and consumerism.[19] All of these films have been high-profile releases catering to massive audiences. Moreover, their commercial success is not limited to box-office profits. Successfully connecting consumption and moviegoing, Disney's animated films provide a "marketplace of culture," a launching pad for products and merchandise, including videocassettes, sound-track albums, children's clothing, furniture, stuffed toys, and new theme park rides.[20]

For example, *The Little Mermaid* and *Beauty and the Beast* videocassettes have combined sales of over 34 million. *Aladdin* has earned more than "$1 billion from box-office income, video sales and such ancillary baubles as Princess Jasmine dresses and Genie cookie jars"[21] and as a video interactive game sold more than 3 million copies in 1993. Similar sales are expected for the video and interactive game version of the film *The Lion King,* which had grossed $253.5 million in profits by August 24, 1994.[22] In fact, the first few weeks after *The Lion King* videocassette was released, it had sales of more than 20 million, and Disney's stock soared by $2.25 a share based on first-week revenues of $350 million. Jessica J. Reiff, an analyst at Oppenheimer and Company, says that "the movie will represent $1 billion in profits for Disney over two or three years."[23]

At the launching of *The Hunchback of Notre Dame,* Disney Records shipped 2 million sing-along home videos and seven *Hunchback* audio products, including the soundtrack CD and cassette and a toddler-targeted *My First Read–Along.* Tie-in promotions for the film included Burger King, Payless Shoes, Nestle, and Mattel.[24] While *The Hunchback of Notre Dame* did not fare well at the box office, generating a disappointing $99 million in North American revenue, it is expected, according to *Adweek* magazine, "to generate $500 million in profit (not just revenues), after the other revenue streams are taken into account."[25] Similarly, Disney characters such as Mickey Mouse, Snow White, Jasmine, Aladdin, and Pocahontas have become prototypes for toys, logos, games, and rides that fill department stores all over the world. Disney theme parks, which made more than $4 billion in revenues in 1997, produced a sizable portion of their profits through the merchandising of toys based on characters from the animated films.

The Lion King has been one of Disney's biggest commercial successes and provided a model for marketing its future animated films, including Mulan and Hercules (with its blatant commercial built into the movie itself). The Lion King produced a staggering $1 billion in merchandising profits in 1994 alone—the year of its release—not to mention the profits made from spin-off products. For example, when The Lion King was first released, Disney shipped out more than 3 million copies of the sound track. Disney's culture of commercialism is big business and the toys modeled after Disney's animated films provide goods for the more than 365 Disney Stores worldwide. "The merchandise—Mermaid dolls, Aladdin undies, and collectibles like a sculpture of Bambi's Field Mouse—account for a stunning 20 percent of Disney's operating income."[27]

One of Disney's biggest promotion campaigns began with the summer 1995 release of Pocahontas. A record lineup of tie-in merchandise included Pocahontas stuffed animals, sheets, pillowcases, toothbrushes, games, moccasins, and more than forty "picture and activity books."[28] A consortium of corporations spent an estimated $125 million on cross-marketing Pocahontas. Two well-known examples include Burger King, which was converted into an advertisement for the film and gave away an estimated 50 million Pocahontas figurines, and the Mattel Corporation, which marketed more than fifty different dolls and toys.

But Disney's attempt to turn children into consumers and to make commodification a defining principle of children's culture should not suggest a parallel vulgarity in its aesthetic experiments with popular forms of representation. Disney has shown enormous inventiveness in its attempts to reconstruct the very grounds on which popular culture is defined and shaped. For example, by defining popular culture as a hybridized sphere that combines genres and forms and that often collapses the boundary between high and low culture, Disney has pushed against aesthetic form and cultural legitimacy. When Fantasia appeared in the 1930s, it drew the wrath of music critics, who, holding to an elite view of classical music, were outraged that the musical score drew from the canon of high culture. By combining high and low culture, Disney opened up new cultural possibilities for artists and audiences alike. Moreover, as sites of entertainment, Disney's films work because they put both children and adults in touch with joy and adventure. They present themselves as places to experience pleasure, even when we have to buy it. And yet Disney's brilliant use of aesthetic forms, musical scores, and inviting characters can only be read in light of the broader conceptions of reality shaped by these films within a wider system of dominant representations about gender roles, race, and agency that are endlessly repeated in the visual worlds of television, Hollywood film, and videocassettes.

A number of the films mentioned draw upon the talents of songwriters Howard Ashman and Alan Menken, whose skillful arrangements provide the emotional glue of the animation experience. The rousing calypso number "Under the Sea" in The Little Mermaid, and "Be Our Guest," the Busby Berkeley-inspired musical sequence in Beauty and the Beast, are indicative of the musical talent at work in Disney's animated film. Fantasy abounds, as Disney's animated films produce a host of exotic and stereotypical villains, heroes, and heroines. The Beast's enchanted castle in Beauty and the Beast becomes magical as household objects are transformed into dancing teacups and silverware and a talking teapot. And yet tied to the magical fantasy and lighthearted musical scores are stereotypes characteristic of Disney's view of childhood culture.

For example, Ursula, the large, oozing, black and purple squid in The Little Mermaid, gushes with evil and irony, and the heroine and mermaid, Ariel, appears as a cross between a typical rebellious teenager and a Southern California fashion model. Disney's representations of evil women and good women appear to have been fashioned in the editorial office of Vogue. The wolflike monster in Beauty and the Beast evokes a combination of terror and gentleness. Scar, in The Lion King, is a suave feline who masterfully portrays evil and betrayal. Disney's evocation of war and battle in *Mulan* is expansive and provocative. The animated objects and animals in these films are of the highest artistic standards, but they do not exist in an ideology-free zone. They are tied to larger narratives about freedom, rites of passage, intolerance, choice, greed, and the brutalities of male chauvinism.

Enchantment comes at a high price, however, if the audience is meant to suspend judgment of the films' ideological messages. Even though these messages can be read from a variety of viewpoints, the assumptions that structure these films restrict the number of cultural meanings that can be brought to bear on these films, especially when the intended audience is mostly children. The role of the critic of Disney's animated films, however, is not to assign them a particular ideological reading but to analyze the themes and assumptions that inform these films, both within and outside of the dominant institutional and ideological formations. Such analyses allow educators and others to understand how such films can become sites of contestation, translation, and exchange.

And beyond merely recognizing the plurality of readings such films might foster, there is also the pedagogical task of provoking audiences to reflect upon the ways in which Disney's themes function as part of a broader public discourse, privileging some definitions or interpretations over others. The conservative values that Disney films promote assume such force because of the context in which they are situated and because they resonate so powerfully with dominant perceptions and meanings. Pedagogically, this suggests the need for educators, parents, and others to analyze critically how the privileged dominant readings of Disney's animated films generate and affirm particular pleasures, desires, and subject positions that define for children specific notions of agency and its possibilities in society.

Contexts mold interpretations; but political, economic, and ideological contexts also produce the texts to be read. The focus on films must be supplemented with an analysis of the institutional practices and social structures that work to shape such texts. Such analysis should suggest pedagogical strategies for understanding how dominant regimes of power limit the range of views that children might bring to reading Disney's animated films. By making the relationship between power and knowledge visible, while simultaneously referencing what is often taken for granted, teachers and critics can analyze Disney's animated films pedagogically so that students and others can read such films within, against, and outside of the dominant codes that inform them.

There is a double pedagogical movement here. First, there is the need to read Disney's films in relation to their articulation with other dominant texts in order to assess their similarities in legitimating particular ideologies. Second, there is the need to use Disney's thematization of America and America's thematization of Disney as referents to make visible—and to disrupt—dominant codings and to do so in a space that invites dialogue, debate, and alternative readings. For instance, one major pedagogical challenge is to assess how dominant ideas that are repeated over time in these films and that are reinforced through other popular cultural texts can be taken as referents for engaging children in defining themselves within such representations. The task here is to provide readings of such films to serve as pedagogical referents.[29] By providing a theoretical referent for engaging Disney films, it becomes possible to explore pedagogically how we both construct and defend the readings we actually bring to such films, providing an opportunity to expand the dialogue regarding what Disney's films mean while simultaneously challenging the assumptions underlying dominant readings of these films. Taking a position on Disney's films should not degenerate into a doctrinaire reading or legitimate a form of political or pedagogical indoctrination with children or anybody else. Rather, such an approach should address how any reading of these films is ideological and should be engaged in terms of the context, the content, and the values and social relations it endorses. Moreover, engaging such readings politically and ideologically provides the pedagogical basis for making the films problematic and, thus, open to dialogue, rather than treating them uncritically, as mere entertainment.

What Children Learn from Disney

The construction of gender identity for girls and women represents one of the most controversial issues in Disney's animated films.[30] In both *The Little Mermaid* and *The Lion King,* the female characters are constructed within narrowly defined gender roles. All of the female characters in these films are ultimately subordinate to males and define their power and desire almost exclusively in terms of dominant male narratives. For instance, modeled after a slightly anorexic Barbie doll, Ariel, the mermaid in *The Little Mermaid,* at first glance appears to be engaged in a struggle against parental control, motivated by the desire to explore the human world and willing to take a risk in defining the subject and object of her desires. But, in the end, the struggle to gain independence from her father, Triton, and the desperate striving that motivates her dissolve when Ariel makes a Mephistophelian pact with the sea witch, Ursula. In this trade, Ariel gives away her voice to gain a pair of legs so that she can pursue the handsome prince, Eric.

Although girls might be delighted by Ariel's teenage rebelliousness, they are strongly positioned to believe, in the end, that desire, choice, and, empowerment are closely linked to catching and loving a handsome man. Bonnie Leadbeater and Gloria Lodato Wilson explore the pedagogical message at work in the film: "The 20th-century innocent and appealing video presents a high-spirited role for adolescent girls, but an ultimately subservient role for adult women. Disney's 'Little Mermaid' has been granted her wish to be part of the new world of men, but she is still flipping her fins and is not going too far. She stands to explore the world of men. She exhibits her new-found sexual desires. But the sexual ordering of women's roles is unchanged."[31] Ariel becomes a metaphor for the traditional housewife in the making. When Ursula tells Ariel that taking away her voice is not so bad because men don't like women who talk, the message is dramatized when the prince attempts to bestow the kiss of true love on Ariel even though she has never spoken to him. Within this rigid narrative, womanhood offers Ariel the reward of marrying the right man for renouncing her former life under the sea. It is a cultural model for the universe of female choices in Disney's world view.

The rigid gender roles in *The Little Mermaid* are not isolated instances in Disney's filmic universe; on the contrary, Disney's negative stereotypes about women and girls gain force through the way in which similar messages are consistently circulated and reproduced, to varying degrees, in many of Disney's animated films. For example, in *Aladdin* the issue of agency and power is centered primarily on the role of the young street tramp, Aladdin. Jasmine, the princess he falls in love with, is simply an object of his immediate desire as well as a social stepping-stone. Jasmine's life is almost completely defined by men, and, in the end, her happiness is ensured by Aladdin, who is finally given permission to marry her.

Disney's gender theme becomes a bit more complicated in *Beauty and the Beast, Pocahontas,* and *Mulan.* Belle, the heroine of *Beauty and the Beast,* is portrayed as an independent woman stuck in a provincial village in eighteenth century France. Seen as odd because she always has her nose in a book, she is pursued by Gaston, the ultimate vain, macho male typical of Hollywood films of the 1980s. To Belle's credit, she rejects him, but in the end she gives her love to the Beast, who holds her captive in the hope that she will fall in love with him and break the evil spell cast upon him as a young man. Belle not only falls in love with the Beast, she "civilizes" him by instructing him on how to eat properly, control his temper, and dance. Belle becomes a model of etiquette and style as she turns this narcissistic, muscle-bound tyrant into a "new" man, one who is sensitive, caring, and loving. Some critics have labeled Belle a Disney feminist because she rejects and vilifies Gaston, the ultimate macho man.

Less obviously, Beauty and the Beast also can be read as a rejection of hypermasculinity and a struggle between the sensibilities of Gaston and the reformed sexist, the Beast. In this reading, Belle is less the focus of the film than a prop or "mechanism for solving the Beast's dilemma."[32] Whatever subversive qualities Belle personifies in the film, they seem to dissolve when focused on humbling male vanity. In the end, Belle simply becomes another woman whose life is valued for solving a man's problems.

Disney's next femme fatale, Pocahontas, appears to both challenge and reproduce some of these stereotypes. Rather than a young adolescent, Pocahontas is made over historically to resemble a shapely, contemporary, high-fashion supermodel. Bright, courageous, literate, and politically progressive, she is a far cry from the traditional negative stereotypes of Native Americans portrayed in Hollywood films. But Pocahontas's character, like that of many of Disney's female protagonists, is drawn primarily in relation to the men who surround her. Initially, her identity is defined in resistance to her father's attempts to marry her off to one of the bravest warriors in the tribe. But her coming-of-age identity crisis is largely defined by her love affair with John Smith, a blond colonist who looks like he belongs in a Southern California pinup magazine of male surfers. Pocahontas's character is drawn primarily through her struggle to save John Smith from being executed by her father. Pocahontas exudes a kind of soppy romanticism that not only saves John Smith's life but also convinces the crew of the British ship to rebel against its greedy captain and return to England.

Of course, this is a Hollywood rewrite of history that bleaches colonialism of its genocidal legacy. No mention is made of the fact that John Smith's countrymen would ultimately ruin Pocahontas's land, bring disease, death, and poverty to her people, and eventually destroy their religion, economic livelihood, and way of life. In the Disney version of history, colonialism never happened, and the meeting between the old and new worlds is simply fodder for another "love conquers all" narrative. One wonders how this film would have been viewed by the public if it had been about a Jewish woman who falls in love with a blond Aryan Nazi while ignoring any references to the Holocaust.

The issue of female subordination returns with a vengeance in *The Lion King*. All of the rulers of the kingdom are men, reinforcing the assumption that independence and leadership are tied to patriarchal entitlement and high social standing. The dependency that the beloved lion king, Mufasa, engenders in the women of Pride Rock is unaltered after his death, when the evil Scar assumes control of the kingdom. Lacking any sense of outrage, independence, or resistance, the women felines hang around to do Scar's bidding.

The gender stereotyping is somewhat modified in *Mulan*. The lead character of the same name is presented as a bold female warrior who challenges traditional stereotypes of young women. But for all of her independence, in the end, the film is, as the film critic Janet Maslin points out, "still enough of a fairy tale to need a Mr. Right."[33] Mulan may be an independent, strong-willed young woman, but the ultimate payoff for her bravery comes in the form of catching the handsome son of a general. And if the point is missed, when the heroine's grandmother first sees the young man as he enters Mulan's house, she affirms what she (the audience?) sees as Mulan's real victory, which is catching a man, and yells out: "Sign me up for the next war!" And there is another disturbing side to Mulan as an alleged strong woman. Rather than aligning herself against the patriarchal celebration of war, violence, and militarism, Mulan becomes a cross-dresser who proves that when it comes to war she can perform as well as any male. By embracing a masculine view of war, Mulan cancels out any rupturing of traditional gender roles. She simply becomes one of the boys. But lest the fantasy be taken too far, Disney reminds us at the conclusion of the film that Mulan is still just a girl in search of a man, and as in so many other Disney animated films, Mulan becomes an exoticized version of the All-American girl who manages to catch the most handsome boy on the block, square jaw and all.

Given Disney's purported obsession with family values, especially as a consuming unit, it is curious that, with the exception of *Mulan,* there are no strong mothers or fathers in these films.[34] Not only are powerful mothers absent, but with the exception of the fathers of Pocahontas and Mulan, all of the father figures are portrayed as weak or stupid. Only the mermaid has a domineering father. Jasmine's father is outwitted by his aides, and Belle's father is an airhead.

Jack Zipes, a leading theorist on fairy tales, claims that Disney's animated films reproduce "a type of gender stereotyping . . . that has an adverse effect on children, in contrast to what parents think. . . . Parents think they're essentially harmless—and they're not harmless."[35]

Racial stereotyping is another major issue in Disney films. There is a long history of racism associated with Disney, tracing back to *Song of the South,* released in 1946, and *The Jungle Book,* which appeared in 1967.[36] Moreover, racist representations of Native Americans as violent "redskins" were featured in Frontierland in the 1950s.[37] In addition, the main restaurant in Frontierland featured an actor representing the former slave Aunt Jemima, who would sign autographs for the tourists outside of her "Pancake House." Eventually, the exhibits and the Native Americans running them were eliminated by Disney executives because the "Indian" canoe guides wanted to unionize. They were displaced by robotic dancing bears. Complaints from civil rights groups got rid of the degrading Aunt Jemima spectacle.[38]

One of the most controversial examples of racist stereotyping facing the Disney publicity machine occurred with the release of *Aladdin* in 1992, although such stereotyping reappeared in full force in 1994 with the release of *The Lion King. Aladdin* is a particularly important example because it was a high-profile release, the winner of two Academy Awards, and one of the most successful Disney films ever produced. The film's opening song, "Arabian Nights," begins its depiction of Arab culture with a decidedly racist tone. The lyrics of the offending stanza state: "Oh I come from a land/From a faraway place/Where the caravan camels roam./Where they cut off your ear/If they don't like your face./It's barbaric, but hey, it's home." A politics of identity and place associated with Arab culture magnified popular stereotypes already primed by the media through its portrayal of the Gulf War. Such a racist representation is furthered by a host of grotesque, violent, and cruel supporting characters.

Yousef Salem, a former spokesperson for the South Bay Islamic Association, characterized the film in the following way: "All of the bad guys have beards and large, bulbous noses, sinister eyes and heavy accents, and they're wielding swords constantly. Aladdin doesn't have a big nose; he has a small nose. He doesn't have a beard or a turban. He doesn't have an accent. What makes him nice is they've given him this American character. . . . I have a daughter who says she's ashamed to call herself an Arab, and it's because of things like this."[39] Jack Shaheen, a professor of broadcast journalism at Southern Illinois University, Edwardsville, along with the radio personality Casey Kasem, mobilized a public relations campaign protesting the anti-Arab themes in *Aladdin.* At first, Disney executives ignored the protest, but responding to the rising tide of public outrage agreed to change one line of the stanza in the subsequent videocassette and worldwide film release. Disney did not change the lyrics on its popular CD release of *Aladdin.*[40]

Disney executives were not unaware of the racist implications of the lyrics when they were first proposed. Howard Ashman, who wrote the title song, submitted an alternative set of lyrics when he delivered the original lines. The alternative lyrics, "Where it's flat and immense/And the heat is intense" eventually replaced the original verse, "Where they cut off your ear/If they don't like your face." Though the new lyrics appeared in the videocassette release of Aladdin, the line "It's barbaric, but hey, it's home" was not altered. More important, the mispronunciation of Arab names in the film, the racial coding of accents, and the use of nonsensical scrawl as a substitute for an actual written Arabic language were not removed.[41]

Racism in Disney's animated films is also evident in racially coded language and accents. For example, *Aladdin* portrays the "bad" Arabs with thick, foreign accents, while the Anglicized Jasmine and Aladdin speak in standard American English. A hint of the racism that informs this depiction is provided by Peter Schneider, president of feature animation at Disney at the time, who points out that Aladdin was modeled after Tom Cruise.

Racially coded representations and language are also evident in *The Lion King.* Scar, the icon of evil, is darker than the good lions. Moreover, racially coded language is evident, as the members of the royal family speak with posh British accents while Shenzi and Banzai, the despicable hyena storm troopers, speak with the voices of Whoopi Goldberg and Cheech Marin in the jive accents of a decidedly urban black or Hispanic youth. Disney falls back upon the same racial formula in *Mulan.* Not far removed from the Amos 'n' Andy crows in *Dumbo* is the racialized low-comedy figure of Mushu, a tiny red dragon with a black voice (Eddie Murphy). Mushu is a servile and boastful clown who seems unsuited to a mythic fable about China. He is the stereotype of the craven, backward, Southern, chitlin-circuit character that appears to feed the popular racist imagination. Racially coded language can also be found in an early version of *The Three Little Pigs,* in *Song of the South,* and in *The Jungle Book.*[42] These films produce representations and codes through which children are taught that characters who do not bear the imprint of white, middle-class ethnicity are culturally deviant, inferior, unintelligent, and a threat.

The racism in these films is defined by both the presence of racist representations and the absence of complex representations of African Americans and other people of color. At the same time, whiteness is universalized through the privileged representation of middle-class social relations, values, and linguistic practices. Moreover, the representational rendering of history, progress, and Western culture bears a colonial legacy that seems perfectly captured by Edward Said's notion of orientalism—a particular form of Western imperialism that shapes dominant thinking about the Orient—and its dependency on new images of centrality and sanctioned narratives.[43] Cultural differences are expressed through a "natural" racial hierarchy, which is antithetical to a viable democratic society. There is nothing innocent in what kids learn about race as portrayed in the "magical world" of Disney. Even in a film such as *Pocahontas,* in which cultural differences are portrayed more positively, there is the suggestion in the end that racial identities must remain separate. *Pocahontas* is one of the few love stories in Disney's animated series in which the lovers do not live together happily ever after. It is also one of the few love stories that brings lovers from different races together.

Another feature common to many of Disney's recent animated films is the celebration of antidemocratic social relations. Nature and the animal kingdom provide the mechanism for presenting and legitimating caste, royalty, and structural inequality as part of the natural order. The seemingly benign presentation of celluloid dramas, in which men rule, strict discipline is imposed through social hierarchies, and leadership is a function of one's social status, suggests a yearning for a return to a more rigidly stratified society, one modeled after the British monarchy of the eighteenth and nineteenth centuries. In Disney's animated films, "harmony is bought at the price of domination. . . . No power or authority is implied except for the natural ordering mechanisms" of nature.[44] For children, the messages suggest that social problems such as the history of racism, the genocide of Native Americans, the prevalence of sexism, and the crisis of democracy are simply willed through the laws of nature.

Conclusion

Given the corporate reach, cultural influence, and political power that Disney exercises over multiple levels of children's culture, Disney's animated films should be neither ignored nor censored by those who dismiss the conservative ideologies they produce and circulate. There are a number of issues to be addressed regarding the forging of a pedagogy and a politics responsive to Disney's shaping of children's culture. Below, I suggest how cultural workers, educators, and parents might critically engage Disney's influence in shaping the "symbolic environment into which our children are born and in which we all live out our lives."[45]

First, it is crucial that the realm of popular culture that Disney increasingly invades to teach values and to sell goods to children be taken seriously as a site of learning and contestation. This means, at the very least, that those cultural texts that dominate children's culture, including Disney's animated films, should be incorporated into school curricula as objects of social knowledge and critical analysis. This would entail a reconsideration of what counts as useful knowledge and offer theoretical suggestions for addressing the ways in which popular media aimed at shaping children's culture are implicated in power/knowledge relationships. This is not simply a call for making media literacy a part of what kids gain from school (as crucial as such a pedagogy is)[46] but a reconsideration of what counts as school knowledge. In simple terms, this means making popular culture an essential object of social analysis in schools.

Second, parents, community groups, educators, and other concerned individuals must be attentive to the diverse messages in Disney films in order both to criticize them when necessary and, more important, to reclaim them for more productive ends. At the very least, we must be attentive to the processes whereby meanings are produced in these films and how they work to secure particular forms of authority and social relations. At stake pedagogically is the issue of paying "close attention to the ways in which [such films] invite (or indeed seek to prevent) particular meanings and pleasures."[47] In fact, Disney's films appear to assign, quite unapologetically, rigid roles to women and people of color. Similarly, such films generally produce a narrow view of family values coupled with a nostalgic and conservative view of history that should be challenged and transformed. Educators need to take seriously Disney's attempt to shape collective memory, particularly when such attempts are unabashedly defined by one of Disney's imagineers in the following terms: "What we create is a sort of 'Disney realism,' sort of Utopian in nature, where we carefully program out all the negative, unwanted elements and program in the positive elements."[48] Disney's rendering of entertainment and spectacle, whether expressed in Frontierland, Main Street, USA, or its video and film productions, is not merely an edited, sanitary, and nostalgic view of history, one that is free of poverty, class differences, and urban decay. Disney's writing of public memory also aggressively constructs a monolithic notion of national identity that treats subordinate groups as either exotic or irrelevant to American history, simultaneously marketing cultural differences within "histories that corporations can live with."[49] Disney's version of U.S. history is not innocent, nor can it be dismissed as simply entertainment.

Disney's celluloid view of children's culture often works to strip the past, present, and future of diverse narratives and multiple possibilities, a rendering that needs to be revealed as a historically specific and politically constructed cultural "landscape of power." Rustom Bharacuha argues that "the consumption of . . . images . . . can be subverted through a particular use in which we are compelled to think through images rather than respond to them with a hallucinatory delight."[50] The images that pervade Disney's production of children's culture, along with their claim to public memory, need to be challenged and rewritten, "moved about in different ways," and read differently as part of the script of democratic empowerment.[51] It is within the drama of animated storytelling that children are often positioned pedagogically to learn what subject positions are open to them and what positions are not. Hence, the struggle over children's culture should be considered as part of a struggle over the related discourses of citizenship, national identity, and democracy itself.

Third, if Disney's films are to be viewed as more than narratives of fantasy and escape, becoming sites of reclamation and imagination that affirm rather than deny the long-standing relationship between entertainment and pedagogy, it is important to consider how we might insert the political and pedagogical back into the discourse of entertainment. In part, this points to analyzing how entertainment can be addressed as a subject of intellectual engagement rather than as a series of sights and sounds that wash over us. This suggests a pedagogical approach to popular culture that asks how a politics of the popular works to mobilize desire, stimulate imagination, and produce forms of identification that can become objects of dialogue and critical investigation. At one level, this suggests addressing the utopian possibilities in which children often find representations of their hopes and dreams. But it also suggests recognizing the pedagogical importance of what kids bring with them to the classroom (or to any other site of learning) as crucial both to decentering power in the classroom and to expanding the possibility of teaching students multiple literacies, as part of a broader strategy of teaching them to read the world critically.

We must pay attention to how these Disney films and visual media are used and understood differently by different kids. We must talk to children about these films so we can better understand how kids identify with them and what issues they raise, developing a language of pleasure and criticism. This suggests that we develop new ways of critically understanding and reading electronically produced visual media. Teaching and learning the culture of the book is no longer the staple of what it means to be literate.

Children learn from exposure to popular cultural forms, which provide a new cultural register of what it means to be literate. This suggests a cultural pedagogy, rooted in cultural practices, that utilizes students' knowledge and experience of popular cultural forms. Students should be taught to critically analyze the messages produced by the electronically mediated popular culture, but they must also be able to master the skills and technology to produce these forms, making their own films, videos, and music. Thus a cultural pedagogy also requires more resources for schools and other sites of learning, providing the conditions for students and others to become the subject, not simply the object, of pedagogical work. Asserting their role as cultural producers is crucial if students are to become attentive to the workings of power, solidarity, and difference.

Fourth, Disney's reach into the spheres of economics, consumption, and culture suggest that we analyze Disney within a broad and complex range of relations of power. Eric Smoodin argues that the American public needs to "gain a new sense of Disney's importance, because of the manner in which his work in film and television is connected to other projects in urban planning, ecological politics, product merchandising, United States domestic and global policy formation, technological innovation, and constructions of national character."[52] This suggests undertaking analyses of Disney that connect, rather than separate, the various social and cultural formations in which the company engages. Clearly, such a dialectical practice not only provides a more theoretically accurate understanding of the reach and influence of Disney's power but also contributes to forms of analysis that discount the notion that Disney is primarily about the pedagogy of entertainment.

Questions of ownership, control, and public participation in deciding how cultural resources are used should become a central issue in addressing the world of Disney and other corporate conglomerates that shape cultural policy. The control, production, and distribution of such films should be analyzed as part of a wider circuit of power. In this context, Disney's influence in the shaping of children's culture cannot be reduced to critically interpreting the ideas and values Disney promotes. Any viable analysis of Disney must also confront the institutional and political power Disney exercises through its massive control over diverse sectors of what Mark Crispin Miller calls the "national entertainment state."[53] The availability, influence, and cultural power of Disney's children's films demand that they become part of a broader political discourse regarding who makes cultural policy. Issues regarding how and what children learn could be addressed through public debates about how the distribution and control of cultural and economic resources ensure that children are exposed to alternative narratives about themselves and the larger society.

When the issue of children's culture is taken up by—and shaped in—the public schools, it is assumed that this is a matter of public policy and intervention. But when children's culture is shaped in the commercial sphere, the discourse of public intervention gets lost in abstract appeals to the imperatives of the market and free speech. Free speech is only as good as the democratic framework that makes possible the extension of its benefits to all individuals, groups, and public spheres. Treating Disney as part of a media sphere that needs to be democratized and held accountable for the ways in which it wields power and manufactures social identities needs to be part of the discourse of pedagogical analysis and public policy intervention. This type of analysis and intervention is perfectly suited for cultural theorists and community activists willing to employ an interdisciplinary approach to such an undertaking, to address popular culture as an object of serious analysis, to make the pedagogical a defining principle of such work, and to insert the political into the center of such projects.[54]

This suggests that cultural workers need to readdress a politics of representation and the discourse of political economy, treating their varied interrelations as a form of cultural work that rejects the material/cultural divide. The result would be an understanding of how such modalities inform each other within different contexts and across national boundaries. It is particularly important for cultural workers to understand how Disney films work as teaching machines within and across public cultures and social formations. Within this type of analysis, the messages, emotional investments, and ideologies produced by Disney can be traced through the circuits of power that both legitimate and insert "the culture of the Magic Kingdom" into multiple and overlapping public spheres. Disney films need to be analyzed not only for what they say but also for how they are apprehended by audiences within their national and international contexts. That is, cultural workers need to study these films intertextually and from a transnational perspective. Disney is not ignorant of different contexts; on the contrary, its power, in part, rests with its ability to address different contexts and to be read differently in different transnational formations. Disney engenders what Inderpal Grewa and Caren Kaplan call "scattered hegemonies."[55] It is precisely by addressing how these hegemonies operate in particular spaces of power, specific localities—in different transnational locations—that we will be able to understand the agendas and the politics at work.

The defeat in 1995 of Disney's proposed 3,000-acre theme park in Virginia suggests that Disney can be challenged and held accountable for the so-called Disnification of American culture. In this instance, a coalition of historians, community activists, educators, and other concerned groups mobilized against the land developers supporting the project, wrote articles against Disney's trivializing of history and its implications for the park, and aroused public opinion enough to generate an enormous amount of adverse criticism against the Disney project. What was initially viewed as merely a project for bringing a Disney version of fun and entertainment to hallowed Civil War grounds in historic Virginia was translated by opposition groups into a cultural struggle. And Disney lost.

What the Virginia cultural civil war suggests is that, although it is indisputable that Disney provides both children and adults with entertainment and pleasure, Disney's public responsibility does not end there. Rather than being viewed as a commercial venture innocently distributing pleasure to young people, the Disney empire must be seen as a pedagogical and policy-making enterprise actively engaged in the cultural landscaping of national identity and the "schooling" of the minds of young children. This is not to suggest that there is something sinister behind what Disney does. It points only to the need to address the role of fantasy, desire, and innocence in securing particular ideological interests, legitimating specific social relations, and making a claim on the meaning of public memory. Disney needs to be held accountable, which will require that parents, educators, and others challenge and disrupt both the institutional power and the images, representations, and values offered by Disney's teaching machine.

Notes

1. For a critical engagement of commercialization, popular culture, and children's culture, see Marsha Kinder, *Playing with Power in Movies, Television, and Video Games* (Berkeley: University of California Press, 1991); Doug Kellner, *Media Culture* (New York: Routledge, 1995); David Buckingham and Julian Sefton-Green, *Cultural Studies Goes to School* (Washington, D.C.: Taylor and Francis, 1994).

2. Michiko Kakutani, "This Mouse Once Roared," *New York Times Magazine,* January 4, 1998, p. 8. Compare Kakutani's analysis with Matt Roth, "A Short History of Disney-Fascism," *Jump Cut,* no. 40 (1996), pp. 15–20.

3. Michael D. Eisner, "Letter to Shareholders," *The Walt Disney Company 1997 Annual Report* (Burbank, Calif.: Walt Disney Company, 1997), p. 2.

4. There is a growing list of authors who have been pressured by Disney either through its refusal to allow copyrighted materials to be used or through its influence on publishers. Examples can be found in Jon Wiener, "In the Belly of the Mouse: The Dyspeptic Disney Archives," *Lingua Franca* (July/August 1994), pp. 69–72. Also Jon Wiener, "Murdered Ink," *Nation,* May 31, 1993, pp. 743–50. One typical example occurred with a book in which one of my own essays on Disney appears. While editing a book critical of Disney, Elizabeth Bell, Lynda Haas, and Laura Sells

requested permission from Disney executives to use the Disney archives. In response, the editors received a letter from one of Disney's legal assistants asking to approve the book. The editors declined, and Disney forbade the use of its name in the title of the book and threatened to sue if the Disney name was used. Indiana University Press argued that it did not have the resources to fight Disney, so the title of the book was changed from *Doing Disney* to *From Mouse to Mermaid*. In another instance, Routledge publishers omitted an essay by David Kunzle on the imperialist messages in Disney's foreign comics in a book entitled *Disney Discourse*. Thinking that Disney would not provide permission for the use of illustrations from the Disney archives, Routledge decided they could not publish the essay. Discouraged, Kunzle said, "I've given up. I'm not doing any more work on Disney. I don't think any university press would take the risk. The problem is not the likelihood of Disney winning in court, it's the threat of having to bear the cost of fighting them." Wiener, "In the Belly of the Mouse," p. 72.

5. This figure comes from Michael Meyer et al., "Of Mice and Men," *Newsweek*, September 5, 1994, p. 41.

6. The mutually determining relationship of culture and economic power is captured in Sharon Zukin, *Landscapes of Power: From Detroit to Disney World* (Berkeley: University of California Press, 1991), p. 221:

> The domestication of fantasy in visual consumption is inseparable from cen-tralized structures of economic power. Just as the earlier power of the state illu-minated public space—the streets—by artificial lamplight, so the economic power of CBS, Sony, and the Disney Company illuminates private space at home by electronic images. With the means of production so concentrated and the means of consumption so diffused, communication of these images becomes a way of controlling both knowledge and imagination, a form of corporate social control over technology and symbolic expressions of power.

7. For a listing of public service programs that Disney has initiated, see Jennifer J. Laabs, "Disney Helps Keep Kids in School," *Personnel Journal* (November 1992), pp. 58–68.

8. Disney executives, quoted in Mark Walsh, "Disney Holds Up School as Model for Next Century," *Education Week* 39, (1994), p. 1.

9. Tom Vanderbilt, "Mickey Mouse Goes to Town(s)," *Nation*, August 28/September 4, 1995, p. 199.

10. Jean Baudrillard, *Simulations* (New York: Semiotext(e), 1983), p. 25. Also see Baudrillard, "Consumer Society," in Mark Poster, ed., *Jean Baudrillard: Selected Works* (Stanford: Stanford University Press, 1988), pp. 29–56.

11. Alan Bryman, *Disney and His Worlds* (New York: Routledge, 1995), p. 26.

12. Eric Smoodin, "How to Read Walt Disney," in Smoodin, ed., *Disney Discourse: Producing the Magic Kingdom* (New York: Routledge, 1994), p. 18.

13. Jon Wiener, "Tall Tales and True," *Nation*, January 31, 1994, p.134.

14. Disney's animated film *The Lion King* may be the most financially successful film ever made. Disney's animated films released since 1990 are all among the ten top-grossing films. *The Lion*

King ranked first, with $253.5 million; Aladdin ranked second, with $217.4 million; and *Beauty and the Beast* ranked seventh, grossing $145.9 million. See Thomas King, "Creative but Unpolished Top Executive for Hire," *Wall Street Journal,* August 26, 1994, p. B1.

15. Elizabeth Bell, Lynda Haas, and Laura Sells, "Walt's in the Movies," in Bell, Haas, and Sells, eds., *From Mouse to Mermaid* (Bloomington: Indiana University Press, 1995), p. 3.

16. The celebrations of Walt Disney are too numerous to mention in detail, but an early example is Bob Thomas, *Walt Disney: An American Original* (New York: Simon and Schuster, 1976). Thomas's book followed on the heels of a scathing attack on Disney by Richard Schickel, *The Disney Version* (New York: Simon and Schuster, 1968). A more recent version of the no-holds-barred critique of Disney is Carl Hiassen, *Team Rodent: How Disney Devours the World* (New York: Ballantine, 1998). The more moderate position is Steven Watts, *The Magic Kingdom* (New York: Houghton Mifflin, 1998). Schickel's book is one of the best critiques of Disney.

17. Barbara Foley, "Subversion and Oppositionality in the Academy," in Maria-Regina Kecht, ed., *Pedagogy Is Politics: Literary Theory and Critical Teaching* (Urbana: University of Illinois Press, 1992), p. 79. See also Roger I. Simon, "Forms of Insurgency in the Production of Popular Memories,'" in Henry A. Giroux and Peter McLaren, eds., *Between Borders: Pedagogy and the Politics of Cultural Studies* (New York: Routledge, 1994).

18. A number of authors address Disney's imagined landscape as a place of economic and cultural power. See, for example, Zukin, *Landscapes of Power*; Michael Sorkin, "Disney World: The Power of Facade/the Facade of Power," in Sorkin, ed., *Variations on a Theme Park* (New York: Noonday, 1992); and see the especially impressive Stephen M. Fjellman, *Vinyl Leaves: Walt Disney World and America* (Boulder, Colo.: Westview, 1992).

19. In his brilliant book, Norman M. Klein argues that Disney constructed his expanded cartoons as a form of animated consumer memory. As Klein puts it, "The atmospheric lighting of Disney epic cartoons is very similar to the reverie of shopping, to shopping arcades, even to the permanent dusk of a room illuminated by television. It takes us more to the expanded shopping mall than a planned suburb, to a civilization based on consumer memories more than urban (or suburban) locations. . . . Disney showed us how to stop thinking of a city as residential or commercial, but rather as airbrushed streets in our mind's eye, a shopper's nonscape. If we can make a city remind us of animated consumer memory, it removes the alienation of changing cities, and replaces it with a cloud of imaginary store windows." *7 Minutes: The Life and Death of the American Animated Cartoon* (London: Verso, 1993, reprinted in 1998), p. 144.

20. The term "marketplace of culture" comes from Richard de Cordova, "The Mickey in Macy's Window: Childhood Consumerism and Disney Animation," in Eric Smoodin, ed., *Disney Discourse,* p. 209. Disney was one of the first companies to tie the selling of toys to the consuming of movies. Challenging the assumption that toy consumption was limited to seasonal sales, Disney actively created Mickey Mouse Clubs, advertised its toys in storefront windows, and linked its movies directly to the distribution of children's toys.

21. Richard Corliss, "The Mouse that Roars," *Time,* June 20, 1994, p. 59.

22. Richard Turner, "Walt Disney Presents: Forward to the Future," *Wall Street Journal,* August 26, 1994, p. B1.

23. Sallie Hofmeister, "In the Realm of Marketing, the 'Lion King' Rules," *New York Times,* July 12, 1994, p. D1.

24. Moira McCormick, "'Hunchback' Soundtrack Tie-ins Abound," *Billboard,* May 25, 1996, p. 10.

25. Robert W. McChesney, *Corporate Media and the Threat to Democracy* (New York: Seven Stories Press, 1997), pp. 20-21.

26. For a summation of the merchandising avalanche that accompanied the movie theater version of *The Lion King,* see Hofmeister, "In the Realm of Marketing."

27. Karen Schoemer,. "An Endless Stream of Magic and Moola," *Newsweek,* September 5, 1994, p. 47.

28. Tom McNichol, "Pushing 'Pocahontas,'" *USA Weekend,* June 9–11, 1995, p. 4.

29. Tony Bennett touches on this issue through an explication of the concept of reading formation. He argues, "The concept of reading formation is an attempt to think of context as a set of discursive and inter-textual determinations, operating on material and institutional supports, which bear in upon a text not just externally, from the outside in, but internally, shaping it—in the historically concrete forms in which it is available as a text-to-be-read—from the inside out." "Texts in History: The Determinations of Readings and Their Texts," in Derek Atridge et al., eds., *Poststructuralism and the Question of History* (Cambridge: Cambridge University Press, 1987), p. 72.

30. Critiques of Disney's portrayal of girls and women can be found in Bell, Haas, and Sells, eds., *From Mouse to Mermaid;* Susan White, "Split Skins: Female Agency and Bodily Mutilation in *The Little Mermaid,*" in Jim Collins, Hilary Radner, and Ava Preacher Collins, eds., *Film Theory Goes to the Movies* (New York: Routledge, 1993), pp. 182–95.

31. Bonnie J. Leadbeater and Gloria Lodato Wilson, "Flipping Their Fins for a Place to Stand: 19th- and 20th-Century Mermaids," *Youth and Society* 27:4 (1993), pp. 466–86.

32. Susan Jefford, *Hard Bodies: Hollywood Masculinity in the Reagan Era* (New Brunswick: Rutgers University Press, 1994), p. 150.

33. Janet Maslin, "Disney Turns to a Warrior of the East in 'Mulan.'" *New York Times,* June 19, 1998, p. B10.

34. I thank Valerie Janesick for this insight.

35. June Casagrande, "The Disney Agenda," *Creative Loafing,* March 17-23, 1994, pp. 6–7.

36. Upon its release in 1946, *Song of the South* was condemned by the National Association of the Advancement of Colored People for its racist representations.

37. For a historical context in which to understand Frontierland, see Fjellman, *Vinyl Leaves.*

38. These racist episodes are highlighted in Wiener, "Tall Tales and True."

39. Richard Scheinin, "Angry over 'Aladdin,'" *Washington Post,* January 10, 1993, p. G5.

40. Howard Green, a Disney spokesperson, dismissed the charges of racism as irrelevant, claiming that such criticisms were coming from a small minority and that "most people were happy" with the film. Scheinin, "Angry over Aladdin."

41. Jack Shaheen, "Animated Racism," *Cineaste* 20:1 (1993), p. 49.

42. Susan Miller and Greg Rode, "The Movie You See, the Movie You Don't: How Disney Do's that Old Time Derision," in Bell, Haas, and Sells, *From Mouse to Mermaid*.

43. Edward Said, *Culture and Imperialism* (New York: Knopf, 1993).

44. Susan Willis, "Fantasia: Walt Disney's Los Angeles Suite," *Diacritics* 17 (Summer 1987), pp. 83–96.

45. George Gerbner, Larry Gross, Michael Borgan, and Nancy Signorielli, "Growing Up with Television: The Cultivation Perspective," in Jennings Bryant and Dolf Zillmann, eds., *Media Effects: Advances in Theory and Research* (Hillsdale, N.J.: Erlbaum 1995), p. 17.

46. See, for instance, Andrew Hart, ed., *Teaching the Media: International Perspectives* (Hillsdale, N.J.: Erlbaum, 1998).

47. David Buckingham, "Conclusion: Re-Reading Audiences," in David Buckingham, ed., *Reading Audiences: Young People and the Media* (Manchester, U.K.: Manchester University Press, 1993), p. 211.

48. Cited in Zukin, *Landscapes of Power,* p. 222. While this quotation refers to Disney's view of its theme parks, it is an ideological view of history that shapes all of Disney's cultural productions. For a comment on how this view affects Disney's rendering of adult films, see Henry A. Giroux, *Disturbing Pleasures: Learning Popular Culture* (New York: Routledge, 1994), esp. pp. 25–45.

49. Fjellman, *Vinyl Leaves*, p. 400.

50. Rustom Bharacuha, "Around Ayodhya: Aberrations, Enigmas, and Moments of Violence," *Third Text,* no. 24 (Autumn 1993), p. 51.

51. Bennett, "Texts in History," p. 80.

52. Smoodin, "How to Read Walt Disney," pp. 4–5.

53. Mark Crispin Miller, "Free the Media," *Nation,* June 3, 1996, pp. 9–15.

54. For an example of such an analysis, see Stanley Aronowitz, *Roll over Beethoven* (Middletown: Wesleyan University Press, 1993); Giroux, *Disturbing Pleasures.*

55. Inderpal Grewal and Caren Kaplan, "Introduction: Transnational Feminist Practices and Questions of Postmodernity," in Inderpal Grewal and Caren Kaplan, eds., *Scattered Hegemonies* (Minneapolis: University of Minnesota Press, 1994).

Questions for Discussion

1. In the opening paragraph of this selection, Giroux comments that at one time he "accepted the largely unquestioned assumption that animated films stimulate the imagination and fantasy, create a feeling of innocence and healthy adventure, and in general are 'good' for kids." Despite this

opinion, Giroux goes on to critique Disney films, perhaps the most technologically and aesthetically advanced in the industry. Why? What elements of these films does he critique? In what ways are they problematic, according to Giroux?

2. Giroux argues, in part, that the power of the Disney appeal is a result of the unparalleled skill of the "imagineers," that Disney films are successful means of manipulation because of their technological achievement. The apparent transparency of the films hides racism, sexism, and an "anti-democratic ethos." Reflect on the specific evidence Giroux provides to support his claim. Extend his argument to other Disney films or other films intended for children. In what ways do the claims Giroux makes apply to these other films?

3. Take a close look at the way that Giroux constructs his argument. What are the parts of it? How are those parts put together? When, for example, does he concede Disney's aesthetic effectiveness? Why do you believe he made that particular strategic decision? In what ways does Giroux anticipate this audience's position and/or construct his arguments to meet their needs or expectations?

Explorations

1. David Theo Goldberg has commented that Giroux "links the cultural messages promoted by Disney Inc. to the corporate economy, exploitative and exclusionary practices it at once represents and pushes." What kinds of evidence does Giroux provide to illustrate his claims of exploitation and exclusion?

2. The immense entertainment value of Disney productions, combined with the innocent subject matter of its films, form a transparent form of valuing. Giroux, in response, encourages viewers to question the "diverse messages that constitute Disney's conservative view of the world." What, according to Giroux, are some of the elements of this world view? Comment in your exploration on the Disney corporate culture beyond film (e.g., theme parks, planned communities).

3. Animated films, Giroux claims, are the "new 'teaching machines'" because they teach children about "roles, values, and ideals" even more effectively than "more traditional sites of learning." Compose an informal response in which you explore the impact of film on your cultural education. What have films taught you? In what ways have films articulated your understanding of your roles, values, and ideals?

Formal Writing Assignments

1. Our "public visual space," Giroux argues, is not free from "ideology, politics, and power." Like other sites—homes and universities—the public sphere is saturated with competing ideologies and belief systems. Select another cultural text, institution, or medium (e.g., advertising billboards, Nickelodeon television) and discuss and analyze the means by which it presents and packages its messages.

2. Giroux focuses in particular on the treatments and representations of race, gender, and democracy in Disney films. Compose an essay in which you briefly summarize his claims about these issues and then extend his arguments to encompass other more recent Disney films. Do these films continue the pattern identified by Giroux? If so, in what ways? If not, in what ways have Disney films changed to address substantively, Giroux's claims?

Call and Response: Sports, Talk Radio, and the Death of Democracy

David Theo Goldberg

As Director of the School of Justice Studies at Arizona State University, David Theo Goldberg oversees interdisciplinary undergraduate and graduate programs related to law and social justice in U.S. society. In those programs, as in "Call and Response," Goldberg focuses attention on gender, race, economics, and class in the public sphere. He has also published extensively on race, ethics, social issues, Jewish identity, multiculturalism, and postcolonialism. One of his most recent books, *Ethical Theory and Social Issues: Historical Texts and Contemporary Readings,* is a college text intended for courses in which students examine ethics from both historical and contemporary perspectives, using their knowledge to examine such issues as AIDS, hate speech, affirmative action, and capital punishment.

"Call and Response: Sports, Talk Radio, and the End of Democracy" appears in David Sladen and Rita Whillock's *Soundbite Culture: The Death of Discourse in a Wired World.*

Writing Before Reading

1. Take a quick look at the title of Goldberg's essay: "Sports, Talk Radio, and the Death of Democracy." Knowing that Goldberg writes frequently about race, gender, and class, what predictions would you make about his approach to the subject of sports and talk radio?

2. If you've ever listened to sports radio, take a few minutes to describe it. Who calls in? What kinds of callers are most appreciated by hosts? What are the rules of engagement? What are the topics of discussion?

3. Make some generalizations about the kinds of people who attend sporting events. Your goal is not to stereotype but to work conscientiously from your own experiences to create a kind of demographic profile of the kinds of people who attend sporting events. (You may even want to compare and contrast fans of different sports.)

Call and Response: Sports, Talk Radio, and the Death of Democracy

Dog Dayz

Midweek morning rush hour. Car radio tuned to the talking head haute culture of NPR morning news, the highway of informed democracy. Volume turned up hard enough to be heard above the air-conditioning humdrum, drowning out the dissonance of a disinformed public as it washes out the surround-sound traffic noise. The self-encasement that keeps democracy safe, (public) radio as privat(ized) consumption. Alone in and with my-world-in-22-minutes, as rubber rocks the road.

Static, then silence. The digital display blinks blank. Panic stations. This is *not* a test of the Emergency Broadcasting System. The mediated thoughts that fill my mind about current events dissolve along with the radio signal. The radio, my mind and word-world, democracy, at once at risk. Noise swirls about as cars swish by, horns honk, jets vaporize overhead, men curse, sirens scream, rock and roll of all the insults thumps in from someone else's car audio. There's something wrong with my radio, goddammit. Fiddling frantically with the dial doesn't help any. I inadvertently knock the AM button. The drone that before had split the silence of an informed public radio audience is displaced by the shrill shrieking of local talk. My dial is fixed on AM! Top of the morning to the meat market of ideas in America, Democracy Inc.

A psychoanalyst friend once insightfully suggested to me, as I prepared to drive from Philadelphia to Phoenix, that I would have no better sense of place, of the vast differences in (between) America, than to listen to AM radio on the road. Local is to radio what states rights are to federalism. On more waves than one, I was about to discover how right my doctor of the unconscious was.

Lost on the AM airwaves, I sampled each station. Talk radio: political, religious, do-it-yourself psychology, more local politics, Randy Weaver talks with the local Viper militia, more local religion, CBS oldies nostalgia (postmodernism lives even—especially—on local radio), more griping, more religion.

Radio On

And then . . . then sports talk. Talking about sports. Twenty-four hours. If the spanking new stadia that mark cities are the new cathedrals (a town doesn't get to be a city, isn't marked on the map, without one, as I've argued elsewhere), sports radio is the bully pulpit, the MTV of/for sports. Call and response in the church of athletic self-opinion. MTV sells as it entertains, markets as it broadcasts. So, too, sports talk radio. It announces, informs, pontificates, moralizes, politicizes, commercializes, and commodifies— as it entertains. It should come as no surprise, then, that MTV Sports should be a popular prime-time Monday evening program hosted by none other than Scott Ferrall, the Dennis Rodman of sports talk radio. Ferrall is the quintessential Gen-Xer who speaks a mile a minute with a raspy gargling in an ironic "I-don't-give-a-fuck" in-your-face self-promoting style. In a nod to the ratings effects of surface social consciousness, he growls, "Get involved, get deep, go up the mountain to Lake Tahoe to support the snowboarders' benefit for breast cancer. It'll make you feel good." No doubt, you've got a four-wheel drive and a Working Assets car phone calling card to take you to a freedom winter mountaintop. This is a feel-good social consciousness, pleasure as im-politic(s).

Sports talk radio, as talk radio generally, is all about entertainment. Yesteryear's sports radio was principally concerned with play-by-play, player and team stats, the season's progress. Radio days: Take me out to the ball game even if I can't actually go. This function has been taken over in any case by ESPN. For sports talk radio, the romance with numbers counts only superficially if at all. Today, sports talk radio concerns itself overwhelmingly, if not exclusively, as an arena for voicing opinion—about sports, of course, but about sports as a surrogate for almost anything. Sports talk radio is both symbol and expression of the "democratizing" of opinion, equal opportunity beliefs, evidence or its lack notwithstanding. Shout, shout, let it all out, these are the things we're thinking (and not thinking) about. If I can vent more entertainingly than the next guy, if I can shout louder and longer (and what better training than being a sports fan), I'm king not for a day but for my 15 seconds of self-elevated and self-promoting fame Jim Rome, Mad Dog Russo, and Scott Ferrall have made their reputations on that stage, the kings of sports talk rap. Howard Stern meets The Last Poets, Rush reaching out to touch Geraldo. Good callers give good phone, imitating the style (if not the substance) of their hosts. Even if the unfed baby is screaming for food in the background. "It's a jungle out there, man." First-time callers be warned: Say something disagreeable, and you're radio-actively flushed down the toilet, thrown through shattering glass, subjected to a drug test, even shot. Click, you're off the air, baby. Life's over. Your 15-second soapbox just got swept away. Democratic consumption calls for public sphere police officers.

Talk radio is marked by class. Public radio in the talking head formats represents the intellectually inclined, upmarket, and somewhat more fiberally oriented audience. Here, Diane Reams (in political reverse) is to public radio what Cornel West or Noam Chomsky are to C-Span, the exception that proves the rule. By contrast, AM talk radio reaches (out to) a more conservative, white male clientele. In 1960, only two radio stations—KABC in Los Angeles and KMOX in St. Louis—were devoted to talk formats. Through the 1960s, AM turned increasingly to talk as the explosion of rock and roll enabled the transmission muscle of FM to dominate music stations. Talk radio stations mushroomed in the 1980s, prompted by a confluence of inexpensive satellite capabilities, deregulation, sophisticated niche marketing, and dramatic localism spurred by growing antistatist sentiments. In a single decade, talk radio stations quadrupled remarkably to 800. This represents a new talk station every 4 or 5 days! That's a whole lot of jawing going on.

By 1996, more than 4,000 talk shows were on 1,200 stations and networks, a more than tenfold increase in less than two decades. Today, talk radio "captures" one fifth of the male audience over age 18, mainly middle and working class. In 1994, 20 million people were rushing each week to laugh along with Limbaugh on 659 stations. Talk radio listeners and participants are largely men who, in the midterm elections of 1994 (and probably still), tended (significantly more so than women listeners) to vote Republican, disaffected Reagan-Rush acolytes. Between 5% and 10% of the African American audience tune in to talk radio, mostly to shows offered on the 189 black-owned stations. Interestingly enough, white and black men listen to talk radio in roughly the same proportions (about 20% of each group), although listening to talk radio has no demonstrable bearing on African American male voting patterns in the ways it has on white male voting patterns (Coleman, 1996). Talk radio, to refashion William Rusher's (1995) characterization only slightly, has become a white male "conservative precinct" (Bolce, DeMaio, & Muzzio, 1996; Hutchby, 1992; Page & Tannenbaum, 1996).

Class of the '90s

Sports talk radio likewise is all about class formation, even as it represents itself as classless—as class blind or class transcendent. How could it escape class formation in a market where 7-year contracts run from $50m to $120m, where a 21-year-old golfer earns $40m on a promise before winning a professional tournament from a company able to pay him only because its product is made by those it barely pays at all. And yet, the audience for sports talk radio ranges from the un- or under- or lowly-employed at one end of contemporary class structure to the beeper/cellular phone/beamer generation at the other. By the mid-1990s, there were 100 24-hour sports talk stations: all sports talk, all the time. There are sports talk stations that serve sports franchises, cheerleading owners' commitments, apologists for "what it takes" for a franchise to get a city to subsidize its activities (a new stadium or arena, downtown revitalization, sales tax subsidy, selling the public on a trade of popular players). KMVP in Phoenix, the new CBS affiliate, for instance, is user friendly to Jerry Colangelo, mega sports overlord of the Phoenix Suns (basketball), the Phoenix Coyotes (hockey, formerly the Winnipeg Jets), the Arizona Diamondbacks (the expansion baseball team), and the Arizona Rattlers (Arena football team). Not only do these radio stations broadcast franchise games, but the likes of Al McCoy ("voice" of the Suns) and Greg Schulte ("voice" of the Diamondbacks) run regular daytime byline commentaries, homeboy Peter Vecseys or Frank Giffords. Radio callers here tend to be the cellular phone clientele, wishful clients or hopeful subcontractors, community partners or sky box inhabitants of their "home" teams.

Downmarket, by contrast, one finds (I think more interestingly) sports radio talking to and for, about and with, the little guy, sewing him into the seamless web of American consumptive practice, giving him a place he can call his own while dropping a buck in its name. The bleacher bums (Whoopi's whooping

Eddie, the dawg pound masochists, collars and all), pooling resources for pay-per-view simulcasts where tickets for the game are out of reach. More vocally opinionated, more locally knowledgeable than the coach about the team's woes, longer suffering than anyone should be and still prepared to pay for it. The quintessential Cubs or Cleveland Browns fan. Upscale audio, down to earth radio; man in the car talking to himself on his car phone (never a moment alone), man in the street ranting at anyone who will listen (forced by circumstance to be alone); "good guy" radio, "bad dude" radio. Brent Musberger and Mad Dog.

Pamela Haag, nevertheless (or precisely consequently), thinks there is something inherently democratizing about sports talk radio, for she thinks it fashions civil talk in public space as an alternative to "hate radio," as well as giving local color to the all but hegemonic "corporate voice" of media representation: playful offense in the face of both hate speech and humor less homogenized commercialized blandness. Local living color rather than nationally syndicated sameness, civil disagreement rather than anarchic militia disobedience, playful projection rather than put-upon politics. Giving in to the thin romance of the local in the face of the homogeneity of the multinational, Haag concludes that sports talk radio fulfills people's desires to be "thrown together in unexpected, impassioned, even random social relations and communities." They do? No segregation in this vision. Folks want "to mix with people they have nothing (but sports) in common with. They want to be *from* somewhere again, to be part of a heterogeneous tribe rather than a narrowly defined political cabal" (Haag, 1996, p. 467). Across class, irrespective of race, against the grain of gender. That's a different sports talk radio than the one I'm stuck with.

Haag's romantic longing suggests a telling point, although not quite the one she has in mind to project. Sports is productive of a sort of *uni*formity, and sports talk radio helps fashion it. Uniforms encourage, enable, establish sameness, identity, and identification. They throw together almost indistinguishably the large and small, fat and thin, dark and fair, large-chested and lanky, fat cats and working stiffs, high rollers and the tightfisted. The magnification of sports in our culture thus has massive ramifications for democracy, although otherwise than in the idealized sense Haag would have it. Public sphere exchange is mediated through the trading off of commitments to sports franchises, endless debates about who's better than whom, who should be MVP, who "belongs" in the Hall of Fame. In the end, it adds up now to little more than the commitment to purchase marketed merchandise, to root for the same team no matter how exploitative of fan sentimentality. The professional sports franchises in cities, owned by mega-capital conglomerate interests, establish their indispensability to civic life by fabricating the consciousness that they are "your Chicago Bulls/Phoenix Suns/New York Knicks/etc." This enacts at once a team loyalty exhibited through the purchase of a team T-shirt or baseball cap. We're all dancing to the same tune here, watching the same cheerleading dancers high-stepping, dressed identically, shouting in unison, "Let's go . . . !" "De-fense!" We're closer here to the mass psychology of fascism with a human face than to a democratic public sphere.

Sports talk radio plays a central role in producing this uniformity—a uniformity in style of expression, of opinion, of team support. Giving away team T-shirts and caps, tickets and corporate promotions. Getting fans to line up behind team players and chemistry, product development and consumption, trades and waivers, benchings and discipline, rationalization and exoneration through individualized charities that cover (up) for corporate profits. Something is abstractly ethno-nationalistic about the enterprise. Supporting one's team today has taken the place of what it was once like supporting one's country, right or wrong. Sports talk radio is the propaganda machine of the new fan-aticism.

The demographic and commercial makeup of professional sports in America has always reflected, as it has reified, prevailing social relations. Think of Jesse Owens or Joe Louis in 1936, the Negro League and the Women's League, Jackie Robinson and President Truman's desegregation of the military, free agency and deregulation, affirmative action and Al Campanis. Why should sports be any (in)different now? And why should sports talk radio make a social difference, rather than represent prevailing social relations? Sports reflects the divide between rich and poor; the stylized and improvisational; the incessant commercialized shifting of the fashionable required by commodified professionalism in the face of the necessary repetition of the everyday; the physically demanding, aggressive violence of daily life hidden behind the veneer of an exhilarating, breathtaking aesthetic beauty; the rule-bound, repetitive, task-oriented nature of so much in late modern life in the face of the entrepreneurial need to push the limits, break the bounds, defy regularity, the norm(al), the law(s) of nature). Made for and imitative of, yet imitated by, television. Sport imitates life, which ironically has come to follow the lead of sports fashion.

We are encouraged by sports and sports talk to remember the winners and stars, and we forget all too quickly the role players and losers (this latter word itself drips pejoratively off the tongues of sports radio hosts: In a world where winner takes all, we couldn't be caught losing, now, could we?). The star phenomenon individualizes sport, hiding the collective efforts of producing competitiveness (even in the case of radically individualized giants like Muhammad Ali, or Carl Lewis, Michael Johnson or Michael Jordan, FloJo or Martina), elevating the pleasures of success while deriding the pains of their preparation, dismissing all too quickly the disappointments of their failures, blind to the hidden costs of life in retirement as the smile of the professional spotlight fades too often to a grimace of a life faced with physical suffering. Muhammad Ali has been resurrected in the public eye only now that his politics are deemed no longer relevant.

Men/to/Ring Boyz, Airing Race

Talk on sports radio ranges across the political, more than occasionally explicitly about race in sports, always implicitly about race in America. And it invariably represents men's interests. For example, the local sports talk downmarket station runs a weekly segment, "What's Your Beef?" encouraging callers to gripe, not just about sports and sports character concerns, but about "anything" and "anyone" in one's life one might want to chew or stew upon. This furnishes, in other words, a forum for letting, off steam, for venting venom(ously). It effectively opens a channel for the performativity of angry white males (who are overwhelmingly its performers). "The worst thing a woman can have is lip hair." "Women should not be allowed to broadcast men's sports." "Women's professional basketball, what a joke. You wouldn't catch me dead watching it." Sports talk radio provides a covert political stage for those who think of themselves as nonpolitical or (what in the age of self-proclaimed political correctness amounts to the same thing) as politically disenfranchised. Like Limbaugh, though more discretely, sports talk radio enables white men to express themselves white and male.

David Roediger (1996) remarks, in an interesting read of Rush Limbaugh's cultural resonance in America, that "banality can carry much more social power than genius where white consciousness is concerned" (p. 42). Whiteness silently produces and reproduces itself behind the vocality of loudmouthed, flaccid ranting. Sports talk similarly enacts its whiteness through the banal, no longer through the micro details of sports statistics (in itself banal enough, though relatively harmless) but via the disputational and contentious, the licensed arrogance of self-opinionated expression where anything goes so long as one is heard to say it forcefully and angrily enough. Sports radio discussion overwhelmingly infantilized concerns raised about Fuzzy Zoeller's disparately arrogant references to Tiger Woods as "that little boy" likely to serve "fried chicken and collard greens" at the "green jacket dinner" in the wake of Woods's record-breaking win at the Augusta Masters, dismissing them as choices of the politically correct unable (once again) to take a joke. No surprise that no mention was made of the Internet appearance soon after of the call to boycott K-mart because, by dropping Zoeller as its spokesman in the wake of his remarks about Woods, the chain had chosen to cater to a "black clientele," thereby ignoring the interests of whites. By contrast, two local hosts on the sports station that for a while ran a daily segment of Howard Stern's morning show spent all hour talking about the virtues for men of tight-fitting but uncomfortable women's lingerie. Sports talk is to radio what the Wide World of Wrestling is to television. These are marriages made at the polls of the lowest common denominator of whitemaleness.

503

Men invest in mediated sports as a down payment on the (reproduced) pervasiveness of male domination. It is obviously not that all men are better than all women in sports, only that the best male athletes on the established physical criteria outstrip the best women. And this is the point: Men's investment in spectator sports accordingly becomes investment in their own projected superiority through the superiority of the best athletes (who "just happen to be" men) (Messner, 1989). Sports talk radio facilitates this (masculine) self-elevation, the ideological reproduction of hegemonyrisk- and cost-free but for the price of the toll call.

A caller the other day to Jim Rome's "In the Jungle" trashed what he called "the Trailgangsters"—referring to the off court criminal troubles of the Portland Trailblazers—for "all they can beat up is women." Notice the rhetorical force of *all* here, which effeminizes "the Trailgangsters" even as it demonizes them for physically assaulting women (as one of the team members was, in fact, accused). Another caller to another program positively gushed, "My estimation of Marv Albert [NBC basketball play-by-play analyst accused of assaulting a woman in a hotel room, biting her repeatedly, forcing her to commit fellatio, and then sodomizing her] just went up." The caller indicated in his remarks that he had hitherto assumed Albert sexually inept, a conclusion he had derived with impeccable logic from the "fact" of Albert's supposed (self-evident, it seems) toupee. Apparently, Albert hadn't heeded the exhortation, in this caller's estimate, of the ads run regularly on all sports talk radio stations to seek out (the presidency of) The Men's Hair Club. The charge of sexual abuse, its innuendo, is payment sufficient for white men to offset the sin of (covering up) baldness (black men apparently don't need to, as they "clearly" have no hair to speak of, as evidenced by the likes of Michael Jordan and Charles Barkley).

Behind the projection of masculinity here obviously lurks race. Many of the best, the most high-profile athletes in the most high-profile sports are—or at least are considered to be—people of color, as the euphemism would have it, whereas the players—hosts and callers alike—in sports talk radio are almost invariably white men. (The one very notable exception among sports talk hosts is the Fabulous Sports Babe, Nanci Donnellan, the dominatrix of sports talk; she who knows more and kicks butt harder than her competitors.) Here we find risk-free identification with the superiority of black men in sports—the action-at-a-distance of being born-to-it assumption—while rhetorically reenacting technologically and technophonically that segregating divide of black folk residentially, educationally, socioeconomically, and culturally marking America throughout the 20th century.

Sports talk has become a leading forum for expressing "whitemaleness." Whitemaleness traditionally has taken itself as the arbiter of rationality, of intelligence, reduced impotently to reflecting on and about what signifies overwhelmingly as physical activity. Sports talk manifests a peculiar version of this. Isaiah Thomas complained at the beginning of the 1990s about white basketball commentators gushing on about "the genius" of white players, whereas black talent was characterized merely as physically gifted. Everyone "knows" that "white men can't jump," so they must cut it through superior intelligence and work ethic. In this context, sports talk radio mediates the racialized gaze on the (black) body in and through sports. A colleague, a self-declared radical feminist, once blurted out in my company, "Oh, Shawn Kemp, he's gorgeous, from the neck down." Sports talk radio enables white men to imagine the black body in a sense without being in its presence, unthreatened by it racially or homoerotically, unchallenged by the sexuality projected onto it imaginatively by the racialized fantasies of ("their") white women. In that sense, Dennis Rodman's cross-dressing is radical, certainly more risky—as it is more risqué—than the safety of the reflexive metatalk about it on sports talk radio by the likes of Scott Ferrall. Rodman's performance in acting out or up expresses the audacity of speaking back, for which he inevitably gets endlessly spoken about—paraded and oddly parroted—by radio talkers and stalkers.

Interpellated Selves, Invisible Subjects

Sports has become not only big business but also the arbiter of fashion, and fashion increasingly has been set/led by black stylin'. The baggy shorts craze that has swept youthful America leapt first from the street of black youths into high fashion projected by the antics of Michigan Wolverines' Fab Five and kid rappers Kris Kross. Sports crosses over commercially with rap in the bank account of the Shaq Attack. The market meets the street, where "the street" floats signifyin'ly between the sign for the stock market ("Wall St.") and the culture of hip hop, the former an investment in being "up," the latter in being "down." Whitemaleness finds a place for self-expression through fandom, the market of youthful parents and their doted kids with disposable cash in hand and the mentorship of fan-aticism, through consumptive apparel. I recently sat next to a father and his 8-year-old son at a Phoenix Suns game. The child, sporting the mandatory Kevin Johnson vest, quietly sipped on a soft drink and munched tacos through much of the game, until late in the fourth quarter when, buoyed by his father's increasingly aggressive support for the team, he began screaming in tune with his dad. Here in the flesh, I thought, I was witnessing sports (talk radio's) interpellating power at work. Sports radio fashions a clientele, filling the unconscious with desires less and less of its own making. It molds subjects as seekers of spectatorial excitement, instantaneous gratification, consumers of newly fashioned and packaged merchandise, releasing expressions of commitment the force of which leave the cool reflectiveness of a thoughtful democracy in the public sphere quite chilled (out). Sport is the perfect medium for this fanatical consumptive power. It is all about winners and losers, excitability and excitement, releasing nervous energy that is at once manic yet for the most part socially controllable. It is unpredictable within predictable parameters, sensuously stimulating, open almost constantly to new configuration, therefore perfectly conducive to fashionable commodification and commodifiable fashion.

Beyond this, sport and sports talk radio have proved conducive also—a medium well fitted—to the "advancement" of the new racism over the past two decades: racist expression coded as race neutrality, racialized exclusions as color blindness, racist discrimination as market choices, as commodity preferences. If I fanatically support a team that is all black, how can I be racist in trashing welfare state policies? Indeed, my freedom to support that team is identical to my preference against welfare for anybody. It "just happens to be" that the racially marginalized lose out by welfare divestment. Racial neutrality is sustained only by historical amnesia, political erasure, and moral ignorance. The public disinvestment in the welfare state means I have more disposable cash in hand to spend on my team's merchandise, should I so choose. It's a win-win situation, only by virtue of rendering the losers invisible. We never hear their voices on democratically arranged sports talk radio.

Anne McClintock (1995, pp. 31–36) demonstrates the late 19th-century shift that emerged in dominant forms of racist expression from scientific racism to commodity racism. *Commodity racism* manifests in consumer spectacles: advertising, expositions, museum exhibitions. It could be added that today commodity racism finds its principal expression in and through the hyperconsumptive spectacle of sports. Sports sneakers like Nike promote their market superiority through the physical prowess of their overwhelmingly black sports superstars. The megasalaries associated with the racialized bodies of sports heroes hide from view the exploitative conditions marking racialized bodies elsewhere that precisely make such spectacular salaries possible. At the height of the controversy over Nike's exploitative labor practices in Indonesia and Vietnam, sports talk callers to a person dissed the concern: "Those countries should do something about it if they are so concerned, but they're getting good jobs. . . . It's not happening in America, so who cares." We might call this, without too much conceptual twisting, "commodity neo-colonialism." At the same time, the whiteness of sports talk radio is reflected in the music it advertises: Clapton, the Eagles, Country, as its class commitments are reflected in commercials for the likes of Sears and Home Depot.

Racialized commodity neo-colonialism hides in good part behind the feel-good color blindness of sports talk hosts: "We don't care whether someone is white, black, yellow, pink, or green." Color may not matter, but race surely does. So Scott Ferrall growls menacingly that Patrick Ewing's nostrils are wide enough for a basketball to fit. Sufficiently conscious that he has silently invoked the "r" word in a way that might get his radio balloon popped, he quickly adds, "This is not a race thing, it's a nose thing." Must be the nose thing that allows him to play so well, huh. Perhaps he can take in more air, thus allowing him to elevate more easily in the drive to the rim. I now understand that it's the aerodynamics of the nose, not the Nikes, that explain how black men get to jump so high. This is not so far a cry from the restaurant remarks about slavery and thigh bones that got Jimmy the Greek fired from CBS Sports.

Fanatic Communities

Talk radio creates new communities, or at the least the artifice of old communities anew. *Sports* talk radio re-creates the artifice of a white male community of like-minded, like-thinking souls, gated circles of virtual friends whose virtuality is reflected by the abstractness, the irreality of the friendships and the ephemerality, the ethereality, of the community. But irreality and ethereality notwithstanding, it reproduces the artifice, the sense of whitemaleness, by offering if only informally an apparatus of ideological interpellation, the hailing to be part of a subjectivity larger than oneself, a member of a body (politic) enactive of (self-)elevation and (social) mobility via racialized and (en)gendered exclusions.

This is, if only by indirection, the death of civil discourse, of a discourse of civility, as social control through fan–aticism takes over. It is prescient in this context to note that there is more on-field/on-court/on-ice violence in American sport than there is among fans. And noteworthy as well, the altogether white sport of ice hockey has shown such growth in fan and sports radio support. Against this icy uncool background, I end by emphasizing that "I love this game" reduces all too quickly to "Life is a game. Play hard." Life is sport, as (my) sport is life (on the whole, "I'd rather be . . ."). Winner takes all. No fear. As long as the Dow is climbing, my team's winning, my mutual funds are soaring. I can retire to . . . the living room to watch the next world final whatever. Drinking Miller Lite or Bud, eating nachos or tacos, my newest model Nikes thumping the couch, the fantasy of my leased Lexis or Nissan in the garage, the car audio and cellular phone safely out of reach of all those nonwhite vultures I see on *Cops* (when I'm watching sport of another kind), who if they didn't make it into professional sports are prowling my streets looking to commit a crime. And the homeless are not camped outside my suburban home, not selling their newspaper on my highway to work, not raiding my garbage can, not living off the tax I'm no longer paying. Talk radio makes me just do it, at least in the intervals when television isn't gripping me.

Ahh, Our America. A commercial time-out for the dream (on) team. I believe I can fly, I believe I can touch the sky. Lite me up another. Life is good. Don't worry, be happy. I love what you do for me. Enjoy the ride.

As the game fades noisily to black. Welcome to the real terrordome.

Author's Note

I thank my colleagues Gray Cavender and David Altheide for their helpful suggestions in thinking about sport and talk radio, and my research assistant Sam Michalowski for knowing the score.

Notes

1. KMVP recently took over sports from KTAR, now a 24-hour talk radio format, hiring many of the latter's sports personnel, no doubt, with the blessing of the father figure. KMVP has stations in major sports markets nationwide, the sports talk version of AutoNation. Wayne Huizenga's "blockbuster" new "discount" auto franchise. Huizenga owns the Miami Dolphins (football), the Florida Marlins (baseball), and the Florida Panthers (hockey) teams in three of the four major league professional sports covering the country's third largest television market. Colangelo and Huizenga are to sports perhaps what Turner and Murdoch are to broadcasting. They represent the new entrepreneurship in the rapidly expanding southern/southwestern demographic markets of Arizona and Florida, respectively. They offer to late modernity what Ford once made available to the immigrant *driven* expansion into the Midwest, or Mayer and Selznick to the movie industry, capturing the popular imagination of their times.

2. Cerullo, Ruane, and Chayko (1992) make out a similar line of argument regarding talk radio more generally—namely, that it offers "technological ties that bind," "time efficient ways to enjoy social interaction," a perfect form of community for the times. Similarly, Bolce, DeMaio, and Muzzio (1996) suggest the emergence of a "hyper-" version of "cyberdemocracy": "Talk radio can create instantaneous communities of coexistent interest and passion over continental distances."

References

Bolce, L., DeMaio, G., & Muzzio. D. (1990). Dial-in-democracy: Talk radio and the 1994 election. *Political Science Quarterly.* 111(3). 457–48 1.

Cerullo, K., Ruane, J., & Chiyko, M. (1992). Technological ties that bind: Media-generated primary groups. *Communication Research,* 19, 102–129.

Coleman, T. (1996). Black talk. *Emerge.* 8(2), 50–57.

Haag. P. (1996). "50,000 watt sports bar": Talk radio and the ethic of the fan. *South Atlantic Quarterly,* 95(2), 453–470.

Hutchby, 1. (1992). The pursuit of controversy: Routine skepticism in talk on "talk radio." *Sociology.* 26(4), 673–694.

McClintock, A. (1995). *Imperial leather: Race, gender, amd sexuality in the colonial contest.* New York: Routledge.

Messner, M. (1989). Masculinities and athletic careers. *Gender & Society,* 3. 71–88.

Page, B., & Tannenbaum, 3. (1996). Populistic deliberation and talk radio. *Journal of Communication,* 46(2), 33–54.

Roediger, D. (1996). White looks: Hairy apes, true stories, and Limbaugh's laughs. *Minnesota Review,* 47.

Rusher, W. (1995). The importance of talk radio. *Newspaper Enterprise Association,* 3.

Questions for Discussion

1. Goldberg uses headings strategically in this essay. In a small group, review the headings and try to determine the allusions Goldberg is making through the headings. Next, determine the relationship between the headings and the material that follows them. Under what kinds of circumstances might you elect to use headings in your own writing?

2. White men make up the majority of listeners of sports talk radio. Why is this the case and what are its potential consequences for U.S. culture?

3. Goldberg points out that the argumentative styles and strategies of callers and hosts are "disputational and contentious," that the speakers are arrogant and "self-opinionated." Sports talk radio, in other words, is a cultural site in which "anything goes so long as one is heard to say it forcefully and angrily enough." This is a style markedly different from the argumentative strategies privileged in the university. Why is it the case that this particular context allows, even demands, a significantly different argumentative style and form?

Explorations

1. Racism, Goldberg argues elsewhere in his work, is far more than hate speech or even stereotyping. It is better understood, he claims, as those relations of power that function to exclude. In what ways can sports talk radio, according to Goldberg, be considered racist? Classist? Sexist?

2. Both Goldberg and Patricia Williams ("Radio Hoods") comment upon how the public space is constructed over the radio waves. Compare and contrast their representations of the communities that form in this virtual space. To what varying uses is the radio put?

3. The racialized body, the bodies of black men, are objectified in sports talk radio while white men, Goldberg argues, construct an ethos through "fandom." Outline Goldberg's understanding of fandom and its impact on spectatorship and consumerism.

Formal Writing Assignments

1. Goldberg, throughout this essay, writes about the relationship between race and sports talk radio. Familiarize yourself with the fine details of his argument and then spend several hours listening to a sports talk radio program seeking examples of the kinds of subtle but insidious racism that infiltrate the conversation. Write up your findings in the form of an informative essay.

2. Identify and write about a forum in which other groups defined generally by race or gender meet—virtually or face to face. In what ways do they use language to include some or exclude others? Compose an essay in which you describe and analyze the language practices and discourses you find at the site. (Internet chat rooms, bulletin boards, or listservs are often informative virtual communities.)

Society Writes Biology

Ruth Herschberger

A native of New York state, Ruth Herschberger has spent her professional life as a poet, playwright, and theatrical producer. Winner of many awards, including the Avery and Jule Hopwood Award in poetry and the Harriet Monroe Memorial Prize of *Poetry Magazine,* Herschberger has been described by Selden Rodman as one of the five most "outstanding woman-poets alive." Hershberger began publishing her work in the 1940s and in 1948, under the pseudonym Josephine Langstaff wrote what was to become her most successful work, *Adam's Rib.* Most recently, Herschberger has turned to investigating the possible relationships between poetry and visual media, including film.

Writing Before Reading

1. The "'hard"sciences—physics and chemistry, for example—are often considered more objective than other disciplines. Spend a few minutes identifying why this is the case. What is it about the hard sciences that make them less vulnerable to interpretation or question?

2. Reflect on a time when you found yourself frustrated by the ways that an author represented facts. How did the person manipulate language? What was the effect of the strategy?

3. When you consider "scientific" discourse, what comes to mind? What elements are most characteristic of scientific discourse?

Society Writes Biology

> well, here's looking at ourselves
> —E. E. Cummings

There is a prevalent belief that scientists are unprejudiced. It is true that they of all citizens make the most stirring attempt at objectivity, but in realms close to the social structure, as in the biological sciences, it is easy for the scientist and popularizer of science to slip into hidden evaluations in their reports on organic fact. If we like their bias, we contentedly ignore it. In accounts of sexual processes, however, there is a painfully persistent tendency to award the female a derogatory role.

By capturing the mood, and an occasional phrase, from various widely selling sex books, we shall piece together a typical account entitled *A Patriarchal Society Writes Biology.* The outstanding device for entering opinion under the guise of objective the other. The male cell acts, voluntarily, yet with a teleological sense of destiny, while the female reacts, involuntarily, taking her cues from him.

For in the patriarchal account, the male sperm is by all odds the central character. We watch his actions with breathless suspense. He is an independent little creature, single-minded, manly, full of charm, resourcefulness and enterprise, who will make his own minute decision to swim toward the egg.

The female egg is portrayed as the blushing bride, ignorant but desirable who awaits arousal by the gallant male cell. The egg, like the human female, is receptive. In most accounts of the physiology of sex, the writer becomes rhapsodic over the relaxed and nutritious condition of the waiting ovum. Since the egg is not known to be capable of self-motion, it is regarded as helpless.

The sperm is the purposeful agent in reproduction; the egg learns direction and purpose only after union with the sperm. Thus the human ovum is a country cousin until entered by the worldly male cell; the human female is only half alive until she is pregnant.

In choice of terms the patriarchal biologist makes liberal use of the word *vestigial,* as applied to any organ in the female which is similar to an organ in the male but not quite like it. The uterus escapes being called a vestigial prostate because it bears sons, but the clitoris has never thrown off the label of vestigial penis.

The patriarchal biologist employs *erection* in regard to male organs and *congestion* for female. Erection of tissue is equivalent to the filling of the local blood vessels, or congestion; but erection is too aggressive-sounding for women. Congestion, being associated with the rushing of blood to areas that have been infected or injured, appears to scientists to be a more adequate characterization of female response.

While robbing us of some of our illusions about father science, the discussion may have a salutary effect upon poets, who have expressed fears that the language was losing its flavor and its myth-creating qualities. Opinions are still hiding out among us, but less often in such naïve adjectives as good and bad, superior and inferior. Opinion finds just as adequate shelter, and a wider market, by adopting the dress of the times–the lingo of Science, its vocabulary and its accent.

A Patriarchal Society Writes Biology

Embrology

Male. The human embryo first passes through an indifferent or asexual stage in which it is not possible to distinguish male from female. In the second month, however, nature prepares for the great differentiation which is to come.

The genital projection, later the penis, is joined by a large genital fold, a sort of collar. This collar later becomes the scrotum.

Along the genital projection is a cleft, a median slit which leads to the kidneys and internal genital glands.

As development proceeds, the penis grows rapidly, and the genital cleft closes to form the urethra which opens temporarily at the base of the glans.

In the third month the glans splits and forms a groove which recloses, continuing the urethra to its proper place at the tip of the penis.

Just before or after birth the testes progress from their position within the pelvic region to their definitive place in the scrotum.

Thus the male human being has utilized the asexual embryonic projection (or genital tubercle) to develop the organs of penis and scrotum.

Female. The female, we find, does not develop in any important way from the asexual or early embryonic state. Her sexual organs remain in an infantile condition, displaying an early arrest of development.

Whereas in the male the genital tubercle progresses rapidly toward the mature penis form, the genital tubercle in the female embryo slowly regresses until it forms the clitoris, or vestigial penis, a minute glans hidden in an upper depression of the vulva.

Similarly, the genital cleft which successfully closes in the male remains as a pronounced unsealed slit in the female, forming the inner lips of the vulva. The outer lips are the vestigial scrotum; the inner are the vestigial raphe.

Biologically the woman occupies an intermediate position between the man and the child.

She remains related to the child in order to be able to serve better as a mother.

Various malformings of the female system may take place, due to embryonic development suddenly ceasing. This leads to many kinds of infantilisms in the organic construction of the female.

The conditions of female development are negative rather than positive that is to say . . . they depend on the absence of male hormone rather than the presence of female hormone . . . The female may therefore be regarded as the basic type of the mammalian species, and the male as the more highly differentiated type derived from it by the action of the male hormone.

Physiology

The Male Sexual Mechanism. The simple and elementary fact behind human reproduction is that a fertile female egg awaits impregnation in the fallopian tube, and the active male sperm must find this egg and penetrate it.

The female sex apparatus is a depression to receive the sex cells; the male organs are advanced in order to expel the cells.

When the male becomes sexually excited by internal stimuli, his sexual mechanism is called into play. There is a spontaneous erection of the penis, and the passageway from the testicles is thrown open. The sperm has a long way to travel through the vas deferens, through the penis, through vagina and uterus, and finally into the tiny tube where the female egg is waiting.

Nature has provided for this purpose an aggressive and active male cell. Each sperm manufactured in the complex tissues of the testes is composed of very rich and highly specialized material, and is equipped with a fine wriggling tail which gives it the power of self-locomotion.

No less than 225,000,000 cells are emitted from the man's body with each ejaculation—and every cell is a human being![1]

The male seminal fluid, which accompanies the sperm, has a characteristic faint odor, remarkably like that of the flowers of the Spanish chestnut.[2]

When coitus and ejaculation take place, the male sperm, millions in number and each one swimming like a fish, begin their concentrated search for the female egg.

The instant that one of the sperm penetrates a receptive egg, the creation of a new human being has occurred.

The male system differs markedly from that of the female, for the male produces billions of sperm without interruption for forty or fifty years, whereas the girl child is born with ova already present. It merely follows that each month one ovum is discharged from an ovary.

It is of the utmost importance to make clear that reproduction and the sex act are far more closely allied in the man's case than in the woman's, for in the normal man the sex act is by Nature's design specifically a reproductive act as well.

A woman produces an egg usually only once a month, and it may be viable—capable of being fertilized—for perhaps no more than twenty-four hours. . . . Intercourse at all other times has no reproductive significance to the female.[3]

The Female Reproductive Function. The coordinated system of the female is merely the negative reflection of the positive features of the male. It functions to receive the male sperm, and to provide shelter for the growing embryo. When the male has sufficiently aroused the female, the organs of vulva and vagina become flushed and congested, while various glands secrete mucus in order to permit the entrance of the erect penis. This moisture is the signal that the female is ready to receive the male cells.

The female egg is incapable of self-motion. It is dependent on mechanical means for transportation from the ovary to the fallopian tube, where it is fertilized by the male sperm. It is significant that only one egg is provided each month in the female, while billions of active sperm are produced in the male for the purposes of reproduction.

If an egg is not fertilized, the currents of moisture that are always present in the female sweep it out of the body.

As an inducement to sexual union and procreation, nature has provided both men and women with sensitive pleasure-producing zones. In the male the source of pleasure is outside of his body, whereas in the female it is inside. In a fully developed woman, the strongest sexual feeling will be in the vagina. The female's vestigial penis, the clitoris, has its function in the transmission of external stimuli to the internal generative organs.

Many women say that they do not experience either pleasure or orgasm, and some have come to regard orgasm as a luxury.

And from the point of view of function, it may be said that they are right; an orgasm is for them a luxury. Whereas for the satisfactory discharge of the male function of fertilization an ejaculation, and therefore an orgasm, is indispensable, for the female function of conception an orgasm is unnecessary.

Frigidity. Frigidity is a condition in females in which sexual desire or the ability to reach a climax is lacking. This is very frequent, and the theory may be advanced that the cause of this, more frequently than usually realized, is an actual organic inadequacy in the human female, perhaps resulting from the rigors of evolution. The frigidity of a wife should not interfere any more than necessary with the normal gratification of the man's sexual impulse.

Impotence. Impotence is the occasional inability of a man to obtain an erection or to carry out intercourse, either because of revulsion to the woman, indifference, or because of a psychological barrier.

We will now watch the Matriarchal biologist take over the facts of biology, producing a mirror-image of the Patriarchal account, as true and as false.

Through patriarchal eyes we observed the Tom Mix bravado of the male cell and the flower-like receptivity of the female egg. In the matriarchal account, we are not surprised to discover that the egg has become overnight the smart little administrator of fertilization, ringleader and lion-tamer, led on by destiny and a sense of right.

The male semen, on the other hand, is laboriously put together by one doubtful function after another. It begins to seem a miracle that it stays intact as long as it does, in time for the capable egg to extend a helping hand to the faltering sperm that comes so reluctantly to the bridal hour.

The matriarchal account is by no means a fair account. It is invented for the purpose of illustrating the emotional connotations of words thought by science to be objective and unprejudiced. Since the matriarchal version has not found previous expression, we will allow it a little more space and a louder grasp of adjectives.

A Matriarchal Society Writes Biology

Embryology

Female. The human embryo first passes through an indifferent or asexual stage in which it is not possible to distinguish female from male. In the second month, however, nature prepares for the great differentiation that is to come.

The genital projection, later the clitoris, is joined by a large genital fold, a sort of collar. This collar later becomes the outer lips of the vulva.

Along the genital projection is a cleft, a median slit which leads to the kidneys and internal genital glands. This cleft widens to form the inner lips of the vulva.

As development proceeds, the vestigial human tail, which projects from the body just as the genital tubercle does, begins to recede, taking its proper place at the base of the spine.

In like manner—but only in the female—the genital tubercle also progresses to its proper place at the head of the labia minora, or inner lips of the vulva. This interesting development of the clitoris is accompanied in the female by an extensive development of the genital fold, which becomes the pubis and outer lips of the vulva.

Thus the female human being utilizes the asexual embryonic projection (or genital tubercle) to develop the distinctive organs of clitoris and vulva.

Male. The male, we find, does not develop in any important way from the asexual or early embryonic state. His sexual organs remain in an infantile condition, displaying an early arrest of development.

Whereas in the female the genital tubercle becomes the complex and highly differentiated organ, the clitoris, in the male the infantile genital projection remains, merely thickening and growing larger. The penis is best described as a vestigial clitoris which has lost much of its sensitivity.

The genital cleft, which normally remains open to form the vulva, closes regressively in the male. During the third month nature, as though dissatisfied with her work, rips out the stitches of the original seam and begins again; that is to say, the glans splits and forms a groove which closes so that the urethra opens at the top of the penis.

The so-called raphe is the gathering line (almost like a sewn thread) which runs longitudinally down penis and scrotum. The raphe is the vestigial vulva, here functionless.

Before or after birth, the male scrotum descends outside of the body, since sperm are incapable of tolerating the high body temperatures that the female ova find congenial. The scrotum, in which the testes reside, is the vestigial labia majora.

Biologically the male occupies an intermediate position between the woman and the child, or—embryonically—between the fish and the human being (for the young embryo very much resembles an amphibious animal).

Various malformings of the male system may take place, due to embryonic development suddenly ceasing. This leads to many kinds of infantilisms in the organic construction of the male.

When the sealing of the genital cleft ceases prematurely, leaving the urethral opening somewhere between the glans and the base of the penis, an abnormality called *hypospadias* is produced. If the inguinal canals fail to close, a part of the intestine may find its way through in later life, causing *hernia*. Sometimes one or both testes fail to descend. The testis retained in the body is then sterile: *cryptorchidism,* a relatively common condition.[4]

The conditions of male development are derivative rather than positive, dependent rather than independent. This is scientifically proven by the fact that if ovaries are removed from new-born mammals, the development of the female organs is not perceptibly affected; the female retains her sexual identity.

But if we remove the testicles of young rats, we find not only the growth of all the male structures in the body arrested, but female traits soon begin to appear.

It is clear that the female is the dominant human form, while the male is a more or less anomalous and accidental variation on that of the female.

Physiology

The Female Sexual Mechanism. The simple and elementary fact behind human reproduction is that the active female egg must obtain a male sperm before it can create new life.

The male sex apparatus is a tiny factory which continually manufactures sex cells for the female reproductive system.

When the female becomes sexually excited by internal stimuli, the pressure of hormones and mental images, her highly coordinated sexual mechanism is called into full play. There is a spontaneous erection of the clitoris, and a flow of blood into the fine sensitive tissues of the vagina. This causes a similar erection of this region and of the vulva, while the involuntary musculature of the vagina begins rhythmically to contract.

Secretions begin to flow which have a characteristic faint odor remarkably like that of the peach-tree blossoms of Mara, a small island off the coast of New Zealand.

Because of its central importance in reproduction, the female egg has been provided with a size much greater than that of the male sperm. This contributes to its greater resistance and independence. The female egg is actually visible to the naked eye, and is the largest cell in the female body and larger than any cell in the male body. The male germ cells are unbelievably tiny, and must be magnified one hundred times in order to be visible at all.

The male sperm is produced in superfluously great numbers since the survival of any one sperm or its contact with an egg is so hazardous, and indeed improbable. The egg being more resilient, and endowed with solidity, toughness, and endurance, can be produced singly and yet effect reproduction.

In the complex tissues of the ovary one egg each month attains maturity. The ovum is composed of very rich and highly specialized material. By the active pressure of its growth, it produces a slit in the wall of the ovary and escapes into the abdominal cavity. From here it works its way into the fallopian tube aided by active cilia and moisture.

The sperm are provided with a continuous enclosed passageway from the testes to the penis, thus making their conveyance as simple as possible. For the female, however, there is a remarkable gap between ovary and tube, a gap which the egg must traverse alone. When we consider that an egg never gets lost on its route, we realize the striking efficiency of the female sexual mechanism.

When the female's impulse inclines her to sexual intercourse, she must arouse the male in order to produce distension of the male organ of reproduction, the penis. This organ is composed of three sacks whose walls are riddled with blood vessels. When the male has been sufficiently stimulated, the vessels relax, thus receiving blood which causes congestion and a consequent swelling of the organ.

This response serves as a signal to the female that the male is ready for coitus. In a fully developed male, moisture will be present at the time of erection, but if this does not occur, adequate secretion is supplied by the numerous specialized glands of the female, particularly the well-known Bartholin's glands.

It is essential that the female take the initiative in the sex act, since she may have multiple orgasms and must secure contact for the clitoris. The male, on the other hand, needs only the rhythmic contractions of the vagina. If the woman obtains an orgasm before he obtains his, it is absolutely essential that she see that he too receives an orgasm. This is especially true if fertilization is desired (and the time of month propitious), but also for humanitarian reasons, in order to relieve the congestion of the penis.

At the height of the orgasm the uterus contracts maximally, becomes erect, prolongs its neck downwards, and now the external os, which, owing to the prolongation of the neck, dips into the seminal fluid, carries out snapping movements like the mouth of a fish. By means of these movements it laps up the semen. . . .

While the external os thus draws certain spermatozoa into the uterus, it leaves still others in the vagina. These are killed by the acids of the vagina and then swept out of the body.

The weakened or dead sperm cells are ingested by scavenger cells that creep out of the vaginal walls.

After the sperm are drawn to the vicinity of the egg, the egg by some little-known mechanism selects one cell from the many present. Sometimes none of the sperm suits the egg, in which case there is no fertilization.

When an egg does select a male sperm, the sperm is required to shed its wisp-like tail. Whatever temporary means the male cell had for locomotion, it is no longer to be retained. Nature seems to be insisting that the sperm sacrifice its independence for the larger destiny of the female egg.

For the future of the new human being now depends wholly upon the courage and acumen with which the egg establishes its placenta and obtains food for the active embryo.

It is clear that the sperm plays a very small and hesitant part in this larger panorama of the creation of life. We must not assume, however, that the sperm is any less essential than the egg; it is a difference in function. There is no question of superiority or inferiority.

The female system differs from that of the male in that the female egg is produced once each month with timely regularity and therefore with greater chance of being fertilized, while a margin of several million sperm is required for the fertilization of one mature egg.

Reproduction and the sex act are more closely allied in the female than in the male, because no matter how many male sperm are present, unless the female provides an ovum the sex act cannot result in fertilization. Only once each month, when the female egg is present, does intercourse have any reproductive significance for the male.

The Male Reproductive Function. The coordinated system of the male is merely the negative reflection of the positive features of the female. The male functions to produce sperm to give to the female.

The sperm are manufactured by the testes and stored away. At this time they have wispy thread-like projections but are totally incapable of any motion. When the female induces a sexual response in the male, passive sperm are forced up the tubes and receive a milky secretion from the prostate. It is this secretion which gives the sperm a limited capacity for self-locomotion.

The motility of the sperm should not be exaggerated. It is the contractions of muscular tissues which force the semen from the penis. The sperm have no capacity for motion until they are supplied with the milky fluid from the prostate during ejaculation; under this influence they move jerkily about. So abortive are their movements, however, that it is no wonder millions of spare sperm are necessary.

The movement of the sperm is neither swift nor certain. Not all sperm have effective tails, and if the prostatic secretion is deficient, there may be no movement whatever. Those sperm which do move cover about one millimeter in three minutes or one centimeter in a half hour.

The mature female egg is obliged to bide its time, not without impatience, until one of the tiny snail-like cells manages to reach it. No wonder the complicated sexual system of the female undertakes as one of its principal tasks the helpful encouragement of the dependent male cell. The fatal acids of the vagina are neutralized as much as possible by sexually stimulated glands. Active moistures supply a milieu without which the sperm would soon dry up and die.

Nature, in order to induce the male to consent to sexual union, has provided him with a sensitive pleasure-producing zone. This zone is the penis, especially the glans. The male differs from the female in that his source of pleasure is only outside the body, while the female's is both outside and inside.

Many men say that they do not experience pleasure during orgasm, and some have come to regard pleasure as a luxury.

From the point of view of function, it may be said that they are right; pleasure for men is indeed a luxury. No woman in a matriarchal society will consent to intercourse unless pleasure is involved, and therefore there can be no conception without female pleasure and satisfaction. But for the male function of supplying sperm, an emission, whether accompanied by pleasure or not, will serve to supply the egg with its needed fertilization.

Frigidity. Frigidity is a condition in males in which sexual desire or the ability to reach a climax is lacking. This is very frequent, and the theory may be advanced that the cause of this, more frequently than usually realized, is an actual organic inadequacy in the human male, perhaps resulting from the rigors of evolution. The frigidity of a husband should not interfere any more than necessary with the normal gratification of the woman's sexual impulse.

Impotence. Impotence is the occasional inability of a woman to obtain erection or to enjoy intercourse, either because of revulsion to the man, indifference, or because of a psychological barrier.

Someday, perhaps, a democratic account of the physiology of sex will be written, an account that will stress both the functional and organic aspects of reproduction. . . .

Notes

1. The sperm itself is only 1/2 a human being, but such fractional qualification would ruin the esthetic veracity of the statement.

2. From Van de Velde's description of semen, quoted by Parshley.

3. If we assume, and one would not like to assume otherwise, that the male in question is monogamous as well as normal, intercourse at times other than when his wife is fertile will have no reproductive significance for him either.

4. The matriarchal biologist realizes that it is not necessary to state that the male system is more *likely* to have disorders than the female. She simply restricts her interest to the disorders of the opposite sex, communicating the impression that they are somehow more fallible.

Questions for Discussion

1. As Hershberger's title suggests, she believes that the discourses of biology do not come to us as objective illustrations of fact. Instead, that discourse is "written" by society. What does Herschberger mean by this claim?

2. Read both of Herschberger's accounts carefully, noting the kinds of adjectives and verbs she uses to characterize sperm and egg as either active or passive agents. What kinds of patterns do you see as you construct the list? What is the effect of her revision?

3. Why does Herschberger provide such extensive examples of both the "patriarchal" and "matriarchal" perspectives on biology? What, in the end, is her purpose in providing these?

Explorations

1. Hershberger's account was originally published in 1948. What kind of reception do you think the piece received when it first appeared? In what ways do you believe today's audiences will respond differently? Why?

2. What are the societal effects of Herschberger's revision? Society may write biology, but biology in turn writes society. What are the social or cultural effects of a biology that is, in Herschberger's understanding, written in such a patriarchal, undemocratic fashion?

3. In what ways does Herschberger establish her own ethos and reliability as an author in this piece? How might she have developed and established her ethos differently?

Formal Writing Assignments

1. Locate a section of a science text in which you find the same kinds of slanting that Herschberger describes in "Society Writes Biology" and rewrite the passage with a different slant. Then, go one step beyond Herschberger and attempt to compose a third, "democratic account" of the same passage.

2. As a variation on the formal writing assignment above, find another public text—a non-scientific text—and compose a similar kind of revision.

What's in a Package

Thomas Hine

Thomas Hine has been a practicing journalist since before his graduation from Yale University in 1968. He reported for the *Chicago Sun Times* in the late sixties and then moved on to the *Old Saybrook* (CT) *Recorder*. He began work at the *Philadelphia Inquirer* in 1970 as a feature writer and then as architecture and design critic. He is still with the *Inquirer* as a writer. Hine's books include *Populuxe: The Look and Life of America in the '50s and '60s from Tailfins and TV Dinners to Barbie Dolls and Fallout Shelters* (1986), *Facing Tomorrow: What the Future Has Been, What the Future Can Be* (1991), *The Total Package: The Evolution and Secret Meanings of Boxes, Bottles, Cans, and Tubes* (1995), and *The Rise and Fall of the American Teenager* (1999). In these last two works in particular, Hine approaches his subjects—consumerism and teenagers—from a multidisciplinary perspective, engaging them as anthropologist, psychologist, sociologist, and journalist. In reflecting on his writing, Hine often cites his own experiences as a teenager, reader, and budding news writer as formative elements in his later writing. A self-described Internet "troller," Hine hosted until recently an MSN bulletin board and chat room on design and architecture.

"What's in a Package" is taken from *The Total Package*.

Writing Before Reading

1. Visualize the items currently in your kitchen cupboard or medicine cabinet. What items do you recall? What elements of their packaging are most memorable?

2. Select one brand name item that you purchase regularly. Examine carefully the reasons behind your choice to purchase this item as opposed to another. Make every effort to look beyond value, comfort, or quality to the lifestyle implied by packaging.

3. Write about a time when you felt that you needed consciously to "package" yourself. What was the situation? What was at stake? In what ways did your "packaged" self differ from your typical manner, dress, or discourse style?

What's in a Package

When you put yourself behind a shopping cart, the world changes. You become an active consumer, and you are moving through environments—the supermarket, the discount store, the warehouse club, the home center—that have been made for you.

During the thirty minutes you spend on an average trip to the supermarket, about thirty thousand different products vie to win your attention and ultimately to make you believe in their promise. When the door opens, automatically, before you, you enter an arena where your emotions and your appetites are in play, and a walk down the aisle is an exercise in self-definition. Are you a good parent, a good provider? Do you have time to do all you think you should, and would you be interested in a shortcut? Are you worried about your health and that of those you love? Do you care about the environment? Do you appreciate the finer things in life? Is your life what you would like it to be? Are you enjoying what you've accomplished? Wouldn't you really like something chocolate?

Few experiences in contemporary life offer the visual intensity of a Safeway, a Krogers, a Pathmark, or a Piggly Wiggly. No marketplace in the world—not Marrakesh or Calcutta or Hong Kong—offers so many different goods with such focused salesmanship as your neighborhood supermarket, where you're exposed to a thousand different products a minute. No wonder it's tiring to shop.

There are, however, some major differences between the supermarket and a traditional marketplace. The cacophony of a traditional market has given way to programmed, innocuous music, punctuated by enthusiastically intoned commercials. A stroll through a traditional market offers an array of sensuous aromas; if you are conscious of smelling something in a supermarket, there is a problem. The life and death matter of eating, expressed in traditional markets by the sale of vegetables with stems and roots and by hanging animal carcasses, is purged from the supermarket, where food is processed somewhere else, or at least trimmed out of sight.

But the most fundamental difference between a traditional market and the places through which you push your cart is that in a modern retail setting nearly all the selling is done without people. The product is totally dissociated from the personality of any particular person selling it—with the possible exception of those who appear in its advertising. The supermarket purges sociability, which slows down sales. It allows manufactures to control the way they present their products to the world. It replaces people with packages.

Packages are an inescapable part of modern life. They are omnipresent and invisible, deplored and ignored. During most of your waking moments, there are one or more packages within your field of vision. Packages are so ubiquitous that they slip beneath conscious notice, though many packages are designed so that people will respond to them even if they're not paying attention.

Once you begin pushing the shopping cart, it matters little whether you are in a supermarket, a discount store, or a warehouse club. The important thing is that you are among packages: expressive packages intended to engage your emotions, ingenious packages that make a product useful, informative packages that help you understand what you want and what you're getting, Historically, packages are what made self-service retailing possible, and in turn such stores increased the number and variety of items people buy. Now a world without packages is unimaginable.

Packages lead multiple lives. They preserve and protect, allowing people to make use of things that were produced far away, or a while ago. And they are potently expressive. They assure that an item arrives unspoiled, and they help those who use the item feel good about it.

We share our homes with hundreds of packages, mostly in the bathroom and kitchen, the most intimate, body-centered rooms of the house. Some packages—a perfume flacon, a ketchup bottle, a candy wrapper, a beer can—serve as permanent landmarks in people's lives that outlast homes, careers, or spouses. But packages embody change, not just in their age-old promise that their contents are new and improved, but in their attempt to respond to changing tastes and achieve new standards of convenience. Packages record changing hairstyles and changing lifestyles. Even social policy issues are reflected. Nearly unopenable tamperproof seals and other forms of closures testify to the fragility of the social contract, and the susceptibility of the great mass of people to the destructive acts of a very few. It was a mark of rising environmental consciousness when containers recently began to make a novel promise: "less packaging."

For manufacturers, packaging is the crucial final payoff to a marketing campaign. Sophisticated packaging is one of the chief ways people find the confidence to buy. It can also give a powerful image to products and commodities that are in themselves characterless. In many cases, the shopper has been prepared for the shopping experience by lush, colorful print advertisements, thirty-second television minidramas, radio jingles, and coupon promotions. But the package makes the final sales pitch, seals the commitment, and gets itself placed in the shopping cart. Advertising leads consumers into temptation. Packaging *is* the temptation. In many cases it is what makes the product possible.

But the package is also useful to the shopper. It is a tool for simplifying and speeding decisions. Packages promise, and usually deliver, predictability. One reason you don't think about packages is that you don't need to. The candy bar, the aspirin, the baking powder, or the beer in the old familiar package may, at times, be touted as new and improved, but it will rarely be very different.

You put the package into your cart, or not, usually without really having focused on the particular product or its many alternatives. But sometimes you do examine the package. You read the label carefully, looking at what the product promises, what it contains, what it warns. You might even look at the package itself and judge whether it will, for example, reseal to keep a product fresh. You might consider how a cosmetic container will look on your dressing table, or you might think about whether someone might have tampered with it or whether it call be easily recycled. The possibility of such scrutiny is one of the things that make each detail of the package so important.

The environment through which you push your shopping cart is extraordinary because of the amount of attention that has been paid to the packages that line the shelves. Most contemporary environments are landscapes of inattention. In housing developments, malls, highways, office buildings, even furniture, design ideas are few and spread very thin. At the supermarket, each box and jar, stand-up pouch and squeeze bottle, each can and bag and tube and spray has been very carefully considered. Designers have worked and reworked the design on their computers and tested mock-ups on the store shelves. Refinements are measured in millimeters.

All sorts of retail establishments have been redefined by packaging. Drugs and cosmetics were among the earliest packaged products, and most drugstores now resemble small supermarkets. Liquor makers use packaging to add a veneer of style to the intrinsic allure of intoxication, and some sell their bottle rather than the drink. It is no accident that vodka, the most characterless of spirits, has the highest-profile packages. The local gas station sells sandwiches and soft drinks rather than tires and motor oil and in turn, automotive products have been attractively repackaged for sales at supermarkets, warehouse clubs, and home centers.

With its thousands of images and messages, the supermarket is as visually dense, if not as beautiful, as a Gothic cathedral. It is as complex and as predatory as a tropical rain forest. It is more than a person can possibly take in during an ordinary half-hour shopping trip. No wonder a significant percentage of people who need to wear eyeglasses don't wear them when they're shopping, and some researchers have spoken of the trancelike state that pushing a cart through this environment induces. The paradox here is that the visual intensity that overwhelms shoppers is precisely the thing that makes the design of packages so crucial. Just because you're not looking at a package doesn't mean you don't see it. Most of the time, you see far more than a container and a label. You see a personality, an attitude toward life, perhaps even a set of beliefs.

The shopper's encounter with the product on the shelf is, however, only the beginning of the emotional life cycle of the package. The package is very important in the moment when the shopper recognizes it either as an old friend or a new temptation. Once the product is brought home, the package seems to disappear, as the quality or usefulness of the product it contains becomes paramount. But in fact, many packages are still selling even at home, enticing those who have bought them to take them out of the cupboard, the closet, or the refrigerator and consume their contents. Then once the product has been used up, and the package is empty, it becomes suddenly visible once more. This time, though, it is trash that must be discarded or recycled. This instant of disposal is the time when people are most aware of packages. It is a negative moment, like the end of a love affair, and what's left seems to be a horrid waste.

The forces driving package design are not primarily aesthetic. Market researchers have conducted surveys of consumer wants and needs, and consultants have studied photographs of families' kitchen cupboards and medicine chests to get a sense of how products are used. Test subjects have been tied into pieces of heavy apparatus that measure their eye movement, their blood pressure or body temperature, when subjected to different packages. Psychologists get people to talk about the packages in order to get a sense of their innermost feelings about what they want. Government regulators and private health and safety advocates worry over package design and try to make it truthful. Stock-market analysts worry about how companies are managing their "brand equity," that combination of perceived value and consumer loyalty that is expressed in advertising but embodied in packaging. The retailer is paying attention to the packages in order to weed out the ones that don't sell or aren't sufficiently profitable. The use of supermarket scanners generates information on the profitability of every cubic inch of the store. Space on the supermarket shelf is some of the most valuable real estate in the world, and there are always plenty of new packaged products vying for display.

Packaging performs a series of disparate tasks. It protects its contents from contamination and spoilage. It makes it easier to transport and store goods. It provides uniform measuring of contents. By allowing brands to be created and standardized, it makes advertising meaningful and large-scale distribution possible. Special kinds of packages, with dispensing caps, sprays, and other convenience features, make products more usable. Packages serve as symbols both of their contents and of a way of life. And just as they can very powerfully communicate the satisfaction a product offers, they are equally potent symbols of wastefulness once the product is gone.

Most people use dozens of packages each day and discard hundreds of them each year. The growth of mandatory recycling programs has made people increasingly aware of packages, which account in the United States for about forty-three million tons, or just under 30 percent of all refuse discarded. While forty-three million tons of stuff is hardly insignificant, repeated surveys have shown that the public perceives that far more than 30 percent—indeed, nearly all—their garbage consists of packaging. This perception creates a political problem for the packaging industry, but it also demonstrates the power of packaging. It is symbolic. It creates an emotional relationship. Bones and wasted food (13 million tons), grass clippings and yard waste (thirty-one million tons), or even magazines and newspapers (fourteen million tons) do not feel as wasteful as empty vessels that once contained so much promise.

Packaging is a cultural phenomenon, which means that it works differently in different cultures. The United States has been a good market for packages since it was first settled and has been an important innovator of packaging technology and culture. Moreover, American packaging is part of an international culture of modernity and consumption. At its deepest level, the culture of American packaging deals with the issue of surviving among strangers in a new world. This is an emotion with which anyone who has been touched by modernity can identify. In lives buffeted by change, people seek the safety and reassurance that packaged products offer. American packaging, which has always sought to appeal to large numbers of diverse people, travels better than that of most other cultures.

But the similar appearance of supermarkets throughout the world should not be interpreted as the evidence of a single, global consumer culture. In fact, most companies that do business internationally redesign their packages for each market. This is done partly to satisfy local regulations and adapt to available products and technologies. But the principal reason is that people in different places have different expectations and make different uses of packaging.

The United States and Japan, the world's two leading industrial powers, have almost opposite approaches to packaging. Japan's is far more elaborate than America's, and it is shaped by rituals of respect and centuries-old traditions of wrapping and presentation. Packaging is explicitly recognized as an expression of culture in Japan and largely ignored in America. Japanese packaging is designed to be appreciated; American packaging is calculated to be unthinkingly accepted.

Foods that only Japanese eat—even relatively humble ones like refrigerated prepared fish cakes—have wrappings that resemble handmade paper or leaves. Even modestly priced refrigerated fish cakes have beautiful wrappings in which traditional design accommodates a scannable bar code. Such products look Japanese and are unambiguously intended to do so. Products that are foreign, such as coffee, look foreign, even to the point of having only Roman lettering and no Japanese lettering on the can. American and European companies are sometimes able to sell their packages in Japan virtually unchanged, because their foreignness is part of their selling power. But Japanese exporters hire designers in each country to repackage their products. Americans—whose culture is defined not by refinements and distinctions but by inclusiveness—want to think about the product itself, not its cultural origins.

We speak glibly about global villages and international markets, but problems with packages reveal some unexpected cultural boundaries. Why are Canadians willing to drink milk out of flexible plastic pouches that fit into reusable plastic holders, while residents of the United States are believed to be so resistant to the idea that they have not even been given the opportunity to do so? Why do Japanese consumers prefer packages that contain two tennis balls and view the standard U.S. pack of three to be cheap and undesirable? Why do Germans insist on highly detailed technical specifications on packages of videotape, while Americans don't? Why do Swedes think that blue is masculine, while the Dutch see the color as feminine? The answers lie in unquestioned habits and deep-seated imagery, a culture of containing, adorning, and understanding that no sharp marketer can change overnight.

There is probably no other field in which designs that are almost a century old—Wrigley's gum, Campbell's soup, Hershey's chocolate bar—remain in production only subtly changed and are understood to be extremely valuable corporate assets. Yet the culture of packaging, defined by what people are buying and selling every day, keeps evolving, and the role nostalgia plays is very small.

For example, the tall, glass Heinz ketchup bottle has helped define the American refrigerator skyline for most of the twentieth century (even though it is generally unnecessary to refrigerate ketchup). Moreover, it provides the tables of diners and coffee shops with a vertical accent and a token of hospitality, the same qualities projected by candles and vases of flowers in more upscale eateries. The bottle has remained a fixture of American life, even though it has always been a nuisance to pour the thick ketchup through the little hole. It seemed not to matter that you have to shake and shake the bottle, impotently, until far too much ketchup comes out in one great scarlet plop. Heinz experimented for years with wide-necked jars and other sorts of bottles, but they never caught on.

Then in 1992 a survey of consumers indicated that more Americans believed that the plastic squeeze bottle is a better package for ketchup than the glass bottle. The survey did not offer any explanations for this change of preference, which has been evolving for many years as older people for whom the tall bottle is an icon became a less important part of the sample. Could it be that the difficulty of using the tall bottle suddenly became evident to those born after 1960? Perhaps the tall bottle holds too little ketchup. There is a clear trend toward buying things in larger containers, in part because lightweight plastics have made them less costly for manufacturers to ship and easier for consumers to use. This has happened even as the number of people in an average American household has been getting smaller. But houses, like packages, have been getting larger. Culture moves in mysterious ways.

The tall ketchup bottle is still preferred by almost half of consumers, so it is not going to disappear anytime soon. And the squeeze bottle does contain visual echoes of the old bottle. It is certainly not a radical departure. In Japan, ketchup and mayonnaise are sold in cellophane-wrapped plastic bladders that would certainly send Americans into severe culture shock. Still, the tall bottle's loss of absolute authority is a significant change. And its ultimate disappearance would represent a larger change in most people's visual environment than would the razing of nearly any landmark building.

But although some package designs are pleasantly evocative of another time, and a few appear to be unchanging icons in a turbulent world, the reason they still exist is because they still work. Inertia has historically played a role in creating commercial icons. Until quite recently, it was time-consuming and expensive to make new printing plates or to vary the shape or material of a container. Now computerized graphics and rapidly developing technology in the package-manufacturing industries make a packaging change easier than in the past, and a lot cheaper to change than advertising, which seems a far more evanescent medium. There is no constituency of curators or preservationists to protect the endangered package. If a gum wrapper manages to survive nearly unchanged for ninety years, it's not because any expert has determined that it is an important cultural expression. Rather, it's because it still helps sell a lot of gum.

So far, we've been discussing packaging in its most literal sense: designed containers that protect and promote products. Such containers have served as the models for larger types of packaging, such as chain restaurants, supermarkets, theme parks, and festival marketplaces. . . . Still, it is impossible to ignore a broader conception of packaging that is one of the preoccupations of our time. This concerns the ways in which people construct and present their personalities, the ways in which ideas are presented and diffused, the ways in which political candidates are selected and public policies formulated. We must all worry about packaging ourselves and everything we do, because we believe that nobody has time to really pay attention.

Packaging strives at once to offer excitement and reassurance. It promises something newer and better, but not necessarily different. When we talk about a tourist destination, or even a presidential contender, being packaged, that's not really a metaphor. The same projection of intensified ordinariness, the same combination of titillation and reassurance, are used for laundry detergents, theme parks, and candidates alike.

The imperative to package is unavoidable in a society in which people have been encouraged to see themselves as consumers not merely of toothpaste and automobiles, but of such imponderables as lifestyle, government, and health. The marketplace of ideas is not all agora, where people haggle, posture, clash, and come to terms with one another. Rather, it has become a supermarket, where values, aspirations, dreams, and predictions are presented with great sophistication. The individual can choose to buy them, or leave them on the shelf.

In such a packaged culture, the consumer seems to be king. But people cannot be consumers all the time. If nothing else, they must do something to earn the money that allows them to consume. This, in turn, pressures people to package themselves in order to survive. The early 1990s brought economic recession and shrinking opportunities to all the countries of the developed world. Like products fighting for their space on the shelf, individuals have had to re-create, or at least represent, themselves in order to seem both desirable and safe. Moreover, many jobs have been reconceived to depersonalize individuals and to make them part of a packaged service experience.

These phenomena have their own history. For decades, people have spoken of writing resumes in order to package themselves for a specific opportunity. Thomas J. Watson Jr., longtime chairman of IBM, justified his company's famously conservative and inflexible dress code—dark suits, white shirts, and rep ties for all male employees—as "selfpackaging," analogous to the celebrated product design, corporate imagery, and packaging done for the company by Elliot Noyes and Paul Rand. You can question whether IBM's employees were packaging themselves or forced into a box by their employer. Still, anyone who has ever dressed for success was doing a packaging job.

Since the 1950s, there have been discussions of packaging a candidate to respond to what voters are telling the pollsters who perform the same tasks as market researchers do for soap or shampoo. More recently, such discussions have dominated American political journalism. The packaged candidate, so he and his handlers hope, projects a message that, like a Diet Pepsi, is stimulating without being threatening. Like a Weight Watchers frozen dessert bar, the candidate's contradictions must be glazed over and, ultimately, comforting. Aspects of the candidate that are confusing or viewed as extraneous are removed, just as stems and sinew are removed from packaged foods. The package is intended to protect the candidate; dirt won't stick. The candidate is uncontaminated, though at a slight remove from the consumer-voter.

People profess to be troubled by this sort of packaging. When we say a person or all experience is "packaged," we are complaining of a sense of excessive calculation and a lack of authenticity. Such a fear of unreality is at least a century old; it arose along with industrialization and rapid communication. Now that the world is more competitive, and we all believe we have less time to consider things, the craft of being instantaneously appealing has taken on more and more importance. We might say, cynically, that the person who appears "packaged" simply doesn't have good packaging.

Still, the sense of uneasiness about encountering packaged people in a packaged world is real, and it shouldn't be dismissed. Indeed, it is a theme of contemporary life, equally evident in politics, entertainment, and the supermarket. Moreover, public uneasiness about the phenomenon of packaging is compounded by confusion over a loss of iconic packages and personalities.

Producers of packaged products have probably never been as nervous as they became during the first half of the 1990s. Many of the world's most famous brands were involved in the merger mania of the 1980s, which produced debt-ridden companies that couldn't afford to wait for results either from their managers or their marketing strategies. At the same time, the feeling was that it was far too risky to produce something really new. The characteristic response was the line extension—"dry" beer, "lite" mayonnaise, "ultra" detergent. New packages have been appearing at a rapid pace, only to be changed whenever a manager gets nervous or a retailer loses patience.

The same skittishness is evident in the projection of public personalities as the clear, if synthetic, images of a few decades ago have lost their sharpness and broken into a spectrum of weaker, reflected apparitions. Marilyn Monroe, for example, had an image that was, Jayne Mansfield notwithstanding, unique and well defined. She was luscious as a Hershey's bar, shapely as a Coke bottle. But in a world where Coke can be sugar free, caffeine free, and cherry flavored (and Pepsi can be clear!), just one image isn't enough for a superstar. Madonna is available as Marilyn or as a brunette, a Catholic schoolgirl, or a bondage devotee. Who knows what brand extension will come next? Likewise, John F. Kennedy and Elvis Presley had clear, carefully projected images. But Bill Clinton is defined largely by evoking memories of both. As our commercial civilization seems to have lost the power to amuse or convince us in new and exciting ways, formerly potent packages are recycled and devalued. That has left the door open for such phenomena as generic cigarettes, President's Choice cola, and H. Ross Perot.

This cultural and personal packaging both fascinates and infuriates. There is something liberating in its promise of aggressive self-creation, and something terrifying in its implication that everything must be subject to the ruthless discipline of the marketplace. People are at once passive consumers of their culture and aggressive packagers of themselves, which can be a stressful and lonely combination.

Questions for Discussion

1. In what ways has the act of buying changed over time? What kinds of physical changes have products and the sites of purchasing undergone in the past 100 years?

2. Hine argues that package serves both practical and expressive functions. What kinds of distinctions is he drawing in defining packaging in this fashion? Can you think of other functions that packaging serves?

3. Hine describes Japanese product packaging as "shaped by rituals of respect and centuries-old traditions." U.S. packaging, on the other hand, is shaped by "inclusiveness." What do you think Hine means by this? By what other principles do you believe U.S. packaging is shaped?

Explorations

1. Like Giroux and Jones, Hine writes about the ways that packaging becomes transparent. In this transparency, they argue, rests an item's invidiousness and power. Compare and contrast the arguments that these three authors construct about culture and consumerism.

2. Products are packaged. People package themselves. Ideas, as well, are packaged through the language that we use to describe them. (This is a point that Herschberger makes in "Society Writes

Biology.") Examine the ways that language is used to package a particularly controversial idea. What kinds of value-laden language are used to illustrate a point or argue a position?

3. Bring to class a product that you believe is effectively packaged. What elements of the packaging most contribute to its effectiveness? Remember to comment on both its functionality and its expressiveness. (Alternative activity: As a group, identify a kind of item to search for. Have everyone bring in what they believe to be the most effectively packaged item and compare packaging and reasons for selecting each as the most effective.)

Formal Writing Assignments

1. Visit two or three department or specialty stores and compose an essay that develops a comprehensive comparative analysis of the ways that the stores package merchandise, salespeople, and even the store itself. Refer to ideas in Giroux, Hine, and/or Jones to develop your analysis and interpretation. You may even work within a single store and examine how similar merchandise (e.g., clothing, cologne, shoes) are packaged differently for men, women, and children. What conclusions can you draw based on your observations?

2. Do some investigative work in your local library or historical society. Leaf through magazines from ten, twenty, and fifty years ago, examining the print advertisements for the same kind (or even the same brand) of item. What kinds of changes do you see over time? In what ways are other cultural changes or preferences reflected in the packaging? (Automobile and cigarette advertisements are often very good products for such an analysis.)

Looking for Mariah

Lisa Jones

Jones, a columnist for the *Village Voice* since 1984, is the author of *Bulletproof Diva: Tales of Race, Sex, and Hair* (1995), which, the publisher reports, addresses how "race, sex, identity, and the politics of style speaks to a young generation of blacks who were raised in an integrated society and are now waiting for America to deliver on its promises of equality." Described variously as forceful, audacious, and unapologetic, Jones writes in *Bulletproof Diva* and "Looking for Mariah" about the politics of raced and de-raced bodies and racial identity.

In addition to her column, "Skin Trade," Jones has co-authored, with film producer Spike Lee, *Do the Right Thing: The New Spike Lee Joint, Uplift the Race: The Construction of School Daze,* and *Variations on the Mo'Better Blues.* The daughter of writers Amiri Baraka and Hettie Jones, Jones was educated at Yale and New York University.

Writing Before Reading

1. In what various ways do you define or name yourself? Is your decision to identify yourself in this manner related to a cultural or ethnic heritage?

2. Reflect on an experience during which you became aware that others had labeled, identified, or named you in a way you prefer not to be named. What was your response to having others take this right from you?

3. We often think of people "passing" as one race or another, as one gender or another, or as hearing people. What does it mean to "pass" as someone other than you are? What are the consequences of attempting to pass? Of failing to pass?

Looking for Mariah

They came to see the nose. The nose never lies. Even the missing nose of Egypt's great Sphinx tells a story. Legend has it that Napoleon gave the Sphinx a nose job in the eighteenth century during the Battle of the Nile—too Negroid, too strong? An Egyptologist friend of mine told me it wasn't Napoleon after all, but Egyptian pharaohs, who made a practice of smashing noses off the statues of their predecessors so the old kings couldn't "breathe," meaning exert influence from the afterworld. Murphy's Law: You can never find a good racial conspiracy theory when you need one.

The nose in question is Mariah Carey's. The twenty-year-old pop singer with a seven-octave vocal range. Mother sang with the New York City Opera. At six, little Mariah could do *Rigoletto* in Italian. Later she discovered gospel, then rhythm and blues, Aretha, Minnie Riperton, and things have never been quite the same. Just before Thanksgiving, two dozen media types gathered at an invitation-only luncheon to meet Carey. The singer's debut album, released last June on Columbia/CBS, was now double platinum. Two singles, "Vision of Love" and "Love Takes Time," had topped the pop and R&B charts.

At the luncheon, held at Lola's, another vibe cafe hovering just above Fourteenth Street, all the guests save two or three were black. Seated at linen-clad tables were folks like Janine McAdams, *Billboard's* black-music editor, *City Sun* arts editor Armond White (who said, on record, he came to see the nose), and a writer from a dance music trade publication who admitted that "for once race wasn't an issue," he had come for the food. (Fried chicken was served.) Apparently the guest of honor was most interested in meeting writer Nelson George, who had sized Carey up in *Playboy*. George's comments, having nothing to do with her body, had all to do with her soul, or more specifically, her marketing profile. George had dubbed Carey a "white girl who can sing."

It was all over the press that Columbia/CBS had rolled out hordes of money for the Carey project. One questions whether the company would have made the same investment in a black vocalist of comparable talent working in the soul idiom. Take Carey's labelmate Regina Belle. Critically acclaimed voice. But Columbia had waited for a good response from the R&B sector on Belle's debut record before selling her, second time around and without fanfare, to the pop market. Carey, on the other hand, was put out as pop product from jump.

Columbia certainly, didn't, for Belle, scrap a video and shoot a new one, putting the combined cost of both at $450,000, or so an inside source told Rob Tannenbaum for *Rolling Stone*. (This figure was later dismissed by the company as "total bullshit.") Or give Belle, as they gave Carey, a "promotional blitz equal to the push given Bruce Springsteen in 1975," says Tannenbaum, securing her an appearance on "Arsenio" even before the CD was released. ("We don't look at her [Carey] as a dance-pop artist," Columbia prez Dou Ienner told *Rolling Stone*. "We look at her as a franchise.")

Did it matter that Regina Belle is a brown-skinned black woman sans weave? Did it matter ultimately, in Columbia's decision to go all out like this for a new artist, that Carey looks the way she does (long blondish hair, pale skin), and that she is what the press had said she is—white? But is she really?

Though at times Carey's voice on her CD is swallowed by a virtual solar system of twinkling synthesizers, it does have its own guttural integrity. Not the life-experience soul power of a Miki Howard, but Carey is young yet. No question, it's a voice with more emotional grip than Lisa Stansfield's, the white Brit, who *Entertainment Weekly* had crowned the new queen of soul. The girl really *could* sing.

And what *about* that nose? In the CD's cover photo, one curly strand of auburn-blonde hair is strewn across Carey's plump nose, casting it in high relief. Shot from another angle, the nose might have been fuller still. Sign of the tar brush? Said a friend framing the CD box in his large brown hands, "saw her videos, but honestly, I can't call this one. Don't know if she's dating Negroes or what, but I tell you one thing, if she herself is not a Negro, there's definitely a Negro component up in there." *Maybe she isn't white, or all white, or . . . ? What is she, or what isn't she?* And since Carey's record company hadn't found it worth mentioning, did only her hairdresser know for sure?

Turned out Mariah Carey was ready to answer just this question at the Mariah Carey luncheon. A vision of loveliness in, how apropos, a two-tone cat suit (black from middrift down, white up top), Carey appeared even taller and leaner than on video. She planted herself opposite George and calmly set the record straight. "My father is black and Venezuelan. My mother is Irish and an opera singer. I am me." The *New York Post's* gossip page added some spice the next day. Below the caption, CAREY: MIXED ANCESTRY, it was reported that "rocker" Carey wanted to "sock" George for calling her a "white girl who can sing." As I was sitting at the next table, I can confirm: Things weren't dramatic as all that.

The *Post* managed to bungle up Carey's mixed-race résumé, calling her half "black-Brazilian" instead of half "black-Venezuelan." *USA Today* carried the story the following week with the caption MARIAH CAREY, MISUNDERSTOOD. Courtesy information supplied by a Columbia publicist, it was noted that the *Post* had "blown out of proportion" Carey's anger at George and that George and Carey were friends. Before leaving Lola's, George did stop to pose for a photo with Carey, but the luncheon was the first time the two had met.

How's this for a racial conspiracy theory?: Had Columbia/CBS been engaging in a little nineties-style "passing" of Carey? Did the company profit, especially in the first few months of the record's release, from having Carey's racial dossier remain under wraps? (White soul singers being more lucrative pop meal tickets than black ones.) And now that Mariah's background was the source of speculation, was the company interested in smoothing out the edges so as not to alienate any market group? Carey conducting her mixed-race confessional at a fried-chicken confab with George, McAdams, and other influential black-music journalists played like a media maneuver of high order. Soon stories embracing Carey and her biracial identity appeared in the black press. And compared to her first music videos, those that aired post-luncheon showcased a decidedly black presence. (Black bit players, missing before, were cast in endearing roles.) Perhaps higher-ups in Columbia marketing had decided it was time to "come out" with the Carey story before the company was charged with running some sort of cover-up.

I had frustrating conversations with two publicity reps in Columbia's pop division and two in black music. (Ever wonder how offices are set up at these record companies? Is there the pop big house, and then, a few flights down, the black music shanties?) All were adamant that no attempt had been made to mask Carey's background. Though not one wanted to address this on the record and not one would comment on who had organized the shindig at Lola's and why.

Each conversation I had became twisted in the cobwebs of racial semantics. One publicist said the label had never pronounced Carey "one hundred percent white or one hundred percent black"; that "Carey's heritage has nothing to do with her voice." And why should Carey have to "broadcast her racial background"? When asked, Carey "will answer, but she's not gonna bring it up."

Another suggested that the record company wasn't responsible; "It's a personal thing, not a label thing." And that, if Carey's race wasn't as important to her as it was to other people, this was not a political issue, but a testament to her marketing savvy: "All entertainers like to be viewed as universal."

One told me I was the only person in America interested in Carey's race (or lack of one) and the connection between her look and her marketing budget: "Mariah had a number one black single and a number three black album. Obviously, the black population is identifying with this woman. So is the white population. White or not, no one cares what her background is."

All judgments about Carey's race, said yet another publicist, came from the press based on photos. Both the *New York Times* and *Musician* had fawned over Carey as a "white soul singer." Nelson George told the *Post* that he judged Carey white based on information supplied in a press release from Columbia and the CD photo. When *Voice* critic Vince Aletti described Carey as a white singer who could "pass for Whitney Houston," he received the following letter from a reader:

Yo! Vince,

You'd better take another look or get yourself some glasses. Not only can Mariah Carey pass for black, she is black! She's just a lighter Whitney Houston. You can't claim this one.

Aletti says he came to his conclusion from the "gungho marketing" of Carey "It doesn't happen as often with black artists. Especially coming from a company like Columbia."

Last August Rob Tannenbaum arrived at a rehearsal studio to interview Carey for *Rolling Stone.* Tannenbaum asked the publicist on the scene if Mariah was black, because the "way she's photographed, it's hard to tell what her background is," and in person, he was getting a less ambiguous picture. According to Tannenbaum, the publicist "assured" him that Carey was white. Tannenbaum questions why, when the press started calling Carey "the white Whitney Houston," no one from the company came forward to correct this, to mention that she's half black, if not black period. "If they [Columbia] didn't deliberately create a misimpression," says Tannenbaum, "they didn't go out of their way to clear one up."

As the Carey luncheon was wrapping up, the singer posed with two journalists, deep brown and dashing in black suits. Set against them, the darker hues of her skin seemed all the more prominent, seemed to glow. (I remembered the photo of Carey on her CD's inner sleeve, her ample nose hidden behind song credits.) In person, Carey came across, quite clearly, as a rainbow baby of African descent, skin toasted almond and hair light brown. The ivory-airbrushed, blonde-hair-blowing-at-the-beach fantasy on view in her publicity shots appeared to be entirely a studio creation.

So Carey has declared herself to be a person of color. Whether or not there is a political dimension to that identity in her mind is a different story. Is she, as Nelson George had tagged Renee Tenison, *Playboy's* 1990 Playmate of the Year, another not so much color-blind, but "race-neutral," mixed-race child? Carey was born in 1970, which means she didn't turn ten years old until 1980. She might well be ignorant of the political importance of affirming a black identity, of the role this has played in the African-American freedom struggle.

Along with her declaration, Carey said this: "It seems that most people don't know much about interracial children." What don't people know? I itched to ask, at this most polite of gatherings. That they exist? That they have options? That they can't be blamed for America's subtle and not so subtle forms of apartheid? That they are the solution? That they *just want to be me* until America forces them to declare an allegiance?

Several months before the Carey luncheon, an article titled "Who's Black and Who's Not?" appeared in *Ebony*. Penned by Lynn Norment, the piece was illustrated with snapshots of actress Jennifer Beals and singers Paula Abdul, Jody Watley, and Prince. Under each photo, readers were invited to check boxes labeled "black" or "white." *Ebony* and *Jet* are known for their campy coverage of interracial identity (geez Louise, look at those half-white, half-black twins!), but this piece had critical gut: "The issue . . . is not mixed parentage and the increasing number of children from such unions. The issue is the downplaying or a denial of a Black parent or Black heritage for economic, social, or career gain by a descendant of mixed or even unmixed marriage." What makes the current trend so "fascinating and provocative," Norment continues, is that "media and moguls, particularly in the entertainment industry, seem to be encouraging crossoverism, especially by *ethnically ambiguous females*" (emphasis hers).

Walking home from Lola's, the questions piled up: By marketing themselves as anything but black, do light-complexioned entertainers such as Carey become, in the eyes of most Americans, de facto whites? And do Carey and other people of color who feel more at ease representing themselves by their combination ethnic heritages, and not by race (making use of a privilege to remain outside), teach the world how to be "raceless"? Or are they positioning themselves as a separate class along the lines of South African "coloreds"? And why aren't Carey et al., if they know or care how racism operates, more willing to take a racial stance? Or have we arrived at a point in history when "black" and "white" have become, to quote bell hooks, "definitive no-nos, perpetuating what some folks see as stale and meaningless binary appositions"; a time when such stances/affirmations/commitments serve little purpose?

Ebony's known for trafficking in paradox. Two months after chiding racially ambiguous entertainers for hauling tail to the bank without paying their black dues, the magazine published a piece by the same writer, Lynn Norment, on Paula Abdul. Norment praises Abdul for giving "expanded definition to the term 'multiple,' for being "multitalented, multifaceted, and multiethnic." "Syrian-Brazilian-Canadian-American" is how the singer describes herself. Norment tells us that Abdul acknowledges African-American culture as her most profound influence and is often mistaken for black and Hispanic (or accused of passing for anything but). Yet the singer refuses to be badgered into declaring for any race, for "she is what she is [Syrian-Brazilian-Canadian-American] and stardom will not change that." This time around, Norment has turned multiculti cheerleader, and she congratulates Abdul for working her hybridity for a bigger market share. Why does racial ambiguity get applause in this case? Apparently, to read *Ebony*, what makes the difference is who orchestrates the sell. If it's people of color, it's about *getting paid*. If it's the entertainment industry, it's a sin of omission. Keep that in mind.

I'm on the other side of the spectrum from race-neutral rainbow babies who claim a multitude of heritages but no race. My older sister and I, born in fifty-nine and sixty-one respectively, never explored an option other than black, never wished to. Blackness has always been this wide and miraculous world of people and places and passions and histories and *stances*. Of course, stances. Honorable stances that gave you dignity, that made you part of a much larger world. By all means, stances.

Race politics, the us versus them of it, were spelled out for us early. Growing up on the ethnic Lower East Side (before it became the fashionable multiculti East Village, and New York the gorgeous mosaic), kids from the Ukrainian school on Sixth Street threw evil looks at us and eventually bottles. To be half white, in my mind, in 1965, meant being half *them*. And why should I claim something that wanted no part of me?

There were the aesthetic and intellectual dimensions as well. After seeing Sly and the Family Stone at the Fillmore East just as puberty hit, who didn't want to be Cynthia Robinson, the funky light-skinned sister on trumpet? Later my idols became "highyella" race women like Angela Davis, Kathleen Cleaver, and Nikki Giovanni. I joined the post-civil rights generation of collegians who took Afro-American history and lit and fashioned ourselves black leaders on campus. We remembered at least the chorus of "Say It Loud—I'm Black and I'm Proud" and clung to fond memories of African dance classes at the New Afrika Houses of our childhood. These signposts stuck in our minds, even when Bakke struck a match under affirmative action and radio melted rhythm and blues down to urban contemporary. And black became less "political vocation" and more "ethnic option."

What does this have to do with Mariah Carey? To value freedom and liberty is to respect the choices others make in identifying themselves, be it by sexual preference, culture, or race. Yet the Careys of the new world have shown me the weight history lays on my open mind. I can't resist comparing them to bisexuals swinging on the closet door in an America in which an "out" gay identity still means a helluva lot. Perhaps I haven't yet figured out what "I am me" solves more than "I'm black and, I'm proud." One thing I'm clear on: If we can't find a way to make *multi*ethnic stand for *anti*racism, then I'll pass on it.

The ironies of racial identity and cultural province in the nineties are making popular culture the best sideshow in town. Cultural mulattos (Prince, Madonna, George Michael, Michael Jackson) rule the marketplace. Rainbow baby girls (Mariah, Sade, Jasmine Guy) rule the mirror. Ethnicity is often presented as an open-invitational participatory sport (Vanilla Ice, New Kids on the Block, white female rapper Tarrie B. from Compton). "Separated from a political and historical context," bell hooks writes, "ethnicity is being reconstituted as the new frontier, accessible to all, no passes or permits necessary." Hence my anger when a publicist told me that Mariah Carey's voice had nothing to do with her heritage. I like to think it does, so that people of African descent might still have some sort of title to black culture. Yet this might be romantic, even retrograde, of me in an age when exchange cross culture, cross race happens at a dizzying pace.

The politics of race somersault all around us: More talented-tenths, middle-class blacks, are coming of age in integrated neighborhoods, being educated at majority-white institutions, and laying down roots outside of African-American communities. Pop culture positions blacks center frame as racially motivated violence chokes urban America; President Bush vetoes civil rights legislation as Miss America 1990, a black woman, passes the crown to Miss America 1991, also a black woman; illiteracy, teen pregnancy, and drug slavery dog the underclass, while a new black conservative lobby gains power by showing little sympathy for poor blacks.

How will the expanding pool of mixed-race people figure into this new world? On one hand, our presence could force all Americans to take a hard look at race as political construction, its utilities and its dead ends. On the other, mixed-race people could remain invisible, our numbers having little impact. The white world invites us to be privy to white privilege. In the black world, specifically in black intellectual communities, we shy away from challenging stereotypes of "the black experience" with our particular histories. These days the race-neutral Mariah Careys seem to be multiplying faster than the heirs of Davis, Cleaver, and Giovanni.

I wonder what message the cautionary tales of the passing novels could send to rainbow babies of the nineties. These novels were written by African Americans in the early part of the century. For all their melodrama, tinny plots, and soapbox politicking, they've always resonated with me. The costs of abandoning black culture and community is one of the genre's central themes, and it's a theme that hits me, as they say, where I live. Though for reasons you might not expect. When my mother married my father, she was deserted by her white family and embraced by his black family. I have always been made to feel, in part because of her stories, that black communities and black cultures are a steady home. A home that is still quick to remind me, in ways material and ethereal, that it keeps the lights on for me. To abandon this home, as my mother's stories whispered, would mean to swim with sharks.

James Weldon Johnson's *Autobiography of An Ex-Coloured Man* (1912) is often called the thinking-colored person's passing novel, as it speaks its truth minus the violins. The closing passage hits deepest. Not because it describes in experience I have lived, but because it tells of one that I ache to believe in, despite how the world around me splinters in ways I don't recognize.

The ex-coloured man goes to hear Booker T. Washington speak at a benefit for Hampton Institute. Though Mark Twain and others share the podium, Washington has the audience in his hand:

"Not because he so much surpassed the others in eloquence, but because of what he represented with so much earnestness and faith. It is this that all of that small but gallant band of coloured men who are publicly fighting the cause of their race have behind them. Even those who oppose them know that these men have the eternal principles of right on their side, and they will be victors even though they should go down in defeat. Beside them I feel small and selfish. I am an ordinarily successful white man who has made a little money. They are men who are making history and a race. I, too, might have taken part in a work so glorious.

". . . I cannot repress the thought that, after all, I have chosen the lesser part, that I have sold my birthright for a mess of pottage."

Is it true what those labels say, NO SALE IS EVER FINAL?

Questions for Discussion

1. What is the significance of Jones' title for this essay? Who is "looking for Mariah"? What is it someone might be looking for, in particular, when s/he looks for Mariah?

2. If asked to identify Jones' thesis, how would you respond? To what particular sentence or sentences would you point? What in the organization or content of the essay leads you to these as the sentence or sentences that articulate the thesis?

3. How does Carey define, locate, or name herself? What is Jones' response to Carey's self-definition?

Explorations

1. Jones reports that Don Ienner, president of Columbia Records, once commented (in referring to Carey) that the company "look[ed] at her as a franchise." This comment suggests that Columbia was quite aware of the marketing possibilities for Carey. In what ways has she been packaged (to use a term from Hine)? What are the cultural and economic implications of this franchising?

2. Jones is skeptical about both Columbia's and Carey's choices in representing her race. What leads Jones to her skepticism?

3. One reader, in response to a *Village Voice* writer's comment that Carey was white but could "'pass for Whitney Houston'" chastised, noting that "You can't claim this one." Why, as this comment suggests, would white culture gain by "claiming" Carey as white? Alternatively, what do other ethnic or racial groups gain (or lose) from claiming her?

Formal Writing Assignments

1. Update Jones' examination of Mariah Carey in an essay by exploring the ways that Carey has been "packaged" in the ten years (1990–2000) since the publication of "Looking for Mariah." Have the packaging methods and outcomes changed? If so, how? And, more important, why?

2. Undertake a researched essay project in which you investigate the various ways younger multi racial performers or sports figures are franchised and packaged. Do they continue to face the same kinds of ridicule and questioning as Carey? If so, why do you believe this is the case? If not, what cultural, social, or economic changes have influenced such a shift?

AIDS, Ads and Us vs. Them

Greg Meyers

Greg Meyers is a professor in the Department of Linguistics and English Language at Lancaster University in the United Kingdom. His research has explored the way society is shaped by the discoveries and publications of science scholars. He is currently working with the Center for the Study of Environmental Change (CSEC) studying the social and cultural production of environmental knowledge, and the values, identities, and areas of human possibility that are emerging from the environmental agenda. Meyers is working to untangle the cultural restraints that hinder the public's understanding of environmental issues. Through this project Meyers is able to play an active role in the shaping of public environmental policy. "AIDS, Ads and Us vs. Them" is taken from Meyers' book "Words in Ads." It shows his interest in the way language shapes people's working knowledge of important issues like AIDS and ecology.

Writing Before Reading

1. Write a short explanation of AIDS. What is it? How do you get it? What do you think about those who have it and those that don't? Think about where you learned this information and how you developed your opinion.

2. Try to remember the last time that you saw an ad about AIDS. Write out its message. Who was it addressed to? Did it speak to you? How did it make you feel about yourself or others who have AIDS?

3. How would you like to advertise information for AIDS awareness? What kind of argument do you think would affect people the most?

AIDS, Ads and Us vs. Them

A sign on the door in the toilet of a local family centre says:

> Have it on before you have it off.

How do people know what it means? The fact that the notice could leave out so much and still be understood suggests widespread awareness of AIDS and safer sex. On the other hand, the fact that the local health authority paid for the ad suggests this awareness has not always led to the change in behavior it wants: the use of the condoms. Indeed, despite huge advertising and public health campaigns, there remains persistent ignorance about some basic facts about the transmission of the AIDS virus; this is indicated, for instance, by the bigotry towards HIV positive people.

There is a vast literature on AIDS and society (for a start, see the references at the end of this chapter). People have heard so much about AIDS that they may think they know all about it. It helps to make it strange again. One way of doing this is to look closely at the texts of AIDS ads. I will make two main points:

1. The way we talk about AIDS, in medical journals, in ads, and in everyday talk, structures ideas of AIDS, of what it is, who is affected, and what should be done.

2. AIDS structures ideas of society, the way we divide people into groups and relate them, who we consider 'at risk' and who consider as part of 'the general population', normal, neutral, unmarked.

To illustrate these points, I will look first at the choices of words we use to talk about AIDS, and then at some advertising campaigns that illustrate the ways different audiences are addressed, and that assume different views of society. Finally I will show how AIDS talk is used in ads for products that have nothing to do with AIDS, just as products that have nothing to do with saving the environment may be sold with environmental discourse.

Words for AIDS

One leaflet from the San Francisco AIDS Foundation is headed

Straight Talk about Sex and HIV

The heading shows how thinking about and dealing with AIDS is tied up with language issues. First, it promises straight talk—frank information—about taboo matters. It also addresses a specific group: heterosexuals who might consider themselves safe from any risk. (Other booklets from the Foundation include *Man to Man, Condoms for Couples,* and *AIDS and Lesbians*). Also, the leaflet uses the abbreviation *HIV* throughout, rather than *AIDS*, and begins with a technical sounding definition:

HIV stands for <u>H</u>uman <u>I</u>mmunodeficiency <u>V</u>irus. This virus damages the immune system and eventually causes AIDS.

Why So Much Care with Terminology?

Names of epidemic diseases have always had social meanings; syphilis, for instance, was 'The French disease' in England and Germany (the French name said it came from Naples; Europeans traced it to the New World, while Americans said it came from Europe). Let's start with the name of AIDS itself (here I'm drawing on a good article, Jan Zita Grover's 'AIDS: Keywords'). AIDS was first called 'Gay Related Immune Deficiency' when it was diagnosed in 1981, because it was diagnosed in gay men. This had to be changed when it was found that haemophiliacs, intravenous drug users, and Haitians also had it. The name was changed in 1982 to AIDS (Acquired Immune Deficiency Syndrome), which was meant to be neutral, to avoid stigmatization of victims.

AIDS activists point out the importance of the last letter of this name. AIDS is not a disease, it is a *syndrome*. People with AIDS are killed by various ailments that may be ubiquitous but that are kept under control by healthy immune systems. These illnesses differ in different parts of the world. The activists stress this because AIDS itself is not a disease like syphilis or hepatitis. What is transmitted is not the syndrome but the virus that attacks the immune system. People who test positive for the antibodies may take a long time to develop any of the AIDS diseases. But because of the stigma attached to AIDS, their lives will be treated as effectively over, even if they live without major health problems for years. This is why the leaflet I quoted talks about *HIV,* and AIDS activists and official leaflets talk about HIV tests, or HIV virus, not about an AIDS virus. Some AIDS activists believe that changes in the words we use can change attitudes; they reject the popular term, 'AIDS victim' as implying helplessness, and they reject 'AIDS patient' because they are only occasionally under medical care. They prefer the term 'People with AIDS'.

This is deliberately awkward. One can't say it without reminding oneself that they are people first, they have an identity separate from their medical condition.

Tabloids no longer refer to 'the gay plague', but the bigotry and fear remain in subtler forms. One key distinction made in many texts is between 'risk groups' and 'the general population'. The distinction as it is usually made assumes that the reader is heterosexual, monogamous, probably middle-aged, is European or North American, and doesn't inject drugs. That is defined as the 'general population', unmarked. Much of the discussion in the press is about whether or not it looks likely that the disease will spread from 'risk groups' to 'us'. The assumption underlying such worry (sometimes stated explicitly) is that it wouldn't matter much if AIDS just affected gay men, drug users, and Africans. Another assumption in talk about 'risk groups' is that these categories are definite and visible. For instance, when some doctors say that they will not treat people from risk groups, they are assuming there is some way of easily distinguishing 'them' from 'us'. The use of the phrase 'general population' constructs social barriers that dissolve when one thinks of specific cases.

The stigmatization of gay people and other members of so-called 'risk groups', is, I believe, evil in itself. But it also has public health consequences, because it encourages people to believe that AIDS comes only to certain kinds of people, rather than stressing that it is transmitted through certain kinds of practices. Let me give you an example. One survey (by Mykol C. Hamilton) shows that a class of US university students thought lesbians a high risk group, just after male homosexuals, a head of heterosexuals. Even some medical professionals share this belief: there were moves in California to block lesbians giving blood, and there was serious discussion of this issue in *The Lancet,* a British medical journal. A little thought about how HIV is transmitted would suggest that lesbians are a relatively low risk group (though not risk-free, as public health leaflets directed at them point out). This example shows how categories encoded in language shape our assumptions about reality. What seems to have happened is that straight students (and doctors) got in their minds that AIDS is a disease of stigmatized groups; lesbians were categorized in their minds with gay males, so they too must be 'high risk'. If people do not see themselves as members of these groups, they consider themselves safe, and anyone from a stigmatized group at risk.

Susan Sontag pointed out, in her book on AIDS, the way the metaphors around AIDS shape our perceptions of it. One of the metaphors that Sontag and others trace is that of AIDS as battle. The body has its defenses; these are sabotaged from within, allowing invasion. This metaphor not just used of AIDS, it runs through the biomedical vocabulary of our time. When a friend of mine told me in a letter that he had cancer, he used the phrase 'I've been invaded.' This vocabulary helps explain to the patient why the treatment can be so brutal, as chemotherapy can be for cancer, and as AZT, a drug currently used, can be for AIDS. Powerful poisons can be justified as would the bombing of one of one's own cities in wartime. Sontag points out that this may be a dangerous way of thinking of one's own body, as a terrain divided between good and evil, defenders and enemy.

Another common metaphor has to do with what the press calls 'carriers': that is, people with the HIV virus who have not yet developed AIDS, so 'we' cannot recognize 'them'. A UK television ad showed a woman inviting a man to her flat for coffee. Below this apparently ordinary encounter between ordinary people, subtitles warned of AIDS. It is interesting that a parallel ad, showing an attractive man at a disco, had much less successful recall. Both ads assume that the audience is HIV negative, and incarnate the HIV positives as attractive and threatening, as agents of the disease. But the ad that made the man the threat had less effect. In fact there are for more cases of men transmitting to women than women transmitting to men. But given these paired ads, audiences response continued a long tradition that makes women the cause of venereal diseases like syphilis. As read by men, these ads again divide 'us' from 'them'.

One response to these metaphors of battle in the body or vampire-like carriers is to try to reject them and stick to the scientific facts. That is Susan Sontag's position, and she speaks with considerable authority, because when she was being treated for cancer she saw the brutal moral effect of the various metaphors on people who were already suffering from physical pain and grief. But AIDS activists who analyze culture have tended to take a different line; they say that there is no going beyond metaphors, that the scientific facts themselves are based on metaphors, and that activists should focus on the struggle to define which metaphors will circulate. They examine and criticize popular newspapers and media representations, and offer their own alternative metaphors and language.

AIDS Ads and Taboos

One reason AIDS ads attract so much attention is that official institutions—such as public health authorities—must often breach taboos in public use of language. Most public health ads are aimed at getting people to modify their practices so that the virus does not pass from one person to another—getting both gay and straight people to practice safer sex and getting drug users not to share needles. Earlier ads, which only talked vaguely about a threat, seem to have been very unsuccessful at getting people to change. In contrast, a very explicit campaign developed in and directed at the gay community led to very dramatic changes in behavior.

In the British TV ads that most people remember best, there are two versions, one with a iceberg and one with a tombstone. The text at the end in both cases was the same:

AIDS: DON'T DIE OF IGNORANCE

Let's look a little closer at the iceberg message. It involves a metaphor, that of a lurking hidden threat. It is addressed at a 'general' audience, but this general audience is assumed to be unaffected (and ignorant) at the moment. There is no recognition of the diversity of audiences that make up the public. This ad has been much criticized because it emphasized the threat but gave no explicit information. Historians, public health officials, and advertising professionals have all pointed out that fear does not work well at changing behavior. People have to have some sense of getting what they desire, not just of avoiding what they fear. (Think of how unsuccessful anti-smoking campaigns have been). There are some features of such ads that are specific to British culture—for instance, the rather abstract verbal/visual pun of the iceberg. But it does seem that the first wave of ads in almost every country involved both fear and vagueness, with very little information.

One difficulty in including any specific information about safer sex is that talk about condoms or masturbation or penetration or semen or vaginal fluids challenges taboos. For instance, a student group at my university protested about the inclusion of safer sex information in the handbook for new students; they said it was using public money to promote homosexuality. These taboos are rather flexibly defined: AIDS campaigners point out that great latitude is allowed in the pornography available at the newsagents W. H. Smith, or even in *Cosmopolitan,* but not in leaflets aimed at public health. The other interpretation of the vagueness of information is more subtle. Talk about safer sex focuses on what you do, not on who you are. Safer sex is the same for heterosexuals and homosexuals, drug users and non-users, men and women. For heterosexuals who feel they are far from the problem, such talk about specific practices denies the boundaries that make them feel safe.

The National AIDS Manual, a publication for UK professionals who deal with HIV and AIDS, stresses that plain language is crucial in addressing such personal behavior. Both jargon and euphemism put off the intended audience. They make the advertiser or advisor sound like a distant authority. Their remarks recall some of the discussions earlier in this book about associative meanings, forms of address, and everyday talk. The suggestions were made by public health workers, but they could have been made by experienced writers of advertising for any product.

Language that is remote, too formal, or that sounds like scientific jargon tends to alienate most people. By contrast, language that is common and plain tends to involve most people and encourage their active participation. . . .

—frankly, most people neither understand nor use terms like 'frottage,' 'digital intercourse,' 'brachioproctal stimulation,' 'fellatio,' 'cunnilingus' etc.

—Terms like 'making love,' 'sexual intercourse,' 'sleeping together' are much too imprecise and fail to distinguish between safe and unsafe activities . . .

—It's worth asking why Latin and Greek words are supposed to make something sound less offensive than plain English words? Because they misleadingly make the activities sound more remote . . .

To oppose these taboos, Simon Watney, who works with the Terrence Higgins Trust, insists on referring to *fucking,* not using any of the hundreds of possible euphemisms. But if one chooses to use colloquial words, one finds they are highly variable, and the choice of the wrong colloquial form is also likely to make the advisor seem remote. Consider this range of choices:

prophylactic, condom, sheath, french letter, johnny, rubber.

It's clear that *prophylactic* is a word real people never use. But what of the others? Any choice risks sounding absurdly coy or dated, on the one side, or clinical and remote, on the other.

Dramatizing Condoms

The representation of condoms is a problem of taboo images that corresponds exactly to this problem of taboo language. Douglas Crimp mocks the coyness about condoms in ads for the mass media. 'An [advertising] industry that has used sexual desire to sell everything from cars to detergents suddenly finds itself at a loss for how to sell a condom.' The sales pitch is needed for condoms because there is apparently strong resistance by men to using them. One approach is to be clinical but informative. Leaflets for some public health agencies explain with diagrams how to put it on and take it off, and respond rationally to arguments that they make sex too conscious, or that they are too small, or too fragile. The people who make these leaflets argue that one must be explicit to respond to these fears.

The other approach to encouraging the use of condoms is to be coyly amusing about them. Until recently, condoms could only be shown in their wrappers in UK ads, but the ads from other countries in Jasper Carrott's annual reviews of television ads include an astonishing range of animated condoms jumping into holes, or being used to snap bums like elastics, or being blown up like balloons, or being stuck suggestively on fingers. An Australian ad has a woman breaking off an embrace and telling the man

It will be much better if I get my mates.

He looks hopefully at a photograph of her with her friends, but she is actually making the standard advertising pun, in which she mentions the name of the product (Mates™) rather than using the word to mean 'friends'.

The most recent UK television campaign just mentions HIV, and focuses instead on the condoms themselves, with older people talking about them in a matter of fact tone. The fact that the speakers are two generations older than the target audience suggests that these things can be talked about even by those the audience might expect to be more prudish. Both employ the sorts of indications of everyday talk. In one, 'Fred Brewster, age 81' tells about the difficulties he faced with the tough reusable condom of his youth, which he called 'Geronimo'. The message is

If Mr Brewster put up with Geronimo, you can use a condom.

The other ad has a woman in her fifties or sixties sitting at a machine in a condom manufacturing plant. She says:

> Of course, working here we were the first to notice the change in people's behavior. We're making more of these things than ever before. Obviously it's down to AIDS and HIV. Young people can't afford to take chances these days. It seems they've got their heads screwed on though. After all, I've never been so busy.

The on-screen text at the end says, coyly,

KEEP MRS DAWSON BUSY

Sheila Dawson is identified as an ordinary person, talking to us as she might talk to friends. She talks about, but not to, young people; that's what makes her grandparental in her concern rather than nagging like a parent. She still remains euphemistic, talking about 'these things'. But the pictures make it clear enough what they are. Perhaps they show the testing machines to respond to the worries of women that they will leak, thus allowing a possible pregnancy, while incidentally demonstrating to men that a fairly large object will fit in them.

One effect of all this attention is that the taboos are challenged, whatever the ads actually say, just by putting the condoms on TV. And this is part of their aim; Chris Powell, Chief Executive of the ad agency responsible for the Health Education Authority AIDS campaign, says in defense of the ads:

> Advertising has played an important part in the process of the normalization of condom usage. It has helped bring the subject out into the open and make it acceptable. This enables young people to talk about it, and take what can be socially difficult action. (*Campaign* 10/9/93, p. 31).

One strategy of familiarization is apparent in a sticker apparently designed by a local campus entrepreneur, advertising a machine the dispenses 'Streetwise' brand fruit-flavored condoms:

> If you get lucky, get Streetwise.
> Don't be silly, stick fruit on your willy.

This ad positions the reader as a sexually aggressive male. The breaking of language taboos and the ridiculous rhyme are part of this rude macho defiant image; condoms are treated as part of the kit, like beer at a football match.

Ads and Audiences

I have argued that AIDS ads make assumptions about the audience as 'general public', and sometimes reinforce the 'us' vs. 'them' view of the disease. We can see the contrast by looking at some ads that challenge these divisions. Ads aimed at the gay community are particularly important because the British gay community is something of a public health success story; in the early years after the first diagnoses of AIDS, even before the isolation of the retrovirus, the gay community developed a very effective unofficial campaign, so that new cases among gay men in Britain after that point were much fewer than they might otherwise have been.

One ad from the Terrence Higgins Trust, a non-governmental AIDS information service, has a black and white picture of a young man pulling his jumper over his head, thus baring his torso. (The ad is a version of one produced by the Dutch public health service). The text reads:

SAFER SEX
KEEP IT UP
antibody positive & negative
—it's the same for all
The Terrence Higgins Trust
Helpline
01-242 1010

As Simon Watney of the Terrence Higgins Trust points out in one of his articles the emphasis in their ads is on desire: the picture is meant to be erotic. But it does not present the erotic as a threat; rather, it is in occasion for safer sex. The pun of the title, 'keep it up', refers both to an erection and to the gay community's efforts already. The audience is assumed not to be ignorant or foolish. Crucially, the ad addresses both antibody positive and negative people. Watney has argued that the strongest persuasion is to say that one must protect the people one loves; one assumes one might be affected oneself, and acts accordingly. That, he says, is stronger than threatening that any new sexual experience is deadly. There is no point is attacking casual sex, he says; many strong relationships were casual and uncertain at the beginning. This line of persuasion depends on there being a strong community in which people care about each other. So Watney and others argue that attacks on the gay community actually hinder the most effective public health campaign. As long as male gays are treated as total outcasts, already damned, there is no motivation for them practicing safe sex. Changed behavior emerges only from a sense of worth and trust.

It is interesting that almost all these features advocated by the Terrence Higgins Trust have been adopted in a recent HEA ad; the government-sponsored campaign is learning from the gay community's own campaign. Again there is a suggestive picture, an almost abstract close-up of two men's faces. It is suggestive because on the left we see the man looking over his shoulder, on the right we see the man much more closely than we could in casual encounters, and the men are looking aside as if glancing at each other. The text says:

THEY DON'T HAVE SAFER SEX JUST BECAUSE IT'S SAFER
Sex.

We all know how much we enjoy it.

So why should our attitudes change when it comes to safer sex?

After all, people were enjoying it long before the discovery of HIV or AIDS.

Safer sex means any activity where blood, semen, or vaginal fluid can't enter your body.

Mutual masturbation, fingering, massage or body rubbing are just a few examples you may have heard of.

But there are plenty of others you won't have, and half the fun is finding new ways to enjoy each other.

Anal sex, however, is still the highest risk activity and even using a condom won't make it completely safe.

If you'd like more information or advice, pick up a safer sex leaflet (available from gay bars and clubs), or ring your local helpline. Alternatively call the National AIDS Helpline free of charge on 0800 567 123. It's open 24 hours a day and it's completely confidential.

The voice in the ad is 'we', identifying with the gay community. The information, unlike that in UK ads aimed at the 'general' population, is quite explicit about sexual practices. Safer sex is tied to erotic exploration (as in US ads developed by the gay community). If this health authority ad doesn't surprise you, ask yourself if five years ago you could have imagined the national government would pay for ads that encourage masturbation, or even for ads that use the word.

Ads for the London Lighthouse, which provides help for people with HIV and AIDS, are among the few I have seen that directly challenge stereotypes about HIV positive people, the way other campaigns challenge stereotypes about people with cancer or cerebral palsy. In one of their ads, the visual effect is plain, with black and white paintings of a phone, brushes, a cup of coffee, and a large headline saying:

HOW I SURVIVED AIDS

The copy again gives the effect of everyday talk, by referring to specifics and mutual knowledge, a cyclical conception of time, and a local sense of place.

At 9:37 am, on Monday the 8th of June (which also happened to be my birthday), my doctor told me I had AIDS. The first person I went to was my brother. I told him I was thinking of killing myself. 'Why bother,' he said, 'You already have.'

That was six years ago.

You see, the problem at that time was that no-one—not the doctors, nor their hospitals, not the media nor their public—really knew enough about HIV infection or AIDS. Or even if there was a difference. The only thing they were certain of was that if you caught it, you were dead.

One year later, I wasn't dead.

The ad goes on in this powerful, personal fashion, telling about his first call to the London Lighthouse. It is not just the choice of words that is informal; the form is directly addressed to some hearer:

I was amongst new friends (well let's face it, most of the old ones scarpered in the time it takes to say Acquired Immune Deficiency Syndrome).

This ad also illustrates the concern with language choices that I mentioned at the beginning of the chapter: the careful distinction of HIV and AIDS, the joking about the technical name, and later an insistence that the person faces AIDS

not as a victim dying but as a person living.

Good copy-writing like this makes me wish the same issues of attitude change towards people with AIDS could be addressed on television, alongside the HEA prevention campaign.

Most countries in the world have some AIDS advertising campaign, some of them more extensive and effective than that in the UK. (The country with the most reported cases, the US, has excellent campaigns from local and private groups, but still has no national government campaign.) There is a striking similarity in the ads in the European press, except that the source of infection is displaced to other countries, as syphilis once was. (UK ads in airline terminals warn travellers abroad to take condoms; an ad in the SAS flight magazine, in English, warns Danish businessmen visiting London.) But it is worth comparing the ads in a country like Uganda, which not only has a high incidence of HIV, but is immeasurably poorer than the UK, and must face this public health problem in the aftermath of a civil war. Gill

Seidel, who has an important article on the Uganda AIDS campaigns, points out that there were two campaigns, somewhat different in focus, as suggested by their slogans.

Love Carefully
Love Faithfully

The secular authorities produced a campaign based on 'Love carefully', emphasizing the condom. The religious groups, who provide most of the health care in Uganda, produced a campaign treating AIDS as a moral issue of faithfulness in marriage. The two campaigns were based on different definitions of the disease, but they were able to work together. Seidel points out that a later campaign for World AIDS Day

'Thank God I said No to AIDS'

seemed to stress moral aspects. At this point her article takes an interesting turn. She says it is not enough for European analysts to bring their own frameworks to Uganda—they should look at local interpretations of the ads. And she quotes a Uganda newspaper article that criticizes the ads for failing to recognize the brutal social and economic facts that led to people 'choosing' behaviors that spread AIDS.

The differences in perspective on the disease in different countries was brought home to me by a 6 shilling stamp on a package sent to me from Kenya. It says

AIDS has no cure.

Below a picture of a man in a bubble, there are pictures of pills, capsules, syringes, and sachets crossed out. People in the UK to whom I showed it thought it was discouraging intravenous drug use. But a moment's thought will tell you that there isn't much of that in a country as poor as Kenya. I asked about this when I went to Kenya and was told it is aimed at the many locally marketed products that claim to cure AIDS. Many Kenyans believe the cure has been discovered but is being withheld from Africans by powerful western drug companies. The public health authorities, it seems, are worried that people might engage in unsafe sexual behavior, hoping to be cured later, just as nineteenth century men contracted syphilis casually thinking that mercury treatments would cure them. The stamp illustrates how we need social as well as linguistic analysis to understand a text; this stamp changed its apparent meaning as it went from the country in which it was mailed to the country in which it was delivered.

AIDS in Discourse

Just as military and vampire metaphors, drawn from other discourses, shape our sense of AIDS, AIDS becomes a metaphor used in discourses besides that of public health. The most famous example is the notorious Benetton poster that showed a man dying of AIDS, with the only text being

United Colours of Benetton.

Whatever else you think about the use of that image of suffering for commercial purposes, it is a striking example of the omnivorousness of advertising discourse—anything can become material for an ad.

Those who were so appalled about Benetton—including the editor of *Campaign*—may not have noticed how many other ads joke about AIDS—or more accurately, about AIDS ads. A poster in the Netherlands for Love Jeans says

> Love Safely

and shows a couple in a sexual embrace—but still prudently wearing their jeans. Posters for Piz Buin sun cream were the subject of controversy recently because of the nudity in them, but I have heard no criticism of their parody of the public health slogan:

> Practice safe sun.

A Seat car ad with the headline

> Safe Sex

was withdrawn in Northern Ireland when criticized as sexist and crude, but again it was not criticized for playing with a disease. The creative director of the ad agency, Steve Grimes, said in *Campaign* that it could be taken literally: 'The Ibiza is one of the safest cars in its class and when you see it in the flesh one of the most sexy' (29 October 1993).

Some ads for products play on the vagueness and euphemism that characterizes some AIDS ads. A computer firm, Total Control Ltd., plays on the ambiguity of *virus*.

> Before you put it in . . . make sure you know where it's been!
> Protect yourself now with VIS anti-virus facilities

The language of computer viruses carried over from public health to information technology long before this ad, but computer users may hardly remember the origin of the term. This ad for Confident tampons uses the advice about safer sex to sell another product, a tampon with a cover:

> These days shouldn't anything that goes inside you be wearing a sheath?

The key of course is the vagueness of the 'anything that goes inside you'. The ad can work, linking the two discourses, because of the vagueness of both AIDS ads and tampon ads.

Ourselves and Other Bodies

Struggles over how to respond to AIDS are in part struggles over what can be said in public, what cannot be said, and what can go without saying. These struggles did not begin in 1981, and they will not end when, as we hope, better treatments for AIDS or preventives for HIV are found. I will end with a story from an earlier epidemic, the Victorian writer Thomas Carlyle writing in *Past and Present* (1843).

> A poor Irish widow, her husband having died in one of the lanes of Edinburgh, went forth with her three children, bare of all resource, to solicit help from the Charitable Establishments of that City. At this Charitable Establishment and then at that she was refused; referred from one to the other, helped by none;—till she had exhausted them all; till her strength and heart failed her: she sank down in typhus fever; died, and infected her Lane with fever, so that 'seventeen other persons' died of fever there in consequence . . . Very curious. The forlorn Irish Widow applies to her fellow creatures, as if saying, 'Behold I am sinking, bare of help: ye must help me! I am your sister, bone of your bone; one God made us: ye must help me!' They answer, 'No; impossible; thou art no sister of ours.' But she proves her sisterhood; her typhus fever kills them: they actually were her brothers, though denying it!

As in earlier epidemics, AIDS is seen in terms of existing social boundaries, and public health measures reinforce these boundaries. In Carlyle's example the boundaries are Irish/Scottish, male/female, rich/poor. Then as now people who suffered from a disease could be treated as the cause of that disease, and one response was to try to keep barriers, physical and psychological, between the sufferers and one's own group. The people who turn her away see her as part of a foreign and threatening group. But the typhus has its own networks (we now know it is spread through body lice). Similarly the HIV virus makes its own links, through sex, needles, or blood supplies. One response is to try to strengthen the boundaries between gay/straight, men/women, natives/foreigners. But the maintenance of social boundaries can have public health consequences for everyone. Some of the beliefs people hold that make them feel safe ('I'm in the general population; they are in a risk group') lead to dangerous behavior. Besides, these boundaries can victimize those who fall on the wrong side, not just those who are HIV positive, but those deemed to be 'at risk', or those who can become symbols of the danger. And such boundary drawing also has consequences for the way anyone, gay or straight, thinks of themselves, their bodies, pleasure, and fear.

I have argued that close attention to the texts of ads, the words and the pictures, can help us see how AIDS ads represent society, and in particular, how they categorize people:

- Choices of terms suggest blame and fear.

- Metaphors of invasion or carrier/vampires reflect hostility to people with AIDS, and to stigmatized groups.

- Taboos keep the focus of campaigns on people, rather than practices.

- Some campaigns in the gay community and for HIV positive people attempt to redraw the social boundaries.

- Ads in other countries may require a different sense of the issues to be comprehended.

- AIDS itself becomes a metaphor to be used in ads for other products.

All this analysis of language should not make us forget that AIDS is, among other things, a disease with a concrete cause that causes terrible suffering, nor to forget those who carry the burdens of caring for this suffering. But we cannot understand HIV and AIDS just by studying the virus and its effects. We must trace how its signs and meanings are used in culture, to reinforce social boundaries, draw new ones, or perhaps someday, to break them down.

FURTHER READING

AIDS and Culture

This chapter draws largely from articles in Douglas Crimp. ed., *AIDS: Cultural Analysis, Cultural Activism*, especially the essays by Jan Zita Grover, Paula Treichler, and Simon Watney. This is a special issue of a magazine of art theory; it is high-flying critical stuff, but passionate and readable, and well-illustrated. There is another excellent collection, rather more popular in its style, edited by Erica Carter and Simon Watney, *Taking Liberties: AIDS and Cultural Politics;* see especially the pieces by Erica Carter, Judith Williamson, Lynne Segal, Keith Alcorn, and Simon Watney again. Other recent collections include Peter Aggleton and Hilary Homans, eds., *The Social Aspects of AIDS*, especially the pieces by Alcorn, Wellings, Aggleton and Homans, and Watney yet again, and a whole issue of *Social Research* with rather scholarly pieces, of which the most relevant is Allan M. Brandt, 'AIDS and Metaphor: Toward the Social Meaning of Epidemic Disease'. Gill Seidel's article, discussed here, is "Thank God I Said No to AIDS": On the Changing Discourse of AIDS in Uganda'. It has fascinating illustrations of leaflets that are worth further discussion. If you can't find the Crimp collection, Jan Zita Grover also has a piece called 'AIDS, Keywords, and Cultural Work', in Lawrence Grossberg, Cary Nelson, and Paula Treichler, *Cultural Studies*.

Despite this flood of material, one of the most powerful studies of these issues was written before the first diagnoses of AIDS, Susan Sontag's 1978 essay *Illness as Metaphor*, which is mostly about tuberculosis and cancer. It appeared first in sections in the *New York Review of Books*—that is, it's the sort of thing non-academics might sit down to read. Sontag wrote the book after her treatment for cancer, and she is ferocious in her attack on the ways the popular metaphors of illness heap blame and suffering on patients already in physical pain. If you do read it, don't be put off by the casual literary allusions; you don't need to have read as much as Sontag has to understand her argument. She later wrote a later essay called *AIDS and Its Metaphors*, but most of the ideas in that were already there in the earlier book.

The creative response to AIDS is a different story from that of the construction of AIDS in ads, but it is important. Two particularly moving accounts that raise issues of language are Thom Gunn's collection of poems, *The Man with the Night Sweats*, and Derek Jarman's movie, *Blue*. A benefit video, *Red, Hot, and Blue* showed how the romantic lyrics of Cole Porter Could take on new meanings in the age of AIDS.

Questions for Discussion

1. Meyers' essay includes a personal narrative called "How I survived AIDS." How does using a personal narrative help or hinder the message and effectiveness of the ad? Consider the three illustrations that accompany the narrative, the telephone, two paintbrushes, and a steaming cup of coffee. How do these images interact with the narrative?

2. Every ad wants to arrest the spread of AIDS, but how they accomplish this purpose, according to Meyers, is shaped by another agenda that is embraced by the author. How does he describe the way the author/organization that writes an ad shapes its text? How does Meyers explain the effect of audiences on the construction of an advertisement?

3. If you asked Greg Meyers, "What makes an ad change people's behavior?" What would he say? Support this with passages from his article.

Explorations

1. Using Meyers' bulleted list of the ways AIDS represents society and categorizes people, analyze other kinds of ads. Apply this approach to the ads in Cynthia Selfe's essay "Lest We Think the Revolution IS a Revolution."

2. Meyers very specifically talks about the way word choice shapes the tacit message of an ad. Write your own 10–20-word advertisement, including images, if you like. It does not have to be about AIDS. Then, alter the word choices in your ad to address different purposes, audiences and cultural beliefs. How does the kind of language you choose to use change an ad's message?

3. Meyers and Miller believe that mass media causes formerly taboo or offensive material to become normal and acceptable in society. He says, "Advertising has played an important part in the process of the normalization of condom usage." Can you think of other advertising campaigns that have familiarized other products or practices?

Formal Writing Assignments

1. Choose two AIDS advertisements that were produced by different organizations. Compare their approach to audience, their choices of words and metaphors, and their use of images (or lack of images)? Finally, determine what the "unspoken message" of each ad really is, and how it can shape a culture's view of AIDS.

2. Construct your own advertisement for AIDS, or any other informative and controversial issue (Like gun laws or environmental conservation). Then in an essay, describe your composition process, analyzing your choices of words, metaphors, and images, in the context of your purpose, intended audience and beliefs.

How TV Covers War

Mark Crispin Miller

Mark Crispin Miller is one of the leading media critics in the United States, and is Professor of Media Ecology in the Department of Culture and Communication at New York University. His scholarship has enhanced our understanding of the role of the media in controlling our psychic habits, our social relations, and our political ideas. His latest book *A History of Modern Propaganda* (forthcoming 2000) examines the operation of modern propaganda in world cultures. Miller is the director of The Project on Media Ownership. PROMO was established in 1996 to provide the American people with the facts about who owns the media—TV, radio and movies, books and music, newspapers and magazines—and to explain the impact of such concentrated ownership. Also, Miller is the director of research for the National Campaign for Better TV; he is researching and promoting ways that television can positively contribute to society. In concert with Miller's interests in television culture and propaganda, "How TV Covers War" discusses how television reporters construct news stories.

Writing Before Reading

1. Write a short description of a soldier. Include how she fights, what she stands for and how she thinks. As you write think about how you learned what a soldier is like.

2. Remember the latest military recruiting advertisements you were exposed to. Write a narrative of that advertisement that includes a description of its message and the way it made you feel.

3. Write your own TV news story about a war or violent event. You can choose to write about either a fictional or actual event. When you read this essay, think about the way you arranged your story and the language you chose to use.

How TV Covers War

In its latest TV ad campaign, devised to attract recruits, the U.S. Army offers us a potent jingle, the impression of fast action, and an unintended glimpse of truth. We hear the usual piercing voices pipe the following refrain: "Be—all that you can be!—in the Army!" Meanwhile, we see a series of young soldiers, each confidently doing his crucial job: one mans a tank, one sits in a jet, one charts a course, etc. The stirring pitch suggests that Army life is not just fun—it's an adventure in self-fulfillment. Once we tune out its stimulants, however, the ad presents us with a prospect both more accurate and less exciting. What it shows, in fact, is not an assortment of young men "being all they can be," but a succession of intricate machines, each one tended by a placid figure in a uniform. The hardware is imposing: the soldiers are completely blank, wearing headphones, starting engines, staring into computer terminals.

For all its high-pitched jubilance, the ad depicts a grim situation: the dead end of the history of modern war. Five hundred years of technological advance have reduced the soldier to a minor implement, fixed and simple, like a spark plug, used to fire off those spirited engines that now do nearly all the slaughtering. This demotion of the warrior seems to have begun in the fifteenth century, when the first guns were used to shatter the preening cavalries of Europe. "The musket is a weapon invented in Germany in our time,'" wrote Pius II in the early 1460s. "Powder made of charcoal from the fig or willow, mixed with sulphur and nitre, is poured into it; then a small ball of lead, the size of a filbert, is inserted in the front end." This new device could easily dispatch the bravest man on horse or foot, as the Pope suggests in a tone of indignant wonder: "No armor can withstand the force of this engine, and it also pierces wood."

Thenceforth, as the West proceeded slowly to industrialize, war moved ever further from the grasp of its participants, becoming more autonomous, not so much a human conflict as a gross conjunction of victims and machines. By the early nineteenth century, this process seemed to have become complete, eliciting applause from those who considered it a sign of progress. Hegel, for example, saw this mechanization as a step that purified warfare of its savagery:

> Only through this instrumentality [i.e., the use of guns] could that superior order of valor be called forth, that valor in which the heat of personal feeling has no share; for the discharge of firearms is directed against a body of men—an abstract enemy, not individual combatants.

Others were less idealistic, more nostalgic. "The new way of fighting, the variation of weapons, the artillery, have robbed military life of that which is most attractive about it," wrote Benjamin Constant in 1813.

> One no longer tastes that keen delight in the will, in action, in the strengthening of mind and body, which made the ancient heroes and medieval knights love hand-to-hand combat.

If *l'artillerie* were enough to degrade the craft of war in 1813, how can we begin to appreciate the soldier's insignificance in 1915, when machine guns, fragmentation bombs, poison gas, and depth charges first began to express themselves in force? What of the impact of such later innovations as the land mine, radar, automatic rifle, guided missile, napalm, nerve gas, Agent Orange? Since the Great War, "the new superfluity of killing agents," John Keegan tells us, has transformed "the very environment of the battlefield into one almost wholly—and indiscriminately—hostile to man."

In such a killing zone, there is not much need for prowess or practiced abilities. Crack marksmanship, for instance, is no longer a desideratum at the front, where the atmosphere itself is so explosive that the meticulous blasts of the sharpshooter have become redundant. "Hitting the target," Keegan writes, "for centuries the principal military skill, is henceforth to be left to the law of averages." For that matter, the sudden use of a nuclear "device" would quickly invalidate all the special talents of the battlefield, along with "the battlefield" itself.

Nor is it only in time of war that arms displace the man. Even now, reports James Fallows, our soldiers are actually kept idle by their weaponry, most of which is too fragile and expensive to be used much. The army's gunners stationed in Europe and Korea, "where they would presumably be charged with stopping the Soviet tanks with TOW missiles, get to fire at most once a year with a live round," because "the rounds now cost $6,000 apiece." And in the Air Force, "the main barrier to the formation of a cadre of experienced pilots is that so many of them quit" because they don't do much flying, since their temperamental jets are usually out of commission.

Along with this progressive degradation of the soldier there has been a new kind of estrangement, enforced by the technology of war. Since World War I, the enormous scale of mass combat has forced even the ablest general off the field and into the armchair, to be guided by mere reports of the violence raging somewhere else. Throughout this century, this distance has been growing, as the representation becomes more precise. In the Great War, the "front" was, for the first time, far too big and vague to be overseen by the individual leaders, who therefore had to stay behind the lines, studying maps and messages. And now, those who supervise the next catastrophe will be able, theoretically, to follow every development as it occurs, with the help of satellites that can track missiles and warships, locate nuclear explosions, forecast inconvenient weather, and photograph in clear detail any visible area, however tiny or remote.

All these mediating gadgets, however sensitive, must blunt the sense of war in those who use them. Translated into so many blips and telecasts, the fact of war becomes no more than a pressing abstraction, charged with suspense but not noticeably bloody. The same effect obtains for many individual soldiers, those elite technicians encased in the finest jets and tanks, which are built to devastate a countryside and its inhabitants without themselves sustaining any damage. Raised above the crawling infantry, these men are accoutred to approach a battle as their superiors are equipped to gauge it—in a mood of perfect equilibrium and snug detachment. Suspended in this state of artificial infancy—the same state that attracts us all to the promise of advanced technology—the soldier would seem to become psychologically incapable of spoiling for a fight, of closing with some tough opponent, but wants instead to search and destroy without risk, to translate his belligerence into his buttons and extensions, and simply let his fingers do the warring.

In short, it is the intended function of our weaponry to keep war at a distance, even while sustaining it. The overestimation of our hardware, for example, makes the human enemy seem alien, a freak of nature. Our jets and tanks become the indisputable proof of our superiority, things of supreme, self-evident value, so that any destructive counterattack strikes us, not as a worthy challenge, but as downright effrontery, a gross insult to the sacred weapons carrying "our boys." Those guerrillas who fight in person, on the ground, showing their teeth and hacking away in the old-fashioned manner, now seem uncanny, either subhuman or superhuman, as they threaten our machinery with atavistic skills; while the Soviets, more fitting adversaries, are utterly nonhuman, a nation of secret sites and proliferating warheads.

And, as it seems to cancel out the breathing enemy, so does our hardware seem to distance us from what wars really do, to friend and foe alike. Long immersion in technology can make war seem as safe for those who enter it as it looks to those who plan or conduct it from afar. The concept of warfare in outer space, which our military now prepares to realize at vast expense, represents the absolute fulfillment of the technocratic vision. Herman Kahn, the *New York Times* reports, "foresee[s] the day when 'clean wars' could be fought in outer space," with "intense light rays," "space mines and decoys," and "robot warrior craft." Inspired by (among others) Daniel O. Graham and Lyndon LaRouche, the Reagan Administration finds this Atari program irresistible. In outer space, that great playground for bureaucratic speculation, there will apparently be none of the "petty circumstances which cannot be properly described on paper," none of those "difficulties" which, Clausewitz reminds us, "accumulate and produce a friction which no man can imagine exactly who has not seen war." Apparently beyond the reach of chance, outer space offers the deft consultant a realm where, yes, it finally will be possible to deploy machines that enable a kind of war "in which the heat of personal feelings has no share," a place where battle can flash silently, decisively, without leaving any bloody mess.

Up, up, and away–and yet the higher we soar above the scene of battle, trying to transcend the pangs of war in and through the very weapons used to fight it, the more gruesome, more protracted, more extensive war becomes.[1] Since warfare first became pervasively industrialized, no major war has been either brief or "clean"—quite the contrary. The place-names of premodern military history—Thermopylae, Issus, Philippi, Hastings, Agincourt, Pavia, Yorktown, Waterloo—exert a fascination that is essentially dramatic, evoking the key moments of reversal, recognition, and climax in what we still nostalgically interpret as a global story; whereas the great place-names of modern war often generate a different order of association, each denoting an event of such prodigious and explosive horror that it defeats all impositions of narrative, all spectatorial projection, all attempts at evocation, which can never seem to say as much as the mere word "Passchendaele," or "Ypres Salient," "Stalingrad," "Dresden," "Hiroshima."

Thus, through a dark kind of synecdoche peculiar to this era, some proper nouns are now taken to memorialize remote atrocities. But at the times when those atrocities took place, language was used, not to convey the horrors of war, but to put them at a distance: official words were issued as just one more type of authorized materiel. Like submachine guns, or gas, or atomic bombs, certain misleading terms and phrases have been devised and mass-produced by warring governments, in order to conceal the novel agonies of battle from civilian populations ill-equipped to tolerate them. Here again, the Great War marks a starting point: the first extensive, systematic use of propaganda by a government (the British, whose achievement in this area made a big impression on young Adolf Hitler); and the gray dawn of official euphemism, which now imbues our fragmentary culture like polluted air. "Public euphemism as the special rhetorical sound of life in the latter third of the twentieth century," suggests Paul Fussell, "can be said to originate in the years 1914–18," the years that inaugurated an age of apocalyptic violence whose outcome we are still awaiting, at a distance.

Are we helpless to survive within this process? After all this, is it possible to break down these distances? The outlook is bleak; and yet, perhaps, our salvation may be in our midst already, unnoticed until now. Technology, which has made war both invisible and all-consuming, has also blessed us, many think, with the means to remember what's at stake, by giving us television.

Is TV in fact a potent force for peace? It would appear to rediscover precisely what those long-range weapons do, what those euphemisms actually refer to. It reminds the man who's dropped the bomb just what that bomb is meant to do to men and women, children, neighborhoods; and it deftly undercuts the pose of objectivity implicit in a government's bureaucratese: "incursion," "protective reaction strike," "limited nuclear exchange," "political infrastructure," etc. When such unsuggestive language fills the newspapers, George Orwell wrote in 1946, "a mass of Latin words falls upon the facts like snow"; that snow doesn't stick on television, which always homes in on the dead, allowing no excuses.

Modern war clearly demands this kind of plainness, as we learn from the recent history of literary style: our machinery has helped us to commit atrocities, yet has simultaneously enforced the sort of diction needed to describe them. The Civil War and "the mechanical age," Edmund Wilson points out combined to simplify American prose demanding "lucidity, precision, terseness"; and the later, larger wars honed down still more the language of those many writers—journalists as well as novelists and poets—who have struggled to convey the horror, paradoxically, by understating it, rendering it with photographic coolness and exactitude. Through such unflinching reporting, it might be argued, the best war correspondents, and writers like Hemingway, Remarqué, Céline, and Mailer, have aspired, *avant l'image*, to replicate in words the bleak and graphic vision of TV.

The TV coverage of the war in Lebanon seems to have persuaded some that the medium, with its direct and unadorned depictions, may someday usher in an Age of Peace. Confronted with the image of the dead, the viewer can only see and sorrow, and never stand for war again. That, at any rate, is the conclusion drawn by some well-known commentators, who agree about the fact, but differ on the question of its value. A war usually has a purpose, writes George F. Will, of greater moment than the suffering of its victims. Will therefore distrusts TV's inherent pacifism, suggesting that, "had there been television at Antietam on America's bloodiest day (September 17, 1862), this would be two nations," since Americans "might have preferred disunion at the price of union, had they seen the price, in color in their homes in the evening." Ellen Goodman, on the other hand, sees this "price" as all important, and so asserts that TV, "intrinsically anti-war," "brings home what war is all about: killing, wounding, destroying. It doesn't film ideas, but realities," and "this is our greatest hope."

Both of these responses take for granted the idea that television does indeed, as the cliché has it, "bring war into our living rooms." We often hear the same assertion from the figureheads of television, who venerate their medium for having pulled us out of Vietnam. "For the first time," writes Dan Rather, "war was coming into our homes," and William S. Paley too recalls that "television news brought the war into American living rooms almost every night." These observers are only speaking metaphorically, but they present the metaphor as fact: they identify war footage with war itself, as if, after watching each night's newscast in the 1960s, the average viewer had to count his dead, and vacuum the shrapnel out of his couch.

It is, in fact, the great myth of television that the medium somehow gives us an immediate impression, conveying not images, but actualities; and its coverage of war is supposedly the most compelling example of such supreme truthfulness. This pretense of objectivity makes TV's many actual distortions—whether inherent or imposed—all the more insidious, because their camouflage is perfect, fooling not only the viewer, but even most of those who work within the medium, naively claiming to reveal "the way it is."

But what do we see when we sit at home and watch a war? Do we experience an actual event? In fact, that "experience" is fundamentally absurd. Most obviously, there is the incongruity of scale, the radical disjunction of locations. While a war is among the biggest things that can ever happen to a nation or people, devastating families, blasting away the roofs and walls, we see it compressed and miniaturized on a sturdy little piece of furniture, which stands and shines at the very center of our household. And TV contains warfare in subtler ways. While it may confront us with the facts of death, bereavement, mutilation, it immediately cancels out the memory of that suffering, replacing its own pictures of despair with a commercial, upbeat and inexhaustibly bright.

While it thus surrounds its painful images with buffers, TV also mitigates them from within. The medium may pose as the purveyor of raw history, but if war weren't suitably processed for the domestic market, if each disaster didn't have its anchorman and correspondent to introduce it, gloss it, and pronounce its simple moral, we wouldn't stand for it, any more than we could take those football games that played in 1981 without the usual commentary. The TV newsman comforts us as John Wayne comforted our grandparents, by seeming to have the whole affair in hand. This hero functions as the guardian of our enclosed spectatorship. Therefore, when we see a newsman shot to death, as happened in Guyana and El Salvador, we react with an especial horror, because we realize that TV is not, in fact, immune to the events which it observes, but that the protective apparatus can be shattered; and if the medium does not confer invincibility on those who manage it, it surely can't safeguard its helpless viewers.

It is only this kind of violence—extraordinary, unexpected, fully visible, and inflicted on the viewer's alter ego—which can make a strong (if brief) impression on TV. For, despite all we have heard about the harrowing plainness of the footage, we simply can't and don't respond to televised violence as intensely as we would if we were right there on the scene. If we did away with all the ads and newsmen, in other words, the experience would still, necessarily, be mediated, and its impact ultimately slight. Even in extreme close-up, the medium maintains a subtle distance between viewer and victim, presenting every pang and ruin with an ineradicable coolness. Over the years we have seen, not only wars, but assassinations, executions, drownings, beatings, shoot-outs, fatal brawls, and nearly every other kind of cruelty—but how much of this do we remember vividly? If we had actually been present at the many horrible events that we have seen take place on television we would all be as hard and wise as the Wandering Jew, or a nation of quivering shut-ins.

Because the TV image is intrinsically restrained, then, it is not the newsman's purpose to take the edge off an unbearable confrontation. His illusory control performs a different function, necessitated not by the nastiness of actual events, but by TV itself. What upsets us most about those images of aftermath is not so much their painfulness as their apparent randomness; we suddenly arrive upon this unexpected scene and ask ourselves, "Why this?" Watching the news, we come to feel, not only that the world is blowing up, but that it does so for no reason, that its ongoing history is nothing more than a series of eruptions, each without cause or context. The news creates this vision of mere anarchy through its erasure of the past, and its simultaneous tendency to atomize the present into so many unrelated happenings, each recounted through a sequence of dramatic, unintelligible pictures.

In short, the TV news adapts the world to its own commercial needs, translating history into several mad occurrences, just the sort of "story" that might pique the viewer's morbid curiosity. Thus political events appear as lurid crimes: the wars in Lebanon, El Salvador, Guatemala come to seem as chilling and mysterious as the Manson killings, Patty Hearst's kidnapping, and the Tylenol affair. Everything begins to seem the work of chance, so that "chance" begins to lose its meaning; and the news itself, while fostering this impression, at the same time purports to comprehend the chaos. And so we have the correspondent, solemnly nattering among the ruins, offering crude "analysis" and "background," as if to compensate us for the deep bewilderment that his medium created in the first place.

While TV confuses us precisely through its efforts to inform us, so it only numbs us through its mechanical attempts to work us up. If it can't convey some sense of a war's origins or purposes, then perhaps, as Ellen Goodman thinks, it must at least enable us to apprehend war's personal results— "killing, wounding, destroying." But the medium's immanent remoteness won't permit such revelation; and so TV's custodians struggle desperately to overcome this reserve, trying to find a technical method of arousing the very sympathy that their technology inhibits to begin with. They invariably zoom in tight on the mourner's face, as if we can feel more intensely for another by looking deep inside his nose; and they cut hectically from one appalling image to another, trying to force revulsion through a sort of photographic overkill.

And while television keeps us unenlightened and unmoved, it fails to evoke the conflicts that it covers. As a means of conveying the realities of war, TV is all but useless, precisely because of that very quality which some think makes TV the perfect instrument for just such communication: its uninflected vision. For war is, above all, intense, whereas television is too detached to convey intensities. Passion, for instance, rarely registers on television except as something comical or suspect. The medium therefore undercuts the warrior's ardor: crusaders, patriots, and revolutionaries all seem equally insane on television, and the will to power seems nothing but an aberration, a recrudescence of "machismo" or a burst of "deviance." This, according to the liberal argument, is all to the good, since all "aggression" is unnatural and ought to be exposed as such. But TV also strains out the intensity of suffering, flattening the martyr as it ridicules the persecutor, trivializing both victim and tormentor. "Television especially is supposed to reveal the real tragedy of war," Peter Jennings complained from West Beirut last August, "but the camera has not adequately captured the misery this battle between ideologies has produced."

But that camera can't record "real tragedy," because death has no finality, no poignancy, on television. Because the medium cancels out the living presence of its figures, homogenizing all identity, whether individual or collective, it can't restore the impact of a single loss, or express the decimation of a people. Since no one seems to live on television, no one seems to die there. And the medium's temporal facility deprives all terminal moments of their weight.

The uniformity of TV's view includes not just war's victims, but wars themselves. As the medium subverts all overpowering commitment, all keen belief and pain, so it equates jihad, class struggle, imperialist assault, blood feud, and border strife, never capturing whatever is peculiar to specific conflicts, and thereby reducing all wars to a vague abstraction known as War. The medium gave us a "keyhole view" of Vietnam, writes Michael Arlen, reducing that war to a mere handful of unilluminating images, rarely gruesome, never evocative. Similarly, the war in Lebanon was nothing but a lot of sunny rubble, explosions amid tall white buildings, dark women railing at the camera; the wars in Central America, nothing more than rumpled guerrillas doing push-ups in the woods. In short, TV expresses War largely through a few aesthetic images; and even these impressions are unsuggestive. The medium's eye is too jaundiced, its on-the-scene equipment much too cumbrous, its scope too limited, to permit the full delivery of the particular atmosphere—frightening, unique, and fatally arresting—of a given war at a certain time and place.

While the writer or filmmaker can recreate the ambience of a war long finished, the correspondent can't evoke the war that's going on around him. Here again, some presumed advantages of television turn out to be mere hindrances. TV's celebrated presence-on-the-scene only prevents its commentators from arriving at a larger sense, a more informed impression, the sort of grasp that viewers need in order to be moved themselves. Perhaps we can't expect a working journalist thus to transcend his own assignment, when he has a daily deadline; but there is one kind of detachment that doesn't necessitate long reflection, and that is the ex post facto reconstruction that the writing journalist must perform. However, even this achievement is beyond the TV newsman, whose expressive faculties have been supplanted by his footage: if he can show you what he sees, then he needn't labor to express it, and so his eloquence recedes, his perceptions coarsen, as all he has to do is make authoritative noises for the soundtrack, and stand there for the visual cadence, mike in hand. In covering modern war, the newsman is no less reduced by his equipment than the soldiers flying overhead, or rumbling past in tanks. Thus diminished, the newsman is not only incapable of sounding like Hemingway, but can't even reach the descriptive level of earlier war correspondents like Philip Gibbs, Herbert Matthews, Webb Miller, or Edward R. Murrow.

Unable to evoke or analyze, the TV newsman, we would think, ought at least to live up to the claims of his medium, and tell us what he knows (if anything) objectively. But TV may be the least objective medium, because it makes its loaded points from behind an apparently neutral mask: "The camera doesn't lie." While the news report is more or less devoid of atmosphere or telling information, that seeming vacuum is in fact filled up with expressions of the televisual world view, which is the intellectual equivalent of the broadest, coarsest visual image. This world view is a heavy distillation of our general ideological assumptions, which are often dangerously simple to begin with. Further simplified to make a bold impression on the little screen, our ideology comes back to us in especially crude, delusive hunks, disguised, of course, as straightforward reportage.

According to this televisual reality, in a war there are no issues, and only two sides: the bullies and the little guys. Since TV brings us conflicts ahistorically, an attack must necessarily be unjustified and unexpected, its victims innocent, its authors brutal. The purpose of this melodrama is not to "awaken public opinion"—TV can't properly be said to awaken anything—as to treat the viewer to an easy dose of rage and pity. This kind of manipulation may seem quite noble, a cry of honest indignation meant to halt a heinous crime, but it is actually expressive of the subtlest bigotry, the most self-serving moralism.

For the TV news loves a good victim; and while this attitude suggests a most enlightened, charitable impulse, it is not conducive to an activist response, because this love is fatally possessive of its broken object: "Stay as you are!" it tells the oppressed. "Your battered face has earned you our esteem!" Within this schema, the worst thing that can happen to the underdog is not to die or go on suffering, but to become unpitiable, to stand up strong. Because the news allows no categories between those of the noble weakling and the ugly victor, any group that does attempt to shed its lowly status zips straight from subjugation into villainy. Whenever this occurs, the journalists turn indignant; yet they wouldn't have it otherwise, as long as the new configuration yields fresh victims for the sympathetic camera.

This sentimental strategy relies on and perpetuates the oldest stereotypes, and is therefore the expression of mere bigotry, largely unconscious, frequently well meaning, and therefore worse than any overt hatred. Blacks and Jews, the most despised of peoples, have been the major objects in this scheme, shifting from handsome victim to pariah, from one debased status to the other, according to how autonomous they seem to those who work on television. As long as blacks abided by the principles of King and Gandhi, they were aestheticized as Eternal Losers, eyes soulfully pitched upward; but as soon as they acted on their anger, whether as rioters or Black Panthers, the news took back that holy glow and cast them as an unexpected menace, only to reinstate their wings and halos in these quiescent times. And now the Jews of Israel have forfeited their saintliness by acting as Americans used to, expropriating land that isn't theirs, teaching their enemies an atrocious lesson, and doing some harm to innocents as well.

According to the news, the real crime of the Israelis was not their invasion per se, but their willful abandonment of the Jew's historic role as martyr. This was the dominant theme of TV's coverage of the war in Lebanon. Israel, said Richard Threlkeld from Beirut, "has confounded its enemies and . . . commanded fear and respect, but it is not the Israel that its first Prime Minister, Ben-Gurion, always imagined it would be. That Israel, that light unto the nations." Despite the denials of the networks' presidents, it was indeed the case that the coverage of that war was heavily biased against Israel, although not in a way that ought to comfort the Palestinians. The news did consistently inflate the casualty figures, dwell on atrocities, stress heavily the fact of censorship, and otherwise depict Israel as the only guilty party. The Palestinians have also suffered at others' hands—for example, King Hussein's—but the TV news never trumpeted that outrage.

This is hardly meant to justify what Israel did in Lebanon, but merely to define the real animus behind TV's characterization of that war. For the Palestinians too have been diminished by the coverage. As Israel was excoriated for having shed her crown of thorns, the Palestinians were suddenly ennobled, playing the erstwhile Jewish role of victim. As such, they were translated into total helplessness, mere bleeding figures with no grievance, no threatening aims, no voice other than the networks' voices. "In the news," writes Ellen Goodman in approval of the TV coverage, "the sides are not divided into good guys and bad guys, but aggressors and victims." This nondistinction actually equates the "victims" with the "good guys" and thereby cancels out the complicated history in Lebanon, along with the PLO, which doesn't really fit in either TV category.

This omission preserves the simple-minded opposition that the medium imposed upon that conflict. And which side benefits from this reduction? Certainly not the Israelis, who, once the PLO have been erased, appear to have invaded Lebanon simply for the fun of killing Lebanese civilians; and the Palestinians too have been distorted by the TV fiction, which presents them as disorganized, unrepresented, politically unconscious, and therefore fit for pity, in dire need of the medium's own illusory protection. As in El Salvador and Northern Ireland, so here TV created a beleaguered and pathetic mass, "caught in the middle," completely apolitical, and therefore in no shape to strike back later: TV, in short, will only champion those groups whom it can sentimentalize. It has no interest in a stoic people, or in a population that takes careful steps toward self-possession. For when the Palestinians fight again, their belligerence will, as usual, appear as unexpected; and if they eventually find that they too "command fear and respect," they may also find themselves portrayed, therefore, as evil.

What can television tell us, then, about a war? Here is a rich example of the medium's expressiveness, chosen at random from last summer's coverage. On the "NBC Nightly News" on 2 August 1982 Roger Mudd delivered the following introduction: "Watching the shelling and the panic and the smoke and the death in Beirut on television night after night can have a powerful impact. But, as John Chancellor's commentary tonight reveals, seeing it in person is of quite a different magnitude." Chancellor then appeared from overseas, and gave us this:

> What will stick in the mind about yesterday's savage Israeli attack on Beirut is its size and its scope. This is one of the world's big cities. The area under attack is the length of Manhattan Island below Central Park. Five hundred thousand people live here. One in a hundred is a PLO fighter. And it went on for such a long time: before dawn [sic] until five in the afternoon. Systematic, sophisticated warfare. The Israeli planes just never stopped coming. For an entire day, Beirut rocked and swayed to the rhythm of the Israeli attack. The Israelis say they were going after military targets with precision. There was also the stench of terror all across the city.

> Nothing like it has ever happened in this part of the world. I kept thinking yesterday of the bombing of Madrid during the Spanish Civil War. What in the world is going on? Israel's security problem on its border is fifty miles to the south. What's an Israeli Army doing here in Beirut? The answer is that we are now dealing with an imperial Israel which is solving its problems in someone else's country, world opinion be damned. Nobody knows how the

battle of Beirut is going to end. But we do know one thing. The Israel we saw here yesterday is not the Israel we have seen in the past.

Chancellor clearly wanted to convey his own experience of bombardment, but his language is dead, its function having long since been usurped by videotape. What was it like? Well, "it went on for such a long time," the "planes just never stopped coming"; and these colorless phrases culminate in an image both impersonal and feebly aesthetic: "Beirut rocked and swayed to the rhythm of the Israeli attack." This image, which reduces the bombardment to a sort of urban jitterbug, does not convey a strong impression of the citizens' fear, as Murrow's London broadcasts did so well. All that the clause does, in fact, is reproduce the viewer's detached perspective; Chancellor might just as well have watched the bombing on TV, which is equally incapable of expressing others' fears and sorrows. The report's one reference to the vivid human presence is a mere cliché, thrown in as an afterthought: "There was also the stench of terror all across the city."

"What in the world is going on?" Chancellor asks. "What's an Israeli Army doing here in Beirut?" These are good questions, but he's supposed to answer them, not pose them. Rather than provide some history, he merely bolsters our incomprehension with his own, thereby turning the event into a mystery, which, like a priest, he can seem to grasp and solve by uttering a well-known moral formula: "The Israel we saw here yesterday is not the Israel we have seen in the past."

Thus, into the descriptive void of the report there drops the familiar clod of ideology, disguised as an objective fact: "But we do know one thing." At once "savage" and "imperial," Chancellor's Israel has undergone a sudden, terrifying metamorphosis. "I kept thinking of the bombing of Madrid during the Spanish Civil War." Why? Was little Johnny Chancellor, age nine, in Madrid when it was bombed in 1936? Probably not. Then is the Spanish Civil War in any way comparable to "the battle of Beirut"? Not noticeably. What Chancellor actually means by comparing this war to one he's only read about is that Israel has indeed become its opposite, has jumped straight into that other category, since Madrid was bombed, for Franco's sake, by the Junkers 52 of Hitler's Condor Legion.

As this report is typical of television, we must conclude that the medium does not "bring home what war is all about," but rather what TV is all about. Television's seeming transparency is in fact the medium's cleverest fiction, offering what seems a clear view of the world, yet in a way that only makes us more familiar with, more dependent on, TV.

But let's set aside all these distortions—the shrinkage, the implicit distancing, the illusory containment, the imperceptible mist of ideology—and grant that TV does tend to present, as Goodman puts it, "less glory and more gore." Does this also mean that TV is "intrinsically anti-war"? There is no reason to think so; and this belief in television's salutary bias is not only unfounded, but intolerant, positing only one morally acceptable response. To assert, with Ellen Goodman, that on TV "the sides are not divided into good guys and bad guys, but aggressors and victims," is to say that the viewer, when he sits down to watch TV, is suddenly cleansed of all personal identity, all preconception, and can now apprehend the conflicts of the world from an exalted, unimpeachable standpoint, seeing reality through God's own eyes, or Ellen Goodman's. Far from conducive to a world of peace, such "objective" certainty is probably more dangerous than any archaic faith, because it reflects, and has at its disposal, the most enormous system of technology that has ever choked the world.

For not even the most sophisticated Sony has a perfect moral faculty built into it. We usually see what we want to see on television; and TV complicates this tendency by helping to determine that original desire. If it thinks that we want war, it sells us war. The medium can easily circumvent the pacific influence (if any) of its graphic images. Like radio or the yellow press, TV too can beat the drum. "Granted, television helped get us out of Vietnam," writes Michael Arlen, "but it also helped march us in."

And even if the medium weren't influential, the images per se dictate no automatic pacifism. Confronted with those pictures of the slaughtered Palestinians, a Phalangist viewer, or a member of Gush Emunim, would surely smile at the sight of all those dead "aggressors"; nor would the televised corpses of Israelis draw tears from any fervent anti-Zionist. And it isn't only foreigners who take sides. Had there been television at Antietam on America's bloodiest day, this country might indeed still be two nations; but not necessarily, as George Will supposes, two nations frightened into peace, but two nations still at war, each side still watching every battle, and still finding, on the screen, excuses for refusing to negotiate.

And, had the Civil War been thus prolonged by television, the newsmen would, of course, continue to lament it, crying automatically for peace while shooting everything in sight. Truth is indeed the first casualty in any war, and our journalists have never been less honest than in this sentimental era. In his memoirs published in 1946, Herbert Matthews wrote this sentence:

> The urge to go out and fight, to pit one's strength and wits against the forces of nature, to seek adventure, risk life and take joy in comradeship and danger—these are deep feelings, so deep that even I who love life and family and luxury and books have yielded to them.

And, of course, that stirring list of hard inducements implies another, which Matthews took for granted: "the urge for a terrific story." No TV newsman would make such a frank avowal: Matthews's "deep feelings" have become, not only difficult to gratify, but entirely taboo; and the old craving for a scoop now comes concealed in journalistic pieties about "the public's right to know." In a recent *TV Guide*, Dan Rather, asked what event he'd most like to report in the year 2000, came up with this: "Good evening, from CBS News. Peace and good will toward all living things prevails [sic] everywhere on earth and throughout the cosmos."

Now what would Dan Rather do, deprived of war and ill will in the cosmos? His utopian pronouncement, as frightening as it is disingenuous, does not reflect the sentiments of a living human being, but the contradictory longings of the medium that has consumed him. TV has us automatically deplore or ridicule all anger, fear, political commitment, deep belief, keen pleasure, exalted self-esteem, tremendous love; and yet, while making all these passions seem unnatural, the medium persistently dwells on their darkest consequences, teasing the housebound spectator with hints of that intensity that it has helped to kill. In fact, despite its pleas for universal calm, what TV depends upon is something else: brutal wars abroad, and an anxious peace in every living room.

How TV Covers War

Afterword

Arguing that TV's "images per se dictate no automatic pacifism," I used a number of hypothetical examples: Phalangist, anti-Zionist; Yankee or Rebel. It is now possible to point to actual cases—for, after 1982, TV became the primary rhetorical medium of the ultraright, whose militarism was in no way softened by that experience. Indeed, TV accommodates their paranoia, for while its visual coolness tends to subvert the passion of their fanaticism, its melodramatic bias suits their motivating vision of a world divided between Us and Them.

Thus Ronald Reagan, although a product of TV, displayed a medieval fondness for the Apocalyptic face-off. In 1984, the *New York Times* observed that "he usually refers to Christians as 'we' and the adherents of all other religious faiths as 'they'"—a verbal tic made poignant by his frequent references to Armageddon. Such bellicose piety is, of course, common among Reagan's natural constituents: "Sometimes," Mrs. Oliver L. North told *Life* in August 1987, "I feel like 'they're' up there, they've got all the guns—and then there's 'us.' It's very comforting to know there will be an ultimate judgment." Col. North himself promoted the same dichotomous world view: not only as an anticommunist zealot, but as a gifted TV actor, playing the earnest David overcoming the Congressional Goliath—a spectacle that sent his partisans into Manichaean raptures: "It's absolutely classic," exulted G. Gordon Liddy, having watched the hostilities between North and House counsel John Nields: "A lean, hard, strong, battle-ready Marine Corps officer locked in mortal combat with a 60's residue with long hair. The hard jaw versus the soft jaw."

Despite such bloodlust (or lust, perhaps, in Liddy's case), TV is not a rabble-rousing medium—unless the rabble (like those above) are already eager to be roused. "TV," it is true, "can beat the drum," but it tends not to, because its only purpose is to keep us watching, buying, watching—a point that bears reemphasizing, and updating, through the analysis of another, later bit of TV's coverage of the Middle Eastern conflict:

> Good evening. This is the "CBS Evening News," Dan Rather reporting. First: amazement. Then: outrage. Tonight: above all, confusion. Who—if anyone—has custody of the four Achille Lauro hijack/murderers, those young men who took partly paralyzed 69-year-old American Leon Klinghoffer from his wheelchair, shot him, killed him, and tossed him overboard? Who—if anyone—will bring the murderers to justice?

This opening performs in no way like the first paragraph of a standard newspaper article, which—however biased—would still affect to orient the reader. On the contrary: Rather's purpose here was wholly televisual—i.e., to *dis*orient the viewers, and to react on their behalf. At first a mere sequence of explosive nouns, followed by a question so long, garbled, and repetitious that its precise point finally disappears, Rather's lead-in functions only to spread darkness, and fear within that darkness. The plaintive phrase "Who—if anyone?" reveals nothing, but was meant to lead us in a cry of pain; Rather spoke it twice, giving us nothing but anaphora. And the subsequent catalog of atrocities merely amplifies the murder, making the account as hideous as possible in a few seconds. Ignoring what little evidence was then available, Rather referred to all four suspects as active "hijack/murderers," and then further hyped the crime by absurdly multiplying it: "those young men" first "took" the victim "from his wheelchair," then "shot him" and "killed him" and "tossed him overboard." It was as if the killing of "partly paralyzed 69-year-old American Leon Klinghoffer" might not have seemed quite horrible enough if it had happened only once.

Whereas, in 1982, TV cast the Israelis as the Nazis, now—three years later—it was some of Israel's enemies who were apparently acting out of motiveless malignity. Now there was no mention of the earlier atrocity—the invasion of Lebanon—which was, at least in part, the reason for this new one. And so, again, the crime seemed pointless, baseless: its facts misrepresented, its history suppressed, and only for TV's sake.

The real point of the anchorman's lurid rhetoric, then, is to frighten us into depending on the apparatus of the newscast, himself included—and this aim points us toward the actual focus, the secret content, of the TV news. Backed by a map of the seven continents, and—it is implied—in constant contact with dozens of reporters flying in and out of every hot spot, the anchorman sits before us as if exquisitely attuned to the whole world; and yet he is in fact attuned exclusively to us, uses his reporters' data only to promote our continual discomposure as we sit before him. His prefaces need not be accurate, therefore, because their true referent is not the day's events but we who must be made to keep on sitting, keep on sweating:

"First, amazement. Then: outrage." Thus the "report" began as if by slapping us across the face, and then proceeded to disturb us even further with the hint that we were all in danger, because "the four Achille Lauro hijack/murderers" were still at large. This alarmist strategy surely explains why Rather chose automatically to say that Leon Klinghoffer had first been taken "from his wheelchair" and then shot, despite the evidence that the victim had been shot while sitting: Rather's image of someone forced out of a chair before being murdered makes it easier for us to fear, deep down, for our own lives, since we too, as we watch TV, are chairbound Americans (and "partly paralyzed" at that).

Such terrorism makes us grateful to the terrorist—grateful, finally, for our ostensible release at newscast's end, when the anchor suddenly grins us through some little item cute or quaint, to leave us chuckling optimistically after all that pointless torment.

Notes

1. A few years after this essay was written, Ronald Reagan gave succinct expression to this fantasy of universal rescue by some final supramilitary mechanism: "Advancing technology, which originally gave us nuclear weapons, may one day make them obsolete," he told an audience of high school students. "The currents of progress are sweeping us to safety." (Quoted in "Reagan Sees More Teachers in Space," *New York Times*, 8 February 1986)

Questions for Discussion

1. How does the way we write construct the "truth" about an event? Does Miller think that writing can be more accurate than TV reports? How does the commercial pressure to sell a story shape the way it is told? Does Miller believe that a hidden agenda controls the composition of TV new reports?

2. George Will claims that "had there been television at Antietam, the country might, indeed, still be two nations" (page 550). Do you believe that television shapes the ideology of an audience or does an audience shape television broadcasts?

3. In the "Afterword," Miller includes a news report by Dan Rather that is crafted to keep us "watching, buying, watching." What makes this report "televisual?" What kind of audience is TV news written for? How do you think Rather intended his audience to respond? Does his report react for you, or tell you how to think? What rhetorical strategies does he use to capture and maintain his audience's attention?

Explorations

1. Postman and Powers' essay, "How to Watch TV News," suggests some ways to "read" what we see in a TV news report. Miller also wants us to realize that news reports are a construction of an event and not the event itself. Think about a recent news report and list the ways an event has been reported. Include issues of language and image. Then re-present the report in a way that produces another message. As you do this keep a record of the reason you chose to include or exclude certain information. Also, note the way you negotiated decisions about your desired message, affective drama, and audience response.

2. Arrange images and text to create a 3-minute report of some event. Then, replace the text with an appropriate picture or drawing, and the picture with a textual representation. What are the advantages and disadvantages of images and texts?

3. What different insights would Scholes and O'Neill contribute to Miller's discussion about reading television news reports? Would they view television reporting as propaganda, social commentary or as a method of communication that has its own rules of conduct?

Formal Writing Assignments

1. Select either a military recruiting advertisement or a news report and analyze it according to Miller's approach. What makes these reports "televisual?" How does their arrangement call on a consumer audience? What is the message and what is its hidden agenda? Be sure to describe your ad or report and include an analysis of the way it influences audience through the arrangement of language and images.

2. Miller says, "For not even the most sophisticated Sony has a perfect moral faculty built into it. We usually see what we want to see on television; and TV complicates the tendency by helping to determine that original desire. If it thinks we want war, it sells us war." What responsibility do television news teams and their viewers have in the composition of a report? In other words, compare the roles of the creators of a news report and their viewers.

The Language of Advertising

Charles A. O'Neill

Because Charles O'Neill is a very successful independent marketing consultant, he provides an insider's view of the advertising community. O'Neill's years of experience in producing advertisements for industry, and his awareness of what critics say about the effects of advertising on society, are the source of his argument. This essay was originally written for *Exploring Language* and was updated for publication in *Advertising: Feeding Our Fantasies*, where it served as an example of the way advertisers view their own work. O'Neill defends advertiser's use of images to persuade and motivate consumers. This article refutes the arguments of advertising critics who view advertisers as hucksters and contributors to the moral decay of society. O'Neill believes that audiences easily separate the purposeful craft and savvy of advertisements from other more meaningful messages.

Writing Before Reading

1. Write a paragraph or two describing the last advertisement you can remember thinking about. Why do you remember the ad? What was its message? Was it entertaining or informative?

2. Write about an advertisement that has changed your behavior, or that of someone you know. How did that ad influence your thinking or buying practices? Did that ad improve you or not? Do you think advertising can change the way people behave?

3. Imagine that you are an advertiser in the process of composing an ad. What are your goals? What will you use to convince people to buy the product?

The Language of Advertising

The figure on the billboard and in the magazine ads looked like a rock singer, perhaps photographed in the midst of a music video taping session. He was poised, confident, shown leaning against a railing or playing pool with his friends. His personal geometry was always just right. He often wore a white suit, dark shirt, sunglasses. Cigarette in hand, wry smile on his lips, his attitude was distinctly confident, urbane.

He was so successful, this full-lipped, chiquitoas dromedary, that his success quite literally killed him. By mid-1997, with such people and agencies as President Clinton and the Federal Trade commission harassing him at every turn, his masters had no choice. Camel market share reportedly climbed from 3.9 percent in 1989 to 4.4 percent by 1990. According to the FTC, six years after Joe was introduced, more than 13 percent of all smokers under the age of 18 chose Camels as their nicotine delivery system of choice. Finally, the president lent his weight to what had already become a raging debate. "Let's stop pretending that a cartoon camel in a funny costume is trying to sell to adults, not children." New rules, introduced largely as a result of the debate about Joe, prohibit the use of cartoon characters in advertisements.

The obvious topic of the debate that finally killed Joe is cigarette advertising, but beneath the surface it signals something more interesting and broad based: the rather uncomfortable, tentative acceptance of advertising in our society. We recognize the legitimacy—even the value—of advertising, but on some level we can't quite fully embrace it as a "normal" part of our experience. At best, we view it as distracting. At worst, we view it as dangerous to our health and a pernicious threat to no less an authority than the Vatican. In 1997, the Vatican issued a document prepared by the Pontifical Council, titled

561

"Ethics in Advertising." Along with acknowledgment of the positive contribution of advertising (e.g., provides information, supports worthy causes, encourages competition and innovation), the report states, as reported by the *Boston Globe,* "In the competition to attract ever larger audiences . . . communicators can find themselves pressured . . . to set aside high artistic and moral standards and lapse into superficiality, tawdriness and moral squalor."

How does advertising work? Why is it so powerful? Why does it raise such concern? What case can be made for and against the advertising business? In order to understand advertising, you must accept that it is not about truth, virtue, love, or positive social values. It is about money. Ads play a role in moving customers through the sales process. This process begins with an effort to build awareness of a product, typically achieved by facts designated to break through the clutter of competitive messages. By presenting a description of product benefits, ads convince the customer to buy the product. Once prospects have become purchasers, advertising is used to sustain brand loyalty, reminding customers of all the good reasons for their original decision to buy.

But this does not sufficiently explain the ultimate, unique power of advertising. Whatever the product or creative strategy, advertisements derive their power from a purposeful, directed combination of images. Images can take the form of words, sounds, or visual, use individually or together. The combination of images is the language of advertising, a language unlike any other.

Everyone who grows up in the Western world soon learns that advertising language is different from other languages. Most children would be unable to explain how such lines as "With Nice 'n Easy, it's color so natural, the closer he gets the better you look!" (the once-famous ad for Clairol's Nice 'n Easy hair coloring) differed from ordinary language, but they would say, "It sounds like an ad." Whether printed on a page, blended with music on the radio, or whispered on the soundtrack of a television commercial, advertising language is different.

Over the years, the texture of advertising language has frequently changed. Styles and creative concepts come and go. But there are at least four distinct, general characteristics of the language of advertising that make it different from other languages. They lend advertising its persuasive power.

1. The language of advertising is edited and purposeful.
2. The language of advertising is rich and arresting; it is specifically intended to attract and hold our attention.
3. The language of advertising involves us; in effect, we complete the message.
4. The language of advertising is a simple language; it holds no secrets from us.

Edited and Purposeful

In his famous book *Future Shock,* Alvin Toffler describes various types of messages we receive from the world around us each day. As he sees it, there is a difference between normal "coded" messages and "engineered" messages. Much of normal, human experience is "uncoded"; it is merely sensory. For example, Toffler describes a man walking down a street. Toffler notes that the man's sensory perceptions of this experience may form a mental image, but the message is not "designed by anyone to communicate anything, and the man's understanding of it does not depend directly on a social code—a set of agreed-upon signs and definitions." In contrast, Toffler describes a talk show conversation as "coded"; the speakers' ability to exchange information with their host, and our ability to understand it, depend upon social conventions.

The language of advertising is coded. It is also language of carefully engineered, ruthlessly purposeful messages. When Toffler wrote *Future Shock,* he estimated that the average adult was exposed to 560 advertising messages each day. Now, with the advent of 200-channel, direct-broadcast satellite television, the internet, and other new forms of mass media Toffler could not have contemplated, this figure is surely exponentially higher today. None of these messages would reach us, to attract and hold our attention, if it were completely unstructured. Advertising messages have a clear purpose; they are intended to trigger a specific response.

Rich and Arresting

Advertisements—no matter how carefully "engineered'—cannot succeed unless they capture our attention. Of the hundreds of advertising messages in store for us each day, very few will actually command our conscious attention. The rest are screened out. The people who design and write ads know about this screening process; they anticipate and accept it as a premise of their business.

The classic, all-time favorite device used to breach the barrier is sex. The desire to be sexually attractive to others is an ancient instinct, and few drives are more powerful. A magazine ad for Ultima II, a line of cosmetics, invites readers to "find everything you need for the sexxxxiest look around . . . ." The ad goes on to offer other "sexxxy goodies," including "lipsexxxxy lip color, naked eye color . . . . Sun sexxxy liquid bronzer." No one will accuse Ultima's marketing tacticians of subtlety. In fact, this ad is merely a current example of an approach that is as old as advertising. After countless years of using images of women in various stages of undress to sell products, ads are now displaying men's bodies as well. A magazine ad for Brut, a men's cologne, declares in bold letters, "MEN ARE BACK"; in the background, a photograph shows a muscular, shirtless young man preparing to enter the boxing ring—a "manly" image indeed; an image of man as breeding stock.

Every successful advertisement uses a creative strategy based on an idea that will attract and hold the attention of the targeted consumer audience. The strategy may include strong creative execution or a straightforward presentation of product features and customer benefits.

- An ad for Clif Bars, an "energy bar," is clearly directed to people who want to snack but wouldn't be caught dead in a coffee house eating ginger spice cake with delicate frosting, much less ordinary energy bars—the kind often associated with the veggie and granola set: the central photograph shows a gristled cowboy-character, holding a Clif Bar, and asking, in the headline, "What in the hell's a carbohydrate?" Nosiree. This here energy bar is "bound to satisfy cantankerous folk like you."

- Recent cigar ads attract attention through the use of unexpected imagery. An ad for Don Diego cigars, for example, shows a bejeweled woman in an evening dress smoking a cigar, while through the half-open door her male companion asks, "Agnes, have you seen my Don Diegos?"

- A two-page ad for Diesel clothing includes a photo showing the principal participants in the famous Yalta conference in 1945 (Churchill, Roosevelt, and Stalin) with one important difference. Young models in Diesel clothing have been cleverly added and appear to be flirting with the dignitaries. The ad is presented as a "Diesel historical moment" and "the birth of the modern conference." This unexpected imagery is engaging and amusing, appealing to the product's youthful target audience.

Even if the text contains no incongruity and does not rely on a pun for its impact, ads typically use a creative strategy based on some striking concept or idea. In fact, the concept and execution are often so good that many successful ads entertain while they sell.

Consider, for example, the campaigns created for Federal Express. A campaign was developed to position Federal Express as the company that would deliver packages, not just "overnight," but "by 10:00 a.m." the next day. The plight of the junior executive in "Presentation," one TV ad in the campaign, is stretched for dramatic purposes, but it is, nonetheless, all too real: The young executive, who is presumably trying to climb his way up the corporate ladder, is shown calling another parcel delivery service and all but begging for assurance that he will have his slides in hand by 10:30 the next morning. "No slides, no presentation," he pleads. Only a viewer with a heart of stone can watch without feeling sympathetic as the next morning our junior executive struggles to make his presentation *sans* slides. He is so lost without them that he is reduced to using his hands to perform imitations of birds and animals in shadows on the movie screen. What does the junior executive *viewer* think when he or she sees the ad?

1. Federal Express guarantees to deliver packages "absolutely, positively overnight."

2. Federal Express packages arrive early in the day.

3. What happened to that fellow in the commercial will absolutely not happen to me, now that I know what package delivery service to call.

A sound, creative strategy supporting an innovative service idea sold Federal Express. But the quality and objective "value" of execution doesn't matter. A magazine ad for Merit Ultra Lights made use of one word in its headline: "Yo!" This was, one hopes, not the single most powerful idea generated by the agency's creative team that particular month—but it probably sold cigarettes.

Soft drink and fast-food companies often take another approach. "Slice of Life" ads (so-called because they purport to show people in "real-life" situations) created to sell Coke or Pepsi have often placed their characters in Fourth of July parades or other family events. The archetypical version of this approach is filled-to-overflowing with babies frolicking with puppies in the sunlit foreground while their youthful parents play touch football. On the porch, Grandma and Pops are seen quietly smiling as they wait for all of this affection to transform itself in a climax of warmth, harmony, and joy. Beneath the veneer, these ads work through repetition: How many-times-can-you-spot-the-logo-in-this-commercial?

More subtly, these ads seduce us into feeling that if we drink the right combination of sugar, preservatives, caramel coloring, and a few secret ingredients, we'll fulfill our yearning for a world where young folks and old folks live together in perfect bliss.

If you don't buy this version of the American Dream, search long enough and you are sure to find an ad designed to sell you what it takes to gain prestige within whatever posse you do happen to run with. As reported by *The Boston Globe*, "the malt liquor industry relies heavily on rap stars in delivering its message to inner-city youths, while Black Death Vodka, which features a top-hatted skull and a coffin on its label, has been using Guns N' Roses guitarist Slash to endorse the product in magazine advertising." A malt liquor company reportedly promotes its 40-ounce size with rapper King T singing, "I usually drink it when I'm just clowning, me and the home boys, you know, be like downing it . . . I grab me a 40 when I want to act a fool." A recent ad for Sasson jeans, is a long way from Black Death in execution, but a second cousin in spirit. A photograph of a young, blonde (they do have more fun, right?") actress appears with this text: "Baywatch actress Gena Lee Nolin Puts on Sasson. OO-La-La. Sasson. Don't put it on unless it's a Sasson."

Ads do not often emerge like Botticelli's Venus from the sea, flawless and fully-grown. Most often, the creative strategy is developed only after extensive research. "Who will be interested in our product? How old are they? Where do they live? How much money do they earn? What problem will our product solve?" Answers to these questions provide the foundation on which the creative strategy is built.

Involving

We have seen that the language of advertising is carefully engineered; we have discovered a few of the devices it uses to get our attention. R.J. Reynolds has us identifying with Joe in one of his many uptown poses. Coke and Pepsi have caught our eye with visions of peace and love. An actress offers a winsome smile. Now that they have our attention, advertisers present information intended to show us that their product fills a need and differs from the competition. It is the copywriter's responsibility to express, exploit, and intensify such product differences.

When product differences do not exist, the writer must glamorize the superficial differences—for example, differences in packaging. As long as the ad is trying to get our attention, the "action" is mostly in the ad itself, in the words and visual images. But as we read an ad or watch it on television, we become more deeply involved. The action starts to take place in us. Our imagination is set in motion, and our individual fears and aspirations, quirks, and insecurities superimpose themselves on that tightly engineered, attractively packaged message.

Consider, once again, the running battle among the low-calorie soft drinks. The cola wars have spawned many "look-alike" advertisements, because the product features and consumer benefits are generic, applying to all products in the category. Substitute one cola brand name for another, and the messages are often identical, right down to the way the cans are photographed in the closing sequence. This strategy relies upon mass saturation and exposure for impact.

Some companies have set themselves apart from their competitors by making use of bold, even disturbing, themes and images. For example, it was not uncommon not long ago for advertisers in the fashion industry to make use of gaunt, languid models—models who, in the interpretation of some observers, displayed a certain form of "heroin chic." Something was most certainly unusual about the models appearing in ads for Prada and Calvin Klein products. A young woman in a Prada ad projects no emotion whatsoever; she is slightly hunched forward, her posture suggesting that she is in a trance or drug-induced stupor. In a Calvin Klein ad, a young man, like the woman in the Prada ad, is gaunt beyond reason. He is shirtless. As if to draw more attention to his peculiar posture and "zero body fat" status, he is shown pinching the skin next to his navel.

Just as he publicly attacked Joe Camel, President Clinton took an aggressive position against the depiction of heroin chic. In a speech in Washington, D.C. the president commented on the increasing use of heroin on college campuses, noting that "part of this has to do with the images that are finding their way to our young people." One industry observer agreed, asserting that "people got carried away by the glamour of decadence."

Do such advertisers as Prada and Calvin Klein bear responsibility—morally, if not legally—for the rise of heroin use on college campuses? Emergency room visits connected with heroin use reportedly grew from 63,200 in 1993 to 76,000 by 1995, echoing a strong rise in heroin addiction. Is this a coincidence? Does heroin chic and its depiction of a decadent lifestyle exploit certain elements of our society—the young and uncertain, for example? Or did these ads, and others of their ilk, simply reflect profound bad taste? (In fact, on one level, all advertising is about exploitation: the systematic, deliberate identification of our needs and wants, followed by the delivery of a carefully constructed promise that Brand X will satisfy them.)

Symbols offer an important tool for involving consumers in advertisements. Symbols have become important elements in the language of advertising, not so much because they carry meanings of their own, but because we bring meaning to them. One example is provided by the campaign begun in 1978 by Somerset Importers for Johnnie Walker Red Scotch. Sales of Johnnie Walker Red had been trailing sales of Johnnie Walker Black, and Somerset Importers needed to position Red as a fine product in its own right. Their agency produced ads that made heavy use of the color red. One magazine ad, often printed as a two-page spread, is dominated by a close-up photo of red autumn leaves. At lower right, the copy reads, "When their work is done, even the leaves turn to Red." Another ad—also suitably dominated by a photograph in the appropriate color—reads: "When it's time to quiet down at the end of the day, even a fire turns to Red." Red. Warm. Experienced. Seductive.

As we have seen, advertisers make use of a great variety of techniques and devices to engage us in the delivery of their messages. Some are subtle; making use of warm, entertaining, or comforting images or symbols. Others, like Black Death Vodka and Ultima II, are about as subtle as MTV's "Beavis and Butt-head." Another common device used to engage our attention is old but still effective: the use of famous or notorious personalities as product spokespeople or models. Advertising writers did not invent the human tendency to admire or otherwise identify themselves with famous people. Once we have seen a famous person in an ad, we associate the product with the person: "Joe DeMaggio is a good guy. He likes Mr. Coffee. If I buy a Mr. Coffee coffee maker and I use it when I have the boss over for dinner, then maybe she'll think I'm a good guy, too." "Guns 'N Roses rule my world, so I will definitely make the scene with a bottle of Black Death stuck into the waistband of my sweat pants." "Gena Lee Nolin is totally sexy. She wears Sasson, if I wear Sasson, I'll be sexy, too." The logic is faulty, but we fall under the spell just the same. Advertising works, not because Joe DiMaggio is a coffee expert, Slash had discriminating taste, or Gena knows her jeans, but because we participate in it. In fact, we charge ads with most of their power.

A Simple Language

Advertising language differs from other types of language in another important respect; it is a simple language. To determine how the copy of a typical advertisement rates on a "simplicity index" in comparison with text in a magazine article, for example, try this exercise: Clip a typical story from the publication you read most frequently. Calculate the number of words in an average sentence. Count the number of words of three or more syllables in a typical 100-word passage, omitting words that are capitalized, combinations of two simple words, or verb forms made into three-syllable words by the addition of *-ed* or *-es*. Add the two figures (the average number of words per sentence and the number of three-syllable words per 100 words), then multiply the result by 4. According to Robert Gunning, if the resulting number is 7, there is a good chance that you are reading *True Confessions*. He developed this formula, the "Fog Index," to determine the comparative ease with which any given piece of written communication can be read. Here is the complex text of a typical cigarette endorsement:

> I demand two things from any cigarette. I want a cigarette with low tar and nicotine. But I also want taste. That's why I smoke Winston Lights. I get a lighter cigarette, but I still get a real taste. And real pleasure. Only one cigarette gives me that: Winston Lights.

The average sentence in this ad runs 7 words. *Cigarette* and *nicotine* are three syllable words, with *cigarette* appearing four times; *nicotine* once. Consider *that's* as two words, the ad is exactly 50 words long, so the average number of three-syllable words per 100 is ten.

7	words per sentence
+10	three-syllable words/100
17	
× .4	
6.8	Fog Index

According to Gunning's scale, this ad—which has now been consigned to the dustbin of advertising history thanks to government regulations—is written at about the seventh-grade level, comparable to most of the ads found in mass-circulation magazines.

It's about as sophisticated as *True Confessions*; that is, harder to read than a comic book, but easier than *Ladies Home Journal*. Of course, the Fog Index cannot evaluate the visual aspect of an ad—another component of advertising language. The headline, "I demand two things from my cigarette," works with the picture (that of an attractive woman) to arouse consumer interest. The text reinforces the image. Old Joe's simple plea, "Try New Camel Lights," is too short to move the needle on the Fog Index meter, but in every respect it represents perhaps the simplest language possible, a not-distant cousin of Merit Ultra Lights' groundbreaking and succinct utterance, "Yo!"

Why do advertisers generally favor simple language? The answer lies with the consumer: consider Toffler's speculation that the average American adult is subject to some 560 advertising or commercial messages each day. As a practical matter, we would not notice many of these messages if length or eloquence were counted among their virtues. Today's consumer cannot take the time to focus on anything for long, much less blatant advertising messages. In effect, Toffler's "future" is here now, and it is perhaps more "shocking" than he could have foreseen at the time. Every aspect of modern life runs at an accelerated pace. Overnight mail has moved in less than ten years from a novelty to a common business necessity. Voice mail, pagers, cellular phones, e-mail, the Internet—the world is always awake, always switched on, and hungry for more information, now. Time generally, and TV commercial time in particular, is now dissected into increasingly smaller segments. Fifteen-second commercials are no longer unusual.

Toffler views the evolution toward shorter language as a natural progression: three-syllable words are simply harder to read than one or two-syllable words. Simple ideas are more readily transferred from one person to another than complex ideas. Therefore, advertising copy uses increasingly simple language, as does society at large. In *Future Shock*, Toffler speculates:

> If the [English] language had the same number of words in Shakespeare's time as it does today at least 200,000 words—perhaps several times that many—have dropped out and been replaced in the intervening four centuries. The high turnover rate reflects changes in things, processes, and qualities in the environment from the world of consumer products and technology.

It is no accident that the first terms Toffler uses to illustrate his point ("fast-back," "wash-and-wear," and "flashcube") were invented not by engineers, or journalists, but by advertising copywriters.

Advertising language is simple language: in the ad's engineering process, difficult words or images—which in other forms of communication may be used to lend color or fine shades of meaning—are edited out and replaced by simple words or images not open to misinterpretation. You don't have to ask whether King T likes to "grab 40" when he wants to "act a fool," or whether Gena wears her Sassons when she wants to do whatever it is she does.

Who Is Responsible?

Some critics view the advertising business as a cranky, unwelcomed child of the free enterprise system—a noisy, whining, brash kid who must somehow be kept in line, but can't just yet be thrown out of the house. In reality, advertising mirrors the fears, quirks, and aspirations of the society that creates it (and is, in turn, sold by it). This fact alone exposes advertising to parody and ridicule. The overall level of acceptance and respect for advertising is also influenced by the varied quality of the ads themselves. Some ads, including a few of the examples cited here, seem deliberately designed to provoke controversy. For example, it is easy—as President Clinton and others charged—to conclude that Joe Camel represented a deliberate, calculated effort by R.J. Reynolds to encourage children to smoke cigarettes. But this is only one of the many charges frequently levied against advertising:

1. Advertising encourages unhealthy habits.

2. Advertising feeds on human weaknesses and exaggerates the importance of material things, encouraging "impure" emotions and vanities.

3. Advertising sells daydreams—distracting, purposeless visions of lifestyles beyond the reach of the majority of the people who are most exposed to advertising.

4. Advertising warps our vision of reality, implanting in us groundless fears and insecurities.

5. Advertising downgrades the intelligence of the public.

6. Advertising debases English.

7. Advertising perpetuates racial and sexual stereotypes.

What can be said in advertising's defense? Advertising is only a reflection of society. A case can be made for the concept that advertising language is an acceptable stimulus for the natural evolution of language. Is "proper English" the language most Americans actually speak and write, or is it the language we are told we should speak and write?

What about the charge that advertising debases the intelligence of the public? Those who support this particular criticism would do well to ask themselves another question: Exactly how intelligent is the public? Sadly, evidence abounds that "the public" at large is not particularly intelligent after all. Johnny can't read, Susie can't write. And the entire family spends the night in front of the television, channel surfing for the latest scandal—hopefully, one involving a sports hero or political figure said to be a killer or a frequent participant in perverse sexual acts.

Ads are effective because they sell products. They would not succeed if they did not reflect the values and motivations of the real world. Advertising both reflects and shapes our perception of reality. Consider several brand names and the impressions they create: Ivory Snow is pure. Federal Express won't let you down. Absolut is cool. Sasson is sexxy. Mercedes represents quality. Our sense of what these brand names stand for may have as much to do with advertising as with the objective truth.

Advertising shapes our perception of the world as surely as architecture shapes our impression of a city. Good, responsible advertising can serve as a positive influence for change, while generating profits. Of course, the problem is that the obverse is also true: Advertising, like any form of mass communication, can be a force for both "good" and "bad." It can just as readily reinforce or encourage irresponsible behavior, ageism, sexism, ethnocentrism, racism, homophobia, heterophobia—you name it—as it can encourage support for diversity and social progress. People living in society create advertising. Society isn't perfect. In the end, advertising simply attempts to change behavior. Do advertisements sell distracting, purposeless visions? Occasionally. But perhaps such visions are necessary components of the process through which our society changes and improves.

Joe's days as Camel's spokesman are over. His very success in reaching new smokers was the source of his undoing. But standing nearby and waiting to take his place is another campaign; another character, real or imagined; another product for sale. Perhaps, by learning how advertising works, we can become better equipped to sort out content from hype, product values from emotions, and salesmanship from propaganda.

Questions for Discussion

1. O'Neill mentions two occasions when the American President intervened in the production of advertising: the Joe Camel ads' appeal to young people, and the "heroin chic" appeal of Prada and Calvin Klein. Can advertising act as an enemy of the state? Should the authors of ads be responsible for the way audiences respond to their ads?

2. According to O'Neill, advertising works because "we participate in it." Therefore, what role does the audience play in the construction of an ad? Does the ad shape the audience or does the audience shape the ad? What kinds of audiences does O'Neill's approach to advertising address? Intelligent beings, social activists, solipsistic capitalists . . . ?

3. Look at the last section of this essay, "Who IS Responsible?" to find an answer to this question. Are ads that reinforce irresponsible behavior, ageism, sexism, ethnocentrism, racism, homophobia, and heterophobia "necessary components of the process through which our society changes and improves"? Is advertising a place to argue for positive changes in society or should it be relegated to the world of monetary competition?

Explorations

1. Postman and Powers, and Samuels discuss the power of stereotypes and cultural myths in advertising. What kind of myths, or commonly held beliefs, do the ads O'Neill writes about call upon? Are those myths, like the American dream, worth repeating and reinforcing for the sake of sales figures? Do the beliefs of an audience justify their use for advertising ends?

2. O'Neill claims that advertising audiences are able to differentiate between fact and fiction, advertising ploys and real life events. Do you agree with him? How do the arguments by Meyers regarding "AIDS talk," and Selfe's discussion on the persistent presence of cultural bias in technology ads, comment on the audience's ability to separate the reality from the fiction in a marketing program?

3. O'Neill claims that advertising is a product of society and is not the force that predominantly shapes our culture. Do you think Meyers, who argues for the naturalization of taboo subjects for the good of a society, would agree with O'Neill? Why or why not? Does the subject of an ad direct the way it is presented to the public?

Formal Writing Assignments

1. In an essay take a position regarding the moral effect of advertising on individuals or societies. Refer to the essays by O'Neill, Postman and Powers, and any others you find relevant to your argument. Also, refer to an actual advertisement. Support your argument and address counter-arguments to your claims about "responsible advertising practices.

2. Locate two advertisements, one that, in your opinion, is "responsible" and another that is "irresponsible." Compare the two ads, noting the language they use, the cultural images that they elicit, the kind of argument they employ (emotional, logical, ethical), and the kind of audience they try to reach. Conclude with suggestions about the way that irresponsible advertisers should deal with their product. Is there a way to advertise these products responsibly? How should audiences react to the advertising methods you discuss?

How to Watch TV News

Neil Postman and Steve Powers

Neil Postman is chairman of the Department of Communication Arts at New York University and is the founder of its program in Media Ecology. Postman has been a leader in the study of the way media interacts with individuals in societies. Steve Powers is an award-winning television journalist who has worked for Fox Television News and the ABC Information Radio Network. Powers is currently a professor of journalism and communication at St. John's University. This chapter from their book, *How to Watch TV News,* combines Postman's renowned theoretical knowledge of social implications of trends in mass media and Power's extensive practical knowledge of what television actually does, how it does it and what it can do.

Writing Before Reading

1. Write a paragraph that describes the job of a television news team. What are they expected to report about? How do they choose their subjects? How are they expected to deliver the report?

2. What was the last television news report you can remember? Write a synopsis of the report. Describe any images/pictures the reporter used with the text of the report. How did they compliment each other? Why do you think you remember the report so well? Did the report cause you to form an opinion about the issues it discussed?

3. Write a report about the last significant event in your life for a television new presentation. Decide what pictures you will include, who you will quote, and how you want to be represented in the report. As you do this, think about why you made the choices you did and how accurately your story will be understood by the audience.

How to Watch TV News

The Bias of Language, The Bias of Pictures

When a television news show distorts the truth by altering or manufacturing facts (through re-creations), a television viewer is defenseless even if a re-creation is properly labeled. Viewers are still vulnerable to misinformation since they will not know (at least in the case of docudramas) what parts are fiction and what parts are not. But the problems of verisimilitude posed by recreations pale to insignificance when compared to the problems viewers face when encountering a straight (no-monkey-business) show. All news shows, in a sense, are re-creations in that what we hear and see on them are attempts to represent actual events, and are not the events themselves. Perhaps, to avoid ambiguity, we might call all news shows "re-presentations" instead of "recreations." These re-presentations come to us in two forms: language and pictures. The question then arises: what do viewers have to know about language and pictures in order to be properly armed to defend themselves against the seductions of eloquence (to use Bertrand Russell's apt phrase)?

Let us take language first. Below are three principles that, in our opinion, are an essential part of the analytical equipment a viewer must bring to any encounter with a news show.

1. Whatever anyone says something is, it isn't.

This sounds more complex—and maybe more pretentious—than it actually is. What it means is that there is a difference between the world of events and the world of words about events. The job of an honest reporter is to try to find words and the appropriate tone in presenting them that will come as close to evoking the event as possible. But since no two people will use exactly the same words to describe an event, we must acknowledge that for every verbal description of an event, there are multiple possible alternatives. You may demonstrate this to your own satisfaction by writing a two-paragraph description of a dinner you had with at least two other people, then asking the others who were present if each of them would also write, independently, a two paragraph description of the "same" dinner. We should be very surprised if all of the descriptions include the same words, in the same order, emphasize the same things, and express the same feelings. In other words, "the dinner itself" is largely a nonverbal event. The words people use to describe this event are not the event itself and are only abstracted re-presentations of the event. What does this mean for a television viewer? It means that the viewer must never assume that the words spoken on a television news show are exactly what happened. Since there are so many alternative ways of describing what happened, the viewer must be on guard against assuming that he or she has heard "the absolute truth."

2. Language operates at various levels of abstraction.

This means that there is a level of language whose purpose is to *describe* an event. There is also a level of language whose purpose is to *evaluate* an event. Even more, there is a level of language whose purpose is to *infer* what is unknown on the basis of what is known. The usual way to make these distinctions clear is through sentences such as the following three:

> Manny Freebus is 5'8" and weighs 235 pounds.
>
> Manny Freebus is grossly fat.
>
> Manny Freebus eats too much.

The first sentence may be said to be language as pure description. It involves no judgments and no inferences. The second sentence is a description of sorts, but is mainly a judgment that the speaker makes of the "event" known as Manny Freebus. The third sentence is an inference based on observations the speaker has made. It is, in fact, a statement about the unknown based on the known. As it happens, we know Manny Freebus and can tell you that he eats no more than the average person but suffers from a glandular condition which keeps him overweight. Therefore, anyone who concluded from observing Manny's shape that he eats too much has made a false inference. A good guess, but false nonetheless.

You can watch television news programs from now until doomsday and never come across any statement about Manny Freebus. But you will constantly come across the three kinds of statements we have been discussing—descriptions, judgments, and inferences. And it is important for a viewer to distinguish among them. For example, you might hear an anchor introduce a story by saying: "Today Congress ordered an investigation of the explosive issue of whether Ronald Reagan's presidential campaign made a deal with Iran in 1980 to delay the release of American hostages until after the election." This statement is, of course, largely descriptive, but includes the judgmental word "explosive" as part of the report. We need hardly point out that what is explosive to one person may seem trivial to another. We do not say that the news writer has no business to include his or her judgment of this investigation. We do say that the viewer has to be aware that a judgment has been made. In fact, even the phrase "made a deal" (why not "arranged with Iran"?) has a somewhat sleazy connotation that implies a judgment of sorts. If, in the same news report, we are told that the evidence for such a secret deal is weak and that only an investigation with subpoena power can establish the truth, we must know that we have left the arena of factual language and have moved into the land of inference. An investigation with subpoena power may be a good idea but whether or not it can establish the truth is a guess on the journalist's part, and a viewer ought to know that.

3. Almost all words have connotative meanings.

This suggests that even when attempting to use purely descriptive language, a journalist cannot avoid expressing an attitude about what he or she is saying. For example, here is the opening sentence of an anchor's report about national examinations: "For the first time in the nation's history, high-level education policymakers have designed the elements for a national examination system similar to the one advocated by President Bush." This sentence certainly looks like it is pure description although it is filled with ambiguities. Is this the first time in our history that this has been done? Or only the first time that high-level education policymakers have done it? Or is it the first time something has been designed that is similar to what the President has advocated? But let us put those questions aside. (After all, there are limits to how analytical one ought to be.) Instead, we might concentrate on such words as "high-level," "policymakers," and "designed." Speaking for ourselves, we are by no means sure that we know what a "high-level policymaker" is, although it sounds awfully impressive. It is certainly better than a "low-level policymaker," although how one would distinguish between the two is a bit of a mystery. Come to think of it, a low-level "policymaker" must be pretty good, too, since anyone who makes policy must be important. It comes as no surprise, therefore, that what was done was "designed." To design something usually implies careful thought, preparation, organization, and coherence. People design buildings, bridges, and furniture. If your experience has been anything like ours, you will know that reports are almost never designed; they are usually "thrown together," and it is quite a compliment to say that a report was designed. The journalist who paid this compliment was certainly entitled to do it even though he may not have been aware of what he was doing. He probably thought he had made a simple description, avoiding any words that would imply favor or disfavor. But if so, he was defeated in his effort because language tends to be emotion-laden. Because it is people who do the talking, the talk almost always includes a feeling, an attitude, a judgment. In a sense, every language contains the history of a people's feelings about the world. Our words are baskets of emotion. Smart journalists, of course, know this. And so do smart audiences. Smart audiences don't blame anyone for this state of affairs. They are, however, prepared for it.

It is not our intention to provide here a mini-course in semantics. Even if we could, we are well aware that no viewer could apply analytic principles all the time or even much of the time. Anchors and reporters talk too fast and too continuously for any of us to monitor most of their sentences. Besides, who would want to do that for most of the stories on a news show? If you have a sense of what is important, you will probably judge most news stories to be fluff, or nonsense, or irrelevancies, not worthy of your analytic weaponry. But there are times when stories appear that are of major significance from your point of view. These are the times when your level of attention will reach a peak and you must call upon your best powers of interpretation. In those moments you need to draw on whatever you know about the relationship between language and reality; about the distinctions among statements of fact, judgment, and inference; about the connotative meanings of words. When this is done properly, viewers are no longer passive consumers of news but active participants in a kind of dialogue between a news show and themselves. A viewer may even find that he or she is "talking back to the television set" (which is the title of a book by former FCC commissioner Nicholas Johnson). In our view, nothing could be healthier for the sanity and well-being of our nation than to have ninety million viewers talking back to their television news shows every night and twice on Sunday.

Now we must turn to the problem of pictures. It is often said that a picture is worth a thousand words. Maybe so. But it is probably equally true that one word is worth a thousand pictures, at least sometimes—for example, when it comes to understanding the world we live in. Indeed, the whole problem with news on television comes down to this: all the words uttered in an hour of news coverage could be printed on one page of a newspaper. And the world cannot be understood in one page. Of course, there is a compensation: television offers pictures, and the pictures move. Moving pictures are a kind of language in themselves, but the language of pictures differs radically from oral and written language, and the differences are crucial for understanding television news.

To begin with, pictures, especially single pictures, speak only in particularities. Their vocabulary is limited to concrete representation. Unlike words and sentences, a picture does not present to us an idea or concept about the world, except as we use language itself to convert the image to idea. By itself, a picture cannot deal with the unseen, the remote, the internal, the abstract. It does not speak of "man," only of *a* man, not of "tree," only of *a* tree. You cannot produce an image of "nature," any more than an image of "the sea." You can only show a particular fragment of the here-and-now—a cliff of a certain terrain, in a certain condition of light; a wave at a moment in time, from a particular point of view. And just as "nature" and "the sea" cannot be photographed, such larger abstractions as truth, honor, love, and falsehood cannot be talked about in the lexicon of individual pictures. For "showing of" and "talking about" are two very different kinds of processes: individual pictures give us the world as object; language, the world as idea. There is no such thing in nature as "man" or "tree." The universe offers no such categories or simplifications; only flux and infinite variety. The picture documents and celebrates the particularities of the universe's infinite variety. Language makes them comprehensible.

Of course, moving pictures, video with sound, may bridge the gap by juxtaposing images, symbols, sound, and music. Such images can present emotions and rudimentary ideas. They can suggest the panorama of nature and the joys and miseries of humankind.

Picture—smoke pouring from the window, cut to people coughing, an ambulance racing to a hospital, a tombstone in a cemetery.

Picture—jet planes firing rockets, explosions, lines of foreign soldiers surrendering, the American flag waving in the wind.

Nonetheless, keep in mind that when terrorists want to prove to the world that their kidnap victims are still alive, they photograph them holding a copy of a recent newspaper. The dateline on the newspaper provides the proof that the photograph was taken on or after that date. Without the help of the written word, film and videotape cannot portray temporal dimensions with any precision. Consider a film clip showing an aircraft carrier at sea. One might be able to identify the ship as Soviet or American, but there would be no way of telling where in the world the carrier was, where it was headed, or when the pictures were taken. It is only through language—words spoken over the pictures or reproduced in them—that the image of the aircraft carrier takes on specific meaning.

Still, it is possible to enjoy the image of the carrier for its own sake. One might find the hugeness of the vessel interesting; it signifies military power on the move. There is a certain drama in watching the planes come in at high speeds and skid to a stop on the deck. Suppose the ship were burning: that would be even more interesting. This leads to an important point about the language of pictures. Moving pictures favor images that change. That is why violence and dynamic destruction find their way onto television so often. When something is destroyed violently it is altered in a highly visible way; hence the entrancing power of fire. Fire gives visual form to the ideas of consumption, disappearance, death—the thing that burned is actually taken away by fire. It is at this very basic level that fires make a good subject for television news. Something was here, now it's gone, and the change is recorded on film.

Earthquakes and typhoons have the same power. Before the viewer's eyes the world is taken apart. If a television viewer has relatives in Mexico City and an earthquake occurs there, then he or she may take a special interest in the images of destruction as a report from a specific place and time; that is, one may look at television pictures for information about an important event. But film of an earthquake can be interesting even if the viewer cares nothing about the event itself. Which is only to say, as we noted earlier, that there is another way of participating in the news—as a spectator who desires to be entertained. Actually to see buildings topple is exciting, no matter where the buildings are. The world turns to dust before our eyes.

Those who produce television news in America know that their medium favors images that move. That is why they are wary of "talking heads," people who simply appear in front of a camera and speak. When talking heads appear on television, there is nothing to record or document, no change in process. In the cinema the situation is somewhat different. On a movie screen, close-ups of a good actor speaking dramatically can sometimes be interesting to watch. When Clint Eastwood narrows his eyes and challenges his rival to shoot first, the spectator sees the cool rage of the Eastwood character take visual form, and the narrowing of the eyes is dramatic. But much of the effect of this small movement depends on the size of the movie screen and the darkness of the theater, which make Eastwood and his every action "larger than life."

The television screen is smaller than life. It occupies about 15 percent of the viewer's visual field (compared to about 70 percent for the movie screen). It is not set in a darkened theater closed off from the world but in the viewer's ordinary living space. This means that visual changes must be more extreme and more dramatic to be interesting on television. A narrowing of the eyes will not do. A car crash, an earthquake, a burning factory are much better.

With these principles in mind, let us examine more closely the structure of a typical newscast, and here we will include in the discussion not only the pictures but all the nonlinguistic symbols that make up a television news show. For example, in America, almost all news shows begin with music, the tone of which suggests important events about to unfold. The music is very important, for it equates the news with various forms of drama and ritual—the opera, for example, or a wedding procession—in which musical themes underscore the meaning of the event. Music takes us immediately into the realm of the symbolic, a world that is not to be taken literally. After all, when events unfold in the real world, they do so without musical accompaniment. More symbolism follows. The sound of teletype machines can be heard in the studio, not because it is impossible to screen this noise out, but because the sound is a kind of music in itself. It tells us that data are pouring in from all corners of the globe, a sensation reinforced by the world map in the background (or clocks noting the time on different continents). The fact is that teletype machines are rarely used in TV news rooms, having been replaced by silent computer terminals. When seen, they have only a symbolic function.

Already, then, before a single news item is introduced, a great deal has been communicated. We know that we are in the presence of a symbolic event, a form of theater in which the day's events are to be dramatized. This theater takes the entire globe as its subject, although it may look at the world from the perspective of a single nation. A certain tension is present, like the atmosphere in a theater just before the curtain goes up. The tension is represented by the music, the staccato beat of the teletype machines, and often the sight of news workers scurrying around typing reports and answering phones. As a technical matter, it would be no problem to build a set in which the newsroom staff remained off camera, invisible to the viewer, but an important theatrical effect would be lost. By being busy on camera, the workers help communicate urgency about the events at hand, which suggests that situations are changing so rapidly that constant revision of the news is necessary.

The staff in the background also helps signal the importance of the person in the center, the anchor, "in command" of both the staff and the news. The anchor plays the role of host. He or she welcomes us to the newscast and welcomes us back from the different locations we visit during the filmed reports.

Many features of the newscast help the anchor to establish the impression of control. These are usually equated with production values in broadcasting. They include such things as graphics that tell the viewer what is being shown, or maps and charts that suddenly appear on the screen and disappear on cue, or the orderly progression from story to story. They also include the absence of gaps, or "dead time," during the broadcast, even the simple fact that the news starts and ends at a certain hour. These common features are thought of as purely technical matters, which a professional crew handles as a matter of course. But they are also symbols of a dominant theme of television news: the imposition of an orderly world—called "the news"—upon the disorderly flow of events.

While the form of a news broadcast emphasizes tidiness and control, its content can best be described as fragmented. Because time is so precious on television, because the nature of the medium favors dynamic visual images, and because the pressures of a commercial structure require the news to hold its audience above all else, there is rarely any attempt to explain issues in depth or place events in their proper context. The news moves nervously from a warehouse fire to a court decision, from a guerrilla war to a World Cup match, the quality of the film most often determining the length of the story. Certain stories show up only because they offer dramatic pictures. Bleachers collapse in South America: hundreds of people are crushed—a perfect television news story, for the cameras can record the face of disaster in all its anguish. Back in Washington, a new budget is approved by Congress. Here there is nothing to photograph because a budget is not a physical event; it is a document full of language and numbers. So the producers of the news will show a photo of the document itself, focusing on the cover where it says "Budget of the United States of America." Or sometimes they will send a camera crew to the government printing plant where copies of the budget are produced. That evening, while the contents of the budget are summarized by a voice-over, the viewer sees stacks of documents being loaded into boxes at the government printing plant. Then a few of the budget's more important provisions will be flashed on the screen in written form, but this is such a time-consuming process—using television as a printed page—that the producers keep it to a minimum. In short, the budget is not televisable, and for that reason its time on the news must be brief. The bleacher collapse will get more time that evening.

While appearing somewhat chaotic, these disparate stories are not just dropped in the news program helterskelter. The appearance of a scattershot story order is really orchestrated to draw the audience from one story to the next—from one section to the next through the commercial breaks to the end of the show. The story order is constructed to hold and build the viewership rather than place events in context or explain issues in depth.

Of course, it is a tendency of journalism in general to concentrate on the surface of events rather than underlying conditions; this is as true for the newspaper as it is for the newscast. But several features of television undermine whatever efforts journalists may make to give sense to the world. One is that a television broadcast is a series of events that occur in sequence, and the sequence is the same for all viewers. This is not true for a newspaper page, which displays many items simultaneously, allowing readers to choose the order in which they read them. If newspaper readers want only a summary of the latest tax bill, they can read the headline and the first paragraph of an article, and if they want more, they can keep reading. In a sense, then, everyone reads a different newspaper, for no two readers will read (or ignore) the same items.

But all television viewers see the same broadcast. They have no choices. A report is either in the broadcast or out, which means that anything which is of narrow interest is unlikely to be included. As NBC News executive Reuven Frank once explained:

> A newspaper, for example, can easily afford to print an item of conceivable interest to only a fraction of its readers. A television news program must be put together with the assumption that each item will be of some interest to everyone that watches. Every time a newspaper includes a feature which will attract a specialized group it can assume it is adding at least a little bit to its circulation. To the degree a television news program includes an item of this sort . . . it must assume that its audience will diminish.

The need to "include everyone," an identifying feature of commercial television in all its forms, prevents journalists from offering lengthy or complex explanations, or from tracing the sequence of events leading up to today's headlines. One of the ironies of political life in modern democracies is that many problems which concern the "general welfare" are of interest only to specialized groups. Arms control, for example, is an issue that literally concerns everyone in the world, and yet the language of arms control and the complexity of the subject are so daunting that only a minority of people can actually follow the issue from week to week and month to month. If it wants to act responsibly, a newspaper can at least make available more information about arms control than most people want. Commercial television cannot afford to do so.

But even if commercial television could afford to do so, it wouldn't. The fact that television news is principally made up of moving pictures prevents it from offering lengthy, coherent explanations of events. A television news show reveals the world as a series of unrelated, fragmentary moments. It does not—and cannot be expected to—offer a sense of coherence or meaning. What does this suggest to a TV viewer? That the viewer must come with a prepared mind—information, opinions, a sense of proportion, an articulate value system. To the TV viewer lacking such mental equipment, a news program is only a kind of rousing light show. Here a falling building, there a five-alarm fire, everywhere the world as an object, much without meaning, connections, or continuity.

Questions for Discussion

1. Powers and Postman say that the television screen occupies only 15% of the visual field in a viewer's living space and therefore must display extreme and dramatic visual changes to gain a viewer's attention. What kinds of changes do Postman and Powers call attention getters? According to your experience, what gets your attention? Does the need to capture the awareness of an audience change the "truth" that a story represents? Why? When you write, does the way you attract your reader affect the way your essays are understood?

2. This essay argues that television broadcasts are written for a different audience than newspaper articles. Locate a newspaper article in your local newspaper and compare it to a television report about the same story. List the difference in the two reports. Is one more detailed than the other? Why? Do they use images differently? Do they seek to evoke different reactions from their audience? What different ways do they use to persuade their readers or viewers?

3. According to Postman and Powers verisimilitude is difficult, if not impossible, to achieve in a new report. "There is a difference between the world of events and the world of words about events." Choose a major event and construct an outline of a report about it remaining as true to the "facts" as you can. Then, add the dramatic embellishments necessary to gain the attention of a television audience. How does it change? Adjust your outline once again to evoke the kind of emotional or practical response you want your audience to have. How far did you have to skew the "facts" to create these affects?

Explorations

1. Compare the way O'Neill discusses the use of language in advertising with Postman and Powers description of television news reports. What similarities do they describe in ads and news reports? What differences exist between ads and news reports? What creates these differences and similarities, media, audience, purpose, length, vocabulary? What constraints and freedoms does each genre levy upon its authors? Should ads and newscasts be read in the same way? If not, how do we read these texts differently? How do these genres ask you to read them?

2. In what ways do images contribute to evaluative statements about events or products? Refer to the work on AIDS by Meyers and the work on technology by Selfe. What kind of meanings do images add to reports and advertisements? Are there events where the text of a report or ad is contradicted or neutralized by the image that accompanies it? Show some examples.

3. Charles O'Neill, speaking of advertising, believes that the kind of images and messages that ads use are the product of the beliefs of a society. Do these kind of beliefs control the production of news reports?

Formal Writing Assignments

1. Write an essay that analyzes a specific television news report according to the issues raised by Postman and Powers. How does the report establish its credibility? Is the language used to describe the event evaluative? Does the report persuade its viewers to assume a political position? Did the report re-present "reality" or was it limited to a specific point of view?

2. Using actual news reports discuss the way music and images affected the audience response to the story. In each case describe the report well enough to familiarize your reader with the specific report, analyze the way music and images affected it. Then, suggest specific changes in the music or images that were presented in the report and explain how your choices would change its meaning or persuasive effect.

The Rap on Rap: The Black Music That Isn't Either

David Samuels

David Samuels is a journalist and cultural critic who has published many articles in both avant-garde and intellectual publications including, *Rolling Stone*, *Harper's* and *The New York Times*. His work often engages issues of public policy, global relations, electoral politics and popular culture. Like the following article, Samuels' writing is activistic; he seeks to influence American society by informing his readers and changing their opinions. "The Rap on Rap: The Black Music That Isn't Either" was published in *The New Republic*. It challenges the idea that rap music represents "actual urban culture" and asks readers to think about the implications of marketing rap music's image of the black urban male.

Writing Before Reading

1. List your favorite two rap artists. Then, write a short biographical paragraph on each one describing the member's lives. Where did they grow up? What kind of families did they have? What social class did they belong to? How much education did they receive? What kind of role model are they? What is the central message of their music?

2. Why do you, or don't you, listen to and enjoy rap music? What makes it appealing or repulsive to you? How would you characterize people who listen to rap music?

3. Try to remember a piece of rap music and write out its message? What does it say about the relationship between the artist, her audience, and society?

The Rap on Rap: The Black Music That Isn't Either

This summer Soundscan, a computerized scanning system, changes *Billboard* magazine's method of counting record sales in the United States. Replacing a haphazard system that relied on big-city record stores, Soundscan measured the number of records sold nationally by scanning the bar codes at chain store cash registers. Within weeks the number of computed record sales leapt, as demographics shifted from minority-focused urban centers to white, suburban, middle-class malls. So it was that America awoke on June 22, 1991, to find that its favorite record was not *Out of Time*, by aging college-boy rockers R.E.M., but *Niggaz4life*, a musical celebration of gang rape and other violence by N.W.A., or Niggers With Attitude, a rap group from the Los Angeles ghetto of Compton whose records had never before risen above No. 27 on the Billboard charts.

From *Niggaz4life* to *Boyz N the Hood*, young black men committing acts of violence were available this summer in a wide variety of entertainment formats. Of these none is more popular than rap. And none has received quite the level of critical attention and concern. Writers on the left have long viewed rap as the heartbeat of urban America, its authors, in Arthur Kempton's words, "the preeminent young dramaturgists in the clamorous theater of the street." On the right, this assumption has been shared, but greeted with predictable disdain.

Neither side of the debate has been prepared, however, to confront what the entertainment industry's receipts from this summer prove beyond doubt: although rap is still proportionally more popular among blacks, its primary audience is white and lives in the suburbs. And the history of rap's degeneration from insurgent black street music to mainstream pop points to another dispiriting conclusion: the more rappers were packaged as violent black criminals, the bigger their white audiences became.

If the racial makeup of rap's audience has been largely misunderstood, so have the origins of its authors. Since the early 1980s a tightly knit group of mostly young, middle-class, black New Yorkers, in close concert with white record producers, executives, and publicists, has been making rap music for an audience that industry executives concede is primarily composed of white suburban males. Building upon a form pioneered by lower-class black artists in New York between 1975 and 1983, despite an effective boycott of the music by both black and white radio that continues to this day, they created the most influential pop music of the 1980s. Rap's appeal to whites rested in its evocation of an age-old image of blackness: a foreign, sexually charged, and criminal underworld against which the norms of white society are defined, and, by extension, through which they may be defied. It was the truth of this latter proposition that rap would test in its journey into the mainstream.

"Hip-hop," the music behind the lyrics, which are "rapped," is a form of sonic bricolage with roots in "toasting," a style of making music by speaking over records. (For simplicity, I'll use the term "rap" interchangeably with "hiphop" throughout this article.) Toasting first took hold in Jamaica in the mid-1960s, a response, legend has it, to the limited availability of expensive Western instruments and the concurrent proliferation of cheap R&B instrumental singles on Memphis-based labels such as Stax-Volt. Cool DJ Herc, a Jamaican who settled in the South Bronx, is widely credited with having brought toasting to New York City. Rap spread quickly through New York's poor black neighborhoods in the mid- and late 1970s. . . .

Although much is made of rap as a kind of urban streetgeist, early rap had a more basic function: dance music. Bill Stephney, considered by many to be the smartest man in the rap business, recalls the first time he heard hip-hop: "The point wasn't rapping, it was rhythm, DJs cutting records left and right, taking the big drum break from Led Zeppelin's 'When the Levee Breaks,' mixing it together with 'Ring My Bell,' then with a Bob James Mardi Gras jazz record and some James Brown. You'd have 2,000 kids in any community center in New York, moving back and forth, back and forth, like some kind of tribal war dance, you might say. It was the rapper's role to match this intensity rhythmically. No one knew what he was saying. He was just rocking the mike."

Rap quickly spread from New York to Philadelphia, Chicago, Boston, and other cities with substantial black populations. Its popularity was sustained by the ease with which it could be made. The music on early rap records sounded like the black music of the day: funk or, more often, disco. Performers were unsophisticated about image and presentation, tending toward gold lamé jumpsuits and Jericurls, a second-rate appropriation of the stylings of funk musicians like George Clinton and Bootsy Collins.

The first rap record to make it big was "Rapper's Delight," released in 1979 by the Sugar Hill Gang, an ad hoc all-star team drawn from three New York groups on Sylvia and Joey Robinson's Sugar Hill label. Thanks to Sylvia Robinson's soul music and background, the first thirty seconds of "Rapper's Delight" were indistinguishable from the disco records of the day: light guitars, high-hat drumming, and hand-claps over a deep funk bass line. What followed will be immediately familiar to anyone who was young in New York City that summer:

I said, hip-hop, de-hibby, de-hibby-dibby,

Hip-hip-hop you don't stop.

Rock it out, Baby Bubba to the boogie de-bang-bang,

Boogie to the boogie to be.

Now what you hear is not a test,

I'm rapping to the beat

I said, "By the way, baby, what's your name?"

She said, "I go by the name Lois Lane

And you can be my boyfriend, you surely can

Just let me quit my boyfriend, he's called Superman."

I said, "he's a fairy, I do suppose

Flying through the air in pantyhose

You need a man who's got finesse

And his whole name across his chest"

Like disco music and jumpsuits, the social commentaries of early rappers like Grandmaster Flash and Mellie Mel were for the most part transparent attempts to sell records to whites by any means necessary. Songs like "White Lines" (with its anti-drug theme) and "The Message" (about ghetto life) had the desired effect, drawing fulsome praise from white rock critics, raised on the protest ballads of Bob Dylan and Phil Ochs. The reaction on the street was somewhat less favorable. "The Message" is a case in point. "People hated that record," recalls Russell Simmons, president of Def Jam Records. "I remember the Junebug, a famous DJ of the time, was playing it up at the Fever, and Ronnie DJ put a pistol to his head and said, 'Take that record off and break it or I'll blow your fucking head off.' The whole club stopped until he broke that record and put it in the garbage."

It was not until 1984 that rap broke through to a mass white audience. The first group to do so was Run-DMC, with the release of its debut album, *Run-DMC*, and with *King of Rock* one year later. These albums blazed the trail that rap would travel into the musical mainstream. Bill Adler, a former rock critic and rap's best-known publicist, explains: "They were the first group that came on stage as if they had just come off the street corner. But unlike the first generation of rappers, they were solidly middle class. Both of Run's parents were college-educated. DMC was a good Catholic schoolkid, a mama's boy. Neither of them was deprived and neither of them ever ran with a gang, but on stage they became the biggest, baddest, streetest guys in the world." When Run-DMC covered the Aerosmith classic "Walk This Way," the resulting video made it onto MTV, and the record went gold.

Rap's new mass audience was in large part the brainchild of Rick Rubin, a Jewish punk rocker from suburban Long Island who produced the music behind many of rap's biggest acts. Like many New Yorkers his age, Rick grew up listening to Mr. Magic's Rap Attack, a rap radio show on WHBI 1983, at the age of 19, Rubin founded Def Jam Records in his NYU dorm room. (Simmons bought part of Def Jam in 1984 and took full control of the company in 1989.) Rubin's next group, the Beastie Boys, was a white punk rock band whose transformation into a rap group pointed rap's way into the future. The Beasties' first album, *Licensed to Ill*, backed by airplay of its authentic fratparty single "You've Got to Fight for Your Right to Party," became the first rap record to sell a million copies.

The appearance of white groups in a black musical form has historically prefigured the mainstreaming of the form, the growth of the white audience, and the resulting dominance of white performers. With rap, however, this process took an unexpected turn: white demand indeed began to determine the direction of the genre, but what it wanted was music more defiantly black. The result was

Public Enemy, produced and marketed by Rubin, the next group significantly to broaden rap's appeal to young whites.

Public Enemy's now familiar mélange of polemic and dance music was formed not on inner-city streets but in the suburban Long Island towns in which the group's members grew up. The children of successful black middle class professionals, they gave voice to the feeling that, despite progress toward equality, blacks still did not quite belong in white America. They complained of unequal treatment by the police, of never quite overcoming the color of their skin: "We were suburban college kids doing what we were supposed to do, but we were always made to feel like something else," explains Stephney, the group's executive producer.

Public Enemy's abrasive and highly politicized style made it a fast favorite of the white avant-garde, much like the English punk rock band The Clash ten years before. Public Enemy's music, produced by the Shocklee brothers Hank and Keith, was faster, harder, and more abrasive than the rap of the day, music that moved behind the vocals like a full-scale band. But the root of Public Enemy's success was a highly charged theater of race in which white listeners became guilty eavesdroppers on the putative private conversation of the inner city. Chuck D denounced his enemies (the media, some radio stations), proclaimed himself "Public Enemy #1," and praised Louis Farrakhan in stentorian tones, flanked onstage by black-clad security guards from the Nation of Islam, the SIWs, led by Chuck's political mentor, Professor Griff. Flavor Flav, Chuck's homeboy sidekick, parodied street style: oversize sunglasses, baseball cap cocked to one side, a clock the size of a silver plate draped around his neck, going off on wild verbal riffs that often meant nothing at all.

The closer rap moved to the white mainstream, the more it became like rock 'n' roll, a celebration of posturing over rhythm. The back catalogs of artists like James Brown and George Clinton were relentlessly plundered for catchy hooks, then overlaid with dance beats and social commentary. Public Enemy's single "Fight the Power" was the biggest college hit of 1989:

> Elvis was a hero to most
> But he never meant shit to me, you see
> Straight-up racist that sucker was simple and plain
> Motherfuck him and John Wayne
> 'Cause I'm black and I'm proud
> I'm ready and hyped, plus I'm amped
> Most of my heroes don't appear on no stamps
> Sample a look back, you look and find
> Nothing but rednecks for 400 years if you check.

After the release of "Fight the Power," Professor Griff made a series of anti-Semitic remarks in an interview with *The Washington Times*. Griff was subsequently asked to leave the group, for what Chuck D termed errors in judgment. Although these errors were lambasted in editorials across the country, they do not seem to have affected Public Enemy's credibility with its young white fans.

Public Enemy's theatrical Black Nationalism and sophisticated noise ushered in what is fast coming to be seen as rap's golden age, a heady mix of art, music, and politics. Between 1988 and 1989 a host of innovative acts broke into the mainstream. KRS-One, now a regular on the Ivy League lecture circuit, grew up poor, living on the streets of the South Bronx until he met a New York City social worker, Scott La Rock, later murdered in a drive-by shooting. Together they formed BDP, Boogie Down Productions, recording for the Jive label on RCA. Although songs like "My Philosophy" and "Love's Gonna Get 'Cha (Material Love)" were clever and self-critical, BDP's roots remained firmly planted in the guns-and-posturing of the mainstream rap ghetto.

The ease with which rap can create such aural cartoons, says Hank Shockee, lies at the very heart of its appeal as entertainment: "Whites have always liked black music," he explains. "That part is hardly new. The difference with rap was that the imagery of black artists, for the first time, reached the level of black music. The sheer number of words in a rap song allows for the creation of full characters impossible in R&B. Rappers become like superheroes. Captain America or the Fantastic Four."

By 1988 the conscious manipulation of racial stereotypes had become rap's leading edge, a trend best exemplified by the rise to stardom of Schoolly D, a Philadelphia rapper on the Jive label who sold more than half a million records with little mainstream notice. It was not that the media had never heard of Schoolly D: white critics and fans, for the first time, were simply at a loss for words. His voice, fierce and deeply textured, could alone frighten listeners. He used it as a rhythmic device that made no concessions to pop-song form, talking evenly about smoking crack and using women for sex, proclaiming his blackness, accusing other rappers of not being black enough. What Schoolly D meant by blackness was abundantly clear. Schoolly D was a misogynist and a thug. If listening to Public Enemy was like eavesdropping on a conversation, Schoolly D was like getting mugged. This, aficionados agreed, was what they had been waiting for: a rapper from whom you would flee in abject terror if you saw him walking toward you late at night.

It remained for N.W.A., a more conventional group of rappers from Los Angeles, to adapt Schoolly D's stylistic advance for the mass white market with its first album-length release, *Straight Out of Compton*, in 1989. The much-quoted rap from that album, "Fuck the Police," was the target of an FBI warning to police department across the country, and a constant presence at certain college parties, white and black:

"Fuck the Police" coming straight out the underground
A young nigger got it bad 'cause I'm brown
And not the other color. Some police think
They have the authority to kill the minority . . .
A young nigger on the warpath
And when I'm finished, it's gonna be a bloodbath
Of cops, dying in L.A.
Yo, Dre I've got something to say: Fuck the Police.

Other songs spoke of trading oral sex for crack and shooting strangers for fun. After the release of *Straight Out of Compton*, N.W.A.'s lead rapper and chief lyricist, Ice Cube, left the group. Billing himself as "the nigger you love to hate," Ice Cube released a solo album, *Amerikkka's Most Wanted*, which gleefully pushed the limits of rap's ability to give offense. One verse ran:

I'm thinking to myself, "why did I bang her?"
Now I'm in the closet, looking for the hanger.

But what made *Amerikkka's Most Wanted* so shocking to so many record buyers was the title track's violation of rap's most iron-clad taboo—black on white violence:

Word, yo, but who the fuck is heard:
It's time you take a trip to the suburbs.
Let 'em see a nigger invasion
Point blank, on a Caucasian.
Cock the hammer and crack a smile:

"Take me to your house, pal . . ."

Ice Cube took his act to the big screen this summer in *Boyz N the Hood*, drawing rave reviews for his portrayal of a young black drug dealer whose life of crime leads him to an untimely end. The crime-doesn't-pay message, an inheritance from the grade-B gangster film is the stock-in-trade of another L.A. rapper-turned-actor, Ice-T of *New Jack City* fame, a favorite of socially conscious rock critics. Taking unhappy endings onto glorifications of drug dealing and gang warfare, Ice-T offers all the thrills of the form while alleviating any guilt listeners may have felt about consuming drive-by shootings along with their popcorn.

It was in this spirit that "Yo! MTV Raps" debuted in 1989 as the first national broadcast forum for rap music. The videos were often poorly produced, but the music and visual presence of starts like KRS-One, LL Cool J, and Chuck D proved enormously compelling, rocketing "Yo!"to the top of the MTV ratings. On weekends bands were interviewed and videos introduced by Fab Five Freddie; hip young white professionals watched his shows to keep up with urban black slang and fashion. Younger view-ers rushed home from school on weekdays to catch ex-Beastie Boys DJ Dr. Dre, a sweatsuit-clad moun-tain of a man, well over 300 pounds, and Ed Lover, who evolved a unique brand of homeboy Laurel and Hardy mixed with occasional social comment.

With "Yo! MTV Raps," rap became for the first time the music of choice in the white suburbs of middle America. From the beginning, says Doug Herzog, MTV's vice president for programming, the show's audience was primarily white, male, suburban, and between the ages of 16 and 24, a demographic profile the "Yo!"'s success helped set in stone. For its daytime audience, MTV spawned an ethnic rain-bow of well-scrubbed pop rappers from MC Hammer to Vanilla Ice to Gerardo, a Hispanic actor turned rap star. For "Yo" itself, rap became more overtly politicized as it expanded its audience. Sound bites from the speeches of Malcolm X and Martin Luther King became de rigueur introductions to formulaic assaults on white America mixed with hymns to gang violence and crude sexual caricature.

Holding such polyglot records together is what *Village Voice* critic Nelson George has labeled "ghet-tocentrism," a style-driven cult of blackness defined by crude stereotypes. P.R. releases, like a recent one for Los Angeles rapper DJ Quik, take special care to mention artists' police records, often enhanced to provide extra street credibility. When Def Jam star Slick Rick was arrested for attempted homicide, Def Jam incorporated the arrest into its publicity campaign for Rick's new album, bartering exclusive rights to the story to *Vanity Fair* in exchange for the promise of a lengthy profile. Muslim groups such as Brand Nubian proclaim their hatred for white devils, especially those who plot to poison black babies. That Brand Nubian believes the things said on its records is unlikely: the group seems to get along quite well with its white Jewish publicist, Beth Jacobson of Electra Records. Anti-white, and, in this case, anti-Semitic, rhymes are a shorthand way of defining one's opposition to the mainstream. Racism is reduced to fash-ion, by the rappers who use it and by the white audiences to whom such images appeal. What's signifi-cant here are not so much the intentions of artist and audience as a dynamic in which anti-Semitic slurs and black criminality correspond to "authenticity," and "authenticity" sells records.

The selling of this kind of authenticity to a young white audience is the stock-in-trade of *The Source*, a full-color monthly magazine devoted exclusively to rap music, founded by Jon Shecter while still an undergraduate at Harvard. Shecter is what is known in the rap business as a Young Black Teenager. He wears a Brooklyn Dodgers baseball cap, like Spike Lee, and a Source T-shirt. As editor of *The Source*, Shecter has become a necessary quote for stories about rap in *Time* and other national magazines.

An upper-middle-class white, Shecter has come in for his share of criticism, the most recent of which appeared as a diatribe by the sometime critic and tinpot racist Harry Allen in a black community newspaper, *The City Sun*, which pointed out that Shecter is Jewish. "There's no place for me to say any-thing," Shecter responds, "Given what I'm doing, my viewpoint has to be that whatever comes of the black community, the hip-hop community which is the black community, is the right thing. I know my place. The only way in which criticism can be raised is on a personal level, because the way that things are set up, with the white-controlled media, prevents sincere back and-forth discussion from taking place." The latest venture in hip-hop marketing, a magazine planned by Time Warner, will also be edited by a young white, Jonathan van Meter, a former Condé Nast editor.

In part because of young whites like Shecter and van Meter, rap's influence on the street continues to decline. "You put out a record by Big Daddy Kane," Rubin says, "and then put out the same record by a pop performer like Janet Jackson. Not only will the Janet Jackson record sell ten times more copies, it will also be the cool record to play in clubs." Stephney agrees: "Kids in my neighborhood pump dance hall reggae on their systems all night long, because that's where the rhythm is. . . . People complain about how white kids stole black culture. The truth of the matter is that no one can steal a culture." Whatever its continuing significance in the realm of racial politics, rap's hour as innovative popular music has come and gone. Rap forfeited whatever claim it may have had to particularity by acquiring a mainstream white audience whose tastes increasingly determined the nature of the form. What whites wanted was not music, but black music, which as a result stopped really being either.

White fascination with rap sprang from a particular kind of cultural tourism pioneered by the Jazz Age novelist Carl Van Vechten. Van Vechten's 1926 best seller *Nigger Heaven* imagined a masculine, criminal, yet friendly black ghetto world that functioned, for Van Vechten and for his readers, as a refuge from white middle-class boredom. In *Really the Blues*, the white jazzman Mezz Mezzrow went one step further, claiming that his own life among black people in Harlem had physically transformed him into a member of the Negro race, whose unique sensibility he had now come to share. By inverting the moral values attached to contemporary racial stereotypes, Van Vechten and Mezzrow at once appealed to and sought to undermine the prevailing racial order. Both men, it should be stressed, conducted their tours in person.

The moral inversion of racist stereotypes as entertainment has lost whatever transformative power it may arguably have had fifty years ago. MC Serch of 3rd Bass, a white rap traditionalist, with short-cropped hair and thick-rimmed Buddy Holly glasses, formed his style in the uptown hip-hop clubs like the L.Q. in the early 1980s. "Ten or eleven years ago," he remarks, "when I was wearing my permanent-press Lee's with a beige campus shirt and matching Adidas sneakers, kids I went to school with were calling me a 'wigger,' 'black wanna-be,' all kinds of racist names. Now those same kids are driving Jeeps with MCM leather interiors and pumping Public Enemy."

The ways in which rap has been consumed and popularized speak not of cross-cultural understanding, musical or otherwise, but of a voyeurism and tolerance of racism in which black and white are both complicit. "Both the rappers and their white fans affect and commodify their own visions of street culture," argues Henry Louis Gates, Jr., of Harvard University, "like buying Navajo blankets at a reservation roadstop. A lot of what you see in rap is the guilt of the black middle class about its economic success, its inability to put forth a culture of its own. Instead they do the worst possible thing, falling back on fantasies of street life. In turn, white college students with impeccable gender credentials buy nasty sex lyrics under the cover of getting at some kind of authentic black experience."

Gates goes on to make the more worrying point: "What is potentially very dangerous about this is the feeling that by buying records they have made some kind of valid social commitment." Where the assimilation of black street culture by whites once required a degree of human contact between the races, the street is now available at the flick of a cable channel—to black and white middle class alike. "People want to consume and they want to consume easy," Hank Shocklee says. "If you're a suburban white kid and you want to find out what life is like for a black city teenager, you buy a record by N.W.A. It's like going to an amusement park and getting on a roller coaster ride—records are safe, they're controlled fear, and you always have the choice of turning it off. That's why nobody ever takes a train up to 125th Street and gets out and starts walking around. Because then you're not in control anymore: it's a whole other ball game." This kind of consumption—of racist stereotypes, of brutality toward women, or even of uplifting tributes to Dr. Martin Luther King—is of a particularly corrupting kind. The values it instills find their ultimate expression in the ease with which we watch young black men killing each other: in movies, on records, and on the streets of cities and towns across the country.

Questions for Discussion

1. In his discussion of rap music, Samuels discusses the construction of black identity as a social phenomenon and as a consumer product. How do social stereotypes and consumer desires interact? Does consumer pressure sustain oppressive ideas about race or does it work toward racial respect? How does consumerism shape popular beliefs about black culture? Also discuss the way audience shapes the acceptable message in a text.

2. "The Rap on Rap" counts on two contrasting black images. One of these images approaches reality, accounting for the differences of upper, middle and lower class black cultures. The other is constructed from public stereotypes, traditions and fantasies. List the characteristics of each image and discuss alternative ways they represent these characteristics.

3. Samuels says that when white Jewish editor John Schecter was questioned about his magazine *The Source*, he replied "There's no place for me to say anything. Given what I am doing, my viewpoint has to be that whatever comes of the black community . . . I know my place. The only way in which criticism can be raised is on a personal level, because the way that things are set up, with the white-controlled media, prevents sincere back and forth discussion from taking place." If the white controllers of media can't speak, and the black community is silenced in their publications and marketing practices, then, who can speak? Why is it important that Schecter is Jewish? Who actually gets a voice in the marketing of rap music? Why? How is a space for individual voices made in the rhetoric of advertising and marketing programs?

Explorations

1. Peggy Macintosh discusses the backpack of privileges that white people carry in this society. What does Samuels believe fills the backpack of African Americans?

2. Samuels argues that commercial forces can hinder cross-cultural understanding. What other forces work for and against cross-cultural understanding? Choose another author that addresses this phenomenon, (like Jean Anyon, Keith Gilyard, or Sherman Alexie), and discuss how cross-cultural understanding can be assisted.

3. Samuels writes, "The ways in which rap has been consumed and popularized speak. . . . of a voyeurism and tolerance of racism in which black and white are both complicit." Would Miller and Postman also believe that television news equally caters to the voyeuristic desires of their consumers? Do any of these authors believe that their audiences want to see the "real" thing? Compare the way Tim O'Brien explains "How to Tell a True War Story" with the way rap musicians might truly represent black culture.

Formal Writing Assignments

1. Using the lyrics from a popular rap artist, discuss how the text transmits its message to its audience. What words are used and what connotative meaning do they carry? How do audiences respond to these messages? How does including taboo topics affect audiences? What do the lyrics say about the character of its artist and the character of its audience?

2. Rap music is only one form of racial representation in commercial media. Compare the way that race is presented in ads, TV commercials, film, or news reports with the way it is displayed in rap music. What do the differences say about their audiences and the purpose of these media productions?

Technology in Reverse

Robert J. Samuelson

Robert J. Samuelson is an award-winning journalist and writer. Since 1977, he has been a commentator and columnist for *Newsweek* magazine, the *Washington Post*, and other national newspapers. Though his columns most frequently focus on economic and business trends, he typically analyzes these trends from the perspective of those people in the general population who are affected by them. A sampling of other writings by Samuel can be found at http://washingtonpost.com/wp-dyn/opinion/columnns/samuelsonrobert/

Writing Before Reading

1. Describe in a paragraph the reasons you could not imagine your life without some form of digital technology (such as a personal computer, cellular phone, or pager). In a second paragraph, describe how the generation of people before you accomplished many of the same everyday activities without technology. Which world would you rather live in? Why?

2. If there came a time when newspapers, magazines, or even books were available on on-line, what would be lost? What would be gained? Does a printed newspaper have any advantages over its electronic counterpart?

3. If you lived in a time before electronic word processing became a standard for preparation of academic work, create a list of the ways expectations have changed for that work. Do professors expect more? Has the length of time required to prepare work been lessened by technology? Increased by technology?

Technology in Reverse

Let me introduce you to retarded technology. It's the opposite of advanced technology. Advanced technology enables us to do useful new things or to do old things more efficiently. By contrast, retarded technology creates new and expensive ways of doing things that were once done simply and inexpensively. Worse, it encourages us to do things that don't need doing at all. It has made waste respectable, elaborate, alluring and even fun.

Just the other week, *Newsweek* reported a boom in electronic books. The idea is to put books onto discs that you can plug into your customized book-displaying computer. Here's a swell idea of retarded technology. On the one hand, you can buy a $900 or $9,000 book-reading computer that you can feed with $30 discs of your favorite books. It's cumbersome. If you take it to the beach, it gets clogged with sand. You can't use it as a pillow. If it slips off the kitchen counter, it smashes.

On the other hand, you can buy an old-fashioned book. It's cheaper, more mobile, less fragile and more durable. You can lend it, even to casual friends. If you don't like it, you can stop reading without hating yourself for ever buying it. Losing it is not a traumatizing event.

The pro-technology comeback is that computers will someday compress entire libraries onto chips or discs and, thereby, open vast vistas of information to almost anyone. The trouble with this is arithmetic and common sense. A school library with 2,000 books can theoretically serve 2,000 readers simultaneously.

A school library with one computer terminal that can call up 200,000 books can serve only one reader at a time. The computers creates a bottleneck. Sure, the library can buy more computers, but they're costlier and bulkier than books. Finally, there's common sense: do most people really need access to, say, the entire collection of the New York Public Library?

Here's another example of technology racing backward: the video press release. In my business, we're bombarded with press releases for products, politicians and policies. And now there are promotional videos. Instead of a 10-cent press release that took two days to prepare and 29 cents to mail, I get a $4.50 tape that cost $2 to mail and two months to prepare. I can read standard press releases in 10 or 15 seconds before tossing 99 percent of them. But the videos get tossed immediately. To view them would require finding a VCR and wasting five to 10 minutes watching. Sorry, no sale. The video costs more and does less.

I am not about to argue that all technology is bad. Heavens, no. Ours is an era of conspicuous technological upheaval. But the purported gains of new technology—rising incomes, greater productivity—seem to elude us. Somehow, the paradox must be explained. One theory holds that we're still in the primitive stages of, say, the computer revolution, whose full benefits will soon burst upon us. Maybe. (A corollary is that techno-dopes like me are holding back progress.)

But to this theory, I would add the notion of retarded technology. Yup, the gains from new technologies are plentiful and real. But the benefits are being crudely offset by a lot of technology-inspired waste. Technology is often misused because the reasons people embrace it can be fairly frivolous. To wit:

- *Social Status.* Suppose your brother in Honolulu gets a car phone. He might even need it for work. Can you then be without one? Obviously not. Need isn't an issue. (Since 1985, the number of cellular subscribers has leaped from 34,000 to about 8 million.)

- *Adult Play.* New machines are often grown-up toys, successors to Legos and dolls. A woman I know well (my wife) recently exulted after creating invitation cards on her personal computer. (I dared not ask how long this took.) "But I'm so proud of myself. I'm thrilled." In the office, computer mail has transformed idle chitchat into an all-day affair.

- *The Mount Everest Effect.* Every new technology inspires the temptation to see what it will do—no matter how inane or time-consuming the task. This is the technological equivalent of "We're climbing that mountain because it's there." Hence, the video press release. Entire areas of academic life (political science, economics and even history) are now increasingly given over to number crunching. Computers allow numbers to be easily crunched; so they are. Genuine thought is discouraged. The same thought-deadening process afflicts American managers.

The survival of stupid technology is ordained by ego and money. New technologies often require a hefty investment. Once investments are made, they can't easily be unmade. To do so would be embarrassing. Old and inexpensive ways of doing things are eliminated to help pay for new and expensive methods. Retarded technology becomes institutionalized and permanent.

This is routinely denied, because people won't admit they're frivolous or wasteful. One survey of cellular-phone owners found that 87 percent said their phones raised their productivity by an average of 36 percent. More than half (54 percent) said the phone had improved their marriages. Imagine if these gains were generalized to the entire population: our economy's output would instantly leap from $6 trillion to $8 trillion; divorce rates would plunge, and "family values" would triumph. What we need are cellular subsidies so everyone can have one.

The beat goes on. Apple Computer recently announced Newton, the first of a generation of handheld "personal digital assistants." Newton will, Apple says, recognize your handwriting when you scribble something on its small display screen. This seems impressive. You scrawl "Joe Smith," and Newton calls up "Joe Smith" from its memory and tells you Joe's phone number and anything else you've put in Joe's tiny file. Just like a Rolodex.

Hey, maybe a Rolodex is better. It's cheaper. How about a standard notebook or address book? They already accept handwriting. Even fancy address books cost only $15 or $20. Apple says Newton (which will also act as a pager and send messages over phone lines) will be priced "well under $1,000." It should be a smashing success.

Questions for Discussion

1. What does Samuelson mean in the second paragraph of this essay when he writes that electronic books are a "swell idea"? What does this word choice—and others that you can identify—say about the ethos that Samuelson wants to establish in this essay?

2. Can you think of examples of technologies that once seemed to be luxuries but are now considered to be necessities? In the 1950s and 60s, for example, car radios and air conditioning were luxury items included on only a few vehicles. Do you feel that the items mentioned by Samuelson—particularly cellular phones—have moved from the category of luxury to that of necessity? Do cellular phones still carry with them the aura of status they did when this article was written in 1995?

3. If, as Samuelson suggests, technology often impedes real accomplishment, why then are we so quick to adopt each new advance as it becomes available?

Explorations

1. You are exposed to advertising each day touting the latest technology advancement, from wireless internet access to in-car satellite navigational devices. How do advertisers battle the perception that the technology is not really necessary to customers' lives? Or do they need to establish this at all?

2. The argument could be made that each email sent saves a sheet of paper, and thus a valuable natural resource is preserved. Does this claim hold up to scrutiny? Consider all of the resources necessary to the maintenance of an electronic communication, then speculate on environmental consequences of the technological revolution. Which takes a greater toll on the environment—old technologies or new?

3. Consider Samuelson's essay in light of the claims made by Cynthia Selfe in "Lest We Think the Revolution is a Revolution." Selfe is interested in the ways in which computer technology has changed only the expression—but not the substance—of biases and destructive attitudes that have been part of our society for decades. Samuelson, in a lighter tone, seems to make a similar point. Do the attitudes toward technology described by Samuelson tend to support Selfe's argument? Undermine it?

Formal Writing Assignments

1. Choose a recent non-game software application and write a review of that software that could be published in either a technology trade magazine or a more general interest magazine such as *Wired*. As part of your review, consider Samuelson's essay and determine whether or not the soft-

ware accomplished something new and valuable or, rather, complicates a process that could be achieved more simply before this software was developed.

2. In an essay, compare the lives of people on each side of the so-called "technological divide" in our society. What are the distinctions between the lives of the digital haves and have-nots? Are there ways, as Samuelson suggest, that those who opt out of the technological revolution are better off? How do aspects of their lives compare to the lives of those who have no access to technology for economic or social reasons?

On Reading a Video Text

Robert Scholes

Robert Scholes is a Professor of Humanities at Brown University. There are few university professors who have been as honored as Robert Scholes for research, writing, and teaching. Over the course of his career, he has published more than thirty books. His most recent one, *The Rise and Fall of English,* has created controversy by claiming that English departments at universities across the country must reassess their goals and, among other things, place greater emphasis on teaching students to understand a diverse body of texts, including those outside the standard literary canon. In this essay, from the earlier book *Protocols of Reading,* Scholes helps readers understand that video images can indeed be "read" in much the same way as the printed word.

Writing Before Reading

1. The phrase "a picture is worth a thousand words" has been part of the American culture for many years. In a paragraph or two, speculate on the origin of this phrase and its resonance with the public. Why do we believe that a picture is worth a thousand words?

2. Very soon after the technology of film was created, film makers began to develop means of controlling the images they produced. They did this both on the scene and in the darkroom, where the images could be altered to suit the maker's purpose. Digital technology has allowed such image manipulation to become nearly undetectable. Given this, is a picture still worth a thousand words? List reasons the public might have for distrusting the video or photographic images it sees daily on TV, in magazines, or at the movies.

3. Think of the last advertisement you saw on TV that was meant to "tell a story." In your own words, re-tell that story then write a paragraph explaining the connection between the narrative and product the narrative is meant to sell.

On Reading a Video Text

The moments of surrender proposed to us by video texts come in many forms, but all involve a complex dynamic of power and pleasure. We are, for instance, offered a kind of power through the enhancement of our vision. Close-ups position us where we could never stand. Slow motion allows us an extraordinary penetration into the mechanics of movement, and, combined with music, lends a balletic grace to ordinary forms of locomotion. Filters and other devices cause us to see the world through jaundiced or rose-colored optics, coloring events with emotion more effectively than verbal pathetic fallacy and less obtrusively. These derangements of normal visual processing can be seen as either constraints or extensions of visual power—that is, as power over the viewer or as extensions of the viewer's own optical power, or both. Either way they offer us what is perhaps the greatest single virtue of art: change form the normal, defense against the ever-present threat of boredom. Video texts, like all except the most utilitarian forms of textuality, are constructed upon a base of boredom, from which they promise us relief.

Visual fascination—and I have mentioned only a few of its obvious forms—is just one of the matrices of power and pleasure that are organized by video texts. Others include narrativity and what I should like to call, at least tentatively, cultural reinforcement. By narrativity, of course, I mean the pleasures and powers associated with the reception of stories presented in video texts. By cultural reinforcement, I mean the process through which video texts confirm viewers in their ideological positions and reassure them as to their membership in a collective cultural body. This function, which operates in the ethical-political realm, is an extremely important element of video textuality and, indeed, an extremely important dimension of all the mass media. This is a function performed throughout much of human history by literature and the other arts, but now, as the arts have become more estranged from their own culture and even opposed to it, the mass media have come to perform this role. What the epic poem did for ancient cultures, the romance for feudalism, and the novel for bourgeois society, the media—and especially television—now do for the commodified, bureaucratized world that is our present environment.

It is time, now, to look at these processes as they operate in some specific texts. Let us begin with a well-known Budweiser commercial which tells—most frequently in a format of twenty-eight seconds, though a longer version also exists—the life story of a black man pursuing a career as a baseball umpire. In this brief period of time, we are given enough information to construct an entire life story—provided we have the cultural knowledge upon which this construction depends. The story we construct is that of a young man from the provinces, who gets his "big break" his chance to make it in the big city, to rise to the top of his profession. We see him working hard in the small-time, small-town atmosphere of the minor leagues, where the pace of events is slower and more relaxed than it is "at the top." He gets his chance for success—the voice-over narrator says, "In the minors you got to make all the calls, and then one day you *get* the call"—after which we see him face his first real test. He must call an important and "close" play correctly and then withstand the pressure of dispute, neither giving ground by changing his mind (which would be fatal) nor reacting too vigorously to the challenge of his call by an offended manager. His passing of this test and being accepted is presented through a later scene in a bar, in which the manager who had staged the protest "toasts" the umpire with a bottle of Budweiser beer, with a chorus in the background singing, "You keep America working. This Bud's for you." From this scene we conclude that the ump has now "made it" and will live happily ever after. From a few scenes, then, aided by the voice-over narration and a music track, we construct an entire life. How do we do this? We draw upon a storehouse of cultural information that extends from fairy tales and other basic narrative structures to knowledge about the game and business of baseball.

In processing a narrative text we actually construct the story, bringing a vast repertory of cultural knowledge to bear upon the text that we are contemplating. Our pleasure in the narrative is to some extent a constructive pleasure, based upon the sense of accomplishment we achieve by successfully completing this task. By "getting" the story, we prove our competence and demonstrate our membership in a cultural community. And what is the story that we "get"? It is the myth of America itself, of the racial melting pot, of upward mobility, of justice done without fear or favor. The corporate structure of baseball, with minor leagues offering a path for the talented to the celebrity and financial rewards of the majors, embodies values that we all possess, we Americans, as one of the deepest parts of our cultural heritage or ideology. It is, of course, on the playing field that talent triumphs most easily over racial or social barriers. Every year in baseball new faces arrive. Young men, having proved themselves in the minors, get their chance to perform at the highest level. Yale graduates and high-school dropouts who speak little or no English are judged equally by how well they hit, run, throw, and react to game situations. If baseball is still the national pastime, it is because in it our cherished myths materialize—or appear to materialize.

The commercial we are considering is especially interesting because it shows us a black man competing not with his body but with his mind, his judgment and his emotions, in a cruelly testing public arena. Americans who attend to sports are aware that black athletes are just beginning to find acceptance at certain "leadership" positions, such as quarterback in professional football, and that there is still an active scandal over the slender representation of blacks at baseball's managerial and corporate levels. The case of the black umpire reminds viewers of these problems, even as it suggest that here, too, talent will finally prevail. The system works, America works. We can take pride in this. The narrative reduces its story to the absolutely bare essentials, making a career turn, or seem to turn, on a single decision. The ump must make a close call, which will be fiercely contested by a manager who is deliberately testing him. This is a story of initiation, in that respect, an ordeal that the ump must meet successfully. The text ensures that we know this is a test, by showing us the manager plotting in his dugout, and it gives us a manager with one of those baseball faces (Irish? German?) that have the history of the game written on them. This is not just partisan versus impartial judge, it is old man against youth, and white against black. We root for the umpire because we want the system to work—not just baseball but the whole thing: America. For the story to work, of course, the ump must make the right call, and we must know it to be right. Here, the close-up and slow motion come into play—just as they would in a real instant replay—to let us see both how close the call is and that the umpire has indeed made the right call. The runner is out. The manager's charge from the dugout is classic baseball protest, and the ump's self-control and slow walk away from the angry manager are gestures in a ritual we all know. That's right, we think, that's the way it's done. We know these moves the way the contemporaries of Aeschylus and Sophocles knew the myths upon which the Greek tragedies were based. Baseball is already a ritual, and a ritual we partake of mostly through the medium of television. The commercial has only to organize these images in a certain way to create a powerful narrative.

At the bar after the game, we are off stage, outside that ritual of baseball, but we are still in the world of myth. The manager salutes the ump with his tilted bottle of beer; the old man acknowledges that youth has passed its test. The sword on the shoulder of knighthood, the laying on of hands, the tilted Bud—all these are ritual gestures in the same narrative structure of initiation. To the extent that we have wanted this to happen we are gratified by this closing scene of the narrative text, and many things, as I have suggested, conspire to make us want this ending. We are dealing with an archetypal narrative that has been adjusted for maximum effect within a particular political and social context, and all this has been deployed with a technical skill in casting, directing, acting, photographing, and editing that is of a high order. It is very hard to resist the pleasure of this text, and we cannot accept the pleasure without, for the bewildering minute at least, also accepting the ideology that is so richly and closely entangled with the story that we construct from the video text. To accept the pleasure of this text is to believe that America works; and this is a comforting belief, itself a pleasure of an even higher order—for as long as we can maintain it. Does the text also sell Budweiser? This is something only market research (if you believe it) can tell. But it sure sells the American way first and then seeks to sell its brand of beer by establishing a metonymic connection between the product and the nation, a national beer for the national pastime.

An audience that can understand this commercial, successfully constructing the ump's story from the scenes represented in the text and the comments of the narrative voice, is an audience that understands narrative structure and has a significant amount of cultural knowledge as well, including both data (how baseball leagues are organized, for instance, and how the game is played) and myth (what constitutes success, for example, and what initiation is). At a time when critics such as William Bennett and E.D. Hirsch are bewailing our ignorance of culture, it is important to realize that many Americans are not without culture; they simply have a different culture from that of Bennett and Hirsch. What they really lack, for the most part, is any way of analyzing and criticizing the power of a text like the Budweiser commercial—not its power to sell beer, which is easily resisted, especially once you have tasted better beer—but its power to sell America. For the sort of analysis that I am suggesting, it is necessary to recover (as Eliot says) from the surrender to this text, and it is also necessary to have the tools of ideological criticism. Recovery, in fact, may depend upon critical analysis, which is why the analysis of video texts needs to be taught in all our schools.

Before moving on to the consideration of a more complex textual economy, we would do well to pause and consider the necessity of ideological criticism. One dimension of the conservative agenda for this country has been conspicuously anticritical. The proposals of William Bennett and E.D. Hirsch, for instance, different as they are in certain respects, are both recipes for the indoctrination of young people in certain cultural myths. The great books of past ages, in the eyes of Bennett, Hirsch, and Allan Bloom, are to be mythologized, turned into frozen monuments of Greatness in which our "cultural heritage" is embodied. This is precisely what Bloom does to Plato, for instance, turning the dialectical search for truth into a fixed recipe for "greatness of soul." The irony of this is that Plato can only die in this process. Plato's work can better be kept alive in our time by such irreverent critiques as that of Jacques Derrida, who takes Plato seriously as an opponent, which is to say, take him dialectically. In this age of massive manipulation and disinformation, criticism is the only way we have of taking something seriously. The greatest patriots in our time will be those who explore our ideology critically, with particular attention to the gaps between mythology and practice. Above all, we must start with our most beloved icons, not the ones we profess allegiance to, but those that really have the power to move and shake us.

Questions of Discussion

1. Robert Scholes' essay focuses on a single video text, that of a Budweiser commercial that tells the story of an African-American baseball umpire passing a crucial test and joining the ranks of the initiated in the baseball community. He also writes that all video texts present the viewer with a complex dynamic of power and pleasure. What is the power we experience in watching this video? What is the pleasure?

2. Why, in Schole's view, is it important that the umpire in the video story be African-American? How would the narrative be different if the races of the principal players—the umpire and the team manager—were reversed? Would the reader experience the same "cultural reinforcement," as Scholes describes it?

3. Recall other advertisements you have seen recently that require you to "draw upon a storehouse of cultural information" to understand the connection the ads' creators want you to make. Discuss the ads and the stories they present. Does bringing that cultural knowledge to a conscious level in your thoughts change your impression of the advertisement?

Explorations

1. Other essays in this collection, including Mark Crispin Miller's "How TV Covers War" and Neil Postman and Steve Powers' "The Bias of Language, The Bias of Pictures" address issues of media manipulation of images and words. Postman and Powers particularly make the point that video images not only limit the message they intend to convey, but also limit that message in the particular manner that best suits the purposes of the images' makers. How would Postman and Powers analyze the manner in which language and image have been limited in the Budweiser commercial? another commercial?

2. After reading this essay, what questions would you ask the author? At the time of this writing, Robert Scholes' web site, http://www.modcult.brown.edu/people/scholes, lists his current research and teaching activities, with links to book excerpts and course schedules. Write to professor Scholes, then share his response with your peer group or class.

3. At one point in the essay, Scholes admits that he has no idea whether or not the Budweiser commercial is successful at selling beer, saying that "this is something only market research (if you believe it) can tell." There are several well-known examples of award-winning commercials that failed in their attempt to sell a product. Why do commercials that sell "the American way" or another value work to sell a product? Under what circumstances would an advertiser actually find that to focus on the qualities of the product itself would be detrimental to sales?

Formal Writing Assignments

1. In an essay, analyze a commercial message that calls on the viewer to understand a broad range of cultural information. In particular, choose an advertisement that teems with narrative elements—one that "tells a story." Be sure to summarize the content of the message sufficiently for a reader to understand your point without actually seeing the commercial.

2. Focus on ways that symbols of the United States such as the U.S. flag, the bald eagle, or the images of early presidents such as George Washington and Abraham Lincoln have been used as sales tools. In this essay, provide examples of instances of this marketing practice, and analyze the effect of such practices on our perception of these symbols.

Lest We Think the Revolution Is a Revolution: Images of Technology and the Nature of Change

Cynthia L. Selfe

Cynthia L. Selfe is a professor of Composition and Communication at Michigan Technological Institute. Her most recent scholarship has focused on the relationship between technology and literacy, including her 1999 book *Technology and Literacy in the Twenty-First Century: The Perils of Not Paying Attention.* During her career at Michigan Tech, Professor Selfe has divided her time between teaching, research, and administration, but in each of these roles has sought to be an activist and advocate. She served on the committee, for example, that promoted the first African-American woman professor in the history of Michigan Tech, and created initiatives to boost salaries and improve workplace quality for clerical and professional staff. She has been recognized by her colleagues in the field of composition studies as an innovator and leader.

The intended audience for the essay included here is, in fact, composition instructors. You will see, however, that her thoughts on technological progress and societal change have broad application to our understanding of technological literacy.

Writing Before Reading

1. It is tempting to believe that technological innovation always benefits those who take advantage of that technology. Think of an example of such an innovation that has been widely hailed as beneficial—such as the telephone, vaccines, or air-conditioning—and create a list of the **detrimental** effects to individuals or society of these advances in technology.

2. What are some of the events or phenomena that may have made us less trusting in the value of scientific or technological advancement in the past ten years? the past fifty years? Choosing an item from the list you created in the previous exercise, write a paragraph that states the reason for your mistrust.

3. Do you remember the first time you accessed the internet? What were your impressions? Did they match your expectations? Describe in writing one of your first encounters with the net.

Lest We Think the Revolution Is a Revolution: Images of Technology and the Nature of Change

When English studies teachers get together to talk about technology we generally end up talking about change. It is common sense, after all to link computers with change when microprocessors, according to Moore's law, double in speed every eighteen months, when biomemory, superscalar architecture, and picoprocessors become feature stories for National Public Radio; and when media generations flash by in less time than it takes to uncrate a faculty workstation and get rid of the styrofoam packing.

And, at some level, English Departments have come to terms with technological change—we have adjusted diminishing supplies and equipment budgets to accommodate an ongoing program of purchases and upgrades, accepted computer studies as a new area of scholarly focus, integrated technology into various curricula, and modified many programs to include technology training and use (c.f., Selber, 1994; McDaniel, 1990; Schwartz, Selfe, Sosnoski, 1994; Wahlstrom and Selfe, 1994).

Like most Americans, however, even though educators have made these adaptations, we remain decidedly undecided about technology and change. At one level, we believe in the pairing; we believe in the computer's power, and we believe strongly in the beneficial ways that technology promises to improve our lives (Bump, 1990; Delany and Landow, 1991; Snyder, 1996). At other levels, we fear the effects of technology, and the potent changes that it introduces into familiar systems. (Apple, 1986; Kramarae, 1988; Hawisher and Selfe, 1993; Selfe and Selfe, 1994).

These contradictory impulses are the focus of this chapter, especially as they affect the work of English studies specialists and educators. In addition, these attitudes shade subtly into one another at multiple levels of a larger collective social experience, and they are worth exploring for that reason as well.

Change Technology, and the Status Quo: Some Background

Because our culture subscribes to several powerful narratives that link technological progress closely with social progress, it is easy for us—for Americans, in particular—to believe that technological change leads to productive social change.

Indeed, the narratives linking technological change to social change are part of the reason that English studies teachers—like many other educators—have come to embrace computer technology so enthusiastically over the past decade.

Quite simply put, like many Americans, we hope computers can help us make the world a better place in which to live. In the profession of English studies, for example, we hope computers can help make us, and the students with whom we work, more productive in the classroom and other instructional settings (Hafer 1996; Coogan 1995; Clark 1995; Tornow 1997; Sirc 1995) more effective as communicators (Blair 1996; Minock and Shor 1995; Sproull and Kiesler 1991), and more responsibly involved as literate citizens in world affairs (Schuler 1994; Selfe 1996; Geren 1996).

We are not alone in these stories that we tell ourselves—indeed, they are echoed for us constantly and in a variety of versions. Vice President Albert Gore (1994) has noted that the Global Information Infrastructure (GII) would increase opportunities for intercultural communication among the peoples of the world. Howard Rheingold, in *The Virtual Community* (1993), describes how computer networks can support more citizens in their efforts to communicate with government agencies, corporations, political groups, and information resources. Nicholas Negroponte, in *Being Digital* (1995), sketches a picture of electronic landscapes that provide individuals new ways of making personal contributions to public deliberations and decision making. Dale Spender, while more careful in her perspective in *Nattering on the Nets* (1995), speculates on what it will take to establish new kinds of electronic forums that will support women and other groups now often left out of—or kept out of—public discussions in other venues.

This optimism about technology often masks in a peculiar way, however, a contrasting set of extremely potent fears. Moreover, and perhaps more importantly, an exclusive focus on the positive changes associated with technology, often serves to distract educators from recognizing how existing social forces actually work to resist change in connection with technology; how they support the status quo when technology threatens to disrupt the world in any meaningful way; how our culture, and the social formations that make up this culture, react with a special kind of conservatism to technology, even as we laud the changes it promises to bring.

This chapter will attempt to illustrate the ways in which change is modulated and complicated by forces of stasis by focusing attention on a series of images that come from commercial advertisements about technology. These advertisements reflect a portion of our collective American cultural imagination about technology. Like most images, they tell rich and powerful stories about the social contexts in which they are produced. Like snapshots—of weddings and graduations, of Christmas and family reunions, they reveal us, as Americans, to ourselves. They are laden with cultural information, shot through with the values, ideological positions, and social understandings that comprise our shared experience. Indeed, it is because we recognize the common cultural symbols in these snapshots so clearly, because we commonly construct meaning with and through them, because they are so loaded with social significance to us, that such images are powerful communication devices.

These are also the reasons that the ads included in this chapter can reveal to us the complications of our feelings toward technology and illustrate how these feelings are played out in the shared landscapes of our lived experience.

Narrative #1: The "Global Village" and the "Electronic Colony"

One of the most popular narratives Americans tell ourselves about computers is that technology will help us create a global village in which the peoples of the world are all connected—communicating with one another and cooperating for the commonweal. According to this popular social narrative, the computer network that spans the globe will serve to erase meaningless geopolitical borders, eliminate racial and ethnic differences, re-establish a historical familial relationship which binds together the peoples of the world regardless of race, ethnicity, or location. As Nicholas Negroponte (1995) re-tells the story to us, "a new generation is emerging from the digital landscape free from many of the old prejudices. . . . Digital technology can be a natural force, drawing people into greater world harmony" (230) within a landscape where "we are bound to find new hope and dignity" (231).

This story, as you can imagine, is appealing at a romantic level to many Americans. It is also, incidentally, quite terrifying. Becoming just another member of the tribe, just another citizen of the global village, suggests the possibility that Americans could be asked to relinquish their current privileged status in the world where, as Negroponte (1995, 230) also reminds us, twenty percent of the population currently consumes eighty percent of the resources. Being just one among many village members also suggests the possibility of losing the economic benefits that have accrued to us as citizens in one of the most highly technological nations of the world and the possibility of functioning within a new global context in which classism and racism arc unacceptable because so many members of the connected human family are poor and of color.

In fact, we find ourselves, as a culture, ill equipped to cope with the changes that the "global village" story necessitates, unable, even, to imagine, collectively, ways of relating to the world outside our previous historical and cultural experiences. As a result, in the advertisements included here, we revise the script of the narrative to fit within the historically determined contexts that are familiar and comfortable. In doing so, we also limit our cultural vision of the technological changes that are acceptable and possible for us as a culture.

The first series of images presented in this chapter reveals how our cultural imagination deals with the radical changes that the Global Village Narrative implies, by re-constituting technological change within the boundaries of these more historically and socially familiar contexts. In the global village narrative, for example, while we maintain the vision of linking peoples around the world, we imagine ourselves, not as simple members of this electronically constituted village, but rather as discoverers of the village, explorers of its remote corners, and even colonizers of its exotic peoples.

In the revised narrative, the global village retains its geographical reach, but it becomes a world in which different cultures, different peoples, exist to be discovered, explored, marveled at—in a sense, known and claimed—by those who can design and use technology. Inhabitants of this electronic global village, in turn, become foreigners, exotics, savages, objects to study and, sometimes, to control.

This revision is a familiar imaginative context for us—we have, after all, a history of experiencing the world as missionaries, as colonists, as tourists, as representatives of multinational companies. The revised story leaves no doubt about our own role—Americans are the smart ones who use technological expertise to connect the world's peoples, to supply them with technology and train them to use it. Nor does the revised story leave us in doubt about the roles of other peoples in the world—they are the recipients of technology and its benefits, those who use the technology that we control. This story is so familiar because it has happened before and in ways that Americans like to remember. We have a long and admirable history of exporting technological expertise to less fortunate neighbors—through the Lend-Lease, the Peace Corps, and the Space Program among other routes.

This re-telling or re-vising of the Global Village story—we can now call it the Electronic Colonial narrative—happens very naturally within the discursive venues available to our culture—on television, in our classrooms, in books, and articles, and in corporate settings—often without anyone noticing because the elements of revised Electronic Colonial narrative are so much more familiar and acceptable to us than were those of the original Global Village story.

The following pair of images reveals these themes (figures 1 and 2). Especially fascinating in terms of this revised narrative is the use in these two ads, by Virgin Sound and Records, of the "one tribe" motto.

In the first image (figure 1) we get a glimpse of both stories we have described. The text here narrates the Global Village story, "For the world to have a future, we must work together as one tribe" because "encroaching civilization, disease" and "epidemics" are threatening some of the world's people with "near extinction." Virgin, the ad tells us, has donated a portion of their profits from their CD atlas, entitled *One World*, to assist the Yanomami tribe in the Amazon Basin as they establish health care programs in their villages.

The second, revised story—the Electronic Colonial narrative—is revealed most clearly in the visual image represented in the ad, the picture of the Yanomami man. In accordance with the themes of the revised narrative, the Yanomami is shown in ritual dress with feathers and face paint, presented as a wondering savage, vulnerable to the crueler effects of civilization, and obviously unaware, in a critical or informed sense, of the power of the technology being used to his benefit. He is connected to Americans as "a member of the tribe," but the also remains a world away from us—the people who are creating the CD technology and donating the money to health care projects.

The second ad (figure 2), again for Virgin Sound and Records, announces two products and provides us another version of the revised Electronic Colonial story. In this story, Americans use technology to become world travelers, to learn about—and acquire knowledge of—other cultures, while remaining comfortably situated within their own living rooms and, thus, comfortably separated from the other inhabitants of the global village.

On the left side of the page, the One Tribe CD is described, in which "MTV star Pip Dann takes you on a journey exploring the people and cultures of our world, from the origin of the Maori islanders to the rituals of a Tibetan monk." As the ad says, "One Tribe takes you further than you can imagine—right from your own Home." On the right side of the page, the *One World* atlas offers "A stunningly rich trek around the earth," and a "wealth of maps and information all set to a culturally rich music track." The non-Americans featured in this ad are identified as exotic, albeit inviting, co-habitants of the global village. At the top left, are representations of two youngsters, spliced together to present a bizarre tribal image; on the left margin scattered among postcards from exotic destinations and lists of foreign vocabulary words, two picturesque French men sport the requisite berets and a veiled Middle Eastern woman with mysterious eyes is portrayed.

To complement the textual representation of the electronic colony narrative, the picture in the bottom left of this ad reveals the source of this world gaze—a white, blond woman sits in a well appointed living room that is chock full of artifacts from around the world; several big-screen viewing areas in front of her feature images of exotic peoples and far-off locations, a large computer with a world map on the screen, and a globe complete the representation. Virgin provides an interesting case study of the Electronic Colonial narrative. As a company, it has roots in Great Britain, but, given its marketing and advertising targets, it has acquired a decidedly American flavor, thus, joining the two countries under the potency of a single colonial gesture.

And, these are the tasteful and more subtle advertisements that are associated with the Electronic Colony narrative. The other end of the spectrum is represented in the next two images (figures 3 and 4).

Figure 3, entitled "Unexpected" shows an Indian woman, bone picks through her nose, feathers attached to her ear, beads around her neck, nursing a baby on one breast and a monkey on the other. The ad, for a color scanner, begins with a large dollar sign. The person in the image, the message suggests, is another inhabitant of the global village, but one important to Americans only as the unexpected exotic, an image that we can use to sell a piece of technology.

The next ad (figure 4), for Polyglot International software, provides yet another version of the electronic colony story. In this image, a male, of undefined indigenous origins, with gold teeth, a broad smile, and a Carmen Miranda kind of bonnet made up of roses and topped by either a radio antenna or a birthday candle. The ad's designers have superimposed a set of aviator's goggles over the man's eyes, and, across these goggles, are printed a series of 1s and 0s, denoting binary code.

In this ad, the text provides the background story for the image, "You need a team of software . . . experts who can help you culturally adapt every aspect of your software for global markets. What you need for what they want." The members of the global village, the ad implies, are indeed different from Americans, and strange, but we can, given the know-how that characterizes the American free enterprise system, identify what these people are seeking in terms of desirable software and provide it to them in a language that they can understand, even with a simplistic notion of our technology products.

These four advertisements—like the travelogue images we look at in National Geographic, like the tourist brochures we pore over in the travel agency, like the slides we view after a friend's trip abroad— are representations of exotic places and exotic peoples now available to Americans as new global markets, multiplied, as Fredric Jameson (1991) and Jean Baudrillard (1983) would say, to the point of dizzying accessibility and specificity. And it is the wondering native, the silly Indian, the veiled woman that is the object of our collective technological, cultural, and capitalist gaze. Americans, in these four ads, you'll notice, go almost un-represented in terms of images. Instead, Americans are the canny and sophisticated minds behind the text, behind the image, behind the technology. We are the designers, the providers, the village benefactors. We are cybertourists and cybercapitalists who both understand and represent the world as a private standing reserve.

This next pair of advertisements (figures 5 and 6) from IBM entitled "Solutions for a small planet" also tells the electronic colony story, illustrating how generous Americans can be in providing other needier countries with useful technology, and providing the story a potent cumulative power. A small map portrayed in each ad helps to orient viewers to the particular area of the world that IBM and American influence have reached.

In the first ad (figure 5), for example, with the tone of an old master, IBM provides the 3-D rendering technology needed to rebuild the Frauenkirche, a church destroyed during the allied firebombing of Dresden in 1945. The ad notes that this technology, along with the experience of talented stonemasons, allows the reconstruction to proceed, linking the power of a "21st century tool" with the imagination of " 18th century craftsmanship."

In the next IBM ad, this set in South Africa, IBM helps the smiling driver of a South African Breweries truck "slake the thirst of . . . far flung customers . . . so precisely that no one's ever short a drop."

If the previous series reduces the world to a series of tourist destinations, this pair of ads—representative of a much more extensive series of technological "solutions for a small planet"—reduces the world's problems to a set of embarrassingly quick fixes. American technology and technological know-how, these images imply, can provide reparations for the cultural damage caused by the firebombing of Dresden, recreate the painstaking artistic achievement of a destroyed eighteenth-century cathedral, and serve as a corrective for decades of apartheid. These implications, of course, are not only absurd; they are humiliatingly small-minded. Nothing can provide redress for the millions of human lives, the art, the history, the beauty lost in Dresden; nothing can totally ameliorate the pain and the lingering inequities of South African apartheid. As much as Americans might like to think it; technology is not the solution for all of the world's problems—and, indeed, it might well be a contributing cause to many of them.

Technology, in these ads, is an American tool. And what we use this tool for reveals all too clearly our values as *homo faber*—the tool maker. In these images, I'm afraid, we see reflected not those fundamental and much needed changes we talked about pursuing earlier; not improvements in the world situation, nor the elimination of hunger or pain or suffering or war; not, in other words, an improved life for our fellow inhabitants in the global village or an improved understanding of their cultures and concerns, but, rather, the all too familiar stories of how to multiply our own markets, how to increase our own cultural profits at the expense of others, how to take more effective advantage of need and difference whenever we identify them, and how to reduce the cultures of other people to inexcusable simplifications.

Narrative #2: "Land of Equal Opportunity" and "Land of Difference"

A second favorite cultural story that we tell ourselves in connection with computers and change focuses on equity, opportunity, and access—all characteristics ascribed to the electronic landscape we have constructed on the Internet and to computer use, in general.

This landscape, Americans like to believe, is open to everybody—male and female, regardless of color, class, or connection. It is, in fact at some level a romantic re-creation of the American story and the American landscape themselves—a narrative of opportunity in an exciting land claimed from the wilderness, founded on the values of hard work and fair play. It is a land available to all citizens, who place a value on innovation, individualism, and competition, especially when tempered by a neighborly concern for less fortunate others that is the hallmark of our democracy. If you recognize this story, it is because it has been told so many times. It is the same story that Alexis DeToqueville (1735) told us in *Democracy in America* and one that we've been telling ourselves ever since—in *Horatio Alger* and *Huck Finn,* in *Nancy Drew* and in episodes of "Father Knows Best."

This next series of advertisements play on this narrative, emphasizing, in particular, our fascination with—and strong faith in—these traditional American values; in this case, specifically as they have the enduring power to inform and temper technological innovations. The first is an ad (figure 7) for Bob, Microsoft's friendly operating system. These images are all ripe with references to the 1950s, a time when America was entering the very beginning of an accelerated push toward technological growth and innovation. Although Sputnik, launched by the Russians on the 4th of October in 1957, weighed heavily on our collective minds, the fifties were chock full of optimism. We were still fresh from our successes in World War II, invigorated by the promise of the space program, tantalized by the bright future that the new world order seemed to hold for those who were innovative and farsighted, ready to help the world realize the promise of democracy and technology through special projects like the Peace Corp.

This cultural memory is a potent one for Americans, and these ads resonate with the values that we remember as characterizing that golden time—recalling for example, the down-home, no-nonsense comfort associated with a good dog, a good pipe, a warm fire, a comfortable pair of shoes (figure 7), and the other very American comforts accruing from a good salary and hard work in a culture where effort is rewarded with capital gain, regardless of race, color, creed, or class.

Indeed, we tell ourselves this clearly American tale—which I'll refer to as the Land of Equal Opportunity narrative—often and in many different versions. The next two images (figures 8 and 9) also play on it, for instance.

The first, for Cisco Systems, uses a picture that could have come right out of a Dick and Jane reader (figure 8). It shows another very American scene, also harkening back to the magic time of the fifties. This time, the focus is on landscape inhabited by smiling people who point to airplanes as evidence of the technological progress because these machines characterize what American know-how can accomplish in the land of equal opportunity when circumstances are right. The text notes, "With wide-eyed optimism, you thought technology was going to let you set information free. You were going to put power into the hands of the people." The ad goes on to explain that technology uninfluenced by traditional American values can run amuck, especially in a postmodern world characterized by "conflicting standards," "rival companies," "incompatibilities," and inefficient work habits.

The second image (figure 9) tells a bit more of the Land of Equal Opportunity narrative. It speaks for a piece of software by CINet called "The Ultimate Internet Tour," showing what looks like a frame from an old home movie. From a wide angle shot of a fifties suburban tract home development, we get a magnified perspective on a typical American family—three smiling kids, two smiling, upwardly-mobile parents posing in front of a spanking new, functionally designed, split-level home, with all the optimism characteristic of the Eisenhower era. The message, which urges readers to "keep up with the Joneses, the Gates and your kids," suggests that citizens of the twenty-first century can achieve the same kind of happy security and personal well being that was enjoyed by citizens of the fifties—by purchasing a software package rather than a new home.

Unfortunately, if Americans have no collective imaginary context for, or historical experience of, a real global village, nor do they have any real experience with an undifferentiated land of opportunity. Our cultural experience, indeed, tells us something very different—that America is the land of opportunity only for some people. The history of slavery in this country, the history of deaf education, women's suffrage, immigration, and labor unions remind us of this fact; as do our current experiences with poverty, the differential school graduation rate for blacks and whites and Hispanics, the fact that we have never had a woman President, and the presence of border guards and the razor-wire fences over the Rio Grande. All these things remind us that opportunity is a commodity generally limited to privileged groups within this country.

Thus, the revised story in the case of these last five ads—which we can call the Land of Difference narrative—is present not in what they show, but what they fail to show. These ads are what my grandmother would call "mighty white." There is a remarkable absence in all the images of people of color, and poor people, and people who are out of work, and single-parent families, and gay couples, and foreigners. If citizens of all kinds are to have access to technology and the opportunities it provides, we do not see such a narrative imagined in the Land of Difference narrative; if technology is to improve the lives of all Americans regardless of race and class and other differences, our collective ability to envision such a world is not evident in these images.

Narrative #3: "The Un-Gendered Utopia" and "The Same Old Gendered Stuff"

A third potent narrative that Americans tell ourselves about technology and change focuses on gender—specifically, this story claims that computers and that computer-supported environments will help us create a utopic world in which gender is not a predictor of success or a constraint for interaction with the world. This narrative, the Un-gendered Utopia story, encourages educators to see and understand computers as educational allies that can support efforts to create new kinds of educational and economic opportunities for students—regardless of gender. The potency of this narrative persists despite evidence to the contrary. It is clear, for instance, that fewer girls use computers in public secondary schools than do boys, especially in the upper grades, fewer women enter the advanced fields of computer science than do males, that the computer industry continues to be a space inhabited by and controlled primarily by males. Computer games are still designed for boys; computer commercials are still aimed mainly at males; computing environments are still constructed by and for males (cf., Spender 1995; Kramarae 1988; Jessup 1991). Computers, in other words, are complexly socially determined artifacts that interact with existing social formations and tendencies—including sexism, classism, and racism—to contribute to the shaping of a gendered society.

This situation, complexly overdetermined as it is within our cultural context, is nowhere more visible than in gendered images of technology use—especially, but not limited to, commercial images. In these richly textured images, the elaborately woven fabric of social formations that supports the male focused computer industry is coded ideologically at numerous visual and discursive levels for consumers and users. This fabric is so tightly woven, that for many computer users and consumers, for many students in our schools, it represents what Pierre Bourdieu (1977) would term "doxa"—ideological systems of belief so consistent with popular beliefs, and therefore so invisibly potent, that they preclude the consideration of other positions altogether. At the same time, all such fabrics have gaps, lacunae, that provide the space for resistance; and this one is no exception. Indeed, it is exactly because this ideological system is so densely and consistently coded that these images provide such rich sites of analysis and strategic information. In Andrea Dworkin's (1974) words, an analysis of these images can provide us the chance to unthink current discourses about technology and to transform the dialogues we hold with ourselves about gender and computers in new and productive, heterodoxic ways.

Like the Land of Equal Opportunity narrative, the Un-Gendered Utopia story can appeal at a romantic level to many Americans, while, at the same time, terrifying us on a practical level. Creating an electronic ungendered utopia means that we might have to learn how to understand people outside of the limited gender roles that we have constructed for them in this country, that we may have to abandon the ways in which we have traditionally differentiated between men's work and women's work in the marketplace, that we may have to provide men and women with equitable remuneration for comparable jobs, that we may have to learn to function within new global contexts that acknowledge women as Heads of State as well as heads of households.

In fact, we find ourselves, as a culture, ill equipped to cope with the changes that this Un-gendered Utopia narrative necessitates. We cannot, indeed, even imagine, collectively, ways of relating to gender outside the context of our familiar historical and cultural set of experiences. As a result, we revise the script of the narrative to fit more snugly within the historically determined contexts that are familiar and comfortable to us. In doing so, however, we also limit our cultural vision of gender within technological landscapes—constraining roles and expectations and possibilities to those we have already constructed as a culture, limiting the potential for change by subscribing to a conventional framework for our imagination.

In this revision, for example, while we maintain the vision of an electronic landscape that is open to all innovative and hardworking people, regardless of their gender, we also limit the actual participation of women and men within this landscape to the more traditionally determined gender roles we have already constructed within our culture. In the revised narrative—the Same Old Gendered Stuff narrative—the new electronic landscape retains a value on innovation, hard work, and the individual contributions of people of both genders, but only as they are practiced appropriately—within the traditionally gendered contexts we have historically and culturally ratified for women and men in our culture.

In such a landscape, women use technology within a clearly constrained set of appropriate settings: to enrich the lives of their family and to meet their responsibilities at home—as wife, as mother, as seductress, as lover; within a business setting, women use computers to support the work of their bosses—as secretaries, executive assistants, and loyal employees. There are, of course, exceptions to this story, as we shall see, but this narrative, as Anthony Giddens (1984, p. 22) would say, is "deeply sedimented" in habit, historically determined practices, in tradition, in our imaginations, and, thus, it exerts a strong influence on even these alternative stories. Men, in contrast, use computers at home to expand their personal horizons beyond current limits—for excitement, for challenge, to enhance their own private lives as explorers, pioneers, and builders. Within the business world, men use computers to support their historically constructed roles as bosses, leaders, decision makers.

This re-telling or re-vising of the Un-Gendered Utopia story happens very naturally. A good portion of our collective imagination is constructed by history and sedimented in past experience and habit. Indeed, many of the images appearing in the next series have a distinctive "retro" look that harkens back to the fifties—for many of the same reasons as those ads telling the Land of Equal Opportunity narrative discussed earlier in this chapter.

In that optimistic time, women were no longer encouraged to maintain a presence in the workplace. At the close of WWII, they were displaced from the workplace by men returning home from the European and Pacific theaters (May, 1988). Women, faced with this eventuality, became the savvy managers of the private sphere—especially when they were assisted by technological innovations. These women were urged to serve their families frozen foods and TV dinners, and to acquaint themselves with the scientific principles of eating so that they could be effective nutritional advisors to the family; they were expected as well to heed the advice of Dr. Spock, take advantage of the Salk vaccine for polio, and keep abreast of advances in antibiotics and modern theories of behaviorism to become effective health advisors; and they were expected to use the newly developed and improved technologies of electric vacuum cleaners, dishwashers, washing machines, televisions, cleaning products, and station wagons to be increasingly effective housekeepers.

The fact that this previous era of technological optimism provides the context for Americans' collective imagination about the current cultural project of technological expansion is both interesting and important. The results are evident in numerous advertisements about computers and women that use a retro look to link women's roles in the 50s to those in the 90s—in which each gender assumes their appropriate role in connection with technology. Men use technology to accomplish things; women benefit from technology to enhance the ease of their lives or to benefit their families.

And to understand how these traditionally gendered roles of the fifties are projected directly on the technological context of the nineties, readers can focus on the living room in figure 10, where images from the television-era of the fifties are overlaid by those of the computer-era of the nineties. Despite this fact, however, despite the fact that families in the nineties must maintain a dual presence in the work force, despite the fact that the rising incidence of divorce at the end of this century makes single-parent families the norm rather than the exception, despite the fact that the optimism of the fifties and sixties as articulated by John Kennedy has given way to the paranoia of the nineties as expressed by Pat Buchanan—the images of gender, the narratives they tell in connection with technology remain relatively stable, disturbing intact except for the imposition of a computer keyboard—held and operated by the father—and a computer menu—admired and enjoyed by the woman and children.

And so the revised narrative—the Same Old Gendered Stuff narrative—remains current. Its resonance is also demonstrated in figure 11, an advertisement for Reveal, and in figure 12, where we meet a thoroughly modern woman, Celeste Craig of Pontiac Illinois. Celeste, we learn, is finally achieving her dream of "going to college by staying home." The invention of a sophisticated distance-education computer network has allowed Celeste to undertake a course of study from her home in Pontiac Illinois while, at the same time, continuing to fulfill her role as a single mother supporting a family, parenting her children, and maintaining a household.

The gender roles of the fifties also translate into workplace roles for women in the nineties. In figure 13, for example, Irma—like a good, upscale, personal business assistant in the nineties—speaks "fluent Internet" much like her fifties counterpart would have spoken French. In figure 14, Fran, a fifties secretary with "just another pretty face" has been transmogrified, into a "multi-talented" nineties cyborg/robot assistant that "makes your website look good." And finally in figure 15, which suggests only a slightly revised version of the Same Old Gendered Stuff narrative, a nineties woman-as-boss, also portrayed in sepia tones against a fifties-style restaurant banquette, remains as decidedly cool, relaxed, and elegant despite the fact that she has also required the title of "hotshot," "collector," "workhorse," and "nomad."

But the roles of parent, housewife, and secretary/boss are not the only ones open to women in the new cyberlandscape represented by the Same Old Gendered Stuff narrative. Figure 16, for example, shows an ad for Nokia monitors, and in doing so, portrays a woman in the traditional role of "beauty." In the advertisement, a sophisticated woman draped with jewels, decked out in a chic black dress, washed in sepia tones and softened by a grainy texture gazes into a computer monitor. Although the text accompanying this image ostensibly outlines the capabilities and design of the monitor, the language itself leaves no doubt of the picture's focus or intent. As it notes, the "European passion for beauty" is quickly "winning the hearts and eyes of Americans too" by seductive means. The woman pictured in this advertisement, it should be noted, gazes longingly into a monitor, but lacks a keyboard with which she could act on the computer.

Finally, the 1990s retro series offers Americans the role of seductress—also a traditionally defined role for women, and one that has retained enormous strength even in cyberspace where change is expected to affect so many areas of our lives. Figure 17, representing a narcissistic seductress for Samsung, illustrates the potency of these traditionally constrained roles.

In these ads, we see reflected the roles that our culture can imagine women playing in relation to technology. And they are familiar roles—the seductress, the beauty, the mother—all relationships ratified by our historical experience, easily accessible to our collective imagination, and informed by traditional social values. These roles exist, and are reproduced, within a set of over determined social formations that makes radical change hard to imagine and even harder to enact—especially when technology is involved.

The revision of the Un-Gendered Utopia narrative into the Same Old Gendered Stuff narrative deals no less traditionally with men's roles, it should be noted. In connection with workplace technologies, men are allowed essentially the same tie-and-oxford-cloth look in the nineties (figure 18) as they were in the fifties (figure 19), although slight variations of this role—the impatient-and-rebellious young entrepreneur on the go sans tie (figure 20) or the successful architect-net-cruiser (figure 21) sporting a turtle neck—are also permitted. Out of the workplace (figures 22–24), men are shown to adopt the equally traditional and retrograde roles of bikers, nerds, and sex maniacs.

These ads, of course, are only one expression of our collective experience—and I would not want to claim that they tell a totalizing story. They do indicate, however, that it will be exceedingly difficult for Americans to imagine an electronic landscape in which individuals enjoy new kinds of opportunities to relate to each other and new kinds of opportunities to make positive changes in their lives. It takes energy and careful thinking to create a landscape in which women can participate in roles other than those of seductress, beauty, or mother; and in which men don't have to be bikers or abusers or rabid techno geeks or violent sex maniacs. It is far easier and more comfortable simply to re-construct for ourselves those traditional narratives that tell the same old gender stories over and over again, and that re-create the status quo ever more clearly in their re-telling.

Confronting Revised Narratives

The images in this chapter illustrate the richly textured narrative fabrics within which computer technology and other communication technologies are situated in the American cultural scene. Our work as teachers, the curricula we fashion, the corporate and public environments our students enter as professionals, the schools that make up the educational systems—these social formations are also shaped by the same sets of culturally determined values, the same complexities, the same ambiguities, the same contexts for our imaginations.

Such a realization can serve to remind teachers that technology does not necessarily bring with it social progress, and that educators had better make sure that students recognize and understand this fact if we want them to be able to make contributions of which they can be proud. Within the English studies programs that we design and administer, and participate in, we place everyone in jeopardy if we limit our understanding of technology and change to one dimension, if we teach students only one part of this complicated picture.

A good English studies curriculum will educate students robustly and intellectually rather than narrowly or vocationally. It will recognize the importance of educating students to be critically informed technology scholars rather than simply expert technology users. Graduates of English studies programs will face an increasingly complex set of issues in the workplace and in the public sphere, and our failure to provide the intellectual tools necessary to understand and cope with these issues at multiple levels signals our own inability to lead productively as professionals and as citizens.

Finally the images can serve to remind educators that even though productive changes are hard to make—with or without technology—our responsibility to work for change, especially as educators, remains undiminished in its urgency and importance. Like Paulo Friere, we need to be optimistic enough to believe that in teaching ourselves and others to recognize the inequities that challenge humanity in our world—the ethnocentrism, racism, classism, sexism—we have begun the difficult work of addressing these problems.

Questions for Discussion

1. Cynthia Selfe claims in her essay that we are guided in our response to new technologies by powerful "cultural narratives" that condition us to equate technological progress with social progress. However, she claims that there is an equally powerful cultural narrative that causes us to resist this technological change and even work to subvert its impact. Identify in the text some of the examples she uses to support this claim. Do further examples of this seeming contradiction occur to you?

2. Describe the structure of this essay. How does the author present the contradictions she finds in the differing versions of cultural narratives? Selfe believes that the images in advertising are particularly revealing of the forces behind societal beliefs. Why do these consumer-oriented messages carry particular weight in her arguments? Critique Selfe's argument. Can a case be made that this technology is truly revolutionizing the culture of the United States and our relationship with the rest of the world?

3. This essay was intended for an audience of English teachers. Why do you believe it might be important for teachers of English and composition to understand Selfe's ideas? What are some of the connections between technology and writing?

Explorations

1. Seek out advertisements for technology-based companies in magazines or other media, and analyze them from Cynthia Selfe's perspective. Do the ads you have discovered fit into any of the categories of narrative she has created? Do they tend to support her argument, or have you found evidence that the "revolution" is real?

2. Cynthia Selfe argues in this essay that technology hailed as revolutionary is simply putting a new face on the cultural biases that have plagued our society for decades. Robert J. Samuelson, in the essay "Technology in Reverse" included in this book, argues that in many cases technical progress itself is not really progress, but rather a complication of everyday activities that could be accomplished with ease in a low-tech manner. In some cases he even believes that advances in technology are making information accessible only to a privileged elite. Do you find other connections between these phenoma described in these two essays?

3. Talk to someone who became an adult before the advent of the technology addressed in Selfe's essay. Does that person's experience tend to back up Selfe's claims that nothing has changed in society at the fundamental level?

Formal Writing Assignments

1. Choose as a text for analysis one of the recent advertisements that you discovered in the Exploration above. In an essay, summarize and describe the content of the ad, evaluate its effectiveness in selling the product, and analyze the rhetoric of the ad from a cultural perspective. What is the "cultural narrative" behind the message of the ad?

2. In this essay, use your own experience as a basis for exploring the gender gap in computer technology. Selfe writes that "computer games are still designed for boys; computer commercials are still aimed mainly at males; computing environments are still constructed by and for males." Why are these observations important, and what impact do they have for you or for others you know?

Electronic Intimacies

Peter Steinhart

Peter Steinhart is a writer and editor for *Audubon* magazine, the publication of the National Audubon Society, an organization dedicated to wilderness conservation and endangered species protection. He has written several books, including *The Company of Wolves* in 1995. The essay that follows was originally published in *Audubon*.

Writing Before Reading

1. Create a list of differences between the experience of seeing wildlife on television and the experience of seeing wildlife in a natural setting.

2. Recall a memorable encounter with wildlife and write a paragraph describing the moment. This encounter may have taken place in or near your home or in a natural setting such as a park or wilderness area.

3. Record your view of the nature of the relationship between humans and wild animals. Are animals in nature to be feared? controlled? Has your opinion been influenced by images of wildlife you have seen on television?

Electronic Intimacies

In Yellowstone National Park a man trotted up to a lone buffalo. The buffalo didn't seem to be doing anything, so the man sought to improve its day by posing it for a picture. The buffalo became annoyed and bluff-charged. Undaunted, the man approached to within a few feet. The buffalo tossed him in the air and gored him.

A dozen visitors are injured by buffalo and a few more by bears or elk or moose every year in Yellowstone. Most of them are trying to snuggle up for a photograph. These encounters suggest something about the way we view wild animals today: We expect them to be available, accessible, and capable of intimacies.

Little in our actual experience of wildlife supports that expectation. In real life, our view of most creatures is abrupt and flickering, shadowed and blurred. Much of the content of our encounter comes from imagination or convention. And, since most of the park adventurers who end up in bandages are city slickers, it seems quite likely that they have learned their conventions by viewing wildlife on television.

Television has become our chief means of seeing wild creatures. Our living rooms are livelier than any national park. Any day you can switch on *Nature* or the *National Geographic Specials* and watch monkeys cavorting in trees or lions slinking through the grass. Britain's Survival Anglia keeps twenty-two crews in the field around the world. One-third of the programming on The Discovery Channel is wildlife. It's the biggest single subject for nonfiction video.

Wildlife film has a relatively short history. In the first decade of this century, Cherry Kearton filmed birds in nests and showed the footage with lectures. Lenses and films were not fast enough to allow telephotos or shots in dim light, so the filmmakers were happy simply to get a shot of, say, a cheetah sauntering along the veldt several hundred yards away. Until the 1950s most wildlife film consisted of simple identification shots—a gazelle grazing in the distance, a zebra running the other way. Most were shown in lecture halls rather than movie theaters. "When color film came out," recalls Karl Maslowski, a filmmaker who for forty years toured on National Audubon's lecture circuit, "if you had a red bird, a yellow bird, and a sunset, people stood up and cheered."

In the 1950s Walt Disney changed the field forever. He sought to bring nature to the movie screen and hired cameramen with studio-quality equipment to film close-ups, sustained action, and whole sequences of behavior from several camera angles. Disney brought the animals closer, and his films were immensely popular. But they changed the nature of the animals. Movies dramatize. In a darkened theater, character is everything. In the Disney version, and virtually all the theater films that followed, wildlife was presented as distorted humanity, as bumbling bears, square-dancing tarantulas, adolescent beavers running away from home, or the leering monsters of *Jaws* and *Grizzly*.

The big screen has seldom shown animals with what we might consider scientific integrity. Hollywood is a dream factory and it values emotional intensity over factual accuracy. Modern wildlife filmmakers are quite critical of the Hollywood version. But Disney's popularization combined with increasingly faster films and lenses, lighter equipment, and cheap travel to remote areas to allow other filmmakers to go out into the wild for months on end and compile intimate biographies. Bill Burrud began filming wildlife in 1959, and Mutual of Omaha sent out crews in 1962. And they sold their films to television.

In the 1960s commercial television hadn't yet sought to displace Hollywood as our dream merchant. It still focused much on fact and event. So television's wildlife descended from the traveling wildlife lecture and the science films produced by the BBC's natural-history unit, whose programs explained how birds navigate or fish live in water. American television borrowed from the movies by weaving humans into the story, for example having Marlin Perkins help a scientist anesthetize a rhino. And there was much emphasis on action, on hunting and being hunted. The British tradition was much enriched when, in the 1960s, Survival Anglia sent crews to live in the field for two or three *years* at a time, to film great cradle-to-grave epics of wildebeest and caribou and elephant. That ushered in a golden age of wildlife film. Today we enjoy hour-long portraits, rich with insight and intimacy. The appetite for such films is enormous.

Despite the popularity of wildlife films, they have a way of seeming repetitious. In part, the repetition is real: Much of the stock footage produced by Bill Burrud in the 1960s is still being screened today. Old footage gets dated as better equipment and more skillful photographers raise the level of clarity and intimacy. And new films often recall what we have seen in the old ones. Christopher N. Palmer, executive producer of the *Audubon Television Specials,* cautions, "It takes an enormous amount of time and creativity to make them look fresh."

Cameramen are driven to find new species and places to film, and ways to get closer to the animals. Heinz Sielman cut away the side of a tree trunk and installed a window and a blind to film nesting woodpeckers. Dieter Plage disguised a camera as a pelican and swam underwater to film waterfowl. The Oxford Scientific Films unit built a forty-foot-long indoor trout stream, with pumps to create currents and all the aquatic organisms needed to film a life history of trout.

Novelty doesn't come easy. Since the 1960s it has grown harder to make films overseas, because travel is now more expensive and many of the countries are politically unstable or simply hostile. There are fewer places in which animals survive, and so there is competition for the unobstructed view. Des and Jen Bartlett spent four years filming in Namibia's Etosha National Park in part because the wildlife in the more accessible parks of Kenya is always ringed with tour buses.

Filming is also more expensive. A complete portrait may take years in the field, and that time costs money. Belinda Wright and Stanley Breeden spent two years and $500,000 filming *Land of the Tiger.* That's more than television will pay for a wildlife film. To cut costs, some filmmakers use trained animals and staged shots.

Still, there is a sameness. A local newspaper columnist complains that every time he turns on PBS, he expects to see a show about insects.

The problem is not that we're seeing the same creatures over and over again, but that there is an orthodoxy to wildlife films. The organizing idea is almost invariably that a creature struggles to survive the hardships of nature and civilization. Says Bayer, "The typical life story of, say, the mountain lion is a story about survival, and it becomes repetitious."

The new orthodoxy is clearly not in interest in science, for the films show a marked preference for mammals and birds, for creatures that are warm-blooded and seemingly approachable, rather than for spiders, jellyfish, or lizards. Nor is the main interest conservation. The films seldom do a good job of explaining who is responsible for a species decline or what a viewer can do about it. It's not because the filmmaker doesn't care. It's because he wants the film to last long enough to pay back its costs in video rentals and television syndication, so he does not delve into legal or regulatory issues which may be out of date by the time the film is edited and released, let alone rerun in syndication.

The focus of survival probably has more to do with television's growing envy of Hollywood than with wildlife's problems. Thinking about survival allows us to personify animals without seeming as anthropomorphic as Disney. And even the most exacting filmmakers have doubts about science and survival as themes. Says James Murray, executive producer of *The Nature of Things*: "you're peering inside and looking at everything in detail, and you're missing the emotional part of it." Photographer and filmmaker Jeff Foott says, "A lot of what's happening in wildlife films is terribly cerebral. I'd love to see films that let people just feel rather than learn."

Our real interest is empathy. Humans are designed to mythologize. Give us acres of science and we'll still plant gardens of rhyme. We'll look for spirit anywhere it offers to blossom, and it seems to beckon from the eye shine of the tiger and the flight of the sparrow. We want honesty, but we don't want it to get in the way of vision. That's why, I suspect, the spine of many wildlife films is evolution. It is so abstract that, after a few repetitions, we can conveniently ignore it.

If we ignore the message and look for myths, the films may mislead us. For wildlife films suffer from the chief curse of television: They make experience seem accessible and well-organized when it fact it is not. Nature doesn't reveal itself in thirty minutes or in an hour. To see wild creatures one needs to train one's senses, to exercise imagination and temper it with effort and experience.

To film a red fox and her cubs, Karl Maslowski built a blind forty feet above a den in a black locust tree and then spent four or five days in the blind every spring for twelve years, waiting for a shot of the vixen and her pups. Only twice in those years did he get a shot. Filmmaker Wolfgang Bayer waited three days in a mine shaft, motionless behind a blind, for wild horses to come in to drink, and once waited three weeks for a coyote to come out of its den.

The patience and resourcefulness of the wildlife filmmaker are enormous. But they never appear on the screen. In the comfort of our living rooms we escape the cold feet, the mosquito bites, the uncertain glimpses that are part of our real relationship with the wild. And we miss the surges of impulse and imagination that flow out of these gaps in our vision. Still photographs elicit those surges because they usually leave the context of the shot unexplained and let the viewer imagine what has preceded and what follows the shot. But film organizes the experience, sets a context, a place, a meaning. There is at times too little for a viewer to do.

By taking the waiting out of watching, wildlife films also make wild creatures appear less modest and retiring than they really are. Animals become almost promiscuously available on television. We get lingering close-ups. The animals are fully revealed. There are no empty landscapes. That, I suspect is why visitors to our national parks expect wildlife to be accessible. Says National Park Service naturalist Glen Kaye, "Whatever the hour of the day, the question is, 'Which meadow do I go to see the deer or the elk or the bear *right now?'* There's no sense that the animals may not be available."

Films also make the animals seem confiding. Television's close-ups leap across centuries of evolution by taking us within the fight and flight distances that normally separate individuals. That probably explains why we assume a familiarity with movie stars and politicians that we wouldn't attempt with neighbors. We have been electronically intimate, close enough to hear them breathe and see their eyelids flutter. Among real people such things imply familiarity. So we'll barge in on them and demand autographs or recitations, though we are perfect strangers.

The same thing is true for wildlife. Filmmakers have taken us into the range of eye shine and body heat and personified the creature by telling us of its struggle. We're apt to feel the same cheap familiarity we feel with Tom Selleck or Oprah Winfrey. Says Mary Meagher, a Yellowstone biologist, "I don't think people have too much sense of flight distance in buffalo or bear, although humans have flight distances themselves. Even when I see that something dangerous is about to happen, if I explain to people that the animal is dangerous, I usual get the finger for my trouble. People can have all the warnings and disregard them."

Modern life seems tainted more and more with the expectation of gratification without effort, revelation without knowledge, feeling without understanding. Television is one of the culprits. Too often it absolves us of the responsibility to look to ourselves and sort the real from the perceived. Look at the animals in the wild and you get an uncertain image, full of blur and shadow, which requires large measures of imagination and judgment. Look at them on film and you lose the responsibility to organize what you see.

Television brings wildlife into our hearts and minds. It makes us aware of humanity's aggrandizement of the Earth. But celluloid is not a substitute for experience. With or without television, we still make much use of animals in our minds. We let them symbolize virtues and vices, carry thoughts and feelings. If wildlife films ever become our only access to wild animals, we may be the less intelligent, perceptive, and imaginative for it.

Questions for Discussion

1. To anthropomorphize is to alter our perception of an object or creature—such as a wild animal—by assigning it human characteristics. For example, a film maker might imply that a doe who has lost her fawn to predation experiences grieving emotions like those experienced by a human parent faced with the loss of a child. Why are film makers and audiences tempted to anthropomorphize? In what way is this phenomenon a potential disservice to wildlife? Do animals benefit or suffer when we describe their lives in human terms?

2. The intended audience for this essay is likely to consist largely of already dedicated environmentalists and conservationists. Why is it important for them to hear this message? What is Steinhart's purpose?

3. What do you believe the author means when he writes "we'll look for spirit anywhere it offers to blossom, and it seems to beckon from the eyeshine of a tiger and the flight of the sparrow"? What do you believe he intends to say about the consequences of this attitude toward the natural world?

Explorations

1. Neil Postman and Steve Powers, in "The Bias of Pictures, the Bias of Language," argue that "whatever anyone says something is, it isn't." In addition, they argue that this truth extends to video images as well. Can their claim be applied to wildlife films? How? In making choices about how to present images, do wildlife film makers show us what "isn't"?

2. Your local video store or public library is likely to have a selection of wildlife films. Choose one of

these films and analyze it from a perspective you have developed as a result of reading this essay. For example, consider how the experience of the wildlife photographer in filming the animals differs from your experience of viewing, and describe those differences.

3. Consider other examples of situations in which television or film "make experience seem accessible and well-organized when in fact it is not," as Steinhart writes. How about films on war? films depicting other work situations you are familiar with? films depicting human emotional responses?

Formal Writing Assignments

1. In an essay, take a stand on the following statement: Though it is important for animal species to be preserved in zoos and parks, human needs should take priority in land that could be used for human habitation or exploited for its commercial value. Consider whether or not your own viewing of wildlife films has influenced you determining your position on this issue.

2. Write an essay in the form of an extended review of wildlife video of your choice. Summarize, evaluate, and analyze the video from perspectives that include production values, your sense of the scientific accuracy of the film, and whether or not the film's stated or implied agenda has been achieved.

Who Am We?

Sherry Turkle

Sherry Turkle is highly regarded for her ground-breaking studies of how people are changed by their interaction with computers. She was educated at Radcliffe, Harvard, and the University of Chicago and is a licensed clinical psychologist. Currently, she is a professor at the Massachusetts Institute of Technology.

Turkle has studied and written widely about the relationships between people and computers, and as a result is regularly featured in magazine articles and television programs meant for general audiences. This essay is from her book Life on the Screen: Identity in the Age of the Internet. The chapter focuses on how our understanding of who we are is affected by the creation of new identities in interactive digital environments, or more accurately, "multi-user dungeons" or MUDs.

Writing Before Reading

1. Have you ever represented yourself to others on the internet or in a computer chat room as someone other than who you are in RL (real life)? Describe this experience. Did you feel as if you were being dishonest?

2. Do you believe that computer technology has the power to change the identity of those who use it? It is widely held that our interaction with other people—family members, friends, enemies, loved ones, co-workers—leaves permanent changes in us. Do you believe that our interaction with computers leaves similar traces? List some examples of this phenomenon.

3. In your real life, your words and actions have consequences. Is this also true in the virtual world? Does the anonymity provided by the Internet shield you from the consequences of your "virtual" choices?

Who Am We?

In the early 1970s, the face-to-face role-playing game *Dungeons and Dragons* swept the game culture. The term "dungeon" persisted in the high-tech culture to connote a virtual place. So when virtual spaces were created that many computer users could share and collaborate within, they were deemed Multi-User Dungeons or MUDs, a new kind of social virtual reality. (Some games use software that make them technically MUSHes or MOOs, but the term MUD has come to refer to all of the multiuser environments.)

MUDs are a new kind of virtual parlor game and a new form of community. In addition, text-based MUDs are a new form of collaboratively written literature. MUD players are MUD authors, the creators as well as consumers of media content. In this, participating in a MUD has much in common with scriptwriting, performance art, street theater, improvisational theater, or even commedia dell'arte. But MUDs are something else as well.

As players participate, they become authors not only of text but of themselves, constructing new selves through social interaction. Since one participates in MUDS by sending text to a computer that houses the MUD's program and database, MUD selves are constituted in interaction with the machine.

Take it away and the MUD selves cease to exist: "Part of me, a very important part of me, only exists inside PernMUD," says one player. Several players joke that they are like "the electrodes in the computer," trying to express the degree to which they feel part of its space.

All MUDS are organized around the metaphor of physical space. When you first enter a MUD, you may find yourself in a medieval church from which you can step out into the town square, or you may find yourself in the coat closet of a large, rambling house. For example, when you first log on to LambdaMoo, one of the most popular MUDs on the Internet, you see the following description:

> The Coat Closet. The Closet is a dark, cramped space. It appears to be very crowded in here; you keep bumping into what feels like coats, boots, and other people (apparently sleeping). One useful thing that you've discovered in your bumbling about is a metal doorknob set at waist level into what might be a door. There's a new edition of the newspaper. Type "news" to see it.

In the MUDS, virtual characters converse with each other, exchange gestures, express emotions, win and lose virtual money, and rise and fall in social status. A virtual character can also die. Some die of "natural" causes (a player decides to close them down), or they can have their virtual lives snuffed out. This is all achieved through writing, and this in a culture that had apparently fallen asleep in the audiovisual arms of television. Yet this new writing is a kind of hybrid: speech momentarily frozen into artifact, but curiously ephemeral artifact. In this new writing, unless it is printed out on paper, a screenful of flickers soon replaces the previous screen.

The anonymity of MUDs gives people the chance to express multiple and often unexplored aspects of the self, to play with their identity and to try out new ones. MUDs make possible the creation of an identity so fluid and multiple that it strains the limits of the notion. Identity, after all, refers to the sameness between two qualities, in this case between a person and his or her persona. But in MUDs, one can be many.

A 21-year-old college senior defends his violent characters as "something in me; but quite frankly I'd rather rape on MUDs where no harm is done." A 26-year-old clerical worker says, "I'm not one thing, I'm many things. Each part gets to be more fully expressed in MUDS than in the real world. So even though I play more than one self on MUDs, I feel more like 'myself' when I'm MUDding." In real life, this woman sees her world as too narrow to allow her to manifest certain aspects of the person she feels herself to be. Creating screen personae is thus an opportunity for self-expression, leading to her feeling more like her true self when decked out in all array of virtual masks.

MUDs imply difference, multiplicity, heterogeneity, and fragmentation. Such all experience of identity contradicts the Latin root of the word, *idem*, meaning "the same." But this contradiction increasingly defines the conditions of our lives beyond the virtual world. MUDs thus become objects-to-think-with for thinking about postmodern selves. Indeed, the unfolding of all MUD action takes place in a resolutely postmodern context. There are parallel narratives in the different rooms of a MUD. The cultures of Tolkien, Gibson, and Madonna coexist and interact. Since MUDs are authored by their players, thousands of people in all, often hundreds at a time, are all logged on from different places; the solitary author is displaced and distributed. Traditional ideas about identity have been tied to a notion of authenticity that such virtual experiences actively subvert. When each player can create many characters in many games, the self is not only decentered but multiplied without limit.

As a new social, experience, MUDs pose many psychological questions: If a persona in a role-playing game drops defenses that the player in real life has been unable to abandon, what effect does this have? What if a persona enjoys success in some area (say, flirting) that the player has not been able to achieve? Slippages often occur in places where persona and self merge, where the multiple personae join to comprise what the individual thinks of as his or her authentic self.

* * *

Doug is a Midwestern college junior. He plays four characters distributed across three different MUDs. One is a seductive woman. One is a macho, cowboy type whose self-description stresses that he is a "Marlboros rolled in the T-shirt sleeve kind of guy." The third is a rabbit of unspecified gender who wanders its MUD introducing people to each other, a character he calls Carrot. Doug says, "Carrot is so low key that people let it be around while they are having private conversations. So I think of Carrot as my passive, voyeuristic character." Doug's fourth character is one that he plays only on a MUD in which the characters are furry animals. "I'd rather not even talk about that character because my anonymity there is very important to me, Doug says. "Let's just say that on FurryMUDs I feel like a sexual tourist." Doug talks about playing his characters in windows and says that using windows has made it possible for him to "turn pieces of my mind on and off.

"I split my mind . . . I can see myself as being two or three or more. And I just turn on one part of my mind and then another when I go from window to window. I'm in some kind of argument in one window and trying to come on to a girl in a MUD in another, and another window might be running a spreadsheet program or some other technical thing for school and then I'll get a real-time message that flashes on the screen as soon as it is sent from another system user, and I guess that's RL. RL is just one more window, and it's not usually my best one."

Play has always been an important aspect of our individual efforts to build identity. The psycho-analyst Erik Erikson called play a "toy situation" that allows us to "reveal and commit" ourselves "in its unreality." While MUDS are not the only "places" on the Internet in which to play with identity, they provide an unparalleled opportunity for such play. On a MUD one actually gets to build character and environment and then to live within the toy situation. A MUD can become a context for discovering who one is and wishes to be. In this way, the games are laboratories for the construction of identity.

Stewart, a 23-year-old physics graduate student, uses MUDs to have experiences he can't imagine for himself in RL. His intense online involvements engaged key issues in his life but ultimately failed to help him reach successful resolutions.

Stewart's real life revolves around laboratory work and his plans for a future in science. His only friend is his roommate, another physics student whom he describes as even more reclusive than himself. For Stewart, this circumscribed, almost monastic student life does not represent a radical departure from what has gone before. He has had heart trouble since he was a child; one small rebellion, a ski trip when he was a college freshman, put him in the hospital for a week. He has lived life within a small compass.

Stewart is logged on to one MUD or another for at least 40 hours a week. It seems misleading to call what he does there playing. He spends his time constructing a life that is more expansive than the one he lives in physical reality. Stewart, who has traveled very little and has never been to Europe, explains with delight that his favorite MUD, although played in English, is physically located on a computer in Germany and has many European players.

On the German MUD, Stewart shaped a character named Achilles, but he asks his MUD friends to call him Stewart as much as possible. He wants to feel that his real self exists somewhere between Stewart and Achilles. He wants to feel that his MUD life is part of his real life. Stewart insists that he does not role play, but that MUDs simply allow him to be a better version of himself.

On the MUD, Stewart creates a living environment suitable for his ideal self. His university dormitory is modest, but the room he has built for Achilles on the MUD is elegant and heavily influenced by Ralph Lauren advertising. He has named it "the home beneath the silver moon." There are books, a roaring fire, cognac, a cherry mantel covered with pictures of Achilles's friends from around the world.

"You look up . . . and through the immense skylight breathtaking view of the night sky. The moon is always full over Achilles's home, and its light fills the room with a warm glow."

Beyond expanding his social world, MUDs have brought Stewart the only romance and intimacy he has ever known. At a social event in virtual space, a "wedding" of two regular players on a German-based MUD I call Gargoyle, Achilles met Winterlight, a character played by one of the three female players on that MUD. Stewart, who has known little success in dating and romantic relationships, was able to charm this desirable player.

On their first virtual date, Achilles took Winterlight to an Italian restaurant close to Stewart's dorm. He had often fantasized being there with a woman. Stewart used a combination of MUD commands to simulate a romantic evening—picking Winterlight up at the airport in a limousine, driving her to a hotel room so that she could shower, and then taking her to the restaurant and ordering veal for her.

This dinner date led to others during which Achilles was tender and romantic, chivalrous and poetic. The intimacy Achilles experienced during his courtship of Winterlight is unknown to Stewart in other contexts. "She's a very, she's a good friend. I found out a lot of things, from things about physiology to the color of nail polish she wears." Finally, Achilles asked for Winterlight's hand. When she accepted, they had a formal engagement ceremony on the MUD.

At the engagement, Winterlight gave Achilles a rose she had worn in her hair; Achilles gave her 1,000 paper stars.

Although Stewart participated in this ceremony alone in his room with his computer and modem, a group of European players actually traveled to Germany, site of Gargoyle's host computer, and got together for food and champagne. Many of the 25 guests at the German celebration brought gifts and dressed specially for the occasion. Stewart felt as though he were throwing a party. This was the first time that he had ever entertained, and he was proud of his success. In real life, Stewart felt constrained by his health problems, his shyness and social isolation, and his narrow economic straits. In the Gargoyle MUD, he bypassed these obstacles, at least temporarily.

The psychological effects of life on the screen can be complicated: a safe place is not all that is needed for personal change. Stewart came to MUDding with serious problems, and for Stewart, playing on MUDs led to a net drop in self-esteem. MUDs did help Stewart talk about his troubles while they were still emotionally relevant, nevertheless, he is emphatic that MUDding has ultimately made him feel worse about himself. MUDding did not alter Stewart's sense of himself as withdrawn, unappealing, and flawed.

While Stewart has tried hard to make his MUD self, the "better" Achilles self, part of his real life, he says he has failed. He says, "I'm not social. I don't like parties. I can't talk to people about my problems." The integration of the social Achilles, who can talk about his troubles, and the asocial Stewart, who can only cope by putting them out of mind, has not occurred. From Stewart's point of view, MUDs have stripped away some of his defenses but have given him nothing in return. In fact, MUDs make Stewart feel vulnerable in a new way. Although he hoped that MUDs would cure him, it is MUDs that now make him feel sick. He feels addicted to MUDs: "When you feel you're stagnating and you feel there's nothing going on your life and you're stuck in a rut, it's very easy to be on there for very large amounts of time."

Stewart cannot learn from his character Achilles's experience and social success because they are too different from the thing of which he believes himself capable. Despite his efforts to turn Achilles into Stewart, Stewart has split off his strengths and sees them as possible only for Achilles in the MUD. It is only Achilles who can create the magic and win the girl. In making this split between himself and the achievements of his screen persona. Stewart does not give himself credit for the positive steps he has taken in real life. Like an unsuccessful psychotherapy, MUDding has not helped Stewart bring these good experiences inside himself or integrate them into his self-image.

Relationships during adolescence are usually bounded by a mutual understanding that they involve limited commitment. Virtual space is well suited to such relationships, its natural limitations keep things within bounds. As in Thomas Mann's *The Magic Mountain,* which takes place in the isolation of a sanatorium, relationships become intense very quickly because the participants feel isolated in a remote and unfamiliar world with its own rules. MUDs, like other electronic meeting places, can breed a kind of easy intimacy. In a first phase, MUD players feel the excitement of a rapidly deepening relationship and the sense that time is speeding up. "The MUD quickens things. It quickens things so much," says one player. "You know, you don't think about it when you're doing it, but you meet someone on the MUD, and within a week you feel like you've been friends forever."

In a second phase, players commonly try to take things from the virtual to the real and are usually disappointed.

Gender-swapping on MUDs is not a small part of the game action. By some estimates, Habitat, a Japanese MUD, has 1.5 million users. Habitat is a MUD operated for profit. Among the registered members of Habitat, there is a ratio of four real-life men to each real-life woman. But inside the MUD the ratio is only three characters to one female character. In other words, a significant number of players, many tens of thousands of them are virtually cross-dressing.

What is virtual gender-swapping all about? Some of those who do it claim that it is not particularly significant. "When I play a woman I don't really take it too seriously," said 20-year-old Andrei. "I do it to improve the ratio of women to men. It's just a game." On one level, virtual gender-swapping is easier than doing it in real life. For a man to present himself as female in a chat room, on an IRC channel, or in a MUD, only requires writing a description. For a man to play a woman on the streets of an American city, he would have to shave various parts of his body; wear makeup, perhaps a wig, a dress, and high heels; perhaps change his voice, walk and mannerisms. He would have some anxiety about passing, and there might be even more anxiety about not passing, which would pose a risk of violence and possibly arrest. So more men are willing to give virtual cross-dressing a try. But once online as female, they soon find maintaining this fiction is difficult. To pass as a woman for any length of time requires understanding how gender inflects speech, manner, the interpretation of experience. Women attempting to pass as men face the same type of challenge.

Virtual cross-dressing is not as simple as Andrei suggests. Not only can it be technically challenging, it can be psychologically complicated. Taking a virtual role may involve you in ongoing relationships. You may discover things about yourself that you never knew before.

Case, a 34-year-old industrial designer who is happily married to a co-worker, is currently MUDding as a female character. In response to my question, "Has MUDding ever caused you any emotional pain?' he says, "Yes, but also the kind of learning that comes from hard times.

"I'm having pain in my playing now. Mairead, the woman I'm playing in MedievalMUSH, is having an interesting relationship with a fellow. Mairead is a lawyer, and the high cost of law school has to be paid for by a corporation or a noble house. She fell in love with a nobleman who paid for her law school. [Case slips into referring to Mairead in the first person.] Now he wants to marry me although I'm a commoner. I finally say yes. I try to talk to him about the fact that I'm essentially his property, I'm a commoner . . . I've grown up with it, that's the way life is. He wants to deny the situation. He says, 'Oh no,no,no . . . We'll pick you up, set you on your feet, the whole world is open to you.' But every time I behave like I'm going to be a countess some day . . . as in, 'And I never liked this wallpaper anyway,' I get pushed down. The relationship is pull up, push down. It's an incredibly psychologically damaging thing to do to a person. And the very thing that he liked about her, that she was independent, strong, said what was on her mind, it is all being bled out of her."

Case looks at me with a wry smile and sighs, "A woman's life." He continues: "I see her [Mairead] heading for a major psychological problem. What we have is a dysfunctional relationship. But even though it's very painful and stressful, it's very interesting to watch myself cope with this problem. How am I going to dig my persona's self out of this mess? Because I don't want to go on like this. I want to get out of it. . . . You can see that playing this woman lets me see what I have in my psychological repertoire, what is hard and what is easy for me. And I can also see how some of the things that work when you're a man just backfire when you're a woman."

Case further illustrates the complexity of gender-swapping as a vehicle for self-reflection. Case describes his RL persona as a nice guy, a "Jimmy Stewart type like my father." He says that in general he likes his father and he likes himself, but he feels he pays a price for his low-key ways. In particular, he feels at a loss when it comes to confrontation, both at home and in business dealings. Case likes MUD-ding as a female because it makes it easier for him to be aggressive and confrontational. Case plays several online "Katharine Hepburn types," strong, dynamic, "out there" women who remind him of his mother, who says exactly what's on her mind and is a take-no-prisoners sort.

For Case, if you are assertive as a man, it is coded as "being a bastard." If you are assertive as a woman, it is coded as "modern and together."

Some women who play male characters desire invisibility or permission to be more outspoken or aggressive. "I was born in the South and taught that girls didn't speak up to disagree with men," says Zoe, a 34 year-old woman who plays male and female characters on four MUDs.

"We would sit at dinner and my father would talk and my mother would agree. I thought my father was a god. Once or twice I did disagree with him. I remember one time in particular when I was 10, and he looked at me and said, "Well, well, well, if this little flower grows too many more thorns, she will never catch a man."

Zoe credits MUDs with enabling her to reach a state of mind where she is better able to speak up for herself in her marriage ("to say what's on my mind before things get all blown out of proportion") and to handle her job as the financial officer for a small biotechnology firm.

"I played a MUD man for two years. First I did it because I wanted the feeling of an equal playing field in terms of authority, and the only way I could think of to get it was to play a man. But after a while, I got very absorbed by MUDding. I became a wizard on a pretty simple MUD. I called myself Ulysses and got involved in the system and realized that as a man I could be firm and people would think I was a great wizard. As a woman, drawing the line and standing firm has always made me feel like a bitch and, actually, I feel that people saw me as one, too. As a man I was liberated from all that. I learned from my mistakes. I got better at being firm but not rigid. I practiced, safe from criticism."

Zoe's perceptions of her gender trouble are almost the opposite of Case's. While Case sees aggressiveness as acceptable only for woman. Zoe sees it as acceptable only for men. These stories share a notion that a virtual gender swap gave people greater emotional range in the real. Zoe says: "I got really good at playing a man, so good that whoever was on the system would accept me as a man and talk to me as a man. So, other guys talked to Ulysses guy to guy. It was validating. All those years I was paranoid about how men talked about women. Or I thought I was paranoid. Then I got the chance to be a guy and saw that I wasn't paranoid at all."

Irony is about contradictions that do not resolve into larger wholes . . . about the tension of holding incompatible things together because both or all are necessary and true.

—Donna Haraway

As we stand on the boundary between the real and the virtual, our experience recalls what the anthropologist Victor Turner termed a liminal moment, a moment of passage when new cultural symbols and meanings can emerge. Liminal moments are times of tension, extreme reactions, great opportunity. When Turner talked about liminality, he understood it as a transitional state, but living with flux may no longer be temporary. Technology is bringing postmodernism down to earth itself; the story of technology refuses modernist resolutions and requires an openness to multiple viewpoints.

Multiple viewpoints call forth a new moral discourse. The culture of simulation may help us achieve a vision of multiple but integrated identity whose flexibility, resilience, and capacity for joy comes from having access to our many selves. But if we have lost reality in the process, we shall have struck a poor bargain. In Wim Wenders's film *Until the End of the World,* a scientist develops a device that translates the electrochemical activity of the brain into digital images. He gives this technology to his family and closest friends, who are now able to hold small battery–driven monitors and watch their dreams. At first, they are charmed. The see their treasured fantasies, their secret selves. The see the images they would otherwise forget, the scenes they otherwise would repress. As with the personae one can play in a MUD, watching dreams on a screen opens up new aspects of the self.

However, the story turns dark. The images seduce. They are richer and more compelling than the real life around them. Wenders's characters fall in love with their dreams, become addicted to them. People wander about with blankets over their heads the better to see the monitors from which they cannot bear to be parted. They are imprisoned by the screens, imprisoned by the keys to their past that the screens seem to hold.

We, too, are vulnerable to using our screen in these ways. People get lost in virtual worlds. Some are tempted to think of life in cyberspace as insignificant, as escape or meaningless diversion. It is not. Our experiences there are serious play. We belittle them at our own risk. We must understand the dynamics of virtual experience both to foresee who might be in danger and to put these experiences to best use. Without a deep understanding of the many selves that we express in the virtual, we cannot use our experiences there to enrich the real. If we cultivate our awareness of what stands behind our screen personae, we are more likely to succeed in using virtual experience for personal transformation.

The imperative to self-knowledge has always been at the heart of philosophical inquiry. In the 20th century, it found expression in the psychoanalytic culture as well. One might say that it constitutes the ethic of psychoanalysis. From the perspective of this ethic, we work to know ourselves in order to improve not only our own lives, but those of our families and society. Psychoanalysis is a survivor discourse. Born of a modernist world view, it has evolved into forms relevant to postmodern times. With mechanistic roots in the culture of calculation, psychoanalytic ideas become newly relevant in the culture of simulation. Some believe that we are at the end of the Freudian century. But the reality is more complex. Our need for a practical philosophy of self-knowledge has never been greater as we struggle to make meaning from our lives on the screen.

Questions for Discussion

1. Sherry Turkle writes that "without a deep understanding of the many selves that we express in the virtual, we cannot use our experiences there to enrich the real." What do you believe she means by this statement? If you identify this statement as her thesis for the essay, discuss the means she has employed in support of her argument.

2. The MUDding activity that Turkle describes in the essay involves the literal creation of alternative personalities and identities. Though this type of role-playing certainly has an impact on the lives of those who participate, relatively few computer users engage in these games. Can you create an argument that the identities of all computer users are affected by their everyday interaction with "the screen"?

3. In follow-up to the previous question, in what ways is a society accustomed to email different from the pre-email world? How has email changed the manner in which we communicate with one another? the people with whom we communicate? ourselves as communicators?

Explorations

1. Though Sherry Turkle argues that our relationship with computers has profound meaning for individuals, Cynthia Selfe in "Lest We Think the Revolution is a Revolution" argues that in many ways the digital "revolution" has merely resulted in a new way of dressing up the same societal prejudices that have been with us for decades. Is it possible that Turkle is wrong, and that the escapism she describes in her essay does not represent a break with the past, but simply a new means of expression for that desire to escape "real life"?

2. Turkle draws comparisons to Thomas Mann's classic novel *The Magic Mountain,* claiming that the virtual community exhibits the social characteristics of a small, enclosed community such as a sanitarium. How does Turkle describe these social dynamics? Can you think of other examples, perhaps from your own experience, of communities that parallel MUDs?

3. If you found yourself in a situation where you were absolutely unknown and able to invent for yourself a new identity, would you? Why or why not? What would the advantages be? the disadvantages?

Formal Writing Assignments

1. In an essay take a position either in support or in disagreement with the following statement: Computers are a humanizing element in our society, allowing people to communicate with each other more frequently and directly. Our society has benefited from the free flow of ideas that computer technology has created.

2. Take an ethnographic approach to analyzing an online community that you are familiar with. In so doing, you might want to answer some of the following questions: Who makes up this community, and why have they chosen to be part of it? How has the community changed or evolved over its existence? Could this community exist outside of virtual space? Why or why not?

Radio Hoods

Patricia J. Williams

Patricia J. Williams is a writer and educator who is a professor of law at Columbia University in New York. She was born in Boston in 1951. The experience of growing up in that city during a time of great racial tension, as well as her experiences as a student at Wellesley College and the Harvard University Law School, has inspired her to write on many occasions about the relationship between white Americans and African Americans. The essay "Radio Hoods" is part of a book entitled *The Rooster's Egg: On the Persistence of Prejudice,* in which she examines events of the first half of the 1990s with implications for race relations. She explores the significance of occurrences such as the nomination hearings for Supreme Court Justice Clarence Thomas and, in this essay, the growing influence of politically conservative talk radio programs.

Writing Before Reading

1. Have you ever realized that you have resented assumptions that have been made about you because of your ethnic background, sex, or presumed membership in any particular group of people? Describe this moment of awareness and your reaction to it.

2. Though talk radio and call-in programs have been around for decades, there has been a resurgence in the popularity of this format in recent years. Why do you think talk radio has grown so much in the past decade? Provide at least three points of support for your claim.

3. The First Amendment to the U.S. Constitution guarantees freedom of speech to all Americans, with limited exceptions (such as the prohibition of shouting "Fire!" in a crowded theater). In what ways does this freedom strengthen the democratic system? Are there ways in which this freedom could actually threaten our democracy?

Radio Hoods

> It is a hallmark of Limbaugh's commentary to provide blue-collar translations of white-collar conservatism, and in doing so to inflect them with tones of anger and outrage that articulate the resentment of a newly disenfranchised social formation, one that had its wallets emptied by Reaganomics while Reaganism massaged its egos.
> —John Fiske, *Media Matters: Everyday Culture and Political Change*

Four years ago, I stood at my sink, washing the dishes and listening to the radio. Howard Stern was a popular deejay in New York City but I had never heard of him; he was not the national celebrity he has since become. I was listening to rock'n'roll so I could avoid thinking about the big news from the day before: George Bush had just nominated Clarence Thomas to replace Thurgood Marshall on the Supreme Court. I was squeezing a dot of Lemon Joy into each of the wineglasses when I realized that two smoothly radio-cultured voices, a man's and a woman's, had replaced the music.

"I think it's a stroke of genius on the president's part," said the female voice.

"Yeah," said the male voice. "Then those blacks, those African-Americans, those Negros—hey, 'Negro' is good enough for Thurgood Marshall—whatever they can't make up their minds they want to be called—I'm gonna call them Blafricans. Black Africans. Yeah I like it. Blafricans. Then they can get all upset because now the president appointed a *Blafrican!*"

"Yeah, well, that's the way those liberals think. It's just crazy."

"And then after they turn down his nomination the president can say he tried to please 'em, and then he can go ahead and appoint someone with some intelligence."

Back then, this conversation seemed so horrendously unusual, so singularly hateful, that I picked up a pencil and wrote it down. I was certain that a firestorm of protest was going to engulf the station and purge those foul radio mouths with the good clean soap of social outrage.

I am so naive. When I finally rolled my dial around to where everyone else had been tuned while I was busy watching Cosby reruns, it took me a while to understand that there's a firestorm all right, but not of protest. In the four years since Clarence Thomas has assumed his post on the Supreme Court, crude, in-your-face racism, sexism, anti-semitism, and homophobia have become commonplace, popularly expressed, and louder in volume than at any time since the beginning of the civil rights movement. Snide polemical bigotry is everywhere—among my friends, on the street, on television in toned-down versions. Unleashed as the new freedom of "what people are really thinking," it has reached its highest pitch in the wildly proliferating phenomenon of right-wing radio shows. Blaring the battle hymn of the First Amendment, these radio programs enshrine a crude demagoguery that makes me heartsick; I feel more and more surrounded by megawatted expressions of hate and discrimination—the coded epithets, the mocking angry glee, the endless tirades filled with nonspecific, nonempirically based slurs against "'these people" or "'those minorities" or "feminazis" or "liberals" or "scumbags" or "pansies" or "jerks" or "sleazeballs" or "loonies" or "animals" or "foreigners." American popular culture has suddenly been given a megadose of childish turnaround faced with a very adult kind of verbal brutality.

At the same time I am not so naive as to suppose that this is something new. In clear-headed moments I realize I am not listening to the radio anymore; I really am listening to a large segment of white America think aloud and ever louder-resurgent thoughts that have generations of historical precedent. It is as if the radio has split open like an egg, Morton Downey's clones and Joe McCarthy's ghost spilling out, broken yolks, a great collective of sometimes clever, sometimes small, but uniformly threatened brains—they have all come gushing out. Just as they were about to pass into oblivion, Jack Benny and his humble black sidekick, Rochester, get resurrected in the ungainly bodies of Howard Stern and his faithful black henchwoman, Robin Quivers. The culture of Amos 'n' Andy has been revived and reassembled in Bob Grant's radio minstrelsy, radio newcomer Darryl Gates's sanctimonious imprecations on behalf of decent white people, and Jerry Springer's racially and homophobically charged Punch and Judy shows. and in striking imitation of Father Coughlin and of Jesse Helms's nearly forgotten days as a radio host, the far right has found its undisputed king in the personage of Rush Limbaugh—a polished demagogue with a daily radio audience of at least twenty million, a television show that vies for the top ratings with David Letterman and Jay Leno, a newsletter with a circulation of 360,000, and two best-selling books whose combined sales exceed seven million copies.

While it is probably true that the media are a reflection of America in general, I resist the temptation to say that they are just a mirror. From Churchill to Hitler to the old Soviet Union, it is quite clear that radio and television have the power to change the course of history, have the power to proselytize and to coalesce not merely the good and the noble but also the very worst in human nature. When Orson Welles made his famous radio broadcast "witnessing" the landing of a spaceship full of hostile Martians, America ought to have learned a lesson about the power of radio to appeal to mass instincts and crowd panic.

Radio remains a peculiarly powerful medium even today, its visual emptiness in a world of six trillion flashing images allowing one of the few remaining playgrounds for the aural subconscious. Perhaps its power is attributable to our need for an oral tradition, sonic conveying of stories, feelings, myths of ancestors, epics of alienation and the need to rejoin ancestral roots, even the ignorant bigoted roots. Perhaps the visual quiescence of radio is related to the popularity of electronic networking. It encourages some deep imaginative blindness of which we are barely aware, the busy embodiment being eliminated from view. Only the voice made manifest, the masked and hooded words that can not—or dare not?—be seen. Just yet. Nostalgia crystallizing into a dangerous future. The preconscious voice erupting into the expressed, the prime time.

The shape of this electronic voice could be anything. What comes out of the modern radio mouth could be the *Iliad,* the *Rubáiyát,* the griot's song of our times. If indeed radio is a vessel for the American Song of Songs, then what does it mean that a manic, racist, penis-obsessed adolescent named Howard Stern is number one among radio listeners, that Rush Limbaugh's wittily smooth sadism has gone the way of prime-time television, and that these men's books tie for the number one slot on all the best-seller lists—Stern's book having had the largest first printing in publishing history. Professor Andy Herz of Touro College Law School sent me this anecdote:

> In my Jurisprudence class this semester, we were discussing John Stuart Mill's notion that the speech of eccentrics should be protected, even if the majority widely frowns upon their unconventional ideas, because their "ravings" against orthodoxy could ultimately lead society to some deeper understanding. Names like Galileo, Darwin, Pearl S. Buck and other early environmentalists were mentioned as good examples. Then someone (seriously) suggested that Howard Stern might fit the same category: a man who also "rants against orthodoxy" and whose views are looked down upon and even censored by some in the majority. What a vision: Howard Stern as the seer of our future society.

I smiled when I first received this letter. But a few weeks later Citizen Stern became the Libertarian Party's candidate for governor of New York—a candidacy cut blessedly short only by Stern's refusal to disclose his personal finances.

What to make of the stories being told by our modern radio evangelists, and their tragic unloved choruses of "dittohead" callers? Is it really just a collapsing economy that spawns this drama of grown people sitting around scaring themselves to death with fantasies of black feminist Mexican able-bodied gay soldiers earning $100,000 a year on welfare who are so criminally depraved that Hillary's hen-pecked husband or the Anti-Christ-of-the-moment had no choice but to invite them onto the government payroll so they can run the country?

As I spin the dial on my radio, I can't help thinking that this stuff must be related to that most poignant of fiber-optic phenomena, phone sex with Jessica Hahn (who now has her own 900 number). Oral sex. Radio racism with a touch of S&M. High-priest hosts with the power and run-amok ego to discipline listeners, to smack with the verbal back-of-the-hand, to smash the button that shuts you up for once and for all. "Idiot!" shouts Bob Grant—and then the sound of a droning telephone emptiness, the voice of dissent dumped out some trapdoor in the aural space. Rush Limbaugh's "splendidly awful taste" and "delightful offensiveness" have been celebrated in the *National Review.* And Howard Stern remains on the air by popular demand at the highest levels of the FCC, thanks to a seemingly insatiable national appetite for blam! and ker-pow! and make-a-big-bathroom-sound and the earth shakes and you get to giggle afterward.

As I have listened to a range of such programs around the country what has struck me as the most unifying theme of this genre is not merely the specific intolerance of such hot topics as race and gender but a much more general contempt for the world, a verbal stoning of anything different. It is like some unusually violent game of "Simon Says," this mockery and shouting down of callers, this roar of incantations, the insistence on agreement. A disrespect so deep as to be satisfying, I suppose, all those shouted epithets and dashed receivers, like a car crash in a movie except you can stay on the safe side of it if only you agree.

But, ah, if you *will* only agree, what sweet and safe reward, what soft enfolding by a stern and angry radio god, oh leader of a righteous nation. And as an added bonus, the invisible shield of an AM community, a family of fans who are Exactly Like You, to whom you can express, with sheltering call-in anonymity, all the filthy stuff you imagine "them" doing to you. The comfort and relief of being able to ejaculate, to those who understand, about the dark imagined excess overtaking, robbing, needing to be held down and taught a good lesson, needing to be put in its place before the ravenous demon enervates all that is true and good and pure in this life.

The panicky exaggeration reminds me of a child's fear . . . *And then, and then, and then, a huge lion jumped out of the shadows and was about to gobble me up and I can't ever sleep again for a whole week, it was the biggest most dangerous lion in the whole world* . . . The irresistible thread of a good story line; a trail of breadcrumbs to an inevitable ending. Yet the panicky exaggeration is not that of a child but that of millions of adults. And the trail of that story line reminds me of nothing so much as the quietly epic subtitles in that great American cornerstone of the silent screen, *The Birth of a Nation: Drunk with wine and power* . . . *the negroes and carpetbaggers sweep the state* . . . *men, who knew nothing of the uses of authority, except its insolences* . . . *want to marry a white woman* . . . *the town given over to crazed negroes* . . . *the helpless white minority* . . . *victims of the black mobs* . . . *a veritable overthrow of civilization.*

If the statistics are accurate, the audience for this genre of radio flagellation is mostly young, white, and male. (For example, 96 percent of Rush Limbaugh's audience is white, about two-thirds of it white men, and 75 percent of Howard Stern's listeners are white men.) Yet it is hard to take the call-in conversations as a genuine barometer of social relations in any sense other than as a measure of nonrelation and just plain ignorance. Most of the callers, by their own testimony, have spent their lives walling themselves off from any real experience with feminists and gays, they certainly don't have any black neighbors, and they avoid and resent all manner of troublesome "types" in the workplace.

In this regard, it is probably true, as former Secretary of Education William Bennett says, that Rush Limbaugh "tells his audience that what you think inside you can talk about in the marketplace." If only that quality of exorcising "what's inside" were the highlighted feature of that statement. Unfortunately "what's inside" is then mistaken for what's outside, treated as empirical and political reality. The *National Review* extols Limbaugh's conservative leadership as no less than that of Ronald Reagan, and the Republican Party provides Limbaugh with books, stories, angles, and public support. "People were afraid of censure by gay activists, feminists, environmentalist—now they are not because Rush takes them on," says Bennett. Hooray for the cavalry of bad-boy smash-'em-up audacity, for the cruel cowboy hero gone political.

Our history in the United States has been marked by cycles in which brands of this or that hatred come into fashion and go out again, are unleashed and restrained. If racism, homophobia, jingoism and woman-hating have been features of national life in pretty much all of modern history, it's probably not worth spending much time wondering if right-wing radio is a symptom or a cause. For at least four hundred years, prevailing attitudes in the West have considered blacks less intelligent than whites. When recent statistics show 53 percent of Americans agreeing that blacks and Hispanics are less intelligent and a majority believing that they are lazy, violent, welfare-dependent, and unpatriotic, it's not as though it's ever been a lot better than that. In other words, it's not as though dittoheads needed Rush Limbaugh to tell them what to think—they can be pretty creative on their own. (Once upon a time, I went on Wisconsin public radio to talk about statistics that showed college-educated black men earning much less than similarly qualified white men. Promptly a male caller phoned in to explain that this was because it took a college degree to bring a black man up to the level of a white high school graduate.)

I think that what has made life more or less tolerable for out-groups has been those moments in history when those "inside" feelings were relatively restrained, when angry or bigoted people more or less kept their feelings to themselves. In fact, if I could believe that right-wing radio were only about idiosyncratic, singular, rough-hewn individuals thinking those inside thoughts, I'd be much less concerned. If I could convince myself, as the Columbia University professor Everette Dennis proclaims, that "Stern and Limbaugh make [radio] a more interactive, more personal experience . . . They make it a better, more vibrant medium. It's the triumph of the individual"—then I'd be much more inclined to agree with *Time* magazine's bottom line that "the fact that either is seriously considered a threat . . . is more worrisome than Stern or Limbaugh will ever be." If, moreover, what I were hearing had even a tad more to do with real oppression, with real depression, with real white and black levels of joblessness and homelessness, or with the real problems of real white men, then I wouldn't have bothered to slog my way through hours of Howard Stern's miserable obsessions.

Yet at the heart of my anxiety is the worry that Stern, Limbaugh, Grant, et al. represent the very antithesis of individualism's triumph. As the *National Review* said of Limbaugh's ascent, "It was a feat not only of the loudest voice but also of a keen political brain to round up, as Rush did, the media herd and drive them into the conservative corral." "Rush is God / Rush in '96" reads the body paint slathered across the bare backs of two young male fans pictured in *Time* magazine. And when asked about his political aspirations, New York radio demagogue Bob Grant gloated, "I think I would make rather a good dictator."

Were this only about "conservative" politics, I would not be quite so worried, but Limbaugh's so-called dittohead fans are not really conservative in the best sense of that word. The polemics of right-wing radio are putting nothing less than hate onto the airwaves, into the marketplace, electing it to office, teaching it in schools, and exalting it as freedom. What worries me, in other words is the increasing-to-constant commerce of retribution, control, and lashing out, fed not by fact but by fantasy and very powerful myth. (The media watchdog organization Fairness and Accuracy in Reporting has issued a series of lists of substantial factual errors purveyed by Limbaugh's show. But is anybody listening to that?)

What worries me is the reemergence, more powerful than at any time since the founding of the Ku Klux Klan and the institution of Jim Crow, of a socio-centered self that excludes "the likes of," well, me for example, from the civic circle, and that would rob me of my worth and claim and identity as a citizen. Dittoheadedness has less the character of individualism (or at least what the conventional political imagination would wish individualism to be) than of a mass-produced group identity that knows itself by denunciation and racialized nationalism. As the *Economist* observes, "Mr. Limbaugh takes a mass market—white, mainly male, middle class, ordinary America—and talks to it as an endangered minority."

I worry about this identity whose external reference is neither family nor religion nor the Constitution but a set of beliefs, ethics, and practices that exclude, restrict, and act in the world on me, on mine, as the perceived if not real enemy. I (that is, the likes of me) am acutely aware of losing my mythic shield of protective individualism, in the dittohead cosmos, to the surface shapes of my mythic group fearsomeness as black, as female, as left-wing. "I" merge not fluidly but irretrievably into a category of "them"; I become a suspect self, a moving target of loathsome properties, not merely different but dangerous. And it is precisely this unacknowledged contest of groupness—an Invisible Nation of whites locked in mortal combat with an Evil Empire of rascally carpetbaggers and Know-Nothing Negros—for which the dominant ideology of individualism has no eyes, no vocabulary, and certainly no remedy that worries me most.

It is interesting, moreover, to note what has happened as Rush Limbaugh has moved from being a small-time talk-show host with lots of noisy callers to a big-time radio host with twenty million listeners willing to be summed up by a pair of ditto marks, to a television personality, seated behind a school master's desk with an American flag planted on it, with only an applause-metered audience of onlookers and no call-in voices at all. This is, arguably, a progression away from a conversation among those who styled themselves the Little Guys, on to a mean-spirited populism, and finally to an embodiment of Rush Limbaugh as Über-Little-Guy. And this seems dangerously close to those moments when populism passes into fascism, when the common man is condensed into an aggregation, a mass united in one driving symbol. Limbaugh is hardly just an "irreverent individual" under such circumstances; in invoking the name of the common man, he mines a power that is the "addition of all oneness" and uses it to affirm great, coordinated, lock-step political power.

What happens to the lives of those not in lock step with all this translated license, this permission to be uncivil? What happens to the social space that was supposed to have been opened up by the Reconstruction Amendments' injunction against the badges and incidents of institutionalized stigma, the social space that was supposedly at the sweet mountaintop of the civil rights movement's trail? Can I get a seat on the bus without having to be reminded that I should be standing? Did the civil rights movement guarantee us nothing more than the freedom to use public accommodations while surrounded by raving bigots? "They didn't beat this idiot [Rodney King] enough," says Howard Stern in the background.

Not long ago I had the misfortune to hail a taxicab in which the driver was listening to Howard Stern undress some woman. After several blocks, I had to get out. I was, frankly, afraid to ask the driver to turn it off—not because I was afraid of "censoring" him, but because the driver was stripping me too as he leered into the rearview mirror. "Something the matter?" he demanded, still leering, as I asked him to pull over and let me out at the next corner, well short of my destination. (I'll spare you the full story of what happened from there—trying to get another cab, having lots of trouble as cabs speed by me while stopping for all the white businessmen who so much as scratch their heads near the curb; a nice young white man seeing my plight, giving me his cab, having to thank him, he hero, me saved-but-humiliated, cab driver peeved and surly. I fight my way to my destination, arriving in a bad mood, militant black woman, cranky feminazi, gotta watch out for my type, no pleasing that kind.)

When Yeltsin blared rock'n'roll music at his opponents holed up in the Parliament building in Moscow, in imitation of the Marines trying to torture Manuel Noriega in Panama, it occurred to me that it must be like being trapped in a crowded subway car when all the Walkmen are tuned to Bob Grant or Howard Stern. With Howard Stern's voice a tinny, screeching backdrop, with all the faces growing dreamily mean as though some soporifically evil hallucinogen were gushing into their bloodstreams, I'd start clawing at the doors, begging to surrender, for sure.

Surrender to what? Surrender to the laissez-faire resegregation that is the metaphoric significance of the hundreds of Rush Rooms that have cropped up in restaurants around the country; broadcasting Limbaugh's words, rooms for your listening pleasure, rooms where bigots can capture the purity of a Rush only lunch counter, rooms where all those unpleasant others just "choose" not to eat? Surrender to the naughty luxury of a room in which a Ku Klux Klan meeting could take place in orderly, First Amendment fashion? Everyone's "free" to come in (and a few of you outsiders do), but mostly the undesirable nonconformist non-dittoheads are gently repulsed away. It's a high-tech world of enhanced choice, you see. Whites choose mostly to sit in the Rush Room; feminists, blacks, and gays "choose" to sit elsewhere. No need to buy black votes, you just pay blacks not to vote; no need to insist on white-only schools, you just sell them on the desirability of black-only schools. No need for signs and police to enforce the separation of gay from straight; nonconformist troublemakers will herd themselves nicely in the face of a din of racist, sexist, homophobic babble. Just sit back and watch it work, like those invisible shock shields that keep dogs cowering in their own backyards.

How real is the driving perception behind all the Sturm und Drang of this genre of radio harangue— the perception that white men are an oppressed minority, with no power and no opportunity in the land that they made great? While it is true that power and opportunity are shrinking for all but the very wealthy in this country (and would that Limbaugh would take that issue on), white men remain this country's most privileged citizens and market actors, firmly in control of almost all major corporate and political power. In contrast, according to the *Wall Street Journal,* "Blacks were the only racial group to suffer a net job loss during the 1990–91 economic downturn, at the companies reporting to the Equal Employment Opportunity Commission. Whites, Hispanics and Asians, meanwhile, gained thousands of jobs." Three years of black gains were wiped out between July 1990 and March 1991, the dates of the last recession. "While whites gained 71,144 jobs at these companies, Hispanics gained 60,040 and Asians gained 55,104, blacks lost 59,479." And while right-wing radio deejays complain that unqualified minorities are taking all the jobs in academia, that white men need not apply, they ignore the degree to which, as a result of the economy, the pool of available academic jobs itself is what has been shrinking, and not just in the United States. Moreover, the number of minority undergraduate and graduate students is declining dramatically: Stanford University, for example, has suffered a 10 percent decline in minority Ph.D. enrollments since 1988, and that statistic reflects a national decline. In fact, there aren't enough people of color in the world to do justice to that expanding balloon of fear felt by white men who think that they have been dispossessed by hordes of the "less qualified."

It certainly cannot be said that minorities are taking over the jobs of radio disc jockeys. In 1993 the *Los Angeles Times* found only 12 full-time weekday hosts who are members of minority groups among the 1000 or so general-market talk stations. Three of them are on public radio, which tends to be more liberal." And of that small number, a good portion are conservative blacks, although even conservative blacks have trouble in such a race-conscious market: Ken Hamblin, a conservative disc jockey in Denver who rails against "blacks," "black leaders," and the entire civil rights movement, "mentioned on air he was black. The phone lines suddenly went dead, and he had to filibuster his remaining four hours on air."

I think this reaction may be related to the rather fixed way in which all blacks are seen as allied with "radical" causes, no matter what right-wing claptrap they spout. How else call it be that City College of New York professor Leonard Jeffries, who teaches that blacks are sun people and whites are colder, harder, ice people, was held up to be such a symbol of multiculturalism, for example, when his theories revealed him as nothing if not a committed *mono*culturalist? When Khalid Muhammad (the Nation of Islam's national representative) indulged in his notorious anti-Semitic "bloodsucker" rantings, I was curious about why the mainstream media did not just condemn his words, as of course was proper, but condemned them as symbolic of a fearsome black radical Left–this when, except for the fact that he was black, his message was indistinguishable from that of far right-wingers like David Duke.

Similarly, I wonder why Charles Murray's or Richard Herrnstein's or Michael Levin's Nazi-like sociobiological theories of the inferiority of blacks are always so protected from the political vagaries of either Right or Left and graced as "science." And if we can understand what is so upsetting about Louis Farrakhan's famous excesses, one wonders why Senator Ernest Hollings's calling Africans cannibals—in the *Congressional Record* no less—should, be received with barely a ho-hum.

What if whites understood Leonard Jeffries not as a "radical" but as a mirror image of a more general American right-winger with a taste for the delicious power of racial pornography? Perhaps some dawning but wrong-headed recognition of this connection motivated *Time* magazine's odd characterization of the call to black leaders to denounce black anti-Semitism as "'just another kind of bigotry'"— not because such calls single out only black leaders and only when it is black prejudice that is at issue, but because such efforts are purportedly attempts to "enforc[e] racial correctness." My guess is that the author of this astounding bit of moral dismissiveness also might feel that speaking out against white fraternity brothers who stage a slave auction is just another attempt at "enforcing political correctness." As A. M. Rosenthal observed in the *New York Times,* "Not a word did *Time* print to indicate that it ever crossed its collectivized-journalism mind that black leaders who denounced [anti-Semitic] speech really might despise it, that maybe they stood up because they liked that stance in life." Rather than a movement to pressure the full leadership structure of our entire society to look at itself and condemn all forms of bigotry, the intense reductionism in discourse about First Amendment rights in recent years seems to have resulted in an odd formula according to which groups have a *right* to be as racist as they wannabe, and no one else has a *right* to be offended unless they actually get hit.

Questions for Discussion

1. Patricia Williams claims that "the unifying theme of [talk radio] is not merely the specific intolerance of such hot topics as race and gender but a much more general contempt for the world, a verbal stoning of anything different." If you have ever listened to these programs, do you believe this characterization is accurate? Why or why not?

2. One of Patricia Williams' points is that radio has an unusual power because of the anonymity it provides to both speaker and listener. She goes on to describe radio's power as that of "the voice made manifest, the masked and hooded words that cannot—or dare not?—be seen." What images are evoked by the phrase "masked and hooded"? Can you find other examples in the text of equally evocative language? To what end is Williams using this language? How does Williams choose language to advance her persuasive goals?

3. Some might claim that the impact of this variety of talk radio programming—particularly that of Rush Limbaugh and Howard Stern—has declined since this essay was written. Evidence for this claim might be that Rush Limbaugh's syndicated television program is no longer produced and Howard Stern's program is no longer broadcast in many markets. Could this change indicate a shift in the public attitudes that Williams decries in her essay?

Explorations

1. At one point in this essay, Williams refers to D. W. Griffith's film *Birth of a Nation,* which in one regard is considered a masterpiece for its groundbreaking use of cinematic techniques. However, this movie is often criticized for overt racism. Consider other films you have seen with implications for race relations in our society—either intended or unintended—and discuss the impact of those works on you or your peers.

2. A media watchdog group called FAIR (Fairness & Accuracy in Reporting) has published a list of what it believes to be factual errors propogated by Rush Limbaugh in support of his political stance (http://www.fair.org/press-releases/limbaugh-debatesreality.html). This list of factual errors is available at many web sites devoted to Rush Limbaugh. After you have read some of FAIR's claims, reflect on the importance of "accuracy" in Limbaugh's radio program.

3. In your study of rhetoric, you may have learned of the weakness of arguments based on such logical fallacies as the *ad hominum* attack on a person rather than an engagement with that person's ideas. Williams claims that talk radio hosts such as Rush Limbaugh employ the *ad hominum* attack regularly in what she calls a "verbal stoning" and "mockery and shouting down of callers." If she is correct, what then accounts for the persuasive impact of these programs? Does she weaken her argument by calling Howard Stern a "manic, racist, penis-obsessed adolescent" in the same essay?

Formal Writing Assignments

1. The talk radio hosts most referenced by Patricia J. Williams in this essay have both written books. Rush Limbaugh's book, *The Way Things Ought to Be,* was a national best seller for months. Howard Stern has written two autobiographical books, *Private Parts* and *Miss America.* Read one of these books and write a review that summarizes the work, evaluates it as writing, and analyzes the contents of the book from a political perspective.

2. In this essay, Williams describes her concern about a set of beliefs that has as its point of reference the existence of an "enemy" of those values. In other words, the values of those in agreement with talk radio hosts such as Rush Limbaugh are based not so much on their intrinsic merits, but on the notion that someone is always attempting to tear those values down. In an essay, describe what you believe to be a set of "American" values based on the inclusion of all who share this citizenship.

Ethos - Ethics, speaker credibility
Pathos - feeling & emotion, Sympathetic (A of security systems)
Logos - Logic / intellect